BUSINESS LAW IN CANADA

ELEVENTH EDITION

RICHARD A. YATES
SIMON FRASER UNIVERSITY

TERESA BEREZNICKI-KOROL
THE NORTHERN ALBERTA INSTITUTE OF TECHNOLOGY

TREVOR CLARKE
AURORA COLLEGE

PEARSON

Toronto

Editorial Director: Claudine O'Donnell
Acquisitions Editor: Carolin Sweig
Marketing Manager: Jessica McInnis
Program Manager: Karen Townsend
Project Manager: Kimberley Blakey and Pippa Kennard
Developmental Editor: Leona Burlew
Manager of Content Development: Suzanne Schaan
Production Services: iEnergizer Aptara®, Ltd.
Permissions Project Manager: Joanne Tang
Text Permissions Research: iEnergizer Aptara®, Ltd.
Interior Designer: iEnergizer Aptara®, Ltd.
Cover Designer: Alex Li
Cover Image: © venimo / Shutterstock

Vice-President, Cross Media and Publishing Services: Gary Bennett

10 9 8 7 6 5 4 3 2 1 V058

Library and Archives Canada Cataloguing in Publication

Yates, Richard, author
     Business law in Canada / Richard A. Yates (Simon Fraser University), Teresa Bereznicki-Korol (The Northern Alberta Institute of Technology), Trevor Clarke (Aurora College).— Eleventh edition.

Includes bibliographical references and index.
ISBN 978-0-13-384713-0 (paperback)

     1. Commercial law—Canada. I. Bereznicki-Korol, Teresa, 1957–, author II. Clarke, Trevor, 1952–, author III. Title.

KE919.Y376 2015   346.7107   C2015-906144-X
KF889.Y383 2015

PEARSON

978-0-13-384713-0

Brief Contents

Contents

PART 4
Methods of Carrying on Business 307

Chapter 10
Agency and Partnership 307

Chapter 11
Corporations 345

Chapter 12
Employment 381

PART 5
Property and Information Technology 429

Chapter 13
Intellectual Property 429

Preface

In order to ensure that *Business Law in Canada* continues to be a valuable resource to post-secondary instructors and students, the 11th edition has undergone a thoughtful revision, incorporating changes based on the increased importance of the Internet, information technology, and intellectual property. It also incorporates the large amount of feedback and many thoughtful suggestions provided by users of the 10th edition.

CHANGES TO THE 11TH EDITION

The following pedagogical changes have been made to the 11th edition:

- Content from the previous edition's Chapter 14, "Information Technology and the Internet," has been updated and integrated into relevant chapters to better address the pervasive presence of the digital world when making everyday business decisions.
- An increased number of CanLII citations have been incorporated into the text to provide readers with quick access to online materials.
- An increase in the number of visuals, such as tables and checklists, to make content more visually appealing and more accessible to visual learners.

The key changes for each chapter are listed below:

Chapter 1: Managing Your Legal Affairs: Revisions include a Case Summary on the Supreme Court of Canada decision in *Cojocaru v. British Columbia Women's Hospital and Health Centre*, in which the Court discussed the presumption of judicial integrity and impartiality, as well as an expanded discussion in the Ethics section regarding corporate social responsibility.

Chapter 2: Introduction to the Legal System: The Case Summaries in this chapter have been updated significantly, including one that discusses *R. v. Caron*. Case Summary 2.2 now focuses on *Craig v. Canada*. A summary of the Supreme Court's decision on physician-assisted suicide (in *Carter v. Attorney General of Canada*) has been added. A summary of *Simpson v. Oil City Hospitality Inc.* is introduced, and the *Campbell River* case has been replaced with *Canada (Attorney General) v. Johnstone*. New Case Summaries examine *Vaughan (City) v. Tsui*, *R. v. Keshane*, and *Smith v. St. Albert (City)*. Table 2.1 has been updated, and material concerning the Mounted Police Association case has been removed.

Chapter 3: The Resolution of Disputes: The Courts and Alternatives to Litigation: The section on Alternatives to Court Action has been moved to the beginning of the chapter. Information relating to jurisdiction from the previous edition's "Information Technology and the Internet" chapter has also been incorporated into this chapter.

Chapter 4: Intentional Torts and Torts Impacting Business: Revisions to this chapter include the refinement of the "unlawful means" tort, as clarified lately by the Supreme Court of Canada, and the effect of the Internet on tort law and privacy from the previous edition's chapter "Information Technology and the Internet."

Chapter 5: Negligence, Professional Liability, and Insurance: The chapter is introduced with a new Case Summary dealing with negligence. The *Crocker v. Sundance* case has been retained, but is located in the section dealing with defences to negligence. In direct response to reviewers' comments, the *Design Services v. Canada* Case Summary has been replaced by a recent product liability case, *More v. Bauer*. A chart detailing what needs to be established to prove negligence has been added. Analysis of strict liability and occupiers' liability has been rearranged, while analysis of the *Hercules* case has been expanded.

Chapter 6: The Elements of a Contract: Consensus and Consideration: A discussion on the Supreme Court of Canada decision in *Bhasin v. Hrynew* has been added to the chapter. The case creates a new "general organizing principle of good faith contractual performance," and also a common law duty of parties to a contract "to act honestly in the performance of contractual obligations." Material from the previous edition's "Information Technology and the Internet" chapter relating to Internet transactions, consensus, and ecommerce legislation has been incorporated into this chapter.

Chapter 7: The Elements of a Contract: Capacity, Legality, and Intention: Material from the previous edition's "Information Technology and the Internet" chapter relating to Internet transactions, capacity, writing, and ecommerce legislation has been incorporated into this chapter.

Chapter 8: Factors Affecting the Contractual Relationship: Case Summaries have been updated and, in response to reviewer input, the *Ron Engineering* case is addressed. Other additions include two tables on rescission of contract and exceptions to operation of the privity rule.

Chapter 9: The End of the Contractual Relationship: A Case Summary describing the *Tercon* decision has been added together with further marginal notes as needed. Reviewers asked for a detailed review of the status of fundamental breach in contract law, so the approach taken by the courts "before and after" the *Tercon* case has been detailed. Table 9.2, on the effect of the *Frustrated Contracts Act*, has been clarified. The analysis of exclusionary clauses and their enforceability has also been updated.

Chapter 10: Agency and Partnership: The discussion of agency has been carefully delineated from partnership, with the importance of choosing an agent emphasized and fiduciary duty clarified. The discussion of sole proprietors and partnership has been expanded and a summary of items that could be included in a partnership agreement added. The status of a partner being an employee was clarified with a discussion of the Supreme Court of Canada case *McCormick v. Fasken Martineau DuMoulin LLP*. The discussion of limited liability partnerships has been clarified and a section on joint ventures added. Content pertaining to undisclosed principals has been reduced.

Chapter 11: Corporations: Case Summaries have been refreshed with new content and a short section entitled "Shareholder Agreements" has been added to the chapter.

Chapter 12: Employment: Relevant material from the previous edition's "Information Technology and the Internet" chapter has been incorporated into this chapter. In response to reviewers' requests, the *Tree Savers* case has returned as Case Summary 12.6. The *R. v. Cole* Case Summary has been updated to include the new ruling from the Supreme Court of Canada. The recent Supreme Court decision in *Potter v. New Brunswick Legal Aid Services Commission* dealing with constructive dismissal has been summarized. Employment law is an area undergoing constant change, so further new cases summarized or discussed include

- *Crisall v. Western Pontiac Buick GMC (1999) Ltd.*,
- *Jardine Lloyd Thompson Canada Inc v Harke-Hunt*,
- *Payette v. Guay Inc.*,
- *Pate Estate v. Galway-Cavendish and Harvey (Township)*
- *Hicks v. HRSDC*
- *Canada (Attorney General) v. Johnstone*
- *Ontario (Attorney General) v. Fraser*

This case is addressed under the Cases and Discussion Questions section:

- *Goudie v. Ottawa (City)*

Chapter 13: Intellectual Property: This new chapter covers relevant material taken from the previous edition's chapter "Real, Personal, and Intellectual Property" and "Information Technology and the Internet," including a discussion on copyright, patents, trademarks, and other forms of intellectual property. The chapter also looks at the protection of private and confidential information and how these subjects intersect with changing technology and the expansion of the Internet.

Chapter 14: Real and Personal Property and Protection of the Environment: In general the chapter content has been condensed and clarified where possible and a major section on the protection of the environment added. Intellectual property has been moved to Chapter 13, as indicated above. The discussion on joint tenancy and tenancy in common has been expanded, as has the discussion of mortgages. In the area of residential tenancies, a list of areas often changed by provincial legislation has been included.

Chapter 15: Priority of Creditors: The section entitled "Alternatives to Bankruptcy" has been moved to the end of the chapter so that the material on bankruptcy would flow more smoothly.

Chapter 16: Sales and Consumer Protection: Discussion of the *Sale of Goods Act* has been simplified. Thus the requirement of writing discussion has been removed and the discussion of FOB, CIF, COD, and bill of lading contracts has been condensed. However, discussion of sales made online and the *International Sale of Goods Act* has been expanded with material from the previous edition's chapter "Information Technology and the Internet." Discussion of the *Federal Competition Act* and the subject of mergers have been reduced. A discussion of identity theft has been added, as well as an examination of the 2001 *Internet Sales Contract Harmonization Template* and an extended discussion of electronic money based on material from the previous edition's chapter "Information Technology and the Internet."

FEATURES

You will find the following text features in the 11th edition:

Learning Objectives provide an overview of the chapter content.

Learning Objective icons appear where the discussion of each learning objective begins.

Case Summaries appear throughout each chapter. They are used to introduce topics and to provide concrete examples that help students understand key legal issues. Many of the Case Summaries also include Discussion Questions, which help promote a more thorough understanding of the relevant issues, or Small Business Perspectives, which identify the relevant legal issues facing small business owners.

Marginal notes summarize adjacent paragraphs and highlight key points.

Reducing Risk boxes are featured throughout the text. Each Reducing Risk box describes what the sophisticated client would do in the business situation the box presents.

Provincial content is available on MyBusLawLab.

Diagrams illustrate cases with complex fact patterns.

Key legal terms appear in bold and full definitions appear in the Glossary.

Summaries in point form promote quick review and reference.

Finally, we remind all who use this text that it is designed as a tool for learning business law and not as an authoritative source of legal advice. When faced with a specific legal problem, the reader is advised to seek the assistance of a lawyer.

Student Supplements

MyBusLawLab (www.pearsonmylabandmastering.com). MyBusLawLab is an online study tool for students and an online homework and assessment tool for faculty. MyBusLawLab provides students with an assortment of tools to help enrich the learning experience, including

- pre- and post-tests with study plan,
- mini-cases with assessment questions,
- simulations (new),
- provincial material,
- CBC videos with assessment questions, and
- a Pearson eText electronic version of the textbook.

The Pearson eText gives students access to their textbook anytime, anywhere. In addition to note-taking, highlighting, and bookmarking, the Pearson eText offers interactive and sharing features. Instructors can share their comments or highlights, and students can add their own, creating a tight community of learners within the class.

An access code for MyBusLawLab is included with every new printed textbook or can be purchased separately at **www.pearsonmylabandmastering.com**.

Instructor Supplements

Business Law in Canada, 11th Edition, is accompanied by a complete package of instructor supplements. Some of the following items are available for download from a password-protected section of Pearson Canada's online catalogue at **http://catalogue.pearsoned.ca**; see your Pearson Canada sales representative for details and access.

Instructor's Resource Manual. This supplement contains summaries of each chapter, answers to the questions found at the end of each chapter in the text, and solutions to the cases, plus their full citations.

Computerized Test Bank. Pearson's computerized test banks allow instructors to filter and select questions to create quizzes, tests, or homework. Instructors can revise questions or add their own, and may be able to choose print or online options. These questions are also available in Microsoft Word format.

PowerPoint Presentations. Over 400 slides highlight key concepts featured in the text.

CBC Video Cases. Segments from CBC programs complement the text and enhance learning by bringing practical applications and issues to life. These videos are available on MyBusLawLab for this text.

Learning Solutions Managers. Pearson's Learning Solutions Managers work with faculty and campus course designers to ensure that Pearson technology products, assessment tools, and online course materials are tailored to meet your specific needs. This highly qualified team is dedicated to helping schools take full advantage of a wide range of educational resources, by assisting in the integration of a variety of instructional materials and media formats. Your local Pearson Canada sales representative can provide you with more details on this service program.

Acknowledgments and Dedications

As has been the case in every new edition of *Business Law in Canada*, reviewers have played an important role in correcting, reshaping, and updating the book, and we would like to acknowledge their invaluable contributions. In addition to providing encouragement and insight into what instructors want and need, they provide an important connection to the people this book is designed to serve.

We thank all those who have patiently gone over the text and made suggestions for revision, including Lorrie Adams, MacEwan University; Michael Bozzo, Mohawk College; Douglas Kennedy, NAIT; Daniel Le Dressay, Langara College; Douglas Peterson, University of Alberta; Joseph Radocchia, University of Waterloo; Mark Schwartz, York University; Don Valeri, Douglas College.

I am grateful for the opportunity to continue contributing to *Business Law in Canada* and wish to express my gratitude to my co-writers, Trevor and Teresa, for their leadership and dedication to the text. The writing and publishing of a textbook requires a coordinated effort by many people. Pearson Canada provided us with a team of enthusiastic and knowledgeable people, all of whom willingly helped us in many ways. I appreciate and acknowledge the assistance and support received from Carolin Sweig, Karen Townsend, Jessica McInnis, Leona Burlew, Kimberley Blakey, and Alex Li at Pearson Canada.

Finally, I would like to thank my wife, Ruth, who continues to lend her support to this effort. I would like to dedicate this edition of the text to her, our children, their partners, and our grandchildren.

—*Richard A. Yates, LLB, MBA*

Allow me to acknowledge my colleagues and the students at NAIT. Working within such a supportive environment has been a real pleasure. I value the positive energy of Anna Beukes, chair of the School of Finance, and Tad Drinkwater, Peter Nissen, and Perri Sinal, dean and associate deans, respectively, for the JR Shaw School of Business. My colleagues who teach business law, Douglas Kennedy, Kim Watamaniuk, Anne Henderson, Craig Grubisich, Angus Ng, Chelsea-Evans Rymes, Justin Matthews, and Robin Kaulback, have all contributed to the success our course has had in creating sophisticated clients. Thank you for all your efforts.

I would like to dedicate the 11th edition to my husband, Rick, and my supportive family, whose plans were frequently adjusted to accommodate my work. Have I told you lately that I love you?

—*Teresa Bereznicki Korol, BA, JD*

I would like to dedicate the 11th edition to all of the students I have taught using *Business Law in Canada*. My interactions with my students have always been inspiring, and watching them develop into sophisticated clients continues to be incredibly satisfying and motivating. Given that, it only seems right to dedicate this edition of the textbook to all of them, wherever they are and whatever they are doing.

I would like to thank one of those former students in particular, Sherry Baxter. Now a practising lawyer, Sherry did the research required to update the legislation and case law relevant to the chapters in the 11th edition for which I was responsible. This task is time consuming and demanding. Sherry did an excellent job and provided comments, insights, and suggestions that were extremely helpful. Thank you once again, Sherry.

I would also like to acknowledge the unwavering support of my wife, Peggy. The saying "Behind every successful man is a great woman" is definitely true. Preparing a business law textbook is an onerous project. I could not have completed the work required to prepare the 11th edition without Peg's continued patience, tolerance, understanding, and encouragement. Thank you very much, Peg!

—*Trevor Clarke, BSc, MBA, LLB*

1 Chapter

Managing Your Legal Affairs

LEARNING OBJECTIVES

1. Explain the meaning of "sophisticated client"
2. Examine the role of the lawyer
3. Identify when to hire a lawyer and when to represent yourself
4. Explain how to find an appropriate lawyer
5. Review how lawyers bill their clients
6. Describe legal aid
7. Outline the procedure to follow to complain about your lawyer
8. Discuss the ethics of lawyers and of clients

Defendant: Before I plead guilty or not guilty, I would like to ask if a lawyer could be appointed to defend me.

Judge: You were caught robbing a convenience store, holding the stolen goods with a gun in your hand, standing over the store clerk who was lying on the floor. What could a lawyer possibly say in your defence?

Defendant: That's just it—I'm really curious as to what he could possibly say.

Lawyers constantly hear lawyer jokes at parties and receive them via email. Some business law students tell lawyer jokes in class. This is often a humorous attempt to embarrass the lawyer who is teaching the class.

Students tell lawyer jokes . . .

"I THINK I NEED LEGAL ADVICE . . ."

Sometimes a student who has told a lawyer joke in class (or a friend or relative of the student) becomes involved in a "legal situation" during the semester. She may have been charged with a criminal offence. She may have become eligible to apply for a pardon for a crime for which she was previously convicted. She may have received a traffic ticket, or been charged with a drinking-and-driving offence. She may have been involved in a car accident and be facing charges, or be having difficulty dealing with her insurance company in obtaining benefits. She may not have received her damage deposit from her former landlord or be in some sort of dispute with her landlord. She may be unable to collect from someone to whom she lent money. She may have been involved in a house deal that has collapsed. She may be involved in divorce proceedings or a custody dispute. She may have been served with a restraining order. She may have a business idea involving a

. . . but when involved in a "legal situation" . . .

product she has invented. She may have written a song or a software program for a computer game. She may be thinking of setting up a business with one of her friends or relatives.

All of the above situations (and many more) have been experienced by students of the authors of this textbook during recent semesters. (Some of these situations have in fact been going on for extended periods of time.) In every case, the involved student approached her business law instructor to ask for advice. That is, while the typical student may publicly participate in the criticism of lawyers, when faced with a personal problem involving legal aspects she will unashamedly seek advice from a lawyer.

The student often approaches the instructor because she has suddenly realized that the situation in which the student (or her friend or relative) is involved relates to legal issues or requires decisions that require legal input if they are to be dealt with appropriately. The student often says, "My parents don't know that I am speaking to you about this issue." Alternatively, she may say, "My friend heard me talking about the business law course I'm taking and asked me to ask you about this issue."

This usually indicates that the student has been listening during her business law classes and has been reading the relevant course materials. She has begun to realize that many decisions in today's world involve legal issues, and that good decisions can be made only if appropriate attention is paid to the relevant legal advice. She therefore puts aside the bias against lawyers she started the course with and approaches a lawyer (her business law instructor) to obtain the relevant legal advice.

This textbook attempts to help the student develop the attitude that it is often best to obtain legal advice before making business decisions. Obtaining relevant legal advice on a timely basis requires putting aside the usual derision and public mistrust of lawyers and instead building a good long-term relationship with a lawyer. We will refer to someone who understands the importance of the solicitor–client relationship and who knows how to form and use such a relationship to make good business decisions as a "sophisticated client." This textbook chapter will try to help business law students become sophisticated clients so that they can manage their legal affairs more efficiently and effectively.

> **... they seek advice from a lawyer**

> **The objective is to help students become sophisticated clients**

LO ❶ BECOMING A SOPHISTICATED CLIENT

> **Meaning of "sophisticated client"**

The first step in becoming what is known as a "sophisticated client" is to understand what is meant by the phrase. The dictionary meaning of "sophisticated"[1] would suggest that a sophisticated client is confident, knowledgeable, and up to date on legal trends. A **sophisticated client** understands the role of the lawyer and of the client. She knows when to represent herself, when to hire a lawyer, and how to hire a lawyer. She understands the costs associated with hiring a lawyer. A sophisticated client also knows what can be done if she is dissatisfied with the conduct of her lawyer. All of these topics will be discussed in this chapter.

Taking a business law course often helps students understand the significance of becoming a sophisticated client. It also marks the beginning of their development into sophisticated clients. One of the authors of this textbook has asked the question "Explain the meaning of 'sophisticated client' and discuss whether the objective of helping you develop into a sophisticated client has been achieved during the course" on the final exam for a business law course. Many students answer the question by describing a situation that they (or their friends or relatives) faced while they were taking the course. They explain that they dealt with the situation in a quite different manner from what they had done in similar

---

1. See, for example, *Canadaspace.com English Online Dicitonary:* http://dictionary.canadaspace.com.

situations in the past. They attribute this difference to what they had learned in the business law course.

A business law course, with its practical emphasis on general legal principles as they apply to many different areas of business, often serves as a catalyst in the development of students. It provides a spark that results in a sense of empowerment. Students come to realize that business decisions are made all the time and usually have serious consequences. Therefore, they begin to understand that it is critical that good decisions be made.

Business law course a catalyst

The business law course also makes it obvious that good business decisions cannot be made without consideration of the appropriate laws. The students start to appreciate that sometimes, through their own research, they can find the legal information required to enable them to make sound business decisions, but that other times the necessary information must be obtained from a lawyer. This understanding of the importance of having a good lawyer on your team is a critical component of being a sophisticated client.

Need a lawyer on the team

A useful example illustrating how students come to understand the advantages of considering the relevant laws when making business decisions involves the importance of evidence. Students learn that the burden of proof borne by the plaintiff in a civil lawsuit is that he must prove his case on a balance of probabilities. The students see that evidence is introduced during the trial through the testimony of witnesses on direct examination, cross-examination, and re-examination. They learn that the evidence can be a tangible object ("the bloody knife"), a piece of documentation ("the contract"), or simply an eyewitness account. They learn that hearsay (second-hand) evidence is not admissible. Once the students learn about the importance of evidence in satisfying the relevant burden of proof and the different types of admissible evidence, their behaviour changes. They will take pictures after a car accident, for example, and get the names and telephone numbers of any witnesses. They will also understand the significance of having a written contract for a business transaction. They know that they may not win a case based on a verbal contract, when the evidence will consist of their word against the word of the other party. They then realize that the lawyer is not advising her clients to "Get it in writing!" simply to generate legal work for which the lawyer will be paid. They will instead understand that the lawyer has provided legal advice to help them make good business decisions. They are now approaching the situations that they encounter as sophisticated clients.

The author mentioned above frequently encounters former students several years after they took the business law course. They usually indicate that they have constantly used what they learned in the course in making their personal and business decisions. They specifically mention contract, employment, consumer, and intellectual property law, and the research they have done (usually online) about relevant legal topics. It is clear that many business law students do indeed become sophisticated clients!

Evidence shows that business law students become sophisticated clients

THE ROLE OF THE LAWYER

LO ❷

One of the reasons for the general lack of respect for lawyers is that many people do not understand the role of the lawyer in the solicitor–client relationship. This misunderstanding is shown by the student who, after consulting with a lawyer, claims, "My lawyer told me to do this." This statement implies that the decision maker in the relationship is the lawyer, not the client.

The better approach is to see the client as the decision maker. She has encountered a problem and must make a decision. She needs to collect certain information before she can make an informed decision. In this regard, she consults her "experts"— namely, her accountant, marketing manager, human resources officer . . . anyone who can provide relevant information. She gathers all of the useful information, which she then takes into consideration when she makes her decision.

Client is decision maker

Lawyer is an expert providing advice

The lawyer is simply one of the experts the businessperson consults. The lawyer provides legal advice relevant to the client's situation. The client is, of course, free to ignore the legal advice she receives, just as she is free to ignore any other advice she receives. Sometimes it would be unwise to ignore the lawyer's advice. ("If you do this, you will be committing a crime for which you will go to jail if you are convicted.") But the businessperson makes her decisions in light of all the relevant factors. She may therefore choose to accept some legal risk because she deems some other business factors to be of greater importance.

A clear understanding of the nature of the solicitor–client relationship will demystify the role of lawyers. While they typically are experts in their area of practice and can provide invaluable assistance to their clients, lawyers are simply providers of advice. They are hired by the client, who provides them with instructions. The lawyer is bound to follow these instructions, provided that they are lawful.

A client's information must be kept confidential

There is one aspect of this relationship that must be emphasized. A lawyer's advice to his client will not be of any value unless the client has provided all relevant information to the lawyer. If the client does not have confidence that her information will be kept confidential, she may not divulge all the relevant information to the lawyer. **Solicitor–client privilege** refers to the duty of the lawyer to keep the information provided by the client confidential. Solicitor–client privilege is therefore fundamental to our legal system, since without it access to justice would be significantly reduced. Most lawyers will advise their clients about solicitor–client privilege and encourage their clients to disclose all relevant information. A sophisticated client will understand that the value of the legal advice will vary in direct proportion to the completeness of the information provided to the lawyer.

CASE SUMMARY 1.1

Can Solicitor–Client Privilege Be Ignored? *Canada (Privacy Commissioner) v. Blood Tribe Department of Health*[2]

The Privacy Commissioner requested records from an employer with respect to an employee requesting access to her personal employment information. The employee, who had been dismissed, suspected that the employer had improperly collected inaccurate information and used it to discredit her before its board of directors. At the time of dismissal, the employer had sought legal advice from its lawyers. The employer claimed solicitor–client privilege for certain records and refused to provide them. The Federal Court ordered that these records be provided to the Privacy Commissioner so that she could fulfill her statutory investigative role. The Federal Court of Appeal reversed this decision and ordered that the records did not have to be provided. The Supreme Court of Canada upheld this decision on the basis that the relevant legislation did not expressly allow the Privacy Commissioner to "pierce" the solicitor–client privilege. Given the fundamental importance of the privilege, clear and explicit language is required to allow it to be breached.

SMALL BUSINESS PERSPECTIVE

A businessperson seeking legal advice must be completely honest with his lawyer or the legal advice provided by the lawyer will not be appropriate for the situation. The client need not worry that the information provided will be made public because the lawyer is obligated to maintain confidentiality by the solicitor–client privilege. Are there any exceptions to the general rule that solicitor–client privilege attaches to all communications between a client and a lawyer?

---

2. [2008] 2 SCR 574, 2008 SCC 44 (CanLII).

SHOULD I HIRE A LAWYER?

When to Hire a Lawyer

It is useful to examine the solicitor–client relationship in the context of a small business. From start-up to the selling of the business, the owner has many decisions to make. As a sophisticated client, when should the small business owner consult his lawyer for advice?[3]

Business owners make many different decisions

The first thing the owner should do is consider how he will organize his business. Will he operate as a sole proprietor? Will he have a partner? Should he incorporate? Will the business be operated as a franchise? The decision as to the form of business organization is significant and has many implications (including liability, income taxes, and estate planning). The lawyer can provide information and advice that will help the owner make decisions appropriate for achieving his objectives.

Examples of business decisions and how a lawyer can help

If the owner is buying an existing business, the lawyer can provide advice and information that will enable the owner to minimize his potential risk and liability. What if the current owner has unsatisfied judgments against her? What if the assets of the current business have mortgages registered against them? Can the owner make good business decisions in these situations without receiving appropriate legal advice?

Anyone starting a business should ensure that all relevant laws will be complied with. How will the owner of the business determine which laws are relevant to his business? Can he understand the laws and whether his business plan will result in compliance with these laws? The lawyer can, of course, determine which municipal, provincial, and federal laws are relevant to the business and provide advice as to what is required to ensure compliance with them. This could cover everything from obtaining a business licence to complying with municipal noise bylaws to satisfying provincial and federal environmental standards.

Most businesses require a physical location, which usually means that there will be a lease to be negotiated. As is the case with all contracts, the owner should read the form of lease provided by the landlord. What if the owner doesn't understand various clauses of the document? Should he just sign the lease anyway, or should he consult his lawyer as to the meaning of the clauses before he signs?

The same questions apply to the documents provided by the bank or other lending institution. The owner of a small business usually must finance the start-up of the business or the purchase of an existing business. In particular, the extent of the personal liability of the owner for losses incurred by the business should always be carefully analyzed and understood by the owner before he signs the relevant documentation. This may require the provision of legal advice by the owner's lawyer.

There are other contracts that may need to be prepared in connection with the business. Examples include contracts with employees, suppliers, and customers. Can the owner of the business draft these documents himself? Would he be wise to do so without obtaining legal advice from his lawyer?

Most businesses today have intellectual property issues. These vary from the naming of the business to the protection of the business's intellectual property, such as patents, trademarks, and copyrights, to ensuring that the business is not infringing on someone else's property rights. This is a very complicated area that is changing rapidly. Is it prudent for the business owner to make decisions involving intellectual property without obtaining relevant legal advice?

Legal advice will enable better decisions

Even when selling his business the owner may need to seek legal advice from his lawyer. Should the sale involve the assets of the business or the shares of the corporation that owns the assets? What are the income tax implications? Is there any potential future liability for the seller to consider? How does the seller ensure that he will get paid? It is clear that there are many issues for which a business owner should consult his lawyer to ensure that he makes good business decisions, even when he is selling his business.

---

3. This approach was used in Glenna Erikson, "Pay Me Now or Pay More Later," *LawNow* (March 1993): 19.

When to Represent Yourself

The above section suggests that a good approach to understanding the solicitor–client relationship is to view the client as the decision maker. The lawyer is one of the "experts" that the client approaches in his efforts to collect the information necessary for him to make good business decisions. This approach assumes that good business decisions will be based, at least in part, on relevant legal information and advice.

Not always necessary to retain a lawyer

It is not, of course, necessary (or desirable) for the client to seek legal advice for every decision he must make. To do so would not only be prohibitively expensive, but it would also result in delays in the client's decision making. The crucial question, then, is "When should you hire a lawyer?"

Best to research relevant law

If you need to make a business decision and you do not retain a lawyer, then you will either not be considering relevant legal information when you are making your decision or you will be obtaining the legal information yourself. For small, insignificant decisions it may be appropriate to proceed without taking the time to find the relevant legal information. But in most cases it would be prudent to proceed only after completing some research of the relevant law.

Sophisticated clients may be able to find legal information

A sophisticated client will understand this and will know how to find the relevant information. This is helped along, of course, by the availability of legal information online. In the past, lawyers were "the keepers" of legal information. It was necessary to consult a lawyer to access legal information. This added to the "mystique" of (and the resentment against!) lawyers. This has recently changed: Now anyone with a computer and access to the Internet can find legal information online. A sophisticated client will capitalize on this; he will do his own legal research whenever he requires legal information to make a business decision and it is not appropriate to hire a lawyer to find the necessary information.

Legal information is now readily available . . .

This textbook will help students realize that legal information is readily accessible and will assist them in overcoming their fear of the law. It will also serve as a valuable resource with many references to online legal information and specific legal websites. The MyBusLawLab that accompanies this textbook also emphasizes the availability of online legal information by providing relevant provincial law and legal information as well as direct links to significant legal websites.

. . . but may be incorrect or incomplete

For perceptive clients, the availability of an abundance of easily accessible legal information is a positive development. Not only do they understand the need for legal input when business decisions are being made, but they know how to access relevant legal information. This is an important aspect of the empowerment that business law students experience as they start to develop into sophisticated clients. It is important, however, that they develop an understanding and appreciation that not all online information is correct or complete, and that their research may be incomplete if, for example, they do not consider a relevant issue.

Sophisticated clients need to know when to seek legal advice

The question asked earlier in this chapter, "When should you hire a lawyer?" is therefore more difficult to answer than it was in the past. As always, the businessperson must consider the time and the cost that will be incurred if a lawyer is consulted for assistance in making a particular business decision. But there is now another alternative—namely, the businessperson doing his own research and finding the relevant legal information himself.[4] If this approach is used, the time it takes to find the information must be considered. Furthermore, if the businessperson is unable to find the relevant information, or if he is unable to understand

---

4. There now appears to be a third alternative, at least in some jurisdictions. Ontario, for example, allows the licensing of paralegals. Like lawyers, they are regulated by the Law Society of Upper Canada. Licensed paralegals are authorized to represent clients in small claims court, the provincial offences court, the summary conviction court, and before various administrative tribunals. In 2012, the Law Society of British Columbia approved rule changes that allowed designated paralegals to perform certain duties under a lawyer's supervision. A two-year pilot project allowing designated paralegals to appear in specified family law proceedings was undertaken. See www.lawsociety.bc.ca/page.cfm?cid=2582&t=Paralegals.

the information he does find, then he should call his lawyer for advice. This is an important attribute of a prudent client—knowing when it is necessary to consult a lawyer.

One example that illustrates the above discussion involves small claims court litigation. Each of the provinces has set a monetary jurisdiction for small claims court. (The limit in Alberta, for example, is \$50 000.[5]) A sophisticated client will understand that any litigation involving an amount greater than the small claims court maximum limit will take place in a superior court and that a lawyer should therefore be retained.[6] A careful client, however, will also appreciate that while a case may involve an amount of money less than the monetary jurisdiction of small claims court, a lawyer may still need to be retained because of the complexity of the case.

Small claims court litigation

Another example showing how a sophisticated client will manage his legal affairs in an appropriate manner involves the collection of accounts receivable. Assume that all of the accounts involve amounts less than the monetary jurisdiction of small claims court. One form of contract is used for all credit sales. A perceptive client would realize that it is not necessary to retain a lawyer to secure judgment against customers who don't pay their accounts. The client, or one of his employees, can go to small claims court on behalf of the business. The client could hire a lawyer to train him or his employee with respect to how to conduct a trial in small claims court. The lawyer can be consulted if there are any complications on any particular collection file.

Collection of accounts receivable

There is one issue that always needs to be considered when someone is deciding whether to represent herself. If you break the law and harm someone else, there will likely be two different legal proceedings. First, there will be a criminal prosecution in which you will be charged by the government with committing a crime. If you are convicted, you will be punished and you will have a criminal record. Given this, it is wise to always retain legal counsel when you are facing criminal charges.

Best to retain counsel for criminal charges

If the person you harmed sues you, you may be liable for damages whether you were convicted of a crime or not. The civil litigation may take place in small claims court; in most of these cases you could represent yourself. If the litigation involves an amount of money greater than the monetary jurisdiction of small claims court, then you should hire a lawyer to represent you because the trial will take place in a superior court. Given the growing complexity of the law and the resulting specialization of lawyers, you may even have two lawyers: one to represent you in your criminal trial and the other to represent you in your civil trial.

May be liable even if not convicted of a crime

 REDUCING RISK 1.1

This textbook will help students become sophisticated clients so that they can better manage their legal affairs. Such management involves managing legal risk, which is therefore a primary focus of this textbook. This emphasis will be highlighted by the inclusion of "Reducing Risk" boxes throughout the textbook. These boxes will contain suggestions as to how sophisticated clients can manage legal risk.

Sophisticated clients understand that success ultimately depends on making good business decisions, and that good business decisions can be made only if they are based on appropriate information. One type of information required for good decision making is legal information. Sophisticated clients have the skills and the confidence to find basic legal information. Sophisticated clients will, however, understand that there will be situations in which it is necessary to retain a lawyer to obtain the required legal information. Sophisticated clients will not be afraid to request legal advice from a lawyer in such situations. They will then incorporate the legal advice received into their decision-making process, thereby reducing their legal risk.

---

5. *Provincial Court Civil Division Regulation*, Alta. Reg. 329/89.
6. This is subject to the abandonment of small amounts over the limit.

LO **4** # HOW TO FIND AN APPROPRIATE LAWYER

Assume that you are going to start a small business. You have decided that you need to retain a lawyer to help you. How do you find a good lawyer?

This question deals with an important issue, but it is not worded correctly. It would be better to ask, "How do you find an *appropriate* lawyer?" This emphasizes that a lawyer may be very knowledgeable and successful, but may not be appropriate for you. What, then, makes a lawyer "appropriate" for a particular client?

Make a list of possible lawyers . . .

The first step in finding an appropriate lawyer is to make a list of lawyers. There are many possible sources of lawyers' names. The first source most students think of is the telephone book, specifically the *Yellow Pages* and its online

. . . from telephone listings

companion. This source can be overwhelming. For example, on August 1, 2014, there were 965 lawyers and 953 corporate lawyers listed on YellowPages.ca for Edmonton! It is possible to tell where a lawyer's office is located, and perhaps what type of law the lawyer practises, but there is definitely not sufficient information in the *Yellow Pages* advertisements to help you decide whether a particular lawyer is appropriate for you. The same limitation applies to any advertisement, regardless of the medium used.

. . . or from friends or relatives

Another important source of lawyers' names involves getting referrals from friends or relatives. It is important that the referral be given by someone whose judgment you trust. Also, it is important that the referral be provided by someone who had the same type of legal problem that you are now facing. Being referred to a highly recommended real estate lawyer is not much help if you have just been charged for committing a serious crime. If you are considering setting up a small business, you want a referral from someone who operates a small business and is willing to recommend the lawyer who has provided legal advice to him in this context.

. . . or from a provincial law society

Another possible source of lawyers' names is the provincial **law society**. These organizations are self-governing bodies for lawyers. Their mandate usually involves regulating the legal profession in the public interest.[7]

. . . or from a lawyer referral service

Some of the provincial law societies (such as the Law Society of Alberta and the Law Society of Upper Canada) offer a lawyer referral service. These services provide the names and phone numbers of lawyers who practise in the relevant area of law. This service is offered by the law societies free of charge. The lawyers who are referred will provide up to 30 minutes of free consultation.

In British Columbia, the Lawyer Referral Service is operated by the BC Branch of the Canadian Bar Association (CBA).[8] The CBA is a professional organization that represents judges and lawyers. One of its purposes is to enhance the profession and the commercial interests of its members. The Lawyer Referral Service is offered by the BC Branch free of charge. The lawyer to whom you are referred will charge you $25 (plus tax) for up to 30 minutes of consultation.

Call for an initial consultation

Once you have the name of a lawyer near you who practises the type of law relevant to your situation, you should set up a meeting for an initial consultation. It is best to confirm the cost (if any) of this meeting when you are setting it up. You do not want any unpleasant surprises, such as receiving an unexpected bill from the lawyer after the meeting.

Mutual trust is key

The primary purpose of the initial consultation is for you to decide whether to retain the lawyer. At the same time, the lawyer will decide whether to agree to represent you. Both of these decisions should be made on the basis of trust, as the solicitor–client relationship will not function as it should unless there is mutual trust between the lawyer and the client. Unfortunately, there are no objective

---

[7] This discussion will refer to three of the provincial law societies: the Law Society of Alberta (www.lawsociety.ab.ca), the Law Society of British Columbia (www.lawsociety.bc.ca), and the Law Society of Upper Canada (www.lsuc.on.ca). All of the information in the chapter referring to these law societies may be accessed through these websites.

[8] Canadian Bar Association, "Lawyer Referral Service," http://cbabc.org/For-the-Public/Lawyer-Referral-Service.

criteria to measure "trust." Both you and the lawyer must use your instincts in deciding whether to form a solicitor–client relationship. Relevant factors may include whether you believe you can work with the lawyer; whether you feel comfortable discussing all relevant information, no matter how personal or sensitive, with her; and whether you want that particular lawyer to negotiate on your behalf or represent you in court. The lawyer will be concerned about whether the client will be honest and disclose all relevant information.

With respect to someone who is setting up a small business, the best approach to follow is to assume that the lawyer you choose to assist you in the start-up of the business will continue to represent you even after the business has been set up and commences operating. There are several advantages to maintaining an ongoing relationship with your lawyer. She will know and understand you and your business, which will enable her to provide you with legal advice more efficiently, reducing your legal costs. It will also enable her to customize the legal advice so that it will be even more useful to you when you are making your decisions. And because you are her client, she will give you and your requests for legal advice priority. This can be very important when you are facing matters that must be dealt with urgently. Finally, the more you deal with your lawyer, the more comfortable you will become with her, which means that you will be more likely to call her when you require legal advice.

Advantages of an ongoing relationship

HOW LAWYERS BILL THEIR CLIENTS

LO ⑤

One of the reasons people don't retain lawyers even when they clearly require legal advice is that they are afraid of the cost. While the provision of legal services is not cheap, an understanding of how lawyers bill their clients will help someone determine whether to retain a lawyer. In this regard, the issue of fees should be discussed during the initial consultation with the lawyer.

Discuss fees with the lawyer

Every legal problem is unique. Also, there are many factors a lawyer will consider when calculating the fee to charge a client. It is therefore important that the client understand from the beginning exactly how the lawyer will bill him for providing assistance with his particular problem. It is prudent to confirm this understanding in a fee agreement with the lawyer.

Have a fee agreement with the lawyer

Each of the provincial law societies provides online information on lawyers' fees.[9] It appears that there are three main ways that lawyers calculate their fees. First, the lawyer may charge a **fixed fee** for the work required, regardless of the time involved. This method of billing is often used for specific tasks, such as preparing a will, purchasing a house, or incorporating a business.

Lawyer may bill on basis of a fixed fee . . .

Second, the lawyer may bill the client for all of the time she spends working on his file using her hourly rate. Hourly rates vary with the number of years that the lawyer has been practising law. A senior lawyer may have a higher hourly rate than a junior lawyer, but the experience of the senior lawyer may enable her to complete the required legal work more efficiently, perhaps resulting in a fee lower than that charged by the relatively inefficient junior lawyer, who will be learning as she does the work.

. . . or on basis of time spent and hourly rate

Third, the lawyer may receive a percentage of the amount the client collects, either through a settlement or a court judgment. If the client does not collect anything, then the lawyer does not receive anything. This is a **contingency fee** agreement, which is often appropriate in personal injury claims or product liability cases when the client does not have any funds to pay the lawyer at the beginning of the case. The provincial law societies may restrict the use of contingency fee agreements or set a maximum contingency fee for certain types of cases. The Law Society of

. . . or as a contingency fee

---

9. See the Law Society of Alberta, *supra* note 7 at www.lawsociety.ab.ca/public/public_fees.aspx; the Law Society of British Columbia, *supra* note 7 at www.lawsociety.bc.ca/page.cfm?cid=141&t=Common-billing-practices; and the Law Society of Upper Canada, *supra* note 7 at www.lsuc.on.ca/with.aspx?id=2147490124.

British Columbia, for example, does not permit contingency fee agreements for family cases involving child custody or access. The maximum contingency fee allowed in claims for personal injury or wrongful death resulting from a motor vehicle accident is one-third of the amount received; for all other personal injury or wrongful death cases the limit is 40 percent of the amount received.[10]

Client responsible for disbursements

The client is also responsible for paying the out-of-pocket costs incurred by the lawyer on the client's behalf. These costs are called **disbursements**. Disbursements usually include costs such as the court fees for filing documents, long-distance telephone charges, courier charges, the fee charged by an expert for testifying or preparing a report, and photocopying costs.

A retainer is a deposit

If a client decides to hire a lawyer, and the lawyer agrees to represent the client, the lawyer will usually request that a **retainer** be paid before she commences work on the matter. A retainer works as a deposit. The amount paid by the client is deposited into a trust account, to the credit of the client. When the lawyer bills the client, the amount owed will be paid from the retainer. The lawyer may require the client to "top up" the retainer as funds are withdrawn from the trust account.

LO ⑥ LEGAL AID

Legal aid may be available . . .

You may be eligible for **legal aid** if you have a legal problem and you can't afford a lawyer. The provision of legal aid varies from province to province. If you believe that you are eligible for legal aid, it is best to check the website of the organization in your province that administers the legal aid program.[11]

In British Columbia, the Legal Services Society (LSS), an independent, non-profit organization, provides legal aid for people with low incomes.[12] LSS may pay for a lawyer if the client has a legal problem involving serious family, child protection, or criminal law issues, or for some immigration, mental health, and prison law issues. To receive legal aid, a client must meet certain financial guidelines involving household income and assets. If the client doesn't qualify for legal representation but meets other financial guidelines involving household income, he may be eligible to receive legal advice. Anyone in British Columbia can obtain legal information provided through a toll-free telephone service, LSS publications, a family law website, and links to other sources identified as reliable.

. . . but usually not for owners of a small business

It must be emphasized that not everyone qualifies for legal aid, and even some of those who do qualify may have to pay some of the legal costs incurred. Furthermore, if you collect money as a result of a settlement or judgment, you will probably have to repay some or all of the benefits you received from legal aid. Finally, not all types of cases are covered by legal aid. Legal Aid Alberta, for example, states that legal aid will be provided most often for serious criminal charges, charges laid under the *Youth Criminal Justice Act*, family law, child welfare, civil law (e.g., employment, tenant, income support), and immigration issues (e.g., refugee claims).[13] It is clear that the owner of a small business will usually not be able to receive legal aid with respect to the legal issues involving the business.

LO ⑦ HOW TO COMPLAIN ABOUT YOUR LAWYER

Law societies deal with complaints about lawyers

As indicated above, the provincial law societies are self-governing bodies for lawyers. Their mandate involves regulating the legal profession. Part of this regulation involves dealing with complaints regarding a lawyer's conduct.

---

10. Ibid.

11. In Alberta, legal aid is administered by Legal Aid Alberta, www.legalaid.ab.ca. In Ontario, legal aid is administered by Legal Aid Ontario, www.legalaid.on.ca/en.

12. Legal Services Society, www.lss.bc.ca.

13. *Supra* note 11, at www.legalaid.ab.ca/help/eligibility/Pages/default.aspx.

In general, the law societies do not assist clients with complaints about the fees being charged by their lawyers. In such cases, the client is usually advised to first discuss her concern about the fee with her lawyer. Some law societies offer a fee mediation service.[14] Participation in such a program is voluntary. These programs usually involve a neutral mediator who tries to facilitate a mutually acceptable resolution of the dispute.

Fee mediation may be available

If the client cannot resolve the fee dispute directly with the lawyer, and if any mediation is unsuccessful, then the client can have her lawyer's bill reviewed by a court official. In Alberta, for example, the review is conducted by a review officer of the Court of Queen's Bench.[15] In Ontario, the review is conducted by an assessment officer of the Superior Court of Justice.[16] Court officials, such as review officers and assessment officers, have the power to decide that the lawyer's bill is fair and does not need to be changed. Alternatively, they can decide that the bill is too high and reduce it accordingly.

Lawyer's bill can be reviewed by a court official

For complaints regarding a lawyer's conduct other than fee disputes, each of the law societies has a complaint resolution process.[17] This process usually begins with an attempt at mediating the dispute between the client and the lawyer. If mediation fails and the law society decides that the complaint is valid, then there will usually be a more formal investigation. This could result in a hearing before a panel. This hearing will involve the testimony of witnesses, the entering of other evidence, and submissions by the legal counsel for the lawyer and for the law society. If the panel finds the lawyer guilty of misconduct, the penalty could include a reprimand, fine, suspension, disbarment (termination of membership in the law society), and costs of the hearing.

Complaints may be investigated and there may be a hearing

It is important to note that the complaint resolution process does not result in compensation being paid to the client who made the complaint. If the client believes that he has suffered a financial loss because of his lawyer's misconduct (negligent or deliberate), it is necessary for the client to take other steps, such as commencing legal action against the lawyer. (All lawyers are required to purchase professional liability insurance to protect them if they are found liable for negligence or deliberate misconduct.) This may require the client to seek legal advice from another lawyer. Clients should not procrastinate with respect to these matters since limitation periods may exist, meaning that they may not be able to pursue their claims after a certain period of time.

Complainant does not receive compensation

ETHICS

LO **8**

Ethics of Lawyers

While understanding how to complain about a lawyer is important, it is equally important to know when to complain about a lawyer. In this regard, the website for the Law Society of British Columbia contains the following statement:

> High ethical standards are a hallmark of the legal profession—and a reason that people place their confidence and trust in lawyers. The Law Society sets standards of professional responsibility for B.C. lawyers and articled students and upholds those standards through a complaints and discipline process.[18]

---

14. One that does is the Law Society of British Columbia, *supra* note 7 at www.lawsociety.bc.ca/page.cfm?cid=143&t=Disputes-involving-fees.

15. See James Christensen and Joe Morin, "Review of a Lawyer's Charges," November 29, 2010, https://albertacourts.ca/docs/default-source/default-document-library/review-of-a-lawyer's-bill-sample-forms-(november-2010).pdf?sfvrsn=0.

16. See the Law Society of Upper Canada, *supra* note 7 at www.lsuc.on.ca/with.aspx?id=640.

17. See the Law Society of Alberta, *supra* note 7 at www.lawsociety.ab.ca/lawyer_regulation/complaints.aspx, the Law Society of British Columbia, *supra* note 7 at www.lawsociety.bc.ca/page.cfm?cid=25&t=Complaints, and the Law Society of Upper Canada, *supra* note 7 at www.lsuc.on.ca/with.aspx?id=644.

18. See the Law Society of British Columbia, *supra* note 7 at www.lawsociety.bc.ca/page.cfm?cid=42&t=Complaints-and-Discipline. Used by the permission of The Law Society Of British Columbia.

Lawyers have ethical obligations

All of the provincial law societies have mandates to govern the conduct of lawyers in the public interest. The professional and ethical obligations of lawyers are set out in rules of professional conduct.[19] Lawyers who fail to satisfy these obligations will be subject to the complaint resolution process, as discussed in the previous section. As the rules of professional conduct consistently emphasize the need for ethical behaviour, it is important to know what is meant by **ethics** and ethical behaviour.

Difference between law and ethics

Law provides a set of rules for behaviour. If these rules are not complied with, the person breaking the rules will be punished. Law therefore tells us what we must do. Ethics, on the other hand, tells us what we should do. When a person breaks the law, he has also acted unethically. However, if a person acts unethically, he may not have broken the law. Ethical behaviour therefore implies integrity, honesty, and professionalism. This is illustrated by a dictionary definition of "ethics" as "rules of behavior based on ideas about what is morally good and bad."[20] Ethics thus relates to issues of right and wrong; these depend on a person's conscience, rather than on what the law says.

Some lawyers don't satisfy professional and ethical standards

Referring back to the lawyer joke at the beginning of this chapter, and how many people tell lawyer jokes to deride lawyers, it seems that many people today do not trust or have confidence in lawyers because members of the legal profession do not appear to meet the standards of professional responsibility set by their governing bodies. A review of the website for the Law Society of Alberta, for example, shows that between January 1, 2014, and June 16, 2014, there were seven suspensions and three disbarments of Alberta lawyers.[21] The reasons for these penalties included the following:

- disclosing confidential information
- assisting a client in an improper purpose
- lying to, misleading, and failing to provide thorough and timely service to a client
- engaging in a business transaction with a client who did not have independent legal representation
- acting for more than one party in a potential conflict situation where all parties had not consented
- failing to serve and protect the interests of clients
- failing to be candid with clients
- misappropriating trust funds
- failing to advance a client's matter
- failing to transfer a client's file to the successor lawyer
- breaching a trust condition
- failing to follow the trust accounting rules
- breaching a court order
- fabricating a court order
- failing to properly supervise support staff
- failing to respond to counsel on a timely basis

---

[19] See the Law Society of Alberta, *supra* note 7 at www.lawsociety.ab.ca/lawyers/regulations/code.aspx; the Law Society of British Columbia, *supra* note 7 at www.lawsociety.bc.ca/page.cfm?cid=2578&t=Code-of-Professional-Conduct-for-British-Columbia; and the Law Society of Upper Canada, *supra* note 7 at www.lsuc.on.ca/with.aspx?id=671.

[20] By permission. From *Merriam-Webster's Collegiate® Dictionary, 11th Edition* © 2015 by Merriam-Webster, Inc. (www.Merriam-Webster.com).

[21] See the Law Society of Alberta, *supra* note 7 at www.lawsociety.ab.ca/lawyer_regulation/hearings_outcomes/notices.aspx.

- unwittingly engaging in conduct that enabled others to achieve an improper purpose
- demonstrating lack of candour in dealings with others
- failing to be candid with the law society

The law society is required to refer these cases to the minister of justice and the attorney general whenever there are reasonable and probable grounds to believe that a lawyer has committed a criminal offence.

While the vast majority of lawyers are completely honest and ethical, it only takes a few well-publicized cases involving lawyers being penalized for unethical behaviour to taint the reputation of the entire profession. The case involving Martin Wirick is a good example. Wirick was a Vancouver lawyer who, along with one of his clients, defrauded clients and lenders of close to $40 million. This amount was covered by the lawyers in British Columbia through their Special Compensation Fund. Wirick was disbarred in December 2002, and criminal charges were laid against him and his client in August 2008; Wirick pleaded guilty to fraud and was sentenced to seven years in prison.[22] Needless to say, this case has damaged the image of lawyers even though the Law Society of British Columbia and its members took responsibility for Wirick's actions.[23]

For sophisticated clients, there are a few important points to keep in mind. First, lawyers operate under strict rules governing their professional and ethical obligations. You can therefore place your confidence and trust in your lawyer. But, second, there are some lawyers who unfortunately do not meet the standards of the profession. It is necessary therefore to understand the types of behaviour that are unacceptable and the steps that can be taken if your lawyer violates your trust and confidence by breaching the professional standards. Third, as is the case with all professionals it is necessary to be vigilant with respect to your lawyer and, if he breaks the rules he should be following, to take whatever action is appropriate on a timely basis.

Clients should watch their lawyers and take action when appropriate

Ethics of Clients

The discussion on the ethical behaviour of lawyers emphasized the need for lawyers to comply with the relevant rules of professional conduct. Unfortunately, there is not an equivalent set of rules for businesspeople. That is, there is not a "Code of Professional Conduct" for businesspeople in Canada, or even in any of the provinces.

No code of conduct for businesspeople

There have been many recent cases involving influential and powerful people being charged with and in some cases convicted of crimes relating to the ownership and operation of businesses. The situations involving Martha Stewart[24] and Conrad Black[25] are two well-known examples. There have been several other recent high-profile cases involving individuals who have been entangled in questionable situations:

Many people are not making good ethical choices

- Rob Ford, the mayor of Toronto, had his powers restricted by Toronto City Council after his much-publicized behaviour that included him admitting to having smoked crack cocaine and to having purchased illegal drugs while serving as mayor.[26]

---

22. "Disbarred Vancouver Lawyer Gets 7-Year Jail Sentence for Fraud," June 9, 2009, *CBC News*, www.cbc.ca/news/canada/british-columbia/story/2009/06/09/bc-martin-wirick-sentencing.html.

23. See the Law Society of British Columbia, *supra* note 7 at www.lawsociety.bc.ca/page.cfm?cid=486&t=What-Martin-Wirick-left-in-his-wake.

24. For a timeline of the events that took place after Martha Stewart sold her shares in ImClone Inc. in 2001, see "Timeline," *CBC News*, January 6, 2006, www.cbc.ca/news2/background/stewart_martha/timeline.html.

25. For a timeline of the events that led to Conrad Black going to prison, see "Conrad Black through the Years," *CBC News*, July 5, 2010, www.cbc.ca/news/canada/conrad-black-through-the-years-1.868133.

26. "Rob Ford Promises 'Outright War' as Powers Further Restricted," *CBC News*, November 18, 2013, www.cbc.ca/news/canada/toronto/rob-ford-promises-outright-war-as-powers-further-restricted-1.2430150.

- The Canadian Senate suspended three senators (Patrick Brazeau, Mike Duffy, and Pamela Wallin) for having claimed inappropriate expenses. It was the first time a senator had been suspended over expenses without being convicted of a criminal offence.[27]

- One of the suspended senators, Mike Duffy, was subsequently charged by the RCMP with 31 charges relating to Senate expenses, the awarding of consulting contracts, and the acceptance of a payment from the prime minister's former chief of staff.[28]

- The mayor of Detroit was sentenced to four months in jail and five years of probation after pleading guilty to obstruction of justice charges. He denied having an affair with his aide but was sentenced after he admitted that he had lied. He was also sentenced to a year in jail for violating his probation. He was subsequently convicted of corruption charges, including racketeering conspiracy, and sentenced to 28 years in prison.[29]

- The Dean of the Faculty of Medicine and Dentistry at the University of Alberta resigned after apologizing for plagiarizing his convocation speech.[30]

- Several Ontario police officers were caught cheating on exams that were part of the promotion process.[31]

- A Calgary stockbroker was fired for soliciting a prostitute and taking her back to his office after hours.[32]

- Bernard Madoff pleaded guilty to 11 charges (including securities, wire, and mail fraud; money laundering; and perjury) with respect to a Ponzi scheme (in which existing investors were paid with the money of new investors) involving as much as $65 billion. He was sentenced to 150 years in jail.[33]

- The Chinese government ordered the execution of the director of the State Food and Drug Administration for approving untested medicine in exchange for cash.[34]

The increasing occurrence of cases such as these caused Gwyn Morgan, former CEO of EnCana Corp., to cite Transparency International's 2005 Corruption Perceptions Index, which showed that Canada ranked fourteenth among countries perceived as free of corruption:[35]

Businesspeople should act ethically

There can be nothing more crucial to the integrity and prosperity of our country than to protect Canada from the proliferation and acceptance of

---

27. Leslie MacKinnon, "Senate Votes to Suspend Brazeau, Duffy, Wallin," *CBC News*, November 5, 2013, www.cbc.ca/news/politics/senate-votes-to-suspend-brazeau-duffy-wallin-1.2415815. The auditor general completed a comprehensive review of Senate spending in June 2015. He indicated that he was "struck by the overall lack of transparency and accountability" exercised by the Senate and by some individual senators. See Chloe Fedio, "Auditor General Cites Lack of Oversight for Senate Spending Mess," *CBC News*, June 9, 2015, www.cbc.ca/news/politics/auditor-general-cites-lack-of-oversight-for-senate-spending-mess-1.3106022.

28. "Mike Duffy Faces 31 Charges Including Bribery, Fraud, Breach of Trust," *CBC News*, July 17, 2014, www.cbc.ca/news/politics/mike-duffy-faces-31-charges-including-bribery-fraud-breach-of-trust-1.2709500.

29. "Ex-Detroit Mayor Leaves Prison," *CBC News*, September 4, 2008, www.cbc.ca/news/canada/windsor/story/2011/08/02/wdr-kwame-kilpatrick-leaves-prison.html; "Ex-Detroit Mayor Kwame Kilpatrick Gets 28 Years for Corruption," *CBC News*, October 10, 2013, www.cbc.ca/news/world/ex-detroit-mayor-kwame-kilpatrick-gets-28-years-for-corruption-1.1958983.

30. "Alberta Medical Dean Accused of Plagiarism Resigns," *CBC News*, June 17, 2011, www.cbc.ca/news/canada/edmonton/story/2011/06/17/edmonton-dean-medicine-resigns.html.

31. Dave Seglins, "Niagara Police Officers Caught Cheating on Exam," *CBC News*, June 13, 2011, www.cbc.ca/news/canada/story/2011/06/13/niagara-police-test.html.

32. "Disgraced Banker Loses Fight with Former Employer," *CBC News*, June 6, 2006, www.cbc.ca/news/canada/edmonton/story/2006/06/06/ca-bankerloses-20060606.html.

33. "Will Society Forgive Bernie Madoff?" *CBC News*, October 27, 2011, www.cbc.ca/newsblogs/yourcommunity/2011/10/will-society-forgive-bernie-madoff.html.

34. "China Executes Former FDA Chief amid Product Safety Crisis," *CBC News*, July 10, 2007, www.cbc.ca/world/story/2007/07/10/china-tainted-products.html.

35. See Transparency International, "Corruption Perceptions Index, 2005," www.transparency.org/research/cpi/cpi_2005/0.

corruption. . . . When it comes to business and government, there is an especially heavy responsibility that comes with leadership. . . . It's up to Canadian business leaders to act as role models with strong ethical values. . . . If you don't have a moral compass, haven't got the discipline to steer in a direction of strong values, it doesn't matter whether you're rich or poor, you're still going to act unethically.[36]

CASE SUMMARY 1.2

Is Plagiarism by a Judge Acceptable? *Cojocaru v. British Columbia Women's Hospital and Health Centre*[37]

A baby and his mother sued a hospital, some of its nurses, and some of its doctors for negligence relating to brain damage suffered by the baby during his birth. The trial judge awarded $4 million damages to the plaintiffs. The reasons for his decision included large portions of the submissions of the plaintiffs' lawyer. The Court of Appeal held that the decision should be set aside because of the extensive copying.

The Supreme Court of Canada stated that there is a presumption of the integrity and impartiality of judges. This presumption must be rebutted by a party seeking to set aside a judicial decision because the judge included the material of others in his reasons for decision. The issue that must be addressed is whether the evidence shows that a reasonable person would conclude that the judge did not perform his duty to review and consider the evidence with an open mind. The key is whether the reasons reflect the judge's thinking. If the copying is such that a reasonable person would conclude that the judge did not address his mind to the evidence and issues, and therefore did not render an impartial, independent decision, then the judge's decision should be set aside.

In this case, the Court ruled that, while it would have been preferable for the trial judge to have used his own words in his reasons, the presumption was not rebutted. The trial judge had rejected some of the plaintiffs' key submissions, showing that he had addressed his mind to the issues on which he had to rule.

DISCUSSION QUESTIONS

Do you agree that there should be a presumption of judicial integrity and impartiality? Explain your reasons. If you don't agree, what is the appropriate presumption?

Code of Business Conduct

For a sophisticated client who is starting a business, the best approach would appear to be to make a commitment to ethical behaviour. This would involve being a role model for employees, showing them by example the type of behaviour that is expected of all employees. As British Columbia lawyer Alison Dempsey has said:

Commitment to ethical behaviour

> A more proactive approach for public sector, private, and non-profit organizations is to foster internal cultures that make ethical values, individual and collective accountability, integrity, and trust explicit priorities. . . . As demonstrated by the transgressions that have shaken the corporate world and these lessons being learned with the public sector, an organization's continued good reputation and respectability depends on building and maintaining a culture founded on ethical values, integrity, and trust.[38]

[36.] "Corruption Threatens Our Values, EnCana Exec Says," *Business Edge News Magazine,* March 1, 2006, www.businessedge.ca/archives/article.cfm/corruption-threatens-our-values-encana-exec-says-12066. Used by the permission of Business Edge News Magazine.

[37.] [2013] 2 SCR 357, 2013 SCC 30 (CanLII).

[38.] Alison L. Dempsey, "Build an Ethical Organizational Culture before the Whistle Blows," *LawNow* (February/March 2005): 9 at 10.

Prepare a code of conduct for business and its employees . . .

A tangible step that can be taken in this regard is to prepare and communicate to employees a statement of values and principles of ethical conduct. Such statements are usually referred to as a "Code of Conduct" or a "Code of Ethics." In a recent article, Julie Walsh provides an overview of codes of conduct and ways to make them effective:[39]

> A **code of business conduct** is a formal statement adopted by a company that sets out its values and standard of business practices. It essentially codifies a company's organizational values and establishes procedural norms and standards of expected behaviour for all employees, officers, and directors involved with that particular company. There is no prescribed format—it can be a short mission statement or a sophisticated declaration of business practices with articulated values, standards, and compliance required as a term of employment.

. . . to ensure ethical behaviour by the employees

Even a sophisticated client starting a small business can follow this approach. In fact, this is probably the best way to ensure the long-term adoption of ethical behaviour by employees of the business. Organizations that have top management who practise ethical behaviour are those that are most likely to experience compliance with a code of ethics.

Ethical values and principles

Walsh goes on to suggest that at least the following issues (taken from a policy proposed by the Canadian Securities Administrators) should be included in a code of ethics:[40]

- conflicts of interest
- protection and proper use of corporate assets and opportunities
- confidentiality of corporate information
- fair dealing with the issuer's security holders, customers, suppliers, competitors, and employees
- compliance with laws, rules, and regulations
- the reporting of any illegal or unethical behaviour

The remaining question is to determine the content of the code of ethics. What should the code say, for example, about the proper use of corporate assets and opportunities? While these sorts of decisions are very personal, the Josephson Institute of Ethics identified the six core values and supporting ethical principles shown in Table 1.1.[41]

Table 1.1   Core Values and Ethical Principles

Core Ethical Values	Supporting Ethical Principle
Trustworthiness	truthfulness, sincerity, candour, integrity, promise keeping, loyalty, honesty
Respect	respect, autonomy, courtesy, self-determination
Responsibility	responsibility, diligence, continuous improvement, self-restraint
Fairness	justice, fairness, impartiality, equity
Caring	caring, kindness, compassion
Citizenship	citizenship, philanthropy, voting

[39.] Julie Walsh, "Setting the Tone at the Top," *LawNow* (February/March 2005): 16 at 16.

[40.] Ibid. at 17.

[41.] Keith Seel, "Values, Ethics and Civil Society," *LawNow* (April/May 2005): 9 at 9. Used by the permission of LawNow Magazine.

These core values are fundamental to the relationships that individuals have with the people they come into contact with. It is apparent that they could form the basis of a code of conduct for a small business. It would therefore appear that a sophisticated client who starts a small business could enhance the success of the business by personally adopting these core values and then incorporating them into a code of conduct for the business.

Incorporate core values into code of conduct

Social Responsibility

There has been an increasing awareness in recent years of the need for and the benefits of socially responsible behaviour, by both individuals and organizations. The International Organization of Standardization has prepared a voluntary standard on this matter, "ISO 26000:2010, Guidance on social responsibility."[42] This is an attempt to help organizations operate in a socially responsible manner and to facilitate sustainable development. ISO 26000 addresses seven core subjects of social responsibility: organizational governance, human rights, labour practices, the environment, fair operating practices, consumer issues, and community involvement and development.

Industry Canada also provides a number of resources on social responsibility for Canadian businesses.[43] Canadian Business for Social Responsibility (CBSR), a non-profit organization, has prepared a document entitled "CSR Governance Guidelines," which outlines a best practice approach for boards of directors of corporations.[44] The definition of **corporate social responsibility** in this document is "a company's environmental, social and economic performance and the impacts of the company on its internal and external sytakeholders."[45]

In addition to a code of conduct, a sophisticated client starting a small business may want to adopt the best practice approach developed by the CBSR. Doing so would demonstrate a commitment to social responsibility. One aspect of this is to understand that transparency about why you are engaging in transactions relating to social responsibility will lead to ethically better outcomes.[46] Admitting, for example, that the donation of money to an organization is not just to "do good" for the organization and its community, but also to improve the organization's image, will reduce community mistrust and disillusionment about the organization. This will result in a better relationship with the community.

MyBusLawLab Be sure to visit the MyBusLawLab that accompanies this book to find practice quizzes, province-specific content, simulations and much more!

42. International Organization for Standardization, "Discovering ISO 26000," 2014, www.iso.org/iso/discovering_iso_26000.pdf.

43. See Industry Canada, "Corporate Social Responsibility," www.ic.gc.ca/eic/site/csr-rse.nsf/eng/home.

44. CBSR, "CSR Governance Guidelines," "Corporate Social Responsibility: An Implementation Guide for Canadian Business. Copyright© 2011 by Industry Canada. Reproduced with the permission of the Minister of Industry." www.cbsr.ca/sites/default/files/file/CBSR%20CSR%20Governance%20Guidelines_29Jun_10(2).pdf.

45. Ibid. at 2.

46. This point was made by Janet Keeping in "Ethics of Corporate Social Responsibility," *LawNow* (July/August 2012): 13.

SUMMARY

Becoming a sophisticated client
- Knowledgeable, up to date, and confident
- Understands the role of lawyer and of client

The role of the lawyer
- Client is decision maker
- Lawyer is an expert who provides legal advice
- Information provided to lawyer must be kept confidential

Should I hire a lawyer?
- Small businesses face many issues on which a lawyer can advise
- Lawyer can help client make better business decisions
- Client makes many business decisions without consulting a lawyer (time, cost)
- Sophisticated client can find relevant legal information
- Sophisticated client knows when to retain a lawyer (e.g., criminal law)

How to find an appropriate lawyer
- Many sources of lawyers' names
- Initial consultation
- Importance of mutual trust

How lawyers bill their clients
- Fixed fee
- Time spent and hourly rate
- Contingency fee
- Disbursements must be reimbursed by client
- Retainer is a deposit

Legal aid
- Available for certain types of legal problems
- Client eligible if meets financial requirements
- Even if client qualifies for legal aid, may have to pay some or all of legal costs
- Usually not available to owners of small businesses

How to complain about your lawyer
- Mediation may be available to resolve fee disputes
- Lawyer's bill can be reviewed by a court official
- Other complaints made to law society
- Investigation may be followed by a hearing
- Penalties range from reprimand to disbarment
- Process does not provide compensation to the client

Ethics
- Rules of professional conduct contain professional and ethical obligations of lawyers
- If rules broken, lawyer may be penalized
- There are many recent cases involving legal/ethical situations
- Sophisticated client will make a commitment to ethical behaviour
- May prepare a code of conduct for business
- Should be based on ethical values and principles
- May also adopt a best practice approach to social responsibility

QUESTIONS FOR REVIEW

1. Explain the meaning of "sophisticated client."

2. Why should the owner of a small business have a lawyer on "the team"?

3. Distinguish the role of the client from the role of the lawyer.

4. "The elimination of 'solicitor–client privilege' would significantly undermine the integrity of the Canadian legal system." True or false? Explain your answer.

5. What are some examples of the decisions that owners of small businesses make? What role can a lawyer play with respect to making these decisions?

6. What role has the computer played with respect to the solicitor–client relationship?

7. "It is a good idea to hire a lawyer when you have been charged with a crime." True or false? Explain your answer.

8. When you are trying to find a lawyer to help you, what are some sources of lawyers' names?

9. What is the primary purpose of an initial consultation with a lawyer?

10. Briefly explain three ways lawyers bill their clients. Which of the three is most commonly used?

11. "Legal aid is available to anybody with a legal problem." True or false? Explain your answer.

12. What can a client do if she is unhappy with the bill she received from her lawyer?

13. "Should a client lose money because of the carelessness of his lawyer, he will be compensated for his losses if he makes a complaint to the law society." True or false? Explain your answer.

14. When will a lawyer be disbarred?

15. "When a person acts unethically, she will also have broken the law." True or false? Explain your answer.

16. What is a code of business conduct? Should such a code be used by a small business?

17. What is "corporate social responsibility"? What is a benefit of being transparent about the reasons why you are engaging in socially responsible behaviour?

CASES AND DISCUSSION QUESTIONS

1. *Ontario (Public Safety and Security) v. Criminal Lawyers' Association*, [2010] 1 SCR 815, 2010 SCC 23 (CanLII)

A stay of proceedings was ordered by the trial judge because of abusive conduct by government officials. The Ontario Provincial Police investigated the local police and the Crown attorney. It exonerated them of misconduct but did not give reasons for its decision. The Criminal Lawyers' Association (CLA) made a request under the provincial *Freedom of Information and Protection of Privacy Act* for disclosure of the records relevant to the investigation. Some of these documents contained legal advice. The legislation exempts documents subject to solicitor–client privilege from disclosure. The legislation provided for a review to determine whether a compelling public interest in disclosure outweighs the reason from the exemption, but this review did not apply to the solicitor–client exemption. The CLA claimed that its right to freedom of expression under the Canadian *Charter of Rights and Freedoms* was breached because the solicitor–client privilege was not subject to the compelling public interest in disclosure.

The Court of Appeal agreed with this position. This decision was appealed to the Supreme Court of Canada.

Should the Supreme Court reverse the decision of the Court of Appeal? Does s. 2(b) of the *Charter* guarantee access to all government documents? Should documents protected by solicitor–client privilege ever be disclosed because of the public interest?

2. *Wayne v. Wayne*, 2012 ABQB 763 (CanLII)

A woman suffering from dementia sold her house for less than half its assessed value. Her son was subsequently appointed trustee of her estate. He asked for an order for production of the law firm's estate file relating to his mother, as he had concerns regarding her mental capacity at the time of the real estate transaction. The relevant legislation provided that a trustee was entitled to access collateral or other personal information about the adult he was representing "that was relevant to the exercise of the authority and the carrying out of the duties and responsibilities of the trustee." The legislation did not expressly allow for the waiving of the solicitor–client privilege of a represented adult.

Should the Court grant access to the mother's estate file of the law firm? If it should, what is the justification for piercing the solicitor–client privilege?

3. *University of Alberta v. Chang*, 2012 ABCA 324 (CanLII)

Two actions were dismissed because of the delay in prosecution of the actions. The decision was appealed on the ground that the chambers judge failed to engage in a meaningful analysis of the issues and failed to provide reasons that disclosed his interpretation. The reasons for judgment included nothing but paragraphs that had been copied and pasted from the briefs filed by the parties' lawyers. There was no independent authorship; even spelling mistakes in the briefs were included in the reasons. Also, the reasons included the wording "it is submitted that," which is appropriate for a party's brief but not a judicial analysis. The headings in the reasons were numbered incorrectly and were out of order. A rule was quoted twice, apparently because the judge copied from the briefs of two of the parties.

Should the Court of Appeal overturn the decision of the chambers judge and order a new trial? What presumption must be rebutted before an appellate court can overturn a decision of a lower court?

Introduction to the Legal System

2
Chapter

LEARNING OBJECTIVES

1. Define "law" and identify the types of law that exist in Canada
2. Distinguish between the civil law and common law legal systems found in Canada
3. Identify the sources of Canadian law
4. Isolate the three elements of Canada's Constitution
5. Explain how legislative power is divided in Canada
6. Detail how legislation is created in the parliamentary system
7. Describe the rights and freedoms protected by the *Charter of Rights and Freedoms*
8. List the areas and grounds upon which human rights legislation prohibits discrimination

WHAT IS LAW?

Most of us recognize the rules and regulations that are considered law and understand that law plays an important role in ordering society, but knowing that does not make it easy to come up with a satisfactory, all-inclusive definition of "law." Philosophers have been trying for centuries to determine just what **law** means, and their theories have profoundly affected the development of our legal system. Law has been defined in moral terms, where only good rules are considered law (natural law theorists). Others have defined law by looking at its source, stipulating that only the rules enacted by those with authority to do so qualify as law (*legal positivists*). And some have defined law in practical terms, suggesting that only those rules that the courts are willing to enforce qualify as law (*legal realists*). Legal positivism helped shape the concept of law in Canada, where **parliamentary supremacy** requires that we look to the enactments of the federal Parliament or provincial legislatures as the primary source of law. In the United States, however, a more pragmatic approach to law based on legal realism has been adopted. It allows judges to factor in current social and economic realities when they make their decisions.

For our purposes, the following simplified definition is helpful, if we remember that it is not universally applicable. **Law is the body of rules made by government that can be enforced by the courts or by other government agencies**. In our daily activities, we are exposed to many rules that do not qualify as law. Courtesy demands that we do not interrupt when someone is speaking. Social convention determines that it is inappropriate to enter a restaurant shirtless or shoeless. Universities and colleges often establish rules of conduct for their students and faculty. These rules do not fall into our definition of law because the courts do not enforce them. But when there is a disagreement over who is responsible for an accident, a question as to whether a crime has been committed, or a difference of opinion about the terms

LO **1**

There is no wholly satisfactory definition of law

Definition

of a contract or a will, the participants may find themselves before a judge. Rules that can be enforced by the courts govern these situations; thus, they are laws within the definition presented here.

A person dealing with government agencies, such as labour relations boards, workers' compensation boards, or city and municipal councils, must recognize that these bodies are also able to render decisions in matters that come before them. The rules enforced by these bodies are also laws within this definition. The unique problems associated with government agencies and regulatory bodies will be discussed in Chapter 3 in the section entitled "Dealing with Regulatory Bodies."

While the definition of law as enforceable rules has practical value, it does not suggest what is just or moral. We must not assume that so long as we obey the law we are acting morally. As discussed in Chapter 1, legal compliance and ethical behaviour are two different things, and people must decide for themselves what standard they will adhere to. Many choose to live by a personal code of conduct demanding adherence to more stringent rules than those set out in the law, while others disregard even these basic requirements. Some think that moral values have no place in the business world, but in fact the opposite is true. As was pointed out in Chapter 1, there is now an expectation of high ethical standards in business activities, and it is hoped that those who study the law as it relates to business will appreciate and adhere to those higher standards. We must at least understand that whether we are motivated by divine law, conscience, moral indifference, or avarice, serious consequences may follow from non-compliance with the body of rules we call law.

Categories of Law

Law consists of rules with different but intersecting functions. The primary categories are substantive and procedural laws. **Substantive law** establishes not only the rights an individual has in society, but also the limits on his or her conduct. The rights to travel, to vote, and to own property are guaranteed by substantive law. Prohibitions against theft and murder as well as other actions that harm our neighbours are also examples of substantive law. **Procedural law** determines how the substantive laws will be enforced. The rules governing arrest, investigation, and pre-trial and court processes in both criminal and civil cases are examples.

Law can also be distinguished by its public or private function. **Public law** includes constitutional law, which determines how the country is governed and the laws that affect individuals' relationships with government—such as criminal law and the regulations created by government agencies. **Private law** involves the rules that govern our personal, social, and business relations, which are enforced when one person sues another in a private or civil action. Knowing the law and how it functions allows us to structure our lives as productive and accepted members of the community and to predict the consequences of our conduct. Business students study law because it defines the environment of rules within which business functions. In order to play the game, we must know the rules.

ORIGINS OF LAW

Nine of the ten Canadian provinces and the three territories have adopted the common law legal system developed over the past millennium in England. For private matters, Quebec has adopted a system based on the *French Civil Code*. Although this text focuses on common law, understanding it may be assisted by briefly examining the basic differences between the common law and civil law legal systems. It is important to note that the term "civil law" has two distinct meanings. The following discussion is about the **civil law legal system** developed in Europe and now used in many jurisdictions, including Quebec. The terms "civil court," "civil action," and "civil law" are also used within our **common law legal system** to describe private law matters and should not be confused with the *Civil Code* or civil law as used in Quebec.

Civil Law Legal System

Modern civil law traces its origins to the Emperor Justinian, who had Roman law codified for use throughout the Roman Empire. This codification became the foundation of the legal system in continental Europe. Its most significant modification occurred early in the nineteenth century when Napoleon revised it. The *Napoleonic Code* was adopted throughout Europe and most of the European colonies. Today, variations of the civil code are used in continental Europe, South America, most of Africa, and many other parts of the world including Quebec. The most important feature of French civil law is its central code—a list of rules stated as broad principles of law that judges apply to the cases that come before them. Under this system, people wanting to know their legal rights or obligations refer to the *Civil Code*.

Quebec courts rely on the rules set out in the *Civil Code* to resolve private disputes in that province. While civil law judges are influenced by decisions made in other cases, and lawyers will take great pains to point out what other judges have done in similar situations, the key to understanding the civil law legal system is to recognize that ultimately the *Civil Code* determines the principle to be applied. Prior decisions do not constitute binding precedents in a civil law jurisdiction. The most recent *Civil Code of Quebec* came into effect on January 1, 1994.[1] One-quarter of the 1994 *Civil Code* is new law, making its introduction a significant event in the evolution of the law in Quebec.

One of the effects of the updated *Civil Code of Quebec* was to make the doctrine of good faith (recently developed in common law and discussed in Chapter 7) part of Quebec's contract law. Prior to this the law was similar to the common law, where the obligation to act in good faith toward the person you are dealing with applied only when special relationships existed. Article 1375 of the new *Civil Code* states that contracting parties "shall conduct themselves in good faith both at the time the obligation is created and at the time it is performed or extinguished."[2] This means that the parties can no longer withhold important information or fail to correct erroneous assumptions that they know have been made by the other side without exposing themselves to an action for violating this obligation of good faith.

To illustrate how the law is applied in a civil law legal system as opposed to a common law legal system, consider the situation involving a person suffering injury because of the careless act of another. If a person was seriously burned in Quebec, as a result of being served overly hot coffee in a pliable paper cup at a fast-food restaurant drive-through, the victim would turn to the *Civil Code* to determine his or her rights. Articles 1457 and 1463 of the *Civil Code of Quebec* state the following:[3]

> 1457. Every person has a duty to abide by the rules of conduct incumbent on him, according to the circumstances, usage or law, so as not to cause injury to another. Where he is endowed with reason and fails in this duty, he is liable for any injury he causes to another by such fault and is bound to make reparation for the injury, whether it be bodily, moral or material in nature. He is also bound, in certain cases, to make reparation for injury caused to another by the act or fault of another person or by the act of things in his custody.
>
> 1463. The principal is bound to make reparation for injury caused by the fault of his agents and servants in the performance of their duties; nevertheless, he retains his remedies against them.

Thus, applying article 1457 the server may be held liable to the customer. But if in a subsequent identical case the court applied both articles 1457 and 1463, the employer could be held liable in addition to the employee, increasing the

Variations of the civil code are used throughout much of the world

A civil code provides predictability

Quebec uses the *Civil Code* to resolve private disputes

The *Civil Code* recognizes doctrine of good faith

The *Civil Code* also applies to tort cases

Consistency is reduced where preceding court decisions can be ignored

---

1. *Civil Code of Quebec*, SQ 1991, c. 64.
2. *Civil Code of Québec*, S.Q. c. 64, a. 1375. Copyright © 1991 by Government of Québec. Used by the permission of Government of Québec.
3. Ibid., art. 1457, 1463. Copyright © 1991 by Government of Québec. Used by the permission of Government of Québec.

likelihood that the customer would actually recover any damages awarded by the court. Since the courts in a civil law jurisdiction are not required to follow each other's decisions, two very similar cases may be decided differently. The end result is shaped by the specific "law" or article of the *Civil Code* that is applied to the facts of a case.

Following precedent increases consistency and predictability

In a common law jurisdiction, liability may also be imposed on both the employer and the employee who caused injury by the application of the principles of negligence and vicarious liability(see Chapter 5). But in a common law jurisdiction, the doctrine of following **precedent** would demand that the courts look to similar cases for the principles to be applied. Thus, if a litigant can point to a case similar to her own, where a superior court imposed liability on both the employee (server) and the employer (restaurant), it is likely that a similar decision will be delivered in her case.

There are many important differences between civil law and the principles of common law. In this text, we have limited the discussion to common law. While there are many similarities, care should be taken not to assume that the same principles apply to Quebec or other civil law jurisdictions.

Common Law Legal System

Common law grew from the struggle for power

As Roman civil law was taking hold in Europe, relations between the existing English and French kingdoms were frequently strained. It has been suggested that this strain is the reason England maintained its unique common law system of justice rather than adopting the more widely accepted Roman civil law. The early Norman kings established a strong feudal system in England that centralized power in their hands. As long as they remained strong they maintained their power; but when weak kings were on the throne, power was surrendered to the nobles. The growth of the common law legal system was affected by this ongoing struggle for power between kings and nobles and later between kings and Parliament.

Henry II established travelling courts

Common law principles came from the common people—their traditions and customs

During times when power was decentralized, the administration of justice fell to the local lords, barons, or sheriffs who would hold court as part of their feudal responsibility. Their courts commonly resorted to such practices as trial by battle or ordeal. Trial by battle involved armed combat between the litigants or their champions, and trial by ordeal involved some physical test. The assumption was made that God would intervene on behalf of the righteous party. Strong kings, especially Henry II, enhanced their power by establishing travelling courts, which provided a more attractive method of resolving disputes. As more people used the king's courts, their power base broadened and their strength increased. The fairer the royal judges, the more litigants they attracted. Eventually, the courts of the nobles fell into disuse. The function of the royal courts was not to impose any particular set of laws but to be as fair and impartial as possible. To this end, they did not make new rules but enforced the customs and traditions they found already in place in the towns and villages they visited. The judges also began to look to each other for rules to apply when faced with new situations.

STARE DECISIS

Judges follow decisions—if made within that court's hierarchy

Gradually, a system of justice developed in which the judges were required to follow each other's decisions. This process is called *stare decisis*, or "following precedent." Another factor that affected the development of *stare decisis* was the creation of appeal courts. Although the process of appeal at this time was rudimentary, trial judges would try to avoid the embarrassment of having their decisions overturned and declared in error. Eventually, the practice of following precedent became institutionalized.[4]

---

4. See Department of Justice, "Canada's System of Justice," accessed December 2014, www.justice.gc.ca/eng/csj-sjc/index.html.

CASE SUMMARY 2.1

Inconsistent Interpretations—The Significance of Having a Supreme Court: *R. v. Keegstra*[5] and *R. v. Andrews*[6]

Each province in Canada has its own hierarchy of courts. Thus a ruling from the highest court in one province may conflict with decisions from other courts. Consider the dilemma faced by the police in enforcing Canada's *Criminal Code* following the decisions in the *Keegstra* and *Andrews* cases. Both cases involved charges laid under section 319(2) of the *Criminal Code*, which prohibits wilful promotion of hatred against identifiable groups.

Keegstra had been teaching students in Eckville, Alberta, that the Holocaust was a hoax. Andrews was also spreading anti-Semitic, white supremacist hate literature. In the *Keegstra* case, the charges were set aside when the Alberta Court of Appeal declared section 319 to be unconstitutional because it violated the *Charter*. Keegstra successfully argued that the *Criminal Code* prohibition violated his freedom of expression as guaranteed by the *Charter of Rights and Freedoms*. But in the *Andrews* case, the Ontario Court of Appeal upheld the constitutionality of the same charges even though it had the benefit of the Alberta decision. It simply chose not to follow that decision.

Courts from different provinces are not bound to follow each other's decisions. Consequently, Canadians may face situations where charges cannot be laid in one province but similar conduct will result in criminal prosecution in others. The police could not pursue hate crimes in Alberta because the Alberta Court of Appeal had ruled the law unconstitutional; yet in Ontario similar conduct drew charges.

Fortunately, both cases were appealed to the Supreme Court of Canada, which ruled on the *Keegstra* and *Andrews* appeals simultaneously. It declared section 319 constitutional, finding that although it violates freedom of expression, this infringement is justifiable under section 1 of the *Charter*. Prohibiting hateful and harmful communications was found to be justifiable for the good of society as a whole. Keegstra was thus tried for inciting hatred and was eventually convicted.

SMALL BUSINESS PERSPECTIVE

These cases demonstrate that one law may be interpreted and enforced differently from province to province. You cannot assume that the law in one province is identical to that in another. Laws—and their interpretation—may differ across the country.

The most significant feature of the common law legal system today is that the decision of a judge at one level is binding on all judges in the court hierarchy who function in a court of lower rank, provided the facts in the two cases are similar. For example, in the *Toronto Star* case[7] the Court referred to the necessity to follow precedent, even though the applicants argued that the Court could depart from an earlier 1984 decision of the Ontario Court of Appeal that upheld mandatory publication bans. The judge declared that

> the question put to the Court of Appeal in *Global* is indistinguishable from the one I am asked to consider. I find I have no authority to reconsider *Global*. Until such time as the Court of Appeal or the Supreme Court of Canada finds that *Global* was wrongly decided, it remains the law in Ontario.

---

5. [1988] A.J. No. 501 (C.A.), rev'd [1990] 3 SCR 697.
6. [1988] O.J. No. 1222 (C.A.), [1990] 3 SCR 870.
7. *Toronto Star Newspapers Ltd. v. The Queen*, [2007] 84 O.R. (3d) 766 (Ont. H.C.J.). It is interesting to note that this case did make its way to the Supreme Court of Canada; see [2010] 1 SCR 721, 2010 SCC 21. Mandatory publication bans were again upheld as constitutional.

A judge today hearing a case in the Court of Queen's Bench for Alberta would be required to follow a similar decision laid down in the Court of Appeal for Alberta or the Supreme Court of Canada, but would not have to follow a decision involving an identical case from the Court of Appeal for Manitoba.[8] Such a decision would be merely persuasive, since it came from a different jurisdiction. Because the Supreme Court of Canada is the highest court in the land, its decisions are binding on all Canadian courts.

CASE SUMMARY 2.2

Lower Court Must Follow Decision of Higher Court: *Canada v. Craig*[9]

This was a case where the minister of national revenue reassessed the taxpayer's income taxes, placing a limit (or cap) on the farm losses that were deductible. In doing so, the minister applied the interpretation of the *Income Tax Act* made by the Supreme Court of Canada in *Moldowan v. The Queen*.[10] The taxpayer appealed to the Tax Court of Canada, which decided to follow a different interpretation of section 31 of the Act, as made in the *Gunn* case,[11] a decision of the Federal Court of Appeal. Based on this interpretation, the taxpayer was successful and the limit on deductions was removed. The minister appealed to the Federal Court of Appeal, which also chose to follow the *Gunn* precedent. The preliminary issue was thus whether the Federal Court of Appeal was entitled to disregard the Supreme Court's precedent in *Moldowan*.

The Supreme Court reiterated the importance of following precedent. One of the fallouts from *Gunn* was that it left lower courts in the difficult position of facing two inconsistent precedents and having to decide which one to follow. This led to uncertainty, which the application of precedent is intended to preclude. There may have been justification for arriving at a different interpretation, "But regardless of the explanation, what the Court in this case ought to have done was to have written reasons as to why *Moldowan* was problematic, in the way that the reasons in *Gunn* did, rather than purporting to overrule it."[12]

The Supreme Court then addressed whether it should overrule *Moldowan*. It stated that overturning its own precedent was a step not to be taken lightly, but only based on compelling reasons. Courts must balance two important values: correctness and certainty, assessing whether it is preferable to adhere to an incorrect precedent to maintain certainty or to correct the error. In this case, the Supreme Court was satisfied that relevant considerations justified overruling *Moldowan*, which it did, and the minister's appeal was dismissed.

SMALL BUSINESS PERSPECTIVE

A sophisticated businessperson will appreciate the predictability of the common law. If in doubt as to what the law may be, a lawyer will review precedents from similar cases and, with some degree of certainty, be able to predict a likely outcome.

Stare decisis **provides predictability**

The role *stare decisis* plays in the English common law legal system is similar to the role the *Civil Code* plays in the French system. It allows the parties to predict the outcome of the litigation and thus avoid going to court. However, a significant

---

8. Strictly speaking, a judge is not bound to follow decisions made by other judges in a court at the same level in that province. However, the practical effect is the same, since these judges must follow their colleagues' decisions "in the absence of strong reason to the contrary." *R. v. Morris*, [1942] O.W.N. 447 (Ont. H.C.J.).

9. 2012 SCC 43, [2012] 2 SCR 489, 2012 SCC 43 (CanLII).

10. [1978] 1 SCR 480, 1977 CanLII 5 (SCC).

11. *Gunn v. Canada*, 2006 FCA 281 (CanLII), [2007] 3 F.C.R. 57.

12. *Supra* 9, para. 21.

disadvantage of following precedent is that a judge must follow another judge's decision even though social attitudes may have changed. The system is anchored to the past, with only limited capacity to make corrections or to adapt and change to meet modern needs. Opposing legal representatives present a judge with several precedents that support their side of the argument. The judge's job is to analyze the facts of the precedent cases and compare them with the case at hand. Since no two cases are ever exactly alike, the judge has some flexibility in deciding whether or not to apply a particular precedent. Judges try to avoid applying precedent decisions by finding essential differences between the facts of the two cases if they feel that the prior decision will create an injustice in the present case. This process is referred to as **distinguishing the facts** of opposing precedents. Still, judges cannot stray very far from the established line of precedents.

One drawback is inflexibility

SOURCES OF LAW

LO ❸

Common Law

At an early stage in the development of common law, three great courts were created: the Court of Common Pleas, the Court of King's Bench, and the Exchequer Court, referred to collectively as the **common law courts**. The rules developed in the courts were called "common law" because the judges, at least in theory, did not create law but merely discovered it in the customs and traditions of the people to whom it was to be applied. However, the foundation for a complete legal system could not be supplied by local custom and tradition alone, so common law judges borrowed legal principles from many different sources. Common law borrows from **Roman civil law**, which gave us our concepts of property and possessions. **Canon or church law** contributed law in relation to families and estates. Another important European system that had an impact on common law was called the **law merchant**. Trading between nations was performed by merchants who were members of guilds (similar to modern trade unions or professional organizations), which developed their own rules to deal with disputes between members. As the strength of the guilds declined, common law judges found themselves dealing increasingly with disputes between merchants. The law merchant was then adopted as part of the English common law, and it included laws relating to negotiable instruments such as cheques and promissory notes.

Customs and traditions are major sources of common law
Common law borrows from
- **Roman civil law**
- **Canon law**
- **Law merchant**

Equity

Common law courts had some serious limitations. Parties seeking justice before them found it difficult to obtain fair and proper redress for the grievances they had suffered. Because of the rigidity of the process, the inflexibility of the rules applied, and the limited scope of the remedies available, people often went directly to the king for satisfaction and relief. The burden of this process made it necessary for the king to delegate the responsibility to the chancellor, who in turn appointed several vice-chancellors. This body eventually became known as the **Court of Chancery**, sometimes referred to as the **Court of Equity**. It dealt with matters that, for various reasons, could not be handled adequately or fairly by the common law courts. The Court of Chancery did not hear appeals from the common law courts; rather, it provided an alternative forum. If people seeking relief knew that the common law courts could provide no remedy or that the remedy would be inadequate, they would go to the Court of Chancery instead.

Initially, the Court of Chancery was unhampered by the requirement to follow precedent and the rigidity that permeated the common law courts and could decide a case on its merits. The system of law developed by the Court of Chancery became known as the **law of equity**. This flexibility, which was the most significant asset of **equity**, was also its greatest drawback. Each decision of

Common law is rigid

Court of Chancery provided relief

Resulted in the law of equity

Conflict resulted in rigidity in chancery as well

the Court of Chancery appeared arbitrary—there was no uniformity within the system, and it was difficult to predict the outcome of a given case. This caused friction between the chancery and the common law judges, which was solved, to some extent, by the chancery's adopting *stare decisis*. Finally, the two separate court systems were amalgamated by the *Judicature Acts of 1873–1875*.[13] This merger happened in Canada as well, and today there is only one court system in each of the provinces.

Equity today does not simply mean fairness

Equity supplements the common law

Although the two court systems merged, the bodies of law they had created did not, and it is best still to think of common law and equity as two distinct bodies of rules. Originally, the rules of equity may have been based on fairness and justice, but when a person today asks a judge to apply equity they are not asking for fairness—they are asking that the rules developed by the courts of chancery be applied to the case. Equity should be viewed as a supplement to rather than a replacement of common law. Common law is complete—albeit somewhat unsatisfactory—without equity, but equity would be nothing without common law. The courts of chancery were instrumental in developing such principles in law as the **trust** (in which one party holds property for another) and also provided several alternative remedies, such as injunction and specific performance, which will be examined later in the text.

The common law provinces in Canada administer both common law and equity, and judges treat matters differently when proceeding under equity as opposed to common law rules. Of course, judges must always be alert to the fact that any applicable parliamentary statute will override both.

Statutes

Statutes and regulations override judge-made law

In many situations, justice was not available in either the common law or chancery courts, and another method was needed to correct these inadequacies. The English Civil War of the seventeenth century firmly established the principle that Parliament, rather than the king, was supreme, and from that time on Parliament handled any major modification to the law. Parliamentary enactments are referred to as **statutes** or legislation and take precedence over judge-made law based on either common law or equity.

It is important to remember that government has several distinct functions: legislative, judicial, and administrative. The **legislative branch** consists of Parliament, which legislates or creates the law, as do each of the provincial legislatures. The **judicial branch** is the court system, and the judiciary interprets **legislation** and makes case law. The **executive branch** and its agencies administer and implement that law. Organizations such as the RCMP, the Employment Insurance Commission, and the military are part of the executive branch of government. Often legislation creating such bodies (the enabling statute) delegates power to them to create regulations (the subordinate legislation). Through those **regulations** government agencies implement and accomplish the goals of the enabling statute and enforce its terms. Similarly, municipal bylaws operate as subordinate legislation. A provincial statute, such as Ontario's *Municipal Act, 2001*,[14] may enable municipalities to pass bylaws, but only with regard to matters stipulated in the Act.

For the businessperson, these statutes and regulations have become all-important, setting out the specific rules governing business activities in all jurisdictions. Although judge-made law still forms the foundation of our legal system, it is statutes and regulations that control and restrict what we can do and determine what we must do to carry on business in Canada today. See Table 2.1 for a summary of the sources of law in Canada.

---

13. *Judicature Acts* (1873–1875), 31 Geo. III.
14. S.O. 2001, c. 25.

Table 2.1 Sources of Law in Canada

Branch of Government	Legislative	Executive	Judicial
Who fills these positions?	Federally: Parliament	Prime minister and cabinet ministers together with each department's civil servants/bureaucrats	Judges appointed by the various provinces and federally appointed justices
	Provincially: Legislative Assemblies	Premier and the cabinet together with each department's civil servants/bureaucrats	
Type of law made	Statute law (legislation)	Subordinate legislation • regulations made by order-in-council or as authorized by legislation • bylaws made by municipal governments	Case law
Examples	**(Federal)** • *Income Tax Act* • *Immigration and Refugee Protection Act* • *Criminal Code*	**(Federal)** • *Income Tax Regulations* • *Immigration and Refugee Protection Regulations* • *Criminal Appeal Rules*	**(Federal)** The decision of the Supreme Court of Canada in *R. v. Keegstra*
	(Provincial) • *Workers' Compensation Act* • *Traffic Safety Act* • *Business Corporations Act*	**(Provincial)** • *Workers' Compensation Regulations* • *Traffic Control Device Regulation* • *Business Corporations Regulation*	**(Provincial)** The decision of the Ontario Court of Appeal in *Halpern v. Canada (Attorney General)*

LAW IN CANADA

LO ❹❺❻

Confederation

Canada came into existence in 1867 with the federation of Upper and Lower Canada, Nova Scotia, and New Brunswick. Other provinces followed, with Newfoundland being the most recent to join **Confederation**. Every jurisdiction except Quebec adopted the English common law legal system. Quebec elected to retain the use of the French civil law legal system for private matters falling within provincial jurisdiction.

Confederation was accomplished when the British Parliament passed the *British North America Act* (*BNA Act),* now renamed the *Constitution Act, 1867.*[15] The *BNA Act*'s primary significance is that it created the Dominion of Canada; divided power between the executive, judicial, and legislative branches of government; and determined the functions and powers of the provincial and federal levels of government. The preamble to the *BNA Act* says that Canada has a constitution "similar in principle to that of the United Kingdom"; that is, we claim as part of our Constitution all the great constitutional institutions of the United Kingdom, such as the *Magna Carta* (1215) and the *English Bill of Rights* (1689). Also included are such unwritten conventions as the **rule of law**, which recognizes that although Parliament is supreme and can create any law considered appropriate, citizens are protected from the arbitrary actions of the government. All actions of government and government agencies must be authorized by valid legislation. In addition, our Constitution includes those acts passed by both the British and Canadian Parliaments subsequent to the *Constitution Act, 1867* that have status beyond mere statutes, such as the *Statute of Westminster* (1931) and the *Constitution Act, 1982,*[16] which includes

The *BNA Act* created Canada and divided powers

[15.] *Constitution Act, 1867* (U.K.), 30 & 31 Vict., c. 3, reprinted in R.S.C. 1985, App. II, No. 5 (formerly the *British North America Act, 1867).*

[16.] *Constitution Act, 1982,* being Schedule B to the *Canada Act 1982* (U.K.), 1982, c. 11.

the *Charter of Rights and Freedoms*. Section 52(2) of the *Constitution Act, 1982*, clarifies that it and the *Canada Act 1982*, together with the 30 enactments listed in its schedule, collectively form the Constitution of Canada.[17]

There is more to the Canadian Constitution than the *BNA Act* and *Charter*

Canada's Constitution is, in essence, the "rulebook" that government must follow. It comprises three elements: (1) statutes, such as the *Constitution Act, 1982*, and the statutes creating various provinces; (2) case law on constitutional issues, such as whether the federal or provincial government has jurisdiction to create certain statutes; and (3) conventions, which are unwritten rules dictating how the government is to operate and include the rule of law.

CASE SUMMARY 2.3

The Impact of Convention: Deciding Whether to Prorogue Parliament[18]

Since the King–Byng Affair in 1926,[19] the convention (unwritten rule) has been that the governor general is expected to take the advice of the sitting prime minister. This convention arose on the heels of the then governor general's (Lord Byng's) decision to ignore the wishes of the prime minister (Mackenzie King) to dissolve Parliament. Instead, Lord Byng called upon the leader of the opposition to lead Parliament, which proved to be futile since the opposition did not have the support of the House of Commons. The minority government was soon defeated and an election had to be called anyway.

In December 2008, the leaders of the Liberal and New Democratic parties formed a coalition and, with the support of the Bloc Québécois, planned to defeat Stephen Harper's Conservatives during the first sitting of Parliament. Harper thus asked Governor General Michaëlle Jean to prorogue Parliament until a new budget could be presented. In deciding to heed the prime minister's request, the governor general followed convention. Her decision to prorogue Parliament, however, dealt a death blow to the coalition and provided the Conservatives with a chance to win back the confidence of the House.

DISCUSSION QUESTION

Since the King–Byng Affair the role of the governor general has been largely ceremonial, yet when political division impedes the function of government, the head of state may be called upon to make tough decisions. Under what circumstances might it be acceptable for the governor general not to follow the advice of a prime minister?

For the person in business, it must be remembered that the effect of Confederation was not simply to create one country with one set of rules. Each province was given the power to establish rules in those areas over which it had jurisdiction. As a consequence, businesses operating within and between provinces must comply with federal, provincial, and municipal regulations. In spite of the opportunity for great divergence among the provinces, it is encouraging to see how similar the controls and restrictions are in the different jurisdictions.

Constitution and Division of Powers

The *Constitution Act* and *Charter* limit power of federal and provincial governments

In Canada, as in Britain, Parliament is supreme and traditionally has had the power to make laws that cannot be overruled by any other body and are subject only to the realities of the political system in which they function. But in Canada, the *Constitution*

---

17. See the Schedule to the *Constitution Act, 1982*, listing the *Alberta Act, Saskatchewan Act, Newfoundland Act*, and numerous *Constitution Acts* as parts of Canada's Constitution.

18. For more information on this constitutional spectacle, see Robert Sheppard, "The Delicate Role of the Governor General," *CBC News*, December 2, 2008, accessed December 2014, www.cbc.ca/news/canada/the-delicate-role-of-the-governor-general-1.701974.

19. To view a video clip summarizing the King–Byng Affair, see "The King–Byng Affair," *CBC Digital Archives*, accessed December 2014, www.cbc.ca/archives/entry/political-scandals-the-king-byng-affair.

Act, 1867 and the *Charter of Rights and Freedoms* place some limitations on this supremacy. Unlike the United Kingdom, Canada has a federal form of government with 11 different legislative bodies, each claiming the supreme powers of Parliament.

Refer to the MyBusLawLab for links to the federal and various provincial government sites for current legislation.

The *Constitution Act, 1867* assigned different legislative powers to the federal and provincial governments. The powers of the federal government are set out primarily in section 91 of the *Constitution Act, 1867*, and those of the provincial governments are set out in section 92. The federal government has exclusive power over such matters as banking, currency, the postal service, criminal law (although not its enforcement), and the appointment of judges in the federal and higher-level provincial courts. The federal government passes considerable legislation affecting such matters as the regulation of all import and export activities, taxation, environmental concerns, money and banking, interprovincial and international transportation, as well as important areas of intellectual property, such as copyrights, patents, and trademarks. The provinces, on the other hand, have exclusive jurisdiction over such matters as hospitals, education, the administration of the courts, and commercial activities carried on at the provincial level.

Thus, most business activities that are carried on within the province are governed by provincial legislation or municipal bylaws, including statutes dealing with the sale of goods, consumer protection, employment, workers' compensation, collective bargaining, secured transactions, incorporation, real estate, and licensing. For industries that fall within federal jurisdiction, such as banking and the railways, there are corresponding federal statutes. Under the "Peace, Order, and good Government" (POGG) clause (found in the introduction to section 91), the federal government has residual power to make law with respect to things not listed in the *Constitution Act, 1867*, such as broadcasting and air travel. Under section 92(16), the provinces are given broad powers to make law with respect to all matters of a local or private nature. It is important to note that these assigned areas of jurisdiction are concerned with the nature of the legislation being passed rather than the individuals or things affected. Thus, the federal government's power to pass banking legislation allows it to control anything to do with banking, including interest rates, deposits, and how those deposits are invested. See Table 2.2 for a summary of the division of powers.

> The *Constitution Act, 1867* divides powers between the federal and provincial governments
>
> Federal powers set out in section 91
>
> Provincial powers set out in section 92

> Sections 91 and 92 deal with areas of jurisdiction

Table 2.2 Division of Powers

Federal—Section 91	Provincial—Section 92
Trade and commerce	Municipal institutions
Employment insurance	Hospitals (and health care)
Raising monies by any mode of taxation	Direct taxation within the province
Criminal law (although not its enforcement)	Administration of justice within the province
Banking, currency, postal service	Property and civil rights
Residual power under the "POGG" clause	Generally, matters of a local or private nature

The division of powers accomplished by sections 91 and 92 of the *Constitution Act, 1867* has been important in the development of Canada as a nation and, until the recent entrenchment of the *Charter*, was the main consideration of courts when faced with constitutional questions. In these jurisdictional disputes between governments, where competing governments claim to control a particular activity, the courts are called upon to act as a referee.

When determining the constitutional validity of legislation, the courts often resolve the issue by looking at the "pith and substance" of the challenged law. In other words, what is the main purpose of the law? Then the court examines whether the government that enacted the law has the constitutional jurisdiction to regulate that concern.

> Courts examine the essence of laws in constitutional challenges

CASE SUMMARY 2.4

National Securities Regulator Declared Unconstitutional: *Reference Re Securities Act*[20]

Should Canada have a single national securities regulator? Proponents have argued that a national regulator would help discourage white-collar crime by making enforcement much tougher. Currently, each province and territory has its own securities regulator, making enforcement more costly and potentially less effective.

But the Supreme Court was not asked to make an economic decision. It was asked to determine the constitutional validity of a national *Securities Act*. The federal government claimed it had jurisdiction based on its power to regulate trade and commerce under section 91(2) of the *Constitution Act, 1867*. Several provinces countered that regulating securities falls under the provincial power over property and civil rights (under section 92(13) of the *Constitution Act, 1867*) and pertains to matters of a merely local or private nature (section 92(16)), namely the regulation of contracts and property.

The Supreme Court conducted a pith and substance analysis to ascertain the purpose and effects of the law. It determined that the purpose of the *Securities Act* is to implement a comprehensive Canadian regime to regulate securities with a view to protect investors; to promote fair, efficient, and competitive capital markets; and to ensure the integrity and stability of the financial system. However, its effects would be to duplicate and displace the existing provincial and territorial securities regimes.

The Court declared that while Parliament's power over the regulation of trade and commerce under section 91(2) is, at face value, broad, it cannot be used in a way that denies the provincial legislatures the power to regulate local matters and industries within their boundaries.

Accordingly, the Court ruled that "The *Securities Act* as presently drafted is not valid under the general branch of the federal power to regulate trade and commerce under s. 91(2) of the *Constitution Act, 1867*."

QUESTION FOR DISCUSSION

Has the Supreme Court left the door open for another version of a national *Securities Act*? What options does the federal government have? How has the federal government introduced national standards over other areas falling under provincial control, such as health care?

A pith and substance analysis was also the approach taken in the *Reference re Firearms Act (Can.)* case.[21] In 1995, Parliament amended the *Criminal Code* by enacting the *Firearms Act*.[22] The amendments require all holders of firearms to obtain licences and register their guns. Alberta, backed by Ontario, Saskatchewan, Manitoba, and the territories, challenged the law, arguing it was a brazen intrusion on private property and civil rights, a provincial power according to section 92(13) of the *Constitution Act, 1867*. The opponents argued that the new law would do no more to control gun crimes than registering vehicles does to stop traffic offences.

Laws are upheld if interference with another jurisdiction's power is incidental

The Supreme Court of Canada upheld the *Firearms Act* as *intra vires* Parliament, meaning that it was within its power. It found that the Act constitutes a valid exercise of Parliament's jurisdiction over criminal law because its "pith and substance" is directed at enhancing public safety by controlling access to firearms. Because guns are dangerous and pose a risk to public safety, their control and regulation as dangerous products were regarded as valid purposes for criminal law. In essence,

---

20. [2011] 3 SCR 837, 2011 SCC 66 (CanLII).
21. [2000] 1 SCR 783, 2000 SCC 31 (CanLII).
22. S.C. 1995, c. 39.

the law was determined to be criminal in focus. The Act impacted provincial jurisdiction over property and civil rights only incidentally. Accordingly, the *Firearms Act* was upheld as a valid exercise of federal power under section 91(27) of the *Constitution Act, 1867*.

Nonetheless, the *Firearms Act* and the gun registry it created were later denuded, not by a court decision but by a change of government. Prime Minister Harper's Conservative Party had opposed the legislation from the outset, and once in a majority position it introduced Bill C-19 to end the controversial long-gun registry. Further amendments to the *Firearms Act* continue to be brought forward, as evidenced by the introduction of the proposed *Common Sense Firearms Licensing Act* in October 2014.[23]

It is interesting to note that constitutional challenges are not undertaken just by governments. Individuals affected by laws may choose to challenge their validity as well.

CASE SUMMARY 2.5

Individual Challenges Validity of Forfeiture Laws:
Chatterjee v. Ontario (Attorney General)[24]

Chatterjee, a university student, was being arrested for breach of probation when the police coincidentally found $29 000 in cash and items associated with drug trafficking in his car, but no drugs. No charges were laid relating to the money, nor was Chatterjee charged with any drug-related activity. Nonetheless, the attorney general applied for and obtained an order allowing the Crown to keep the money and equipment as proceeds of unlawful activity under Ontario's *Remedies for Organized Crime and Other Unlawful Activities Act*, also known as the *Civil Remedies Act (CRA)*. Chatterjee challenged the constitutional validity of the *CRA*, arguing that the province did not have the right to seize proceeds of crime because criminal law is a matter of federal, not provincial, jurisdiction.

The Supreme Court of Canada unanimously upheld the provincial law, since the dominant feature related to "property and civil rights," a provincial matter. While its provisions may incidentally overlap with criminal law, "the fact that the *CRA* aims to deter federal offences as well as provincial offences, and indeed, offences outside of Canada, is not fatal to its validity." As stated by Justice Binnie for the Court,

> The *CRA* was enacted to deter crime and to compensate its victims. The former purpose is broad enough that both the federal government (in relation to criminal law) and the provincial governments (in relation to property and civil rights) can validly pursue it. The latter purpose falls squarely within provincial competence. Crime imposes substantial costs on provincial treasuries. Those costs impact many provincial interests, including health, policing resources, community stability and family welfare. It would be out of step with modern realities to conclude that a province must shoulder the costs to the community of criminal behaviour but cannot use deterrence to suppress it.

SMALL BUSINESS PERSPECTIVE
Although this constitutional challenge was unsuccessful, the lesson is that if you find yourself confronted by a particular law you might solve the issue by challenging the constitutional validity of the enactment.

---

[23] You can track the progress of Bill C-42, the *Common Sense Firearms Licensing Act*, on Parliament's website, accessed October 2014, www.parl.gc.ca/LegisInfo/Home.aspx?language=E&ParliamentSession=41-2.

[24] [2009] 1 SCR 624, 2009 SCC 19 (CanLII).

Conflicting Powers

On occasion, one level of government passes legislation that may infringe on the powers of another. For example, municipal governments have tried to control prostitution or pornography, using their zoning or licensing power, when in fact these matters are controlled by criminal law, a federal area.[25] Such bylaws have been struck down as *ultra vires* (beyond one's jurisdiction or power) by the courts as veiled attempts to control moral conduct, matters to be dealt with under criminal jurisdiction. Municipalities sometimes try to dramatically increase the licensing fee charged to a business to accomplish the same purpose, often with the same result.

One level of government cannot invade the area given to another by trying to make it look like the legislation is of a different kind. This is called "colourable legislation" and the court simply looks at the substance of what the governing body is trying to do, as opposed to what it claims to be doing, and asks whether or not it has that power.

Validity of a statute determined by its true nature

CASE SUMMARY 2.6

Municipal Bylaw Addressing Morality: *Vaughan (City) v. Tsui*[26]

A pith and substance analysis was used in the *Tsui* case, where a bylaw prohibited body rub parlours from being open after 10:00 p.m. on weekdays and after 5:00 or 6:00 p.m. on weekends. Faced with losing his licence for staying open after hours, the owner of a body rub parlour challenged the validity of the bylaw, arguing that its object was to curtail prostitution, an activity allegedly occurring at body rub parlours. Evidence established that the city did not want the criminal element associated with prostitution to be in residential neighbourhoods, so it enacted laws relocating body rub parlours to industrial neighbourhoods and set restrictive hours of operation. The Court concluded that the pith and substance of the impugned sections of the bylaw was criminal and therefore *ultra vires* the City of Vaughan.

The sections prescribing hours of operation were an attempt to legislate prostitution; the sections dealing with nudity also fell within the scope of the criminal law. Since these matters lay within the federal government's scope of power, the impugned sections of the bylaw were quashed.

DISCUSSION QUESTION

In light of the division of powers, can you think of other laws that may be characterized as colourable legislation? Who can challenge such legislation and how is this done?

Double aspect doctrine leads courts to uphold laws where the provincial and federal aspects are of equal importance

What if, after reviewing the pith and substance of the challenged legislation, it is not possible to determine which aspect is dominant? The provincial and federal aspects of the impugned legislation are occasionally of equal importance. In such cases, the courts may apply the double aspect doctrine of judicial restraint and conclude that the legislation is constitutionally valid. In *R. v. Keshane*,[27] for example, the constitutionality of Edmonton Bylaw 14614 was challenged. It made fighting in a public place punishable by a fine and applied both to consensual and non-consensual fights. The Court found the dominant purpose of the bylaw had both federal and provincial aspects of roughly equal importance. The provincial aspect was protection of public spaces and reducing nuisance; the federal aspect was preservation of public peace and order. The double aspect doctrine of judicial restraint was applied, and the validity of the bylaw was upheld.

---

25. *R. v. Westendorp*, [1983] 1 SCR 43, 1983 CanLII 1 (SCC).

26. 2013 O.N.C.J. 643 (CanLII); See also [2000] B.C.J. No. 1154 (B.C.S.C.), where a municipal bylaw prohibiting topless sunbathing was similarly struck down.

27. 2012 A.B.C.A. 330 (CanLII).

Likewise, in *Smith v. St. Albert (City)*,[28] Chad Smoke Shop challenged the validity of a bylaw restricting the sale and display of items associated with illicit drug consumption. The pith and substance of the bylaw provisions fell under multiple heads of power: federal power over criminal law under section 91(27) and provincial power over licensing and regulating businesses in the community under sections 92(9) and 92(13). The double aspect doctrine was again applied and the bylaw was upheld.

The powers of the federal and provincial governments can overlap considerably. If the overlap between provincial and federal legislation is merely incidental, both are valid and both are operative. An individual must obey both by adhering to the higher standard, whether provincial or federal. But there are occasions where the laws truly conflict and it is not possible to obey both. In those situations, the principle of **paramountcy** may require that the federal legislation be operative and the provincial legislation go into abeyance and no longer apply.

> **When provincial and federal laws conflict, follow federal**

CASE SUMMARY 2.7

Another Challenge Goes Up in Smoke: *Rothmans, Benson & Hedges Inc. v. Saskatchewan*[29]

The federal *Tobacco Act* permitted manufacturers and retailers to display tobacco products and to post signs setting out availability and prices. Saskatchewan passed the *Tobacco Control Act* prohibiting all advertising, display, and promotion of tobacco products in any location where they might be seen by someone under 18. Rothmans, Benson & Hedges Inc., preferring the provisions of the federal statute, challenged the provincial law, arguing that it was in conflict with the federal Act and that because of the principle of paramountcy it could not stand. The federal legislation was valid and within the competency of the federal government under its criminal law power described in section 91(27) of the *Constitution Act, 1867*. The provincial legislation was likewise valid under the provincial powers set out in section 92 of the *Constitution Act, 1867*. The problem was to determine whether the provincial Act could stand given the federal intrusion into the area.

The Supreme Court of Canada found that the two statutes were not in conflict; one simply went further than the other. It was possible for the retailers and manufacturers to obey them both by following the higher standard set out in the provincial Act. Thus if young people were prohibited from coming into a place, such as a bar or pub, the merchant could still display tobacco products and be in compliance with both the federal and the provincial Act. Thus, finding no conflict, the Court found the provincial Act valid and binding.

SMALL BUSINESS PERSPECTIVE

The above case demonstrates an interesting tactic—if a particular law restricts the profitability of a person's business, he may be able to challenge its constitutionality. If the challenge is successful, the courts can strike the law down, resolving the problem for the business owner. But note: Paramountcy only applies when there is a true conflict between valid federal and valid provincial legislation.

Delegation of Powers

Since neither the federal nor the provincial levels of government are considered inferior legislative bodies, both are supreme parliaments in their assigned areas. Over the years, for various reasons, these bodies have sometimes found it necessary

> **Direct delegation is prohibited**

---

28. 2014 A.B.C.A. 76 (CanLII).
29. [2005] 1 SCR 188, 2005 SCC 13 (CanLII).

to transfer the powers given to them to other levels of government. However, direct delegation between the federal and provincial governments is prohibited. For example, during the Depression of the 1930s, it became clear that a national system of unemployment insurance was needed. The provinces, having jurisdiction in this area, may have preferred to delegate their power to the federal government. The Supreme Court held that they could not do so since it was an "abdication" of the "exclusive powers" given to the provinces under the *Constitution Act, 1867*. To make unemployment insurance an area of federal responsibility, the British Parliament needed to amend the Constitution. This amendment is now incorporated in section 91, subsection (2A) of the *Constitution Act, 1867*.

Indirect delegation is permitted

Although direct delegation is prohibited, it is possible for the federal and provincial governments to delegate their powers to inferior bodies, such as boards and individual civil servants; in fact, this is usually the only way that governmental bodies can conduct their business. It is thus possible for the federal government to delegate its power in a particular area to a provincial board or a provincial civil servant. Similarly, a province can give powers to federal boards, since these are also inferior bodies. In this way, governments overcome the prohibition against delegation.

Agreements to Share Powers

Federal government exerts influence by providing funding—with strings attached

Another means used to circumvent the constitutional rigidity created by the 1867 division of powers is through federal and provincial agreements to share powers. These agreements may consist of *transfer-payment schemes*, or conditional grants under which the transfer of funds from the federal government is tied to conditions on how the money is to be spent. Through such schemes, the federal government can exercise some say as to how a provincial government operates programs that fall under the province's constitutional area of control. The federal government may set certain national standards to which the funding is tied and in this fashion ensure that all Canadians have access to similar levels of service.

Transfer-payment schemes in the areas of health, social programs, and education are examples of provincial areas where the federal government provides considerable funding along with the imposition of national standards or other conditions on the provinces. At the time of Confederation, government spending on these services was minuscule. Now these areas may account for two-thirds of all government spending. The provinces, with their restricted taxing powers, would have difficulty providing these services without federal funding.

Legislative Power

Statutes must receive royal assent

Canada's Constitution divides legislative power between the federal and provincial governments, but it also requires legislation to proceed through a sequence of introduction, debate, modification, and approval that is referred to as first, second, and third readings. When a **bill** is finally enacted, it has the status of a statute (although it may still be referred to as a bill or an act). Such a statute does not have the status of law until it receives the approval of the governor general at the federal level or the lieutenant-governor in a province, a process referred to as receiving **royal assent**. The governor general and the lieutenant-governors are the Queen's representatives in Canada and can grant royal assent (sign) on behalf of the Crown. Current convention (practice) in Canada directs the Queen's representatives to sign as the government in power directs them, and such approval is therefore usually a formality. The government may use this requirement to delay a piece of legislation from coming into effect, and care should therefore be taken when examining an Act to make sure that it has received royal assent. The statute itself may provide that different parts of it will come into force at different times. There are many examples where whole acts or portions of them have no legal effect for these reasons. See Figure 2.1 for a summary of the traditional process for passing bills.

The Government of Canada publishes a compilation of these statutes annually; the collection can be found in most libraries under *Statutes of Canada*. The federal

Figure 2.1 Traditional Passage of Bills

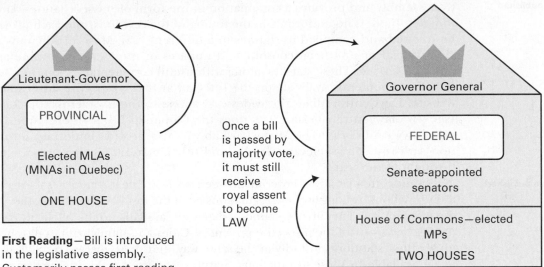

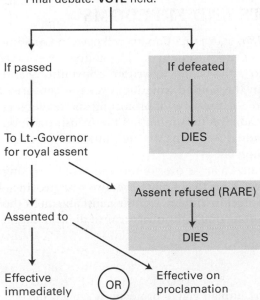

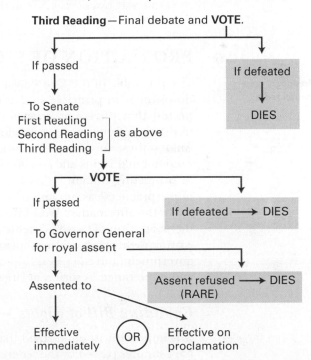

First Reading—Bill is introduced in the legislative assembly. Customarily passes first reading without debate.

Second Reading—Bill is read again. Now it is debated. After approval, it may go to committee of the whole for review and amendment. Committee of the whole must approve all bills before they can receive a third reading.

Third Reading—Bill is read again. Final debate. **VOTE** held.

Once a bill is passed by majority vote, it must still receive royal assent to become LAW

First Reading—Introduction (by government, by private member, or possibly by all-party committee*¹). Bill is printed. May go to all-party committee after approval.*²

Second Reading—Bill is debated. After approval in principle, the bill goes to all-party committee, which may recommend amendments.

Third Reading—Final debate and **VOTE**.

The federal government now allows for two variations from the "traditional" passage of bills.*¹ A motion may be tabled for a committee to prepare and introduce a bill.*² Bills may now be referred to committee *before* second reading. In any event, a bill goes to committee only *once*.

government has summarized and published all current statutes in the *Revised Statutes of Canada* of 1985, cited as R.S.C. (1985). It is not necessary to go back any earlier than this compilation to find current legislation. Federal legislation can be accessed online at http://laws-lois.justice.gc.ca. As of June 1, 2009, all consolidated acts and regulations on the Justice Laws Website are "official," meaning that they can be used for evidentiary purposes.

Federal and provincial statutes are compiled and published

Similarly, each province annually publishes the statutes passed by its legislative assembly and provides a compilation in the form of revised statutes. Unfortunately, there is no uniformity in the timing of the revisions, and each province has revised and compiled its statutes in a different year. Most jurisdictions provide official or unofficial consolidated updates of their statutes online as an ongoing service. These statutes, along with useful commentary about new legislation, are currently available on the Internet at their respective government's website. LawCentral Alberta provides easy access to the laws across the country (see www.lawcentralalberta.ca) as does the Canadian Legal Information Institute (www.canlii.org). The MyBusLawLab will also provide important information with respect to relevant statutes and other material as they are discussed throughout the text.

Regulations are also published

Statutes often empower government agencies to create further rules to carry out their functions. As long as these regulations meet the terms of the statute, they have the effect of law. They are also published and are available to the public as *Regulations of Canada* or of the respective provinces. Cities and municipalities pass bylaws under their statutory authority in the same way, and these too are published and made available by those jurisdictions. Statutes (if passed within the power of the respective government's constitutional authority) override any previous law in place, whether judge-made law (common law or equity) or prior legislation.

Judges interpret and apply statutes

Decisions create precedents for future interpretations

When judges are required to deal with a statute, they must first determine what it means. The judge must then determine whether, under the *Constitution Act, 1867* and other constitutional provisions, the legislative body that passed the statute in question had the power to do so. When a judge interprets and applies a statute, that decision becomes a precedent, and henceforth the statute must be interpreted in the same way by courts lower in the court hierarchy.

LO ⑦ PROTECTION OF RIGHTS AND FREEDOMS

Rights and freedoms were historically protected by convention

The preamble of the *Constitution Act, 1867* states that Canada will have "a Constitution similar in principle to that of the United Kingdom." The courts have interpreted that phrase as importing into Canada the unwritten conventions and traditions of government developed in the United Kingdom over the centuries. Among those unwritten conventions are the practices of protecting and preserving fundamental rights and freedoms. Canada has thus inherited the British tradition of protecting human rights and individual freedoms through unwritten conventions (practices) as supported by common law.

In the aftermath of World War II, concern arose over the adequacy of entrusting the protection of personal rights and freedoms to common law. Two streams of legislation developed: one dealing with protecting human rights against abuses by the government and the second aimed at protecting individuals against discrimination and intolerance by society at large.

Canadian Bill of Rights

It is important to understand that basic human rights protections set out in ordinary statutes passed by the federal or provincial governments may not protect people from abuses by government. Because Canada adopted the British method of government, which is based on the supremacy of Parliament, the provincial and federal governments were free to interfere at will with civil rights through legislation. We need look no further than the way Japanese Canadians were treated during World War II to conclude that it could be dangerous for Canadians to leave the protection of their basic rights to the political process.[30]

---

30. During World War II, Japanese Canadians were forcibly relocated to internment camps across the country because they were deemed a "threat" to national security.

The first attempt at limiting the federal government's power to pass legislation that violates basic human rights was the passage (in 1960) of the *Canadian Bill of Rights*.[31] Because it was not entrenched in the Constitution, the courts viewed the *Canadian Bill of Rights* as just another statute that could be repealed, amended, or simply overridden by any subsequent federal statute. Furthermore, when asked to apply the *Canadian Bill of Rights*, the courts approached its provisions in the same narrow, restrictive way that they did any other legislation, thus significantly limiting its scope and effect. For example, when subsequently passed federal legislation was found to be in conflict with the provisions of the *Canadian Bill of Rights*, instead of applying the *Canadian Bill of Rights* and limiting the operation of the new statute, the courts would treat the new legislation as overriding the old and would disregard the provisions that conflicted with the new legislation. This, of course, effectively defeated the purpose of the *Canadian Bill of Rights*, and while it is still considered law in Canada its effectiveness is extremely limited. Something more was needed.

The Canadian Bill of Rights was viewed as just another statute

Charter of Rights and Freedoms

A constitutional guarantee of basic rights and freedoms arose in 1982 following a series of constitutional conferences. The *Constitution Act, 1982*[32] was simultaneously enacted in Canada and the United Kingdom. In the latter, it was contained in a statute called the *Canada Act 1982*.[33] One effect of these enactments was to make a significant addition to the Canadian Constitution in the form of the *Canadian Charter of Rights and Freedoms*.

The effect of including the *Charter* in our Constitution is twofold. First, neither the federal government nor the provinces have the power to modify or otherwise interfere with the basic rights set out in the *Charter* except through constitutional amendment. Ordinary legislation will not override the *Charter* simply because it is passed after the *Charter*. The provisions are said to be entrenched in the Constitution and are, as declared in section 52 of the *Constitution Act, 1982*, "the supreme law of Canada." Section 52 goes on to state "any law that is inconsistent with the provisions of the Constitution is, to the extent of that inconsistency, of no force or effect." In other words, the *Charter* and the rights protected by it come first.

The Constitution includes the *Charter*; together they are the SUPREME law of Canada

Second, the burden of protecting those rights has shifted from politicians to judges. Now an individual who feels that her rights have been interfered with by legislation or other forms of government action can seek redress from the courts, relying on the provisions of the *Charter*. The courts can remedy a violation of rights by excluding evidence improperly secured and can grant any remedy deemed to be just in the circumstances.[34] The courts can even strike down statutes that infringe on those rights. Hence, the doctrine of parliamentary supremacy has been restricted, and the courts are able to check the power of both Parliament and the legislatures in those areas covered by the *Charter*.

Courts are empowered to strike down offending statutes

LIMITATIONS

There are three important limitations on the entrenchment of these basic rights. Section 1 of the *Charter of Rights and Freedoms* allows "reasonable limits" to be placed on those rights and freedoms when limiting them can be "demonstrably justified in a free and democratic society." This gives the courts the power to uphold a law even if it violates rights so as to avoid an unreasonable result.

The rights and freedoms set out in the *Charter* are, therefore, not absolute. For example, the *Charter* guarantees freedom of expression, but there would be

Government cannot interfere with basic rights and freedoms except if it is justifiable to do so

---

31. S.C. 1960, c. 44.

32. Schedule B to the *Canada Act 1982* (U.K.), 1982, c. 11.

33. *Canada Act 1982* (U.K.), 1982, c. 11.

34. *Canadian Charter of Rights and Freedoms*, s. 24, Part I of the *Constitution Act, 1982*, being Schedule B to the *Canada Act 1982* (U.K.), 1982, c.11.

little dispute that libel, slander, or hard-core pornography must be controlled. In *Hill v. Church of Scientology of Toronto*,[35] the Supreme Court was asked to give effect to the freedom of expression provision of the *Charter* by dismissing a defamation action against the church and its representative, especially where the remarks were directed at a government official or Crown prosecutor. The Court found that the laws of defamation were, under section 1, a reasonable limitation on the operation of the freedom of expression clause of the *Charter*. Similarly, in the *Sharpe* case[36] the accused argued that since freedom of expression was protected by the *Charter*, charges making it an offence to possess child pornography should be struck down since the material (in this case, photos in the possession of and stories written by the accused) may have artistic merit. The Supreme Court upheld most of the pornography law on the basis that it was needed to protect children from harm.

The interests of the public are considered when applying section 1. Nonetheless, a law that restricts *Charter* rights, though apparently justified, will be rejected if it goes too far. In the *Oakes* case,[37] the Supreme Court created a framework for assessing whether a law that violates rights should be upheld. First, it must be established that the impugned legislation relates to a pressing and substantial concern in a free and democratic society. Second, the means must be reasonable and demonstrably justified. This involves a proportionality test to be applied between the legislative objective and the disputed legislation. The more severe the deleterious effects of a measure, the more important the objective must be. Furthermore, the means should impair the right in question as little as possible.

CASE SUMMARY 2.8

Polygamy and Crime: *Reference re Section 293 of the Criminal Code of Canada*[38]

Investigations into polygamous practices in Bountiful, British Columbia, including allegations of trafficking young girls between Canada and the United States, raised concerns regarding the constitutional validity of section 293 of the *Criminal Code*. It declares polygamy to be an indictable offence punishable by imprisonment. Before proceeding with prosecutions under section 293, the BC government decided to put this question to the Court: Is section 293 of the *Code* consistent with the *Charter*, and if not, in what particulars and to what extent?

Those challenging the law submitted that it was a product of anti-Mormon sentiment and constituted an unacceptable intrusion upon the freedoms of religion, expression, association, and equality as protected by the *Charter*. They argued that those infringements were not justified under section 1 of the *Charter*.

The Court conceded that the *Criminal Code* restriction against polygamy infringes on certain sections of the *Charter*, but the key issue was whether the prohibition was justifiable. In its 335-page decision, the Court ruled that section 293 is constitutionally sound because prevention of the collective harms associated with polygamy, including sexual exploitation of young women and expulsion of young men from polygamous communities, was a pressing and substantial concern in a free and democratic society. The impairment of religious freedom was minimal and, since the provision was proportional in its effect, the violation of religious freedoms was justified as reasonable. The benefits of banning polygamy far outweighed the detriments.

[35.] [1995] 2 SCR 1130, 1995 CanLII 59 (SCC).

[36.] *R. v. Sharpe*, [2001] 1 SCR 45, 2001 SCC 2 (CanLII).

[37.] *R. v. Oakes*, [1986] 1 SCR 103, 1986 CanLII 46 (SCC).

[38.] 2011 BCSC 1588 (CanLII).

DISCUSSION QUESTION

As is evident in this decision, the Court determined that the legislation banning polygamy related to a pressing and substantial concern. Second, the infringement of religious freedom was assessed as proportionate when compared with the greater harm caused by polygamous practices. What other laws that may violate *Charter* rights or freedoms would you evaluate as being reasonable and justifiable?

The second limitation is contained in section 33 and is referred to as the "notwithstanding clause." It allows each of the provinces and the federal government to override the basic rights contained in section 2 and sections 7 through 15 of the *Charter* simply by stating that the new legislation operates "notwithstanding" (regardless of) the *Charter*. The sections that can be overridden in this way include **fundamental freedoms** (provisions such as freedom of conscience and religion, of thought and belief, of opinion and expression, and of assembly and association); **legal rights** (the right of life, liberty, and security of person; security against unreasonable search and seizure, arbitrary imprisonment, and detention); and **equality rights** (the right not to be discriminated against on the basis of gender, age, religion, race, or colour; and the guarantee of equality before the law).

It would appear that section 33 weakens the *Charter of Rights and Freedoms* considerably and restores the supremacy of Parliament, at least in relation to the designated sections. It was originally hoped that most politicians would find the political cost too great to override the *Charter* in this way and, as a result, would refrain from doing so. For the most part, this has been the case. Quebec, however, used the notwithstanding clause to support language legislation restricting the use of English on business signs in that province. This legislation clearly violates the *Charter*'s guarantee of freedom of expression, but the Quebec government gambled that the majority of the electorate would favour such protection of the French language. Refer to the MyBusLawLab for details.

There are few other examples of the notwithstanding clause being used, and Alberta's experiments with invoking the clause have been controversial.[39] The notwithstanding clause does not apply to sections guaranteeing democratic rights (the right to vote and to elect members to Parliament and the legislative assemblies), mobility rights (the right to enter and leave Canada), or language rights (the right to use both official languages). In addition, the rights of Aboriginal people and the rights guaranteed to both genders cannot be overridden by the federal or provincial governments.

A "sunset clause" is applied to the operation of section 33. If the notwithstanding clause is invoked, the statute must be re-enacted by that legislative body every five years. This forces a re-examination of the decision to override the *Charter* after the intervening event of an election where the use of the notwithstanding clause can be made an issue. New legislators may not be as willing to pay the political cost of using the notwithstanding clause.

The third limitation is the restriction of the operation of the *Charter* to government and government-related activities. Section 32(1)(a) declares that the *Charter* applies only to matters falling within the authority of "the Parliament and Government of Canada" and the territories, and section 32(1)(b) makes the *Charter* apply "to the legislature and government of each province." A serious problem facing the courts is determining just where government stops and government institutions acting in a private capacity begin. Are government

The use of the notwithstanding clause may be a political gamble

A sunset clause causes legislation to expire

The Charter *applies only to the government—but where does government stop?*

---

39. Alberta used the notwithstanding clause to override equality rights when it passed the *Marriage Act* provisions restricting marriage to a man and a woman. The clause was used to deny same-sex couples the ability to marry. The sunset clause caused that override to expire in 2005. See *Marriage Act*, R.S.A. 2000, c. M-5, s. 2.

institutions—universities, schools, hospitals, and Crown corporations like the Canadian Broadcasting Corporation—affected?

The *Charter* probably applies to private institutions acting as arms of government

While there are still many questions, it does seem clear that when such institutions are acting as an arm of government, the *Charter* applies. Certainly the *Charter* applies to the legislation creating these institutions and to the services provided directly by government departments, including the police and military. When government agencies act in their private capacity (for example, in employee relations), the appropriate federal or provincial human rights legislation applies; such legislation must, in turn, comply with the provisions of the *Charter*. If a section of a statute is in conflict with the provisions of the *Charter*, the offending section may be declared void. Courts may strike down the void law or grant a remedy that is appropriate. In the *Vriend* case[40] (discussed in Case Summary 2.17), the Supreme Court of Canada showed its willingness to interpret into the Alberta statute a provision prohibiting discrimination on the basis of sexual orientation rather than overturning the statute. Occasionally, the courts have declared legislation invalid but have stayed (held in abeyance) their decision to give the legislators an opportunity to amend the statutes themselves.[41]

While the *Charter* directly affects an individual's relationship with government, it only indirectly affects the relationships between individuals and between individuals and private institutions. Human rights legislation impacts these latter relationships, but these federal and provincial human rights codes must comply with the *Charter*. It is also important to remember that the provisions of the *Charter* apply not only to the regulations and enactments of these government bodies and institutions but also to the conduct of government officials employed by them. These officials derive their authority from provincial or federal enactments. If they are acting in a way that violates the provisions of the *Charter*, either they are not acting within their authority or the statute authorizing their conduct is itself in violation of the *Charter*. In either case, such offending conduct can be challenged under the *Charter*.

Charter Provisions

A brief summary of the types of rights and freedoms Canadians now enjoy because of the *Charter of Rights and Freedoms* follows. The *Charter* sets out several rights that are available in some cases only to citizens of Canada and in other cases to everyone in the nation. The extent of these rights and freedoms, their meaning, and the limitations on those rights are still being defined by court decisions. Recourse is available through the courts if the declared rights are interfered with by laws or by the acts of government agents. The courts have been empowered under section 24 of the *Charter* to "provide such remedies as the court considers appropriate and just in the circumstances." These powers are in addition to the inherent power of the court to declare that the offending legislation or conduct is of no effect. This provision allows the courts to award damages, injunctions, and other remedies when otherwise they would have had no power to do so. Section 24 also gives a judge the power in a criminal matter to exclude evidence that has been obtained in a way that violates the *Charter* rights of the accused if its admission "would bring the administration of justice into disrepute."

FUNDAMENTAL FREEDOMS

Everyone in Canada has the right to freedom of conscience and religion; of thought, belief, and opinion; of the press; of peaceful assembly; of association.

Section 2 of the *Charter* declares certain underlying fundamental freedoms available to everyone in Canada. These are freedom of conscience and religion; freedom of belief, opinion, and expression; and freedom of assembly and association. The *Charter* protects the right to believe in whatever we wish, to express

---

40. *Vriend v. Alberta*, [1998] 1 SCR 493, 1998 CanLII 816 (SCC).
41. See *Haig v. Canada*, 1992 CanLII 2787 (ON CA).

that belief, and to carry on activities associated with it free from interference. When the expression of those freedoms or the activities associated with them interferes with the freedoms of others, the courts may restrict those freedoms by applying section 1 of the *Charter*.

CASE SUMMARY 2.9

Sunday Shopping: Does It Prevent Corporations from Going to Church? *R. v. Big M Drug Mart Ltd.*[42]

Big M Drug Mart Ltd. was charged with violation of the *Lord's Day Act*, which required that commercial businesses be closed on Sunday. This statute was enacted by the federal government under its criminal law power long before the enactment of the *Charter*. It compelled the observance of a religious duty by means of prohibitions and penalties. The Supreme Court of Canada held that the *Lord's Day Act* was invalid and of no effect because it interfered with freedom of conscience and religion. It did not matter that the applicant was a corporation incapable of having a conscience or beliefs. Section 2 states that "everyone," be it a corporation or an individual, enjoys fundamental freedoms. And section 24 states "Anyone whose rights or freedoms, as guaranteed by this Charter, have been infringed or denied" may apply to a court to obtain a just remedy.

Communities seeking to maintain a day of rest can look to the decision in *London Drugs Ltd. v. Red Deer (City)*.[43] It involved a requirement that businesses close one day a week. In that case, however, the bylaw simply required businesses to be closed any day during a week. The bylaw specified Sunday as a default, but allowed the business to specify another day if it wished. That made the law secular rather than religious, its object being to give workers one day in the week free of work. This treated all businesses equally since they had a choice as to when to close.

SMALL BUSINESS PERSPECTIVE

Ironically, businesses have raised violation of religious freedoms to increase their profits. These cases illustrate that the *Charter* can be used to strike down laws even when the true motive has little to do with asserting rights.

Freedom of conscience and religion was likewise raised in the *Hutterian Brethren* case,[44] where a regulation requiring that all drivers' licences include a photo of the driver was challenged. The Hutterian Brethren took the position that requiring a photograph to be taken violated the respondents' religious freedoms and equality rights under the *Charter*. The courts refused to strike down the regulation. The objective of the impugned regulation, namely maintaining the integrity of the licensing system in a way that minimizes the risk of identity theft, was clearly a goal of pressing and substantial importance, justifying limits on rights. Thus, if Albertans wish to drive, they will need to submit to having their photos taken despite any religious reservations.

Freedom of expression, which includes freedom of the press, is an extremely important provision for preserving the democratic nature of Canada, and our courts are careful to uphold these freedoms. Still, there are many limitations on them, such as the laws of defamation and obscenity.

---

42. [1985] 1 SCR 295, 1985 CanLII 69 (SCC).

43. [1987] A.J. No. 815 (Q.B.); appeal dismissed [1988] A.J. No. 701 (C.A.); leave to appeal to the Supreme Court refused [1988] S.C.C.A. No. 246.

44. *Alberta v. Hutterian Brethren of Wilson Colony*, [2009] 2 SCR 567, 2009 SCC 37 (CanLII).

CASE SUMMARY 2.10

When Does Expressing One's Opinions Contravene the Law?
Saskatchewan (Human Rights Commission) v. Whatcott[45]

Whatcott distributed four anti-gay flyers to homes in Saskatoon and Regina in 2001 and 2002. Several recipients filed complaints with the Saskatchewan Human Rights Commission, alleging the material in the flyers "promotes hatred against individuals because of their sexual orientation" in violation of section 14(1)(b) of the *Saskatchewan Human Rights Code*. A tribunal hearing was convened and it concluded that the material did violate the *Code*. Whatcott appealed, claiming that the *Code* provisions violated his freedoms of expression and religion because they prevented him from expressing his religious beliefs about homosexual conduct. Ultimately, the case was heard by the Supreme Court of Canada.

Section 14(1)(b) of the *Code* prohibited the publication or display of any representation "that exposes or tends to expose to hatred, ridicules, belittles or otherwise affronts the dignity of any person or class of persons on the basis of a prohibited ground." The Supreme Court of Canada concluded that section 14(1)(b) infringed on section 2(a) (freedom of religion) and section 2(b) (freedom of expression) of the *Charter*, but the infringement was justified under section 1 of the *Charter*.

The Court held that a prohibition of any representation that "ridicules, belittles or otherwise affronts the dignity of" any person or class of persons on the basis of a prohibited ground was not a reasonable limit on freedom of expression or religion, thus these words were severed. But the remaining prohibition of any representation "that exposes or tends to expose to hatred" any person or class of persons on the basis of a prohibited ground was a reasonable limit and demonstrably justified in a free and democratic society.

DISCUSSION QUESTION

In protecting individuals from discrimination, human rights legislation causes a conflict between freedom of expression and the right to equal treatment free from discrimination. What factors should guide the courts in balancing these conflicting rights?

The *Charter* also protects freedom of association. The Supreme Court of Canada has stated that collective bargaining is the "most significant collective activity through which freedom of association is expressed in the labour context."[46] Laws that restrict collective bargaining rights are thus subject to *Charter* scrutiny. But in *Fraser v. Ontario (Attorney General)*,[47] the Supreme Court was less expansive in its interpretation of freedom to associate. In 2002, the Ontario government introduced the *Agricultural Employees Protection Act (AEPA)*, thus excluding farm workers from the provisions of the *Labour Relations Act*. Farm workers claimed the new Act offered fewer protections and failed to adequately protect their *Charter* freedom of association rights. Specifically, the new legislation failed to provide for meaningful collective bargaining and provided no right to strike. In a divided decision, the Court stated that the *AEPA* did not violate section 2 because the freedom to associate does not guarantee access to any particular model of labour relations. The freedom protects the right to associate to achieve workplace goals through collective action, and since employers were obligated to listen to representations from an employee association implicitly in good faith, the *AEPA* satisfied this constitutional obligation. Essentially, the Court found that an individual's freedom of association under section 2(d) simply imposes an obligation on employers to bargain in good faith on workplace issues.

---

45. [2013] 1 SCR 467, 2013 SCC 11 (CanLII).

46. *Health Services and Support-Facilities Subsector Bargaining Assn. v. British Columbia*, [2007] 2 SCR 391, 2007 SCC 27 (CanLII), at p. 66.

47. [2011] 2 SCR 3, 2011 SCC 20 (CanLII).

When employer rights are interfered with by inappropriate trade union activity, limits may be imposed on the right to peaceful assembly. The rights to peaceful assembly and freedom of association have likewise been limited when riots may occur.

Note that section 2 is one of the areas of the *Charter* that can be overridden by the use of the notwithstanding clause (section 33).

DEMOCRATIC RIGHTS

Sections 3, 4, and 5 protect our rights to vote and to qualify to be elected to the House of Commons or the provincial legislative assemblies. Reasonable limitations can be put on the right to vote, restricting those who are underage and, most likely, those deemed mentally incompetent. But the abuses of the past, where racial groups were denied the vote, are now prohibited. Before 1982, these rights were protected by constitutional convention, but now they are enshrined in the *Charter*. Section 4 ensures there will be an election at least every five years, except in times of war, and section 5 requires that the elected body be called into session at least once every 12 months. The government in power still has the right to decide when to call an election within that five-year period and also whether to call the session into sitting more often than the "once every 12 months" minimum. The government also has the power to determine what that session will consist of, which also provides some potential for abuse. These sections cannot be overridden by the notwithstanding clause (section 33), a distinction of which the courts have taken notice (see Case Summary 2.11).

Maximum duration before the next election is five years unless crises loom

***Charter* enshrines the right to vote, to be elected; requirement to have government sit annually**

CASE SUMMARY 2.11

Ballot Boxes in Jails: *Sauvé v. Canada (Chief Electoral Officer)*[48]

All prison inmates were prohibited from voting in federal elections by the former provisions of the *Canada Elections Act*. That Act was held unconstitutional as an unjustified denial of the right to vote, guaranteed by section 3 of the *Charter*, in *Sauvé v. Canada (Attorney General)*.[49] Parliament responded to this litigation by changing the Act, denying the right to vote to a smaller group—those inmates serving sentences of two years or more. The issue in this case was whether the new provisions were likewise unconstitutional. It was argued that they violated the right to vote (section 3) and equality rights as protected by section 15. The Crown conceded that the Act contravened section 3 of the *Charter*. The key issue was thus whether this restriction could be demonstrably justified under section 1.

The Court decided that the violation was not justified. As stated by Chief Justice McLachlin, "The right to vote, which lies at the heart of Canadian democracy, can only be trammeled for good reason. Here the reasons do not suffice . . . Charter rights are not a matter of privilege or merit, but a function of membership in the Canadian polity that cannot be lightly set aside. This is manifestly true of the right to vote, the cornerstone of democracy, exempt from the incursion permitted on other rights through s. 33 override."[50]

DISCUSSION QUESTIONS

The fact that the notwithstanding clause cannot be used to override democratic rights was emphasized in the above decision. But what about 17 year olds and other youths? Shouldn't the right to vote be extended to them as well?[51] And what does this suggest about the inviolability of mobility rights and language rights?

[48.] [2002] 2 F.C. 119 (C.A.), rev'd [2002] 3 SCR 519, 2002 SCC 68 (CanLII).

[49.] [1993] 2 SCR 438, 1993 CanLII 92 (SCC).

[50.] Inmates finally secured the right to vote in provincial elections in Alberta in 2010 with passage of the *Election Statutes Amendment Act, 2010*, S.A. 2010, c. 8.

[51.] See *Fitzgerald v. Alberta*, 2004 A.B.C.A. 184 (CanLII), where 17 year olds, denied the right to vote in provincial and municipal elections, challenged the *Elections Act* and the *Local Authorities Act* for violating their *Charter* rights under section 3 and section 15(1), respectively.

MOBILITY RIGHTS

Citizens enjoy the right to enter and leave Canada

Section 6 of the *Charter* ensures that Canadians can travel and live anywhere within the geographic limitations of Canada as well as enter and leave the country at will. It also ensures that all Canadians have the right to earn a livelihood in any part of Canada. But again, these assurances are qualified. Programs that are of general application in a province or region can be valid even though they appear to interfere with these rights. In the field of employment, for instance, provincial licensing and educational requirements may prevent people trained and licensed in other parts of the country from carrying on their chosen profession without requalifying in that province. Section 6(4) specifically allows for programs that are designed to better the condition of those "who are socially or economically disadvantaged," even when those programs interfere with the mobility rights of other Canadians who might want to take advantage of the programs but are prohibited from doing so.

CASE SUMMARY 2.12

Non-Resident Asserts the Right to Earn a Living: *Basile v. Attorney General of Nova Scotia*[52]

Under the *Direct Sellers' Licensing and Regulation Act*,[53] anyone involved in the activity of direct selling (door-to-door sales) in Nova Scotia had to be a resident of that province. Mr. Basile was a bookseller and a resident of Quebec. He applied for a licence to sell in Nova Scotia and was refused because he was not a permanent resident, as required by the statute. He challenged this decision as a violation of his mobility rights under the *Charter of Rights and Freedoms*. This was clearly an infringement of the mobility rights under the *Charter*, which gave any Canadian the right to travel to and earn a living in any part of the country. The main difficulty was to decide whether this fell into one of the exceptions set out in either section 6(3)(a) (laws of general application) or the reasonable limitation clause in section 1 of the *Charter*. The Court held that this did not qualify as a law of general application, since it was directed at one specific group—non-residents. Further, since no evidence had been presented that would support the argument that this was a reasonable limitation as required under section 1 of the *Charter*, Mr. Basile was successful, and the offending section was declared by the Court to be "of no force and effect."

SMALL BUSINESS PERSPECTIVE

Mr. Basile was successful in asserting his mobility rights and in having the restricting legislation struck down. But would a business or corporation be able to raise a similar argument? Consider to whom mobility rights are extended.

LEGAL RIGHTS

The rights listed under this heading are intended to protect individuals from unreasonable interference from the government or its agents and to ensure that when there is interference it is done in a way that is both procedurally fair and consistent with basic principles of fundamental justice. It is important to note that the protections provided under this heading do not extend to interference with property rights. There is no specific reference to property rights in the *Charter*.

Everyone has a right to life, liberty, and security of person

Section 7 states that we have the right to life, liberty, and the security of person and the right not to have these rights taken away except in accordance with the "principles of fundamental justice." In the *Baker* case, where the Supreme Court examined the procedure followed at deportation hearings, Justice L'Heureux-Dubé

---

52. [1984] N.S.J. No. 337 N.S.S.C. (App. Div.).
53. S.N.S. 1975, c. 9.

summarized what is required by the principles of **procedural fairness**: "The values underlying the duty of procedural fairness relate to the principle that the individual or individuals affected should have the opportunity to present their case fully and fairly, and have decisions affecting their rights, interests, or privileges made using a fair, impartial, and open process, appropriate to the statutory, institutional, and social context of the decision."[54] The requirements of fundamental justice include procedural fairness but go further. Certain underlying principles considered basic to our legal system, such as the rule of law, would also be included.

Everyone is entitled to procedural fairness

Sections 8 and 9 prohibit such activities as unreasonable search and seizure and arbitrary imprisonment.[55] Subsequent sections provide for the right to be informed of the reason for an arrest, the right to retain counsel, the right to be tried within a reasonable time, the right to the presumption of innocence, the right not to be tried twice for the same offence, and the right not to be subjected to any cruel or unusual punishment. The common theme here is the protection of people from abusive, arbitrary, or unequal application of police and prosecutorial power. Not only is the individual protected in the event of such an abuse, but the provisions also serve to discourage the police and prosecutors from acting outside the law. The powers given to the courts further help to persuade the law-enforcement community to act properly by allowing the court to exclude evidence obtained in violation of these provisions, where not to do so "would bring the administration of justice into disrepute" (see section 24(2)). These basic legal rights can be overridden by the invocation of the notwithstanding clause.

Everyone is to be secure from unreasonable search, seizure, detention, or imprisonment

---

CASE SUMMARY 2.13

A Right to Die? *Rodriguez v. British Columbia (Attorney General)*;[56] *Carter v. Canada (Attorney General)*[57]

Does the right to life as guaranteed by section 7 of the *Charter* also protect the right to die? Sue Rodriguez, a terminally ill patient, sought the assistance of a physician to commit suicide. The *Criminal Code of Canada*, however, prohibits aiding a person to commit suicide, so Rodriguez argued that this violated her rights under sections 7, 12, and 15(1) of the *Charter*. Rodriguez argued that the guarantee of "security of person" found in section 7 protected her right to decide what would happen to her body. Control over her body would be violated if she could not choose to die. Rodriguez claimed that forcing her to live in a degenerated body would be cruel and unusual treatment, in violation of section 12. Finally, she claimed that the *Code*, by barring a terminally ill person from a "physician assisted suicide," in effect creates inequality. It prevents individuals who are physically unable to end their lives without assistance from choosing suicide; yet that option is, in principle, available to other members of the public without contravening the law. Commission of suicide is not a punishable offence or a crime.

In a split decision, the Supreme Court of Canada determined that the right to security of person also had to be viewed in light of the sanctity of life, the right to life also being specifically guaranteed under section 7. Section 12 was not violated by the *Code*, as a prohibition of assisted suicide is not a form of "treatment" by the state. Finally, the majority determined that if equality rights were violated by the *Code*, this violation would be justifiable under section 1. Criminalizing assisted suicide protects the sanctity of life and prevents abuses. Concern that decriminalization of assisted suicide might lead to abuses

---

54. *Baker v. Canada (Minister of Citizenship and Immigration)*, [1999] 2 SCR 817, 1999 CanLII 699 (SCC) at 841.

55. See *Sivia v. British Columbia (Superintendent of Motor Vehicles)*, 2011 B.C.S.C. 1639 (CanLII), where British Columbia's drunk driving laws, providing for automatic roadside prohibition, were successfully challenged for violating section 8 of the *Charter*.

56. [1993] 3 SCR 519, 1993 CanLII 75 (SCC).

57. [2015] 1 SCR 331, 2015 SCC 5 (CanLII).

prevented the Court from taking the first step down the slippery path toward it. "Active euthanasia," or doctor-assisted suicide, thus remained illegal in Canada.

Two decades later the same issue was before the Supreme Court in the *Carter* and *Taylor* appeals. Gloria Taylor set about ending her life following a diagnosis of Lou Gehrig's disease. She launched a "right to die with dignity" lawsuit. In June 2012, the B.C. Supreme Court agreed that existing laws did deny Taylor the right to control her own life. She was given an exemption so she could get help ending her own life, but she died before that could happen.[58]

Lee Carter also sought the right to die; the Supreme Court of Canada heard the appeal in October 2014.[59] The Court reversed its earlier position and declared that insofar as the law prohibits physician-assisted dying for competent adults who seek such assistance as a result of a grievous and irremediable medical condition that causes enduring and intolerable suffering, sections 241(b) and 14 of the Criminal Code deprive these adults of their right to life, liberty, and security of the person under section 7 of the Charter. The declaration of invalidity, however, was suspended for 12 months.

DISCUSSION QUESTIONS

Should the issue of decriminalizing euthanasia be determined by the courts or by Parliament? As Sue Rodriguez asked, "Whose life is it anyway?" The courts have clearly put the issue back into Parliament's hands, within a time frame. It remains to be seen whether politicians will seek public input on this complex ethical issue.

EQUALITY RIGHTS

Every person is to be equal before and under the law

The equality rights set out in section 15 of the *Charter* prohibit discrimination in the application of the law on the basis of gender, religion, race, age, or national origin and ensure that all people in Canada have the same claim to the protection and benefits of the law. This means that the various provisions of the federal and provincial laws must be applied equally to all. Any time a distinction is made in any provincial or federal law or by a government official on the basis of one of these categories, it can be challenged as unconstitutional.

CASE SUMMARY 2.14

Age Discrimination Justified: *Withler v. Canada (Attorney General)*[60]

The plaintiffs, widows whose supplemental death benefits were reduced because of the age of their husbands at the time of death, complained of unequal treatment under the law. The *Public Service Superannuation Act* (PSSA) and the *Canadian Forces Superannuation Act* (CFSA) provide a supplementary death benefit of twice the salary of the participants upon their death, subject to a reduction for age. Under the *PSSA*, public servants' benefits are reduced by 10 percent for each year of age in excess of 65; under the *CFSA*, Canadian Forces members' benefits are reduced 10 percent for each year of age beyond 60. The plaintiffs claimed that those provisions constitute age discrimination and thus violate section 15 of the *Charter*. They sought a declaration that the provisions are inconsistent with the *Charter* and of no force and effect and claimed judgment for the amount by which benefit payments had been reduced (an amount exceeding $2 billion for the class).

---

58. See *Carter v. Canada (Attorney General)*, 2012 B.C.S.C. 886 (CanLII), where the laws prohibiting physician-assisted suicide were declared to unjustifiably infringe on sections 7 and 15 of the *Charter*.

59. A webcast of the hearing (Case #35591), held on October 15, 2014, is available on the Supreme Court's website, www.scc-csc.gc.ca/case-dossier/info/webcast-webdiffusion-eng.aspx?cas=35591.

60. [2011] 1 SCR 396, 2011 SCC 12 (CanLII).

The Supreme Court concluded that the approach to be taken when addressing equality rights is one that takes account of the full context of the claimant group's situation, the actual impact of the law on that situation, and whether the impugned law perpetuates disadvantage to or negative stereotypes about that group.

Clearly, the reduction provisions at issue in this case were age related; they thus constituted an obvious distinction on an enumerated ground. Next, the Court addressed whether the distinction creates a disadvantage by perpetuating prejudice or stereotyping. To answer this question, the focus must be on the nature of the benefit. A contextual assessment revealed that the age-based benefit reduction did not breach section 15 because the benefit reductions reflected the reality that different groups of survivors have different needs. For younger employees, it acts as group life insurance by insuring against unexpected death at a time when the surviving spouse would not be protected by a pension. For older employees, whose spouses' long-term income security is guaranteed by the survivors' pension coupled with the public service's health and dental plans, it is intended to assist with the costs of terminal illness and death. Rather than causing disadvantage, the reduction provisions actually furthered the goal of the scheme—to provide for surviving spouses according to their needs. Accordingly, the court challenge to these provisions failed.

DISCUSSION QUESTION

Distinctions as to who qualifies for government assistance are often based on age or some other ground that may be protected by the *Charter*. What factors may lead a court to conclude that a program violates the *Charter* because of unequal treatment?

Section 15 contains a general prohibition against discrimination, so even where the discrimination relates to a category not specifically listed, victims will generally be protected. The courts interpret the Constitution and its provisions broadly. Thus, even though section 15 makes no reference to sexual preference or orientation, the courts have had no difficulty in concluding that a denial of benefits to same-sex couples is prohibited because it discriminates against applicants on the basis of their sexual orientation. See the MyBusLawLab for further details.

CASE SUMMARY 2.15

Courts Prompt Significant Legislative Changes: *Halpern v. Canada (Attorney General)*[61]

The Ontario Court of Appeal was asked whether the exclusion of same-sex couples from the common law definition of marriage as "one man and one woman" breached sections 2(a) or 15(1) of the *Charter*. It declared the definition of marriage to be invalid as it offends equality rights. It reformulated the definition to the "voluntary union for life of two people to the exclusion of all others" and declared this definition to have immediate effect. Consequently, numerous same-sex couples rushed to secure marriage licences. The federal government responded by referring a proposed bill on same-sex marriage to the Supreme Court of Canada for review.[62] After the Supreme Court affirmed the validity of the proposed legislation and the authority of the federal Parliament to define marriage, Parliament proceeded to redefine marriage to include same-sex couples.[63]

[61.] 2003 CanLII 26403 (ON CA).

[62.] *Reference re Same-Sex Marriage*, [2004] 3 SCR 698, 2004 SCC 79 (CanLII).

[63.] *Civil Marriage Act*, S.C. 2005, c. 33.

It is important to note that section 15(2) provides for affirmative-action programs. When a provision is intentionally introduced that has the effect of discriminating against one group of people, it may still be allowed if its purpose is to correct an imbalance that has occurred through discrimination in the past. Thus, the government may intentionally set out to hire women or specific ethnic minorities to get a better balance in the civil service. This is permissible even though it will have the effect of preventing people of other groups, such as white men, from having an equal opportunity to obtain those same jobs. Universities often have similar programs to encourage minorities to enter faculties or professions to correct historical imbalances.

In addition to the provisions set out in section 15, there are other provisions in the *Charter* setting out equality rights. Section 28 guarantees that the provisions of the *Charter* apply equally to males and females. Equality rights (protected by section 15) can be overridden by the operation of the notwithstanding clause, but section 28 cannot be overridden.

Section 35 states that the *Charter* in no way affects the rights (including treaty rights) of the Aboriginal peoples of Canada. Although this last provision may have the effect of preserving inequality rather than eliminating it, the objective of this section is to ensure that during the process of treaty negotiations and land claim disputes between the provincial governments and Aboriginal groups, nothing in the *Charter* would interfere with the special-status rights associated with that group. Section 33 cannot be used to override the protection given to the position of the Aboriginal peoples of Canada.

Although these *Charter* provisions apply only in our dealings with government, it is important for businesspeople to remember that these equality provisions are the essence of most provincial and federal human rights legislation. Since those statutes must comply with the *Charter* provisions, the *Charter* indirectly controls business practices (see Case Summary 2.17, *Vriend v. Alberta*). In addition, there are many examples of provincial and federal legislation that require all those working on government-funded projects to comply with special federal and provincial programs aimed at correcting past injustices. These special requirements may range from fair-wage policies (where non-union businesses must pay wages comparable with union-negotiated wages) to programs requiring the hiring or promotion of disadvantaged minorities or the correction of gender imbalances in the workforce.[64]

LANGUAGE RIGHTS

French and English have equal status—Canada and New Brunswick are officially bilingual

The part of the *Charter* headed "Official Languages of Canada" and outlined in sections 16 to 22 ensures that French and English have equal status and that rights of minorities to use those languages are protected.[65] Of the Canadian provinces, only New Brunswick is officially bilingual, so section 16 of the *Charter* declares that English and French are the official languages of Canada (federally) and of New Brunswick. All federal government activities, including court proceedings, publications, and other services where numbers warrant, must be available in both official languages. Similar rules are established for New Brunswick. Note that some language rights are set out in the *Constitution Act, 1867*. For example, section 3 requires that Quebec provide court services in English as well as French. The *Constitution Act, 1867* also requires that Manitoba provide many government services in both English and French.

---

[64] See, for example, the federal *Employment Equity Act*, S.C. 1995, c. 44.

[65] See *R. v. Beaulac*, [1999] 1 SCR 768, 1999 CanLII 684 (SCC), where the accused successfully appealed his conviction on murder charges and a new trial was ordered because the B.C. trial judge refused his request for a trial before a bilingual judge and jury. Although the accused could express himself in English, his own official language was French.

CASE SUMMARY 2.16

Traffic Ticket Challenge Could Necessitate Translation of Alberta's Laws: *R. v. Caron*[66]

It is amazing what fighting a traffic ticket might lead to. Gilles Caron, a francophone truck driver, challenged a $54 traffic ticket, arguing that the law was invalid as it had not been published in French. Alberta's 1988 *Languages Act* revoked French language rights, but Caron argued this law was unconstitutional.

Expert testimony was introduced and revealed that a key piece of historical evidence was missing when the *Languages Act* was passed. Records established that Rupert's Land (from which Alberta was carved) agreed to join Canada only if French language rights were protected. Judge Leo Wenden ruled the *Languages Act* unconstitutional and stated that Alberta was constitutionally required to enact all of its legislation in English and French. Caron was found not guilty of the traffic violation.

The decision was appealed. The Court of Appeal was asked to consider two questions: (1) Must the statutes of the province of Alberta be printed and published in English and French; and (2) is the *Languages Act*, R.S.A. 2000, c. L-6, *ultra vires* to the extent that it abrogates Alberta's constitutional obligation to print and publish its statutes and regulations in English and French? The Court's answer to these questions was "no." Justice Rowbotham stated,

> Even with the application of the constitutional principles of protection of minorities, and the need to interpret the relevant language in a large and liberal manner, I cannot ignore certain realities. Parliament clearly entrenched language rights in Manitoba about the same time as it enacted the 1870 Order. Parliament and the Imperial Parliament knew full well how to entrench language rights. Yet, neither elected to do so in any constitutional document relating to what is now Alberta. In the result, I conclude that this is an insurmountable obstacle to the appellants' claim.[67]

Justice Slatter, who concurred with the result, did so on the basis that the decision of whether legislation needed to be published in French had already been decided in *R. v Mercure*,[68] which addressed identical issues with respect to whether laws need be published in French in Saskatchewan.

A final appeal was heard by the Supreme Court of Canada on February 13, 2015. The judgment was reserved, so the province awaits word as to whether it will need to publish its laws in French.

DISCUSSION QUESTION

Who should bear the cost of *Charter* challenges? Caron obtained an order directing the Crown to provide approximately $94 000 to him for legal costs incurred during the trial. While the traffic ticket charges were minor, the trial raised the issue of French language rights and proceeded over 80 days. The government appealed the funding order but lost.[69] The legal costs, however, will be trivial compared to the potential cost of translating and publishing Alberta's laws in French.

Minority-language educational rights, outlined in section 23, are guaranteed for the citizens of Canada, ensuring that those whose first language is English or French and who received their primary education in English or French, or have had one of their children educated in English or French, have the right to have their other

---

[66] 2014 A.B.C.A. 71 (CanLII); appeal heard by the Supreme Court of Canada on February 13, 2015; judgment reserved. See Case #35842.

[67] *Supra* note 65, at para. 20.

[68] [1988] 1 SCR 234, 1988 CanLII 107 (SCC).

[69] [2011] 1 SCR 78, 2011 SCC 5 (CanLII).

children educated in that language. People who are immigrants to Canada have no such rights, no matter what their native language may be. Note that the right to be educated in English or French applies only where community numbers warrant the expense of setting up such a program. Language rights and minority-language educational rights cannot be overridden by section 33 of the *Charter.*

SECTION 52

The *Constitution Act, 1982* made other important changes to Canada's Constitution. In addition to declaring that the Constitution is the "supreme law of Canada," section 52 also sets out all the statutes that have constitutional status in an attached schedule. Important amendments were also made to the *Constitution Act, 1867,* creating section 92A, which expands the power of the provinces to make law with respect to non-renewable natural resources, including the generation of electric power and forestry resources.

The Importance of the Changes to the Constitution

The significance of the 1982 additions to the Constitution cannot be overemphasized. The *Charter of Rights and Freedoms* will continue to affect the development of Canadian law over the next century. Traditionally, Canadian courts had adopted the position that their function was to apply the law as it existed. If the law needed to be changed, the judiciary left the job to Parliament and the legislative assemblies. It is clear that the courts have been forced to play a more active role and create new law through their interpretation and application of the provisions of the *Charter.* The broad, generalized nature of the *Charter* provisions contributes to this more expansive role of the courts. Statutes have traditionally been interpreted in a narrow way, and because of this they are always carefully and precisely worded. But the *Charter* provisions are generalizations, and the courts must therefore interpret these broad statements by filling in the gaps and thus making new law.

The *Constitution Act, 1982* also eliminated the requirement that any major change involving Canada's Constitution had to be made by an act of the Parliament of Great Britain. Because the original *BNA Act* was an Act of the British Parliament, any changes to it had to be made by that body. When the provinces and the federal government agreed on a formula for amending the Constitution at home in Canada (a process known as "repatriation"), the British Parliament passed the *Canada Act,*[70] making Canada completely independent of Britain. It should be emphasized that although Canada's ties to the British Parliament have been severed, our relationship with the monarch remains. The Queen remains the Queen of Canada, just as she is the Queen of the United Kingdom, Australia, New Zealand, and other independent nations.

Quebec did not agree with patriating the Constitution

Quebec, however, did not assent to this document. Subsequently, another important agreement that attempted to change this amending formula was drawn up—the Meech Lake Accord. However, the Accord did not receive the required unanimous approval by the provinces within the specified time limit. Its failure and the failure of the subsequent Charlottetown Accord (which went to a national referendum) have created a constitutional crisis in Canada, with Quebec seeking independence. The pro-separatist government in Quebec took the question of sovereignty to a provincial referendum in 1996, which failed by a margin of only 1 percent. Thereafter, the federal government submitted a Reference to the Supreme Court of Canada[71] to determine whether Quebec could unilaterally secede from Canada. Discussions regarding granting Quebec distinct status in Canada have occasioned much debate and dissension within the federation. The question of whether Quebec will remain in Canada continues to be an important and troubling issue for Canada.

---

70. *Canada Act 1982* (U.K.), 1982, c. 11.
71. *Reference re Secession of Quebec,* [1998] 2 SCR 217, 1998 CanLII 798 (SCC).

HUMAN RIGHTS LEGISLATION

LO ❽

Whereas the *Canadian Bill of Rights* and the *Charter of Rights and Freedoms* address protecting individuals' rights from abuses by government, various federal and provincial statutes have been enacted with the aim of protecting an individual's rights from abuse by other members of the public. Initially, human rights legislation was designed to stop discrimination against identifiable minority groups in specific areas, such as hotels and restaurants (see the *Racial Discrimination Act, 1944* of Ontario[72]). Today's statutes are broader in scope, protecting individuals against human rights violations by the public at large in a variety of settings. The *Canadian Human Rights Act*[73] is one example. Refer to the MyBusLawLab for details and provincial variations.

The *Canadian Human Rights Act (CHRA)* applies to abuses in sectors regulated by federal legislation, such as the broadcast and telecommunication industries; similar provincial statutes apply only in areas controlled by provincial legislation.[74] For example, if you were employed by a bank, any human rights complaints concerning activities at work would be brought before the Canadian Human Rights Commission (CHRC) because banks are federally regulated; however, if you were employed by a provincially regulated retailer, those human rights complaints would be addressed by the provincial human rights commission. These statutes aim at ensuring that individuals have access to employment (including membership in professional organizations and unions) without facing barriers created through discrimination. Access to facilities and services customarily available to the public, as well as to accommodation (tenancies), is likewise addressed. In addition, the legislation targets discriminatory publications and signs that expose individuals to hatred or contempt.

Human rights legislation prohibits discrimination in certain prescribed areas

Human rights acts prohibit discrimination based on various protected grounds, including gender, religion, ethnic origin, race, age, and disabilities. The *CHRA* now specifically protects against discrimination on the grounds of sexual orientation and pardoned criminal conviction, but not all provincial legislation goes so far. Where protection against discrimination on the basis of sexual orientation has been left out of human rights legislation, the courts have shown a willingness to imply the existence of this protection. The principle applied is that under the *Charter of Rights and Freedoms* every individual is entitled to the "equal protection and equal benefit of the law"; therefore, such rights ought to have been included. In the process, the courts are effectively rewriting statutes.

Human rights legislation addresses discrimination on certain prohibited grounds

---

CASE SUMMARY 2.17

Equality Issues Resolved by the Courts: *Vriend v. Alberta*[75]

In 1987, Delwin Vriend was employed at King's College, a private religious school. His job performance was not in question, but he was dismissed after he "disclosed his homosexuality." He tried to file a complaint under Alberta's *Individual's Rights Protection Act (IRPA)* but was advised that sexual orientation was not a ground upon which discrimination was prohibited by the Act.

---

72. S.O. 1944, c. 51.

73. R.S.C. 1985, c. H-6.

74. See *Human Rights Code*, R.S.O. 1990, c. H-19; *Charter of Human Rights and Freedoms*, R.S.Q. c. C-12; *Alberta Human Rights Act*, R.S.A. 2000, c. A-25.5; *Human Rights Code*, R.S.B.C. 1996, c. 210; *Saskatchewan Human Rights Code*, S.S. 1979, c. S-24.1; *The Human Rights Code*, C.C.S.M. c. H175; *Human Rights Act*, R.S.N.B. 2011, c. 171; *Human Rights Act, 2010*, S.N.L. 2010, c. H-13.1; *Human Rights Act*, R.S.N.S. 1989, c. 214; *Human Rights Act*, R.S.P.E.I. 1988, c. H-12; *Human Rights Act*, S.N.W.T. 2002, c. 18; *Human Rights Act*, S. Nu. 2003, c.12; *Human Rights Act*, R.S.Y. 2002, c. 116.

75. [1998] 1 SCR 493, 1998 CanLII 816 (SCC).

The case went to the Supreme Court of Canada, which agreed with the trial court that the protections given by the Act were under-inclusive, protecting some but not all from discrimination. The Supreme Court essentially rewrote the provincial statute so that it complied with section 15 of the *Charter of Rights and Freedoms* by reading "sexual orientation" into the impugned provisions of the *IRPA*. It reasoned that this was the most appropriate way of remedying the under-inclusiveness. In light of the Act's preamble and stated purpose, if the legislature had the choice of having no human rights statute or having one that extended protection to those historically facing discrimination—like homosexuals—the latter option would be chosen.

This case is interesting because it raises the issue of how far the courts can go in shaping the law. Here the Supreme Court effectively rewrote provincial legislation so as to make it consistent with the *Charter*.

DISCUSSION QUESTIONS

What do you think? Is "judicial legislating" proper under Canada's Constitution? Or should the courts merely declare whether legislation is constitutional or not, and then allow the legislators time to amend any contravening legislation?

Human rights protections continue to evolve

It is interesting to reflect on the evolution of human rights protection. Three decades ago discrimination based on sexual orientation was not specifically prohibited. Passage of the *Charter* enabled individuals to challenge laws that denied equal treatment. Cases like the *Vriend* decision brought the issue of discrimination based on sexual orientation to the attention of the public. As public sensitivity increased, the protection given to same-sex relationships expanded. The denial of marriage licences was held to be unconstitutional; eventually, the federal government was pressured to redefine marriage and sought the Supreme Court's input in the *Reference re Same-Sex Marriage* case.[76] Now the protections extended to same-sex marriages equal those extended to traditional marriages. See the MyBusLawLab for details.

Complaints are resolved through mediation—or tribunal hearings

Both the federal and the provincial governments have set up special human rights tribunals authorized to hear complaints of human rights violations, to investigate, and where appropriate to impose significant sanctions and remedies. There are time limits to consider: A complaint before the CHRC, for example, must be filed within 12 months of the alleged incident. The commission then proceeds to attempt settlement of the complaint through mediation and investigation. If all else fails, a tribunal hearing is convened.

For businesspeople, knowledge of the human rights codes applicable to their industry is essential. These codes not only govern how employees are to be treated but also apply to the treatment of customers and those with whom business is conducted. In fact, a significant number of cases before human rights commissions deal with complaints arising from business interactions, usually because of questionable customer relations practices.

CASE SUMMARY 2.18

Nightclub's Racial Policies Exposed: *Randhawa v. Tequila Bar & Grill Ltd.*[77]; *Simpson v. Oil City Hospitality Inc.*[78]

In the *Randhawa* case, the complainant had already been refused entry by another establishment before joining the lineup to enter the Tequila Bar. He asked the doorman whether he too would be turning the complainant away because he was wearing a turban. The first

---

76. [2004] 3 SCR 698, 2004 SCC 79 (CanLII).
77. 2008 A.H.R.C. 3 (CanLII).
78. 2012 A.H.R.C. 8 (CanLII).

doorman indicated that it was not going to be an issue. But then another doorman came over and told Randhawa to save his time as he would not be admitted that night. The club would require that Randhawa produce three pieces of government-issued ID, and if he did manage to produce that, the club would insist on five or ten pieces.

When Randhawa objected that such discrimination was wrong and asked why the doorman was doing this, the doorman replied that it being Calgary Stampede week the owners wanted to maintain a certain image. The lineup was being monitored by management via security camera; management had instructed the doormen to deny the complainant and his friends entry so as not to have too many "brown" people inside.

Similarly, in the *Simpson* case the complainant was denied entry to a nightclub because he was Asian.

In each case the Human Rights Tribunal found the evidence of the complainants and their witnesses credible, whereas the respondents failed to take the complaints seriously. Simpson was awarded general damages of $15 000; Randhawa was awarded $5000 for his pain, suffering, and loss of self-respect and dignity plus interest and travel costs. The respondents were each required to issue apologies, implement specific policies on racial discrimination in the workplace, and their management and staff were ordered to participate in an education seminar conducted by the commission. Oil City was also required to post signs stating "THIS ESTABLISHMENT WELCOMES PATRONS OF ALL RACES."

SMALL BUSINESS PERSPECTIVE

These cases highlight the necessity of being familiar with human rights legislation as a provider of services or accommodation. Failure to treat customers equally may lead to a finding of unlawful discrimination. The consequences may be costly and the negative publicity embarrassing.

Discrimination may involve singling out individuals and treating them differently than others. Harassment is an action addressed by human rights legislation. The offending conduct usually involves the misuse of a position of power or authority to obtain a sexual or some other advantage. Protection against sexual harassment exists because sexual harassment is regarded as a form of discrimination on the basis of gender. Protection against other forms of harassment, even where not specifically addressed by legislation, is now being addressed by employers in their policy manuals and in collective agreements.

Remedies are available for harassment upon a prohibited ground

Human rights decisions recognize that when there is a duty not to discriminate there is a corresponding duty to take reasonable steps to accommodate any person who may be discriminated against. This may require anything from creating wider spaces between workstations to accommodate a wheelchair to providing a digital reader for a blind person. Failure to accommodate religious beliefs may result in the employer being required to take reasonable steps to rearrange work schedules so that employees are not obligated to work on their day of worship. The field of employment is impacted significantly by human rights legislation. This will be treated as a specific topic in Chapter 12.

Duty to accommodate—unless causing undue hardship

CASE SUMMARY 2.19

Duty to Accommodate Those Facing Discrimination: *Ontario Human Rights Commission et al. v. Simpsons-Sears Ltd.*[79]

Salesclerks employed at a particular branch of Simpsons-Sears Ltd. were required to work some Friday nights and two out of every three Saturdays. Mrs. O'Malley, a member of the Seventh-day Adventist Church, informed her manager that she could no

---

79. [1985] 2 SCR 536, 1985 CanLII 18 (SCC).

longer work on their Sabbath day (Friday night to Saturday night). Her employment was terminated, and she was hired back part time to accommodate these restrictions. She wanted to continue working full time and laid a complaint with the Ontario Human Rights Commission on the basis of discrimination against her because of her creed. The matter was eventually appealed to the Supreme Court of Canada, which held that discrimination had, in fact, taken place.

It was not necessary to show that there was an intention to discriminate, only that there was discrimination in fact. Even where the rule or practice was initiated for sound economic and business reasons, it could still amount to discrimination if it impacted individuals negatively based on one of the protected grounds. The employer was required to take reasonable steps to try to accommodate the religious practices of this employee, short of creating undue hardship on the business. Since the business had failed to show any evidence of accommodation or that to accommodate would have created undue hardship, the complaint was upheld. Simpsons-Sears was required to pay Mrs. O'Malley the difference in wages between what she had made as a part-time employee and what she would have made as a full-time employee.

SMALL BUSINESS PERSPECTIVE

Human rights legislation forces employers to be sensitive to the diverse needs of employees and accommodate their differences. Employers may complain about this added inconvenience or added obligation, but unless it imposes an undue hardship accommodation will be required.

Since the adoption of the *Charter of Rights and Freedoms*, an issue that often arises is whether these human rights acts go far enough. The protections extend only to certain areas as identified by the specific federal or provincial legislation—typically employment, tenancies, public facilities and services, and public signs and notices. Private clubs can still discriminate as to who they will admit as members because discrimination by private facilities is not prohibited by the legislation. This explains why some golf clubs, for example, do not have female members. Furthermore, the grounds upon which discrimination is prohibited vary from one jurisdiction to another; so even though pardoned criminals may be protected by the federal law, the same is not true under each province's legislation.

CASE SUMMARY 2.20

Accommodating Family Status Includes Considering Childcare Obligations: *Canada (Attorney General) v. Johnstone*[80]

Ms. Johnstone was employed by the Canadian Border Services Agency (CBSA), as was her spouse. Both worked variable shift schedules. After their second child was born, Ms. Johnstone sought a fixed schedule at Pearson International Airport because finding childcare was difficult when both parents worked variable schedules.

In the past, the CBSA had accommodated some employees who had medical issues or constraints due to religious beliefs by providing them with a fixed work schedule on a full-time basis. However, the CBSA refused to accommodate employees' childcare obligations on the ground that it had no legal duty to do so. Instead, the CBSA had an unwritten policy allowing an employee with childcare obligations to work fixed schedules, but only if the employee agreed to work part time. Part-time employees, however,

---

[80]. 2014 F.C.A. 110 (CanLII).

enjoyed fewer employment benefits, notably with regard to pension entitlements and promotion opportunities.

Ms. Johnstone was not satisfied with the requirement to accept part-time employment in return for obtaining static shifts. She filed a complaint with the Canadian Human Rights Commission alleging discrimination on the basis of family status contrary to sections 7 and 10 of the *Canadian Human Rights Act.*

Note that the CBSA did not refuse to provide static shifts to Ms. Johnstone on a full-time basis on the grounds that this would cause it undue hardship. Instead it took the position that accommodation of childcare obligations was not required of an employer.

The Federal Court of Appeal affirmed that family status incorporates parental obligations such as childcare obligations. Accommodation is required for parental obligations "which engage the parent's legal responsibility for the child, such as childcare obligations, as opposed to personal choices," such as choosing to enrol their children in extracurricular activities.

The Court set out the following tests to be applied:

[I]n order to make out a *prima facie* case where workplace discrimination on the prohibited ground of family status resulting from childcare obligations is alleged, the individual advancing the claim must show (i) that a child is under his or her care and supervision; (ii) that the childcare obligation at issue engages the individual's legal responsibility for that child, as opposed to a personal choice; (iii) that he or she has made reasonable efforts to meet those childcare obligations through reasonable alternative solutions, and that no such alternative solution is reasonably accessible, and (iv) that the impugned workplace rule interferes in a manner that is more than trivial or insubstantial with the fulfillment of the childcare obligation.

The employer was thus required to accommodate Ms. Johnstone.

SMALL BUSINESS PERSPECTIVE

It will be interesting to see if provincial human rights legislation is enforced using these tests. If so, employers will face further demands to adjust workplace policies in light of employees' childcare obligations.

Part of the mandate of human rights commissions is to promote knowledge of human rights and to encourage people to follow principles of equality. The prohibition of discriminatory signs and notices assists in that end. The federal *CHRA* goes even further and deems it a discriminatory practice to communicate hate messages "telephonically or by means of a telecommunication undertaking within the legislative authority of Parliament."[81] In 2002, Ernst Zündel's Internet site was found to have contravened section 13 of the Act. This was Canada's first-ever human rights complaint involving an Internet hate site. The Canadian Human Rights Tribunal concluded that the site created conditions that allow hatred to flourish.[82]

Amendments to the *CHRA* impacting First Nations governments came into force in June 2008. Since 1977, the *CHRA* did not apply to the federal government and First Nations governments for decisions authorized by the *Indian Act.* Complaints arose largely from First Nations women who married non-status Indians and were thus exposed to discriminatory treatment; these women were not able to seek remedies under the *CHRA.* This exemption from the *CHRA* was removed and gender equality stipulations were expressly protected.[83]

---

81. *Canadian Human Rights Act*, R.S. 1985, c. H-6, s. 13.

82. *Citron and Toronto Mayor's Committee v. Zündel*, 2002 CanLII 23557 (CHRT).

83. Section 67 of the *Canadian Human Rights Act* restricted the ability of First Nations people living on reserve to file a complaint against band councils or the federal government. It was repealed by Bill C-21 effective June 18, 2008.

REDUCING RISK 2.1

Sophisticated clients understand that it is wise to be familiar with the human rights legislation in place where they do business and to make sure that their activities comply with these laws. In addition to requiring offenders to pay compensation and damages to those aggrieved, human rights commissions often require public apologies when discriminatory practices have been condoned. The resulting damage to the goodwill and reputation of a business is simply too great to ignore.

MyBusLawLab Be sure to visit the MyBusLawLab that accompanies this book to find practice quizzes, province-specific content, simulations and much more!

SUMMARY

A workable definition of "law"

- Law is the body of rules made by government that can be enforced by courts or government agencies

Categories of law

- Substantive law governs behaviour
- Procedural law regulates enforcement processes
- Public law comprises constitutional, criminal, and administrative law
- Private law involves one person suing another

Origins of law

- Civil law jurisdictions rely on principles found within a civil code
- Common law jurisdictions rely on principles established by judge-made laws (precedents)

Sources of Canadian law

- Common law
- Equity from chancery courts
- Statutes—legislation of federal and provincial governments

Constitution of Canada

- Various statutes that have constitutional status
  - *Constitution Act, 1867 (BNA Act)*
  - *Constitution Act, 1982,* including the *Charter of Rights and Freedoms*
  - Statutes listed in the Schedule to the *Constitution Act, 1982*
- Conventions and traditions
- Case law on constitutional issues

Constitution Act, 1867

- Created the Dominion of Canada and established its structures
- Divides power between federal and provincial governments
- Legislative powers are set out largely in sections 91 and 92
- Courts interpret and rule on constitutional issues

Charter of Rights and Freedoms

- Entrenches the rights of individuals in Canada
- All legislation must be compliant with the *Charter*
- Applies to relationships with government
- Limited by sections 1, 32, and 33

Human rights legislation

- Federal—provides protection against discrimination by businesses that fall under federal jurisdiction
- Provincial—addresses discriminatory practices by parties under provincial regulation

---

QUESTIONS FOR REVIEW

1. Why is it difficult to come up with a satisfactory definition of law?

2. Where do we look to predict the outcome of a legal dispute:
   a. in a common law system?
   b. in a civil law system?

3. Explain how the use of previous decisions differs in civil law and common law jurisdictions.

4. Describe what is meant by the following statement: "Common law judges did not make the law, they found it."

5. Describe the advantages and the disadvantages of the system of *stare decisis*.

6. Describe the problems with the common law system that led to the development of the law of equity.

7. Detail what was accomplished by the *Judicature Acts of 1873–1875*.

8. Explain what is meant by the phrase "the supremacy of Parliament."

9. What effect will a properly passed statute have on inconsistent judge-made law (case law)?

10. Outline how a parliamentary bill becomes law.

11. Using the principle of *stare decisis*, explain how judges determine whether they are bound by another judge's decision in a similar case.

12. What is included in Canada's Constitution?

13. What is the effect of sections 91 and 92 of the *Constitution Act, 1867*, formerly the *British North America Act*?

14. How did the *Constitution Act, 1867* limit the power of the federal and provincial governments? How is it possible, given the division of powers, to have identical provisions in both federal and provincial legislations and have both be valid?

15. Explain what is meant by the doctrine of paramountcy. When does the doctrine apply?

16. Describe the limitations on the federal and provincial governments' powers to delegate their authority to make laws.

17. Identify the limitations of human rights legislation. Does it address all discrimination?

18. Explain how the *Constitution Act, 1982*, including the *Charter of Rights and Freedoms*, affects the doctrine of supremacy of Parliament.

19. Explain any limitations that apply to the rights and freedoms listed in the *Charter*.

20. Give examples of democratic rights, mobility rights, legal rights, and equality rights as protected under the *Charter*. Give examples of three other types of rights protected under the *Charter*.

21. How do human rights codes differ in their application from the *Charter of Rights and Freedoms*?

CASES AND DISCUSSION QUESTIONS

1. *R. v. Clough*, 2001 BCCA 613 (CanLII)

Ms. Clough was convicted in a B.C. Provincial Court of possession of cocaine for the purposes of trafficking and possession of a small amount of marijuana. At the time of sentencing, the provincial court judge had to decide whether this was an appropriate case to impose a conditional sentence on Ms. Clough or whether a harsher sentence involving a jail term was warranted. He was asked to take into consideration the Supreme Court of Canada decision in *R. v. Proulx*, setting out certain guidelines for sentencing in these circumstances, and the British Columbia Court of Appeal decision in *R. v. Kozma*, which upheld the imposition of a conditional sentence in a similar matter. The trial judge decided that *Kozma* was wrongly decided and imposed a jail sentence instead.

If Clough was to appeal her sentence, what argument could she make?

2. *R. v. Spratt*, 2008 BCCA 340 (CanLII); application for leave to appeal to the Supreme Court dismissed June 18, 2009

Spratt and Watson were charged under sections 2(1)(a) and 2(1)(b) of the provincial *Access to Abortion Services Act* as a result of their activities outside of a Vancouver health clinic. Signs stating "You shall not murder" and "Unborn Persons Have the Right to Live" were waved within a "bubble" or access zone outside the abortion clinic. The law aims to protect women from interference in this zone. The accused argued that the law violates their freedom of expression.

Whose rights should be paramount in cases such as this?

3. *McKay-Panos v. Air Canada*, [2006] 4 FCR 3, 2006 FCA 8 (CanLII)

The appellant, a morbidly obese passenger, was subjected to offhand remarks and laughter when she expressed concern over whether an economy class seat would accommodate her. She was told she would not have to purchase two seats, but suffered bruising and indignation when she tried to fit into a standard seat. The issue brought before the Canadian Transportation Agency was whether obesity was a disability that airlines needed to accommodate.

Is obesity a disability that demands accommodation? To what extent should an airline have to accommodate large passengers?

3 Chapter

The Resolution of Disputes: The Courts and Alternatives to Litigation

LEARNING OBJECTIVES

1. Examine the alternative dispute resolution (ADR) methods: negotiation, mediation, and arbitration
2. Describe the court system in Canada
3. Outline the process of civil litigation
4. Explain the nature and function of regulatory bodies

In addition to hearing criminal matters, the courts have been charged with the duty of adjudicating civil or private disputes, including assessing liability for injuries and awarding compensation when someone has been harmed by the actions of another. But having the court settle those claims can be an expensive and time-consuming process.

The first part of this chapter outlines a variety of alternatives to the litigation process, along with a review of the reasons why businesspeople might choose negotiation, mediation, or arbitration over courts in resolving their disputes. If they are unsuccessful using these approaches, they can turn to the courts to adjudicate a resolution. We examine the structure of the courts in Canada and then look at the litigation process, from the initial claim to the enforcement of a judgment. Finally, we discuss the important area of **administrative law**, which concerns itself with decisions made by an expanding government bureaucracy that affect businesses and individuals. These decision-making bodies often look like courts, though they are not, and their decision-making powers are sometimes abused. Restrictions on the powers of such decision makers and how those decisions must be made as well as what we can do when those restrictions are violated will also be reviewed.

LO ❶ ALTERNATIVES TO COURT ACTION

Need for alternatives

Businesspeople involved in private disputes are well advised to avoid litigation whenever possible because of the high costs, long delays, and likelihood of dissatisfaction with the results. In this section we will discuss the various alternatives that can be used instead of—or in conjunction with—the litigation process. Many jurisdictions are now questioning the efficiency of the present civil justice system and are looking for better alternatives. Compulsory mediation, for example, has been incorporated as part of the litigation system in several jurisdictions. (In Ontario, the mandatory mediation component of the case management system was successful in increasing the resolution rate of disputes before trial and in reducing costs to the parties.[1])

ADR can be used at any time

Alternative dispute resolution (ADR) and litigation can work hand in hand, with the threat of one encouraging the parties to take advantage of the other. (For example, the collaborative family law process involves an ADR approach in which the parties and their lawyers sign a contract agreeing not to go to court.[2]) Even if the matter does go to court, negotiation and mediation can be used at any stage in the litigation process, including post-judgment when the parties wish to avoid an appeal. Note that the comments below with respect to the value of ADR apply equally to processes before administrative tribunals and other government decision-making bodies.

What Is Alternative Dispute Resolution?

Negotiation

Mediation

Arbitration

Any strategy that is used as a substitute for court action qualifies as a method of ADR, but there are three main approaches:

1. **Negotiation**: When the decision making is left in the hands of the disputing parties to work out for themselves

2. **Mediation**: When a neutral third party assists the parties in coming to a resolution on their own

3. **Arbitration**: When a third party makes a binding decision in the matter under dispute

Table 3.1 compares these methods with litigation. They are discussed in more detail later in this section.

Table 3.1	Summary and Comparison of Litigation and ADR Methods			
	Litigation	**Arbitration**	**Mediation**	**Negotiation**
Control	Low	Low	High	Highest
Delay	Lengthy	Moderate	Brief	Briefest
Cost	High	Moderate	Low	Low
Privacy	Low	Moderate	High	Complete
Flexibility	Low	Moderate	High	Highest
Goodwill	Unlikely	Possible	Likely	Ensured
Predictability	Low	Low	Reasonable	High
Appealability	Usually	Low	None	None
Visibility	High	Moderate	None	None

---

[1] See Helen Burnett, "Pilot Project Meets Many of Its Goals," *Law Times*, April 21, 2008, www.lawtimesnews.com/200804213999/Headline-News/Pilot-project-meets-many-of-its-goals. For an article that examines the advantages and disadvantages of mandatory mediation, see Martin Svatos, "Mandatory Mediation Strikes Back," Mediate.com, November 2013, www.mediate.com/articles/SvatosM1.cfm.

[2] See the discussion at www.collaborativepractice.ca.

ADVANTAGES OF ADR VERSUS LITIGATION

There are some significant advantages to choosing an alternative to litigation. One is the retention of control of the matter by the people most affected by it. Rarely does a court judgment compensate the parties for all their time, money, and personal and business resources expended. It is therefore vitally important that businesspeople maintain control over the problem-solving process and appreciate the disadvantages of placing the matter in the hands of lawyers and the court system when doing so can be avoided.

ADR leaves control in the hands of the parties

Most of the delays in litigation occur because of the lengthy pre-trial process and the problems of scheduling court personnel and facilities. When other resolution processes are used, there are fewer procedural and scheduling delays because these matters are controlled by the parties themselves.

Less delay with ADR

In addition, an ongoing court battle can be very distracting to a corporation's directors, managers, and employees. Key people may find themselves involved over a considerable period of time in overseeing the process, providing information, or preparing to testify. Much of this can be avoided by looking to an alternative method of resolving these disputes.

Less distraction with ADR

The fact that there is faster resolution of the matter with a simplified process involving fewer parties and fewer lawyers but with continued access to expert witnesses if needed contributes to a significant cost savings.[3] Also, indirect considerations, such as the fact that the matter can be kept private, avoiding negative publicity and the disclosure of sensitive information, as well as the reduced risk of an adverse judgment, make an ADR approach more attractive.

Less expense with ADR

An American case against fast-food chain McDonald's illustrates the risk of insisting on litigation. In that case, a woman was injured when a cup of extremely hot coffee spilled on her as she removed the lid to add sugar. She suffered serious burns and spent some time in hospital. She had asked for some small compensation from McDonald's and was rebuffed. When the matter went to trial, the jury awarded more than $2.7 million in punitive damages. (Note that the trial judge later reduced the punitive damages to $480 000; the $160 000 compensatory damages award remained intact.) This could have been avoided had the representatives of McDonald's simply negotiated reasonably with the complainant in the first place.[4]

Risk of adverse judgment is reduced

One of the costs of a protracted conflict is the breakdown in the relationship between the parties. Litigation—in which questioning the opposition's credibility and honesty is routine—is adversarial in nature, often resulting in bitterness and animosity between the parties, thereby poisoning any future business relationship. In contrast, a quick settlement using ADR techniques may actually strengthen the relationship.

Good relationship can be retained with ADR

Another attractive feature of ADR is its flexibility. The parties remain in control, allowing them to accommodate the needs of multiple parties and competing interests. Even cultural differences can be taken into consideration. ADR can even be used to resolve internal disputes within an organization, often in an informal atmosphere with a quick resolution that is satisfactory to all.

ADR provides more flexibility

It should also be noted that when international trade is involved ADR methods are much more common, especially when dealing with businesses that are in a civil law jurisdiction. Organizations have been established throughout Canada to assist

ADR can resolve conflicts between businesses operating internationally

---

3. See "Nortel Bankruptcy Mediation Begins with $9 Billion on the Table," *Toronto Star*, April 24, 2012, www.thestar.com/business/article/1167146–nortel-bankruptcy-mediation-begins-with-9-billion-on-the-table. In this example, the mediator warned the parties that litigation "would delete much of the money now available to creditors" and encouraged the parties to settle their claims through mediation.

4. *Liebeck v. McDonald's Restaurants, P.T.S. Inc.*, 1995 WL 360309 (N.M. Dist. Ct. 1994). For an interesting article that summarizes the case and the details of the settlement negotiations, see Jim Dedman and Nick Farr, "The Stella Liebeck McDonald's Hot Coffee Case FAQ," January 25, 2011, http://abnormaluse.com/2011/01/stella-liebeck-mcdonalds-hot-coffee.html.

in conducting such processes.[5] Legislation enabling the enforcement of arbitrated awards strengthens their usefulness.[6]

DISADVANTAGES OF ADR VERSUS LITIGATION

ADR cannot ensure a fair hearing

ADR does little to overcome a power imbalance

It must also be emphasized that there are many situations in which ADR should be avoided. The qualities of judicial fairness and impartiality associated with the litigation process are not always present in ADR. The court has no prior interest in the parties or their problems, but it does have extraordinary powers to extract information from the parties—powers that do not exist outside of the litigation process. A mediator cannot ensure that all relevant information has been brought forward. In the court system, there are safeguards and rules in place to ensure that each side gets a fair hearing. Because there are few rules or required procedures, ADR may not be able to provide this assurance. The court strives to balance the process so that neither side can take unfair advantage of the other, although this balance may be compromised when only one side can afford extensive legal help. If parties are using ADR and there is a power imbalance, there is the danger that the stronger party will take advantage of the weaker. In contrast, the discovery process does much to level the playing field where such inequality exists.

ADR cannot ensure consistent outcomes

ADR decisions are usually not appealable

Other advantages of litigation are that the decision will be based on or will set a precedent, and the decisions will normally be made public and thus be an effective deterrent to similar behaviour. (In fact, concern has been expressed by judges and academics that case law will not develop because mediation and arbitration are becoming much more popular than litigation, and ADR approaches are private.[7]) There are also effective tools available for enforcing the judgment. Finally, there is a right to appeal a court's decision.

It must always be remembered that what is a disadvantage to one party may be the most attractive feature of the chosen process to another. As in all business decisions, sound, properly informed judgment is needed in deciding between ADR and litigation in any given situation.

ADR Mechanisms

Upon concluding that ADR is a viable option, the businessperson must then decide which of the various strategies would be most effective in resolving the dispute.

NEGOTIATION

Negotiation should be tried first

Negotiation should be the first recourse for people who find themselves in a disagreement—too often, it is the last. Negotiation involves the parties or their representatives meeting to discuss the problem to come to an agreement as to how it should be resolved. Both sides must be willing to enter into negotiations, and the goal must be to find a solution even if that means making concessions. Negotiation can be as simple as a phone conversation, an exchange of correspondence, or sitting down together in a private meeting; any meeting with the goal of resolving a dispute qualifies as a negotiation.

Parties can withdraw from negotiation

Because the process is cooperative and non-binding, either side can withdraw from the negotiations if the other is being unreasonable or intransigent; the parties may then elect to move on to some other means of dealing with the matter. An understanding of the law surrounding the dispute will help the parties recognize the consequences of a failure to settle as well as the relative strength or weakness of the position they are taking.

[5.] The British Columbia International Commercial Arbitration Centre is one example of this type of organization: www.bcicac.com.

[6.] See, for example, *International Commercial Arbitration Act*, R.S.B.C. 1996, c. 233.

[7.] See Daryl-Lynn Carlson, "Family Lawyers Flocking to ADR," *Law Times*, June 11, 2007, www.lawtimesnews.com/200706182260/Headline-News/Family-lawyers-flocking-to-ADR.

Successful negotiation requires an understanding of the issues and a willingness to cooperate and compromise. A competitive approach that tries to best the other party will likely not resolve underlying issues. Similarly, there is danger in being too willing to accommodate demands from the other side. It may not always be possible to reach a win–win solution, but satisfactory results often involve both sides cooperating to minimize their losses. Of course, there is always the danger of being subjected to unethical behaviour or coercion, and since not everyone can be a skilled negotiator, any decision to take this course of action must be made by weighing all of the advantages and disadvantages.

Negotiation requires cooperation and compromise

When one of the parties lacks skill or experience or when one party is in a more powerful position, it is often wise to negotiate through a representative. While this involves extra costs and a certain amount of loss of control, it has the advantage of overcoming the lack-of-skill problem and creates a buffer between the parties so that a more powerful personality can be resisted. When lawyers are used, care must be exercised to choose one that is skilled in negotiation and not simply predisposed to litigation. There is a further advantage since lawyers better understand the legal issues involved, and if the matter does proceed to litigation the lawyer is already involved in the process. It should also be kept in mind that any legal concession, admission, or compromise made during these negotiations when made **without prejudice** will not hurt the parties if the negotiations fail and litigation results. And it may also be true that successful negotiation, when there has been concession and compromise between the parties, can actually improve the business relationship.

Representatives may conduct negotiation

Relationship may be enhanced

MEDIATION

Mediation also has a long history in resolving disputes. Its use in labour relations has been mandated by statutes for most of the last century, and its mandated use has been expanded to other areas of litigation in various jurisdictions.[8] Alberta, Ontario, and Saskatchewan have introduced mandatory dispute resolution for litigation unless the court says otherwise.

A neutral third party facilitates communication but does not make a decision

Mediation has always played a role in commercial relations but has become much more vital in recent years. The main difference between negotiation and mediation is that mediation involves a neutral third party, hopefully properly trained, who assists the parties to come to an agreement. The **mediator** does not make decisions but facilitates the discussion, making sure that each side has the opportunity to put their side forward, eliciting information, finding areas of possible compromise, identifying potential problems and solutions, and encouraging settlement.

The mediation process can be very informal or it can be carefully structured with rules of procedure and a set time frame. Often only a few meetings are necessary, with the main objective of the mediator being to find some common ground between the parties. The mediator will meet with both parties together and separately, using a variety of techniques to find some area of agreement and developing compromises between the parties, which can be used to encourage a settlement. It is this degree of flexibility and creativity that makes the process effective in the hands of a skilled mediator. Mediation has been so successful because the persuasiveness, skills, and neutrality of a trained third party are introduced, while control over the problem is retained by each party. While the parties are not bound by any solutions suggested by the mediator, once an agreement is reached it can be enforced just like any other contract.

Mediator finds common ground

---

8. Ontario has introduced a mandatory mediation pilot project, which requires that a mediation session take place after a statement of defence has been filed. See *supra* note 1 and "Public Information Notice—Ontario Mandatory Mediation Program," www.attorneygeneral.jus.gov.on.ca/english/courts/manmed/notice.asp. In several provinces, including Alberta and British Columbia, parties involved in small claims litigation may be required to attempt mediation before a trial date will be fixed. See *Mediation Rules of the Provincial Court—Civil Division*, Alta. Reg. 271/1997 and *Small Claims Rules*, B.C. Reg. 261/93 Rule 7.2.

Mediators are trained

Successful mediators require considerable specialized training. There are organizations that provide membership and certification and set recognized professional standards.[9] The disputing parties will normally choose a mediator who is a member in good standing with such an organization. They may, in fact, choose a mediator from a list provided by the organization.

When mediation is appropriate

Mediation works well when highly confidential or sensitive information that should not be disclosed to the public is involved, a speedy resolution is vital, good ongoing relations must be maintained, there is some trust involved, or both parties are desirous of reaching a settlement.

Disadvantages of Mediation

Mediation may be inappropriate in some situations

Mediation depends on cooperation and goodwill between the disputing parties. When there has been some wrongdoing involved or blame needs to be assigned it is unlikely that proper disclosure will be made and crucial information may be withheld. Mediators have little power to compel parties to produce evidence and documentation when they are unwilling to do so.

Successful mediation requires balance of power and a willingness to act in good faith

Also, when one of the parties is weaker, mediation may just exacerbate that weakness. This can be a serious problem in family disputes, when the weakness of one of the parties—or his desire to accommodate—leads to an unbalanced result. Also, when one of the parties is suspected of acting in bad faith, mediation is simply inappropriate, because trust is such an important component of the mediation process.

REDUCING RISK 3.1

There are a variety of circumstances in which mediation might be preferable to and more productive than other means of dispute resolution. One example would be when the benefits of a continuing relationship outweigh the benefits of securing a damage award. In the construction industry, for example, it may appear that a contractor is about to fail to complete the building on time or on budget, leading to a dispute with the owner. Rather than expending time, energy, and expense on litigation, with the likelihood of further delaying the project, it may be more reasonable to call in a mediator who has knowledge of the construction industry. This mediator could help the parties arrive at an understanding of the problems each has faced, such as unexpected illness, increased costs, or the unavailability of materials. This could lead to a solution acceptable to both sides, resulting in the completion of the building and the maintenance of the relationship. In fact, in the construction sector it is reported that millions of dollars are saved annually in jurisdictions where the first recourse in the event of problems is to mediate rather than to litigate. A sophisticated client working in any industry will be aware of the potential advantages of mediation whenever she is faced with a disagreement that could end up in litigation.

ARBITRATION

Arbitration involves a third-party decision maker

The third major category of alternative dispute resolution involves surrendering the decision-making authority to a third party. In most cases arbitration is voluntary, but in some situations, such as labour relations, the parties are required by statute to agree to some arbitration mechanism as part of the collective agreement process.[10] In some instances, arbitration is agreed upon before any dispute has arisen by including a requirement to arbitrate in the original contract. Often, however, the parties agree to arbitrate after a dispute arises. Arbitration can be very effective when external disputes arise with creditors, suppliers, or customers, and even internally with employees and shareholders or between departments. Arbitration is commonly used in resolving disputes arising from international trade agreements.[11]

---

9. One example of such an organization is the ADR Institute of Canada, www.adrcanada.ca.

10. See, for example, s. 48 of Ontario's *Labour Relations Act, 1995*, S.O. 1995, c. 1, Sch. A.

11. See the discussion of the "International Arbitration Process" at www.bcicac.com/about/international-arbitration-process.

Typically, the **arbitrator** is chosen from a pool of trained and certified professionals, often with expertise in the subject matter of the dispute. Organizations of professional arbitrators have been established, and the members offer their services like any other professionals.[12] These organizations not only provide training and certification, but also set professional and ethical standards requiring that their members be properly trained, avoid conflicts of interest, be free of bias, and keep in strict confidence all information they obtain. In more formal instances, retired judges are hired to hold what is essentially a private trial, rendering a decision much like a court but without the attendant publicity or delay.

Parties can stipulate in their contract the requirement for arbitration, how the arbitrator is to be chosen, and, if they want, that provincial arbitration legislation apply to the process. The specific process to be followed may be left to the arbitrator or, alternatively, the procedure may be set out in the agreement,[13] but such procedures, whether determined by the parties or by the arbitrator, must be fair.

Usually, before an arbitration hearing takes place there is a requirement that information relating to the matter be disclosed by both sides. At the hearing itself lawyers or other representatives of the parties usually examine witnesses, present documents, make arguments, and summarize their cases. Formal rules of evidence need not be adhered to, nor is the arbitrator required to follow precedent in reaching the decision. When the process is mandated by statute, as in labour disputes, the requirements are much more stringent and more closely resemble an actual court hearing. An arbitrator's decision is binding on the parties and is generally not appealable, but it is important to remember that the courts still have the right to supervise and review the decision-making process, as discussed below under the heading "Dealing with Regulatory Bodies."

The unique feature of arbitration is that a third party makes the decision. To be effective, it is vital that the parties be required to honour that decision. Most jurisdictions provide that the decisions reached by arbitrators are binding and enforceable.[14] As a result, arbitration is usually an effective process.

Arbitration is, however, still essentially adversarial in nature. In this sense, it is like litigation, with the attendant danger that bitterness and hard feelings may be aggravated. Arbitration is more costly than other forms of ADR because it is more formal and involves more people, but it is still much less expensive than the litigation process.

Ideally, arbitration should be voluntary, but clauses requiring arbitration are finding their way into standard form contracts at an alarming rate. These contracts often cover consumer transactions, with the consumer unaware that he has surrendered the right to a court hearing until the dispute arises. Because the decision is binding and non-appealable, the disgruntled party may challenge the validity of the arbitration clause in court, compounding an already complex resolution procedure.

Arbitration may look much like litigation, but it is still private and still usually within the control of the parties. When expertise is important, an arbitrator with that expertise can be chosen. Arbitration is faster, less costly, and more private than litigation, but it also has disadvantages. Arbitration is still more costly and likely more time consuming than other forms of ADR. Also, there may be little certainty or predictability, as precedents are usually not binding and animosity between the parties may actually increase as a result of this adversarial process.

Arbitrators are chosen by the parties

Arbitrators may be experts in the field

The procedure must be fair

Evidence is presented and cases are summarized

Decision cannot be appealed, but the process may be reviewed by a court

The third party makes a decision that is binding

Similar to litigation, but cheaper

Mandatory arbitration is more common now

Arbitration has some advantages . . .

. . . and some disadvantages

---

12. One such organization is the ADR Institute of Canada, *supra* note 9.

13. The ADR Institute of Canada has published Arbitration Rules, which the parties can agree to use to resolve their contractual disputes: www.adrcanada.ca/rules/arbitration.cfm.

14. See, for example, *Arbitration Act, 1991*, S.O. 1991, c. 17, ss. 37, 50.

Mediator may become an arbitrator

It should be noted that these ADR mechanisms are not mutually exclusive. Sometimes the tools of mediation and arbitration will be brought together when the outsider starts out as a mediator and, if it grows clear that the parties cannot reach a settlement even with the mediator's help, she becomes an arbitrator, making a decision that is binding on both parties. Of course, such a change of roles must be agreed upon by the parties.

ADR used in online disputes

Finally, mediation and arbitration are becoming more common in resolving online disputes.[15] There are many advantages to using ADR in the context of e-commerce. Many Internet transactions involve relatively small amounts of money, so litigation is not practical. Using ADR for online disputes overcomes geographical issues, reduces costs, and enables a quick resolution of disputes. Confidentiality is often important to online businesses, which do not want publicity about problems with their sites or security systems.

ODR programs are becoming more common

Online dispute resolution (ODR) programs have been developed to help resolve disputes between parties.[16] Such programs will continue to improve and become more cost effective. Over time, this may enable businesses to impose mandatory ODR systems that would be effective and acceptable to consumers.[17] Consumer Protection BC is conducting a pilot project designed to enable consumers and businesses to resolve their disputes using ODR.[18]

Legislated ODR

British Columbia recently incorporated ODR into its law in the *Civil Resolution Tribunal Act*.[19] This legislation creates an online tribunal for small claims and condominium disputes. The tribunal is expected to begin operating in 2016. It remains to be seen whether the implementation of ODR in the justice system is successful, leading to more widespread utilization of the approach.

REDUCING RISK 3.2

ADR services are now being offered online. Such services can be helpful in attempting to mediate between corporations and their customers; when information, services, or products do not meet expectations; or when customers have not fulfilled their obligations. In addition, such intermediaries may serve to set standards, monitor compliance, and warn potential customers when problems exist. As there is little regulation controlling ADR generally, it is likely that there will be even less in the electronic environment. A sophisticated businessperson making purchases online should therefore ensure that the online ADR services are being offered by qualified professionals and be aware that he may have little recourse if things go wrong.

LO ❷ # THE COURTS

Procedures vary with jurisdiction

The process described below outlines the various procedures used at the trial level of the superior courts; students should note that the actual procedure may vary with the **jurisdiction**. Procedural laws ensure that the hearing will be fair, that all litigants have equal access to the courts, and that parties have notice of an action against them and an opportunity to reply.

---

15. See Derek Hill, "ADR Picking up in Internet and E-commerce Law," *Law Times*, August 1, 2008, www.lawtimesnews.com/200808014192/Headline-News/ADR-picking-up-in-internet-and-e-commerce-law. The online dispute resolution system used by eBay is credited with resolving approximately 60 million cases each year, as reported in "Will Online Dispute Resolution Gain a Foothold in the Canadian Justice Landscape?" CBA Legal Futures Initiative blog, April 28, 2014, www.cbafutures.org/FoL-Blog/Blog/April-2014/Will-online-dispute-resolution-gain-a-foothold-in.

16. Glenn Kauth, "ODR in Canada Getting a Boost," *Law Times*, December 8, 2008, www.lawtimesnews.com/200812084400/Headline-News/ODR-in-Canada-getting-a-boost.

17. See Fahimeh Abedi and Sakina Shaik Ahmad Yusoff, "Consumer Dispute Resolution: The Way Forward," *Journal of Global Management* 2, no. 1 (July 2011), www.academia.edu/839830/Consumer_Dispute_Resolution_The_Way_Forward, for an informative discussion about the emergence of e-commerce and the resolution of the resulting online disputes.

18. See the Online Dispute Resolution Portal: www.consumerprotectionbc.ca/odr.

19. SBC 2012, c. 25.

As a general rule, Canadian courts are open to the public. The principle is that justice not only must be done but also must be seen to be done; no matter how prominent the citizen and no matter how scandalous the action, the procedures are open and available to the public and the press. There are, however, important exceptions to this rule. When the information coming out at a trial may be prejudicial to the security of the nation,[20] the courts may hold **in-camera hearings**, which are closed to the public. When children are involved, or in cases involving sexual assaults, the more common practice is to hold an open hearing but prohibit the publication of the names of the parties.[21]

Trials are open to the public

The courts in Canada preside over criminal prosecutions or adjudicate in civil disputes. While civil matters are the major concern of this text and criminal law is discussed only incidentally, it should be noted that there are some important differences between civil and criminal actions. In civil actions, two private persons use the court as a referee to adjudicate a dispute, and the judge (or in some cases the judge with a jury) chooses between the two positions presented. The decision will be made in favour of the side advocating the more probable position. The judge, in such circumstances, is said to be deciding the matter on the *balance of probabilities*, which requires the person making the claim to show the court sufficient proof so that there is a greater than 50 percent likelihood that the events took place as claimed.

Courts have both criminal and civil functions

Civil test—balance of probabilities

Criminal prosecutions are quite different. When a crime has been committed, the offence is against the state and the victims of the crime are witnesses at the trial. The government pursues the matter and prosecutes the accused through a Crown prosecutor. Since the action is taken by the government (the Crown) against the accused, such cases are cited as, for example, "*R. v. Jones.*" (The "*R.*" stands for either Rex or Regina, depending on whether a king or queen is enthroned at the time of the prosecution.) While a civil dispute is decided on the balance of probabilities, in a criminal prosecution the judge (or judge and jury) must be convinced beyond a reasonable doubt of the guilt of the accused. This is a much more stringent test in that even when it is likely or probable that the accused committed the crime, the accused must be found "not guilty" if there is any reasonable doubt about her guilt.

Criminal test—beyond reasonable doubt

As illustrated by Case Summary 3.1, a person might be faced with both a civil action and a criminal trial over the same conduct and, as occurred here, even though a person was acquitted at the criminal trial, he may still be found liable in the civil action. While there may not be enough proof to establish beyond a reasonable doubt that the accused committed the crime, there may be enough evidence to show that he probably committed the wrong. Another recent example involves a woman in British Columbia who won a $50 000 civil judgment against the man she accused of raping her, even after a criminal prosecution had acquitted him of sexual assault.[22]

May face both a criminal and a civil trial for the same matter

---

CASE SUMMARY 3.1

What Is the Appropriate Burden of Proof? *Rizzo v. Hanover Insurance Co.*[23]

Rizzo owned a restaurant that was seriously damaged by fire. When he made a claim under his insurance policy, the insurer refused to pay on the basis of its belief that Rizzo had started the fire himself. It was clear that the fire was intentionally set and that it was

---

20. See *Ruby v. Canada (Solicitor General)*, [2002] 4 SCR 3, 2002 SCC 75, for a discussion by the Supreme Court of Canada of the issue of open courts.

21. *A.B.C. v. Nova Scotia (Attorney General)*, 2011 NSSC 476 (CanLII), provides a concise summary of the law on this issue.

22. *J.L.L. and S.R.H. v Ambrose*, 2000 BCSC 0351, 2000 CanLII 13679 (BC SC). The criminal prosecution is unreported in case reports, but was reported in the *Vancouver Sun*, February 25, 2000. See also The National Crime Victim Bar Association, "Civil Justice for Victims of Crime," 2008, www.victimsofcrime.org/docs/NCVBA/standard-cj-bro-final.pdf?sfvrsn=2. Part IV of this booklet examines the difference between civil and criminal justice.

23. (1993), 14 O.R. (3d) 98 (C.A.), 1993 CanLII 8561, leave to appeal to S.C.C. refused, [1993] S.C.C.A. No. 488.

done with careful preparation. Because the restaurant business had not been doing well and Rizzo was in financial difficulties, the finger of blame was pointed at him. Other evidence damaged his credibility. The Ontario High Court in this case had to decide what burden of proof the insurer should meet. Because the conduct that Rizzo was being accused of was a crime, he argued that it should be proved "beyond a reasonable doubt." The Court held that because this was a civil action, it was necessary only that the insurer establish that Rizzo was responsible for setting the fire "on the balance of probabilities" and that it had satisfied that burden. "I have found on balance that it is more likely than not that the plaintiff did take part in the setting of the fire." As a result, Rizzo's action against the insurer was dismissed. Note that the fact that Rizzo had been acquitted of arson in a criminal proceeding was inadmissible in a civil proceeding as proof that he had not committed the arson.

DISCUSSION QUESTIONS

Should there be two different standards of proof? Wouldn't it be better to require the higher standard of proof even in civil matters? What effect would that have on the amount of civil litigation taking place in our courts?

Regulatory offences

Criminal law is restricted to the matters found in the *Criminal Code*, as well as certain drug control legislation and a few other areas under federal control that have been characterized as criminal matters by the courts. There is a much broader area of law that subjects people to fines and imprisonment but does not qualify as criminal law. This involves regulatory offences, sometimes referred to as quasi-criminal matters, and includes such areas as environmental, fishing, and employment offences as well as offences created under provincial jurisdiction, including motor vehicle, securities, and hunting offences. See MyBusLawLab for examples.

Constitutional authority

The provincial and federal governments have authority to create enforcement provisions, including fines and imprisonment, for laws that have been enacted under the powers they have been given under the *Constitution Act, 1867*. These regulatory offences are manifestations of the exercise of that power. Only the federal government has the power to make criminal law, and although people may be punished with fines, and sometimes even imprisonment, for violations of these regulatory offences, the violations do not qualify as criminal acts. People charged under these provisions usually go through a process similar to prosecution of a summary conviction offence under the *Criminal Code*.[24]

Trial Courts of the Provinces

Provincial courts

The nature and structure of the courts vary from province to province—see MyBusLawLab to view the court structures in each province—but there are essentially four levels, including the Supreme Court of Canada. (Figure 3.1 provides an outline of Canada's court system.) At the lowest level are the provincial courts (their titles may be different in some provinces or territories). These courts have a criminal jurisdiction over the less serious criminal matters that are assigned to magistrates and judges under the *Criminal Code*.

As a separate body, but usually as a division of the provincial courts, most jurisdictions also have small claims courts and family courts. Small claims courts deal with civil matters that involve relatively small amounts of money, between $10 000 and $50 000, depending on the province.[25] Family courts handle family matters, such as custody

---

24. To view a flowchart depicting the criminal justice process followed when adults are prosecuted for commission of a crime, see Justice and Solicitor General of Alberta, "Criminal Justice Process for Adults," http://justice.alberta.ca/programs_services/criminal_pros/Pages/process_adults.aspx.

25. In Alberta, the monetary jurisdiction of the small claims court is $50 000. In British Columbia, Newfoundland and Labrador, Nova Scotia, Ontario, and Yukon, the monetary jurisdiction is $25 000. In Saskatchewan it is $20 000, and in Manitoba it is $10 000.

issues that arise once the parents have separated. Enforcement of maintenance and alimony can also be dealt with by these courts, but they have no jurisdiction to issue divorces, which must be obtained in the province's superior trial court.[26]

Some provinces maintain separate youth justice courts while others designate the family court to fulfill this function. These deal with offences under the *Youth Criminal Justice Act*.[27] In Canada, youth offenders between 12 and 18 years of age are subject to the same *Criminal Code* provisions as adults, but they are subject to a different level of punishment, and so the role of youth courts is very important.

Figure 3.1 Outline of Canada's Court System[28]

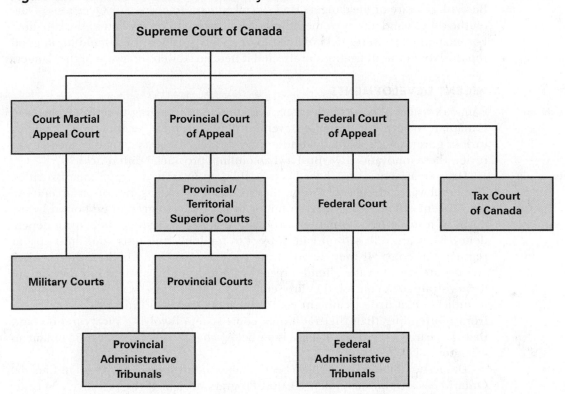

The judges in the provincial courts are appointed and paid by the relevant provincial government. The mandatory age of retirement varies from province to province. For example, in Ontario judges must retire upon reaching the age of 65; in Alberta, upon reaching the age of 70; and in New Brunswick, upon reaching the age of 75.[29]

The highest trial level court, referred to generally as the *superior court* of a province (the specific name varies with the jurisdiction), has an unlimited monetary jurisdiction in civil matters and deals with serious criminal issues. Some provinces (such as Nova Scotia) have also retained specialized courts, referred to as **surrogate** or **probate courts**, dealing with the administration of wills and estates. In most jurisdictions, however, this is now just a specialized function of the superior court. Similarly, bankruptcy courts operate within the superior court system. These courts deal with the legal aspects of bankruptcy and must comply with the procedural rules set out in the *Bankruptcy and Insolvency Act*.[30]

Provincial judges

Superior courts

---

26. *Divorce Act*, R.S.C. 1985 (2nd Supp.), c. 3, s. 2(1), under "court."

27. S.C. 2002, c. 1. This legislation replaced the *Young Offenders Act* on April 1, 2003.

28. Department of Justice Canada, "Canada's Court System: How the Courts Are Organized," www.justice.gc.ca/eng/csj-sjc/ccs-ajc/page3.html. Note: The Federal Court Trial Division changed its name to Federal Court on July 2, 2003. See explanation below, under "Courts at the Federal Level."

29. See *Courts of Justice Act*, R.S.O. 1990, c. 43, s. 47; *Provincial Court Act*, R.S.A. 2000, c. P-31, s. 9.22; and *Provincial Court Act*, R.S.N.B. 1973, c. P-21, s. 4.2. In Ontario and Alberta, judges can be reappointed for a term of one year up to the age of 75.

30. R.S.C. 1985, c. B-3.

Questions of law and fact

It is before the trial courts that the disputing parties in a civil case first appear and testify, the witnesses give evidence, the lawyers present arguments, and judges make decisions. (The trial itself is discussed in more detail below, under "The Process of Civil Litigation.") When both a judge and a jury are present, the judge makes findings of law and the jury makes findings of fact. When the judge is acting alone, which is much more common, especially in civil matters, the judge decides both matters of fact and matters of law. Matters of fact are those regarding the details of an event. For example, was Erasmus at the corner of Portage and Main in the city of Winnipeg at 7:00 a.m. on March 5, 2007? Did a portion of the building owned by Bereznicki fall on Erasmus? Was he paralyzed as a result of his injury? Was Bereznicki aware of the danger? Had she taken steps to correct it? Questions of law, on the other hand, concern the rules or laws that are to be applied in the situation. For example, was Bereznicki obliged to keep the outside of her building in good repair? Would this obligation be affected if Bereznicki were unaware of the danger?

RECENT DEVELOPMENTS

Court reforms dictate change

Canada's system of courts is dynamic; it is constantly changing to reflect changes in Canadian society. For example, several innovations have recently been made by various governments. For a full understanding of the court system, it is necessary to review these innovations. MyBusLawLab outlines provincial differences.[31]

Drug treatment courts

Drug treatment courts have been established in several large Canadian cities. The emphasis in these courts is on the treatment of addicts, not on incarceration. Non-violent offenders involved in minor drug offences agree to be bound by the terms of a structured outpatient program designed to reduce their drug dependency. They are released on bail, subject to random drug tests, and must appear regularly in court. If they demonstrate control of their addiction, the criminal charges are stayed or the offender receives a non-custodial sentence. If they cannot demonstrate such control, they are sentenced in the normal way. Research appears to indicate that drug treatment courts are more successful in preventing addicts from reoffending than the traditional court system involving incarceration, and that the yearly cost per participant is far below what it costs per year to maintain an offender in jail.[32]

Domestic violence courts

Domestic violence courts have been established in several provinces in Canada. Ontario has a Domestic Violence Court Program in each of the province's 54 court jurisdictions.[33] These courts deal with spousal, elder, and child abuse. While the structure and jurisdiction of these courts vary from province to province, most of them offer specialized investigations by police, counselling for first-time offenders, prosecution of repeat offenders by specialized prosecutors, and support services for victims.

Unified family courts

Unified family courts have jurisdiction over all legal issues related to the family and do not deal with any other types of cases. Such courts have been created in several provinces. This simplifies the court process, which can be extremely complicated because of overlapping jurisdictions of the federal government and the provincial governments. In addition, the court procedures and rules for family cases have been simplified. As is the case with all specialized courts, judges in unified family courts develop expertise in family law.

[31.] Inspiration and information for this section came from a series of articles included in "Feature on Evolution of the Courts," *LawNow* 26, no. 4 (February/March 2002); a series of articles included in "Feature Report on Specialized Courts," *LawNow* 33, no. 2 (November/December 2008); and Department of Justice Canada, "Canada's Court System," www.justice.gc.ca/eng/csj-sjc/ccs-ajc/page5.html.

[32.] "Canada's First Drug Court Breaks the Cycle of Drugs and Crime," *LawNow* 26, no. 4 (February/March 2002); "Drug Treatment Court: Not a Free Ride," *LawNow* 33, no. 2 (November/December 2008). The federal government provided funding to establish drug treatment courts in several provinces. See the website for the Canadian Association of Drug Treatment Court Professionals: www.cadtc.org.

[33.] Ontario Ministry of the Attorney General, "Domestic Violence Court (DVC) Program," www.attorneygeneral.jus.gov.on.ca/english/about/vw/dvc.asp. See also Ontario Court of Justice, "Integrated Domestic Violence Court (IDV Court)," www.ontariocourts.ca/ocj/integrated-domestic-violence-court.

As health-care services involving mentally ill persons have declined in recent years, the criminal justice system has seen an increase in the number of accused persons with mental illnesses. As criminal courts are not designed to identify and address the mental health concerns of accused persons, several of the provinces have implemented mental health courts. These are specialized courts that focus on the treatment and rehabilitation (rather than the punishment) of those who have committed criminal acts because of mental disorders. Judicially monitored programs involving a multidisciplinary team (judges, lawyers, psychologists, nurses, community caregivers) encourage voluntary treatment over punishment. This gives accused persons with mental disorders the opportunity to access appropriate resources and services while ensuring public safety.[34]

Mental health courts

The Nunavut Court of Justice, established in 1999, is Canada's first single-level court. Judges in this court are given the powers of both the superior trial courts and the territorial courts. These judges can, therefore, hear all of the cases that arise in the territory. The court is a "circuit court" that travels throughout the territory hearing cases.

Nunavut Court of Justice

Sentencing circles are found in several provinces and are used primarily at the provincial court level for cases involving Aboriginal offenders and victims. Sentencing circles are not courts. They involve all interested persons meeting in a circle to discuss the offence, including sentencing options. The circle may suggest restorative community sentences, including restitution to the victim and treatment or counselling of the accused. The judge is not bound to accept a circle sentence. A judge in Saskatchewan created controversy when he granted a sentencing circle in a high-profile case involving two young children who froze to death.[35]

Sentencing circles

Aboriginal persons have been overrepresented in Canadian prisons in recent years. An initiative to try to remedy this situation involves the establishment of specialized courts dedicated to serving Aboriginal persons. In these courts, cultural sensitivity and respect are incorporated into the criminal justice process. Alberta, British Columbia, Ontario, and Saskatchewan have established Aboriginal courts.[36]

Aboriginal courts

The criminal justice system is constantly under scrutiny by many different groups in our society, from governments and their employees, to defence lawyers, victim service workers, and the media. There are many problems, such as a significant backlog of cases, that need to be addressed. One example of this type of scrutiny was the formal review of British Columbia's criminal justice system undertaken by BC Justice Reform Initiative.[37] The objective of this and other initiatives is to identify and recommend reforms to improve the efficiency and effectiveness of the criminal justice system. The federal Department of Justice monitors trends in criminal law, develops and implements options for criminal law reform, and advises the justice minister on criminal justice issues.[38]

Criminal justice reform

It is clear that the Canadian court system will continue to evolve in an effort to improve its success in helping Canadians resolve their disputes fairly. These reforms are taking place with respect to the structure of the courts themselves, as well as the processes involved at both the criminal and civil level. It must be clearly understood, however, that many of the suggested reforms are strenuously resisted on the grounds that they threaten to damage an effective system that is the envy

Not all are in favour of reforms

[34.] See the website for the Toronto Mental Health Court: www.mentalhealthcourt.ca.

[35.] See "Father of Girls Who Froze to Death Gets Sentencing Circle," *CBC News*, January 7, 2009, www.cbc.ca/news/canada/saskatchewan/father-of-girls-who-froze-to-death-gets-sentencing-circle-1.791241; and Kevin Libin, "Sentencing Circles for Aboriginals: Good Justice?" *National Post*, February 27, 2009, www.nationalpost.com/news/story.html?id=1337495.

[36.] For a research paper that examines the jurisdiction of Aboriginal courts, existing Aboriginal courts, and related issues, see Karen Whonnock, "Aboriginal Courts in Canada," April 2008, http://scow-archive.libraries.coop/library/documents/Aboriginal_Courts.pdf.

[37.] See the final report of the review: D. Geoffrey Cowper, "A Criminal Justic System for the 21st Century," August 27, 2012, www.ag.gov.bc.ca/public/justice-reform/CowperFinalReport.pdf.

[38.] See Department of Justice, "Criminal Justice Program," www.justice.gc.ca/eng/cons/rt-tr/index.html.

of much of the world. Retired Supreme Court Justice Frank Iacobucci has urged caution before we embark on such reforms: "We must not take what we have for granted, and we must be particularly vigilant so that in our quest for improvement, we don't desert the values and procedures that have brought us to this level of excellence."[39]

Provincial Courts of Appeal

Appellate courts

Each province's appellate court hears appeals from the lower courts of that province. They must hear a matter before it can go to the Supreme Court of Canada. In most cases, this is the court of last resort. When one of the parties is dissatisfied with the decision of a provincial trial court, he may commence an **appeal** of the decision. If an error in law or procedure is identified, the appeal will be successful. As a general rule, an appeal court will consider a case only when questions of law are in dispute, not questions of fact. But many appeals are based on questions of mixed law and fact, where the rules that are applied are inseparably connected to the facts that are found. Whether a person lived up to the standards of a reasonable person in a given situation would be an example of such a question of mixed law and fact. Refer to MyBusLawLab to determine specific provincial structures and jurisdiction.

Not a new trial

The court exercising an appellate jurisdiction does not hold a new trial. The assumption is that the judge (or judge and jury) who saw and heard all of the evidence presented at trial is (are) best qualified to determine questions of fact. The appeal court judges (usually three) read the transcript of the trial as well as the trial judge's reasons for the decision. They then deal with the specific objections to the trial judge's decision submitted by the appellant's lawyers, hearing the arguments of both the appellant and the respondent.

Superior court judges

The judges who serve on provincial superior and appeal courts are appointed by the federal government from a list of candidates supplied by the provinces.[40] Once appointed, the judges have tenure until they retire (by age 75) or are appointed to new positions. They can be removed from the bench only for serious misconduct,[41] but not as the result of making an unpopular decision or one that is unfavourable to the government.

Courts at the Federal Level

Federal Court and Federal Court of Appeal

The Federal Court and the Federal Court of Appeal serve a function similar to that of the provincial superior courts. Until July 2, 2003, the Federal Court of Canada had a trial division and an appellate division. On that date, the *Courts Administration Service Act*[42] came into effect, making the two divisions of the Federal Court separate courts. The Trial Division became the Federal Court, a trial court. It hears disputes that fall within the federal sphere of power, such as those concerning copyrights and patents, federal boards and commissions, federal lands or money, and federal government contracts. The Federal Court of Appeal kept its previous name; it is an appellate court. It hears appeals from the Federal Court. Both of the federal courts can hear appeals from decisions of federal regulatory bodies and administrative tribunals. The role of these quasi-judicial bodies will be discussed later in the chapter under the heading "Dealing with Regulatory Bodies." An appeal from the Federal Court of Appeal goes directly to the Supreme Court of Canada.

[39.] *Lawyers Weekly* 24, no. 9 (July 2 2004).

[40.] Part VII of the *Constitution Act, 1867*.

[41.] *Judges Act*, R.S.C. 1985, c.J-1, s. 65(2). For an interesting article that discusses the history of the process involving complaints about judicial misconduct, see Michael McKiernan, "Judging the Judges," *Canadian Lawyer*, February 6, 2012, www.canadianlawyermag.com/4030/Judging-the-judges.html.

[42.] S.C. 2002, c. 8.

The Tax Court of Canada is another specialized court that was established in 1983 to hear disputes concerning federal tax matters. This body hears appeals from assessment decisions made by various federal agencies enforcing taxation statutes, such as the *Income Tax Act*, the *Employment Insurance Act*, and the *Old Age Security Act*. Pursuant to the *Courts Administration Service Act*, the Tax Court of Canada became a superior court on July 2, 2003, although its powers and jurisdiction did not change. The courts that hear cases involving the military are also specialized courts, but a discussion of these courts is beyond the scope of this text.

Tax Court of Canada

The Supreme Court of Canada is the highest court in the land. It has a strictly appellate function as far as private citizens are concerned. There are nine judges appointed by the Government of Canada according to a pattern of regional representation.[43] A quorum consists of five judges, but most appeals are heard by a panel of seven or nine judges. There is no longer an automatic right of appeal to the Supreme Court of Canada (except in criminal cases where a judge in the appellate court dissents on a point of law or when an appellate court sets aside an acquittal and enters a verdict of guilty).[44] In all other cases, leave to appeal must be obtained from the Supreme Court, and such leave will be granted only if a case has some national significance. The Supreme Court hears both criminal and civil cases. In addition, it is sometimes asked to rule directly on constitutional disputes involving federal and provincial governments. For example, the federal government submitted a Reference to the Supreme Court of Canada in February 1998 asking whether Quebec could unilaterally secede from Canada.[45] Decisions of the Supreme Court are binding precedents for all other courts in Canada.

Supreme Court of Canada

Supreme Court decisions set binding precedents

THE PROCESS OF CIVIL LITIGATION

LO ❸

Most of this text deals with matters of substantive law (law that summarizes rights and obligations of the "you can" or "you can't" variety) rather than procedural law (law that deals with the process by which we enforce those rights and obligations). But it is important to be familiar with the procedures involved in bringing a dispute to trial, if only to understand the function of lawyers and the reasons for the expense and delay involved. Before a decision is made to sue someone, all avenues for settling the dispute outside of litigation ought to be exhausted. Alternative methods for resolving legal disputes, including negotiation, mediation, and arbitration, have been developed and were discussed at the beginning of this chapter. Often the court requires the disputing parties to have tried these dispute resolution mechanisms before a trial procedure will be instigated. The litigation procedures may vary somewhat from province to province, but they are substantially the same in all common law jurisdictions. They apply to most superior courts. (One of the distinguishing characteristics of small claims courts is that this involved procedure has been streamlined significantly, eliminating many of the steps described.) Figure 3.2 sets out the process of **civil litigation**. Refer to MyBusLawLab for the procedures used in each of the provinces.[46]

Parties should try to settle a dispute

---

43. Three of the judges must be from the province of Quebec, pursuant to the *Supreme Court Act*, R.S.C. 1985, c. S-26, s. 6.

44. *Criminal Code*, R.S.C. 1985, c. C-46, s. 691.

45. *Reference re Secession of Quebec*, [1998] 2 SCR 217. Another reference to the Supreme Court was submitted to determine whether the federal government had the power to authorize same-sex marriage. That positive decision was rendered on December 9, 2004. *Reference re Same-Sex Marriage*, [2004] 3 SCR 698, 2004 SCC 79.

46. Alberta, British Columbia, and Ontario recently made significant changes to their rules of civil procedure. The new Alberta *Rules of Court* (Alta. Reg. 124/2010) came into force on November 1, 2010. The *Supreme Court Civil Rules* (B.C. Reg. 168/2009) came into effect on July 1, 2010. Significant changes to Ontario's *Rules of Civil Procedure* (R.R.O. 1990, Reg. 194) were effective as of January 1, 2010. Saskatchewan's revised *Rules*, *The Queen's Bench Rules* (Chapter Q-1.01 Reg. 1, as amended), came into force on July 1, 2013.

Figure 3.2 Process of Civil Litigation

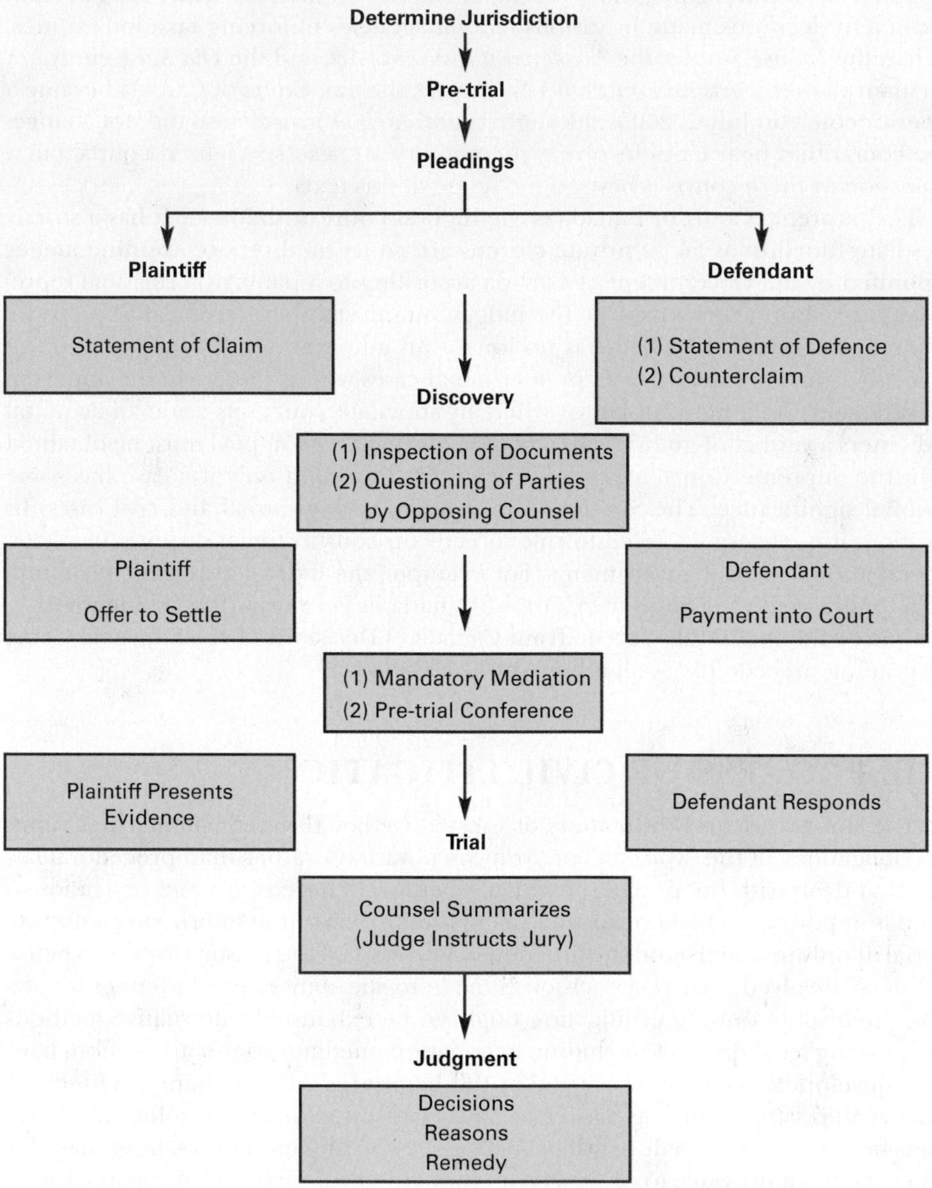

Determine Jurisdiction

↓

Pre-trial

↓

Pleadings

Plaintiff

| Statement of Claim |

Defendant

| (1) Statement of Defence |
| (2) Counterclaim |

Discovery

| (1) Inspection of Documents |
| (2) Questioning of Parties by Opposing Counsel |

Plaintiff

Offer to Settle

Defendant

Payment into Court

| (1) Mandatory Mediation |
| (2) Pre-trial Conference |

Plaintiff Presents Evidence

Defendant Responds

Trial

| Counsel Summarizes (Judge Instructs Jury) |

↓

Judgment

| Decisions |
| Reasons |
| Remedy |

Limitation Periods

Timely start to action is necessary

Whether to remove ongoing uncertainty or to ensure fairness when memories fade or witnesses become unavailable, court action must be brought within a relatively short period of time from the event giving rise to the complaint. This time is referred to as a **limitation period**. In most provinces, for example, a person who is owed money from a simple sale of goods transaction must bring an action against the debtor within six years of the failure to pay the debt.[47] The plaintiff must commence an action by filing the appropriate pleading (the writ of summons, the

---

[47.] But in Alberta, the *Limitations Act* (R.S.A. 2000, c. L-2), in s. 3(1), states that most lawsuits (including those for breach of contract and tort) must be commenced within two years of discovering the claim, or within ten years from the date when the claim arose, whichever period expires first. British Columbia and Ontario have similar systems, except that the ultimate limitation period is 15 rather than 10 years, pursuant to the *Limitation Act* (S.B.C 2012, c. 13, s. 21) and the *Limitations Act, 2002* (S.O. 2002, c. 24, s. 15(2)). The Alberta legislation (ss. 8–9), the BC statute (s. 24), and the Ontario legislation (s. 13) carry forward the rule that a written acknowledgment or part payment of a debt before a limitation period expires revives the limitation period, which begins again at the time of the acknowledgment or part payment. The Alberta legislation (s. 7) also allows the parties to extend a limitation period by agreement.

statement of claim, or the notice of civil claim) with the appropriate court. Failure to fulfill that step within the limitation period will result in the plaintiff being barred from pursuing the action. This time limitation will vary depending on the jurisdiction and the nature of the complaint involved and may be embodied in several different statutes in a province. Refer to MyBusLawLab.

With the expiry of the limitation period and the threat of court action removed, the potential defendant is not likely to settle out of court and the plaintiff is left with no recourse. For this reason, it is important for a person involved in a potential lawsuit to get the advice of a lawyer quickly regarding the relevant limitation period. Whether the limitation period had expired is the problem facing the Court in the Canada's Wonderland case discussed in Case Summary 3.2. This case shows that a person not only has to sue for the right thing—in this case, negligence—but also has to do so in a timely manner.

Expiration of the limitation period prohibits suing, making settlement unlikely

---

CASE SUMMARY 3.2

Does a Judge Have Discretion to Extend a Limitation Period? *Joseph v. Paramount Canada's Wonderland*[48]

Joseph suffered an injury at Paramount's amusement park. His lawyer prepared a statement of claim, but his assistant did not file it before the limitation period expired. She believed that the relevant limitation period was six years. However, in Ontario the *Limitations Act, 2002* established a basic two-year limitation period and an ultimate limitation period of 15 years. (The basic limitation period runs from when the claim is discovered.) When the lawyer realized the error that had been made, he filed and served the statement of claim. The defendant applied for a ruling that the action was barred since the limitation period had expired. A judge of the Superior Court of Justice held that the action was barred by the two-year limitation period provided by the new Act. The judge also held, however, that he had discretion under the common law doctrine of special circumstances to extend the time to commence an action as long as there was no prejudice to the defendant that could not be compensated for with either costs or an adjournment.

The Court of Appeal briefly discussed the aim of the new Act ("to balance the right of claimants to sue with the right of defendants to have some certainty and finality in managing their affairs"). It also discussed some of the reforms introduced by the new Act, such as the doctrine of discoverability. With respect to the special circumstances doctrine, the Court held that the Ontario legislature did not intend that the courts would continue to have discretion to extend the limitation periods under the new Act, which was intended to be comprehensive.

DISCUSSION QUESTIONS

If the special circumstances doctrine no longer applies and a claim is not filed prior to the expiration of the limitation period because of a mistake by a lawyer's assistant, is the plaintiff out of luck? Is there anyone who could be held liable for the damages she may have recovered if her lawsuit had proceeded? If there is an ultimate limitation period, claims that have not been discovered prior to the expiration of the period can never be pursued. Is that fair?

Jurisdiction

The first step when suing is to determine which court should hear the action. The proper geographic jurisdiction in which to bring an action can be a difficult question, but generally the plaintiff or person bringing the action can choose a court in the area where the defendant resides or in the area where the matter complained

Where to sue?

---

48. (2008), 90 O.R. (3d) 401 (C.A), 2008 ONCA 469 (CanLII).

Special link or connection is needed to give court jurisdiction

about arose. If a traffic accident that happened in Alberta involved one driver from British Columbia and one from Ontario, the Ontario driver would have to sue in British Columbia or Alberta.

Jurisdiction with respect to the Internet is an important area of concern.[49] The body of existing rules (referred to as the **conflict of laws**) may require modification to effectively handle these disputes. The problem is to determine which court will have the right to hear a case when the parties reside in different jurisdictions. When a retail business advertises or offers a product or service over the Internet, does it face the risk of being sued or prosecuted in every area that the Internet message is seen? Is it subject to the variations of contract, consumer protection, criminal, and tort law in all of those jurisdictions? Web messages are transmitted into every jurisdiction in the world, but it is now generally accepted that there has to be something more than information delivery or mere advertising to give a particular court jurisdiction to hear a complaint. A passive website will not usually create a problem in any particular jurisdiction where it is read.[50] There must be a special link, connection, or degree of interactivity before a local court will take jurisdiction. Without that real and substantial connection the courts in a particular province may refuse to hear a case. This principle has now been incorporated into legislation in several jurisdictions.[51]

CASE SUMMARY 3.3

Canadian Court Had No Jurisdiction: *DesJean v. Intermix Media, Inc.*[52]

Lack of any "real and substantial connection" to the jurisdiction may well doom a claim. An action was commenced in the Federal Court against Intermix, a publicly traded Delaware corporation with its principal offices in Los Angeles. DesJean alleged that Intermix violated the provisions of the federal *Competition Act* by bundling "spyware" or "adware" with the free software that it offered on various websites, without disclosing the bundling to consumers. The spyware would infect the consumers' computers when they downloaded the free screensavers. DesJean alleged that Intermix thus engaged in deceptive, fraudulent, and illegal practices and false advertising in the distribution of spyware and adware. Intermix enabled third parties to expose consumers to all sorts of schemes and often caused computers to crash.

Intermix challenged the jurisdiction of the Federal Court to hear the action. Evidence was submitted establishing that Intermix was not registered in any Canadian jurisdiction, did not have any offices or employees in Canada, had no bank accounts in Canada, and did not pay taxes in Canada. Furthermore, Intermix did not engage in direct advertising, marketing, or solicitation directed at the Canadian market. Their solicitations contained no specific references to Canada, no specialized content for a Canadian audience, and no French-language content. Intermix also had no servers in Canada; MyCoolScreen.com was hosted on a server located in California. Further, before downloading Intermix applications, consumers accepted the licence agreement, which contained a jurisdiction and choice-of-law clause providing that the laws of the State of California would govern the agreement.

---

49. For a website that discusses jurisdiction and the Internet, see www.michaelgeist.ca/tech-law-topics/jurisdiction.

50. The leading and most cited case in this area is *Braintech, Inc. v. Kostiuk*, 1998 CanLII 953 (BC SC), which involved the refusal of the BC Court of Appeal to enforce a Texas judgment for Internet defamation. This was the first Canadian appellate decision to address the issue of Internet jurisdiction. In it, the Court adopted the "passive versus active" test.

51. For example, see BC's *Court Jurisdiction and Proceedings Transfer Act*, S.B.C. 2003, c. 28, ss. 3, 4, and 10.

52. 2006 FC 1395 (CanLII), [2007] 4 FCR 151, 28 BLR (4th) 315, appeal dismissed 2007 FCA 365 (CanLII), 41 BLR (4e) 78.

Earlier case law identified eight factors that courts should look to when determining jurisdiction:

1. The connection between the forum and the plaintiff's claim
2. The connection between the forum and the defendant
3. Unfairness to the defendant in assuming jurisdiction
4. Unfairness to the plaintiff in not assuming jurisdiction
5. Involvement of other parties to the suit
6. The court's willingness to recognize and enforce an extra-provincial judgment rendered on the same jurisdictional basis
7. Whether the case is interprovincial or international in nature
8. Comity and the standards of jurisdiction, recognition, and enforcement prevailing elsewhere

The application of these factors clearly indicated that the connection between the forum and the defendant or subject matter was not substantial enough to warrant the Federal Court's intervention. The action was thus dismissed.

SMALL BUSINESS PERSPECTIVE

When doing business over the Internet, it is prudent to insert a forum selection clause into any electronic contract. The above case demonstrates, however, that this clause will be just one of the factors considered when a court's jurisdiction to hear a case is challenged. There must be some real and substantial connection to a particular jurisdiction before the court will have the authority to hear the case.

Adding to the problem of establishing jurisdiction is the fact that the origin of the service provider or the business is not always obvious. Furthermore, it is also complicated to take a judgment obtained in one jurisdiction and enforce it in another (specifically where the offender resides or may have assets). Treaties often allow for the enforcement of one court's orders in another jurisdiction, but generally, as a prerequisite, the conduct complained of must be actionable in both areas. Offshore gambling over the Internet exemplifies the problem with respect to jurisdiction. Is the activity happening in this country or where the operators reside? Or where the bet is made? While the activity may be criminal in Canada it is usually permitted in the jurisdiction where the operators reside, making enforcement of Canadian laws and extradition impossible.

Location of parties is not always clear in online transactions

To avoid battles over jurisdiction, the parties should make their own rules, specifying in their contract what law is to apply. When business is solicited, disclaimers similar to product warranties should be included, such as "Void where prohibited by law," or "Only available to residents of Canada." If a website is created to do business in another jurisdiction, the law of that jurisdiction will likely apply to the transactions unless it is clearly stated otherwise in the contract. But even with that precaution, if the content of the website offends the laws of another jurisdiction prosecution may follow. A cautious businessperson will take proactive steps to anticipate and provide for these contingencies before they happen: "The nightmare of costly and difficult multi-jurisdictional conflict of laws disputes demands a creative solution, particularly for the mid-size to small business person or individual."[53]

Parties should specify what court has jurisdiction and what law applies

---

[53.] Victoria Carrington, "Internet Needs Fast, Fair Dispute Resolution Process," *Lawyers Weekly* 20, no. 27, November 17, 2000, QL.

REDUCING RISK 3.3

A business that offers services or products over the Internet, the legality of which is at all questionable, should offer them only in jurisdictions in which they are permitted. It is also prudent to declare which jurisdiction's law applies to the transaction. It makes sense to establish the contracting process such that the contract is actually formed in the jurisdiction in which the business is located. Care should also be taken to include appropriate disclaimers of liability in the contracts. Another key factor is to preclude any degree of interactivity in those prohibited jurisdictions. A sophisticated client will initiate all of these steps to reduce risk as much as possible. Still, if the material is perceived as offensive some localities may try to prosecute; thus, if it is available, insurance to cover such a risk may be a wise investment.

Must choose which court to use

Small claims court is simple, but only minimal costs are recoverable

Once the province has been chosen, the plaintiff must then choose the court in which to commence the litigation. In a civil action, this is either the province's small claims court or its superior court. The monetary jurisdiction of the small claims court varies from province to province, as discussed above. Although it is simpler and less expensive to bring an action in small claims court, a disadvantage is that the court is restricted in the costs it can award. The costs incurred for representation by a lawyer usually cannot be recovered. On the other hand, the procedure followed at the small claims court has been significantly streamlined. It is designed to enable ordinary people to present their legal problems without the need to hire a lawyer. Hiring a lawyer, asking a friend to assist in court, or handling the action on one's own are all options.

Pre-Trial Procedures

Writ of summons

Statement of claim

Statement of defence

The traditional way to commence an action in a superior court was for the plaintiff to issue a **writ of summons**. However, this process has been abandoned. British Columbia, for example, passed the *Supreme Court Civil Rules*,[54] eliminating writs of summons effective July 1, 2010. An action in a superior court is now commenced by filing a **statement of claim** (called a **notice of civil claim** in British Columbia) with the court clerk. The relevant document must then be served on the defendant. It sets out in detail the plaintiff's allegations. The defendant must then prepare and file a **statement of defence** (called a **response to civil claim** in British Columbia), in which he provides answers to the claims of the plaintiff, stating areas of agreement, disputed claims, and contrary allegations.

Counterclaim

If the defendant believes that he is the real victim, he can also file a **counterclaim**. This is similar to a statement of claim. A counterclaim requires the filing of a statement of defence from the plaintiff in response.

Pleadings

The documents used to start and defend a lawsuit constitute the **pleadings**. The purpose of the pleadings is not to argue and justify positions; rather, the parties are merely stating the claims giving rise to the dispute and establishing the required elements of the legal action. If either party believes that the documents do not make the other party's position completely clear, she may ask for clarification or further information. Once the pleadings have closed, the parties have the right to apply to set a date for trial and begin the process of discovery. Throughout the pre-trial process, the parties have the right to—and often do—make **applications for directions** to the court regarding what details have to be disclosed, what questions have to be answered, and other matters that may arise.

The process of **discovery** has two distinct parts:

Documents may be used at trial

1. **Discovery of documents**: Each party has the right to inspect any document in the possession of the other party that may be used as evidence in the trial. This includes email and computer files on a disk or a hard drive.

---

54. *Supra* note 46.

2. **Examination for discovery:**[55] The parties (with their lawyers) meet before a court reporter and, under oath, are asked detailed questions relevant to the problem to be tried. The parties are required to answer these questions fully and truthfully. Everything said is recorded and may be used later at the trial. This examination process generally applies to only the parties to the action, not to witnesses. When corporations are involved, a representative who has personal knowledge of the matter may be examined. As part of a general reform of the litigation process in some provinces, and in an attempt to reduce the costs of an action, the examination for discovery has been eliminated in actions involving smaller amounts.[56] Other provinces have limited the amount of time given to the examination process.[57]

Statements made under oath may be used at trial

In most jurisdictions, a pre-trial conference must be scheduled. This is a meeting of the parties, their lawyers, and the judge. It is held to determine which issues remain to be tried and whether the parties can themselves resolve the dispute. In fact, most disputes are resolved by the parties during these pre-trial processes.

Pre-trial conference

Another tool often available to parties before a trial is an **offer to settle**. Either party can make an official offer to settle; if it is accepted, that ends the matter. If it is refused and the judgment at the trial is different from the offer made, the costs awarded are adjusted to punish the parties for failing to act more reasonably.

Offer to settle

If Jones was claiming $200 000 against Smith for an automobile accident, Smith could make an offer to settle (a "payment into court") of $150 000. The judge would know nothing about such a payment. If the eventual judgment was for more than $150 000, costs would be awarded as normal, since Jones acted reasonably in refusing to accept the offer. But if the judgment was for less than $150 000, obviously Jones would have been better off accepting the payment. Because he acted unreasonably in not doing so, he would be denied compensation for the legal expenses incurred from the time of his refusal of the offer. The plaintiff can also make an offer to settle, showing a willingness to take less than originally claimed. If this is unreasonably refused by the defendant, he will be required to pay greater costs due to his failure to accept a fair settlement.

Payment into court

REDUCING RISK 3.4

The discovery stage is an extremely important part of the litigation process; cases are often won or lost at this point. When parties testify under oath at discovery, they often make admissions or incorrect statements that come back to haunt them at the trial. Admissions of fact that may not seem important at the time may become crucial at the actual trial, and a party is bound by those admissions. A false claim can be investigated before trial, and the party can be forced to recant at the trial, bringing her credibility into question. This means that what is said at the discovery stage often determines the outcome of the case, compelling the parties to come to a settlement. A sophisticated client will understand the role that the discovery process plays in litigation. She will know that documents must be produced during the discovery of documents and will appreciate the importance of her testimony and its potential impact on the legal action. She will therefore ensure that she is very well prepared.

RECENT INITIATIVES

While it is obvious that the purpose of this long, involved, and expensive pre-trial process is to encourage the parties to reach a settlement and thereby avoid a trial, it is also clear that such a process results in frustrating delays for the parties. For this reason, provinces have implemented reforms to speed up the litigation process, especially

Recent initiatives

[55.] In Alberta, Part 5 of the new *Rules of Court* (*supra* note 46) refers to the discovery of documents as "disclosure" and the examination for discovery as "questioning," which may be done orally under oath or through written questions by affidavit.

[56.] Under Ontario's simplified procedure, for example, examination for discovery is not permitted for actions involving less than $100 000 (*Rules of Civil Procedure* [*supra* note 46], r. 76).

[57.] In British Columbia, for example, there is a two-hour limit on examinations for discovery for fast track litigation (*Supreme Court Civil Rules* [*supra* note 46], r. 15-1).

when smaller amounts are involved. Alberta and British Columbia, for example, allow for summary trials in which evidence is adduced by **affidavit** instead of by the testimony of witnesses.[58] British Columbia also provides for fast track litigation for trials that can be completed within three days.[59] Ontario has a simplified procedure for claims of $100 000 or less,[60] New Brunswick[61] and Prince Edward Island[62] have procedures for quick rulings, and Manitoba has implemented expedited trials and expedited actions.[63] Some provinces, including Ontario and Saskatchewan, have introduced mandatory mediation.[64] Several provinces, including Ontario, have started mandatory case management, which involves judicial supervision of the specific steps in the litigation process.[65] Ontario now also regulates paralegals, which provides people involved in disputes with an alternative to hiring lawyers.[66] The objectives of reducing costs and delay—and of making the justice system more accessible—have motivated all jurisdictions to create small claims courts where the procedures have been dramatically simplified and costs reduced accordingly. (Refer to MyBusLawLab for provincial variations.) It is important for businesspeople to understand that these changes, and all of the other changes to the justice system discussed above, have provided them with increased opportunities to use the system when necessary.

The Trial

Plaintiff presents its case first; defendant cross-examines

Because the burden of proof at trial rests with the plaintiff, the plaintiff's case and witnesses are presented first. The plaintiff's lawyer assists witnesses in their testimony by asking specific questions, but the types of questions that may be asked are restricted. For example, the plaintiff's lawyer is prohibited from asking leading questions in which the answer is suggested (such as, "You were there on Saturday, weren't you?").

When the plaintiff's lawyer completes this direct examination of the witness, the defendant's lawyer is given the opportunity to cross-examine the witness. In cross-examination, the defence has more latitude in the types of questions asked and is permitted to ask leading questions. When the opposing lawyer believes that the lawyer questioning the witness is abusing the process by asking prohibited questions, he can object to the question. The judge rules on the objection, deciding whether to permit the question or order the lawyer to withdraw it. The rules governing the type of testimony that can be obtained from witnesses—and, indeed, from all other types of evidence to be submitted at a trial—are referred to as the **rules of evidence**. (These rules are complex and beyond the scope of this text.) If something new arises from the cross-examination, the plaintiff's lawyer may re-examine the witnesses on those matters.

When the plaintiff is finished, the defence then presents its case

When the plaintiff has completed presenting evidence, the lawyer for the defence will then present its case, calling witnesses and presenting evidence that supports its side, and the plaintiff cross-examines. After both sides have finished calling witnesses, the plaintiff's lawyer and then the defendant's lawyer are allowed to summarize the evidence and make arguments to the court. Again, if anything new comes up the other party is given a chance to respond to it.

---

58. Alberta, *Rules of Court, supra* note 46, Part 7, Div. 3, and British Columbia, *Supreme Court Civil Rules, supra* note 46. r. 9-7.

59. *Supreme Court Civil Rules, supra* note 46. r. 15 1.

60. *Rules of Civil Procedure, supra* note 46, r. 76.

61. New Brunswick, *Rules of Court*, Rule 77.

62. Prince Edward Island, *Rules of Civil Procedure*, Rule 75.

63. Manitoba, *Court of Queen's Bench Rules*, Man. Reg. 553/88, Rule 20 and Rule 20A.

64. Ontario, *Rules of Civil Procedure, supra* note 46, r. 24.1, and Saskatchewan, *Queen's Bench Act, 1998*, S.S. 1998, c. Q-1.01, s. 42.

65. Ontario, *Rules of Civil Procedure, supra* note 46, r. 77.

66. Paralegals are regulated by the Law Society of Upper Canada. See the Ontario Paralegal Association website at http://ontarioparalegalassociation.com/cpages/homepage. See the material for paralegals on the Law Society's website at www.lsuc.on.ca.

Judgment

If a jury is involved (which is not very common in civil cases), the judge will instruct it on matters of law. The jury then retires to consider the case and returns to announce its decision to the judge. The function of the jury is to decide questions of fact; the judge decides questions of law. Where the matter is heard by a judge alone, a decision may be delivered immediately; however, it is more common for the judge to hand down a judgment in writing some time later that includes reasons for the decision. These reasons can form the basis for an appeal.

Role of judge and jury

COSTS

The cost of retaining a lawyer to sue someone is often prohibitive; some creditors may decide to write off a debt rather than incur this outlay. In small claims courts, the presence of a lawyer is the exception rather than the rule, mainly because the winning party usually will not recover the costs of obtaining the services of a lawyer from the losing party. In higher-level courts, lawyers are usually essential, although parties do have the right to represent themselves. Although legal fees are usually the greater part, other expenses are often incurred, such as the costs of obtaining transcripts from the discovery process and the fees paid to secure specialized reports from experts.

Litigation costs are high

Even the winning party must pay her own legal expenses. She may, however, obtain as part of the judgment an order for "costs." This means that the defendant will be required to compensate the successful plaintiff for at least a portion of her legal expenses. While a judge always has discretion when awarding costs, **party and party costs** are usually awarded to the victorious party in a civil action. Party and party costs are determined using a predetermined scale and normally fall short of the actual fees charged.[67] Consequently, the plaintiff will usually have to pay some legal expenses even when she is successful. There is, of course, always the risk that a party may lose the action and have to pay all of her own legal expenses as well as the winning party's costs. If the judge finds the conduct of the losing party objectionable (e.g., if an action is "frivolous and vexatious"), he may award the winning party the higher **solicitor and client costs**, making the losing party liable for all of the legal expenses of the winning party.

Losing party usually pays costs

Legal expenses are usually not completely recoverable

REDUCING RISK 3.5

The delay and costs associated with litigation, as well as the lack of control over the process and outcome, have contributed to its decreasing popularity. For sophisticated clients, finding themselves in court should normally be viewed as a failure. Considerable care should be taken to avoid disputes or to attempt to settle them before litigation becomes necessary. When a settlement cannot be reached by the parties, and both parties are willing, it is sometimes advantageous to explore some of the alternatives to litigation that are available. (These were discussed above.) However, in some situations—especially when it may be necessary to enforce the court's decision—even a sophisticated client may decide that litigation is the best option.

REMEDIES

One of the things that must be decided when a civil suit is begun is what the plaintiff will ask the court to do. The most common remedy requested in a court action is monetary payment in the form of **damages**, which are designed to compensate the victim for any loss suffered. **General damages** are based on estimates, such as when the court awards compensation to a litigant for pain and suffering or for future lost wages. **Special damages**, on the other hand, are calculated to reimburse the litigant for expenses or costs incurred before the trial. **Punitive damages** or **exemplary damages** are intended not to compensate the victim but rather to punish the

Damages involve payment of money

[67.] In Alberta, for example, party and party costs are usually awarded for actions in the Court of Queen's Bench pursuant to Schedule C of the *Rules of Court, supra* note 46.

wrongdoer for outrageous or extreme behaviour. This may result in a windfall for the victim. Punitive damages will be awarded only in very serious cases, such as a sadistic physical attack or when an insurer pursued an unfounded allegation of arson against a vulnerable insured.[68]

Other remedies

In rare cases, remedies other than damages may be awarded. The court can order money incorrectly paid to the defendant to be restored to the rightful owner. In some circumstances, it is also possible to obtain an **accounting**, which results in any profits derived from the defendant's wrongful conduct being paid over to the victim. The court also has the power to order an **injunction** to stop wrongful conduct or correct some continuing wrong. The court may compel proper performance of a legal obligation by **specific performance**. In some situations, it may be appropriate for the courts to simply make a **declaration** as to the law and the legal rights of the parties.

CASE SUMMARY 3.4

Is Specific Performance Always an Appropriate Remedy for Land Transactions? *Semelhago v. Paramadevan*[69]

Although damages or monetary compensation is the common remedy in a civil action, sometimes the court will order the equitable remedy of specific performance. In land transactions, it was thought that because all land is unique, specific performance would always be available—at least until this case was decided by the Supreme Court of Canada. Semelhago agreed to purchase a house from Paramadevan that was under construction, for $205 000. When it was time to perform the contract, Paramadevan refused, and this action was brought. Semelhago asked for the remedy of *specific performance*—or, as permitted by statute, damages in lieu of specific performance. At the trial he elected to receive damages, and the Court awarded him $125 000 damages in lieu of specific performance. The reason for this high award was that the market value of the house had risen from the $205 000 agreed upon at the time the contract was made to $325 000 at the time of trial. Paramadevan appealed the award, and the Appeal Court reduced it by the amount of the interest that Semelhago would have had to pay to finance the purchase of the house over the period from when the contract was entered into until the trial, saying that damages should reflect not only the increase in the value of the house from the time of the contract but also the interest that would have been paid out had the deal closed as required by the contract. This reduced the damages to just less than $82 000.

The purpose of such damages is to put the victim in the position he would have been in had the contract been properly performed—so the interest he would have had to pay should have been taken into consideration. The Supreme Court of Canada stated that specific performance should not always be considered the appropriate remedy in such land transaction disputes. It then refused to further reduce the award, and also refused to take into consideration the increased value of the house that Semelhago had intended to sell to acquire the one in question, but which he had instead retained. This case shows the factors that will be taken into consideration when assessing damages to be paid. An important statement that came out of the case was that it should no longer be thought that all land is unique, so specific performance is therefore not always appropriate in a land transaction.

DISCUSSION QUESTIONS

Consider the remedies available to a court in a civil action. Here the Court refused to grant specific performance but took into consideration the increasing value of the

---

68. See, for example, *Whiten v. Pilot Insurance Co.*, [2002] 1 S.C.R. 595, 2002 SCC 18 (CanLII).
69. [1996] 2 S.C.R. 415, 1996 CanLII 209 (SCC).

property and the interest costs that would have been incurred when awarding damages. Were these appropriate considerations in the circumstances? Should remedies be limited to monetary compensation in most cases? Should damages always simply compensate, or are there situations where punitive damages should be awarded?

Enforcement

Even when the litigation process is completed and judgment is obtained, there is no guarantee that the amount awarded will be paid. There may no longer be a dispute over liability, but if the **judgment debtor** refuses to pay, steps must be taken by the plaintiff, now the **judgment creditor**, to enforce the judgment. If the judgment debtor cannot pay and owns no assets (a "dry judgment"), it was likely unwise to have pursued the action in the first place. The successful plaintiff will not only get nothing from the defendant, but will also have to pay her own legal expenses. On the other hand, if the judgment debtor has prospects of owning future assets, the judgment does remain enforceable for several years and could be enforced in the future. The plaintiff must consider all of these factors—as well as the risk of losing the action—when deciding whether to proceed with an action against the defendant.

A judgment does not ensure payment

ENFORCING JUDGMENT

The process to follow when enforcing a judgment is set out in Figure 3.3. Once judgment has been obtained, most provinces provide for a further hearing, sometimes called an **examination in aid of execution**,[70] to determine the judgment debtor's assets and income that can be seized or garnished to satisfy the judgment. The plaintiff

Hearing to enforce judgment

Figure 3.3 Enforcement of Judgment

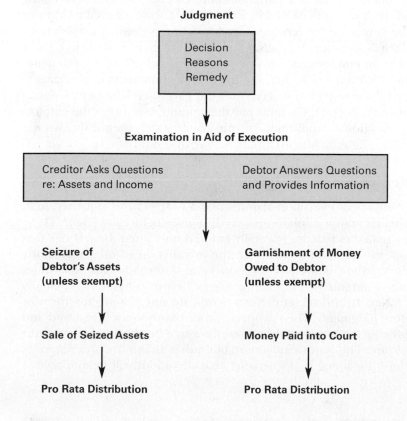

---

[70] In Alberta, this hearing is called an "examination in aid of enforcement." Instead of conducting an examination, the plaintiff may attempt to determine the information by requiring the judgment debtor to complete a financial report, verified by statutory declaration. See *Civil Enforcement Regulation*, Alta. Reg. 276/95, Part 1.3.

can question the judgment debtor (who is under oath) about his property, income, debts, recent property transfers, and present and future means of satisfying the judgment. At the conclusion of the process, the plaintiff can take appropriate steps to execute against particular property or income to recover the judgment.

SEIZURE OF PROPERTY

Property may be seized and sold

Proceeds of sale are shared by all creditors

The execution process allows for the **seizure** and eventual sale of the debtor's property to satisfy the judgment. The property is seized by a government official (or in some provinces by a private business designated for that purpose[71]) who, after deducting a fee, sells it, usually through public auction. The proceeds are distributed first to secured creditors, then to preferred creditors, and finally, on a pro rata or proportionate basis, to the remaining unsecured creditors, including the judgment creditor. A **secured creditor** used the property in question as security for a loan or other indebtedness, and so has first claim to the proceeds from its sale, up to the amount secured. **Preferred creditors** are those who, by legislation, must be paid before other unsecured creditors. Landlords owed unpaid rent and employees owed unpaid wages (both for a limited number of months) are examples of preferred creditors.

Some properties are exempt from seizure

Not all property is subject to seizure. The "necessities of life" are exempt from seizure. Exempt assets vary from province to province, but generally include—within specified limits—food, clothing, household furnishings, tools or other personal property needed to earn income, motor vehicles, and medical and dental aids. It should be noted that real property (land and buildings) can be seized to satisfy a judgment, but that the method employed varies with the jurisdiction. Often, registering the judgment against the real property is enough to pressure the debtor to pay. But when this is not enough the property can be sold to satisfy the judgment.

Funds owed to a debtor can be garnished

Garnishment (also called **attachment of debt**) involves the interception of funds owed to the judgment debtor and the payment of those funds into court. A creditor may garnish funds such as wages earned by the debtor but not yet paid to him, or the balance of the debtor's bank account. The legislation governing garnishment varies from province to province. Typically, when wages are garnished the judgment debtor is entitled to an employment earnings exemption, which will vary depending on such factors as the amount earned and the debtor's number of dependants.[72] Once the required documentation is served on the garnishee (the person owing money to the judgment debtor), she must pay the amount owing (less the employment earnings exemption, if applicable) to the court, which then disburses the funds to the creditors. Refer to MyBusLawLab for provincial variations.

Judicial Remedies before Judgment

Prejudgment remedies are limited

Although most methods of execution require that a judgment be obtained first, some judicial remedies may be available to a creditor even before judgment. These are extraordinary remedies that are normally granted only when there is risk that the debtor's property will be removed from the jurisdiction or otherwise made unavailable to the creditor. While bank accounts and other debts can sometimes be attached before judgment, garnishing wages before judgment is usually not permitted.[73] New Brunswick and Nova Scotia do not permit any form of garnishment before judgment. When property other than money is involved and there is risk of its being removed or sold, the creditor may be able to obtain a court order allowing seizure. This is not a judgment, but rather an interim order granted by the court before the actual trial to ensure that the goods will be available to

---

71. In Alberta, these businesses are called "civil enforcement agencies" pursuant to the *Civil Enforcement Act*, R.S.A. 2000, c. C-15.

72. In Ontario, for example, 80 percent of a person's wages are usually exempt from garnishment; *Wages Act*, R.S.O. 1990, c. W. 1, s. 7.

satisfy a judgment if one is ultimately granted. Another remedy available in some situations is an injunction to a third party from paying out money owed to the debtor. This remedy does not direct those funds to the creditor, but it does prevent them from going to the debtor—who may dissipate or abscond with them.[74]

REDUCING RISK 3.6

The process of collection and enforcement of judgments as described above may appear cumbersome, but it can be quite effective because of the diversity of options available. The process can be expensive, however, and may therefore not be justifiable economically depending on the amount of the debt and the likelihood of recovery. Note that when property has been used to secure a debt and the security has been properly registered, the creditor has a right to seize the property upon default, without recourse to the courts. Bankruptcy will also affect the debtor's obligation to pay. (Secured transactions involving personal property as well as the bankruptcy process are dealt with in Chapter 15.)

A businessperson should consider the various ways to structure a transaction ("Should I take security or not?" or "Should I take a personal guarantee from the corporation's principal?") before he enters into a business arrangement. This will require an analysis of whether the other party will be able to fulfill her obligations ("Is her business plan reasonable?"), and if not, whether it will be possible to collect any resulting shortfall through the litigation process ("What other assets does she own that could be used to satisfy the debt?"). An understanding of the process of collection and the enforcement of judgments will enable a sophisticated client to make better decisions, thereby reducing the risk associated with his business arrangements.

Class Actions

One definition of **class action** is "a lawsuit in which many people join together to sue because they all say they were harmed by the same person or group."[75] Class actions (also called *class proceedings*) allow individuals to pool their resources and hire lawyers who will represent all of them. This reduces the number of lawsuits, thereby lowering the total cost and avoiding inconsistent results. Consumers often commence class proceedings against businesses.[76]

Class actions reduce the number of lawsuits

All of the provinces allow class proceedings.[77] Typically, a court must certify the litigation as a class proceeding and appoint a representative plaintiff. There must be an identifiable class of persons with common issues. A judgment by the court on these issues binds every member of the class.

DEALING WITH REGULATORY BODIES

LO ❹

Most people are aware of the significant growth of government regulation and bureaucracy over the last 50 years. Sometimes these government **regulators** abuse their positions or go beyond their authority when making decisions that affect individuals or businesses. This section deals with an examination of our rights before these regulatory bodies.

Government can be divided into three different functions: legislative, judicial, and executive. The legislative branch in Canada consists of the federal Parliament and its provincial counterparts. The judicial branch consists of the courts at both the federal and provincial levels. The executive branch includes the prime minister, the premiers of the provinces, the cabinet ministers, and all of the civil

Government consists of the legislative branch, judicial branch, and executive branch

Executive branch is also known as the Crown

[73.] See, for example, s. 3(4) of the *Court Order Enforcement Act*, R.S.B.C. 1996, c. 78.

[74.] In Alberta, the *Civil Enforcement Act*, *supra* note 71, Part 3, enables claimants to apply for attachment orders, which can allow both seizure and garnishment before a judgment is obtained.

[75.] By permission. From *Merriam-Webster's Collegiate® Dictionary, 11th Edition* © 2015 by Merriam-Webster, Inc. (www.Merriam-Webster.com).

[76.] See, for example, "Regina Lawyer Launches Facebook Class-Action Lawsuit," *CBC News*, June 8, 2012, www.cbc.ca/news/canada/saskatchewan/story/2012/06/08/sk-facebook-class-action-120608.html, which discusses the lawsuit against Facebook relating to its initial public offering.

[77.] See, for example, *Class Proceedings Act*, S.A. 2003, c. C-16.5; *Class Proceedings Act*, R.S.B.C. 1996, c. 50; and *Class Proceedings Act, 1992*, S.O. 1992, c. 6.

servants in the various government departments. In Canada, the theoretical head of the executive branch is the Queen, so this aspect of government is often referred to as "the Crown."

Government objectives are achieved through rule enforcement, economic incentives, and education

Civil servants, or the bureaucracy of the executive branch at both the federal and provincial levels, assist people in their dealings with government. They provide service functions such as security, education, health, and welfare; they administer departments such as customs and revenue; and they manage government affairs generally. They also regulate such matters as human rights, the environment, and employment. Government agents exercise their powers directly through the enforcement of rules and the imposition of penalties, and indirectly through funding or education.

Tribunals implement and enforce policies

Government departments establish regulatory bodies or **administrative tribunals** such as labour relations boards, human rights commissions, and workers' compensation boards to implement and enforce their policies. These bodies may look and act like courts, but it is important to keep in mind that they are not part of the judicial branch and therefore are not subject to the same regulations that govern the courts. Because administrative tribunals make decisions that profoundly impact businesses and individuals and have powers of enforcement that can be abused, the courts have some jurisdiction, albeit limited, to supervise their actions.

Advantages of tribunals

It is important to keep in mind that there are some significant advantages to administrative tribunals. Government employees who make up these decision-making panels usually have specific expertise in the matter being decided, and the tribunals generally have more discretion than a judge. This flexibility creates a more efficient, quicker, and less costly process.

When powers are abused, judicial review is available

To protect the public interest, courts are empowered to review the process by which these decisions are made. When a decision is challenged, the court determines whether the decision maker acted within his authority and whether the procedure used to come to the decision was fair. It is a review, rather than an appeal, of the decision. In fact, the Supreme Court of Canada has established a standard that significantly restricts when the decision of such a body can be challenged. As long as the administrative decision maker acted within the authority granted to him, and any discretion was exercised in a fair and honest way so that the decision can be said to be reasonable, the decision will stand.[78]

Procedural Fairness in Tribunals

To determine our rights before administrative tribunals, there are three questions that must be addressed:

1. From where did the tribunal derive its authority?

2. Was the decision-making process fair?

3. What recourse is there if there has been a failure in jurisdiction or procedure?

1. THE AUTHORITY OF THE DECISION MAKER

The decision maker must have authority

Decision makers cannot act arbitrarily. They must be able to point to some statutory authority that empowers them to make a decision. Authority is granted by statute or by a regulation created pursuant to that statute. Either can be the source of authority for the decision maker, but the provisions must clearly authorize the conduct.

Rules of statutory interpretation

The statutes usually start out with a definition section, which must be used to interpret the terms used in the statute. Most jurisdictions provide a general **interpretation statute** to provide further guidance. Usually, the application of a little common sense with reliance on the statutory definitions and the rules of interpretation provided solves most difficulties. The words of a statute are read in their

---

[78.] In *Dunsmuir v. New Brunswick*, [2008] 1 S.C.R. 190, 2008 SCC 9 (CanLII), the Supreme Court reconsidered the approach to judicial review and decided that there will be only two (instead of three) standards of review: correctness and reasonableness.

ordinary grammatical sense unless it is clear from the overall statute that a different meaning was intended. The words should then be read in such a way as to be in harmony with the objective and other provisions of the statute. (Note that these rules apply to courts as well as administrative tribunals.)

Remember that the *Constitution Act, 1867* divides powers between the provincial and federal governments. If the statute goes beyond the powers of the level of government enacting it, whether federal or provincial, it will be void and will not support the actions of the decision maker who relied on it. Similarly, if the statute, the regulation, or the conduct of the decision maker is found to violate a provision of the *Charter of Rights and Freedoms*, the decision can be successfully challenged. A court may determine that a statute has the effect of discriminating on the basis of gender, religion, or ethnic origin, or that it restricted freedom of the press or religion and is, therefore, invalid. And even when the statute is valid, if the decision maker, in reaching that decision, has violated a provision of the *Charter* the decision can be set aside.

Statutes must be passed by the appropriate level of government

Statutes and regulations must comply with the *Charter*

2. THE FAIRNESS OF THE PROCESS

Once it is determined that the decision maker acted under proper authority, the next question to be considered is whether that authority was exercised properly. Essentially, the decision maker is required to act fairly when making a decision. What constitutes fair treatment will vary with the circumstances, but the minimum standards of procedural fairness, otherwise known as the **rules of natural justice**, set a basic standard. The first requirement is a **fair hearing**. The person affected by the decision must be notified that a decision was going to be made and she must be given an opportunity to respond.

Administrator must act fairly

There is no fair hearing without notice that includes the disclosure before the hearing of any evidence or information that will affect the decision so that an effective defence can be prepared. There must also be an opportunity to cross-examine witnesses presenting material evidence, to refute written declarations, and to present supporting evidence and arguments. But again, what constitutes fairness will be dictated by the circumstances. The strict rules of evidence need not be followed, nor is there a general right to be represented by a lawyer (unless provided for in legislation or when criminal charges can result). The decision maker is not required to give reasons for the decision unless required by the supporting statute. The test is reasonableness and in some cases the right to submit a letter for consideration by the decision maker is sufficient to satisfy the requirement of procedural fairness.

Notice must be given and all information must be disclosed

Another requirement of the rules of natural justice is that the decision be made by the persons hearing the evidence. If, for example, a panel of five is hearing a case and one member has to leave because of illness, that person cannot be replaced by another partway through the proceedings because the replacement would not have heard all of the evidence.

Decision must be made by persons hearing all evidence

A third requirement is that the decision makers must be impartial. As shown by Case Summary 3.5, any indication of **bias** will normally be sufficient grounds to have the decision overturned. Even the appearance of bias must be avoided, and any indication of hostility or bad feelings, or the involvement of a relative, friend, or business acquaintance of the decision maker, will taint the decision. Of course, when it can be demonstrated that the decision maker has an interest (especially a financial interest) in the matter being decided, or where he has already made his decision before the hearing, the decision can be challenged. Note, however, that in some types of panels a bias seems to be built in. For example, in labour matters such panels are often composed of three members, one with a union background, one from the business side, and a third (who normally becomes the chair) chosen by the two of them. Thus any appearance of bias is balanced by both sides being represented.

Decision maker must be free of bias

Sometimes these basic procedural standards will be modified by statute, either increasing or decreasing the requirements. Thus a statute will often require a written decision or set out specific procedural requirements and time limits that must be met. When a statute attempts to remove or significantly reduce these basic rights, certain requirements set out in the *Charter of Rights and Freedoms* may come

Principles of fundamental justice

into play. Section 7 of the *Charter* states that everyone has the right to "life, liberty and the security of person," and it requires that all decisions depriving a person of them must be made "in accordance with the principles of fundamental justice." The **principles of fundamental justice** include the procedural fairness and natural justice rules set out above, but go even further. Even when a proper hearing has taken place with appropriate notice and all other procedural requirements have been met, if the statute offends our basic concepts of justice, such as offending the rule of law or requiring the imposition of retroactive penalties, it is likely to offend the principles of fundamental justice and be overturned.

CASE SUMMARY 3.5

Was There a Fair Hearing? *Baker v. Canada (Minister of Citizenship and Immigration)*[79]

A woman was ordered deported. She applied, on humanitarian and compassionate grounds, for an exemption from the rule that an application for permanent residency had to be made from outside of Canada. Her application was supported by letters about the availability of medical care in her home country and the effect of her departure on her Canadian-born children. An immigration officer refused her application by letter, without providing reasons for his decision.

The Supreme Court indicated that the duty of procedural fairness is flexible and variable. The extent of the duty depends on several factors, including the nature of the decision (the more an administrative tribunal is designed like a court, the higher the duty of fairness), the relevant legislation (greater procedural fairness is required if there is no appeal process, the decision is determinative/final, and there are no further requests that can be made of the tribunal), the importance of the decision to the individual affected (the higher the stakes, the higher the requirement of fairness), and the procedure followed in making it (legitimate expectations of the party[ies] regarding the level of procedural fairness that ought to be part of the decision-making process). Here the claimant had to have an opportunity to present evidence and to have it fully and fairly considered. An oral hearing was not required; the chance to provide written documentation was sufficient. Written notes prepared by a junior officer that were provided to the claimant's lawyer were a sufficient explanation of the decision. The claimant was successful, however, because these notes gave rise to a reasonable apprehension of bias. The decision appeared to be based on the fact that the claimant was a single mother with several children and had been diagnosed with a psychiatric illness. This was inappropriate; decisions of this nature should instead be made impartially, based on the evidence. The Court ordered that another hearing be held in front of a different immigration officer.

DISCUSSION QUESTIONS

Are the standards imposed on administrative tribunals too onerous? Should the courts ever have the power to interfere with the operation of statutory tribunals in the execution of their function? Should such tribunals remain unfettered from the restrictions of rules and procedures found in the court process? What do you think?

---

3. REVIEWING A DECISION

Judicial review can follow from . . .

Many statutes establishing administrative boards and panels provide for appeals of their decisions to another level of decision maker. The rights under any such appeal process must be exhausted before the courts are asked to exercise their right to review the decision. Remember that **judicial review** is not an appeal on the merits of

---

[79.] [1999] 2 S.C.R. 817, 1999 CanLII 699 (SCC).

the case, but instead refers to the court's right to supervise the process by which the decision was reached. For the courts to exercise their right of judicial review, one of the following must be present:

1. When the validity of the statute or regulation (or provision under it) relied on by the decision maker is in question. This usually relates to a challenge of the statute or regulation based on the *Charter of Rights and Freedoms* or the division of powers under the *Constitution Act, 1867*.

   • **invalid statute or regulation**

2. When the decision maker has acted outside his authority under the statute or regulation. Sometimes a decision maker will act beyond his jurisdiction in deciding to deal with the matter in the first place, or render a decision or impose a penalty not authorized under the statute.

   • **action outside the prescribed jurisdiction**

3. When an **error of law** on the record has been made. The record consists of the decision and any documents associated with the process of reaching that decision. The courts will not tolerate such an error and will generally overturn a decision based on it.

   • **error of law on record**

4. When the decision-making process itself has failed to follow the requirement of procedural fairness (the rules of natural justice), as discussed above.

   • **failure to follow procedural fairness**

5. When there has been an **abuse of power** (including discretionary power) by the decision maker. Any decision directed by malice, dishonesty, or fraud is reviewable by the courts. A decision must not be made for an improper purpose and the exercise of any discretion must be a genuine exercise. For example, a decision maker in exercising discretionary power cannot merely follow the direction of a superior.

   • **abuse of discretionary power**

CASE SUMMARY 3.6

Was There a Breach of Natural Justice? *Odia v. Canada (Citizenship and Immigration)*[80]

The applicant was a citizen of the Democratic Republic of Congo. The Refugee Protection Division (RPD) of the Immigration and Refugee Board of Canada determined that she was not a refugee or person in need of protection on the basis that she lacked credibility. She appealed for judicial review on the basis that the RPD member breached the requirement of procedural fairness by failing to consider Guideline 4: Women Refugee Claimants Fearing Gender-Related Persecution ("Gender Guidelines") in a meaningful way. She also claimed that the member's assessment of her credibility was unreasonable.

The applicant had claimed that her in-laws exerted pressure on her to marry the brother of her deceased husband, who was believed to be HIV positive. The pressure included death threats. Prior to fleeing to Canada, the applicant had taken refuge on her property (which was 40 square metres in size and surrounded by high walls) for 15 months.

The Court granted the application for judicial review. The decision of the RPD was quashed and the matter was to be remitted to a different member of the RPD.

DISCUSSION QUESTIONS

What is the standard of review for the issue of procedural fairness? What did the Court indicate about the sensitivity of the RPD member in assessing the applicant's testimony? Was the requirement of procedural fairness satisfied?

What is the standard of review for the issue of assessing the credibility of the applicant? Did the Court find the member's assessment reasonable? Can the Court substitute its opinion for that of the member with respect to the credibility of the applicant?

---

80. 2014 FC 663 (CanLII).

Methods of Judicial Review

Prerogative writs

Judicial review only if a decision is "incorrect" or "unreasonable"

Historically, the right to judicial review of the decision of a board or tribunal involved obtaining a **prerogative writ** (an order used to control lower courts) from the court. The three main writs are the writs of *certiorari* (an order that quashes and sets aside a tribunal's decision as void and of no effect), **prohibition** (an order that prohibits a tribunal from proceeding), and *mandamus* (an order compelling a government to perform its duties). In addition, the courts always had the right to declare the law in these situations, making a **declaratory judgment**, and then providing remedies such as damages or an injunction to enforce that declaration. Today, some provinces have consolidated and simplified this procedure by statutory enactment.[81] Whether the person challenging the tribunal proceeds by statute or by writ, it must be kept in mind that any remedy provided by the court is completely discretionary when judicial review is involved. There is a reluctance to exercise this discretion except in situations in which the decisions of the tribunal can be demonstrated to be "incorrect" or "unreasonable."[82]

Governments use privative clauses

Governments are naturally reluctant to have the courts interfere with boards that they have empowered to make such decisions. To prevent such judicial review, they will include statutory provisions that are designed to stop the courts from reviewing the board's decision. A **privative clause** can take several different forms, but a typical example is found in the current Ontario *Labour Relations Act*:

> No decision, order, direction, declaration or ruling of the Board shall be questioned or reviewed in any court, and no order shall be made or process entered, or proceedings taken in any court, whether by way of injunction, declaratory judgment, certiorari, mandamus, prohibition, quo warranto, or otherwise, to question, review, prohibit or restrain the Board or any of its proceedings.[83]

Courts resist operation of privative clauses . . .

The intent of this kind of provision is obvious, but the courts interpret it to apply only when the board is acting within its jurisdiction. Thus, the original question as to whether the administrator has jurisdiction is still open to review. In fact, the way the courts have interpreted this type of privative clause varies with circumstances. If the courts wish to review a decision, they will often find a way to do so, despite the presence of a privative clause. And, of course, such privative clauses cannot remove rights given under the *Charter of Rights and Freedoms*, such as the right that the rules of fundamental justice be followed when a person's right to "life, liberty and the security of person" is compromised.

. . . but are reluctant to conduct judicial review

It must be remembered that, because of recent Supreme Court of Canada decisions, courts today are generally reluctant to exercise their right of judicial review even when there is no privative clause involved. As stated by the Supreme Court of Canada, "Courts, while exercising their constitutional functions of judicial review, must be sensitive not only to the need to uphold the rule of law, but also to the necessity of avoiding undue interference with the discharge of administrative functions in respect of the matters delegated to administrative bodies by Parliament and legislatures."[84]

Challenging administrative decisions may be futile and costly

Finally, it must be emphasized that anyone adversely affected by the decision of an administrative board or tribunal should think long and hard before attempting to exercise any of the rights outlined above. It is generally very expensive to go through the process of judicial review, and often the resulting remedy is hollow. For example, when an order of *certiorari* is obtained, quashing a board's decision, that board will often simply reconvene, making sure that it does everything right, and make the same decision again. The result of this approach is that the whole process of challenging a decision becomes futile. Also, when a government agency is

---

81. See, for example, *Judicial Review Procedure Act*, R.S.B.C. 1996, c. 241; and *Judicial Review Procedure Act*, R.S.O. 1990, c. J-1.

82. These words are explained in *Dunsmuir v. New Brunswick, supra* note 78.

83. Labour Relations Act, S.O. 1995, CH-1, Schedule A. Copyright © 1995 by Queen's Printer for Ontario. Used by the permission of Queen's Printer for Ontario.

84. *Dunsmuir v. New Brunswick, supra* note 78 at 27.

involved, it can usually afford to pay the legal costs involved, and it may prefer to incur those costs rather than face an embarrassing court decision. There is more than a little truth in the old adage that "You can't fight city hall." For these reasons, even when rights have been clearly violated, it is often more appropriate, especially when dealing with government, to turn to the alternative methods of dispute resolution that were described above.

Alternative dispute resolution may provide a better resolution

REDUCING RISK 3.7

It is vital that businesspeople remember that challenging government regulators and administrators should be done only as a last resort. As with litigation, an administrative proceeding can be a frustrating, costly, and often fruitless exercise that should be avoided if at all possible. Further, this is a specialized field in which the costs incurred may be even higher than the expense of litigation. The complainant must deal with officials who have access to government funds and who may be more than willing to spend those funds to save themselves the embarrassment of being found in the wrong. A sophisticated client will carefully consider all of the costs and benefits before making a complaint against a government body.

 Be sure to visit the MyBusLawLab that accompanies this book to find practice quizzes, province-specific content, simulations and much more!

SUMMARY

Alternative dispute resolution (ADR)

- Alternative dispute resolution is a recent trend to avoid costs and delays associated with litigation
- Advantages:
  - Control, timeliness, productivity, cost, privacy, good will, flexibility
- Disadvantages:
  - Unpredictable, no precedents set, cannot deal with complex legal problems
- Must be voluntary, must have a balance of power between the parties
- Parties must cooperate to ensure agreement and resolution
- ADR mechanisms:
  - Negotiation—direct discussion between parties
  - Mediation—neutral third party facilitates discussion
  - Arbitration—neutral expert makes a binding decision

The courts

- Procedural rules govern structure and function, which may vary with jurisdiction
- Open to the public, with some exceptions
- Both criminal and civil functions are found at trial and appellate levels
- All but lower-level provincial court judges are appointed by the federal government

Provincial courts

- Handle less serious criminal offences, civil matters under a set amount, custody and maintenance in family divisions, youth offenders
- Provinces have recently created new specialized courts to deal with societal changes and problems

Superior courts

- Handle serious criminal offences, civil matters with unlimited monetary jurisdiction, divorces

Appellate courts

- Deal with appeals of law from trial courts, usually have three judges, do not rehear the facts, usually hold final hearing for most criminal and civil matters

Federal courts

- Tax Court hears cases involving federal tax matters
- Federal Court hears disputes within federal jurisdiction and appeals from some administrative tribunals
- Federal Court of Appeal hears appeals from the Federal Court, Tax Court, and some administrative tribunals

Supreme Court of Canada

- Highest-level appeal court
- Deals primarily with constitutional and *Charter* matters, as well as cases of national importance

Process of civil litigation

- Limitation periods are set by statute
- Jurisdiction:
  - Must be a real and substantial connection
- Pre-trial procedures:
  - Plaintiff files writ of summons (if required) and statement of claim
  - Defendant responds with appearance (if required) and statement of defence
  - Discovery of documents and questioning of parties by opposing counsel
  - Payment into court or offer of settlement to encourage reasonable demands and offers
  - Purpose is to bring information to light and encourage settlement
- The Trial
  - Examination of witnesses and presentation of evidence
  - Judgment
  - Jury decides questions of fact
  - Judge decides questions of law
  - Loser usually pays some legal costs
- Remedies
  - Damages—general, special, punitive
  - Accounting, injunction, specific performance, declaration
- Enforcement
  - Examination in aid of execution
  - Seizure of property
  - Garnishment

Dealing with regulatory bodies

- Decisions of government bureaucrats are reviewable by the courts
- Enforce government policies and resolve disputes
- Act within the jurisdiction granted by the enabling statute
- Comply with the *Charter of Rights and Freedoms*
- Maintain a minimum standard of procedural fairness
- Rules of natural justice require:
  - Fair hearing with adequate notice
  - Decision made by the person who heard the evidence
  - Absence of bias in process
- Methods of judicial review:
  - Courts can review administrative decisions when the administrative tribunal did not have jurisdiction or did not follow the rules of natural justice
  - Can issue prerogative writs, including *certiorari*, *mandamus*, and prohibition

- Can make a declaration or order an injunction
- Privative clauses are statutory provisions that attempt to prevent judicial review, which sometimes are resisted by the courts

---

QUESTIONS FOR REVIEW

1. List and describe the principal advantages of alternative dispute resolution.

2. Distinguish between negotiation, mediation, and arbitration, and discuss the advantages and disadvantages of each of them.

3. Explain online dispute resolution.

4. Describe the court hierarchy in Canada, including provincial and federal courts.

5. Distinguish between questions of law and questions of fact, and explain why this distinction is significant.

6. Who appoints provincial superior court judges? Provincial court judges?

7. How would the expiration of a limitation period affect the rights of parties to litigate a matter in dispute?

8. In cases involving the Internet, what are some of the factors the courts examine when they are determining if there is a real and substantial connection to a jurisdiction?

9. What are the pleadings used to commence an action in the superior trial court in your jurisdiction?

10. How does the discovery process take place, and what is its significance in civil litigation?

11. Explain how an offer to settle can affect the judgment award made by the court to the plaintiff.

12. Describe the recent initiatives taken in your jurisdiction to "speed up" the litigation process.

13. Explain the trial process.

14. Compare party and party costs with solicitor and client costs. To whom are these costs generally awarded?

15. Distinguish among the various remedies available to a successful plaintiff in a civil action.

16. Explain the role of the examination in aid of execution in enforcing remedies (from Question 15), and indicate what methods are available to enforce a judgment against a debtor who is trying to avoid payment.

17. Explain the value of an injunction as a prejudgment remedy. Discuss other prejudgment remedies available to aid in the collection of debt.

18. Under what circumstances will the courts review a decision made by a government bureaucrat or administrative tribunal?

19. What must be examined to determine whether a decision maker has acted within her authority?

20. What are the requirements for a fair hearing, and what is necessary to satisfy the rules of natural justice?

21. Distinguish between *certiorari*, prohibition, *mandamus*, and a declaration.

22. What is a privative clause? How do courts usually react to them?

CASES AND DISCUSSION QUESTIONS

1. *M. v. C.*, 2014 ONSC 567 (CanLII)

The applicant was a 14-year-old girl who claimed that the respondent was her biological father. She claimed child support. She indicated that her birth parents signed an agreement by which the respondent paid a lump sum to her mother in full satisfaction of child support obligations. The applicant wanted to attend a private school and asked for financial assistance from the respondent. The respondent was married to someone other than the applicant's birth mother and they had three young children who did not know about the applicant. The respondent asked the Court to seal the file and order that the names of the parties be initialized to protect these three children from psychological harm.

The Court acknowledged that the value of the principles of openness and transparency must be weighed against the goal of protecting children who may be adversely affected by litigation. Should the Court extend this concern to children who are not parties to the litigation, as was the case here? What evidence is relevant to determining if children will suffer harm from the litigation or if it is made public? Discuss the arguments for giving the public access to personal and private matters such as those in this case. What did the Court decide?

2. *Windrem v. Couture*, 2008 SKQB 33 (CanLII)

The plaintiff claimed that he was physically assaulted by the defendant, suffering significant pain and injury. He asked for general and special damages. The defendant was charged with assault causing bodily harm but was acquitted of the charge. On the basis of his acquittal, the defendant applied for an order striking the paragraphs of the statement of claim that referred to the assault and the injuries suffered by the plaintiff. He claimed that permitting these allegations to remain in the statement of claim would be an abuse of process.

Did the Court order the removal of the indicated paragraphs from the statement of claim? Is an acquittal in a criminal trial admissible in a subsequent civil trial as proof that the party did not commit the offence? Why or why not?

3. *Wolff v. Momentus.ca*, 2014 ONSC 1195 (CanLII)

The plaintiff (and defendant by counterclaim) sought dismissal of the counterclaim against him that was issued by one of the defendants, Zip. The application was based on the argument that filing the counterclaim was not done in compliance with the *Limitations Act*. Almost three years after the plaintiff commenced the litigation, Zip filed its statement of defence and counterclaim on April 25, 2012. The allegations in the counterclaim were almost identical to the allegations raised in a statement of claim filed by Zip more than three years before on January 26, 2009. The plaintiff was therefore aware, in 2009, of the issues raised by the allegations in the counterclaim. Zip's 2009 action was ultimately dismissed by the Court on March 15, 2012, because the action had been commenced in the wrong jurisdiction.

The relevant limitation period set out in the *Limitations Act* was two years after the claim was discovered. Zip argued that the limitation period was inapplicable in this case since the plaintiff was aware of the issues raised in the counterclaim.

Did the Court accept Zip's argument? Did it have the discretion to refuse to apply the statutory limitation period because of the special circumstances of the case? Is it appropriate for limitations legislation to eliminate the discretion of the courts to extend the limitation periods set by the legislation?

4. *Angelo's Gold Factory Inc. v. Anthony Pipolo Incorporated*, 2007 CanLII 80119 (ON SC)

The plaintiff had been unsuccessful in its attempts to serve the defendants by personal service. The plaintiff's lawyer then served the statement of claim on a lawyer who was representing the defendants in other matters. The lawyer had not obtained his clients' authorization to accept service of the statement of claim. None of the defendants responded to the statement of claim, so the plaintiff obtained default judgment against them.

In this action, the defendants applied to have the default judgment set aside. Explain the nature of their complaint and the likely outcome. In your answer consider the role of fairness in the administration of justice and whether practical requirements should be permitted to overrule this requirement of procedural fairness within court processes or when dealing with government tribunals.

5. *Community Panel of the Adams Lake Indian Band v. Adams Lake Band*, 2011 FCA 37 (CanLII)

Dennis ran for election to the band council but was unsuccessful. He appealed the election result, alleging irregularities and improprieties. The election rules required the community panel (which handles any appeals) to have five persons "to govern and decide all proceedings . . ." On the last day of deliberations of the panel, after deliberations had been completed and halfway through the voting process, one of the five members of the panel resigned. His reasons for resigning related to the merits of the appeal; it was clear that he had made a decision on the appeal and that he knew he was going to be outvoted by the other four members of the panel. The remaining members completed the voting process and dismissed the appeal. The Federal Court held that the panel did not have jurisdiction to rule on the appeal because it did not have a five-person quorum. The decision of the panel was quashed. The panel appealed.

What was the decision of the Federal Court of Appeal? Should a member of an administrative tribunal be allowed to frustrate the work of the tribunal by resigning at an inopportune time?

6. *Black v. Canada (Advisory Council for the Order)*, 2013 FCA 267 (CanLII)

Black was convicted of fraud and obstruction of justice in the United States. The advisory council for the Order of Canada proposed to review his appointment to the Order. Black requested an in-person oral hearing to enable him to demonstrate that the American prosecutors had not acted appropriately in handling his case and that he would not have been convicted of the crimes in Canada. The council refused his request and indicated that he could make written representations in support of his position that his appointment to the Order of Canada should not be terminated because of his conviction. Black applied for judicial review on the ground that the duty of fairness required that he be given an opportunity for an oral hearing. The Federal Court dismissed his application.

Did the Federal Court of Appeal uphold Black's appeal? Do the factors set out in *Baker v. Canada* (see Case Summary 3.5) indicate a duty of fairness so high that it required the council to give Black an oral hearing?

7. *Cabrera v. Canada (Citizenship and Immigration)*, 2010 FC 709 (CanLII)

The Immigration Division (ID) of the Immigration and Refugee Board issued an exclusion order against the applicant who had come to Canada on a caregiver visa. Two years later she applied for permanent resident status. A date for a hearing was set. Prior to the hearing, the applicant filed a notice of constitutional question (NCQ). The timing of the filing was not in compliance with the relevant notice requirement. The applicant asked for an adjournment of the hearing to comply with the NCQ requirements. The ID refused her request and the hearing proceeded. The ID issued an exclusion order against the applicant because she stated that she had never been married when in fact she had been. The applicant applied for judicial review of the decision on several grounds, one of which was that her right to procedural fairness was breached because her request for an adjournment was refused.

The Court allowed the application on the basis that the ID's decision on the request for an adjournment did not take into account all of the material factors and considerations as required by the relevant regulation. What were these factors? What is the justification for ordering another hearing when it was clear that the applicant had made a material misrepresentation in her application for permanent residency?

8. *GNWT v. Beaulieu*, 2014 NWTSC 63 (CanLII)

Beaulieu applied on a competition for a position with the Government of the Northwest Territories (GNWT). His application was screened out by the selection committee on the basis that he did not meet the screening criteria. Another applicant was selected. Beaulieu appealed the decision to screen him out of the competition. After a hearing, a staffing review officer (SRO) granted Beaulieu's appeal and directed that the competition be rerun. She ruled that the selection committee used two separate combinations of education and experience to evaluate Beaulieu's résumé when only one combination should have been used. The GNWT applied for judicial review of the decision. It claimed that the SRO erred in interpreting the GNWT's human resource manual.

The screening criteria included completion of the third level of a recognized accounting program or equivalent postsecondary education, and three years of varied accounting/ budgeting and contracting administration experience. Beaulieu had a business administration diploma and three years of varied accounting experience. As this was not three years' experience in a budgeting and contracting environment, the selection committee concluded that he did not satisfy the requirements of the screening criteria.

Was the SRO correct in screening Beaulieu in on the basis of his diploma and his varied accounting experience? Would her approach be appropriate in competitions for which there are several screening criteria? Why did the Court consider whether her error was "reasonable"?

4

Chapter

Intentional Torts and Torts Impacting Business

LEARNING OBJECTIVES

1. Describe the role of tort law

2. Distinguish torts from crimes and breaches of contract

3. Identify remedies awarded to redress torts

4. Explain vicarious liability, indicating when it may be imposed

5. Distinguish the torts of assault, battery, and trespass to land, listing the relevant defences

6. Describe three torts that deal with wrongful interference with goods (chattels)

7. Contrast the torts of false imprisonment, malicious prosecution, private and public nuisance, defamation, and injurious falsehood

8. Identify issues surrounding torts committed in the online environment

9. Delineate the following torts: inducing breach of contract, unlawful interference with economic relations, conspiracy to injure, fraudulent misrepresentation (deceit), passing-off, misuse of confidential information, and intrusion upon seclusion

10. Detail how privacy is protected in Canada

11. Outline security and privacy concerns arising as a result of computer use

The law of torts involves private disputes decided in the civil courts. When one person harms another, either intentionally or carelessly, a tort has likely been committed. A civil action can be brought seeking compensation for injuries suffered from the person who committed the wrong. In this chapter, we examine the nature of tort law and discuss the distinctions between intentional torts and negligence, focusing primarily on intentional torts and their business counterparts. We also examine the defences that the person being sued may raise and the conditions that must be met for the plaintiff to be awarded compensation.

THE NATURE OF TORTS

Finding a wholly satisfactory definition for torts is difficult because of the different kinds of conduct that may be considered tortious. Some general principles, however, do apply. A **tort** is committed when one person causes injury to another, harming his person, property, or reputation. The right to sue for redress arises when the injurious conduct falls below a minimal social standard. In other words, a tort is a social or civil wrong that gives rise to the right to sue and to seek one of several remedies. Such remedies may include an injunction (a court order stopping certain conduct) or even punitive damages (an extra award intended to punish the wrongdoer) but normally will be limited to a monetary award of general damages intended to compensate the victim for the loss suffered.

A tort is a civil or social wrong

The role of tort law is multifaceted. It aims to compensate victims, requiring the party at fault to bear the burden of the loss suffered. In so doing, it deters the occurrence of such wrongful behaviour and educates society by "making someone pay." Further, it serves a psychological function by providing some appeasement to those injured by wrongful conduct. Essentially, tort law is a body of law that aims to provide remedies wherever wrongful conduct is involved. It is also continually evolving, with the courts declaring new torts to exist as the need arises. (See the discussion at the end of this chapter concerning invasion of privacy and spoliation.)

Tort law compensates victims and deters wrongful conduct

Crimes must be distinguished from torts. Harmful conduct that is so serious that it poses a threat to society generally is said to be criminal in nature. The prosecution for such acts is carried out by the state in a criminal court where the goal is to punish the wrongdoer, not to compensate the victim. A tort is considered a private matter where the victim of the injurious conduct sues the person responsible for the injury. With many crimes the victim has the right to sue for tort, even if the prosecution results in an acquittal. Thus, wrongful conduct is often both a crime and a tort. Most of the torts discussed in this chapter have a *Criminal Code* counterpart. For example, a driver who is racing on city streets and causes an accident resulting in injury could be charged with criminal negligence and face a fine and imprisonment. But regardless of whether the criminal charges result in a conviction or acquittal, that driver could also be sued in a civil action for the tort of negligence. If found liable, the driver would be ordered to compensate the injured parties. It is much easier to successfully sue for tort, because the standard of proof is based on a "balance of probabilities" test. In a criminal action, the standard is "beyond a reasonable doubt," which is a much higher standard than required in a civil action. (See the discussion under the heading "The Courts" in Chapter 3.)

Crimes are wrongs that affect society as a whole

A tort must also be distinguished from a **breach of contract**. An act that breaches a contract may not be inherently wrong, but the contractual relationship makes the violation of its terms unacceptable. A tort, on the other hand, is inherently wrongful conduct that is either deliberate or falls below a minimal social standard. When the victim sues, the court examines who was at fault, who caused the injury, and determines who should bear the loss for the injuries suffered. Ultimately, the court assesses the amount that should be paid to the victim.

Torts differ from actions based on breach of contract

Two categories of tortious activity are *intentional* (or deliberate) acts and *unintentional* (or careless) negligent acts. Businesspeople can find themselves liable for both. One important difference between deliberate torts and negligence is in the remedies that the courts are willing to grant to the injured party. When the interference has been intentional, the courts may be persuaded to grant punitive damages in addition to the more common general and special damages. General damages compensate for estimated future losses, including both future pecuniary losses (such as loss of earning capacity) and non-pecuniary losses (such as pain and suffering). Special damages are awarded to cover actual expenses and calculable pre-trial losses. Punitive or exemplary damages are designed to punish the wrongdoer and do not relate to the injury suffered. To avoid excessive awards, the Supreme Court of Canada has placed an upper limit of approximately $328 000 on damages that can be awarded to compensate for non-pecuniary losses, including pain and suffering and

Torts may involve intentional or inadvertent conduct

loss of enjoyment of life.[1] Occasionally, the court will also order the return of property or grant an injunction to stop some offending activity.

It is important for businesspeople to keep the concept of **vicarious liability** in mind while studying tort law. An employer can be held liable for the tortious act an employee commits while at work. This liability is limited to torts committed while carrying out employment duties. The employer will not be vicariously liable when the employee is off doing his or her own thing, even if done during working hours, instead of doing the employer's business. The importance of vicarious liability in the business world cannot be overemphasized.

An employer may be vicariously liable for employees' torts

A detailed examination of the master–servant (employer–employee) relationship and vicarious liability can be found in Chapter 12. Several provinces have imposed vicarious liability by statute on the owners of motor vehicles, making them liable for damage and injury caused by the people they allow to drive their cars. Refer to the MyBusLawLab for provincial variations.

 REDUCING RISK 4.1

Perhaps the most valuable thing to gain from the study of tort law—or, for that matter, any of the rules discussed in this text—is the habit of mind that anticipates and avoids legal problems. This is called *risk avoidance* or *risk management*. Businesspeople have a responsibility to manage their legal affairs in the same way they manage the production, marketing, and distribution of their products. Too often, managers wait for something to go wrong, then put the matter into the hands of a lawyer and wait for the results of a lawsuit. Managing risk responsibly means avoiding the problem in the first place. A sophisticated business manager would reflect upon the conditions and practices that pose a danger to the public, customers, suppliers, or employees and consider how they should be corrected. This might be as simple as checking the creditworthiness of customers, keeping a record of emails, putting a warning sticker on a plate-glass window, or lighting a dark stairwell. It saves money to adopt an attitude of risk avoidance and to promote this attitude throughout one's organization. Holding risk evaluation meetings, ensuring adequate insurance coverage, developing policies, and providing incentives that encourage risk avoidance can reduce exposure to costly and time-consuming legal actions.

INTENTIONAL TORTS

LO ⑤ ⑥ ⑦ ⑧

Intentional physical interference

The following discussion is concerned with torts where the conduct involved was intended or deliberate, as opposed to the following chapter's discussion of negligence, where the conduct is inadvertent. The term *intentional* does not mean that the wrongdoer intended to do harm, only that the conduct itself was wilful as opposed to inadvertent. As with all forms of actionable torts, fault on the part of the wrongdoer must be demonstrated, but when we examine intentional torts as discussed here, that fault is embodied in the wilful act of the wrongdoer.

Trespass to Person: Assault and Battery

Actual contact—battery

Fear of contact—assault

Assault and battery (or **trespass to person**) involve the intentional physical interference with another person. These torts are a concern particularly to businesses whose employees serve the public. Conduct that makes a person think he is about to be struck is an **assault**. If someone fakes a punch, points a gun, or picks up a stone to threaten another person, an assault has been committed. A **battery** takes place when someone intentionally makes unwanted physical contact with another person. Since battery almost invariably involves an assault, the term *assault* is often used to refer to both assault and battery. Assault and battery are actionable, even where there is no injury: "the least touching of another in anger is battery."[2] The

---

1. The Supreme Court of Canada established a cap of $100 000 for non-pecuniary damages for personal injury actions in the 1978 "trilogy": *Andrews v. Grand & Toy Alberta Ltd.*, [1978] 2 SCR 229; *Thornton v. Prince George School District No. 57*, [1978] 2 SCR 267; *Arnold v. Teno*, [1978] 2 SCR 287. Due to inflation, the amount is approximately $330 000 (as of 2014).

2. *Cole v. Turner* (1704), 6 Mod. 149, 87 E.R. 907.

purpose of the tort of trespass to the person is to recognize the right of each person to control her body and who touches it. Damages are awarded when this right is violated.

The test to determine whether an assault has taken place is to look to the victim and ask whether he was fearful of or anticipated unwanted physical contact. If the defendant's conduct would cause a reasonable person to feel threatened with imminent harm or even simply unwanted contact, it constitutes an assault. Even threats made online can constitute an assault. In *Warman v. Grosvenor*,[3] for example, the defendant waged a "campaign of terror" against the plaintiff. The personal emails and postings on the Internet were threatening and intimidating. By virtue of their repetitiveness, their level of malevolence, and their detail regarding the plaintiff's whereabouts, the postings made the plaintiff apprehensive of imminent physical harm. Damages were assessed at $175 000, but since the plaintiff proceeded summarily, his award was capped at $50 000.

The anticipated contact might be anything from a physical blow to unwanted medical treatment to a kiss. The motive or goodwill of the person attacking is not relevant. The words are taken into consideration as well as the gestures and actions. The action of a person walking toward another can be an assault when accompanied by threatening words, whereas words such as "How nice to see you again" remove the threat.

CASE SUMMARY 4.1

Bouncers Beware! *Tardif v. Wiebe*;[4] *Tootoosis v. John Doe*[5]

There is no dispute that Tardif was drunk when he was refused further service and was asked to leave the hotel on the Friday night in question. He was not usually a fighter but did get obnoxious and rude when intoxicated. In the process of leaving the bar with his girlfriend, he got into an altercation with a woman who made some offensive remarks about the two of them. This scuffle resulted in the hotel bouncers, Wiebe and Poburn, being called to intervene and eject Tardif. On the landing above the outside steps of the hotel, Poburn held Tardif while Wiebe struck him twice. As a result of the second blow, Tardif was thrown off the landing and fell down four steps onto the concrete sidewalk below, causing serious injuries. Tardif has no recollection of this, but Poburn testified that his head "cracked like an egg."

While Poburn was a professional bouncer, Wiebe was untrained, and both were considerably larger than Tardif, who posed no threat to them. Excessive and unjustified force was clearly used against Tardif.

The bouncers may have had a right to eject Tardif with force if he had been refusing to leave, but that was not the case here. And even if use of some force to remove Tardif were justified, delivery of such forceful blows when Tardif was already outside the hotel certainly was not.

Because of considerable brain and nerve damage and other injuries, Tardif was unable to return to work. The award against the hotel and bouncers exceeded $1 million.

Because no malice was involved, there was no award for punitive damages. By contrast, in the *Tootoosis* case, where the Vibe Nightclub operator permitted the plaintiff to be viciously beaten and humiliated by some of his employees, who left the unconscious plaintiff on the street with his pants pulled down, the Court added an award of exemplary damages in the sum of $10 000.

[3.] 2008 CanLII 57728 (ON SC).

[4.] 1996 CanLII 1703 (BC SC).

[5.] 2006 SKQB 75 (CanLII).

> **SMALL BUSINESS PERSPECTIVE**
>
> Numerous similar cases demonstrate the potential liability faced by businesses dealing with the public. The fact that a business instructed its employees not to use force does not operate as a defence—because of vicarious liability, employers will nonetheless remain liable. Since investing in training one's staff will not totally eliminate the risk, it is prudent to secure adequate insurance.

DEFENCES

There are several defences that can be raised against an assault or battery claim. Normally, doctors escape liability for their actions when operating on or otherwise treating patients through the principle of consent. Essentially, a person who expressly or implicitly consents to conduct that would otherwise constitute an assault or battery loses the right to sue. This is the reason why injured boxers cannot sue their opponents. **Consent**, when informed and voluntary, operates as an effective defence to many of the torts discussed in this chapter and the next.

Consent is a defence

It is important to remember that the level of interference cannot exceed the consent. Excessive violence in a sporting activity will constitute the tort of battery despite the consent. For example, Mike Tyson faced liability after biting his opponent during a boxing match. Excessive violence may also be a crime, as Todd Bertuzzi discovered when he was charged and subsequently convicted of assault causing bodily harm for a vicious hit to Steve Moore during an NHL game in 2004.[6]

Also, the consent must be *informed consent*—people must know what they are consenting to. In the *Halushka v. University of Saskatchewan* case,[7] medical researchers were unable to establish that the consent obtained was informed. The plaintiff student had agreed to participate in a drug experiment in exchange for $50 but was not fully informed of the risk. When the drug was administered his heart stopped. He had to undergo emergency surgery to restart it. Halushka was paid $50 four days later when he regained consciousness. His battery action against the university was successful.

Physical touching beyond that consented to is a battery

People may refuse or give only limited consent to medical treatment. In *Malette v. Shulman*,[8] the physician administered a blood transfusion, which likely saved the patient's life, yet the plaintiff successfully sued for battery. The plaintiff carried a card in her purse stating that as a Jehovah's Witness she refused consent to receive any blood products. Since this refusal of consent was drawn to the doctor's attention and he administered the blood anyway, the doctor was found to have committed a battery.[9] Patients have a right to control interference with their bodies and can refuse treatment, even when they may die without it. This often puts physicians in an unsettling position. Patients now can indicate what treatments they do and do not consent to by creating an advance directive.[10]

Individuals may outline and limit consent in advance

---

[6]. *R. v. Bertuzzi*, [2004] B.C.J. No. 2692, (B.C.P.C.). Note: A civil action was also commenced by Moore. See *Moore v. Bertuzzi*, [2012] ONSC 597 (CanLII). It was eventually settled out of court; details were not made public.

[7]. 1965 CanLII 439 (SK CA).

[8]. 1990 CanLII 6868 (ON CA).

[9]. When parents refuse treatment needed to save the lives of their children for religious reasons, applications may be made to the courts to intervene and direct treatment. See *R.B. v. Children's Aid Society of Metropolitan Toronto*, 1995 CanLII 115 (SCC).

[10]. Examples of legislation validating these directives include the *Personal Directives Act* of Alberta (R.S.A. 2000. c. P-6), Nova Scotia (S.N.S. 2008, c. 8), or the Northwest Territories (S.N.W.T. 2005, c.16). See also *Advance Health Care Directives Act*, SNL 1995, c. A-4.1; *Health Care Directives Act*, CCSM c. H27; *The Health Care Directives and Substitute Health Care Decision Makers Act*, SS 1997, c. H-0.001; *Health Care Consent Act, 1996*, SO 1996, c. 2, Sch A; *Health Care (Consent) and Care Facility (Admission) Act*, RSBC 1996, c. 181.

Reasonable force is permitted to defend self

Reasonable force is permitted to eject trespassers

Self-defence can also be raised to counteract an assault and battery accusation. The law entitles people who are being attacked to use necessary force to defend themselves. The test asks whether the force used was reasonable. An attack is not a licence to respond with unrestrained violence. Of course, the skill and experience of the person being attacked will be taken into account in determining what is reasonable. Thus, a boxer is held to a higher standard than an ordinary person not accustomed to such violence. When a bouncer ejects an unruly patron from a bar, the same principle applies. If a patron refuses to leave when asked, she becomes a trespasser and reasonable force can be used to eject her. But as seen in Case Summary 4.1, use of excessive force may result in liability on the part of both the bouncer and the occupier of the premises.

Trespass to Land

Trespass: Deliberately going onto someone's land without authority

Trespass to land involves going onto another person's property without having either the lawful right or the owner's permission to do so. Such a trespass is an actionable wrong, even when no damage or injury takes place and even if the intruder does not know he is trespassing. Ignorance of the location of the property line is no excuse. Only if the intruder had no control of where he was would there be a defence. Thus, if he was struck by a car and thrown on the property, there would be no trespass. But if he was running away and went onto the property to escape a threat, it is still a trespass and he would be responsible for any damage caused. A mere "bruising of the grass" is trespass; but if only nominal damages are likely, why sue? In some provinces, legislation has been passed enabling occupiers to have trespassers apprehended and fined.[11]

Permission to be on the property may be implied

People acting in an official capacity, such as postal workers, meter readers, municipal inspectors, and the police, have the right to come on private property and are not trespassing. In shopping malls and other premises where the public is welcome, visitors have an implied right to be there even when they have not come to shop. Permission is also implied when visitors have been allowed on the property over time without steps being taken to remove them. If such visitors become unruly or dangerous to other patrons they can be asked to leave. In fact, visitors can be required to leave even though they have done nothing wrong, so long as the reason does not violate human rights legislation (such as refusing entry to persons based on their race or religion). In *Russo v. Ontario Jockey Club*,[12] for example, a private racetrack was able to exclude a gambler from the premises simply because she was very successful. But if visitors refuse to leave they become trespassers, and reasonable force can be used to eject them.

Permanent incursions constitute a continuing trespass

Trespass can also occur indirectly. When a person leaves or throws some item on another's property, or erects a sign without the occupier's permission, a trespass has taken place. Trespass can also involve a permanent incursion onto the property of another. This is referred to as a **continuing trespass** and can take the form of a building or other structure that encroaches on the property of another. The remedy requested would likely include an injunction. Where multi-storeyed buildings are involved, the costs of correcting the problem can be enormous. Of course, consent (in the form of permission to come onto the property or build the encroaching structure), if there has been full disclosure, will be a complete defence to an action for trespass.

Occupiers' liability legislation outlines duties owed to trespassers

Trespassers who cause damage while on private property bear responsibility for any injury or loss caused. This is the case whether injury was foreseeable or not. But what if the trespasser is the one injured? Under common law, the injured trespasser generally has no claim against the occupier. Provincial occupiers' liability legislation

---

11. See Alberta's *Petty Trespass Act*, R.S.A. 2000, c. P-11, and *Trespass to Premises Act*, R.S.A. 2000, c. T-7, both of which enable the arrest without warrant of individuals caught trespassing. Fines range from $2000 to $5000 (for subsequent violations).

12. [1987] O.J. No. 1105.

generally reiterates this rule, requiring only that the occupier of property not wilfully or recklessly cause harm to a trespasser or someone on the property for a criminal purpose. A greater duty is owed, however, to minors who trespass. If it is foreseeable that minors who trespass may be harmed, a duty may arise to take reasonable steps to ensure safety. Check the appropriate provincial statutes through the MyBusLawLab to determine the exact nature of the duties owed.

CASE SUMMARY 4.2

Trespasser's Temper Ignited: *G.T. et al. v. D. Saunders et al.*[13]

The plaintiffs owned a piece of forested property that they maintained as a nature sanctuary. They were distressed when they discovered that the defendants were constructing a portion of road that encroached substantially on their property. The slope of the land was altered, and many trees were cut down in the process. When the plaintiffs tried to stop further work on this road, relations between the neighbours quickly deteriorated.

Armed with the survey proving the incursion, the plaintiffs served a notice of trespass upon the defendant, Daniel Saunders, pursuant to the *Trespass to Property Act*, R.S.O. 1990, and gave their neighbours one week's notice that they intended to close the road. The plaintiffs were then subjected to acts of vandalism and threats. Tires were slashed and property damage incurred.

Subsequently, the plaintiffs obtained a court order enjoining the defendants from further trespass. This too was breached, because the road met the defendants' needs. The plaintiffs thus brought this action seeking a permanent injunction against further trespass by the defendants, damages for trespass, and punitive damages.

The Court found that the defendants repeatedly trespassed on the plaintiffs' property. It was probable that, to avoid objections from the Ministry of Natural Resources, a road constructed on the defendants' land was too close to the creek and might disrupt fish habitat, so the defendants deliberately selected this route for their road (driveway). They continued with the construction and defended it even when presented with a survey establishing the property line. Even after a court order was issued requiring that they cease trespassing, they violated the court order and continued to use the road. The Court found the plaintiffs' claim for punitive damages of $10 000 to be modest in the extreme, and had they asked for more, more would have been awarded.

A permanent injunction was thus granted to restrain further trespass, and the defendants were ordered to pay to the plaintiffs pecuniary, non-pecuniary, and punitive damages in the amount of $103 031.95.

SMALL BUSINESS PERSPECTIVE

In light of the considerable damages payable should a trespass occur, particularly for a continuing trespass, doesn't obtaining a survey to clarify where property lines lie seem a small price to pay?

Trespass to Chattels, Conversion, and Detinue

Trespass to chattels, conversion, and detinue are three torts that deal with the wrongful interference with goods. The decision to assert one tort and not another may impact the remedies available. Any direct intentional interference causing damage to the goods of another is a **trespass to chattels**. Where the plaintiff has possession or an immediate right of possession and that right or possession is wrongfully interfered with physically by the defendant, a trespass to chattels has occurred.

Trespass to chattels is actionable

---

13. 2014 ONSC 4422 (CanLII).

Generally, the remedy for trespass to chattels is compensatory damages. When vandals smash the windshield of a car or kick the door in, they have committed trespass to chattels and are liable to pay compensation and possibly punitive damages to the victim. They may also face criminal charges.

Conversion involves one person intentionally appropriating the goods of another person for her own purposes. In essence, it is a wrongful taking, using, or destroying of goods or asserting control over them. There must be intent to deprive the owner of title.

In *Robertson v. Stang*,[14] for example, the plaintiff sued for conversion after the managers of her apartment removed her property and placed it in storage. The plaintiff, a compulsive shopper, had crammed her unit with so many purchases that it was difficult to walk through the unit. This hazardous state of affairs was discovered when the unit flooded. The managers told the plaintiff she would have to move her belongings, and they assisted her in removing items to storage. After an identified third party broke in and stole some property, the plaintiff asserted conversion by the managers. The Court determined that since the managers moved the goods not to claim them for their own but only to remove a fire hazard, there was no conversion. The plaintiff had failed to show any intent on the part of the managers to deprive the plaintiff of title. Similarly, in *Chow v. Gershman Transport International Ltd.*,[15] where a wrongful seizure of property was claimed, the bailiff who seized the vehicle was not liable in conversion because his conduct did not demonstrate an intention to exercise dominion over the truck. While the bailiff did take possession of the truck and did cause it to be transported to a storage facility, it could not be said that he converted the chattel to its own use. As such, the bailiff's actions did not constitute conversion.

In addition to being crimes, theft of goods or acquiring possession of goods through deceit are also actionable under the tort of conversion. Conversion takes place when someone sells or otherwise wrongfully disposes of goods belonging to someone else. When goods are damaged or destroyed to the extent that they are no longer of any value to the rightful owner, the wrongdoer should have to pay the market value at the time of the tort. Effectively, conversion consists of interference with the plaintiff's chattels in such a way that a forced sale is justified. In such circumstances the person converting the goods is forced to purchase them. In exchange for payment, the defendant acquires the property. The courts also have the power to order the return of the goods if that is a more appropriate remedy.

Unfortunately for the unsophisticated buyer, if one purchases an item from someone other than the true owner, one may later be sued by the rightful owner for conversion. The court may require the buyer to return the goods to the rightful owner or pay damages equal to the market value of the goods when misappropriated. In the end, the buyer may end up paying the price twice—once to the seller who misrepresented ownership and again to the true owner.

The third tort involving wrongful interference with goods is called **detinue**. Like conversion, it involves the wrongful possession of someone else's goods. But where conversion requires wrongfully taking control of the goods through some intentional act, detinue deals with situations where the person is wrongfully retaining the goods. The defendant may have come into possession of them legally but is now, after a proper request, refusing to return them. As the name of the tort suggests, it is the wrongful detention that gives the plaintiff the ability to sue. For example, if Nicole lends Henry her lawnmower and Henry refuses to return it, Nicole could bring an action in detinue for compensation.

Like conversion, the calculation of damages essentially amounts to a forced sale of the goods, but since detinue is a continuing tort, damages are calculated as at the date of the trial. This distinction proved to be significant in the *Steiman* case,[16]

Conversion involves the defendant treating the plaintiff's goods as his own

Theft of or wrongful sale of another's property is conversion

Damages for conversion equal the value of the goods taken

Refusal to return goods enables the owner to assert detinue

---

14. [1997] B.C.J. No. 2022 (B.C.S.C.).
15. 2000 ABQB 360 (CanLII).
16. *Steiman v. Steiman*, [1982] M.J. No. 21 (C.A.).

where the defendants were found liable in conversion for taking the plaintiffs' jewellery. Damages were initially assessed at $186 787 based on the value of the jewellery at the time of trial. But on appeal, the defendants successfully argued that the proper date of valuation was back in 1976, since that was when the loss or taking occurred. Had the plaintiffs claimed in detinue instead of conversion, the Court would have been able to order the return of the goods or payment of their value at the time of trial. Since the jewellery had appreciated in value, the plaintiffs would have been better off to sue in detinue.

CASE SUMMARY 4.3

Conversion of an Entire Business: *Klewchuk v. Switzer*[17]

Switzer and Klewchuk were pioneers in the emerging casino industry in Calgary. Switzer owned a hotel and provided facilities to charities on a per-event basis, while Klewchuk provided the charities with dealers and portable gaming equipment. Years later, Switzer built a new facility to which he relocated the casino operation in 1989, and Klewchuk continued to supply the dealers and equipment. Each party was paid by the charities for his particular contribution.

In 1996, the rules governing the conduct of casinos were changed by the government such that charities could contract only with a "casino facility licensee," which would in turn provide an entire package of services. Klewchuk and Switzer thus entered a new business arrangement, whereby Klewchuk secured the casino facility licence and, as licensee, would alone contract with the charities. In turn, Klewchuk paid Switzer a "per casino" fee for the facility rental.

Things turned sour when Klewchuk ran into financial difficulty. He found a buyer, but the deal fell through. Thereafter, Switzer prepared a Landlord's Distress Warrant for rent and, through a bailiff, seized all Klewchuk's gaming equipment and supplies. Switzer evicted Klewchuk from the property, secured a temporary casino facility licence, and continued operations.

The Court determined that Switzer carried out a secret plot to expropriate Klewchuk's business and to reap the profits for himself. Switzer and Klewchuk were not landlord and tenant but licensor and licensee; thus Switzer had no right to levy distress for rent. Damages for conversion were awarded in the amount of $2.2 million, based on lost income, but that sum was reduced on appeal to $500 000.

DISCUSSION QUESTIONS

In determining damages, the Court of Appeal considered the value of the business at the time of its conversion. Would the price offered to Klewchuk by the purchaser, mentioned above, be relevant to this determination? What other factors should a court consider in assessing damages for conversion of an ongoing business?

False Imprisonment

False imprisonment, including false arrest, occurs when people are intentionally restrained against their will and the person doing the restraining has no lawful authority to do so. This may be in the form of complete imprisonment, where the person is held in a cell or room, or in the form of an arrest. In either case, the person's liberty to go where he pleases must be totally restrained. Even a person who submits to authority or threat can be considered imprisoned, since in his mind he has been restrained. The second requirement is that the restraint be unlawful. When a security guard arrests someone found shoplifting, there has been no false imprisonment. Generally, a private person has the power to make

Restraint without lawful excuse is false imprisonment

Submission to authority can constitute imprisonment

---

17. 2003 ABCA 187 (CanLII); leave to appeal refused [2003] S.C.C.A. No. 392.

an arrest, but only when she finds someone in the process of actually committing a crime, such as shoplifting. A citizen's powers of arrest are set out in section 494 of the *Criminal Code*:[18]

> 494(1) Any one may arrest without warrant
>
> (*a*) a person whom he finds committing an indictable offence; or
>
> (*b*) a person who, on reasonable grounds, he believes
>
>   (i) has committed a criminal offence, and
>
>   (ii) is escaping from and freshly pursued by persons who have law-ful authority to arrest that person.
>
> (2) The owner or a person in lawful possession of property, or a person authorized by the owner or by a person in lawful possession of property, may arrest a person without a warrant if they find them committing a criminal offence on or in relation to that property and
>
> (*a*) they make the arrest at that time; or
>
> (*b*) they make the arrest within a reasonable time after the offence is committed and they believe on reasonable grounds that it is not feasible in the circumstances for a peace officer to make the arrest.
>
> (3) Any one other than a peace officer who arrests a person without warrant shall forthwith deliver the person to a peace officer.

Damage awards for false imprisonment can be significant

A charge of false imprisonment is a significant risk for any business involved in serving the public. This risk is great when, either because of store policy or inexperience on the part of staff, customers are detained when suspected of wrongdoing. If the customer has not in fact stolen any goods, there is no justification for holding him. A sophisticated manager will often discourage employees from apprehending shoplifters, since the potential loss from goods stolen is far outweighed by the danger of losing a false imprisonment action. Of course, this may encourage more shoplifting. The answer is to carefully select and train security people to deal with these matters and have the other employees only inform the security people of what they observe. Case Summary 4.4 demonstrates the difficulties a retail store or other business may encounter.

The risk of acting outside one's authority when arresting another and thereby committing an offence oneself is real, as Case Summary 4.4 demonstrates. But the person restrained may not be satisfied with pressing criminal charges. Damages may also be sought for the tort of false imprisonment.

CASE SUMMARY 4.4

Toronto Shopkeeper Grabs Thief and National Headlines: *R. v. Chen*[19]

When David Chen, his cousin, and nephew were charged with assault and forcible confinement after chasing, restraining, and tying up a man who had stolen plants from Chen's Lucky Moose Food Mart, the nation took notice. The *Vancouver Sun* noted, "The case has captivated Toronto with most observers demanding to know why an honest grocer struggling to make a buck and protect his merchandise has become a target of punishment." The prime minister responded to the storm by announcing the introduction of the *Citizen's Arrest and Self-Defence Act*,[20] which would purportedly strike a better balance between allowing citizens to protect themselves and their property on the one hand and guarding against vigilantism on the other.

---

18. R.S.C. 1985 c. C-46, s. 494.

19. 2010 ONCJ 641 (CanLII).

20. S.C. 2012, c. 9.

The case highlighted the limits on citizen's arrest. The thief was not caught "in the act" but rather was grabbed an hour later. Further, there was concern about the amount of force used. Police acted in response to four calls made to the 911 operator. They were told that up to four individuals had grabbed a person, tied him up, and placed him in the back of a white van. The first two officers on scene found a male (Bennett) tied up on the floor of a white van; a cursory search also produced some X-acto knives. The police therefore arrested Chen and his two co-accused for assault and unlawful confinement.

The difficulty was that the *Criminal Code* provision that set the rules for a citizen's arrest stipulated that one "may arrest without warrant a person whom he finds committing a criminal offence on or in relation to that property." Since Bennett was caught after the fact, there were fears that Chen and the co-accused acted outside of the law. Bennett, however, admitted he had returned to Chen's store to steal more. Ultimately, the Court concluded that Bennett's two offences would be viewed together as one transaction, and therefore the requirements of section 494 of the *Criminal Code* were met. As to the matter of excessive force used, the trial judge stated: "The only conclusion that I can come to is that I have a reasonable doubt. All such doubts must always be resolved in favour of the defence." Accordingly, Chen and his co-accused were acquitted of all charges.

DISCUSSION QUESTIONS

Chen claimed he had to forcibly restrain the thief because the police were too busy to respond promptly to complaints of shoplifting. In light of the Court's broad interpretation of citizen's arrest, was there any need to pass the *Citizen's Arrest and Self-Defence Act*? Nonetheless, the *Criminal Code* was amended and section 494(2) was broadened in scope.

In *Hanisch v. Canada*,[21] $25 000 was awarded as general damages for false imprisonment. The plaintiff pursued civil action, as he was understandably incensed by his arrest. Having braved frigid waters in a storm to rescue a Zodiac boat that had broken away from a Parks Canada vessel, the plaintiff contacted the parks warden and informed him that he had secured the Zodiac and was claiming compensation (salvage). Not wanting to pay the plaintiff, the parks warden called the RCMP, requesting police assistance. Then, instead of telling the officer that the boat was secure, the parks warden stood by as the officer arrested and imprisoned Hanisch for mischief for allegedly refusing to return the Zodiac. There were absolutely no grounds for the parks warden to believe that the offence of mischief had occurred—he simply sought to regain the boat without paying Hanisch's claim—and he took advantage of the young, inexperienced RCMP officer in pressing for the arrest and charges. Consequently, both the officer who performed the arrest and the parks warden who encouraged it were found liable for false imprisonment and arrest.

Malicious Prosecution

Sometimes the criminal justice system is improperly used. When this happens, the victim may be able to sue for the tort of **malicious prosecution**. The defendant in the tort action must have initiated a criminal or quasi-criminal prosecution in which the accused was subsequently acquitted or the prosecution was abandoned. In addition, the plaintiff must establish that the prosecution was motivated by malice and that there were no reasonable grounds to proceed with the criminal action in the first place. Successful malicious prosecution actions may involve prosecutors who have chosen to ignore important evidence or complainants who have lied or manufactured evidence used to improperly support the charges.

Malicious prosecution is available where charges have been unjustifiably laid

---

21. 2004 BCCA 539 (CanLII).

A successful claim for malicious prosecution involved a patron at a restaurant who disputed his obligation to pay for liquor. He had been served the drinks but couldn't consume them before they had to be removed from the table under provincial liquor law.[22] The restaurant detained the patron. When the police arrived he was arrested, charged under the *Criminal Code* with fraudulently obtaining food, and imprisoned. There was no basis for the criminal charge as this was, at worst, a civil dispute between the parties. The restaurant owner and police were liable for false arrest, but the restaurant owner was also liable for malicious prosecution. The charge was initiated at the restaurant owner's request; since there was no basis for the charge, it was dismissed. The fact that a threat of criminal charges was used to pressure the patron to pay for the drinks was enough to constitute malice. All the elements required for malicious prosecution were thus established.

CASE SUMMARY 4.5

Suppression of Evidence Establishes Malicious Prosecution: *McNeil v. Brewers Retail Inc.*[23]; *Pate Estate v. Galway-Cavendish and Harvey (Township)*[24]

The employer, Brewers Retail Inc. (BRI), fired Douglas McNeil from his job for allegedly stealing $160 from the till. BRI handed over surveillance tapes to the police that incriminated McNeil, but suppressed parts of the tapes that would have exonerated him. Initially McNeil was convicted, but these convictions were quashed on appeal. McNeil and his wife, Terry, commenced a civil action, and a global award exceeding $2 million was granted.

The Court of Appeal upheld the trial decision, finding that all four elements of malicious prosecution were established:

1. The proceedings must have been commenced by the defendant
2. The criminal proceedings must have been terminated in favour of the plaintiff
3. There must have been an absence of reasonable and probable cause
4. There must be malice (or a primary purpose other than that of carrying the law into effect)

The assessment of damages was also upheld. The jury awarded $100 000 for general damages, $188 000 for aggravated damages, $500 000 in punitive damages, $240 000 in pecuniary damages for future loss of income, $308 000 in special damages for past loss of income and legal expenses, and McNeil's wife was awarded $50 000 in damages for loss of her spouse's companionship. The Court of Appeal found that the award of damages, while generous, was not in error.

Similarly, the suppression of exonerating evidence resulted in a sizable award of punitive damages in the *Pate* case. The trial judge determined there was ample evidence establishing that the township initiated the criminal proceedings against Pate, its building inspector and former chief building officer, without reasonable and probable grounds to believe that he had committed the thefts; it did so maliciously to avoid civil liability for the termination of his employment. Pate was dragged into the public spotlight and after a four-day trial was acquitted. Throughout the ordeal, the employer kept the exonerating evidence from the police. Ultimately, Pate was successful in establishing wrongful dismissal (damages of 16 months' pay were awarded) as well as malicious prosecution (special damages of $7500 for Pate's criminal trial defence

---

22. *Perry et al. v. Fried et al.* (1972), 32 D.L.R. (3d) 589 (N.S.S.C. Trial Div.).

23. 2008 ONCA 405 (CanLII).

24. 2013 ONCA 669 (CanLII).

costs, general and aggravated damages of $75 000, punitive damages of $450 000, prejudgment interest of $74 032, and costs, including those of the appeal, of $84 149 were also awarded).

SMALL BUSINESS PERSPECTIVE

Such awards could cripple a small business. A sophisticated client may thus wish to consult a lawyer before initiating criminal charges against an employee or other party.

Private Nuisance

The tort of **private nuisance** is committed when an individual or business uses property in such a way that it interferes with a neighbour's use or enjoyment of her property. Such interference is usually ongoing and continuous. When a commercial building, such as a mill, is built near a residential neighbourhood, and the resulting odour and noise interfere with the neighbours' enjoyment of their yards, it is appropriate for them to sue for nuisance. Such an action is possible only where the property is being used in an unusual or unreasonable way and the problem caused is a direct consequence of this unusual activity. A finding of nuisance depends on the following findings of fact: that the conduct of acts complained of substantially interfered with the use and enjoyment of property, and that the interference was unreasonable in light of all the surrounding circumstances.[25] Consequently, even homeowners whose properties have been barraged by misdirected golf balls have successfully sued the adjacent golf courses in nuisance cases.[26]

A person living in an industrial section of a city cannot complain when a factory begins operating in the neighbourhood and emits noise, smoke, and dust. Nor could the residents of a rural area complain about the normal odours associated with farming. But if the odours create a significant disturbance, far beyond what one would expect from farming operations, liability may follow. For example, in the *Pyke* case a plaintiff complained about the odours emanating from the composting phase of the defendant's mushroom farm.[27] The odours were described in graphic terms, including "nauseating and like rotten flesh," "worse than a pig farm," and "like an outhouse, ammonia, sour, putrid, rotten vegetables." The Court considered the proximity of the neighbours and the fact that the plaintiff was there first. The degree and intensity of the disturbance exceeded that of a "normal farm practice," and thus damages exceeding $260 000 were awarded.

Normally, the properties would need to be in close proximity for private nuisance to apply and for a nuisance action to be brought. However, in an Alberta case a telephone was used to harass people on the other side of the city, interfering with the enjoyment of their property. The Court found this to be a private nuisance, even though the two parties were kilometres apart.[28]

Can one sue in nuisance to control unwanted spam? One hopes that Canada's Anti-Spam Legislation (*CASL*)[29] will be effective in combating unwanted email communications. The legislation requires that the recipient consent to any type of

> **Private nuisance is when the use of property interferes with a neighbour**

> **Private nuisance at a distance**

> **CASL aims to control spam and other Internet abuses.**

---

25. *Sutherland v. Attorney General of Canada*, 1997 CanLII 2147 (BC SC), at para 21.

26. *Carley v. Willow Park Golf Course Ltd.*, 2002 ABQB 813 (CanLII); *Cattell v. Great Plains Leaseholds Ltd.*, 2008 SKCA 71 (CanLII).

27. *Pyke v. TRI GRO Enterprises Ltd.* (2001), 55 O.R. (3d) 257 (Ont. C.A.), leave to appeal to S.C.C. refused, [2001] S.C.C.A. No. 493.

28. *Motherwell v. Motherwell*, 1976 ALTASCAD 155 (CanLII).

29. Oddly, the title of the legislation is *An Act to Promote the Efficiency and Adaptability of the Canadian Economy by Regulating Certain Activities that Discourage Reliance on Electronic Means of Carrying Out Commercial Activities, and to Amend the Canadian Radio-television and Telecommunications Commission Act, the Competition Act, the Personal Information Protection and Electronic Documents Act and the Telecommunications Act* (S.C. 2010, c. 23) and although many refer to it as "CASL" or "Canada's Anti-Spam Legislation," this short title is not an official one. View the *Act* at http://laws-lois.justice.gc.ca/eng/acts/E-1.6/page-1.html.

repetitive emails, that a method be provided for the recipient to unsubscribe, and that the sender identify themselves and provide contact information. Also, the secret installation of spyware and other software that the recipient is unaware of is prohibited without consent, and to obtain such consent there must be disclosure of any possible negative effects of the installation of the program. Further, the interception, modification, or redirection of an electronic message is prohibited without consent. Significant penalties have been imposed for violation, and the *Act* also provides for private actions to be brought by victims.

For a private nuisance to be actionable, the consequences must be reasonably foreseeable to the defendant. Reasonable foreseeability will be discussed in the next chapter, but essentially it requires that an ordinary, prudent person in the same circumstances would have anticipated the risk.

Because nuisance often involves offending substances, it is one of the few common law tools that can be used to enforce environmental protection. In *St. Lawrence Cement Inc. v. Barrette*, the Supreme Court of Canada summarized the common law of nuisance thus:

- At common law, nuisance is a field of liability that focuses on the harm suffered rather than on prohibited conduct . . .
- Nuisance is defined as unreasonable interference with the use of land . . .
- Whether the interference results from intentional, negligent or non-faulty conduct is of no consequence provided that the harm can be characterized as a nuisance . . .
- The interference must be intolerable to an ordinary person . . .
- This is assessed by considering factors such as the nature, severity and duration of the interference, the character of the neighbourhood, the sensitivity of the plaintiff's use and the utility of the activity . . .
- The interference must be substantial, which means that compensation will not be awarded for trivial annoyances.[30]

Significantly, the Court held that the term *neighbour* must be construed liberally, opening the door to class action suits for private nuisance. Residents in the greater Quebec City area who endured dust, smoke, and noise pollution generated by the cement plant during the 1990s were awarded damages despite the fact that St. Lawrence Cement had met environmental standards and had spent more than $8 million to collect the dust emitted by its plant. Liability was nonetheless imposed because the interference was unreasonable because neighbours had been exposed to excessive and abnormal annoyances, contrary to article 976 of the *Civil Code of Quebec*.

CASE SUMMARY 4.6

Disruption by Construction: A Nuisance if Unreasonable: *Antrim Truck Centre Ltd. v. Ontario (Transportation)*[31]

Antrim Truck Centre Ltd. owned a truck stop complex property along Highway 17 near Antrim, Ontario, that included a restaurant and gas bar. The respondent opened a new highway in 2004, the construction of which significantly restricted access to the appellant's land. Without direct access, motorists no longer stopped at the truck stop, so the new highway effectively put Antrim Truck Centre out of business at that location. The appellant brought a claim for damages for injurious affection before the Ontario Municipal Board under the *Expropriations Act* and was awarded $58 000 for business loss and $335 000 for

---

30. *St. Lawrence Cement Inc. v. Barrette*, [2008] 3 SCR 392, 2008 SCC 64 (CanLII), at para. 77.
31. 2013 SCC 13 (CanLII).

loss in market value of the land. This decision was later set aside by the Court of Appeal on the basis that in assessing whether the use was unreasonable the board failed to consider that the interference was the product of an essential public service.

The Supreme Court, however, allowed the subsequent appeal. The main question was how to decide whether an interference with the private use and enjoyment of land is unreasonable when caused by a project that serves an important public purpose. The reasonableness of the interference must be determined by balancing the competing interests, as it is in all other cases of private nuisance. One must examine whether, in all of the circumstances, the individual claimant has shouldered a greater share of the burden of construction than it would be reasonable to expect individuals to bear without compensation. Here, the construction of the new highway inflicted significant and permanent loss to the appellant.

Nuisance consists of an interference with the claimant's occupation or enjoyment of land that is both *substantial and unreasonable*. A *substantial* interference is one that is non-trivial, amounting to more than a slight annoyance or trifling interference. This threshold screens out weak claims. Once met, the next question is whether it was also unreasonable—in all of the circumstances—to justify compensation.

When assessing unreasonableness, courts and tribunals focus on whether the interference is such that it would be unreasonable, in all of the circumstances, to require the claimant to suffer it without compensation. Generally speaking, the acts of a public authority will be of significant utility. Once a claimant passes the threshold test of showing harm that is substantial in the sense that it is non-trivial, there ought to be an inquiry into whether the interference is unreasonable. In the circumstances here, it was unreasonable to expect the appellant to endure permanent interference with the use of its land and a significant diminution of its market value in order to serve the greater public good.

SMALL BUSINESS PERSPECTIVE

Difficulties are often encountered when land is redeveloped, especially in a highly urbanized environment. Renewal requires a certain amount of give and take by all affected parties. If aggrieved parties feel particularly short-changed, litigation may be the only remaining option. Recently, class actions have become more popular so that all affected parties facing a common affliction or nuisance can band together to find a more cost-effective solution.

It should also be noted that private nuisance as discussed here is different from **public nuisance**. Only rarely is an action for public nuisance brought, and then usually by the government. A public nuisance takes place when some public property is interfered with. Protesters blocking a road or park, or a mill polluting a river, would be examples. The Supreme Court of Canada found that such a public nuisance had occurred when a forest company in British Columbia allowed a controlled burn to escape.[32] The resulting forest fire caused damage to environmentally sensitive streams, and the attorney general of that province brought an action for public nuisance against the company. The Supreme Court adopted the language of an earlier decision, stating "any activity which unreasonably interferes with the public's interest in questions of health, safety, morality, comfort or convenience" is capable of constituting a public nuisance.[33] Note that a private individual can bring an action of public nuisance only if he is able to show that the conduct harmed him particularly and more than other members of the general public.

32. *British Columbia v. Canadian Forest Products Ltd.*, 2004 SCC 38 (CanLII).

33. *Ryan v. Victoria (City)*, 1999 CanLII 706 (SCC), at para. 52

Defamation

Defamation: statements that are derogatory, false, and published

Defamation is a published false statement that is to a person's detriment. It is a primary concern for businesses involved in media communications, but all commercial enterprises face some risk over defamation, even if it is only from a carelessly worded letter of reference. For the statement to be an actionable defamation, it must be derogatory, false, and published and must refer to the plaintiff. If the false statement causes people to avoid or shun someone, it is derogatory. In the *Youssoupoff* case, Lord Justice Scrutton said that a statement was defamatory if it was "a false statement about a man to his discredit."[34] A complimentary statement about a person, even if it is false, is not defamation. Thus, if a manager were to say of an employee that she was the best worker in the plant, it would not be defamation even if false. Once the plaintiff establishes that a derogatory statement was made, he need not prove it was false. This is assumed, and it is up to the defendant to prove it true if she can. If the statement can be shown to be true, it is an absolute defence to a defamation action.[35]

Member of a defamed group may not be personally defamed

It is not possible to defame a dead person; however, it is possible to defame a corporation, which is a person in the eyes of the law, and it is possible to defame a product. (See the discussion of product defamation, trade slander, and injurious falsehood below.) For a statement to be actionable, it must be clear that it refers to the person suing. Thus, a general negative reference to a group, such as the faculty or student body of a university, will not qualify. In *Bou Malhab v. Diffusion Métromédia CMR Inc.*,[36] a group defamation action brought against a shock radio host who made negative racist comments against taxi drivers of Arab and Haitian descent was dismissed. The Court found that because the statements did not target any specific individuals, individual members could not claim their reputation had been damaged by comments aimed at large groups. A group defamed by racist comments may, however, file a complaint under human rights legislation.

Statement must be published

Further, the false statement must be published. In this sense, "to publish" means that the statement had to be communicated to a third party. Publication could have occurred in a newspaper, in the broadcast media, on the Internet,[37] or simply by word of mouth. It is sufficient publication if just one person other than the plaintiff hears or reads the defamatory statement.

Significant damages are available

In those situations where legislation does not specifically restrict damages payable, the damages for defamation can be substantial. The courts will not only compensate the victim for actual losses as well as for a damaged reputation, but will go further, awarding damages to rehabilitate the victim's reputation. For this reason, the Supreme Court of Canada upheld a decision to award a Crown prosecutor defamed by a church $1.6 million in damages—far in excess of what would be awarded for general damages in a normal tort action.[38] Justice Cory stated that, unlike non-pecuniary losses in personal injury cases, general damages in defamation are not capped.

The decision in *Bernstein v. Poon*[39] warns, however, that courts will not be sympathetic to claims characterized as being "more about ego than injury." Drs. Bernstein and Poon were physicians who each marketed weight-loss books and plans. Dr. Poon's website contained certain "preview" passages from his book,

---

34. *Youssoupoff v. Metro-Goldwyn-Mayer Pictures Ltd.*, (1934), 50 T.L.R. 581 at 584 (C.A.).

35. *Elliott v. Freisen et al.*, 1984 CanLII 1922; leave to appeal refused May 3, 1984.

36. 2011 SCC 9 (CanLII).

37. See *Buckle v. Caswell*, 2009 SKQB 363 (CanLII), where an online blog was found to be defamatory. Damages were only $50000 because the plaintiff chose to proceed by summary procedure, but costs of $5000 were also awarded. The defendant was ordered to make all reasonable efforts to remove any postings referring to the plaintiff, and injunctions were issued restraining publication of any further defamatory statements.

38. *Hill v. Church of Scientology of Toronto*, 1995 CanLII 59 (SCC).

39. 2015 ONSC 155 (CanLII).

which included criticisms of the Dr. Bernstein diet; it also posted a video of an interview conducted in Cantonese where Dr. Poon had made similar statements. Poon's criticisms were largely excused under the defence of fair comment. But malice, if shown, defeats the defence of fair comment, and malice includes "any indirect motive or ulterior purpose" that conflicts with the sense of duty being put forward in commenting on a matter of public interest. Poon demonstrated improper motive in discrediting the Bernstein Diet to promote his own clinics and, thereby, gain an economic advantage. Thus defamation was established with regard to two of the false statements made. The defamation action tied up court time and resources for almost seven years and ultimately led to a paltry $10 000 award of damages for Bernstein—and a scathing indictment from the judge.

Earlier case law suggested that a corporation's reputation deserved less protection than that of a person. However, *Jameel v. Wall Street Journal Europe SPRL*[40] confirms that all plaintiffs, be they corporations or real persons, are to be treated equally in the assessment of damages. Recognition of the potential damage to a corporation's reputation is evident in *WeGo Kayaking Ltd. v. Sewid*,[41] where a competitor posted defamatory statements about rival kayak tour operators on the Internet. The defendant created a "bad kayak companies" list and refused to take the plaintiffs' names off. The plaintiffs relied heavily on the Internet to attract customers. Evidence establishing that the defendant published the list to punish the plaintiffs for not continuing to do business with him, and evidence suggesting he also wanted to remove the competition, supported the finding of malice. The two corporate plaintiffs were thus awarded general damages totalling $250 000, together with punitive damages of $7500.

> **Damage to the good name of a corporation is also compensable**

Statements often contain **innuendo**, which is an implied or hidden meaning. A statement may appear perfectly innocent on the surface, but when combined with other information it may take on a more sinister meaning. It is no excuse to say that the person making the statement thought it was true or did not know of the special facts that created the innuendo. Such a mistake is no defence, and the offending party can be held liable for the defamatory remark.

> **Innuendo can be defamatory**
> **Mistake is no excuse**

CASE SUMMARY 4.7

CBC Painfully Discovers Innuendo Is Actionable: *Myers v. Canadian Broadcasting Corp.*;[42] *Leenen v. Canadian Broadcasting Corp.*[43]

In an episode of *The Fifth Estate*, the CBC interviewed Dr. Myers on his views about a certain heart medication; Myers had conducted a study on behalf of the pharmaceutical company, Bayer, concerning the drug. The broadcast clips from the interview distorted Myers's statements and conveyed the impression that Myers promoted the interests of pharmaceutical companies over the interests of patients. The innuendo suggested that Myers was dishonest, recommending medication he knew to be harmful.

The CBC tried to establish the defences of fair comment and qualified privilege (see the "Defences" section below), without success. The Court determined that the distortion of Myers's words invited viewers to make false inferences. The defence of qualified privilege failed because the CBC did not have a duty to communicate the information. The defence of fair comment failed because the trial judge found malice based on the

---

40. [2006] UKHL 44; this decision can be viewed at www.bailii.org/uk/cases/UKHL/2006/44.html.

41. 2007 BCSC 49 (CanLII)

42. 2001 CanLII 4874 (ON CA), leave to appeal to S.C.C. dismissed February 7, 2002, (S.C.C. File No. 28775).

43. 2001 CanLII 4997 (ON CA), leave to appeal to S.C.C. dismissed February 7, 2002, (S.C.C. File No. 28774).

CBC's decision not to include reference to other doctors who concurred with Myers. General damages of $200000 plus aggravated damages of $150000 were awarded.

Even greater damages ($950000) were awarded against the CBC in the *Leenen* case. Again through innuendo, the CBC called into question the plaintiff doctor's honesty, integrity, and credibility as a research scientist. Malice defeated the defences of qualified privilege and fair comment because the Court found that the CBC had invented or misstated the facts.

DISCUSSION QUESTION

Professionals guard their reputations carefully, so before one expresses comments critical of their competence, performance, or integrity, should legal advice be sought?

Libel and Slander

Slander is spoken; libel is written

Defamation can be either **slander**, which is spoken defamation, or **libel**, which is usually written defamation. The significance of finding a defamatory remark to be libelous rather than slanderous is that libel is easier to prove because there is no requirement to show that special damages have been sustained. Libel is seen to be more deliberate, more premeditated, and also more permanent than slander, thus causing more harm. However, modern means of mass communication give slander a potentially huge audience, so the rationale for distinguishing between libel and slander is breaking down. In fact, this distinction has been eliminated altogether in some provinces, while in others legislation has simply declared that all broadcast defamation will constitute libel whether spoken or written.[44]

Apology reduces damages

While defamation is primarily governed by common law, most provinces have passed statutes modifying those common law provisions in light of the needs of a modern society. Should defamation by the media occur, for example, legislation may reduce the damages plaintiffs can claim where material was published in good faith. If the publisher shows that the damage was done by mistake or misapprehension of the facts, and a full apology or retraction has been made, damages may be restricted to special damages (the actual losses and expenses incurred).[45] Refer to the MyBusLawLab for provincial variations.

These statutes will need even more modification to take into account the new problems associated with defamation on the Internet. It is often difficult to trace the original source of defamation in an Internet message because it can be so easily copied and transferred by intermediate parties. Nevertheless, the injury caused by such transmission of defamatory information can be extensive. Another problem is that in a traditional communication environment there is usually a broadcaster or publisher that can be held responsible for the damaging words, but in online communication there is often no intermediary who checks and authorizes material, nor is there any clear way of determining just how far a message has been spread or even who wrote it in the first place.

CASE SUMMARY 4.8

Is Posting a Link Publication? *Crookes v. Newton*[46]

To prove the publication element of defamation, a plaintiff must establish that the defendant had, by any act, conveyed defamatory meaning to a single third party who has received it. Wayne Crookes brought a number of lawsuits against those responsible for

---

44. See *Libel and Slander Act*, R.S.O. 1990, c. L-12, s. 1(1) and s. 2.

45. See, for example, Alberta's *Defamation Act*, R.S.A. 2000, c. D-7, s. 16, or New Brunswick's *Defamation Act*, S.N.B. c. D-5, s. 17.

46. *Crookes v. Newton*, 2011 SCC 47 (CanLII).

an allegedly defamatory "smear campaign."[47] A website owned by Newton contained commentary on numerous issues, including free speech. One of the posted articles, "Free Speech in Canada," contained hyperlinks to other websites, which in turn contained information about Crookes. The critical issue in the appeal was whether one has published any defamatory material present on a linked site by posting a hyperlink to it.

The Supreme Court of Canada ruled that posting a hyperlink does not in itself constitute publication of any material found therein. The Court likened hyperlinks to footnotes, since they communicate that information can be found elsewhere but do not by themselves communicate their content. On the other hand, where someone presents content from the hyperlinked material in a manner that repeats the defamatory content, such party can be considered a publisher and is at risk of being sued for defamation.

Applying the traditional publication rule (that it is irrelevant to consider the form the defendant's act takes and the manner in which it assists in causing the defamatory content to reach the third party) to hyperlinks would have the effect of creating a presumption of liability for all hyperlinkers. Justice Abella considered this negative impact:

> The Internet cannot, in short, provide access to information without hyperlinks. Limiting their usefulness by subjecting them to the traditional publication rule would have the effect of seriously restricting the flow of information and, as a result, freedom of expression. The potential "chill" in how the Internet functions could be devastating, since primary article authors would unlikely want to risk liability for linking to another article over whose changeable content they have no control. Given the core significance of the role of hyperlinking to the Internet, we risk impairing its whole functioning.[48]

Accordingly, the Court ruled that nothing on Newton's webpage itself was defamatory, and since the mere inclusion of hyperlinks did not constitute publication of their content, Crookes's action against Newton was dismissed.

DISCUSSION QUESTIONS

In light of the foregoing decision, when might an author be held liable for defamatory content found on a third party's website? If one posts material on the Internet that includes links to other sites, should one avoid making any associated commentary?

Legislation has clarified that any broadcast defamation, even if spoken, constitutes libel and special rules apply to broadcast defamation. Thus, in the *Bahlieda* case,[49] the Ontario Court of Appeal held where postings on the Internet qualified as broadcasts, the legislation required notice. Those notice requirements had not been complied with. One might well ask, is Internet broadcasting more like radio or television broadcasting or just a personal message? Does it make a difference whether a blog, website, or simply an email is involved? Note that in the *Crookes* case the courts, including the Supreme Court of Canada, consistently referred to the defamation contained on the linked website as libel, but this was clearly written information that was visually communicated.

When determining damages, the size of the audience has been regarded as relevant, as in *Ross v. Holley*.[50] Holley emailed statements about an archeologist, accusing her of grave robbing. Ross was awarded general ($75 000) and aggravated damages ($50 000) because Holley urged recipients to republish the accusations. Similarly, in *Barrick Gold Corp. v. Lopehandia*,[51] the defendant made hundreds of

Defamation on the Internet— libel if broadcast

Size of audience impacts the injury suffered and the damage award

47. See also *Crookes v. Wikimedia Foundation Inc.*, 2008 BCSC 1424 (CanLII); aff'd 2009 BCCA 392 (CanLII). See footnote 48.
48. *Supra* note 46, at para. 36.
49. *Bahlieda v. Santa*, 2003 CanLII 2883 (ON CA).
50. (2004), 28 C.C.L.T. (3d) 83 (Ont. S.C.J.).
51. 2004 CanLII 12938 (ON CA).

Internet postings accusing Barrick of fraud, tax evasion, money laundering, and genocide. On appeal, Barrick was awarded $75000 in general damages, $50000 in punitive damages, and a permanent injunction. The Court considered the Internet's unique ability to cause instantaneous and irreparable harm. On the other hand, the BC Court of Appeal awarded only $3000 when the plaintiff was rudely attacked and called an "idiot" in an email distributed to the local community in a dispute with respect to the development of a sports facility.[52] A cautious user of the Internet will take all of these risks into consideration and not only avoid making disparaging remarks, but also limit all communications to only those who need to know.

Another problem relates to whom an injured party can sue. If the author is known and lives in the same jurisdiction there is little difficulty, but where the author is unknown, uses a false name, or resides in another jurisdiction with different rules, where does one sue? If one doesn't have access to the author, can one sue the service provider (ISP) or website operator for defamation? What happens where an offensive email is intercepted and sent to others? It is now clear that an ISP or website host can be forced to disclose the sources of such material,[53] but even that may not be helpful where they are in a different jurisdiction or without resources. It is likely that these intermediaries will be liable for the defamation only if they encouraged the offending behaviour or if they knew or ought to have known of it and failed to remove it after notification.[54]

ISP can be forced to disclose source

ISP will be liable only where it fails to remove defamatory material after notification

---

CASE SUMMARY 4.9

When Will a Court Hear a Case Involving Defamation on the Internet? *Black v. Bredden*[55]

Conrad Black controlled a huge media empire through Hollinger International Inc., but he lost that control when he was convicted of fraud in the United States and spent significant time in jail. After Black was ousted as chief executive officer, the directors and officers of Hollinger International reported in press releases and published on the Hollinger website that Black was involved in wrongdoing against the company amounting to fraud. The report includes the statement "[t]he Special Committee knows of few parallels to [Black's] brand of self-righteous, and aggressive looting of Hollinger to the exclusion of all other concerns or interests"; that "Black as both CEO and controlling shareholder . . . created an entity in which ethical corruption was a defining characteristic of the leadership team"; that "the evidence . . . establishes an overwhelming record of abuse, overreaching and violations of fiduciary duties by Black"; and that he made it his business to "line [his] pockets at the expense of Hollinger almost every day, in almost every way." Black filed this action in Ontario, alleging libel by those officers of Hollinger International.

An issue was raised questioning whether the Ontario Court had jurisdiction to hear the action. The statements were made in the United States, as was the press release on the Hollinger website. But the Ontario Court noted that Black resided in Ontario and that the alleged injury took place there. Further, the press releases and reports were downloaded and read in Ontario, they were reprinted in several Ontario papers, and the intent of the press release was that they would be republished in Canada. These factors created a connection between Black's claims and Ontario.

---

52. *Best v. Weatherall*, 2010 BCCA 202 (CanLII).

53. *Mosher v. Coast Publishing Ltd.*, 2010 NSSC 153 (CanLII); and *York University v. Bell Canada Enterprises*, 2009 CanLII 46447 (ON SC).

54. See *Society of Composers, Authors and Music Publishers of Canada v. Canadian Association of Internet Providers*, 2004 SCC 45 (CanLII). In this case the Supreme Court treated the ISP like a postal or delivery service and they were found not to be liable for the material delivered. Note that in the US case of *Louis Vuitton Malletier, S.A. v. Akanoc Solutions, Inc. et al.* (C 07-03952 JW [N.D. Cal., August 28, 2009]), the ISP was held liable of contributing to trademark and copyright infringement where they ignored repeated notices of the infringement. This may well indicate what will happen in a similar case in Canada.

55. *Black v. Breeden*, Ont. C.A., 2010 ONCA 547 (CanLII); appeal to S.C.C. dismissed, 2012 SCC 19 (CanLII).

> The Supreme Court of Canada found that there was a real and substantial connection with Ontario, giving the Ontario Court jurisdiction to hear the libel action. The tort of defamation had been committed in that province. Defamation occurs where publication takes place, and the offending statements were read, downloaded, and republished by three different newspapers in that province. A trial in Ontario could thus proceed.
>
> Arguably, Black gained an advantage by having the matter tried in Ontario. Canadian defamation law is much more favourable to his position, and a Canadian jury may have been more sympathetic to his position since this is where his reputation was primarily injured.

DEFENCES

Once it has been established that a defamatory statement has been made, several defences are available to the defendant. **Truth**, also called the defence of **justification**, is an absolute defence. But even when a statement is technically true, it can still be derogatory if it contains an innuendo or is capable of being interpreted as referring to another person about whom the statement is false. Note also that substantial truth is sufficient. If the defendant claimed that the plaintiff had stolen $300 000 when in fact he had stolen only $250 000, justification would still be an effective defence.

Truth is an absolute defence

The second defence is called **absolute privilege**. Anything discussed as part of parliamentary debate on the floor of the legislature, in Parliament, or in government committees, and statements made or documents used as part of a court procedure cannot give rise to a defamation action, no matter how malicious, scandalous, or derogatory they are.

Absolute privilege

The rationale for this defence is that there are certain forums where, for the good of society, people should be able to exercise freedom of expression without fear of being sued. For example, even statements made to an investigator in the context of a *Human Rights Act* investigation are privileged.[56] Absolute privilege has also been extended to documents used in the process of a complaint before the College of Physicians and Surgeons of British Columbia.[57]

The most significant defence for businesspeople is called **qualified privilege**. When a statement is made pursuant to a duty or special interest, there is no action for defamation so long as the statement was made honestly and without malice and was circulated only to those having a right to know. A manager reporting to a superior about the performance of a worker, or members of a professional organization describing the performance of an officer of that organization to other members, would be instances protected by qualified privilege. When a manager sends a defamatory email specifically to someone with a shared interest in the matter, such as his superior or the particular group of employees he supervises, that may be protected by qualified privilege, but that privilege would be lost if the defamatory message were sent to a website available to everyone. Since anyone could access the website, the publication would be too broad and privilege could no longer be claimed. Thus, in *Egerton v. Finucan*, a community college professor's claim for wrongful dismissal was complicated by the fact that his supervisor sent a highly critical performance evaluation to all the professors in the institution via email. The Court found that the plaintiff had grounds for a defamation suit against his superior.[58] Note that when reporting on matters of public interest newspapers and other media often claim this defence, but it is normally denied them on the grounds that although they claim

Qualified privilege requires duty

---

[56] *Ayangma v. NAV Canada*, 2001 PESCAD 1 (CanLII), leave to appeal to S.C.C. refused, [2001] S.C.C.A. No. 76.

[57] *Schut v. Magee*, 2003 BCCA 417 (CanLII).

[58] [1995] O.J. No. 1653 (Gen. Div.).

Fair comment

that they have a duty to report and that the public has a right to know, there is no legal duty on them to report matters to the public and so no qualified privilege.

A further defence available in the field of defamation is the defence of **fair comment**. When people put their work before the public, as with movies, plays, artwork, books, and the like, they invite public criticism and run the risk that the opinions expressed may not be complimentary. Even when these opinions amount to a vicious attack and may be unreasonable, artists cannot sue for defamation. The defence raised here is fair comment. Public figures are also open to such criticism. To successfully use this defence, the critic or editorial writer must be able to show that what was said was a matter of opinion, drawn from true facts that were before the public, and was not motivated by malice or some ulterior motive. A food critic expressing a negative opinion of a restaurant[59] and a theatre critic attacking a play or movie are examples of fair comment. The same defence should apply where a play, photograph, or musical performance is put on the Internet and made available to a wide audience.

CASE SUMMARY 4.10

Supreme Court of Canada Recognizes New Defence: *Grant v. Torstar Corp.;*[60] *Cusson v. Quan*[61]

Public interest responsible journalism defence

In a pair of decisions issued consecutively, the Supreme Court recognized a new defence that the media can raise. The **public interest responsible journalism defence** operates to protect the media from liability so long as it acts responsibly in communicating on matters of public interest. In the *Grant* case, Grant and his company sued the *Toronto Star* for defamation over an article concerning a proposed private golf course development. The story relayed views critical of the development. Local residents were suspicious that Grant had exercised political influence in securing government approval for the new golf course. The reporter attempted to verify the allegations in the article, but Grant refused comment. In the *Cusson* case, Cusson, an Ontario Provincial Police constable, voluntarily went to New York City following the September 11 attack on the World Trade Center to assist with rescue operations. Initially, he was portrayed in the media as a hero, but a newspaper later published three negative articles about him. At issue in both cases was whether the media could raise a defence previously unknown in Canada.

The Supreme Court agreed that in light of freedom of expression, the defence of public interest responsible journalism ought to be available. The Court adopted the rationale of the House of Lords in *Reynolds v. Times Newspapers Ltd.*,[62] which identified 10 factors that courts might consider in applying the public interest responsible journalism defence:

1. The seriousness of the allegation. The more serious the charge, the more the public is misinformed and the individual harmed if the allegation is not true.

2. The nature of the information and the extent to which the subject matter is a matter of public concern.

3. The source of the information. Some informants have no direct knowledge of the events; some have their own axes to grind or are being paid for their stories.

4. The steps taken to verify the information.

5. The status of the information. The allegation may have already been the subject of an investigation that commands respect.

---

59. Fair comment was successfully raised in *Sara's Pyrohy Hut v. Brooker,* 1993 ABCA 95 (CanLII).
60. 2009 SCC 61 (CanLII).
61. 2009 SCC 62 (CanLII).
62. [1999] 4 All ER 609, [2001] 2 AC 127 (H.L.); see www.bailii.org/uk/cases/UKHL/1999/45.html.

6. The urgency of the matter. News is often a perishable commodity.

7. Whether comment was sought from the plaintiff. She may have information others do not possess or have not disclosed. An approach to the plaintiff will not always be necessary.

8. Whether the article contained the gist of the plaintiff's side of the story.

9. The tone of the article. A newspaper can raise queries or call for an investigation. It need not adopt allegations as statements of fact.

10. The circumstances of the publication, including the timing.

This list is not exhaustive, and the weight to be given to these and any other relevant factors will vary from case to case. But in the *Grant* and *Cusson* cases, the Supreme Court determined that new trials were warranted where the defendants could raise the defence that they had communicated the respective stories responsibly.

DISCUSSION QUESTION

These cases establish that the traditional media may avoid liability if they act responsibly when reporting on matters of public interest. Should non-traditional journalists, such as bloggers and others posting to websites, also be able to seek the benefit of this defence?

Product Defamation (Injurious Falsehood)

Is the goodwill associated with a product entitled to protection, much like the good reputation of a person or corporation? The tort of **injurious falsehood** addresses attacks on the reputation of another's product or business. When a person spreads a false rumour that the wine manufactured by a competitor is adulterated with some other substance, or that a rival's business is about to become bankrupt, he has committed an injurious falsehood. Although this tort is often called **trade slander** or **product defamation**, it must be distinguished from the tort of defamation that involves injury to the personal reputation of the injured party. Injurious falsehood deals with the reputation and value of a person's property; it addresses attacks on the quality of the product or upon the title held by another. When a person falsely claims that the seller does not own what she is selling or that the product is in violation of patent or copyright, he has uttered an actionable injurious falsehood.

Injurious falsehood is actionable

CASE SUMMARY 4.11

Unfounded Accusations Can Be Costly: *Procor Ltd. v. U.S.W.A.*[63]

Procor Ltd., a manufacturer that exports much of its product to the United States, was involved in a serious and difficult labour dispute with its employees. In the air of hostility created by the labour dispute, members of the union accused the company of customs fraud, saying that it was exporting Japanese products into the United States (marked as products made in Canada) without disclosing the fact. This caused an intensive and disruptive investigation into the operations of the company, even stopping production for a time. In addition, there was considerable negative publicity.

The investigation exonerated the company, showing the union members to be wrong and the accusations to be unfounded. Procor Ltd. then sued the union and the members who had made the accusations for injurious falsehood. These defendants knew or should have known that the statements they made to customs agents, which instigated the investigation, were false.

[63.] 1990 CanLII 6637 (ON SC).

In addition to the presence of a false statement made to a party causing damage, it is also necessary to establish malice to succeed in an injurious falsehood action. "Malice" is usually described as a dishonest or improper motive. While the judge did not find that they lied outright, he did find that the union officials were "willfully blind to the truth" when they made these false statements to the customs officials. That was enough to establish malice. In addition, their motive was not to act as good citizens but to further their labour dispute and vent their frustrations and hostility toward the company. This was an improper purpose, supporting the finding of malice. The judge also found that the defendants had participated in a conspiracy to accomplish these goals and were, as a result, liable to pay $100 000 general damages and a further $100 000 punitive damages. In a society like ours, we have to be careful about what we say about others. This case is an example of the difficulties that a few misguided words can cause.

DISCUSSION QUESTION

Especially during a heated labour dispute, things may be said that may be regretted. What would a sophisticated businessperson do to avoid having words come back to bite her later?

Successfully Establishing a Tort Claim

When a plaintiff commences a tort action, he bears the burden of establishing each of the required elements or *ingredients* of that tort. Failure to prove an ingredient should result in the action being dismissed. See Table 4.1 for a simplified list of ingredients for the torts examined thus far.

Table 4.1 Simplified Ingredients for Torts

Assault	1. Deliberate threat creating fear of imminent harm 2. No consent
Battery	1. Deliberate physical interference (contact. with one's body 2. No consent
Trespass to Land	1. Deliberate interference with property 2. No consent/permission/lawful right to be there
Trespass to Chattels	1. Deliberate interference with goods of another 2. No consent
Conversion	1. Deliberate appropriation of the goods of another 2. The act is committed in such a way that a forced sale is justified
Detinue	1. Deliberate possession (detaining) of another's goods 2. Wrongful refusal to return the goods to the owner
False Imprisonment	1. Deliberate restraint 2. Lack of lawful authority
Malicious Prosecution	1. Initiation of prosecution on criminal or quasi-criminal charges 2. Subsequent acquittal of the plaintiff 3. Prosecution was motivated by malice
Private Nuisance	1. Unusual use of property 2. Interference caused to neighbour's enjoyment/use of property 3. Foreseeable consequences
Defamation	1. False statements made 2. Derogatory to the plaintiff's reputation 3. Publication or communication to a third party
Injurious Falsehood (trade defamation)	1. Publication of false statements 2. Derogatory to the reputation of the product or business of another 3. Statements were made with malice, without just cause or excuse

OTHER TORTS IMPACTING BUSINESS

LO **9**

Intentional torts are more common in some businesses

People involved in business activities can find themselves faced with tortious liability for their conduct or the conduct of their employees and agents. Businesses that deal directly with the public, such as restaurants, hotels, and retailers, may find their employees becoming involved in conflicts with customers in the course of their work. Vicarious liability for assault and battery, negligence, trespass, and even false imprisonment may follow. When business premises are visited by customers or the public, there can be actions for negligence based on occupiers' liability.

Negligence will be the primary focus of the following chapter. Those providing consulting services to businesses and individuals, such as bankers, accountants, auditors, lawyers, financial advisers, engineers, and architects, are increasingly vulnerable to damage actions for both tort and breach of contract.

Unfair competition may result in tortious behaviour

In addition to the torts already discussed in this chapter, there are other unique torts that can be important to businesses: inducing breach of contract, interference with economic relations, intimidation, deceit, conspiracy, passing-off, breach of confidence, and invasion of privacy. Most of these are associated with unfair or overly aggressive competition.

CASE SUMMARY 4.12

Cold and Calculated: *Polar Ice Express Inc. v. Arctic Glacier Inc.*[64]

The trial judge found that the defendant, Arctic Glacier, used threats and bribery to get customers to stop doing business with the plaintiff, Polar Ice. In so doing, it committed the torts of inducing breach of contract and unlawful interference with economic relations.

Arctic Glacier had a virtual monopoly over ice sales in Alberta to grocery stores, liquor stores, service stations, small confectionary stores, and concrete supply companies. Polar Ice, a fledgling company, adduced evidence revealing that Arctic Glacier made offers to match or undercut Polar Ice's price, but only to the liquor outlets and Sobeys stores that Polar Ice supplied. In addition to being actionable torts, these direct and deliberate attempts to induce those targeted businesses to breach their contracts with Polar Ice breached the *Competition Act*. Damages for inducing breach of contract were thus awarded.

Arctic Glacier also threatened to refuse further delivery of ice to Inland Cement at a critical time unless Inland Cement stopped buying ice from Polar Ice. A bribe was also offered to Inland Cement's employee to secure an exclusive contract. To establish the tort of interference with economic relations, the plaintiff had to prove that (1) the defendant had an intention to injure, (2) the means employed by the defendant to accomplish this were unlawful, and (3) the plaintiff suffered economic loss or a related injury as a result. All three requirements were met, and damages of $50 000 were awarded.

The Court of Appeal upheld the decision and found that an award of solicitor and client costs to the plaintiff was justified. The defendant's employee had lied under oath, which impeded earlier settlement of the action and necessitated a longer trial.

SMALL BUSINESS PERSPECTIVE

Competition is encouraged in Canada, but within ethical guidelines. Businesses need to teach their employees that certain lines are not to be crossed to "make a deal."

---

64. 2007 ABQB 717 (CanLII), aff'd 2009 ABCA 20 (CanLII).

Inducing Breach of Contract

There are several ways that one can interfere with the operation of another's business. **Inducing breach of contract** usually involves an employer persuading an employee of another business to leave that employment and work for him. This practice is more common when that employee has special knowledge about trade secrets or customer lists, or has a special relationship with customers that enables her to bring them to the new job. If the employee is contractually committed to stay in that position of employment for a period of time or to not disclose secret information, she will breach that contractual obligation if she submits to the enticement to make the move and make the disclosure. A party that persuades someone else's employee to commit such a breach, usually with financial incentives, violates a duty not to intervene in that relationship. As a result, that party may face the tort action of inducing breach of contract.

For the victim to sue for inducing breach of contract, he must be able to establish that there was a contract that was breached and that the person being sued knew about the contract and intentionally induced the breach. The victim likely has the right to sue the employee for breach, but it is often preferable to sue the other employer because it tends to have "deeper pockets" (the funds to make the action worthwhile), and legal action may deter the defendant from luring other employees away and causing the plaintiff such losses again.

Inducing breach of contract can also be committed when one business induces severance of contractual relations with someone else, as when a supplier is persuaded to abandon one customer in favour of another, or a customer is persuaded to breach its contract with a competing supplier. Another interesting application of this tort is to sue a director of a corporation for inducing the corporation to breach a contract it had with the plaintiff. See Case 3 (*369413 Alberta Ltd. v. Pocklington Holdings Inc.*) at the end of this chapter.

CASE SUMMARY 4.13

The Consequences of Inducing Breach: *Ahmad v. Ontario Hydro*[65]

Dr. Ahmad was an engineer working for Atomic Energy Canada Limited (AECL) as head of the advanced engineering branch. He was working on a project to get the nuclear reactors to work at a higher efficiency, which was of great interest to Ontario Hydro, AECL's primary customer. Each percentage rise in efficiency would reap a reward of $20 million in income. Ahmad was working on a process that would lead to such results, but stated in his report that further study was required. Ontario Hydro needed a more positive report to take before the controlling board, so it persuaded Ahmad's employer to transfer him and put someone more "supportive" in charge. Ontario Hydro threatened to withdraw from future joint research projects unless Ahmad was reassigned.

AECL complied, assigning Ahmad to a project where he was no longer in contact with Ontario Hydro. The result was that he could no longer work in his area of expertise and went from managing 24 employees to being in a one-person office with nothing to do. Ontario Hydro produced a press release stating that Ahmad was reassigned because of research delays and inadequate research, accusations that were repeated in the *Globe and Mail*. Ahmad sued Ontario Hydro, and when AECL failed to supply documents he needed for his action, he added them to the action. As a result he was terminated. In this action Ahmad sought remedies against Ontario Hydro for defamation and inducing breach of contract.

---

65. 1997 CanLII 899 (ON CA).

This is a classic example of one company putting extensive pressure on another to breach its employment relationship with a long-term employee. The Court awarded damages of $488 525 for inducing breach of contract and another $40 000 for defamation against Ontario Hydro. The Court further awarded the plaintiff his solicitor and client costs. It found that there had been a valid contract between AECL and Ahmad, which Ontario Hydro was aware of, and that Ontario Hydro had intentionally and wrongfully induced AECL to breach that contract, causing substantial damage to Ahmad. In a separate action, Ahmad was awarded $102 000 against AECL for wrongful dismissal.

SMALL BUSINESS PERSPECTIVE

Unethical practices, such as pressuring a party to breach its contractual obligations, cannot be justified on the basis that one was merely removing an obstacle to profits. Before taking steps to optimize profits, a wise manager will ask whether the courts would find that the end justifies the means.

When one business intentionally interferes with the operation of a competitor, problems can develop. When this is done through ordinary competition there is no complaint, but sometimes that competition becomes unfair. Examples of improper interference in business and unfair competition include one business seeking confidential information from the employees of another, intimidation to discourage someone from opening a business in an area, or one business positioning its employees near the door of its competitor to redirect customers to the first. Most of these kinds of problems are dealt with by the federal *Competition Act*.[66]

Unlawful Interference with Economic Relations

Unlawful interference with economic relations is actionable whether or not a breach of contract has taken place, but there must be some other unlawful conduct associated with the complaint, such as bribery or defamation. That unlawful conduct must have been intended to cause harm and, in fact, harm must have resulted (as in the *Polar Ice* case discussed above). In the *Sagaz* case,[67] a company had supplied seat covers to a retailer for over 30 years when that business arrangement was abruptly terminated. A competitor bribed a key employee of the retailer with a 2 percent kickback for every seat cover the competitor supplied. The key employee accepted the bribe and arranged for the change in suppliers. The bribe was sufficient illegal activity to support the claim of illegal interference with the supplier's economic relations.

The Supreme Court has now clarified what must be proven to establish what it called the "unlawful means" tort, emphasizing that it extends civil liability without creating new actionable wrongs.

Unlawful interference with economic relations

CASE SUMMARY 4.14

Supreme Court clarifies the "Unlawful Means" Tort: *A.I. Enterprises Ltd. v. Bram Enterprises Ltd.*[68]

Several family members, through their companies, owned an apartment building and the majority wanted to sell it. One brother did not, and he took action to thwart the sale, turning interested buyers away. Ultimately, the building was sold to the dissenting

2014 CASE SCC

---

66. R.S.C. 1985, c. C-34.
67. *671122 Ontario Ltd. v. Sagaz Industries Canada Inc.*, 2001 SCC 59 (CanLII).
68. 2014 SCC 12 (CanLII).

brother's company, but at a significantly lower price than what had been offered by outside parties. The majority sued to recover this loss, and a key issue was whether the dissenting family member and his company were liable for the tort of unlawful interference with economic relations. The Supreme Court took this opportunity to clarify and narrow the scope of the "unlawful means" tort.

Justice Cromwell clarified that it is an intentional tort that allows a plaintiff to sue a defendant for economic loss resulting from the defendant's unlawful act against a third party. It creates a type of "parasitic" liability in a three-party situation, because liability to the plaintiff is based on (or parasitic upon) the defendant's unlawful act against the third party. And for conduct to constitute the required "unlawful means," the conduct must give rise to a civil cause of action by the third party (or would do so if the third party had suffered loss as a result of that conduct). Essentially, the unlawful means tort extends an existing right to sue from the immediate victim of the unlawful act to another party whom the defendant intended to target with the unlawful conduct.

The gist of the tort is the defendant's targeting of the plaintiff by committing unlawful acts against a third party.

In this case, however, the dissenting brother and his company did not commit a tort by obstructing the sale, thus the unlawful means tort was not applicable. But the dissenting brother and his company did not escape liability. The trial judge imposed liability based on finding that the brother breached his fiduciary obligations as a director of the family companies that initially owned the subject building. Since that brother was the sole director and shareholder of the defendant company, it too was liable because it had knowingly assisted in the breach of fiduciary duty and had knowingly received the proceeds of the breach.

SMALL BUSINESS PERSPECTIVE

The basic ingredients of the unlawful means tort are unlawful conduct that is deliberately done with intent to harm the plaintiff's business and resulting in harm. The underlying rationale is to "stretch liability," extending an existing right to sue from the immediate victim of the unlawful act to another party whom the defendant intended to target with the unlawful conduct. Accordingly, it extends civil liability without creating new actionable wrongs, yet it enables the targeted victim to secure a remedy.

Intimidation

Intimidation

Just the threat of violence or some other illegal activity, such as an illegal strike, can constitute the tort of **intimidation** if it forces a party to do something that harms it. For example, a trade union threatening an illegal strike if a particular employee was not terminated amounted to the tort of intimidation and was actionable in England.[69] Of course, if a union was in a legal strike position, the threat of such a strike would not amount to intimidation since the necessary element of a threat to do an illegal act would be missing. Intimidation is often associated with the tort of unlawful interference with economic relations. Note that a related tort of **intentional infliction of mental suffering** (or nervous shock) will often also be alleged where such threats and harassing behaviour is involved. Examples include harassing behaviour associated with wrongful dismissal, such as harassing an ill employee for justified absences after he has already been given notice of termination.[70] Another example involves the improper activities of a collection agency, including harassment and the threat of physical violence, to encourage repayment of a loan.[71]

Intentional infliction of mental suffering

---

69. *Rookes v. Barnard*, [1964] 1 All E.R. 367 (H.L.).

70. *Prinzo v. Baycrest Centre for Geriatric Care*, 2002 CanLII 45005 (ON CA).

71. *Tran v. Financial Debt Recovery Ltd.*, 2000 CanLII 22621 (ON SC).

Deceit (Fraudulent Misrepresentation)

The tort of **deceit** involves the fraudulent and intentional misleading of another person causing damage. This is where one person lies to another, causing loss. Deceit is an intentional tort and one of the few situations where the court will entertain an application for punitive damages. The case of *Derry v. Peek*[72] established that deceit did not require actual knowledge that what was stated was incorrect. It was enough that the person making the statement did not believe it to be true. This is a common wrong committed in business[73] and will be dealt with in Chapter 8 under the "Fraudulent Misrepresentation" section.

Conspiracy

A **conspiracy to injure** takes place where two or more persons act together using unlawful means to injure the business interests of another. For example, in the *Sagaz* case mentioned above, where the key employee was given kickbacks to change to a new supplier of seat covers, the actions of that employee and the supplier together also constituted a conspiracy. Similarly, when union officials made false statements to customs officials to spite the employer in the *Procor* case (see Case Summary 4.11), a conspiracy was found. When a group of employees work together to get another employee fired, a conspiracy is involved. In *Meehan v. Tremblett*,[74] the plaintiff worked as a corrections officer. His immediate supervisor and the superintendent got together and created a false performance evaluation report that led to the plaintiff's forced resignation. This conspiracy to injure involved the wrongful act of creating false and misleading documents and was thus an actionable tort. Not only were the parties to it liable, but due to vicarious liability the New Brunswick government (as employer) was held liable as well.

Conspiracy involves concerted actions aimed at injuring another

An interesting case where an insurer alleged conspiracy to injure is *Insurance Corp. of British Columbia v. Husseinian*.[75] The plaintiff (ICBC) alleged that the defendants staged motor vehicle accidents to obtain insurance monies for personal injuries and property damage. Most of the motor vehicle accidents involved a stolen car either rear-ending another vehicle or hitting a parked car. The driver of the stolen vehicle would flee the scene of the accident on foot without ever being caught. The insurer established that the defendants either knew each other or shared acquaintances. The Court concluded there was conspiracy to injure. Further, this extensive scheme to defraud an insurer of significant monies was the type of reprehensible conduct that warranted an award of punitive damages.

For there to be a conspiracy, however, there must be an agreement to act in concert (either lawfully or unlawfully) with the purpose of harming the plaintiff. In *Bernstein v. Stoycheva-Todorova*,[76] the Todorovas alleged that the Bernstein defendants conspired to eliminate the Todorovas' clinic as competitors in the weight-loss industry. Failure to establish that Dr. Bernstein acted in combination with others caused the conspiracy claim to be dismissed.

Passing-Off

A **passing-off** action is appropriate when a business or product is presented to the public in such a way as to lead the public to believe that the product is being provided by another business. When imitation Rolex watches are sold as the real thing, or when a restaurant adopts the golden arches logo leading the public to

Passing-off is actionable

---

72. (1889), 14 App. Cas. 337 at 374 (H.L.); see www.bailii.org/uk/cases/UKHL/1889/1.html.

73. See *Usenik v. Sidorowicz*, 2008 CanLII 11373 (ON SC), where the plaintiffs purchased a home from the defendants after being assured there were no problems with moisture and flooding. These statements were untrue. The defendants were ordered to redress the water damages suffered.

74. 1996 CanLII 4811 (NB CA).

75. 2010 BCSC 217 (CanLII).

76. 2007 BCSC 14 (CanLII).

believe it is part of the McDonald's chain when it is not, the tort of passing-off has been committed. The court can award damages in these circumstances, but an injunction or an order that the offending product be delivered to the plaintiff for destruction may be a more appropriate remedy. This will be discussed in more detail in Chapter 13 under the heading "Trademarks."

CASE SUMMARY 4.15

Prank Backfires: *Inform Cycle Ltd. v. Draper*[77]

Inform Cycle operated a high-end bicycle business and created its website using the domain name InformCycle.ca. The defendant, Draper, a former employee, may have thought that redirecting customers of his former employer to a gay porn website was amusing—but the plaintiff was not amused. Draper accomplished this by purchasing the domain name InformCycle.com and registering it in the name of his new employer, Rebound Cycle. Customers looking for Inform Cycle's website who mistakenly clicked on the .com site instead of the .ca site were initially redirected to Rebound's website, where Rebound displayed its goods and services. But after several weeks, Draper changed the forwarding from the Rebound website to a gay pornographic website and then went on vacation. When customers of Inform Cycle brought the matter to Inform Cycle's attention, it discovered that the .com site was registered in Rebound's name and demanded corrective action. Rebound contacted Draper in Costa Rica, and he cited an outstanding debt owed to him by Inform Cycle as an excuse for his actions.

In addition to finding defamation, the Court determined that the tort of passing-off had been established. For several weeks, anyone who typed in "InformCycle.com " would have been redirected to Rebound Cycle's website, where similar services and products were offered. The actual loss in sales was difficult to adduce, but since damages are presumed as flowing from passing-off, damages were assessed at $5000 for this tort. Ultimately, Inform Cycle obtained judgment for $15 000: $5000 for defamation, $5000 for passing-off, and a further $5000 in punitive damages because Draper's actions were deemed malicious.

DISCUSSION QUESTIONS

Could Rebound Cycle, as employer, have been held vicariously liable for Draper's actions? What would Inform Cycle have to prove for vicarious liability to be imposed?

Misuse of Confidential Information

Misuse of confidential information is actionable

Wrongful disclosure of **confidential information**, which will also be discussed more extensively in Chapter 13, can also be a problem. A company's trade secrets and other forms of confidential information, including customer lists and future plans, are some of the most important assets a business can have, and their improper disclosure to a competitor can do that business great harm. Key employees, agents, and others that do business with that company have a duty not to disclose its confidential information to others or to use it for their own purposes. Persons can be sued where they fail in that duty. An action can also be brought against anyone who induced them to breach that confidence. This duty to maintain confidentiality may be imposed through contract or may arise simply because the information has been provided in confidence. Often it exists because of the fiduciary relationship existing between the parties. A fiduciary duty arises when one party places a considerable amount of trust in another, making himself particularly vulnerable to any wrongful actions of that

---

[77.] 2008 ABQB 369 (CanLII).

trusted party. A fiduciary duty may arise, for example, if a client puts his business affairs in an adviser's hands. Fiduciary duty will be one of the topics discussed under the heading "Liability of Professionals and Other Experts" in the next chapter.

An example of the misuse of such confidential information is found in *Enterprise Excellence Corporation v. Royal Bank of Canada.*[78] The plaintiffs approached the bank with a promotional idea, including the sponsorship of a radio program and the use of the phrase "Today's Entrepreneur." The bank rejected their proposal and instead went ahead with its own promotion, using the phrase "Today's Entrepreneur" constantly over a one-year period while the promotion ran. The Court found that this was a misuse of information that had been given to the bank in confidence and awarded damages of over half a million dollars to the plaintiff. The judge found that such a breach of confidence took place where (1) the information was of a confidential nature, (2) it was given in confidence, and (3) it was misused by the person to whom it was conveyed. In this case all three requirements had been met.

CASE SUMMARY 4.16

Guarding Confidences: *Walter Stewart Realty Ltd. v. Traber*[79]

A 200-acre tract of undeveloped land beside a housing development was thought to be unserviceable—at least until the plaintiff, Walter Stewart, discovered a method to service it. Stewart approached Traber, a real estate developer, with his plan to service and develop this land, but disclosed it to him only after receiving a promise (1) that the information would be kept secret and confidential and (2) that Stewart would receive 30 percent of the profits from the venture. Traber then acquired the property and developed it, but refused to give Stewart the funds promised. Stewart sued, claiming that the project amounted to a joint venture and that there had been a breach of confidentiality.

At trial the judge found that the agreement for a joint venture, while discussed, had never been finalized. Nonetheless, the conduct of the developer amounted to a breach of confidentiality, and Stewart was awarded 15 percent of the profits. On appeal, the Court agreed that there had been a breach of confidentiality but determined that the appropriate damages should be based on 30 percent of the profits from the development, as originally promised.

SMALL BUSINESS PERSPECTIVE

It is risky to assume that others will behave ethically. One must learn to protect assets, especially intangible ones such as knowledge or intellectual property. Insisting that a confidentiality agreement be signed before the information is shared is a prudent practice.

PRIVACY

LO **10**

Privacy protection initially found only in statutes

Invasion of a person's **privacy** may take the form of a physical intrusion, surveillance, misuse of an image or name, or access to information. Businesses often use information that people would like to keep private. They sometimes use images or likenesses to promote products without permission. Until very recently, there was no tort of invasion of privacy in common law, but several provinces made interfering with a person's privacy a statutory tort.[80] These statutes enabled claimants to sue if, for example, their likeness or voice was used without their consent. In *Heckert v. 5470 Investments Ltd.,*[81] a tenant sued her landlord for invasion of privacy by video

---

78. 2002 CanLII 49637 (ON SC).

79. 1995 ABCA 307 (CanLII); supplementary reasons given in 1995 ABCA 418 (CanLII).

80. See *Privacy Act*, R.S.B.C. 1996, c. 373; *The Privacy Act*, R.S.S. 1978, c. P-24; *The Privacy Act*, C.C.S.M. c. P125; *Privacy Act*, R.S.N.L. 1990, c. P-22.

81. 2008 BCSC 1298 (CanLII).

surveillance; she was awarded $3500 in damages. British Columbia's *Privacy Act* was relied upon. Similarly, in *L.A.M. v. J.E.L.I.*,[82] the defendant videotaped the plaintiff and her daughter in the bathroom through a peephole; general and punitive damages were awarded. Pursuant to *Privacy Acts*, remedies ranging from damages to injunctions and accounting for profits may be awarded. Often, consent of the claimant operates as a defence.

Because of the courts' reluctance to recognize invasion of privacy as a tort, parties have tried to characterize the action as another kind of tort. For example, where a business uses a person's image, name, or likeness to promote its product without permission, there is an innuendo communicated that the person has endorsed the product. That is a false statement and is actionable as defamation. Obviously, it would be much clearer if parties could simply sue for breach of privacy.

The courts recognized a need to expand tort law. In *Somwar v. McDonald's Restaurants of Canada Ltd.*,[83] the plaintiff, Somwar, sued his employer for invasion of privacy, and the defendant applied to have the case dismissed because the pleadings disclosed no known cause of action. The Court refused the application, stating "The traditional torts such as nuisance, trespass, and harassment may not provide adequate protection against infringement of an individual's privacy interests. Protection of those privacy interests by providing a common law remedy for their violation would be consistent with *Charter* values and an 'incremental revision' and logical extension of the existing jurisprudence. . . . Even if the plaintiff's claim for invasion of privacy were classified as 'novel' (which, in any event, is not a proper basis for dismissing it) the foregoing analysis leads me to conclude that the time has come to recognize invasion of privacy as a tort in its own right."

Judicial recognition of the tort of invasion of privacy continued to be divided. In *Nitsopoulos v. Won*,[84] the judge voiced his endorsement: "I agree with counsel for the plaintiffs that *Somwar* is a strong endorsement for the development of a common law remedy consistent with *Charter* values." But later, in *Jones v. Tsige,* the Ontario Superior Court of Justice reached the opposite conclusion. Ultimately, the Ontario Court of Appeal recognized, for the first time, a tort called "intrusion upon seclusion" (see Case Summary 4.17).

CASE SUMMARY 4.17

Time to Recognize Invasion of Privacy as a Tort—Under a Different Name: *Jones v. Tsige*[85]

Sandra Jones sued Winnie Tsige for invasion of privacy after learning that Tsige had inappropriately used her workplace computer to access Jones's personal account information at least 174 times. Both ladies worked at the same bank, and both were personally involved with the same man. Tsige was living with Jones's former husband; she wanted to find out if her common law spouse was actually paying child support to Jones.

The trial judge dismissed the action on the basis that he was bound by the Court of Appeal decision in the *Euteneier v. Lee*,[86] which predated the *Somwar* and *Nitsopoulos* decisions. There the appellant had "properly conceded in oral argument before this court that there is no free standing right to dignity or privacy under the *Charter* or at common law."

---

82. 2008 BCSC 1147 (CanLII).

83. 2006 CanLII 202 (ON SC).

84. *Nitsopoulos v. Wong*, 2008 CanLII 45407 (ON SC).

85. 2011 ONSC 1475 (CanLII); reversed on appeal, 2012 ONCA 32 (CanLII).

86. 2005 CanLII 33024 (ON CA).

Now, however, the Court of Appeal allowed the action, awarding Jones $10 000 in damages (there being no financial loss). The Court conceded that the law had to evolve to protect individuals from unreasonable intrusion into their private lives. The new tort, "intrusion upon seclusion," was described thus:

> One who intentionally intrudes, physically or otherwise, upon the seclusion of another or his private affairs or concerns, is subject to liability to the other for invasion of his privacy, if the invasion would be highly offensive to a reasonable person.

The key features of this cause of action are (1) the defendant's conduct must be intentional or reckless; (2) the defendant must have invaded, without lawful justification, the plaintiff's private affairs or concerns; and (3) a reasonable person would regard the invasion as highly offensive, causing distress, humiliation, or anguish. However, proof of harm to a recognized economic interest is not an element of the cause of action.

DISCUSSION QUESTIONS

Based on your understanding of *stare decisis*, does this decision establish the tort of intrusion upon seclusion across Canada? What level of judicial recognition is required before one can say with certainty that the tort of intrusion upon seclusion exists in its own right?

The introduction of computers has only heightened concerns over privacy and confidentiality. Digital information has become much easier to access, accumulate, and sort. Internet transactions usually require the exchange of private information, and the misuse or resale of this information without consent is a growing concern. The hope of self-regulation in this area was misplaced. It is clear that as the value of intercepted, confidential data taken from stored computer files or from online communications increases, so too does the temptation to acquire that data in any way possible.[87] The data can reveal a person's browsing and buying habits as well as other personal information. Steps are now being taken in most jurisdictions to increase the level of business and consumer protection in this area. In Canada, legislation has been enacted at both the federal and provincial levels to control the collection, use, and distribution of such personal information.

Internet poses new problems

Private data are often sold for profit

The federal *Privacy Act*[88] gives people the right to access their personal information held by the government and government agencies and severely restricts how that information can be disseminated to others. The *Personal Information Protection and Electronic Documents Act (PIPEDA)*[89] applies to personal information held by private organizations. It applies in all jurisdictions in Canada, except where a province has passed substantially similar legislation. At the time of writing, Quebec, British Columbia, and Alberta have passed such legislation,[90] and Ontario, New Brunswick, and Newfoundland and Labrador have privacy legislation that applies to health information. These acts have been declared substantially similar to *PIPEDA* with respect to health information custodians.[91]

The *Privacy Act* regulates government collection and use of private information

***PIPEDA* regulates the collection and use of private information by the private sector**

---

87. See *Autosurvey Inc. v. Prevost*, 2005 CanLII 36255 (ON SC), where the plaintiff sued a former business partner over misappropriation of intellectual property and business opportunities. The plaintiff, however, in anticipation of a hearing, infiltrated the defendant's computer server, copied documents, and then deleted computer logs to hide the infiltration. A permanent stay of the civil action was granted to compensate the defendants for the unauthorized, invasive access and download.

88. R.S.C. 1985, c. P-21.

89. S.C. 2000, c. 5.

90. *Personal Information Protection Act*, S.A. 2003 c. P-6.5; *Personal Information Protection Act*, S.B.C. 2003, c. 63; *An Act Respecting the Protection of Personal Information in the Private Sector*, CQLR c. P-39.1.

91. *Personal Health Information Protection Act, 2004*, S.O. 2004, c. 3; *Personal Health Information Privacy and Access Act*, S.N.B. 2009, c P-7.05; *Personal Health Information Act*, S.N.L. 2008, c. P-7.01.

PIPEDA contains a requirement of notice and consent

PIPEDA requires private organizations to account for their activities, identify the purposes for which the information is being collected, inform and get the consent of the individuals involved; and limits the use, disclosure, and retention of the information. The organization concerned must ensure the accuracy of the information, protect it with security safeguards, and be open about policies and practices relating to the management of the information. The Act requires that organizations make available to individuals, upon request, the nature of the information and how it is being used. It also outlines how an individual would proceed to have a complaint reviewed and empowers a privacy commissioner to impose fines for violations.

Model Code approved as a national standard for privacy protection

PIPEDA has attached as its central core the code of the Canadian Standards Association (CSA). The CSA code, entitled the "Model Code for the Protection of Personal Information," sets out 10 privacy protection principles. The European Union enacted legislation to protect privacy in this area some time ago, and the passage of this Act provides similar protection in Canada, removing a major barrier that threatened to interfere with international business. It must also be emphasized that while the rights, obligations, and remedies set out in these statutes are important with respect to safeguarding private information, they do not create a general right to sue in tort for a violation of those provisions.

Collection and use of private information without consent may violate statutory rights

Businesses may be tempted to extract private information from their employees or even to use surveillance techniques to obtain information about them. Secret surveillance of computer users is a major problem, especially in the work environment, where employers claim to have the right to read employees' emails and monitor their Internet use on their office computers. Telephones and email are sometimes also monitored. Medical information, political or religious affiliations, treatment for alcohol or drug-related problems, even mental conditions all may be of considerable interest. Surveillance for detecting theft and monitoring other security concerns is also common. This is dangerous territory, as it may violate statutory rights to privacy in that jurisdiction. It may also be a violation of human rights legislation, depending on the kind of information being sought and the methods used to obtain it.

Concern over privacy is increasing in Canada

Canadians are beginning to realize that information from email and other Internet communications can easily be intercepted, made public, or redirected to others who might misuse it. A survey commissioned by the Office of the Privacy Commissioner of Canada in 2014 found that nine out of ten Canadians were concerned about privacy. One in three (34 percent) said they were *extremely* concerned—up significantly from 25 percent in 2012.[92] In the past there was some anonymity in the vast amounts of data collected, but today this information can be sorted and arranged in such a way that individuals can be identified and targeted, not only by advertisers or others seeking to do business with them, but also by those committing identity theft or fraud.

REDUCING RISK 4.2

Protecting privacy is an immense challenge, and computer users ought to refrain as much as possible from giving out their private information online. Users of social networking sites such as Facebook and Twitter can expose themselves to significant loss of personal information. Encryption of the information or data communicated is advisable, but even then there is no guarantee that it will be secure from a motivated hacker. A further problem relating to privacy is the unauthorized interception of communications between individuals. This is now a criminal offence in Canada.[93] Users should remember that the information stored in computers is traceable, and even when information is deleted, someone with the appropriate expertise can readily recover it.[94]

---

92. Office of the Privacy Commissioner of Canada, "News Release: Concern for Privacy Has Jumped, Survey of Canadians Finds," January 28, 2015, www.priv.gc.ca/media/nr-c/2015/nr-c_150128_e.asp.

93. *Criminal Code*, R.S.C. 1985, c. C-46, s. 184.

94. Additional information is available at the Office of the Privacy Commissioner at www.priv.gc.ca.

Evolution of Tort Law

As stated at the beginning of this chapter, tort law is continually evolving, with the courts declaring new torts to exist as the need arises. The tort of intrusion upon seclusion, for example, is recognized in the United States and has been recently asserted in Ontario. Similarly, the tort of spoliation is finding its way north of the border. Spoliation would provide a remedy where one party has deliberately spoiled or destroyed the evidence needed by the plaintiff to establish a civil case. In *Spasic Estate v. Imperial Tobacco Ltd.*,[95] the Ontario Court of Appeal found that in the proper circumstances a trial judge might find that the tort of spoliation did exist; pre-trial dismissal of the action on the grounds that no cause of action was disclosed was therefore inappropriate.

Computer data are vulnerable

The Canadian law of spoliation was summarized by the Alberta Court of Appeal in *McDougall v. Black & Decker Canada Inc.* thus:[96]

Spoliation summarized—remedy to be left to trial judge

1. Spoliation currently refers to the intentional destruction of relevant evidence when litigation is existing or pending.

2. The principal remedy for spoliation is the imposition of a rebuttable presumption of fact that the lost or destroyed evidence would not assist the spoliator. The presumption can be rebutted by evidence showing the spoliator did not intend, by destroying the evidence, to affect the litigation, or by other evidence to prove or repel the case.

3. Outside this general framework other remedies may be available—even where evidence has been unintentionally destroyed. Remedial authority for these remedies is found in the court's rules of procedure and its inherent ability to prevent abuse of process, and remedies may include such relief as the exclusion of expert reports and the denial of costs.

4. The courts have not yet found that the intentional destruction of evidence gives rise to an intentional tort, nor that there is a duty to preserve evidence for purposes of the law of negligence, although these issues, in most jurisdictions, remain open.

5. Generally, the issues of whether spoliation has occurred and what remedy should be given if it has are matters best left for trial where the trial judge can consider all of the facts and fashion the most appropriate response.

6. Pre-trial relief may be available in the exceptional case where a party is particularly disadvantaged by the destruction of evidence. But generally this is accomplished through the applicable rules of court, or the court's general discretion with respect to costs and the control of abuse of process.

The evolution of tort law, with new torts being recognized as the need arises, certainly makes tort law interesting from an academic perspective. From a businessperson's perspective, this constant evolution of law underscores the importance of having an ongoing relationship with a lawyer to keep abreast of changes in the law.

ONLINE TORTS

LO ⑪

Regulation poses unique challenges

Creating laws to regulate the Internet presents some unique challenges. Abuses with respect to security and privacy create concern over how to protect the vast amounts of personal and business data stored digitally in clouds and being transferred online. A significant difficulty with online transactions is that often the identity and location of the person or business being dealt with are uncertain. This makes it difficult to determine not only who to sue but also the jurisdiction where the contract was made and what law applies.

[95.] 2000 CanLII 17170 (ON CA).

[96.] *McDougall v. Black & Decker Canada Inc.*, 2008 ABCA 353 (CanLII).

CASE SUMMARY 4.18

Torts in Cyberspace: *Braintech, Inc. v. Kostiuk*[97]

This precedent serves to clarify the approach to be taken to resolve jurisdictional issues in Internet-related disputes. A Vancouver firm sued a Vancouver investor for defamation over comments he made about the company in a chat room at Silicon Investor. The lawsuit was filed in a Texas Court (even though both litigants were in Vancouver and there was no active presence of the plaintiff in Texas) primarily because courts in that jurisdiction have a reputation for making huge damage awards. The defendant did not defend himself, believing that the Court had no jurisdiction in the case. The plaintiff was awarded US$300 000 in damages. When the successful plaintiff took the judgment to the British Columbia Court to have it enforced, the defendant argued that the Texas Court had no jurisdiction in the matter and was not the appropriate forum to hear the case. He lost at the trial level, but the Appeal Court agreed with the defendant and reversed the decision.

It was argued that the case should have been heard where there was a "real and substantial connection" to the matter in dispute. The only connection with Texas was that a Texas resident could have logged on to an out-of-state Internet site and read the alleged libel. But that was true of any location in any country, and to allow any location to have jurisdiction would have a "crippling effect" on the Internet and freedom of expression. The danger is having several different parallel actions going on at the same time. The action should be brought according to American law in a jurisdiction where there was a "real and substantial presence," or according to Canadian law if that was the jurisdiction having a "real and substantial connection" to the case. The Court found that the connection was to British Columbia and not Texas. The Supreme Court of Canada refused leave to appeal. The decision is important because it spells out under what conditions a given jurisdiction can rule on an Internet dispute and, by extension, which set of laws ought to apply to cyberspace behaviour.

Note, however, that the use of the Internet here was passive. An active use of the Internet occurs where the parties use the Internet to communicate while engaging in commercial transactions.

DISCUSSION QUESTIONS

Where the Internet is used actively, should a different rule apply in determining which courts have jurisdiction? Could several jurisdictions then have a "real and substantial" connection to the case? What impact would that have on the practice of business over the Internet? Is it prudent to specify which laws apply and which courts have jurisdiction over disputes when one creates an active website?

This question over which courts have jurisdiction has been amplified by disputes involving communication over the Internet. The *Burke v. NYP Holdings, Inc.*[98] case is another example. Following the NHL game in which Steve Moore was injured by Todd Bertuzzi, the *New York Post* published an article critical of the plaintiff, Brian Burke, who was general manager of the Vancouver Canucks when the incident occurred. The alleged defamatory article suggested that Burke personally challenged the Vancouver Canucks to "get" Steve Moore and that Burke was a participant in the plot to retaliate against Moore. Burke sued in British Columbia, but the defendants brought an application to have the action stayed,

---

97. 1999 BCCA 169 (CanLII); leave to appeal to S.C.C. refused, [1999] S.C.C.A. No. 236.
98. 2005 BCSC 1287 (CanLII).

arguing that the BC Court did not have jurisdiction. The defendants argued that the majority of the 431 000 copies of the *Post* were delivered to subscribers in the New York area and no copies were delivered to newsstands in British Columbia. The article, however, also appeared on the *Post*'s website, and the *Post* admitted it had no way to determine the geographic origin of the hits accessing the website. In determining whether the BC Court should assume jurisdiction, the judge stated the following:

> In cases of multi-state defamation, it is the publication, not the composition of the libel, that is the actionable wrong. Defamation is to be located at the place where the damage to reputation occurs . . .
>
> In considering the real and substantial connection test, in the context of allegedly false and injurious communications over the Internet, the location of the plaintiff is a key factor that receives greater weight than other factors. This is the case because damage to the reputation and actual pecuniary loss is the key element in such an action, and a plaintiff will experience damages most keenly in the jurisdiction in which they reside. Moreover, those who publish via the Internet are aware of the global reach of their publications, and must consider the legal consequences in the jurisdiction of the subjects of their articles.[99]

Not only did the incident at the hockey game occur in British Columbia, the witnesses to what was or was not said or done by Burke all resided in British Columbia. Burke suffered damage to his reputation in British Columbia. While the defendants had little or no business connection in British Columbia, the *Post* is a major newspaper that established a website available on the Internet worldwide. It was foreseeable that the story set out in the column would follow Burke to where he resided. Accordingly, the Court determined that a BC Court would have jurisdiction to hear the case.

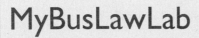 **MyBusLawLab** Be sure to visit the MyBusLawLab that accompanies this book to find practice quizzes, province-specific content, simulations and much more!

SUMMARY

Intentional torts

- Assault and battery involve deliberate interference with one's person; defences are consent or self-defence (reasonable force)
- Trespass is the temporary or permanent intrusion on someone else's property without lawful right or consent
- Trespass to chattels, conversion, and detinue involve deliberate interference with another's goods
- False imprisonment is the restraint of a person by someone without authority
- Malicious prosecution is pursuing criminal charges in the absence of evidence
- Private nuisance is the unusual use of property causing foreseeable disturbance to a neighbour

---

[99] This summary is taken from the judgment in *TimberWest Forest Corp. v. United Steel Workers*, 2008 BCSC 388 (CanLII), in its analysis of the *Burke v. NYP Holdings, Inc.* decision.

- Defamation is a false, published statement that discredits a person
  - Libel is written defamation; slander is spoken
  - Defences include truth, absolute privilege, qualified privilege, fair comment, and public interest responsible journalism
- Injurious falsehood (product defamation or trade slander) is false, published statements that damage the goodwill associated with a product or business

Other business torts

- Inducing breach of contract, which is knowingly causing the breach of a contract that exists between two other parties
- Unlawful interference with economic relations is causing damage by the use of unlawful means to disrupt the business of another
- Intimidation is using threats to cause another person or business to act against their interests
- Deceit is deliberately misleading another with false statements
- Conspiracy is acting in concert with others to damage a third party
- Passing-off is misleading the public to think one's goods or services are those of another
- Misuse of confidential information is the wrongful use or disclosure of trade secrets and other confidential information
- Intrusion upon seclusion is the violation of a person's reasonable expectation of privacy
- Spoliation is the destruction of evidence to hide proof of wrongdoing

Online torts

- Present problems with jurisdiction and with enforcement

QUESTIONS FOR REVIEW

1. Explain what is meant by the statement "A tort is a civil wrong."

2. Distinguish between assault and battery.

3. How do doctors avoid liability for the tort of battery when operating on or otherwise treating patients?

4. What limitations are there on the right of self-defence when people are defending themselves against an attack?

5. Describe the situations in which battery may be justified.

6. What are the necessary elements that must be present for a person to be classified as a trespasser?

7. What may the proprietor of a business do when faced with an unruly patron?

8. Distinguish between trespass to chattels, conversion, and detinue.

9. Imprisonment can take the form of confinement, arrest, or submission to authority. Explain.

10. What must be established to sue successfully for false imprisonment?

11. How is malice typically established by a plaintiff who sues in malicious prosecution?

12. Distinguish between libel and slander, and explain the significance of the distinction.

13. Define the terms *innuendo* and *qualified privilege*.

14. Distinguish between defamation, trade slander, and deceit, indicating in what situations each would be used.

15. Explain the nature of the tort of inducing breach of contract and what circumstances would give rise to such an action.

16. How does the tort of unlawful interference with economic relations differ from the tort of inducing breach of contract?

17. Differentiate between conspiracy and intimidation.

18. List the remedies that may be appropriate to redress misuse of confidential information.

19. Privacy concerns are becoming more problematic in the technological age. What statutes protect the rights of individuals in this area?

20. How do the courts determine if they have jurisdiction over a tort action where the Internet is the means of communicating a defamatory message?

CASES AND DISCUSSION QUESTIONS

1. *Chopra v. Eaton (T.) Co.* (1999), 240 A.R. 201 (Q.B.); 1999 ABQB 201 (CanLII)
Chopra went to Eaton's department store seeking a refund. An argument ensued. Frauenfeld (from security) told Chopra that he would have to leave; Frauenfeld took Chopra's elbow and started to escort him out of the store. Near the doors, Chopra pushed Frauenfeld away, presumably wishing to go through the doors unassisted. Frauenfeld reacted quickly and violently, putting Chopra into a headlock. Chopra's glasses were knocked off and his lip was cut; he was handcuffed, detained in the security office, and subjected to racial slurs. Chopra asked to leave, asked to call his wife, and asked Frauenfeld to call the police; all of these requests were refused. After Chopra had been detained for four hours or more, the police arrived and charged Chopra with assaulting Frauenfeld and causing a disturbance. All charges were later dismissed.

Identify what causes of action are available to Chopra to address the wrongs done to him.

2. *Banfai v. Formula Fun Centre Inc.* (1984), 19 D.L.R. (4th) 683 (Ont. H.C.)
Ontario Hydro leased property to the defendant, who ran a small racetrack operating scaled-down Grand Prix cars from 11 a.m. to 11 p.m. each day during the summer season. The noise generated from the motors and screeching tires seriously interfered with the plaintiffs' operation of their motel located adjacent to the amusement park.

Indicate the nature of the plaintiffs' complaint, the likelihood of success, and what would be an appropriate remedy if they were successful in their action. How would you balance the interests of the two businesses?

3. *369413 Alberta Ltd. v. Pocklington* (2000), 194 D.L.R. (4th) 109, 271 A.R. 280, (Alta. C.A.); 2000 ABCA 307 (CanLII)
Gainers, an Alberta corporation, turned to the provincial government for funding. The agreed-upon terms required Gainers not to sell or dispose of its assets without the prior written consent of its major creditor, the Alberta government. When Gainers fell upon financial difficulty, its sole director, Peter Pocklington, signed a director's resolution transferring certain shares owned by Gainers (valued in the millions) to his own company, Pocklington Holdings Ltd., for $100. This transfer took place one day before Alberta gave notice of its intention to exercise its rights under their security agreement. As a result of the share transfer, Gainers was without sufficient resources to repay the government.

What is the nature of the creditor's complaint? What tort action is most appropriate in the circumstances? What would be the appropriate remedy?

4. *Duke v. Puts* **(2004), 21 C.C.L.T. (3d) 181, [2004] 6 W.W.R. 208 (Sask. C.A.); 2004 SKCA 12 (CanLII)**

Duke, a pharmacist, operated a successful pharmacy in Saskatchewan for 20 years.

Dr. Puts developed a suspicion about Duke's association with a physician in another town; Puts accused Duke of conspiring with that physician to cheat the health-care system by claiming for false prescriptions and double billing. In a letter of complaint sent to the College of Physicians and Surgeons of Saskatchewan, Puts alleged professional misconduct against Duke. He told other people that Duke was a crook. These accusations greatly harmed the pharmacist's reputation and business and caused him to sell his business at a reduced price.

Assuming all the allegations were false, what tort actions could Duke bring against Dr. Puts? What defences, if any, could the defendant assert?

5
Chapter

Negligence, Professional Liability, and Insurance

LEARNING OBJECTIVES

1. Identify the four elements of a negligence claim

2. State when a duty of care arises, explaining how courts determine whether it is owed

3. Describe breach of the standard of care, identifying the test used to determine if a breach has occurred

4. Explain how both physical and legal causation and damage are proven

5. Distinguish the defences applicable to the tort of negligence

6. Examine legislation that affects when liability may be imposed

7. Distinguish among strict liability, vicarious liability, and product liability

8. Describe the circumstances where professional liability may arise

9. Describe four types of insurance businesses commonly need

10. Identify when an insurable interest exists

11. Explain the significance of insurance being a contract of utmost good faith

12. Identify the duties imposed on the insured and insurer

The torts discussed in the previous chapter involved intentional conduct. The fact that the tortfeasor's acts were deliberate or "intentional" established the required degree of fault necessary to constitute an actionable wrong or tort. In this chapter we will examine the law of negligence, which, unlike intentional torts, involves inadvertent conduct causing injury or damage to others. The required fault is found in the failure of the wrongdoer to live up to the degree of skill or care required in the circumstances. We will also examine defences that can eliminate or reduce a tortfeasor's liability. Then product and professional liability will be explored, two applications of the law of negligence that are of particular interest to businesspeople.

In the last part of this chapter, insurance will be discussed. While not related specifically to the subject of tort law, insurance is used primarily as a method of spreading the risk of injury and loss. Several different types of insurance will be discussed, including liability insurance, which is uniquely designed to provide insurance coverage for the liability that individuals or businesses may face when a tort action is brought against them.

CASE SUMMARY 5.1

Road Rage Leads to Liability: *Davies v. Elston*[1]

The plaintiff, an experienced cyclist, was out for a ride with his son. They passed a parked truck and the son remarked loudly on how its mirrors protruded into the bike lane. Overhearing them, the truck owner jumped into his Ford F-350 truck and drove after the cyclists to confront them. The plaintiff initially thought the motorist pulling up beside him was seeking directions; instead angry words were exchanged. The cyclists and the truck were travelling fast and the truck came so close that the plaintiff placed his hand on the passenger side window. As the truck drove away the plaintiff lost control of his bicycle, crashed into the curb, and fractured his pelvis.

At trial, the defendant argued that the plaintiff was at fault for the incident and that his son was negligent for riding abreast of his father. The trial judge disagreed and found the defendant fully responsible. In reaching this conclusion, the Court provided the following reasons:

> As for whether Mr. Elston's conduct was negligent, I find that the defendant fell below the standard of care of a reasonable and prudent driver, in driving alongside the two cyclists and yelling at them, while so close to the bike lane that it made it intimidating, threatening and unsafe for the cyclists; and then in addition in pulling away quickly, without warning, with Mr. Davies so close by and with his hand on the truck.

> It is obvious as a matter of common sense that such driving conduct was without reasonable care for the safety of the cyclists and was negligent.[2]

The judge concluded that but for the defendant's aggressive and negligent conduct, the plaintiff would not have fallen from his bike. Elston's negligence therefore caused the accident and the resultant injuries. The plaintiff, a former national athlete who was 77 years old at the date of the crash, was awarded damages of $100 162.69 plus additional damages for cost of future care.

SMALL BUSINESS PERSPECTIVE

Note that in this case there was a second defendant, Pajo's (Garry Point) Restaurant Ltd. It had been conceded that if Elston was liable in negligence, the corporate defendant, being the owner of the vehicle, would be jointly and severally liable. The *Motor Vehicle Act* of British Columbia, like legislation elsewhere in Canada, dictates that when a vehicle is driven in contravention of the law, liability may also be imposed on the owner of the vehicle. In light of this, owners should ensure they have appropriate insurance if they allow others to drive their vehicles.

LO **1** # NEGLIGENCE

The A, B, C, and D of Negligence

Negligence is by far the most important area of tort liability for businesspeople and professionals. It involves inadvertent or unintentionally careless conduct that causes injury or damage to another person or his property. Four required elements or ingredients must be established by the plaintiff to succeed in a negligence action.

---

1. [2014] B.C.J. No. 3172.
2. Ibid., at paras. 167–168.

Failure to establish any one of these four will lead to dismissal of the plaintiff's action. See Table 5.1, which sets out those ingredients and lists the tests used by the courts to determine whether these elements have in fact been proven.

Table 5.1 Negligence: The Required Ingredients

Ingredients	What Needs to Be Established	Tests Used
A A duty of care is owed to the plaintiff	That the proximity of the parties created an obligation to exercise caution or care	1. Foreseeable plaintiff test (reasonable foreseeability test) 2. Policy considerations—may negate existence of a duty
B Breach of that duty; breach of the standard of care	That the defendant was not careful enough	Reasonable person test
C Causation	1. That the defendant directly or physically caused the injury; and 2. That the injury was reasonably foreseeable	1. Physical: "but for" test 2. Legal: remoteness test
D Damage	That the plaintiff suffered injury or loss	Refer to precedents—has this type of loss been recognized by courts as compensable?

A: A Duty to Exercise Care Must Exist

Negligence involves a failure on someone's part to live up to a **duty** to be careful to someone else. We do not have a duty to be careful to everyone. The court must determine whether the defendant owed a **duty of care** to the plaintiff. The court uses the **reasonable foreseeability test**, also called the *foreseeable plaintiff test*, to determine the existence of such a duty. Based on the proximity of the parties, if it were reasonably foreseeable that the conduct complained of would cause harm to the plaintiff, a duty to be careful exists. It seems almost self-evident today that we should act carefully toward people whom we can see are put at risk by our behaviour, but this was not always the case.

LO ❷

Reasonable foreseeability test establishes duty

CASE SUMMARY 5.2

"Neighbours" Are Owed a Duty of Care: *Donoghue v. Stevenson*[3]

The reasonable foreseeability test was developed in *Donoghue v. Stevenson*, one of the most significant cases of the twentieth century. Mrs. Donoghue went with a friend into a café, where the friend ordered a bottle of ginger beer for her. After consuming some of it, Donoghue discovered part of a decomposed snail at the bottom of her bottle. She became very ill as a result of drinking the contaminated beverage. In the process of suing, she discovered that she had some serious problems. She could not successfully sue the café that had supplied the ginger beer for breach of contract; she had no contract with the establishment, since her friend had made the purchase. Similarly, she could not successfully sue the café for negligence since it had done nothing wrong—the ginger beer was bottled in an opaque container and served to her in the bottle. Her only recourse was to sue the manufacturer for negligence in producing the product, but the bottler claimed it owed her no duty to be careful. The Court had to determine whether a duty to be careful was owed by the manufacturer to the consumer of its product. In the process of finding that such a duty was owed, the House of Lords developed the reasonable foreseeability test. Lord Atkin, one of the judges in the case, made the following classic statement when discussing how to determine to whom we owe a duty:

---

3. [1932] A.C. 562 (H.L.); see www.bailii.org/uk/cases/UKHL/1932/100.html.

> The rule that you are to love your neighbour becomes in law, you must not injure your neighbour; and the lawyer's question "Who is my neighbour?" receives a restricted reply. You must take reasonable care to avoid acts or omissions which you can reasonably foresee would be likely to injure your neighbour. Who, then, in law, is my neighbour? The answer seems to be—persons who are so closely and directly affected by my act that I ought reasonably to have them in contemplation as being so affected when I am directing my mind to the acts or omissions which are called in question.[4]

SMALL BUSINESS PERSPECTIVE

Risk management involves asking whether one's actions put others at risk. If injury is foreseeable, then a duty to take care may be owed. Liability could follow unless reasonable precautions are taken to avoid causing harm.

Foreseeable plaintiff test
(a) injury to plaintiff is foreseeable
(b) proximity suggests defendant should have considered the plaintiff

Policy aspect applies to new situations

Policy aspect: only relevant where a duty of care has never been imposed in the past

Duty owed to anyone who could foreseeably be harmed

We owe a duty, then, to anyone whom we can reasonably anticipate might be harmed by our conduct. The reasonable foreseeability test was further refined in the English *Anns* case.[5] The *Anns* case created a two-stage test for determining the existence of a duty of care. The first question to ask is whether there was a degree of neighbourhood or **proximity** between the parties such that if the person being sued had thought of it she would have realized that her actions posed a risk of danger to the other. Essentially, this question restates the *Donoghue v. Stevenson* reasonable foreseeability test. Note that this test has two requirements. First, that injury to the plaintiff was *reasonably foreseeable*, but also that there is a *relationship* between them such that the plaintiff was of a class of "persons who are so closely and directly affected by my act" that the defendant should have had them in mind when committing the act in question.

The second set of policy questions probes deeper, providing for exceptions or modifications to the primary test. Was there any reason that the duty should not be imposed? Should the scope of the duty be reduced? Should the class to whom the duty is owed be limited, or should the damages be reduced? These questions allow the court to consider social policy, rather than strict legal rules, when looking at special situations and relationships. Essentially, the courts try to avoid situations where a defendant may be exposed to "liability in an indeterminate amount for an indeterminate time to an indeterminate class."[6] The English have abandoned the principles set out in the *Anns* case, but the Supreme Court of Canada has made it clear that it is good law in Canada.[7] It is important to note, however, that this second policy aspect of the *Anns* test will only be applied to those new situations that don't fit into a category of negligence where a duty of care has already been recognized by the courts.

In Canada, then, the existence of a duty of care is established, by the reasonable foreseeability test set out in the *Donoghue v. Stevenson* case; however, in new situations or classes of cases where a duty of care has not already been established, the court can apply the second half of the *Anns* case test negating or modifying that duty on the basis of policy considerations.

This approach was evident in the *D'Amato v. Badger* case,[8] where a corporation's key employee was injured in a motor vehicle collision and the corporation sought to recover its economic loss from the party at fault. It is

---

4. Ibid. at 580.

5. *Anns v. Merton, London Borough Council*, [1977] 2 All E.R. 492 (H.L.); [1977] UKHL 4; see www.bailii.org/uk/cases/UKHL/1977/4.html.

6. *Ultramares Corp. v. Touche* (1931), 174 N.E. 441 at 444 (N.Y.C.A.); www.uniset.ca/other/cs3/174NE441.html.

7. *Canadian National Railway Co. v. Norsk Pacific Steamship Co.*, 1992 CanLII 105 (SCC).

8. 1996 CanLII 166 (SCC).

conceivable that an employer corporation will suffer economically if its employee(s) are unable to work; thus, employers can be "foreseeable plaintiffs." But will the party who caused injury to an employee be held liable for the economic loss suffered by the employer? Applying the *Anns* policy test, the Supreme Court held there were policy reasons to prohibit recovery by employers for losses resulting from injuries to employees. Allowing such recovery could lead to indeterminate liability to an unlimited number of potential plaintiffs. The Court reasoned that employers/corporations could plan for the risk of physical injury to their employees/shareholders through insurance or other means. Essentially, the Supreme Court reasoned that it made more social sense to put this duty onto the shoulders of employers rather than to cause motorists and their insurers to bear this additional risk.

In many negligence cases, the existence of a duty is obvious and the court need not deal with the problem at length. Still, it is a required element in a negligence action and is important in those cases where the existence of a duty of care is brought into question. Requiring that policy considerations be taken into account before a duty of care is recognized in "new" situations weakens the predictability of case law—but how else can "new" situations be adequately addressed?

Scope of duty can be reduced where appropriate

CASE SUMMARY 5.3

"Policy Considerations" Negate Finding a Duty of Care: *Dobson v. Dobson*[9]; *Childs v. Desormeaux*[10]

When determining whether a new duty of care should be imposed, policy considerations come into play. Two cases involving negligent operation of vehicles demonstrate this. In the *Dobson* case, a pregnant mother drove a snowmobile negligently, crashed, and caused injury to her unborn child. The child was mentally and physically disabled, and the child's grandfather sought recovery from the negligent parent (who was insured). Presumably, if the mother was found at fault her insurer would be required to pay benefits to the injured child. The Court decided that the existence (or absence) of insurance should not to be a factor. Instead, the Court focused on whether a duty of care existed. Due to the proximity of the parties, the mother did owe her unborn child a duty of care. Injury to one's fetus is foreseeable if one is pregnant and drives without due care. However, the Supreme Court was loath to impose a new duty of care as between a pregnant mother and her fetus, because doing so would severely impair the mother–child relationship. The purpose of tort law—compensation and deterrence—would not be furthered if pregnant mothers could be liable to their children. Further, imposing such liability on pregnant women would involve severe intrusions into their bodily integrity, privacy, and autonomy rights, as it would subject every aspect of pregnant women to judicial scrutiny. Thus, on policy grounds, the action was dismissed.

In the second case, Childs was severely injured when a drunk driver struck her vehicle in the early hours of New Year's Day. Childs sought to add as defendants the social hosts who served alcohol to Desormeaux and then allowed him to drive while impaired. Applying the foreseeability test, the trial judge determined that hosts may owe a duty of care to their guests and to other users of the road that they might encounter. But on policy grounds, the Court cautioned that Canadians were not ready for the imposition of social host liability. Insurance to protect against such liability was not yet readily available, if at all.

---

[9] 1999 CanLII 698 (SCC).

[10] 2006 SCC 18 (CanLII).

> **SMALL BUSINESS PERSPECTIVE**
>
> In the *Childs* case, the Court sent the signal that social host liability may become a reality in the future.[11] Note that many insurers now provide this type of coverage. Businesses that rent out facilities for parties, weddings, and other social events where alcohol is served are well advised to require the host to purchase social host liability coverage. It may also be prudent to require that the facility owner be named as a co-insured.

MISFEASANCE AND NONFEASANCE

Unacceptable action— misfeasance

Failure to act—nonfeasance

The law imposes a duty on people to carry out their activities carefully so as to not cause harm to others. Where **misfeasance** or wrongful conduct is involved, the courts are ready to impose liability on the wrongdoer. But the courts are reluctant to provide a remedy in a case of **nonfeasance** (when a person fails to do something). Such reluctance was demonstrated in the *Childs* case;[12] the Court was reluctant to hold social hosts liable for their failure to intervene and prevent an intoxicated guest from driving.

Usually there is no duty in the case of nonfeasance

People who see a child drowning have no duty in tort law to rescue that child. Apparently, unless it can be established that a special relationship exists, such as in the case of a swimmer and a lifeguard or a child and a guardian, a duty of care will not be established and nonfeasance will not draw liability. Such a special relationship does exist between a commercial establishment that profits from the sale of alcohol and its customers. The courts have also extended that duty to third parties who might foreseeably be injured by intoxicated customers.[13]

Once a person starts to help, he must take reasonable care

Doctors have no legal duty to come to the aid of an accident victim when they pass a car crash. But once someone does start to help, he has an obligation to continue to do so in a reasonable way. Stopping midway may lead to a claim of abandonment, which can draw liability in itself. Similarly, when someone attempts to repair a car of a friend he has no legal duty to help, but if he does he is responsible for any damage caused by his carelessness. These rules discourage people from coming to the aid of others. In an attempt to alleviate such harsh consequences, some jurisdictions have introduced legislation either creating a duty to assist or at least protecting rescuers from liability for injuries arising out of their rescue efforts.[14] Refer to MyBusLawLab for details.

LO ❸ ## B: Breach of the Standard of Care

Reasonable person test establishes standard

In a negligence action, once the existence of a duty is established the second issue is whether the defendant demonstrated sufficient care. How careful need one be to avoid liability? The **reasonable person test** is used by the court in many areas of law to establish standards of socially acceptable behaviour. Faced with the problem of having to decide if certain conduct is socially acceptable, the courts ask, "What would a reasonably prudent person, in possession of all the facts of the case, have done in this situation?"

Reasonable care, not perfection, is required

It is important to understand that the standard determined using the reasonable person test is not what would be expected of an average person. A reasonable

---

11. Recently, in *Sidhu v. Hiebert*, 2011 BCSC 1364, the social host brought an application to have the case against him dismissed, arguing that as a social host he owed no duty of care to the public users of the highway who might be injured by an intoxicated guest. The application failed. Similarly, in *Lutter v. Smithson*, 2013 BCSC 119 (CanLII), the Court refused a motion for dismissal and allowed an action against a social host to proceed. Once these matters proceed to trial, a judgment on social host liability may follow.

12. *Supra* 10, at paras. 31–41.

13. *Stewart v. Pettie*, 1995 CanLII 147 (SCC).

14. *Emergency Medical Aid Act*, R.S.A. 2000, c. E-7; *Good Samaritan Act*, R.S.B.C. 1996, c. 172; *Good Samaritan Act*, 2001, S.O. 2001, c. 2; *The Good Samaritan Protection Act*, C.C.S.M. c. G65.

person is expected to be "prudent" or particularly careful, demonstrating a level of behaviour considerably better than average. On the other hand, the conduct is not required to be perfect. If one draws an analogy to the game of golf, a standard score, called *par*, is set for each hole on the course. If par for a particular hole is 3, the average golfer would likely score 4 or 5. On the other hand, 3 is not the best possible score. Rather, par is the score you would expect from a good golfer playing well. Similarly, the reasonable person test represents the standard of care expected from a prudent person who, in light of the circumstances, acts with reasonable care. To avoid liability for negligence, the standard of care is reasonableness as opposed to average or perfection. If the conduct of the defendant is found to have fallen below this standard, she is negligent and liable for any injury or loss thus caused.

What is reasonable conduct will vary with the circumstances. For example, the court will take into account the risk of loss. In *Blyth v. Birmingham Water Works, Co.*,[15] the plaintiff's home was flooded when a water main serving a fireplug froze and burst during a severe winter cold spell. The Court rejected the plaintiff's claim that the water works company was negligent for not having placed the pipes deeper. Considering the risk, one could not justify the great costs of digging the pipes in deeper. The risk was low—the system had been in place for 25 years and this was the coldest winter in 50 years. The judge in the case said, "Negligence is the omission to do something which a reasonable man, guided upon those considerations which ordinarily regulate the conduct of human affairs, would do, or doing something which a prudent and reasonable man would not do."[16]

Surrounding circumstances are relevant to the degree of care

Similarly, a person driving a truck or car on a busy freeway must be more careful than a person driving down an open country road because of the increased risk of significant injury. Or a teacher must exercise greater vigilance when supervising students engaged in risky exercises, especially if students are unfamiliar with the equipment.[17] Thus, in *Hussack v. Chilliwack School District No. 33*,[18] the gym teacher was found to have breached the requisite standard of care when he allowed the plaintiff (a 13-year-old student) to participate in a field hockey game despite his absence from earlier classes in which progressive skills had been taught. The plaintiff was struck in the face with a stick, suffered a concussion, and developed somatoform disorder; thus, damages were significant.

Risk of injury affects standard, as does cost

CASE SUMMARY 5.4

Police Chases Found to Violate Standard of Care Required: *Radke v. M.S. (Litigation Guardian of)*[19]; *Burbank v. R.T.B.*[20]

The attorney general of British Columbia appealed two findings of negligence on the part of its police officers. In the *Radke* case, the constable spotted a parked car that had been reported as stolen. M.S., then 15 years old, was later seen entering the vehicle with two others. The constable followed him, and when he engaged the lights and sirens M.S. fled, ultimately colliding with the vehicle driven by Radke.

---

15. (1856), 156 E.R. 1047 (Ex. Ct.).

16. Ibid., p. 1049.

17. See *MacCabe v. Westlock Roman Catholic Separate School District No. 110*, reversed in part 2001 ABCA 257 (CanLII), where liability was imposed partly on the teacher for failing to adequately supervise a gym class at which a student was rendered quadriplegic.

18. 2011 BCCA 258 (CanLII).

19. 2007 BCCA 216 (CanLII).

20. 2007 BCCA 215 (CanLII).

In assessing whether the officer acted with sufficient care, the trial judge considered the constable's failure to follow police policy when initiating the pursuit. The crime, possession of stolen property, was not serious, and there was no one in position to assist the officer, which raised the risk to the public significantly. Further, once the officer put on his lights and saw that the driver's response was to accelerate in a residential area and drive through stop signs while heading toward a busy street, a proper risk assessment would have warned him of the significant danger to the public posed by continuing the pursuit. The failure to conduct proper risk assessments at two critical times led the judge to conclude that the constable did not act within the standard of the reasonable police officer, acting reasonably and within the statutory powers imposed upon him in the context of all of the circumstances of this case.

Similarly, in the *Burbank* case, the officer had been chasing a stolen vehicle, driven by a suspected impaired driver, when it sped through a stop sign and collided with a third automobile. The collision claimed the life of one child; others were seriously injured. The trial judge determined that in conducting the pursuit, the officer had breached the requisite standard of care. Although the impaired driver was found to be 85 percent at fault, the officer was also negligent and fault was assessed at 15 percent.

The Court of Appeal affirmed both trial decisions, finding that the officers had each breached the required standard of care. In addressing whether the risk of pursuit was justified, the evidence revealed that the officers had no specific information that any serious offence had been committed. Further, there was no justification for pursuing a suspect through a residential area where it was expected that there would be a high volume of pedestrian and vehicular traffic.

As to causation, the "but for" test required a finding of causation when it could be said that but for the impugned conduct, the injury would not have been suffered. Here, the collisions would not have occurred but for the pursuits by the police officers.

SMALL BUSINESS PERSPECTIVE

These two cases exemplify that the amount of care is dependent on and shaped by the risks inherent in the activity. As risk increases, so does the requisite amount of care.

Expenses or costs will also be taken into consideration in determining the required standard of care. It may be possible to design and build an automobile that would suffer minimal damage in a high-speed accident, but the costs involved would be prohibitive. No one could afford such a car; therefore, it would be unreasonable to hold a manufacturer to such a standard. But even here care must be taken, because saving money will not excuse the production of a defective or dangerous product. A balance must be struck.

Standard depends on expertise

What constitutes reasonable behaviour will also vary with the expertise of the person being sued. A doctor is expected to function, at least as far as medical matters are concerned, at a higher level than a non-medical person, and so is held to a higher standard. The test asks: Was the person's conduct up to the standard expected of a reasonable person in the same circumstances? Did he conduct himself as a reasonable doctor, reasonable lawyer, reasonable accountant, reasonable plumber, or reasonable driver? This has special implications for professionals and other experts as the standard is not lowered because of inexperience; the novice is required to perform at the same standard as the reasonably prudent practitioner.

The required standard of care does not diminish in the case of an elderly person. Thus, in *McKee (Guardian ad litem of) v. McCoy*,[21] the standard of care required for a driver was that of an ordinary driver, not that of a person whose capacities are reduced by age. Initially the defendant was found 100 percent liable, but on appeal it was determined that the plaintiff was struck in an "unmarked crosswalk"; since the plaintiff was found partly at fault, the defendant's liability was reduced to 80 percent.

---

21. (2001), 9 C.C.L.T. (3d) 294 (B.C.S.C.).

The opposite is true when children are involved. The courts recognize that a 13-year-old cannot be expected to act at the same level of responsibility as an adult. Children are liable for their torts, but the standard required of them is the level of conduct that would be expected of a reasonable child of the same age. Thus, a small child playing with matches may not be liable for a resulting fire, whereas a teenager doing the same thing could very likely be held responsible. At this point, attention usually turns to the parents. Although many people do not realize it, parents are not, as a general rule, vicariously liable for the torts committed by their children. In the absence of a statute to the contrary (and these are becoming much more common[22]) parents are liable only if it can be established that they were negligent in their own right by failing to properly train, control, or supervise their children. Refer to MyBusLawLab for information on the provinces that have passed such statutes.

Liability may vary with age

REDUCING RISK 5.1

It has been suggested that risk avoidance is the most appropriate course of action for businesspeople to reduce the likelihood of being sued. Professionals should examine not only the condition of their premises, tools, cars, and other physical objects used in the course of business, but also the habits and practices that may give rise to a complaint. Medical professionals such as doctors, nurses, podiatrists, chiropractors, and the like run some risk of being sued in tort for battery and negligence. Since the nature of their practice depends on physical contact with their clients and patients, securing proper consent is a vital component of risk management. Problems may also arise when physical injury is caused by an error in judgment or a mistake in practice. People involved in sports, education, training, and recreational activities face such a risk. The main thing to remember is that the standard of care demanded of such experts is that of the reasonable person operating in similar circumstances. A sophisticated client will periodically review his or her practices, physical premises, services, and advice to make sure that potential misinformation or misdirection and foreseeable dangers are anticipated and avoided.

It is not always necessary for the plaintiff to show that the defendant was careless. This can sometimes be implied from the surrounding circumstances. For example, if a piano were to fall into the street from a fourth-floor apartment injuring a passerby, those facts by themselves seem to say more eloquently than anyone could that the people who were handling the piano were careless in the way they moved it. From the evidence of the falling piano, the court can conclude that the handlers were negligent.

This type of situation used to be dealt with under a special provision of the law of negligence called *res ipsa loquitur* ("the thing speaks for itself"), but the Supreme Court of Canada has said that it is better approached as a matter of circumstantial evidence.[23] The new approach is somewhat more flexible, but the effect is similar. The court can find that the circumstantial evidence establishes a *prima facie* ("on the face of it") case and then turn to the defendants to produce evidence that they were not negligent. Without such evidence from the defendants, the plaintiff will be successful. In *Jordan v. Power*,[24] for example, the Court stated that in discharging the plaintiff's primary burden of proving negligence, circumstantial evidence can be used with or without direct evidence. Then, to avoid liability, the defendant need only neutralize or negate the inference of negligence with evidence explaining the occurrence of injury without the defendant's negligence.

Liability may be established by circumstantial evidence

C and D: Causation and Damages

Unlike intentional torts, which may be actionable even without any specific damage, negligence requires that some sort of loss to person or property be suffered. When a customer slips and falls on a wet floor in a store but suffers no injury there is no right to sue, even though the store employees have been careless. However, if the

LO ❹

Damage or loss is critical to a negligence claim

---

22. See, for example, Manitoba's *Parental Responsibility Act*, C.C.S.M. c. P8; British Columbia's *Parental Responsibility Act*, S.B.C. 2001, c. 45, s. 3; and Ontario's *Parental Responsibility Act, 2000*, S.O. 2000, c. 4, s. 2.

23. *Fontaine v. British Columbia (Official Administrator)*, 1998 CanLII 814 (SCC).

24. 2002 ABQB 794 (CanLII).

customer breaks a leg, this would be a tangible, physical injury that would provide grounds for an action.

No injury—no negligence claim

O.E.X. Electromagnetic Inc. v. Coopers & Lybrand[25] confirms that without damages negligence cannot be established. The action concerned a failed stock promotion. The plaintiffs claimed the defendants negligently prepared a technical report on a company and business venture that the plaintiffs sought to take public on the Vancouver Stock Exchange. Ultimately, the company promoted by the plaintiffs was listed on the Vancouver Stock Exchange, but trading was suspended in the spring of 1988 when it was revealed that a manufacturing facility in Arkansas, which was the company's only asset, was a sham. The Court determined that although the plaintiffs had been misled by the negligently prepared report and suffered damages as a result, they also made money on the initial offering of shares. Since they gained more than they lost, their negligent misrepresentation action was dismissed.

Economic loss and mental distress are recognized as compensable injuries

In the past, there had to be some actual physical damage or bodily injury for the plaintiff to successfully sue for negligence. Today, the courts are willing to provide a remedy even in cases of pure economic loss or where the negligence has caused a recognized mental disorder, such as depression. Some parents have even successfully sued physicians for the "wrongful birth" of their child. It is a matter of considerable controversy, but where a physician fails to advise parents of a potential genetic defect and the pregnancy is allowed to continue, the cost of raising a child born with severe defects may be awarded.[26]

"BUT FOR" TEST: PHYSICAL CAUSATION

Conduct must be the cause of injury

For negligence to apply, not only must there be damage, but that damage must also be a direct result of the careless conduct. If the operator of a motor vehicle knowingly drives at night without tail lights, the driver can be said to be careless. However, if the vehicle is involved in a head-on collision, the driver of the other car could not rely on the first driver's failure to have tail lights to support a negligence action. The test usually applied in such situations is called the **"but for" test**. The plaintiff must prove to the court's satisfaction that *but for* the conduct complained of, no injury would have resulted. In this illustration, the plaintiff cannot say that but for a failure to have properly functioning tail lights, no collision would have occurred.

Courts may look for material cause

The "but for" test is the general test for **causation**. Where this test is unworkable, as where multiple causes bring about a single harm, the courts will look for material causation (whether the conduct complained of materially contributed to the injury or loss). If the defendant is part of the cause of an injury, the defendant may be liable even though her act alone was insufficient to cause the injury. For example, with respect to tainted blood, the Red Cross was found negligent in employing certain donor screening procedures. Even though others, such as the blood donors, may have been part of the cause of the injury, the Red Cross was held liable because the Court found that its carelessness was a material cause of injury to the recipients of tainted blood.[27]

CASE SUMMARY 5.5

Material Contribution Test Only Applied in Exceptional Cases: *Resurfice Corp. v. Hanke*[28]

Ralph Hanke suffered severe burns in an explosion at an ice arena in Edmonton. The ice resurfacing machine he was operating had both a gasoline tank and a water tank, which unfortunately were situated adjacent to each other. Hanke mistakenly placed the hot

---

25. 1995 CanLII 2602 (BC CA).
26. *Zhang v. Kan*, 2003 BCSC 5 (CanLII); and *Jones v. Rostvig*, 2003 BCSC 1222 (CanLII).
27. *Walker Estate v. York-Finch General Hospital*, 2001 SCC 23 (CanLII).
28. 2007 SCC 7 (CanLII).

water hose into the machine's gasoline tank, resulting in the release of vaporized gasoline into the air, which then ignited.

Hanke sued the manufacturer and distributor of the ice resurfacing machine claiming negligent design: It was too easy to confuse the gasoline tank and the water tank, given their appearance and proximity. The trial judge dismissed the action, concluding that Hanke was not confused and that the design of the machine had not caused the accident. On appeal, the Court concluded that rather than apply the "but for" test, the trial judge should have considered the comparative blameworthiness of the parties and applied the material causation test. Since the design was one cause leading to the explosion, the defendant was held liable.

But the Supreme Court of Canada reversed the Alberta Court of Appeal's decision; it asserted that "the basic test for determining causation remains the 'but for' test. This applies to multi-cause injuries. The plaintiff bears the burden of showing that 'but for' the negligent act or omission of each defendant, the injury would not have occurred. Having done this, contributory negligence may be apportioned . . ." The "but for" test thus remains the fundamental rule as it recognizes that compensation for negligent conduct should only be made where a substantial connection between the injury and the defendant's conduct is present.

The Supreme Court conceded that there are exceptions to the basic "but for" test where a "material contribution" test is to be used, but stated that generally two requirements are to be satisfied for the material contribution test to be properly applied:

> First, it must be impossible for the plaintiff to prove that the defendant's negligence caused the plaintiff's injury using the "but for" test. The impossibility must be due to factors that are outside of the plaintiff's control; for example, current limits of scientific knowledge. Second, it must be clear that the defendant breached a duty of care owed to the plaintiff, thereby exposing the plaintiff to an unreasonable risk of injury, and the plaintiff must have suffered that form of injury. In other words, the plaintiff's injury must fall within the ambit of the risk created by the defendant's breach. In those exceptional cases where these two requirements are satisfied, liability may be imposed, even though the "but for" test is not satisfied, because it would offend basic notions of fairness and justice to deny liability by applying a "but for" approach.[29]

> Evidently, the existence of multiple causes is not enough to relax the test. To find the defendant liable in negligence, the plaintiff generally will need to establish that "but for" the defendant's negligence, injury would not have occurred.

SMALL BUSINESS PERSPECTIVE

This decision may offer good news to manufacturers, because it is insufficient that one's product may have contributed to an injury. Unless the product or its design directly caused the injury, the manufacturer will not be held liable.

REMOTENESS TEST—LEGAL CAUSATION

Once the plaintiff has established that the defendant owed a duty to be careful to the plaintiff, that the defendant's conduct fell below the standard of care required in the situation, and that the conduct complained of caused some injury or loss to the plaintiff, negligence is established. Problems sometimes arise, however, when the connection between the conduct complained of and the injury seems tenuous or where the nature of the injury suffered is unusual or unexpected. For example, if a careless driver were to damage a power pole, causing an interruption of power to a business and thereby resulting in considerable economic loss, should the driver be held responsible for such an unexpected result? The suggestion is that the con-

Problem of remoteness

---

29. *Resurfice Corp. v. Hanke*, [2007] 1 SCR 333, 2007 SCC 7 (CanLII).

nection between the conduct complained of and the actual damage suffered is too remote. In Canada today, our courts will impose liability only when the defendant could have reasonably anticipated the general nature of the injury or damage suffered. Liability is avoided if the injury is too remote or too unforeseeable. As Justice Dickson in *Ontario v. Coté* explained, "It is not necessary that one foresee the precise concatenation of events; it is enough to fix liability if one can foresee in a general way the class or character of injury which occurred."[30]

Foreseeability of the type of injury is critical

The **remoteness test** is often confused with the test to determine whether a duty of care exists, since both are based on reasonable foreseeability. However, with duty of care the test is used to determine whether *danger to the plaintiff* should have been anticipated, whereas with remoteness it is the *type of injury* itself that must have been foreseen.

CASE SUMMARY 5.6

Fly Phobia Not Foreseeable: *Mustapha v. Culligan of Canada Ltd.*[31]

Mustapha was replacing an empty bottle of drinking water with a full one when he saw a dead fly and part of another dead fly in the unopened replacement bottle. His reaction was surprisingly severe. The incident caused him so much distress that he developed a major depressive disorder, phobia, and anxiety. At trial, he was awarded an amount that shocked many—$80000 in general damages, $24174 in special damages, and $237600 in damages for loss of business.

On appeal, the Supreme Court of Canada agreed that there was a duty owed to Mustapha that had been breached. Injury had indeed been caused. But what Mustapha failed to show was that it was foreseeable that a person of ordinary fortitude would suffer injury from seeing flies in a bottle of drinking water he was about to install. Such an injury, even if imaginable, was too remote. Accordingly, the claim was dismissed.

SMALL BUSINESS PERSPECTIVE

The above decision indicates that unusual or excessive reactions to events caused by negligence are not reasonably foreseeable. If a *type* of injury is too unlikely or too remote to foresee, then even if such a loss is suffered liability will not be imposed. Thus, even where one's negligence directly causes an injury, liability will not be imposed if the type of injury is unforeseeable.

Anns case is applied to determine the existence of duty

The problem of remoteness may arise twice in a negligence action. The proximity of the parties is considered when determining if a duty of care is owed. Further, when applying the second half of the *Anns* test, the courts ask, Was there any reason that the duty should not be imposed? Should the scope of the duty be reduced? Should the class to whom the duty is owed be limited, or should the damages be reduced? In addressing these issues the courts will sometimes be influenced by the remoteness of the injuries or damages suffered. Second, remoteness is a factor in determining causation.

We take our victims as we find them

Nonetheless, where the *nature* or type of injury is foreseeable but not the *extent* or gravity of a personal injury the rule is clear: *We take our victims as we find them.* If personal injury is a foreseeable consequence of a motor vehicle collision, then one is liable for the full extent of injuries suffered. If a person has osteoporosis, brittle bones, or an "egg-shell-thin skull," we cannot avoid responsibility by claiming that we could not reasonably be expected to foresee the special condition. If a

---

30. 1974 CanLII 31 (SCC), [1976] 1 S.C.R. 595 at 604.
31. 2008 SCC 27 (CanLII).

person experiences greater injury from our conduct than would be expected because of a unique physical condition, there is nonetheless a responsibility to compensate for all consequences of the injury.[32] This principle is often referred to as the **thin skull rule**.

Thus, if through our negligence we cause a concert pianist to lose the use of his hand, we can't escape liability for the greater loss by claiming we could not have anticipated that the person we would hurt would be a concert pianist. But we must not take this principle too far. If the concert pianist had a deteriorating condition in his hand such as arthritis, and in a short time would have lost the use of it anyway, we are not responsible for the lost career since those damages would have taken place in any case. This has been dubbed the **crumbling skull rule** and must be used in conjunction with the thin skull rule.[33] When a court applies the crumbling skull rule, it recognizes the pre-existing frailties and the award of damages aims at restoring the plaintiff to that (original) position.[34]

Not responsible for inevitable loss

Defences

LO ⑤

VOLUNTARY ASSUMPTION OF RISK

Historically, where a plaintiff voluntarily assumed the risk of injury this operated as a complete bar to recovery of damages. An example might be knowingly getting into a car with a drunk driver. This is referred to as *volenti non fit injuria*. Today the principle is much more restrictive. To escape liability the defendant must show that the plaintiff not only assumed the physical risk but also the legal risk. As stated by Justice Estey, *volenti* will arise "only where there can truly be said to be an understanding on the part of both parties that the defendant assumed no responsibility to take due care of the plaintiff, and the plaintiff did not expect him to."[35] This essentially requires that the person assuming the risk make it clear that she is also completely absolving the other party of any responsibility—something that is rarely done. Thus, a successful claim of *volenti* is rare today.

The law will not assist those who volunteer to bear the risk

But assumption of legal risk must also be clear

The courts now usually deal with such foolhardy behaviour under the heading of **contributory negligence**, which permits the courts to apportion the loss between the parties—a much more satisfactory result. This rejection of *volenti* in favour of contributory negligence was evident in the *Crocker v. Sundance* case discussed in Case Summary 5.7.

CASE SUMMARY 5.7

Defences to Negligence: *Crocker v. Sundance Northwest Resorts Ltd.*[36]

Crocker went to the Sundance Mountain Resort and participated in an inner tube race run by the resort for the entertainment of its patrons. The competition involved going down a steep portion of the ski hill containing many moguls, which caused the inner tubes and participants to be bounced around like "rag dolls."

Crocker entered the competition by signing, but not reading, an entry form that contained a waiver absolving the resort of responsibility. The first time he went down the hill

---

32. *Tsalamandris v. MacDonald*, 2011 BCSC 1138 (CanLII).

33. *Athey v. Leonati*, 1996 CanLII 183 (SCC).

34. For example, see *Whitfield v. Calhoun*, 1999 ABQB 244 (CanLII), where the plaintiff developed antisocial, paranoid, and schizoid behaviour and depression as a result of a motor vehicle collision. His pre-existing personality traits contributed to these psychological problems and the reduced damages reflected this original predisposition.

35. *Dube v. Labar*, 1 SCR 649 Supreme Court Judgments. Copyright © 1986 by Supreme court of Canada. Reproduced by the permission of the Supreme Court of Canada.

36. 1988 CanLII 45 (SCC).

he won his heat, but by the second heat it was clear he had been drinking and the operators suggested he not compete. He had consumed several drinks at the bar and some brandy given to him by the driver of the beer van. Crocker insisted on continuing in the competition and when he dropped his tube down the hill, the operators supplied him with another. On his second run he was thrown from the inner tube and seriously injured.

The Supreme Court of Canada found that the resort organized a dangerous competition for commercial gain. It owed a duty to be careful, especially to visibly intoxicated participants where the potential for injury was great—potentially more so than with sober individuals. Although Crocker was initially cautioned not to proceed with the second run, Sundance later supplied him with a replacement tube. The resort thus failed its duty to keep intoxicated contestants from competing and injuring themselves, and because of its negligence was liable for the injuries suffered.

Sundance asserted the defence that Crocker had voluntarily assumed the risk, pointing to the signed waiver. The Court rejected the *volenti non fit injuria* argument. By voluntarily participating in the race, Crocker had assumed only the physical risk, not the legal risk. The signed waiver didn't apply since he had not read it and insufficient steps were taken to alert Crocker of its presence in the entry form. However, Crocker had also been negligent. Because of his contributory negligence Crocker was held responsible for 25 percent of the loss.

This case illustrates the requirement of the existence of a duty of care, use of the reasonable person test to determine whether sufficient care was exercised, and the operation of contributory negligence in reducing the award of damages. It further illustrates the significant restriction on the defence of *volenti non fit injuria*, which can only be used where there is an assumption of both the legal risk and the physical risk.

DISCUSSION QUESTIONS

So what should an event organizer do to eliminate its potential liability? Is it ever safe to rely solely on waivers? What further steps should be taken to ensure participants know and accept the risks as their own? Is backup protection in the form of insurance a virtual necessity?

CONTRIBUTORY NEGLIGENCE

Previously, when a defendant could show that the plaintiff was also careless, contributing to his own loss, it was a complete bar to recovery. This was an all-or-nothing result and was clearly unfair. The courts then developed the **last clear chance doctrine**, which held the person who had the last opportunity to avoid the accident and failed to do so completely responsible. This wasn't much better, so most jurisdictions have since adopted a legislated compromise where both parties are held responsible.

Legislation allows apportionment of responsibility

Alberta's *Contributory Negligence Act*[37] and Ontario's *Negligence Act*[38] are examples of this compromise; the all-or-nothing approach is abandoned and the courts are directed to apportion responsibility between the parties who contributed to the loss. Compensation must be paid in proportion to that assigned responsibility. Thus if a collision is caused where one driver fails to stop at a light and the other is adjusting his radio and not paying attention, both have contributed to the accident. The courts assign a degree of fault to each party (for example 80 percent on one driver and 20 percent on the other) and liability is apportioned accordingly. Refer to MyBusLawLab for specific provincial details.

---

[37] R.S.A. 2000, c. C-27.
[38] R.S.O. 1990, c. N.1.

Some jurisdictions have included provisions in their occupiers' liability acts absolving the occupier of responsibility where the visitor has voluntarily assumed the risk. Ontario's *Occupiers' Liability Act*, for example, stipulates that the duty to exercise reasonable care "does not apply in respect of risks willingly assumed by the person who enters on the premises."[39] The Supreme Court of Canada has interpreted this provision in the same restrictive way; the occupier will be absolved of responsibility only where it is clear that the visitor has assumed the legal risk as well as the physical risk.[40]

Occupier is not liable if the visitor voluntarily assumed all risks

REDUCING RISK 5.2

Businesses may require customers to sign waivers, counting on these waivers to prove that the customer voluntarily assumed the risks. As is evident from the case law, however, the onus is on the party trying to claim protection under the waiver to show that the customer knew the physical risks and accepted them. Second, the customer must appreciate that she is releasing the business from legal liability. A sophisticated client knows that unless the waiver is brought to the customer's attention, it may not be worth the paper it's written on. To be effective, waivers should also be explained and assented to. Even then, if the customer does not fully appreciate the physical risks (as with novice students who are learning a new physical activity), the waiver will be insufficient. Insurance to cover against liability may be a necessary backup.

Does *volenti* apply to remove liability to a rescuer? If the rescuer gets hurt, can it be said that he voluntarily assumed the risk? A mother who is injured when she jumps in front of a train to save her child can hold the railway responsible for failing to have proper barriers. If the rescuer is injured, the author of the danger cannot escape liability by claiming the rescuer voluntarily assumed the risk. If the potential danger was reasonably foreseeable, so was the potential need for a rescue. The person who caused the danger must pay compensation to both the victim and the injured rescuer.[41] Similarly, the principle of *volenti* does not apply to work-related accidents, even if the work being performed is inherently dangerous. The employer cannot avoid liability, arguing that the employee voluntarily participated in the work.

Duty is owed to rescuers

ILLEGALITY (*EX TURPI CAUSA*)

Plaintiffs harmed while acting illegally or immorally may be denied recovery in tort law. The maxim *ex turpi causa, non oritur actio* suggests that "an action does not arise from a base cause." In simple terms, the courts should refuse to entertain a lawsuit brought by a party who engaged in unlawful activity. Generally, the illegal conduct must cause the loss to the plaintiff before the defence will operate.[42]

There is little judicial enthusiasm for this defence and cases where a tort action has been defeated by the *ex turpi causa* maxim are rare. Yet it was recently used successfully in the *Zastowny* case,[43] where a former inmate sued for wages lost while imprisoned. As stated by the Court, the only justification for the application of *ex turpi causa* is preservation of the integrity of the legal system. To allow an inmate to recover lost wages while incarcerated would constitute a rebate of the natural consequence of the penalty provided by criminal law. Thus, *ex turpi causa* prevented an award of damages for lost wages from being made.

***Ex turpi causa* is applied to prevent injustice**

39. *Occupiers' Liability Act*, R.S.O. 1990, c. O.2, s. 4. Copyright © 1990 by Queen's Printer for Ontario. Used by the permission of Queen's Printer for Ontario.
40. *Waldick v. Malcolm*, 1991 CanLII 71 (SCC).
41. *Videan v. British Transport Commission*, [1963] 2 All E.R. 860 (C.A.).
42. *Cement LaFarge v. B.C. Lightweight Aggregate*, 1983 CanLII 23 (SCC).
43. *British Columbia v. Zastowny*, 2008 SCC 4 (CanLII).

CASE SUMMARY 5.8

Contributory Negligence Preferred over *Ex Turpi Causa* and *Volenti*: *Hall v. Hebert*[44]

Hebert owned a "souped-up muscle car." After consuming a large amount of alcohol with Hall, Hebert stalled that vehicle on an unlit gravel road and proceeded to lose the keys. Hebert suggested they attempt a rolling start and Hall asked to take the wheel. Both men were clearly drunk, and in the process of rolling the car to start it Hall lost control of the vehicle. It rolled over into a gravel pit and Hall was severely injured. Clearly, Hebert owed Hall a duty to be careful, which he breached by letting his intoxicated friend drive the car. The issue before the Supreme Court of Canada was whether *volenti non fit injuria* or *ex turpi causa* would operate as a complete bar to recovery of damages.

For *volenti* to apply, the Court would have to find that it was clear to both parties that "the defendant assumed no responsibility to take care for the safety of the plaintiff and the plaintiff did not expect him to do so." The Court found that the plaintiff assumed the physical risk, but there was no indication that he had assumed the legal risk as well.

As to the application of *ex turpi causa*, Justice McLachlin, writing for the majority, stated:

> [T]here is a need in the law of tort for a principle which permits judges to deny recovery to a plaintiff on the ground that to do so would undermine the integrity of the justice system. The power is a limited one. Its use is justified where allowing the plaintiff's claim would introduce inconsistency into the fabric of the law, either permitting the plaintiff to profit from an illegal or wrongful act, or to evade a penalty prescribed by criminal law. Its use is not justified where the plaintiff's claim is merely for compensation for personal injuries sustained as a consequence of the negligence of the defendant.

Since neither *ex turpi causa* nor *volenti* applied, the Court was then free to apply the principle of contributory negligence and apportion the loss between the parties.

DISCUSSION QUESTION

The defences of *volenti* and *ex turpi causa* are rarely successful today. Instead, the courts demonstrate a preference toward apportioning the loss on the basis of contributory negligence. Is this a better approach or should people assume the whole loss when they are foolish enough to put themselves in harm's way?

LO **6** ## Legislation Impacting Duty of Care

Although the foreseeability test and reasonable person standard discussed in the context of negligence are extremely important, there are many situations where the obligation to exercise care has been changed by statute. Examples include the *Occupiers' Liability Acts* and *Innkeepers' Acts* discussed below. The *Motor Vehicle Acts* of the provinces also create special categories of duty that make people responsible for the condition of their car even if they were not aware of a defect. Such statutes may also impose liability upon the owner of a vehicle if their vehicle is involved in an offence even when the owner was not driving the vehicle. Alberta's *Traffic Safety Act*,[45] for example, provides that unless the vehicle was driven without the owner's expressed or implied consent, the owner of the vehicle will be held guilty of any offence committed by the driver.

---

44. 1993 CanLII 141 (SCC).
45. R.S.A. 2000, c. T-6, s. 160.

As a general rule, however, these statutes do not create new categories of tort unless they specifically say so. Thus, *Human Rights Acts* and privacy legislation may impose new obligations on people, but violations of these obligations do not amount to a tort unless the Act says they do. Some jurisdictions have also changed tort law with respect to automobile collisions. Because of the devastating losses and injuries associated with this area, many provinces have turned to compulsory insurance schemes. Some jurisdictions have gone further, instituting **"no fault" programs** by which people are treated the same and compensated for their injuries whether they were at fault or not. Ontario, in the face of exploding settlements, has passed controversial legislation setting a threshold for physical injury that must be met before **non-pecuniary damages** (damages based on non-monetary factors) for such things as pain and suffering can be awarded. Refer to MyBusLawLab to determine regional differences.

Modifications imposed by statute

The trend away from fault

It is also possible to create a duty of care by statute where none existed before. In common law, a mother owes no duty of care to an unborn child, and this has caused tragic results when an unborn child was injured in an automobile accident caused by the negligence of the mother. Owing no duty to the unborn child, the mother could not be held liable for the fetus's injuries; but because the mother's insurer would pay only if the mother was held liable, no insurance proceeds were payable to cover the injuries to the unborn child. (See the *Dobson* case in Case Summary 5.3). Alberta has passed legislation that overcomes this difficulty by creating a duty of care between the mother and the unborn child where there is such insurance coverage.[46]

Statutes may create duty of care

OCCUPIERS' LIABILITY

In common law, people who occupy property have a special obligation to people who are injured on their property. Note that this obligation rests with the occupier, not the owner; thus, where the property is leased the duty falls on the tenant, not the landlord.

Occupiers owe a special duty of care

In common law, the obligation to look out for the welfare of visitors varies with their status. A person coming onto a property for a business purpose is referred to as an **invitee**. A person on the property with permission but for a non-business purpose is a **licensee**. A person there without permission is a **trespasser**. The occupier must take reasonable steps to protect invitees from unusual dangers. This may extend to putting up a fence around an elevator shaft or providing a hard hat. The duty toward licensees is lower, requiring the occupier only to take reasonable steps to warn of hidden dangers on the property; here, a sign would suffice. The only duty to a trespasser is not to wilfully or recklessly cause her harm.

Most provinces have passed legislation eliminating the distinction between invitees and licensees, imposing an obligation on occupiers to take reasonable steps to protect all classes of visitors to their property. The definition of *occupier* varies; often it is broad enough to include both the tenant and landlord, with liability being imposed upon the party responsible for or in control of the premises.[47] As for trespassers, most jurisdictions retain the common law minimum obligation not to wilfully or recklessly cause them injury. In some provinces, this minimal duty also applies to those visitors who voluntarily assume the risk of dangerous conditions on the property. But for trespassers who are children, the duty of care may well equate that extended to visitors. When assessing whether an occupier was careful enough, the age of the child, their ability to appreciate the danger, and other such factors may be considered. These rules vary from province to province, so refer to MyBusLawLab for provincial variations.

Invitee/licensee distinction may no longer be important

---

46. *Maternal Tort Liability Act*, S.A. 2005, c. M-7.5.
47. See *Taylor v. Allen*, 2010 ONCA 596 (CanLII), where in addition to the tenant the landlord was held liable for the injuries suffered by the plaintiff who fell into an outdoor fire pit. Because the landlord was found responsible for the "maintenance or repair of those premises" he owed the plaintiff a duty of care.

Generally, the legislation requires that occupiers of premises owe a duty to take such reasonable care that people will be reasonably safe in using the premises; this duty may also extend to any property brought onto the premises. Further, that duty to exercise care applies in relation to (1) the condition of the premises, (2) the activities on the premises, or (3) the conduct of third parties on the premises. In other words, it is not necessary to apply the foreseeability test to establish whether a duty is owed; instead, the legislation imposes and describes this duty.

CASE SUMMARY 5.9

Fun Fraught with Risk: *Hutchison v. Daredevil Park Inc.*[48]; *Christensen v. Calgary*[49]; *Galka v. Stankiewicz*[50]

Fun is great, except when it exposes you to lots of liability! Hutchison, a 49-year-old father, took his family to the water park and broke his ankle the first time he used the serpentine waterslide. He did not receive instruction from the attendant on how to enter the slide. Relying on the *Occupiers' Liability Act*, liability was imposed on the operator of the park because it failed to install signs or lines in the entry section warning not to step beyond the line. Pursuant to the Act, an occupier owes visitors a duty to take reasonable steps to ensure visitors will be safe. General damages of $45 000 were awarded to Hutchison, but as the Court found contributory negligence, damages were reduced by the 20 percent attributed to his lack of care.

Similarly in the *Christensen* case, the City was held liable to inline skaters; it failed to take reasonable precautions to ensure inline skaters would be reasonably safe in using park paths. Evidence established that the City knew the paths were used for inline skating, yet it never consulted inline skaters in designing the path. The path included a steep hill—making it difficult for skaters to control their speed—followed by a sharp curve. In light of the gravity of the danger posed, the design and signage were found to be inadequate. Once again, damages were reduced by the percentage attributed to the skaters' contributory negligence.

But on occasion the occupier is excused of liability simply because the accident was so unpredictable that the occupier could not have been reasonably expected to foresee or prevent it. That was the finding in the *Galka* case, where the City, as operator of an archery range, escaped liability after the plaintiff was shot with an arrow that pierced his eye and lodged itself in his brain. The plaintiff put himself in danger by going downrange of the target to look for lost arrows, conduct that was expressly prohibited by rules posted at the range. Applying the "but for" test, the plaintiff failed to establish that any alleged negligence by the City effectively caused his losses.

SMALL BUSINESS PERSPECTIVE

These cases underline the importance of considering risk of harm when designing or operating recreational spaces. Waivers can be used, but their usefulness is questionable where participants are novices and may not appreciate the physical risks inherent in the activities engaged in.

A special problem arises when alcohol is served. The courts are willing to hold commercial dispensers of alcoholic beverages at least partially responsible when a patron becomes intoxicated and is injured or injures others.[51] Businesses supplying liquor at company activities have also been liable for subsequent drinking-

---

48. [2003] O.J. No. 1570 (S.C.J.).

49. [2011] A.J. No. 923 (C.A.).

50. [2010] O.J. No. 2046 (S.C.J.).

51. See *Holton v. MacKinnon*, 2005 BCSC 41 (CanLII), where the Court held that the bar's employees should have foreseen the risk that one of the three drunk friends would drive and should have taken steps to intervene.

related injuries,[52] but the Supreme Court of Canada has so far refused to extend this responsibility to social hosts holding private parties (see the *Childs* case in Case Summary 5.3). It should be noted that the door is still open to a more compelling case, possibly where the hosts actually supplied the liquor to someone they knew was driving and they knew was getting drunk. For example, in *Kim v. Thammavong*, a negligence action was brought against a 20-year-old who held a party in her parents' home while they were on vacation. One of the guests was injured by an intoxicated guest. The Court refused to dismiss the action summarily as against the host:

> In the case at bar, in terms of foreseeability and proximity, the relationship between the defendant Tracy and the plaintiff Mr. Kim is somewhat closer than the relationship between the parties in *Childs*, because Mr. Kim was a guest at the party and not a third-party passenger in a car some distance away. In my opinion, whether there is "something more" in the circumstances of the party hosted by Tracy that led to the injuries suffered by Mr. Kim is a genuine issue for trial.[53]

Commercial hosts' liability is a reality

Social host liability is on the horizon

It is reasonable to anticipate social host liability being imposed in the near future.

INNKEEPERS' LIABILITY

At common law, an innkeeper—being in a unique position—was required to protect his guests from the wrongful acts of others, even when the innkeeper or servant was not at fault. Only when the damage or loss to a guest's property was caused by that guest's own negligence was the innkeeper relieved of this responsibility. Again, most jurisdictions have modified this obligation by statute and impose liability only when the innkeeper or his servants are negligent. Note that this reduction in liability is available only where the innkeeper has carefully complied with the statute by placing notices at designated locations. (Refer to MyBusLawLab to review the specific legislation and note how it is applied.)

 REDUCING RISK 5.3

Even where there is no physical contact between the business, its staff, and the client, care should be taken to ensure that the premises and the activities thereon are safe and secure. The best method of risk avoidance is to carefully inspect the premises and examine the practices of the business, anticipating what might go wrong and taking steps to correct the problems. A sophisticated client may thus charge an individual or committee with the responsibility of finding such dangers or risks and removing them. Occupational health and safety laws already impose duties on employers to conduct audits to determine what the hazards are in a workplace and provide safety training. Providing similar training for staff and management in the area of risk awareness and avoidance is likewise a smart move.

Strict Liability

LO **7**

Tort law generally requires the demonstration of fault, but there are some situations where liability will be imposed even where there is no fault on the part of the defendant who has acted completely reasonably. Note that this discussion of **strict liability** must be distinguished from those situations where fault is required but the standard imposed is extremely high, such as where dangerous products, processes, or animals are involved. The liability of food handlers, for example, approaches strict liability because extreme care is demanded by law in light of the potential for illness or contamination.

---

52. *Jacobsen v. Nike Canada Ltd.*, 1996 CanLII 3429 (BC SC).
53. [2008] O.J. No. 4908 (S.C.J.), affirming 2007 CanLII 52791 (ON SC) [para. 25].

When dangerous things escape

The case of *Rylands v. Fletcher*,[54] however, established that strict liability arises in certain circumstances where liability will be imposed regardless of absence of fault. The defendant had built a reservoir on his property, but under the surface there was a shaft from a coal mine leading to his neighbour's property. The water escaped, flooding his neighbour's mine. The defendant was in no way negligent, having no knowledge of the underground shaft. Still, the Court held him liable for the damage. The principle applied was that if a person brings something inherently dangerous, such as stored water or explosives, onto his property and it escapes, the occupier is liable for any damage.

Must be an unusual use of property

It must be noted that strict liability will not be imposed unless the use of the property is unusual. Today, electricity and plumbing are part of normal operations for modern buildings, and damage caused by these conveniences will normally not support a claim of strict liability. On the other hand, the escape of flammable gases because of an unusual use of land can lead the court to impose strict liability. The escape of methane gas from a municipal landfill site in the *Gertsen v. Municipality of Metropolitan Toronto*[55] case demonstrates the application of this rule. There it was reasonably foreseeable that the decomposition of organic material would create methane gas. The gas filled a garage located on a nearby property and an explosion was ignited when the plaintiff tried to start his car. The municipality was held strictly liable for the personal injury and property damage caused.

VICARIOUS LIABILITY

Vicarious liability of employer

Vicarious liability is also a form of strict liability in that the employer is being held responsible for the wrongful acts of an employee even though the employer has done nothing wrong. The imposition of vicarious liability is limited to those situations where the employee is carrying out her employment responsibilities. Vicarious liability was introduced in the previous chapter and will be discussed in more depth in Chapter 12 under the heading "Liability of Employer."

Product Liability

Breach of duty must be shown for product liability

Manufactured products are often dangerous, either because of some inherent defect or because of their nature, such as in the case of chemicals, tools, or explosives. In the United States it is often enough to show that the product was defective and that the defect caused the injury. This is a strict liability approach requiring no demonstration of fault on the part of the manufacturer. In Canada, however, it is still necessary to establish fault when suing manufacturers for some injury or loss caused by their product. Not only is it necessary to establish that there was a duty to be careful, it is also necessary to prove that there was a failure to live up to that duty. Either the manufacturer or an employee must be shown to have been negligent or careless.

Lack of intervening inspection confirms duty rests with manufacturer

Donoghue v. Stevenson, discussed in Case Summary 5.2, had a significant impact on **product liability** in tort law. Historically, if there was no privity of contract between the manufacturer and the party injured by the product, an action for breach of contract could not succeed. Further, because there were usually several intervening parties between the manufacturer and the ultimate consumer of a product, it was thought that the manufacturer owed no duty of care to the ultimate consumer. The *Donoghue* case established that if a product was designed in such a way as to get into the hands of the consumer without intervening inspection or modification, a duty of care did exist. Now with the prevalence of prepackaged and complicated manufactured goods, there is even less likelihood that a problem will be disclosed by intermediate inspection. It is thus much more difficult for a manufacturer to deny the existence of a duty of care. This duty, if coupled with evidence of a breach of that duty, will impose liability on the producer of the product.

---

54. (1868), L.R. 3 H.L. 330.
55. 1973 CanLII 606 (ON SC).

Over time the obligation to exercise care has been extended so that those repairing or assembling a product, in addition to those manufacturing the product, may all owe a duty of care to the consumer. Further, it is not just the purchaser who is owed a duty of care. Where the purchaser buys the product for a third party, the courts may regard the purchaser as the agent for the ultimate consumer. In this way, a child who eats a spoiled food item purchased by his parent can nonetheless maintain an action against the manufacturer. The parent will be regarded as the child's agent in making the purchase.

The *Donoghue* case suggested that a duty is owed by the manufacturer to the consumer if a product was designed in such a way as to get into the hands of the consumer without intervening inspection or modification.[56] But what if there is opportunity for intervening inspection, or worse, for tampering? Does the onus fall on the consumer to prove that there was no tampering? It appears that the courts prefer to put the onus on the manufacturer to prove tampering or interference—if that party hopes to avoid liability.

Onus is on the manufacturer to establish tampering or interference

On the other hand, where there has been intermediate inspection or modification of a product it is unlikely that the courts will find that the manufacturer still owes a duty of care to the ultimate consumer. The rationale for this rebuttal of duty is that where intermediate inspection is contemplated and has occurred, it is no longer reasonably foreseeable that the product would be used and cause harm despite the discovery of a defect. If harm is not foreseeable, a duty does not arise. Thus, in *Viridian Inc. v. Bovar Inc.*,[57] the manufacturer was able to avoid liability to the end user. The manufacturer was to supply a stock item (iron diaphragms) and the distributor was to inspect the same and, if approved, deliver them to customers for use in their plants. It was the clear intention of all parties that there was to be intermediate inspection of the product before use, and inspection did, in fact, take place. The manufacturer was entitled to rely on that inspection to ensure that the product was not defective for the intended use and was used properly. The Court decided that in these circumstances the manufacturer did not owe the end user a duty of care.

Intermediate inspection rebuts the existence of duty

Note, however, that the manufacturer may not be able to rely on the principle of intermediate examination where the product it supplies is not significantly different from that delivered to the end user, as in the case discussed in Case Summary 5.10.

CASE SUMMARY 5.10

Foam Party Flops—Manufacturer and Supplier Jointly Liable: *376599 Alberta Ltd. v. Tanshaw Products Inc.*[58]

Back Alley, a popular nightclub, held a foam party with disastrous results. Its patrons suffered significant skin and eye irritation from the chemical concentrate used to make the bubbles; many were hospitalized. The party promoter had used a Texan supplier of the chemicals in the past but had turned to the defendant Tanshaw seeking to save costs. Tanshaw provided a sample of the Texan product to its supplier, Debro, which in turn created and supplied Tanshaw with the chemical concentrate used at the party. A successful trial party was held at the Back Alley, but before the second party Debro supplied Tanshaw with undiluted concentrate that was different from that used at the test party.

After paying out close to half a million dollars to settle claims, Back Alley sued Tanshaw and the manufacturer, Debro, seeking contribution and indemnity. Back Alley claimed it suffered continued lost profits on top of the sums paid out to those injured.

---

56. *Supra* note 3, at 599.
57. 2002 ABCA 173 (CanLII).
58. 2005 A.J. No. 670 (Q.B.); for the judgment on costs, see *Matthews v. Landex Investments Ltd.*, 2006 ABQB 470 (CanLII).

The Court held that the occupier, Back Alley, had exercised sufficient care by holding a test run to ensure patrons would be safe. The injuries were not reasonably foreseeable in light of the successful test party; thus, Back Alley was not liable to its patrons. The issue that remained was whether the manufacturer, Debro, and distributor, Tanshaw, should be held liable for the injuries caused to Back Alley's patrons. Both were aware of the intended use.

Debro claimed that intermediate examination by Tanshaw relieved the manufacturer of owing a duty of care to the party patrons. But the Court determined that the appropriate test was whether it was reasonable that the intermediate party would examine or test the product and whether it was reasonably foreseeable this testing would be of a nature that would reveal the defect. Here Debro knew that Tanshaw was relying on Debro's expertise in producing and recommending a product for use at foam parties. Debro made a specific recommendation to Tanshaw and did not couple that recommendation with a clear caution regarding irritability, nor did it suggest that it would be advisable for Tanshaw to conduct irritation tests. Not only was it readily apparent that Tanshaw possessed a lesser degree of expertise in chemical formulations than Debro, it was well understood by both parties that Debro's recommendations would be relied upon. In these circumstances, it was not reasonable to expect that Tanshaw would independently test or examine the product; in fact, Tanshaw used it as supplied by Debro. Accordingly, the principle of intermediate examination could not be relied upon. As the Court found negligence on the part of both Tanshaw and Debro, liability was equally divided.

SMALL BUSINESS PERSPECTIVE

To escape liability, a manufacturer must show it was reasonable to assume intermediate inspection would be done skillfully and reveal any hidden defects. If a manufacturer is not comfortable with the diligence or skill of the inspector, it must turn to other means to reduce risk. Detailed warnings and employing well-designed waivers may assist in this regard.

Shared liability is preferred

The introduction of contributory negligence legislation has often led to the courts finding shared liability. Both the negligent manufacturer and the negligent inspector may be held jointly liable to the injured consumer. Businesses must thus remain vigilant and not assume that others will eliminate risks for them. Similarly, if it is the plaintiff who has failed to adequately inspect a product before its use, or uses a product despite an apparent defect, she may be held partly responsible. The courts seem to prefer this shared liability approach over finding that the plaintiff's failure to inspect negated the manufacturer's duty to exercise care.[59]

Defective warnings draw liability

Defective products may cause manufacturers to be held liable; liability may also be imposed for negligent designs or negligent warnings. The fact that a design defect only causes injury when coupled with the wrongdoing of the consumer does not preclude manufacturer liability. The onus rests with the manufacturer to post warnings, and these warnings must be reasonably communicated. The warning must also be adequate. The required explicitness of the warning will vary with the danger likely to be encountered. In assessing whether a warning was adequately worded and disseminated, the courts will give weight to the difference in knowledge and expertise of the parties.

---

59. See, for example, *Orlando Corp. v. Bothwell Accurate Co.*, [2001] O.J. No. 1946, (S.C.J.); aff'd [2003] O.J. No. 2036 (C.A.), where the defendant manufacturer and the plaintiff were both held liable for the cost of replacing corroded steel roofs. The plaintiff negligently failed to use a vapour barrier and the manufacturer negligently failed to warn of the likelihood of corrosion if moisture was present. Both partiers thus contributed to the loss.

CASE SUMMARY 5.11

Warning Inadequate in Light of Defective Design: *Nicholson v. John Deere Ltd.*[60]

The Nicholsons purchased a second-hand riding lawnmower manufactured by John Deere Ltd. One day when the lawnmower was being filled with gas, the gas cap rolled off the tank where it had been placed, hitting the exposed battery cable and causing a spark that ignited the gas fumes. The resulting blast burned down the plaintiffs' house.

This was not the first time such an explosion had happened, and John Deere had a program in place to correct the defective design and warn of the problem. The company had placed a warning decal on the gas tank and supplied a battery cover safety kit to owners to remove the danger. There were also several warnings in the operating manual about the danger, but the Nicholsons had purchased the mower used and had not received the manual or been told about the safety kit by the dealer when they had it serviced. The Court held that these efforts on the part of John Deere were inadequate. The manufacturer should have taken much more positive action to make sure the defects were corrected. In addition, the dealer, who had failed to tell the Nicholsons about the danger and the safety kit, was also liable for negligence.

This case is interesting in that it shows the great responsibility placed on a manufacturer when such a defective and dangerous product is produced. Once it had been established that the design was defective and dangerous, it was difficult if not impossible for the manufacturer to show that it was not negligent, despite its stringent efforts to correct the situation.

SMALL BUSINESS PERSPECTIVE

The duty to warn is a continuing one. Once a manufacturer learns of a defect, the duty to warn consumers arises, and this includes both future and past purchasers. Product recalls can be very costly, but failure to take adequate steps to warn and otherwise protect consumers invites liability—and bad publicity.

A particularly difficult problem in product liability cases is to show that someone was "careless" in the manufacturing process. In Canada, the courts are willing to draw, from the circumstantial evidence of the injury or loss, a conclusion that someone must have been negligent, leaving it to the defendant to then produce evidence to the contrary. As discussed above, this **circumstantial evidence** method replaces the *res ipsa loquitur* approach used in the past and also seems more appropriate for product liability cases.[61]

Since it is not easy for a consumer to prove negligent design or production, plaintiffs have often chosen to allege negligent warning as an additional basis for the action. The manufacturer may find itself in a no-win situation. On the one hand, where warnings, cautions, and procedures are in place such that if followed no injury could happen, then they must not have been followed if injury did occur. On the other hand, where communicated precautions were followed and injury still occurred, this suggests the warnings or policies were not adequate. Either way, negligence is established.

Consider the figurative snail in the bottle; once negligence has been inferred from the circumstances of the injury, it will be difficult for the manufacturer to avoid liability unless it can show that it was not careless. Even then, if injury has occurred despite the absence of negligence in its production, does the fact of injury alone suggest that the warning, if any, was inadequate?

Breach of duty can be implied from the circumstances

Inference of negligence demands that the manufacturer prove it was not negligent

Manufacturers must warn and act reasonably to make dangerous products safer

---

60. 1986 CanLII 2502 (ON SC).
61. *Fontaine*, supra note 23.

Where the products are inherently dangerous, as is the case with chemicals, explosives, tools, and pharmaceuticals, the requirements are more stringent. Manufacturers must do all they can to make the products as safe as reasonably possible given the risks. They must also provide appropriate warnings and instructions. In Canada, the courts thus examine whether the warnings and instructions were clear, as well as whether everything reasonably possible had been done to reduce the risk. Adding childproof caps to pharmaceutical products is an example, as is the practice of adding a double-switching mechanism to power tools so they can't be turned on accidentally. Where this has been done effectively and sufficient warnings are included, the manufacturer will likely escape liability. It may be self-evident that the misuse of a knife or table saw might result in injury, but a prudent manufacturer will still include warnings to that effect.

CASE SUMMARY 5.12

Injury Alone Does Not Establish Liability: *More v. Bauer Nike Hockey Inc.*[62]

Darren More, a 17-year-old playing for a AAA midget hockey team, hit the back of his head against the boards during a game. At first he appeared fine, and More made his way to the bench. But his condition deteriorated rapidly; he began to vomit, and his trainer immediately recognized that More had suffered a serious head injury.

More suffered a subdural hematoma. The swelling of his brain caused irreversible and catastrophic damage. Why hadn't his CSA (Canadian Standards Association) Bauer helmet protected him?

A lawsuit was brought forward naming several parties, but eventually only the manufacturer of the helmet and CSA remained as defendants. More's legal team argued that Bauer did not make an adequate helmet and that the CSA's standards were not sufficient. The trial spanned 33 days, where evidence from various experts was presented. It was established More's type of injury was virtually unheard of in Canadian hockey, so the manufacturer was not found liable. The helmet's design did not cause or materially contribute to the injury. As stated by the trial judge, safety devices are inherently dangerous if they fail to provide reasonable protection when in normal use. On the other hand, Bauer was not obligated to design an "accident-free" helmet. It is not an insurer nor should it be held to a standard of perfection.

As to the claim of negligent warning, the CSA, by certifying helmets for public use, must exercise reasonable care to safeguard users of certified helmets by informing them that injury can occur while playing hockey despite wearing a certified helmet. The warning on the helmet was clear that serious injury may occur despite wearing the helmet. As highlighted by the trial judge:

> Equally important, before his accident Darren was aware that people suffer head injuries while playing hockey despite wearing the CSA approved helmets. Darren himself suffered two concussions prior to the accident and at least one other teammate had suffered a concussion while wearing a CSA approved helmet. Darren was clearly aware of the risks associated with playing hockey, even while wearing a helmet, and like hundreds of thousands of other Canadians, chose to play anyway.[63]

More's case was dismissed. It serves as a reminder that injury, no matter how substantial, does not guarantee that others will be held liable. Negligence (or some other tort) must still be proven.

---

62. 2010 BCSC 1395 (CanLII), aff'd. 2011 BCCA 419 (CanLII).
63. *More v. Bauer Nike Hockey Inc.*, 2010 BCSC 1395 (CanLII), at para. 244.

SMALL BUSINESS PERSPECTIVE

Those who manufacturer products for consumers use must sit back and analyze how injuries might occur, both by their use and misuse. Then warnings need to be adequately designed to address foreseeable injuries. Even though More's case failed, manufacturers can and will be held liable where there is sufficient evidence to substantiate a claim of negligent design or manufacture.

Liability for damage or injury caused by products may also be based on contract. When there is such a contract between the parties, there is no need to establish fault. Liability will follow simply by showing the contract has been breached through the sale of the defective product. Contracts will be the subject of the following four chapters. Note that some jurisdictions have passed legislation extending this contractual liability of the seller and manufacturer to injured consumers even where they were not the direct purchaser of the product. For a more complete discussion of contractual product liability, refer to "Consumer Protection" in Chapter 16. New Brunswick and Saskatchewan have gone even further, imposing strict liability for consumer loss upon manufacturers of defective products.[64]

> **Contractual liability exists if the product is defective**

LIABILITY OF PROFESSIONALS AND OTHER EXPERTS

> LO **8**

For business students who are planning to enter professions or who intend to do consulting work, the subject of **professional liability** may be one of the most important covered in this chapter. Experts are simply people who hold themselves out to have some specialized knowledge or skill not generally available. Professionals belong to professional organizations and practise in a specific area of service. These definitions are obviously imprecise. For the purposes of this discussion, the term *professional* should be interpreted expansively rather than restrictively. Whether we are talking about doctors or accountants, designers or building contractors, litigation by clients injured as a result of their services or disgruntled over the quality of their work has had a major impact on professional practice. Not only have the occurrences of such malpractice actions increased dramatically, so too have the damages awarded by the courts. Today, an important consideration for many professionals is the amount of **liability insurance** they must obtain at a very high cost.

> **Professional liability and insurance costs are important aspects of business**

The liability of professionals may be founded in contract law or based on fiduciary duty, but the recent expansion of liability has been in the area of tort law, specifically negligence. Professionals must also adhere to the rules and standards set by their governing bodies. Failure to comply with the rules or unskilled or unprofessional conduct may result in disciplinary action with the potential consequence of losing the right to practise.

> **Liability is based on tort law, contract law, or breach of fiduciary duty**

Contract

In the past, the liability of accountants, bankers, lawyers, business consultants, and other professionals was based on the contract they had with their clients. Contracts will be discussed in the next chapters, but briefly, when professionals provide substandard service they are liable for the losses resulting from the breach of the contract. The actual standard of service expected is normally implied; it is implied that the professional will provide a *reasonable level of performance* given his claimed expertise. Often professionals attempt to limit that liability with terms to that effect included in the contract.

> **Tort standard is implied in a contract, but note the disclaimer**

[64.] See *Consumer Product Warranty and Liability Act*, S.N.B. 1978, c. C-18.1, s. 27; *Consumer Protection Act*, S.S. 1996, c. C-30.1, s. 64.

Tort liability extends beyond the parties to a contract

Because professionals' liability is based on the contract with the client, their liability is also restricted to that client. An outsider has no rights under the agreement. Thus, an accountant's contractual liability for improperly prepared financial statements is limited to the company for which they were prepared. The shareholders and investors have no claim. But in tort law, the courts are willing to expand liability beyond these immediate (contractual) parties. This expansion of potential plaintiffs has had an important impact on the risks faced by accountants and other experts.

Negligence

Extension of tort liability to third parties

The expansion of tort liability has introduced considerable uncertainty into the area of professional liability. The standard of care expected of a professional is reasonably straightforward and will be discussed below. What has changed in recent times is who can sue. Expansion of the duty of care has increased the potential liability of most experts far beyond what it has been. Is an architect liable to a person injured in a collapsed building when errors are found in her designs? Is an accountant liable to shareholders or investors because of erroneous financial statements prepared for a specific corporate client? The extension of liability to these third parties has greatly expanded the risks faced by professionals who provide these services.

TO WHOM IS A DUTY OWED?

Liability may extend beyond the immediate parties

In the past, professionals and other experts faced liability to their clients only for shoddy work (based on contract law) and to their colleagues and clients on the basis of a breach of a fiduciary duty. Liability to strangers or third parties arose only where physical damage or bodily injuries resulted. For example, experts such as architects and engineers, whose services produce physical structures that could cause injury if they failed, might be subject to liability to strangers. On the other hand, if those injured were not immediate parties and their loss (whether caused by physical acts or words) was purely economic, there was considerable reluctance on the part of the courts to extend the professional's liability to them.

The problem with words: economic loss caused by negligent words is recoverable

Today, however, accountants, bankers, lawyers, business consultants, and other professionals giving financial advice may be sued in tort even when their negligent words cause only economic loss. Only in the past few years have courts been willing to grant compensation for this kind of loss.

A. NEGLIGENT MISSTATEMENT

Negligent conduct and negligent words are both actionable

Initially, liability for negligence was limited to *conduct* that fell below an acceptable standard of care. Then, in 1963, the House of Lords in the United Kingdom indicated its willingness to expand this liability to *careless words* (or **negligent statements**) causing economic loss.[65] The Supreme Court of Canada adopted a similar approach in the case of *Haig v. Bamford*.[66] An accounting firm negligently prepared financial statements for a company, knowing that the statements would be used to entice potential investors to purchase shares. Haig relied on these statements in his decision to purchase a number of shares; later he found the company to be considerably less profitable than the incorrect financial statements had led him to believe. As a result, he suffered a financial loss and sued. The Court found that a duty was owed by the accounting firm to the victim, even though there was no contract between them. The services were contracted to the company. Haig was just a potential investor, but it was foreseeable that potential investors would rely on the financial statements when making their decision to buy. Since Haig fell within the class of "foreseeable plaintiffs," a duty of care was owed to anyone that fell within that class of claimants.

---

65. *Hedley Byrne & Co. v. Heller's Partners Ltd.*, [1963] 2 All E.R. 575 (H.L.).
66. 1976 CanLII 6 (SCC).

The case of *Haig v. Bamford* was the first in Canada where accountants were found liable to third-party investors for their negligence in preparing audited financial statements. This decision opened the door to other claims of negligent misstatement. Its impact on the law of negligence in this country has been great, especially with regard to experts such as accountants and lawyers whose liability for economic loss has been extended beyond the actual clients they serve.

Once the Court decided to provide liability for economic loss caused by negligent words, it then had to decide just how far this liability would extend. In fact, the judges in the *Haig* case stopped short of adopting the reasonable foreseeability test, but said that a duty of care was owed only when the person making the misleading statement actually knew it was to be used by an individual or a limited class of people. The problem was that the reasonably foreseeable test as developed in *Donoghue v. Stevenson* was simply too broad when it came to negligent words. The argument was that words were much more volatile, and if that test for duty was used it would expose professionals and other experts to considerably greater liability than would be appropriate. A defendant might be exposed to "liability in an indeterminate amount for an indeterminate time to an indeterminate class." Where does one draw the line?

Negligent misstatement is actionable by third parties even where the loss is purely economic

Reasonable foreseeability test was deemed too broad for negligent words

---

CASE SUMMARY 5.13

Closing the Floodgates: *Hercules Management Ltd. v. Ernst & Young*[67]

The plaintiffs (already shareholders) relied on incorrect financial statements to make further investments in a company. The shareholders were clearly a group that the accountants knew would rely on the statements so, using the *Haig* case, a duty would be owed. But these financial statements were prepared not to encourage further investment. The statements were prepared as required by statute—for review at the annual shareholders' meeting to evaluate the capabilities of the management team. Should accountants' liability extend beyond the purpose for which the statements were prepared?

The Supreme Court of Canada confirmed that the two-part *Anns* test is to be used to determine the existence of a duty of care. First one determines (1) whether a *prima facie* duty of care is owed, and if so (2) one must ask whether it is negated or limited by policy considerations.

In negligent misrepresentation cases, a *prima facie* duty of care exists if the parties were in such proximity or neighbourhood that *reliance* was not just *foreseeable* but *reasonable* as well. A *prima facie* duty arises when (1) the defendant ought reasonably to have foreseen that the plaintiff would rely on his representation, and (2) reliance by the plaintiff would, in the particular circumstances of the case, be reasonable.

The Court stated that reliance by a plaintiff on a defendant's representation will not always be reasonable. The reasonable foreseeability/reasonable reliance test reduces the scope of a representor's potentially infinite liability. Adding the reasonable reliance requirements provides a means of assessing whether the defendant should be compelled to compensate the plaintiff for losses suffered.

The Court recognized that in the area of auditors' liability, the problem of indeterminate liability often arises because the reasonable foreseeability/reasonable reliance test may be satisfied in many if not all such cases. On the facts of this case, the respondents clearly owed a *prima facie* duty of care to the appellants.

Additional factors such as (1) whether the defendant knew the identity of the plaintiff (or the class of plaintiff) and (2) whether the defendant's statements were used for the *specific purpose or transaction* for which they were made ought properly to be considered in the "policy" branch of the test once the first branch concerning "proximity" has been found to be satisfied.

---

67. 1997 CanLII 345 (SCC).

Applying the second part of the *Anns* case test, the Court stated that the accountants' duty extended only to the purpose for which the financial statements were prepared—in this case to assist the collectivity of shareholders of the audited companies in their task of overseeing and evaluating management. The respondents did not prepare the audit reports to assist the shareholders in making personal investment decisions or, indeed, for any purpose other than the standard statutory one. The accountants therefore escaped liability because the plaintiffs failed to establish a duty of care.

DISCUSSION QUESTION

Does the introduction of the reasonable reliance test remove the problem of indeterminate liability to an indeterminate class?

Tort liability of professionals extends beyond clients

Clearly, the *Anns* case remains important in Canadian law, allowing the courts to apply social policy to limit duty and liability where it seems appropriate to do so. It is vital to understand that a duty to be careful exists not only toward one's clients but also toward others who may reasonably rely on the advice or service given. That duty may be reduced or restricted by the application of the second test set out in the *Anns* case, but it is risky to count on the courts applying the *Anns* case test to excuse liability.

Duty is determined by reasonable reliance

To determine the existence of a duty, the courts are now asking whether the plaintiff's reliance on these representations was reasonable. This is especially true where the defendants may have tried to eliminate or reduce their liability by using disclaimers or exculpatory words. To determine if there was "reasonable reliance," courts will consider whether:

1. the defendant had a direct or indirect financial interest in the transaction in respect of which the representation was made;

2. the defendant was a professional or someone who possessed a special skill, judgment, or knowledge;

3. the advice or information was provided in the course of the defendant's business;

4. the information or advice was given deliberately, and not on a social occasion;

5. the information or advice was given in response to a specific inquiry or request.

These indicators have been accepted as helping to distinguish those situations where reliance on a statement is reasonable from those when it is not. In the *Micron Construction* case discussed in Case Summary 5.14, the Court applied these five indicators. Since four of the five were present, the Court concluded that there was "reasonable reliance" on the statements by the plaintiff, establishing that a duty of care did exist in these circumstances.

CASE SUMMARY 5.14

Bank Liable for Careless Words: *Micron Construction Ltd. v. Hong Kong Bank of Canada*[68]

In the process of converting a large office building to another use, the contractors approached the developer's bank for assurances that the developer had funding in place to support the project. The bank responded in writing and in a telephone conversation

---

68. 2000 BCCA 141 (CanLII); leave to appeal to SCC dismissed [2000] S.C.C.A. No. 193.

that the project was well financed and that there were no problems. In fact, at the time of these assurances the developers had failed to advance sufficient security to support the bank loan. Without the security there was no bank loan and the project failed, causing the plaintiff contractors considerable losses.

The plaintiffs sued the bank in question for negligent misrepresentation. The bank had included a disclaimer in its written letter of recommendation and relied on that disclaimer as its main defence. The Court found that it was reasonable for the plaintiffs to rely on the representations of the bank in this matter. They had no other source of information, and the bank supported the project in a very positive manner. The disclaimer was held not to apply because it was reasonable for the contractors to rely on the very clear and explicit representation despite the disclaimer; further, the exact meaning of the disclaimer was not clear except to a banker. A second important factor was that there was no disclaimer associated with the telephone conversation. Since reliance on the statements was found to be reasonable, a duty of care was owed to the contractors.

Applying the second part of the *Anns* case test, the Court found that "no policy concerns arose to impede the assessment of liability." The bank was aware of the developer's failure to provide sufficient securities at the time it made these representations, which it knew were being relied on by the plaintiffs. That conduct amounted to a failure to live up to the required standard of care in the circumstances. Accordingly, the bank was held liable for its employee's negligent misrepresentation.

SMALL BUSINESS PERSPECTIVE

This case nicely illustrates the modern approach to negligent misrepresentation in commercial relationships. How thoroughly must one train employees if their careless statements can lead to liability?

Actions based on negligent misrepresentations can arise in a multitude of settings; it is not just bankers or accountants who may face liability if parties are mislead. In the *Marlin v. Interbrooks Ltd.* case,[69] for example, a negligent misstatement action was successful against a server at a restaurant. The plaintiff, due to his nut allergy, asked the server whether the dessert contained nuts. The server assured him that the cheesecake was nut free. After one bite, the plaintiff was in trouble and needed medical attention. The Court determined that the server owed the plaintiff a duty of care, which he breached by failing to ascertain the cake's contents, something he could have easily done by checking the packaging. Negligent misrepresentation was established because the plaintiff had relied on the server's assurance and suffered injury as a result. General damages of $25 000 plus special damages of $1535 were awarded, for which the hotel owner and restaurant were vicariously liable.

Businesses, particularly those whose staff interact with the public, should impress on their employees the impact their careless words may potentially have. Carelessly made recommendations, when relied upon, can have costly repercussions.

Practices should be adapted to avoid risk

B. BREACH OF STANDARD OF CARE

The standard of care expected from an expert is a little different from that expected from a non-expert. Experts must live up to the standard of a reasonable person *in the circumstances*. There are two problems here: first, the level of skill they must have, and second, how they exercise that skill. Essentially, these people are required to have the skills and abilities that one would expect from an expert or professional in that field. If a person professes to be a medical doctor, he had better have the training and skills of a medical doctor. The same applies to a chartered accountant or investment counsellor; she has to have the training and skills expected of someone in that profession.

Standard is that of a reasonable member of the profession

---

69. [2011] S.J. No. 404 (Q.B.)

GAAP and GAAS set standards for accountants

The accounting professions, for example, have established standards of practice for their members: GAAP (generally accepted accounting principles) and GAAS (generally accepted auditing standards). Where it can be shown that an accountant has failed to live up to these standards, that failure generally will be enough to establish negligence.

Standard of care is set by one's peers

The second problem relates to how that skill is exercised. In assessing liability, the court determines what a reasonable person possessed of the same skills and abilities as the defendant would have done in the circumstances. For a doctor, the test is that of a reasonable doctor; for an accountant, a reasonable accountant. Often the degree of care to be exercised is described by others in one's profession who are called on to testify as to what a reasonable, prudent professional would have done in the circumstances. The standard of care is thus defined by one's peers.

Standard is not lowered for novices

It must be emphasized that a client or patient is not required to tolerate ineptitude on the part of professionals because of inexperience. It may be true that a doctor or mechanic in the first month of employment is more likely to make a mistake, but these people have represented themselves as proficient members of their profession. They must, therefore, live up to the level of competence one would expect of a normal member of their profession functioning in a reasonably prudent manner.

Common practice may not measure up to reasonable standard

It can be helpful to the defendant to show that what he did was common practice among his colleagues. Such common practice in the profession is generally an indication of competent professional service. But this is not always the case. The test is that of a *reasonable* person, not an *average* person. Although one would hope that the average standard of practice in the skilled professions would coincide with the practice one would expect from a reasonable person, this is not always so. When it is obvious that the common practice is dangerous or careless, then such sloppy practice will not be tolerated. The court, in such circumstances, is not reluctant to declare that the common practice falls below the standard of a reasonable person and is, therefore, negligent. This principle was reinforced by the Supreme Court of Canada in the *Waldick v. Malcolm* case, where Justice Iacobucci, quoting Professor Linden, states: "Tort courts have not abdicated their responsibility to evaluate customs, for negligent conduct cannot be countenanced, even when a large group is continually guilty of it." In short, no amount of general community compliance will render negligent conduct "reasonable . . . in all the circumstances."[70] It is clear, however, that to find such negligence in the face of common practice in a profession would happen only in extraordinary circumstances.

CASE SUMMARY 5.15

Not Enough to Follow GAAP: *Kripps v. Touche Ross Co.*[71]

The British Columbia Court of Appeal held that even where accountants follow GAAP (the standard used at the time by the Canadian Institute of Chartered Accountants), they cannot be sure they are acting with sufficient care. In this case, the company Kripps raised funds from investors and then invested those funds in mortgages. In fact, more than $4 million of its mortgages (about one-third of the company's entire investment portfolio) were in default, and this was not disclosed in the 1983 financial statements even though the auditors were aware of the situation. The unpaid interest on those mortgages was added to the principal, inflating the apparent value of the asset. The Court held that the investors were misled by the accounting statements, and the accountants were held liable even though they had carefully followed GAAP. They did

---

70. 1991 CanLII 71 (SCC).
71. 1992 CanLII 923 (BC CA); leave to appeal dismissed (1993), 78 B.C.L.R. (2d) xxxiv (note) (S.C.C.).

not disclose this information (that the mortgages were in default) because the GAAP rules then in place did not require such disclosure. The Court said, in effect, that the accountants could not hide behind the GAAP standards to escape liability.

SMALL BUSINESS PERSPECTIVE

Following a standard practice, even one established by a professional body, will not act as a shield against liability. If a practice leads to deception or a misrepresentation of the facts, liability for misrepresentation may follow. This case emphasizes that poor excuses, such as abidance to common practice, will not suffice if in the end the courts conclude that parties were harmed by one's failure to be diligent and professional.

C. CAUSATION AND RELIANCE

Finally, it should be emphasized that to succeed in any negligence action the plaintiff must show that the negligent conduct (or words) *caused* the loss. If the professional can show that the negligent words were not relied on, that the investment or action involved would have taken place in any case, there is no liability. It will be interesting to follow the *Silver v. Imax Corporation* case,[72] where the Ontario courts have certified a class action against Imax Corporation and its directors for negligent and fraudulent misrepresentation. The novel aspect of that case is whether alternative forms of reliance will be actionable. The argument is that individual reliance by each investor on specific statements would be too burdensome in a class action. Rather, one can infer reliance from the fact that investors purchased the corporation's securities following Imax's misstatement of financial results.

In summary, when an expert conveys erroneous information, carelessly causing economic loss, this constitutes negligent misrepresentation for which the professional can be held liable. Even disclaimers may not protect the professional from liability if the court determines that she should have been aware of the error. Where the expert knowingly makes a false statement, she can be sued for deceit and may have to pay not only compensation to the victim but punitive damages as well. In many cases a professional's insurance will not cover such intentional fraud.

Fiduciary Duty and Breach of Trust

When a person places trust in a professional, the professional has a **fiduciary duty** to act in the client's best interests. In the past the principle was narrower, but the Supreme Court in *Hodgkinson v. Simms* (see Case Summary 5.16) extended this obligation to any situation where one person advises another and reliance is placed on that advice. This is, in effect, a relationship built on the trust placed in the professional by the client. The resulting duties of the fiduciary (the person being relied on) are significant.

Loyalty and **good faith** on the part of the professional are demanded. Further, the fiduciary is required to act in the best interest of the client, putting the client's interests ahead of his own and avoiding any situation where his self-interest conflicts with that duty. Any opportunity to acquire property or some other business interest or benefit that arises as a result of that relationship belongs to the client. Even when taking advantage of the opportunity will not harm the client, the fiduciary should refrain from doing it. It would be risky to take advantage of the opportunity even with the client's consent; at a minimum, the fiduciary should insist that the client obtain independent legal advice before granting consent. Furthermore, any information coming to the fiduciary because of his position must remain confidential, must not be disclosed, and must not be used by the fiduciary for his own benefit.

> Fiduciary duty exists in many relationships built on trust

> Fiduciary is required to act in the best interest of the client

---

72. 2011 ONSC 1035 (CanLII).

CASE SUMMARY 5.16

Conflict of Interest: *Hodgkinson v. Simms*[73]

Perhaps the most difficult and common violation of a fiduciary duty is the conflict of interest. This case is a classic example, where an accountant advised a client to invest in a real estate development while also acting for the developers. Such a conflict would require the accountant to at least disclose his role in the development to the investors. The defendant's failure to disclose his financial interest in the investment to those putting their trust in him was a breach of fiduciary duty. It resulted in a judgment against him for more than $350 000. Since the investor made his own decision to invest, the vulnerability normally present in fiduciary relationships was not present here. Still, the Supreme Court found that "the presence of loyalty, trust and confidence" were the identifying features of a fiduciary relationship; since they were present, a fiduciary duty was imposed.

DISCUSSION QUESTIONS

Within a fiduciary relationship, should the existence of a conflict of interest be enough to draw liability? Or should liability be restricted to those situations where the fiduciary is shown to have acted in his own interest to the detriment of the person to whom that duty was owed?

Fiduciary duty is owed by directors and officers to the company, and by partners to the firm

Real estate agents, travel and insurance agents, professionals giving advice, bankers, and financial planners are all likely to find themselves in a fiduciary relationship. People acting as agents sometimes have the opportunity to take a commission from both the seller and the buyer. This may constitute a breach of fiduciary duty unless the situation is disclosed to and permitted by both sides.

Any situation where people put their affairs in the hands of a trusted adviser or employee can give rise to a fiduciary duty. Even within organizations fiduciary duty is common. Partners owe fiduciary duties to the firm. Directors, officers, and managers owe a fiduciary duty to the company. Generally, ordinary employees, as opposed to those in executive or managerial positions, do not owe fiduciary duties to the employer, but a fiduciary duty may be imposed because of the function they assume. Even where no fiduciary duty exists, specific aspects of it, such as the obligation to keep information confidential, may rest on the employees.

Trust funds are strictly controlled

Often, funds from transactions or property are left in the hands of professionals for periods of time. Real estate agents, accountants, lawyers, and financial planners, for example, often find themselves in possession of large amounts of their clients' money. Any misuse of such property or funds is actionable as a breach of trust. Struggling professionals may be tempted to borrow from such funds, with every intention of paying the money back. No matter how sincere the intention, this is a serious violation and the professional is not only liable for any loss but will also be subject to disciplinary action within her professional organization. Criminal penalties may also be imposed.

The fiduciary duty goes far beyond the avoidance of negligence and can be the greatest potential risk to a business if it is not taken seriously. The subject of fiduciary duty will be discussed again in the chapters devoted to employment, agency, and business organizations.

Petrasky
Alberta
Trust fund issue.

Professional Insurance

Premiums are increasing in response to the greater number of claims

Professional associations (such as the law society or society of professional accountants) require their members to carry specialized liability insurance, sometimes called **errors and omissions insurance**. The premiums associated with such

---

73. 1994 CanLII 70 (SCC).

insurance can be a significant cost of carrying on business, and some may be tempted to avoid the cost. With the increased risk caused by the expansion of liability to third parties for negligent words and for economic loss, it is not surprising that the premiums have been rising.

Lawyers and accountants may be required to carry insurance as a condition of practice. (Law societies often arrange for coverage for their members, and a lawyer cannot practise without it.) Insurance is also required for professionals practising in limited liability partnerships (see Chapter 12 for more details). Such liability insurance will normally cover negligence but will not cover **fraud** or **breach of trust**. This may cause serious problems for a professional being sued for the frauds committed by a partner. Another problem occurs when the policy covers only claims made during the period of coverage. If the coverage is allowed to lapse and claims are then made, even for events that happened during the period of coverage, the insurer will likely not be required to pay.

Liability insurance is often required by one's professional association

Normally, an insurer will provide legal representation for insured parties when they are sued. This is, of course, in the insurer's own self-interest since it will have to pay out on the policy if the court imposes liability. The courts have recently been stricter in interpreting insurers' obligations. Because of the significant costs of litigation, malpractice actions involving professionals are a financial strain, even if the professional wins. It has been suggested that professional malpractice is an ideal area to be handled by the mechanisms for alternative dispute resolution (discussed in Chapter 3).

Mediation of malpractice actions may be more suitable

INSURANCE

LO ⑨

A recurring theme of this text is to encourage risk management and to promote an attitude of risk avoidance. A sound strategy for risk management is to learn the law, recognize potential pitfalls, and correct them before any harm takes place. A second aspect of risk management is to reduce the effect of risk by acquiring appropriate insurance.

Insurance transfers the risk from the insured to the insurer. When property is insured against fire, for example, the risk of loss shifts from the insured to the insurer. The insurer calculates the risk and assesses premiums based on the amount of coverage and the amount of risk involved. As risk increases, so too should the premiums charged. In essence, insurance spreads the loss across a great number of parties in exchange for the payment of a premium.

Insurance transfers risk to the insurer

The industry is tightly regulated by the federal *Insurance Companies Act*.[74] This statute requires all non-provincial insurance corporations to be registered and sets out the amount of reserves that must be retained to cover eventual claims. All provincial jurisdictions have similar insurance legislation. These provincial and federal statutes can be viewed as a type of consumer protection legislation in the field of insurance.

Industry is regulated by statutes

The Insurance Industry

Most insurance is purchased through an agent or a broker. Both are agents in the technical sense, but the broker operates an independent business, usually dealing with several different insurance companies in the course of finding the best deal for his client, the insured. Agents and **brokers** owe significant duties to the people they represent, so it can be important to determine whether that party is acting for the insurance company or for the insured. While **insurance agents** owe important obligations to their principals (the insurance corporations), they still owe a duty of good faith to the customer; thus, agents will be held liable if they fail to provide the insurance coverage asked for or otherwise fail to properly service the client's needs. The general topic of agency will be discussed in Chapter 10.

Insurance can be acquired through agents and brokers

74. S.C. 1991, c. 47.

An adjuster values the loss for the insurance company after the insured-against event takes place

Adjusters are employees or representatives of the insurance corporation charged with investigating and settling insurance claims against the corporation after the insured-against event takes place. It is important to remember when dealing with adjusters that they are normally looking after the interests of the insurance corporation rather than those of the person making the claim. Independent adjusters may also be engaged when problems arise with respect to claims.

Insurance companies often reinsure

Often businesses need the assistance of a broker to ensure adequate coverage. In the event of a large risk, a broker may further spread the risk by involving two or three insurance companies, each taking a percentage of the total. The primary company may take 60 percent, the second company 30 percent, and the third company the final 10 percent. Often one company will carry the risk on paper, but turn to the reinsurance market where the risk is divided among a larger number of secondary market companies. Many of these companies operate only behind the scenes so that the policyholder has to deal with only one adjuster in the event of a claim.

Types of Insurance

A. LIABILITY INSURANCE

Liability insurance covers negligence by self or employees

The insurance industry is divided between commercial and personal insurance, with the commercial line offering a variety of products. *Liability insurance* is the type of insurance most closely associated with torts. The main objective of tort law is to determine who should pay when wrongful conduct causes injury and loss, while the function of insurance is to spread that loss. It is important for businesspeople to maintain appropriate insurance coverage to avoid potentially devastating claims against them or their employees.

Coverage only when insured is at fault and only to the extent of coverage

Liability insurance is normally designed to cover not only the loss suffered but also the legal defence and court costs. Should the policyholder purchase an insufficient amount of coverage she will have to cover any shortfall. It is thus a good idea to follow a broker's advice and insure for an amount that will cover most eventualities. Note that liability insurance will not cover wilful acts, such as assault, theft, arson, or fraud. Nor will it provide coverage where the insured is not the one at fault. There must be negligence or some other basis for liability on the part of the insured for the insurer to pay out on the policy.

Liability insurance takes many forms. Professionals, such as lawyers and accountants, who exchange their expertise for money should carry **professional liability insurance**. A contractor should have a **builder's risk policy** in place. Anyone shipping goods should carry insurance that protects the goods while they are in his care. A recent innovation in the industry is **umbrella liability**, where several types of liability are bundled together, allowing the insured higher limits of coverage for a more economical premium.

CASE SUMMARY 5.17

Policy's Terms Determine Coverage: *Omega Inn Ltd. v. Continental Insurance Co.*[75]

There was both fire insurance and business interruption insurance coverage on the Omega Inn when it burned down in 1985. Because the insurance company suspected arson, however, it refused to pay, and with no funds available the insured was not able to rebuild. Finally, after six months of investigation where no evidence of arson was discovered, Continental agreed to pay. The reconstruction took another four months, resulting in a total of 10 months' delay in reopening the business. The insurance com-

---

[75.] 1988 CanLII 3371 (BC CA).

pany claimed that the policy obligated it to pay only for the four-month delay caused by the actual rebuilding. The policy stated that Omega was covered only for the length of time it was actually in the rebuilding process.

At trial the Court held that because the delay had not been caused by the insured, Continental had to pay for the whole 10-month period. But on appeal that decision was reversed.

The policy was clear and required payment only for the time the business would be interrupted while diligent effort was being made to rebuild. That obligation should not be affected by the fact that the insured did not have the funds to rebuild. As stated in the decision, "the impecuniosity of the plaintiff cannot be laid at the door of the insurer because it failed to pay more promptly. Its obligation and the full extent of its obligation, with respect to the business loss interruption coverage under the policy, was to pay for such length of time as would be required with the exercise of due diligence and dispatch to rebuild."[76]

SMALL BUSINESS PERSPECTIVE

Fire insurance and business interruption insurance usually go together, and this case demonstrates how they work. It also highlights the necessity to get back into business as soon as possible, despite any delays attributable to the insurer. The need to read one's policy and be clear on what is covered and what is not is likewise critical.

B. PROPERTY INSURANCE

The predominant form of property insurance covers losses to buildings and their contents due to fire or other named perils. **Comprehensive policies** cover everything except what is specifically excluded. Typical exclusions are acts of war, riots, or illegal activity. Insurance companies often set limits on what the company will pay in the event of a loss or apply a higher deductible. Most insurance contracts require insured parties to maintain certain safety and security standards to protect themselves against the risk of fire and theft.

There are problems with arranging for more or less coverage than is needed. If you take out more insurance than required, you are wasting money since you can collect only on what is actually lost. Carrying too little insurance is also a problem since companies normally include **co-insurance clauses** in most property insurance policies requiring that the insured parties maintain a certain percentage of coverage or bear some of the risk of loss themselves.

REDUCING RISK 5.4

A business that has been categorized as high risk or undesirable because of a claims history, late payments, or generally poor practices may not be able to acquire insurance or may be forced to pay high premiums for limited coverage. A sophisticated client will develop strategies to avoid such a consequence. Insurance companies and brokers may assist in identifying ways to diminish or eliminate losses.

C. BUSINESS INTERRUPTION INSURANCE

Often a business suffering a loss from a fire will have insurance to cover the property damage, but there will be nothing to cover the losses the business suffers during the period it is closed down for repairs. **Business interruption insurance** is designed to cover that gap, providing coverage not only for lost profits but also any additional expenses incurred to bring the business back into production. Compre-

Business interruption insurance covers lost profits

---

76. Ibid., at para. 10.

hensive property insurance and business interruption insurance together are an attempt to put the insured in the same financial position it would have been in had the fire or other damage not occurred.

D. LIFE AND HEALTH INSURANCE

Life insurance is used in business to cover key personnel

Life insurance provides security for a family or business against the death of the insured. Death is inevitable, so premiums are calculated on the basis of a prediction of how long a person of a certain age and health can be expected to live. Businesses often take out life insurance against the death of key personnel to cover losses incurred from any disruption that may result from the death or illness of an executive partner or key employee.

CASE SUMMARY 5.18

Consent Given—Insurable Interest Requirement Satisfied: *Chantiam v. Packall Packaging Inc.*[77]

Chantiam was working as the plant manager for Packall Packaging Inc. when he consented to the company's taking out an insurance policy on his life (called a "keyman" policy). Later he left the company and started another business in competition with it. When he discovered that the insurance policy on his life was still in place, he demanded that it be terminated or transferred to him; when his former employer refused, he brought this action against the company.

Like all forms of insurance there must be an insurable interest to support such a policy. There was no question that an insurable interest for the employer existed in Chantiam's life at the time the policy was taken out, but he argued that conditions had changed, the insurable interest had ended, and it was against the public interest for a business to maintain an insurance policy on the life of a competitor.

The trial Court agreed, ordering that the policy be cancelled. But on appeal the Court held that the appropriate time for determining whether an insurable interest existed or not was at the time the policy was taken out. It was clear that an insurable interest existed at that time; thus, the company was entitled to continue the policy regardless of termination of employment, even where the subject of the policy became a competitor. Furthermore, the applicable legislation stipulated that where the insured consents in writing to the creation of the policy, as happened here, that satisfies the insurable interest requirement. Since there was an insurable interest at the time the policy was created, there were no grounds to challenge the continuation of the policy.

With life insurance, the question of insurable interest relates only to when the policy is taken out. Note that Manitoba has changed its legislation, allowing a person to bring an application to the court to have the policy cancelled when that insurable interest is no longer present.[78] But in this case, Ontario (like other provinces) had no similar provision.

SMALL BUSINESS PERSPECTIVE

It is necessary to refer to the applicable provincial legislation for clarity as to when one has an insurable interest in the life of another. Having "something to lose" suggests that an insurable interest may exist. So would a business have an insurable interest in the life of a debtor? Should the size of the debt matter?

There are various forms of life insurance to meet the needs of different individuals. Term insurance provides only a benefit upon death, and the premiums are lower than whole life insurance, which provides coverage in the event of death as

---

[77] 1998 CanLII 3218 (ON CA); leave to appeal to SCC refused, [1998] S.C.C.A. No. 358.
[78] *Insurance Act*, R.S.M. 1987, c. I-40, s. 155(4).

well as investment potential and retirement income. These are just two of several variations of life insurance available.

Health and disability insurance provides coverage during the life of the insured and is designed to pay health-care expenses and provide an income for a person who is unable to earn a living because of illness or accident. Medical insurance can be arranged individually or as part of group coverage. Health-care services in Canada are funded through the government-sponsored medical system, which is often supplemented by plans providing extended coverage.

In most Canadian jurisdictions, disability insurance can be obtained on an individual basis with an insurance corporation, but it is more often acquired by large organizations as part of an employee benefits package. See MyBusLawLab for provincial variations.

Health and disability insurance are usually part of group coverage

Sometimes, where the husband and wife are both working, there will be overlapping extended benefits coverage such as dental and disability. Usually there is a deductible amount that must be paid or a limitation on the coverage. When there are two policies, often one can be used to cover the shortfall of the other, but they cannot be used to overpay. Today these policies often include a provision declaring them to be "excess coverage" when another policy is in place, with the result that the first policy will cover up to the deductible or the limit of the coverage and only then will the other kick in and pay the rest. Where both policies declare themselves to be excess coverage, the two insurers will split the cost of the coverage.[79]

Contract governs coverage, but where they conflict both share equally

E. BONDING

While insurance coverage is not generally available for intentionally wrongful acts, such as assault, many businesspeople insist on some protection against losses brought on by their employees or the people they deal with who may act wrongfully, even wilfully so. Bonding is available in these circumstances, and it takes two forms. Usually, an employer will pay a fee to have an employee bonded against that employee's own wrongful conduct (**fidelity bond**). If the employee steals from the employer or a customer, the bonding corporation will compensate the employer for that loss. It must be emphasized, however, that this does not relieve the bonded employee of responsibility. The bonding corporation can turn to the employee and collect from that party, which is what distinguishes bonding from normal insurance arrangements.

Bonded parties are still liable

The second form of bonding, a **surety bond**, occurs when the bonding is designed to provide assurance that a party to a contract will perform its side of the contract. For example, in a large construction project, the corporation doing the foundation may be required to put up a performance bond that it will finish the job at a specified level of quality and by a certain time. If it fails to complete or does not complete on time, the bonding company will be required to pay compensation.

Insurable Interest

LO

For insurance not to be considered a wager, the insured must be able to demonstrate an **insurable interest** in what is insured. That means that when the insured-against event happens, the insured must have suffered a loss for which the insurance payout provides compensation and no more. The contract for insurance is a contract of indemnity. Consequently, except in the case of life insurance, the insured can recover only what she has actually lost, up to the limit set out in the policy. When the payout becomes a windfall, the insurance agreement is void as an illegal contract.

There must be an insurable interest to avoid illegality

The insurable interest, then, is the amount an insured stands to lose if the insured-against event takes place. If Masson owned a half-interest in a painting worth $150 000, he would have an insurable interest of $75 000. If Masson carried an insurance policy of $150 000 on the painting and it was stolen, he would be able to collect only $75 000 for himself, even though he had insured it for the higher amount. (Were the painting

---

79. See *Family Insurance Corp. v. Lombard Canada Ltd.*, 2002 SCC 48 (CanLII).

to be stolen, he would likely collect the entire $150 000 but be required to hold the other $75 000 in trust for the person who owned the other half-interest in it.)

CASE SUMMARY 5.19

Insurance Void Due to Lack of Insurable Interest? *Milos Equipment Ltd. v. Insurance Corp. of Ireland Ltd.*[80]

Milos Equipment Ltd. (Milos), a dealer in logging equipment, sold to Upland Logging Ltd. (Upland) a new piece of equipment for the sum of $310 000, of which $130 000 was to be paid by way of a trade-in of an older unit. Since the new unit would not be ready immediately, Milos allowed Upland continued use of the trade-in. Milos insured the trade-in even though Upland continued its insurance on the unit. When the trade-in was damaged by fire, Milos's insurer refused to compensate Milos, claiming Milos had no insurable interest in the unit.

The Court of Appeal held that whether title had passed to Milos or not did not determine whether Milos had an insurable interest in the trade-in. Instead, the Court applied the rationale in the *Kosmopoulos* case: If an insured can demonstrate to have benefit from the insured property's existence, or suffer prejudice from its destruction, the insured has an insurable interest in it.[81]

In the *Kosmopoulos* case, the insured transferred ownership of his business to a corporation in which he was the sole shareholder, but the fire insurance remained in his name. The corporation's assets were damaged by fire, and the insurer argued that because a corporation was a separate legal entity the shareholder could not insure its assets because of a lack of insurable interest. The Supreme Court of Canada, however, decided that shareholders may have an insurable interest in those assets even though they don't have a direct legal claim to them. The fact that this shareholder would suffer a loss (damage, detriment, or prejudice) if the insured assets were damaged may be enough to establish insurable interest in that property.

In the *Milos* case, it was established that Milos would suffer a loss if the trade-in unit was destroyed. Consequently, Milos did have an insurable interest and its insurer was required to pay.

SMALL BUSINESS PERSPECTIVE

This case illustrates the significance of an insurable interest. Insurance policies are invalid without it. Sometimes following incorporation of a family business owners fail to distinguish between assets owned individually and assets owned by the corporate entity. To preclude one's insurer from denying coverage, it is prudent to get coverage in the name of the actual owner of the asset.

Legislation may determine in whose life one has an insurable interest

It should be noted that when life insurance is involved, people have an insurable interest in their own life and in the lives of their spouse and other close relatives. A loss—economic, emotional, and otherwise—is assumed if a close relation dies. Depending on the jurisdiction, where the lives of key business personnel are insured, the written consent of that person may be required, as was the case in the *Packall* case discussed in Case Summary 5.18. The value of that insurable interest will be the amount of insurance coverage contracted for.

Limitation Clauses

Ambiguities in a contract are interpreted in favour of the insured

Insurance contracts take a standard fixed form and often contain limitation clauses favouring the insurer. Where there is ambiguity in the meaning of such clauses, the *contra proferentum* **rule** allows the court to choose an interpretation that favours the

---

80. 1990 CanLII 634 (BC CA).

81. *Kosmopoulos v. Constitution Insurance Company of Canada Ltd.*, 1987 CanLII 75 (SCC).

insured. Coverage will be broadly construed while exclusions will be narrowly interpreted. Thus, courts will apply an interpretation that favours the insured since it was the insurer that chose the language to use.

CASE SUMMARY 5.20

Contra Proferentum Rule Applied: *Heitsman v. Canadian Premier Life Insurance Co.*[82]

The insured's widow sued for death benefits under a policy of accidental death and dismemberment insurance. The insured died after suffering a heart attack while trying to free himself from an overturned tractor-trailer following a motor vehicle accident. Medical experts testified that the heart attack was brought on by the stress, emotional and physical, resulting from the accident. The stress would not have been fatal were it not for the deceased's pre-existing heart problems. The Court determined that both the pre-existing condition and the stress caused by the accident contributed to the death. Neither one was the proximate cause. The insurance policy included an exclusion of liability for loss of life caused by sickness or disease. The Court found the clause ambiguous. It was not clear whether the parties had excluded payment for a death where one of its causes was accidental and the other a pre-existing disease. The *contra proferentum* rule was applied, and the exclusion was narrowly interpreted; thus, judgment was issued to the widow.

DISCUSSION QUESTIONS

This case illustrates that one's insurer may try to avoid payment, relying upon an "exclusion" to justify its actions. Do you think that this rule of interpretation is sufficient to protect the interests of the insured? What if the clause is clear but unfair?

Contract of Utmost Good Faith

A relationship of *trust* exists between the insured and insurer, creating an *obligation to act in good faith*. An important aspect of that obligation is the duty on the part of the insured to disclose pertinent information, especially where it affects the *risk* assumed by the insurer. After all, it is the insured that knows, has possession of, or has access to the information relevant to that risk. Even after the contract is made, there is often a duty to notify the insurance company when circumstances change, as when an occupied building becomes unoccupied for a length of time.[83]

LO ⑪,⑫

Insured has a duty to disclose changes in risk

CASE SUMMARY 5.21

Failure to Notify of Change Voids Policy: *Mueller v. Wawanesa Insurance Co.*[84]

The fire insurance policy in question was taken out by the landlord when the house was rented as a residential family dwelling. The "family" never moved in—instead, the building was occupied by three members of a motorcycle gang. Despite notice from the police that the property was being used as a clubhouse, the landlord did not terminate the lease. The rent cheques were kept current, so the landlord felt unable to terminate the lease. The property was eventually destroyed by fire, and the police suspected arson at the hands of a rival gang.

---

82. 2002 BCSC 1080 (CanLII).

83. See, for example, *528852 Ontario Inc. v. Royal Insurance Co.*, 2000 CanLII 22715 (ON SC), where the insured's failure to disclose a change of use, namely that the premises were left unoccupied, was a material non-disclosure that entitled the insurer to deny coverage.

84. [1995] O.J. No. 3807 (Ont. Ct. [Gen. Div.]).

> The insurance company refused to honour the policy, and in this action the Court agreed, finding that the use of the house was not the residential use envisioned under the policy and that there had been a material change in risk. The failure to notify the insurer of the change voided the policy and the insurance company did not have to pay.

SMALL BUSINESS PERSPECTIVE

The case shows how important it is to inform the insurer of any material changes that take place. Could leaving a building vacant, even for a limited period of time, constitute a material change? To be on the safe side, advance notification of changes to risk should be given to the insurer and a written record of the notice should be retained.

Insured must disclose relevant information

When applying for property insurance, the insurer will want to know what the property will be used for, whether it is for a business, whether it will be vacant for extended periods, and what kind of security and safety equipment is in place. For life, disability, or medical insurance, any injury, disease, or other health problems that may affect that person's health must be disclosed.

These factors affect eligibility or the rates charged for insurance, and since the insurer usually has no way of determining this information by itself it must depend on the honesty of the insured to disclose it. Failure to disclose information material to the loss may be misrepresentation and may result in the loss being unrecoverable. Even where it is not relevant to the loss, if it is a material misrepresentation it may cause the entire policy to be void. Legislation in some provinces upholds the insurance where the misrepresentation was innocent; but even in those jurisdictions the policy will be unenforceable if the misrepresentation or failure to disclose was done knowingly. An all-too-common misrepresentation involves representations as to who owns and who is driving an automobile. The insured may be tempted to misrepresent who the primary driver will be, hoping to thus secure a lower premium. Such misrepresentations have enabled many insurers to avoid payment following collisions.[85] See MyBusLawLab for provincial legislation and cases.

CASE SUMMARY 5.22

Perilous Non-Disclosure: *Agresso Corp. v. Temple Insurance Co.*[86]

Since insurance contracts are contracts of utmost good faith, parties must err on the side of caution when completing applications for coverage. The insured software company, Agresso Corp., applied for information technology errors and omissions insurance from the defendant insurers for the period of February 28, 2002, to February 28, 2003. Prior to that time, the insured had signed a software licence, implementation, and maintenance agreement with the third party, pursuant to which maintenance was to continue until 2005. By January 20, 2003, the insured was aware that the third party was dissatisfied with the insured's progress on solving a major problem with the software. But when the insured applied for a second policy, it did not disclose that there was a potential claim from the third party to the defendant insurers. In April 2003, the third party abandoned the software agreement and retained legal counsel. The insured notified the insurers on January 20, 2004, of a potential claim.

The insurers took the position that the insured had no coverage due to non-disclosure of a potential claim in the application form of February 21, 2003. Questions

---

85. See *Demontigny v. Insurance Corp. of British Columbia*, [1989] B.C.J. No. 2475; *Schoff v. Royal Insurance Company of Canada*, 2004 ABCA 180 (CanLII).
86. 2007 BCCA 559 (CanLII).

in the application for insurance required the insured to attach a list and status of all "claims, disputes, suits or allegations of non-performance" made during the past five years against the insured. Further, the insured was asked to advise whether it was aware of any "facts, circumstances or situations that may reasonably give rise to a claim other than advised in the previous question." Negative answers to both of these questions were given.

The Court of Appeal concluded that the insured's failure to disclose a potential claim from the third party constituted a material non-disclosure. There was "ample" evidence that the insured had knowledge of a "dispute" and of "allegations of non-performance." Accordingly, the insurer was able to have the insurance policy set aside.

SMALL BUSINESS PERSPECTIVE

This case underlines the need to be open and forthright with one's insurer. The consequences of keeping silent or failing to disclose information relevant to risk can be disastrous.

Just as the insured has a duty to be honest in its dealings with the insurer, the insurer has a duty to process claims fairly. Damages, punitive damages, and solicitor and client costs have been awarded to the aggrieved insured where insurers have withheld payments without justification. In the *Whiten* case,[87] the insurer's rejection of proof of loss (without explanation) was regarded as a failure of its duty of good faith. The insured had fled their burning house in their nightclothes, suffering frostbite as they watched their house burn down. After paying their living expenses for only a brief time, the insurer abruptly cut off payments. It raised a weak claim of arson, which was wholly discredited at trial. Punitive damages of $1 million were awarded by the jury, which evidently regarded the insurer's conduct as reprehensible.

Insurer has a duty to process claims fairly

The largest punitive award against an insurance company in Canadian history was made in the *Branco* case.[88] Luciano Branco, a 62-year-old immigrant to Canada, fought his insurers for over a decade. Branco, a welder, took on an assignment in Kyrgystan for his Canadian employer. He was disabled permanently when a steel plate fell on him on the job. The insurer, American Home Assurance Company, withheld his benefits and repeatedly pressured him to accept an unreasonably low settlement. The Court found this insurer to have demonstrated this pattern of conduct in other cases. A punitive award of $1.5 million was granted. As to the other insurer, Zurich, it was shown that despite approving Branco's claim at an early stage, this information was kept from Branco. Instead, the insurer brought several court applications forward in an effort to defeat the admitted claim. Callously, the insurer also defied court orders to pay Branco's legal fees. For putting Branco through this trauma, the Court awarded punitive damages of $3 million against Zurich.

Normally the insurer also has a duty to arrange for legal representation and a defence for the insured. One reason for purchasing liability insurance is to avoid such costs. But this duty does not extend to funding a defence where intentional or criminal acts are involved. In the *Scalera* case,[89] where the insured had a comprehensive general liability policy, the insurer was not required to defend the insured against charges of sexual assault. Also, in *Hodgkinson v. Economical Mutual Insurance Company*[90] there was no obligation to provide a defence when the defendant was sued for defamation for making a deliberate verbal attack on the plaintiff on the Internet.

Duty to defend

87. *Whiten v. Pilot Insurance Co.*, 2002 SCC 18 (CanLII).

88. *Branco v. American Home Assurance Company*, 2013 SKQB 98 (CanLII).

89. *Non-Marine Underwriters, Lloyd's of London v. Scalera*, 2000 SCC 24 (CanLII).

90. 2003 CanLII 36413 (ON CA).

Subrogation

Subrogation enables the insurer to assume remedies and redress of the insured

The right of **subrogation** gives the insurance corporation, once it has paid out a claim, the right to take over the rights of the insured in relation to whoever caused the injury or loss. The insurer steps into the shoes of the insured and can then sue whoever caused the loss as if it were the insured. Thus, where a neighbour carelessly allows a bonfire to get out of control, causing Columbo's house to burn down, Columbo would normally claim on her insurance and receive compensation. Her insurance corporation would then sue the neighbour for negligence and recoup what it can. In fact, if the neighbour had liability insurance, it would likely be his insurer that would ultimately pay. One should not assume when involved in an accident, however, that just because the other person has insurance one is protected. If it is your fault, that person's insurance company will normally seek to recover its loss from you.

Depreciated rather than replacement value

Insurance corporations will also normally have the choice to rebuild, repair, or replace what is damaged so that they can minimize their cost. They also have the **right of salvage**. If stolen goods are recovered, for example, insurers can sell those goods to recover their costs. When personal property has been lost, the insurer usually has to pay only the depreciated value of the goods, not the replacement cost, unless it has agreed otherwise. Most personal household insurance policies today provide for the replacement of destroyed or stolen goods at their full retail value. When a loss does take place, there is a general requirement on the part of the insured to report that loss to the insurance corporation right away so that the insurance corporation can take steps to minimize the damage. There might also be an obligation to report the matter to the police if a crime is involved or if the loss resulted from an automobile accident.

Insured can't profit from wilful misconduct

It should also be pointed out that the insured is not permitted to profit from her wilful misconduct. If the insured deliberately causes the loss, she will not be able to collect. Thus, if Fagan burns down her own house, killing her husband in the process, she will not be able to collect on the fire insurance and she will not be able to collect on her husband's life insurance, even where she is named as beneficiary. The **forfeiture rule** (that a criminal should not be permitted to profit from a crime) also extends to those who claim through the criminal's estate. In the above example, if Fagan were also to die in the house fire, her estate would not be able to collect on either policy.

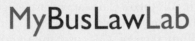 Be sure to visit the MyBusLawLab that accompanies this book to find practice quizzes, province-specific content, simulations and much more!

SUMMARY

Negligence
- Inadvertent conduct falling below an acceptable standard of behaviour
- Plaintiff must establish:
  - **A** duty of care was owed using the reasonable foreseeability test; in new situations, the court may also refer to policy considerations
  - **B**reach of duty by conduct falling below the level expected from a reasonable person
  - **C**ausation using the "but for" test, which establishes a physical link; remoteness test used to determine if the injury or damage was unforeseeable
  - **D**amage must have resulted from the conduct

- Defences to negligence:
  - If there is contributory negligence, courts may apportion the losses
  - If the plaintiff voluntarily assumed the legal risk, the defendant has a complete defence
  - If the plaintiff was hurt while engaged in illegal activity, he may be denied a remedy
- Special situations:
  - Statutes may impose a duty of care where none exists at common law, or may create liability in the absence of fault
  - Strict liability means that liability is imposed even where there is no fault on the part of the defendant
  - Vicarious liability means that liability is imposed on one party for the wrong committed by another; employers are held vicariously liable for torts committed by their employees
  - Occupiers' liability refers to legislation that imposes a duty on occupiers to people who are injured on their property
- Product liability:
  - Unlike in the United States, strict liability is not imposed on manufacturers in Canada
  - Manufacturers owe a duty of care to consumers of their products, but the plaintiff consumer must establish breach of that duty, causation, and damage

Professional liability

- Usually based on negligence
- Professionals may be liable for:
  - False or inaccurate information that causes economic loss
  - Breach of fiduciary duty or of contractual obligations

Insurance

- Designed to spread the risk of loss
- Liability, property, business interruption, life, and health are the primary forms of insurance available
- Insured must have an insurable interest in the subject matter; recovery is limited to the extent of that insurable interest
- *Contra proferentum* rule: the policy's ambiguities are interpreted in the insured's favour
- Insurance is a contract of utmost good faith
- Insured has a duty to act fairly, fully disclose material facts, and be honest
- Misrepresentation of material facts enables the insurer to have the insurance contract rescinded
- When a claim is paid, the insurance company has salvage rights and is subrogated to the rights of the insured

---

QUESTIONS FOR REVIEW

1. List and explain what a plaintiff must establish to succeed in a negligence action.

2. When a tort is committed intentionally, what remedies are available that may not be available when the conduct is unintentional?

3. Explain what is meant by the reasonable person test.

4. What test do courts use to determine whether the defendant owed to the plaintiff a duty to be careful?

5. Explain how the adoption of the *Anns* case test by the Supreme Court of Canada modified the approach to duty of care established in *Donoghue v. Stevenson*.

6. Distinguish between misfeasance and nonfeasance, and explain the significance of the difference in tort law.

7. Describe the test used in determining the appropriate standard of care demanded of the defendant in a negligence action.

8. How has an occupier's liability to persons using the property changed in recent years?

9. How does the "but for" test help to satisfy the requirements of causation?

10. Distinguish between the thin skull rule and the crumbling skull rule and explain how they relate to the question of remoteness.

11. Explain how the effect of contributory negligence has been modified in recent years.

12. Explain why the defence of *volenti non fit injuria* is difficult to establish.

13. Explain the obligations that are imposed on the producer of a product and to whom that obligation is owed.

14. Why is the case of *Haig v. Bamford* important in the development of tort law?

15. Describe how the *Anns* case test can impact the establishment of a duty of care in cases involving professional liability.

16. Identify the principle established in *Rylands v. Fletcher*. When will it be applied?

17. What is vicarious liability? Are there any restrictions on its availability?

18. How does the standard of care required from professionals or other experts differ from the standard of care required generally?

19. Explain the nature of a fiduciary duty and under what circumstances it arises.

20. Explain the source and nature of the powers of a professional organization. List the rights a member of that organization has when facing disciplinary proceedings.

21. Distinguish between business interruption insurance and fire insurance. Why might a businessperson want to have both forms of coverage?

22. What is meant by an insurable interest, and how does it apply to the various types of insurance discussed in the chapter?

23. What remedies does an insurer have if the insured misrepresented material facts when applying for insurance coverage?

24. Explain what is meant by the right of subrogation. How may subrogation affect not only the insured but also the person who has caused the injury or damage? Indicate what other means insurance corporations have to keep their damages as low as possible.

CASES AND DISCUSSION QUESTIONS

1. *Roper v. Gosling*, 2002 ABCA 71 (CanLII)
Roper and Jensen had consumed beer and smoked marijuana before going with Gosling for the evening to a bar, where they all consumed a considerable amount of alcohol. They were drunk when they left and got into Roper's car so that he could drive them home. A single-car accident caused by his impairment occurred in which Roper rolled the car and Gosling was seriously injured. She sued Roper for negligence.

Indicate what arguments can be raised in his defence and what factors the courts will take into consideration in determining liability. Would it make any difference to your answer if the Court determined as a finding of fact that although a reasonable person would have been aware that Roper's ability to drive was impaired, Gosling wasn't in fact aware of this when she got into the vehicle with him? What if she didn't have any other way home? If she did know, should her conduct be a complete bar to recovery?

2. *Dixon v. Deacon Morgan McEwan Easson*, 1989 CanLII 2786 (BC SC)

Dixon was an investor who chose to invest $1.2 million in National Business Systems when the share price was $12.89 per share. These shares went up in price somewhat, but before he could sell the Securities Commission suspended trading. When trading resumed, the shares sold at about $3 each. Dixon had invested on the strength of financial statements, including one marked "Consolidated Statements of Income and Retained Earnings (Audited)," which had been audited by the defendants. In fact, these statements were based on fraudulent information supplied by the management of National Business Systems to indicate annual profits of $14 million when the company had in fact lost $33 million. There is no question that the accounting firms involved in the audit were negligent for not detecting the inaccuracy. Dixon sued the accounting firm for negligence. Nothing on the document indicated who the auditors were, and the statements had been prepared without the auditors' knowing that they would be used by an investor such as Dixon.

Did the auditors owe a duty to Dixon to be careful? If the auditors had known that the statements were being prepared to attract investors, would this affect your answer? Is this a just way of treating liability for professionals, or should they only be liable to the clients they have contracted with?

3. *Schoff v. Royal Insurance Company of Canada*, 2004 ABCA 180 (CanLII)

Charles Goyan, an underage driver, was driving his 1966 Malibu when he caused an accident injuring the driver and passenger in another car (the Schoffs). They successfully sued him, obtaining a judgment totalling almost $500 000. They then sought to collect this amount from the insurance company that had insured the Malibu. The insurance company refused to pay, claiming that it was not bound by the policy contract because of misrepresentations made when the policy was made. Goyan had transferred ownership of the vehicle to his mother at the time the policy was taken out, and on the application she claimed that she was the only licensed driver in her household and she would be the only person driving the Malibu. She also claimed that there had been no accidents in relation to any vehicle she owned in the past six years and that she owned three vehicles at the time of the policy. In fact, of her four sons living with her, three had valid driver's licences and the fourth had his suspended. Also, the three with licences were under the age of 25. She owned five vehicles, not the three claimed, and her accident record had also been incorrectly stated. Obviously, her son Charles was driving the Malibu.

Do you think that the insurance company should be required to pay the Schoffs? Would it affect your answer to know that the insurance company had learned that the statement she gave about having no accidents in the last six years was incorrect before it issued the policy, and it was issued anyway?

6
Chapter

The Elements of a Contract: Consensus and Consideration

LEARNING OBJECTIVES

1. Discuss the fundamentals of the contractual relationship
2. Explain consensus and the significance of a "meeting of the minds"
3. Describe a valid offer
4. Describe an effective acceptance
5. Examine electronic transactions and the formation of contracts
6. Define "consideration" and the significance of "the price one is willing to pay"
7. Discuss the irrelevance of the adequacy of consideration
8. Consider why gratuitous promises are not consideration
9. Present some examples of valid consideration
10. Outline two exceptions to the general rule that consideration is required if a promise is to be enforceable

Along with torts, the second area of private law affecting businesspeople—and by far the most important—is the law of contracts. The world of commerce and most business relationships are based on contracts. In this and the following three chapters we will discuss how a contract is formed, various factors that affect those contracts, and how they can come to an end. This chapter introduces the first two of the five essential elements necessary for valid contracts: consensus and consideration. The other three elements (capacity, legality, and intention) will be discussed in the next chapter.

Business is based on contracts

THE CONTRACTUAL RELATIONSHIP

LO ❶

Definition of a Contract

Knowledge of contract law is vital to all businesspeople because most commercial transactions are built on contractual relationships. A good starting point would be a practical definition of a contract. We will define a **contract** as a voluntary exchange of promises creating obligations that, if defaulted on, can be enforced and remedied by the courts.

Exchange of promises are enforceable in court

It is important to understand that when agreeing to the terms of a contract, people are creating and defining their own rules and obligations. This differs from other areas of the law, such as torts, where rules and obligations are imposed on them. A valid contract creates a situation in which parties to the contract can predict, with some certainty, their future relationship because each party knows that the courts will hold them to their agreement.

Parties determine the obligations

While the courts will enforce a valid contract after it has been created, what the parties agree to in the first place is generally unrestricted. This approach is referred to as the freedom of contract. People can enter into almost any kind of contractual agreement they want to, as long as the contract meets the common law requirements that will be discussed in this and the following chapter. Although the law of contracts is found primarily in the common law, there are a number of specialized areas in which legislation that modifies, restricts, or replaces these common law principles has been enacted, thereby interfering with the freedom to contract. Examples include employment, partnerships, corporations, real property, the sale of goods, and consumer protection, all of which will be the subjects of later chapters.

But freedom to contract is restricted by common law and by legislation

When we study contract law, the focus is usually on the problems that can arise. It may therefore appear that most contractual relationships experience difficulties. In fact, most contracts are honoured or resolved to the mutual satisfaction of the parties. The courts become involved in a small proportion of contractual agreements, when an irresolvable dispute arises.

Elements of a Contract

Not all agreements are contracts. To qualify as a valid contract, an agreement must contain certain elements:

The elements of a valid contract

1. **Consensus.** Parties to a contract must have reached a mutual agreement to commit themselves to a certain transaction. They are assumed to have negotiated the agreement from equal bargaining positions. The process by which the agreement is reached usually involves an offer and an acceptance, although consensus can be implied.

2. **Consideration.** There must be a commitment by each party to do something or to abstain from doing something. The consideration is the price each is willing to pay to participate in the contract.

3. **Capacity.** Parties to a contract must be legally capable of understanding and entering into the agreement. Limitations in contracting capacity have been placed on infants, insane or intoxicated persons, aliens (persons who are not Canadian citizens), and, in some instances, Indians (pursuant to the *Indian Act*), and corporations.

4. **Legality.** The object and consideration involved in the agreement must be legal and not against public policy.

5. **Intention.** Both parties must be serious when making the agreement, and both must intend that legally enforceable obligations will result from it.

It should be noted that the general rule is that an agreement reached verbally between parties is every bit as binding as a written one. However, legislation (the *Statute of Frauds*) has been passed requiring that certain types of agreements be

Sometimes contracts must be evidenced in writing

supported by evidence in writing before they will be enforced in the courts. For convenience, this limited requirement of writing will be discussed along with the five elements of a contract.

Important Terms and Definitions

Before addressing the elements of a contract in more detail, it is necessary to outline some basic terminology that is used in the discussion of contractual obligations.

FORMAL AND SIMPLE CONTRACTS

The use of a seal

A **formal contract** is one that is sealed by the party to be bound by it. Traditionally, a seal involved making an impression in sealing wax. A modern seal normally consists of a paper wafer affixed to a document, but any mark or impression will do. A **simple contract**, also called a **parol contract**, may be verbal or written but is not under seal.

EXPRESS AND IMPLIED CONTRACTS

Contracts may be implied

An **express contract** is one in which the parties have expressly stated their agreement, either verbally or in writing. An **implied contract** is inferred from the conduct of the parties. When people deposit coins in vending machines, it can be inferred that they intend to create a contractual relationship, and thus an implied contract is in force. Portions of an express contract may also be implied.

VALID, VOID, AND VOIDABLE CONTRACTS

– contract with minor voidable (handwritten)

A void contract is no contract

A voidable contract is valid, but one party has the right to escape

Distinction between void and voidable

Voidable with mental incapacity (handwritten)

A **valid contract** is one that is legally binding on both parties. A **void contract** does not qualify as a legally binding contract because an essential element is missing. If the parties to a void contract thought they were bound and followed the agreement, the courts would try to put the parties back to their original positions. A **voidable contract** exists and has legal effect, but one of the parties has the option to end the contract.

The distinction between void and voidable can have important implications for outsiders to the contract who have acquired an interest in the subject matter of the contract. If the original contract is void, the goods must be returned to the seller. If the original contract is voidable, the outsider has acquired good title to the goods and can keep them.

UNENFORCEABLE AND ILLEGAL CONTRACTS

Courts won't enforce unenforceable contracts

An example of an **unenforceable contract** is one that is required to be in writing under the *Statute of Frauds* but does not meet that requirement. It may be valid in all other respects, but the courts will not force a party to perform such a contract. As well, if an unenforceable contract has been performed, the courts will not help a party to escape the contract.

An illegal contract is void

An **illegal contract** is one that involves the performance of an unlawful act. An illegal contract is void. The parties to such an agreement cannot be required to perform it. If an illegal contract has been performed or partially performed, the court, because of the moral taint, normally will not assist the parties by returning them to their original positions. This would usually be done if the contract was void. For example, if there is an illegal contract and a deposit has been paid, the court will not order its return. Neither will the court require property to be returned if the contract is illegal, even when one of the parties has been enriched at the other's expense. There is, however, an exception to this general approach—the courts will help a person who is innocent of any wrongdoing even when the contract is illegal.

BILATERAL AND UNILATERAL CONTRACTS

Unilateral contract— performance is acceptance

A **bilateral contract** is one in which both parties make commitments and assume obligations. There is no exchange of promises in a **unilateral contract**. This type of contract comes into effect when one party actually performs what has been requested by the other. For example, a person may offer a reward for the return of a lost item. It is not until the lost item is returned that the offer is accepted and the contract created. Thus, a bilateral contract involves an exchange of promises, whereas a unilateral contract involves a promise followed by an act.[1]

CONSENSUS

A Meeting of the Minds

LO **2** **3** **4** **5**

The essence of a contract is, at least in theory, a meeting of the minds of the contracting parties. The two parties must have a common will in relation to the subject matter of their negotiations, and they must have reached an agreement. They must share an understanding of the bargain struck and be willing to commit themselves to the terms of that contract.

> **Meeting of the minds of the parties**

In practice, however, it is not necessary that both parties fully understand, or even have read, all the terms of the contract. Few people thoroughly read the major contracts they enter into, such as insurance policies, leases, and loan agreements. Of those who do, few fully understand the specific meaning of the documents. The law does not recognize the excuse that one of the contracting parties did not read the contract or that he did not understand it.

> **Agreement reached—contract formed**

Both parties must have had an opportunity to read and understand the contract for it to be valid. The terms of the agreement must be clear and unambiguous. If the terms of the contract are ambiguous, then the court will decide that there has not been consensus between the parties and it will declare the contract void. Case Summary 6.1 provides an example of a court declaring a contract void because of a lack of consensus.

> **Terms must be clear and unambiguous**

CASE SUMMARY 6.1

No Consensus, No Contract! *Wallace v. Joughin*[2]

A row of trees separated properties owned by the parties. The trees were located on Joughin's property but some of the branches extended over Wallace's property. The parties tried at various times to reach an agreement about the trees. Wallace removed some of them, pursuant to oral agreements she thought had been reached by the parties. Joughin denied the existence of such agreements. When Wallace removed some of the overhanging branches, Joughin called the RCMP. An officer facilitated an agreement between the parties, but Joughin refused to comply with it. Wallace removed more of the overhanging branches and left them on Joughin's property. Wallace filed a claim on four occasions asking that the trees be removed as agreed to by a verbal contract. Joughin denied the existence of any verbal contract and counterclaimed for damages on several grounds.

The Court held that none of the verbal discussions between the parties resulted in an enforceable contract, as Wallace had not proved on a balance of probabilities that there was consensus. In particular, the agreement facilitated by the RCMP officer was only an agreement to continue negotiations. The claim for breach of contract was therefore rejected by the Court.

SMALL BUSINESS PERSPECTIVE

Courts make their decisions based on the evidence presented to them. What types of evidence will a court consider in cases in which the existence of a contract is at issue? In light of this, what can parties involved in contractual negotiations do to ensure that a court will reach the correct decision as to whether there was a meeting of the minds of the parties?

---

[1]. See *Speidel v. Paquette* (1979), 20 A.R. 586 (Q.B.), which involved a promise to convey title to a house if the other party moved into the house, looked after it, and paid rent for five years. The Court ruled that a unilateral contract was formed when the other party performed all of the stipulated terms.

[2]. 2014 BCPC 73 (CanLII).

Consensus may be implied

Obviously mistakes happen, and some very complex rules, which we will discuss later, have been developed to handle them. Nevertheless, contract law is based on the assumption that the culmination of the bargaining process occurs when one party states its position in the form of an offer in the expectation that the other party, through acceptance, will make a similar commitment to be bound by the terms of that offer. It should be stressed that a valid offer and an acceptance are not always obvious and yet, from the conduct of the parties or other factors, it is clear that the parties have a mutual understanding. In such circumstances, the courts are willing to imply the existence of a contract, and no evidence of a specific identifiable offer and acceptance is required.

Offer

Offer—tentative promise

A valid **offer** contains all of the terms to be included in the contract; all that is required of the other party is to give its consent or denial. The offer is a tentative promise on the part of one party to do whatever is set out, providing that the other party consents to do what is requested in return. When a salesperson offers to sell a car to a customer for $5000, the offer is a tentative promise by the seller to deliver the car contingent on the customer's willingness to pay the $5000. The process of making an offer is the communication of a willingness to be bound by the terms and conditions stated in that offer.

Contract is formed when offer is accepted

This aspect of the offer can be confusing to those involved in commercial activities. People often have documents placed before them and are asked to sign "the contract" (e.g., in transactions involving insurance policies or leases). In fact, at that stage, the document is not a contract; it is merely an offer. Only after it is accepted and signed can it be said to be the "contract," and even then it is probably only the written evidence of the contractual relationship between the parties.

Offer must include all important terms

Some terms can be implied

The offer must contain all significant terms of the proposed contract. The parties, the subject matter of the contract, any price to be paid, as well as any other important terms should all be stated in the offer. The courts do have the power to imply into contracts the insignificant terms that the parties may not have considered, such as time of delivery, time of payment, and so on. Such terms must be incidental to the agreement but consistent with the apparent intention of the parties. Courts will often turn to the common practice of the trade or industry for assistance in deciding which terms should be implied. As discussed in Chapter 16, when goods are sold the *Sale of Goods Act* sets out the terms to be implied if they are not in the contract of sale. Sometimes, as mentioned above, it is even possible for the courts to imply the entire contract from the conduct of the parties, but if it is clear that important terms have been left out or are to be negotiated later the courts will rule that there is no contract.

CASE SUMMARY 6.2

An Agreement to Enter into a Contract Is Not Good Enough: *Beacock v. Wetter*[3]

Wetter owned a house. She and Beacock discussed his renting the house for $950 per month and eventually buying it for $200 000. No written contract of purchase and sale was signed by the parties. Beacock moved into the house and paid rent of $950 per month. He made improvements to the house that were worth $23 000. During further discussions, Beacock increased his offer to $215 000. However, he could not obtain

---

3. 2006 BCSC 951 (CanLII), aff'd 2008 BCCA 152 (CanLII).

funding, and Wetter would not agree to take back a second mortgage. He filed a build-er's lien for the cost of the improvements. Wetter served him with a notice to vacate the house. Beacock sued for specific performance of his agreement with Wetter or, in the alternative, damages for breach of contract. Wetter denied entering into an agreement to sell the house to Beacock.

The Court ruled that there was no consensus or meeting of the minds regarding the terms of the alleged agreement. The discussions between Wetter and Beacock resulted in "an agreement or intention to enter into a contract of purchase and sale at some unspeci-fied date in the future." There was no definite offer that contained the specific terms of an agreement that could be accepted. The Court quoted from *Bawitko Investments Ltd. v. Kernels Popcorn Ltd.* (1991) CanLII 2734 (ON CA), 53 O.A.C. 314, at 327:

> [W]hen the original contract is incomplete because essential provisions intended to govern the contractual relationship have not been settled or agreed upon; or the contract is too general or uncertain to be valid in itself and is dependent on the making of a formal contract; or the understanding or intention of the parties, even if there is no uncertainty as to the terms of their agreement, is that their legal obligations are to be deferred until a formal contract has been approved and executed, the original or preliminary agreement cannot constitute an enforceable contract. In other words, in such circumstances, the "contract to make a contract" is not a contract at all.

The Court also held that there was no option-to-purchase agreement since there was no consideration for such an agreement. Finally, the Court denied Beacock's claim for the cost of the improvements because they had not been requested by Wetter and she did not accept them.

SMALL BUSINESS PERSPECTIVE

Do you think that this is a fair result from Beacock's perspective? What about the expectations that were created? What should he have done to protect himself?

REDUCING RISK 6.1

There are many reasons why a court may hold that there is no consensus between two parties. The essential terms may not have been agreed upon, or the agreement may be dependent on the making of a formal contract, or the agreement may have been nothing but "an agreement to agree." A sophisticated client will understand the need to avoid these common pitfalls. This will require the ability to recognize when a transaction is so complex that legal advice should be sought to ensure that the desired agreement will be enforced by the courts.

Interim agreements are binding

It must be emphasized that the parties can make it clear that, while they intend to put the agreement into a more formal document later, they intend to be bound before the contract is formalized as long as all of the important terms have been agreed upon. This is called an **interim agreement**; an agreement of purchase and sale in a real estate transaction is an example of such a contract. It is binding even though a more formal document will follow. A letter of intent will also be binding if all significant terms are included in it. If a person does not want to be bound by such a letter, she should clearly state this in the document.[4] A court will consider the common practice of a particular industry when deter-mining whether a particular agreement constitutes a valid contract and at what stage it is considered binding.

---

4. For a case in which an enforceable contract was found, despite an argument that it had been a mere "agreement to agree," see *Knappett Construction Ltd. v. Axor Engineering Construction Group Inc.* (2003), 25 C.L.R. (3d) 120 (B.C.S.C.), 2003 BCSC 73 (CanLII).

Contract is not binding until conditions are satisfied

It should also be noted that **subject-to clauses** often raise the same concerns. An offer may include a term making the contract conditional on some future event. A person may offer to purchase a house "subject to" the sale of his house. These types of provisions are not necessarily uncertain or ambiguous, unless the subject-to clause itself is uncertain. If the terms of the offer are clear and nothing is left to be negotiated or agreed upon, the parties are bound to perform as agreed once the subject-to term has been satisfied.[5]

Note exception for request for goods or services

Some types of contractual relationships, often referred to as **quasi-contracts**, must be viewed as exceptions to the rule that important terms must be clear. These contracts involve requests for goods and services. They will be discussed later in this chapter, as *quantum meruit*, under the heading "Request for Services."

INVITATION TO TREAT

An invitation to treat is not enforceable

An offer is usually made to an individual or to a group of people, but it is also possible to make an offer to the world at large, such as by posting a notice offering a reward for information or the return of a lost item. Most newspaper, radio, television, and Internet advertisements, however, are just **invitations to treat**. They are simply invitations to potential customers to engage in the process of negotiation. As part of the pre-negotiation process, invitations to treat have no legal effect. The typical process to create a contract is illustrated in Figure 6.1.

Figure 6.1 Typical Process to Create a Contract

	Invitation		Negotiations		Offer		Counteroffer		Acceptance	
A	→	B	↔	A	→	B	↔	A	→	B
	No obligation		No obligation		No obligation		No obligation		Contract	

Invitation to treat is not an offer

Goods displayed on a shelf are an invitation only

It is sometimes difficult to distinguish between an offer and an invitation to treat. A newspaper advertisement stating "Automobile tires for sale, two for the price of one" is not an offer. The advertisement is meant to encourage the reader to visit the store and then make an offer to purchase some tires. Catalogues and personal advertisements in the classified section of a newspaper are also invitations to treat. According to the famous English case *Pharmaceutical Society of Great Britain v. Boots Cash Chemists (Southern), Ltd.*,[6] goods displayed on the shelves of self-serve stores are also mere invitations to treat, even though the price of the items may be clearly marked.

With the display of such goods being merely an invitation to treat, a customer might be tempted to switch the prices on items displayed for sale in a store. To do so, however, is a crime.[7] The use of scanners and bar codes has made this crime more difficult to commit.

OFFER BY CONDUCT

Offer may be implied by conduct

A customer in a self-serve store takes the goods to be purchased to a cashier and places the goods and money on the counter. A person hails a cab by the gesture of raising a hand and calling, "Taxi!" These are both examples of offers being made by conduct. However, an auctioneer's comment "Do I hear $50?" is merely an invitation to the people in the audience to make an offer. When

---

[5.] See *McIntyre v. Pietrobon* (1987), 15 B.C.L.R. (2d) 350 (S.C.), 1987 CanLII 2612 (BC SC), in which a sale was made "subject to purchaser obtaining satisfactory personal financing." The Court held that the clause was vague, that there was therefore no contract, and that the deposit paid by the purchasers was to be repaid. This decision was distinguished in *Young v. Fleischeuer*, 2006 BCSC 1318 (CanLII), in which the condition precedent was "Subject to the Buyer . . . receiving . . . financing satisfactory to the Buyer." The Court held that this condition was not void for uncertainty. This area of the law is not settled. Each subject-to clause must be drafted carefully to ensure it will be enforced.

[6.] [1953] 1 All E.R. 482 (C.A.), aff'g [1952] 2 All E.R. 456 (Q.B.).

[7.] Obtaining goods by false pretences, *Criminal Code*, R.S.C. 1985, c. C-46, ss. 361, 362.

one of them raises a hand or makes some other acceptable gesture, that is an offer. The auctioneer is free to accept or reject it. A further question, "Do I hear $60?" is another invitation for offers. The statement "Sold!" is an acceptance of a person's offer.

COMMUNICATION OF AN OFFER

Before you can accept an offer, it must be communicated to you. You can accept only an offer that has been communicated to you as an individual, to you as a member of a group, or to the world at large. You cannot accept an offer made to someone else, no matter how you learn about it. Also, you cannot accept an offer you did not know about. If you return a lost item unaware that a reward has been offered, you have no claim to the reward because the offer was not communicated to you.

Offer must be communicated

Even where two offers cross in the mail with both parties of the same mind there is no contract. If one party sent a letter offering to sell and the other, in another letter sent at the same time, offered to buy a particular car for $500, there would not be a contract. Neither letter could be an acceptance, since neither party was aware of the other's offer.

It should be noted that, for a contract to be binding, all important terms must have been disclosed to the offeree. This is especially important with respect to exemption clauses. In contracts with customers, merchants will often include clauses that favour their own position or limit their liability. There are usually signs disclaiming responsibility for theft or damage to cars or contents posted in parking lots. Tickets to athletic events or for the use of sporting facilities will often include terms disclaiming responsibility for injury, damages, or loss of personal property by theft. In cases such as these, an exemption clause will be binding only when it has been reasonably brought to the attention of the customer at the time the contract is made. For example, the sign in the parking lot must be placed in a well-lit location where the driver will see it before or at the time the contract is made; this is usually at the cashier's booth or vending machine, as well as at other strategic locations on the lot. When the clause is on the back of a ticket, there must be a reference to it on the front of the ticket for it to be binding. Also, the ticket must be given to the customer at the time the contract is made, not afterwards. Even if these precautions are taken, consumer protection legislation may restrict the effect of an exemption clause. This issue will be discussed in Chapter 16.

Important terms must be disclosed, especially exemption clauses

REDUCING RISK 6.2

Whether terms are set out in signs or included in written agreements, it is vital that any unusual terms be reasonably brought to the attention of the other party, especially if they limit the liability of the party who created the terms. It is no longer good enough for the term to appear in small print in a document, or to be put on a receipt so that it can be seen only after the contract has been created. It is likely that those terms will simply not be considered part of the contract and therefore not binding on the other party. Sophisticated clients will therefore take steps to ensure that customers are made aware of all relevant exemption clauses.

Exemption clauses are also commonly found in written contracts. When people sign contracts, they are generally taken to have read the entire document. Even then, when an exemption clause is unusually restrictive the court may hold that there was a requirement to specifically bring the clause to the attention of the other contracting party and that the obligation was not met. Even when the clause was brought to the attention of the other party, if the merchant's failure to perform amounts to a fundamental breach she still may not be able to rely on the exemption clause for protection. The topic of fundamental breach will be discussed in Chapter 9.

Fundamental breach may avoid exemption clause

CASE SUMMARY 6.3

An Offer Can't Be Accepted After You Know the Offeror Has Changed His Mind: *Dickinson v. Dodds*[8]

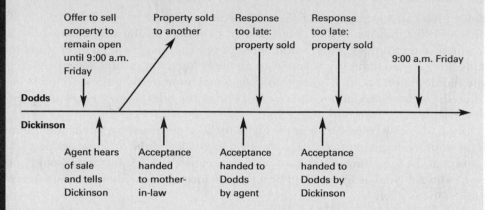

Dickinson v. Dodds, an old case from the latter part of the nineteenth century, remains one of the best cases to illustrate how offer and acceptance work. Dodds made an offer to sell certain property to Dickinson for £800, stating "This offer to be left over until Friday, 9:00 a.m." Before the expiration of that deadline, Dickinson learned through his agent that Dodds had been trying to sell or had sold the property to someone else.

He quickly went to Dodds's home and left a written acceptance with Dodds's mother-in-law. The next morning, Dickinson and the agent went down to the train station to intercept Dodds as he arrived in town. The agent found him first and handed him a written acceptance. Dodds replied that it was too late and that he had already sold the property. This scenario was repeated a few minutes later when Dickinson intercepted Dodds, with the same response—all before the stated deadline.

This case is important because it illustrates the nature of an offer. The offer is a tentative commitment on the part of the person making it. Until the other party accepts it, there is no obligation on the offeror. Dodds was free to withdraw his offer any time before it was accepted. Even though he had promised to hold the offer open, he was not obligated to do so. He could change his mind and sell the property to someone else, but he had to let the other party know he had changed his mind. In this case Dodds was extremely lucky, because although he didn't tell Dickinson directly that he had changed his mind, Dickinson found out indirectly. He couldn't accept an offer he knew was no longer available. Had Dickinson not found out about the sale, his acceptance would have been valid and Dodds would have been bound in contract to sell the property to two different purchasers.

SMALL BUSINESS PERSPECTIVE

Do you think that Dodds should have been bound by his promise to hold the offer open? Should a sale to someone else automatically end the offer? Why would a businessperson want to keep his promise, even if he doesn't have to?

THE END OF AN OFFER

Offer ends . . .

For the acceptance of an offer to be effective, the offer must be in force at the time of the acceptance. There are several ways for an offer to come to an end before acceptance.

---

8. (1876), 2 Ch. D. 463 (C.A.).

1. End of a specified time. The offer will end at the time stated in the offer. Note that the offeror is still free to revoke the offer before this time expires, unless an option has been purchased. Option agreements will be discussed below.

. . . when specified

2. Expiration of a reasonable time. If no time is specified in the offer, it will expire at the end of a reasonable time. What is reasonable depends on the circumstances. Thus, an offer to sell a ship would likely last longer than an offer to sell a load of ripe peaches.

. . . after a reasonable time

3. Death or **insanity** of the offeror. The offer will end even if the offeree is unaware of the death or insanity.

. . . upon death or insanity of the offeror

4. **Revocation** of offer. The offeror may revoke an offer any time before acceptance, but the revocation must be communicated to the offeree to be effective. (When letters are used, the revocation is effective only when received by the offeree.) Until the revocation is communicated to the offeree, the offeree can still accept the offer. The offeror should therefore not contract with another party until she is sure that the message that she has revoked the offer has been received by the offeree. While it is possible for the revocation to be communicated indirectly, as in *Dickinson v. Dodds* (see Case Summary 6.3), reliance on such a method would be foolish in the extreme. Dodds was extremely lucky in that case.

. . . when revoked (revocation must be communicated)

5. Rejection and **counteroffer**. During the bargaining process, several different proposals may be put forward, rejected, and then followed by counterproposals. Each counteroffer or rejection ends the offer before it. For example, when a car is offered for sale for $5000 and the customer replies "I'll give you $4500," a counteroffer has been made and the original offer is thereby ended. If the seller rejects the counteroffer, it is too late for the purchaser to reconsider and accept the original offer, as it no longer exists. Under such circumstances, an attempt to accept the original $5000 offer constitutes a new offer, which the seller is free to accept or reject.

. . . when rejected or a counteroffer is made

Note that a simple request for information or clarification, such as an inquiry as to whether the sale of a car includes the stereo, does not constitute a counteroffer or a rejection. It therefore does not end the offer. On the other hand, a counteroffer that is worded like a question will end the offer (such as "Will you take $4500?").

Request for information is not a counteroffer

The existence of an offer can be affected by other factors as well. For example, the offer will be ended if the activity contemplated by the contracting parties becomes illegal before acceptance. Also, if the goods forming the subject matter of the contract are destroyed without the parties being aware of it, the offer is ended.

Other factors can end an offer

OFFERS THAT CANNOT BE REVOKED

Often businesspeople find the uncertainty associated with the offeror's right to revoke any time prior to the point of acceptance inconvenient, especially when they are arranging their business affairs to take advantage of the offer.

For example, when assembling land, a land developer will get offers from several sellers. He will not accept any of them until he is sure that all of the required properties can be obtained. The right of each of the sellers to revoke is inconsistent with this process. The developer will therefore acquire an option on each property. An **option agreement** is a subsidiary contract, with separate consideration given to the offeror in exchange for a commitment to keep the offer open for a specific length of time. The developer thereby gains the certainty necessary to accomplish his goal. Such arrangements are quite common; they are found in all areas of finance and business. (Options can also be put under seal; the use of the seal will be discussed below, under the heading "Consideration.")

Option keeps offer open

A similar problem exists when dealing with tenders, a normal practice in the construction industry. A purchaser issues a request for bids to get the best possible price on a required product or service. The request for bids is an invitation to treat, and

Tendered bids cannot be revoked

each submitted bid is an offer. The problem is that normally there would be nothing to stop the offeror from withdrawing her offer if she realizes she has made a mistake or, if upon seeing the other bids, she realizes that hers is too low. The Supreme Court of Canada has decided that in some circumstances such tendered bids cannot be revoked.[9] When the original request for tenders made it clear that bids would be considered only when the offeror agreed that the offer could not be withdrawn once submitted, a subsidiary contract exists and the offer then cannot be revoked. As above, the problem is also avoided when the tendered bid is made under seal.

Unilateral offer can't be revoked once performance begins

It is likely that the same principle will apply in any situation in which a unilateral contract is involved and performance of the act requested has begun. Thus, when an employer promises to give his business to an employee if she stays until he retires, the acceptance is made simply by the employee's staying on. With such an implied subsidiary contract, the employer could not wait until just before his retirement and then revoke the offer.

CASE SUMMARY 6.4

The Tendering Process and the Duty to Be Fair: *Martel Building Ltd. v. Canada*[10]

The Department of Public Works issued a call for tenders, pursuant to which it did not have to accept the lowest bid. Martel submitted the lowest bid. However, the department conducted a financial analysis of the bids and added certain costs to Martel's bid. The tender was then awarded to another bidder.

After reviewing the general principles of the law of tender, the Court stated that a call to tender is an offer to contract and a binding contract may arise when a bid is submitted. The Court held that the parties intended to include an implied term that all bids were to be treated fairly and equally. Pursuant to the call for tenders, which included a "privilege clause," the department did have some discretion in evaluating the bids. (A privilege clause states that the lowest or any tender will not necessarily be accepted.) It added fit-up costs (leasehold improvements undertaken by a tenant) to all of the bids, using the same approach. This was not a breach of the duty to act fairly. The department was entitled to add another specific cost to Martel's bid, as this was an express requirement to which all of the bidders had to comply. The department did, however, breach its duty to treat all bidders fairly and equally; it added this cost only to Martel's bid. As this addition did not cause Martel to lose the tender, Martel's claim for damages was dismissed.

DISCUSSION QUESTIONS

Given the duty to treat all bidders fairly, can a party calling for tenders protect itself simply by including a "privilege clause" in the tender documents, stating that the lowest or any tender will not necessarily be accepted? Can a privilege clause be used to attach an undisclosed condition to the offer of the party calling for tenders?

STANDARD FORM CONTRACT

Bargaining is difficult with a standard form contract

The law assumes that the two parties to an agreement are in equal bargaining positions and that both will negotiate the terms of the agreement until a consensus, which represents a fair bargain, is reached. In actual fact, most large businesses do not negotiate with their customers. Rather, they present an offer with fixed terms that the customer is invited to accept. A passenger purchasing an airline ticket is an example. These are called **standard form contracts** and usually contain one-sided

---

9. *R. (Ont.) v. Ron Engineering*, [1981] 1 S.C.R. 111.
10. [2000] 2 S.C.R. 860, 2000 SCC 60.

terms favouring the business. Exemption clauses, discussed earlier, that attempt to limit the liability of the business are examples of such one-sided terms.

In an effort to correct the imbalance in bargaining power and to alleviate some of the unfairness, consumer protection legislation has been enacted in most jurisdictions to control the worst abuses. Consumer protection is covered in Chapter 16. Also, when the courts deal with exemption clauses they interpret them strictly so that any ambiguity is read in favour of the disadvantaged party. Thus, a business that includes in its contracts terms disclaiming responsibility for "damage" to goods left on the premises would still be held responsible for goods that were stolen. Even when exemption clauses are clear, the courts have shown a willingness to set them aside on the basis of fairness and good faith.

Statutes and attitude of courts mitigate this

DUTY OF GOOD FAITH

While the courts have set aside exemption clauses on the basis of fairness and good faith, they have not recognized a "stand-alone" duty of good faith in the performance or enforcement of commercial contracts, as have the courts in Quebec and the United States. It was thought that such a duty would interfere with the freedom to contract. Canadian common law courts have therefore only been willing to imply a duty of good faith that ensures the parties do not act in a way that defeats the objectives of the agreement that they have entered into.[11]

No stand-alone duty of good faith . . .

That approach changed with a recent decision of the Supreme Court of Canada.[12] In that decision, the Court created a general organizing common law principle—namely, the need for good faith contractual performance. This includes the need for a party to a contract to have regard to the legitimate contractual interests of the other party. The Court also recognized that, as part of the organizing principle of good faith, there is now a common law duty to act honestly in the performance of contractual obligations.

. . . until a recent Supreme Court case

This decision will no doubt have a huge impact on the interpretation and performance of all contracts in the future. At this time it is impossible to predict the effect of the organizing principle of good faith and the duty of honesty. As one commentator stated soon after the decision was delivered, "It will probably take decades for the full implications of the decision in *Bhasin v. Hrynew* to be worked out."[13]

Common law will develop slowly

CASE SUMMARY 6.5

The Extent of the Duty of Good Faith: *Bank of Montreal v. No. 249 Seabright Holdings Ltd.*[14]

The bank provided financing to several parties, secured in part by guarantees, for the purpose of building a real estate development. Due to cost overruns and a shortage of capital, the bank made a formal demand for payment in full of the loans. There were then many steps that were taken by the bank and the parties, but ultimately the borrowers advised the bank that they could not comply with all of its conditions. The bank obtained an order appointing a receiver-manager, awarding judgment against the borrowers, and granting a foreclosure order. The receiver-manager completed the construction and sold all of the units. This action involves a claim for $24 million against the guarantors of the loans.

---

11. For a good discussion on this approach, see *Transamerica Life Canada Inc. v. ING Canada Inc.* (2003), 68 O.R. (3d) 457 (C.A.), 2003 CanLII 9923 (ON CA).

12. *Bhasin v. Hrynew*, 2014 SCC 71.

13. Barry Sookman, "Good Faith and Honesty Contractual Obligations Says Supreme Court: *Bhasin v. Hrynew*," *Computer and Internet Law Weekly*, November 16, 2014, www.barrysookman.com/2014/11/16/good-faith-and-honesty-contractual-obligations-says-supreme-court-bhasin-v-hrynew.

14. 2014 BCSC 1094 (CanLII).

The guarantors argued that the bank had acted in bad faith with respect to providing further funding. The Court referred to *Transamerica* and the duty of the parties to act in good faith only in the performance of their contractual obligations. There was no general duty of good faith on the bank to negotiate the terms and the timing of the proposed funding.

DISCUSSION QUESTIONS

This case was heard prior to the Supreme Court deciding that there is a "stand-alone" duty of good faith requiring a party to consider the legitimate contractual interests of the other party. Would the above decision be different if the case were heard again? Will the good faith principle change the behaviour of sophisticated businesspeople?

Acceptance

Acceptance must be complete and unconditional

At the heart of contract law are the concepts of consensus and mutual commitment. The manifestation of an intention to commit on the part of the offeror is found in the offer; the offeree's intention to commit is found in the **acceptance**. The contract is formed and the parties are bound by it at the point of acceptance. The key to understanding acceptance is that the commitment must be total. If a condition or qualification is put on the acceptance, it becomes a counteroffer and is not an acceptance. If a salesperson offers to sell a car and a trailer to a customer for $5000 and $3000, respectively, and the response is "I accept, provided you include new tires," that response is a counteroffer. Nor is it possible to accept only part of an offer. In this example the purchaser cannot say, "I accept your offer, but I want only the car." For an acceptance to be valid, it must be an all-or-nothing proposition.

Exchanging order forms

A serious problem can arise when customers and suppliers exchange order forms. Sometimes instead of filling in the supplier's order form, the customer simply sends his own, which may include different terms. This is not an acceptance but a counteroffer. If the supplier simply sends the product in response, she has accepted and is bound by the new terms. Suppliers often do not realize the difference, and such a mistake is easily made. Sophisticated businesspeople will watch for such substituted forms.

An incomplete offer cannot be accepted

Even a clear acceptance cannot correct an incomplete offer. When the wording of an offer is unclear, the courts will interpret the agreement to find the most reasonable construction. They will not, however, go so far as to strike a bargain on behalf of the parties. As mentioned, there is no such thing as a contract to enter into a contract.

CASE SUMMARY 6.6

An Incomplete Offer Can't Be Accepted: *Middleton v. Howard*[15]

Mitchell was told by his doctors that he had only months to live. Prior to his death, he had discussions with his best friend, Howard, regarding Mitchell purchasing a floating home owned by Howard. Mitchell paid Howard $140 000. The issue was whether Mitchell and Howard had reached an agreement prior to Mitchell's death.

The Court referred to the paragraph in the *Bawitko* case quoted in Case Summary 6.2. Mitchell had offered to buy the floating home for $140 000, but the Court held that there was not an agreement on all of the important terms prior to his death. There was not

---

15. 2012 BCSC 1089 (CanLII).

even an agreement as to what assets were being sold and what the purchase price was. Mitchell intended that there would be a written agreement negotiated between the parties in respect of the transaction, but that was not done. There was simply "an agreement to agree to a later agreement to be negotiated and documented." The $140000 was viewed as a deposit and was ordered to be repaid to Mitchell's estate.

DISCUSSION QUESTION

In this case, the offer was incomplete and therefore could not be accepted. No matter how definite the acceptance was, it could not overcome the defect of an incomplete offer. How can parties ensure that the agreements they enter into will be enforceable?

COMMUNICATION OF ACCEPTANCE

Acceptance of an agreement is usually accomplished by communicating it to the offeror. It is possible, however, for an offer to be accepted by conduct. If the offeror has indicated particular conduct to specify acceptance, the offeree must comply with that stipulation for it to be effective. Acceptance may also be implied from conduct as when, for example, a purchaser leaves a deposit on a car she has purchased.

Offer may be accepted by conduct, where specified or implied

A unilateral contract is accepted by performance of the act specified in the offer.[16] If a prize were offered for the first human-powered flight across the English Channel, acceptance would be by making the flight. Starting the flight would not qualify; only the completion of the cross-Channel flight would constitute effective acceptance of the offer. But what if the offeror tried to revoke his offer when the flight was only partially performed? In theory, an offer can be revoked any time before acceptance. As discussed already, a Canadian court would likely follow the American example and find a subsidiary contract requiring that once the performance starts the offer cannot be revoked. In any case in which acceptance is by conduct, there is no requirement to communicate the acceptance to the offeror, although there may still be a need to notify the offeror that the required conduct has taken place when this is not self-evident.

Unilateral contract is accepted by completion of performance

Merchandisers often send unsolicited goods to people along with an invoice stating that if the goods are not returned within a specified time the customer will have purchased them. But silence, as a general rule, does not constitute acceptance. When goods are supplied in this way, the customer can normally ignore them and just put them away. If the customer uses the goods, she is receiving a benefit and is deemed to have accepted the offer. Consumer protection legislation in many provinces outlaws "negative option practices," reinforcing the common law. Consumer protection legislation is discussed in Chapter 16.

An unsolicited offer is not accepted by silence

An important exception to silence not being an acceptance occurs when there is an ongoing business relationship between the parties. It is quite common for a supplier to send materials used by a business on a regular basis with the understanding that they will continue to be sent unless the supplier is informed otherwise. A relationship of trust has developed, and the purchaser now has a duty to inform the supplier when he changes his mind. When a person joins a book-of-the-month club a similar duty is created, and return of the book is likely required to escape obligation. But such clubs sometimes continue to send products when there has not been a request, or even after they have been told to stop. As mentioned above, there is now consumer protection legislation in place in most provinces dealing with negative option practices in an attempt to prevent this kind of abuse.

But silence can be acceptance if the parties have had prior dealings

When acceptance is not by conduct, the general rule is that it is not effective until it has been communicated to the offeror in the manner stipulated in the offer. The result of this general rule is that the contract is formed when and where the

Acceptance is effective when and where received

---

16. See *Speidel*, *supra* note 1, for an example of a case involving a unilateral contract.

offeror learns of the acceptance. If a supplier of lumber products in Halifax makes an offer to a customer in Winnipeg and the offeree accepts over the telephone, the contract comes into existence in Halifax when the offeror hears the acceptance. Where the contract is formed can be an important factor in determining which court has jurisdiction and which jurisdiction's law will apply to the contract.

CASE SUMMARY 6.7

Where Contract Is Formed Reason for Conviction: *R. v. Schulz*[17]

Schulz operated a stucco business. He had a municipal business licence that entitled him to carry on business from his residence. He did not have a licence under the *Fair Trading Act* that would have allowed him to carry on a prepaid contracting business. He twice attended at the home of a couple and discussed the work they wanted done. Negotiations about the terms of the contract took place during these meetings. The wife delivered a cheque for the deposit to Schulz's residence. She later called and accepted his estimate of the cost of the work. Schulz commenced work a couple of days later but did not complete the work satisfactorily. The couple complained to the provincial government pursuant to the *Fair Trading Act*. Schulz was charged with engaging in a prepaid contracting business without being the holder of an appropriate licence.

The Court ruled that the couple accepted the offer Schulz made at their residence. He was therefore guilty of the offence because he entered into a contract out of his office.

SMALL BUSINESS PERSPECTIVE

Would Schulz have been convicted if the Court had concluded that the contract was made when the wife called him at his office and accepted his offer? Is it important for a small businessperson in Schulz's position to be a sophisticated client and to understand the consequences of soliciting business outside of his office as well as when and where a contract is formed?

THE POSTBOX RULE

Mailed acceptance is effective when and where dropped in a mailbox

Difficulties arise when parties deal with each other over long distances using non-instantaneous forms of communication. Because neither party can be absolutely sure of the other's state of mind at a given time, there can be no certainty of the contract's status. The **postbox rule** was developed to solve this problem. When use of the mail is reasonable, an acceptance is effective when and where it is deposited in the mailbox. This is a clear exception to the general rule discussed above, which states that an acceptance is not effective until the offeror learns of it. Figure 6.2 illustrates how the postbox rule works.

Figure 6.2 Postbox Rule

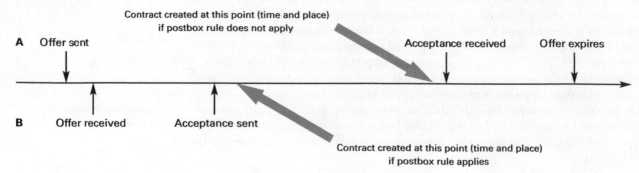

Contract created at this point (time and place) if postbox rule does not apply

A   Offer sent   Acceptance received   Offer expires

B   Offer received   Acceptance sent

Contract created at this point (time and place) if postbox rule applies

---

17. (2003), 331 A.R. 96 (P.C.), 2003 ABPC 13 (CanLII).

One problem—determining the point of consensus—is solved by the postbox rule, but another is created. For a period of time, while the letter of acceptance is still in the mail, the offeror is bound in contract but unaware of that fact. Note that the offeror can avoid this problem by stipulating a different means of communication. When use of the mail is inappropriate, or if another method of acceptance was specified by the offeror, the acceptance will be effective only when received.

Applies only when response by mail is appropriate

Response by mail when an offer is sent by mail is normally reasonable. The problem arises when a means of communication other than mail is used to make the offer, but acceptance is then made by mail. This was illustrated in *Henthorne v. Fraser*.[18] Henthorne was handed an offer in Fraser's office, which was to remain open for 14 days. He took the offer home to think about it and, after several days, posted a letter of acceptance. In the meantime, Fraser sold the property to another party and wrote a letter to Henthorne revoking the offer. The two letters crossed in the mail. The Court decided that even though the offer had been handed to Henthorne, use of the post for acceptance was reasonable. The acceptance was therefore effective when sent. Note that the letter of revocation was not effective until Henthorne received it.

When is response by mail reasonable?

CASE SUMMARY 6.8

Should the Postbox Rule Be Extended? *R. v. Commercial Credit Corp.*[19]

This case dealt with whether a creditor had lost its priority by failing to properly register a security interest as required by Nova Scotia law. If the contract was formed within the province, the creditor would lose any claim to the assets because of the failure to register; however, if it was formed outside the province, the creditor would have a valid claim. The original offer had been sent by courier by Commercial from its Nova Scotia office to the offeree, which was outside of the province. The offer was accepted, and the acceptance was also sent by courier.

The Court held that this communication was akin to using the mail, so the postbox rule applied. This meant that the acceptance was effective where sent, which was outside the province. Referring to the offeror, Commercial, the Court said that "They were the ones that chose the method of communication, and having done so on behalf of both parties, the mailbox doctrine was brought into play. Its extension to a courier service was sound in principle and, in my opinion, the contracts were therefore made outside of Nova Scotia when their acceptances were sent back to Commercial Credit." This is one of the few cases in which the postbox rule has been extended beyond communication by mail or telegram. The case has not yet been followed in other jurisdictions in Canada.

DISCUSSION QUESTIONS

Is there any justification to extend the postbox rule to other forms of communication? Should it even be in effect today?

The question must also be asked whether the postbox rule applies to any other form of communication. The postbox rule has been extended to include telegrams, but it has not been applied to instantaneous forms of communication, such as telex or fax.

Postbox rule extends to telegrams

---

18. [1892] 2 Ch. 27 (Eng. Ch. D.).
19. (1983), 4 D.L.R. (4th) 314 (N.S.C.A.).

CASE SUMMARY 6.9

Limitation of the Postbox Rule: *Entores Ltd. v. Miles Far East Corp.*[20]

An American company contracted with a British company through a Dutch subsidiary for the purchase of electronic components. The British company wanted to sue the American company in England, but the British courts would have jurisdiction only if the contract came into existence in the United Kingdom. It was argued that since the Dutch company sent the acceptance by telex (similar to a modern fax machine), the postbox rule should apply, meaning that the contract came into existence where the acceptance originated in Holland. The Court rejected this argument. The Court found that because telex was instantaneous, like the telephone, there was no need to extend the postbox rule exception to that form of communication. Therefore, the general rule applied and the acceptance was effective in the United Kingdom, when and where it was received. The contract thus came into existence in the United Kingdom, and the courts there had jurisdiction.

DISCUSSION QUESTION

This case illustrates the operation of the postbox rule and its limitations. There is some question whether there is any justification for the postbox rule in this day of modern high-tech communication. Should the postbox rule be eliminated by legislation so that it is not possible for a court to apply the rule to any contract, no matter how the acceptance is communicated?

Should the postbox rule be extended?

Today it is becoming much more common to use electronic means of communication, such as email and fax, rather than the postal service. The question arises whether the postbox rule will be extended to these methods of doing business. Since these new electronic communications are instantaneous or near-instantaneous, it is not likely that the postbox rule will be extended to them. This conclusion was confirmed, at least with respect to communication by fax, in *Eastern Power Ltd. v. Azienda Comunale Energia and Ambiente*,[21] in which it was decided that an acceptance sent by fax was effective only when it was received by the offeror.

REDUCING RISK 6.3

People often make the mistake of thinking that if they make an offer to sell something to several people and then sell it to one of them their other offers are automatically ended. Normally you must notify the other parties that you have sold the item to revoke the offers. If you fail to do so, you face the risk of one of these parties accepting your offer. You would then be bound to sell the same item to two different people.

To avoid the problem of being bound in contract without knowing it because of the postbox rule, the offeror who is a sophisticated client would be careful to specify the method of acceptance and to clearly state in the offer that it will not be considered accepted until the acceptance is actually received by the offeror. Of course, when a long-term business relationship is involved this may not be a problem.

---

20. [1955] 2 All E.R. 493 (C.A.).

21. (1999), 50 B.L.R. (2d) 33 (O.C.A.), 1999 CanLII 3785 (ON CA); leave to appeal to S.C.C. refused, [1999] S.C.C.A. No. 542.

It should be noted that there are still significant advantages to using the mail. The use of the mail involves the exchange of a permanent tangible record of the transaction and its terms. Electronic communication like email may be convenient, but it suffers from a lack of permanency or certainty. Such records can be lost through the crash of a system or simply altered in an undetectable way, making written records and communications through the mail still—and likely to remain—an attractive option as a common aspect of future business transactions.

Mail still has some advantages

As mentioned above, where a contract is formed can also determine which law applies or whether a court has jurisdiction. These things may therefore be determined by the postbox rule. In the *Entores* case, the British Court had jurisdiction because the postbox rule did not apply to an acceptance by telex and the contract was thus made in England. In the *Commercial Credit Corp.* case, the transaction was not subject to Nova Scotia law because the postbox rule was held to apply to a couriered acceptance, meaning that the contract was made outside the province.

Postbox rule can also determine which law applies to the contract

It must be stressed that the postbox rule is an exception to the requirement that an acceptance must be communicated to be effective. It does not apply to the offer or to a revocation of an offer. In the *Henthorne v. Fraser* case, discussed above, the postbox rule applied only to the letter of acceptance, not to the letter of revocation, which had to be received before it could have any effect on the transaction.

Postbox rule does not apply to an offer or a revocation

Electronic Transactions

CONSENSUS

The applicability of the postbox rule to electronic communications is just one example of how the law of contracts must adapt to the rapid growth of electronic transactions. All aspects of contract law will have to be reconsidered as electronic transactions grow in importance.

Law of contracts must adapt to new technology

For example, most electronic transactions involve contracts, whose validity should not be affected by the fact that they were made electronically. The *Uniform Electronic Commerce Act (UECA)*,[22] a model statute created by the Uniform Law Conference of Canada, has largely been adopted in whole or in part by every legislative body in Canada.[23] The *UECA* clearly states that an offer may be made and accepted electronically.[24]

Contracts can be made electronically

Electronic transactions do, however, create some special problems. An advertisement is normally just an invitation to treat, but if the terms are clear, certain, complete, and are communicated to the offeree, and provision is made for the reader to click on a button on the screen to actively accept those terms and make the purchase, it will likely qualify as an offer. If the retailer wants the advertisement to remain an invitation to treat, it must demonstrate that clearly in the advertisement. This will enable the retailer to retain control over the process and avoid being found to be carrying on business in a particular jurisdiction and being subject to that jurisdiction's law.

Internet ad with "click-wrap" may be an offer

An offer accepted on a website or by electronic communication will also be effective as long as the basic requirements of acceptance are met. A purchaser of a product, whether in a store or online, will be bound only by those terms of the agreement of which she has notice. When purchasing software in a store, it is common to find the actual product sealed in shrink wrap, which when opened indicates acceptance of the terms set out on the package itself. When people buy software over the Internet or purchase a licence to use it, the purchasers are usually required to indicate that they have read and accepted the seller's terms and conditions before accepting.

Clicking "I Accept" button accepts terms

[22.] For an annotated version of this statute, see *Uniform Electronic Commerce Act* (Consolidation, 2011) at www.ulcc.ca/images/stories/Uniform_Acts_EN/Uniform%20Electronic%20Commerce%20Act%20Consolidation%202011.pdf.

[23.] See, for example, the *Electronic Commerce Act*, S.O. 2000, c. 17.

[24.] *UECA, supra* note 22, s. 20.

Clicking the "I Accept" button is the equivalent of removing the shrink wrap. This is called "click-wrap," and the contract is binding as soon as that button is clicked.[25]

Form of acceptance affects enforceability

Two issues seem particularly important when the courts are deciding whether to enforce an electronic contract. One is the form of assent. Did the offeree really know and accept the terms? In *Ticketmaster Corp. v. Tickets.com, Inc.*,[26] the Court held that the terms and conditions were unenforceable because the user was not required to click "I Agree" or otherwise confirm that the customer read the terms. In *Canadian Real Estate Association v. Sutton*,[27] users of a website were not required to click on an "I Agree" button to agree to the terms of use of the website. The Court nonetheless granted an injunction preventing Sutton from violating the terms of use. This decision suggests that conduct—using a website with knowledge of the terms of use—may constitute acceptance of these terms. The result is a binding contract.

Reasonableness of terms is also relevant

The reasonableness of the actual terms is the second issue. Several courts have refused to enforce electronic contracts when the terms have been found to be unreasonable. For example, in *Mendoza v. AmericaOnline*,[28] the Court refused to enforce AOL's online forum-selection clause. The Court noted that "it would be unfair and unreasonable because the clause in question was not negotiated at arm's length, was contained in a standard form contract, and was not readily identifiable by the plaintiff due to the small text and location of the clause at the conclusion of the agreement."

Postbox rule will likely not apply to online communications

As discussed in *Eastern Power Ltd. v. Azienda Comunale Energia and Ambiente*,[29] the Court held that when acceptance is made using instantaneous communication the contract is formed when and where the acceptance is received. But what of email and web-based communications where there can be some delay before transmission or reading? What if the offeror receives the email on his BlackBerry while travelling abroad? What if the email is received on December 1 but the offeror does not read it until December 15? Determining where and when Internet transactions are created is made more difficult (1) because electronic communication is asynchronous and (2) because electronic communication is mobile—it can be received at multiple locations. Recent statutes in various jurisdictions provide that such communication will be effective when it reaches the information system of the recipient, even though there may be some time before it is actually read.

ECOMMERCE LEGISLATION

Legislation determines when electronic communications are "sent" and "received" . . .

Ecommerce legislation (in common law provinces) specifies how the time and place of the formation of electronic contracts, including contracts negotiated via email, are to be determined. Ontario's *Electronic Commerce Act, 2000*[30] splits the risks of failed communications between the parties. It does so by prescribing a time when the message is deemed to be sent and by creating a presumption of reception. Under this Act, electronic information is deemed "sent" when it enters an information system that lies outside the sender's control. The message is presumed to have been "received" when it enters the addressee's information system such that it can be retrieved and processed. If the addressee has not designated or does not use the information system for the purpose of receiving such information, then the receipt only occurs when the addressee becomes aware of the information in the addressee's information system.[31]

. . . and where it is sent from and received

The Ontario legislation deems electronic information sent in the context of an electronic transaction to have been sent from the sender's place of business and to

---

25. The landmark decision in this area was *Rudder v. Microsoft Corp.*, 1999 CanLII 14923 (ON SC), 2 CPR (4th) 474, in which an Ontario Court upheld the validity of a "click-wrap agreement." See Martin P.J. Kratz, "So I Clicked 'I Agree'—Am I Bound?" *LawNow* (March/April 2008), in which the author notes that the courts apply traditional contract law principles in "click-wrap" cases.

26. (C.D. Cal. 2000), www.internetlibrary.com/cases/lib_case393.cfm.

27. [2003] J.Q. no 3606.

28. (Cal. Sup. Ct. 25 September 2000), upheld on appeal 90 Cal. App. 4th 1 (Cal. App. Ct. 21 June 2001).

29. *Supra* note 21.

30. *Supra* note 23.

31. Ibid., s. 22.

have been received at the addressee's place of business. Accordingly, the actual physical location of the device or the person receiving the information becomes irrelevant to the place of contract formation.

It remains open to the parties to agree to modify any rule pertaining to electronic information. The retailer or other businessperson can specify in the offer or website advertisement that an acceptance will not be effective until the information is actually received, no matter what form of communication is used. The parties can also agree as to which jurisdiction's laws shall apply to the transaction.[32] Such a forum-selection clause was upheld in *Rudder v. Microsoft Corp.*[33] If a forum is not specifically selected, the contract is formed and is governed by the laws of the jurisdiction where the acceptance is received, which is usually where the offer is made. The issue of electronic documents and signatures will be discussed in Chapter 7.

But parties can override legislation

CONSIDERATION

The Price One Is Willing to Pay

LO ⑥⑦⑧⑨⑩

Central to contract law is the bargaining process in which people trade promises for promises and all parties derive some benefit from the deal. That benefit, essential to the existence of a contract, is called *consideration*, which is defined as the price one commits to pay for the promise of another. Consideration is not restricted to the exchange of money. A bargain may involve the exchange of anything the parties think is of value. For example, when Brown purchases a computer from Ace Computers Ltd. for $2000, there is valid consideration on both sides. The promise to deliver the computer is valid consideration, as is the promise to pay $2000. Note that before the parties actually exchange the computer for the cash they are bound in contract because the consideration given is the exchange of commitments or promises, not the actual money or goods. If one of the parties fails to honour that commitment, the other can successfully sue for breach of contract.

Consideration—not necessarily money

Because it is sometimes difficult to determine the value a person is getting from a deal, it is often better to look at what the parties are giving or paying. For example, if a public-spirited business agrees to pay someone to clean up a public park, the commitment is still binding even though it might have been made out of a sense of civic responsibility and may result in no actual benefit to the business. Both sides have exchanged promises or commitments. Normally the promise to make a charitable donation is not enforceable because it is a one-sided promise or gift, but when the charity makes a commitment in return—such as a promise to name a building after the donor or to use the money in a certain way—it has made a commitment, and both parties will be bound.

Promise of a charitable donation is usually not enforceable

Similarly, a contract is just as binding if the consideration involved is a commitment not to do something as opposed to a promise to do something. For example, if a business promises to pay its employees $500 to quit smoking, such an arrangement is a valid, binding contract. The consideration on the one side is the promise to pay $500, and the consideration on the other side is the promise to refrain from doing something the party has a legal right to do (i.e., smoke). Consideration is a benefit or a detriment flowing between the parties to an agreement as the result of the striking of a bargain (see Figure 6.3).

Consideration can be a benefit or a detriment

Figure 6.3 Consideration Involves the Exchange of Promises or Commitments

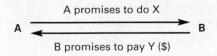

A promises to do X

A ⟶ B

B promises to pay Y ($)

[32.] Ibid.

[33.] *Supra* note 25.

**Courts will not enforce
gratuitous promises**

If the agreement is one sided and only one of the parties is getting something from the deal it is called a **gratuitous promise** or a gift, and the courts will not enforce it. It may well be that such gratuitous promises ought to be honoured from an ethical point of view, but there is no legal obligation to do so. Once the gift has been given, however, the courts will not assist the giver in getting it back. Also, when services are performed gratuitously, there is still an obligation to do a proper job. If, through the negligence of the person performing the gratuitous service, damage or injury results, she can be sued in tort. For example, if a skilled carpenter, out of the goodness of her heart, helps her neighbour repair a roof, and because of her negligence the roof leaks and causes damage to furniture and belongings, the neighbour will be successful in suing in tort for compensation.

CASE SUMMARY 6.10

Promise to Pay Was Gratuitous: *NAV Canada v. Greater Fredericton Airport Authority Inc.*[34]

NAV provided aviation services and equipment to the Authority. The Authority decided to extend one of its runways and requested that NAV relocate its instrument landing system. NAV decided that it made economic sense to replace part of the system rather than move it. The cost of the replacement part was $223 000. NAV asked the Authority to pay for the part. The Authority refused, saying it was not contractually bound to do so. Eventually the Authority agreed to pay to ensure that the extended runway became operational. The payment was made "under protest." NAV installed the part, but the Authority refused to pay for it. An arbitrator held that there was nothing in the agreement between NAV and the Authority that required the Authority to pay for the cost of the part. He held, however, that the subsequent correspondence between the parties resulted in a contract, which required the Authority to pay.

The Court of Appeal held that the Authority was not required to pay for the part because the subsequent correspondence did not create a valid contract. It ruled that the variation of the existing agreement between the parties was not supported by consideration. Performance of a pre-existing obligation does not qualify as valid consideration. NAV had not promised anything in return for the Authority's promise to pay for a part for which it was not legally obligated to pay.

DISCUSSION QUESTIONS

What step could NAV have taken to ensure that the Authority would be bound by its promise to pay for the part, even if the Court held that there was no consideration given by the Authority for its promise? Should a gratuitous promise to vary an existing contract be enforceable as long as it was not procured under economic duress? If that were the law, would the Court have held the Authority liable to pay for the part?

Adequacy of Consideration

**The courts will not bargain for
the parties**

Consideration need not be fair. The court will not interfere with the bargain struck, even when it is a bad deal for one of the parties. If a person agrees to sell someone a brand new Cadillac for $100, this becomes a valid, binding contract. When businesses deal with each other, the value of a particular deal to the parties is not always apparent, and the wisdom of the courts not reviewing the fairness of the consideration is clear. But when businesses deal with consumers, the courts are much more concerned with fairness. They are therefore sometimes willing to assist consumers who have been taken advantage of by merchants. They have developed concepts

---

34. (2008), 229 N.B.R. (2d) 238 (C.A.), 2008 NBCA 28 (CanLII).

such as unconscionability, fraud, and mistake (to be discussed in Chapter 8), which give them power to review these transactions. The courts will also examine the fairness of consideration when insanity, drunkenness, or undue influence may have affected the transaction. This power to intervene is now also often found in legislation, such as consumer protection statutes.

Inadequate consideration may indicate fraud, insanity, etc.

CASE SUMMARY 6.11

Both Sides Must Make Commitments: *Gilbert Steel Ltd. v. University Construction Ltd.*[35]

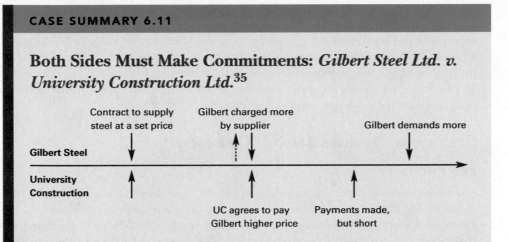

Gilbert had supplied construction steel to University for a number of its projects. For one particular project, it had a contract for a specified amount of steel to be provided at a set price. But Gilbert's costs for the steel increased, and it requested that University pay a higher price for the steel supplied for that project. University agreed to pay the higher price.

The steel was delivered, but the payments made were never enough to cover the increased price. When Gilbert demanded payment, University refused to pay the amount over the original price, claiming it didn't get anything in return for its promise to pay more. It had agreed to pay more, but Gilbert's position hadn't changed; it still had the same obligation to deliver steel that it had under the original agreement. Such a one-sided agreement was not a binding contract. For a contract to exist, there must be an exchange of promises or commitments between the parties—a one-sided agreement is not enforceable.

The lawyers for Gilbert argued that University received consideration in that Gilbert promised to give University a "good price" on a subsequent project. The Court found that this promise was not specific enough and that there was no commitment involved. Gilbert also argued that because University did not have to pay for 60 days after the price went up it was getting free credit, but the Court also rejected that argument. The Court therefore held that there was no bargain struck. Only one side made a commitment, and thus there was no obligation to pay the higher price even though there was a promise to do so. (Note that Gilbert also argued that there was promissory estoppel in this case, but this position was rejected by the Court. See page 210.)

DISCUSSION QUESTION

What could Gilbert have done to ensure that the promise of University to pay more would be enforced by the Court?

Although the consideration paid does not need to be fair, it must have some legal value. The promise of "love and affection" is not good enough, nor is a promise to stop "bothering" someone's father.[36] Whatever the parties have bargained for must have some material value for the courts to enforce the bargain.

Consideration . . .

. . . need not be fair but must have legal value

---

35. (1976), 12 O.R. (2d) 19 (C.A.).
36. *White v. Bluett* (1853), 23 L.J. Ex. 36 (C.E.).

. . . must be specific, particularly if money is involved

In addition, the parties must agree to a specific consideration or price. Suppose someone agrees to exchange a car for another's promise to "do some work around the house." Such a promise would not be enforceable because the work to be done is not specified. This was the problem in the *Gilbert Steel* case discussed in Case Summary 6.11, when Gilbert promised to give University a "good price" on a future project. This problem becomes acute whenever monetary consideration is involved. It is not sufficient to promise to give "some money" as payment for the promise of another. Such a commitment must refer to a specific or calculable amount of money. When the parties agree to pay the "market value" of an item, or when some other objective method or formula for pricing a product at some time in the future is used, the consideration is calculable and is sufficiently specific to be binding, thus overcoming the problem. Even then, great care must be taken to make sure the price at that time will be clear.[37]

Gratuitous Promises Are Not Consideration

EXISTING DUTY

No consideration where extra pay is offered to do the same work

Sometimes people enter into agreements to do what they are already legally obligated to do. This raises a problem concerning the adequacy of consideration. For example, Olsen agreed to paint Chang's house for $1500. When the painting was three-quarters finished, Olsen demanded $500 more to finish the job on time. Even if Chang agreed, there would be no binding obligation because Chang got nothing in exchange for the promise to pay more. Olsen was obligated to finish painting the house before the promise to pay the extra $500 was made, and after the promise the obligation remained the same. Olsen's legal position did not change; therefore, there was no consideration. These types of problems often arise in the construction industry, when unforeseen factors may increase the costs significantly, as in the *Gilbert Steel* case discussed in Case Summary 6.11. This is just one more reason for the parties to take great care to predict all costs that are likely to arise and to build into their agreement provisions for resolving conflicts over these unexpected eventualities.

A new bargain requires new consideration

When a duty to act exists but that duty is owed to a third party, a promise to do the same thing for someone else is enforceable. In the situation above, if Chang's tenant Adams promised to pay Olsen the extra $500 to ensure the job was finished on time, that agreement would be binding. Before Adams's promise to pay the extra $500, Olsen was legally obligated to Chang to finish painting the house. After the promise to Adams, Olsen is now legally obligated to Adams as well as to Chang to paint the house. Olsen's legal position has changed because Olsen now runs the risk of having to pay Adams's damages as well as Chang's if the contract is breached. There is valid consideration here, and the contract would be binding.

No additional consideration for public duty

When a public duty is involved, a demand for further compensation will not be tolerated. A police officer, firefighter, or other public servant can't demand more money to do his job. A firefighter cannot arrive at a blaze and extract a promise from the victim to pay an extra $500 to put out the fire. Such a contract would be against public policy and void. But paying police personnel in their off-duty hours to provide security at a rock concert or celebration is valid, as they are on their own time and not otherwise obligated to help.

PAST CONSIDERATION

Past consideration is no consideration

There are situations in which there is no consideration even though it appears to be present. One of these is when the consideration was given in the past; that is, the bargain is struck after the price agreed on has been paid. An employer's promise to pay a bonus in recognition of good work already performed by the employee

---

[37.] *Foley v. Classique Coaches* (1934), 2 K.B. 1 (C.A.).

would not be binding—the work has already been done. Although it may appear that both parties have given something (the employer the promised bonus and the employee the good work), such a promise is not enforceable. The key to this problem is in the timing. When the promise to pay the bonus was made the work had already been performed, so where is the bargain? In fact, the employee is in exactly the same legal position before the promise as afterward. Thus, it is often said, "**past consideration** is no consideration."

CASE SUMMARY 6.12

Past Consideration Is No Consideration:
Fox v. Blood Tribe[38]

Fox was the chief of the Blood Tribe for several years until 1996. Prior to his last meeting as chief, Fox asked the band manager to draft a resolution creating a lifetime pension for Fox. He announced his retirement at the meeting and asked the band council to pass the resolution, which it did. Fox received pension payments until 2007, when the council decided to rescind the resolution and stop making the payments. Fox sued for damages for unpaid pension benefits and for future pension benefits.

The Court held that the resolution was passed because the council wanted to recognize Fox's past service. The consideration for the pension was therefore past consideration, so there was not a valid contract. Fox also pleaded estoppel, but the Court ruled that he did not rely upon the resolution to his detriment since he had decided to retire for other reasons. His claim was dismissed.

DISCUSSION QUESTION

Is there anything that Fox could have done to ensure lifetime payments of the pension?

PAYING LESS TO SATISFY A DEBT

A creditor will often agree to take less in full satisfaction of a debt. Such agreements also raise problems with respect to consideration. After a $5000 debt becomes due, a creditor who agrees to take $3000 from the debtor as full payment has received no consideration for the reduction in the debt. In fact, the reduction of the debt is gratuitous. It is quite clear that, under the common law, such a one-sided promise is not binding and that the creditor can therefore sue for the remaining $2000. Even if the partial payment is actually made, the creditor can still turn around and sue for the remainder.[39]

> **Common law states that an agreement to take less to satisfy a debt is not binding**

But, as a practical business matter, such an arrangement to accept less is often beneficial to the creditor as well as the debtor. The creditor might otherwise have to sue to recover, and then runs the risk of not collecting anything. Many jurisdictions have passed legislation providing that when a creditor has agreed to take less in full satisfaction of a debt and has actually received the lesser sum, the creditor is bound by the agreement and cannot sue for the difference.[40]

> **Legislation may overrule common law if there is payment of the lesser sum . . .**

When the creditor has agreed to take less but none of the money has yet been paid, the creditor is still free to change her mind and insist on the entire amount being paid. Of course, when the debtor has agreed to pay the lesser amount early or to do something in addition to the payment, such as pay a higher rate of interest, there is consideration on both sides to support the new arrangement. In cases like these, the creditor is bound by her promise to accept less.

> **. . . and payment has been made**

[38.] 2013 ABQB 653 (CanLII).

[39.] *Foakes v. Beer* (1884), 9 App. Cas. 605 (H.L.).

[40.] See, for example, *Law and Equity Act*, R.S.B.C. 1996, c. 253, s. 43.

ILLEGAL CONSIDERATION

Illegal or impossible consideration is no consideration

There are some policy restrictions on what constitutes good consideration. For example, when illegal drugs are sold there is **illegal consideration** and the agreement is therefore void. Contracts between businesses to interfere with free competition and unduly restrain trade may also be void due to illegality. In addition, for consideration to be valid it must be possible to perform the consideration promised. An agreement to change lead into gold for a fee would also be void because of the impossibility of performance (at least at this time).

REDUCING RISK 6.4

The old adage that you cannot get something for nothing has been enshrined in the law of contract in the form of the requirement of consideration. In all contracts (with a couple of exceptions, discussed below) there must be a bargain in which both parties make a commitment to each other. The lack of such consideration is often difficult to see, especially in business deals in which pre-existing obligations are being modified. In such circumstances, sophisticated clients will be especially vigilant in their dealings to ensure that the deals they make are legally binding and not simply one-sided gratuitous agreements that can be ignored by the other party.

Examples of Valid Consideration

SETTLEMENT OUT OF COURT

Consideration exists in out-of-court settlements

When the parties to a dispute settle the matter outside of court, there is also valid consideration on both sides. When a litigant learns later that he would likely have won, it may look like there is no consideration. In fact, as both parties have given up their right to have the court determine the matter, there is consideration on both sides. As a result, the release signed in such situations is a binding contract.

REQUEST FOR SERVICES

Must pay reasonable amount for services

When services are requested from providers, such as lawyers or mechanics, the parties often do not agree on a specific price before the service is performed. When you ask a lawyer for assistance in resolving a contractual dispute or a mechanic to fix your car, you are often not given a firm price for the service. In these circumstances, the courts will impose an obligation to pay a reasonable price. This is an application of the principle of *quantum meruit*, sometimes called a *quasi-contract*. *Quantum meruit* means "as much as is deserved." The courts use this principle to impose an obligation to pay a reasonable price when services are requested. Provincial statutes have also applied the requirement to pay a reasonable price to the sale of goods when no specific price has been agreed upon.[41]

Used even if person is not allowed to finish a job

The courts will also use *quantum meruit* to determine how much should be paid when a person providing the services is not allowed, by a breaching party, to finish the job. For example, when a person has agreed to paint a house and, before the job is finished and payment is due, the other party refuses to allow completion, the court will use the *quantum meruit* principle to require the breaching party to pay a reasonable price for the benefit she has received. The same is not true if the breaching party is the one seeking payment. In the example above, if the painter were the one who refused to finish the job, he could not demand partial payment for what he had done.

---

41. See, for example, Alberta's *Sale of Goods Act*, R.S.A. 2000, c. S-2, s. 10.

Exceptions to the General Rule

PROMISSORY ESTOPPEL

Another exception to the rule that a promise is enforceable only if consideration is present is based on the principle of **promissory estoppel**, sometimes referred to as **equitable estoppel**. The more common or ordinary use of the term *estoppel* involves statements of fact, which will be discussed in Chapter 10. Promissory estoppel, in contrast, deals with a person making a promise or a commitment to do something in the future. As we have discussed, an exchange of such promises or commitments constitutes consideration, and the result is a binding contract. But when the promise is one sided or gratuitous, it is normally not enforceable. (Figure 6.4 illustrates how promissory estoppel works.)

Gratuitous promises are usually not enforceable . . .

Figure 6.4 Promissory Estoppel

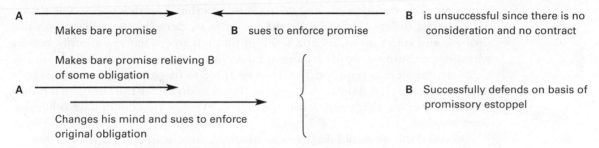

A ⟶ Makes bare promise   ⟵ B sues to enforce promise   B is unsuccessful since there is no consideration and no contract

A ⟶ Makes bare promise relieving B of some obligation / Changes his mind and sues to enforce original obligation   B Successfully defends on basis of promissory estoppel

But sometimes the promisee, in anticipation of the promise being performed, incurs expenses or other obligations that otherwise could have been avoided. In the presence of such reliance, unique remedies have been developed to compensate for significant loss. In the United States, when such reliance is placed on a gratuitous promise and injury results, it is possible to sue for compensation. In the United Kingdom and Canada, however, such an unfulfilled promise can be used only as a defence to an action initiated by the person who made the promise.

. . . but sometimes can be used as a defence

In London, England, just before World War II, High Trees leased an apartment building from Property Trust under a 99-year lease, with the intention of renting out the individual flats in the building.[42] The two parties agreed to a set yearly rent of £2500. Because of the outbreak of the war, it soon became apparent that High Trees would not be able to rent out all of the flats. Therefore, in 1942, Property Trust agreed to lower the yearly rent to £1250. After the war, it changed its mind and demanded payment of all of the rent owed under the original lease, including back rent for the portion that had not been paid since 1942. It argued that the promise to take less rent was one sided and, as a gratuitous promise, was not binding. The Court agreed that, for the period after the war, High Trees had to again pay the full rent. With respect to the back rent, however, Property Trust was bound by its promise to take the lower amount. The key to understanding this is to realize that High Trees was not suing to enforce the promise; rather, Property Trust was suing for the higher amount in spite of its promise. High Trees was using the plaintiff's promise as a defence to the plaintiff's claim. Thus, in the United Kingdom, the principle of promissory estoppel is remedial in nature. In *Combe v. Combe*, Lord Denning made it clear that "it does not create new causes of action where none existed before,"[43] and Lord Asquith, in his concurring judgment, said that promissory estoppel could be used only as "a shield but not as a sword."[44]

Promissory estoppel cannot be used as a sword

---

[42] *Central London Property Trust, Ltd. v. High Trees House, Ltd.*, [1947] 1 K.B. 130.

[43] [1951] 1 All E.R. 767 (C.A.) at 769.

[44] Ibid. at 772.

Canada has followed the English example, limiting the use of promissory estoppel to a defence. That is why, in the case of *Gilbert Steel* (discussed in Case Summary 6.11), the argument of promissory estoppel failed. Gilbert Steel argued that because University Construction promised to pay more and Gilbert Steel relied on the promise, it created an "estoppel" and University Construction should be required to pay the higher amount. But Gilbert Steel was not using the promise as a defence; it was suing, claiming payment on the basis of that promise. Since it was using the promise as a sword instead of a shield, it failed. Note that if University Construction had made the higher payments and then sued Gilbert Steel to get them back, promissory estoppel would have been available to Gilbert Steel as a defence.

There must also be reliance placed on the promise

In fact, in almost every case where promissory estoppel has been successfully used as a defence there was an existing legal relationship, usually contractual, that was modified by a promise. The promisor was attempting to enforce the original terms of the agreement, ignoring the relied-upon promise to alter the terms. The disappointed promisee was using the promise as a shield, or defence, to the action. To raise this defence successfully, the victim must demonstrate reliance on the promise and suffer an injury as a result of that reliance. That was another reason why the promissory estoppel argument raised in the *Gilbert Steel* case failed. True, it delivered the steel as required, but it was required to do so under the original contract in any case. It did only what it was required to do under the contract; it didn't take on any extra obligation or incur any extra expense that could have otherwise been avoided.

Do you think we would do better to adopt the American approach and allow an action for compensation whenever someone relies on a gratuitous promise to her detriment?

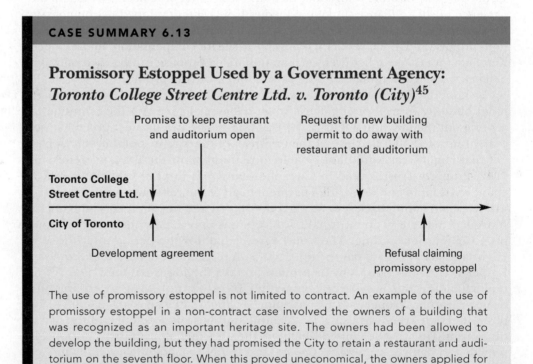

CASE SUMMARY 6.13

Promissory Estoppel Used by a Government Agency:
Toronto College Street Centre Ltd. v. Toronto (City)[45]

The use of promissory estoppel is not limited to contract. An example of the use of promissory estoppel in a non-contract case involved the owners of a building that was recognized as an important heritage site. The owners had been allowed to develop the building, but they had promised the City to retain a restaurant and auditorium on the seventh floor. When this proved uneconomical, the owners applied for a building permit to change the use of the seventh floor to rental units. The permit was refused, and that decision was challenged by way of judicial review of administrative action (see Chapter 3 for a discussion of this process). The Court based its

---

[45.] (1986), 56 O.R. (2d) 522 (C.A.).

decision partly on promissory estoppel. The owners of the building had promised to maintain the seventh floor as a restaurant and auditorium, and the City had refused to grant a permit to do otherwise. The owners were estopped by their promise. Note that the promise of the owners of the property was being used as a defence by the City; it was clear that the City had relied on the promise when allowing them to do other things with the building. The case is interesting in that it involves the enforcement of the doctrine in a non-contract situation and to the benefit of a government entity rather than an individual.

SMALL BUSINESS PERSPECTIVE

In light of this case, businesspeople must be careful in making promises to government agencies while seeking government approval or permission. What should government agencies do to ensure that such promises will be enforced against the promisors?

SEALED DOCUMENTS

The last major exception to the requirement of consideration involves the use of a seal. Seals were originally made by placing melted wax on a document and impressing a signet ring in it, thus lending authenticity or authority to the document. When the parties went to so much trouble to indicate they were serious, they were bound by their commitment. This practice—which predates modern contract law—has been retained; thus, when a seal is used it is not necessary to show consideration for the contract to be binding. Today, instead of a wax impression, the seal normally takes the form of a paper wafer, although almost any form of marking on the document that the parties have identified as a seal can be used. A sealed contract is a formal contract, or a deed. The court will not entertain any suggestion that the promise contained in a formal contract is not supported by consideration. Although it is not necessary to look for consideration when a seal is present, the existence of the seal does not eliminate the need for the other elements of a valid contract.

Sealed documents do not require consideration

To summarize, consideration (the price one is willing to pay for a promise) is one of the required elements of a contract. There must be some form of valid consideration in the form of a benefit or detriment flowing between the parties for a court to enforce a contract. Only when the document embodying the agreement is sealed, or on those rare occasions when the promise of the promisor is being raised as a defence by the promisee, will the court enforce an agreement without requiring consideration to be established.[46]

MyBusLawLab   Be sure to visit the MyBusLawLab that accompanies this book to find practice quizzes, province-specific content, simulations and much more!

---

[46]. See *Romaine Estate v. Romaine* (2001), 95 B.C.L.R. (3d) 95 (C.A.), 2001 BCCA 509 (CanLII), in which gift documents with wafer seals were enforced as sealed contracts.

SUMMARY

The contractual relationship

- A contract is an exchange of promises enforceable in court
- There are five elements of a valid contract: consensus, consideration, capacity, legality, and intention
- There are many important terms and definitions relevant to the contractual relationship

Consensus

- A contract requires "a meeting of the minds"
- An offer is a tentative promise by the offeror contingent upon an acceptance by the offeree
- All the essential terms of the contract must be contained in the offer; non-essential terms will be implied by the courts
- An invitation to treat, or an invitation to negotiate, is not an offer
- An offer must be communicated to the offeree before it can be accepted
- An offer will end at a specified time, but it may be revoked earlier by notice to the offeree, unless an option agreement has been entered into
- If there is not a specified time limit, an offer will lapse after a reasonable time
- A counteroffer, a rejection of the offer, or the death or insanity of the offeror will also cause an offer to lapse
- A standard form contract is interpreted strictly against the party who drafted it
- There is now a need for good faith contractual performance and a duty to act honestly in the performance of contractual obligations
- An acceptance is an indication of a willingness to be bound; a contract is formed when an offer is accepted
- An acceptance must be complete and unconditional
- An acceptance must be communicated in the manner required by the offer; it is effective when and where it is received
- Silence may be acceptance if there is an existing business relationship
- The postbox rule says that an acceptance by mail (when reasonable) is effective when and where it is dropped in the mailbox
- The postbox rule has been extended to telegrams, but not to instantaneous forms of communication
- The law of contracts has evolved with respect to electronic transactions and will no doubt continue to do so as ecommerce continues to grow in importance

Consideration

- Consideration is the price paid for another party's promise and can be anything of value
- Both parties must have experienced some benefit; a gratuitous promise is not enforceable
- Consideration must be specific, but it need not be fair; courts will not review its adequacy
- A promise to do what you are already legally obligated to do is unenforceable
- Past consideration is no consideration
- An agreement to accept less in full satisfaction of a debt is unenforceable in common law, but may now be binding under legislation
- Illegal consideration and impossible consideration are not valid consideration
- An out-of-court settlement is enforceable, as there is valid consideration
- *Quantum meruit* is used when there is a request for services with no agreement as to the amount; a reasonable price must be paid
- Promissory estoppel enables a gratuitous promise to be used as a defence
- When a contract is sealed, consideration is not necessary

QUESTIONS FOR REVIEW

1. What is meant by "freedom of contract"? Explain the impact of this principle on the development of contract law. What are two types of restrictions on this principle?

2. List and explain the elements that must be present for an agreement to qualify as a valid contract.

3. Explain the difference between a formal contract and a parol contract.

4. Explain the difference between void and voidable. What is a practical result of this difference?

5. Distinguish between unenforceable contracts and illegal contracts.

6. Explain the difference between a bilateral contract and a unilateral contract.

7. What practical concepts does contract law use to determine if "a meeting of the minds" has happened?

8. At what stage in the process of forming a contract are the significant terms of the contract clearly set out?

9. Explain the role of implied terms in a contract. Who has the power to imply terms into a contract? When will that power be used?

10. Is an "agreement to agree" binding? Explain your answer.

11. Distinguish between an offer and an invitation to treat.

12. Can you accept an offer that was made to someone else? Explain your answer.

13. List and explain the various ways an offer can come to an end.

14. What is the effect of the offeror stating in an offer that the offer will remain open for acceptance until a specific date? What can an offeree do to protect himself from the offer being revoked?

15. What risks are faced when a person offers to sell certain goods to A and then sells them to B instead? How can this problem be avoided?

16. Explain the two types of contracts that result from the tendering process.

17. What do the courts do, when interpreting standard form contracts, to correct the imbalance in bargaining power between the parties?

18. Do parties to a contract have a duty to act honestly in the performance of their contractual obligations? Explain your answer.

19. What qualities must an acceptance demonstrate to be effective?

20. When is a contract formed?

21. When will silence be considered an acceptance of an offer?

22. What is the general rule regarding acceptance? What is a practical result of this rule?

23. Explain the effect of the postbox rule on the principles governing acceptance.

24. Discuss the role the postbox rule plays when modern communication methods are used.

25. What is "click-wrap?" How is an online offer to sell a software licence usually accepted?

26. What two factors do the courts consider when deciding whether to enforce an electronic contract?

27. Define consideration and explain what is meant by the term "the exchange of consideration."

28. Explain under what circumstances a person who fails to properly perform a gratuitous promise can be held legally liable for that failure.

29. Does consideration have to be fair? Explain your answer.

30. What difficulty might be faced by a person who has already agreed to do a specific job and then extracts a promise of more pay from the other party?

31. If a person who is rescued promises to pay the rescuer $1000 but doesn't pay, will the rescuer be successful in suing for breach of contract? Explain your answer.

32. "A creditor is bound by her promise to take less in full satisfaction of the debt." True or false? Explain your answer.

33. Explain why a contract dispute settled out of court is considered binding even though one party would have obtained more if the action had been taken to court.

34. Explain a person's obligation regarding payment when he has requested a service without specifying a particular fee.

35. Describe what is meant by promissory estoppel and the circumstances in which it will arise in contract disputes.

36. How does the presence of a seal affect the requirement that consideration must be present in a contract?

CASES AND DISCUSSION QUESTIONS

1. *Wembley Marketing Ltd. v. ITEX Corp.*, [2008] O.J. No. 5194 (S.C.), 2008 CanLII 67425 (ON SC)

Wembley claimed it did not receive goods and services from ITEX for which it had paid. ITEX argued that the action should not proceed because the relevant contract said that any actions must be brought in California. Wembley had completed an application, providing relevant information, two different times. The application included the word *AGREEMENT* in bold letters. The section below that required a separate signature and referred to "the most recent Membership Agreement and Operating Rules." The rules required that any action arising under the agreement "shall lie only in the courts of Sacramento, California." A copy of the agreement and rules had been provided to Wembley; they were also available on ITEX's website. The person who signed the application on behalf of Wembley testified that he would not have signed it had he read the agreement and rules. He admitted that he "did not bother to read the small print on the Application."

Was there a contract between Wembley and ITEX? Does it matter if the person who signed the contract did not read all of it? Would the clause giving jurisdiction to California courts be enforced?

2. *Bigstone v. Bigstone*, 2013 SKCA (CanLII)

A separated couple negotiated an agreement under which the wife waived her rights to her husband's pension benefits. The husband signed the interspousal agreement on October 9, 2010. The wife signed it on October 13. Unfortunately, the husband died unexpectedly on October 12. The wife claimed not to be bound by the interspousal agreement and made a claim under the husband's pension plan. She was denied benefits. She applied to have the Court nullify the interspousal agreement so she would qualify as the beneficiary of the pension benefits.

Should the Court enforce the interspousal agreement, even though the wife signed it after the husband died? Was this a case in which the parties did not intend to be bound by their agreement until the written contract was signed by both of them?

3. *Ayerswood Development Corp. v. Hydro One Networks Inc.*, [2004] O.J. No. 4926 (S.C.), 2004 CanLII 45463 (ON SC)

Ontario Hydro published information about an incentive program designed to promote energy efficient initiatives. The stated deadline for applications was March 31, 1993. Just before this date, Ontario Hydro announced that the program was suspended. Ayerswood applied under the incentive program on March 30, 1993, but its application was not even processed. It therefore sued for the incentive payment that it would have been entitled to under the incentive program.

Should the Court order that the incentive payment be made? If there was a contract, what type was it?

4. *IGM U.S.A. Inc. (Bucci Industries U.S.A. Inc.) v. Linamar Holdings Inc.*, 2007 CanLII 38942 (ON SC), aff'd ONCA 256 (CanLII)

Industrial machines designed and manufactured in Italy by IGM were installed in Linamar's facility in Ontario. Linamar claimed that the machines were not ready on time and that they were not made pursuant to the agreed-upon specifications. It sued for $17 million. IGM claimed that the contract required that all disputes between the parties were to be determined under Italian laws, in Italian courts.

The Court determined that the contract was formed by extensive negotiations and an exchange of documents between the parties. IGM then issued an invoice for an advance payment, which Linamar paid. The following clause was on the back of the invoice:

> For all disputes arising directly or indirectly from the supply contract regardless of where this agreement took place or where the goods were delivered, the Forum of Ravenna will have jurisdiction, without exception whatsoever.

Assuming there were no other provisions in the contractual documents that dealt with the jurisdictional issue, does the clause apply? If it doesn't, would Linamar's standard terms (that the Ontario courts would have jurisdiction) apply?

5. *Leonard v. GC Surplus*, 2014 CanLII 18980 (ONSCSM)

Leonard lived in Toronto. He made an Internet bid on a vehicle and received an email confirming that his bid was the winning bid. The email was sent from Nova Scotia. The Court would only have jurisdiction if the subject matter of the claim arose in the City of Toronto. The defendant claimed that the cause of action arose in Nova Scotia because that is where the parties entered into the contract.

Where was the contract formed?

6. *Stadnyk v. Dash*, 2007 SKQB 443 (CanLII)

The parties were negotiating a settlement agreement. On July 5 Stadnyk's lawyer sent a proposal for settlement to Dash's lawyer with a note that said, in part, "I would appreciate it if you could provide me with a response to this proposal within the next 10 days." Dash's lawyer replied on August 15 and indicated that the proposal was acceptable to Dash. He enclosed an amended agreement that has to be signed by Stadnyk. On August 28, prior to being advised of the August 15 acceptance by her lawyer, Stadnyk instructed him to revoke the offer.

The Court was faced with three issues: Was acceptance unconditional, clear, and absolute? Was the quoted sentence from the letter of July 5 sufficient to impose a time limit for acceptance? Was the offer contained in the letter of July 5, 2007, revoked? What should the Court decide?

7. *MacMillan Estate v. Hoffman*, 2011 BCSC 141 (CanLII)

Hoffman rented a house. He and the owner signed a document entitled "Lease to Purchase." The only relevant term of this agreement read as follows: "The Vendor hereby grants to the Purchaser an exclusive option to purchase, free and clear the lands and premises for the sum of SIXTY THOUSAND DOLLARS ($60,000.00)." Hoffman claimed that the lease to purchase was an agreement for sale.

What type of agreement is the lease to purchase? This agreement was not signed under seal. Is it valid?

7 Chapter

The Elements of a Contract: Capacity, Legality, and Intention

LEARNING OBJECTIVES

1. Explain the capacity of minors
2. Compare the capacity of the insane and the drunk
3. Review the law for others of limited capacity
4. Discuss the law relating to contracts performed illegally
5. Discuss the law relating to contracts formed illegally
6. Review the contractual element of intention
7. Examine the requirement that contracts be in writing
8. Explain the principle of part performance

In addition to consensus and consideration (discussed in the previous chapter), contracting parties must have the capacity to contract, the contract must be legal and be performed legally, and both parties must have intended that legal consequences would follow from their agreement. Each of these elements will be discussed in this chapter. Although it is always a good idea to put a contract in writing, the general principle is that a verbal contract is as binding as a written one. There are several situations, however, for which contracts are required by statute to be evidenced in writing. These will also be discussed in this chapter.

CAPACITY

Lawmakers have always recognized that some people are more vulnerable than others and thus require special protection. Over the years, several categories of people have been identified as needing protection. These categories have been protected by having their freedom to enter into contracts limited or, in some cases, eliminated completely.

 LO **1** **2** **3**

Some groups are given legal protection

Minors/Infants

The age of majority was 21 at common law, but it has been reduced by statute to 18 or 19, depending on the province. The general principle is that persons under the age of majority, called **infants** or **minors**, are not bound by their agreements, but the adults with whom they contract are bound. The courts try to balance protecting the minor against the objective of not imposing undue hardship on the adult. It is important to distinguish between the actual incapacity of a child who is incapable of understanding what is happening, and the artificial incapacity imposed on a youth who is a functioning member of society.

Most problems relating to minors and contracts they have entered into arise in situations involving young people who are approaching the age of majority. The test for capacity is objective. When an adult deals with a person who is a minor, it does not matter if the adult was under the impression that the other person was an adult, or even that the minor clearly understood the terms of the contract. The only question is whether the other person was under the statutory age of majority at the time the contract was created. As a general rule, whenever a minor enters into a contract with an adult, the adult is bound by the contract, but the minor can choose not to be bound by it.

For example, when a sales representative of a car dealership offers to sell a car for $2500 to a minor who accepts the offer, the dealership will be bound by the contract. If the young person has not yet taken delivery of the car, she has the choice as to whether to go through with the deal or not. If she takes delivery of the car and then chooses not to pay for it, she would have to return the car. She could not, however, be forced to pay or otherwise go through with the contract even if she wrecks the car or it is stolen.

In most provinces, these principles are based on English and Canadian case law. British Columbia, however, has a unique *Infants Act*.[1] This legislation states that, in most cases, a contract made by a minor is unenforceable against him. The minor may, however, enforce the contract against an adult party to the contract. The result, then, is the same as in the provinces that rely on the common law. Other provinces may also have legislation dealing with the contractual capacity of minors. For example, Alberta's *Minors' Property Act*[2] allows a court to confirm a contract entered into by a minor if it believes it is in the best interests of the child to do so.

Special problems arise when dealing with contracts made online. The law with respect to capacity will be determined by the jurisdiction where the contract is created, which is sometimes not clear. Also, there is no way for online merchants to know the personal characteristics of the parties with whom they are dealing. For example, children and people who are mentally incompetent often have access to computers and the Internet. As it is not possible to determine the capacity of persons with whom they are dealing, it is important that online merchants include appropriate restrictions and disclaimers in their online contracts. Any business engaged in Internet transactions with parties in the United States should be aware of the *Children's Online Privacy Protection Act*.[3] This legislation includes restrictions on marketing to children under 13 years of age.

NECESSARIES AND BENEFICIAL CONTRACTS OF SERVICE

Except in British Columbia, minors are bound by contracts for the acquisition of necessaries and by contracts of employment, or for service, that benefit the minor. **Necessaries** are things required to function in society, such as food, clothing, lodging, and transportation. What constitutes a necessary will vary with the particular needs of a minor and her status. If the young person is purchasing clothing but already has a sufficient supply, then that clothing will not be considered a necessary.

Age of majority varies with provinces

Test for capacity is objective

Minors are not bound by their contracts, but adults are

Legislation supplements common law

Online contracts should include restrictions

Minors are bound by contracts for necessaries . . .

What is a necessary depends on the circumstances

---

1. R.S.B.C. 1996, c. 223.
2. S.A. 2004, c. M-18.1, s. 3.
3. 15 U.S.C. 6501.

Minors must pay only a reasonable price for necessaries

When a minor is married or is living on his own, what constitutes a necessary will be broader than would be the case if he were single and dependent on his parents. The courts have held that medical, dental, and legal services, along with toiletries, uniforms, and even a house, will be considered as necessaries in different situations. It is unlikely, however, that they will find that a car qualifies as a necessary, since other alternative forms of transportation are generally available. Even when the subject of the contract is determined to be a necessary, it does not guarantee that the merchant will get paid full price, as the minor is obligated only to pay a reasonable price for such necessaries.[4]

Minors must repay money borrowed and used for necessaries

When a minor borrows money to buy necessaries, there is an obligation to repay the debt only if the funds advanced are actually used for necessaries. For this reason, a creditor cannot recover money loaned to a minor to pay for school tuition if it is used instead for gambling. Government student loans are exceptions, because they are supported by legislation requiring repayment regardless of what the money is used for and regardless of the age of the borrower.

Minors are bound by contracts of employment or for services that benefit them

Contracts of employment for service are binding if it can be demonstrated that, taken as a whole, the contract is for the benefit of the minor. If it becomes apparent that the minor is being taken advantage of or the contract is not in the minor's best interests, the minor will not be bound. Today, these kinds of relationships are usually controlled by legislation.[5]

Note the BC exception

Note that in British Columbia's *Infants Act*, all contracts, including contracts for necessaries and beneficial contracts of employment or for service, are unenforceable against an infant. Only contracts made specifically enforceable by legislation will be binding on infants.[6] An example of such a contract is a student loan agreement.[7]

ON BECOMING AN ADULT

Minor can ratify a contract at age of majority

If a minor agrees to a contract (other than a contract for necessaries or a beneficial contract of service) he is not bound by it. If, however, he ratifies the contract after becoming an adult, he loses the right to avoid the contract. That is, ratifying the contract makes a voidable contract binding. For example, if a minor agrees to pay $5000 for an automobile in a series of instalment payments, he cannot be forced to pay. If, however, the minor, after becoming an adult, makes an instalment payment or provides a written statement indicating that he intends to be bound, the contract will then be binding. Ratification can be in writing[8] or it can be implied. Ratification must be complete; a minor cannot affirm the beneficial provisions of the contract and repudiate the rest.

CASE SUMMARY 7.1

What Amounts to Ratification? *Bayview Credit Union Ltd. v. Daigle*[9]

Daigle was a minor when he borrowed a considerable sum from the Bayview Credit Union. He used his motorcycle as security for the loan. While still a minor, he stopped making payments and hid the motorcycle. After reaching the age of majority, he disclosed the location of the motorcycle. The credit union repossessed and sold the motorcycle, but there was still $4100 owing on the loan. The credit union sued Daigle. It claimed that his

---

4. Some provinces have legislation dealing with the purchase of necessaries by minors. See, for example, Alberta's *Sale of Goods Act*, R.S.A. 2000, c. S-2, s. 4, which states that minors need only pay a reasonable price for necessaries, and that necessaries are goods suitable to the "condition in life" of the minor and to the minor's actual requirements.

5. See, for example, Alberta's *Apprenticeship and Industry Training Act*, R.S.A. 2000, c. A-42.

6. *Supra* note 1, s. 19.

7. See, for example, the *Canada Student Loans Act*, R.S.C. 1985, c. S-23, s. 19, which states that a lender may recover a student loan made to a minor as if the minor "had been of full age at the time the loan was made."

8. In some provinces, ratification must be in writing and be signed by the minor to be effective. See, for example, Nova Scotia's *Statute of Frauds*, R.S.N.S. 1989, c. 442, s. 9.

9. (1983), 3 D.L.R. (4th) 95, 52 N.B.R. (2d) 436, 137 A.P.R. 436 (N.B.Q.B.).

disclosure of the location of the motorcycle when he was an adult amounted to ratification of the contract, making it enforceable against him.

The Court held that Daigle was not liable. His action was not ratification. He was merely assisting the credit union in realizing its security. The Court commented, "Surely the acts of the defendant here, in co-operating as he did to the benefit of the plaintiff, should not place him in a worse position than a person who would refuse co-operation to reduce the plaintiff's loss." The case illustrates the danger of businesspeople dealing with minors as if they were adults. It also shows the implications of a minor ratifying a contract after becoming an adult.

DISCUSSION QUESTIONS
What are some policies a sophisticated client could adopt to reduce the risk associated with entering into contracts with minors? Should a minor lose the protection of the law when, whether out of ignorance or a sense of obligation, he chooses to continue to pay or acknowledges a debt after becoming an adult?

There are certain contracts that a minor must repudiate within a reasonable time after becoming an adult to avoid obligations (or, as some cases suggest, a failure to repudiate can be evidence of ratification). These situations tend to involve contracts through which a minor acquires some interest of a permanent and continuous nature—for example, those involving land, shares in corporations, partnerships, and marriage settlements. The cases in this area tend to be very old, with little in the way of recent case law.[10]

Some contracts must be repudiated

Although these principles may seem reasonably straightforward, their application has created a good deal of confusion. To appreciate the reasons for this confusion, it is necessary to understand how the contractual relationship progresses through prescribed stages. At the first stage, when the parties have entered into the contract but the minor has not yet obtained any benefit from it and has not yet paid, the minor is not bound by the contract. This is an **executory contract**. If the minor has received the goods but has not yet paid for them, she is not necessarily bound by the contract. This is a **partially executed contract**. When the goods are in the minor's possession, she will be required to return them or pay for them, and upon return is entitled to a refund of any money already paid. If the minor has passed the goods on to a third party or the goods have been destroyed, the merchant will not be entitled to payment and the merchant also cannot insist that the party to whom the goods have been given return them.

Description of contractual relationships

Conflict may arise when the contract has been **executed**. Once minors have obtained the benefit under a contract, can they change their minds and insist on the return of their money? In Canadian law, the conclusion seems to be that minors are bound by the contract unless it can be demonstrated that what was received was of no value at all. That is, a minor can insist that payment be refunded if there is a total failure of consideration and the minor gained nothing from the deal. In general, if the contract is prejudicial to the interests of the minor, it is void.

When a contract gives no benefit, a minor can escape even an executed contract

REDUCING RISK 7.1

Merchants run a great risk when they deal with even mature youths as if they were adults. Contracts cannot be enforced against them and, while security can be taken in goods, even that may not be much protection when the goods used as security are destroyed or otherwise made unavailable, as illustrated by Case Summary 7.1. When dealing with minors, a sophisticated client will not only take security for the loan, but also have the parents of the minor co-sign the contract or have them give a personal guarantee. Secured transactions will be discussed in Chapter 15.

---

10. See, for example, *R. v. Rash* (1923), 53 O.L.R. 245; *Saunders v. Russell*, [1902] B.C.J. No. 65, 9 B.C.R. 321 (S.C.); *Lovell and Christmas v. Beauchamp*, [1894] A.C. 607 (H.L.); and *Edwards v. Carter*, [1893] A.C. 360 (H.L.).

PARENTS' LIABILITY

Parents are not responsible for minors' contracts

There is a popular misconception that liability will rest with the parents if a child fails to pay a debt. As a general rule, parents are not responsible for the torts of their children, nor are they responsible for the contractual obligations of their children in the absence of specific legislation creating such a responsibility. If a minor enters into a contract, he alone is responsible to perform the contract. The adult contracting with the minor cannot turn to the parents if the minor does not perform as required by the contract.

Legislation may make parents liable

Parents may be responsible where there is agency or a guarantee, or where goods are necessaries

Many jurisdictions have passed legislation making parents liable for the torts, contracts, and even criminal activities of their children.[11] In the absence of such legislation, parents can be held liable for their children's contracts only under specific conditions. Parents can be liable when the minor is acting as an agent having the appropriate authority to bind the parent in contract. (Agency will be discussed in Chapter 10.) Parents will also be bound if they guarantee the minor's obligation at the time the contract is entered into. A guarantee is a written commitment whereby the guarantor agrees to pay the debt if the debtor does not. Since the very purpose of the guarantee is to encourage the merchant to enter the contract, these guarantees have been held to be binding on the parents. Also, because parents are responsible to provide for their minor children, they can be held responsible by the merchant for contracts their children enter into for necessaries.[12]

INFANTS' LIABILITY FOR TORTS

Minors may be liable in tort

Adults cannot avoid protection given to minors under contract law by suing in tort . . .

A merchant will occasionally try to get around the protection given to a minor in contract law by suing in tort instead. Sometimes the act that constitutes the breach of contract will also qualify as negligence or some other tort, as discussed in Chapters 4 and 5. It is a basic tenet of tort law that a minor is as liable as an adult for torts committed, although the standard of behaviour expected may differ. But the courts will not allow adults to bring a tort action just to get around the incapacity problem in contract law. If the minor used the subject matter of the contract in a way that would be expected under the contract, then the adult must sue in contract, not tort, despite the protection given to the minor by the law of contracts.

. . . except when tort arises independent of a contract

On the other hand, if the minor used the subject matter of the contract in a way that was not contemplated in the contract, carelessly causing injury or damage to those goods, the adult would be able to sue for negligence and the minor would not be protected by the defence of infancy. For example, if a minor rents a two-wheel-drive automobile and then damages it while off-roading, the merchant would be able to sue the minor for negligence because the use to which the automobile was put was outside what was anticipated in the contract.

However, if the minor had an accident while driving the rented automobile on a highway, the adult could not sue in tort, even if the minor was clearly negligent, because that activity would be expected when a car is rented. In short, the adult cannot circumvent the protection afforded to the minor in contract law by suing in tort instead. (This explains why car rental agencies will not rent to minors, but when a minor misrepresents herself as an adult and contracts to rent a vehicle, the agency may be able to get damages from the minor by suing for the tort of fraudulent misrepresentation.) Nor are the parents responsible, since parents are not liable for the torts of their children unless they can be said to have been negligent in their own right, or when there is a statute in place imposing such liability.

---

11. Several provinces have enacted legislation to this effect. See, for example, Ontario's *Family Law Act*, R.S.O. 1990, c. F.3, s. 45(2).

12. See, for example, Manitoba's *Parental Responsibility Act*, C.C.S.M. c. P8, which makes parents liable if their child "deliberately takes, damages or destroys the property of another person." The parents' liability is limited to $10 000. The parents may avoid liability by showing that they were exercising reasonable supervision and that they made reasonable efforts to prevent or discourage the child from engaging in the kind of activity that resulted in the property loss.

CASE SUMMARY 7.2

Minor Liable for Tortious Acts Not Contemplated by Contract: *Royal Bank of Canada v. Holoboff*[13]

Holoboff, a minor, entered into an agreement for a savings account with the bank. He then sold his client card and his personal identification number (PIN) to a third party. The third party proceeded to defraud the bank by making a "fake" deposit to Holoboff's account and then withdrawing money from the account. Holoboff was convicted of fraud. He was then sued by the bank.

Holoboff claimed that he should not be found liable because of the common law that allows minors to avoid contracts that are not for necessaries. The bank argued that the fraudulent use of the debit card by a third party with Holoboff's assistance was not contemplated by the terms of the contract. The Court found that the contract required Holoboff to keep his PIN confidential and to restrict the use of his debit card to his personal use only. Therefore, Holoboff selling his card and revealing his PIN were outside the contemplation of the contract. The Court thus allowed the bank's claim and found Holoboff liable for the tort of conspiracy to commit fraud.

DISCUSSION QUESTIONS

Is the distinction between liability in tort and in contract artificial? Is it appropriate that an infant may be found liable in tort but not in contract? Should the law be made consistent so that an infant cannot be found liable for any of his actions?

Insanity and Drunkenness

The law extends its protection to those incapacitated because of insanity or mental incompetence in a way similar to the protection given to minors. To qualify for this protection, it must be shown that the person could not understand the nature of the act being performed. To take an extreme example, if a man thinks that he is Napoleon and that he is selling his horse when, in fact, he is selling his car, he would be declared to lack the capacity to contract because he does not understand the nature of the transaction. The burden of proving incapacity on the basis of insanity or mental incompetence rests with the person claiming to be incapacitated. That person must lead evidence showing that he did not understand the consequences of his actions.

> Insanity or mental incompetence applies if a person did not understand . . .

To escape contractual liability on the basis of insanity or mental incompetence, the person (or a representative) must prove not only insanity or mental incompetence, but also that the person he was dealing with knew or ought to have known of the incapacity. This is the point illustrated in Case Summary 7.3.

> . . . and if other party knew or ought to have known of incapacity

---

CASE SUMMARY 7.3

Bank Must Know or Ought to Have Known of Insanity: *Canadian Imperial Bank of Commerce v. Milhomens*[14]

Milhomens executed a Visa application agreement in favour of CIBC and was issued a Visa card. He used the card and, eventually, had an outstanding balance owing of $18 104.29 plus interest at the rate of 18.5 percent. CIBC sued for non-payment of the debt. Milhomens claimed that "he was of unsound mind and incapable of appreciating

---

13. (1998), 221 A.R. 192 (Q.B.).
14. 2004 SKQB 168 (CanLII).

[handwritten margin note: Ct stated under no obligation to ascertain, and could not be expected to know if spending pattern changed.]

or understanding the meaning and effect of the Visa application agreement when he signed it." The evidence showed that Milhomens had a long psychiatric history. However, there was no evidence showing that CIBC ever knew or ought to have known about his condition.

DISCUSSION QUESTIONS

Should CIBC be awarded judgment for the amount claimed? Is there an obligation on a bank to monitor the spending patterns of its credit card holders to determine if they change and, if they do, the reason for the change? Is there anything else Milhomens could have done with respect to the purchases he made with his Visa card?

Provincial legislation applies to people who are mentally incompetent

A person may be declared mentally incompetent by a court. In such cases, a trustee will be appointed to handle that person's affairs. To understand the precise rights and obligations of a trustee and the care and use of that person's property, the appropriate provincial legislation should be carefully examined.[15]

Drunkenness is treated like insanity

Must repudiate upon becoming sober

People who lose their ability to reason through intoxication, whether from alcohol or drugs, are treated in the same way as people incapacitated by insanity or mental incompetence. As is the case with insanity, for the contract to be avoided the person must have been so intoxicated that she didn't know what she was doing, and the other person must have known or ought to have known of the incapacity. The person trying to escape a contract on the basis of drunkenness must also be able to show that, on reaching sobriety, the contract was repudiated. For example, an intoxicated person who purchases shares is not permitted, on becoming sober, to wait and see whether the stocks go up or down before repudiating the contract. Hesitation to repudiate makes the contract binding. This requirement of **repudiation** also applies to insane people who regain their sanity. As with minors, the insane, mentally incompetent, or intoxicated person is also required to pay a reasonable price for necessaries.

A person who is of weakened intellect, or otherwise vulnerable, but not insane or mentally incompetent, is still to some extent protected. Unconscionable transactions, the legal principle providing this protection, will be discussed in Chapter 8.

Others of Limited Capacity

Corporate capacity—usually no longer a problem

Corporations have their capacity to contract determined by the legislation under which they are incorporated. In some jurisdictions, corporations can limit their capacity to contract by so stating in their incorporating documents. Otherwise, corporations incorporated under these general statutes have "all the power of a natural person" to contract. Even in those jurisdictions where the capacity of a corporation can be limited, people dealing with those corporations are affected by that limitation only if they have notice of it.

CASE SUMMARY 7.4

Unincorporated Business Has No Capacity: *Maple Engineering & Construction Ltd. v. 1373988 Ontario Inc.*[16]

Maple submitted a bid to be the general contractor of a project. One of the defendants, Bisson, was the director and sole shareholder of 1373988, which carried on business using the trade names "AC" and "ACI." Bisson submitted a bid to Maple for subcontract work on behalf of ACI. After winning the contract for the project, Maple

15. See, for example, Alberta's *Adult Guardianship and Trustee Act*, S.A. 2008, c. A-4.2.
16. [2004] O.J. No. 5025 (S.C.J.), 2004 CanLII 46655 (ON SC).

provided Bisson with plans and specifications of the project. Maple received a new bid from Bisson, also on the letterhead of ACI. It forwarded a formal contract to ACI for review. ACI eventually advised Maple that an agreement between them could not be reached. Maple entered into a contract with another subcontractor and sued Bisson for the difference in price.

Maple did not know of the existence of 1373988. Maple argued that a contract between it and ACI came into existence when it accepted the second bid. The Court agreed. It held that an unconditional contract was formed when ACI submitted its second bid and it was accepted by Maple. When ACI refused to perform, Maple lost profits by having to hire a second subcontractor at a greater cost. Bisson was personally liable for the damages, as he had signed the bid on behalf of ACI, an unincorporated business, and had then induced Maple to enter into a contract by representing himself as an agent of ACI.

This case shows that it is important that businesspeople understand the status of the businesses they are representing. A corporation has the capacity to enter into contracts; an agent will therefore not incur personal liability if a contract is breached by the corporation. If a business is unincorporated, it does not have the capacity to enter into contracts and a person representing the business may thus be personally liable for breaches of any contracts entered into. A sophisticated client will avoid such liability by ensuring that the business is incorporated before a contract is created.

SMALL BUSINESS PERSPECTIVE

How can a person determine whether the business she is contracting with is incorporated? If it is, is there any way to ensure that the person representing the corporation will be held responsible for the liabilities of the corporation if it breaches the contract?

Other corporate bodies are created by special legislation. These include some private companies, Crown corporations, and other government bodies that have been created to accomplish particular government purposes. The Business Development Bank of Canada, Canada Revenue Agency, Canada Mortgage and Housing Corporation, Canada Post Corporation, Canadian Air Transport Security Authority, and Canadian Tourism Commission are some examples. The capacity of these entities depends on the legislation that created them. Their power to contract is often limited by that legislation. If they have not been given the capacity to enter into a particular type of contract, any agreement of that type will be void. Outsiders dealing with these corporations or government bodies would be well advised to determine ahead of time the validity of any such dealings. This is especially true when the contract involved is unusual in any way.

Capacity of Crown corporations and government bodies is limited by legislation

CASE SUMMARY 7.5

When a Minister Lacks Capacity: *Andrews v. Canada (Attorney General)*[17]

A group of crab fishermen sued the federal government for breach of contract relating to an arrangement agreed upon by the minister of fisheries and oceans. The minister had indicated that the crab quota allocated to the fishermen would not be reduced unless

17. 2009 NLCA 70 (CanLII); leave to appeal to S.C.C. refused, 2010 CanLII 27731 (SCC). Note that, in subsequent litigation (*Andrews v. Canada (Attorney General)*, 2014 NLCA 32 (CanLII)), the Court allowed a similar case to proceed to trial on the basis that litigation after 2009 had raised questions as to the scope of the "anti-fettering doctrine." *Stare decisis* therefore does not apply and it is necessary that the litigation proceed so that the scope of the doctrine can be determined.

conservation required overall reduction. The minister reduced the quota in violation of his commitment. The government stated that its decisions were within the exclusive discretion of the minister and therefore could not be the subject of a contract.

The Court held that a public authority cannot contract in a manner that would fetter its statutory conferred legislative or executive discretion. That meant that the minister did not have the capacity to agree to not reduce the quota. He could reduce the quota provided his decision was made in good faith.

SMALL BUSINESS PERSPECTIVE

This case illustrates how important it is to determine the power of government bodies before dealing with them. How can a businessperson do this? What should he do if he can't determine whether the government body he is dealing with has the power to enter into the contract that is being negotiated?

REDUCING RISK 7.2

Since Crown corporations and government bodies acting under statutory authority may have their power to contract limited by legislation, a sophisticated client dealing with them will determine, before entering into the contract, whether any contemplated dealings are within their statutory power. This would enable her to avoid incurring losses that usually result if the dealings are not within the entity's statutory power and the resulting contract is declared void.

Capacity of enemy aliens is limited in times of war

Dealing with aliens and representatives of foreign governments also gives rise to capacity issues. When at war, any contract with a resident of an enemy country is void if detrimental to Canada. If not detrimental, the contract is merely suspended for the duration of the hostilities. Note that the government usually passes special legislation covering this area whenever hostilities break out.

Contracts with foreign governments may or may not be enforceable

Even in times of peace, contracts with foreign governments or their representatives were traditionally thought to be unenforceable because of that government's sovereign immunity. The principle is that the sovereignty of the foreign government would be lost if subjected to the jurisdiction of our courts. This provision was particularly important when dealing with matters of state that were of diplomatic importance. However, since foreign governments are now more frequently involved in simple commercial activities that have nothing to do with matters of state, the courts have been willing to treat them as any other party to commercial transactions. These principles are now embodied in legislation.[18]

Foreign diplomats have immunity

Representatives of foreign governments, such as ambassadors and their families, have traditionally been immune from prosecution in our criminal courts and continue to be. In civil matters, a court will not allow a lawsuit to proceed against such persons, and their property is immune from seizure. Of course, these representatives can waive this immunity, if they wish, but anyone dealing with persons who have diplomatic immunity ought to be aware of the protection they have been given.[19]

Trade unions have capacity to contract for union activities

A problem may also arise with respect to the capacity of trade unions. While they are not incorporated as such, it is likely safe to conclude that they at least have the capacity to enter into contracts that relate to their trade union activities. The capacity of trade unions is governed by legislation.[20]

---

18. *State Immunity Act*, R.S.C., 1985, c. S-18.

19. To review the law relating to the privileges and immunities of foreign diplomats, see the *Foreign Missions and International Organizations Act*, S.C. 1991, c. 41.

20. See, for example, s. 25 of Alberta's *Labour Relations Code*, R.S.A. 2000, c. L-1, which states, "For the purposes of this Act, a trade union is capable of (a) prosecuting and being prosecuted, and (b) suing and being sued."

Bankrupts also have their capacity to contract limited. A bankrupt is a person who has made an assignment in bankruptcy or been forced into bankruptcy through a court order obtained by a creditor and who has not been discharged from bankruptcy. Bankruptcy will be discussed in Chapter 15.

Capacity of bankrupts is limited

Finally, the capacity of Indians is limited to some extent by the *Indian Act*.[21] Section 89, for example, says that the property of an Indian on a reserve "is not subject to charge, pledge, mortgage, attachment, levy, seizure, distress or execution in favour or at the instance of any person other than an Indian or a band." Although provisions such as these may seem discriminatory, they remain because section 35 of the *Constitution Act, 1982* recognizes and affirms existing Aboriginal and treaty rights. Section 25 of the *Charter of Rights and Freedoms* states that the *Charter* should not be construed to abrogate or derogate from these rights. Businesspeople contracting with Indians must therefore be aware of their limited contractual capacity.

Indians are protected under the *Indian Act*

REDUCING RISK 7.3

As a general rule, the capacity to enter into contracts is not a problem facing most businesspeople. Still, a sophisticated client will be aware of the problem and be alert to the possibility that the law may protect the person being dealt with so that appropriate steps can be taken. For example, the difficulty in dealing with minors can be avoided through the use of cash, without the extension of credit.

LEGALITY

LO **4** **5**

An agreement must be legal and not contrary to public interest to qualify as a binding contract. It is easy to understand that a contract to commit a crime would be void. But contracts involving activities that, while not illegal, are considered immoral or contrary to public interest may also be void. The courts have taken several different approaches when faced with the problem of illegal or immoral contracts.

Contracts Performed Illegally

When discussing legality, it is necessary to distinguish between illegality as to formation of the contract (the contract itself is illegal) and illegality as to performance (the contract is performed in an illegal way). The Supreme Court of Canada explained this distinction in a case in which a man died when a cocaine-filled condom burst in his stomach.[22] The beneficiaries of his life insurance policy were found to be entitled to the proceeds of the policy. The Court held that the insurance policy was lawful and that the innocent beneficiaries should not be disentitled to the insurance benefits because the insured accidentally died while committing a criminal act. The Court stated: "If the insurance contract purported to cover an illegal activity, the contract would be unlawful and could not be enforced."[23] But, as the case involved a lawful contract that was performed in an illegal manner, the Court enforced the contract. There was no **public policy** reason to prevent the beneficiaries from receiving the insurance proceeds.

Difference between contracts formed illegally and contracts performed illegally

The response of the courts to the illegal performance of a lawful contract will vary. In making their decisions, the courts will consider many factors, such as the intent of the parties, the actions of the parties, and public policy. The case discussed in the previous paragraph shows that in such situations the court may even enforce the contract, in appropriate circumstances.

Lawful contracts performed illegally may be enforced

The illegal performance of a lawful contract often involves a breach of legislation that is regulatory in nature. Such legislation may contain provisions declaring that a breach of the legislation will result in the relevant contract being void or

Legislation may render a lawful contract void

[21.] R.S.C. 1985, c. I-5.

[22.] *Oldfield v. Transamerica Life Insurance Co. of Canada*, [2002] 1 S.C.R. 742, 2002 SCC 22 (CanLII).

[23.] Ibid. at para. 54.

other specified consequences. The courts will apply these statutorily mandated outcomes whenever a contract is performed contrary to the legislation.

Sometimes, however, regulatory legislation does not indicate the result of a violation of the legislation. In such cases, the courts may make a variety of decisions. They may treat the contract as void but not illegal. They will then restore the parties to their original positions, ordering the return of any deposits advanced and property that has been transferred. If the illegal performance can be separated from the rest of the performance of the contract, then they may rule that only that part of the contract is void. If the violation of the legislation is more one of procedure than of substance, the courts may enforce the contract. The current judicial approach is illustrated by Case Summary 7.6.

Several possible results when performance breaches regulatory legislation

---

CASE SUMMARY 7.6

Illegally Performed Contract Enforced: *Horizon Resource Management Ltd. v. Blaze Energy Ltd.*[24]

There was complicated litigation involving the abandonment of a sour gas well and the drilling of a new well. Blaze did not pay Roll'n for the services it provided, so Roll'n sued Blaze for breach of contract. One of the issues was whether Roll'n failed to comply with relevant legislation such that its contract was unenforceable due to illegality. After reviewing the law relating to illegal contracts and contracts performed illegally, the Court set out the following approach, at para. 522:

> Synthesizing the foregoing cases and doctrines into a coherent and useable set of rules is difficult, but I take from the authorities the following approach:
>
> 1. If the very formation of the contract is obviously and expressly prohibited by statute, or the contract is for an unlawful purpose, then it is void *ab initio*, and only in exceptional circumstances will a party be entitled to relief.
>
> 2. If it seems that the formation of the contract may be *impliedly* prohibited by a statutory scheme (for example, certain conduct is prohibited), then the court should engage in a policy-oriented analysis, considering the "effect on the parties for whose protection the law making the bargain illegal exists". If the policy underlying the legislation would not be advanced by treating the contract as void, then the court should hesitate to do so.
>
> 3. Where the purpose of the contract is not impugned, but the method of its performance is, the court should consider the good faith of the parties, the intention to perform the contract in a legal manner, and the relative importance of the infringement compared with the hardship that would be suffered by treating the contract as void. In performing this balancing, the court must remember the presumption of legality.

The Court concluded that the contract was not prohibited, expressly or impliedly. Also, the breaches of legislation by Roll'n were not wilful or intentional. The contract was therefore not void for illegality. While Roll'n did breach the contract, in some respects its liability was limited by exclusion clauses in the contract. It was awarded judgment of $946 590 against Blaze.

DISCUSSION QUESTIONS

Is the modern approach, which may result in enforcement of a contract performed illegally, appropriate? Does this introduce uncertainty into the law? Would it be better to follow the traditional approach, which makes all illegally performed contracts unenforceable? Wouldn't this encourage the parties to comply with all relevant laws?

---

24. 2011 ABQB 658 (CanLII).

Contracts Formed Illegally

As discussed above, the Supreme Court has distinguished between illegality as to formation of the contract (the contract itself is illegal) and illegality as to performance (the contract is performed in an illegal way). A reference to an "illegal contract" is to a contract that is illegal at the time it was formed. As the Supreme Court observed, an illegal contract will not be enforced; it is void. Usually, when faced with a void contract, the court will restore the parties to their original position, ordering them to return any deposits advanced and property that had been transferred. But an illegal contract involves unacceptable or immoral conduct. Under such circumstances, while the contract is void, the courts will not assist the parties by restoring them to their original position unless one of them is innocent of any wrongdoing.

An illegal contract usually involves the commission of some prohibited conduct, such as the sale of a controlled substance or the commission of some violent or antisocial act. The conduct may be identified as wrongful and specifically prohibited by the *Criminal Code* or some other statute, or it may simply be inconsistent with the provisions of such a statute. The common law, however, goes even further, and assumes that some types of immoral conduct are unacceptable and against public policy. Even though the immoral conduct is not a crime or does not result in a violation of a statute, when people make agreements involving such conduct the agreements are treated like illegal contracts. One example involves an agreement with a prostitute; prostitution is not illegal, but it is considered immoral and against public policy.

> **Illegal contracts are illegal when formed**
>
> **Illegal contracts are void and courts will not assist parties**
>
> **An agreement involving immoral conduct is an illegal contract**

CASE SUMMARY 7.7

Contracts with Criminal Rates of Interest—An Exception to the Rule? *Transport North American Express Inc. v. New Solutions Financial Corp.*[25]

The parties entered into a credit agreement that included many payments other than the principal and interest: a monthly monitoring fee, a standby fee, royalty payments, payment of legal and other fees, and a commitment fee. The trial judge held that the agreement contained an interest component greater than the 60 percent allowed by section 347 of the *Criminal Code*. He applied "notional severance" to reduce the effective annual interest rate to 60 percent. The Court of Appeal allowed the appeal and struck out the interest clause, leaving in place the other payments, which amounted to an effective annual rate of 30.8 percent when computed as interest.

The Supreme Court of Canada overturned the Court of Appeal decision. It held that all of the various payments under the agreement were "interest" under section 347. The Court stated, "There is broad consensus that the traditional rule that contracts in violation of statutory enactments are void *ab initio* is not the approach courts should necessarily take in cases of statutory illegality involving s. 347 of the Code. Instead, judicial discretion should be employed in cases in which s. 347 has been violated in order to provide remedies that are tailored to the contractual context involved."[26]

These remedies range from declaring the contract void if it is very objectionable to severing the illegal clause if the contract is otherwise unobjectionable. The courts should consider "the specific contractual context" and the illegality involved when determining an appropriate remedy.

The Supreme Court ruled that notional severance was appropriate in this case. It therefore affirmed the decision of the trial judge. The Court outlined four factors to be

---

25. [2004] 1 S.C.R. 249, 2004 SCC 7 (CanLII).

26. Ibid. at para. 4.

considered when deciding whether to declare an illegal contract void or to partially enforce it and cited the following:

> In Thomson, at p. 8, Blair J.A. considered the following four factors in deciding between partial enforcement and declaring a contract void *ab initio*: (i) whether the purpose or the policy of s. 347 would be subverted by severance; (ii) whether the parties entered into the agreement for an illegal purpose or with an evil intention; (iii) the relative bargaining positions of the parties and their conduct in reaching the agreement; and (iv) whether the debtor would be given an unjustified windfall. He did not foreclose the possibility of applying other considerations in other cases, however, and remarked (at p. 12) that whether "a contract tainted by illegality is completely unenforceable depends upon all the circumstances surrounding the contract and the balancing of the considerations discussed above and, in appropriate cases, other considerations."[27]

DISCUSSION QUESTIONS

Does the approach of the Supreme Court lead to uncertainty since it can result in partial enforcement of an illegal contract? Does it provide the courts with too much discretion, in that they can choose from a variety of remedies when they make their decisions? Would it be better to limit the courts to the simple remedy of severance, rather than to enable them to apply "notional severance," which in effect allows them to rewrite the contract?

New judicial approach to illegal contracts

It appears that the approach followed in the *Transport* case applies in all cases, not just those involving section 347 of the *Criminal Code*. The classic approach of declaring every illegal contract void was viewed as harsh and inequitable since it could result in a windfall to one of the parties. The modern approach means that an illegal contract may be partially enforceable. The courts may sever the illegal provisions of the contract, leaving the balance of the contract enforceable. In the *Transport* case, the Supreme Court said that the severance can even be "notional," meaning that the courts can, in effect, rewrite part of the contract.

EXAMPLES

Examples of illegal contracts

The following is a list of some of the types of contracts that have been determined to be illegal. The list includes contracts that are in violation of legislation as well as contracts that are against public policy.

1. **Contracts to commit a crime.** Agreements involving murder, drug dealing, or even charging a high rate of interest are contrary to the *Criminal Code* and are therefore illegal contracts.

2. **Contracts to commit a tort.** If Mullins offers Nowak $100 to falsely claim that Abercromby did a poor job of repairing his house, that would be defamation. The contract to pay Nowak to defame Abercromby would be illegal.

3. **Contracts involving immoral acts.** As indicated above, prostitution is not illegal in Canada. However, a prostitute could not expect the courts to enforce an agreement made with a client. Prostitution is considered immoral, and the contract would therefore be illegal.

4. **Contracts that are bets and wagers.** Historically, the courts would not enforce contracts related to gambling activities, because they were against public policy. Now this area is covered by statute, and the rules vary from province to province. The statutory provisions are designed primarily to limit and regulate gambling activities. The courts will enforce only contracts for which the activities have statutory approval or are licensed.

---

27. Ibid. at para. 24.

Insurance is like a wager. A person owning property pays for insurance to insure against the destruction of the property. If the property is destroyed, the insurer compensates the owner for the loss. This requirement of loss is called an insurable interest. It must be present for the insurance contract to be valid. Insurance is discussed in Chapter 5.

Insurance contracts are valid when there is an insurable interest

Contracts for the sale of shares have the same difficulty. If the contract merely requires the parties to pay each other the difference when the share price goes up or down, it is void as a wager. To avoid this problem, the contract must provide that the shares will actually change hands. Commodities traded in a similar fashion suffer the same problem.

Contracts for sale of shares are valid when shares are transferred

5. **Contracts in restraint of marriage or in favour of divorce.** Any contract that has as its object the prevention or dissolution of marriage is against public policy. An agreement to pay someone $100 000 in return for a promise never to marry would be an illegal contract.

6. **Contracts that promote litigation.** An agreement in which one person, to satisfy some ulterior motive, pays another to sue a third party would be an illegal contract and therefore void because it promotes litigation. An exception is a lawyer's contingency fee. In such an agreement, the lawyer agrees to proceed with an action without payment in return for a share of the judgment (often amounting to 30 or 40 percent). This agreement appears to be permissible because it does not promote litigation and it serves to make the courts more accessible to those who normally could not afford to proceed.[28]

Contingency fee agreements are permissible because they make the courts accessible

7. **Contracts that obstruct justice.** If the effect of a contract is to interfere with the judicial process, it is against public policy. An agreement that encourages criminal activity by providing to pay a person a salary whenever he is in jail would involve such an obstruction of justice.

CASE SUMMARY 7.8

An Agreement Made to Avoid Prosecution Is Void:
Newell v. Royal Bank of Canada[29]

A woman forged her husband's signature on 40 cheques totalling more than $58 000. He tried to protect her from prosecution by signing a letter prepared by the bank agreeing to assume "all liability and responsibility" for the forged cheques. The Court found that this was "an agreement to stifle a criminal prosecution which is an illegal contract and unenforceable." Because the contract was illegal, the husband's agreement to accept responsibility for the cheques was void. He was therefore entitled to get his money back. A merchant may find an arrangement such as the husband's letter very appealing. Such an agreement, however, smacks of blackmail and tries to cover up a criminal act. It may even be considered an obstruction of justice. Any such agreement will therefore be an illegal contract and void.

DISCUSSION QUESTIONS

Was the Court's decision appropriate? Should the parties be free to make their own arrangements in these circumstances? Explain your reasoning.

---

8. **Contracts that injure the state.** An example is a contract to sell secret military information.

---

28. For a case in which a contingency fee agreement that allowed an arbitrator to resolve any disputes was held to not be contrary to public policy, see *Jean Estate v. Wires Jolley LLP*, 2009 ONCA 339 (CanLII).

29. (1997), 156 N.S.R. (2d) 347 (C.A.), 1997 CanLII 9871 (NS CA).

9. **Contracts that injure public service.** Bribing a public official to vote a certain way is an example of an illegal contract.

Undue restriction of competition is prohibited

10. **Contracts between businesses to fix prices or otherwise reduce competition.** These types of contracts are controlled by the federal *Competition Act*.[30] This statute specifically prohibits agreements that restrict competition:

> 45. (1) Every person commits an offence who, with a competitor of that person with respect to a product, conspires, agrees or arranges (a) to fix, maintain, increase or control the price for the supply of the product; (b) to allocate sales, territories, customers or markets for the production or supply of the product; or (c) to fix, maintain, control, prevent, lessen or eliminate the production or supply of the product. (2) Every person who commits an offence under subsection (1) is guilty of an indictable offence and liable on conviction to imprisonment for a term not exceeding 14 years or to a fine not exceeding $25 million, or to both.

Clauses often restrict competition

Thus, if two merchants agreed not to sell a particular commodity below a certain price, or not to open up branches that would compete with each other in specified communities, and they were the only ones selling the products in that community, such agreements would likely be illegal contracts and void. Such a conspiracy may also be punishable as a criminal act. This is another example of a contract in restraint of trade. The *Competition Act* prohibits a number of other unacceptable business practices, some of which will be discussed in Chapter 16.

Restrictive covenants must be reasonable

11. **Contracts that unduly restrain trade.** When a business is sold, the contract often includes a clause prohibiting the seller from opening another business in competition with the business she is selling. If such a provision is reasonable and necessary to protect the interests of the parties it is enforceable. If the provision is unreasonably restrictive or against public interest, it will be void. An agreement is against the public interest when it interferes with free trade, drives up prices, decreases service, or has any other effect whereby the public may be harmed.

Assume Fiona purchases a barbershop from Ahmed for $50 000. A considerable portion of the purchase price may be for the customer relations established by Ahmed. This is called **goodwill**. If Ahmed opens another barbershop next door to the business he sold Fiona, it would destroy the goodwill value of the contract. It would be reasonable for the buyer to include a provision in the contract prohibiting the seller from carrying on a similar business for a specified time (e.g., three years) and within a specified geographical area (e.g., five kilometres). If the time and distance restrictions agreed to are not excessive, the agreement would be considered a reasonable restraint of trade. The contract would be valid.

CASE SUMMARY 7.9

Helping a Business Owned by Daughter-in-Law Is a Breach of Sale of Goodwill Agreement and Non-Competition Agreement: *Ascent Financial Services Ltd. v. Blythman*[31]

Carolyn and Don Beveridge agreed to combine their financial services business with that of Anna and Art Blythman. Carolyn and Don were told that Anna and Art's son, Brad, and his wife, Marilyn, were not entering the financial services business. Ascent was incorporated; Anna, Art, Carolyn, and Don were its directors and shareholders. Anna and

---

30. R.S.C. 1985, c. C-34, as amended.
31. (2006), 276 Sask. R. 23 (Q.B.), 2006 SKQB 28 (CanLII), aff'd (2002), 302 Sask. R. 118 (C.A.), 2007 SKCA 78 (CanLII).

Art sold the goodwill in their business to Ascent. They were to retire over the next five to ten years, with Carolyn and Don taking over the business. Anna and Art signed a non-competition agreement that required that they not compete with the business nor solicit any suppliers or customers of the business.

The relationship between the couples broke down quickly. Carolyn and Don exercised their right to purchase Anna and Art's shares. Art was upset. He asked clients to pick up their files instead of giving them to Carolyn and Don. He encouraged clients to transfer their business to Lifestyle, a new financial services corporation owned by Marilyn. Art also provided client information to Marilyn. Carolyn and Don sued for breach of the sale of goodwill agreement and the non-competition agreement.

The Court decided that Anna and Art were in breach of both the sale of goodwill agreement and the non-competition agreement, as well as their fiduciary duty because they did not do what they could have to have the clients stay with the business. The Court assessed damages at $150 000, based on a decrease in the book value of the clients' portfolios transferred from Ascent to Lifestyle.

DISCUSSION QUESTIONS

In cases such as this, who has the burden of proof? What presumption do the courts make in cases involving restrictive covenants? Which party has to rebut this presumption to be successful in litigation regarding the enforceability of restrictive covenants?

When a restriction is excessive and is deemed to be an unreasonable restraint of trade, normally only that provision will be void. It will be severed and the rest of the agreement will be enforced. The effect would be that the purchase price and all other terms of the agreement would be the same, but the seller would have no restrictions at all; he would be free to open a similar business anywhere at any time. In the example above, if the provision in the contract for the purchase of the barbershop prohibited Ahmed from opening another shop anywhere in Canada or imposed an unreasonably long period of time, such as 10 years, the provision would likely be void. Ahmed would then be free to open a new barbershop wherever and whenever he wanted. Great care must therefore be taken to avoid the purchaser's normal inclination to make the restriction on competition as broad as possible. It is best that such a clause go no further than necessary to protect the interests of the purchaser.

Restrictive covenants will be void if too broad

An employer will often impose a similar restrictive covenant requiring employees to promise not to compete during or after their employment. Although the same test of reasonableness is used, the courts are much more reluctant to find such restrictive covenants valid. It is only when the employee is in a unique position to harm the company (e.g., by having special access to customers or secret information) that these provisions will be enforced. This will be discussed in more detail in Chapter 12.

Law applies to employers as well

CASE SUMMARY 7.10

Too Broad to Be Enforced: *Martin v. ConCreate USL Limited Partnership*[32]

Martin worked for ConCreate for 20 years, during which he acquired an interest in ConCreate and a related business, SDF. Both businesses were sold, and Martin retained an interest in both. In conjunction with the sale, Martin signed agreements with ConCreate and SDF. Each of the agreements contained restrictive covenants that would end two years after he disposed of his interest in the business. Martin could only sell those interests with the approval of others, including ConCreate, SDF, the board of the business that bought ConCreate and SDF, and others, including lenders, who could change from time to time. Martin applied for an order that the restrictive covenants were unenforceable. The Court dismissed his application, and Martin appealed.

The Court indicated that the main issue was whether the restrictive covenants were ambiguous or otherwise unreasonable. It held that the covenants were unreasonable because they had no fixed, outside limit on their terms. The duration of the restrictions depended on the approval of third parties and was therefore for an indeterminate period of time. Also, some of the parties who had to give their approval were unascertainable at the time the covenants were agreed to, while some of them may have a commercial interest in limiting Martin's competition with ConCreate and SDF. The Court also ruled that the restrictions on competition and on soliciting employees, customers, and dealers were unreasonable because they restricted activities that ConCreate and SDF were not engaged in at the time of the transaction. This was beyond what was necessary to protect their reasonable commercial interests.

SMALL BUSINESS PERSPECTIVE

What should the owner of a small business do to ensure that a restrictive covenant in an employment contract that has been signed by an employee will not be struck down by the courts? Is it a good idea to simply draft the provision as broadly as possible?

The Court in the *Martin* case referred to the judgment of the Supreme Court of Canada in *Shafron v. KRG Insurance Brokers (Western) Inc.*[33] The headnote of that case contains the following:

> Restrictive covenants generally are restraints of trade and contrary to public policy. Freedom to contract, however, requires an exception for reasonable restrictive covenants. Normally, the reasonableness of a covenant will be determined by its geographic and temporal scope as well as the extent of the activity sought to be prohibited. Reasonableness cannot be determined if a covenant is ambiguous in the sense that what is prohibited is not clear as to activity, time, or geography. An ambiguous restrictive covenant is by definition, *prima facie*, unreasonable and unenforceable. The onus is on the party seeking to enforce the restrictive covenant to show that it is reasonable and a party seeking to enforce an ambiguous covenant will be unable to demonstrate reasonableness. Restrictive covenants in employment contracts are scrutinized more rigorously than restrictive covenants in a sale of a business because there is often an imbalance in power between employees and employers and because a sale of a business often involves a payment for goodwill whereas no similar payment is made to an employee leaving his or her employment. In this case, the restrictive covenant arises in an employment contract and attracts the higher standard of scrutiny.

The Court went on to say that notional severance (reading down a contractual provision to make it legal and enforceable) is not appropriate to apply to an unreasonable restrictive covenant. This approach would encourage employers to draft overly broad restrictive covenants. "Blue-pencil" severance (removing part of the restrictive covenant) may be used when part of the restrictive covenant is severable, trivial, and not part of the main purpose of the restrictive covenant.

---

33. [2009] 1 S.C.R. 157, 2009 SCC 6 (CanLII).

REDUCING RISK 7.4

There is a great temptation for employers and purchasers of businesses to protect themselves from competition, as they are particularly vulnerable to competition. They can include terms in their contracts that restrict that competition, but such provisions must not go too far. There is a tendency for the person who is advantaged by such a clause to make it much broader than is necessary to prevent unfair competition. Such clauses, however, must be reasonable in the circumstances and must not be against the public interest. They must go no further than is necessary to prevent unfair competition. They should have a geographical limit and a time limit to their operation. A clause restricting competition within a 500-kilometre radius, when 50 kilometres would be sufficient, is void. A clause with a five-year restriction, when one year would be enough, is also void. Great care should be exercised in negotiating these non-competition clauses. A sophisticated client will seek legal advice to ensure that the resulting clause will be enforceable.

The list above describes some of the types of contracts restricted by statute or held to be against public policy. This list is neither complete nor exhaustive. It may well be that new types of activities made possible by changing technology could also be controlled by statute or be declared as being against public policy in the future. Special care should be directed to activities on the Internet. Gambling and pornography account for a large portion of Internet use; the validity of the activity depends on the jurisdiction involved, which often is not clear. Several jurisdictions have passed or will soon enact statutes controlling these activities. Great care should be taken, by both businesses and consumers who become involved in such activities, to determine the legality of that involvement.

List of illegal contracts will continue to grow

INTENTION

LO 6

Not all agreements are contracts. Often people enter into arrangements or undertakings never intending that legal consequences will flow from them. For example, if a person invited a friend over for dinner and the friend failed to show up for some reason, the delinquent guest would probably be quite surprised if the would-be host were to sue for breach of contract. The law requires that for an agreement to be a binding contract, the parties must have intended that legal obligations and rights would flow from it. Since neither the host nor the guest intended to create a legal obligation, the host's legal action would fail.

Parties must have intended legal consequences from an agreement

When determining intention, the courts do not look to the state of mind of the person making the promise. Rather, they look to the reasonable expectations of the promisee. The test is objective. Would a reasonable person have thought that the person making the promise was serious and that the agreement was legally binding? If so, it is not going to help the person making the promise to say, "I was only kidding."

Courts will enforce reasonable expectations

CASE SUMMARY 7.11

When Friends Fall out over Money: *Osorio v. Cardona*[34]

Osorio and Cardona went to the horse races together and bought tickets on the "Sweep Six" (betting on six races where they had to predict all six winners). After the third race, they discovered that both their tickets were still eligible to win. They made an agreement that if either of them won they would split the winnings. Cardona went on to win $735 403 but refused to honour the deal. Because of the odds involved, Osorio was entitled to $147 000. Cardona refused to pay, offering Osorio "$60 000 or nothing." Osorio took the $60 000 and then sued for the remainder.

34. (1984), 15 D.L.R. (4th) 619 (B.C.S.C.), 1984 CanLII 364 (BC SC).

The Court held that the agreement was not a bet or a wager; rather, it was an agreement to pool the winnings, so there was no problem regarding legality. The Court then decided that there was an intention to be bound and thus a valid contract. The fact that they had adjusted the split to reflect the odds indicated that they were serious. Cardona had always acted toward Osorio in a way that led Osorio to believe that he was serious and that he intended the agreement to be in force. Note that because there were threats involved, the agreement to take $60 000 was held to be unconscionable and not binding as a settlement. Osorio was able to collect the other $87 000.

This case illustrates not only the requirement of intention, but also that the test whereby the court seeks to determine the intention of the parties is objective.

DISCUSSION QUESTIONS
When friends enter a contest and agree to divide the prize if they win, and then they disagree as to the division of the prize when they do in fact win, who will have to convince the court that there was an intention to be bound by the agreement? What is the most convincing evidence to use in this regard? What advice would you therefore give to friends who are entering a contest together?

The following examples illustrate situations in which the issue of intention arises and indicate the courts' probable responses:

Courts will enforce the stated intention

1. **Stated intention of the parties.** If the parties clearly state that they do not wish to be legally bound by their agreement, or that their agreement is not to be enforceable in any court, that instruction will be honoured. Such a statement must be embodied in the terms of the contract and be very clear as to the intention not to be bound. Often, in commercial relationships, the parties will make agreements that are convenient but which they don't want to be legally binding. Sometimes the parties are in pre-contract negotiations and are not yet ready to be bound. "Letters of intention" are examples of such communications; they clearly do not create legal obligations for the parties.

Courts will presume intention in commercial transactions

2. **Commercial relations.** If the relationship between the contracting parties is primarily commercial in nature, the courts will presume that the parties intended to be legally bound by their agreement. The contract will be binding on them in the absence of any evidence or clear instructions to the contrary.

Courts will presume no intention in domestic and social relations

3. **Domestic and social relations.** When an agreement is between members of a family, or friends involved in domestic (non-business) activities, there is a presumption that the parties do not intend legal consequences to flow from their agreement. For example, if members of a family informally agree to make payments to each other, such as a child agreeing to pay room and board or parents agreeing to pay an allowance, the courts would assume that there is no intention to be legally bound and would therefore not enforce the agreement. However, if the parties had gone to the trouble of having a lawyer draw up a formal contract, then the courts would be satisfied that the parties did intend that legal consequences would flow from their agreement, so they would enforce the contract. The presumption of no intention would have been rebutted.

Reasonable person test is applied when social and business relations mix

4. **Social and business relations.** Problems occur when the relationship involved is a mixture of social and commercial relations. Such an example arises when friends jointly enter a contest and then disagree on the distribution of the prize. This problem could become more common in Canada with the increase in the number of lotteries with large prizes. In such cases, the courts must judge each situation on its individual merits. The courts use the reasonable person test to determine whether it is reasonable for the parties trying to enforce the agreement to think that a legally binding contract had been created.

5. **Exaggerated claims.** Merchants often exaggerate the qualities of their products in advertisements or when they talk to customers. They may, for example, claim that their product is "the biggest" or "the best." To some extent, this enthusiasm is expected and is not taken seriously by the customers or the courts. The problem is where to draw the line, and the courts again apply the reasonable person test to determine whether, in the circumstances, the customer should have taken the exaggerated claim seriously. Note, however, that even when the exaggeration is obvious it may still be prohibited by statute as misleading advertising or an unfair trade practice. Such consumer protection legislation will be discussed in Chapter 16.

Reasonable person test is also applied when dealing with exaggerated claims

CASE SUMMARY 7.12

Are Businesses Permitted to Exaggerate? *Carlill v. Carbolic Smoke Ball Company*[35]

The defendants manufactured a product that they claimed would protect users from influenza. They offered £100 to anyone who used their product as prescribed and still contracted influenza. They stated, in an advertisement, that £1000 had been deposited in the Alliance Bank, Regent Street, and that this showed their sincerity in the matter.

Carlill used the product, got influenza, and claimed the money. The company refused to pay, stating that the advertisement was an advertising puff that merely indicated enthusiasm for the product and that it was not meant to be taken seriously by the public. The Court held that depositing money to back up the claim had taken it out of the category of an advertising puff. It was determined that a reasonable person would have thought that the advertisement was serious, so there was intention. The offer was held to be valid, and Carlill's use of the product and contracting of the illness were appropriate forms of acceptance. There was therefore a valid contract.

Misleading advertising has become a serious problem and is now controlled by consumer protection legislation, which will be discussed in Chapter 16.

DISCUSSION QUESTIONS

Should merchants ever be allowed to make exaggerated claims about their products?

FORM OF THE CONTRACT

LO **7** **8**

We have established that the essential elements of contracts are consensus, consideration, capacity, legality, and intention (as summarized in Table 7.1 at the end of this chapter). Next we will examine the form of the contract.

The Requirement of Writing

Historically, the form of the contract was very important. Promises were enforceable because they were contained in sealed documents called *deeds*. Today, there is no general rule that a contract must take a certain form, although most jurisdictions have statutory requirements regarding the transfer of land.[36] Contracts may be in writing, they may be under seal, they may simply be verbal, or they may even be implied from the conduct of the parties.

No specified form of contract

People are often surprised to discover that most verbal agreements have the same legal status as written ones, provided they meet the requirements described in this and the previous chapter.

Verbal contracts are binding . . .

[35.] [1893] 1 Q.B. 256 (C.A.).

[36.] See, for example, s. 155 of Alberta's *Land Titles Act*, R.S.A. 2000, c. L-4, which requires a transfer of land to be signed in front of a witness, who must swear an affidavit of attestation of an instrument.

. . . but written contracts are
advised

The importance of a written contract is practical, not theoretical. It is always a good idea to put the terms of an agreement in writing, so that if a dispute arises there is something permanent that establishes the terms to which the parties agreed. In the absence of such a document, it is surprising how differently even well-intentioned people remember the terms of their agreement. If a dispute between the parties does end in litigation, each of the parties will be in a better position to prove his case if he can produce written evidence to support his claim.

WHEN WRITING IS REQUIRED

Statute of Frauds requires
writing for enforcement of
some contracts

In some limited circumstances, a contract is required by statute to be evidenced in writing to be enforceable. These requirements for writing are found primarily in the *Statute of Frauds*. There are also, however, some other statutes that set out similar requirements.

Statute of Frauds in force in
some provinces

The first *Statute of Frauds* was enacted in England in the seventeenth century. It was adopted with some variation by the Canadian provinces. The *Statute* requires that certain types of contracts be evidenced in writing to be enforceable. The *Statute* has been criticized as causing as much abuse as it was intended to prevent. As a result, many important changes have been made by the provinces to the *Statute*. Manitoba[37] and British Columbia have repealed the *Statute* altogether, although British Columbia retains some of its provisions in its *Law and Equity Act*.[38]

CASE SUMMARY 7.13

Writing Still Needed in Manitoba: *Megill Stephenson Co. v. Woo*[39]

Two parties negotiated by telephone. At the conclusion of their conversation, an agreement was reached regarding the purchase and sale of a parcel of land. However, before any documents were prepared the vendor changed his mind. The purchaser sued. The Court held that, despite the fact that the *Statute of Frauds* had been repealed in Manitoba, there was the usual expectation of the parties that a contract dealing with the sale of land would not be effective until it was put into writing. The Court honoured that expectation and refused to enforce the agreement.

Note that the Court first had to find that an agreement had been reached. It can be argued that by this decision the vendor was allowed to take advantage of the purchaser for his own profit. It was this type of fraud that led to the adoption of the *Statute of Frauds*.

DISCUSSION QUESTION
Should the requirement of writing be retained for important transactions such as the purchase and sale of land?

The following is a discussion of the types of contracts generally included under the *Statute of Frauds* in Canada. The actual wording varies among provinces.

When a contract cannot be
performed within one year

1. **Contracts not to be performed within one year.** When the terms of the agreement make it impossible to perform the contract within one full year from the time the contract is entered into, there must be evidence in writing for it to be enforceable. For example, if Sasaki Explosives Ltd. agrees in March 2016 to provide a fireworks display at the July 1 celebrations in Halifax in the summer of 2017, that contract must be evidenced by writing to be enforceable. Failure to have evidence in writing will make it no less a contract, but the

---

37. See *An Act to Repeal the Statute of Frauds*, C.C.S.M. c. F158.
38. R.S.B.C. 1996, c. 253, s. 59.
39. (1989) 59 D.L.R. (4th) 146 (Man. C.A.).

courts will refuse to enforce it. Some provinces, including British Columbia (which has repealed the *Statute of Frauds*) and Ontario,[40] have eliminated the requirement of writing in this area. Note that even when it is impossible for one party to complete performance within the year, written evidence is not required when it is clear in the contract that the other party is expected to perform within that year.

2. **Land dealings.** Any contract that affects a party's interest in land must be evidenced in writing to be enforceable. It is often difficult to determine what types of contracts affect interest (or ownership) in land and what types do not. Any sale of land (or part of it, such as the creation of a joint tenancy in land) must be evidenced in writing. Any creation of an easement, right of way, or estate (such as a life estate) is also covered by the *Statute of Frauds*. But contracts for services to the land that do not affect the interest in the land itself are not covered. For example, if a carpenter agrees to build a house, such an agreement may affect the value of the land, but not the interest in the land itself. It therefore need not be evidenced in writing to be enforceable. This provision of the *Statute of Frauds* has also been modified in some jurisdictions. For example, in British Columbia[41] and Ontario[42] a lease for three years or less is exempt from the legislation, but longer leases are treated just like any other interest in land and must be evidenced in writing to be enforceable.

When an interest in land is involved

3. **Guarantees and indemnities.** When creditors are not satisfied with the creditworthiness of a debtor, they may insist that someone else also assume responsibility for the debt. This can be done by using a guarantee or an indemnity. If the third party incurs a secondary liability for the debt, she has given a guarantee. A guarantor promises that, if the debtor fails to pay the debt, she will assume responsibility and pay it. Note that in this type of transaction the obligation is secondary, or contingent; there is no obligation on the guarantor until the debtor actually fails to pay the debt.

When a guarantee is involved

An **indemnity** describes a relationship in which a third party assumes a primary obligation for the repayment of the debt along with the debtor. As a result, both owe the debt, and the creditor can look to either for repayment. When a third party says, "I'll see that you get paid," there is an assumption of a primary obligation, and the promise is an indemnity.

Indemnity involves obligation

The distinction between a guarantee and an indemnity is important, because in most provinces the *Statute of Frauds* requires that a guarantee be in writing, but not an indemnity. If the court classifies the nature of a third-party agreement as an indemnity, there is no requirement of writing. The distinction can be vital when a person has made only a verbal commitment to pay the outstanding loan to the debtor.[43] In British Columbia, the *Law and Equity Act* requires that both indemnities and guarantees be evidenced in writing to be enforceable.[44]

Guarantees must be in writing

4. **Others.** The original *Statute of Frauds* required that whenever the purchase price of goods sold exceeded a specified minimum, there had to be evidence in writing for the sale to be enforceable. This provision has been included in the *Sale of Goods Act* in many jurisdictions in Canada.[45] It is usually sufficient evidence in writing if a receipt or sales slip has been given. The definition of goods and the sale of goods generally will be discussed in Chapter 16.

When goods are sold over a specific value

[40.] See the *Statute of Frauds,* R.S.O. 1990, c. S.19.

[41.] *Supra* note 38, s. 59(2)(b).

[42.] *Supra* note 40, s. 3.

[43.] For a good discussion of guarantees and indemnities, see *MacNeill v. Fero Waste and Recycling Inc.* (2003), 213 N.S.R. (2d) 254 (C.A.), 2003 NSCA 34 (CanLII).

[44.] *Supra* note 38, s. 59(6).

[45.] See, for example, s. 6 of Alberta's *Sale of Goods Act, supra* note 4, which sets a minimum value of $50.

Parliament and the provincial legislatures have passed many statutes that require certain transactions to be in writing to be valid. Some examples are the *Bills of Exchange Act,* insurance legislation, consumer protection legislation, some of the legislation dealing with employment relations, and the carriage of goods and passengers. For example, while there does not seem to be a provision in the Ontario *Sale of Goods Act*[46] requiring that certain transactions be evidenced in writing, other Ontario legislation requires certain types of consumer contracts to be in writing.[47] In many jurisdictions, the *Statute of Frauds* also requires the promises of executors (to be responsible personally for the debts of an estate)[48] and promises made in consideration of marriage[49] to be evidenced in writing to be enforceable.

WHAT CONSTITUTES EVIDENCE IN WRITING

> **Writing must contain all essential terms . . .**
>
> **. . . and may be in more than one document**
>
> **. . . and must be signed by the party to be charged**
>
> **. . . and may arise after an agreement**

Note that it is not the whole agreement that must be in writing to satisfy the *Statute of Frauds*—there need be **evidence in writing** supporting only the essential terms of the agreement. The essential terms are normally an indication of the parties, the subject matter of the contract, and the consideration to be paid. Other terms may become essential, however, depending on the nature of the contract. The evidence in writing can take the form of the actual agreement itself, or simply a receipt or note. It can even come into existence after the creation of the contract referring to it. The writing can be a single document or a collection of documents that taken together provide the required evidence. The document(s) must also be signed, or initialled, but only by the person denying the existence of the contract.

EFFECT OF THE *STATUTE OF FRAUDS*

> **Contract is valid but unenforceable when no writing**

It is vital to remember that if a contract is not evidenced in writing this does not make it void under the *Statute of Frauds*; it is merely unenforceable. The contract is binding on the parties, but the courts will not assist them in enforcing it. If the parties have already performed, or if there is some other remedy available that does not require the court's involvement, the contract will still be binding. The courts will not assist a person who has performed to get out of the contract. Nor will the court order the return of any money paid (see Figure 7.1). In effect, the party has only done what was required under the contract. Similarly, when there is a lien (a right to seize property) or when there is a right to set off a debt against the obligations created by the contract, the parties themselves may be able to enforce the contract without the help of the courts. In that sense, such a contract is binding even though there is no evidence in writing and it won't be enforced by the courts.

Figure 7.1 Effect of *Statute of Frauds*

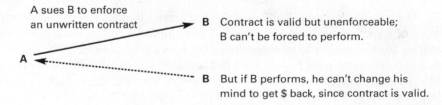

A sues B to enforce an unwritten contract

B Contract is valid but unenforceable; B can't be forced to perform.

A

B But if B performs, he can't change his mind to get $ back, since contract is valid.

---

46. R.S.O. 1990, c. S.1.

47. See the *Consumer Protection Act, 2002,* S.O. 2002, c. 30, Sch. A., which requires future performance agreements, time-share agreements, personal development services agreements, direct agreements, and other consumer agreements to be in writing.

48. See Ontario's *Statute of Frauds, supra* note 40, s. 4.

49. In Alberta, this provision is now subject to the *Matrimonial Property Act,* R.S.A. 2000, c. M-8, s. 37, which deals with prenuptial agreements.

REDUCING RISK 7.5

There are only a few situations in which evidence in writing is required to ensure that a contract is enforceable. However, from a practical business point of view contractual arrangements should always be put into writing (or, as technology develops, some other permanent form). Even people with the best of intentions will remember things differently as time passes. It is vital, therefore, to have a permanent record that can be referred to later so that the terms are certain and the goodwill between the parties is retained. When relations have broken down, there is nothing better than a written document to resolve a dispute that arises over a business transaction that has gone bad. The existence of the document may, by itself, prevent litigation. If it does not, at least there is evidence as to what the parties agreed to that can be used in the lawsuit. So, while in law it may be true that a verbal contract is as binding as a written one, it is poor practice indeed to rely on verbal agreements in business. A sophisticated client will therefore ensure that agreements meant to be binding are put into written form.

ELECTRONIC CONTRACTS

Electronic transactions and ecommerce legislation were discussed in Chapter 6 in the section on consensus. With respect to the requirement of writing, important adaptations have been required because of changing technology. As electronic records and communications have become more common and paper has begun to play less of a role, changes have been made to reflect that reality. Many land registries, for example, have created computer databases of their registration system that now allow lawyers to transfer property and register interests online.[50] Some court documents may also be filed online.[51]

Technological developments have resulted in many changes

In many situations, however, it is still necessary to sign a printed document to provide the required evidence in writing. Online registrations of property transfers and property interests require the submission of applications using the same forms that are used for over-the-counter registrations.[52] As indicated above, the *Statute of Frauds* survives today in most common law provinces. Several provincial *Sales of Goods Acts* similarly contain writing requirements.[53] Furthermore, provincial *Consumer Protection Acts* that comply with the Internet Sales Contract Harmonization Template[54] require that consumers be provided certain information in writing or in an easily printed format. (The law relating to the sale of goods and to consumer protection will be discussed in more detail in Chapter 16.)

Sometimes a paper document is required

We therefore have a situation in which businesses are adapting to the electronic environment, but laws continue to require that certain transactions or documents be in writing. In most cases, it would not appear necessary to require that electronic transactions be put in written form and signed manually. These factors have led to efforts to develop laws that give digital records and electronic signatures the same legal recognition as paper documents and manual signatures.

Statutes to make electronic documents equivalent to written ones

The Uniform Law Conference of Canada has adopted the *Uniform Electronic Commerce Act (UECA)*,[55] a model law designed to implement the United Nations

Canada adopted United Nations' model law

[50.] See, for example, Saskatchewan's *Land Titles Act, 2000*, S.S. 2000, c. L-5.1, s. 29 and 30.

[51.] In British Columbia, for example, e-filing is available for most Supreme Court Civil and Provincial Small Claims documents. See "Court Services Online" at https://justice.gov.bc.ca/cso/index.do.

[52.] *The Land Titles Regulations, 2001*, R.R.S. c. L-5.1, Reg. 1, s. 9.

[53.] See, for example, s. 6 of Alberta's *Sale of Goods Act, supra* note 4, which requires that sales of goods worth more than $50 be evidenced in writing or that there be part performance for the contract to be enforceable. This issue will be discussed in more detail in Chapter 16.

[54.] An agreement entered into by provincial ministers to harmonize their approach toward consumer protection in ecommerce. See Industry Canada, "Internet Sales Contract Harmonization Template," www.ic.gc.ca/eic/site/oca-bc.nsf/eng/ca01642.html. An example of provincial legislation passed pursuant to this agreement is Alberta's *Fair Trading Act*, R.S.A. 2000, c. F-2. Section 35 provides a list of the information that must be included in a direct sales contract. The *Internet Sales Contract Regulation*, Alta. Reg. 81/2001, requires (in s. 4) a supplier to disclose specified information to consumers prior to them entering into an Internet sales contract and (in s. 5) to provide a copy of the Internet sales contract to a consumer after the contract is entered into. The specified information must be included in the contract, which can be provided in writing or in electronic form.

[55.] Uniform Law Conference of Canada, *Uniform Electronic Commerce Act, (UECA)*, August 1999.

Commission on International Trade Law Model Law on Electronic Commerce.[56] This model law was designed to create a more certain legal environment for ecommerce. It sought to provide equivalent treatment for paper-based documentation and computer-based information. It was proposed as the model that Canadian governments could use to develop a harmonized approach to ecommerce.

Electronic documents have legal effect and are enforceable

The governing principle of *UECA* is that information shall not be denied legal effect or enforceability solely because it is in electronic form.[57] No one, however, should be compelled to use electronic documents. A legal requirement that information be in writing is satisfied by information in electronic form if the information is accessible so that it is usable for subsequent reference. The use of electronic signatures is allowed; a signature must be created or adopted by a person with the intent to sign the document.

Federal legislation to recognize electronic documents

The *Personal Information Protection and Electronic Documents Act*[58] adapts federal laws to the electronic environment, recognizing electronic documents and electronic signatures. This statute governs contracts entered into with the federal government. (In general, contracts are regulated by provincial laws.) The legislation provides specifically that electronic documents satisfy a requirement under federal law for a document to be in writing.[59] It also provides a definition of an electronic signature[60] and sets out how electronic signatures may be used in federal government documents.[61] (In some situations, a "secure electronic signature" must be used.)

Provincial and territorial legislation also passed

All provincial and territorial governments have also passed legislation to facilitate ecommerce by clarifying the status of electronic documents, contracts, and signatures.[62] These statues stipulate that an electronic document will satisfy a requirement that a document must be in writing if it is accessible to use for subsequent reference[63] and if it is accessible and capable of being retained by the person to whom it is provided.[64] Electronic signatures will also satisfy a legal requirement for a written signature.[65] The various governments may set standards for electronic signatures as the federal government has done in requiring secure electronic signatures in some situations.[66]

Some documents are not covered by legislation

Many of the provincial and territorial statutes follow the *UECA* and specify that their electronic documents legislation does not apply to wills, trusts, powers of attorneys, land transfers, or negotiable instruments.[67] These documents do not have legal force if completed electronically or are governed by separate legislation restricting the role of electronic communications. Some provinces also exclude documents not excluded by the *UECA*; for example, Alberta's legislation does not apply to personal directives, guarantees, or land transfers involving rights to mines and minerals.[68] Despite these exceptions, it is clear that the trend is for governments to enact laws that govern the use of electronic documents and electronic signatures in an effort to

---

56. United Nations Commission on International Trade Law, *UNCITRAL Model Law on Electronic Commerce with Guide to Enactment, 1996*, New York, 1999.

57. For an excellent discussion on the *UECA* and the legislation enacted by Canada and other jurisdictions, see Alysia Davies, "The Development of Laws on Electronic Documents and E-Commerce Transactions," Background Paper, Legal and Legislative Affairs Division, Library of Parliament Research Publications, December 20, 2008, http://www.parl.gc.ca/content/lop/researchpublications/prb0012-e.htm.

58. S.C. 2000, c. 5.

59. Ibid. s. 41.

60. Ibid. s. 31.

61. Ibid. s. 43.

62. See, for example, Alberta's *Electronic Transactions Act*, S.A. 2001, c. E-5.5.

63. Ibid. s. 11.

64. Ibid. s. 12.

65. Ibid. s. 16.

66. Ibid. s. 22.

67. Ibid. s. 7.

68. Ibid.

facilitate the conduct of online business and the creation of electronic contracts that are of legal effect and are legally enforceable.[69]

CASE SUMMARY 7.14

Can You Sell Your Condo by Email? *Druet v. Girouard*[70]

The parties exchanged seven emails regarding the purchase of a condominium unit. Girouard believed that an agreement had been reached after the sixth email, but Druet advised him in the seventh email that she would not sell the unit at the stated price. Girouard sued, asking for specific performance or damages for breach of contract. The lower Court held that the series of emails contained the essential terms of an agreement and therefore resulted in a binding contract for the purchase and sale of the unit.

The Court of Appeal held that there was not a binding agreement and allowed the appeal. It ruled that the parties reached an agreement with respect to the essential terms (parties, price, property) and to the assumption of the existing mortgage and payment of the closing fees. The Court based its decision that there was no binding agreement on the finding that there was no intention to create a contractual relationship. The Court ruled that this was a transaction with a rebuttable presumption against the intention to create legal relations. Important in this regard was the offer of the purchaser to have a formal agreement prepared for the seller's consideration and the fact that the purchaser had not viewed the property. The presumption was therefore not rebutted.

The Court went on to discuss the requirement of writing. The *Statute of Frauds* states that a contract for the sale of land must be in writing and be signed by the party to be charged if it is to be enforceable. The *Electronic Transactions Act* provides that if a law imposes a requirement that information be in writing, that requirement can be satisfied by the provision of "electronic information." Also, a legal requirement to provide a signature can be met by an "electronic signature." The Court accepted that an exchange of emails can satisfy the writing requirement under the *Electronic Transactions Act*, and therefore the *Statute of Frauds*. The Court questioned, however, whether the seller's method of identifying herself in her emails qualified as an electronic signature.

In an attempt to answer this question, the Court reviewed the definition of "electronic signature." Unfortunately, the meaning of the phrase was not clear. The Court indicated that it would have to review the purpose of the legislation and the provisions relating to electronic signatures. That would require an examination as to whether the objectives of the signature requirement under the *Statute of Frauds* are relevant to the application of the *Electronic Transactions Act*.

The Court then reviewed an English case that held that the automatic insertion of a person's email address in the header did not constitute a signature in the context of the *Statute of Frauds*. As there are American cases that take the opposite view, the Court concluded that there is no consistency in the treatment of email signatures.

The Court went on to identify other issues relevant to the signature requirement. Would the signature required on an Internet standard form agreement be different than that in an exchange of emails? Would the law accept as a valid signature a person's first or last name only? In an exchange of emails, does the signature requirement apply only to the email containing the acceptance, or to the emails which set out the essential terms, or to all of the emails?

It is clear from this case that there is a need for judicial interpretation of the legislation regarding electronic transactions and electronic documents. Until the common law regarding this legislation is developed (a process that will take many years!), there will be uncertainty as to the law regarding electronic transactions and ecommerce.

---

69. For a good discussion on the development of the law relating to the use of electronic signatures in land transactions, see Marg Bruineman, "Signing on the Dotted Line Easy as 1-2 in the Digital World," *Canadian Lawyer*, November 18, 2013, http://www.canadianlawyermag.com/4891/Signing-on-the-dotted-line-easy-as-1-2-in-the-digital-world.html.

70. 2012 NBCA 40 (CanLII).

Part Performance

When part performance is consistent with the contract, writing is not required

The court will waive the requirement of writing if the parties can produce evidence to show that a contract dealing with an interest in land has been partially performed. There are some important limitations to this principle. The part performance must be evidence of the existence of the contract and consistent only with the existence of the contract. The payment of money owed under the contract will therefore not usually be acceptable as proof of part performance, as the payment of money is consistent with any number of different obligations. In British Columbia, however, the payment of a deposit is sufficient part performance with respect to land transactions to make such contracts enforceable.[71] A good example of acceptable part performance when land has been sold is the start of construction. The permission to enter onto the land and start building is consistent with the sale of the land, and so the courts will accept the part performance as sufficient evidence to support the contract.

CASE SUMMARY 7.15

Part Performance Satisfies Statute: *Erie Sand and Gravel Ltd. v. Tri-B Acres Inc.*[72]

Erie bought "the north side property" from Seres' Farms and now wanted to buy "the south side property." This land was subject to a right of first refusal in favour of Tri-B. Erie was aware of this right. Erie and Seres' Farms agreed on the terms for the purchase and sale of the south side property. Seres' Farms agreed to sell the property to Erie unless Tri-B matched the agreed-upon terms. Tri-B made an offer that did not match Erie's offer, but Seres' Farms accepted the Tri-B offer. Erie brought an action for specific performance of its agreement with Seres' Farms. The Court ordered that the property be transferred to Erie.

The Court found that an agreement had been reached between Erie and Seres' Farms, as all of the essential terms had been agreed upon, even though there was no formal written contract. This agreement was subject to Tri-B exercising its right of first refusal. The Court also held that there were acts of part performance to take the agreement outside of the *Statute of Frauds*, including the preparation and delivery of the offer and delivery of a certified cheque for the full purchase price. This finding was necessary because Seres' Farms never signed Erie's offer, so there was not a "sufficient note or memorandum" signed by "the party to be charged."

DISCUSSION QUESTIONS
The *Statute of Frauds* was passed originally to prevent fraudulent transactions. The doctrine of part performance provides an exception to the requirement of writing. Does adoption of the doctrine of part performance therefore increase the likelihood of fraud being committed with respect to transactions involving interests in land?

Table 7.1 summarizes the elements required to make a contract valid and enforceable.

---

71. *Supra* note 38, s. 59(4).
72. 2009 ONCA 709 (CanLII).

Table 7.1 Summary of Contract Formation

No consensus	Contract void	But must pay for requested services
No consideration	Contract void	But note promissory estoppel, gift, and seal
No capacity	Contract voidable	But infants can enforce contracts with adults
		But infants are bound by contracts for necessaries and beneficial contracts of service
	Contract void	But insane persons must show the others knew of insanity
Illegal	Contract void	But depends on statute
No intention	Contract void	Note presumptions
No writing	Valid	But note *Statute of Frauds* exceptions

MyBusLawLab Be sure to visit the MyBusLawLab that accompanies this book to find practice quizzes, province-specific content, simulations and much more!

SUMMARY

Capacity

- For a contract to be binding, each of the parties must have legal capacity
- In most provinces, contracts with minors are not binding on them, except for contracts for necessaries and beneficial contracts of employment or for service
- In British Columbia, all contracts with minors are unenforceable except those that are specifically made enforceable by legislation, such as government student loans
- The test for the capacity of minors is objective
- Parents are not liable for the torts or contractual obligations of their children unless there is legislation making them liable
- A contract with someone who is insane or drunk will be rendered invalid only when the person was so incapacitated as to not know what he was doing, and the other contracting party knew or ought to have known of that incapacity
- Corporations, enemy aliens in times of war, trade unions, Crown corporations and government bodies, bankrupts, and Indians have their capacity to enter into contracts limited to some extent

Legality

- To be binding, a contact must be legal and be performed legally
- If a lawful contract is performed illegally, the courts may rule that the contract is illegal and void, or just void, or they may enforce some or all of the contract
- An illegal contract is illegal at the time it is formed. Illegal contracts include contracts that violate legislation and contracts that are against public policy
- The courts may rule that an illegal contract is illegal and void, or just void, or they may enforce some or all of the contract
- There are many types of contracts that are illegal because they violate legislation or are against public policy
- One example is contracts that unduly restrain trade, which are usually illegal, but contracts in which one party agrees not to carry on business in competition with another are legal if they can be shown to be reasonable in terms of the interests of the parties and the public

Intention

- For a contract to be binding, each of the parties must intend to be bound by it
- The courts will enforce the stated intention of the parties
- In family and other social relationships, there is a presumption of no intention. This presumption can be challenged by evidence that shows an intent to be bound

- In commercial relationships, intention is presumed; this can also be rebutted
- In other situations, the courts use the reasonable person test to determine intention

Form of the contract

- Most verbal contracts are valid if they contain the essential elements of a contract
- Under the *Statute of Frauds*, certain contracts must be evidenced in writing to be enforceable
- The *Statute of Frauds* has been repealed or modified in many jurisdictions
- Most jurisdictions now have legislation requiring certain types of contracts to be in writing
- Legislation now gives electronic documents and electronic signatures the same legal status as paper documents and manual signatures, with some exceptions
- When part performance is established, verbal agreements dealing with interests in land are also enforceable

---

QUESTIONS FOR REVIEW

1. "In determining whether a child has contractual capacity, the court will attempt to determine if she actually understood the transaction." True or false? Explain your answer.

2. Explain the circumstances in which a minor may escape liability for a contract and the circumstances in which a minor is bound by a contract.

3. What is the significance of a minor's contract being designated as a beneficial contract of employment or for service?

4. In addition to debts incurred for necessaries, when will a minor be liable for a debt he incurred?

5. What are the three stages of a contractual relationship? Describe the legal situation of a minor in each of these stages.

6. If there is no relevant legislation, when will the parents of a minor be responsible for the minor's contracts? When will they be liable for the torts of the minor?

7. When can an adult sue a minor in tort even though there is a contract between them?

8. What must an insane or drunk person establish to escape liability under a contract?

9. Explain what care businesspeople must exercise when entering into contracts with government corporations or bodies.

10. Explain four other situations where businesspeople must be careful that those they deal with have the capacity to contract.

11. Explain the difference between a contract that is performed illegally and an illegal contract.

12. What decisions can a court make if performance of a contract violates a regulatory statute?

13. What are the two reasons that can cause contracts to be illegal?

14. How has the law regarding the judicial treatment of illegal contracts changed?

15. Give five examples of contracts deemed by the courts to be against public policy, and describe the effect of such a designation.

16. "All contracts that restrain trade are illegal." True or false? Explain your answer.

17. Describe the test the court will use in determining whether the parties had an intention to be bound when they made an agreement.

18. With respect to the element of intention, explain how the courts' treatment of domestic agreements differs from their treatment of commercial transactions.

19. How will a court determine if there was contractual intention when there is a dispute between a brother and his sister over how to operate their business?

20. What is the significance of a written document in contractual relations?

21. Explain why some people have suggested that the *Statute of Frauds* has led to more frauds than it has prevented.

22. Give examples of the types of contracts currently included under the *Statute of Frauds*.

23. What "evidence in writing" is required to satisfy the requirements of the *Statute of Frauds*?

24. "A contract that does not satisfy the *Statute of Frauds* is void." True or false? Explain your answer.

25. Will a contract formed online with electronic signatures be enforced by the courts? Why or why not?

26. Under what circumstances will a contract falling under the jurisdiction of the *Statute of Frauds* be enforceable even though it is not evidenced by writing?

CASES AND DISCUSSION QUESTIONS

1. *National Money Mart Co. v. Tazmania Auto Sales Inc.*, 2001 ABPC 254
The plaintiff sued Tazmania for the amount of five cheques that were dishonoured upon presentation. It also sued Bannerman, a minor, for the amount of two of these cheques. Bannerman had endorsed these cheques and received their face value, less a fee charge. He immediately gave the funds to his mother and stepfather.

Assuming that the law relating to the capacity to incur liability as an endorser of a cheque is the same as the law relating to the capacity to contract, will the plaintiff succeed in its claim against Bannerman?

2. *Graham v. Capital Cabs Ltd.*, 2005 NWTTC 6 (CanLII)
In July 2004, a group of people, including Graham, decided to set up a taxi-cab business. Graham agreed to assist however she could in setting up the business, by doing such things as arranging telephone hookups and applying for licences. It was agreed that she would be the office manager for the business. It was also agreed that Graham would receive a share in the corporation that was to be set up in return for the work she was doing and for agreeing to work for a reduced salary for the first year the business operated. The corporation (the defendant) was incorporated on August 6, 2004. A meeting was held the next day, and it was agreed that Graham would be paid $2000 for the work she had done, and would continue to do, in setting up the business. There was also an agreement that Graham would receive a share in the corporation only if she invested $5000 in it and provided a car to be used in the business. The business opened on September 1, 2004. Graham resigned on September 3 because the working conditions had deteriorated very quickly. She sued for the $2000, for reimbursement of the expenses she had paid on behalf of the corporation, and for a share in the corporation.

What, if anything, is Graham entitled to judgment for against the Corporation?

3. *Harvey v. Newfoundland and Labrador*, 2005 NLTD 198 (CanLII)
Harvey claimed that Grimes verbally promised to hire him if he voted for Grimes to be the leader of the Liberal Party. Grimes won the election, but he did not hire Harvey, who then sued for breach of contract. Grimes denied that he had agreed to hire Harvey in return for his vote. The Court noted that it is a crime under the *Criminal Code* to "give, offer, agree to give or offer to an official . . . a reward, advantage or benefit of any kind."

If the evidence supported Harvey's allegation, should the Court enforce the contract that he claimed he entered into with Grimes?

4. *Dhingra v. Dhingra*, 2012 ONCA 261 (CanLII)
Dhingra was the beneficiary of his wife's life insurance policy. He was charged with murdering her but was found not criminally responsible because of a mental disorder. He applied to have the insurance proceeds paid to him. The Court refused his application

because of the public policy rule that prohibits a person from benefiting from his criminal acts.

Should the public policy rule apply when the person who has committed the crime is found not criminally responsible for the crime?

5. *Whitrow v. Hamilton*, 2010 SKCA 7 (CanLII)

Whitrow loaned Hamilton $5000 on March 13, 1991. Hamilton's brother signed a promissory note that required full payment on March 23, 1991, with interest at 10 percent per year. Hamilton was also required to pay a $500 processing fee. The money owing was not paid, so a new promissory note was signed, requiring payment of $5500 on March 31, 1991, plus interest at 8 percent per year from March 13, 1991. The debt was not paid, so Whitrow sued. The trial judge held that the processing fee resulted in a criminal rate of interest. She severed the interest portion of the loan (including the processing fee) and awarded judgment for the principal amount of $5000.

Should the Court of Appeal uphold the trial judge's decision and sever all of the interest from the debt obligation? Is there a more appropriate approach that would apply notional severance so that the contract is partially enforced and neither party enjoys a windfall?

6. *Steinke (o/a Muscle Mechanics Massage Therapy) v. Barrett*, 2012 MBQB 49 (CanLII)

Steinke owned and operated a massage therapy clinic in Winnipeg. The defendants were massage therapists who were operating as independent contractors. The agreements entered into by Steinke and the defendants stated that each defendant was not to provide massage therapy services within five kilometres of Steinke's clinic for a two-year period after his or her agreement was terminated. The defendants could not remove any patient files from the clinic, but they could photocopy files of patients they had treated, and they were allowed to contact only patients they had treated.

The defendants gave notice to terminate their agreements. Within a month of the date of termination, the defendants opened their own massage therapy clinic that was located less than five kilometres from Steinke's clinic. Steinke sued the defendants for breaching their agreements and asked for an injunction to stop them from operating their clinic.

Should the Court uphold the restrictive covenant contained in the agreements? What factors will the Court consider in determining whether the covenant was reasonable?

7. *McKnight v. Grant*, 2009 NBCA 4 (CanLII)

Grant executed documents to sell her cottage to her nephew. Six months later, she commenced an action requesting that the transaction be set aside because of misrepresentation and undue influence. The nephew decided to re-convey the cottage to Grant. Her lawyer talked to her nephew a couple of times, and an agreement was made that the cottage would be conveyed if Grant repaid the nephew the deposit he had made and the legal fees he had incurred. They agreed that the lawyers were to "paper" the settlement agreement. Two days later, the nephew changed his mind and advised that he did not want to settle the action. The trial judge found that there was a binding settlement agreement. The nephew appealed on the basis that the *Statute of Frauds* applied and that the settlement agreement should therefore not be enforceable.

Was the agreement to re-convey the cottage subject to the *Statute of Frauds*?

8. *Leoppky v. Meston*, 2008 ABQB 45 (CanLII)

An unmarried couple purchased a house as joint tenants. After they separated, they negotiated a settlement regarding the house. Leoppky claimed that an agreement was reached but that Meston refused to honour it. Meston denied that an agreement was reached and pled the *Statute of Frauds*. Most of the negotiations took place through email. Meston used her sister's email account. She signed all of her emails with her first name only.

Assume that the Court found there was an agreement between the parties as to the essential terms as set out in the emails between the parties. Did the agreement comply with the *Statute of Frauds*?

Chapter

Factors Affecting the Contractual Relationship

1. Distinguish innocent, fraudulent, and negligent misrepresentation
2. Identify the remedies available for each type of misrepresentation
3. Explain the implications of duress and undue influence
4. Identify three types of mistake
5. Describe the effect of mistake upon the enforceability of a contract
6. Outline the rules governing privity and assignment

The two previous chapters examined the process of forming contracts. This chapter examines what happens when a party claims it was misled or pressured into entering an agreement, and the nature and effect of a contract made under mistake. The requirement of privity of contract is discussed, together with how obligations are affected when an innocent third party, or a stranger to the contract, becomes involved.

MISREPRESENTATION

During pre-contract negotiations, people often say things that are designed to persuade the other party to make the deal but that never become part of the contract. When these statements are false, misleading the other party and inducing them to enter into the contract, an actionable misrepresentation has taken place.

Misrepresentation is a false statement of fact; it becomes a material misrepresentation when it persuades someone to enter into a contract. The false statement can be made fraudulently, when the person making the statement knew it was false; negligently, when the person should have known the statement was false; or completely innocently, when the misrepresentation is made without fault. These distinctions are important because they impact the remedies available to the aggrieved party.

LO

Misrepresentation is a misleading statement

Misrepresentation may be fraudulent, negligent, or innocent

CASE SUMMARY 8.1

Evidence of Fraud Opens Door to Extrinsic Evidence:
Metropolitan Stores of Canada Ltd. v. Nova Construction Co.[1]

Nova, upon taking over ownership of the Antigonish Mall, tried to evict Metropolitan. In the process of settling the resulting dispute, a new lease was negotiated for a 20-year term. The lease contained a non-competition clause, such that no stores in competition with Metropolitan would be allowed to be located in the mall. However, the non-competition clause would not apply if there was any expansion to the existing shopping centre.

When questioned about this exception (or exemption clause), the representative of Nova explained that the only expansion that would take place would be within the present boundaries of the mall and that another clause in the agreement protected Metropolitan from competition within those boundaries. The representative knew that this was false. Nova later purchased surrounding property, expanded into that area, leased space to another department store, and claimed that the exemption clause permitted this.

The Court found that a fraudulent misrepresentation had taken place, which induced Metropolitan to enter into the contract. Although the parol evidence rule restricts consideration of any outside or extrinsic evidence that conflicts with the plain meaning of the contract, there are several exceptions. An exception arises if there is evidence of fraud inducing the parties to enter into the contract. Such fraud was found, so the evidence pertaining to the misleading statements was admitted.

This case is unusual because the normal remedies for misrepresentation are rescission or, when fraud is present, rescission or damages. An order to rescind the contract sets it aside and the court focuses on restoring the parties to their pre-contract position. Metropolitan, however, asked for **rectification** of the contract—that is, for the contract to be rewritten to include the terms as it understood them, making leasing space to the rival department store a breach of its lease. Rectification—the rewriting of a contract on behalf of one of the parties at the expense of the other—is a drastic remedy, but because of the fraud it was deemed appropriate.

SMALL BUSINESS PERSPECTIVE

In the heat of closing a deal, individuals may be tempted to hide or misrepresent information so as not to scare the other party away. Sophisticated businesspeople will insist that employees and agents deal with third parties honestly. Not only is this ethical, it also makes good business sense, saving money in the long run.

Allegation of Fact

Misrepresentation must be fact, not opinion or promise

Opinion by expert may be misrepresentation

The statement that forms the basis of the misrepresentation must be an allegation of fact. Only statements made about the current state of things that prove to be incorrect can be considered misrepresentation. "This car has a new motor" is a statement of fact. "I will have the car inspected next year" is not a statement of fact, but a promise to do something in the future. A promise to do something in the future will qualify as a misrepresentation only when it can be clearly shown that the person making the promise had no intention of honouring that promise at the time it was made. Otherwise, for promises of future conduct to be enforceable they must be included as terms in the contract.

Where the misleading statement being complained of was an expression of opinion rather than fact, it too is not actionable unless the person making the statement was an expert. When a person declares that the car he is selling is a "good car" or a "good deal" he is entitled to have that opinion, and the statement is not actionable if the car later breaks down. But if a mechanic makes the same statement and it proves to be false, it can be actionable as misrepresentation because he is an expert.

[1.] [1988] N.S.J. No. 112 (N.S.C.A.).

CASE SUMMARY 8.2

Loss Caused by Reliance on Home Inspection Report:
Semeniuk v. Key Home Inspections Ltd.[2]

The plaintiffs knew that the property they were seeking to buy required work, but to avoid any unpleasant surprises they secured the services of a home inspector. Nonetheless, after taking possession, they discovered there was insufficient insulation in the home's attic, improper grading, cracks in the foundation, and inadequate drainage in part of the basement, among other issues. These defects had not been identified in the inspector's report, and the plaintiffs claimed these omissions demonstrated negligence or a failure to meet the standards of the home inspection profession.

In his analysis, the trial judge stated:

> The five general requirements for establishing liability for negligent misrepresentation are definitively set out in *Queen v. Cognos Inc.*, [1993] 1 SCR 87 at 110 [*Cognos*]:
>
> 1. there must be a duty of care based on a "special relationship" between the representor and the representee;
> 2. the representation in question must be untrue, inaccurate, or misleading;
> 3. the representor must have acted negligently in making said misrepresentation;
> 4. (the representee must have relied, in a reasonable manner, on said negligent misrepresentation; and
> 5. the reliance must have been detrimental to the representee in the sense that damages resulted.

This framework from *Cognos* applies in this claim alleging negligent misrepresentation against the home inspector.

As to whether a duty of care was owed by the inspector to the plaintiffs, the judge cited these indications of whether the reliance was reasonable:

1. The defendant had a direct or indirect financial interest in the transaction in respect of which the representation was made.
2. The defendant was a professional or someone who possessed special skill, judgment or knowledge.
3. The advice or information was provided in the course of the defendant's business.
4. The information or advice was given deliberately, and not on a social occasion.
5. The information or advice was given in response to a specific enquiry or request.

Since the inspection report was a professional service that was requested and paid for, reliance upon it was reasonable and a duty of care was thus owed. It was also breached, causing the plaintiffs substantial injury. Damages of $18 782.41 were awarded.

SMALL BUSINESS PERSPECTIVE

Clearly, if individuals with expertise in a field are asked for their "professional opinion," alarm bells should start to ring. The recipient may well be swayed by them, so extra care must be invested. The expert had better ensure the representations are accurate or are made only after due diligence is exercised.

[2.] 2013 ABPC 254 (CanLII). See also *Alloway v. CMG Engineering Services Ltd.*, 2008 ABPC 88 (CanLII); *Salgado v. Toth*, 2009 BCSC 1515 (CanLII); and *Whighton v. Integrity Inspection Inc.*, 2007 ABQB 175 (CanLII) for similar cases brought against property inspectors.

Silence or Non-Disclosure

For a misrepresentation to take place, there also must be some actual communication of information. Silence or **non-disclosure** by itself is not usually actionable. There are, however, some special situations where the person contracting is required to disclose certain information. For example, insurance contracts require the parties acquiring insurance to disclose a great deal of personal information that affects the policy. People who apply for life insurance are required to disclose if they have had heart attacks or other medical problems in the past. The sale of new shares involves a similar obligation of disclosure to an investor in a prospectus. If the terms require that the parties disclose all information to each other as a condition of the agreement, the contract can be rescinded if they fail to do so. Professionals also have an obligation to disclose certain information at their disposal that might affect the actions of their clients. These are often referred to as **utmost good faith** contracts. This requirement of good faith is being expanded, and it is now much more common for the courts to find that a misrepresentation has taken place where one party withholds information from the other.

Where a person actively attempts to hide information that would be important to the other contracting party, this also might qualify as misrepresentation. It is not necessary that the statement be written or verbal; misrepresentation can occur even if the method of communicating it is a gesture, such as a nod of the head.

But when individuals mislead themselves, *caveat emptor* applies and there is no cause for complaint. In *Hoy v. Lozanovski*,[3] the home Hoy purchased from the Lozanovskis proved to be infested with termites. Hoy sought rescission of the contract, alleging misrepresentation, but the judge determined that since the Lozanovskis did not know of the termites when they sold the house there was no fraudulent misrepresentation. Also, they had remained silent, so no representation had been made. Finally, since Hoy had had the house inspected, he had not relied on any representations from the vendors. In effect, Hoy misled himself about the condition of the building. Accordingly, no remedy against the Lozanovskis was available to Hoy.

False Statement

It is necessary to demonstrate not only that the misleading comment qualifies as an allegation of fact, but also that the statement is incorrect and untrue. Even when a person technically tells the truth but withholds information that would have created an entirely different impression, this can amount to misrepresentation. For example, if a used car salesperson tells a potential purchaser that the transmission of a particular car has just been replaced but fails to say it was replaced with a used transmission, this partial truth can be misrepresentation if it leads the purchaser to believe a new transmission was installed.

Statement Must Be Inducement

A victim of misrepresentation must show that she was induced into entering a contract by a false statement. If the victim knew that the statement was false and entered into the agreement anyway, either because she did not believe the statement or believed that the statement did not make any difference, the misrepresentation is not actionable. For there to be an actionable misrepresentation, the false statement must affect the outcome of the agreement, and the victim must have been misled into doing something that she otherwise would not have done.

[3.] (1987), 43 R.P.R. 296 (Ont. Dist. Ct.).

Franchisee Misled by Inflated and Inaccurate Contentions of Franchisor: *TRC Enterprises v. Tobmar Newstands Inc. (c.o.b. Gateway Newstands)*[4]

Imagine entering a franchise agreement based on information supplied by the franchisor and learning later that this vital information was untrue!

The franchisee was to operate a newsstand near a casino and hotel, on the understanding that the site was suitable, casino traffic was heavy, a conference facility augmented that traffic, and the franchisee would exclusively supply newspapers and tobacco products in this favourable setting. In fact, casino traffic was only 35 percent of that represented and the conference facility for 50 000 people did not exist. Further, other outlets on the property were permitted to sell competing products, so no exclusivity existed. In light of these material misrepresentations, the Court determined that rescission of the franchise agreement, together with a return of all monies paid to the franchisor, was the appropriate remedy.

SMALL BUSINESS PERSPECTIVE

The temptation to paint a bright picture often arises when trying to market one's product or service to others. But as the above case illustrates, making unsubstantiated claims in the heat of zealous marketing can be an expensive mistake.

As a Term of the Contract

Plaintiffs may need to seek special remedies when induced or persuaded, by misleading statements, into a contract. Special (equitable) remedies are needed because the misleading statement usually does not become a term of the agreement itself. If the misleading statement has become incorporated as a term of the agreement, the normal rules of breach of contract apply, providing broader remedies that are easier to obtain. If Mills agreed to sell Lucas a used Nissan automobile, which in the contract was described as a 2015 Nissan Murano, Lucas could sue for breach of contract if the vehicle turned out to be a 2012 Murano. But if Lucas bought a particular vehicle because the vendor Mills said that the Murano had specific fuel efficiency, rarely would such a provision be inserted as a term of the agreement. Because the statement is an inducement to buy, not a term of the contract, the victim must rely on the rules of misrepresentation to obtain a remedy. The remedies available will depend on whether the statement was made inadvertently, fraudulently, or negligently.

> **Breach of contract action may be appropriate if a misleading term is inserted in the contract**

The courts today are more open to the suggestion that such representations have become terms of the contract. Even statements in advertisements can now be taken to be part of the contract. Many provincial consumer protection statutes contain provisions controlling misleading and deceptive trade practices; several specifically state that representations of salespeople are made part of the contract. Refer to MyBusLawLab for particulars. The topic of consumer protection legislation will be discussed in Chapter 16.

Innocent Misrepresentation

An **innocent misrepresentation** is a false statement that is made honestly and without carelessness by a person who believed it to be true. If the person making the misrepresentation is in no way at fault, the misrepresentation is innocent and the remedies are limited. The only recourse available to the victim is to ask for the equi-

> **Innocent misrepresentation— remedy is rescission**

---

4. 2010 MBQB 112 (CanLII).

table remedy of rescission. As soon as the victim realizes what has happened, he can either choose to ignore the misrepresentation and affirm the contract or refute the contract and seek rescission.

Rescission requires property to be returned

Rescission attempts to return both parties to their original positions; the subject matter of the contract must be returned to the original owner, and any monies paid under the contract must also be returned. The courts will also require the party who is returning the subject matter of the contract to return any benefit derived from the property while it was in her possession. Similarly, a person can be compensated for any expenses incurred. Damages are not available as a remedy, because both parties are innocent. Rescission is an important remedy, but because it is equitable it is restricted in its application.

Rescission is not available in certain circumstances:

Rescission of contract is not available in the situations outlined in Table 8.1.

Table 8.1 Situations Where Rescission Is Not Available

Affirmation	Victims of misrepresentation who have affirmed the contract are bound by the affirmation and cannot later insist on rescission. Thus, where a person uses the proceeds of a contract when he knows about the misrepresentation, he has affirmed the contract.
Restoration impossible	The remedy of rescission is not available if the parties cannot be returned to their original positions because the subject matter of the contract has been destroyed or damaged. Since neither party is at fault with innocent misrepresentation, the court will not impose a burden on either one of them but will simply deny a remedy.
Adverse impact on third party	Rescission will not be granted if it will adversely affect the position of a third party. When the subject matter of the contract has been resold by the purchaser to a third party who has no knowledge of the misrepresentation and otherwise comes to the transaction with **clean hands**, the courts will not interfere with that person's possession and title to the goods.
Plaintiff is not blameless	Where the victim comes without clean hands, rescission will not be available. Where the victim has also misled or cheated, or where the victim has caused unreasonable delay, rescission will be denied.

These principles apply to all equitable remedies. (Equitable remedies will be discussed further in the next chapter.)

Note that in those few situations where the misrepresentation causes the victim to make a fundamental mistake about the nature of the contract, the agreement may be void because of failure to reach a consensus. When this happens there is no contract and the victim can recover money or goods supplied despite the effect on third parties or the presence of affirmation.

Fraudulent Misrepresentation

Rescission or damages will be awarded for intentional misrepresentation

If a misrepresentation of fact is intentional and induces another person to enter into a contract, the victim of the **fraudulent misrepresentation** can sue for damages under the tort of deceit in addition to or instead of the contractual remedy of rescission. According to the 1889 decision in *Derry v. Peek*, fraud is established when the false statement was made "(1) knowingly, (2) without belief in its truth, or (3) recklessly, careless whether it be true or false."[5] Essentially, it is fraud if it can be demonstrated that the person who made the false statement did not honestly believe it to be true. The person making the statement cannot avoid responsibility by claiming she did not know for sure that what she said was false, or

---

5. (1889), 14 App. Cas. 337 (H.L.), at 374.

because she did not bother to find out the truth. Fraud exists even if the victim of the misrepresentation could have found out the truth easily but happened to rely on the statement of the defendant.

CASE SUMMARY 8.4

Disguising Used Goods as New: *Kellogg Brown & Root Inc. v. Aerotech Herman Nelson Inc.*[6]

The plaintiff purchased 282 portable heaters from the defendant, Aerotech. Immediately after delivery, it became apparent that the heaters were not new. The plaintiff made some use of the heaters before deciding to discontinue its attempts to service or use them further. It notified Aerotech that the contract was being rescinded and demanded reimbursement. The Court found an obvious intent to mislead the purchaser. Aerotech tried to disguise the used heaters as new by altering hour meters, repainting, cleaning, re-serializing, and changing the manufacturer's plates on the units. The fact that the plaintiff had tried to repair the heaters to make them usable did not operate as a bar to rescission. Victims of fraud do not, as soon as there is an inkling of a misrepresentation, have to make up their minds whether to rescind or not. The plaintiff was found to have repudiated the contract within a reasonable period of time, and the cost of the heaters ($1 359 571) and the cost of shipping ($321 905) *plus* punitive damages ($50 000) were awarded.

SMALL BUSINESS PERSPECTIVE

If one reflects upon all the additional costs incurred—the loss of the sale, the cost of shipping, the punitive damages, and the legal costs—it was hardly a sound business decision to mislead the purchaser just to get a better initial price.

When a person innocently makes a false statement and later discovers the mistake, he must inform the other person of the misrepresentation without delay. Failure to do so will turn an innocent misrepresentation into a fraudulent one. If during the process of negotiating the terms of a contract a person makes a statement that was true but later becomes false because of changing circumstances, she must correct the statement upon finding out the truth. **[margin note: Failure to correct turns innocent misrepresentation into fraud]**

Once it has been established that the false statement was intentional and thus fraudulent, the courts can award rescission or damages:

1. **Rescission.** The victim of fraudulent misrepresentation retains the right to have the parties to the contract returned to their original positions and to be reimbursed for any out-of-pocket expenses. **[margin note: Rescission]**

2. **Damages for deceit.** The victim of fraudulent misrepresentation can seek monetary compensation as well as rescission for any loss incurred as a result of the fraud. The damages are awarded for the tort of deceit. Note that to obtain damages there is no obligation to return property, nor is the court attempting to return both parties to their original positions, as with rescission. Rather, the courts require financial compensation to be paid to the victim by the person at fault. A victim of fraud can seek damages even where rescission is not available. The victim does not lose the right to demand monetary compensation by affirming the contract or where the goods have been resold to a third party. The victim of a fraudulent misrepresentation can also seek punitive damages, that is, damages intended to punish the wrongdoer rather than simply compensate the victim. **[margin note: Damages]**

---

6. 2004 MBCA 63 (CanLII); leave to appeal to S.C.C. refused, [2004] S.C.C.A. No. 344.

The courts do not treat fraud lightly. In *Pirbhai v. Singh (c.o.b. Sarwan Auto Sales)* for example, the purchaser paid the fraudulent vendor $32 913 for a Lexus. The vendor falsified documents, was unblinkingly dishonest, and told "untruths too numerous to catalogue and insulting in their breadth."[7] The Court awarded the plaintiff $33 465 for breach of contract and another $50 000 in punitive damages.

The major hurdle with fraudulent misrepresentation is establishing that the defendant knowingly misled the victim. This is often difficult to do and is not necessary if only rescission is sought.

Negligent Misrepresentation

Damages for negligence may be available in cases of misrepresentation

Negligent misrepresentation may be established where a party carelessly provided false and material information. All four elements of negligence must be established; thus, a duty to exercise care must first be owed. When it is foreseeable that the plaintiff will be relying on this information, such as when she asks an expert for his opinion (as in Case Summary 8.2, where a property inspection report was requested), a duty of care will be owed. A breach of that duty is required, so if the party who delivered false information did not act with reasonable care, breach of the standard will be found. It is necessary to further prove causation and damage, so the recipient of the false information must act on it and suffer a loss.

Note that in tort law the remedy of damages is available for negligent misrepresentation (sometimes called negligent misstatement, as discussed in Chapter 5). When the negligent statement becomes a term of a contract or arises out of a contractual relationship, the plaintiff may have a choice about whether to sue in contract, seeking damages for breach of contract, or sue in tort for negligence. The Supreme Court of Canada made it clear that such "concurrent liability" may exist, subject to limitations that may be included in the contract.[8] Thus, whether the plaintiff can circumvent the protection provided in an exemption clause (which may prevent an action for breach of contract) by suing in tort instead depends on the wording and breadth of the exemption clause.

As stated by Justices La Forest and McLachlin in *BG Checo International Ltd. v. British Columbia Hydro and Power Authority*:[9]

> In our view, the general rule emerging from this Court's decision in *Central Trust Co. v. Rafuse*, [1986] 2 S.C.R. 147, is that where a given wrong *prima facie* supports an action in contract and in tort, the party may sue in either or both, except where the contract indicates that the parties intended to limit or negate the right to sue in tort. This limitation on the general rule of concurrency arises because it is always open to parties to limit or waive the duties which the common law would impose on them for negligence. This principle is of great importance in preserving a sphere of individual liberty and commercial flexibility. . . . So a plaintiff may sue either in contract or in tort, subject to any limit the parties themselves have placed on that right by their contract. The mere fact that the parties have dealt with a matter expressly in their contract does not mean that they intended to exclude the right to sue in tort. It all depends on how they have dealt with it.

Damages are available as a remedy where the misrepresentation has become a term of the contract that is breached, where the misrepresentation is fraudulent, and where there is negligence.[10] Only when the misrepresentation is truly innocent and without fault is the victim restricted to the remedy of rescission.

---

7. *Pirbhai v. Singh et al.*, 2010 ONSC 2446 (CanLII).

8. *Central Trust Co. v. Rafuse*, [1986] 2 SCR 147, 1986 CanLII 29 (SCC).

9. *BG Checo International Ltd. v. British Columbia Hydro and Power Authority*, [1993] 1 SCR 12, 1993 CanLII 145 (SCC).

10. *Beaufort Realties v. Chomedey Aluminum Co.*, [1980] 2 SCR 718, 1980 CanLII 47 (SCC).

DURESS AND UNDUE INFLUENCE

Duress

When people are forced or pressured to enter into contracts against their will by threats of violence or imprisonment, the contract can be challenged on the basis of **duress**. In *Byle v. Byle*,[11] a young man threatened physical harm to his sibling. The parents, fearing that threat would be acted on, conveyed some land and other advantages to the aggressor son. The trial judge declared the transactions void on the basis of duress, but the Court of Appeal reversed this decision, finding contracts made under duress to be only voidable. A void contract is no contract and nothing can save it, but a voidable contract could be revived later by affirmation and be binding on the parties.

Duress involves threats of violence or imprisonment, making the contract voidable

Today, duress includes not only threats of violence and imprisonment, but also threats of criminal prosecution and threats to disclose embarrassing or scandalous information. Duress also includes threats to a person's goods or property:

> The presence of economic duress is often tested by looking for certain indicia or "badges" of duress, [namely]:
>
> (a) whether the party protested at the time the agreement was entered into;
> (b) whether the party had a realistic alternative to entering into the agreement;
> (c) whether the party had the opportunity to speak with independent legal counsel;
> (d) whether, after entering into the agreement, the party took steps to void it within a reasonable period of time; and
> (e) whether the pressure exerted was illegitimate.[12]

To succeed, it may be necessary to show that the threat was the main inducement for entering into the agreement.

Even though the threat of loss of employment and other financial losses can amount to economic duress and be actionable, it is important not to mistake the normal predicaments in which we all find ourselves for improper pressure or duress.[13] If a person has no choice except to deal with the only airline that services a particular area, these accepted conditions of the marketplace do not amount to duress. Likewise, where a person has to pay a high rate of interest because no one else will loan him money at a lower rate, it is not duress. Even the threat of suing when the person doing so has a legitimate right to sue is not duress. Rather, it is the legitimate exercise of the rights of that person.

Economic disadvantage is not enough

Note that duress only causes a contract to be voidable, so the victim of duress may be denied a remedy if it would jeopardize a third party. If someone is forced to sell a gold watch by threat of violence and the watch is then resold to an innocent third party, the watch cannot be retrieved. Because a voidable contract is still a contract, the title has passed on to the third party.

Voidable contracts cannot affect third parties

CASE SUMMARY 8.5

Threats Fail to Amount to Duress: *Braut v. Stec*[14]

Braut brought an action seeking to enforce an equity-sharing agreement allegedly made with Stec. Stec defended the action arguing that Braut, literally, put a gun to Stec's head to force him to sign the agreement.

---

[11]. 1990 CanLII 313 (BC CA) (1990) 65 D.L.R. (4th) 641 (B.C.C.A.).

[12]. *Attila Dogan Construction and Installation Co. Inc. v. AMEC Americas Limited*, 2014 ABCA 74 (CanLII), at para. 20.

[13]. See *Bell v. Levy*, 2011 BCCA 417 (CanLII), where Levy's claim of duress was dismissed. His consent to the loan agreement was obtained as a result of threats "to report his family to the tax authorities" and "to bad mouth him to mutual business contacts."

[14]. 2005 BCCA 521 (CanLII); leave to appeal to SCC dismissed 2006 CanLII 14570 (SCC).

Braut offered to sell certain properties to Stec and offered to arrange the financing. Since Stec was impecunious, they falsely reported his income to lenders. Braut arranged for further financing to be advanced by his friend. After the transfers were complete, Braut presented the equity-sharing agreement to Stec, who refused to sign it. Stec's lawyer also advised Stec not to sign. Stec was to bear all of the risks and any losses related to the property and was to expend considerable work and labour on the properties, yet he was to share only half the profits with Braut. Duress under gunpoint is a serious allegation, and the trial judge stated the amount of proof needed would approach the criminal standard. Such proof was not established.

Nonetheless, the judge had no doubt that Braut threatened Stec, warning he would expose the fact that Stec had lied on the applications for the mortgages (which Braut had completed). Braut, a sophisticated businessperson, evidently sought to dupe Stec, an uneducated immigrant. The equity-sharing agreement was found to be unconscionable. Reference was made to *Harry v. Kreutziger*, (1978), 9 B.C.L.R. 166 (C.A.), where Justice McIntyre said "Where a claim is made that a bargain is unconscionable, it must be shown for success that there was inequality in the position of the parties due to the ignorance, need or distress of the weaker, which would leave him in the power of the stronger, coupled with proof of substantial unfairness in the bargain. When this has been shown a presumption of fraud is raised and the stronger must show, in order to preserve his bargain, that it was fair and reasonable." Since inequality existed yet Braut failed to rebut the presumption of fraud, the Court refused to enforce the equity-sharing agreement.

SMALL BUSINESS PERSPECTIVE

Where an agreement is blatantly unfair or one-sided, courts are drawn to conclude that the deal is unconscionable and thus unenforceable. A presumption of fraud is difficult to dispel. A sophisticated client who hopes to enforce a contract that is one-sided in her favour should insist that the other party seek independent legal advice and record that suggestion.

Undue Influence

The types of pressure brought to bear upon people are often more subtle than those described by duress. When pressure from a dominant, trusted person makes it impossible to bargain freely, it is regarded as **undue influence**, and the resulting contract is also voidable.

In the case of *Allcard v. Skinner*,[15] a woman entered a religious order and gave it all her property. The Court determined that there had been undue influence when the gift was given, even though there was clear evidence that there had been no overt attempt on the part of the religious order to influence this woman. The Court would have set the gift aside, except that she had affirmed it after leaving the relationship.

Undue influence is presumed in certain relationships

CASE SUMMARY 8.6

Undue Influence Presumed: *Rochdale Credit Union Ltd. v. Barney*[16]

Barney was a friend and client of John Farlow, a solicitor. He reluctantly guaranteed Farlow's $50 000 loan from Rochdale Credit Union. Farlow died, and the credit union demanded payment from Barney. The Ontario Court of Appeal found undue influence on the part of Farlow in persuading his client to guarantee the loan. Because Farlow

---

15. (1887), 36 Ch.D. 145 (C.A.).
16. 1984 CanLII 1851 (ON CA); leave to appeal to the SCC refused, February 18, 1985. S.C.C. File No. 19206.

represented both the lender and the guarantor, the credit union was also held responsible for that undue influence. Barney thus did not have to pay the debt.

The relationship of solicitor/client leads to a presumption of undue influence. Unless that presumption is overturned with evidence that the contract was freely entered, the contract may be set aside. It is interesting that the credit union was also affected by that presumption.

SMALL BUSINESS PERSPECTIVE

Depending on the line of work one's business is engaged in, a presumption of undue influence may arise, particularly when contracts are made with clients. To preserve the enforceability of such contracts, extra precautions need to be taken, including a requirement that the client secure independent legal advice.

The court may find undue influence in the following situations:

1. **Presumption based on a special relationship.** In certain categories of relationships the courts will presume the presence of undue influence, and if the presumption is not rebutted the contract will be set aside. Some examples of such relationships include the following:

   - Professionals such as doctors or lawyers contracting with their patients or clients
   - Parents or guardians contracting with infant children in their care
   - Adult children contracting with mentally impaired parents
   - Trustees contracting with beneficiaries
   - Religious advisers contracting with parishioners

   Where undue influence is presumed

   Note that undue influence is not automatically presumed in contracts between parents and adult children and contracts between spouses, but it may be established upon consideration of special circumstances.

2. **Presumption based on unique circumstances.** A presumption of undue influence may arise on the basis of unique circumstances, where one person was in a position to dominate the will of another. A husband or a wife signing a guarantee for a spouse's indebtedness might constitute such a situation. If the court makes that presumption, it falls on the party trying to enforce the contract to show that there was no domination or unfair advantage taken of the other party. In *Bank of Montreal v. Duguid*,[17] for example, the issue was whether an automatic presumption of undue influence arises when one spouse guarantees a loan for the other. Although the bank was concerned about the wisdom of the investment, it did not send Mrs. Duguid to get independent legal advice. A presumption of undue influence might arise in a marriage where one partner is unaware of and not involved in financial decisions. In this case, however, the wife was a sophisticated real estate agent who knew what she was doing, so no such presumption of undue influence evolved. Evidently, for the presumption to arise, there has to be more than just a close relationship—the guarantor has to be vulnerable and the bank has to know of that vulnerability.

   Undue pressure from circumstances

3. **Undue influence is determined from the facts.** In the absence of a relationship that gives rise to the presumption, it is still possible for a victim to produce actual evidence to satisfy the court that undue influence was, in fact, exerted and that there was coercion. This can be difficult to prove, since the victim must show that a relationship of trust developed and that this trust was abused. When the person trying to enforce the contract took advantage of the fact that he was being relied on for advice, the courts may find that there was undue influence.

[17.] (2000) 185 D.L.R. (4th) 458; 2000 CanLII 5710 (ON CA).

Even when undue influence is presumed, the contract will be binding if the person trying to enforce the contract can show that the undue influence was overcome and that the victim either affirmed the contract, which was the situation in the *Allcard* case, or did nothing to rescind it after escaping the relationship. The courts may also refuse a remedy if the person trying to escape the contract is not altogether innocent of wrongdoing.

Of course, if the party accused of undue influence can convince the court that there was no such influence, any presumption is rebutted and the contract is binding. It is thus advisable for contracting parties who are concerned about this problem to ensure that the other party secures independent legal advice before entering into an agreement. This is especially true for professionals who are contracting with clients for matters outside that professional relationship.

Independent legal advice is desirable, but the contract must be fair

Unconscionable Transactions

The concept of **unconscionable transactions** has received a greater acceptance by the courts in recent years. This is an equitable doctrine that permits the court to set aside a contract in which one party has been taken advantage of, because of such factors as desperation caused by poverty or intellectual impairment that falls short of incapacity. To escape from such a contract, it must be shown that (1) there is an inequality in the bargaining positions of the parties arising out of ignorance, need, or distress of the weaker party; (2) the stronger party has consciously used the position of power to achieve an advantage; and (3) the agreement reached is substantially unfair to the weaker party.

CASE SUMMARY 8.7

Insurance Settlements Set Aside When Unconscionable: *Blackburn v. Eager*[18]; *Floyd v. Couture*[19]

Blackburn, who was 42 years old and had a Grade 7 education, was injured in an automobile collision. She commenced an action for damages, and the insurance adjuster offered her $7000 to settle the matter. The adjuster suspected that Blackburn's injuries were far more significant than she realized but withheld sharing that information with her. Blackburn accepted the settlement without seeking prior legal advice; later she discovered that her injuries would be permanent. The settlement was set aside as unconscionable. The Court determined that the adjuster had unconscientiously exploited Blackburn's naivety to achieve an early and unconscionable settlement.

Floyd v. Couture also involved settlement of a personal injury claim. One month after the accident, the insurer offered Floyd a sum to cover the cost of repairs plus $2000 for a release of his claim. Floyd accepted and cashed the cheque. Later Floyd sued, claiming the settlement was unconscionable in light of his continuing pain. In contrast to the *Blackburn* decision, this Court determined that the release was not obtained in an unconscionable manner. No pressure had been exerted on Floyd to sign the release, it detailed that both property and personal injury claims were being settled and in light of known circumstances, and the amount was not so low as to be substantially unfair.

If a contract is reasonable in light of all the risks and contingencies, it is not unconscionable.

DISCUSSION QUESTIONS

When comparing the above two decisions, one differentiating factor was the deception employed by the insurance adjuster in the *Blackburn* case. In light of the dim view the Court took of such behaviour, how should businesses train their employees to conduct themselves? Will one-sided bargains be upheld to favour those who act unethically?

18. 2001 NSSC 30 (CanLII).
19. 2004 ABQB 238 (CanLII).

Simple economic advantage does not, in itself, make a transaction unconscionable. If a person having limited assets cannot get a loan from anyone else and must pay 20 percent interest, this alone will not make the contract unconscionable. There must be evidence that the debtor was taken advantage of because of some problem, such as age, desperation, or lack of sophistication, and then it must be shown that the resulting deal was not reasonable. If the 20 percent interest charged was reasonable given the risk, the contract is not unconscionable.

There is some overlap in the principles of unconscionable transactions and undue influence. Although legislation has been passed in most common law provinces prohibiting unconscionable transactions,[20] in most instances the statutory provisions are limited to loan transactions.[21] The recent acceptance of this equitable doctrine makes the defence of unconscionability available even when the contracts in question do not involve the lending of money. Of course, as with other equitable remedies, the court will not grant a remedy based on undue influence or unconscionability where a third party is negatively affected or where the victim also has unclean hands.

> **A deal must be unreasonable to be unconscionable**

> **Statute law addresses unconscionable loan transactions**

> **Common law broadly addresses unconscionable transactions**

REDUCING RISK 8.1

Businesspeople—especially professionals in service industries, such as lawyers, bankers, and accountants—should be careful when dealing with their clients to avoid situations where an accusation of undue influence or unconscionability can arise. Sophisticated professionals will avoid entering business arrangements with their clients outside of those related to the profession. Even transactions related to the profession should be guarded so that conflicts of interest do not arise. When in doubt, the transaction should be avoided. Insisting that the client obtain independent legal advice is wise. If the deal goes well, chances are no one will complain; but if a loss occurs, the client may have grounds to seek compensation from the professional to cover those losses.

MISTAKE

In limited circumstances, the courts will provide a remedy where one or both of the parties have made a **mistake** with respect to a contract. Where it is clear that because of the mistake the parties have failed to reach a consensus, the contract is void—there is no complete agreement between them. It must be made clear at the outset that the court will not interfere when the parties have simply made a bad bargain; this is an error in judgment and the person who made it must live with it.

Reviewable mistakes in contract involve a person's mind being at odds with the terms, surrounding circumstances, or other factors relating to the contract. Such a mistake can relate to the major terms of the contract, including the identity of the parties. It can relate to an assumption upon which the contract is based, whether that assumption is about (1) a matter of fact, (2) some future event, or (3) the law surrounding the contract. And it can also concern an expected result or consequence of the agreement. The mistake can be made by only one of the parties or by both. When both parties are making a mistake, it can be a *shared mistake* (where both are making the same mistake) or it can be a *misunderstanding* (where each party has a different idea as to the meaning of the terms of the contract). This is a complex and difficult area of contract law to understand. The guiding principle seems to be that the courts will try to do what is necessary to give effect to the reasonable expectations of the parties.

LO

> **A misunderstanding that destroys consensus results in void contract**

> **Mistake must go to the very root of the contract**

> **Courts will try to give effect to the reasonable expectations of the parties**

---

20. See, for example, Alberta's *Unconscionable Transactions Act*, R.S.A. 2000, c. U-2; Nova Scotia's *Unconscionable Transactions Relief Act*, R.S., c. 481; and Manitoba's *Unconscionable Transactions Relief Act*, C.C.S.M. c. U20.

21. See British Columbia's *Business Practices and Consumer Protection Act*, S.B.C. 2004, c. 2, particularly Part 2 (Unfair Practices); and Ontario's *Consumer Protection Act, 2002*, S.O. 2002, c. 30.

CASE SUMMARY 8.8

Bad Advice Does not Void a Contract Made Based on It: *Orrin Irvin Lewis Works v. Rhonda Elaine Works*[22]

The husband had agreed to transfer his interest in the matrimonial home to his wife in settlement of a claim for spousal support. Later, the husband discovered that he had received incorrect tax advice as to the consequences of this settlement and he tried to avoid signing the formal Minutes of Settlement. He now claimed to have entered a contract based on a mistake. The Court held that a consensus had been reached. The husband knew he was transferring his interest in the home for a release from spousal support. The fact that he had made a "bad deal" because the tax advice given to him was erroneous did not void the agreement itself.

The issue of tax deductibility was not discussed between counsel, and the wife's counsel had no reason to believe the agreement was based on that assumption. Where only one party is mistaken about something significant in a contract, the court will exercise its discretion to set aside the contract only if satisfied that, in light of the circumstances, it would be unfair or unjust to enforce the contract. The issue of a tax saving was never a central issue; thus the deal was deemed fair.

SMALL BUSINESS PERSPECTIVE

If there are certain assumptions upon which parties are acting, would it be wise to state those assumptions in the contract itself? This decision suggests that would be prudent.

Mistake must be serious

When the mistake relates to the terms of the agreement itself, such as the identity of the parties or the subject matter of the agreement, the courts are more willing to provide a remedy. The courts also will not interfere with contractual obligations unless the demonstrated mistake is significant or material with respect to the agreement.

Careless party is responsible when mistake is a result of negligence

Finally, where the mistake is caused by the negligence of one of the parties, that party will normally be held responsible for the error. In *Crystal Graphite Corp. (Receiver of) v. Deith*,[23] for example, the Court refused to rectify an agreement for the sale of Crystal's assets to Deith. The receiver had mistakenly believed the guaranteed investment certificate (GIC) in Crystal's name was not to be included in the transfer and accepted Deith's offer on that basis. But the agreement was clear and unambiguous and did include the GIC. There was no evidence to suggest that the mistake was mutual, so Deith got to keep the GIC.

CASE SUMMARY 8.9

Read the Contract or Live with It: *978011 Ontario Ltd. v. Cornell Engineering Co.*[24]

When is it fair to set aside a contract where only one party suffers a mistake? Apparently, the courts will refuse to grant rectification or rescission where the mistaken party is to blame or, as in this case, where the mistaken party contributed to his own mistake.

---

22. 2002 NSSC 159 (CanLII).

23. 2008 BCCA 475 (CanLII).

24. 2001 CanLII 8522 (ON CA), leave to appeal to S.C.C. refused, [2001] S.C.C.A. No. 315.

The shares in Cornell Engineering Co. (Cornell) were owned by Stevens and Bimboga. Bimboga sought to sell his interest, and Stevens suggested that Macdonald, whom Stevens had mentored, buy the shares. Negotiations were held, and eventually the parties agreed that Macdonald would enter a service agreement and demonstrate to Bimboga that Macdonald was capable of carrying on Cornell's business.

Stevens asked Macdonald to prepare the agreement; Macdonald amended a standard form agreement and presented it to Stevens, asking him to read it. The agreement provided for compensation to be paid to Macdonald in the event of termination of his services. Stevens read only the first page, where salary was laid out, and signed the 11-page contract on Cornell's behalf. Later, when Cornell terminated the service agreement, Macdonald claimed compensation pursuant to the termination clause. Stevens took the position that Macdonald should have brought the alteration to the standard contract, specifically the termination clause, to his attention. The trial judge held that since termination had not been discussed by the parties during their negotiations, Macdonald had a duty to draw the termination clause to Stevens's attention. The Court thus rectified the contract by striking out the termination clause entirely.

On appeal, however, no such duty was found to exist. Stevens was a sophisticated businessperson. Macdonald had, in fact, asked Stevens to read the contract. The Court refused to grant an equitable remedy to correct a mistake that Stevens, through oversight, had allowed to occur.

SMALL BUSINESS PERSPECTIVE
Clearly, the message is "Read before you sign!"

The court will be more likely to provide a remedy if the mistake is one about the facts involved, as opposed to a mistake based on an interpretation of the law or its effect. On the other hand, where one party stands to make a windfall at the expense of the other, the courts likely will review the transaction—whether the mistake is one of law or of fact. For example, when one party receives a payment she is not entitled to, because the other has misunderstood his legal obligation, the court will likely order those funds returned on the basis of **unjust enrichment**.

> The courts are less likely to remedy a mistake in law

The area of mistake in contract law is evolving. The discussion that follows is an attempt to summarize the important aspects of the law in this area. The approach taken concentrates on three different ways that a mistake can be made. It should be remembered that if a contract is found to be *void* it is not a contract at all; if it is *voidable* the contract does exist, but one of the parties has the option of getting out of it. Consequently, when an innocent third party has acquired goods that are the subject of a voidable contract, that party gets to keep the goods. But if the previous contract was void—that is, there never was a contract—the person who sold the goods to the third party never had title to them, and those goods must be returned to the original owner.

> Void contract—does not exist

> Voidable contract—exists but may be set aside

Shared Mistake

A **shared mistake** occurs when the two parties are in complete agreement but they have both made the same mistake regarding some aspect of the contract. The courts will review the transaction only where the mistake relates to some fundamental aspect of the subject matter of the contract. The most common example of such a shared mistake resulting in a void contract is where the subject matter of the contract no longer exists at the time the contract is made. Thus, where the parties enter into an agreement for the sale and purchase of the cargo of a ship, without knowing that the ship and cargo were destroyed the night before, the contract is void because of the shared mistake.

> Shared mistake—no consensus, thus no contract

The courts have also found a contract void because of a shared mistake when, unknown to the parties, the property being sold was already owned by the purchaser. In both these instances, the parties have together made the same significant

> Shared mistake as to title voids contract

mistake with respect to a factual aspect of the agreement that has destroyed the basis of the contract. As a result, the contract is void for lack of consensus.

When there is a shared mistake as to value, the contract remains valid

When the shared mistake relates only to the value of what they are dealing with, it normally will not affect the enforceability of the contract. For example, if both vendor and purchaser think that they are dealing with an ordinary violin when, in fact, they are dealing with a rare and valuable Stradivarius, the contract would be binding nevertheless.

RECTIFICATION

Rectification is available where the written agreement does not reflect the actual agreement

If the written document does not reflect the common intention of the parties to the contract, the courts are willing to correct or rectify the document. In the *Pacific Petroleums* case,[25] for example, the two parties had agreed to the sale of butane. The agreed upon price was expressed in US dollars per US gallon. A clerical error made the document read US dollars per Canadian gallon. Rectification was ordered since it was clear that both understood what they were agreeing to, and what was written in the contract was different from that understanding.

CASE SUMMARY 8.10

Damages Awarded as Rectification Not Possible: *Sylvan Lake Golf & Tennis Club Ltd. v. Performance Industries Ltd.*[26]

A verbal agreement had been reached between the parties concerning the purchase and operation of a golf course. One of the terms discussed was the future residential development of lands adjacent to the eighteenth hole. The agreement was reduced to writing by a lawyer acting on instructions from the defendant. The plaintiff proved, beyond any reasonable doubt, that he signed the agreement of December 21, 1989, under a unilateral mistake as to the dimensions of the development property and further that the defendant knew he had signed that agreement by mistake.

The preconditions to obtaining the equitable remedy of rectification of the contract were met:

1. The plaintiff established the existence and content of the prior oral agreement; there was a definite project in a definite location to which both parties had given their definite assent.

2. It was found that the defendant had fraudulently misrepresented the written document as accurately reflecting the terms of the prior oral contract.

3. The precise terms of rectification were readily ascertained. All that was required was to change the word *feet* in the phrase "one hundred ten (110) feet in width" to "yards."

4. There was convincing proof of the plaintiff's unilateral mistake and the defendant's knowledge of that mistake. The plaintiff's version of the oral agreement was sufficiently corroborated on significant points by other witnesses and documents.

The Court held that the defendant's conduct in attempting to take advantage of the plaintiff's mistake was equivalent to fraud—or a misrepresentation amounting to fraud—or sharp practice. It would thus be unjust and unconscionable for the court not to offer redress to the plaintiff in the face of that conduct. Rectification itself was no longer a real option as the lands had been developed by the defendant. Accordingly, damages in lieu of rectification were awarded, compensating the plaintiff for the loss of the opportunity to profit from developing residential lots around the eighteenth hole.

[25.] *Pacific Petroleums Ltd. v. Concordia Propane Gas Marketers Limited*, 1979 ALTASCAD 160 (CanLII).
[26.] [2002] 1 SCR 678, 2002 SCC 19 (CanLII).

It is important to remember that the courts are not rewriting the agreement during rectification—they are simply correcting a written document so that it corresponds to the demonstrated intentions of the two parties. Thus, in *Mills v. Mills*[27] rectification was granted. Both parties had miscalculated what the sale proceeds from their home would be. They believed it would be $65 824, whereas only $22 408 was available for distribution. Nonetheless, the Court found that there was consensus to split the balance equally, so the amounts were rectified but the balance itself was split equally.

Courts will correct an improperly recorded agreement

CASE SUMMARY 8.11

The Case of the Million-Dollar Comma: *AMJ Campbell v. Kord Products Inc.*[28]

This case involved AMJ Campbell's selling the assets of a subsidiary to the defendant, Kord. The transaction included the sale of a significant inventory of plant containers with the value determined by calculating the "average sales price" over the prior eight months. This was to be calculated "net of taxes, freight rebates and discounts," but the solicitors for Kord changed that by inserting a comma between the words *freight* and *rebates*. This change, along with some others, was made in the final contract. Before the change, only freight rebates would be deducted from the average price, but with the insertion of the comma all of the freight costs as well as any rebates would also be deducted. This resulted in a saving to Kord of more than $759 000 (hence the "million-dollar comma").

AMJ Campbell, claiming mistake, asked the Court to rectify the contract by removing the comma. The Court refused, saying that for rectification to take place it had to be clear that both parties had intended the document to read the other way. Here the solicitors for Kord had intentionally inserted the comma and intended that any freight costs be deducted from the purchase price. Only AMJ Campbell had made a mistake by agreeing to the change—and that is not good enough for rectification.

SMALL BUSINESS PERSPECTIVE

In light of the restricted situations where rectification can be used, what should a party do before concluding a contract?

Misunderstanding

A different type of mistake occurs when the parties have a misunderstanding about the terms of the agreement itself and neither party is aware of the other's different understanding. When one party to an agreement thinks that the agreement is to do something else, the courts will usually apply the reasonable person test to determine which interpretation of the contract is more reasonable. The court will then adopt the more reasonable position as the correct interpretation of the contract. This point

Court will enforce the reasonable interpretation

---

27. *Mills v. Mills*, 2004 CanLII 4793 (ON SC).
28. 2003 CanLII 5840 (ON SC), [2003] O.J. No. 329.

is discussed below in more detail under the heading "Rules of Interpretation." Only if the error is a serious one and the court cannot choose between the two positions because both are equally reasonable will the contract be declared void.

If two interpretations are equally reasonable, the contract is void because there is no consensus

The case of *Raffles v. Wichelhaus*[29] is a good example of such a dilemma. In this case, the contract concerned cargo being transported on a ship called *The Peerless*. It happened that there were two ships by this name, both leaving the same port but at different times. The seller intended one of these two ships, and the purchaser had in mind the other. The reasonable person test could not resolve this case, and since the disagreement was fundamental there was no consensus between the parties and the contract was void.

One-Sided Mistake

One-sided mistake—"Let the buyer beware"

A one-sided or **unilateral mistake** takes place where only one of the parties to the contract is making a mistake with respect to the contract. As a general rule, there is no recourse for a person who makes such a one-sided mistake. Thus, when someone buys a computer by name and model thinking it will do a specific job and it turns out that it does not have the required capacity, a mistake has been made by the purchaser but there will likely be no remedy. This is a one-sided mistake, and if there were no reliance placed on the salesperson and no misrepresentation or misleading information supplied in the documentation and brochures, there will be no remedy. In effect, the purchaser has misled himself, and the principle of *caveat emptor* ("Let the buyer beware") applies. But where the unilateral mistake or error has been caused, or at least contributed to, by wrongful behaviour, the courts may be more sympathetic.

Snapping up an offer—contract is rescinded

Note, however, that when the offeror makes an obvious error in relation to her offer the purchaser will not be allowed to take advantage of this obvious error and snap up the offer. Thus, if the merchant selling the computer misquoted it, agreeing to sell it at $25 instead of the normal price of $2500, the purchaser would not be able to ignore such an obvious error and "snap it up" at the bargain price.[30]

CASE SUMMARY 8.12

Unilateral Mistake *May* Lead to Rescission of Contract: *Moss v. Chin*[31]

Moss was left unconscious after being struck by a car driven by Chin. Moss's representative, the public trustee, started a legal action and negotiated with the driver's insurer, ICBC. ICBC made an offer to settle, but Moss died before it was accepted. The public trustee accepted the offer on behalf of Moss without informing ICBC of her death. When ICBC found out what had happened, it applied to have the settlement set aside.

This was a unilateral mistake on the part of ICBC, and normally it would not affect the rights of the other parties. But in this situation, rather than this being a matter of ICBC's misleading itself, the public trustee deliberately set out to make sure ICBC did not discover the mistake. The Court accordingly ordered that the contract be rescinded.

SMALL BUSINESS PERSPECTIVE

Hiding relevant information from a party to ensure they sign an agreement may be regarded as shady practice. It opens the door to the courts doing what is just to "rectify" the situation.

---

29. (1864), 2 H. & C. 906, 159 E.R. 375 (E.D.).

30. See *Ottawa (City) Non-Profit Housing Corporation v. Canvar Construction (1991) Inc.* 2000 CanLII 2004 (ON CA) for a case involving a tender error. Since the error was evident on the face of the tender, the tenderer was not obligated to perform the construction job at the erroneous tender price.

31. 1994 CanLII 1400 (BC SC).

When a one-sided mistake takes place, the person making the mistake usually has a remedy only when he has been misled; then the normal course of action is to claim for misrepresentation with its associated remedies. There are some situations, however, where the one-sided mistake is so fundamental as to destroy consensus between the parties. If consensus is lacking, the contract is void—providing even broader remedies.

Contract is void where the mistake is fundamental

Such a one-sided mistake can occur when there is incorrect identification of one of the parties to a contract. If the person claiming that a mistake has taken place actually thought the deal was with someone else and can demonstrate that identity was an important aspect of the agreement, the court can declare the contract to be void. However, if the error was only about some attribute of the other party, such as her wealth, this will not affect the existence of the contract.[32]

If the mistake goes to identity, the contract is void

NON EST FACTUM

Where one of the parties is unaware of the nature of the document being signed the courts will, in rare circumstances, declare the agreement to be void on the basis of **non est factum** ("It is not my act"). If a person were led to believe he was guaranteeing a note and was, in fact, signing a mortgage agreement on his home, he could argue that there was no consensus between the parties and no contract. In *Ohlson v. Canadian Imperial Bank of Commerce*,[33] an 82-year-old mother signed a "loan agreement" so that the bank would advance money to her son. Since the money had already been advanced, the essence of the arrangement was really a guarantee. The Court found it was unconscionable for the bank not to disclose that the money had already been advanced. Had it presented a guarantee for her signature, independent legal advice would have been required by law. As it stood, she signed without knowledge of the facts and without legal advice. The loan agreement was thus rescinded.

If mistake goes to the nature of the document signed, the contract is void . . .

Non est factum might be a valid defence even against an innocent third party who had acquired rights under the agreement. For this defence to succeed and the contract to be void, it must be shown that the mistake about the document went to the very nature of that document rather than merely to its terms. For example, if the mistake went only to the rates, with the mortgagor thinking she was to pay 10 percent interest when the document actually required 15 percent, she would still be bound because the mistake only concerned some aspect of the document and not the document itself. Today, negligence, such as failure to read the document before signing, can defeat the defence of *non est factum*; successful claims of *non est factum* are thus quite rare.

. . . but not where carelessness is present

CASE SUMMARY 8.13

Non Est Factum Available to Non-English Signatory: *Farrell Estates Ltd. v. Win-Up Restaurant Ltd.*[34]

The landlord brought an action against the defendant, Su-Chen Wu Yang, as guarantor on a commercial lease. The defendant, as the director and shareholder of the tenant corporation, admitted she had signed the lease as co-covenantor, but relied on *non est factum*, asserting that her interpreter told her that the lease did not contain a personal guarantee.

The defence succeeded because the defendant had consistently taken the position that she did not want to provide a personal guarantee and had been assured she was not assuming any personal liability under the lease. The landlord was careless in relying on the translator to communicate its position on a critical term in the lease to a non-English signatory, and the landlord's action on the guarantee was dismissed.

---

32. *Cundy v. Lindsay* (1878), 3 App. Cas. 459 (H.L.).

33. 1997 ABCA 413 (CanLII).

34. 2010 BCSC 1752 (CanLII).

Rules of Interpretation

Reasonable person test applies when there is a misunderstanding

When interpreting contracts, the courts are not concerned with what the parties thought they were agreeing to but rather with what the parties should have been aware of and expected when they made the agreement. The test to determine whether a mistake has taken place is objective. In such instances, the courts use the reasonable person test. Instead of declaring the contract void because one of the parties has made a mistake about the meaning of a term, the courts will look at the wording to determine what a reasonable person would have understood the term to mean. Only in those rare circumstances in which there is no reasonable interpretation of the agreement, or the positions taken by the two parties are equally reasonable, will the courts declare the contract to be void.[36]

Courts apply literal meaning to specific wording

Whenever there is a dispute involving the meaning of a specific term, the courts have a choice of applying the literal meaning of the term or adopting a more liberal approach by trying to determine the parties' intent. Usually, the courts will apply the literal meaning of the wording chosen by the parties if there is no ambiguity. If the term is ambiguous, the court will look at what was behind the agreement and apply the most reasonable meaning of the term to the contract.

Determining the literal meaning of the words is not as simple as it might first appear. Even dictionaries often have several different meanings for particular words. Determining the intention of the parties may also be difficult because of the conflicting positions taken by the parties to the dispute. The court will often look at how the terms are normally used in the particular industry involved. The court will also consider past dealings between the parties as well as their dealings at the time the contract was formed to determine what they intended by the words they used. The key to a court's approach to such ambiguous terms in an agreement is to choose the most reasonable interpretation.

Courts will not permit outside evidence to contradict clear wording

A common rule of interpretation is the **parol evidence rule**. It provides that where the terms used in an agreement are clear and unambiguous, the courts will not allow other outside evidence to be introduced to show a different meaning was intended: "What you see is what you get." If the agreement states that the contract is for the sale of a "2008 Honda Civic automobile," one cannot later try to introduce evidence that a Honda motorcycle was intended. But if the contract only referred to a "2008 Honda" this term is ambiguous, and evidence then could be introduced to show whether a car or a motorbike was intended.

Exceptions to the parol evidence rule

Several exceptions to the parol evidence rule have developed over the years. When the evidence contradicting the terms of the agreement falls into one of these categories, the court can be persuaded to hear it despite the parol evidence rule:

- When the evidence to be introduced is of a *fraud* or some other problem associated with the formation of the contract, such as *duress* or *undue influence*

- When evidence of a *condition precedent* (a condition that has to be met before the obligations set out in the contract are in force) exists

- Where there is evidence of a **collateral contract** (a separate contractual obligation that can stand alone, independent of the written one)

---

35. See *Bank of Montreal v. Fraser*, 2013 BCSC 2328 (CanLII), where the individual thought he was signing as "co-signor" to a student loan to a maximum of $15 000, not guaranteeing a line of credit for the student in question.
36. *Raffles v. Wichelhaus*, *supra* note 29.

- Where there is evidence of a *subsequent agreement* entered into by the parties after the written one

- When there is an *absence of an intention* that all of the contract would be embodied in the written document

When necessary, the courts may imply terms into an agreement. It does not occur to most contracting parties to provide terms in their agreement for every possible eventuality, and the courts are willing to supply these missing terms. Where the parties agree to the purchase of a car, for example, they might not specify the time of delivery or when the price is to be paid. The courts will imply what is reasonable in the circumstances—that delivery must take place within a reasonable time as determined by the nature of the goods, and that the price is to be paid upon delivery. What is reasonable will often be determined by looking at past dealings between the parties or the normal practices and traditions found within that specific industry or trade. Some terms may be implied automatically by statute. *Sale of Goods Acts* set down, in rule form, the terms that are implied in a contract for the sale of goods when the parties have not addressed them. As well, some consumer protection legislation imposes terms in contracts whether or not the parties have agreed to them). The courts have also been known to impose contract terms on the parties and modify obligations, using the principle of fairness[37] and unconscionability.

Courts will imply terms, where appropriate

Statutes may imply terms into a contract

REDUCING RISK 8.2

The interpretation of contracts often leads to confrontation. A deal made on a handshake involves a lot of trust, but this examination of mistake and misrepresentation shows the danger of failing to review contracts carefully. Even the most sincere businessperson can forget just what was agreed to. Two parties may recall the terms quite differently despite feeling they had the same understanding of the terms in the first place. Then there are instances of wilful blindness and convenient memory loss. Putting an agreement into some permanent form, such as writing, is only the first step. A sophisticated client will also ensure that the words used are clear and unambiguous so that there can be no question later of what has been agreed upon.

PRIVITY OF CONTRACT AND ASSIGNMENT

LO ❻

Privity

When two parties enter into a contract, they create a world of law unto themselves. Contracting is a bargaining process, and only those participating in the bargain can be affected by it (see Figure 8.1). It is a fundamental principle of contract law that the parties to a contract do not have the power to impose benefits or obligations on

Contract binds only the parties to it

Figure 8.1

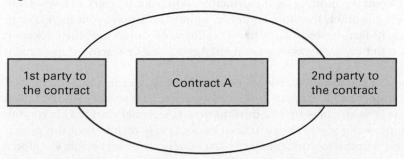

Only the parties to the contract can enforce it, even if outsiders are to benefit from it.

[37.] *Cooper v. Phibbs* (1867), L.R. 2 H.L. 149 (H.L.).

third parties or outsiders who are not parties to the contract. The contracting parties have created a private agreement, and outsiders to it can neither enforce it nor be bound to perform its terms. This principle is called **privity of contract**.

The case of *Donoghue v. Stevenson*,[38] referred to in Case Summary 5.2 illustrates the application of the privity principle. In that case, a woman bought her friend a bottle of ginger beer that contained a decomposed snail. The friend, who consumed the contaminated drink, could not sue the owner of the café for breach of contract because she was not the person who bought it. There was no contract between them. Under normal circumstances, merchants can be sued by the purchaser for breach of contract for selling faulty products, even though they are unaware of the problem. But if there is no contract between the merchant and the individual harmed, the victim can normally sue only the manufacturer in tort.

EXCEPTIONS

Original party to a contract can enforce it where the benefit is to be bestowed on an outsider

There are several exceptions and apparent exceptions to the operation of the privity rule. First it must be emphasized that while a third party designated to receive a benefit cannot enforce the contract, the original parties still have the right to insist on performance. Thus if Currah, who operates a landscaping company, contracts with Husein to mow Kicia's lawn, Kicia cannot enforce the agreement, but Husein certainly can. The court may award Husein either damages or compensation calculated on the basis of what it would cost to have somebody else mow the lawn. See Table 8.2 for other exceptions to the privity rule, which are discussed in detail below.

Table 8.2 Exceptions to the Operation of the Privity Rule

Land	Rights of the parties run with the land
Agents	Contract is between the principal and the other contracting party
Trust	Beneficiary can enforce the rights bestowed
Insurance	Beneficiary can enforce the policy
Constructive trust	Inferred that the beneficiary can enforce rights
Novation	Terms of the former contract are adopted by the parties to the new contract
Principled exception	Third-party benefits were intended

Rights run with the land

Where land is involved, the rights of the parties are said to run with the land. If a person leases a suite in a house and the owner sells the house, the new owner must honour the lease, even though the new owner was not a party to the lease.

Agents create contracts between principals and third parties

When an agent acts on behalf of a principal in contracting with a third party, the actions of that agent are binding on the principal. When a sales clerk in a store sells a magazine to a customer, the store owner is bound. This may seem inconsistent with privity, but in fact the contract is between the store owner and the customer; the sales clerk is merely acting as a go-between. Agency will be discussed in detail in Chapter 10.

Trust allows a third party to benefit from the property of another

Beneficiary can enforce a trust agreement against the trustee

The concept of the **trust** is a little more complicated. This involves one person (the settlor) transferring his property to a second person (the trustee) who in turn is obligated to use it to the benefit of a third person (the beneficiary). This is often done in estate planning where the beneficiaries are family members of the person creating the trust. For this to work, the third-party beneficiary must be able to enforce the contract between the original parties (the settlor and trustee). Since the person creating the trust is often dead and unable to enforce the original contract, it would be an affront to allow the trustee to ignore the obligations set out in the agreement

---

38. [1932] A.C. 562 (H.L.).

and take the benefits for herself. The Court of Chancery developed the equitable principle of the trust to overcome this problem, and the beneficiary now can enforce the terms of the original trust agreement even though he was not a party to it.

Insurance is handled in a similar fashion, with the beneficiary of an insurance contract having the power to enforce it after the death of the insured. Sometimes, when a contract bestows a benefit on a third party, the courts will infer a trust, even though the parties did not specifically create one. This is called a **constructive trust** and provides an important method for the third party to obtain the benefit promised.

Beneficiary can enforce an insurance contract

When the parties to a contract agree to substitute someone new for one of the original parties there is also no problem with privity so long as all three parties agree to the change. This is called a **novation** (see Figure 8.2). If Jones has a contract to provide janitorial services to a college and he sells his business to Brown, there is no problem with Brown taking over that service contract, provided the college agrees. A new contract has been substituted for the old one, and no privity problem arises since all parties have agreed to the change.

Novation involves a new agreement

Figure 8.2

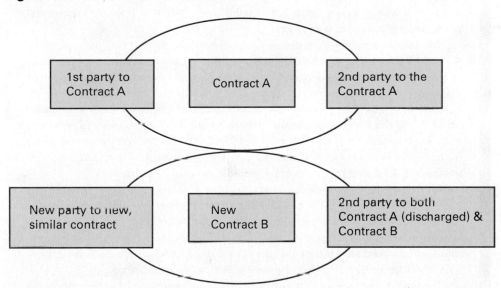

Novation: If the 2nd party agrees to the substitution of the new party, a new contract is formed and Contract A is discharged, replaced by the new Contract B.

There are signs that the doctrine of privity may be breaking down. The Law Reform Commission of Nova Scotia, for example, recommended reform of the law pertaining to privity, particularly as it relates to third-party rights in contract.[39] One of its recommendations is that privity be relaxed by statute to allow third-party beneficiaries to enforce their rights under contracts. New Brunswick abolished the privity rule in favour of the identified beneficiary concept. Section 4(1) of the *Law Reform Act*[40] reads as follows:

> A person who is not a party to a contract but who is identified by or under the contract as being intended to receive some performance or forbearance under it may, unless the contract provides otherwise, enforce that performance or forbearance by a claim for damages or otherwise.

The courts have also been relaxing the privity rule by finding principled exceptions to it.

---

39. Law Reform Commission of Nova Scotia, *Privity of Contract (Third Party Rights): Final Report*, September 2004, www.lawreform.ns.ca/Downloads/Privity_FIN.pdf
40. S.N.B. 1993, c. L-1.2.

CASE SUMMARY 8.14

Principled Exception to Privity Rule Applied: *London Drugs Ltd. v. Kuehne & Nagel International Ltd.*[41]; *Williams-Sonoma Inc. v. Oxford Properties Group Inc.*[42]

When should the protection found in a contract be extended to parties beyond the contracting parties themselves? Kuehne and Nagel contracted to store a large and valuable transformer for London Drugs. The contract between them restricted "warehouseman's" liability for damage to only $40. Unfortunately, two employees were careless in their handling of the transformer, causing significant damage, and London Drugs sued. However, instead of suing Kuehne and Nagel for breach of contract, it sued the employees in tort for negligence. By doing this, London Drugs thought to avoid the protection of the exemption clause limiting any claim to $40, the theory being that the employees were not privy to the contract and therefore not protected by it. The Supreme Court, however, found that the protection of the exemption clause extended to the employees, even though they were not party to the contract; the Court created a "principled exception" to the common law doctrine of privity.

The rationale underlying this decision is that the employees were third-party beneficiaries under the exemption clause. Obviously, since the employer was exempted from liability for negligence by the exemption clause, employees who would actively be doing the storing of the goods were intended to be included under that exemption as third-party beneficiaries. In essence, the protection from liability given to the warehouseman extended not just to the employer that signed the contract, but also to its employees who performed the tasks contemplated by the contract as well. The Court held that in circumstances where the traditional exceptions (such as trust or agency) do not apply, the Court should examine whether the doctrine of privity should be relaxed in the given circumstances.

Similarly, in the *Williams-Sonoma* case, the tenants, Williams-Sonoma (Pottery Barn), suffered losses due to water damage. The damage was caused by a vandal who accessed space used by a general contractor doing renovations on behalf of the mall owner. The lease required the tenant to obtain insurance regarding all water damage, regardless of its cause, and released the landlord (mall owner) and those for whom it was "in law responsible" for all occurrences for which the tenants were to obtain insurance.

The tenant (and its insurer) thus could not sue the mall owner; instead, the tenant sued the general contractor, alleging it was negligent in failing to adequately secure the space it held in the mall. Although the general contractor was not a party to the lease, the Court allowed it to take advantage of the exemption clause in the lease because (1) the landlord (mall owner) and tenant intended to extend the benefit of the release to the general contractor, and (2) the activities that the general contractor was performing were the very activities that were contemplated as coming within the scope of the insurance and exemption clauses.

Accordingly, the Court dismissed the tenant's action against the general contractor.

SMALL BUSINESS PERSPECTIVE

The above decisions demonstrate the willingness of the courts to further extend the benefits of a contract. If the contract demonstrates intent to extend benefits to others, the courts are ready to set aside the restraints of privity.

The rule of privity of contract may also be weakening in the field of product liability. In *Donoghue v. Stevenson*,[43] the consumer of the ginger beer could not sue the merchant for breach of contract because she was not the one who purchased

---

41. [1992] 3 SCR 299, 1992 CanLII 41 (SCC).

42. 2013 ONCA 441 (CanLII).

43. *Supra* note 38.

it. Some provinces have passed legislation allowing the consumer of defective products to sue the seller in contract law, even when the injured person is not the purchaser and not party to the contract. The courts have also extended the right to sue in contract law in product liability cases by finding collateral contracts created by advertising brochures, giving the purchaser a right to seek redress in contract law past the retailer back to the manufacturer. These topics will be discussed in Chapter 16 under the heading "Consumer Protection."

Assignment

Just as a person buying goods under a contract is free to resell them, so can a person entitled to receive a benefit under a contract transfer that benefit to a third party (see Figure 8.3). This is called the **assignment** of contractual rights, and the benefit transferred is known as a **chose in action**. While the practice of transferring such rights was originally not permitted because of privity, it is now an essential aspect of doing business. The principle is that a person who has acquired a right or a benefit under a contract has the right to assign that benefit to another. Where Schmidtke does carpentry work for Nehring and is owed money for those services, Schmidtke is free to assign (sell) that claim (or account receivable) to Green. Schmidtke is referred to as the *assignor*, a party to the original contract, and Green is the *assignee*, a stranger to it. It is common for businesses to assign their accounts receivable (money they are owed) outright to obtain immediate cash.

Contracting parties can assign rights

Figure 8.3

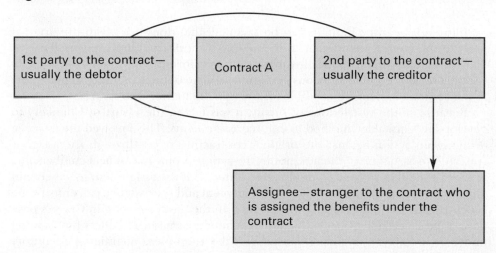

The ability to make such assignments has become a vital component of our commercial world. There are, however, some important qualifications to keep in mind. First, only a benefit can be assigned, not an obligation. In the example above, if Schmidtke has failed to complete the job, he is still obligated to Nehring, despite the assignment. Schmidtke cannot say that it is no longer his problem, as he has assigned the contract to Green. Schmidtke has assigned only the benefits, not the obligations.

Only benefits can be assigned

Of course, if Green tried to collect those benefits (the money payable under the contract) in face of the defaulted contract, he would fail. While it is true that the assignment of the benefits of the contract can be transferred or assigned, Green can be in no better position to collect that benefit than was Schmidtke. If Schmidtke has no claim since he has defaulted, the assignee cannot recover the full account. The principle is that an assignee is "subject to the equities" between the original parties, meaning that the assignee can be in no better position than was the assignor. Schmidtke transferred to Green only what claim he had against Nehring, and that claim was tainted. If the debtor has a good defence against the assignor, he also has a good defence against the assignee.

Assignee in no better position than the assignor

CASE SUMMARY 8.15

Assurances Enhance the Position of the Assignee: *Costco Wholesale Canada Inc. v. Cazalet*[44]

Unfortunately, it is sometimes the innocent who pay for the wrongs of the guilty. Crozier intended to purchase a Costco cash card from an individual but first contacted Costco to verify the card's balance. After receiving assurance that the balance was $500, Crozier paid the cardholder. In essence, that cardholder assigned the benefits of the card to Crozier.

Later it was learned that the assignor had paid Costco for the card with a counterfeit cheque, so Costco froze the remaining balance.

Normally an assignee (Crozier) gets no better rights than the assignor had to give, suggesting that Costco was in the right in freezing the card. But the Court determined that since Costco had made a representation to Crozier, who relied on that representation, Costco should be estopped from freezing the remaining balance on the card. Estoppel is an equitable remedy that is sometimes awarded to a party who comes with clean hands. No blame could be placed on Crozier's shoulders, whereas Costco did, by its actions, allow the fraud to be perpetuated. Accordingly, Crozier was able to keep shopping.

DISCUSSION QUESTION
In hindsight, Costco gave an assurance prematurely. What advice could you offer businesses in light of the above decision?

Contractual obligations can be performed by others

Although only the benefits can be assigned, that does not mean the original party to the contract always has to be the one to perform. Often it is understood that the actual work or service involved will be performed by an employee or subcontractor. This is called **vicarious performance**. The point is that the original party to the contract remains responsible for the work no matter who does it.

Because of the restrictions of privity, it was left to the Court of Chancery to develop an "equitable" method to enforce assignments. This involved the assignee bringing an action against the original contracting party through the assignor (referred to as "joining" the assignor in the action). Joining can be a cumbersome process, and it has since been modified by statute.[45] If the assignment meets certain qualifications, it qualifies as a **statutory assignment** and the assignee can enforce the claim directly without involving the assignor. In the past, someone in Green's position would have had to bring an action in Schmidtke's name to collect funds owing under the contract by Nehring. But today, if the assignment qualifies as a statutory assignment, Green can simply sue Nehring for the money directly.

Qualifications for statutory assignment

The qualifications that have to be met to establish a statutory assignment are as follows: First, the assignment must be *absolute*, meaning that it must be both complete and unconditional. The full amount owed must be assigned (complete) without any strings attached (unconditional). Second, the assignment must be *in writing, signed by the assignor*. And third, the original party obligated to pay must be *notified in writing* of the assignment. Only when all these requirements are met will the assignee be able to sue directly; otherwise, she still must join the assignor in any attempt at collection.

Some things cannot be assigned

Some things cannot be assigned, such as the right to collect support payments (in family matters) or the right to sue another in a tort action. Certain statutes[46] prohibit the assignment of benefits provided under the statute. Note, however, that

---

44. 2008 BCSC 952 (CanLII).

45. See, for example, Alberta's *Judicature Act*, R.S.A. 2000, c. J-2, s. 20.

46. See, for example, Alberta's *Workers' Compensation Act*, R.S.A. 2000, c. W-15, s. 141, which says that benefits may not be assigned without the approval of the Workers' Compensation Board.

although the right to sue cannot be assigned, there is no such restriction on the assignment of the proceeds from such a lawsuit once awarded.

Sometimes an assignor may be tempted to assign the same claim to two assignees. This, of course, is fraud, and the victim has the right to seek redress from the assignor. Often that assignor has fled or has no funds. The original debtor against whom the assignment is made is obligated to pay only once, and one of the two assignees will be out of luck. In such circumstances, it is the first assignee to give the debtor notice of the assignment who will collect. The other assignee will be left to seek remedies against the assignor, which may be worthless. It is, therefore, vital in business to take such assignments with care and then to *immediately notify* the debtor. It is only when the debtor makes the mistake of ignoring such notice and paying either the wrong assignee or insisting on paying the original assignor that it may have to pay twice.[47]

Debtor must pay first assignee who gives notice of assignment

The principles discussed so far relate to voluntary assignments. There are some circumstances in which the assignment of rights can take place involuntarily. For example, rights and obligations are automatically transferred to the administrator or executor of the estate when a person dies. This representative steps into the deceased's shoes and is not restricted by the privity of contract rule, unless the terms of the contract require personal performance by the deceased. The second situation of **involuntary assignment** occurs when a party to a contract goes bankrupt. Under bankruptcy legislation, the bankrupt's assets are transferred to a trustee, called the *receiver*, who will then distribute them to pay the creditors as much as possible. Bankruptcy will be discussed in Chapter 15.

Involuntary assignment in cases of death and bankruptcy

REDUCING RISK 8.3

A sophisticated businessperson should never ignore a notice of assignment and continue paying the original party. The party now entitled to payment is the assignee. A party who assigns an account receivable should realize its obligations do not cease just because it has assigned an account. If a product has been sold and the financing arrangements have been assigned to a finance company, the merchant vendor is still responsible with respect to the performance of the product. If it is defective or dangerous, causing injury or loss, it is the vendor that is responsible, not the finance company. One can assign only the benefits, not one's obligations under such a contract.

Negotiable Instruments

A further exception to the privity of contract rule is the law surrounding **negotiable instruments**. Negotiable instruments (including cheques, promissory notes, and bills of exchange, commonly called "drafts") bestow unique rights on the parties. Cheques are an important method of transferring funds in business, and promissory notes retain their popularity where credit is involved because of the unique advantages they bestow.

Negotiable instruments are true exceptions to privity

Briefly, a negotiable instrument can be freely passed from one person to another, conveying with it all the rights associated with the original agreement between the parties, and no notice of the transfer is required. This flexibility is completely inconsistent with the doctrine of privity of contract and the law of assignment discussed above. The most significant innovation of negotiable instruments was that better rights or claims than those held by the initial parties could be passed on. As discussed under the "Assignment" heading, it is clear that even when it is possible to assign contractual rights the assignee can be in no better position than was the assignor. Thus, if a defence such as deceit or breach of contract was available against the original party to the contract (the assignor), it was available against the assignee as well. This is not the case with negotiable instruments.

Negotiable instruments give better rights to the holder than is the case with assignment

---

[47.] Rights of an assignee and the consequences of notice are also dealt with in provincial legislation. See, for example, Alberta's *Personal Property Security Act*, R.S.A. 2000, c. P-7, s. 41.

When you give a cheque or promissory note to someone (who has deceived or cheated you), once that instrument gets into the hands of an innocent third party who satisfies the qualifications of a "holder in due course" you can be required to pay despite the existence of the fraud. In other words, if Nehring pays Schmidtke by cheque and then Schmidtke endorses the cheque and delivers it to Green, Green is entitled to cash the cheque despite any complaints Nehring might later have with regards to the quality of the work done by Schmidtke.

Although the use of cheques has declined with the popularity of credit cards, debit cards, and direct deposits, payment by cheque is still common in business. From the recipient's perspective, a cheque, once certified, is almost as good as cash.

MyBusLawLab Be sure to visit the MyBusLawLab that accompanies this book to find practice quizzes, province-specific content, simulations and much more!

SUMMARY

Misrepresentation

- A false statement that induces a person to enter a contract

Types	Remedies
• Innocent misrepresentation	• Rescission is the only remedy
• Fraudulent misrepresentation	• Damages (and possibly punitive damages) for the tort of deceit or rescission
• Negligence	• Damages or rescission

Duress, undue influence, or unconscionability

Types	Remedies
• Duress; contract made involuntarily	• Contract is voidable—rescission
• Undue influence	• Contract is voidable—rescission
• Unconscionable	• Contract is voidable—Court may rescind or modify the contract

Mistake

- Must go to the nature of the agreement or the existence of the subject matter, not just to the effect of the agreement when performed

Types	Remedies
• Both parties making a common error	• If serious, there is no contract
• An error in recording the terms	• Can be corrected by rectification
• A misunderstanding between the parties	• Most reasonable interpretation of the contract is enforced
• A one-sided mistake	• *Caveat emptor* applies unless the mistake is so fundamental as to destroy consensus or there is fraud

Privity of contract

- Only the original parties to the contract are bound. Any benefit going to a third party must be enforced by the original party to the agreement
- A trust is a true exception to the privity rule because the beneficiary can enforce it even though he is not a party to the original agreement
- Other exceptions include real estate transactions, contracts of insurance, and various principled exceptions as defined by the courts

Assignment

- Only the benefits, not the obligations, in a contract can be sold (assigned) to a third party, and those benefits are to be enforced through the original contracting party, the assignor
- But when an assignment qualifies as a statutory assignment, the assignee can enforce the assigned rights directly, in its own name

Negotiable instruments

- Negotiable instruments may be enforced by third parties without notification to the original drawer (the party who wrote and signed the cheque) of the instrument
- Negotiable instruments sometimes convey better rights than existed between the original parties

QUESTIONS FOR REVIEW

1. Explain how fraudulent, negligent, and innocent misrepresentations differ. Identify the remedies that are available for each type of misrepresentation.

2. What happens when a misrepresentation becomes a term of the contract?

3. Under what circumstances can silence or a statement of opinion become misrepresentation?

4. What factors may affect the availability of the remedy of rescission?

5. Distinguish among duress, undue influence, and unconscionability and give examples of each.

6. A mistake may result in a contract being declared void or voidable. What difference does it make if a contract is merely voidable?

7. When will a misunderstanding as to the terms of a contract cause that contract to be void?

8. Distinguish among shared mistakes, misunderstandings, and one-sided mistakes.

9. What approach will the courts usually take when the mistake involves disagreement about the meaning of the contract?

10. What must a party to a contract show to obtain rectification of a document?

11. How will the courts respond to ambiguous wording in a contract?

12. Explain what is meant by *caveat emptor*. What is the significance of this principle in relation to a one-sided mistake?

13. Under what circumstances would a person raise a claim of *non est factum*? What restrictions are there on its availability?

14. Explain the parol evidence rule.

15. What is meant by privity of contract?

16. Explain what is meant by the term "novation."

17. Explain how privity of contract is impacted in the context of land transactions, agency, trusts, and assignment.

18. With regard to third-party beneficiaries under a contract, what direction does the law appear to be taking?

19. What qualifications must be realized before there can be a statutory assignment?

20. What is meant by "the assignee takes subject to the equities"?

21. Can a "holder in due course" obtain better rights than an assignee? Explain.

CASES AND DISCUSSION QUESTIONS

1. *Queen (Ont.) v. Ron Engineering*, **[1981] 1 S.C.R. 111; 1981 CanLII 17**

In response to a call for tenders, Ron Engineering submitted both its bid to do the work for $2 748 000, together with the required deposit of $150 000. The tender documents included a term that if a tender was withdrawn the owner could retain the deposit. Once the submitted tenders were opened by the owner, Ron Engineering saw it was the low bidder by a substantial margin. Only then did it discover that they had made a mistake in calculating their total bid price. Ron Engineering informed the owner of the mistake and tried to have the offer changed. The change was refused, the contract was given to another company, and the owner kept Ron Engineering's bid deposit. Ron Engineering sued to get their deposit back, claiming mistake. The owner counterclaimed for costs incurred as a result of having to go with a different bidder.

Should the deposit be returned? Will the Court rectify the bid? Does the mistake made by Ron Engineering enable it to get a remedy from the courts?

2. *RF Real Estate Inc. v. Rogers Telecom Holdings Inc.*, **[2008] O.J. No. 3314 (Ont. S.C.J.); 2008 CanLII 42598 (ON SC), aff'd 2009 ONCA 899 (CanLII)**

The plaintiff real estate brokerage firm brought an action seeking $1.6 million as its commission. It submitted that it had completed four of five stages of a commercial lease project that never came to fruition. Had the project been completed, its commission would have equalled $2 million. The defendant submitted that commission was payable only on a completed deal. (Note: Sprint had been sold to the defendant, Rogers Telecom, after the subject agreement had been made.) The issue before the Court was whether the agreement between the parties was ambiguous, thereby justifying consideration of extrinsic evidence, such as industry norms, by the courts. Rogers argued that real estate commissions were typically payable only once a deal was concluded.

The agreement stipulated: "For purposes of clarification, Sprint may not cancel this agreement arbitrarily. In the event that Sprint terminates RF, Sprint will pay RF a percentage payment based on work completed at the date of termination."

Is the clause ambiguous? Is the termination clause to be given a literal interpretation? Explain how a court would deal with this problem and the likely outcome.

3. *Royal Bank of Canada v. Gill* **(1988), 47 D.L.R. (4th) 466 (B.C.C.A.); 1988 CanLII 2970 (BC CA)**

The younger Mr. Gill was fluent in English and a sophisticated businessperson. He had worked in a credit union for a number of years and had managed his father's berry farm. To take advantage of a business opportunity, he arranged with the Royal Bank to borrow $87 000. During the negotiations, it became clear that he could get a more favourable rate of interest if his father guaranteed the loan. In fact, the son had done a considerable amount of banking on behalf of his father, who was also a customer of the same bank. The elder Gill could not read, write, or speak English and relied on his son in all his business dealings. The documents were prepared, and the son brought his father to the bank to sign. At no time did he explain to his father that he was signing a personal guarantee, and the evidence is clear that the father had no idea what he was signing other than that it was a document associated with a loan transaction. Gill, Sr., had implicit faith in his son's handling of his business affairs. Gill, Jr., on the other hand, was so excited about the deal that he apparently never explained the nature of the documents to his father. It is clear in this situation that at no time was there any misrepresentation to the father or the son on the part of the bank. When the son defaulted on the loan, the bank turned to the father for payment.

Should Gill, Sr., be held responsible for this debt? What precautions should the bank have taken? Identify the best arguments of the father. What arguments should the bank advance?

9
Chapter

The End of the Contractual Relationship

LEARNING OBJECTIVES

1. Illustrate how a contract is discharged by performance
2. Describe when a breach of contract will be sufficient to relieve the opposite party from its obligations
3. Explain how a contract may be discharged by agreement
4. Outline the consequences flowing from frustration of contract
5. Describe how damages for breach of contract are assessed
6. Differentiate the equitable remedies available for a breach of contract

Contracts can come to an end or be discharged by performance, breach, agreement between the parties to end or modify, or frustration. This chapter examines each of these means of discharge and concludes with a discussion of remedies for breach of contract.

DISCHARGE BY PERFORMANCE

LO ①

Contractual obligations are discharged and a contract is ended when both parties have satisfactorily completed their obligations under the contract. Often parties perform their obligations simultaneously. The closing of a sale requires the purchaser to tender the price in exchange for the transfer of title. The purchaser hands over the cash and the seller hands over the goods. With most bilateral contracts, however, one party must complete its side before the other is required to perform. In employment contracts, the employee must perform the work before the employer is obliged to pay wages. If the employee fails to report for a shift, the employer has no obligation to pay the hourly wage. It becomes vitally important, then, to determine whether one party has properly performed its side, thereby obligating the other party to perform in turn. The question that must be asked is, "Will anything short of exact **performance** satisfy the requirement?"

In fact, there are two situations where something short of exact performance of the contract will still be considered proper performance. Contracts usually consist of major terms (called *conditions*) and minor terms (called *warranties*)—see the section "Conditions and Warranties" below. When the failure to perform is relatively

Where warranty is breached, contract is still considered performed

insignificant, or where failure to perform involves only a warranty or minor term, that party is regarded as having performed his side of the agreement. The other party will be required to perform, subject to a claim for compensation for whatever loss was caused by the breach of warranty. Thus, if the new car is delivered but without the ordered fog lights, a minor term or warranty has been breached; the purchaser will still be required to take delivery and pay for the car minus the cost of the fog lights.

On the other hand, where the breach is significant, as when a condition or major term of the contract is breached, the contract is normally considered discharged and the other party is relieved of performing her obligations under it. Still, when a condition is breached in some minor, inconsequential way, the court will usually treat it like a breach of warranty, requiring the other party to perform subject to a claim for the loss caused by the shortfall. This is called **substantial performance**. For example, if a farmer is required to deliver 4000 kilograms of potatoes and delivers only 3987 kilograms, the contract would be considered substantially performed. The farmer would be discharged from further performance, and the purchaser would have to pay for the potatoes that were delivered. Of course, exact performance will be required where only exact performance will do. If a contract with a driller requires a producing well and 25 dry holes are drilled instead, there has been no substantial performance and there is no obligation to pay.

Contract is discharged when contract is substantially performed

But some contracts must be performed exactly

CASE SUMMARY 9.1

If Breach Is Minor, Substantially Performed Contract Is Enforceable: *Sail Labrador Ltd. v. Challenger One (The)*[1]; *1290079 Ontario Inc. v. Beltsos*[2]

Sail Labrador Ltd. leased a ship from Navimar Corp. Ltd. with an option to purchase, but only if every payment was properly made. The contract required cash, but the parties agreed to payment through a series of postdated cheques. One cheque was dishonoured because of a bank error, and despite immediate correction the owner took the position that the option was no longer available because of this failure.

The Supreme Court of Canada decided that the owners had assumed this kind of risk when they agreed to take postdated cheques. Since the error was inconsequential and immediately corrected, the contract had been substantially performed and the option was still available. This case illustrates the doctrine of substantial performance. Here the contract was properly performed except for some minor variation, and the owners had to honour their contractual obligations.

Contrast the above with the outcome of the *Beltsos* case. There the tenant sought a declaration that it validly exercised its right to renew a commercial lease with the landlord. The lease was for an 11-year term, and the tenant could renew for a further 5 years provided it was not in default. When the tenant tried to exercise the right to renew the landlord refused, citing as the cause the subtenant's failure to name the landlord as a co-insured (as required by the lease) in the contract of insurance. This breach continued to subsist at the renewal date.

This failure to properly insure the premises was further complicated by the fact that a third party had fallen on the premises and the landlord now faced potential liability to the injured person. Because the potential liability to the party who fell remained, substantial performance by the tenant could not be maintained—despite the later rectification of insurance coverage. The option to renew was thus lost.

---

[1]. [1999] 1 SCR 265, 1999 CanLII 708 (SCC).

[2]. 2011 ONCA 334 (CanLII).

Tender

The general rule in common law is that when a person has tendered performance of a contract, it counts as if the contract had been performed. **Tender of performance** means that if a person is ready, willing, and able to perform a contractual obligation and attempts to do so, but the other party refuses to accept it or prevents it, the first party is taken to have completed its obligation. The other party is then required to perform. If it fails to do so then it is in breach, not the party who has tendered performance.

Tender of performance ends obligation

Where goods and services are involved and tender of performance is refused, the tendering party has no further obligation and can sue immediately. If Tomas's Irrigation Service contracted with Jedrasik to install lawn irrigation, and when Tomas shows up to do the job he is refused entrance, he has discharged of his obligation and can sue. It is no excuse for Jedrasik to claim that the work was not done.

The effect of tendering proper payment of debt is different. It does not extinguish the debt but simply relieves the debtor of the normal obligation to seek out the creditor to make payment. Once proper payment has been tendered and refused, the debtor can simply wait for the creditor to collect the debt. Any costs associated with that process will then be borne by the creditor.

Where a debt owed and money is refused, the money is still owed but the creditor bears the expense

Proper payment of a debt requires legal tender. Cheques, even certified cheques, are acceptable only when the parties have agreed to allow cheques to be used to pay debts. This may be an actual agreement between the parties, or it may be implied from accepted business practice. If there is any question about the acceptable form of payment, it is advisable to present cash, and then only the exact amount, in proper legal tender. Under the *Currency Act*,[3] creditors can refuse to take more than a limited amount in coins, as set out below:

Payment must be in legal tender

When being paid in coins of this denomination	No more than this need be taken
$2	$40
$1	$25
10, 25, 50 cents	$10
5 cents	$5
1 cent	25 cents

There is no limit on what qualifies as legal tender when paper money is offered, as long as official Canadian banknotes are used. To avoid problems, especially as we move toward a cashless society, the parties should specify the appropriate method of payment in their agreement.

When not specifically addressed in the contract, the tendering of performance must be done at a reasonable time and place.[4] Usually this means during normal business hours at a person's place of business. Thus, if Aronyk has a contract to

Delivery must be as specified or at a reasonable time and place

[3.] R.S.C. 1985, c. C-52, s. 8.
[4.] See Alberta's *Sale of Goods Act*, R.S.A. 2000, c. S-2, s.29, for example.

deliver five tonnes of ripe grapes to Demers by July 10, Aronyk would be expected to make that delivery to Demers's winery rather than to her home or office. The delivery should also take place during the usual working day. Demers would not be obligated to accept delivery at 6:00 p.m. on Saturday, unless such a time was permitted in the contract.

When the parties do specify a time for performance in the contract, the court will have to determine whether it is an important term or not. Where the parties specify (or the court determines) that "time is of the essence," it must be strictly adhered to. Even just a few seconds can make a difference. This was the case in *Smith Bros. & Wilson (B.C.) Ltd. v. British Columbia Hydro and Power Authority,*[5] where a bid was submitted for a job just a few minutes late. Tenders were to be submitted no later than 11:00 a.m. The bid was submitted at 11:01, but could not be considered.

Some obligations continue after discharge

When the contract has been properly performed by both parties, there may still be some continuing obligations. For example, where a product is sold and the purchase price has been paid, title has transferred to the purchaser. Even then, if the product is dangerous or fails to meet the specifications of the agreement the purchaser can turn back to the seller and seek compensation for the breach. This continuing obligation is imposed in the case of sales of goods by legislation. Provincial *Sale of Goods Acts* impose certain implied warranties of fitness and merchantability upon sellers. Breach of these implied warranties can lead to an award of damages. This topic is examined further in Chapter 16.

LO ❷ ## DISCHARGE BY BREACH

Breach may involve failure to perform or repudiation

Breach of contract involves the failure of the breaching party to properly perform its contractual obligations. Such a breach can take place in two ways: (1) by improper or incomplete performance of the obligations set out in the agreement, or (2) by refusal to perform.

Allegations of improper or incomplete performance are quite common. In *Johnson v. Barry,*[6] the plaintiff hired the defendant to sew four bridesmaid dresses and create much of the bridal party's attire. The designer/tailor was extremely late. The bridesmaid dresses were not delivered until the day of the wedding, and the bride's dress was only delivered 48 hours earlier, giving the bride no time to have final alterations done. Because the defendant did not complete his work in a timely manner, the bride missed out on the planned activities the night before, the photographer was unable to take some of the planned photos, and the bride was late for the ceremony itself. All this caused the bride mental distress, for which $1000 in damages were awarded. Damages for breach of contract were also awarded to cover the deficiencies in performance and the cost of retaining another seamstress's help.

CASE SUMMARY 9.2

When Is a Breach Enough to Discharge a Contract?
Baid v. Aliments Rinag Foods Inc.[7]

It is often difficult to determine just how serious a breach must be to discharge a contract. In the *Baid* case, the father of the groom arranged to have the reception catered. The caterer failed to show up and the father hastily arranged to have the reception

---

5. 1997 CanLII 2046 (BC SC).
6. 2012 ABPC 359 (CanLII).
7. 2003 CanLII 49322 (ON SC).

hall supply food and drinks—at nearly twice the cost. The caterer's truck had broken down and its cellphone wouldn't work, so the wedding party was not notified. When the caterer finally arrived five hours late, it served food that hadn't been properly warmed. The father sued for breach of contract, claiming the extra costs plus damages for emotional distress. The caterer counterclaimed, demanding payment of the balance of their unpaid account. Whereas in some situations a five-hour delay in performance would not justify treating the contract as discharged, here the Court determined that the failure to perform was significant. Accordingly, the plaintiff was relieved of paying for the poorly performed task, and the defendant had to pay for the costs that flowed from the breach.

SMALL BUSINESS PERSPECTIVE

Parties who provide services for pay may be surprised to learn that "not getting paid" is just one of the potential consequences of performing a task poorly. As the above case demonstrates, not only was the defendant caterer unable to get paid, it also had to compensate the plaintiff for his costs in hiring a third party to supply the food and drinks. A costly lesson indeed!

Breach by refusal to perform can also lead to discharge of the contract. Refusal to perform will be addressed under the heading "Repudiation."

Conditions and Warranties

Conditions are terms essential to the substantial performance of a contract; **warranties** are minor, insignificant terms or terms that are peripheral to the central obligation of the contract. A breach of warranty will not relieve the other party of the obligation to fulfill his side of the agreement. The victim of such a breach of warranty has the right to sue the other party for whatever it costs to overcome the deficiency in performance, but still must perform his part of the agreement. However, when a condition or important term is breached, so that the victim of the breach is deprived of the major benefit of the contract, the victim can usually treat her obligation as ended and sue for breach of contract. It must be stressed that the breach of condition must be a serious impairment of the performance of the contract. A minor breach of even an important term will not generally allow the victim of the breach to discharge the contract. A common example of this occurs when goods are to be delivered in instalments. A single missed instalment usually will not be enough to discharge the agreement, even though it is the breach of an important term.

Although the breach of a condition normally allows the victim of the breach to treat the contract as discharged, he can elect or choose to treat the contract as still binding. In fact, if the non-breaching party has received some significant benefit under the agreement, he loses the right to discharge and must perform his obligations subject to a claim for compensation for the breach.

It may be tempting for one party to breach a condition of the contract to relieve herself of any further obligation to perform. But the breaching party can't choose how the breach will be treated. It takes both parties to end a contract. If Willoughby provided a sculpture of a moose instead of the flying geese agreed to for the foyer of Kubicki's new office building, this would normally be a breach of a condition and Kubicki would not have to pay. However, if Kubicki liked the moose sculpture he can keep it, but he would have to pay for it—albeit at a reduced value. Thus, when a breach of condition in a contract has been accepted by the other party, it is treated as a breach of warranty.

What is important to one person might seem unimportant to another. Therefore, terms can be designated as either conditions or warranties in the agreement. Normally, when a person orders a new car, the particular shade of red ordered

Breach of warranty—performance is required

Breach of condition—party is relieved

Where the breach is accepted—performance is required

BC's *Sale of Goods Act* allows a specified warranty to be treated as a condition, expanding the remedies available

would be a minor term, and if a car of a slightly different shade were delivered the purchaser would still have to take it. But where the exact shade is important to the purchaser, which might be the case where it is used as a trademark for a business, it can designate the required shade to be a condition and refuse to take the car if a car of any other shade of red is delivered. Similarly, the person supplying goods or services will often designate as a warranty a term that would normally be a condition in the agreement. The BC *Sale of Goods Act* states that in transactions governed by the Act, the court has the option of treating a term as a condition although it is specified as a warranty in the contract.[8]

Exemption Clauses

Exemption clauses attempt to limit liability

Exemption clauses are an attempt by a party to significantly limit or eliminate its liability under an agreement. The courts will generally enforce exemption clauses because their focus in contract law is to enforce whatever the parties have freely bargained to do. But they do so reluctantly, especially where the parties are not in equal bargaining positions. If there is any ambiguity in the terms of the exemption clause, the narrow or restrictive meaning will be applied.

Exemption clauses are strictly interpreted

If a restaurant has a sign above the cloakroom stating that it is "Not responsible for lost or stolen clothing," by bringing this term to the customer's attention the restaurant would make it part of the contract for care of the goods, or bailment. If clothes left were damaged by fire or water, the proprietor would not be protected as that kind of loss was not specified on the sign. Similarly, if a briefcase were stolen the exemption clause would not apply because it was a briefcase and not "clothing" that was stolen.

Clause must be brought to the attention of the party at the time of contract

Exemption clauses can be intricate and involved because the people who draft them try to cover all possible eventualities, knowing that the courts will take a restrictive approach in their interpretation. Such clauses usually form part of a written document, but they could be included in a sign or notice. In any case, the terms cannot be unilaterally imposed and must be brought to the attention of the customer at the time the contract is made. If the clause is on the back of the ticket or receipt, there must be a reference on the front directing the holder to read the back. Where a sign limiting liability is involved, as at a parking lot or bus depot, it must be in clear view so that a reasonable person would notice it when entering the premises or undertaking a contractual obligation. Even when the exemption clause is part of a written contract, if it is in any way unique or unusual it must be brought to the attention of the other contracting party. If it is buried in other insignificant writing, or so small it cannot be read, it is doubtful that it will have any legal effect.[9]

Effect of legislation

When goods or services are sold in consumer transactions, these exemption clauses are usually embodied in terms referred to as "limited warranties." The term is misleading and causes confusion, since these are major terms of the contract (conditions), not minor ones. The courts are likely to be much more sympathetic to the plight of a customer in a consumer transaction who has not read the exemption clause than to the more sophisticated parties in a business transaction. It is important to note that under the *Sale of Goods Act* or other consumer protection legislation, the sellers' rights to restrict their obligations in such sales may be extremely limited. Consumer protection and the sale of goods will be discussed in Chapter 16.

[8.] R.S.B.C. 1996, c. 410, s. 15.

[9.] In *Boutcev v. DHL International Express Ltd.* (2001), 283 A.R. 19 (Q.B.), the defendant was unable to rely on an exemption clause despite the fact that the front of the waybill directed parties' attention to provisions that were printed on the back of the form. The Court found that the exclusion clause was illegible and incomprehensible.

CASE SUMMARY 9.3

Exemption Clauses Are Strictly Interpreted:
Meditek Laboratory Services Ltd. v. Purolator Courier Ltd.[10]; *Zhu v. Merrill Lynch HSBC*[11]

A Purolator employee delivered an expensive medical machine meant for Meditek to the wrong address. To make matters worse, the delivery sheets showing where the goods were delivered had been falsified, and the goods could not be traced. After a long delay the goods were found, but Meditek had in the meantime obtained a replacement machine. It refused delivery and sued Purolator for damages. Purolator relied on an exemption clause in the contract limiting its liability "whether or not from negligence or gross negligence." But the act of the employee in falsifying the documents had been wilful, not negligent, and the Court found that Purolator was not protected by the clause.

In the *Zhu* case, Zhu used Merrill Lynch's Internet trading facility to trade shares from his registered retirement savings account. He cancelled the trade immediately after, and shortly thereafter attempted to make the trade a second time. A problem arose because the first cancellation had not been completed, which resulted in a duplicate trade and a short position in Zhu's account. Merrill Lynch then insisted that Zhu buy back the shares—at a higher price. Zhu argued that he relied on the notation on his computer screen that the trade had been cancelled. Merrill Lynch tried to assert a limitation of liability clause, warning that clients had to confirm cancellations, but the Court would not allow that. The disclaimer was deemed unenforceable because Merrill Lynch could have made it clear that the cancellation was not complete, but it had failed to do so. After all, who would expect one had to telephone to confirm a cancellation where the entire transaction had been conducted online?

SMALL BUSINESS PERSPECTIVE

In light of the restrictive approach taken by the courts when asked to enforce exemption clauses, a party who wishes to limit its liability should realize that simply inserting an exemption clause may not be enough. Steps should be taken to show that the clause was brought to the other party's attention, explained, and assented to.

FUNDAMENTAL BREACH

A **fundamental breach** is a breach that goes to the very root of the contact. Essentially it suggests the innocent party was denied the benefit it had bargained for. Contracting parties often try to limit their liability as much as possible, and sometimes they try to contract out of all obligations and responsibilities. Earlier case law held that when a party breaches its contract in a fundamental way, then that party cannot rely on an exclusion clause in its favour.[12] (This rule was called the *doctrine of fundamental breach*). The Supreme Court of Canada, however, in the *Hunter Engineering* case,[13] made it clear that a properly worded exemption clause can overcome even a fundamental breach—particularly where sophisticated businesspeople are involved (see Case Summary 16.3). Because of the parties' freedom to contract, the courts may enforce an exemption clause that protects the breaching party.

[10.] (1995), 102 Man. R. (2d) 85 (C.A.), leave to appeal to S.C.C. refused, [1995] S.C.C.A. No. 405.

[11.] 2002 BCPC 535 (CanLII).

[12.] See the doctrine of fundamental breach as created by Lord Denning in *Karsales (Harrow) Ltd. v. Wallis*, [1956] 1 WLR 936 (CA), www.bailii.org/ew/cases/EWCA/Civ/1956/4.html.

[13.] *Hunter Engineering Co. v. Syncrude Canada Ltd.*, [1989] 1 SCR 426, 1989 CanLII 129 (SCC); see also *Beaufort Realties v. Chomedey Aluminum Co. Ltd.*, [1980] 2 SCR 718, 1980 CanLII 47.

CASE SUMMARY 9.4

Exemption Clauses Enforced Despite Fundamental Breach: *Selkirk Petroleum Products Ltd. v. Husky Oil Ltd.*[14]

Prairie Petroleum Products Limited and Selkirk Petroleum Products Ltd. both brought actions against their supplier, Husky Oil, alleging breach of contract when Husky unilaterally changed its pricing structure without written consent. (Husky had taken over these contracts from Mohawk.) This price change fundamentally affected the competitiveness of Prairie and Selkirk; they thus claimed this breach entitled them to terminate all business relations with Husky and purchase product from another supplier.

At trial, the judge found Husky Oil breached these contracts in a fundamental manner, and since the exclusionary clauses were unconscionable, unfair, and unreasonable they did not apply to limit Husky's liability. These clauses stated:

> **12.03** Mohawk shall not, by reason of the termination of this Agreement, be liable to Distributor for compensation, reimbursement or damages on account of the loss of prospective profits on anticipated sales or on account of expenditures, investments, leases or commitments in connection with the business or goodwill of Distributor or otherwise.

> **12.04** Mohawk shall not be liable for any special or consequential damages or otherwise from any breach of its obligations under this Agreement.[15]

On appeal, however, the Court rejected the finding of unconscionability. The Court agreed with the Alberta Court of Appeal in *Plas-Tex Canada Ltd. v. Dow Chemical of Canada Ltd.,*[16] where it was held that "unconscionability should be used sparingly to avoid an exclusion clause, but should be applied in such a way as to prevent a party to a contract from acting in an unconscionable manner, secure in the knowledge that no liability can be imposed because of such clause." There was no evidence of coercion, fraud, immorality, or abuse that would constitute an evidentiary basis to unconscionability. There was also no evidence of abuse of inequality of bargaining power. Furthermore, the clauses were not harsh when entered into. In light of the above, Husky was entitled to rely on the exclusion clauses.

SMALL BUSINESS PERSPECTIVE

This case highlights the risks that accompany the freedom to contract. Parties can exclude their liability, even for a fundamental breach. While Canadian courts have refused to enforce exemption clauses where it would be unconscionable, unfair, or unreasonable to do so, absent such complications the courts are likely to enforce the terms agreed upon. One cannot overemphasize the importance of understanding each clause in a contract and its effect before one signs it.

Exemption clauses are ineffective if unconscionable

In 2010, the Supreme Court of Canada laid the doctrine of fundamental breach to rest. In its place, it outlined the analysis to be followed when a plaintiff seeks to escape the effect of an exclusion clause or other contractual terms to which it had previously agreed. The *Tercon* decision (see Case Summary 9.5) focuses on:

a. whether the clause applies to the breach,

b. whether the clause was unconscionable, and finally

c. whether public policy dictates that the clause be set aside.

---

14. 2008 MBCA 87 (CanLII).
15. Ibid., at para. 32.
16. 2004 ABCA 309 (CanLII).

Exemption Clauses May Operate Despite a Significant or "Fundamental" Breach: *Tercon Contractors Ltd. v. British Columbia (Transportation and Highways)*[17]

Parties to a contract should generally be bound by its terms, and a broadly drafted exclusion clause should operate to protect a party from liability for damage it may have caused. The issue in this case centred on the enforceability of an exclusion clause where the government violated the ground rules. It issued a request for proposals (RFP) for highway construction and limited participation to "eligible bidders." Later it knowingly awarded the job to an ineligible bidder and actively took steps to obscure the reality of the situation. *Tercon* was an eligible bidder whose bid was not accepted. It sued and was awarded $3.3 million at trial, representing the loss of profits on the highway project.

The Province appealed on the basis that the exclusion clause sanitized its breach of contract (namely, its intentional acceptance of a bid from an ineligible bidder). The exclusion clause stated:

> Except as expressly and specifically permitted . . . no Proponent shall have any claim for compensation of any kind whatsoever, as a result of participating in this RFP, and by submitting a Proposal each Proponent shall be deemed to have agreed that it has no claim.

In its decision, the Supreme Court of Canada issued a framework to follow in assessing the enforceability of exclusion clauses:

> The first issue, of course, is whether as a matter of interpretation the exclusion clause even applies to the circumstances established in evidence. This will depend on the Court's assessment of the intention of the parties as expressed in the contract. If the exclusion clause does not apply, there is obviously no need to proceed further with this analysis. If the exclusion clause applies, the second issue is whether the exclusion clause was unconscionable at the time the contract was made, "as might arise from situations of unequal bargaining power between the parties" (*Hunter*, at p. 462). This second issue has to do with contract formation, not breach.

> If the exclusion clause is held to be valid and applicable, the Court may undertake a third enquiry, namely whether the Court should nevertheless refuse to enforce the valid exclusion clause because of the existence of an overriding public policy, proof of which lies on the party seeking to avoid enforcement of the clause, that outweighs the very strong public interest in the enforcement of contracts.

Interestingly, the Court was split five to four on the first step of this analysis. The minority concluded that the exclusion clause applied. Their decision is consistent with the notion of freedom to contract: *Tercon* and the other bidders chose to bid on a project based on the terms proposed by the ministry, which included the exclusion clause. Since it agreed to the exclusion clause, it was enforceable unless (1) it was unconscionable or (2) public policy demanded that the clause not be enforced in the circumstances.

The majority, however, held that the exclusion clause did not apply to the breach in question, namely unfairly dealing with a party who was not entitled to participate in the bidding process. Justice Cromwell focused on the need for transparency and fairness in the context of public tenders. It would be senseless to participate in the RFP "if the Province could avoid liability for ignoring an express term concerning eligibility to bid on which the entire RFP was premised." The majority awarded damages to *Tercon* in the amount established by the trial judge.

---

[17] [2010] 1 SCR 69, 2010 SCC 4 (CanLII).

> **SMALL BUSINESS PERSPECTIVE**
> The framework for deciding whether or not an exclusion clause should be enforced still retains some flexibility. Nonetheless, when entering contracts that contain such clauses, a sophisticated client will ask whether it is prudent to secure some additional protection or insurance.

REDUCING RISK 9.1

In business dealings, people may assume that the courts will enforce all the clauses found in their contracts. This is not necessarily so. The courts may refuse to enforce terms found to be unconscionable or oppressive. Public policy may lead the courts to set aside terms. Furthermore, the courts may even take an expansive role by implying obligations that may not be stated.

The duty to act in good faith toward the other contracting party is such a commonly implied obligation. Whereas lawyers may be familiar with the manner in which courts interpret and enforce contracts, most laypeople are not. Getting legal advice on the enforceability of one's standard form contracts is good business practice.

Repudiation

Repudiation is refusal to perform one's obligations

Repudiation occurs when one of the parties to a contract indicates to the other "an intimation or an intention to abandon and altogether to refuse performance of the contract."[18] Repudiation that takes place after performance is due is just one more way that a contract can be breached; but if this refusal occurs before performance is due, it is called an **anticipatory breach** and is treated somewhat differently.

CASE SUMMARY 9.6

Anticipating a Breach: *LeDrew Lumber Co. v. West Point Development Inc.*[19]

The general contractor had agreed to build three houses on three lots for the defendant. The agreement provided for instalments payable at the end of each stage of construction. Invoices were submitted after the first stage was completed on two homes, and the general contractor continued with the construction. But when the defendant failed to pay, work ceased and the general contractor filed liens against all three lots. It alleged that the failure to pay the two invoices led it to conclude there would be no payment on the third job either.

If a party has acted in such a way as to lead a reasonable person to the conclusion that she does not intend to fulfill her part of the contract, there has been an anticipatory breach. There was anticipatory breach of the third contract. Accordingly, the general contractor was entitled to treat all three contracts as terminated by breach. It was further entitled to enforce these liens by sale of these lots.

DISCUSSION QUESTIONS

Anticipatory breach enables the aggrieved party to sue before the due date for completion. Is there any good reason to wait?

In the face of an anticipatory breach, victims have a choice. They can choose to immediately treat the contract as breached, refuse to go through with any further

---

18. Comment of Lord Coleridge, C.J. in *Freeth v. Burr* (1874), L.R. 9 C.P. 208 (Crt. C.P.).
19. [2009] N.J. No. 216 (N.L.S.C.); 2009 NLTD 128 (CanLII).

performance on their part, and sue. However, the repudiation must relate to an important term of the contract and be a clear refusal to perform, not just a disagreement as to the nature of the contractual obligations. Alternatively, the victim of the repudiation can ignore the breach, demand performance, and continue to perform its side of the agreement. If the repudiating party still fails to perform, the innocent party can then sue for breach of contract and the party repudiating will be held responsible for damages incurred even after the repudiation.

> **Victim is discharged and can sue if repudiation occurs before the due date—or demand performance and wait**

Once made, the choice is binding. This can have serious consequences, for if the victim chooses to insist on performance and then in turn cannot perform, she is then in breach herself, as happened in the *Vanderwal* case discussed in Case Summary 9.7.

> **Victim is bound by his choice**

CASE SUMMARY 9.7

Bound by Choice When Faced with Anticipatory Breach: *Vanderwal v. Anderson*[20]

Anderson agreed to purchase property from the Vanderwals, conditional on the purchaser selling her house. This condition precedent was subsequently removed. Anderson's obligation to purchase was thus unconditional when she explained to the vendors, through her lawyer, that she didn't understand what she had done and didn't have the money to complete the transaction. She asked that the condition be reinstated and the time extended. The vendors refused, insisting that the contract was binding on her unconditionally. The vendors then sold the property to another purchaser and sued Anderson for breach. The Court found that the purchaser's claim of insufficient funds and plea for an extension amounted to an anticipatory breach. The vendors had a choice to ignore the breach and insist on performance or treat the contract as discharged. By insisting that the contract was binding unconditionally, they chose to reject the repudiation and insist on performance. But when they sold the property they abandoned the contract—thus they were in breach, not the purchaser. The Vanderwals' action for breach of contract was dismissed.

SMALL BUSINESS PERSPECTIVE

When anticipatory breach occurs, the innocent party has a right to demand performance or to sue for breach, but it would be prudent to seek legal advice before one responds to an apparent breach of contract. If that party demands performance, it had better be prepared to perform its side of the agreement.

Repudiation can be expressed or implied from the conduct of the parties. An express repudiation occurs, for example, when a vendor calls or writes to the purchaser indicating that he refuses to complete the sale. On the other hand, where the goods to be sold are simply sold to someone else, such repudiation will be implied. Also, repudiation may be implied from the failure to properly perform a term of the agreement. As seen, failure to deliver an important instalment can lead to repudiation being implied. Missing just one delivery of goods will normally not be serious enough, but if non-delivery is serious enough to cast doubt on the proper performance of the rest of the agreement, repudiation may be implied. Thus, if Song agreed to deliver 10 loads of gravel to Singh's building site and failed to deliver the first two on the specified days, this might well be considered a repudiation of the contract. Singh could then look for another source. See Table 9.1 for a summary of the results of a failure to perform.

> **Repudiation may be implied from conduct**

---

20. [1999] O.J. No. 2646 (Div. Ct.).

Table 9.1   Results of Failure to Perform

Breach of performance	If minor, or if contract is substantially performed	Contract remains binding and the other party must perform, but can seek damages
	If breach is a major one, as with breach of a condition	Contract ends but victim can seek damages
Repudiation of contract	Victim insists on performance	Contract remains binding on both
	Victim chooses to treat contract as discharged	Contract ends but victim can seek damages

LO ❸ # DISCHARGE BY AGREEMENT

Contracts can be modified or ended by agreement

Just as the parties to a contract can agree to create contractual obligations, they can also agree to end or modify those obligations. This is referred to as **discharge by agreement**. Whether the intention of the parties is to merely modify the old agreement or to end it and substitute a new one, all the ingredients necessary to form a contract, including consensus and consideration, must be present.

Modifications—must have consideration

If both parties have something left to do under the original contract and the agreement to modify relieves them of their respective obligations, there is valid consideration on both sides to support the change. This is called **bilateral discharge** or mutual release. The problem arises where the discharge or modification is one sided. Where one party performs its side, yet allows the other party to get out of all or part of its obligations, the discharge, being unilateral, may not be binding because of lack of consideration. The original contract may still be enforceable. When a significant change is introduced that favours only one party, there may also be a problem with consideration. Lack of new consideration was the reason the limited warranty provision, agreed to later, did not bind *Gregorio* in Case Summary 9.8. Of course, problems surrounding consideration can be avoided by putting the agreement under seal.

CASE SUMMARY 9.8

Must Be Consideration to Support Change: *Gregorio v. Intrans-Corp.*[21]

Gregorio ordered a truck from Intrans conditional upon financing, which was arranged on July 3, 1984. The only condition was thus removed, creating a binding contract. When the truck was delivered on August 2, Gregorio was required to sign a one-year limited warranty that excluded all other implied warranties and other liability for consequential damages for failure to perform.

The truck turned out to be a lemon, and when the company couldn't fix it Gregorio sued to get his money back. It was now 1987. The company claimed to be protected by the limited warranty, but the Court held that this warranty was a modification of the original agreement from May 12. Since Gregorio had received no consideration for the change, he was not bound by it. Thus, the statutory protections set out in the *Sale of Goods Act* still applied to the purchase, and because the vehicle was defective Gregorio was entitled to get his money back. (The *Sale of Goods Act* is discussed in Chapter 16.)

---

21. 1994 CanLII 2241 (ON CA), additional reasons, 1994 CanLII 1890 (ON CA).

Note, however, that even when the discharge is entirely one sided, the person being relieved of her obligation may be able to raise the defence of promissory estoppel if sued under the original agreement. Estoppel would prevent the party who forgave some indebtedness from later turning around and suing for that sum. In fact, a prime example where the principle of promissory estoppel arises is in the context of such one-sided discharges or modifications of contracts.

Promissory estoppel may stop legal action commenced by a promissor

Where the party benefiting from a modification agrees to do something extra to support the change (or discharge) of the contract, this is called **accord and satisfaction**. The **accord** refers to the agreement to change (or end) the old contract, and the **satisfaction** is the extra consideration to be supplied by the party benefiting from the change (or discharge). For example, if Groves was renovating his house and paid Grubisich in advance to paint it, there would be a problem with lack of consideration if he simply allowed Grubisich to abandon the contract. But if Grubisich were to agree to do something extra, such as paint Groves's garage instead, there would be a new agreement (an accord) with added consideration (satisfaction), and the new arrangement would be binding.

Accord and satisfaction overcomes the consideration problem

CASE SUMMARY 9.9

Accord and Satisfaction: *Total Energy Services Inc. (c.o.b. Chinook Drilling) v. Tamarack Valley Energy Ltd.*[22]

Chinook Drilling issued invoices to the defendant, Tamarack Valley Energy, for drilling work performed. The defendant withheld payment, claiming that the plaintiff was responsible for delays and significant damages arising from a drilling pipe fracture. Responsibility was denied by the plaintiff, Chinook Drilling; the parties discussed resolution of the $250 000 owed on the invoices. The defendant sent a cheque to the plaintiff for half of the amount outstanding and enclosed a "without prejudice" letter. It stated that the cheque was in full and final satisfaction of the dispute, and that cashing the cheque constituted waiver of any further claim.

The plaintiff cashed the cheque immediately, but later received a consultant's report confirming that it, Chinook Drilling, was not responsible for the drilling problem. The plaintiff then asserted the right to pursue the balance still owed. It commenced an action for payment of the remaining $125 000.

The defendant secured a dismissal in its favour based on the defence of accord and satisfaction. The plaintiff's contention that the without prejudice letter required a separate step of acceptance in addition to cashing the enclosed cheque was rejected. The letter clearly stipulated that acceptance and cashing the cheque were one and the same. By cashing the cheque, the plaintiff took the positive step contemplated by the letter and expressed acceptance of its terms. A new agreement had been reached, dismissing any further claims.

SMALL BUSINESS PERSPECTIVE

This is an example of the principle of accord and satisfaction with consideration on both sides supporting a new, renegotiated contract.

22. 2011 ABQB 787 (CanLII).

Sometimes the old contract is not simply modified but discharged by agreement and a new contract is substituted for it. Whether a new agreement has been created or the old one modified will be determined by looking at the intention of the parties and what has been changed. The more important the provision changed, the more likely it is that a new agreement has been substituted for the old one. The difference can be important since it may affect whether various terms from the old agreement, such as exemption and penalty clauses, are carried over to the new one. If the original agreement was merely modified (and not discharged and substituted), then the clauses found in the original agreement continue to apply.

When the new agreement involves a new party being substituted for one of the original parties to the agreement, it is called a *novation*. Naturally, both parties must agree to the substitution of one party for there to be a consensus. One party cannot unilaterally impose substitution of a party.

When a debt is assumed by a new debtor, an issue that can arise is whether the original debtor is still liable if the new debtor fails to repay the indebtedness. When a person sells her home and the new purchaser assumes the mortgage, is the original debtor still indebted to the mortgagee? Or has novation occurred, thereby extinguishing the original debtor's obligation to pay? Madam Justice Wilson explains:

[T]he burden of establishing novation is not easily met. The courts have established a three part test for determining if novation has occurred. It is set out in *Polson v. Wulffsohn* (1890), 2 B.C.R. 39 as follows:

1. The new debtor must assume the complete liability;

2. The creditor must accept the new debtor as principal debtor and not merely as guarantor; and

3. The creditor must accept the new contract in full satisfaction and substitution for the old contract.[23]

Clearly, where the terms of the agreement or the parties to it are being changed, or the contract is being discharged, there must be complete agreement among all the parties before the new agreement becomes binding.

Contractual Terms

Most contracts, by their nature, will end upon proper performance. However, sometimes they involve an ongoing relationship, with no provision to bring that relationship to an end. An employment contract for an indefinite term would be an example. In these circumstances, the courts have implied that the contract can be terminated by either party giving the other reasonable notice. Often contracts will provide for their own termination, usually by specifying a particular period of notice that must be given; these notice provisions will be binding subject to contrary legislation. In employment relationships and residential tenancy arrangements, for example, such termination provisions must comply with the governing statutes. Legislation, such as *Employment Standards Acts* and *Residential Tenancies Acts,* render notice provisions void or ineffective unless they satisfy statutory minimums.

When the contract itself specifies that some event or requirement must be satisfied before the parties are bound by it, this is properly referred to as a **condition precedent**, but is more commonly called a **subject-to clause**. For example, if Nishiama were to agree to buy Fafara's house subject to the sale of her own house, the contract is conditional on that event. Thus, if Nishiama fails to sell

---

23. *National Trust Co. v. Mead*, 1990 CanLII 73 (SCC), [1990] 2 SCR 410 at pp. 431–432.

her house she is not obligated to go through with any agreement for the purchase of Fafara's house. When such a condition precedent is not satisfied, there is no contractual obligation.

A **condition subsequent**, on the other hand, is a term that brings the obligations of the parties to an end upon some event or condition taking place. Whereas conditions precedent determine when the obligations between the parties begin, conditions subsequent determine when they end. For example, if Halford agreed to pay Perron $400 per month for security services "until Perron ceases to be a full-time student," this term is a condition subsequent. Halford will be obligated to pay only until Perron finishes school.

Sometimes the contract anticipates some catastrophic event, such as a riot, invasion, earthquake, or flood, that will interfere with the performance of the contract. This is referred to as a *force majeure clause*. Such terms might set out the consequences—such as which party will bear the risk of loss—as in the *Fishman* case discussed in Case Summary 9.10. Alternatively, they may provide for discharge of the contract. When catastrophic events take place and are not anticipated in the contract, they will likely cause the contract to be discharged by frustration.

Of course, when such terms are not included in the contract the parties can always agree to end, modify, or substitute obligations with a new agreement, as discussed above. Contracts can also end by operation of law, as would be the case when one of the parties dies, becomes insane, or is declared bankrupt. Bankruptcy will be discussed in Chapter 15.

Conditions subsequent determine when contractual obligations end

CASE SUMMARY 9.10

Frustration Alleged, But Event Covered by *Force Majeure* Clause: *Fishman v. Wilderness Ridge at Stewart Creek Inc.*[24]

The appellants sought a declaration that their contracts to purchase condominiums from the respondents had been frustrated because a condominium was destroyed by fire. The respondents countered that frustration had not occurred because the project was adequately insured and rebuilding had commenced. The agreements had been signed in January 2007 with possession to be delivered in February 2010, and the fire, which occurred in April 2009, would push the possession date back by a year at most. Further, the contract contained a *force majeure* clause that stipulated the respondents would not be deemed in default for any delay due to causes beyond their control.

The Court determined that "a contract is only frustrated when it becomes incapable of performance, not just because performance might be more onerous, more costly or different from what was anticipated." Although late delivery would be onerous for the appellants, they would still be receiving what they had bargained to buy. As to the delay in possession, there was no doubt that this constituted a breach on the respondents' part, but one that was addressed by the *force majeure* clause. Accordingly, the parties remained bound by the contract.

DISCUSSION QUESTIONS

Here the *force majeure* clause excused the breach of the builder. Consider a purchaser's position. What type of clause might be inserted if a purchaser wants to be able to escape a purchase should the property be consumed by fire?

[24.] 2010 ABCA 345 (CanLII).

LO ❹ DISCHARGE BY FRUSTRATION

Sometimes some unexpected event (out of the control of the parties) makes performance of the contract impossible. For example, where a construction firm agrees to repair a bridge but the bridge is washed away in a storm before the repair work begins, performance has become impossible. In such circumstances the contract is considered discharged through frustration. **Frustration** occurs when some unforeseen, outside event (out of the control of either party) interferes with the performance of the contract, making the basic object of the agreement unobtainable.

Frustrating event may end a contract

It is easy to understand frustration when performance of the contract is made impossible, such as when a person agrees to paint a house that is destroyed in a fire before the job can be performed. Difficulties arise because the courts have expanded the principle to also cover situations where the foundation of the contract is destroyed. Performance may still be technically possible, but the whole nature of the relationship has changed, making performance something essentially different from what the parties anticipated.

For example, in *KBK No. 138 Ventures Ltd v. Canada Safeway Ltd.*,[25] KBK agreed to buy land from Canada Safeway that was zoned for high-density development. When the city rezoned the property to a much lower density, this effectively destroyed KBK's plans for redevelopment. KBK demanded the return of the $150 000 deposit paid, claiming frustration. Safeway argued that the essential nature of the contract was for the purchase of the property, and that remained intact, but the Court found frustration and ordered the return of the deposit. In this case the whole substance of the contract had been radically altered by the unanticipated intervention of the city in rezoning the property. Although performance of the contract was possible in a literal sense, it was no longer possible to obtain the purpose or object of the contract itself. The change struck at the root of the contract, fundamentally changing its nature and thus frustrating it.

Even an injury that causes an employee to be unable to perform his work can be a frustrating event.[26] An employer may regard the employment as terminated since the employee can no longer do the work. Having benefits such as long-term disability coverage is a safeguard that employees should seek to secure, for if the contract is terminated by frustration (illness) and the employment contract is terminated, damages for wrongful dismissal will be unavailable. (Note, however, that human rights legislation may offer some relief as employers have a duty to accommodate disabilities, to some extent.)

Shared mistake is not the same as frustration

It is easy to confuse frustration with shared mistake, discussed in the preceding chapter. With shared mistake, there is no contract because the subject matter had been destroyed before the contract was entered into. Frustration, on the other hand, deals with situations where the problems arise *after* the formation of the contract. If a ship that is the subject of a contract is destroyed before the contract is made, the parties are making a mistake by assuming the ship is still functioning. But if the ship is destroyed after the contract is made, the contract is discharged through frustration.

Circumstances constituting frustration

Frustration commonly arises in the following circumstances:

1. Performance of a contract becomes impossible because the subject matter of the agreement is destroyed or is otherwise unusable. Contracts may be frustrated when a person who has agreed to supply personal services becomes very ill or dies, or when the specific article that formed the object of the contract is destroyed before the agreement can be performed. *Taylor v. Caldwell*[27] concerned the rental of a music hall that burned down six days before the subject performance was to take place. The Court held that the contract was discharged through frustration.

---

25. (2000) 185 D.L.R. (4th) 650 (B.C.C.A.); 2000 BCCA 295 (CanLII).

26. *Demuynck v. Agentis Information Services Inc.*, 2003 BCSC 96 (CanLII).

27. (1863) 3 B. & S. 826 (Q.B.), www.bailii.org/ew/cases/EWHC/QB/1863/J1.html.

2. An event that forms the basis of a contract fails to take place. An example is the cancellation of the coronation parade in *Krell v. Henry*,[28] where the parties agreed to the rental of an apartment from which the tenant could view the coronation parade of Edward VII. It was still possible to occupy the flat, but to require the tenant to do so with no coronation parade to watch would be something essentially different from what the parties had in mind when they entered into the contract.

3. Acts of the government interfere with performance. Government policy can interfere with the performance of a contract in several different ways. A contract with someone in another country may become unlawful or impossible to perform because of a declaration of war; contracts involving the manufacture and production of particular drugs or foodstuffs may become illegal by statute; a contract may anticipate the acquisition of a licence or permit that the government does not grant; or a government may expropriate the property that may form the basis of a contract.

Although the above is not intended to be a complete list, most of the frustrating events that do take place fall into one of these three categories.

Circumstances Not Constituting Frustration

CASE SUMMARY 9.11

When Complications Are Avoidable, Even if Not Foreseen: *Roberts & Webster v. Hobert*[29]

The claimants, Roberts and Webster, bought a building from the defendant for $25 000 with plans to have it moved to their property to be used as a residence. After paying the purchase price, the purchasers sought a permit to have the building moved. The inspector advised that the building could not be moved before significant structural changes (at an estimated cost of $22 000) were made. The claimants brought this action seeking return of the purchase price, arguing that the refusal of the permit frustrated the contract of sale. The Court determined that the contract had not been frustrated. For frustration to occur, a contractual obligation must become incapable of being performed without default of either party. Mere hardship, inconvenience, or material loss is insufficient. Further, the act or event that brought about the complication must not have been foreseen. In this case, the building could still be moved, albeit after a significant expenditure of funds.

But the Court also found that both parties knew the building inspector would have to approve of the move. Although the parties hoped a permit would be issued, a hope is not a certainty. The purchasers could have made the purchase conditional upon securing a permit, but they failed to take that precaution.

SMALL BUSINESS PERSPECTIVE

Good risk management involves addressing reasonably foreseeable risks. The time to do so is before a contract is concluded. Ignorance of the law is not an excuse, so if a party knows that there are permits to secure or conditions to satisfy, then those obstacles should be addressed immediately or the contract be made subject to approvals being received. One cannot simply assume that refusal of a permit will constitute frustration of the contract.

Self-induced frustration involves one of the parties causing—or, if it is within her control, failing to prevent—the frustrating event. It may appear to be frustration, but self-induced frustration is simply treated as a breach of contract.

Self-induced frustration is a breach

---

28. [1903] 2 K.B. 740 (C.A.).
29. 2011 BCPC 275 (CanLII).

Event must be unanticipated to be frustration

Second, where the parties have anticipated the frustrating event or have provided for one of the parties to bear the risk of such an eventuality, these contractual terms (often called *force majeure* clauses) will prevail. Such was the result in the *Fishman* case (see Case Summary 9.10.) There the *force majeure* clause prevailed, and the parties were not be able to claim that their agreement had been frustrated. It is only when the event is an unforeseen interference, not caused by either party, that the courts are willing to find frustration. In *Naylor Group v. Ellis-Don Construction*,[30] for example, the doctrine of frustration was found not to apply because the parties had made specific provision for the problem that materialized. The defendant contractor had inserted a clause in the contract stipulating it could object to awarding the subcontract to Naylor if it had a good reason. It failed to use that option and proceeded to award the contract to Naylor (despite the fact that it knew Naylor's workers were not affiliated with the International Brotherhood of Electrical Workers, IBEW). The defendant contractor could not, in these circumstances, claim that Naylor's inability to hire IBEW union workers was a frustrating event.

Increased difficulty or increased cost is not frustration

Finally, the contract is not frustrated if the unforeseen outside event only makes the performance of the contract more costly or more difficult. In the case of *Tsakiroglou Co. v. Noblee & Thorl GmbH*,[31] delivery of cargo from a port in the Sudan on the east coast of Africa to Germany became more onerous when the Suez Crisis closed the canal. The seller claimed that the contract was frustrated. The Court, however, found the seller liable for breach, holding that although it was more difficult and costly to ship the cargo around Africa, the essential nature of the contract remained intact and frustration did not apply. Note that the result would likely have been different had the parties specified delivery through the Suez Canal, since using that route was now impossible.

To find frustration, performance must be impossible or the foundation or purpose of the contract must be fundamentally or radically changed. Lack of profits or funding will not frustrate a contract. Thus in the *Korol v. Saskatchewan Federation of Police Officers* case[32] the federation's inability to pay wages did not frustrate the contract, so the employer was held liable for wrongful dismissal when it terminated Korol on that basis.

Effect of Frustration

The major problem associated with frustration is to determine who suffers the loss when the contract is discharged. Under common law, the general principle used to be "Let the loss lie where it falls." In other words, the party who had done work or compensation from the other party. Similarly, money already paid was lost. Note, however, that where payment was due before the frustrating event, that payment still had to be paid. This is illustrated by *Chandler v. Webster*,[33] a case that also involved the rental of a flat for viewing King Edward VII's coronation parade. While the entire rent of just over £141 was due and payable in advance, only £100 had actually been paid. Because the principle was that the loss should lie where it fell when a contract was frustrated, the tenant could not get his money back. In addition, because the sum not yet paid was owed before the frustrating event, that sum had to be paid as well.

Problems with deposits

Legislation allows deposits to be split

This position was considered unsatisfactory, and the House of Lords made a significant change in the *Fibrosa* case,[34] where a deposit was paid by a Polish company to a British manufacturer and the outbreak of war frustrated their contract. Because the Polish company had received no benefit under the contract, it was entitled to the return of its deposit. This represents the common law position today, but it still leads to some unsatisfactory results. The whole deposit or nothing has to be returned, depending on whether any benefit was received.

---

30. [2001] 2 SCR 943, 2001 SCC 58 (CanLII).

31. [1962] A.C. 93 (H.L.).

32. 2000 SKQB 367 (CanLII).

33. [1904] 1 K.B. 493 (C.A.).

34. *Fibrosa Spolka Akeyjna v. Fairbairn Lawson Combe Barbouk Ltd.*, [1943] A.C. 32 (H.L.).

Where a benefit has been obtained by one party prior to the frustrating event, legislation in most jurisdictions in the form of the *Frustrated Contracts Act*[35] now permits the court to order that party to pay the other for it.

Where a deposit has been paid, the legislation usually allows the court to take into consideration the costs that have been incurred in preparation to perform the contract, whether or not the other party has received a benefit. The court can now apportion that deposit on the basis of the costs incurred and the benefits received (see Table 9.2). In British Columbia and Yukon, such costs can be apportioned between the parties whether or not a deposit is involved.

Table 9.2 Effect of *Frustrated Contracts Act*

Contract Frustrated	(A) No deposit paid or payable	(B) With deposit
IMPACT	(A) Contract discharged—loss lies where it falls	(B1) Deposit used to pay for benefit received and contract is discharged
		(B2) Deposit is split to cover expenses and contract is discharged
		(B3) No benefit received and no costs incurred, deposit returned and contract is discharged

Other statutes also modify the common law application of the frustration principle. In common law, frustration does not apply to leases, but most jurisdictions have clearly stated that frustration applies to residential leases.[36] British Columbia extends the application of frustration to commercial leases as well. When goods are being sold, the *Sale of Goods Act* provides that if the goods, through no fault of the parties, perish before the risk passes to the purchaser, the contract is voided. The effect is that the contract is not binding on the purchaser, and any monies paid have to be returned.

Statutes may modify the impact of frustration

CASE SUMMARY 9.12

Reimbursement for Expenses Where Contract Is Frustrated: *Can-Truck Transportation Ltd. v. Fenton's Auto Paint Shop Ltd.*[37]

The plaintiff's truck was sent to the defendant for repairs after an accident. Repairs worth some $28 000 were completed when a fire destroyed both the shop and the truck, thus frustrating the repair contract. The Ontario *Frustrated Contracts Act* provided that when funds were paid (as with a deposit) or were payable before the frustrating event took place, they could be used to reimburse for expenses incurred. The Court found that payment for repairs was due prior to the fire, thus the plaintiff had to reimburse the company for the expenses it had incurred in repairing the vehicle even though the vehicle had been destroyed.

DISCUSSION QUESTIONS
Here the plaintiff's truck was destroyed, but it still had to pay for repairs notwithstanding the absence of benefit. Is there a better method for dealing with unforeseen events?

---

35. Such legislation exists in all common law provinces and territories with the exception of Nova Scotia: British Columbia, R.S.B.C. 1996, c. 166; Alberta, R.S.A. 2000, c. F-27; Saskatchewan, S.S. 1994, c. F-22.2; Manitoba, C.C.S.M. c. F190; Ontario, R.S.O. 1990, c. F.34; Newfoundland, R.S.N.L. 1990, c. F-26; Prince Edward Island, R.S.P.E.I. 1988, c. F-16; New Brunswick, R.S.N.B. 2011, c. 164; Yukon, R.S.Y. 2002, c. 96; Northwest Territories, R.S.N.W.T. 1988, c. F-12; Nunavut, R.S.N.W.T. (Nu) 1988, c. F-12.

36. See, for example, Alberta's *Residential Tenancies Act*, R.S.A. 2000 c. R-17.1, s. 40.

37. (1993) 101 D.L.R. (4th) 562 (Ont. C.A.).

LO ⑤ # REMEDIES FOR BREACH OF CONTRACT

Several examples of remedies provided to parties involved in contractual disputes have already been discussed. *Rescission* deals with problems with the formation of a contract and focuses on restoring the parties to their original position. *Rectification* interprets and corrects the terms of contracts, whereas *damages* compensate a victim who has been misled or pressured into the contract. The following discussion looks at remedies available where a party has failed to properly perform its obligations under the contract.

Damages

Damages in contract law are designed to compensate

Victim of breach is compensated as if contract had been properly performed

The most common remedy for a breach of contract is an order that the breaching party pay damages. Damages are amounts of money assessed by the court and designed to compensate victims for their losses. The object is to put the victim, as near as monetary compensation can, into the position he would have been in had the contract been properly performed.[38] Thus in contract law damages look forward, whereas in tort actions damages look backward and try to put the victim in the position he would have been in had the tort never taken place. For example, in a contract action, if a person bought defective paint from a supplier that blistered when put on the walls, necessitating repainting, the court would not only award the cost of the paint as damage, the court would also take into consideration the amount it would cost for a painter to scrape the blistered paint off and repaint the house. The court would then order the vendor to pay a sum sufficient to put the purchaser in the position he would have been in had the subject contract been properly performed.

CASE SUMMARY 9.13

Damages Cover Losses that Flow Naturally from Breach: *Ko v. Gill*[39]

The plaintiff, Ko, purchased a 1999 ML430 Mercedes Benz motor vehicle from the defendant on May 10, 2007, for $19 500. Five days later the plaintiff also paid $445 for the dealership's fee for facilitating the purchase together with the mechanical inspection fee. At the time of the purchase, neither party had any knowledge that the motor vehicle was a stolen vehicle.

The theft was discovered when Ko went to have his car serviced and attempted to have a second key made. It was revealed that the electronic vehicle information number (VIN) had been altered. The vehicle was subsequently seized and removed by Edmonton Police Services in January 2008. By then Ko had already incurred expenditures for various repairs and improvements totalling $6273. He sued, seeking reimbursement for the above sums, special damages of $5000 representing the expenses incurred for the use of rental transportation, and general damages of $10 000 for the loss of use and enjoyment of the motor vehicle.

In assessing damages, reference was made to the decision in *Wertheim v. Chicoutimi Pulp Co.*: "[I]t is the general intention of the law that, in giving damages for breach of contract, the party complaining should, so far as it can be done by money, be placed in the same position as he would have been in if the contract had been performed."[40]

---

38. See *Hamilton v. Open Window Bakery Ltd.*, [2004] 1 SCR 303, 2004 SCC 9 (CanLII), which confirms that where a party who has breached a contract had a variety of ways of fulfilling its obligations, damages will be based on the least expensive method of performance.

39. 2010 ABQB 247 (CanLII).

40. [1911] A.C. 301 at 307 (P.C.), www.bailii.org/uk/cases/UKPC/1910/1.html.

Thus, the plaintiff was entitled to recover the full purchase price of the vehicle since he bargained for title to the vehicle and did not receive it. As to later improvements and expenses, these consequential losses were limited by the principle of remoteness. The buyer's fee, vehicle inspection, repairs to the bumper, and purchase of new tires were all losses that flowed as a consequence of the failure of consideration. But the other expenses claimed, such as the deposit for a second key and purchase of an oil filter, did not represent losses that flowed naturally from the contractual breakdown; these were denied. Also denied was any award for general damages. Further, the claim for transportation rentals did not naturally arise from the contractual failure at hand; thus it too was disallowed.

Ultimately, Ko was awarded damages of $23 081.70 (representing the $19 500 purchase price, the $445.20 for the inspection and buyer's fee, and $3136.50 for the tires and bumper repairs) plus costs.

DISCUSSION QUESTIONS

The vendor unknowingly transferred a stolen car. Not only was he required to reimburse the purchase price, but the purchaser's after-purchase expenditures as well. What steps could a dealership take to prevent such an unfortunate event?

When the damages awarded are to cover specific costs and expenses they are called *special damages*, but when the funds awarded are an estimate of what has been lost or what will be lost they are called *general damages*. The calculation of damages may be based on the shortfall from what was expected with proper performance, so if a vendor fails to deliver goods damages may equal the purchaser's costs of securing such goods elsewhere. Sometimes damages are designed to cover what has been lost because reliance was placed on the performance of the contract, as where a supplier fails to deliver sufficient quantities and the purchaser (retailer) loses the profits she anticipated from their resale. Only in rare circumstances involving particularly vexatious conduct will courts award *punitive damages* for breach of contract.[41] Punitive damages are intended to punish the offending party rather than compensate the injured and may result in a considerably higher award.

Damages awarded may be special, general, or punitive

Limitations on Recoverable Damages

Although damages are designed to compensate a person for injuries suffered, not all losses are recoverable. Remoteness and mitigation are two limitations on the recoverability of damages. As well, the parties are free to place terms in the contract itself limiting the damages recoverable or specifying other courses of action in the event of breach.

Not all losses can be recovered

REMOTENESS

The important case of *Hadley v. Baxendale*[42] involved the shipping of a broken crankshaft from a steam engine to be used as a pattern for the manufacture of a new one. The shipper was asked to send it quickly but failed to do so. Unknown to the shipper, the plaintiff's entire plant was shut down during the wait for the crankshaft. This caused great expense to the plaintiff, who sued the shipper for lost profits. The shipper claimed that he could not be responsible for the unusual loss because he had no knowledge of it. The Court used the reasonable foreseeability test to determine the extent of the shipper's responsibility for damages and held that the shipper was responsible only for the usual damages that could be expected if the contract were breached. The shipper was thus not liable for the plaintiff's lost profits.

---

41. *Whiten v. Pilot Insurance Co.*, [2002] 1 SCR 595, 2002 SCC 18 (CanLII), has become a leading authority on punitive damages. In contract cases, punitive damages should not be awarded in the absence of an independent actionable wrong.

42. (1854), 156 E.R. 145 (Ex. Ct.), www.bailii.org/ew/cases/EWHC/Exch/1854/J70.html.

**Must pay reasonably
anticipated losses**

The principle that has developed from this and other cases is essentially that a breaching party is responsible only for those damages that, at the time the contract was entered into, seem a likely outcome if the contract were breached. Thus, the breaching party is responsible not only for the normally expected damages that flow from a breach, but also for any unusual damages resulting from special circumstances that were communicated to it at the time of the contract. In short, the breaching party is responsible in contract law for any damages that can be reasonably foreseen at the time the contract is entered into.

An area where the problem of remoteness often arises is in a claim for damages to compensate for lost profits. Applying this principle, the breaching party will be responsible only for the loss of ordinary profits that could have been expected given his knowledge of the business. In *Horne v. Midland Ry*,[43] the defendants were one day late in the delivery of a shipment of shoes, causing the merchant to lose an opportunity to sell the shoes at an exceptionally high price. The shipper knew only that the merchant would have to take the shoes back if they were late, not that an exceptional profit would be lost. The defendants were not responsible for the unusually high lost profit since they were not aware of those special circumstances, and such a loss was not reasonably foreseeable.

**General damages compensate
for economic loss and (recently)
for mental distress**

When a contract is breached, damages are awarded to compensate for economic losses. Courts have only recently shown a willingness to award monetary compensation for mental distress. These situations are generally limited to cases where some non-monetary benefit was the subject matter of the contract, such as a disrupted vacation or cruise.[44]

MITIGATION

**Victims must mitigate
their losses**

Victims of a breach are sometimes tempted to do nothing when a contract is breached, allowing damages to accumulate on the assumption that they are the responsibility of—and therefore will be paid by—the breaching party. This is bad practice for several reasons. Victims of breach have a duty to **mitigate** the damages, meaning they must do what they can to keep those damages as low as possible. Also, if they fail to mitigate or minimize losses, courts may actually make a deduction from damages equal to the amount attributable to the failure to mitigate.

**Failure to mitigate may result
in damages**

The failure to mitigate is a common problem in wrongful dismissal actions. A person who has been wrongfully dismissed has a right to sue but must make a reasonable effort to find other employment. If the employer can show that the dismissed employee failed to look for another job, the damages will be reduced by the amount she should have earned during that notice period. (See Chapter 12 for an expanded discussion of wrongful dismissal.)

**Reasonable costs associated
with mitigation are recoverable**

The obligation to mitigate means that the victim of the breach must take all reasonable steps to minimize the losses suffered, but that person is not required to take personal risks or to incur unreasonable expense in the process. Reasonable costs associated with mitigation, such as the cost of flying to another city to attend an interview, can be recovered from the breaching party.

CONTRACTUAL LIMITATIONS

Remedies set out in a contract

It is possible for a contract to set out the consequences in the event of breach and thus avoid the expense and drain of litigation. The consequences may be quite varied. The contract may call for mediation or arbitration to resolve disputes and determine compensation. The contract might state the maximum amount of compensation to be paid by the breaching party. Businesses often post signs indicating that they are not responsible for losses over a specified amount.

---

43. (1873), L.R. 8 C.P. 131 (C.P.).
44. *Jarvis v. Swan Tours Ltd.*, [1973] 1 All E.R. 71 (C.A.), www.bailii.org/ew/cases/EWCA/Civ/1972/8.html. Here the vacationer was awarded compensation for the loss of the enjoyment he had been promised. Awards in the travel industry are normally limited to the cost of the holiday or a portion thereof.

Failure to make an instalment payment will often trigger an **acceleration clause**, which makes the entire outstanding debt due and payable immediately. Where the contract involves a consumer transaction, the operation of acceleration clauses are often restricted by consumer protection legislation,[45] which will be further examined in Chapter 16.

When the contract specifies the amount of damages to be paid they are called **liquidated damages** and the courts will normally enforce such terms once liability has been determined. Where the amount is actually prepaid with the provision that the funds are to be forfeited in the event of a breach it is called a **deposit**. For example, to secure the purchase of an automobile, the vendor will usually require the buyer to pay a substantial deposit when ordering. If the purchaser fails to go through with the deal when the car arrives, the vendor can retain the deposit.

It is important to distinguish between deposits and down payments. Deposits are to be forfeited in the event of a breach, whereas a **down payment** is just the first payment and may have to be returned. Of course, from a practical point of view, once a down payment is made it may be used as a lever to force performance. But if the matter comes to trial, the court will order the return of the down payment, usually setting off the actual damages to be paid against it. Regardless of what the term is called, it is the provision requiring the forfeiture of the prepayment that will cause the court to treat it as a deposit.

The temptation to take a large deposit entails significant risk. To qualify as liquidated damages, a deposit must be an honest attempt by the parties to estimate the damages that would be suffered if the contract were breached. Too large a prepayment becomes an unreasonable penalty rather than liquidated damages and must be returned. A $1000 deposit on a new car might be fair in view of the cost of advertising, the time lost, the extra interest payments, and so on. But a $10 000 deposit on a $15 000 car is no longer an attempt to compensate for possible loss or injury and becomes an attempt to punish the breaching party for failure to go through with the contract.

A penalty clause, if excessive, is unconscionable and void. Such a penalty would have to be returned subject to an action to establish the actual loss. Thus, demanding too large a deposit defeats itself. Even when no prepayment is involved, a liquidated damages clause may be challenged if the amount involved is exorbitant and the object is to unreasonably punish rather than to compensate.

Liquidated damages are specified in a contract

Deposit is forfeited—down payment is not

Deposit must be reasonable to avoid becoming a penalty

CASE SUMMARY 9.14

Initial Instalment Intended as a Forfeitable Deposit:
Trilwood Investments Ltd. v. Bruce Agra Foods Inc.[46]

The defendant approached the plaintiffs seeking to purchase their shares in Sweet Ripe Drinks Ltd. Once the plaintiffs indicated a willingness to sell, things got difficult, with the defendant creating numerous delays. The initial offer was withdrawn, then the price was negotiated down by $7 million. The plaintiffs now doubted whether the purchaser was truly serious. After extended negotiations the parties entered into an agreement at a price of $21.7 million. In response to the plaintiffs' expressed concerns over the delay in arriving at a final agreement, the defendant agreed to pay $5.5 million (described in the agreement as the "initial instalment") as evidence of its good faith. The "initial instalment" was to be compensation to the vendor if the transaction did not close for "*inter alia* lost opportunity and expenses incurred in connection with the transaction."

---

45. See, for example, Alberta's *Fair Trading Act*, R.S.A. 2000, c. F-2, s. 71, which requires written notice of a default to be served on a borrower and the passage of 10 days from such service before the acceleration clause takes effect.
46. 1998 CanLII 14633 (ON SC).

Consent from the government of Nova Scotia to the change of control of Sweet Ripe Drinks Ltd. was a requirement of the share purchase agreement. The plaintiffs were to obtain consent and deliver it to the defendant on or before the date fixed for the closing of the transaction. Shortly before the transaction was to close, the majority owner of the defendant contacted the government officer responsible for issuing the consent, directing him not to send the consent. The official disregarded this intrusion and forwarded the consent; it was received by the plaintiffs' solicitors before closing. The defendant's majority owner, anticipating that the consent would not be received, terminated the agreement on that basis. The plaintiffs thus brought an action for a declaration that they were entitled to retain the $5.5 million as the initial instalment under the share purchase agreement.

The Court concluded that the defendant relied on the expected failure to deliver the consent in an attempt to terminate the agreement and then negotiate a lower price. It declared that the defendant had breached the share purchase agreement by refusing to close on the date and time specified. The $5.5 million was to be paid to the plaintiffs.

The trial judge reasoned that the parties were never in any doubt that the money being put up by the defendant was a non-refundable deposit. They regarded the sum as reasonable and agreed that it was subject to forfeit in the event that the transaction did not close through any breach on the part of the defendant. In the alternative, the trial judge held that the $5.5 million constituted liquidated damages. The amount and manner of payment were arrived at after substantial negotiations between sophisticated businesspeople and their legal representatives. The amount was fairly and reasonably pre-estimated and agreed upon, supporting the conclusion that the $5.5 million was to be forfeited following a breach by the defendant.

DISCUSSION QUESTIONS

It is unusual to see such a large sum declared to be a deposit, especially when it was labelled an initial instalment. What factors were material to the trial judge in his characterization of the large sum as a deposit or, alternatively, as liquidated damages? Did the questionable business practices of the defendant play a role?

Equitable Remedies

The following are examples of remedies that have been developed by the Court of Chancery to deal with special situations in which the ordinary remedy of damages would not be adequate. Note that these remedies are discretionary and will be granted only when the judge thinks it right and fair to do so.

SPECIFIC PERFORMANCE

Court orders defaulting party to perform its obligations if damages are not suitable or adequate

Specific performance occurs when the court orders the defaulting party to live up to the terms of the contract. Where a land developer signs agreements to buy several adjacent properties, and one property owner refuses to go through with the deal, it would be appropriate to obtain a court order for specific performance. The developer won't be assisted by an award of damages if its goal is to build a shopping centre on the total parcel; it wants the court to order that property owner to transfer the property at the agreed-upon price. But if the same developer ordered a number of new trucks from a dealer who then refused to deliver them, specific performance would not be appropriate as equivalent vehicles could be obtained elsewhere. The appropriate remedy would be damages, and they would be assessed on the basis of the extra cost of getting the vehicles from another dealer. Only if the trucks were *unique* and not available from some other source might specific performance be available.

Courts will not force performance of contracts for personal services

The courts will not order the defaulting party to perform a contract that requires personal service. If the above developer were to contract with a famous performer to sing at a concert celebrating the opening of the shopping centre and the performer then refused to perform, the court would not order specific performance. Similarly, the courts will not award specific performance as a remedy in any situation that would require close supervision to ensure that the contract is properly performed. Nor will specific performance be available where it would hurt a third party.

On the theory that all land is unique, the courts in the past have been willing to award specific performance whenever parties to a purchase of land breach their contract. The Supreme Court of Canada has indicated, however, that contracts dealing with the purchase of land will now be treated like any other contract, limiting the availability of specific performance to those situations where damages are inappropriate.[47]

Specific performance only available if damages are inappropriate

---

CASE SUMMARY 9.15

Specific Performance Ordered Despite Presence of Deposit Clauses: *Romfo v. 1216393 Ontario Inc.*[48]

The vendors of several lots appealed an order of specific performance, which demanded that the sales proceed. The prices of these lots had increased substantially, and the vendors made deals with new purchasers to sell the lots at the higher prices. The vendors argued that since the initial contracts contained deposit clauses, stipulating that if a party breached the contract the deposit would be forfeited, the purchasers would have to be content with the return of their respective deposits. In other words, the vendors argued damages were limited by these "liquidated damages" clauses to the deposits paid earlier.

In dismissing the appeal, the Court of Appeal stated that the parties to the contract could not have intended the deposit clauses to apply where the vendors deliberately deceived the purchasers. By holding onto the deposits while they applied for development approval and then breaching the contracts once approval was granted, the vendors had acted with deception. The deposit clauses were severed and the contracts were enforced. The vendors were required to transfer the lots to the initial purchasers at the initial price.

SMALL BUSINESS PERSPECTIVE

Here the vendors fundamentally breached the contracts for self-serving reasons. In light of the vendors' questionable conduct, the purchasers were not restricted to seeking damages. This case demonstrates that equitable remedies may be granted to parties who come to the courts with "clean hands."

INJUNCTION

Specific performance involves a court order to do something (to perform the contract), whereas an **injunction** usually involves an order to refrain from some offensive conduct. In the example involving personal service by a singer, the court would not order the performer to fulfill the contract by singing at the concert; but the aggrieved party may be able to secure an injunction preventing the performer from performing somewhere else on the day he was to sing at the shopping centre's concert. The granting of an injunction is not limited to contractual disputes; it may be available in any situation in which wrongful conduct is involved.

In rare circumstances the courts may issue a mandatory injunction when a person does something to violate a contractual term and thereby creates an ongoing problem. Striking workers involved in an illegal work stoppage are often ordered to stop breaching their contract and return to work. Another example might involve a

Courts may order breaching conduct to stop . . .

---

47. *Semelhago v. Paramadevan*, [1996] 2 SCR 415, 1996 CanLII 209 (SCC).
48. [2008] B.C.J. No. 745 (B.C.C.A.).

party that erects signs exceeding the permitted height limit set out in a restrictive covenant or a municipal bylaw. The courts may order the violator to remove the sign or reduce it to the permitted height.

As with specific performance, there are many instances in which the courts will refuse to issue an injunction. The courts are reluctant to order an injunction that would make it impossible for the person defaulting on the contractual agreement to earn a living. A court might well enforce, by injunction, a term requiring an employee not to work for a competitor for three years upon leaving, but would not enforce a term preventing that employee from working for anyone for three years. Similarly, the courts will not issue an injunction when damages provide a sufficient remedy. An injunction is designed not to punish someone for breaching a contract but to prevent further injury. An injunction will also not be awarded where it will cause harm to a third party.

An injunction is sometimes ordered even before there has been a trial on the issues. If an employee leaves and works for a competitor, it is important to get an injunction right away and sort out the merits of the dispute later. This is called an **interlocutory injunction** and is issued by the court when some ongoing injury will increase the damage done to the person seeking the interlocutory injunction. When waiting for the trial to determine the matter is unacceptable, granting an interlocutory injunction becomes the preferable alternative.

ACCOUNTING

It is often difficult for the victim of a breach to determine just what kind of injuries she has suffered, especially when the offending party has taken advantage of some opportunities or rights belonging to the victim. This can happen when there is a fiduciary relationship between the contracting parties, that is, a relationship in which the person breaching the contract has a duty to act in the best interests of the other party. In these circumstances, the court can order that the defaulting party disclose all financial dealings and records so that the injured party can determine what she is entitled to claim. This is called an **accounting** or **accounting for profits.** In some circumstances the court will then order the offending party to pay over to the injured party all or a portion of the profits made from the wrongful conduct. So the court, instead of awarding damages on the basis of what has been lost by the victim, awards damages on the basis of what has been wrongfully obtained by the breaching party.

QUANTUM MERUIT

In some situations the contract is breached when only part of the work has been done and before the amount agreed to in the contract is due and payable to the injured party. In these circumstances the courts have the power to award compensation for the value of work that has been done on the basis of *quantum meruit.* As discussed in Chapter 6, *quantum meruit* is the principle that allows the supplier of a service to collect a reasonable fee, even when no price had been agreed upon. Note that only the victim of the breach can claim compensation on the basis of *quantum meruit.* The courts are extremely reluctant to grant any compensation for the breaching party's partial performance of the agreement, unless the contractual obligations have been substantially performed. Sometimes partial payment is payable before completion, and in that case even the breaching party can collect.

If a contractor has agreed to build a house with payment due upon completion of the job and refuses to continue after completing half, he will not be successful in claiming compensation for what he has done. He should finish the job. Only where the contract called for partial payments at different stages of completion will the breaching party be able to collect those payments due before the breach. But if he has finished half the project and the owner of the property with whom he has contracted refuses to let him continue, the contractor, being the innocent party, will be able to claim compensation for the work that has been done under the principle of *quantum meruit.*

... but not where a person can no longer earn a living

... or where damages are more appropriate

... or where it would hurt a third party

An interlocutory injunction is issued before the trial

Court may order an accounting and require profits to be paid over

Court may order payment for part performance

Some general requirements must be met before the courts will grant an equitable remedy. If there has been **laches**, an undue delay on the part of the person seeking the equitable remedy, the courts can refuse to grant the remedy. The plaintiff will still be able to pursue any common law remedy, such as damages, without penalty for delay—provided the action is brought within the limitation period. The courts can also refuse to award an equitable remedy in any situation in which it would cause undue hardship to the parties or to some other person or would be inappropriate for any other reason. A person seeking equity must come to the court with clean hands, meaning the remedy will be denied when the person seeking the equitable remedy is also guilty of some wrongdoing. These requirements apply to all equitable remedies.

Equitable remedies are discretionary

• **unavailable if hardship caused**

• **only available if claimant applies with clean hands**

• **unavailable if claim is unduly delayed**

CASE SUMMARY 9.16

Equitable Remedies Are Not Always Available: *Island Properties Ltd. v. Entertainment Enterprises Ltd.*[49]

The vendors arranged to sell property through one real estate agent and then made similar arrangements with another. Two different purchasers acting through the two different agents accepted the offer to sell. When the property was transferred to Pegasus, Island Properties, which had accepted first, sued for specific performance.

The trial judge ordered that the property be returned and transferred to Island Properties, but that decision was reversed on appeal. Pegasus was a completely innocent third party, and an equitable remedy cannot be given where it will cause harm to such an innocent party. Island Properties was thus limited to a remedy of damages for breach.

SMALL BUSINESS PERSPECTIVE
This case illustrates the limitations placed on equitable remedies. Even when one's action is successful, the preferred remedy may not be available.

Another factor that may affect the right of the victim of a breach of contract to obtain any remedy is the limitations legislation discussed in Chapter 3. The limitation periods outlined in these statutes apply to any action brought to court, including contract claims, with the result that once the limitation period has expired, none of the remedies discussed in this chapter will be available to the victim of the breach.

Finally, it should be noted that when a judgment or an equitable remedy has been awarded and a defendant refuses to comply, the defendant may be held in contempt of court and can be jailed for contempt, although this is extremely unlikely. The remedies to enforce a judgment, which were outlined generally in Chapter 3, are available to the victim of a breach of contract as well.

Expiry of limitation period may preclude remedies from being available

Refusal to comply with judgment may constitute contempt of court

---

Be sure to visit the MyBusLawLab that accompanies this book to find practice quizzes, province-specific content, simulations and much more!

---

49. 1986 CanLII 2426 (NL CA).

SUMMARY

Discharge of contracts

- Can come to an end through performance, breach, agreement, or frustration

Discharge by performance

- Substantial performance may discharge a contract unless exact performance is required
- When performance is properly tendered but refused, contract may be discharged
- When payment is tendered but refused, the creditor must bear the cost of its collection

Discharge by breach

- Breached condition—the victim may treat the contract as discharged and sue
- Breached warranty—contract is still binding but the victim can sue for damages
- Anticipatory breach—victim can treat the contract as discharged immediately or wait for performance (and later sue) but is bound by her choice

Discharge by agreement

- Contract may provide for its own end; the agreed-upon method for termination is effective in ending the contract
- Condition precedent—obligations to perform arise if the condition is fulfilled
- Condition subsequent—obligations exist and continue until the condition is fulfilled
- Liquidated damages—parties may agree in advance as to sum payable in event of breach
- Deposit, if forfeitable, is regarded as liquidated damages

Discharge by frustration

- Frustration occurs when performance is impossible or fundamentally changed
- Monies advanced may be apportioned to compensate for expenses or losses incurred
- Self-induced frustration is a breach of contract

Remedies

- Damages paid to compensate the victim
- Damages limited to what was reasonably foreseeable
- Damages must be reduced or mitigated by the victim
- Deposits or liquidated damages set out in contract must be reasonable or they will be treated as a penalty provision—courts do not enforce penalty clauses
- Specific performance requires the breaching party to fulfill the agreement
- Injunction—a court order to stop conduct that breaches the contract
- Accounting—requires disclosure of information so the other party can assess the extent of damages
- *Quantum meruit*—an equitable remedy requiring payment of a fair sum equal to what the goods or services are reasonably worth

QUESTIONS FOR REVIEW

1. Describe the various ways in which a contractual relationship can come to an end.

2. Under what circumstances would a breaching party who had partially performed the terms of the contract be entitled to receive part payment?

3. Describe the differences between a condition and a warranty. Why is the distinction significant?

4. When might the victim of a breach of a condition lose the right to treat the contract as discharged?

5. What constitutes adequate tender of performance?

6. What recourse is available to one party to a contract when performance is made impossible by the other party's conduct?

7. What options are available to the victim of an anticipatory breach? Explain the advantages, disadvantages, and risks associated with these options.

8. What is an exemption clause? When might an exemption clause be unenforceable?

9. What is meant by fundamental breach? What remedy is available to the victim of a fundamental breach of contract?

10. Assume the defendant claims that the contract was discharged or modified by agreement; the plaintiff challenges this conclusion and seeks to enforce the original contract. What will the defendant need to prove to avoid having the initial contract enforced?

11. Explain what happens when a creditor agrees to take less than is owed to settle a debt.

12. How do conditions precedent differ from conditions subsequent?

13. Define frustration. List three ways in which frustration can take place.

14. What is the significance of a court's determination that a contract was frustrated through the fault of one of the parties?

15. Explain how the *Fibrosa* case and subsequent statute law have modified the previously accepted common law rule on the obligations of the parties in the face of a frustrating event.

16. Distinguish between a deposit and a down payment. What is the significance of this distinction?

17. What must be shown for the court to conclude that money paid ought to be categorized as a deposit?

18. In light of the decision in *Hadley v. Baxendale*, how is the recovery of damages limited?

19. Describe what is meant by mitigation. Explain how the obligation to mitigate damages limits the ability of the victim of a breach to obtain damages.

20. Distinguish between specific performance and injunction. Explain the restrictions on their availability.

CASES AND DISCUSSION QUESTIONS

1. *Betker v. Williams*, [1991] B.C.J. No. 3724 (C.A.); 1991 CanLII 1160
Williams owned property in Cranbrook and listed the property for sale with Klinkhammer, a real estate agent. It was advertised as a residential lot in the local newspaper, with a clear indication that a house could be built on it. Betker bought the property after specifically asking Klinkhammer if it would be appropriate for a solar home and receiving a positive reply. Four years after the sale, the Betkers discovered that a house could not be built on the property because it was too small for a septic tank and had no access to the city sewer line.

It turned out that neither Williams nor the real estate agent were aware of this problem. The Betkers brought an action against the agents and Williams. There was a term in the agreement stating that there were no representations other than those contained on the written agreement itself, but this provision had not been specifically brought to the attention of the purchasers.

Explain the arguments available to both parties. Were representations made that were subsequently relied upon? Must a party who wishes to limit its liability have to bring those limitations to the attention of the opposite party? What remedies might be sought by the purchaser in this case?

2. *Teleflex Inc. v. I.M.P. Group Ltd.*, (1996), 149 N.S.R. (2d) 355 (NS CA); 1996 CanLII 5603

Teleflex Inc., an American company manufacturing aircraft components, knew that I.M.P. Group Ltd. was negotiating with the Brazilian government to carry out a program for the turbinization of its Tracker aircraft fleet. Teleflex offered to supply necessary parts, to which proposal I.M.P. responded with a purchase order for 13 quadrant assembly sets at $27 500 each. The shipping schedule was to commence in March 1990. Included was a provision whereby I.M.P. could order a suspension of the work with a reasonable price adjustment, and a further provision whereby I.M.P. could terminate the order with payment to Teleflex for both completed and uncompleted work, according to a formula that factored in lost profits. Thereafter, Teleflex commenced manufacturing the quadrant assembly units.

In September 1989, Teleflex received the first of a series of notices from I.M.P. requesting postponement of delivery of the units. Teleflex acknowledged receipt of these stop-work letters, advising that in the event of termination its termination liability schedule "attached to our original proposal will apply." I.M.P. continued to experience difficulties in closing the deal with the Brazilian government and finally, in 1994, indicated it would not be requiring fulfillment of the purchase order.

Teleflex treated this as a termination notice and advised I.M.P. that it would submit a termination claim based on work performed to date. The claim amounted to US$229 576 for materials, overhead, and profit. I.M.P. countered that no monies were payable because the contract had been frustrated by the Brazilian government, and further, no quadrant assembly units were ever delivered by Teleflex.

Based on these facts, was the contract frustrated? Is any money payable to Teleflex? What factors affect your conclusion?

3. *Meunier v. Cloutier*, 1984 CanLII 1929 (ON SC)

Cloutier returned to Timmins and purchased a hotel only a block away from the one he had sold to Meunier four years earlier. In doing so, he violated a non-competition clause prohibiting him from participating in the hotel business in Timmins for five years following the sale to Meunier. The original contract required him to pay $50 000 for such a breach as liquidated damages, and Meunier brought this action to recover that amount.

Assume that the plaintiff, Meunier, has not provided any evidence of economic loss. What factors will the court consider in light of Cloutier's argument that the clause was a penalty and should not be enforced? When is a non-competition clause unenforceable?

4. *652013 B.C. Ltd. v. Kim*, [2006] O.J. No. 423 (Ont. S.C.J.); 2006 CanLII 2892

The defendant rented six illuminated signs from the plaintiff. Upset that one of the signs was illuminated only sporadically, the defendant stopped payment. Later the defendant also complained that one of the signs was obstructed by trees. After repeated demands for payment, the plaintiff sued. The lease agreement contained an acceleration clause, so the plaintiff claimed the accelerated amount owing under the lease. The plaintiff established that the cause for the interrupted illumination was beyond its control—the power supply was not its responsibility. The acceleration clause, when applied, resulted in an effective rate of interest of 26.8 percent.

Should the plaintiff recover judgment for the accelerated amount? What facts are relevant and what further facts would one need to predict the outcome of this case?

10 Chapter

Agency and Partnership

LEARNING OBJECTIVES

1. Describe the agency relationship, outlining the rights and responsibilities of agents and principals

2. Distinguish between actual authority and apparent authority of agents

3. Explain fiduciary duty and describe when it arises

4. Distinguish the three types of business organization used in Canada, focusing on the method of creation and the rights and obligations of partners specific to each type

5. List the characteristics of a sole proprietorship and explain why sole proprietors face unlimited liability

6. Outline the advantages and disadvantages of operating a business through a partnership, and describe the processes of dissolving partnerships

The subject of agency is a vital component in any discussion of business law. The legal consequences that stem from an agency relationship are of utmost concern to businesspeople because at least one of the parties in most commercial transactions is functioning as an agent. Agency law is the basis of the law of partnership, and an understanding of it is essential for coming to terms with corporate law. Agency and partnership are dealt with in this chapter, and corporations will be the topic of the following chapter.

An agent's function is to represent and act on behalf of a principal in dealings with third parties. Although by far the most common example of agents representing principals is in the creation of contracts, agents also find themselves involved in other types of legal relationships. Real estate agents and professionals such as lawyers and accountants often represent clients where their actions have legal ramifications but where they don't enter contracts on their behalf. The term **agency** refers to the service an agent performs on behalf of the principal. This service may be performed as an employee, as an independent agent, or gratuitously. When an agent is acting independently, the business performing the service is often called an *agency*, such as a travel agency, employment agency, or real estate agency.

What follows focuses on the law of agency generally, and in most cases no distinction will be made between people functioning as agents as part of an employment contract and those acting independently. Note that where employees also act as agents of the employer, their duties and obligations as agents go far beyond the employment relationship and must be understood as a separate function or set of obligations. But keep in mind: Not all employees are agents.

Agency refers to a service performed by an agent

An agent represents and acts for a principal

CASE SUMMARY 10.1

Liability of Principal for Agent's Fraud: *Mignault et al. v. Palmer et al.*[1]

Palmer acted for Great-West Life Assurance Company (GWL) in selling life insurance products to customers. In the contract between Palmer and GWL, Palmer was clearly identified as an independent contractor and later this relationship was changed to a broker. As part of his agency function, he acted for the Mignaults, assisting them to transfer several investment vehicles into GWL products. Later he persuaded the Mignaults and several other clients to cash out their GWL investments and transfer the money to his company (J. D. Raleigh & Company Ltd.) for further investment at a more attractive interest rate. In fact, he used these funds for personal living expenses and to further his own business activities. He led the Mignaults and the other clients to believe these new investments were also GWL investments.

Palmer was convicted of fraud and at the time of this action was in jail. In this action the Mignaults are suing GWL, claiming that they are vicariously liable for the fraud of their agent, Palmer. The Court agreed. Palmer may have been an independent agent, but he worked out of the GWL offices and all of the documentation involved referred to Palmer as their agent. GWL had held out Palmer as their agent and was therefore vicariously liable for the fraud committed by him on the basis of vicarious liability.

DISCUSSION QUESTION

Great-West Life tried to have it both ways. They tried to separate themselves from their representatives to avoid this kind of liability, but then they did all they could to create the impression that the representatives were working for GWL in their dealings with clients. As a result, they found themselves liable for the actions of their representative. Do you think imposing liability in these circumstances places too great a burden on companies like GWL?

LO ❶ # THE AGENCY RELATIONSHIP

The agency relationship can be created by an express or implied contract, by estoppel, by ratification, or gratuitously, the key element being the granting of **authority**.

Formation by Contract

Agency relationship is usually created through contract

Usually, an agency relationship is created through a contract (an **agency agreement**) between the agent and the principal; thus, general contract rules apply. This should not be confused with the contracts agents enter into on behalf of their principals. The agency contract can cover such things as the authority of the agent, the duties to be performed, and the nature of payment to be received (Figure 10.1). It may be embedded in a contract of employment, or the contract may create a more independent relationship between principal and agent. Generally, there are no formal requirements for the creation of such a contract, although putting it in writing is a wise practice and may be required under certain statutes such as the *Bills of*

Figure 10.1 The Agency Agreement

Principal: Grants actual and implied authority

→

Agency Agreement

←

Agent: Agrees to act on behalf of principal

[1.] 2013 MBQB 300 (CanLII).

Exchange Act.[2] When an agency agreement is in writing and under seal it is called a **power of attorney**, although the seal is no longer required in most provincial *Powers of Attorney Acts.*[3] Refer to MyBusLawLab for details. These Acts also provide for the creation of enduring powers of attorney, which will be discussed later in this chapter.

All the elements of a contract, such as consensus, consideration, legality, intention to be bound, and capacity on the part of both parties, must be present for an agency agreement to be binding. The lack of any one of these elements may void the agency contract, but that will not affect the binding nature of any agreement the agent enters into on behalf of the principal. An underage agent may not be bound by his agreement with the principal, but any contracts he enters into with authority on the principal's behalf will still be binding on that principal, unless of course the agent is so young or insane that he doesn't understand what he is doing. Similarly, when an agent is acting gratuitously the resulting contract can be binding on the principal. Only consent in the form of authorization by the principal is required.

Still, most agency relationships are based on contract, either expressly entered into by the parties or implied from their conduct. Often, these are simply employment contracts.

> **Basic rules of contract apply to agency contracts**
>
> **Consent is the only essential requirement of agency**

AUTHORITY OF AGENTS

LO **2**

Many disputes that arise in agency relate to the extent of the authority of the agent in dealing with third parties. An agent's authority can be derived from the principal in several ways.

Actual Authority

The authority specifically given by the principal to the agent and usually set out in the agency agreement is called the agent's **actual authority**. This actual authority may be *expressly* stated by the principal (**express authority**) or *implied* from the circumstances (**implied authority**). A person who is hired as a purchasing agent has the authority by implication to carry out the customary and traditional responsibilities of purchasing agents. Of course, if the principal has specifically stated that the agent does not have certain powers no such authority is implied. Still, even where actual (express or implied) authority is absent, there may be apparent authority.

> **Actual authority can be express or implicit**

Any written agency agreement should carefully set out the authority of the agent, eliminating, as far as possible, the need for any implied authority. An agent who exceeds this actual authority may be liable to the principal for any injury caused by her conduct. But no matter how much care is used in drafting an agent's actual authority, the principal may still be bound by the agent's conduct that falls within her apparent authority.

Apparent Authority: Authority Created by Estoppel

When a principal does something by conduct or words to lead a third party to believe that an agent has authority, the principal is bound by the agent's actions regardless of whether there is actual authority or not. Even when the principal has specifically prohibited the agent from doing what he did, the principal may still be bound because of the agent's **apparent authority**. This is an application of the principle of estoppel. **Estoppel** is an equitable remedy that stops a party from trying to establish a position or deny something that, if allowed, would create an injustice. It would not be fair if a principal could say to a third party, "George has authority to act for me," and then later be able to deny it and escape liability for George's actions. In these circumstances, estoppel applies. If the principal has held out the

> **Apparent authority is presumed from the words or actions of the principal**
>
> **Estoppel applies when the principal indicates that the agent has authority**

---

2. R.S.C. 1985, c. B-4.
3. For example, see the *Powers of Attorney Act*, R.S.O. 1990, c. P.20.

agent to have authority even if no such authority has been granted, the principal is bound. If a third party has relied on this representation, the principal cannot then claim that the agent had no authority.

It is important not to confuse this principle of estoppel with promissory estoppel, as described in Chapter 6. **Promissory estoppel**, sometimes referred to as **equitable estoppel**, involves a promise or commitment to do something in the future. When considering an agent's apparent authority, we are dealing not with a promise but with a claim or a statement of fact made by the principal.

Agent acting on apparent authority will bind the principal

Although the principal may look to the agent for compensation, so long as that agent has acted within her apparent authority, the principal is bound in contract with the third party. If Pedersen employed Mohammed as sales manager of his used car dealership, it would be reasonable for customers to assume that Mohammed had the authority to sell cars and take trade-ins. If after receiving instructions from Pedersen not to accept trades over $2000 without his express approval Mohammed were to give Kim a $5000 trade-in for a 2005 Mercedes, Pedersen would still be bound by the deal. Pedersen put Mohammed in that position, and the agent acted within his apparent authority as sales manager. The contract with Kim would be binding on the principal because of the agent's apparent authority. If, however, the agent had sold Kim the entire car lot, this would be beyond both his actual and apparent authority and would not be binding on Pedersen.

Previous acceptance of agent's actions

Actions of principal create apparent authority

A principal can also be bound by the actions of an agent that would normally be beyond the agent's authority if the principal has sanctioned similar actions in the past. If Kim's chauffeur, Green, had been allowed to buy several cars for Kim from the dealer, Pedersen, in the past, he would have the apparent authority to purchase another one. Even if Kim specifically told him he could no longer do so, if he bought another car the contract would be binding on Kim because of that apparent authority. The existence of this apparent authority is based on the statements and conduct of the principal, not the agent. When the misleading indication of authority comes from the agent rather than the principal, and the action is otherwise unauthorized, the third party will have no claim against the principal.

Reasonable person test is used to determine existence of authority

The **reasonable person test** has a significant role to play in determining the existence of apparent authority. The usual authority associated with the position of an agent is based on this test. The reasonable person test is also used to determine whether the third party was misled by the statements and conduct of the principal into believing that the agent had authority.

Case Summary 10.2 is a good illustration of apparent authority. It shows how important it is, for public and private institutions alike, to carefully define the authority of those acting for them and then take steps to ensure that their agents act within those boundaries.

CASE SUMMARY 10.2

When Is It Reasonable to Conclude Authority Exists?
Gooderham v. Bank of Nova Scotia[4]

The *Gooderham* case demonstrates how apparent authority can result in a principal being bound by the actions of its agent. Gooderham and her husband (now deceased) went to the Bank of Nova Scotia for a $55000 mortgage. They filled in an application for mortgage insurance, but the bank failed to forward it to Canada Life, the insurer. Had the bank done so, Canada Life would have denied coverage because of Mr. Gooderham's poor health. Still, the bank collected premiums until Mr. Gooderham died, at which time Canada Life denied coverage.

---

4. 2000 CanLII 22344 (ON SC), 47 OR (3d) 554.

> Mrs. Gooderham sued and the Court awarded judgment to her, concluding that the bank, through its employee, had apparent authority to represent Canada Life. The bank had the application forms supplied by Canada Life and supplied them to the Gooderhams. The bank, on behalf of Canada Life, sought out prospective policy holders, assisted in completing the applications for insurance, supplied rate information, accepted premiums, forwarded the money and forms to Canada Life, and was paid for this service by Canada Life. Given these factors it was reasonable for the Gooderhams to assume that the bank had authority to represent the insurer.

DISCUSSION QUESTION

Do you think this was enough to find Canada Life liable for the negligence of the bank's employees?

To determine whether a principal is bound in contract with a third party by the actions of an agent, a person must first ask, "Was the agent acting within the actual authority given by the principal?" If the answer is yes, then there is a contract, provided all the other elements are present. If the answer is no, then the question to ask is "Did the principal do anything to lead the third party to believe that the agent had the authority to act?" In other words, was the agent acting with apparent authority? If the answer is yes and the third party relied on that apparent authority, there is a contract between the principal and the third party. It is only when the answer to both these questions is no that there is no contract and the third party must look to the agent for redress.

Was the action of the agent authorized by the principal?

Most people find it difficult to understand the difference between implied and apparent authority, and in most cases the distinction is not important. But to clarify, when a principal has specifically stated that the agent does not have authority, no authority can be implied. In spite of such a declaration, however, there may still be apparent authority because of the principal's comments or conduct in relation to the third party. Where the principal has led the third party to believe that the agent has authority because of the principle of estoppel, the principal cannot deny that fact.

Ratification

A principal can still ratify a contract even if the agent has acted beyond both actual and apparent authority. The first time Kim's chauffeur bought a car on Kim's behalf, there would likely have been no apparent authority, since this is not normally a chauffeur's job. If Kim liked the car, however, she could ratify the contract and the deal would be binding on the dealer. The effect of such **ratification** is to give the agent authority to act on behalf of the principal retroactive to the time of the sale. The result can seem unfair because the principal is not bound when an agent goes beyond the authority given, but if the principal chooses to ratify, the third party is bound and can do nothing to change that.

If the principal ratifies an unauthorized contract, it is binding

In fact, the power of the principal to ratify must meet the following qualifications:

1. The third party has the right to set a reasonable time limit within which the ratification must take place. In the case of a chauffeur buying a car without authority, the dealer might say, for example, "You have until noon tomorrow to decide." Where no specific time limit was set, the power to ratify would expire after a reasonable time.

Third party can set a time for ratification

2. The agent can't make the deal and then search for a principal to ratify it. He must have indicated to the third party that he was acting for a specific stated principal, and that principal must be the one ratifying for the third party to be bound by it.

Agent must have been acting for a specific principal

3. The principal has to be fully capable of entering into the contract at the time the agent was claiming to act on her behalf. If the principal was drunk or insane at the time the agent acted on her behalf she cannot ratify that action.

Principal must be capable of entering into a contract . . .

• when it is entered into

Often promoters will enter into a contract on behalf of a corporation before that company is actually incorporated. Such a pre-incorporation contract cannot be ratified since the company did not exist at the time the agent acted for it. Legislation in some jurisdictions has modified this principle to allow a corporation to ratify such pre-incorporation contracts.[5]

• when it is ratified

4. The parties must still be able to perform the object of the contract at the time of the ratification. For example, if an agent without authority enters into a contract on behalf of a principal to insure a building against fire, the principal cannot ratify the agreement after a fire. Furthermore, the contract the agent enters into must not make any reference to the need for ratification. If the contract includes such terms as "subject to principal's approval" or "subject to ratification" it becomes merely an agreement to enter into an agreement. The contractual requirement of consensus is not satisfied, and there is no contract.

Ratification can take place inadvertently

Ratification is a two-edged sword and can work against the principal. The principal can inadvertently ratify by knowingly accepting some sort of benefit under the agreement or otherwise acting in a way consistent with the existence of the contract. Case Summary 10.3 is an example of such ratification by conduct.

CASE SUMMARY 10.3

Ratification by Conduct: *Selta International Trade Inc. v. Duboff, Edwards, Haight & Schachter*[6]

Selta International Trade Inc. (Selta) was a client of Duboff, Edwards, Haight & Schachter (Duboff), a law firm that held $300 000 in trust for Selta. Murphy was a business associate of Lysenko, the principal shareholder of Selta. He presented a power of attorney purportedly authorized by Lysenko and instructed Duboff to disburse the $300 000 to him, which was done. In fact, Lysenko had not authorized the power of attorney and sued for the return of the $300 000.

Lysenko, Murphy, and Duboff had a history of dubious investment schemes involving Nigerian companies and obsolete gold bonds (various gold bonds from several defunct railways and prewar Germany). It was with respect to the purchase of these gold bonds that the $300 000 was used. The facts were complicated, but on the evidence it was clear that the alleged power of attorney was not authorized and the funds were disbursed without actual or apparent authority. What makes the case interesting is that the lower court decided that the subsequent conduct of Lysenko confirmed the deal. There was no formal ratification, but the conduct of the parties over the following 15 months made it clear that Lysenko was acting as though the transfer had been authorized. This included all three businessmen trying to resell the bonds purchased with the funds, which constituted ratification by conduct. Therefore, Selta's action for the $300 000 failed.

However, Selta's second claim for $30 000 against the law firm did succeed. Lysenko had been persuaded by Duboff to invest the funds in a business (Mr. Tube Steak), but he failed to advise Lysenko that the business was also a client of the law firm. This created a conflict of interest. Duboff should have advised Lysenko to obtain independent legal advice, and his failure to do so amounted to breach of fiduciary duty.

This case is not only a good example of a breach of fiduciary duty but an excellent illustration of inadvertent ratification of an agent's authority to act.

---

5. For example, see the Canada *Business Corporations Act*, R.S.C. 1985, c. C-44, s. 14.

6. 2005 MBCA 137 (CanLII).

Agency by Necessity

In the past, when communications were less reliable, authority was sometimes implied on the basis of **agency by necessity**. For example, an agent might have to sell deteriorating goods to preserve some value for the principal. If the cargo of a ship gets wet, the shipper may be required to have it sold en route, often without getting authorization from the principal. In these circumstances, authority arises on the basis of necessity. Today, with instantaneous forms of communication, it will be rare for an agency by necessity to arise.

In the past, it was also common for a spouse to have the apparent authority to bind his partner for the purchase of necessities even after separation. Today this depends on the legislation in place in the jurisdiction involved, as some provinces have modified or abolished this obligation.[7]

> *Agency by necessity is rarely used today*

REDUCING RISK 10.1

A businessperson who deals through an agent runs a risk of that agent entering into contracts that are not authorized. Whether this is done by mistake or intentionally, the effect on the businessperson can be significant. To avoid the problem, the sophisticated client acting as principal should make the limits of that authority absolutely clear to the agent. Those limitations should be stipulated in a written agency agreement. The principal should also, where practical, make the limits of the agent's authority clear to the customers or third parties with whom that agent will deal. Customers should also be notified immediately upon the termination of that agent's authority, otherwise it will continue because of the principle of apparent authority. Also, great care should be taken in choosing just who to authorize as your agent. Businesspeople generally understand how important it is to vet potential employees, lawyers, and other professionals acting on their behalf. It is just as important to carefully select anyone who will be acting as an independent agent or otherwise representing the company.

THE RIGHTS AND RESPONSIBILITIES OF THE PARTIES

LO ❸

The Agent's Duties

THE CONTRACT

When an agency agreement has been created by contract, the agent has an obligation to act within the actual authority given in that agreement. An agent violating the contract but exercising apparent authority can be sued for breach and will have to compensate the principal for any losses suffered. Failure on the part of the agent to fulfill any other obligation set out in the agreement will also constitute an actionable breach of contract unless the specified act is illegal or against public policy.

> *Agent owes duty of reasonable care*

An agent owes a duty of care to the principal. The agent must not only have the skills and expertise claimed but also must exercise that skill in a reasonable manner. For example, if Khan hires Gamboa to purchase property on which to build an apartment building, and Gamboa fails to discover that the property he finds is not zoned for that use, he would likely be liable to compensate Khan for any loss caused by his mistake. Gamboa's conduct fell below the standard of reasonable performance one would expect from someone in this type of business.

Agents often have considerable discretion in carrying out agency responsibilities as long as they act to the benefit of the principal. However, an agent cannot go against the specific instructions received, even if it might be in the principal's best interests to do so. If a stockbroker is instructed to sell shares when they reach a specific price, the broker must do so even though waiting would bring the principal a better price.

> *Agent must perform as required by the principal*

DELEGATION

Agent cannot delegate responsibility

Generally, the agent has an obligation to perform the agency agreement personally. An agent is not permitted to delegate responsibility to another party unless there is consent to such **delegation**, either express or implied by the customs and traditions of the industry. Even then the primary agent has the responsibility to see that the terms of the agency agreement are fulfilled. The authority of an agent is commonly delegated to subagents when that agent is a corporation or large business organization, such as a law firm, bank, real estate agency, or trust company.

FIDUCIARY DUTY

Because the principal puts trust in the agent, the principal may be vulnerable. Accordingly, the law imposes a **fiduciary duty** obliging the agent to act only in the best interests of the principal. The relationship is often referred to as an **utmost good faith** relationship, requiring the agent to put the interests of the principal ahead of her own.

ACCOUNTING

Agent must account for funds

Agent must turn money over to the principal

The agent must turn over to the principal any monies earned pursuant to the agency function. If the agent acquires property, goods, or money on behalf of the principal, it must be paid over to the principal even where the agent has some claim to the funds. The agent cannot intercept those funds on his own behalf. To facilitate this process, the agent also has an obligation to keep accurate records of all agency transactions.

CASE SUMMARY 10.4

The Existence of Fiduciary Duty: *ICR Brokerage Inc. v. Crescent Restaurants Ltd.*[8]

Danabassis hired Hedemann, a real estate agent, to sell his restaurant. Hedemann failed to get an offer during the listing period but shortly after obtained an offer of $1.5 million from Knibbs. After this deal was in place, however, representatives of the Keg Steakhouse arranged with Knibbs, with the help of Hedemann, to resell the restaurant to them for $1.85 million. But the Keg needed a two-week extension to remove the conditions on their offer, and this in turn caused Knibbs, through Hedemann, to seek a two-week extension on their offer with Danabassis, which was granted. All this time Danabassis knew nothing about the subsequent sale to the Keg. When Danabassis found out about the other deal, he sued Hedemann for breaching his fiduciary duty as agent because of his failure to disclose the subsequent dealings.

The Court of Appeal determined that Hedemann was only required to disclose any information to Danabassis that could affect his decision. Since the sale to Knibbs was already in place, any subsequent dealings with Knibbs and the Keg would not affect that contract, so Hedemann had no fiduciary duty to disclose it. It was a different matter with respect to the request for the extension. When Hedemann approached Danabassis for this extension, the information with respect to the subsequent sale to the Keg might well have affected his decision and Hedemann had a duty to disclose that information. In fact, he was asked point blank the reason for the extension and said nothing. This was a breach of his fiduciary duty.

The Court of Appeal, however, held that Danabassis had suffered no damage. If Danabassis had the knowledge of the other sale, the only thing he could have done was to refuse the extension. He still would have been bound in contract to Knibbs to sell the

---

8. 2010 SKCA 92 (CanLII).

property. That deal would in all likelihood still have gone through, making no difference to Danabassis. Therefore, although a breach of fiduciary duty had taken place, there was no remedy because no damages had been suffered.

DISCUSSION QUESTIONS

Do you feel that this was too lenient an approach and Hedemann should have been required to disclose all of his dealings with Knibbs and the Keg? What about his commission on the first sale?

FULL DISCLOSURE

Agents owe their principal a positive duty of **full disclosure**. The agent cannot arbitrarily decide what would likely influence the conduct of the principal and what would not. For example, in the *Krasniuk* case,[9] the real estate agent failed to disclose verbal offers to the vendor, and because of this breach of fiduciary duty she was denied her commission on the sale. Other examples of fiduciary duty require the agent to do the following:

Agent must disclose all information

- Keep in strict confidence any communications that come through the agency function and communicate that information to the principal

- Act in the best interests of the principal, even if the agent may lose some personal benefit

- Not take advantage of any personal opportunity that may come to her knowledge through the agency relationship

- In addition to information about the agency transactions discussed above, the agent must disclose to the principal any personal benefit the agent stands to gain or any business opportunity that comes to the agent because of her position as agent. Only with the informed consent of the principal can the agent retain any benefit

If there is a failure to disclose these benefits or opportunities, the principal can seek an accounting and have any funds gained by the agent paid over to the principal.

An agent cannot act for both a principal and a third party at the same time. It would be very difficult for an agent to extract the best possible price from a third party on behalf of a principal when the third party is also paying the agent. The common practice of agents accepting gifts, such as holidays, tickets to sporting events, and liquor, is an example of the same problem. If the principal discovers the agent accepting payment from the third party, the principal is entitled to an accounting and the receipt of all such funds, and will likely have just cause to terminate the relationship. Only where full disclosure has been made at the outset and permission given can the agent profit personally in this way.

Agent cannot act for both the principal and a third party without the consent of both

In real estate transactions, the agent usually acts for the seller. This can cause problems for purchasers, who often do not realize this and expect the agent to protect their interests as well. In some western provinces, this difficulty is largely overcome by requiring the purchasers to have their own agent acting for them and splitting the commission.

Another problem sometimes arising in the real estate industry is where the agent obtains property for the purchaser without disclosing that the property being purchased is actually owned by that agent or, inversely, where the agent secretly purchases property for himself sold by the seller he is representing. This is sometimes done through a corporation or some third-party friend of the agent. This is a conflict of interest, and without full disclosure the agent has breached his fiduciary duty and would be required to pay back both profits and the commission to the principal.[10]

Agent must not profit at the principal's expense

---

9. *Krasniuk v. Gabbs*, 2002 MBQB 14 (CanLII), [2002] 3 WWR 364.
10. *G.L. Black Holdings Ltd. v. Peddle*, 1998 CanLII 18149 (AB QB), aff'd 1999 ABCA 264 (CanLII).

Agent must not compete with the principal

It also follows that the agent must not operate her own business in competition with the principal, especially if a service is being offered. Nor can the agent also represent another principal selling a similar product without full disclosure. Also, the agent must not collect any profits or commissions that are hidden from the principal, but must pay over all the benefit resulting from the performance of the agency agreement. Such a breach of fiduciary duty by an agent who is also an employee will likely constitute just cause for dismissal. Note that with senior employees this duty will probably continue after termination of the employment, but for ordinary employees any duty owed ends when they leave. To avoid this problem, employment contracts and contracts with independent agents will often contain terms restricting individuals from working in a similar business after the relationship ends. Note that these restrictive covenants must be carefully worded, going no further than necessary to protect the interest of the employer while preserving the employee's right to earn a living.

Finally, the Supreme Court of Canada has recently made it clear that a fiduciary duty will only arise when, in addition to someone putting his trust in another, that other person accepts the responsibility to act in his best interest.[11] A fiduciary duty can arise in other circumstances, but it is clear that in agency relationships trust and vulnerability exist, so there is no doubt that an agent will have a fiduciary duty toward the principal with all of the obligations described here. In many types of relationships, a fiduciary duty arises automatically, as with doctors, trustees, accountants, and lawyers and their clients.

REDUCING RISK 10.2

When professionals or independent businesses offer their service to others, a relationship of trust is created that leaves a client vulnerable, so a fiduciary duty is usually owed. The person providing the service must put the interests of the client ahead of her own and follow the instructions given. It is sometimes difficult to keep personal interests and the interests of customers and clients separate, but failure to do so is asking for trouble. It is vitally important that sophisticated professionals and businesspeople in such a position learn the nature of their fiduciary duty and make sure they honour it.

The Principal's Duties

THE CONTRACT

Principal must honour the terms of the contract and pay a reasonable amount for services

Principal must reimburse agent's expenses

The principal's primary obligation to the agent is to honour the terms of the contract by which the agent was hired. If the contract is silent as to payment, an obligation to pay a reasonable amount can be implied on the basis of the amount of effort put forth by the agent as well as the customs and traditions of the industry. If the agreement provides for payment only on completion, there is no implied obligation to pay for part performance. Thus, if an agent is to receive a commission upon the sale of a house, even if the agent puts considerable effort into promoting a sale, there is generally no entitlement to commission if no sale occurs. Unless there is agreement to the contrary, or a different custom in the industry, the agent is normally entitled to compensation for reasonable expenses, such as phone bills and car expenses.

Ambiguous authority will be interpreted broadly . . .

. . . except when power to borrow money is in question

If the agency agreement is vague about the extent of the agent's authority, the courts will usually favour an interpretation that gives the agent the broadest possible power. When the power to borrow money is involved, however, the courts take a much narrower approach. Thus, if Klassen were hired as a purchasing agent with "all the authority necessary" to carry out that function he would likely have the authority to purchase even large blocks of product, but if he found it necessary to borrow money to make the purchases, the courts would not imply an authority to borrow without getting additional approval from the principal.

---

11. *Galambos v. Perez*, 2009 SCC 48, [2009] 3 SCR 247, 2009 SCC 48 (CanLII).

Undisclosed Principals

Sometimes agents don't disclose who they are representing to the people they are dealing with. Agents assembling property for a development, for instance, might not want to disclose why they are interested in the property because that might affect the price. These transactions involve an **undisclosed principal**. Where the agent makes it clear she is acting for a principal but does not reveal the identity of that principal, the agent has no liability to the third party and only the principal can enforce the agreement. Sometimes, however, the agent will simply sign in such a way as to be consistent with her being principal or agent or will actually sign as if she were the principal contracting party. If the would-be agent acts as if she were the principal, the third party can sue only her, and only the agent can enforce the contract. Where there is ambiguity the third party has a choice. Once he has determined that the agent was representing someone else, he can either continue to sue the agent or can sue the principal instead. Once the choice is made, however, the third party is bound by it and can't later change his mind.

> Where the agent makes it clear she is acting as agent for an undisclosed principal, the third party cannot sue or be sued by the agent

> Where the agent acts ambiguously as to whether he is the principal or agent, the third party can sue either or be sued by either

Note that there are some types of contracts that cannot be enforced by an undisclosed principal. One example is where the identity of the parties is important. In *Said v. Butt*,[12] a person who had been banned from a theatre because of a disturbance had an agent purchase a ticket on his behalf. When the banned person tried to enter with the ticket, he was refused and brought this action. The action failed because the Court determined that the identity of the purchaser of the ticket was obviously vital to the transaction. For the same reason, you could not go to a job interview and be hired and then claim you were acting as an agent for someone else. Another situation where the undisclosed principal cannot enforce a contract is where apparent authority is claimed. The agent must be acting under actual authority. There can be no apparent authority since the principal is unknown. Nor can the principal later ratify the deal since the agent had no authority to act at the time of the transaction.

> Third party can repudiate when identity of undisclosed principal is important

> Apparent authority does not apply where the principal is undisclosed

> Undisclosed principal cannot ratify

CASE SUMMARY 10.5

When the Agent Has No Responsibility under the Contract: *Sproule v. Atrel Engineering*[13]

The Sunset Cove subdivision was being constructed, and Sproule Powerline Construction Ltd. provided work and material on the site pursuant to an agreement with respect to several streetlights with Limmer Corp. The arrangements for the work had been made through the services of the project manager, Atrel Engineering Ltd., acting through Seguin, and MacDonald acting for Sproule. When the invoice of $23 000 was not paid, Sproule sued Atrel for the funds. Atrel took the position that they had acted at all times as an agent with the knowledge of Sproule and had no responsibility under the resulting contract. The Ontario Court agreed, noting that when Seguin and MacDonald met, Seguin was clearly acting as a subagent for Atrel, which was acting as an agent for Limmer with the knowledge of MacDonald. All parties were sophisticated businesspeople with many years of experience and Atrel, through their representative, had at all times made it clear they were acting as agents. MacDonald knew this and had no claim against them. The contract was between Sproule Powerline Construction and Limmer Corp., and Sproule had to turn to Limmer for payment.

This is a simple case that makes it clear that an agent, so long as he makes it clear he is acting as an agent, has no responsibility under the resulting contract. Note the involvement of subagents here, as is always the case when corporations are involved.

---

12. [1920] 3 K.B. 497.
13. 2011 ONSC 4944 (CanLII).

SMALL BUSINESS PERSPECTIVE

In several industries, businesses are engaged as agents. If personal liability is to be avoided, it is necessary to make it clear that one is acting in a representative capacity.

To further complicate matters, where the contract is made under seal (sealed by the agent), the undisclosed principal cannot be sued. Only parties to a sealed document can have rights or obligations under it.

As can be seen, the responsibilities of the parties in undisclosed principal situations can become very complicated. To avoid the problem of an undisclosed principal, individuals acting as agents should be extremely careful to make it clear that they are acting in an agency capacity. This is normally done by writing "per" immediately before the signature of the agent. For example, if Sam Jones were acting for Ace Finance Company, he would be well advised to sign:

Ace Finance Company

per *Sam Jones*

The Third Party

Third party can sue an agent for unauthorized acts

When an agent does not have the authority claimed, either actual or apparent, that agent may be sued by the third party for breach of "warranty of authority." This action is founded in contract law and is the most common example of an agent being sued directly by the third party. Otherwise, only the principal can enforce the agreement or be sued under it. However, an agent who intentionally misleads the third party into believing that he has authority when he does not may be sued by the third party for the tort of deceit. Furthermore, agents who inadvertently exceed their authority can be sued for negligence.

CASE SUMMARY 10.6

Breach of Warranty of Authority: *Wolfedale Electric Ltd. v. RPM's Systems Automation & Design Quality in Motion Inc.*[14]

Robert Hammond claimed to be an agent acting for RPM Systems Inc. when he arranged for Wolfedale Electric Ltd. to do electrical work for the third party, Meridian. Meridian paid, but there was a shortfall to Wolfedale of $18 367. This action was brought against Hammond personally for that amount. Hammond was a director, shareholder, and officer of 1485777 Ontario Limited and of RPM's Systems Automation & Design Quality in Motion. He took the position that if the money was owed, it was owed by those corporations for which he was acting as agent and not by himself personally. The evidence showed that in all of Wolfedale's dealings and in all of the documentation supplied to Wolfedale, the company they were dealing with was represented as RPM's Systems Inc. In fact, there was no such company in existence, so Hammond, who purported to act for that non-existent company, was personally liable to Wolfedale for the claimed amount on the basis of breach of warranty of authority.

It is likely that the long corporate name RPM's Systems Automation & Design Quality in Motion Inc. was shortened by Hammond for convenience to RPM's Systems Inc. and used in all his business dealings. But that provided misleading information to all those whom Hammond dealt with, and hence he became personally liable for any dealings

---

14. 2004 CanLII 66291 (ON SC), 47 BLR (3d) 1.

done in that name. Businesspeople have to be extremely careful not to fall into the same trap and, when acting as agent, that one specifies accurately the name of the principal being represented.

SMALL BUSINESS PERSPECTIVE

When officers and other employees of corporations negotiate contracts on behalf of the company, they have to be extremely careful to make sure they have authority to do what they are doing and that they properly indicate whom they are representing.

Liability for Agent's Tortious Conduct

As discussed in Chapters 4 and 11, an employer is vicariously liable for the acts an employee commits during the course of employment. When an agent is also an employee of the principal, the principal is vicariously liable for any tortious acts committed by the agent in the course of that employment. The difficulty arises when the agent is not an employee but acts independently. In 1938, the Supreme Court of Canada held that the principle of vicarious liability is restricted to those situations in which a master–servant relationship can be demonstrated.[15] This position was reaffirmed in 2001 in the *Sagaz* case[16] when Major J. of the Supreme Court said, "Based on policy considerations, the relationship between an employer and independent contractor does not typically give rise to a claim in vicarious liability."

Vicarious liability is limited to employment . . .

But that does not end the matter. The courts have been expanding the definition of employment. John Fleming points out that "the employment of a servant may be limited to a single occasion, or extend over a long period; it may even be gratuitous."[17] Even if the relationship involves a person who is essentially an independent agent, that agent may be functioning as an employee or servant in a given situation; thus, the courts may impose vicarious liability on the principal by simply asserting that the agent is also an employee. With such a broad definition of employment, judges will have little difficulty imposing vicarious liability on principals when the circumstances warrant. Still it is only in rare cases that a principal will be found vicariously liable for the acts of an independent agent. Of course, the principal can then look to the agent for compensation for any losses incurred.

. . . but the definition of employment may be broadened

There are some situations in which vicarious liability will apply even if the agent is acting independently. The courts appear willing to hold the principal responsible for theft or fraudulent misrepresentation by an agent, even when no employment exists. It does appear, however, that vicarious liability for the acts of independent agents is limited to those situations where the acts complained of are actually committed in the process of the exercise of that agency function. Also applying the principle of estoppel, where the principal has done something to lead the third party to believe the independent agent is an employee, that third party will be able to rely on that representation. In *Mignault et al. v. Palmer et al.* (see Case Summary 10.1), the Court had no problem finding Great-West Life (GWL) vicariously liable for the acts of a fraudulent agent even though they had taken great care to ensure that he was an independent contractor. The agent, Palmer, acted for GWL in dealings with clients and he persuaded several to cash out those investments and invest in more lucrative GWL investments. In fact, he diverted the funds for his own personal use.

The Court found that by allowing him to use their office, by providing him with documentation, and because of their past dealings with him, these factors led the clients to believe Palmer was an employee of GWL and was acting for them in these

Vicarious liability where the independent agent is deceitful

---

15. *T.G. Bright and Company v. Kerr*, [1939] SCR 63.

16. *671122 Ontario Ltd. v. Sagaz Industries Canada Inc.*, 2001 SCC 59, [2001] 2 SCR 983 at para. 3.

17. John G. Fleming, *The Law of Torts*, 8th ed. (Sydney: The Law Book Co. Ltd., 1990), 371.

dealings and was therefore vicariously liable for the fraudulent acts. The Supreme Court of Canada has stated that in situations like these we are to look to the degree of closeness between the act complained of and the party to be found liable. In that analysis, the Court indicated that the following consideration should be applied:

> [142] The object of the analysis is to determine whether imposition of vicarious liability in a particular case will serve the goals of doing so: imposing liability for risks which the enterprise creates or to which it contributes, encouraging reduction of risk and providing fair and effective compensation.[18]

Vicarious liability—both parties are liable

As is the case with employment law, vicarious liability makes the principal responsible, but it does not relieve the agent of liability for her own tortious conduct. Both can be sued, but the principal can then seek compensation from the agent.

Direct liability if the principal is the origin of fraud

A principal can also be found directly liable for his own tortious conduct. If the agent is following the instructions of the principal and unknowingly passes on false information provided by the principal, it is the principal that is at fault. In the case of *Junkin et al. v. Bedard et al.*,[19] Junkin gave the agent false information with respect to the profitability of the motel being sold and the agent innocently communicated that false information to the purchaser, who, relying on it, bought the property. Bedard sued, and it was the principal, not the innocent agent, who was liable for the loss.

Termination of Agency

Termination as per agreement

An agent's authority ends when notified. If the agent is an employee, the employer can terminate the authority of the employee to act as agent even where the employment continues. Of course, where the employment ends so does the agent's actual authority. Sometimes the authority for the agent to act is given for a specific time or for the duration of a project. Once that time expires or the project ends so does the authority of that agent. Remember, however, that while actual authority may be terminated, the agent's apparent authority may continue depending on the circumstances. The principal should take steps to inform all potential clients and others of the termination of the agent's authority.

Requirement of notification

REDUCING RISK 10.3

Since most business is done through agents, businesspeople must take care to understand the exposure they have to liability for their agents' conduct. That liability may be based in contract or tort, and both are derived from the duties and authority given. Whether the agent is independent or an employee, care should be taken to carefully define her authority and to make sure that the agent stays within those specified parameters. Even then, liability may be incurred when agents do what they are authorized to do in a careless manner. The key here is to minimize exposure, not to eliminate it. In the end, the best practice for a sophisticated client is to ensure that agents are reliable, trustworthy, and well trained.

Frustration may terminate agency, as will requests to perform illegal tasks

When the principal wants to end the agent's authority to act, simple notification is usually sufficient, for there is no requirement that the notice be reasonable, only that it be communicated to the agent. This applies to the termination of authority to enter into new contracts on the principal's behalf, not necessarily to the right to continued payment, which may be based on other contractual considerations. If the activities the agent is engaged to perform become impossible or essentially different from what the parties anticipated, then the contractual doctrine of frustration may apply, terminating the agent's authority. Similarly, an agent's authority to act on behalf of a principal is terminated when the actions the agent is engaged to

---

18. *Fullowka v. Pinkerton's of Canada Ltd.*, 2010 SCC 5, [2010] 1 SCR 132.
19. [1958] SCR 56; 1957 CanLII 23 (SCC).

perform become illegal. If Cantello agreed to act as Jasper's agent to sell products in a pyramid sales scheme, that authority would have been terminated automatically upon passage of the *Criminal Code* provision prohibiting such activities.[20]

An agent's authority to act on behalf of a principal will also end upon the death, bankruptcy, or insanity of the principal (see Table 10.1). When the principal is a corporation, its dissolution will have a similar effect. In these instances both actual and apparent authority will end, although there is some uncertainty with respect to apparent authority where insanity of the principal is involved. In other situations where the principal continues and has simply terminated the agent's authority, the principal is still liable for the agent's conduct on the basis of apparent authority. Therefore, it is vitally important for a principal to take steps to notify current and potential customers as well as other people and businesses that they may have dealings with regarding the termination of the agent's authority.

Death, insanity, or bankruptcy will terminate agency

Table 10.1 Other Ways to Terminate an Agent's Authority

	Impact on Agent's Actual Authority	Impact on Agent's Apparent Authority
Death of principal	Ceases	Ceases
Bankruptcy of principal	Ceases[1]	Ceases
Dissolution of principal corporation	Ceases	Ceases
Insanity of principal	Ceases	Unclear—possibly continues[2]
By mutual agreement	Ceases	Continues until the third party is notified of termination[2]

[1] Other people may assume this authority under the direction of the trustee.

[2] Since apparent authority continues, the principal must actively notify third parties that the agent's authority has been terminated. Only then does apparent authority cease.

Enduring Powers of Attorney

As stated above, loss of sanity on the part of the principal will terminate an agency; consequently, authority to act under a power of attorney terminates when the principal loses capacity. This is problematic, especially where society is aging and many individuals may desire to appoint someone as their agent or decision maker with power to act in the principal's stead after the principal loses capacity. In the past, it was necessary for family members (or others) to apply to the courts for an order appointing them as the trustee of the person who had lost capacity. These applications could be expensive and time consuming, especially if the family was divided as to who should act as trustee. The process could also be a humiliating one for the principal involved, whose loss of mental capacity would be openly examined in a public setting.

CASE SUMMARY 10.7

Abuse of Power of Attorney: *Alcombrack Estate v. Alcombrack*[21]

Barry Alcombrack was given power of attorney by his mother to act for her in the sale of the house she was living in at the time. He later used that power of attorney to sell a cottage and another parcel of land owned by his mother. This was done without her

---

[20] *Criminal Code*, R.S.C. 1985, c. C-46, s. 206.
[21] 2008 CanLII 19202 (ON SC).

knowledge and without her consent. Another son discovered that sale later, and when he brought it to his mother's attention an action was commenced against Barry for fraud and breach of his fiduciary duty. The Court found that he had breached his fiduciary duty and was ordered to account to the estate (Mrs. Alcombrack had died by the time of the trial). He was ordered to pay over $87 000 to the estate plus substantial costs with respect to the action.

The misuse of a power of attorney is a serious matter with significant consequences. This case is typical of the kind of abuse that takes place, especially in family and estate matters, and a wise person will take care in arranging his affairs not to put such temptation into the hands of someone who may not have the strength to resist.

Enduring power of attorney grants power after capacity is lost

To remedy some of these difficulties, provinces have passed legislation to allow individuals to execute enduring powers of attorney,[22] vesting powers similar to those given to trustees to the person chosen to act as one's attorney. The **enduring power of attorney** is created while the principal has full capacity, and the powers typically are exercisable after the principal loses mental capacity. The attorney generally can make all financial decisions on behalf of the donor. Through use of an enduring power of attorney, a person can decide, in advance, who to entrust with the future handling of her financial affairs. It is now also possible for individuals to exercise some control over who will make health-care decisions and similar personal decisions for them.[23] Refer to the MyBusLawLab for provincial variations. These powers of attorney and enduring powers of attorney can be abused, as demonstrated in Case Summary 10.7, and governments are actively taking steps to reduce abuse. The Western Canada Law Reform Agencies (WCLRA) report released in July 2008 deals specifically with recommendations on how to reduce such abuse. The report is available at www.law.ualberta.ca/alri/docs/WCLRA-EPA%20report.pdf.

Specialized Agency Relationships

General principles apply to specialized agencies as well

Many examples of specialized services offered to businesses and the public are essentially agencies in nature, such as those of travel agents, real estate agents, lawyers, accountants, stockbrokers, financial advisers, and insurance representatives. Some of these agents do not enter into contracts on behalf of their clients but negotiate and act on their clients' behalf in other ways. For example, a real estate agent neither offers nor accepts on behalf of a client. In fact, the client is usually the vendor of a property, and the agent's job is to take care of the preliminary matters and bring the purchaser and vendor together so they can enter into a contract directly. Nonetheless, few would dispute that these real estate agents are carrying out essentially an agency function and thus have a fiduciary obligation to their clients. The important thing to remember is that the general provisions set out above also apply to these special agency relationships, although there may be some exceptions. For example, in most of these specialized service professions, the rule that an agent cannot delegate usually does not apply. The very nature of these businesses requires that employees of the firm, not the firm itself, will act on behalf of the client.

Special statutes and professional organizations

Most of these specialized agencies are fulfilling a service function and are governed by special statutes and professional organizations, such as lawyers, accountants, and real estate bodies. The boards and commissions governing these businesses and professions provide licences, training, insurance, and other services to their members. They also hear complaints and provide discipline where abuses occur. Where such abuses do occur victims should know that they have recourse

---

[22.] See, for example, British Columbia's *Power of Attorney Act*, R.S.B.C. 1996 c. 370, and Nova Scotia's *Powers of Attorney Act*, R.S.N.S. 1989, c. 352.

[23.] See, for example, Alberta's *Personal Directives Act*, R.S.A. 2000, c. P-6.

based on the fiduciary duty principles set out here as well as remedies in contract and tort. Such fiduciary duties, in fact, may be imposed on other professional advisers, even when their duties do not extend to being agents.[24]

TYPES OF BUSINESS ORGANIZATION

LO ❹

The law of agency is of particular importance when discussing different methods of carrying on business. These business organizations almost always conduct their business through representatives or agents.

There are essentially three major types of business organization (see Figure 10.2). The first, the **sole proprietorship**, involves an individual carrying on business alone. Employees may be hired and business may be carried on through the services of an employee or agent, but the business is the sole responsibility of one person, the owner. A second method of carrying on business is called a **partnership**, where two or more partners share ownership and responsibilities, along with both profits and losses. As was the case with the sole proprietorship, the partnership may also employ others and act through agents. Also, each partner acts as an agent for the other partners and has a fiduciary duty to them. The third type of business organization is the incorporated company. Any type of business organization involving more than one person can be called a company; a **corporation**, however, is a legal entity. By statute, it has been given an identity separate from the individual members who compose it. Thus, contracts with a corporation are dealings with the corporation itself as if it were a person in its own right. And because the corporation is a fiction, it must conduct all of its affairs through employees and agents.

There are other ways for people to work together to carry on a commercial activity. For example, a **non-profit society** can be set up under legislation such as the Nova Scotia *Societies Act*.[25] This also creates a separate legal entity, but the procedure of incorporation and the obligations of those involved are quite different. There are also several ways in which these various types of business organizations can be combined. A **holding corporation** holds shares in other corporations. A **joint venture** involves several different corporations that band together to accomplish a major project. They may form a separate corporation or a partnership. It must be emphasized at the outset that this is an area where a wise businessperson will obtain

Sole proprietorship involves one person

Partners share responsibilities

Corporation is a separate legal entity

Societies are separate legal entities, but their obligations differ

Figure 10.2 Types of Business Organization

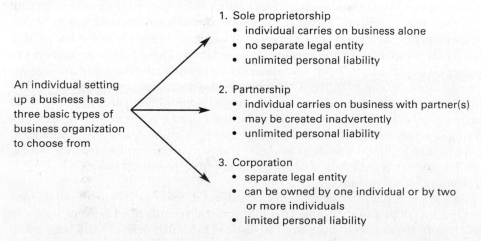

An individual setting up a business has three basic types of business organization to choose from

1. Sole proprietorship
   - individual carries on business alone
   - no separate legal entity
   - unlimited personal liability

2. Partnership
   - individual carries on business with partner(s)
   - may be created inadvertently
   - unlimited personal liability

3. Corporation
   - separate legal entity
   - can be owned by one individual or by two or more individuals
   - limited personal liability

---

24. See *Hodgkinson v. Simms*, [1994] 3 SCR 377, where the Supreme Court held that the relationship of broker and client is not necessarily a fiduciary relationship. However, where the elements of trust and confidence and reliance on skill, knowledge, and advice are present, the relationship is fiduciary and the obligations that attach are fiduciary. It thus remains a question of fact as to whether the parties' relationship was such as to give rise to a fiduciary duty on the part of the adviser.

25. R.S.N.S. 1989, c. 435.

expert advice from professionals such as lawyers, accountants, and bankers. It is a simple matter to start a business as a sole proprietor and not much more complicated to do so as a partnership. While the process of incorporation is more involved, there are self-help books and other mechanisms available to assist in the incorporation process without the necessity of using a lawyer. It is even possible to purchase an already incorporated off-the-shelf company, much like you would purchase a lawnmower or other consumer item. But decisions made at this stage in the attempt to save a few dollars can come back to haunt the proprietor(s) and be very costly later on, especially if the business is successful. The discussion in this chapter will be limited to an examination of sole proprietorship and partnership, while Chapter 11 will deal with corporations.

LO ❺   THE SOLE PROPRIETORSHIP

Sole proprietor carries on business in own right

The sole proprietorship (often shortened to proprietorship) is simply an individual carrying on a business activity on his own. The sole proprietor makes all the decisions associated with the business and is the only one entitled to the benefits derived from the business. A sole proprietor also bears full responsibility for all the costs, losses, and obligations incurred in the business activity. Thus, there is no distinction between the personal assets of the sole proprietor and those of the business. They are all assets belonging to the proprietor and are available to creditors if things go wrong. Small businesses, including professionals practising by themselves, often take this form. As mentioned, a sole proprietor can act through agents or employees. For example, a lawyer or accountant acting as a sole proprietor will usually employ a secretary or clerk, but they are solely responsible for any debts incurred, any contracts entered into, and any torts committed as they carry on their business.

Government Regulations

Sole proprietors must adhere to licensing and governing regulations

The sole proprietor, like all other types of business organizations, must satisfy many federal, provincial, and municipal requirements to carry on business. Usually, the name of the business must be registered if it is different from the sole proprietor's name,[26] and a licence to operate must be obtained from the appropriate level of government. This licensing process is used to gain revenue and control or restrict certain types of businesses, such as door-to-door sales, credit information services, moneylenders, hotels, and cabarets. When professionals are involved they must also be members of their respective professional organizations such as the law society, the dental association, or the accounting association. Those bodies in turn ensure proper qualifications are held, discipline members when necessary, and arrange for appropriate ongoing training. Tradespeople also must have the proper certification. When the handling of food or dangerous commodities is involved, there are further provincial and federal regulations that must be obeyed. Sole proprietors must also satisfy local zoning bylaws, and if they have employees they are subject to employment legislation, such as workers' compensation, employment insurance, and income tax regulations. They are also required to remit taxes (GST or HST, depending on the province).

Sole proprietor is relatively free of outside interference

As a general rule, sole proprietors are subject to fewer government regulations than partnerships and corporations. Only minimal records need be kept, and sole proprietors are usually not required to disclose information about the business to others. They must keep sufficient records to satisfy government agencies, such as the Canada Revenue Agency. In essence, the sole proprietor has complete control and complete responsibility for the business activity.

---

26. See, for example, *Business Names Act*, R.S.O. 1990, c. B. 17, s. 2(2).

Liability

Sole proprietors do not have accountability to others and alone are responsible for making important business decisions. They can look only to their own resources to finance the business operation; they cannot sell shares and are restricted to their own credit standing when borrowing money to finance the business. The sole proprietor owns all the assets, receives all the profits of the business, and is responsible for all its debts and liabilities. This **unlimited liability** can be the most significant disadvantage of the sole proprietorship. When liability is incurred for breached contracts or torts, or where there is insurmountable debt, the whole burden falls on the sole proprietor. Under the principle of vicarious liability, the sole proprietor is responsible for any tort committed by an employee during the course of employment. Although the sole proprietor's entire personal fortune is at risk, insurance may offset that risk. Any profit derived from a sole proprietorship is subject to personal income tax, and some tax advantages available to partnerships and corporations are not available to sole proprietors. These factors alone are often enough to encourage the businessperson to incorporate.

Sole proprietor has unlimited liability, but can purchase insurance

In many jurisdictions, professional individuals such as doctors, dentists, lawyers, and accountants cannot incorporate their practice, and they derive little advantage from doing so in those jurisdictions where professional incorporations are permitted.[27] They carry on business as sole proprietors or band together in a group as partners. (Note that in most jurisdictions limited protection can now be obtained as limited liability partners, discussed below.) These professionals must join the appropriate professional organization, such as the law society or medical association of the province. Note that it is only the practice of the professional service that cannot be incorporated, and so these professionals obtain many of the advantages of incorporation by establishing companies that supply them with management services and equipment, own the building, and employ the office staff.

Professionals are bound by certain rules

PARTNERSHIP

LO ⑥

A partnership is the simplest form of business in which people pool their resources and carry on business together with the object of making a profit. The relationship is based on contract, so basic contract law applies with special provisions to deal with this unique relationship. Unlike a corporation, a partnership is not a separate legal personality from the people in it. However, it is possible for the firm to enter into legal relationships so that it is not necessary to contract with each partner individually. This gives the partnership the convenience of functioning as a single business unit. It can own land, contract with others, employ individuals, and sue or be sued in its own name.

Partnerships are governed by contract law

Partnership—carrying on business together for profit

Legislation

In 1890, as part of a similar trend in other areas of law in the United Kingdom, the vast body of case law governing partnership was summarized into one statute, the *Partnership Act*.[28] This legislation was adopted in all the common law provinces of Canada where it has remained in place to the present day with only a few alterations, such as the creation of limited liability partners. With some minor variations province to province, the law of partnership is basically consistent across Canada. For convenience, this chapter will refer to the Ontario *Partnerships Act*, and the sections discussed will refer to that statute.[29]

The *Partnership Act* is still used today

[27.] See, for example, the *Regulated Accounting Profession Act*, R.S.A. 2000, c. R-12, which, in s. 38, provides that a shareholder or professional corporation is liable as if the business were carried on as a partnership or a sole proprietorship, and that the liability of an accountant is not affected if the practice is carried on by the individual as an employee and on behalf of a professional corporation.

[28.] (1890), 53 & 54 Vict., c. 39 (U.K.).

[29.] *Partnerships Act*, R.S.O. 1990, c. P. 5. Note that Ontario is the only province for which the name of the partnership legislation is in the plural; all of the other provinces have a *Partnership Act*.

Creation of the Partnership

CASE SUMMARY 10.8

Carrying on Business Together: *Prince Albert Co-operative Association Limited v. Rybka*[30]

After the Prince Albert Co-operative Association obtained a judgment for over $50 000 against Mr. Rybka for unpaid debts for the purchase of goods and materials to use in his farming operation, they became aware that Mrs. Rybka had been working with her husband on the farm. This action was an attempt to enforce that judgment against her as a partner in the farming operation. At trial, the judge found that there wasn't enough evidence to establish a partnership. The Saskatchewan Court of Appeal overturned that decision.

Although there was no partnership agreement and the Co-op was not aware of the wife's involvement in the farm at the time the indebtedness arose, it was clear that Mr. and Mrs. Rybka were in partnership in the farm. To establish partnership it is necessary to show that the parties carried on business together with a view toward profit. There is no question that farming is a business and that it was carried on with a view toward profit even though none was made. The couple had also certified that they were in partnership to the Canada Revenue Agency on their tax forms. The main question was whether they were carrying on business in common. While there was no formal agreement to enter a partnership, they clearly intended to engage in a common endeavour, the farm. The bank accounts were held jointly in their names, and she was the farm's bookkeeper and paid all of the bills. Mrs. Rybka stated when examined that when they had a good year they intended to split the profits. Also, from eight years of tax returns it was clear that the couple were in business together, splitting the losses and hoping to split profits, thus satisfying the *Partnership Act* requirement that they were carrying on their farming business together with a view toward profits. Even though they had never entered into any discussion about creating a partnership, they were in partnership and Mrs. Rybka was liable as a partner for this debt.

SMALL BUSINESS PERSPECTIVE

In our business relations we should take care to avoid inadvertently becoming a partner, with this arrangement's inherent potential liability. The existence of such a partnership should never be a surprise to a prudent businessperson, and a carefully drawn up partnership agreement should always characterize such a relationship.

Partnership is created by agreement or inadvertently

A partnership is not always created by formal agreement between the partners. The *Partnerships Act* provides that a partnership is created when two or more people carry on business in common with a view toward profits.[31] A profit does not actually have to be made, but profit is the object of the exercise. It should be noted that the sharing of gross returns from a business activity does not in itself create a partnership. It is the sharing of the net proceeds after expenses have been deducted (the profits) from the enterprise that gives rise to the presumption of a partnership. The splitting of the commission on a sale by two real estate agents does not create a partnership, but when they split what is left after expenses the presumption of a partnership will arise.

The *Partnerships Act* sets out a number of other circumstances that though they involve the sharing of income, by themselves will not establish a partnership:[32]

1. Owning property in common, even when it is rented out for profit.

---

30. 2010 SKCA 144 (CanLII).
31. *Partnerships Act, supra* note 29, s. 2.
32. Ibid., s. 3.

2. When a debt is repaid by the creditors' taking a share of the debtor's profits. For example, Pallas owes Clegg $10 000, and Clegg agrees to let Pallas pay it back by paying 20 percent of the profits of Pallas's furniture store per month until repaid.

3. When the payment of an employee is based on a share of sales or profits, such as commission selling or profit-sharing schemes.

4. When the beneficiary of a deceased partner receives the deceased partner's share of the profits.

5. When a loan is made in relation to a business and payment of interest varies with the profit. For example, Pallas loans Clegg $10 000 to start a furniture business, and Clegg pays interest on that $10 000 principal by paying 10 percent of the store's profits per month.

6. When a business is sold and the payment of the goodwill portion varies with the profitability of the business. For example, Pallas sells Clegg a furniture business for $10 000 for the assets and 50 percent of the first year's profits for goodwill.

The *Partnerships Act* lists exceptions—refer to MyBusLawLab for specific provincial wording

The question remains: What constitutes carrying on business together with a view to profit? Evidence of the following will usually give rise to the presumption of a partnership:

When a partnership is presumed

*   Joint contribution of capital to establish a business
*   Intention to share expenses, profits, or losses
*   Joint participation in the management of a business.

If two people operate a restaurant together by sharing the work and expenses and by jointly making decisions and the business is not incorporated, the relationship will likely be a partnership. It should be further noted that the *Partnerships Act* requires that the parties carry on a continuing business together. A single joint project, for example a school dance put on by two university students who combine their resources, would probably not be classed as a partnership. (If the students put on several dances, they would be in the "business" of providing this type of entertainment and, thus, would be in legal partnership, whether they looked at it that way or not.) Whether a business relationship is held to be a partnership will always depend on the circumstances.

Partnership must carry on continuing business

CREATION BY INADVERTENCE

It is important to realize that the existence of a partnership relationship is a question of fact that a court can imply from the conduct of the parties. A partnership can therefore be created inadvertently. Because of the liability of one partner for the contracts and misdeeds of other partners, the finding of such a relationship can have significant consequences for that person. This must be a consideration whenever someone is involved in any kind of business activity with another. Astute businesspeople will not only take great care in choosing whom they do business with, but also take care to avoid getting involved in this kind of joint project. Failure to appreciate this possibility can have disastrous financial consequences when one partner incurs liability to a third party.

Partnership can be created by conduct . . .

In addition to setting out the responsibilities of partners to third parties, the *Partnerships Act* also sets out the rights and obligations of the partners to each other. But like the *Sale of Goods Act*, the *Partnerships Act* provisions, at least as far as the rights between the partners themselves are concerned, can be modified by the partnership agreement. It is important for the partners to enter into an agreement, preferably in writing, setting out the exact nature of the relationship between them.

. . . but should be created by agreement

CREATION BY CONTRACT

As is the case with most business relationships, it is best to create the partnership through contract. While reducing the agreement to writing is not required, it is always good practice to do so. But the terms of that contract are not always

Written contract is not always conclusive proof of a partnership

conclusive of the relationship. Even where the parties clearly state they are acting in partnership, this may not be enough to create such a partnership. On the other hand, a court may find that a partnership exists even where the parties clearly state in their agreement that they are not partners.[33]

CASE SUMMARY 10.9

Is Professional Continuing Education a Partnership?
Partners in Psychiatry v. Canadian Psychiatric Association[34]

In this unusual case, the Canadian Psychiatric Association entered into an agreement with Partners in Psychiatry to start up an institute to provide continuing professional education opportunities for practising psychiatrists. The institute so created was to be designated the CPA CPD Institute. The agreement provided for shared responsibility for fundraising, content development, program materials, and program delivery. Revenue was collected by the Canadian Psychiatric Association and kept in a separate account (the CPA CPD account). Expenses by both parties were paid out from that account, and profits were shared equally as "management fees." This dispute arose as to who is entitled to the goodwill associated with the CPA CPD Institute and the intellectual property created when the partnership was dissolved.

The Canadian Psychiatric Association took the position that they simply hired the Partners in Psychiatry as an independent contractor, while the Partners in Psychiatry claimed the relationship was one of partnership. The lower court found there was no partnership, determining that a number of elements normally associated with partnership were not present. The Court of Appeal disagreed and overturned the decision. They found that although a number of unusual practices were present, the judge at the lower court failed to look at the basic legal definition of partnership that determined a partnership relationship was present when a "business was carried on in common with a view to a profit." All of these elements were present in this case, so the appeal was allowed and Partners in Psychiatry were entitled to a share in the intellectual property of CPA CPD and the goodwill of the business. The matter was sent back to trial to determine whether this included a claim to the name CPA CPD and to determine the value of the goodwill.

SMALL BUSINESS PERSPECTIVE

Even a non-profit organization like the Canadian Psychiatric Association can find themselves in a unintended partnership when they create an ongoing business relationship where they carry on business in common with a view of sharing any profits they make from that ongoing business.

Rights and obligations of the partners can be modified by agreement

A partnership agreement should deal with all of the matters important to the partnership, such as

- the duties of each partner
- what type of work or talent each is expected to contribute
- the amount of time to be committed to the business
- how the profits are to be shared and how the capital is to be distributed
- any limitations on the powers or authority of each partner

---

33. See *Foothills Dental Laboratory Ltd. v. Naik (c.o.b. Apple Dental Group)*, [1996] A.J. No. 583, (Prov. Ct.). The Court determined a partnership existed despite the contract, which stated "It shall be an express term of this agreement that the Association herein provided for shall, under no circumstances, be deemed to create an employer and employee or partnership relationship between Naik and Goldstein respectively."
34. 2011 ONCA 109.

- methods of resolving any disputes between the partners and how the business is to be managed

- the circumstances in which the partnership will be dissolved.

It must be remembered that the rights of outsiders dealing with the partnership are, without notice, unaffected by any agreement between the partners. Outsiders' rights are determined by the provisions of the *Partnerships Act* and partnership law generally.

It should also be noted that a partnership relationship can arise because of estoppel. If one of the parties represents to a third party, either by words or by conduct, that another person is a partner and that representation is relied on, the existence of a partnership cannot be denied, even if it can be clearly demonstrated that the two were not carrying on a business together. The principle of estoppel applies to partnership just as it does to agency.

Partnership can be imposed by the principle of estoppel

CASE SUMMARY 10.10

Does Holding Someone Out as a Partner Create a Partnership? *Brown Economic Assessments Inc. v. Harcourt Gillis*[35]

Cara Brown provided consulting services to Stevenson and his law firm and submitted a bill for $23 242.59, which was never paid. Since bankruptcy overtook Stevenson in this action, Brown sued the other members of the law firm for what was owed. The other members of the law firm claimed that they were not partners with Stevenson nor with each other, and therefore they were not liable for the claimed amount.

When Brown first met with Stevenson, he introduced himself as "senior litigator and partner" in the firm, presenting her with a business card with the name of the firm listed as "Stevenson, Gillis, Hjelte, Tangjerd, Barristers and Solicitors." She also received correspondence from time to time on a letterhead containing that name.

The Court found that although there was no actual partnership, because the defendant lawyers had allowed themselves to be held out as partners and that holding out had been relied on by the plaintiff, they were estopped from denying that they were partners and were liable to pay the amount owing.

SMALL BUSINESS PERSPECTIVE

This case shows how important it is for a prudent businessperson not to hold or allow herself to be held out as a partner. The risk is that she will not be allowed to deny that fact later.

The Partner As an Agent

Every partner is the agent of the other partners and so has the power to bind them in contract as long as the contract involves the normal business of the partnership.[36] To properly understand the law of partnership, this discussion must be read in conjunction with the material above on agency. Even where the authority of a partner has been limited and the partner exceeds the power given, that contract will be binding if the third party is unaware of the limitation and the contract relates to the partnership business.[37] Assume Akbari and Carlson operated a shoe store in partnership, and Akbari, while visiting his regular supplier in Toronto,

Laws of agency apply to partnership

---

35. 2004 SKCA 89 (CanLII), [2006] 5 WWR 654.
36. *Partnerships Act, supra* note 29, ss. 6, 7.
37. Ibid., ss. 6, 9.

purchased 500 pairs of patent-leather shoes he was unable to resist for $5000. That contract would be binding on Carlson, even if the partnership agreement specifically set out that neither partner could make any purchase over $1000 without the other's approval. However, if Akbari bought a new boat during his trip to Toronto, this purchase would not be binding on his partner because the purchase could not be said to be made pursuant to the partnership business of selling shoes.

Vicarious Liability

Partners are liable for each other's acts

Partners are liable for breach of trust

All partners are also vicariously liable in tort for both careless and intentional conduct of their partners in all business-related activities, including personal injury. Thus, if Agostino and Paradis were partners selling firewood, and Agostino negligently dropped a load of wood on a passing pedestrian, both Agostino and Paradis would be liable to pay compensation for the injury. There are also many cases showing vicarious liability for intentional wrongs, such as an Ontario case in which the partners of a lawyer, even though they were completely innocent, were required to make good the loss when that lawyer fraudulently acquired $60 000 from his client by forging a cheque.[38]

All partners can also be held responsible for the money or property of third parties put into the care of a partner or the firm that is misused or misapplied by a partner. Also, where a partner is appointed as a trustee and improperly uses the trust property entrusted to her, the other partners can be responsible for that loss if they knew of that breach of trust.[39]

Partners are liable for wrongful acts of employees

Since a partnership can employ others, the principles set out in Chapter 12 on employment law apply. Partners are vicariously liable for the misdeeds of their employees committed in the course of their employment. They must also adhere to government regulations on workers' compensation, employment insurance, and income tax.

REDUCING RISK 10.4

For a businessperson, a serious risk associated with the law of partnership is the danger of becoming a partner inadvertently. This can come about by carrying on business together without realizing that a partnership has been created, or by allowing oneself to be held out as a partner by someone else. The danger is the liability imposed by such a partnership both in tort (on the basis of vicarious liability) and in contract (on the basis of each partner being an agent). This unlimited liability means a partner's entire fortune is at risk and can lead to devastating results. A sophisticated client will take care to avoid the risks that might result from the creation of an inadvertent partnership.

Unlimited Liability

Partners share losses equally or proportionally by agreement

Like that of a sole proprietor, a partner's liability is unlimited, and his personal fortune is at risk to satisfy the claims of an injured party. With partners, however, they are liable not only for their own wrongful acts and those of their employees but also for the conduct of their partners. If the assets of a partnership are not sufficient to satisfy the claims of the creditors, the partners must make up the difference out of their own personal assets. This is typically done in the same proportion that they share the profits. Under the *Partnerships Act*, the partners share profits equally, but they can make different arrangements in their partnership agreement.[40] Thus, if a partnership agreement provides that a senior partner gets 40 percent of the profits and each of the three junior partners receive 20 percent of the profits, the senior

38. *Victoria & Grey Trust Company v. Crawford* (1986), 57 O.R. (2d) 484 (H.C.J.).

39. *Partnerships Act, supra* note 29, s. 14.

40. Ibid., s. 24.

partner will bear 40 percent of the loss and the junior partners will each bear 20 percent of the loss.

Note that such a provision in the partnership agreement will affect only the relations between the partners. An outsider is not affected by any term in the partnership agreement that limits the liability of one of the partners and can collect all of what is owed from any partner. If one partner is particularly well off and the other partners have few personal assets, the injured party will look to the partner with significant assets for compensation once the assets of the partnership have been exhausted. Then that partner can seek contributions from the other partners on the basis of the partnership agreement if they have anything left to contribute.

Third party can collect from any partner regardless of agreement

In most provinces, partners are only **jointly liable** for the debts and obligations of the partnership, as opposed to jointly and **severally liable**.[41] This means that for someone to seek a remedy against all the partners, they all must be included in the original action because there is only one cause of action. Thus, if only two of the three partners are sued and it later turns out that they do not have enough assets to satisfy the judgment, it is then too late to sue the third partner. It must be emphasized, however, that when liability arises because of wrongful conduct (tort) or because of misuse of money or property in the custody of the firm, this liability is both joint and several.[42] This means that it is possible for the injured party to sue one partner and still maintain the right to sue the other partners if the claim is not satisfied. In any case, when an action is brought against the partnership in the partnership's name, the plaintiff will be able to enforce the judgment against any of the partners. The result of this vicarious liability is that all the partners are personally responsible for the injuries incurred to the extent of their entire personal fortunes. The liability of partners for each other's conduct is one area where there are some provincial differences. Refer to the MyBusLawLab for further information.

All personal assets are at risk

A retiring partner remains liable for any wrongs committed or liability incurred during the partnership period. This liability also continues for acts committed after the dissolution of the partnership or the retirement of the partner, unless the third party has been given notice that the retiring party has left the firm. The remaining partners or a new partner coming in can agree to take over these obligations in the partnership agreement, but the new partner is not automatically liable for them.[43] This is why cautious partners, when leaving or entering a partnership, take care to notify colleagues and customers of the partnership changes.

Retiring partner remains responsible

Registration

Most provinces require that a partnership be registered. Some provinces, such as British Columbia[44] and New Brunswick,[45] require registration only when the partnerships involve trading, manufacturing, and mining. Alberta also requires registration of partnerships involving contracting.[46] Ontario prohibits partners from carrying on business or identifying themselves to the public unless the firm name has been registered.[47] Registration may also be required when the partners are in limited partnerships or limited liability partnerships, as discussed below. Refer to MyBusLawLab for individual provincial requirements.

Registration is usually required

---

41. Ibid., s. 10.
42. Ibid., ss. 12, 13.
43. Ibid., s. 18.
44. *Partnership Act*, R.S.B.C. 1996, c. 348, s. 81.
45. *Partnerships and Business Names Registration Act*, R.S.N.B. 1973, c. P-5, s. 3.
46. *Partnership Act*, R.S.A. 2000, c. P-3, s. 106.
47. *Business Names Act*, R.S.O. 1990, c. B.17, s. 2.

REDUCING RISK 10.5

All partners are liable to the extent of their personal fortune for the wrongful acts and mistakes of their partners. There are many situations where one partner will be held liable for the wrongful acts of another. Those wrongful acts can range from negligence to fraud. A sophisticated client will use great care in choosing a partner and even then will face considerable risk. This is one reason that incorporation or the creation of a limited liability partnership has become much more popular as a method of doing business.

Failure to register properly can result in the imposition of a fine[48] but typically will prevent the unregistered partnership from maintaining an action[49] and cause joint liability to become joint and several liability.[50] Note that an unregistered partnership can still be sued, so there are pressing reasons to register and no advantage in not doing so.

Rights and Obligations of the Parties

FIDUCIARY DUTY

Fiduciary duty exists between partners

Each partner has a fiduciary duty to act in the best interests of those partners. This duty imposes an obligation to account for any profits that have been made or for any partnership funds or property used. A partner who uses partnership property for personal benefit without the consent of the other partners must pay over any profit made and reimburse the partnership for any deterioration of the property. Property brought into a partnership for the purposes of the business becomes the property of the partnership, even though the title documents might not reflect this ownership. The partner with title is said to hold the property in trust for the partnership.

Partners must account for any profits or use of property

Partners cannot compete with the partnership

If a partner operates a similar business without consent, she will be required to pay over any profits made to the partnership, which will then be distributed normally to all the partners. That partner, however, will not be reimbursed for losses. If a partner in a restaurant in Vancouver were to open another in Victoria without consent, any profits made from the Victoria operation would have to be paid over to the partnership and then be distributed equally among them. However, any losses sustained would be borne by that partner alone.

Information must be disclosed

Information obtained through a person's position as partner must be used to the benefit of the partnership, not for personal use. If Grubisich came across a deal for some mining claims because of his position as a partner in a mining partnership, he would be required to inform his partners about the opportunity. If he bought the claims for himself without his partners' consent, he would have to turn over any profits earned to the partnership but suffer any losses himself. In effect, the information he used was the property of the partnership.

CASE SUMMARY 10.11

Partner Must Account for Income from Other Sources: *McKnight v. Hutchison*[51]

McKnight and the defendant, Hutchison, were partners in a law firm. The partnership agreement stipulated that partners were allowed to conduct business other than the practice of law provided that notice was given to the other partners and that the

---

48. In Alberta, for example, a fine not exceeding $500 can be imposed on each partner who fails to register. See *Partnership Act, supra* note 46, s. 112.

49. Ibid., s. 113.

50. Ibid., s. 115.

51. 2002 BCSC 1373 (CanLII), 28 BLR (3d) 269.

business did not compromise the law practice. Hutchison became a director of a corporation that was a client of the partnership and accepted an honorarium as well as company shares that subsequently returned substantial dividends. McKnight contended that Hutchison breached a fiduciary duty to disclose the activities, giving rise to these and other subsequently revealed privately retained earnings.

Hutchison advised his partners of his directorship, but he did not disclose that he was retaining the honorarium and dividends privately.

The Court held that Hutchison owed his partner duties of disclosure, loyalty, utmost good faith, and avoidance of conflict and self-interest. While Hutchison's acceptance of the directorship and his activities of directorship did not place him in a position of conflict with his partner, his entitlement to the shares and stock options should have been disclosed. Hutchison's silence and his failure to account for the payments received was in breach of his duties. The Court determined that Hutchison's partner was thus entitled to an accounting of these benefits.

SMALL BUSINESS PERSPECTIVE

Again, we see just how important fiduciary duty is. It is present when there is a relationship where one party places trust in another and is vulnerable if that trust is not honoured.

PROVISIONS OF THE *PARTNERSHIPS ACT*

The rights and obligations of partners to each other are set out in the *Partnerships Act*, and these provisions apply except where modified by the partnership agreement.[52] Some of the provisions of the Act are as follows[53] (see MyBusLawLab for provincial variations):

1. The partners will share profits equally between them. Similarly, any losses incurred are shared equally between the partners. This provision is often modified by a partnership agreement, but outside third parties will not be affected by any agreement, as they can recover losses from any partner who has assets. That partner may then look to the other partners for reimbursement.

   Profits and losses are shared equally or modified by agreement

2. The partners are entitled to reimbursement for any expenses they incur in the process of the partnership business. They are entitled to be reimbursed for any money other than capital they have advanced to the partnership before the other partners can claim a share of the profits. In addition, the partner advancing such funds is entitled to the payment of interest on any money loaned to the partnership over and above the capital contribution.

   Partners' expenses are reimbursed

3. All partners have the right to take part in management. This provision is often modified by partnership agreements, which create different classes of partners such as senior and junior partners, particularly in large firms.

   Partners participate in management

4. A partner is not an employee and is not entitled to wages or other remuneration for work done, only to a share of the profits. To provide partners with a steady stream of cash flow, the firm may pay partners a monthly draw against the yet-to-be-calculated profits of the partnership. In a BC case, a partner was also found to be an employee of the partnership by the Human Rights Tribunal, which also determined that he had been the victim of age discrimination. The BC Supreme Court agreed, but this decision was overturned by the Court of Appeal,[54] which found that a partner in a partnership could not

   No salaries are paid to partners

---

52. *Partnerships Act, supra* note 29, s. 20.
53. Ibid., s. 24.
54. *Fasken Martineau DuMoulin LLP v. British Columbia (Human Rights Tribunal)*, 2011 BCSC 713 (CanLII); *Fasken Martineau DuMoulin LLP v. British Columbia (Human Rights Tribunal)*, 2012 BCCA 313 (CanLII); *McCormick v. Fasken Martineau DuMoulin LLP*, 2014 SCC 39 (CanLII).

be an employee of that partnership. The case was further appealed to the Supreme Court of Canada, which upheld the Court of Appeal decision but noted that they were not saying a partner could never be an employee for the purposes of the Human Rights Code, but in this case the equity partner had such a degree of control and input into management decisions that finding him to be an employee would be inconsistent with him being a partner. In most cases a partner will not be an employee, but the Supreme Court left the door open to find otherwise where the arrangement created a relationship of control and dependency.

Unanimous agreement is needed for major changes

5.   No major changes can be made to the partnership business without the unanimous agreement of all the partners. No new partner can be brought into the partnership, nor can a partner be excluded from the firm without the unanimous consent of all the partners.[55] However, for the ordinary matters of the firm a simple majority vote is sufficient, unless the partnership agreement states otherwise.

Assignment requires consent of the other partners

6.   Partners do not have the right to assign their partnership status to some other party without the consent of the other partners. The benefits can be assigned, but the assignee will not be a partner and will not have the right to interfere in the management or administration of the partnership business.[56]

Partners must have access to records

7.   The business records of the partnership must be kept at the partnership office, and all the partners have the right to inspect them.

Elements of a partnership agreement

As can be seen from this summary, the general principle governing a partnership relationship is that the partners function as a unit and have a considerable responsibility to look after each other's interests. When changes are proposed in the partnership agreement, all partners should take great care to consider all of the possible consequences before making such changes. Some provisions that would likely be found in a partnership agreement include the following:

- Names of the partners and the name of the partnership
- What each partner brings to the partnership, including specific duties and responsibilities and the capital contribution of each partner
- Nature of the partnership business and limitations on the authority of the partners
- How profits and losses are to be shared and any right to take a draw against profits
- The decision-making structure and a provision for dispute resolution
- How (and when) changes are to be made to the agreement, such as retirement, adding a new partner, or changing the nature of the business, and under what circumstances the partnership is to be dissolved
- Reference to specific sections of the *Partnership Act* where appropriate

Advantages of Partnership

Insurance coverage is important

Unanimous consent protection

Although the problems associated with a partnership may appear overwhelming, many of these difficulties can be overcome by proper insurance coverage. It should also be noted that a disadvantage to one person might be an advantage to another. For example, the unanimous consent required for important changes in a partnership may appear to interfere with effective management, but it does provide considerable protection to the individual partners—an individual partner cannot be outvoted by the majority, as is the case with a minority shareholder in a

---

55. *Partnerships Act, supra* note 29, ss. 24, 25.
56. Ibid., s. 31.

Chapter 10 Agency and Partnership | **335**

corporation. Similarly, the right of the individual partner to inspect all records of the business confers advantages not shared by minority shareholders in corporations to the same extent.

It may be less expensive to set up a partnership than a corporation and less costly to operate a partnership because there are few formal requirements once the business has been established. For example, a corporation must keep certain types of accounting records and file annual reports with the appropriate government agency. A partnership, on the other hand, has only the needs of the partners to satisfy in this regard. But, as with sole proprietorships and corporations, there are other government regulatory bodies that require records, such as the Canada Revenue Agency, the Workers' Compensation Board, and the Canada Employment Insurance Commission.

Partnership is less costly to form and operate

 REDUCING RISK 10.6

Businesspeople should not be too quick to discard partnership as a valuable method of carrying on business with others. From the individual's point of view, all partners have an equal say, and in all important matters there must be unanimity. This eliminates the "tyranny of the majority" problem usually associated with corporations. The disadvantages, such as unlimited liability, can be overcome to a large extent by obtaining appropriate insurance. Before a decision is made to incorporate, a sophisticated client will also consider the pros and cons of using a partnership to carry on the business instead.

It should not automatically be assumed that, because of the unlimited liability and unwieldy management structure of partnerships, incorporation is a better way of carrying on business. For a small business operating in a "low-risk" industry, for example, it may be advantageous to start up and then carry on business as a partnership until the business becomes profitable. This would enable the partners to personally take advantage of the business losses for tax purposes.

Dissolution of a Partnership

Usually a partnership is easy to dissolve, requiring only notice to that effect by one of the partners.[57] Such notice can be implied, as in the case where a partnership was terminated when Singh, one of two partners driving a shared taxi cab, stopped driving.[58] While it is an advantage to the leaving partner to be able to dissolve the partnership simply by giving notice to the other partners, it can be a considerable disadvantage to the others, requiring the sale of the partnership assets and distribution of the proceeds to the partners. Usually this is overcome by providing in the partnership agreement a mechanism whereby one partner can leave without causing the remainder of the partnership to dissolve.

Dissolution by notice

Subject to the partnership agreement, a partnership is dissolved by the death or insolvency of any partner.[59] This provision varies slightly from province to province.[60] Dissolution can give rise to significant problems in ongoing, long-term partnerships of professional groups. Therefore, professionals will typically set out in partnership agreements that the death or insolvency of one partner will not dissolve the partnership and that, instead, the partner's share will be made available to the heir or creditor of the partner. Insurance coverage is often taken out to cover such a contingency.

Dissolution by death, bankruptcy, or insolvency

---

57. Ibid., s. 32.

58. *Singh v. Taggarh*, 2000 MBQB 53 (CanLII).

59. *Partnerships Act, supra* note 29, s. 33.

60. In Alberta, for example, a partnership is dissolved by the death or bankruptcy of a partner or by an assignment of a partner's property in trust for the benefit of his creditors. See s. 37 of the *Partnership Act, supra* note 46.

British Columbia's partnership legislation is unique because it establishes that, when more than two partners are involved, the partnership will be dissolved only in relation to the partner who has died or become bankrupt. This provision can be modified by agreement, but its unique feature is that the death or bankruptcy of one partner will not bring to an end the whole partnership relationship in the absence of an agreement among the partners.[61]

Partnership established for a specified time will end at expiry

A partnership that has been entered into for a fixed term is dissolved by the expiration of that term.[62] Similarly, a partnership that is entered into for a single venture or undertaking is dissolved by the termination of that venture or undertaking.[63] A partnership is automatically dissolved if the business engaged in by the partnership becomes illegal.[64] In addition, a partner can apply to the court to dissolve the partnership if any of the following factors are present:[65]

1. One of the partners has become mentally incompetent or otherwise incapable of performing partnership responsibilities.

2. The conduct of one partner is prejudicial to the partnership relationship, or the partner is otherwise in breach of the partnership agreement.

3. It is clear that the partnership business can be carried on only at a loss.

4. It is just and equitable that the partnership be dissolved.

Partnership can be dissolved by request to the court

Where partnerships involve corporations, a provision restricting dissolution can become a problem, especially where the nature of the corporation changes (where it is taken over by another corporation and control changes hands). In such circumstances, a wise businessperson will ensure that there is a provision in the partnership agreement allowing a partner to dissolve the partnership when such a change takes place.

CASE SUMMARY 10.12

Court Has Power to Dissolve Partnership: *Ellerforth Investments Limited v. Typhon Group Limited*[66]

A group of physicians and their spouses owned a building through a partnership and rented it out to a medical clinic. After 50 years the clinic decided not to renew the lease, leaving the partners without a tenant. The partnership comprised corporations originally consisting of the founding physicians (Ellerforth) and later bringing in a corporate investor, the Typhon Group Limited. Ellerforth was the major partner with 75 percent interest, and Typhon had a 25 percent interest. It was clear that a considerable amount of renovation was needed before a new tenant could be attracted. The Ellerforth group was unwilling to make further investment and wanted to sell the property, but the Typhon Group refused. They also refused to sell their shares or to buy out the Ellerforth shares. The partnership agreement provided for dissolution upon mutual agreement or upon sale of the assets. Since these conditions were not present, this action was brought for a court order to dissolve the partnership and for the sale of its assets.

In the course of the action, the partner refusing to sell accused the others of being responsible for the loss of the tenant, breach of fiduciary duty, and misleading the

---

61. *Partnership Act, supra* note 44, s. 36(1)(b).
62. *Partnerships Act, supra* note 29, s. 32(a).
63. Ibid., s. 32(b).
64. Ibid., s. 34.
65. Ibid., s. 35.
66. 2009 CanLII 46640 (ON SC); 2010 ONCA 275 (CanLII).

Court. The *Partnerships Act* allows the court to dissolve a partnership where it is "just and equitable to do so".[67] The judge, exercising her discretion under the *Partnerships Act*, ordered the dissolution of the partnership and the sale of the property. She found that there had been a material change in the circumstances of the partnership business that frustrated its purpose, that there was a fundamental disagreement between the partners as to its future direction, and also that the necessary trust between the partners had been lost. These factors made it just and equitable to dissolve the partnership. The decision was appealed, but the Court of Appeal agreed with the trial judge and upheld her decision to dissolve the partnership and liquidate the assets.

SMALL BUSINESS PERSPECTIVE

This case shows when the power of the court can be exercised to dissolve a partnership, but it also illustrates how important it is for parties entering into a partnership agreement to anticipate what can happen when things go wrong. Here the partner with a majority interest was prevented from doing anything without the minority partner's consent.

The effect of dissolution is to end the partnership relationship, oblige the partners to wind up the business, liquidate the assets to pay off any obligations to creditors, and then distribute any remaining assets and funds to the former partners. Individual partners should take care to give public notice of dissolution.[68] The law may require that such notice be filed with the partnership registration office or registrar of corporations, depending on the jurisdiction. For further protection, such notice should be sent to all regular customers of the business. Failure to do so may render each partner liable for the acts of the other partners even after dissolution. Note that although dissolution takes place, the partners still have the authority to act as partners and bind the firm by their actions in doing whatever is necessary to wind up the affairs of the partnership.[69]

Public notice may prevent liability

Distribution of Assets and Liabilities

Subject to the partnership agreement, when dissolving a partnership the debts must be paid first out of profits and, if they are insufficient, out of the capital the partners originally invested. If there is still not enough money to pay the debts, the creditors can then turn to the partners themselves, who are liable in the proportion in which they were entitled to share profits. Remember that all partners are liable to pay the creditors no matter what the partnership agreement says. On the other hand, once all creditors have been paid and the other obligations of the partnership are satisfied, any assets still remaining are applied first to pay back the partners for advances and then to pay back the original capital investment. Any remaining funds are divided among the partners on the established basis for sharing profits.[70]

Debts are paid out of profits first, then capital, then personal assets of partners

The dissolution of the partnership and the distribution of assets may be a problem, especially when some of the partners want to continue the business in a new partnership. To avoid this problem, the partners often agree in the partnership agreement to a different process than that described above. It should be noted that if one partner owes a debt to an outside creditor that has nothing to do with the partnership business, that creditor can claim against only the assets of that partner, including her share of the partnership assets left after all other claims against the partnership are settled.

---

67. *Partnerships Act, supra* note 29, s. 35(f).
68. *Partnerships Act, supra* note 29, s. 37.
69. Ibid., s. 38.
70. See *Partnerships Act, supra* note 29, s. 44, for the rules governing the distribution of assets on final settlement of accounts.

Limited Partnerships

Limited partners are liable only to the extent of their investment

Additions to the legislation governing partnership in every province provide for the creation of **limited partnerships**.[71] This measure gives some of the advantages of incorporation to partnerships. But partners can lose their status as limited partners if they fail to carefully adhere to all the requirements of the governing legislation, with the result that they are then deemed to be general partners with all the consequences inherent in that designation. The main advantage of a limited partnership is that it allows the partners so designated to invest money in a partnership but to avoid the unlimited liability that goes with being a general partner. The only loss a limited partner can incur is the original investment.[72] For example, if Gingras and Gitter were general partners with Leopold, a limited partner, and Gingras negligently injured a customer to the extent of $300 000 damages, Leopold would lose only his investment in the firm. Both Gingras and Gitter would be liable for the entire $300 000, but Leopold's liability would be limited to the amount he invested, even if the combined assets of Gingras and Gitter were not enough to cover the loss.

Unfortunately, it is relatively easy for the limited partner to lose that special status, thus becoming a general partner with unlimited liability. In the preceding example, if Leopold had allowed himself to be represented as a partner in the business, taken part in the control of the business, allowed his surname to be used in the name of the business, contributed services to the partnership, or otherwise failed to followed the statutory requirements set out in the Act, he would have become a general partner and would have been required to pay along with Gingras and Gitter with no limitation on his liability.

Registration is required to become a limited partner

To form a limited partnership it is necessary to file a declaration at the appropriate government registry. This declaration will set out information such as the term of the agreement, the amount of cash and other property contributed, and the way profits are to be shared.[73] The name used by the limited partnership can contain the name of the general partners, but the surname of a limited partner cannot be included in the firm name unless it is also the surname of one of the general partners. It is not possible to form a partnership with only limited partners—there must be at least one general partner in the firm—but it is possible for that general partner to be a corporation, even one without assets (a shell corporation).

REDUCING RISK 10.7

Limited partnerships may be attractive to people because of favourable tax implications. To obtain these tax benefits, limited liability may have to be sacrificed to a considerable extent through modifications set out in the partnership agreement. Often these changes are not brought to the attention of prospective investors. A sophisticated client will take great care before entering into investment vehicles structured as limited partnerships to ensure that she understands exactly what she is getting into.

Limited partners cannot take part in control of the business

A limited partner can contribute money and other property to the business, but not services. A limited partner cannot take part in the control of the business without becoming a general partner. The limited partner is not prohibited from giving the other partners advice as to the management of the business, but since it is often difficult to determine where advice stops and control of the business starts there is a considerable risk in doing so. When a business starts to fail, there is a great temptation for the limited partner to jump in to preserve the investment, but doing so raises the risk of becoming a general partner and should be avoided.

---

71. These additions vary from province to province. In Ontario, see the *Limited Partnerships Act*, R.S.O. 1990, c. L.16. In Alberta, see the *Partnership Act, supra* note 46, ss. 49–80. The discussion in the text refers to the Ontario legislation.

72. *Limited Partnerships Act, supra* note 71, s. 9.

73. In Ontario, the specifics of what is to be included in the declaration are prescribed by the *Limited Partnerships Act* General Regulation, R.R.O. 1990, Reg. 713.

Limited Liability Partnerships

Historically, professionals have not been allowed to incorporate their businesses and have therefore carried on business using partnerships. This has caused increased concern as the size of professional partnerships has grown and the number and size of liability claims against professionals have increased. Ontario addressed this issue in 1998 by introducing the **limited liability partnership (LLP)**.[74] At the time of writing, all provinces except Prince Edward Island and the territories of Nunavut and Yukon have enacted provisions for limited liability partnerships.

An LLP is formed when two or more persons enter into a written agreement that designates the partnership as an LLP and states that the agreement is governed by the *Partnerships Act*.[75] Only professionals belonging to professional organizations permitted to do so in legislation and requiring their members to carry a minimum amount of professional liability insurance coverage[76] can practise their profession through LLPs. They must include "LLP" or "L.L.P." or "Limited Liability Partnership" (or the French equivalent) in their name[77] and be registered as a limited liability partnership.[78] It is common for lawyers and accountants to form LLPs in most jurisdictions, and it is likely that other professions will follow suit. Eligible professions include accountants, chiropractors, dentists, lawyers, optometrists, and physicians.

The main advantage to professionals carrying on business in an LLP is that potential liability is limited. A limited liability partner is not liable for the liability of the partnership arising from the negligent acts or omissions of another partner or an employee, agent, or representative of the partnership.[79] This does not apply to liability caused by the partner's own negligence or the negligence of a person under the partner's direct supervision or control.[80] The result of these provisions appears to be that the partnership's assets are at risk with respect to liability caused by negligent acts or omissions of partners, employees, agents, or representatives of the LLP, but the victim of the negligence may not pursue the individual assets of non-negligent partners.

Unfortunately, the specific legislation with respect to limited liability partnerships varies somewhat from province to province. (See MyBusLawLab for specifics.) In all cases the assets of the partnership are available to satisfy any obligations arising, but once those assets are exhausted there is some variation on how limited the liability of an innocent partner will be. All jurisdictions protect the innocent partner from the negligent acts of other partners and those under their control, but when other torts, breaches of contract, or breaches of trust are involved the liability of the innocent partner depends on the *Partnership Act* of the particular province or territory involved. Also, in Ontario, for instance, a partner will be liable for the negligent acts or omissions of someone she supervises, whereas in Alberta that personal liability will only be imposed where the partner failed to provide adequate supervision.[81] Of course, insurance coverage will be available to satisfy any claims against the negligent partners, who will also be personally responsible for any shortfall. So the main advantage of LLPs is that a non-negligent partner will not face personal liability where the insurance coverage is not sufficient to cover the loss. There are other differences as well.

Keep in mind the distinction between a limited partnership and the more recent limited liability partnership. A limited partner is in effect an investor who does not participate in the partnership business—his liability is limited to losing what he has invested. However, a limited liability partner is an active professional who practises

Limited liability partners must be professionals authorized by statute, maintain minimum insurance coverage, and be registered with LLP in their name

LLPs have unlimited liability only for their own negligent acts and for those they supervise

---

74. The general provisions regarding LLPs are found in the *Partnerships Act, supra* note 29, ss. 44.1–44.4.

75. *Partnerships Act, supra* note 29, s. 44.1. LLP legislation varies from province to province. The discussion in the text is based primarily on the Ontario legislation.

76. Ibid., s. 44.2.

77. Ibid., s. 44.3(3).

78. Ibid., s. 44.3(1).

79. Ibid., s. 10(2).

80. Ibid., s. 10(3).

81. Ibid., s. 12(2).

her profession with other partners and who is liable for her own negligent acts and for those committed by others under her supervision.

Joint Ventures

Often two or more individuals or corporations wish to cooperate in developing a project together. This is called a *joint venture* and may be created in two ways. Where a new corporation is incorporated with each of the parties holding an agreed amount of shares, normal company law will apply to that new company. Company law is the subject of the following chapter.

Joint ventures can also be created through partnership. Sometimes the parties will try to accomplish such a joint venture simply by contract, but because the nature of such an activity is for the parties to join together "carrying on business in common with a view to profits" partnership law will usually apply to these activities even where the parties have specifically stated that the *Partnership Act* will not apply. Like all partnerships, joint ventures should be governed by an overriding partnership agreement that creates the partnership and sets out the rights and obligations of the partners. But remember, even when large corporations enter joint venture agreements the governing partnership agreement will only determine the rights between those parties—it will not affect the rights of outsiders dealing with the joint venture. The principle of unlimited liability also applies. Still, if the parties coming together in the joint venture are corporations, both of those corporations will face unlimited liability but the shareholders of the corporations will have limited liability, as discussed in the following chapter. The joint venture could also take the form of a limited partnership with one or more partners having limited liability so long as there is at least one general partner. Of course, that general partner could also be a corporation.

Joint venture can take the form of a corporation or a partnership

There are all sorts of permutations and combinations of individuals and business entities that could be combined to form a joint venture, and the resulting activities can consist of small business ventures or huge undertakings, such as projects in the airline industry or the Alberta oil sands. Joint ventures are also common in the construction industry and land development.

Refer to Table 10.2 for a comparative summary of the different types of business organizations.

Table 10.2 Comparison of Different Types of Business Organizations

Type of Business Organization	Created by Registration?	Number of Participants?	Separate Legal Entity?	Unlimited Personal Liability?	Vicarious Liability?
Sole proprietorship	No, but registration of business name is usually required	1	No	Yes	Yes, for employees
Partnership	No; can even be created inadvertently	2 or more	No	Yes	Yes, for employees and partners
Limited partnership	Yes	2 or more; must be at least 1 general partner	No	Only general partner	General partners for employees and other general partners
Limited liability partnership	Yes	2 or more members of an eligible profession	No	No, except for own negligence	No except for those supervised

SUMMARY

Agency

- Exists with consent from the principal
- Agents act for a principal in dealings with third parties
- Authority:
  - Actual authority is defined in the contract and may be expressed or implied
  - Apparent authority arises from the position of the agent or from the conduct of the principal
  - Exists when the principal has done something to lead a third party to believe the agent has authority, even when such authority has been specifically withheld
  - Even when the agent has exceeded both the actual and apparent authority, the principal may ratify the agreement
  - When the agent acts beyond all authority he can be sued (breach of warranty of authority)
- Agent's duties:
  - Performing terms of contract without negligence, providing an accounting of funds, and fiduciary duty
  - Normally cannot be delegated
- Principal's duties:
  - To honour terms of contract and reimburse agent's expenses
- Undisclosed principal:
  - Third party's recourse is against agent if existence of principal is not disclosed
  - Third party has a choice to sue the agent or the undisclosed principal to enforce the contract once the existence of the principal is revealed
  - Undisclosed principal cannot ratify contracts
- Vicarious liability:
  - In the absence of an employment relationship, the principal may escape vicarious liability for the acts of the agent, except when fraud or negligent misrepresentation is involved
  - Principal may be vicariously liable if misconduct of agent applies to acts within the agent's actual or apparent authority
- Fiduciary relationship:
  - Exists between the agent and the principal
  - Agent has an obligation to act in the best interests of the principal
  - Full disclosure by the agent is required
- Termination:
  - The agency relationship is typically terminated by simple notification or as agreed upon in the agency contract
  - Bankruptcy, death, or insanity of the principal or, when the principal is a corporation, the dissolution of that corporation will also terminate the agent's authority

Sole proprietor

- An individual carrying on business independently without co-owners
- Must nonetheless deal with some government regulation
- Has unlimited liability for her debts and obligations

Partnership

- Involves two or more partners carrying on business together with a view to profits
- Controlled by partnership legislation and by specific agreement of the partners
- Can be created by agreement, but often comes into existence by inadvertence when people work together in concert in a business activity
- Partners' duties:
  - Each partner is an agent for the partnership, and all partners are liable for the contracts and torts of the other partners and employees. That liability is unlimited, and all the assets of the partners, including personal assets, are at risk to satisfy such debts and obligations

- Fiduciary duty—partners must act in the best interests of the partnership
- Unanimous agreement required to effect major changes, offering partners control over the firm's direction
- Dissolution:
  - Unless the partners have agreed otherwise in their partnership agreement, dissolution occurs:
    - Upon notice to that effect from a partner
    - Upon death or bankruptcy of one of the partners
- Limited and limited liability partnerships:
  - Limited partnerships involve general and limited partners
  - Limited partners are liable only to the extent of the investment made in the business, but must be careful to protect that limited liability status
  - Limited liability partnerships are now available for professionals who cannot incorporate their businesses
  - Qualifying professions include accountants, lawyers, doctors, dentists, and others as identified by legislation
  - Limited liability partners are liable for their own negligence but not that of the partners
- Joint venture:
  - Joint venture can be accomplished through a corporation or a partnership
  - Where partnership is involved normal rules of partnership apply
  - Individuals and corporations can come together to form joint venture partnerships
  - Limited partnerships can be used to form a joint venture, providing there is at least one general partner

---

QUESTIONS FOR REVIEW

1. What is the agent's function? Why is it important to understand the law of agency in business?

2. Explain what effect an agent's limited capacity will have on the contractual obligations created between a principal and a third party. What effect would the incapacity of the principal have on this relationship?

3. Distinguish between an agent's actual, implied, and apparent authority. Explain why this distinction can be important from the agent's point of view.

4. Explain the role estoppel plays in agency law.

5. Explain what is meant by *ratification* and describe the limitations on a principal's right to ratify the actions of his agent. How can the principle of ratification be as dangerous to the principal as it is to the third party?

6. What effect does it have on the relationship between the principal and the third party when an agent writes on an agreement "subject to ratification"?

7. Agents owe a fiduciary duty to their principals. What are the requirements of that duty?

8. What options are open to a third party who has been dealing with an undisclosed principal if the contract is breached?

9. Explain how the doctrine of vicarious liability applies in a principal–agent relationship.

10. Distinguish among a sole proprietorship, a partnership, and a corporation.

11. What advantages and disadvantages are associated with carrying on business as a sole proprietorship? As a partnership?

12. Distinguish between sharing profits and sharing revenues.

13. If two people enter into a business together with the object of making money but lose it instead, can the business still be a partnership?

14. Why must a person understand the law of agency to understand the law of partnership?

15. What danger exists when a third party is led to believe that two people are partners when, in fact, they are not? What legal principle is applied in this situation?

16. What is the significance of the existence of a partnership agreement for outsiders dealing with the partnership? What is the advantage of entering into a formal agreement?

17. Explain the different ways in which a person can become responsible for the acts of her partner and describe the limitations on this responsibility. Describe the liability of retiring and new partners.

18. Partners have fiduciary obligations to each other. Explain what this means and give examples.

19. What events may bring about the end of a partnership prematurely? Under what circumstances might it be necessary to get a court order to end a partnership?

20. What will the normal effect be on a partnership when a partner dies or becomes insolvent? How is the law of British Columbia significantly different?

21. When a partnership is being dissolved and does not have sufficient assets to pay its debts, how is the responsibility for these debts distributed? How are excess assets distributed?

22. What must a person do to qualify as a limited partner? What happens when a limited partner fails to meet one of these qualifications?

23. What is the main advantage of limited liability partnerships? In light of this, what does the law require to protect those who suffer losses through the actions of a partner or an employee of a limited liability partnership?

24. Explain the nature of a joint venture, how it can be formed, and how normal partnership law applies to such a creation.

CASES AND DISCUSSION QUESTIONS

1. *B.P.Y.A. Holdings v. The Innovators Insurance*, 2001 BCSC 836 (CanLII)
Kootney Honda (B.P.Y.A.) agreed to provide a Honda CRV as a prize if a hole-in-one were scored during a golf tournament to take place in June 2000. It was then arranged, as in the past, to have Trimble of Innovators Insurance arrange appropriate coverage. This was normally given to an insurance broker, the Morgex Insurance Group Ltd., to obtain the appropriate policy. The day of the tournament, Nichol faxed the application to Trimble and received a return fax from his office stating that the hole-in-one insurance was in place. In fact, a hole-in-one was scored that day and the Honda CRV was awarded as a prize. But Morgex had never received the application from Trimble and refused to pay out on the non-existent policy. It turned out that the application had never been sent from the Innovators Insurance office.

Explain the arguments, options, and obligations of the parties. Explain the likely outcome.

2. *Ocean City Realty Ltd. v. A & M Holdings Ltd.*, 1987 CanLII 2872, 36 DLR (4th) 94 (BCCA)
Forbes was a licensed real estate salesperson working for Ocean City Realty Ltd. She was approached by Halbauer to find a commercial building in downtown Victoria. After some investigation, Forbes approached the owners of a building to determine whether it might be

for sale. The owner of the property, A & M Holdings Ltd., entered into an arrangement with her whereby they agreed to pay a commission of 1.75 percent if she acted as their agent in selling the building. After some negotiations the sale was concluded for $5.2 million, but unknown to the seller Forbes had agreed to pay back half her commission to the purchaser, Halbauer. When A & M discovered the secret deal between Forbes and Halbauer they refused to pay any commission.

Explain the basis for any complaint A & M holdings might have. Explain any counterargument that might be raised by Forbes and Ocean City Realty. Explain the likely outcome and your reasoning. If the complaint is found to be valid, what would be the appropriate remedy?

3. *3464920 Canada Inc. v. Strother*, 2005 BCCA 384 (CanLII)

A lawyer advised his client (Monarch) that they could no longer participate in a certain business because of changes to the tax laws. He then secretly took advantage of an exception provision in those tax laws to start up his own business doing the same thing. He failed to advise his client of that exception and kept his own participation in the business a secret while continuing to act as their lawyer. When the client found out, he sued both the lawyer and his partners in the law firm.

Explain the nature of the complaint and the appropriate remedy in these circumstances. Should the innocent partners also be liable for the loss?

4. *Tremblett v. Tremblett*, 2012 CanLII 67443 (NL SCTD); appeal, 2013 NLCA 34 (CanLII)

Doug and Bill Tremblett were brothers and, at least in the early stages, owned a fishing boat together. The brothers worked together in the fishing operation from 1988 to 2004 using a crab licence that Bill had acquired through a swap and that was held in his own name. The crab fishing licence was the primary asset of the business and the main subject matter of the dispute. After the brothers stopped working together Bill continued on with the fishing enterprise, relying on the crab licence he had obtained.

Explain any claim Doug might have against Bill in this situation. Would it affect your answer if Bill did more than Doug? If the value of the licence was over $800 000 at the time they stopped fishing together, what would Doug be entitled to if successful given the trial took place in 2012?

11 Chapter

Corporations

LEARNING OBJECTIVES

1. Analyze the separate legal entity principle
2. Describe the advantages and disadvantages of incorporation
3. Explain the process of incorporation
4. Discuss the funding of a corporation
5. Examine the roles of corporate directors, officers, and shareholders
6. Distinguish the ways that a corporation can be terminated

The last half of the previous chapter dealt with the simpler methods of carrying on business: sole proprietorship and partnership. This chapter will examine the third method, the incorporated company. Since incorporation is, by far, the most common means of setting up a large business organization, exposure to the concepts and forms that regulate this important aspect of the commercial world is a vital part of the study of business law. In this chapter we will review the process and effect of incorporation, some features of incorporated bodies, and the rights and responsibilities of the various parties involved.

SEPARATE LEGAL ENTITY

LO **1**

Incorporated companies provide flexibility

The concept of an incorporated company was developed in response to the need to finance large economic projects without the limitations associated with sole proprietorships and partnerships. Those projects required a large number of people to participate financially in a venture without playing active roles in it. The incorporated company was the means to accomplish this end. The most significant feature of an incorporated company is that it has a legal personality separate from the people who own shares in it. An "owner" of an incorporated company owns shares that can be bought and sold; thus, the shareholders can be continually changing, while the company itself remains intact. This structure provides considerably more flexibility for owners and directors, because shareholders need not be involved in the operation of the business and it is a much more effective method of attracting capital.

The *Salomon* case is still cited as an important authority for the existence of the company or corporation as a **separate legal entity**. The case recognized the separate legal existence of even a "one-person company." The decision emphasized that, when the incorporation process is completed, there are two legal persons: the shareholder and an incorporated company, or corporation. Although the corporation does not exist except on paper and is only a "legal fiction," all the forces of law

Corporation is a legal fiction

CASE SUMMARY 11.1

Is a Corporation a Separate Legal Entity?
Salomon v. Salomon & Co.[1]

Salomon ran a successful shoe manufacturing business that he decided to incorporate. He set up a company in which he owned almost all the shares. He then sold the business to that company. Since the company had no assets to pay for the business, he loaned the company enough money to purchase the business from himself, securing the loan with a debenture similar to a mortgage on the company's assets. In short, Salomon loaned the company he "owned" enough money to purchase the business from him and had a mortgage on the assets of the business created to secure the loan.

When the business failed because of labour problems, the creditors turned to Salomon for payment. Not only did he refuse to pay, but as a secured creditor he had first claim on the assets of the company, leaving nothing for the unsecured creditors. In fact, the other creditors had dealt only with Salomon and blamed him for their problems. They sued, claiming that he should not only be prevented from claiming ahead of them, but he should also be responsible for paying them if the company's assets were not enough.

The Court decided that, since the company was a separate legal entity, it had a separate legal existence apart from Salomon and that the debts were those of the company, not Salomon. There was nothing to prevent Salomon from selling his assets to the company and taking security back. The end result was that Salomon was a secured creditor who stood in line ahead of the unsecured creditors. He thus had first claim on the assets of the company and no responsibility for its debts.

This case graphically illustrates not only what is meant by a company or corporation being a separate legal entity, but also the consequences of limited liability on the part of the shareholder. This section will discuss the concept of the corporate entity and the legal benefits and responsibilities that result from the creation of a corporation.

SMALL BUSINESS PERSPECTIVE

Do you agree with this result? Should a major shareholder be able to escape liability for a company's debt in this way? Should a major shareholder be able to acquire priority over other creditors as was done in this case? The separate legal entity principle provides ample justification for a businessperson to operate her business through a corporation.

assume that it does exist as a legal entity separate from the shareholder and that it can function in the commercial world. Shareholders often have difficulty understanding that they do not actually own the assets of the business—the corporation they have incorporated does. Shares held in a corporation bestow the rights of control but give the right to share in the liquidation of the assets (the right to participate in capital) only when the corporation is wound up. See Figure 11.1 for an illustration of the separate legal entity concept.

Figure 11.1 Separate Legal Entity

The shareholders own the shares of the corporation. The corporation (not the shareholders!) owns the assets it purchases.

---

[1] [1897] A.C. 22 (H.L.).

The problem is the opposite when dealing with a large corporation. It is difficult to think of either Sears Canada Inc. or Imperial Oil Limited as a fiction or myth. It is easy to make the mistake of thinking of the corporation's assets (its warehouses and stores) or its shareholders as the entity. But, just as Vandenberg's car is not Vandenberg but an asset owned and used by him, so too is Sears Canada Inc. separate from its stores and its shareholders. The large corporation, just like the small one, is a legal fiction, which is often referred to as the **corporate myth**.

It is also important to recognize that the status of separate legal entity for a corporation is a flimsy one. Businesspeople are often shocked to see the courts cast aside this aspect of the law governing corporations to get at the principals of that corporation. For example, the tax department will often deem several different corporations to be one person for tax purposes. Similarly, when the object of incorporation is to get around some government regulation or to commit a fraud, the courts will ignore the separate legal entity aspect of the corporation and "lift the corporate veil" to get at the directors, shareholders, or officers committing the fraud.

Courts will sometimes ignore separate legal entity

Despite the possibility of a court lifting the corporate veil, the separate legal entity aspect of a corporation is tremendously important for commercial activities. It allows for the acquisition of capital without involving the shareholders in the operation of the corporation. It also allows the purchase and sale of the corporation's shares without interfering with the ongoing operation of the business. Like sole proprietorships and partnerships, a corporation is responsible for contracts made on its behalf and for the torts of its employees under the principle of vicarious liability. The corporation can even be convicted and fined for the commission of a crime. But it is the corporation itself that is liable, not the shareholders, who have **limited liability**. They can lose only their initial investment. It is this principle that protected Salomon in Case Summary 11.1. As a shareholder, he was not liable for the debts of the company. He was even able to claim ahead of the others as a secured creditor of the company.

Many advantages of incorporating

Limited liability is derived from separate legal entity

Today, creditors can protect themselves by requiring directors or shareholders to sign a personal guarantee and become liable for the debt along with the corporation. A significant advantage of incorporation—that of limited liability—is, to a large extent, thereby lost. Furthermore, there are examples in which the courts are willing to lift the corporate veil. But in most cases the status of the corporation as a separate legal entity will be respected. This is an important institution in our commercial world, although it is important that businesspeople not take it completely for granted.

Limited liability can be lost by giving a guarantee

CASE SUMMARY 11.2

Can a Court Lift the Corporate Veil Because It Is Unfair Not To? *Saskatchewan Government Insurance v. Qaisar*[2]

Qaisar and his wife each owned 50 percent of the shares in Asmaq Consulting Inc. All of Asmaq's revenue was generated by Qaisar's consulting work. Qaisar was paid a salary by Asmaq for the services he provided, as was his wife for the bookkeeping services she provided. Qaisar was injured in a motor vehicle accident and was unable to work. He was paid income replacement benefits by the insurer. Qaisar appealed the basis upon which the insurer calculated his benefits. The Automobile Injury Appeal Commission (AIAC) ruled that the corporate veil of Asmaq should be lifted and Qaisar should be treated as though he was self-employed as a sole proprietor.

[2.] 2011 SKCA 37 (CanLII).

The AIAC found that Qaisar's use of a corporation for his business was one of convenience only, for tax planning and income-splitting purposes. As a result of the accident, the loss to Qaisar's family was the entire net income of Asmaq, not the amount reflected as employment income in his personal tax returns. The AIAC held that it was not the intention of the legislation to create financial hardship simply because a family structured its affairs as a corporation for tax purposes. The AIAC therefore ordered the insurer to calculate Qaisar's income based on the corporation's income as if he were self-employed.

The Court of Appeal reviewed the relevant legislation and concluded that it did not allow the lifting of the corporate veil so that an employee of a corporation could be treated as self-employed. The Court also held that the AIAC did not have the power to make a decision based on its perception of the unfairness of the legislation. Qaisar's benefits were therefore to be paid on the basis of his income as an employee of the corporation.

DISCUSSION QUESTION

When, if ever, should a court have the power to "lift the corporate veil?"

REDUCING RISK 11.1

Businesspeople often incorporate their business to maximize their tax savings. There may, however, be other effects of incorporating that have negative results. The decision to incorporate should therefore be made only after considering all of the relevant factors. It may be wise to consult with an accountant and a lawyer before making such a decision; this would be the approach that a sophisticated client would follow.

The Role of Agents

Corporations must act through agents

Since the corporate entity is a legal fiction, all of its activities must be carried out through the services of real people acting as agents. The principles of agency law set out in Chapter 10 are, therefore, extremely important when dealing with corporations. Directors and employees, from officers right down to clerks, may have actual or apparent authority to bind the corporation, depending on the nature of their jobs. Historically, a corporation could be protected from unauthorized action from such employees simply by filing with the incorporation documents a specific limitation on the actual authority of an agent. Today, these limitations on authority are no longer considered notice to the public, even when they are filed with the other incorporating documents.[3]

Filed documents no longer count as notice of limited authority

LO ② PROS AND CONS OF INCORPORATION

Advantages

There are several advantages associated with incorporation, most of which are derived from the concept of the separate legal entity of the corporation.

LIMITED LIABILITY

Liability of shareholder is limited to investment

As illustrated in the *Salomon* case described in Case Summary 11.1, shareholders are not liable for the debts and other obligations of the corporation because the corporation, as a separate legal person, is responsible for its own wrongful conduct. When

---

3. See, for example, *Canada Business Corporations Act*, R.S.C. 1985, c. C-44, s. 17.

the corporation's assets are not enough to pay the unsatisfied creditors, they cannot turn to its shareholders for the difference. Shareholders can lose only what they have invested.

This limited liability, although attractive and often the primary reason for choosing to incorporate, is often only an illusion. When dealing with a closely held corporation, banks and other major creditors will usually insist on a **personal guarantee** from the major shareholders or other principals, which effectively eliminates any advantage of limited liability for those asked to sign such a guarantee.

Limited liability is lost when a guarantee given

Still, limited liability will protect shareholders from unexpected corporate obligations, such as vicarious liability for torts committed by employees or the failure to properly perform contractual obligations. Also, suppliers of materials usually do not obtain any personal commitment from shareholders, so they cannot seek compensation from them if the corporation becomes insolvent. For example, if a person operating a grocery business incorporates a corporation and borrows money from the bank for business purposes, that bank will probably insist on a personal guarantee from the shareholder. A supplier of groceries, however, would normally have no such personal commitment. If the corporation becomes insolvent, the shareholder will have to pay the bank because of the personal guarantee, but the shareholder will not be obligated to the supplier, who must look to the corporation for payment. This is because the contract for the goods supplied was with the corporation, rather than with the shareholder. If an employee of the corporation negligently injured a pedestrian while delivering groceries, the corporation would be vicariously liable for that injury, not the shareholder.

But many debts are not covered by guarantees

Even this amount of limited liability is not certain. In rare cases, the courts are willing to look behind the corporate veil and hold the principals liable for the obligations of the corporation. This is especially true when there is any taint of wrongdoing or avoidance of obligations that ought to be honoured.

In rare cases, the court will lift the corporate veil

CASE SUMMARY 11.3

When Will the Court Lift the Corporate Veil in the Event of Fraud? *N.M. Davis Corp. v. Ross*[4]

Davis, through the plaintiff corporation, loaned money to Ross, through his corporation, to finance the purchase and renovation of properties in Toronto. Ross misled Davis about the true state of affairs; he used the funds to make investments outside Ontario and to fund his lifestyle. When Ross was unable to repay the debt, he arranged to have Davis murdered. Ross pleaded guilty to murder. The plaintiff sued for the funds it was owed.

The Court granted summary judgment. Ross had admitted the facts during his criminal proceedings. The Court referred to case law that says that the separate legal personality of a corporation can be disregarded if it is being used as a shield for fraudulent or improper conduct. The Court concluded that there was fraudulent conduct and that Ross's corporation was interchangeable with him, as they were "indistinguishable" for the purpose of the loan. It was therefore appropriate to pierce the corporate veil, and judgment was entered against Ross personally.

DISCUSSION QUESTIONS

While the facts in this case made the decision obvious, businesspeople are often surprised and react negatively to a court's ability to ignore the fact of incorporation. What do you think? What distinguishes this case from the *Qaisar* case in Case Summary 11.2, in which the Saskatchewan Court of Appeal held that a decision as to whether to lift the corporate veil should not be made on the basis of fairness?

4. 2012 ONSC 1697 (CanLII).

TAXES

Although tax reforms have done away with many of the differences between the federal income taxes paid by sole proprietors, partners, and corporations, because the system is so complex there still may be advantages available to the individual taxpayer through incorporation. At the very least, the shareholder can leave the funds in the corporation and use it as a vehicle of investment, thus deferring some taxes until a later date.[5] In addition, as many provinces have not followed the federal lead, there may still be significant provincial tax advantages to be gained through incorporation.

However, federal and provincial income tax laws are extremely complicated. It is possible that incorporation will backfire and that the process will lead to more income tax being payable rather than less. When losses are experienced, as is normally the case with a new business, the taxpayer is better off if the business is not incorporated so that these losses can be applied directly against personal income. Great care must be exercised in the process of tax planning for any business, and a prudent businessperson will seek expert advice in these circumstances.

SUCCESSION AND TRANSFERABILITY

Because a corporation is a separate legal entity and a mythical person, it does not die unless some specific steps are taken to end its existence. When a partner dies, the partnership will usually come to an end. The death of even a 100 percent shareholder will not affect the existence of the corporation, although the loss may have practical implications, especially when the shareholder is involved in the ongoing operation of the business. The share is simply an asset in the hands of the shareholder. Like any other asset, it therefore forms part of the deceased's estate and, in most cases, is simply distributed to the heirs.

Thus, when two people each hold 50 percent of the shares of a corporation and they are killed in an air crash, the corporation continues and the shares would form part of the estates of the deceased. The heirs, therefore, would normally become the new shareholders. If the two people were carrying on business as partners, however, the partnership would automatically be dissolved.

When a partner leaves a partnership, the process is complex, often requiring the dissolution of the partnership. Shares in a corporation, however, can usually be transferred at will, without reference either to the other shareholders or to the corporate body. This free transferability of shares is one of the attractive features that led to the creation of the corporate entity in the first place. It provides an effective method for the contributors of capital to restrict their relationship with the corporation. When closely held corporations, which often have the same kinds of relationships as partnerships, are involved, this free transferability of shares is significantly restricted.

It is often said that a corporation cannot die, but actually there are several things that can cause a corporation to be dissolved.[6] The ultimate end for a corporation going through the bankruptcy process is dissolution by operation of law. Minority shareholders or creditors can bring an application to the court to have a corporation dissolved because of oppression or some other inappropriate conduct by the other shareholders or directors. The shareholders themselves can vote to bring the corporation to an end when they feel it is appropriate, filing articles of dissolution or a statement of intent to dissolve at the appropriate registry office. But the most common way is for the corporation to simply fail to file the required annual returns. After a year, the corporation will be considered inactive and removed from the registry. Such corporations can later be revived, or restored, by filing the missing returns along with articles of revival and any other required documentation.

[5.] See Tim Kirby, "Tax Law: To Incorporate or Not to Incorporate, That is the Question" *LawNow* (September/October 2006).

[6.] See Part XVIII of the *Canada Business Corporations Act, supra* note 3, for the legislative provisions relating to the liquidation and dissolution of federal corporations.

OBLIGATIONS OF THE PARTICIPANTS

Unlike partners, shareholders are generally free of any obligations or duties to the corporation or other shareholders. There is no fiduciary duty to act in the best interests of the corporation, or even to refrain from carrying on business in competition with the corporation.

No duty on shareholder in a corporation

The extent of this freedom of action can be illustrated by the activities of some environmental groups. They acquire a few shares in the large corporations they consider a threat to the environment for the express purpose of using the special privileges available to shareholders (such as rights to information and to attend shareholders' meetings) in the battle against the polluting corporation. Even when the interests of the environmental group are diametrically opposed to and interfere with the profit-making ventures of the corporation and other shareholders, there is no obligation to act otherwise. Only when people acquire sufficient shares to be classed as insiders, or become directors or officers, or when an individual has a majority of the shares are certain restrictions placed on shareholders' activities. These restrictions usually take the form of rules that prevent the shareholders from abusing their positions of power within the corporation and causing injury to other investors, usually through the misuse of information not available to the general public.

MANAGEMENT

In a sole proprietorship, the business is controlled by the proprietor; in a partnership, each partner is entitled to participate in the business decisions of the partnership; in a corporation, however, it is common to separate the managers from the owners. The shareholders elect a board of directors that controls the business. The directors, in turn, can hire professional managers who have the expertise to make sound business decisions on behalf of the corporation. The shareholders do not have to devote time or attention to managing, but they can change the management if they are unhappy with the decisions being made by electing different people to the board of directors.

Managers and shareholders are separate

Disadvantages

A corporation is not always the best method of carrying on business. Many of the characteristics outlined so far as advantages can just as easily be seen as drawbacks from another person's perspective.

It is helpful to compare incorporation with partnership to illustrate some of the disadvantages of incorporation. Partners who wish to change important aspects of their partnership arrangement need only reach an agreement to that effect. In the case of a corporation, however, the incorporating documents themselves may have to be altered, which is an involved and expensive procedure. A partner in a minority position may have considerable power. In a partnership, one partner can veto a proposal supported by 10 others. On the other hand, a minority shareholder in a corporation may be unable to alter unsatisfactory decisions and may not even be able to sell her shares.

Minority shareholders have a weak position in corporations

In closely held corporations, the free transferability of shares is restricted, either through shareholder agreements or by limitations placed in the incorporating documents themselves. Often, shareholders are required to get approval of a sale of their shares, or offer their shares first to the other shareholders. As with partnerships, the reason people organize themselves into small, closely held corporations is often because of the individual skills each shareholder brings to the corporation. These shareholders are usually employees as well, and their contribution to the operation of the business is often vital to its success. Free transferability of shares in such circumstances might be a significant threat to the corporation, especially if the shareholder withdraws his services when the shares are sold.

Transferability of shares may be restricted

Corporations are more expensive than other forms of business

A corporation is the most expensive way to operate a business. The initial incorporation process is costly, and the ongoing operation of a corporation involves more expense than that of sole proprietorships or partnerships. There are more formal recordkeeping requirements and generally more government control is exercised with a corporation.

But corporations can be used to create a variety of business structures

It is important to note as well that there are many variations on the corporate approach to business. Often, corporations are set up to merely hold shares in other corporations. Corporations may join other corporations or individuals in joint ventures or partnerships, usually for some major project or activity. Corporations may license others to use their products, software, or other forms of **intellectual property**, such as patents or copyrighted materials. Corporations may be part of a larger organization through **franchising**—business arrangements based on contracts of service and the supply of products between the larger and the smaller units (fast-food restaurant chains are often set up this way). Many difficulties can arise in such relationships, and the changing nature of contract law and corporate responsibility is softening the normally narrow approach to these businesses. For example, statutes imposing good faith requirements into business contracts put franchisees in a much more favourable position than they have formerly been.[7]

REDUCING RISK 11.2

Businesspeople usually assume that the best way for them to carry on their business is through incorporation. While that may in fact be the case, consideration should also be given to the alternatives. Sole proprietorship and partnership are the only real alternatives discussed in this text, although if the enterprise is not for profit or does not involve an ongoing business there are other possibilities. For example, societies are used for non-profit activities, such as charities, clubs, and religious organizations, and when property is shared, cooperatives and joint tenancy arrangements might be appropriate alternatives.

Even the choice between partnership and incorporation is not always clear. The unlimited liability of a sole proprietorship or partnership can be overcome by appropriate insurance. The tax advantages of incorporation have, to a large extent, been eliminated, or extended to sole proprietorships and partnerships as

well. The unique power of a single partner to veto the decisions of the other partners can be built into a corporation by a carefully drafted shareholder agreement. Many of the disadvantages that professionals experience because they are required to carry on their profession as partners can be overcome by creating a management corporation to manage the practice or by creating a limited liability partnership.

The point is that there are many different options and many different combinations available to a businessperson when structuring the tools used to carry on the business. Expert advice should be sought and careful consideration given to the options earlier, rather than later, in the process. A sophisticated client will not necessarily choose to incorporate her business; she will do so only if a corporation is the most appropriate form of business organization in the circumstances.

LO ③ THE PROCESS OF INCORPORATION

Royal charters were created for early corporations

An early example of incorporation was the monarch's grant of a royal charter to a town or university, thereby creating a separate legal entity. It was a natural step to extend that practice to commercial ventures. The Hudson's Bay Company was one of the earliest English commercial companies created by royal charter. Parliament also got involved by creating "special-act companies" when ventures were considered important enough to be incorporated by their own legislation.

At this stage, ordinary citizens could not incorporate. They created their own unofficial companies through contracts called **deeds of settlement**. Parliament eventually permitted incorporation for private business activities, but in the process it

---

7. Several provinces, including Alberta (*Franchises Act*, R.S.A. 2000, c. F-23), New Brunswick (*Franchises Act*, S.N.B. 2014, c. 111), Ontario (*Arthur Wishart Act (Franchise Disclosure), 2000*, S.O. 2000, c. 3), and Prince Edward Island (*Franchises Act*, R.S.P.E.I. 1988, c. F-14.1) have enacted legislation governing franchising. See *Apblouin Imports Ltd. v. Global Diaper Services Inc.*, 2013 ONSC 2592 (CanLII), for a case in which the franchisee was allowed to rescind a franchise agreement because the franchisor did not comply with the legislative disclosure requirement.

also had to accommodate the numerous voluntary contractual associations that were already in existence. The resulting legislation gave these companies formal status and the advantages of incorporation by allowing them to register at the appropriate government office and pay a fee.

Citizens were allowed to incorporate companies

Canada adopted many of the features of the British approach to incorporation. Both the federal and provincial governments have created many companies through their power to pass special statutes. For example, the Canadian Broadcasting Corporation (CBC) and the Canadian Pacific Railway (CPR) were created by special acts of Parliament. Some Canadian jurisdictions adopted the British practice of incorporation through **registration**. Other jurisdictions developed their incorporation process from the royal charter approach and created incorporated bodies through the granting of **letters patent**. A third approach, which was borrowed from the United States, is based on the filing of **articles of incorporation**. Although there are technical differences between these three methods of incorporation, it is important to understand that the practical effect of each system is the same. Each method is described in more detail below. Refer to MyBusLawLab for specific provincial variations.

Three general methods of incorporation in Canada

In Canada, it is possible to incorporate a corporation at the federal level or at the provincial level. The choice should be made on the basis of what the corporation will be doing and where it will be done. A sophisticated client will carefully consider these factors before deciding whether to incorporate federally or provincially. If the activity is to be confined to a local area, it is likely that incorporation under the provincial legislation would be appropriate. A business created to operate a restaurant would therefore be provincially incorporated. When the activity involves something that will be carried on in several provinces, such as a chain of restaurants, or generally across Canada, as with some service provided on the Internet, the federal option might be preferable. Cost will be a major consideration. It is possible, even after choosing to incorporate provincially, to carry on business in other provinces as well, but the corporation will have to be registered in all of the provinces in which it does business, with corresponding fees paid in each jurisdiction. If a corporation has been federally incorporated, it can carry on business in any part of the country, although it must go through the formality of registering extra-provincially in each province. Another factor might be the nature of the particular statute involved. For example, Quebec investors might choose to incorporate under the *Canada Business Corporations Act*, which has more favourable shareholder protection and remedies than does the Quebec legislation.[8]

Federal and provincial corporations

Registration

Incorporation through registration recognizes the contractual relationship between its members and grants them corporate status. Nova Scotia is the only jurisdiction in Canada still using the registration system of incorporation. The process involves registering a "memorandum of association" and "articles of association" with the appropriate government agency and paying the required fee. The British Columbia government introduced new corporate legislation[9] moving away from the previous registration system, but retaining significant aspects of it and creating a process of incorporation unique to that province.

Registration accomplished by filing memorandum and articles

The **memorandum of association** serves the same function as a constitution in that it sets out important matters, such as the name of the company, the authorized

Memorandum is like a constitution

8. This may no longer be the case; see Luis Millan, "In Quebec, They Both Praise and Bury," *The Bottom Line*, February 2010, www.thebottomlinenews.ca/index.php?section=article&articleid=432.

9. *Business Corporations Act*, S.B.C. 2002, c. 57. This Act was amended in 2013 to enable community contribution companies to be incorporated. Such a company is a "for profit business that must have a defined 'community purpose.'" At least 60 percent of the annual profits must be directed to the company-designated community purpose.

share capital (the total value of shares that can be sold), and when appropriate the objects of the incorporation. These objects are a list of the purposes for which the company is created. The memorandum can also set out any restrictions on those objects. Historically, these objects were important since they limited the capacity of the corporation to contract, but today, since the corporation has all of the powers and capacity of a natural person,[10] the only ones affected by these objects and any restrictions are those that have specific notice of them. Care should be taken in crafting the memorandum of association, since it is difficult to alter once it has been registered.

Operational rules in articles

The internal procedural regulations for governing the ordinary operation of the company are contained in the **articles of association** (not to be confused with the articles of incorporation used in other jurisdictions—see below). These articles deal with such matters as how shares are to be issued and transferred; requirements for meetings of the board of directors and of shareholders; voting procedures at those meetings; regulations covering borrowing; powers of directors and other officers; requirements dealing with dividends; regulations concerning company records; and how notice will be given to shareholders. The articles also set out the procedures for altering the articles, so there is considerably less difficulty in changing them than in changing the memorandum of association. But because the articles of association are filed along with the other incorporating documents, subsequent changes are more difficult to make than in the jurisdictions where the corresponding bylaws are considered internal documents and need not be filed.

Registrar has no discretion

Because this method of incorporation is accomplished by registration only, the registrar has no discretionary right to refuse incorporation except when the requirements set out in the legislation are not complied with. There is, however, less flexibility in amending the internal procedures for managing the company because of the requirement to file both the memorandum of association and the articles of association in the registration process.

Letters Patent

Use of letters patent method is declining

The letters patent method of incorporation is based on the practice of the monarch granting a royal charter. The process involves an applicant petitioning the appropriate government body for the granting of the letters patent. The government representative, acting by statute, grants a charter of incorporation to applicants who meet certain qualifications. Today, only Prince Edward Island uses this method of incorporation.

Operational rules in bylaws

The letters patent set out the constitution of the new company and contain information such as the purpose for which the company is formed, the name to be used, the share structure, any restrictions on the transferability of shares, and the rights and obligations of the parties. The rules governing the ordinary operation of the company are set out in separate bylaws. In letters patent jurisdictions, companies have always had all the powers of a natural person to enter into contracts.

Articles of Incorporation

Incorporation is accomplished through granting a certificate of incorporation

The other provinces and the federal government have adopted a system of incorporation developed in the United States based on the filing of articles of incorporation and the granting of a certificate of incorporation. The articles of incorporation method has features of both the letters patent and the registration methods. As with letters patent companies, corporations under this system are primarily the creations of government rather than being based on contract. The articles that are filed are similar to a constitution or statute controlling the activities of the parties rather than a binding agreement between them. A corporation is granted a certificate of incorporation by filing the articles of incorporation and paying the

Operational rules in bylaws

---

10. *Companies Act*, R.S.N.S. 1989, c. 81, s. 26 (8).

appropriate fee. The articles of incorporation serve the same function and contain the same types of information as the memorandum of association and the letters patent in the other systems. The day-to-day operation is controlled through bylaws similar to the bylaws in a letters patent system or the articles of association in a registration system. It is not necessary to file these bylaws when applying for incorporation. It is also important to note that in an articles of incorporation system, the government body assigned to grant certificates of incorporation has no general discretion to refuse a request for incorporation. British Columbia made significant changes to its incorporation legislation in 2002, moving much closer to this approach, but it retained some aspects of its old registration system, creating a process of incorporation that is unique to that province. Refer to MyBusLawLab for a more detailed outline of the BC changes.

A considerable amount of confusion is caused by the use of the term "articles." The articles of association used in a registration system are similar to the bylaws in articles of incorporation or letters patent jurisdictions. The "articles" in an articles of incorporation jurisdiction is the main incorporating document and so corresponds most closely to the letters patent in that system or the memorandum of association in a registration jurisdiction. To make matters worse, British Columbia, in reforming its legislation, now accomplishes incorporation through the filing of a "notice of articles." Separate articles have to be kept, but not filed, and so correspond to the bylaws in those other jurisdictions. Table 11.1 will provide assistance in keeping these differences straight.

Terminology is important

Table 11.1   Methods of Incorporation in Canada

Jurisdiction	Charter Documents	Bylaws
Nova Scotia	Memorandum	Articles (filed)
Prince Edward Island	Letters patent	Bylaws (not filed)
British Columbia	Notice of articles	Articles (not filed)
Other provinces and federal	Articles of incorporation	Bylaws (not filed)

Other Incorporated Bodies

Cities, universities, and other public institutions are incorporated legal entities that can sue or be sued in their own right. Under both federal and provincial legislation,[11] it is also possible to establish (incorporate) non-profit bodies, sometimes called "societies" or non-share capital corporations. These bodies are primarily cultural, social, charitable, and religious organizations, such as the BC Society for the Prevention of Cruelty to Animals, the Canadian Red Cross Society, and the Canadian National Institute for the Blind. The one thing these bodies have in common is the non-profit nature of their activities. The legal obligations and technicalities associated with these bodies are much simpler and more straightforward than those associated with corporations generally. Businesspeople often deal with such bodies and so should be aware of them and the statutes by which they are regulated. An examination of these non-profit organizations is beyond the scope of this text.

Societies are also incorporated

Capacity

In provinces using the registration system of incorporation, the capacity of the company to enter contracts was limited. That was more of a nuisance than anything else. Even in Nova Scotia (the only province still using the registration system), the legislation was changed so that all companies now have the capacity of a natural

Most corporations have the capacity of a natural person

---

11. See, for example, Alberta's *Societies Act*, R.S.A. 2000, c. S-12.

person. Under the articles of incorporation statutes, it is stated that a corporation has the capacity and the rights, powers, and privileges of a natural person, subject only to the provisions of the legislation.[12] The problem of capacity to contract still may arise when dealing with corporations created by special acts of the legislature or Parliament, where those acts limit their activities to specified areas. When dealing with such a corporation, it seems that unusual care should be taken to check that there is no restriction on its capacity. Some legislation states that it is possible to set down restrictions on what the corporation can do,[13] but outsiders dealing with that corporation would be affected only in the unlikely event that they had specific notice of the limitation.[14]

LO ❹

FUNDING

Funds are raised by selling shares

An important attraction of the corporation is the ability to acquire capital from a large number of sources through the sale of shares. While the **share** gives the holder an interest in the corporation, that interest falls short of ownership. The corporation remains an independent entity, separate and apart from the shareholders or members who make it up. Owning shares gives the shareholder control of the corporation and, under certain circumstances, a right to the assets of the corporation upon dissolution.

Usually there is no authorized share capital

Registration and letters patent jurisdictions typically require that the authorized share capital be set out in the incorporation documents.[15] This sets an upper limit on the shares that can be sold. This limit is usually set quite high to avoid the problem of having to go back and amend the incorporating documents. It is difficult to justify this limitation, and the articles of incorporation jurisdictions, including British Columbia, no longer require a limitation on the authorized share capital.[16]

Par-Value versus No-Par-Value Shares

Common practice is to issue no-par-value shares

The practice of issuing **par-value shares** is declining. Such practice involves each share being given a specific value, such as $1, at the time of issuance. This can be misleading, as the marketplace quickly sets a value on those shares that is not reflected in the stated par value. The more common practice in Canada and the United States is to not put a value on the share, making it a no-par-value share and allowing the marketplace to determine the value. The articles of incorporation jurisdictions (except British Columbia) have abolished par-value shares.[17] Note that although the use of par-value shares is declining, there may still be some significant tax advantages to using them.[18]

Special Rights and Restrictions

Common and preferred shares

The shares issued by a corporation are normally divided into different classes, usually called common shares and special or preferred shares. If there is only one class of shares, they will be **common shares**. If there are no preferred shares, the

---

12. See, for example, *Canada Business Corporations Act, supra* note 3, s. 15(1).

13. Ibid., s. 16(2).

14. Ibid., s. 17.

15. Nova Scotia now allows no-par-value shares to be issued and does not require a limit on the number of shares of any class. See *Companies Act, supra* note 10, s. 10(a).

16. See, for example, *Canada Business Corporations Act, supra* note 3, in which s. 6(1)(c) gives the incorporators discretion as to whether a maximum number of shares is set. Section 53(b) of BC's *Business Corporations Act, supra* note 9, states that the notice of articles must set out the maximum number of shares for each class or state that there is no maximum number.

17. See, for example, *Canada Business Corporations Act, supra* note 3, s. 24(1). British Columbia currently allows both par-value and no-par-value shares; *Business Corporations Act, supra* note 9, s. 52.

18. Janice Mucalov, "B.C.'s New Business Corporations Act Seen as Better than CBCA," *Lawyers Weekly* 23, no. 21 (October 3, 2003).

common shares must include the rights to vote at shareholders' meetings, to receive dividends declared by the corporation, and to receive the property of the corporation on its dissolution.[19]

The rights and restrictions associated with special shares can be designed to accomplish many diverse objectives. They usually give the shareholder preference when dividends are declared and are, therefore, called **preferred shares**. Usually, a preferred share will bear a promise to pay a specific dividend each year. This is not a debt, and the corporation is not obligated to declare a dividend, but once it does, the **preferred shareholders** have the right to collect first, before the **common shareholders**. These rights may be cumulative and, if they are, when there has been a failure to pay the promised dividend for a number of years, the preferred shareholder has a right to receive any back payments before the common shareholders get any dividends.

> **Preferred shareholders have preference on dividends**

Usually only common shareholders have the right to vote, but a preferred share usually gives the right to vote when the corporation fails to pay the promised dividend. There can be a right to vote even without such a provision when major changes that would materially affect the position of the preferred shareholder are proposed. For example, a proposal to change the rights or nature of the preferred share, or to sell the assets of the corporation, could not be adopted without allowing the preferred shareholders to vote.[20] Also, when a corporation is dissolved, preferred shareholders usually have the right to have those shares repaid before any funds are paid out to the holders of common shares.

> **Other rights of preferred shareholders**

Since a variety of rights and restrictions can be incorporated into preferred shares, depending on the interests of the parties, it is important that these matters be negotiated before the shares are issued. When a closely held corporation is involved, it is common to include a restriction on the transfer or sale of the shares, such as requiring the approval of the directors before the transfer or sale can take place. (Closely held and broadly held corporations are discussed below.)

Special shares are used for other purposes, such as estate planning, when two classes of shares can be created: one with a right to vote and with some control in the affairs of the corporation but no right to dividends or to receive money upon dissolution, and the other with a right to dividends but no right to vote. Such a division allows the holder of the voting shares to maintain control of the operations of the corporation but to surrender the income and the beneficial interests of the corporation to any heirs.

> **Special shares used in estate planning**

 REDUCING RISK 11.3

It is relatively easy to incorporate a business. The process is now simplified to the extent that people can either do it themselves or purchase a simple off-the-shelf corporation, much like they can purchase a suit off the rack. But these approaches may result in a loss of some of the considerable flexibility that is available using the corporate form to carry on business. It is possible—through careful use of common shares, the creation of shares with special rights and restrictions, and shareholders' agreements—to cater to a great variety of different relationships and needs, giving different rights and obligations with unique advantages to the various players. In addition, through holding corporations, corporations working together, and even corporations in partnership there is no limit to the creative solutions that can be designed to deal with a variety of business problems and needs. Businesspeople should be aware that, just as a personally tailored suit has advantages over one off the rack, paying a lawyer to custom design a corporation for their particular needs may well be worth the trouble and expense. Skimping to save a few dollars at the outset may cause expensive problems later on. A sophisticated client will be well aware of this and will therefore seek legal (and accounting) advice before determining the form of business organization best suited to achieving his objectives.

---

19. *Canada Business Corporations Act, supra* note 3, s. 24(3).
20. See s. 176 and s. 189 of the *Canada Business Corporations Act, supra* note 3, which deal with class votes and extraordinary sales or leases of the corporation's assets, respectively.

Borrowing

Corporation can borrow funds

The corporation can also borrow funds, thus accumulating debt. This can be done by borrowing large sums from a single creditor, such as a bank, which usually requires a mortgage on the property of the corporation. It can also be accomplished through the issuing of bonds or debentures, either secured or unsecured, to many different creditors. The result, in either case, is the creation of a debtor–creditor relationship and an obligation that must be repaid. When shares are involved, even preferred shares, there is no legal obligation to pay dividends, but a failure to repay a debt constitutes a breach of the corporation's legal obligation. The creditor can execute against security, bring an action, and once judgment is obtained garnish or seize the assets of the corporation. If the corporation is unable to pay, bankruptcy will likely follow.

Corporation borrows funds by issuing bonds

Usually, the terms "bond" and "debenture" are used interchangeably, but in Canada a **bond** is normally secured by a mortgage, or a floating charge, on all assets of the corporation not already mortgaged or pledged. A **debenture** is more likely to be unsecured. The corporation typically makes a debt commitment to a trustee, who then issues shares in the indebtedness to individual bondholders. These bondholders are entitled to a portion of the repayment at a set rate of interest. They are free to sell such claims to others, sometimes at a premium or discount, depending on the market.

Bondholder has right to payment

Shareholders are participants in the corporation, whereas bondholders are simply creditors. The corporation is in debt to the bondholder for the amount of the bond, but the corporation is not in debt to the shareholder for the price of the share. The bondholder can demand repayment and enforce that right in court, whereas a shareholder, even a preferred shareholder, has no similar right to demand payment of a dividend or repayment of the cost of the share.

Bondholder has no right to vote

On the other hand, while a shareholder can determine the operation of the corporation through the exercise of her voting power, a bondholder has no right to vote and cannot affect management decisions. In the event of a default, however, the bondholders usually have a right to take over the management of the corporation through the appointment of a receiver. This is similar to bankruptcy, but without the requirement of court involvement. While the corporation remains solvent, however, the shareholders retain control through their voting power, and the bondholders have only the right to be paid on a regular basis. From the investor's point of view, the choice among shares at one end, bonds at the other, and preferred shares in the middle is likely to be simply a question of balancing risk and return. To calculate those risks, an understanding of the legal differences between these vehicles and of their different tax implications is essential.

Most large corporations maintain a balance between common and preferred shares and various types of debt instruments, such as large loans and secured and unsecured corporate bonds. To illustrate, suppose Bowman wanted to incorporate a small manufacturing business. There are several ways to transfer the assets of the business to the corporation. Bowman might incorporate a corporation that would acquire the manufacturing business and any property associated with it in return for all the shares of the corporation. A better alternative, however, might be to have the corporation purchase the manufacturing business as well as any property associated with it from Bowman, giving him a bond secured by a mortgage on the property as security for the repayment of the debt.

Bowman owns all the shares of the corporation in either case. However, in the second case, instead of simply owning shares in a corporation with significant assets, Bowman is a creditor of that corporation. Because the debt will be secured, he will be in a better position to get his money back if the corporation eventually runs into financial difficulties. This is similar to the situation in which Salomon found himself in Case Summary 11.1. Before decisions are made with respect to these options, careful consideration must be given to all relevant factors, including the various tax implications of the choices. This, of course, is the approach that a sophisticated client would take. Refer to Figure 11.2 for a summary of the funding of corporations.

Figure 11.2 Funding of Corporations

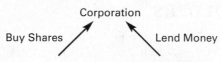

Corporation

Buy Shares   Lend Money

Shareholders
- buy shares from corporation
- common or preferred
- control corporation
- corporation not obligated to declare dividends
- share in liquidation of assets on winding up of corporation, after creditors are paid

Creditors
- lend money to corporation
- secured or unsecured
- no control over management
- corporation has legal obligation to repay loans
- entitled to be paid before shareholders, on winding up of corporation

Closely Held and Broadly Held Corporations

Traditionally, company law statutes in various jurisdictions recognized a distinction between broadly held and closely held companies, which were usually called *public* and *private companies*, respectively. In recent years, statutory provisions relating to these two classes of corporation have received considerable attention and have been significantly modified. In general, a **closely held corporation** is one in which there are relatively few shareholders. There are restrictions on the sale of shares, which cannot be sold to the general public openly or on the stock market. Closely held corporations are usually (but not always!) small corporations that are used to operate a family business. They are usually managed by the shareholders themselves. The closely held corporation is much freer of government regulations and control than the broadly held corporation. The special requirements for **broadly held corporations** are found not only in the appropriate incorporation statutes, but also in the securities legislation of that jurisdiction.

Using Alberta as an example, corporations in that province that offer shares to the public and that have more than 15 shareholders are called distributing corporations.[21] Such corporations have to satisfy the most stringent legislative requirements. For example, section 160 of the Alberta *Business Corporations Act* requires them to file financial statements with the Alberta Securities Commission. They must have an audit committee (section 171); they must provide greater access to corporate records (section 23); they cannot restrict the transfer of their shares, except to non-residents or to enable the corporation to meet any requirement to allow them to obtain a business licence, to become a publisher of a Canadian newspaper, or to acquire shares in a financial intermediary (sections 48, 174); and they must have at least three directors, two of whom must not be officers or employees of the corporation or its affiliates. A non-distributing corporation requires only one or more directors (section 101[2]). Legislative requirements for distributing corporations are found not only in the *Business Corporations Act*, but also in the securities legislation, the *Securities Act*.[22]

Non-distributing corporations with 15 or fewer shareholders have to comply with the least amount of government regulation and control. Non-distributing corporations with 16 or more shareholders that do not offer shares to the public do have to comply with more statutory requirements than those corporations with fewer than 16 shareholders, but not as much as distributing corporations.[23]

Broadly held corporations are more strictly regulated than closely held corporations

Distributing corporations

---

21. *Business Corporations Act*, R.S.A. 2000, c. B-9, s. 1.

22. R.S.A. 2000, c. S-4.

23. Such corporations must, for example, comply with s. 149 and s. 150 of the *Business Corporations Act, supra* note 21, regarding proxies and proxy solicitations, unless they are exempted by the Alberta Securities Commission.

LO ⑤ CORPORATE DIRECTORS, OFFICERS, AND SHAREHOLDERS

Directors (Managers)

WITHIN THE CORPORATION

Shareholders elect directors

The shareholders normally exercise control over a corporation through the election of directors at the annual meeting. Once the directors are elected, the shareholders have little real say in the operation of the corporation until the next election, but the expectation is that if they want to be re-elected, the directors will follow the wishes of the shareholders. Sometimes a shareholders' vote will be held when decisions involving a fundamental change in the corporation are to be made or when required by the incorporating documents. Smaller (closely held) corporations are more often run like partnerships. The shareholders are usually the managers as well as the directors, and they participate in all important decisions.

Qualifications of directors

For a person to serve as a director, he must be an adult of sound mind and cannot be a bankrupt,[24] or in some jurisdictions have been convicted of a crime involving fraud.[25] In most jurisdictions, the director no longer needs to be a shareholder.[26] Because many corporations in Canada are foreign subsidiaries, usually a significant proportion of the directors must be resident in Canada.[27] British Columbia has eliminated the residency requirement for directors altogether.

CASE SUMMARY 11.4

Fraud Disqualifies Director from Serving: *Reeves v. Hart*[28]

Hart was a director and the driving force of Sungold Entertainment Corp. (a publicly traded BC company) and Horsepower Broadcasting Network Inc. (a wholly owned subsidiary of Sungold). An application was brought by Reeves, another director of these companies, to have Hart removed as a director. This was opposed by Hart and the companies themselves. In 2002, Hart had been convicted of tax evasion, having relied on false documents overstating expenses and reducing taxable income. In British Columbia, a criminal conviction involving fraud disqualifies a person from serving as a director in a corporation registered in that province, unless the court exercises its discretion and orders otherwise.

The Court found that the tax evasion conviction involved the submission of false documents, which satisfied the definition of fraud, and disqualified Hart from acting as a director of a BC company. Even though it was suggested that the reason for the application was that Reeves was disgruntled at having lost a valuable consulting contract with Sungold, and that Hart was the driving force behind the companies and his involvement was needed for them to succeed, the Court found that there was not sufficient reason to exercise its discretion and removed Hart as a director of the two companies.

DISCUSSION QUESTIONS

This case illustrates the stringent qualifications that directors are required to not only meet but retain. Are these standards too high? Should the disgruntled shareholder have been permitted to use these provisions for his own ulterior purposes?

---

24. See, for example, *Canada Business Corporations Act*, *supra* note 3, s. 105(1).

25. See, for example, BC's *Business Corporations Act*, *supra* note 9, s. 124 (2) d.

26. See, for example, *Canada Business Corporations Act*, *supra* note 3, s. 105(2).

27. See, for example, ibid. s. 105(3) and (4). Note that the residency requirement for federal corporations was recently reduced from a majority to 25 percent.

28. (2003), 35 B.L.R. (3d) 168 (S.C.), 2003 BCSC 826 (CanLII).

A director owes a significant duty to the corporation to be careful. In common law this duty was minimal, the director being liable only when there was some blatant or gross carelessness on her part. This standard has been significantly raised in most jurisdictions. The federal legislation, for example, now requires directors to exercise the care, diligence, and skill of a "reasonably prudent person" when exercising their powers and discharging their duties.[29]

Director owes duty not to be negligent

Directors also owe a fiduciary duty to the corporation.[30] This duty requires the director to act in the best interests of the corporation, to be loyal, to avoid conflicts of interest, and to otherwise act honestly and in good faith toward the corporation. Directors are not permitted to take personal advantage of opportunities that arise because of their positions as directors, nor can they start a business in competition with the corporation. Any gains made by directors from such dealings must be paid over to the corporation, but any losses must be borne by that director alone. When a director is personally involved in some transaction that the corporation may become involved in, the director must disclose that interest by making a declaration to the board of directors, avoid any involvement in the discussion of the matter, and abstain from voting on it.[31]

Director owes fiduciary duty

A major problem associated with directors' liability is that they owe a fiduciary duty to the corporation itself, not to the shareholders. Only the corporation can sue the director when this duty is violated. Since the directors decide what the corporation does, a decision to sue a director must be made by the directors, and they are not likely to decide to sue themselves. In the *Wise* case discussed in Case Summary 11.5, the Supreme Court clarified that the directors owe a fiduciary duty to the corporation only, and not to other stakeholders such as creditors or shareholders, even when the corporation is insolvent. The Court also made it clear that a duty of care is owed to creditors, and while that is less onerous than a fiduciary duty, a duty of care still imposes on directors a significant exposure to liability for negligence.

Director owes a fiduciary duty to the corporation, not to shareholders

In most circumstances, however, only the corporation can sue the director. To solve this problem, many jurisdictions give even minority shareholders the right to bring what is called a **derivative action** (in some provinces, a **representative action**) against the directors or others on behalf of the injured corporation.[32] This change, along with the change in the nature of the imposed duty to be careful, has significantly enhanced the peril associated with being a director. Refer to MyBusLawLab for province-specific legislation.

Derivative or representative action

CASE SUMMARY 11.5

The Nature of a Director's Duty: *Peoples Department Stores Inc. (Trustee of) v. Wise*[33]

In 1992, Wise Stores Inc. ("Wise") purchased the shares of its rival, Peoples. Lionel, Ralph, and Harold Wise were the majority shareholders, officers, and directors of Wise. They became the sole directors of Peoples. Wise and Peoples were two large department store chains operating in Ontario and Atlantic Canada. For increased efficiency Wise and Peoples instituted a joint inventory and purchasing process. Soon after, both stores were forced into bankruptcy. The trustee in bankruptcy of Peoples, acting for its creditors, brought this action against the three Wise brothers. He claimed that, as directors of Peoples, the brothers had violated their fiduciary duty to Peoples and to Peoples' creditors by favouring the interests of Wise in the joint inventory and purchasing scheme.

---

29. *Canada Business Corporations Act, supra* note 3, s. 122(1)(b).
30. Ibid. s. 122(1)(a).
31. Ibid. s. 120.
32. Ibid. s. 239.
33. [2004] 3 S.C.R. 461, 2004 SCC 68.

The matter went to the Supreme Court of Canada, which made it clear that an honest and good faith attempt to solve a corporation's financial problems does not, if unsuccessful, qualify as a breach of fiduciary duty. The Court held the fiduciary duty of directors was owed only to the corporation and not to its creditors. The fiduciary duty does not change when a corporation is in the nebulous "vicinity of insolvency." Directors owe their fiduciary obligations only to the corporation, not to the corporation's creditors or to any other stakeholder.

The Court also noted that this restriction in the scope of the directors' obligations did not apply to a duty of care and so would not protect them from a negligence action brought by creditors. The case is important because it differentiates between a fiduciary duty owed only to the corporation and a duty of care that can also be owed to other stakeholders. The Court pointed out that the other stakeholders had options, including the right to bring an oppression action against the directors or a derivative action on behalf of the corporation against the directors.

DISCUSSION QUESTIONS

Do you think that the fiduciary duty owed by a director should be limited to the corporation, or should it be extended to the shareholders or creditors? Is even the imposition of a fiduciary duty to the corporation setting too onerous a responsibility on directors? Consider the problems that arise when a director is a director of both a parent and a subsidiary. To whom is the fiduciary duty owed? What should be done when the interests of the two corporations are in conflict?

Directors may face personal liability

In addition to these general duties, statutes in all jurisdictions set out many specific responsibilities and liabilities to which directors are subject when they make specific prohibited decisions. For example, directors become personally liable if they allow shares to be sold for consideration that is less than the fair equivalent of the money that the corporation would have received if the share had been issued for money.[34] Directors will also be personally liable if they allow transactions that are not permitted by the legislation, such as the purchase of shares or the payment of dividends by the corporation if there are reasonable grounds for believing that the corporation would, after carrying out the transaction, be unable to pay its liabilities as they become due, or if the value of its assets would then be less than the value of its liabilities.[35] Finally, directors may be liable if they contravene specific responsibilities as set out in the legislation, such as the calling of annual shareholders' meetings.[36]

Directors are "insiders"

Directors (and officers and others who are deemed to be insiders) are prohibited from using **insider knowledge** to their own advantage or to the advantage of their friends or family. That is, directors who are aware of something about to happen that will materially affect the value of shares, bonds, or other assets of the corporation are prohibited from using that knowledge to their own advantage through dealing in these assets. There are strict disclosure requirements whenever an insider trades in the securities of the corporation. The misuse of insider information is prohibited by securities legislation, and an offender is subject to fines and imprisonment. The *Canada Business Corporations Act* also provides for personal civil liability of a director who commits insider trading.[37]

There are many other statutes that impose duties and responsibilities on directors. Directors of larger corporations, for example, face personal financial liability

---

34. *Canada Business Corporations Act, supra* note 3, s. 118(1).

35. Ibid., s. 118(2).

36. Ibid., s. 133(1).

37. Ibid., s. 131. See *Tongue v. Vencap Equities Alberta Ltd.* (1996), 184 A.R. 368 (C.A.), 1996 ABCA 208 (CanLII), in which the Court found the directors of a corporation personally liable for damages for breach of fiduciary duty and insider trading under the *Canada Business Corporations Act*.

and even imprisonment if information is not provided to the chief statistician of Canada, as required by the *Corporations Returns Act*.[38]

EXTERNAL OBLIGATIONS

Various federal and provincial statutes impose personal liability on the director primarily in three areas. Directors can be held personally liable when a corporation fails while owing workers unpaid wages.[39] Often, when a corporation is in trouble, directors will resign rather than face this risk. Sometimes the corporation will agree to indemnify them, but if the corporation fails such an agreement is useless. Insurance provides the best protection in these circumstances. Directors can also be held personally liable for breaches of employment standards legislation, as well as workers' compensation and occupational health and safety legislation in place in the particular jurisdiction. Refer to MyBusLawLab for specifics.

A second area of personal liability for directors involves unpaid taxes. Under federal income tax legislation, the directors are personally responsible if back taxes are left unpaid.[40] In many jurisdictions in Canada, if foreign firms wish to operate they must have local resident directors.[41] Local businesspeople are often expected to act as token directors and are not actually expected to participate in the decision-making process of the corporation. Many take these positions not realizing their exposure. If the corporation fails, leaving unpaid taxes and other obligations, the personal liability can be ruinous. A sophisticated client would not allow himself to end up in such a situation.

> **Directors have a statutory duty for . . .**
>
> **. . . wages**
>
> **. . . taxes**

CASE SUMMARY 11.6

When Are Directors Liable for Unpaid Taxes?
Lagacé v. Canada[42]

Lagacé, as a director of the corporation, was issued a liability assessment for the corporation's unremitted GST. Lagacé argued that the due diligence defence applied and that she exercised the degree of care, diligence, and skill that a reasonably prudent person would have exercised in the circumstances. She claimed that the failure to remit GST was due to the negligence of the corporation's external tax accountant.

The Court referred to *Canada v. Buckingham*,[43] in which the Federal Court of Appeal indicated that the relevant standard when evaluating a director's due diligence was objective, not subjective as it had been previously. The objective standard is higher than one involving a director's own personal skills, knowledge, abilities, and capacities. This puts pressure on corporations to improve the quality of directors' decisions and discourages the appointment of inactive directors.

The Court stated that the duty of a director is to prevent the failure of the corporation to remit the various types of taxes. A director will not be liable when taxes are not remitted if she established that she exceeded her duty of care, diligence, and skill to prevent a failure by the corporation to make the required remittances.

---

[38] R.S.C. 1985, c. C-43.

[39] See, for example, s. 119 of the *Canada Business Corporations Act, supra* note 3, which makes directors of federal corporations liable for up to six months' wages payable to each employee of the corporation. For a discussion of two cases in which directors of corporations were found liable for unpaid wages, see Glenn Kauth, "Directors on Hook for Unpaid Wages and Benefits," *Law Times*, September 22, 2008.

[40] This includes liability for the corporation's failure to remit any prescribed amounts under the *Income Tax Act*, R.S.C. 1985, c. 1 (5th Supp.), s. 227.1, and the *Excise Tax Act*, R.S.C. 1985, c. E-15, s. 323.

[41] *Canada Business Corporations Act, supra* note 3, s. 105(3) and (4), discussed above in note 26.

[42] 2012 TCC 117 (CanLII).

[43] 2011 FCA 142 (CanLII).

Here the Court held that an arrangement by which the corporation would pay its GST debt as it earned commission income was not due diligence. There was no evidence that the external accountant was negligent. Lagacé was therefore found personally liable as a director of the corporation for the GST owed by the corporation.

SMALL BUSINESS PERSPECTIVE

Do you agree with this outcome? Is there too much responsibility imposed on the directors of corporations? Has the separate legal entity principle been diluted too much?

. . . environment

The third area involves environmental regulation. Complicated statutes impose personal liability on directors for damages caused by the corporation to the environment.[44] Contamination of property, pollution of the air, unexpected spills, and the cost of cleanup are examples of potential sources of a director's personal liability. In addition to potential fines and imprisonment, the directors may also face being personally responsible for the actual damages caused or the costs of cleanup in a civil action.

Usually directors can escape liability only when they can show that they acted with due diligence.[45] What constitutes **due diligence** varies with the situation but, in general, directors must show that they kept themselves informed of what was required of the corporation and what the corporation was doing to comply, and that they did all that was reasonable to avoid the problem.

. . . other

Individual liability has also been imposed on directors for offences under consumer protection legislation, the federal *Competition Act,* securities legislation, and provincial human rights codes. It is important to note that many of these statutes not only contemplate fines but also provide for imprisonment in extreme situations. Both criminal and civil responsibilities may be imposed on the corporation itself, as well as on its directors and officers.

Tort liability

It should also be remembered that when the commission of a tort, such as misrepresentation or deceit, is involved, a director may be held personally liable if he was the one who committed the wrong. The corporate structure sometimes does not provide protection to the person who actually commits the tort. The decisions on this issue have been inconsistent, but the following statement appears to accurately state the law:

> There will be circumstances in which the actions of a shareholder, officer, director or employee of a corporation may give rise to personal liability in tort despite the fact that the impugned acts were ones performed in the course of their duties to the corporation. Where those actions are themselves tortious or exhibit a separate identity or interest from that of the corporation so as to make the act or conduct complained of their own, they may well attract personal liability.[46]

Criminal liability

The *Criminal Code* imposes a duty to take reasonable steps to prevent bodily harm in respect to workplace safety (section 217.1). A corporation can be found liable for

---

[44.] See, for example, s. 280(1) of the *Canadian Environmental Protection Act, 1999,* S.C. 1999, c. 33, which states that when a corporation has committed an offence, any director, officer, or agent of the corporation who "directed, authorized, assented to, acquiesced in or participated in" the commission of the offence is also guilty of the offence and liable to the punishment provided for the offence, whether or not the corporation is prosecuted or convicted.

[45.] Ibid., s. 283. Section 280.1(1) states that a director must take "all reasonable care" to ensure that the corporation complies with the legislation.

[46.] *Blacklaws v. Morrow* (2000), 261 A.R. 28 (C.A.), 2000 ABCA 175 (CanLII); leave to appeal refused, [2000] S.C.C.A. No. 442, para. 41. For a case in which a director was found to be personally liable in tort, see *ADGA Systems International Ltd. v. Valcom Ltd.* (1999), 43 O.R. (3d) 101 (C.A.), 1999 CanLII 1527 (ON CA); leave to appeal refused, [1999] S.C.C.A. No. 124.

criminal negligence if an employee, agent, or contractor is a party to an offence and the responsible "senior officer . . . departs markedly from the standard of care that could reasonably be expected" (section 22.1). (A "senior officer" includes a director, the chief executive officer, and the chief financial officer [section 2].) Corporations can be found guilty of a criminal offence requiring fault (section 22.2) when a senior officer, with the intent to benefit the organization, commits the offence, directs other representatives of the organization so that they commit the offence, or does not take all reasonable steps to stop a representative from committing the offence. Directors (as well as officers and employees) are, of course, liable for the crimes they commit. This would include breaching the duty set out in section 217.1.

Officers and Senior Executives

CASE SUMMARY 11.7

Do Officers Owe a Fiduciary Duty to the Corporation?
Can. Aero v. O'Malley[47]

O'Malley (president and chief executive officer) and Zarzycki (executive vice-president) were senior management officers of Canaero, a wholly owned subsidiary of the US company Canadian Aero Services Ltd. involved in topographical mapping and geophysical exploration.

When an opportunity to pursue a project in Guyana, financed through aid money from the Canadian government, came up, O'Malley and Zarzycki resigned from Canaero and incorporated their own company (Terra Surveys Ltd.) to divert the project from Canaero to Terra. O'Malley and Zarzycki had been involved in other projects for Canaero in the area and knew the local officials. They had been involved in the preparation work for the project for Canaero.

The Supreme Court of Canada found that these senior officers owed a fiduciary duty to Canaero. In the process of incorporating a rival company and diverting the Guyana project away from Canaero to their new company, they had violated that fiduciary duty. The Court held that this duty continued after they had left their position of employment. They were found liable for the damage caused. Note that the Court made it clear that the senior officers owed a fiduciary duty similar to that of a director of the company.

DISCUSSION QUESTIONS
Do you agree that the fiduciary duty owed by directors and senior officers of a corporation should continue after they cease holding their positions?

Although directors are legally responsible for management, in a large corporation they usually appoint a managing director or chief executive officer (CEO), who is given overall responsibility, along with a managing committee of the directors to run the affairs of the corporation. The day-to-day operation of the corporation is assigned to others who report to the CEO. These officers may include a president, treasurer, secretary, and other senior executives, such as vice-presidents and managers, as deemed appropriate for the organization. In general, these officers and managers are in a fiduciary relationship to the corporation, similar to that of directors. They owe the same types of general obligations, duties of care, and competence to the corporation as the directors, but may be held to an even higher standard. In the case of statutory obligations, they may have to pay any wages and taxes owing. They may be held personally liable for judgments against the

Similar duties are owed by senior management

---

47. [1974] S.C.R. 592.

corporation in human rights and consumer complaint actions, as well as costs for cleaning up any environmental damage caused by the corporation.[48] The legislation usually imposes the same obligations on officers as those imposed on directors. The *O'Malley* case in Case Summary 11.7 shows the nature of the fiduciary duty as well as how that duty can continue even after the employment relationship has ceased.

Promoters

Promoters also owe duties . . .

A **promoter** is someone who participates in the initial setting up of the corporation or who assists the corporation in making a public share offering. Provincial securities statutes control the sale of shares to the public, whether through the stock exchange or other means. A **securities commission** is established to prevent fraud and to encourage a free and efficient market in corporate shares and other securities. This requires the complete disclosure of as much information as possible. To accomplish this, a proper prospectus must be issued when shares are to be sold to the public. The purpose of the **prospectus** is to disclose all pertinent information of interest to investors about the corporation and its business operations. The corporation and the promoters are responsible to ensure full disclosure and that there is no misrepresentation in the prospectus. In addition to any civil liability, significant fines and jail sentences may be imposed when there is not full disclosure or when misrepresentations take place.

The securities commission is also charged with controlling other forms of abuse, including insider trading (when officers or people holding significant percentages of the shares of a corporation trade in those shares using their insider knowledge to anticipate a rise or fall in prices). The securities commission also controls abuses by providing for the licensing and regulation of all those involved in the selling and marketing of shares and other securities, including brokers, sales personnel, and the issuers of the shares (the corporations) themselves.

. . . including a fiduciary duty

Whether promoters are officers of the corporation or not, they, like directors and other officers, owe a fiduciary duty to the corporation. This includes, for example, a duty to disclose any personal interest in deals in which the corporation is involved. When a promoter acquires property with the intention of incorporating a corporation and then selling that property to it, she has a duty to act in the best interests of the corporation. The promoter cannot sell the property to the corporation at an excessive profit, she must divulge the original price paid for the property, and she must not participate in the decision of the corporation to purchase the property from her.

CASE SUMMARY 11.8

When Is a Promoter Personally Liable? *1080409 Ontario Ltd. v. Hunter*[49]

Garth Drabinsky incorporated 1080409 to purchase the subject property. He later decided to sell the property. He entered into an agreement with Hunter, but the purchase and sale agreement was in the name "Furama Investments." Furama was not incorporated. Hunter did not have sufficient funds, so the deal did not close. 1080409 later sold the property to a third party but at a lower price than Hunter had agreed to pay. 1080409 sued Hunter for the difference in net proceeds.

---

48. For example, the personal liability described in s. 280(1) of the *Canadian Environmental Protection Act, 1999, supra* note 44, extends not only to directors but also to officers and agents of the corporation.

49. 2000 CanLII 22405 (ON SC).

The Court found that Hunter was personally liable, pursuant to section 21 of the Ontario *Business Corporations Act*, which provided in part that:

21(1) Except as provided in this section, a person who enters into an oral or written contract in the name of or on behalf of a corporation before it comes into existence is personally bound by the contract and is entitled to the benefits thereof.

21(4) If expressly so provided in the oral or written contract referred to in subsection (1), a person who purported to act in the name of or on behalf of the corporation before it came into existence is not in any event bound by the contract or entitled to the benefits thereof.

Hunter had signed the agreement on behalf of a corporation before it came into existence. He could have expressly provided in the purchase and sale agreement that he was not personally bound by the agreement, but he did not do so. Damages were assessed on the basis of what 1080409 would have received had the agreement been performed.

SMALL BUSINESS PERSPECTIVE

Should a businessperson enter into agreements prior to incorporating? If so, what should he do to minimize his potential liability?

 REDUCING RISK 11.4

Promoters will often purchase property on behalf of a corporation before it has been incorporated and then have the corporation ratify the agreement after incorporation. Such ratification of pre-incorporation contracts is invalid in common law, since the corporation did not exist at the time the promoter was claiming to act on its behalf. Although this common law restriction against ratifying pre-incorporation contracts makes logical sense, it causes problems from a business point of view, and many jurisdictions have made legislative changes permitting the later-incorporated corporation to ratify a pre-incorporation contract.[50] The result is that the contract is valid and binding on the corporation once it is so ratified. Of course, if the corporation does not ratify, or if a pre-incorporation contract is signed in a jurisdiction where the corporation cannot ratify, the promoter remains solely liable for any losses since there was no authority to act. Businesspeople should try to avoid personal liability for pre-incorporation contracts. A sophisticated client would achieve this result by ensuring that a provision exempting her from any resulting liability is included in the contract.

Shareholders

One of the main attractions of incorporation is that shareholders have few obligations to the corporation, or to other shareholders, other than to not use insider knowledge for their own purposes. Unlike directors, shareholders usually have no duty to act in the best interests of the corporation or other shareholders. They may have some obligations if they hold enough shares to be classified as "insiders." The number of shares required to qualify as an insider varies from one jurisdiction to another.[51] Shareholders who have been classified as insiders have the same obligation as directors to not use insider information to their own benefit or to the benefit of friends or relatives.

Shareholders have few responsibilities

[50.] See, for example, *Canada Business Corporations Act, supra* note 3, s. 14.

[51.] Section 131(1)(d) of the *Canada Business Corporations Act,* ibid., together with s. 40 of the *Canada Business Corporations Regulations, 2001,* SOR/2001–512, states that any person who beneficially owns or exercises control or direction over at least 10 percent of the outstanding voting shares of a corporation is considered an "insider."

CASE SUMMARY 11.9

Do Shareholders Owe a Fiduciary Duty to Anybody?
Harris v. Leikin Group Inc.[52]

This was a complicated case involving 11 cousins who owned the common shares of a group of closely held corporations. Eight of the cousins decided to "monetize" the value of their interests in some of the corporations' assets. They entered into a share redemption transaction with the corporations. To fund the share redemptions, an equity investor purchased a 50 percent interest in one of the assets. The investor made the price of the interest public. The selling cousins realized the price was much higher than the attributed value of the asset that had determined the share redemption price. Six of the eight selling cousins sued the non-selling cousins. The claim included allegations of breach of fiduciary duty.

The selling shareholders asserted that the non-selling shareholders owed a fiduciary duty to all shareholders that could only be satisfied by the disclosure of the material information, namely, the value of the asset. The non-selling shareholders argued that they disclosed all material information and that there was no fiduciary duty because the transaction pitted one group of shareholders in opposition to the other.

The Court stated that a fiduciary relationship is one that requires the fiduciary to act with absolute loyalty toward the other party. The Court confirmed that there is a *per se* fiduciary relationship between a director and the corporation, but not between a director and a shareholder or between shareholders. The Court also noted that an *ad hoc* fiduciary relationship may arise as a matter of fact out of the specific circumstances of a particular relationship. In such a case, fiduciary duties are imposed on a person because his relationship with another presumes the existence of fiduciary obligations. This depends on the specific circumstances. Fiduciary duties rarely arise in arm's length commercial transactions.

In this particular situation, the Court ruled that there was not even an *ad hoc* fiduciary relationship between the two groups of shareholders. The two groups had negotiated an agreement based on "hard self-interested bargaining," and they did not trust each other. The selling shareholders had relied on their own advisers during the negotiations.

DISCUSSION QUESTIONS
Should a shareholder owe a fiduciary obligation to the corporation or to other shareholders? What if she is a major shareholder?

RIGHTS

Shareholders have the right to see some records and reports . . .

Shareholders do have significant rights and remedies. Certain records must be kept at a designated corporate office and made available to the shareholders.[53] These records include the following:

- the documents of incorporation
- lists of all the shareholders
- lists of transactions or changes in relationship to the shares
- lists of officers, directors, and debenture holders
- minutes of shareholders' meetings.

. . . but not all records

Some corporate records, including the minutes of directors' meetings and the actual financial records ("the books"), are not available to shareholders. Otherwise,

---

[52.] 2013 ONSC 1525 (CanLII).

[53.] *Canada Business Corporations Act, supra* note 3, ss. 20, 21, 138(4).

such information could not be kept from competitors. Nonetheless, much important information is contained in documents that are accessible to anybody who holds a share in the corporation.

Shareholders are entitled to receive copies of annual financial statements of the corporation and the auditor's report, if any.[54] The financial statements of broadly held corporations must be audited.[55] An **auditor** is an unbiased outside accountant whose responsibility it is to ensure that the financial statements use generally accepted accounting practices and are accurate.[56] The auditor's duty is to the shareholders, not to the directors, and the auditors have access to the corporation's books to ensure the accuracy of their conclusions.[57] Shareholders who have some doubts about the accuracy of these audited statements can have an inspector appointed to examine the auditing process.[58]

Financial statements must be provided

The shareholders also have considerable power to affect the decisions made by the corporation. An **annual general meeting** of shareholders must be held at which the shareholders are given an opportunity to vote for the directors of the corporation, making the directors directly answerable to the shareholders for their actions. Advance notice of this meeting, including the appropriate financial statements, must be given to the shareholders. Any major changes that will affect the nature of the corporation must be placed before the shareholders to vote on before the decisions are implemented. If necessary, a special meeting can be called for this purpose.

Annual general meetings must be held

Shareholders have the right to vote

The incorporating documents or bylaws of the corporation may provide for the right of shareholders to vote in other situations as well. Shareholders at these meetings can put forward proposals concerning any matter for the decision of the other shareholders, but management may refuse to submit a proposal if it appears that it is self-serving or is, in some way, an abuse of the process. It must be remembered that each vote is based on the number of shares held. Thus, someone holding a majority of the shares will always be able to outvote minority shareholders.[59]

Votes are based on number of shares

Shareholders can pass their right to vote at the annual general meeting to someone else in the form of a **proxy**. Proxies can be very important when groups of shareholders band together to affect a particular result or to determine which directors are elected at the annual general meeting. The rules for the creation and operation of proxies are quite strict because of the potential for abuse.[60] For example, for federal corporations proxies (with some exceptions) cannot be solicited except by a circular in a form prescribed by regulation.[61] A proxy holder who fails to comply with the directions of the shareholder is liable to a fine of up to $5000 and/or imprisonment for up to six months.[62]

Proxy can be passed to someone else

The bylaws or articles set out how many votes each shareholder is entitled to, but this may vary with the type of shares held. Holders of common shares are usually entitled to one vote per share. Preferred shareholders usually cannot vote unless a promised dividend has not been paid. A shareholder holding a significant portion of

Preferred shareholders may have the right to vote

---

[54] Ibid., ss. 159, 169(1).

[55] Ibid., s. 163.

[56] Ibid., s. 161.

[57] Ibid., s. 170.

[58] Ibid., Part XIX.

[59] Most of the requirements regarding annual general meetings are set out in Part XII of the *Canada Business Corporations Act*, ibid. But see also s. 106(3), requiring the election of directors by shareholders at the annual general meeting of the shareholders, and Part XV, dealing with fundamental changes, which must be approved by special resolution of the shareholders (i.e., by at least two-thirds of the votes cast). It should be noted that the amendments to the federal legislation in 2001 resulted in many changes to the rules governing annual general meetings. In particular, shareholder meetings for federal corporations may now be held by electronic means, and voting can be carried out by using telephonic or electronic communications facilities—see ss. 132 and 141.

[60] The rules relating to proxies are set out in Part XIII of the *Canada Business Corporations Act*, ibid.

[61] Ibid., s. 150.

[62] Ibid., s. 152(4).

the shares can usually force the calling of an extra meeting,[63] while someone with fewer shares, if he has good reason, can apply to the court for the same purpose.[64] However, the majority shareholder is still protected, as a majority vote or greater is necessary to decide all matters once the meeting is held.

Pre-emptive rights entitle shareholders to be offered any new shares first

In many jurisdictions, shareholders have the right not to have their proportion of shares diluted by the sale of more shares to others. If there are 1000 shares outstanding and Pantaz has 500 of them, she owns 50 percent of the corporation. If the directors decide to issue 500 new shares and none are offered to Pantaz, her interest will be reduced to a one-third portion. In smaller corporations this is usually avoided by including, in a separate shareholders' agreement, a provision requiring that a sufficient number of the new shares be offered to the existing shareholders first so that they may retain their proportionate share of the corporation. Such a right is called a **pre-emptive right**. In most jurisdictions in Canada, pre-emptive rights exist only when actually granted in the incorporating documents or shareholders' agreements.[65]

Weak position of minority shareholders

These shareholder rights may seem significant, but to a minority shareholder such power may be an illusion. In large corporations with a great numbers of shares distributed, an individual shareholder's rights may be considerably diluted and the only practical recourse may be to sell the shares. In small, closely held corporations there is usually a restriction on the sale of shares. The "locked-in" shareholder may be unable to sell those shares and unable to influence the course of the corporation because of the overriding control exercised by the majority shareholder.

CASE SUMMARY 11.10

Can a Minority Shareholder Commence a Lawsuit on Behalf of the Corporation? *Sevaal Holdings Inc. v. LCB Properties Inc.*[66]

Bruce and Carman were brothers who succeeded together in business despite an uneasy personal relationship. LCB was a real estate holding corporation whose shares were owned equally by Carman's holding corporation and Bruce's holding corporation, Sevaal. Bruce and Carman were the directors of LCB.

Without Carman's approval, Bruce sold LCB's interest in some property to a corporation owned by another brother. Bruce did not disclose to Carman that he had a formal appraisal of the property. The sale price of the property was more than $1 million below market value.

When Carman learned of the appraisal, he sought leave from the Court to start a derivative action for damages for Bruce's breach of fiduciary duty as a director for selling the property without authorization and for a purchase price that was 34 percent below market value. Bruce claimed that the sale was in the best interests of LCB since he and the other brother needed to make the transaction for estate planning purposes.

The Court held that a resolution signed by both directors was required for the selling of lands owned by the corporation. As Carman was never given an opportunity to approve or disapprove the sale, there was no deadlock. A derivative action is appropriate when a single director, without the approval of the board of directors, sells corporate property for less than market value, thereby reducing the value of the corporation's shares. This was a breach of a director's fiduciary duty to serve the best interests of the corporation. The Court therefore granted leave for a derivative action, as such an action would be in the corporation's best interests.

[63.] Ibid. Section 143 states that the holders of not less than 5 percent of the issued shares may cause a meeting to be called.

[64.] Ibid., s. 144.

[65.] Ibid., s. 28.

[66.] 2014 SKQB 47.

SHAREHOLDER PROTECTIONS

To protect minority shareholders from abuse, the statutes have provided several safeguards. The most important of these is the shareholder's right to sue the directors on behalf of the corporation when the directors have done something actionable. The right to a derivative or representative action exists in British Columbia, Nova Scotia, and those jurisdictions that use the articles of incorporation method of incorporation.[67]

> **Derivative or representative action**

To succeed in a derivative action, a shareholder must show that it is in the interests of the corporation that the action be brought. In the *Sevaal Holdings* case in Case Summary 11.10, one of the directors of the corporation sold corporate assets without authorization for less than market value. This reduced the value of the corporate shares. The Court allowed a shareholder of the corporation to commence a derivative action because it was in the best interests of the corporation.[68]

> **Must be in the interests of the corporation**

In certain circumstances, the shareholder might be able to bring an **oppression action**. Under the federal legislation, current (or past) shareholders, directors, and officers, along with any other person (including a creditor) who, in the discretion of the court, is a proper person, may seek relief from the court on the basis of oppression or unfair prejudice.[69] For example, the directors might arrange for the sale of shares just to weaken the voting position of a particular shareholder or, if the shareholder is also an employee, the directors might fire the shareholder to force the sale of the shares. In some jurisdictions, "complainants" have the right to go to court to seek an order for relief from oppression if this type of abuse has taken place. The court may then make any order it thinks fit, including granting a restraining order, appointing a receiver or receiver-manager, appointing new directors, ordering compensation, or ordering liquidation or dissolution of the corporation.[70] The oppression action is becoming more common because of the wide discretion it allows the courts in granting remedies to complainants.[71]

> **Shareholders have the right to relief from oppression**

CASE SUMMARY 11.11

Oppression Remedy Available to Creditors as Well:
Glasscell Isofab Inc. v. Thompson[72]

Thompson was the sole shareholder, officer, and director of TSL. Glasscell supplied product to TSL. When TSL failed to pay its debt, Glasscell sued. It was awarded default judgment for more than $160 000. It then garnished a bank account of TSL and obtained $15 000. The very next day Thompson's wife incorporated a numbered corporation (1833) and

---

67. See, for example, *Canada Business Corporations Act, supra* note 3, s. 239.

68. See *McAskill v. TransAtlantic Petroleum Corp.* (2002), 332 A.R. 96 (Q.B.), 2002 ABQB 1101 (CanLII), for a useful judicial summary of the case law on derivative actions.

69. *Canada Business Corporations Act, supra* note 3, s. 238.

70. Ibid., s. 241.

71. For a case in which a creditor successfully used the oppression remedy, see *Bird v. Mitchell* (2002), 30 B.L.R. (3d) 107 (Ont. S.C.J.), 2002 CanLII 53226 (ON SC). An employee was granted judgment using the oppression remedy in *Downtown Eatery (1993) Ltd. v. Ontario* (2001), 54 O.R. (3d) 161 (C.A.), 2001 CanLII 8538 (ON CA); leave to appeal refused, [2001] S.C.C.A. No. 397.

72. 2012 ONSC 6423.

became its sole shareholder, officer, and director. The assets of TSL were used by 1833 and some of TSL's customers became customers of 1833.

Glasscell claimed oppression in that Thompson was carrying on the same business through a new corporate entity in an attempt to avoid the financial obligation to Glasscell. The Court agreed and said that the actions of Thompson and TSL were unfairly prejudicial to Glasscell. Thompson's wife and 1833 were also found liable, since Thompson and his wife acted as a partnership in setting up 1833.

DISCUSSION QUESTIONS

Do you agree with this outcome? Should a creditor be allowed to bring an oppression action? Does the threat of an oppression action unduly fetter a corporation's ability to manoeuvre and deal with difficult financial situations?

Dissent provisions provide relief for shareholders

Sometimes a minority shareholder is adversely affected by a decision that is beneficial to the corporation as a whole. In the past when this happened there was no recourse. In many jurisdictions, however, the injured minority shareholder now has the right to dissent and ask that his shares be sold.[73] Such a procedure can be triggered when fundamental changes to the corporation adversely affect the shareholder. The **dissent and appraisal** remedy requires that an appraisal take place and the shareholder's shares be purchased by the corporation at a fair price.

CASE SUMMARY 11.12

When Can Minority Shareholders Force the Corporation to Buy Back Their Shares? *Re 85956 Holdings Ltd. and Fayerman Brothers Ltd.*[74]

For several years, Sidney and Joseph Fayerman operated a merchandising business through Fayerman Brothers Ltd. Because of increased competition and the brothers' failing health it was decided by the directors, and approved by the majority shareholders, not to purchase any more inventory but to simply sell off what the corporation had. The minority shareholders opposed this.

When the decision was made to continue the selloff without replacing inventory, the minority shareholders asked that their shares be purchased at a fair value. The request was refused. This action was brought to force the share purchase at a fair price on the basis that the minority shareholders were dissenting. The Saskatchewan legislation, like many incorporation statutes, had a provision that when "a sale, lease, or exchange of all or substantially all the property of a corporation other than in the ordinary course of business of the corporation" takes place and a shareholder does not approve such a sale, the dissenting shareholder can force the purchase of her shares at a fair price. The problem in this case was whether the choice not to replace the inventory changed this from being a sale done in the ordinary course of business, thus triggering the dissent provision.

The Court held that a sale in the ordinary course of business required the replenishing of the inventory. Not to do so amounted to a sale of all or substantially all the assets

---

73. See, for example, *Canada Business Corporations Act, supra* note 3, s. 190. This is a significant shareholder power, but it is available only in limited circumstances, such as when a decision is being made to amend the articles of incorporation to restrict the issue or transfer of shares, or to restrict the type of business the corporation can carry on. It is also available when amalgamation with another corporation is involved or when a significant portion of the assets of a corporation is going to be sold or leased.

74. (1986), 25 D.L.R. (4th) 119 (Sask. C.A.), 1986 CanLII 160 (SK CA).

of the corporation, and the dissent provisions were triggered. The Court found that the corporation was required to buy out the minority shareholders, paying a fair market price for the shares.

This case illustrates how the dissent provision works and under what circumstances a minority shareholder is entitled to this protection. It is interesting to note that the corporation retained its real estate holdings. Still, this was considered a liquidation of the assets of the corporation, and the minority shareholders were entitled to have their shares purchased by the corporation.

SMALL BUSINESS PERSPECTIVE

It is clear by the nature of the corporation that the majority shareholder has control. Does the right to dissent, and the right to bring an oppression action as discussed above, go too far in weakening this control and pandering to the position of minority shareholders who should have known the risks when they acquired their shares in the first place? Should majority shareholders restrict the sale of shares to others to maintain their control?

DIVIDENDS

Shareholders have no legal right to force the payment of a **dividend**, although they can require payment if one has been declared by the directors. Their recourse is political; if the directors fail to declare a dividend when the shareholders expect one, they are likely to be voted out at the next shareholders' meeting. The shareholders, however, cannot go to court and sue for a dividend even when preferred shares, with the commitment to pay a specific dividend each year, are involved. Such preferred shareholders can force payment before any dividend is paid to the common shareholders (including, when the right is cumulative, the payment of any prior unpaid dividends). The rights associated with the shareholders' position are rights of control, information, and protection, but there is no corresponding right to a specific return on the funds invested. Many provisions are in place to protect the position of shareholders, but it is important to balance these rights against some important drawbacks. In rare circumstances, a shareholder may have the right to sue for oppression when there is an expectation of a regular income flow through dividends and that income flow is stopped.[75]

Shareholders have no right to dividends

SHAREHOLDER AGREEMENTS

The shareholders of a corporation can enter into an agreement that is not within the constitution of the corporation. Such an agreement must relate to the parties' role as shareholders—it cannot restrict their role, if any, as directors of the corporation. Directors, for example, owe a fiduciary duty to the corporation; this duty cannot be compromised by a shareholder agreement.

Partnership law provides more protection to a minority partner than corporate law does to a minority shareholder. This can be overcome with a properly drafted **shareholder agreement**. Such an agreement should, of course, reflect the specific situation. Most shareholder agreements ensure that each of the shareholders will be elected to the board of directors every year. They also ensure that major changes will not take place without the unanimous agreement of the shareholders. The shareholder agreement may also restrict a sale of shares to outsiders and may set a valuation method of the shares if one of the shareholders decides to sell his shares. Other provisions can be included in a shareholder agreement to reflect the concerns of the shareholders in the circumstances.

[75] *Sutherland v. Birks* (2003), 65 O.R. (3d) 812 (C.A.), 2003 CanLII 39961 (ON CA). Note that the remedy in this case was the forced purchase of the shares of the minority shareholder by the corporation.

A unanimous shareholder agreement is usually given special status under legislation governing corporations. The *Canada Business Corporations Act*, for example, allows the powers of the directors to manage the business and affairs of the corporation to be restricted by a unanimous shareholder agreement.[76] In such a situation, the individuals given the power to manage "have all the rights, powers, duties and liabilities of a director of the corporation."[77] The special status of unanimous shareholder agreements makes them very useful to shareholders, especially for closely held corporations.

For an illustration of the concept of the corporate structure, see Figure 11.3

REDUCING RISK 11.5

Small, closely held corporations whose shareholders are also directors and managers of the corporation are often little more than incorporated partnerships. Often the individuals will also be full-time employees of the corporation. When these individuals have a falling out, the problems can go far beyond what can be remedied or even what has been anticipated in the legislation. An individual shareholder may lose not only her job as director and manager, but also her full-time employment, and she may not be able to sell her shares. In such circumstances, the importance of a properly drawn up *shareholder agreement* cannot be overemphasized. Such an agreement should include a provision whereby one shareholder must buy out the other if these types of events or other forms of dissatisfaction occur. Provisions relating to employment are often included in such agreements as well. Shareholder agreements are very important. They can be used to set out many important obligations between the parties, much as a partnership agreement does in a partnership relationship. A sophisticated client entering into a corporate business arrangement with others will ensure that the shareholder agreement is properly drafted, taking into consideration all of the relevant factors. Case Summary 11.13 illustrates the importance of a shareholder agreement, especially a unanimous shareholder agreement.

CASE SUMMARY 11.13

Shareholder Agreement Overrides Other Alternatives: *Hnatiuk v. Court*[78]

Court, Filopoulo, and Hnatiuk were certified management accountants. They entered into a partnership agreement to carry on business. They and their corporations then entered into a unanimous shareholder agreement. The resulting corporation was reorganized into a professional corporation.

Court and Filopoulo decided to terminate the relationship. They served notice on Hnatiuk, advising that the unanimous shareholder agreement was terminated and that the corporation would repurchase Hnatiuk's shares. Hnatiuk applied for liquidation and dissolution of the corporation.

The trial judge referred the dispute to arbitration, as the unanimous shareholder agreement contained an arbitration clause that required disputes of this nature to be arbitrated, not litigated.

SMALL BUSINESS PERSPECTIVE

Shareholders' agreements are important for all corporations, including small, closely held corporations. In light of that, should the members of a family involved in an incorporation of the family business prepare a shareholders' agreement? If they do, is it necessary that each participant retain his or her own lawyer?

---

76. *Canada Business Corporations Act, supra* note 3, s. 146(1).
77. Ibid., s. 146(5).
78. 2010 MBCA 20 (CanLII).

Figure 11.3 Corporate Structure

	Elect		**Appoint**	
Shareholders	→	**Board of Directors**	→	**Officers**

- possibly subject to a shareholders' agreement
- few obligations owed by shareholders to the corporation
- liability limited to amount invested
- many rights and remedies, but no right to be paid dividends

- responsible for management of the corporation
- directors owe duties to the corporation, including fiduciary duty
- personal liability if duties are breached
- due diligence is sometimes a defence

- appointed by the board of directors to run the business
- owe duties to the corporation, including fiduciary duty
- personal liability if duties are breached
- due diligence is sometimes a defence

TERMINATION OF THE CORPORATION

LO ❻

Dissolution may be voluntary or involuntary

Corporations can be dissolved in several ways. Dissolution can take place either voluntarily or involuntarily, and the procedure can be induced internally, by the directors or shareholders, or externally, by the courts or creditors. The process can be voluntary, by following the winding-up procedure found in the corporate law statutes or, in some jurisdictions, in a separate winding-up act.[79] If the corporation owns sufficient assets, it may be worthwhile to follow this process, but often it is not worth the expense.

Occasionally, a court will order a corporation to be dissolved when a minority shareholder has been unfairly treated. If there are more debts owing to the creditors than the corporation has assets to cover, the common procedure is bankruptcy, and the end result is usually the dissolution of the corporation. Under the current bankruptcy legislation, it is possible for the corporation to make a proposal to the creditors and, if accepted and followed, the corporation will continue.

Bankruptcy usually leads to dissolution

One of the most common ways for corporations, especially small, closely held corporations, to come to an end is for the principals simply to neglect to file the annual return. A federal corporation must, for example, file an annual return within 60 days after the anniversary of the incorporation of the corporation.[80] If it fails to do so, a certificate of dissolution may be issued for it one year later.[81]

Dissolution for non-filing of annual return

CASE SUMMARY 11.14

Does It Matter if a Corporation Is Dissolved? *Sutherland Lofts Inc. v. St. Thomas (City)*[82]

The City issued an "order to remedy unsafe building" for a building owned by Sutherland. Engineers then concluded that the building was unsafe for occupancy. The City issued an emergency order and then accepted a tender for demolition of the building. Sutherland obtained a temporary injunction, but the building was partially demolished on July 23, 2008, before Sutherland obtained an order that required the demolition

---

79. The liquidation and dissolution of federal corporations are dealt with in Part XVIII of the *Canada Business Corporations Act, supra* note 3.
80. *Canada Business Corporations Regulations, supra* note 51, s. 5.
81. *Canada Business Corporations Act, supra* note 3, s. 212.
82. 2011 ONSC 5160.

to cease. Sutherland sued, claiming damages for trespass, removing property, and completing demolition unlawfully. The statement of claim was issued on August 16, 2010, but the corporate charter of Sutherland was cancelled on December 29, 2008, for failure to comply with corporate tax regulation.

The Court held that the corporation could be revived, but that it would still be subject to a missed limitation date. Sutherland's claim was therefore dismissed.

This case shows how careful businesspeople must be to make sure they comply with government regulations. In this case, the consequence was dissolution of the corporation. Such a dissolved corporation no longer exists legally and thereby loses the right to bring an action on its own behalf. The case also shows that such a dissolved corporation can be resurrected by following the appropriate procedure, but sometimes even that process may not overcome the consequences of allowing the corporation to become dissolved in the first place.

SMALL BUSINESS PERSPECTIVE

Is this just playing with technicalities? Is the result inconsistent with the purpose of the legislation, which allows for the restoration of the corporation by late filing of the appropriate documents? What steps should a prudent businessperson take to ensure that all relevant laws are complied with?

Selling the shares

Often when a corporation is to go out of business a decision must be made whether to sell the shares of the corporation or to sell its assets. If its shares are sold, the corporation continues as before, but with new shareholders. The debts and other obligations continue, but problems may arise if the purchaser decides to make changes in wages and contracts with suppliers. Because the corporation continues, the contracts stay in place and continue to bind the corporation, even with new ownership.

Selling the assets

When the corporation's assets are sold, on the other hand, the purchaser is not affected by the contractual or other obligations of the corporation selling those assets, unless those assets are encumbered. If the assets in question have been used to secure a debt, the secured creditor has first claim against the assets. Any purchaser of a business would be well advised to search the title of the assets for such liens and charges before entering into the transaction. As explained in Chapter 15, Ontario has a bulk sales statute in place to protect creditors from the sale of all or substantially all the assets of the debtor. Any debts or other obligations that have been incurred by the selling corporation could become liabilities of the purchaser of the assets if it does not pay the proceeds of the sale to the creditors. After the corporation's assets are sold and the corporation no longer has a business, the corporation can be wound up.

The process of distributing the assets upon winding up the corporation is set out in the various statutes and will not be dealt with here.[83] It is important to note, however, that the directors have a considerable obligation not to allow any of the assets of the corporation to get into the hands of the shareholders until the creditors have been satisfied.

MyBusLawLab Be sure to visit the MyBusLawLab that accompanies this book to find practice quizzes, province-specific content, simulations and much more!

[83.] See, for example, Part XVIII of the *Canada Business Corporations Act, supra* note 3.

SUMMARY

Separate legal entity

- The corporation is a separate legal entity
- Shareholders own the shares of the corporation; the corporation owns the assets it buys
- Sometimes the courts "lift the corporate veil" and find directors or officers liable
- Shareholders are not liable for the debts of a corporation; they have limited liability so can lose only what they have invested
- Corporations have the capacity of a natural person, except for special statute corporations whose capacity may be limited

Pros and cons of incorporation

- There are several advantages of incorporation, including limited liability, tax benefits, the ease of transferring shares, few ownership obligations, and the separation of ownership and management
- There are several disadvantages of incorporation, including the cost of incorporating, the difficulty and cost of changing the incorporating documents, the cost of ongoing recordkeeping, and the vulnerability of minority shareholders

The process of incorporation

- Corporations were created because of the need to finance costly projects
- A corporation is a fiction or a myth that has a status as a legal person separate from that of its shareholders
- Methods of incorporation in Canada are registration, letters patent, and articles of incorporation

Funding

- Funding may be derived from the selling of shares (which may be common shares or preferred shares with special rights and restrictions), or through borrowing (which can involve the sale of bonds or debentures, secured or unsecured)
- Shareholders are participants in the corporation, while lenders are creditors
- Broadly held corporations (many shareholders) have more stringent government controls and greater reporting requirements than closely held corporations (few shareholders)

Corporate directors, officers, and shareholders

- Directors are elected by shareholders to manage the corporation
- Directors owe a fiduciary duty and duty to be careful to the corporation
- Directors may be personally liable for decisions they make
- Directors, officers, employees, and the corporation itself may incur criminal liability
- Officers run the affairs of the corporation and owe it a fiduciary duty and a duty of care
- Promoters may be personally liable for pre-incorporation contracts
- Shareholders owe very few duties to the corporation or other shareholders unless they have sufficient shares to be classed as insiders
- Shareholders have significant rights and remedies
- Shareholders do not have a right to sue the directors when they act carelessly or wrongfully in carrying out their duties, as the duty of the directors is owed to the corporation, not to the shareholder
- Shareholders can bring a derivative or representative action against the directors on behalf of the corporation, commence an oppression action, or apply for a dissent and appraisal remedy
- Shareholders do not have a right to demand dividends
- Shareholders can enter into shareholder agreements or even unanimous shareholder agreements

Termination of the corporation

- A corporation can be dissolved in many ways, some voluntary, some involuntary
- The dissolution of a corporation has legal consequences that may not be reversible even if the corporation is revived
- The legal effect of selling a corporation's shares is different than that of selling its assets

QUESTIONS FOR REVIEW

1. What is meant by a corporation having a separate legal identity?

2. Explain how the liability of a shareholder is limited.

3. Explain under what circumstances a court will "lift the corporate veil."

4. Why are the principles of agency law relevant to corporations?

5. Explain how a personal guarantee reduces the limited liability of the principals of a closely held corporation.

6. Explain the advantages of free transferability of shares and how and why this right is often modified by shareholder agreement.

7. Set out and explain some of the disadvantages associated with the corporate method of carrying on business.

8. Distinguish among companies and corporations that have been created by special acts of Parliament, by royal charter, by registration, by letters patent, and by filing articles of incorporation.

9. Explain the significance of the memorandum of association in a registration jurisdiction. Contrast it with articles of incorporation and articles of association.

10. What is a "society" and how does it compare to a corporation?

11. What is the capacity of most corporations? What is the exception to this rule?

12. Explain why the concept of a par-value share is misleading and why the use of such shares has declined.

13. What is meant by a "preferred" share? Contrast this with the "common" share. Explain why the term *preferred shares* is misleading.

14. Does a shareholder, whether preferred or common, have a right to a dividend? Explain.

15. What is the significant difference between a bondholder and a preferred shareholder, both of whom are entitled to a specified payment each year?

16. Distinguish between closely held and broadly held corporations and explain the differences in terms of the provisions in place in your jurisdiction.

17. Set out the nature of the duties owed by a director of a corporation. To whom are these duties owed? Who else in the corporate organization owes similar duties?

18. Explain why it is becoming increasingly difficult to get prominent individuals to serve as directors of Canadian corporations.

19. Who is usually responsible for running the affairs of the corporation?

20. How can a promoter avoid personal liability for pre-incorporation contracts?

21. Explain any duties shareholders assume. Summarize the rights of the shareholders in relationship to other shareholders, the management, and the directors of the corporation.

22. Explain what is meant by a "proxy" and why proxies can be so important at a corporation's annual general meeting.

23. Distinguish among a derivative action, dissent, and oppression. Explain when it would be appropriate to use each of them.

24. Explain the purpose of a shareholders' agreement and why it is important.

25. How can a corporation be terminated?

CASES AND DISCUSSION QUESTIONS

1. *Dynasty Kitchen Cabinets v. Soheili*, 2011 BCPC 414 (CanLII)
The corporate defendant consented to a judgment against it. The issue was whether its owner/director, Soheili, was personally liable. Dynasty provided cabinets for Soheili's personal residence. The transaction was with the corporate defendant. The house went into foreclosure, but Dynasty was owed $250 000. Soheili did not give a personal guarantee; he owed $250 000 to the corporate defendant for the cabinets.

Is this a case in which the Court would "lift the corporate veil"? Why or why not?

2. *BCE Inc. v. 1976 Debentureholders*, [2008] 3 S.C.R. 560, 2008 SCC 69
Bell Canada debentureholders opposed a buyout of BCE, a large Canadian telecommunications corporation, by a group headed by the Ontario Teachers' Pension Plan board. The buyout was financed in part by the assumption, by Bell Canada, a wholly owned subsidiary of BCE, of $30 billion of debt. This would reduce the value of the Bell Canada debentures by about 20 percent. The value of the BCE shares would, on the other hand, increase by about 40 percent as a result of the buyout. The debentureholders therefore opposed court approval of the buyout and claimed that they were entitled to relief under the oppression remedy. The Quebec Supreme Court approved the buyout, but the Court of Appeal allowed the debentureholders' appeal and disallowed the buyout. The case went to the Supreme Court of Canada.

To whom do corporate directors owe a fiduciary duty? What should the directors do if the interests of the corporation and of particular stakeholders do not coincide? What remedies do these stakeholders have if they believe that they have not been treated fairly? Does the law require that business decisions be perfect or they will be overturned by the courts if subsequent events showed that the decisions were not correct?

3. *Kaur v. Canada*, 2013 TCC 227 (CanLII)
Kaur was assessed liability as the sole director of a corporation for its unremitted GST. Kaur left the operational and financial matters of the corporation to the general manager, who did not remit the GST. Kaur claimed that she did not have the expertise, knowledge, or experience to manage the administrative matters of the corporation.

Explain whether Kaur would be able to avoid liability for the unpaid GST because she had shown due diligence in respect of payment of the tax.

4. *Black Fluid Inc. v. Opulence Clothing Inc.*, 2014 ABQB 138 (CanLII)
Two brothers, Taleb and Zoul, were equal shareholders in and the only two directors of two corporations that operated retail clothing businesses. Taleb opened another clothing store. Zoul's wife then opened another clothing store. Zoul advised Taleb that he was not going to order inventory for either of the co-owned stores. Taleb also did not order any inventory for those stores. The landlord terminated the leases for the two co-owned stores for non-payment of rent. Taleb obtained leave to commence a derivative action against Zoul, Zoul's wife, and their corporations. Zoul asked the Court to add Taleb and his corporation as defendants in the derivative action.

The Court denied Zoul's request. On what grounds did it do so?

5. *Salesco Limited v. Lee Paige* **(2007), 61 C.C.E.L. (3d) 279, (2007), 36 B.L.R. (4th) 229 (Ont. S.C.), 2007 CanLII 37463 (ON SC),** *Capobianco v. Paige,* **2009 CanLII 29899 (ON SC)**

C and P decided to buy their employer, Spray-Pak, which was owned by M. They used Salesco (of which P was both a director and officer) to do so. Z loaned $20 000 to Salesco. He received 20 percent of the shares in Salesco, while 40 percent of the shares were allocated to P and C. Salesco obtained two-thirds of the shares of Spray-Pak. M continued to own the other one-third of the shares; he was also a director of the corporation. P was a director and also president of Spray-Pak. He wrote many cheques on Spray-Pak's bank account that benefited him personally, including one for $10 000 as a down payment on a house and another for the purchase of a Jaguar. P, C, and M agreed that each of them would receive $2300 per week from Spray-Pak, and that Spray-Pak would pay M's personal and legal accounting bills.

Spray-Pak experienced financial difficulties, so the payments to M were stopped. P and M then fired C so that the payments to M could resume. M was not providing services to Spray-Pak while C was, so there was no just cause for firing C. Meetings of the shareholders and directors of Salesco were called. P, C, and Z were elected as directors. At a later meeting, C, Z, and M were elected as directors. M then started a lawsuit, asking for a declaration that P could not be removed as a director of Salesco and that Spray-Pak be wound up. C counterclaimed, asking for an injunction preventing depletion of Spray-Pak's assets.

P and M misrepresented Spray-Pak's financial situation to the CIBC and effectively asked it to call in its loan to Spray-Pak, which it did. M incorporated New Spray-Pak and transferred 50 percent of its shares to P. New Spray-Pak acquired the CIBC's security in return for an assignment of Spray-Pak's debt and security. New Spray-Pak continued the business; the customers of Spray-Pak were not advised that they were now doing business with New Spray-Pak. C and Z were not advised of these developments. When they discovered what had happened, they began derivative actions on behalf of Spray-Pak and Salesco, with P, M, and New Spray-Pak as the defendants.

Should the derivative actions succeed? Were the actions of P and M oppressive or unfairly prejudicial? Did they unfairly disregard the interests of C, Z, Salesco, and Spray-Pak? Did P and M breach any fiduciary duties?

6. *Mundy (E.C.) Ltd. v. Canada Safeway Ltd.,* **2004 MBCA 143 (CanLII)**

Mundy sued Safeway for payment of unpaid invoices. Mundy was dissolved when the statement of claim was filed because it had failed to file its annual returns. Mundy was revived as a corporation after the limitation period had expired and after the statement of claim was filed.

Did the Court allow Mundy's claim? Explain your reasoning.

12 Chapter

Employment

LEARNING OBJECTIVES

1 Distinguish employees, agents, and independent contractors

2 Detail common law obligations of employers and employees

3 Outline the purpose of various statutes impacting employment

4 Describe collective bargaining and explain the role of labour unions

A contract for employment is one of the most important contracts in which a person will become involved. This chapter is devoted to exploring the legal ramifications of the employment relationship.

WHAT IS EMPLOYMENT?

LO 1

Not all work is employment

Employment involves one person doing work for another, but not all work relationships are classed as employment. The work of **independent contractors**, such as doctors, lawyers, and plumbers, must be distinguished from employment. Independent contractors work for themselves and act independently, providing a specific service for the person they contract with, whereas an **employee** is said to be in a master–servant relationship, acting under the direction of the master. Agency is a third type of business relationship, in which one person acts as a go-between in relationships between others.

Each of these relationships imposes different legal rights and obligations on the parties; understanding how the courts have defined each relationship enables one to ascertain which rights can be asserted by a worker as well as the obligations that apply. The legal principles governing the independent contractor are embodied in the general rules of contract law already covered in Chapters 6 through 9. Agency is addressed in Chapter 10. This chapter will examine the common law concerning employment, together with the relevant federal and provincial legislation. The chapter concludes with an examination of the trade union movement and collective bargaining.

Characterization of relationship impacts rights of workers and the party paying for services

The Control Test

The traditional method of determining whether an employment relationship exists is to assess the degree of control exercised by the person paying for the service. A person who is told not only what to do but also how to do it is classed as an employee. But if the person doing the work is free to decide how the job should be done, the position is more likely that of an independent contractor. For example, if Felix hires Oscar to paint a house, Oscar could be either an independent contractor or an

Employee is controlled by the employer

employee. If Felix tells Oscar which tools to use, when to work, and how to perform the job, these factors suggest that Oscar is probably an employee. On the other hand, if Oscar does work for several parties and supplies his own tools and determines what time to start work and the best way to perform the job, then he is probably an independent contractor. Other relevant factors include whether the person is paid a wage or salary, or is paid by the job. Courts will also consider who owns the equipment used and who profits or runs the risk of loss from the work performed.

Independent contractor works independently

The employment relationship involves a contract in which the employee agrees generally to serve the employer, who has the right to supervise and direct. On the other hand, an independent contractor agrees to do a particular job, not to enter into a general service relationship. In other words, employees work for their employer, whereas independent contractors work for themselves. As stated by Justice Major of the Supreme Court of Canada:

> [T]he central question is whether the person who has been engaged to perform the services is performing them as a person in business on his own account. In making this determination, the level of control the employer has over the worker's activities will always be a factor. However, other factors to consider include whether the worker provides his or her own equipment, whether the worker hires his or her own helpers, the degree of financial risk taken by the worker, the degree of responsibility for investment and management held by the worker, and the worker's opportunity for profit in the performance of his or her tasks.[1]

CASE SUMMARY 12.1

Level of Control and Wording of Contract Are Not the Only Factors: *TBT Personnel Services Inc. v. Canada*[2]; *Algoma Taxicab Management Ltd. v. M.N.R.*[3]

It is not unusual for the government to challenge the characterization of a worker. The minister of national revenue determined that 96 truck drivers engaged by TBT Personnel Services Inc. were employees, and thus assessed TBT for premiums payable under the *Employment Insurance Act* and contributions payable under the Canada Pension Plan. When TBT appealed those assessments to the Tax Court, it ruled that the 43 drivers whose contracts stipulated that the drivers were engaged as persons carrying on their own businesses were independent contractors. But the Federal Court of Appeal declared that the contracts were just one factor to consider. The other relevant factors were (1) the drivers did not provide their own trucks or equipment; (2) the drivers did not bear any financial risk; (3) the drivers did not negotiate rates of pay; and (4) although the contracts stipulated that drivers could hire a substitute driver at their own cost, there was no evidence suggesting this was ever done. Thus, even though TBT did not supervise the workers the drivers were all found to be employees.

Contrast this with the *Algoma* case, in which Brouillard worked as a taxi driver for Algoma. The contract between Algoma and its drivers entitled the drivers to use Algoma's vehicles and dispatch services. Algoma paid for the vehicle insurance, as well as the maintenance, fuel, oil, and other supplies for the vehicles. The foregoing factors suggested employment. But Algoma did not assign drivers to work at particular times, on particular days, or in specific geographical areas. Instead, drivers could request a vehicle for a specific date and time. Drivers were not required to work any minimum period. They did not

---

[1]. *671122 Ontario Ltd. v. Sagaz Industries Canada Inc.*, 2001 SCC 59 (CanLII), at para. 47.

[2]. 2011 FCA 256 (CanLII); leave to appeal to S.C.C. dismissed, [2011] S.C.C.A. No. 498.

[3]. 2006 SCC 71 (CanLII).

have to be consistently available during a shift. Drivers could have customers call them directly rather than calling the dispatcher. As compensation, the drivers paid Algoma a rental fee that varied from 62 percent to 70 percent of their gross receipts.

It was conceded that the central question is whether the person is performing the services as a person in business on his own account. Still, the level of control the employer has over the worker's activities will always be a factor. The Court concluded that all of Algoma's drivers, including Brouillard, were performing services as independent contractors.

SMALL BUSINESS PERSPECTIVE

Hiring an employee, as opposed to retaining the services of an independent contractor, is generally more costly. If the worker is an employee, several statutes impose responsibilities upon the employer, such as the duty to remit income taxes. The courts thus consider several factors, including the level of control the worker is subject to, when classifying the worker rather than simply deferring to what the relationship is called in the contract.

The Organization Test

The courts supplement the **control test** with the **organization test**. Even if there is little direct control, when the services performed by an individual are an integral part of the organization, the worker is likely an employee. For example, a baker's duties are central to a bakery's operations. Further, if the baker works only for that bakery and is subject to group control, that person is likely an employee.[4] On the other hand, if that person is free to offer services to others and bears the risks of profit or loss when work is not completed in a timely manner, she may be an independent contractor. These factors suggest she is in business for herself.

Individual statutes may provide a definition of employment for the purposes of that statute, but there is no general legislated definition. The Canada Revenue Agency (CRA) often questions the characterization and will require an employer to remit the taxes that were not remitted for certain workers on the grounds that they were not self-employed contractors but really employees. Businesses are thus well advised to familiarize themselves with the interpretation used by the government to avoid paying twice.[5] When a court is deciding whether to impose vicarious liability or determining whether a worker was wrongfully dismissed, it must therefore turn to the principles enunciated in precedents to determine whether an employment relationship exists.

While a person normally cannot be an independent contractor and an employee at the same time, the same is not true of an agent. **Agents** can be independent contractors or employees. A sales clerk in a store is both an employee and an agent; a person selling insurance is likely an independent contractor but is also functioning as an agent for her client. It's important to keep these categories separate, as the liability of the parties will likely be determined by the relationship between them.

Organization test supplements control test

Employment is characterized by the courts through precedents

An employee can be an agent

An agent can be an independent contractor

THE LAW OF EMPLOYMENT

LO ❷ ❸

Over the years, the common law courts developed special rules to deal with the unique problems associated with employment, which used to be referred to as a master–servant relationship. Today, employment law is governed primarily by the general provisions of contract law, supplemented by these special rules as well as by a number of statutes that further define the responsibilities and obligations of the parties.

[4.] John G. Fleming, *The Law of Torts*, 8th ed. (Sydney: The Law Book Co. Ltd., 1992), 372.

[5.] See the following Canada Revenue Agency publication: "Employee or Self-Employed?" www.cra-arc.gc.ca/E/pub/tg/rc4110/rc4110-e.html.

The Employment Contract

Obligations of employer include

- **payment of wages or salary**
- **safe working conditions**

The main responsibility of the employer, in addition to payment of wages, is to provide a safe workplace and good working conditions for the employee. Some types of jobs are inherently dangerous, such as construction, and the employer is obligated to minimize the danger, usually by promoting safe work practices; erecting protective fences, barriers, and nets; and requiring the use of proper safety equipment. The employer must hire competent people. If it can be shown that the employer hired a careless or incompetent worker who caused injury to others, the employer may be held accountable. For example, when an inexperienced crane operator caused the crane to topple, injuring other workers, the employer was responsible because of its failure to ensure that only a competent and experienced worker operated the crane.[6] Job site health and safety requirements and injuries caused by other workers are specialized areas covered by occupational health and safety legislation and workers' compensation legislation; both are discussed below.

The contract of employment usually includes a commitment by the employer to pay a specific wage or salary. That agreement will often also set out bonus arrangements, benefit packages, and promises to repay any reasonable expenses incurred.

Obligations of employee:

- **competent work**
- **honesty and loyalty**
- **punctuality**
- **fiduciary obligations in some cases**

The employee also has obligations to fulfill. The employee must possess the skills claimed and exercise them in a reasonably competent and careful manner. The employee has an obligation to follow any reasonable order pertaining to the employment and must treat the property of the employer carefully. The employee must be honest, loyal, and courteous; an employee who does the work required but acts in an insubordinate or disloyal way can be fired. Similarly, an employee must be punctual and work for the time specified in the contract. If the employee uses the employer's time or facilities without permission he may be disciplined. With some types of jobs, there may also be an obligation to generally act in the best interests of the employer. This is referred to as a fiduciary obligation and is usually imposed only on senior-level employees. For normal employees, unless the employment contract provides otherwise, their obligations to the employer end when that employment is terminated. But for those senior-level employees who have a fiduciary duty, this duty may continue after the employment ends.

An employee who is also a fiduciary is automatically subject to certain obligations toward an employer. These include a duty to act in good faith, make full disclosure, and not take corporate opportunities for one's own benefit. For example, in the *Felker* case,[7] when the employee secretly engaged in negotiations to become the sales agent for a second company and did not advise or offer his employer the opportunity to represent the second company, the Court found just cause for that employee's dismissal. Failure to disclose this activity and to secure prior consent justified the dismissal.

General contract law applies to employment

Employment contracts are often verbal and not formal or written documents. It is, however, a good idea to put the contract in writing, clearly stating the provisions that are important for the parties. Such provisions may include the rate of pay, the hours of work, and a description of what services are required and for what period. As with other contracts, all the ingredients necessary for a contract to exist must be present. Employers often try to impose new, one-sided employment contracts on their employees after the commencement of employment. These contracts often include terms adverse to the employee, such as restrictive covenants or terms limiting the period of notice to be given upon termination. When imposed after the fact, these provisions are often not binding because of a failure of consideration. The employment contract is illustrated in Figure 12.1.

Restrictive covenants must be reasonable

When **restrictive covenants** are included in the original contract, committing the employee not to work in a particular geographical area or a particular industry after leaving the position, they should specify a reasonable time and area. If they are too

---

6. *R. v. A. W. Leil Cranes & Equipment (1986) Ltd.*, 2003 NSPC 60 (CanLII).
7. *Felker v. Cunningham*, 2000 CanLII 16801 (ON CA); leave to appeal to S.C.C. refused, [2000] S.C.C.A. No. 538.

Figure 12.1 The Employment Contract

Employer: Promises to pay wages, provide safe workplace...

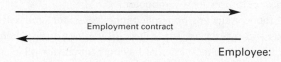

Employment contract

Employee:

| Breach of these major terms may enable the opposite party to treat the contract as discharged |

Promises to be honest, loyal, punctual, competent...

broad, the covenants will not be enforced. Further, such covenants must be the most appropriate way of protecting the employer's interests and not be against the public interest. For example, if an employer invents a special production method, the secrecy of which could be maintained only by requiring that the employees commit themselves not to work in a similar industry for a reasonable period of time after they leave the company, a restrictive covenant in the contract of employment to that effect would likely be valid. But, in general, there is some reluctance on the part of the courts to enforce restrictive covenants in employment contracts because of the danger of denying the employee the ability to earn a livelihood and because of the normally weaker bargaining position of employees.

CASE SUMMARY 12.2

Enforcing Promises Not to Compete: *Herff Jones Canada Inc. v. Todd*[8]; *Globex Foreign Exchange Corporation v. Kelcher*[9]

Todd entered into a sales representative agreement with the respondent whereby he agreed to solicit schools and colleges for the purpose of selling class rings, medals, awards, and yearbooks supplied by the respondent. After six years, Todd severed the relationship and went to work for a competitor, Jostens. By doing so, he breached a promise that he would not compete with his former employer for four years. The respondent sought and obtained an injunction from the trial judge preventing Todd from "soliciting or contacting directly or indirectly any of those schools or accounts who were customers" of the respondent as of May 20, 1994, for a period of four years.

Todd appealed, arguing that the trial judge erred in deciding that the restrictive covenant was valid. Prohibiting an employee from working for a competitor for four years does, at first glance, appear excessive. The Court of Appeal, however, found the trial judge had applied the correct tests: (1) The covenant was reasonable as between the parties. Its duration, four years, was reasonable in light of the fact that Todd would have been entitled to a split commission for three years after leaving the respondent had he not breached the restrictive covenant. Further, Todd had developed a special relationship with the customers, so the proprietary interest of the respondent would be jeopardized if Todd could approach them on the competitor's behalf. Nor did the covenant cover too large a geographical area. Todd had simply promised not to compete in the area formerly serviced by him on behalf of the respondent. (2) Enforcing the covenant would have no negative impact on public interests.

In contrast, the courts refused to enforce restrictive covenants in the *Globex* case, where three employees breached covenants limiting their future activities. Maclean accepted the restrictions on his ability to solicit Globex's clients when hired; Kelcher and Oliviero agreed to the restrictions during their employment but received no new consideration for doing so. When Globex presented them with new employment agreements

---

8. 1996 ABCA 96 (CanLII).

9. 2011 ABCA 240 (CanLII).

that contained even more onerous non-competition and non-solicitation clauses, Kelcher resigned, Maclean was terminated for refusing to sign, and Oliviero resigned shortly thereafter. All three went to work for a competitor.

The Court of Appeal found Kelcher's non-solicitation covenant unenforceable because it was ambiguous and overbroad, regardless of whether or not there was valid consideration. The clause prohibited him from having contact with all clients he ever had "dealings" with. This would prevent him from soliciting Globex clients for any reason, even if unrelated to the currency exchange business.

But since the three employees had been wrongfully dismissed, that in itself made the restrictive covenants unenforceable.

SMALL BUSINESS PERSPECTIVE

Employers may have good reason to include restrictive covenants, particularly non-solicitation covenants, in contracts with their key personnel. Should a former employee breach the covenant and lure clients away, an application can be made to the courts to have the covenant enforced, typically by an injunction.[10] Further, if monetary losses are caused, damages may be sought to compensate for such losses. But as the *Globex* case warns, restrictive covenants cannot be enforced by an employer if it wrongfully dismisses the employee.

It is prudent to obtain legal advice if seeking to include restrictive covenants in contracts. Not only must the non-competition clause be reasonable between the parties (not overly broad geographically or in terms of time), but the party trying to enforce the covenant must show that the clause is necessary to protect some proprietary interest. Otherwise, courts may regard the clause as being unnecessary or too restrictive and simply refuse to enforce it. Note, however, that the Supreme Court of Canada has proclaimed that when restrictive covenants are found in commercial contracts, as opposed to employment contracts, the courts will now presume them to be enforceable.[11] The onus then falls on the party trying to have the clause set aside to show that the clause is unreasonable.

Termination

Contract may stipulate amount of notice to be given . . .

An employment contract may provide for its own discharge (as when the contract is for a fixed term, say one year, and that term expires), or the parties can mutually agree to bring it to an end. However, most contracts of employment are for an indefinite period of time with no reference to notice requirements. In general, such contracts of employment can be terminated (1) by either party giving reasonable notice, (2) by the employer giving the compensation that should have been earned in that notice period (**pay in lieu of notice**), or (3) immediately with just cause.

. . . otherwise, reasonable notice of termination is required of both employer and employee

Just as the employee is not bound to the job and can leave after giving **reasonable notice**, so too is the employer free to terminate the employment relationship for no specific reason as long as sufficient notice is given. Federal and provincial legislation demand that, at a minimum, the statutory amount of notice be given.[12] The employer's right to terminate, even with proper notice, is further

---

10. See *Jardine Lloyd Thompson Canada Inc. v. Harke-Hunt*, 2013 ABQB 313 (CanLII), where an injunction was granted against a former employee engaging in solicitation and competition. Even if the restrictive covenant she had signed was not enforceable, the court declared that as a key employee she owed the company fiduciary obligations not to solicit or compete.

11. See *Payette v. Guay Inc.*, 2013 SCC 45 (CanLII), where an agreement for the sale of assets between the parties contained non-competition and non-solicitation clauses.

12. *Canada Labour Code*, R.S.C. 1985, c. L-2, s. 230; as examples of provincial statutes, see British Columbia's *Employment Standards Act*, R.S.B.C. 1996, c. 113, s. 63, and Alberta's *Employment Standards Code*, R.S.A. 2000, c. E-9, s. 56.

restricted by provincial and federal human rights legislation and by the *Charter of Rights and Freedoms*, which prohibit termination when it amounts to discrimination on the basis of physical or mental disability, gender, religion, colour, or other protected ground.[13]

REASONABLE NOTICE

The problem for employers is that reasonable notice, especially when long-term employees are involved, can be quite significant. The courts impose notice periods on the basis of such factors as length of service; the type of job; the employee's age, experience, training and qualifications; and the availability of similar employment.[14] In some cases involving long-term senior managers, the required notice period may even exceed two years.

CASE SUMMARY 12.3

Bad Faith of Employer Can Draw Damages: *Honda Canada Inc. v. Keays*[15]

Keays had worked for Honda for 14 years but was persistently absent due to chronic fatigue syndrome. He went on long-term disability for a period, but that was terminated (wrongfully, as later determined by the Court) and he had to return to work. There followed a considerable amount of absenteeism caused by his illness. Honda required him to submit an examination by its doctor and, upon his lawyer's advice, Keays refused "pending clarification of the purpose, methodology and the parameters of the assessment." Honda responded by terminating his employment.

Keays sued for wrongful dismissal. At trial, the judge found that Honda had a culture of "lean operation" and production efficiency, which led it to hound Keays because of his absences. It was also clear to the judge that Honda thought Keays's condition was "bogus" and the demand to be examined by Honda's doctor was not made in good faith but as a pretext to fire him. Honda representatives also tried to persuade Keays to reject the advice of his own lawyer. Since these acts amounted to bad faith on the part of the employer, the judge, based on the *Wallace* precedent,[16] extended the normal notice period (15 months) by an additional 9 months. This amounted to an award of $150 000 for wrongful dismissal (24 months' pay). Further, the harassment and discrimination Keays experienced and the denial of his disability benefits constituted a separate wrong. Keays was thus awarded $500 000 in punitive damages.

The Court of Appeal upheld the finding of wrongful dismissal and the awarding of the extra damages because of the manner of dismissal. It did, however, reduce the punitive damages from $500 000 to $100 000.

On further appeal, the Supreme Court of Canada rejected the practice of extending the notice period as a consequence of an employer engaging in bad faith in the manner of dismissal (the "Wallace extension"). The Court indicated that damages for the manner of dismissal will only be available if the employer has acted, during the course of the dismissal, in a manner that is "unfair or is in bad faith by being, for example, untruthful, misleading or unduly insensitive" (para. 57). Such damages should be awarded through an award that reflects actual damages, not by extending the notice period. The Supreme Court overturned the lower courts' findings and ruled that Honda's conduct was not deserving of an award of damages for misconduct in dismissal. Punitive damages are

---

13. *Canadian Charter of Rights and Freedoms*, ss. 15 and 28, Part I of the *Constitution Act, 1982*, being Schedule B to the *Canada Act 1982* (U.K.), 1982, c. 11, and, for example, *Human Rights Code*, R.S.O. 1990, c. H.19, s. 5.

14. *Honda Canada Inc. v. Keays*, 2008 SCC 39 (CanLII).

15. Ibid.

16. *Wallace v. United Grain Growers Ltd.*, 1997 CanLII 332 (SCC).

awarded for deliberate wrongful acts that are malicious and outrageous; Honda's behaviour, although insensitive, was not deserving of punitive damages.

SMALL BUSINESS PERSPECTIVE

While the sympathy of the lower courts was with the dismissed employee, the Supreme Court took a different view. As long as an employer's conduct is not untruthful, misleading, or unduly shameful, the employee will not receive damages for the manner of the dismissal. Aggravated or punitive damages will only be awarded if the employer acts maliciously or outrageously. This decision may be reflective of economic times. Employers are well advised to treat employees fairly in dismissal, or face potential liability.

Even seasonal employees who are fired at the end of a season and then repeatedly rehired may be entitled to reasonable notice if not recalled.[17] In determining whether seasonal employment is in fact employment of indefinite duration requiring notice of termination, relevant factors include the length of the seasonal employment relationship, the pattern of recall or return to work, and the nature of the industry in question.

Short-term or probationary employees may be entitled to extended notice periods if the employee has not been informed of the basis on which her performance will be evaluated or if she was persuaded to leave another job but is then terminated after a short time.[18] Similarly, if an employer fosters employee loyalty by promising job security, that employer may be required to provide even greater notice of termination to its employees than would otherwise be the case.[19] Trade unions generally include terms in their collective agreements as to when an employee can be terminated and what notice is required. Also, minimum statutory notice periods that are set out in employment standards statutes must be satisfied.

REDUCING RISK 12.1

The foregoing discussion highlights that sophisticated clients should seek legal advice before terminating an employee without cause. In such a situation, adequate notice must be given. If the amount of notice has not been agreed upon by the parties, either in the employment contract or through subsequent mutual agreement, then reasonable notice must be given. If the employer has concerns about the employee continuing to work during the notice period, pay in lieu of notice (a severance package) can be given instead. A lawyer can advise as to the length of the required notice, and costly litigation may thus be avoided.

JUST CAUSE

Notice is not required when there is just cause

When there is **just cause** there is no requirement for an employer to give any notice. Any major breach of contract enables the opposite party to treat the contract as discharged or terminated by that breach. In the context of an employment contract, just cause must therefore constitute a serious or fundamental breach of the employee's contractual obligations. An employee can be dismissed without notice for things such as serious absenteeism, open disobedience, misuse of the employer's property including its computers, habitual negligence, incompetence, harassing other employees, drinking on the job, or immoral conduct on or off the job that reflects badly on the employer. The issue is whether the relationship has been

---

17. See *Levy v. Ken-Wo Country Club*, 2001 NSSC 84 (CanLII), where the golf course groundskeeper was not recalled after 24 seasons with that employer.

18. See *Crisall v. Western Pontiac Buick GMC (1999) Ltd.*, 2003 ABQB 255 (CanLII), where a wrongfully terminated employee, who was induced to leave previous secure employment, was entitled to a longer notice period.

19. *Singh v. BC Hydro and Power Authority*, 2001 BCCA 695 (CanLII); leave to appeal to S.C.C. refused, [2002] S.C.C.A. No. 45.

undermined by the wrongful conduct. The employer may rely on such when defending a **wrongful dismissal** action, even if it is discovered after the employee has been dismissed. In the *Dowling* case (see Case Summary 12.4) it was the employee's dishonesty that justified the dismissal. Such dishonesty need not be tolerated by the employer, regardless of the plight of the employee.

DISHONESTY AND MISCONDUCT

For dishonesty or misconduct to justify dismissal, courts consider whether the behaviour violates an essential condition of the contract. Does it breach the bond of trust that is necessary in light of the position the employee holds? In the *Whitehouse* case,[20] where the plaintiff, an investment adviser and vice-president of the defendant company, was abruptly terminated, the Court found his conduct portrayed a lack of integrity, a deficient judgment, dishonesty, untrustworthiness, and a careless disregard for client and corporate confidentiality. Whitehouse, in an intoxicated state, had brought a prostitute to the office after hours. He then left her there, unattended and with access to confidential files, when he stormed out refusing to pay her. The next morning Whitehouse lied about the event, denying it occurred until security tapes were produced. His wrongful dismissal action was dismissed as the court found just cause was established.

Dishonesty or misconduct may not constitute just cause for dismissal if mitigating factors are present. For example, when a bank clerk was found to have stolen $2500 from her employer and then lied about it, her dismissal was overturned by an arbitrator who substituted a 22-month suspension. This decision was upheld when appealed to a Quebec Court.[21] The clerk had an unblemished record of 25 years' employment with the bank. She stole the money because of a pathological addiction to video poker. There was great remorse, along with expert testimony of the family about personal problems she had faced because of the addiction. These factors led the arbitrator, supported later by the Court, to decide that dismissal was too harsh in this instance. Proportionality between the offence and the punishment is the key in such decisions.

Consequences need to be proportionate

CASE SUMMARY 12.4

Honesty Is Still the Best Policy: *Dowling v. Ontario (Workplace Safety and Insurance Board)*[22]

Dowling was a manager of an office of the Workplace Safety and Insurance Board. He had worked for that organization for 25 years. He was terminated for cause, with the employer claiming that Dowling had purchased a computer from one of its clients (an account he supervised), receiving a discount in the process and giving an advantage in return. It was also claimed that he had accepted a payment of $1000 on another occasion from the same client. His employer conducted an investigation and, in the process, Dowling made misrepresentations and provided false documents.

At trial, the judge found that the dishonest conduct was not enough to justify Dowling's termination. On appeal, however, the Court of Appeal found that the receipt of the $1000 payment and the discount with respect to the computers amounted to a conflict of interest. The Court also went on to find that the conduct of Dowling during the investigation, in which he lied and presented false documents, constituted dishonesty and misconduct sufficient to establish a breakdown of the employment relationship. This amounted to cause for termination and was characterized by the Court as

---

20. *Whitehouse v. RBC Dominion Securities Inc.*, 2006 ABQB 372 (CanLII).
21. *Banque Laurentienne du Canada v. Lussier*, 2003 CanLII 14640 (QC CA).
22. 2004 CanLII 43692 (ON CA).

giving rise to a fundamental breach of his employment relationship. In the words of Justice Gillese:

> It was indispensable to the parties' employment relationship that Mr. Dowling exercise the powers of his position with honesty and impartiality, and exclusively in the interests of the Board and the public. The underpinnings of faith and confidence, necessary to the parties' employment relationship, were destroyed by Mr. Dowling's misconduct. When the various acts of misconduct are considered in the context of Mr. Dowling's position, the degree of trust reposed in him and the public nature of the Board's responsibility, it is clear that summary dismissal was a proportionate response.

SMALL BUSINESS PERSPECTIVE

Minor instances of dishonesty may not justify termination, as the courts require that disciplinary measures be proportionate to the wrong, and the context is also important. If that dishonesty relates to some private aspect of the employee's life, for example, the courts may find that a lesser sanction is appropriate. But where the dishonesty undermines the employer's confidence in the integrity of an individual, dismissal may well be warranted.

Employers should document and verify allegations

Great care must be taken when dismissing employees for dishonesty or criminal behaviour such as theft to ensure that the accusations are accurate and the evidence firm. The courts have awarded significant damages for wrongful dismissal, augmented by punitive damages, when such charges have not been substantiated. In the *Pate Estate* case,[23] for example, building inspector Pate was fired when the Township discovered discrepancies between the permits issued and the fees collected. Pate was charged but subsequently acquitted of all criminal charges. The workplace investigation conducted by the employer was seriously flawed; furthermore, the employer failed to disclose relevant evidence to the investigating police officer, namely that the Township knew many of its files had gone missing when its offices were relocated. Pate died before the matter was fully resolved, but his estate was awarded $1 million in damages for malicious prosecution and $450 000 in punitive damages to amply denounce the Township's conduct.

Underlying reasons for termination cannot veil discrimination

Care should also be taken to ensure that when a person is dismissed the real reason for the termination is not discrimination upon a protected ground. Human rights tribunals are very active in prosecuting such violations.

DISOBEDIENCE AND INSUBORDINATION

Although an employee is entitled to refuse to work because of dangerous working conditions, failure to perform a reasonable order is also grounds for dismissal without notice. Disobedience justifies disciplinary measures and, if significant, may justify dismissal. Insubordination is likewise grounds for dismissal, as obedience and a willingness to work collectively is implied in employment relationships. The courts and arbitrators prefer to see employers use progressive discipline to address smaller infractions, but if the misbehaviour is significant or repeated, dismissal may be the proportionate and appropriate remedy.

INCOMPETENCE

Problem when incompetence is tolerated

Incompetence is also just cause for dismissal; however, employers are well advised to let employees know when the level of performance is unacceptable as soon as it becomes apparent and to provide an opportunity for improvement. It may appear

---

23. *Pate Estate v. Galway-Cavendish and Harvey (Township)*, 2013 ONCA 669 (CanLII).

to be easier to let matters go, but the employer may then be faced with the argument that the employer's conduct and tacit acceptance of the employee's performance led that employee to believe that the level of performance was appropriate. This argument will be especially difficult to overcome if bonuses or wage increases were given to the employee in the past despite the poor performance.

ILLNESS AND DISABILITY

In the past, employees who became seriously ill, even though not "at fault," could be discharged without notice if they could no longer perform their job. The employer did not have to pay for work not done. Even though there was no suggestion of fault here, the employment contract was considered to be frustrated. Even today, when the employee can't work termination is justified. However, there is a legislated duty to accommodate disabled workers who are still able to work. Human rights commissions are very willing to rule against employers who fire workers too quickly because of illness or disability. The employer must take great care to accommodate such disabled workers and to otherwise comply with the provisions of both the applicable human rights legislation and the workers' compensation legislation, which are designed to protect disabled or injured workers.

> **Illness may constitute frustration of contract**

In enforcing the prohibition of discrimination against the disabled, the courts have ruled that employers have a legal duty to take reasonable steps to accommodate an employee's individual needs. This legal duty does not apply, however, if the only way to resolve the problem will cause the employer *undue hardship*, which is hardship that is substantial in nature. To deal with this problem, most businesses offer some form of illness and long-term disability insurance or policy as part of their benefits package.

> **Accommodation of employees' disabilities is required by human rights legislation**

LAYOFFS

When an employer simply runs out of work for the employee to do or runs into financial difficulties, that is not just cause for termination; reasonable notice is still required. Even when the layoff is only temporary, the employee may be entitled to treat it as termination and demand the appropriate notice and compensation. In the absence of reasonable notice or just cause, the employee can sue the employer for wrongful dismissal.

Provisions in collective agreements often cover layoffs and recalls, and several provinces have included provisions covering temporary layoffs in their employment standards legislation. Ontario's *Employment Standards Act*,[24] for example, stipulates that if an employee has been laid off for a period longer than the defined "temporary layoff" (generally 13 weeks), employment terminates and the employer must pay the employee termination pay. However, if wages or other payments are made to or for the benefit of the employee during the layoff, the length of the temporary layoff can be extended to 35 weeks. (Each province will have different rules in this area; refer to MyBusLawLab to determine the specific provincial or federal law in effect where the employee is working.) Even so, unpaid layoffs may entitle employees to claim they had been constructively dismissed, so employers should give plenty of advance notice of upcoming layoffs to minimize such claims.

> **Temporary layoffs may be permitted by statute, but common claims of constructive dismissal may still be made**

CONSTRUCTIVE DISMISSAL

When an employer demotes the employee or otherwise unilaterally changes the nature of the job, this may constitute **constructive dismissal**, and the employee may be able to sue for wrongful dismissal. Sometimes the employer does this inadvertently, but at other times the employer does it to make an employee feel uncomfortable or humiliated so that the employee will voluntarily leave. From a contractual perspective, one party cannot simply impose a change in the terms of a

> **Constructive dismissal— employer breaches the contract when the nature of the job or the amount of remuneration is changed without consent**

---

24. S.O. 2000, c. 41, s. 56.

contract without first securing the consent or agreement of the other party. In essence, the employer is simply refusing to perform the original contract when it demotes an employee.

Consider the *Hilton v. Norampac Inc.* case.[25] Hilton had worked for Norampac as a mill worker for 15 years when his conditions of employment were unilaterally changed by the employer. He, along with other foremen, was required to be on call for extensive periods, including weekends, without any extra pay. He explained that he couldn't do this since it required him to be available on the weekends when his wife worked and he had to look after his young children. He offered to be on call during the week or to be demoted to a union position, but these offers were rejected and his employment was terminated for cause—based on his refusal to obey proper instruction. Hilton sued claiming constructive dismissal. The trial Court and the Court of Appeal found that the unilateral changes were material changes in his terms of employment, which amounted to constructive dismissal.

Employer is responsible for behaviour in the workplace

Since the employer is responsible for behaviour at the workplace, failure to address harassment or sexual harassment by management or by other employees may enable a victim to claim constructive dismissal. In the *Stamos* case,[26] for example, an employee suffered stress-related health issues as a result of harassment by another employee. The targeted employee resigned, and the Court found that the employer's failure to defuse the hostile work environment constituted constructive dismissal.

Employee has a duty to mitigate loss—within reason

When there is constructive dismissal, the employee has an obligation to mitigate, possibly to the extent of accepting a new position offered by the employer. The employee is not, of course, obligated to accept such a position when it would cause undue humiliation or otherwise create an impossible working situation, especially if bad relations have been created because of the way the termination took place. The law simply requires reasonable steps to be taken to mitigate damage. One does not have to suffer a substantial loss to mitigate damages.

In the *Weselan* case,[27] the employee was relocated and given a similar position. The new job, however, involved a substantial daily commute at the cost of time and approximately $34 000 per year. This meant that the employee's working conditions and net remuneration would be substantially different, so his claim that he was constructively dismissed was upheld. Unfortunately, the enforcement of his employment contract did not work in his favour. Weselan had been associated with the firm for 29 years. The Court found that if the common law prevailed he would have been entitled to 24 months' notice, or $147 400 in lieu of that notice. Unfortunately for Weselan, his original contract of employment contained a provision requiring only 90 days' notice if dismissed without cause. Since this provision was greater than the statutory minimum it prevailed, and the damage award was limited to only $18 925, representing that 90-day entitlement.[28]

CASE SUMMARY 12.5

Supreme Court Modifies Test for Constructive Dismissal: *Potter v. New Brunswick Legal Aid Services Commission*[29]

When can a non-unionized employee who is suspended with pay claim to have been constructively dismissed? The traditional test of constructive dismissal is whether a unilateral and fundamental change to the terms and conditions of employment has been

---

25. 2003 CanLII 11626 (ON CA).

26. *Stamos v. Annuity Research & Marketing Service Ltd.*, 2002 CanLII 49618 (ON SC).

27. *Weselan v. Totten Sims Hubicki Associates (1997) Ltd.*, 2001 CanLII 9431 (ON CA).

28. *Weselan v. Totten Sims Hubicki Associates (1997) Ltd.*, 2003 CanLII 49300 (ON SC).

29. 2015 SCC 10 (CanLII).

made. Here, the Supreme Court of Canada articulated a new, second test that also determines whether a constructive dismissal has occurred.

Potter was to serve as the executive director of the New Brunswick Legal Aid Services Commission (the Commission) for a seven-year term, but his relationship with the Commission deteriorated to the point where the parties began to negotiate a buyout of the plaintiff's employment contract. Potter went off work on sick leave and the Commission subsequently suspended him indefinitely with pay and delegated his powers and duties to another person. Potter had no knowledge that later that day the Commission recommended to the minister of justice that Potter's employment be terminated for cause.

Potter commenced an action claiming he was constructively dismissed; the Commission responded by terminating his pay and benefits, claiming that the commencement of litigation was equivalent to a resignation.

Overturning the decisions of the lower courts, the Supreme Court of Canada found that the plaintiff was constructively dismissed, clarifying that the test for whether an employee has been constructively dismissed consists of two branches, and a claim for constructive dismissal can be proven through either branch.

First, the employer's unilateral change must be found to constitute a breach of the employment contract and must be found to substantially alter an essential term of the contract. The Commission acted unilaterally when it suspended the plaintiff, as there was no express or implied grant of power in the employment contract to suspend for administrative reasons. Further, it was reasonable for the plaintiff to perceive that the unauthorized unilateral suspension was a substantial change to his employment contract. As such, the plaintiff was constructively dismissed and entitled to damages for wrongful dismissal.

The Supreme Court also introduced a second test. When it can be shown, based on the employer's cumulative actions, that the employer did not intend to be bound by the employment agreement, the employee has been constructively dismissed. This test is an objective one: Would a reasonable person in the same circumstances as the employee conclude the employer intended to no longer be bound by the employment agreement?

Using this second test, employees can argue that they have been constructively dismissed based on past acts by the employer that, viewed objectively, demonstrate an intention not to be bound by the employment contract.

SMALL BUSINESS PERSPECTIVE

Under the new test, courts will ask whether the employer's actions and treatment of the employee leading up to the alleged constructive dismissal demonstrate that the employer did not intend to continue to be bound by the employment contract. If a reasonable person would conclude the employer no longer intended to be bound by the employment agreement given the employer's actions, then a constructive dismissal will be found. In light of this new test, employers should refrain from using suspensions, paid or unpaid, unless the contract specifically provides for them.

Generally speaking, employers will prefer employment contracts that give management broad powers to amend or update the duties of employees. Employees, on the other hand, are better served with job descriptions that are very specific.

REMEDIES FOR WRONGFUL DISMISSAL

A wrongful dismissal is a termination that was improperly done; it is a termination without notice, without pay in lieu of notice, and without cause. In a wrongful dismissal action, the damages awarded are based on what the employee would have received had proper notice been given. If a person is fired and is given only one month's notice when he should have received five months' notice, general damages

Compensation is based on the notice that should have been given

Employee is obliged to mitigate losses

will be awarded to cover the difference, including the value of any benefits and pension rights to which he would have been entitled. The employee does, however, have an obligation to mitigate—he must try to find another job.[30] Any damages awarded will be reduced by what is earned from that other employment. In contrast, money earned from other employment need not be deducted from the statutory termination pay.[31] It is normally the employer, often a corporation, that is sued for wrongful dismissal, but the individual manager implementing the decision may also be sued when defamation or some other actionable wrong has taken place.

Damages for defamation or intentional infliction of mental stress are possible

In rare circumstances, the court will also take into account a person's damaged reputation or mental distress, and sometimes will even award punitive damages where appropriate. In the *Elgert* case,[32] for example, workers made false statements alleging that their supervisor (Elgert) had sexually harassed them, leading to his dismissal. The employer inadequately investigated these claims and fired Elgert without notice. Elgert was awarded 24 months' pay in lieu of notice, and a further $75 000 in punitive damages because of the harsh conduct of the employer ($60 000 in damages for defamation were also awarded against the co-workers who made the false claims).

Employer must have clear evidence of misconduct

It is evident that great care must be exercised when dismissing an employee for incompetence or misconduct. An employer must have clear evidence of the misconduct or incompetence and, with the latter, must demonstrate that the employee has been given a reasonable opportunity to improve. Failure to substantiate just cause will likely result in a successful action by the employee for wrongful dismissal.

REDUCING RISK 12.2

Employers are often surprised to learn of the lengthy notice requirements for termination in Canada. Including specified notice entitlements in the contract of employment will go a long way to solving the problem. But a sophisticated client knows it is vital not to make the contracted notice period less than the minimum specified in the relevant employment standards legislation. If it is for less than the legislated minimum, the contract clause may be void and the employer may be required to pay a much higher amount based on the common law notice period.

Dealing with employees in good faith has benefits

Employers must avoid the temptation to manufacture reasons to justify dismissal without notice or to make an employee so uncomfortable that she will quit. Courts are willing to find constructive dismissal and assess higher damages if there is evidence of false statements, defamation, a poisoned work environment, or damage to the employee's reputation. The sensible way to approach the problem is to negotiate with the employee. Typically, the employee will settle out of court when she realizes that she will thereby avoid the significant legal costs of a wrongful dismissal lawsuit.

Reinstatement remains a rare remedy

Damages are the appropriate remedy for wrongful dismissal. It is rare for a court to order that an employee be given back the job. Reinstatement is more common if collective agreements are involved and when the decision is made by an arbitrator rather than a judge. Some statutes, such as the *Canada Labour Code*,[33] provide for reinstatement in non-union situations. Still, in general, reinstatement is rare.

[30.] Efforts to mitigate damages need only be those expected of a reasonable person. See *Bradbury v. Newfoundland (Attorney General)*, 2001 NFCA 63 (CanLII).

[31.] See *Boland v. APV Canada Inc.*, 2005 CanLII 3384 (ON SCDC), where it was held that amounts paid pursuant to the province's employment standards legislation were not subject to the duty to mitigate. The same conclusion was reached in *E.C. & M. Electric Ltd. v. Alberta (Employment Standards Code)* (1994), 7 C.C.E.L. (2d) 235 (Alta. Prov. Ct.).

[32.] *Elgert v. Home Hardware Stores Ltd.*, 2011 ABCA 112 (CanLII); application for leave to appeal to S.C.C. dismissed November 24, 2011.

[33.] *Supra* note 12.

WRONGFUL LEAVING

Employees are also required to give reasonable notice of their intent to leave, and if the amount is specified in the contract, that is what the courts will enforce. When the contract is silent about notice, reasonable notice is required. Unless the employee is in a key position, such as senior executive or salesperson, it is usually not worth the effort to sue when an employee leaves without giving proper notice. But key employees may be required to give substantial notice, just like employers. When there is a serious breach of the employment contract by the employer, however, an employee is entitled to leave without notice. If the employer gives an unreasonable or dangerous order, if the working conditions are dangerous and the employer refuses to correct them, or if the employer involves the employee in illegal or immoral activities, the employee may be entitled to "quit."

Employees may be sued for leaving without notice

Employees can leave without notice if contract is breached by the employer first

CASE SUMMARY 12.6

Employees Can Be Required to Give Lengthy Notice:
Tree Savers International Ltd. v. Savoy[34]

Savoy and Deringer were employees of Tree Savers, a relatively small company working in the oil industry. After giving Tree Savers' management two weeks' notice, they left and incorporated a company in competition with Tree Savers. Savoy and Deringer had been key employees at Tree Savers, and when they left they took some documents with them, including lists of contacts. Ducharme, who gave them financial aid and advice, and the company they created, Trojan, were also defendants.

The Court had to decide whether Savoy and Deringer were in violation of their fiduciary duty to their former employer. The answer was yes, and an injunction was issued ordering them to stop their offending conduct. The Alberta Court of Appeal decided that because the two men were senior key employees they should have given their employer 18 months' notice, and the damages awarded were calculated on this basis. Ducharme was also found liable for inducing them to breach their contract.

SMALL BUSINESS PERSPECTIVE

Employers may impress upon employees that reasonable notice works both ways—in common law, the employer is entitled to the same notice that the employee is entitled to. Often employees think that they only have to give "two weeks' notice" of their intent to leave, possibly because that is the minimal statutory notice required by employment standards legislation. It may come as a surprise to learn that if the contract is silent as to notice, reasonable notice as determined by common law will be required of each party.

If former employees are sued, it is usually for breach of fiduciary duty or for disclosing confidential information. Ordinary employees do not have a fiduciary duty and, unless there is a valid restrictive covenant in their employment contract preventing them from doing so, they are free to compete with their former employer as soon as they leave.[35] That competition, however, must start after they leave. Employees cannot gather information, copy customer lists, or solicit customers before termination. If they do, they can be sued. Similarly, if the departing employee takes confidential information and misuses it, that conduct is also

Employees may be sued for breach of duty

---

34. 1992 CanLII 2828 (ABCA).

35. See *Gertz v. Meda Ltd.*, 2002 CanLII 49608 (ON SC). Gertz's wrongful dismissal action succeeded, whereas the employer's claims of breach of fiduciary duty and of confidentiality were dismissed. Gertz took certain knowledge about the industry and client needs with him, but the Court held that a mere employee's duty of fidelity to the employer ceases with termination of employment.

actionable.[36] As managers and other executives owe a fiduciary duty to their employer, they may find themselves somewhat restricted in what they can do after they leave their employment. It is preferable for the employer to set out such restrictions clearly in the original employment contract.

CASE SUMMARY 12.7

No General Duty Not to Compete with Former Employer: *RBC Dominion Securities Inc. v. Merrill Lynch*[37]

Virtually all of the investment advisers at the Cranbrook RBC branch left without notice. They went to the branch of a competitor, Merrill Lynch. Delamont, the RBC branch manager, orchestrated the move. RBC sued Delamont, the departing investment advisers, as well as Merrill Lynch and its manager. The trial judge held that (1) Delamont and the investment advisers were not fiduciary employees, (2) the investment advisers breached the implied terms of their employment contracts requiring reasonable notice and prohibiting unfair competition with RBC, and (3) Delamont had breached his contractual duty by organizing the departure. Damages were thus assessed against the investment advisers and Delamont. Because the Merrill Lynch manager had induced the breach of contract and duty not to compete unfairly, Merrill Lynch and its manager were found jointly and severally liable.

The Court of Appeal varied some of these damages, prompting a further appeal. The Supreme Court of Canada reinstated the award of the trial judge, except for the damages payable by the investment advisers for RBC's losses during the notice period. An employee who has terminated employment is not prevented from competing with his employer during the notice period. RBC was restricted to damages for the employees' failure to give reasonable notice ($40 000 for the employees' failure to each give 2.5 weeks' notice).

As to the award against Delamont, the Court ruled that damages should cover losses that arise naturally from the breach, or as may reasonably have been in the contemplation of both parties as the probable result of a breach. An implied term of Delamont's employment contract was the retention of RBC's employees under his supervision. Delamont therefore breached his contractual duty of good faith by organizing the departure of the investment advisers. For this breach, damages were calculated at $1 483 239, being the loss it caused to RBC projected over five years.

SMALL BUSINESS PERSPECTIVE

This case clarifies that unless an employment contract contains an enforceable restrictive covenant, employees are free to compete with their former employer once they leave—even during the notice period. On the other hand, managers may have a duty of good faith or fiduciary duty imposed upon them, the breach of which draws damages. In light of this, what clauses might a business wish to incorporate in its employment contracts?

Liability of Employer

Employer is liable for torts committed by employee while on the job

Although not directly at fault, an employer can be held liable for torts committed by an employee during the course of employment. This is the principle of vicarious liability that was discussed in Chapter 5. Because the employer benefits from the

---

36. See *CRC-Evans Canada Ltd. v. Pettifer,* 1997 CanLII 14943 (AB QB); aff'd 1998 ABCA 191 (CanLII), in which two former key employees set up a competing corporation and used confidential information from the former employer in bidding against that party. They were ordered to pay $305 507.72 in damages for breaching their duty to serve their employer honestly and faithfully, and for breach of their fiduciary duty.
37. 2008 SCC 54 (CanLII).

work of the employee, the employer is held responsible for losses caused by the employee. The employer's liability is limited to those activities that take place during the course of employment. This includes not only incidents arising during working hours, but also any conduct that takes place as part of the employment activity. If Patel, while delivering a letter to her employer's client on her way home, injures a pedestrian, both Patel and her employer would likely be liable. The negligent act occurred during the course of employment, even though it did not happen during working hours. But if Patel injures the pedestrian when she goes out to do her personal banking during working hours, the employer would not be liable. In this case, Patel is "on a frolic of her own," and the injury did not take place in the course of her employment.

As a general rule, there must be an employment relationship for vicarious liability to apply. This is one reason why the tests discussed above for determining whether an employment relationship exists are so important. (Some exceptions to this requirement were discussed in Chapter 10.) Several jurisdictions have legislated vicarious liability in special situations. For example, in Alberta, British Columbia, and some other provinces, the owner of a motor vehicle is vicariously liable for any torts committed by the person driving the vehicle with the owner's consent. The driver is deemed to be "the agent or employee of the owner of the motor vehicle, employed as the agent or employee of the owner of the motor vehicle, and driving the motor vehicle in the course of that person's employment."[38]

Vicarious liability may be imposed on employers—and motor vehicle owners

This section actually expands the potential liability of an employer that allows its employees to drive its vehicles beyond the normal scope of vicarious liability. Under vicarious liability, the employer escapes liability if the employee negligently hurts the plaintiff while "on a frolic of his own." The statute, on the other hand, deems the driver to be driving in the course of his employment, whether he's driving for a job-related purpose or not. For example, in the *Morad* case,[39] the employer was held liable when an employee borrowed the company vehicle and then deliberately ran over some third party who owed him money! Other provinces, like Ontario, simply make an owner liable for any damage negligently caused by a person driving her car with consent without reference to an employment or agency relationship.[40] Refer to MyBusLawLab for provincial variations on this issue.

Vicarious liability is possible for acts of those driving vehicles with consent of the owner

Although the employer has the right to turn to the employee for compensation when it is found vicariously liable, this is usually a hollow remedy since the employee is typically in no financial position to pay such compensation.

Employer is vicariously liable, but can turn to employee for compensation

Employers often try to separate portions of their operations from the actual business they conduct. Cleaning and office management, as well as sales and product service, may be contracted out. This is done to reduce the number of employees, thereby reducing administrative costs, leaving the organization free to concentrate on what it does best. It may also reduce the risk of the employer being found vicariously liable when injuries take place. Avoiding vicarious liability is more likely when great care has been taken to make sure the people doing those jobs are truly independent. But even then the courts may still find a sufficiently close relationship to impose vicarious liability on the employer for the wrongful acts committed by these supposedly independent workers. The risk of such liability should be planned for in the operation of the business. Liability insurance is typically advisable.

Insurance coverage reduces the impact of vicarious liability

Employers are particularly vulnerable to misuse of their computers by employees. Employees may tamper with company data deliberately; more often, they expose the employer to civil and possibly criminal liability in their dealings with outsiders. The employer will be responsible for data transmissions that result in intentional or negligent violations of intellectual property rights, privacy rights, or even the criminal law in local or foreign jurisdictions. To minimize liability, employers should

---

[38]. *Traffic Safety Act*, R.S.A. 2000, c. T-6, s. 187. See also *Motor Vehicle Act*, R.S.B.C. 1996, c. 318, s. 86.

[39]. *Morad v. Emmanouel*, 1993 CanLII 7054 (AB QB).

[40]. *Highway Traffic Act*, R.S.O. 1990, c. H-8, s. 192(2).

Employees' use of computers can expose employers to liability

establish comprehensive communication policies and incorporate these policies into employment contracts. Employees must be taught what they can and cannot do on their computers. In addition, active measures should be taken to protect the business from computer attacks by outsiders or disgruntled former employees.

The ease of communicating by email or text messages can lead to casualness and carelessness; employees may fail to appreciate that their messages may be defamatory, discriminatory, reveal private or confidential information, or expose illegal activity. Even when deleted, a digital trail is created and can be reconstructed. The circulation of confidential, hateful, or defamatory material, or the practice of using computers to harass other employees will also put the employer at risk. Social networking sites, like Facebook and LinkedIn, amplify the potential for harm. Messages intended for one recipient can easily be forwarded and broadly distributed, increasing the potential for damage.

Employers should inform employees of surveillance

Privacy laws require consent when personal employee information is collected, used, or disclosed

Employers may be tempted to monitor employees' email and their Internet use, but this raises privacy concerns. At a minimum, employers should advise employees that their online activities are being monitored. Such notification may encourage employees to use discretion. Still, it is questionable whether advising someone that there is no expectation of privacy constitutes consent; Canada's privacy legislation generally demands that personal information be collected, used, and disclosed only with the consent of the individual.[41]

Although employers have many legitimate reasons to monitor email, employees and the general public are justifiably concerned that allowing monitoring would lead to abuses that undermine privacy rights. The courts and legislatures have tried to be responsive to both sides.

CASE SUMMARY 12.8

Collecting Information Secretly: *Re: Parkland Regional Library Review No. 3016*[42]

An information technology employee made a complaint under the *Freedom of Information and Protection of Privacy Act*[43] when the Parkland Regional Library installed keystroke logging on his computer without his knowledge. The library tried to justify its actions based on concerns over the employee's productivity. Parkland Regional Library was found not to have the authority to collect the employee's personal information in this way, particularly as less intrusive means were available for collecting management information.

SMALL BUSINESS PERSPECTIVE

Employers must be careful to balance liability concerns surrounding possible computer misuse with the employees' rights to privacy. At a minimum, employers should ensure that they collect, use, and disclose personal information about their employees for appropriate purposes only.

Employer must be careful not to violate employees' rights

Employers must consider the impact of the *Personal Information Protection and Electronic Documents Act (PIPEDA)* before monitoring employee email. This Act applies to all private sector organizations that collect, use, or disclose personal information in the course of carrying out a commercial activity. "Personal information" includes "information about an identifiable individual,"[44] and this broad definition likely includes information that would be gleaned from monitoring email, especially

---

41. See the fact sheet from the Privacy Commissioner of Canada, "Privacy in the Workplace," www.priv. gc.ca/resource/fs-fi/02_05_d_17_e.asp.

42. Order F2005-003, 2005 CanLII 78636 (AB OIPC).

43. R.S.A. 2000, c. F-25.

44. *Personal Information Protection and Electronic Documents Act*, S.C. 2000, c. 5, s. 2.

personal email. Thus employers must act in accordance with the privacy principles enunciated in Schedule I of *PIPEDA*. Alberta and British Columbia each have legislation that is "substantially similar" to *PIPEDA*, so in those provinces privacy is protected by these *Personal Information Protection Acts*.[45] (Note that in Alberta and British Columbia, these statutes enable employers to collect, use, or disclose employee personal information without consent if it is reasonably required for the purpose of establishing, managing, or terminating an employment relationship).

Section 32 of the *Charter of Rights and Freedoms* states that the *Charter* applies to government actions—so why should employers in private industry be concerned about safeguards against unreasonable search and seizure? The answer lies in case law. A number of Supreme Court decisions have left room for the *Charter* to impact private disputes indirectly. The Court has made it clear in cases such as *RWDSU v. Dolphin Delivery Ltd.*[46] and *M. (A.) v. Ryan*[47] that the common law must develop in accordance with *Charter* values.

Whereas there had long been no common law right of privacy in Canada, the courts now recognize that invasion of privacy is actionable. In *Somwar v. McDonald's Restaurants of Canada Ltd.*,[48] the Court affirmed that invasion of privacy should be a tort in its own right, pointing to the inadequacy of traditional torts to protect individuals from unauthorized access to personal information. Subsequently, in *Jones v. Tsige*[49] the Ontario Court of Appeal recognized a right of action for intrusion upon seclusion. This expansion of tort law demonstrates that the common law is in fact developing in conformity with the *values enshrined in the Constitution*.

> **Courts are developing rights to privacy**

Before an employer engages in monitoring email, it should also consider the *Criminal Code* prohibition relating to interception of private communications. Section 184(1) stipulates "Every one who, by means of any electro-magnetic, acoustic, mechanical or other device, willfully intercepts a private communication is guilty of an indictable offence and liable to imprisonment for a term not exceeding five years."[50] Whether a communication is "private" depends on the expectation of privacy associated with the nature of the communication. If individuals are told over the phone, for example, that the conversation is being taped, then no reasonable expectation of privacy exists. Without such a caution, telephone conversations are private communications. Similarly, if those exchanging emails are not cautioned that their exchange is being monitored, an expectation of privacy may well arise. However, subsection (1) does not apply to "a person who has the consent to intercept, express or implied, of the originator of the private communication or of the person intended by the originator thereof to receive it." Even though criminal charges are not likely to be brought against an employer, a prudent employer would secure employee consent prior to monitoring to avoid such a risk.

> **Employee should be notified and consent obtained before monitoring**

CASE SUMMARY 12.9

Misuse of Employer's Computer: *R. v. Cole*[51]

Cole, a teacher, was given a laptop computer owned by the school to facilitate his teaching responsibilities, which included supervising school computers used by students. In that capacity, he intercepted a communication between students containing a sexually explicit photo of a Grade 10 student and downloaded it to his laptop computer. The

---

45. *Personal Information Protection Act*, S.A. 2003, c. P-6.5; *Personal Information Protection Act*, S.B.C. 2003 c. 63.
46. 1986 CanLII 5 (SCC).
47. 1997 CanLII 403 (SCC).
48. 2006 CanLII 202 (ON SC).
49. 2012 ONCA 32 (CanLII).
50. *Criminal Code*, R.S.C. 1985, c. C-46.
51. 2012 SCC 53 (CanLII).

laptop (with the school's assent) was used for both work and personal purposes. A school technician performing maintenance activities detected the photo and reported it to the principal, who had copies made onto a CD. The principal seized the laptop, had the temporary Internet files copied to a second CD, and reported the matter to the police. The laptop and CDs were handed over to the police; they also searched the hard drive, including the teacher's web-browsing history, and then laid charges. The issue was whether the evidence obtained from the computer could be used in a prosecution for possession of child pornography or whether it should be excluded as a violation of the teacher's expectation of privacy under the *Charter of Rights and Freedoms*.

The Supreme Court conceded that computers that are reasonably used for personal purposes, whether found in the workplace or the home, contain information that is meaningful, intimate, and revealing. Canadians may thus reasonably expect privacy in the information contained on these computers. While workplace policies can diminish an individual's expectation of privacy on a work computer, they do not in themselves remove the expectation entirely. Ownership of property is also relevant, but to determine whether expectation of privacy is reasonable, the totality of the circumstances must be considered.

The totality of the circumstances, given that use for personal purposes was permitted, supported the reasonableness of the accused's expectation of privacy. While the principal or employer had a statutory duty to maintain a safe school environment, and by implication, the lawful authority to seize and search the laptop, this did not furnish the police with the same power. A reasonable though diminished expectation of privacy is nonetheless protected by section 8 of the *Charter*. Accordingly, it is subject to state intrusion only under the authority of a reasonable law.

Conducting a search of the laptop did violate Cole's expectation of privacy, and the evidence the police obtained by searching the hard drive and Cole's browsing history on the Internet could be excluded under section 24(2) of the *Charter*. But the Supreme Court decided not to exclude the evidence because the conduct of the police did not constitute an egregious breach of *Charter* rights. The officer had reached a sincere but erroneous conclusion as to whether there was a privacy breach. Since the property was owned by the employer and the owner consented to the search, the officer concluded it was unnecessary to secure a search warrant. Further, had an application been made, the officer had reasonable and probable grounds to obtain a warrant; with it, the evidence would necessarily have been discovered. Finally, the exclusion of the material would have a marked negative impact on finding the truth, whereas its admission would not bring the administration of justice into disrepute. The evidence, thus, was not to be excluded and a new trial was ordered.

SMALL BUSINESS PERSPECTIVE

A prudent employer should always guard against the misuse of computers by employees. Even though the computer in this case was the property of the employer, the employee still had a reasonable expectation of privacy. Great care should be taken in balancing these interests and making sure that employees understand that the computers they use are subject to inspection. Although this case involved a breach of *Charter* rights, privacy legislation also gives employees an expectation of privacy when using computers in the workplace, particularly where use for personal purposes is permitted.

Did the employee have a reasonable expectation of privacy?

Employment contracts, by their very nature, create a relationship of subordination. An employer is entitled to exercise direction and control over its employees. Reprimanding an employee who wastes inordinate amounts of time on personal email or surfing on the web would be within an employer's rights. Despite the trend in Canada toward protecting privacy rights, a review of recent case law reveals that employers do have the right to discipline employees for accessing inappropriate sites or improper use of the employer's computer system. The decisions have largely focused on whether, in the circumstances, the employee had a reasonable expectation of privacy. Factors such as whether the employer had an email policy in place, whether the employer had created a permissive culture by turning a blind eye to computer misuse, whether employees were using laptops at home rather than at the workplace, and whether the email was sent during "off hours" are all relevant when assessing whether the employee should have been able to expect privacy. But where an employer has a well-known policy concerning inappropriate email usage, the expectation of privacy is diminished.

As to what sanctions are appropriate for computer misuse, "the penalty must fit the crime." For minor infractions, a reprimand may suffice, whereas graver infractions may warrant dismissal. The content of the email is also an important factor. A more serious penalty is justified where the material is more offensive.

REDUCING RISK 12.3

As in other circumstances, employers can be liable when their employees misuse the Internet. This may involve not only Internet activities at work, but also the use of their own computers at home using the employer's email services. The misuse can range from defamation and harassment of other workers and outsiders to downloading child pornography. The sophisticated employer should have a clear and comprehensive policy prohibiting such use of company resources. The policy should include educating employees with respect to the rules, and notifying them that their use of company resources may be subject to monitoring by the employer.

Legislation Impacting Employment

As a consequence of the relatively weak position of individual employees in the employment relationship, employees have tended to band together to exert greater pressure on the employer. Such collective action is now governed by legislation and will be discussed under "Collective Bargaining" heading later in this chapter.

A considerable amount of legislation has also been passed that is designed to protect employees, whether unionized or not, by setting minimum standards of safety, remuneration, hours of work, and other benefits. Conditions of employment normally fall under provincial jurisdiction. Most provinces have concentrated their employee welfare legislation into one statute, generally called the *Employment Standards Act* or *Labour Standards Act*, which sets minimum standards in connection with

Provincial legislation applies to conditions of employment

- wages,
- overtime, work hours, and rest periods,
- vacation and holiday entitlements,
- maternity and parental leave, and
- termination and severance pay.

Some also provide for bereavement and sick leave.

There are differences in the details because employment standards legislation varies with each jurisdiction. For example, in April 2015 the general minimum wage in Alberta was $10.20 per hour,[52] whereas in Ontario it was $10.30[53] ($9.20 in Alberta and $9.55 in Ontario for liquor servers). Refer to MyBusLawLab for specific information relevant to your particular jurisdiction.

Many workplaces fall under federal jurisdiction, including banks, the military, Aboriginal reserves, the post office, telephone and broadcast companies, airlines, railroads, and steamships. The employment relationship in those sectors is governed by the federal *Canada Labour Code*;[54] Part III sets out employment standards.

[52.] *Employment Standards Regulation*, AR 14/97, art. 9.

[53.] *Exemptions, Special Rules and Establishment of Minimum Wage Regulation*, OR 285/01, art. 5.

[54.] *Supra* note 12.

Since it applies across the country, its provisions will be reviewed here to illustrate employment standards.

EMPLOYMENT STANDARDS

Legislation provides minimal employment standards or protections

Notice periods less than the common law standard can be set out in employment contracts, and as long as they are greater than the minimum statutory requirement they will prevail. This was illustrated in the *Weselan* case, discussed above.[55] If a notice period is shorter than the statutory minimum, it will be void and the employer will then have to comply with the longer "reasonable notice" provisions found in common law. The statutory provisions set a minimum standard, thus agreements that waive the protections or remedies available under the legislation may likewise be declared void. When the parties have agreed to a higher standard, or when a higher standard is imposed by common law, that higher standard will normally prevail.[56] But even the minimum statutory provisions do not treat all employees equally. The government may exempt or modify certain provisions in respect of certain types of employment. In other words, employers may, for example, be excused from paying minimum wage to managers or students, and overtime may be calculated differently for persons engaged in different lines of work. (Note that details as to payment of wages, minimum wage, deductions from pay, hours of work and overtime, vacation and holiday entitlements, maternity and parental benefits, employment of minors, and bereavement and sick leave can be obtained from MyBusLawLab.)

CASE SUMMARY 12.10

Statutory Notice May Not Suffice: *Machtinger v. HOJ Industries Ltd.*[57]

This case involves two employees who were terminated from their employment with only four weeks' notice, despite the fact that they both had been employed for a number of years. The employees each brought a wrongful dismissal action against the employer, demanding compensation. The issue was whether the four weeks' notice was enough. This notice corresponded with the statutory minimum under Ontario's *Employment Standards Act*. The employment contracts required even less notice to be given. If common law applied, each employee would be entitled to more than seven months' notice.

The Supreme Court of Canada held that any contractual term that did not comply with the minimum standards set out in the Act was a nullity. The minimal notice provisions found in the contract were therefore void. The Court then observed that, although the notice given satisfied the requirements of the legislation, this was merely a minimum standard. Since common law required more than seven months' notice in such circumstances, that longer notice requirement prevailed. Complying with the statutory minimum was not good enough in this case.

SMALL BUSINESS PERSPECTIVE

This case illustrates that when enforcing the terms agreed to in an employment contract, courts must also consider whether the terms were enforceable in light of statutory minimums. The risk to employers is that legislated requirements may change, rendering some existing contractual rights or obligations void. Because laws are continually amended or updated, it is important for a small business owner to obtain legal advice when preparing its employment contracts.

[55.] *Supra* notes 27 and 28.

[56.] *Canada Labour Code, supra* note 12, s. 168. Note that similar provisions are found in provincial acts.

[57.] 1992 CanLII 102 (SCC).

TERMINATION

As under common law, the *Canada Labour Code* recognizes that no notice is required when the dismissal is for cause; otherwise, notice of termination is necessary.[58] Where the *Code* and common law differ is in the remedies available for wrongful dismissal. When determining adequate notice and severance pay, the *Code* does not consider the nature of the employment, only its length. Employees who have completed three months or more of continuous employment are to receive two weeks' notice of termination (except when the dismissal is for cause). Additionally, employees who have been employed for more than 12 months are entitled to severance pay of two days' wages for each completed year of service, plus five days' wages. The *Code* also provides that when a person has been laid off for a period longer than three months, he may be able to treat this layoff as a termination and claim termination pay and severance pay. (There are exceptions, as when payments are made to the employee during the layoff.)

Most jurisdictions have passed similar legislation, but the provisions vary substantially; it is thus necessary to review the provisions of the relevant statute to determine the entitlements of a particular employee.

Termination entitlements are determined by length of service

Layoffs may trigger termination pay

ISSUE ESTOPPEL

Employees who face termination have a real concern. Case law makes it imperative that employees seek legal advice before filing a complaint under employment standards legislation. By simply applying for these minimal statutory benefits, an employee may lose the ability to later sue for damages for wrongful dismissal based on common law. If an employment standards officer determines that the complainant was terminated for cause, not only will the complainant's claim for termination pay under the statute fail, but if the employee later tries to sue for damages for wrongful dismissal, the court may decide that the issue was already settled.[59] This is because the employment standards officer has already decided that the termination was not wrongful. **Issue estoppel** may cause the court to dismiss the wrongful dismissal suit altogether, without even hearing the details. Such were the results in the *Fayant* and *Wong* cases,[60] where the pleadings were struck out after issue estoppel was successfully raised.

Choosing to file a complaint may preclude suing later

COMPLAINTS

Employment standards legislation allows employees to file a complaint with a government board; the investigation and determination is then made by civil servants.[61] This process enables the employee to avoid the costs of litigation. Note that time limitations vary between employment standards statutes and may well be as short as a few months (six months from the day on which the subject matter of the complaint arose, or six months from the last day on which the employer was required to pay wages or other amounts under the *Canada Labour Code*). Under the federal legislation, the inspector may dismiss the complaint if it is unfounded, but this determination may be appealed. If the inspector determines that earnings are due to the employee, she may order payment to be made. If the employer is a corporation, the individual directors may be liable personally for up to six months' wages per employee.

Parties who refuse to obey orders made under employment standards legislation my face fines and even imprisonment. In *R. v. Blondin*,[62] the Court sent a clear

Legislated process streamlines the handling of complaints

58. *Supra* note 12, ss. 230–237.
59. *Rasanen v. Rosemount Instruments Ltd.*, 1994 CanLII 608 (ON CA), (1994), 17 O.R. (3d) 267 (C.A.); leave to appeal to S.C.C. refused, [1994] S.C.C.A. No. 152.
60. *Fayant v. Campbell's Maple Village Ltd.*, 1993 CanLII 7216 (AB QB); *Wong v. Shell Canada* (1995), 174 A.R. 287 (C.A.); leave to appeal to S.C.C. refused, [1995] S.C.C.A. No. 551.
61. *Supra* note 12, ss. 249–251.
62. 2012 ONCJ 826 (CanLII).

message to directors: Those who violate obligations under the Ontario *Employment Standards Act, 2000* may be sent to prison. Blondin, a corporate director, was sent to prison for 90 days for repeatedly failing to pay wages; he and his six companies were also fined $280 000 plus a 25 percent victim surcharge and were again ordered to pay outstanding wages.

HUMAN RIGHTS

Federal and provincial human rights legislation prohibit various forms of discrimination in employment

An area of employment law that is becoming much more significant is the protection of employee rights. With the passage of the *Charter of Rights and Freedoms*, as well as federal and provincial human rights legislation, employers are required not only to ensure that they do not discriminate in their hiring and employment practices, but that they take active steps to ensure that these basic rights are protected. Although the *Charter* does not apply directly to most employment situations, it does have an important indirect effect, since federal and provincial human rights statutes must be consistent with the provisions of the *Charter*. Indeed, as evident from the *Vriend* case mentioned in Chapter 2,[63] the courts have gone as far as to read into human rights statutes protection from discrimination based on sexual orientation where no such provision was originally included. Human rights legislation has an impact on employment by prohibiting discrimination on the basis of race, national or ethnic origin, colour, religion, gender, sexual orientation, and in some cases age, marital status, family status, physical or mental disability, and pardoned criminal convictions.

CASE SUMMARY 12.11

Family Needs Must Be Accommodated: *Canada (Attorney General) v. Johnstone*[64]

The complainant and her husband were both employed by the Canada Border Services Agency. She filed a complaint with the Canadian Human Rights Commission following the denial of her request to alter her shift schedule to coincide with available childcare arrangements.

The Federal Court of Appeal agreed that accommodating "family status" included childcare obligations, but rejected the earlier test found in the *Campbell River* case[65] that held there must be "serious interference with a substantial interest." (In the *Campbell River* case, the employer changed the employee's hours, requiring her to work until 6 p.m., but this interfered with her ability to provide the necessary care for her son after school, who had mental disabilities.) Instead, the Court ruled that

> in order to make out a *prima facie* case where workplace discrimination on the prohibited ground of family status resulting from childcare obligations is alleged, the individual advancing the claim must show: (i) that a child is under his or her care and supervision; (ii) that the childcare obligation at issue engages the individual's legal responsibility for that child, as opposed to a personal choice; (iii) that he or she has made reasonable efforts to meet those childcare obligations through reasonable alternative solutions, and that no such alternative solution is reasonably accessible; and (iv) that the impugned workplace rule interferes in a manner that is more than trivial or insubstantial with the fulfillment of the childcare obligation.[66]

---

63. *Vriend v. Alberta*, [1998] 1 S.C.R. 493.

64. 2014 FCA 110 (CanLII). See also the companion case, *Canadian National Railway Company v. Seeley*, 2014 FCA 111 (CanLII).

65. *Health Sciences Assoc. of B.C. v. Campbell River and North Island Transition Society*, 2004 BCCA 260 (CanLII).

66. *Canada (Attorney General) v. Johnstone, supra* note 64, at para. 93.

> Accordingly, a *prima facie* case of discrimination on the basis of family status is made out whenever an employment rule or condition interferes with an employee's ability to meet a parental obligation in a realistic way.

SMALL BUSINESS PERSPECTIVE

With the Court's finding that childcare responsibilities are clearly part of "family status," this ground of discrimination is likely to be asserted more frequently. Employees caring for their aging family members may likewise seek accommodation to attend to eldercare. Employers who fail to treat seriously claims for accommodation based on eldercare responsibilities may face damage awards.[67] Employers may need to become more flexible with shift scheduling and job-sharing arrangements to accommodate these family obligations.

Human rights tribunals have been established to hear complaints about violations of human rights legislation. These tribunals have the power to investigate, levy fines, and even order reinstatement of employees if they find that the employees have been terminated in violation of some human rights provision or forced to quit because of harassment.

Tribunals hear complaints

The *Canadian Human Rights Act*, for example, prohibits discrimination with regard to any term or condition of employment on the basis of a person's race, national or ethnic origin, colour, religion, age, sex, and so on. It specifically prohibits the refusal to hire or the firing of any person on the basis of one of the prohibited grounds.[68] Where the ground of discrimination is pregnancy or childbirth, the discrimination shall be deemed to be on the ground of sex. Employers cannot, therefore, fire or demote an employee because of pregnancy. Also, an employer's refusal to permit an employee to breastfeed in the workplace may constitute discrimination on the basis of gender.[69] Furthermore, employers must refrain from asking women at job interviews whether they are pregnant, or plan to have children, for the legislation also addresses discrimination during pre-employment inquiries.[70]

Impact of prohibiting gender discrimination

Job advertisements and application forms must not directly or indirectly express a limitation or preference based on race, religion, sexual orientation, or other prohibited grounds. The forms used cannot require applicants to furnish information concerning their gender, age, marital status, and so on. Accordingly, unless a bona fide occupational requirement exists that would justify such an inquiry, employers must refrain from requesting photographs or that the applicant's gender, previous name, marital status, date of birth, or religion be provided on the application form.

Restrictions on questions asked on applications and at interviews

Harassment is a form of discrimination that occurs when one subjects another person to unwelcome verbal or physical conduct because of his colour, gender, age, sexual orientation, or other characteristic. Unwanted physical contact, jokes, or insults are harassment when they negatively affect the working environment. Note that interaction between a supervisor and her subordinates, even outside the workplace, can be employment-related harassment. If the supervisor's conduct creates a perception that continued employment is dependent on sexual interaction with that person, then that supervisor has engaged in harassment.[71]

Harassment is also covered

[67.] See *Hicks v. Human Resources and Skills Development Canada*, 2013 CHRT 20 (CanLII), where the complainant was awarded $20 000 because the employer refused to seriously consider his claim for accommodation based on eldercare responsibilities.

[68.] *Canadian Human Rights Act*, R.S.C. 1985, c. H-6, s. 7.

[69.] *Re: Carewest and H.S.A.A. (Degagne)*, (2001), 93 L.A.C. (4th) 129 (Alta.).

[70.] See the Canadian Human Rights Commission, "Policy on Pregnancy & Human Rights in the Workplace," www.chrc-ccdp.ca/eng/content/policy-and-best-practices-page-1.

[71.] *Simpson v. Consumers' Assn. of Canada*, 2001 CanLII 23994 (ON CA); leave to appeal to S.C.C. refused, [2002] S.C.C.A. No. 83.

Sexual harassment is just one example of harassment. When harassment is committed by an employee, the employer can be held responsible if it has failed to take adequate steps to protect the employee who was harassed. It is, therefore, vital for employers to be proactive and to take positive steps to develop anti-harassment and anti-discrimination policies, clarifying that such conduct will not be tolerated.[72] These policies should also spell out what disciplinary steps might be taken if one employee harasses or discriminates against another employee.

CASE SUMMARY 12.12

Should the Employer Be Liable? *Robichaud v. Canada (Treasury Board)*[73]

The Supreme Court of Canada had to determine whether the employer was responsible for the sexual harassment committed by an employee. Robichaud worked as a lead hand in a cleaning operation for the Department of National Defence. A supervisor subjected her to unwanted sexual attention. Such behaviour amounts to discrimination on the basis of gender because it differentiates adversely against an employee on the basis of her gender. The Court held that the employer, under the *Canadian Human Rights Act*, was liable for the discriminatory acts of its employees that were committed in the course of their employment, much like vicarious liability in common law. The case indicates the approach taken by courts when faced with sexual harassment.

In fact, this precedent has been followed when applying provincial legislation to instances of sexual harassment. In the *Katsiris* case,[74] the corporation owning the restaurant was held liable for the harassment committed by its employee. That case also addressed whether the CEO of the corporation should be personally liable. Since it was not shown that he knew of the sexual harassment, liability was not imposed on him personally.

SMALL BUSINESS PERSPECTIVE

What factors should the court consider in determining whether to hold the employer liable for the wrongful conduct of its employee in these circumstances? What can an employer do to minimize its potential liability (and the liability of the directors, if the employer is a corporation) for the actions of its employees? Note that in the *Deluxe Windows* case,[75] the employer was held vicariously liable for the jury's award of $470000 in damages plus $150000 in costs for the repeated sexual assaults of an employee by one of its supervisors!

Duty to accommodate

This positive obligation on the employer to protect vulnerable employees in the workplace has been taken further. As mentioned above, employers now have an obligation to take steps to accommodate employees with disabilities and special needs. This may extend to changing the physical work environment to accommodate visually impaired people or wheelchair users. It includes allowing workers with chronic illness or partial disability to do lighter work or to work only part time. Schedules may require adjustment to accommodate different religious holidays, as long as the request does not cause the employer undue hardship.[76]

[72.] See Canadian Human Rights Commission, "Anti-Harassment Policies for the Workplace: An Employer's Guide," www.chrc-ccdp.ca/eng/content/anti-harassment-policies-workplace-employers-guide.

[73.] 1987 CanLII 73 (SCC).

[74.] *Katsiris v. Isaac*, 2001 SKQB 4 (CanLII).

[75.] *M.B. v. 2014052 Ontario Ltd. (Deluxe Windows of Canada)*, 2012 ONCA 135 (CanLII).

[76.] See *Ontario (Human Rights Commission) v. Roosma*, 2002 CanLII 15946 (ON SCDC), in which it was held that releasing employees from Friday-night shifts to accommodate their religious beliefs would cause undue hardship. Such accommodation was therefore waived.

Workplace policies or rules may be challenged as discriminatory, and if discriminatory impact is established employers may be called upon to make accommodations. Rules requiring employees to be of a certain stature may, for example, discriminate against certain racial groups. Rules requiring uniforms or hard hats to be worn may discriminate against certain religious groups. These rules may, however, be saved if the employer establishes them to be bona fide (genuine) occupational requirements. The hard-hat rule may prevail, even if it violates a religious right to wear a turban, if safety concerns justify its use. But for the requirement to be a bona fide one, it must relate to a necessary part of the job. Also, when a rule adversely affects a particular group, the employer must take reasonable steps to accommodate the disadvantaged group.

Rules to be reviewed in light of human rights

CASE SUMMARY 12.13

Duty to Accommodate and Adverse Effect Discrimination: *"Meiorin" case*[77]

This is a leading case for determining whether a particular occupational requirement is reasonable and justifiable. Meiorin, who worked as a firefighter for over three years, failed a running test designed to measure aerobic fitness. She was therefore terminated. Minimum fitness standards for firefighters had been introduced by the government, and the tests were designed based on the results of a largely male participant group. The issue before the arbitrator was whether the running test component was discriminatory on the basis of gender. It measured aerobic capacity, and women generally have lower aerobic capacity than men. It was argued that this amounted to *adverse effect discrimination* against Meiorin. This type of discrimination involves a *generally applicable rule* that has a *particular adverse effect* on one group (women) because of a prohibited ground (their gender). In these circumstances, when a rule is shown to have a discriminatory effect, the employer can continue to apply the rule only if it is justifiable as a bona fide occupational requirement.

The Supreme Court of Canada stated that the categorization of discrimination as adverse effect or direct effect was no longer appropriate. The Court enunciated a three-part test to evaluate whether an occupational requirement (meeting the fitness standard) is justified. Once the complainant shows that the standard is discriminatory, the employer must prove

1. That there is a rational connection between the test and performance of the job;

2. That the test was adopted under an honest and good faith belief that the standard was necessary; and

3. That the standard is reasonably necessary to accomplish the employer's legitimate purpose.

The third point implies that the employer may need to show that it cannot accommodate the employee without suffering undue hardship.

The test requires employers to accommodate different members' capabilities *before* adopting a "standard" or occupational requirement. Before the aerobic standard is set, and set so high that most women cannot attain it, the employer must show that such a level of aerobic capacity is necessary to do the job. If it is unnecessary, then the standard cannot be saved as a genuine or bona fide occupational requirement.

No credible evidence was shown to establish that the prescribed aerobic capacity was necessary for either men or women to perform the work of a forest firefighter. The employer also failed to show that it would experience undue hardship if a different standard were used. Accordingly, reinstatement of the claimant was ordered, and she was compensated for her lost benefits and wages.

[77.] *British Columbia (Public Service Employee Relations Commission) v. BCGSEU*, 1999 CanLII 652 (SCC).

SMALL BUSINESS PERSPECTIVE

The third part of the test demands that employers consider differing needs when setting a standard or rule. In other words, the question of reasonable accommodation must be taken into consideration from the beginning—as part of establishing the rule. Employers need to be vigilant in setting occupational standards or requirements, for they may be challenged if they have a discriminatory impact on a particular individual or group based upon a protected ground.

Pay equity

Some jurisdictions have passed **pay equity** statutes requiring equal pay for work of equal value.[78] These provisions usually benefit women, who have traditionally been paid less than men for similar jobs, but they may place considerable hardship on the organization that must bear the extra expense. Most notably, in the *Public Service Alliance of Canada* case,[79] the federal government was required to pay more than $3.3 billion to some 230000 current and former employees for 13 years' back pay with interest! The Canadian Human Rights Tribunal ruled that the federal government had failed to abide by section 11 of the *Canadian Human Rights Act* by allowing a wage gap between men and women doing clerical work—work of equal value. Note that this must be contrasted to a Newfoundland case where the government refused to honour such a back pay order on the grounds that it was experiencing a financial crisis. This was challenged under the *Charter*, and the Supreme Court of Canada held that such a financial crisis was a valid reason justifiable under section 1 to continue the inequity.[80]

Correction of past imbalance

Discrimination in the workplace has prompted the passage of various **employment equity** acts as well.[81] Organizations may be required to take steps to correct employment situations where there has been a tradition of racial or gender imbalance, such as in nursing and engineering. This usually means giving preferential treatment to those job applicants or candidates who belong to underrepresented minority groups. The resulting **reverse discrimination** directed at individuals in the overrepresented group is also distasteful to many. Programs that are intended to correct these historical imbalances in the workplace are specifically authorized under section 15(2) of the *Charter of Rights and Freedoms*. They are sometimes referred to using the American terminology **affirmative action**.

Mandatory retirement at 65 used to be permitted

Mandatory retirement also raises human rights issues. Forced retirement at 65 years had been justified as good social policy, opening up new jobs for youth. But from the point of view of the retiree, it could be a disaster. Although discrimination in employment on the basis of age is usually prohibited, retirement at 65 years had been generally exempted in provincial employment standards or human rights statutes. By defining "age" as being "18 or older and less than 65," governments denied those who faced age discrimination (in the form of forced retirement at age 65) a remedy. The Supreme Court of Canada held that where such a mandatory retirement policy was allowed under provincial human rights legislation, it did not violate the provisions of the *Charter of Rights and Freedoms*, being a reasonable exception under section 1.[82]

Mandatory retirement has been abolished across Canada

How things have changed![83] In the last decade, mandatory retirement laws have been set aside, although in some provinces employees may be required to retire if so

---

78. See, for example, *Canadian Human Rights Act*, supra note 68, s. 11; *Alberta Human Rights Act*, R.S.A. 2000, c. A-25.5, s. 6; and Newfoundland's *Human Rights Act*, 2010, S.N.L. 2010, c. H-13.1, s. 16.

79. *Canada (Attorney General) v. Public Service Alliance of Canada*, 1999 CanLII 9380 (FC).

80. *Newfoundland (Treasury Board) v. N.A.P.E.*, 2004 SCC 66 (CanLII).

81. See the federal *Employment Equity Act*, S.C. 1995, c. 44.

82. *Dickason v. University of Alberta*, 1992 CanLII 30 (SCC).

83. See Ontario Human Rights Commission, "Policy on Discrimination Against Older People Because of Age," www.ohrc.on.ca/en/policy-discrimination-against-older-people-because-age.

required by the employer's "bona fide retirement or pension plan."[84] The federal government ended forced retirement by quietly repealing section 9(2) of the *Canadian Human Rights Act* in December 2011.[85]

Clearly, as the rules with respect to discrimination in employment change, employers should be particularly vigilant in developing policies that avoid unjust discrimination against same-sex couples, that accommodate disabled workers, and that prevent the various forms of harassment that can take place in the workplace.

WORKERS' COMPENSATION

Common law was often unable to provide an appropriate remedy for an employee injured on the job. This was especially true when the accident resulted from the employee's own carelessness. All provinces and the federal government have enacted workers' compensation legislation that provides a compulsory insurance program covering accidents that take place on the job.[86] The legislation sets rates of compensation to be paid for different types of injuries and establishes a board that hears and adjudicates the claims of injured employees.[87] The system is essentially a no-fault insurance scheme, in which benefits are paid to injured workers or to their families in the event of death. Careless conduct on the part of the worker will not disqualify an injured employee from receiving compensation. The program is financed by assessments levied by the provincial workers' compensation boards against the employers; the amount levied varies with the risks associated with the industry involved. Some employees, such as casual workers, farmers, and small business employees, are often excluded. British Columbia has, however, extended workers' compensation coverage to almost all workers in the province.[88] Refer to MyBusLawLab for provincial variations.

> **Workers' compensation—compulsory insurance coverage**

A significant aspect of workers' compensation legislation in most jurisdictions is that the worker gives up the right to any other compensation. The worker can no longer sue the employer (or the party who caused the injury, if he also contributed to the plan), being limited to the benefits bestowed by the workers' compensation system. When the injury is caused by someone other than the employer or another employee, the plans usually give the injured worker the choice of receiving workers' compensation benefits or pursuing a civil action.

> **Worker gives up the right to any other compensation and cannot sue**

Compensation is also limited to injury or disease that arises in the course of employment. This can sometimes be a problem when it is difficult to establish that a disease, such as emphysema or a heart condition, was caused by the work of the employee. Compensation is typically paid to the employee, but when an employee dies as a result of injuries sustained on the job, payments are then made to her dependants,[89] which may include same-sex partners or other survivors.[90]

HEALTH AND SAFETY

Related to workers' compensation legislation, in that they work to reduce compensation claims, are statutes controlling health and safety conditions in the workplace. Health and safety requirements are sometimes embodied in general labour

> **Provision of a safe workplace**

---

84. See *New Brunswick (Human Rights Commission) v. Potash Corporation of Saskatchewan Inc.*, 2008 SCC 45 (CanLII), where the Court ruled that to satisfy the requirements of the human rights legislation, a retirement or pension plan must be subjectively and objectively bona fide. More specifically, it must be a legitimate plan adopted in good faith and not for the purpose of defeating protected rights.

85. *Keeping Canada's Economy and Jobs Growing Act*, S.C. 2011, c. 24, s. 165.

86. Further information on workers' compensation in Canada is available through the Association of Workers' Compensation Boards of Canada, www.awcbc.org.

87. See, for example, Alberta's *Workers' Compensation Act*, R.S.A. 2000, c. W-15, and *Workers' Compensation Regulation*, Alta. Reg. 325/2002. The federal legislation is entitled the *Government Employees Compensation Act*, R.S.C. 1985, c. G-5.

88. *Workers Compensation Act*, R.S.B.C. 1996, c. 492, s. 2.

89. *Government Employees Compensation Act*, supra note 87, s. 4.

90. For example, see *Workplace Safety and Insurance Act, 1997*, S.O. 1997, c. 16, s. 2.

statutes, as in the *Canada Labour Code*.[91] Some jurisdictions deal with health and safety in a separate statute, as in Ontario's *Occupational Health and Safety Act*.[92]

Workers generally have the right to refuse work they believe is dangerous to themselves or another worker. Effective October 2014, the federal government redefined *danger* so as to reduce the frequency of work stoppages triggered by workers claiming that danger was imminent.[93] Labour unions have warned that this may lead to a greater number of injuries on the job. Workers also have the right to know about potential hazards to which they may be exposed and the right to participate in the health and safety process, mostly through joint health and safety committees.

The main thrust of occupational health and safety legislation is to

1. provide safer working conditions by requiring fencing of hazardous areas, safety netting, proper shielding of equipment, environmental control, and so on

2. ensure safe employment practices, such as requiring the supply and use of hard hats, goggles, and protective clothing

3. establish programs to educate both the employer and the employee on how to create a safer working environment for all concerned[94]

Safety boards ensure
regulations are adhered to

These objectives are facilitated through the establishment of a board with the power to hear complaints and enforce correction. Officers are empowered to enter the workplace without a warrant. When such officers encounter dangerous conditions (such as lack of fencing or shielding), poor safety practices (such as failure to use hard hats or safety lines), or environmental contamination (caused by hazardous chemicals, fumes, or dust), they can order the problem corrected or, in serious cases, they can shut the job site down. In some jurisdictions, occupational health and safety officers can issues tickets (administrative penalties), much like traffic tickets, for safety violations.[95] Businesses can be prosecuted for violations, especially when injury or death results. These provisions are effective only if the fines are significant. Ontario, for example, has increased the maximum fines levied and extended liability to make directors of corporations personally responsible for harmful and dangerous practices. Other provincial variations are available on MyBusLawLab.

Most jurisdictions now address workplace violence and workplace harassment in their occupational health and safety legislation. Ontario's legislation, for example, requires employers to take precautions to protect workers against workplace harassment, bullying, or violence and includes verbal threats of physical violence in its definition of workplace violence.[96] Consequently, workplace threats can no longer be ignored; they must be reported, investigated, and workplace safety must be considered when assessing the appropriate discipline.

EMPLOYMENT INSURANCE

Employment insurance is under
federal jurisdiction

The federal government was given jurisdiction over insurance coverage for unemployed workers by an amendment to the *Constitution Act, 1867* in 1940.[97] Under the *Employment Insurance Act*,[98] both employers and employees pay into a government-supplemented fund. Laid-off employees are entitled to receive payments for a specific period of time. This is not a fund from which the employee

Employee must meet
qualifications to receive benefits

---

91. *Supra* note 12, Part II.

92. R.S.O. 1990, c. O.1.

93. *Supra* note 12, s. 122.

94. The statutes are supplemented by numerous regulations, such as Ontario's *Confined Spaces Regulation*, O. Reg. 632/05, *Training Programs Regulation*, O. Reg. 780/94, and *X-ray Safety Regulation*, R.R.O. 1990, Reg. 861.

95. *Occupational Health and Safety Act*, R.S.A. 2000, c. O-2, s. 40.3.

96. See Part III.0.1 (Violence and Harassment) of Ontario's *Occupational Health and Safety Act*, *supra* note 92.

97. *Constitution Act, 1940*, 3–4 Geo. VI, c. 36 (U.K.).

98. S.C. 1996, c. 23.

is entitled to get back what she has contributed. Rather, the payments are insurance premiums, and an employee is entitled to receive only what is set out in the statute and regulations. This amount is based on the number of weeks worked before the claim and the amount of wages received. Workers who voluntarily leave their employment or are involved in a strike or lockout are generally not entitled to receive employment insurance benefits. Those who cannot work because others are on strike will receive benefits, provided they otherwise qualify. A severance package from the employer will also limit eligibility, and no benefits will be paid until the severance period is over. Benefits are also paid under the *Employment Insurance Act* to those who are unable to work because of illness, disability, pregnancy, or adoption. Workers may appeal any decisions made, such as entitlement to benefits, to an administrative body set up under the legislation. The rights of individuals before such administrative tribunals were discussed in Chapter 3.

REDUCING RISK 12.4

Adhering to the employment standards legislation and dealing with government regulatory bodies can impose considerable hardship on employers, straining their management resources. Health, safety, and workers' compensation issues are a fact of life, and enforcement provisions usually put enough pressure on the employer so that there is adherence with the legislative requirements. The same is true with respect to employment insurance and taxation. But human rights standards (including provisions against direct and indirect discrimination and harassment) as well as employment standards (such as minimum wage, hours of work, overtime, holidays, maternity leave, and so on) are usually enforced only when someone makes a complaint. Employees who want to keep their jobs usually do not make such complaints. These complaints therefore usually come after the fact, often after the employee or a group of employees have been working in

those conditions, sometimes for years. Penalties imposed can be significant.

Ideally, a sophisticated client will develop carefully crafted policies and develop training for all, especially those in key decision-making positions, to make sure that the many pitfalls are avoided. When jobs are advertised and potential employees interviewed, great care should be taken to avoid stating qualifications or asking questions that could be construed as discriminatory. Questions relating to a person's place of birth, race, religion, age, language, arrest history, gender, sexual orientation, childcare arrangements, marital status, or medications being taken should be avoided. Care should also be taken to avoid practices that could be considered discriminatory in promotions, benefits, and bonuses. Clear policies, designed to prevent harassment or discrimination by other employees, should be designed and implemented, with the policy and penalties being made clear to all.

OTHER LEGISLATION

Many other statutes affect the employment relationship. Most jurisdictions have legislation controlling the apprenticeship process and trade schools.[99] Pension benefits are controlled by legislation. Some jurisdictions have legislation controlling the licensing of private employment agencies and restricting the types of payments they can receive from their clients. And, as will be discussed in Chapter 15, legislation such as the *Bankruptcy and Insolvency Act* and the *Mechanics'* or *Builders' Lien Acts* provide security to the worker in the payment of wages. All jurisdictions have legislation dealing with special categories of employees, such as teachers and public servants.

COLLECTIVE BARGAINING

LO **4**

A significant portion of the legislation affecting employment relates to the collective bargaining process. But because the percentage of unionized workers in Canada has declined over the past few decades, those laws have changed in response to the diminished political strength of the unions. Trade unions today are fighting to hold on to what they have gained and are resisting the further weakening of their position. Since the time of the Industrial Revolution in the United Kingdom,

---

[99.] See, for example, Alberta's *Apprenticeship and Industry Training Act*, R.S.A. 2000, c. A-42, and the *Ontario College of Trades and Apprenticeship Act, 2009*, S.O. 2009, c. 22.

Collective bargaining process is regulated by legislation

workers have banded together in an attempt to overcome poor working conditions and low wages. A considerable amount of confrontation and violence flared up between unions and employers, especially when unions first attempted to organize or unionize the workforce. In North America, earlier governments and courts treated efforts to organize workers as criminal conspiracies, and the activists were severely punished.

***Wagner Act* was a foundational statue of US labour law**

Over the years, trade unions gained grudging acceptance, if not respectability, and legislation passed in the first half of the twentieth century allowed them to play an increasingly significant role in the economy. The first example of important modern legislation was passed by the US Congress in 1935 and was known as the *National Labor Relations Act,* or the *Wagner Act.*[100]

Legislation is designed to reduce conflict

This Act reduced conflict by recognizing an employee's right to be a member of a union and eliminating the employer's power to interfere in any way with the organizational process. A trade union successful in persuading more than 50 percent of the employees to join was recognized as the official bargaining agent for all the employees in that workforce. The employer was then required to negotiate with the trade union in **in good faith**. The primary objectives of the *Wagner Act* were to promote labour peace and to give some stability and structure to the field of labour relations in the United States.

Legislation

Canada followed example of American legislation

After a considerable amount of labour strife in Canada, the federal government passed the *Wartime Labour Relations Regulations* by an order-in-council.[101] This order incorporated most of the provisions set out in the *Wagner Act,* and after the war most Canadian provinces added the provisions of this federal regulation to their provincial statutes. The Canadian legislation, in addition to controlling **recognition disputes** (disputes arising between unions and employers during the organization process), included provisions that reduced conflict in interest disputes and rights disputes. An **interest dispute** is a disagreement between the union and employer about what terms to include in their collective agreement. A **rights dispute** is a disagreement over the meaning or interpretation of a provision included in a collective agreement that is in force. Another type of dispute that can arise is a **jurisdictional dispute**, which is a dispute between two unions over which one should represent a particular group of employees or over which union members ought to do a particular job. For example, should carpenters or steelworkers put up metal-stud walls in an office building? The employer is usually caught in the middle in jurisdictional disputes and has little power to affect the situation.

Types of disputes—recognition, interest, rights, jurisdiction

Both federal and provincial legislation covers collective bargaining

The federal collective bargaining legislation is embodied in the *Canada Labour Code.*[102] This legislation covers those industries over which the federal government has jurisdiction, such as railroads, shipping, air transportation, broadcasting, and dock work. Each provincial government has passed collective bargaining legislation covering sectors over which it has jurisdiction. These acts are variously called the *Labour Code, Labour Relations Code, Trade Union Act, Labour Relations Act, Industrial Relations Act,* and *Labour Act.* The statutes cover most labour relations situations arising within the jurisdiction of the provinces as set out in section 92 of the *Constitution Act, 1867.* Some types of activities, such as public services, schools, and hospitals, have unique federal or provincial legislation specifically designed to cover labour relations within that industry.[103] Refer to MyBusLawLab for particulars.

Labour tribunals regulate the process

In all jurisdictions, labour relations boards have been established to deal with disputes associated with the collective bargaining process. These boards take the

---

[100] (1935), 49 Stat. 449.

[101] 1944, P.C. 1003. (Because of the emergency of war, the federal government had the power to pass general legislation for Canada.)

[102] *Supra* note 12.

[103] See, for example, Alberta's *Public Service Employee Relations Act*, R.S.A. 2000, c. P-43.

place of courts. It is important to remember that although they quite often look and act like courts, they are not. They are part of the executive branch of government and, as such, they can be used as an instrument of government policy. Labour relations boards have the advantage of expertise in labour matters. Resolution of disputes by such tribunals is usually accomplished more quickly than would be the case in the courts. Administrative tribunals were discussed in more detail in Chapter 3.

Important questions arise with respect to union membership, collective bargaining, and the *Charter of Rights and Freedoms*. Is there a constitutional right to belong to a union, to strike, or even to bargain collectively? Earlier, the Supreme Court of Canada held that there was not. These rights had been created by statute, and the limitations imposed by government were held not to have violated section 2(d) of the *Charter* guaranteeing freedom of association. However, recent case law suggests a different direction by the Court. See the Supreme Court of Canada decision in Case Summary 12.14.

No constitutional right to belong to a union

CASE SUMMARY 12.14

Constitutional Right to Bargain Collectively? *Health Services and Support—Facilities Subsector Bargaining Assn. v. British Columbia*[104]

Several unions and some of their members challenged the constitutional validity of the *Health and Social Services Delivery Improvement Act*,[105] claiming it violated the guarantees of freedom of association (s. 2(d)) and equality (s. 15) set out in the *Charter of Rights and Freedoms*. The Act was passed by the BC government to deal with problems in the provincial health-care system. Costs had increased significantly and it was becoming more difficult for the provincial government to provide health-care services. The legislation was designed to resolve both of these issues.

The Act came into force three days after it received first reading. There was no meaningful consultation with the affected unions. The legal challenge related to the provisions dealing with changes to transfers and multi-worksite assignment rights, contracting out, job security programs, and layoffs and bumping rights. These provisions gave health-care employers greater flexibility in dealing with employees. In some cases, they could do so in ways contrary to existing collective agreements and without consultation or notice. The legislation not only overruled existing agreements, it eliminated the need for meaningful collective bargaining on a number of issues. Section 10 of the Act said that "Part 2 prevails over collective agreements."

On this appeal, the Supreme Court held that section 2(d) protects the capacity of union members "to engage, in association, in collective bargaining on fundamental workplace issues." The Court explained that this protects the right of employees to associate in a process of collective action to achieve workplace goals. If the government substantially interferes with that right, it would be in violation of section 2(d).

The Court based its decision on the historic recognition, in Canada and in international law, of the importance of collective bargaining to freedom of association. Canada has ratified international human rights documents that have recognized a right to collective bargaining. Finally, interpreting section 2(d) as including a right to collective bargaining is consistent with and promotes other *Charter* rights, freedoms, and values, including dignity, personal autonomy, equality, and democracy.

The violation of section 2(d) by the Act was not reasonable and justifiable under section 1 of the *Charter*, ruled the Court. The BC government had passed an important piece of labour legislation very quickly and without any meaningful consultation with the

---

104. 2007 SCC 27 (CanLII).
105. S.B.C. 2002, c. 2.

unions and had not considered achieving its goal by less intrusive measures. Further, the violation of the employees' section 2(d) right of collective bargaining was significant. Accordingly, several sections of the Act were declared unconstitutional (with the declaration suspended for a period of 12 months, giving the government an opportunity to amend the legislation).

SMALL BUSINESS PERSPECTIVE

Does this decision impact private sector employers? One can safely assume that since the Supreme Court has affirmed that collective bargaining is essential to freedom of association, labour tribunals will take note of this illumination of *Charter* values.

Following the decision in the *Health Services and Support* case, the Supreme Court revisited freedom of association in a union context in *Ontario (Attorney General) v. Fraser*.[106] It held that people have the right, protected by section 2(d) of the *Charter*, to make collective representations to their employers; employers then have an obligation to consider the representations in good faith and provide a meaningful bargaining process. Later, when Alberta passed the *Public Service Salary Restraint Act (PSSRA)*,[107] imposing wage rate terms for four years on members of the Alberta Union of Public Employees (AUPE), this legislation was challenged. Citing the above two Supreme Court precedents, the Court ruled that the Alberta government did not meet its obligation to bargain in good faith. Negotiations between the government and AUPE were ongoing at the time the legislation capping salaries was passed. Further, the *PSSRA* ended the potential for future collective bargaining for a long period and nullified an existing mandatory consultation process. The Alberta Court thus issued an injunction staying the operation of the *PSSRA*.[108] These cases illustrate that employers need to engage in good faith bargaining and negotiate terms in a meaningful way.

Labour rights have been gained politically, and in the past political action was relied on to retain them. But there is now a constitutional right to bargain collectively. These recent Supreme Court decisions may ensure the continued existence of unions, whose power and influence have dwindled in recent years.

Canadian labour statutes vary considerably from jurisdiction to jurisdiction. Reference herein will generally be made to the federal legislation that has application across the country. Province-specific information is available in MyBusLawLab.

Organization of Employees

CERTIFICATION

Certification of bargaining unit adopted from the *Wagner Act*

While in some Canadian jurisdictions it is possible for employers to voluntarily recognize a trade union as the **bargaining agent** for their employees, the most common method of union recognition in Canada results from the certification process adopted from the *Wagner Act* of 1935. For a union to obtain certification as the bargaining agent for a group of employees, referred to as the **bargaining unit**, it must apply to the appropriate labour relations board for certification and satisfy the board that a certain percentage of the workforce are members of the union. The particular requirements vary with the jurisdiction.

Majority of workers must be members of the union

Under the *Canada Labour Code*, Division III, an applicant can apply for and receive certification if it can show that 50 percent of the workforce has joined the union. If the union has less than 50 percent support but more than 35 percent, a representation vote will be held; to obtain certification it must receive the support

---

[106.] 2011 SCC 20 (CanLII).

[107.] S.A. 2013, c. P-43.5.

[108.] *Alberta Union of Provincial Employees v. Alberta*, 2014 ABQB 97 (CanLII).

of a majority of those that vote, and over 35 percent of the workforce must have participated in that vote. Note that the granting of certification without a vote is unusual. In most provinces, a vote must be taken no matter how much support is included in the initial application. Even in the case of the *Canada Labour Code*, the Canada Industrial Relations Board has the option to order a vote even when the union has over 50 percent support.

BARGAINING AGENT

Once certified, the trade union has exclusive bargaining authority for the employees it represents. A unionized employee loses the right to negotiate personally with the employer, hence the term **collective bargaining**. The resulting contract between union and employer is binding on all the employees in the designated unit. It is important, therefore, to determine whether the workforce the trade union intends to represent is an appropriate bargaining unit before certification is granted. Labour relations boards discourage bargaining units that are either too small or too large, or that contain groups of employees with conflicting interests. Management employees are, thus, excluded. Also, to obtain certification the trade union cannot be guilty of any discriminatory practices. A union that has applied for certification and has failed must wait a specified period before trying again.[109]

Only the union has the right to bargain for employees

UNFAIR LABOUR PRACTICES

The primary objective of labour legislation is to create an orderly process for the organization and recognition of trade unions, eliminating the conflict that often takes place in such circumstances. Prohibited unfair labour practices include threats or coercion of employees by either the union or management. For example, in the *Convergys* case,[110] the employer implemented a policy prohibiting disclosure of employee contact information to union organizers and threatened dismissal for violating this policy. Surveillance cameras positioned near the entry to the workplace enabled the employer to monitor union organizers' activities. Further, a security guard was posted at the entrance whenever union officials appeared to hand out leaflets. The employer was ordered to stop these unfair labour practices and to schedule paid staff meetings where the union could meet with staff, without employer surveillance.

Rules of conduct reduce conflict

The employer cannot threaten dismissal for joining a trade union or require that an employee refrain from joining a trade union as a condition of employment. Once the organization process has begun in most provinces, the employer cannot change conditions or terms of employment to influence the bargaining process. In some jurisdictions, in the face of such an unfair labour practice, if the labour relations board concludes that a vote would not reflect the true feelings of the employees it can grant certification without a vote. This is rarely done and will take place only when there is clear evidence of intimidation interfering with the reliability of the voting process. What constitutes an unfair labour practice can also vary with the jurisdiction. Refer to MyBusLawLab for jurisdiction-specific details.

Threats, coercion, dismissal—unfair labour practices

In some provinces, unfair labour practices can result in certification without a vote

Requiring that an employer not coerce or intimidate employees does not eliminate the employer's right to state his views during the electioneering process that precedes a certification vote. Freedom of expression as set out in the *Charter of Rights and Freedoms* requires that, as long as such statements are merely statements of opinion or fact and do not amount to threat or coercion, they are permitted. But it is an unfair labour practice for an employer to participate in or interfere with the formation or administration of a labour union. Consequently, employers cannot contribute financially or otherwise provide support to a labour union, undermining

Employer retains right of free speech

---

[109] Each jurisdiction may specify a different waiting period. In Alberta, for example, the period is 90 days. See *Labour Relations Code*, R.S.A. 2000, c. L-1, s. 57.

[110] *Convergys Customer Management Canada Inc. v. B.C. Government and Service Employees' Union*, 2003 CanLII 62911 (BC LRB).

the independence of the union. Note that many of these unfair labour practices are also crimes under the *Criminal Code*. For example, when an employer fires, refuses to hire, or threatens an employee with demotion or dismissal because of her union activities, that is a crime punishable with a significant fine or imprisonment.[111]

Employer organizations help employers bargain with unions

Trade unions, even in the process of organizing the workers, do not have the right to trespass on the employer's property or to organize during the employees' work time. However, employers will sometimes allow this so that they can at least know what is going on. Once the trade union has successfully completed the certification process, it becomes the certified bargaining agent for all the employees in the bargaining unit. The employer must recognize it as such and bargain with it. The trade union can then serve notice on the employer requiring the commencement of collective bargaining. Employers often wish to join together to bargain collectively with a trade union. In some jurisdictions, such **employers' organizations** can also be certified (or designated to be the "employer" authorized to bargain with the union),[112] creating bargaining agents that are stronger and better able to negotiate with large unions on behalf of their members. These employers' organizations are usually found where there are a number of small employers, such as in the construction industry. In a similar fashion, local trade union organizations are often affiliated with much larger parent unions, which strengthens the local bargaining units by providing funds to support a prolonged strike and making available research and other expertise to assist in negotiations.

Unfair labour practices are not limited to the organization process. It remains vitally important to ensure that the union remains independent from employer domination even after certification and to ensure that it can carry on its union activities free from harassment by the employer.

Bargaining

COLLECTIVE AGREEMENTS

Bargaining agent has exclusive authority to bargain on behalf of the employees in the unit

Once a union is certified as the bargaining agent for the bargaining unit, it has exclusive authority to bargain on behalf of the employees in the unit. Employees can no longer negotiate "their own deal" with the employer. In the *Toronto Hydro* case,[113] the arbitrator found that an employer program designed to reward good performance by awarding non-cash gifts violated the collective agreement (compensation above scheduled wage) and breached the requirement that the employer recognize the union as the exclusive bargaining agent. By unilaterally implementing this program, the employer was compensating select employees above the wage scales set in the collective agreement. This interfered with the union's exclusive right to negotiate matters of wages, benefits, and other terms of employment.

Either party can give notice to commence collective bargaining

Any time after a trade union is certified, either party can give notice requiring bargaining to commence, usually within 10 to 20 days depending on the jurisdiction.[114] When the union has been certified for some time and a collective agreement is already in place, this notice cannot be given until shortly before (usually three to four months) the expiration of the old agreement.[115]

Parties must bargain in good faith

Once this notice has been given, the parties are required to bargain or negotiate with each other, and in most jurisdictions the bargaining must be "in good faith." This means the parties must at least meet with a willingness to explore compromises and to try to find an area of agreement; it does not mean that either party has to

---

111. *Criminal Code, supra* note 50, s. 425.
112. *Canada Labour Code, supra* note 12, s. 33.
113. *Re Toronto Hydro and Canadian Union of Public Employees, Local 1*, [2002] O.L.A.A. No. 68; (2002), 103 L.A.C. (4th) 289 (On. L.A.).
114. Twenty days under federal legislation, *Canada Labour Code, supra* note 12, s. 50.
115. Four months under federal legislation, Ibid., s. 49.

agree to the other's terms. Some provinces have adopted the wording used in the federal legislation, requiring the parties to "make every reasonable effort to enter into a collective agreement."[116]

CASE SUMMARY 12.15

Employer Must Bargain in Good Faith: *Royal Oak Mines Inc. v. Canada (Labour Relations Board)*[117]

The employer operated a mine in the Northwest Territories. It put forward an offer to contract with its unionized employees. The offer was rejected. A bitter 18-month strike followed in which a number of replacement workers died. Some employees were dismissed, and the employer, when pressured to at least provide for due process in the dismissals, steadfastly refused. After attempts at mediation, an industrial inquiry commission, and intervention by the minister of labour, there was still no settlement to the strike. The union went to the Canada Labour Relations Board, complaining that the employer had failed to bargain in good faith. The board agreed. It ordered the employer to renew the original offer made before the strike. The employer refused and appealed the board's decision. The Supreme Court of Canada upheld the Board's right to find that the employer had not bargained in good faith and upheld its right to impose the settlement.

SMALL BUSINESS PERSPECTIVE

This decision warns that If an employer breaches its duty to bargain in good faith, a collective agreement containing terms it may not like may well be imposed on that employer. While this may constitute interference in the bargaining process to the disadvantage of the employer, the courts view this as an acceptable remedy following bad faith bargaining.

In *Ontario (Attorney General) v. Fraser*,[118] the Supreme Court of Canada examined the constitutionality of Ontario's *Agricultural Employees Protection Act, 2002* (*AEPA*). At issue was whether the *AEPA* infringed on farm workers' rights under sections 2(d) and 15 of the *Charter* by failing to provide effective protection for the right to organize and bargain collectively and by excluding farm workers from the protections accorded to workers in other sectors. The Supreme Court upheld the constitutionality of the Act, stating that while the *AEPA* does not expressly refer to a requirement that the employer consider employee representations in good faith, by implication it includes such a requirement. The employer must not only consider the submission, it must do so in good faith. Consideration with a closed mind would render listening or reading the submission pointless. Evidently, the Supreme Court is clarifying that employees not only have the right to bargain collectively, but that employers have a duty to seriously consider employee submissions in good faith.

RATIFICATION

Once a bargain has been reached, it is presented to the union membership and, when appropriate, to the employer's board or to an employer's organization for ratification. If both sides ratify, there is a binding collective agreement. The agreement is a contract but, because of the modifying legislation, it must be viewed as a special form of contract with unique features, such as the method of its enforcement. In most jurisdictions, while bargaining is ongoing the employer is not permitted to change the terms and conditions of the employment, such as wages,

Agreement must be ratified

---

116. Ibid., s. 50.
117. [1996] 1 SCR 369, 1996 CanLII 220 (SCC).
118. *Supra* note 105.

benefits, or hours of work.[119] When it is clear that the parties cannot reach an agreement, it is possible in some jurisdictions for the labour relations board to impose a first contract, although this option is seldom used.[120]

MEDIATION (CONCILIATION)

Mediation assists the negotiation process

Mediation, sometimes called conciliation, has been provided for in the various Canadian jurisdictions. The subjects of mediation and arbitration were raised in Chapter 3 as part of the discussion on alternative dispute resolution. When negotiations begin to break down, either party has the right to apply to the appropriate government agency for the appointment of a *conciliator* or **mediator**.[121] This person then meets with the two parties and assists them in their negotiations. The hope is that communications between the two parties will be greatly facilitated by this third-person go-between. The parties are prohibited from taking more drastic forms of action, such as a strike or lockout, as long as a conciliator/mediator is involved in the negotiations.

Some provinces provide for a two-tiered process of conciliation with, first, a single officer and, subsequently, a conciliation board consisting of three mediators, but the function is essentially the same. Federally, the minister of labour must choose among a conciliation officer, a conciliation commissioner, or a conciliation board.[122] It is only after the officer, commissioner, or board has checked out of the dispute and filed a report that the parties are allowed to proceed to strike or lockout. In some jurisdictions conciliation is a prerequisite to a strike or lockout.[123] Although conciliators have no authority to bind the parties, they do have the power to make recommendations that will be embarrassing to an unreasonable party. Note that in many jurisdictions conciliation can be imposed on the parties by the labour relations board, even when neither party has requested it.[124] These provisions vary considerably between jurisdictions; see MyBusLawLab for details.

Arbitrators can also play a role in the bargaining process. Arbitration differs from conciliation in that an arbitrator is authorized to make a decision that is binding on the parties. Under federal legislation, the parties can choose to voluntarily submit any matter respecting renewal, revision, or the entry into a new collective agreement to an arbitrator for a binding decision.[125]

Terms of Collective Agreements

Contract must be for at least one year

The completed collective agreement must satisfy certain requirements, such as having a term of at least one year. If the parties have placed no time limit on the agreement, it will be deemed to be for one year.[126] Federally, when the Industrial Relations Board has imposed a collective agreement on the parties its term will be for two years.[127] Collective agreements may have an automatic renewal clause so that if no notice to bargain is given at the appropriate time, the contract will automatically be renewed, usually for another year. Retroactivity is generally a matter to be negotiated by the parties; if the new collective agreement is to apply retroactively, any changes in terms (such as a new rate of pay) will take effect from the date the old agreement expired. The parties often do not reach an

---

[119.] *Canada Labour Code, supra* note 12, s. 50(b).

[120.] Ibid., s. 80; *Labour Relations Code*, R.S.B.C. 1996, c. 244, s. 55; *Labour Relations Act, 1995*, S.O. 1995, c. 1, s. 43.

[121.] *Canada Labour Code, supra* note 12, s. 71.

[122.] Ibid., s. 72.

[123.] Ibid., s. 89.

[124.] Ibid., s. 72(2).

[125.] Ibid., s. 79.

[126.] Ibid., s. 67.

[127.] Ibid., s. 80(4).

agreement until well after the old collective agreement expires. If the new one then takes effect retroactively, even with this one-year minimum requirement in effect, the new contract will last only a few months. It can be readily seen why every province has taken the approach that any agreement for a period shorter than one year is unworkable.

ARBITRATION

All collective agreements must contain provisions for the settlement of disputes arising under the agreement. This is usually accomplished through a **grievance process** that ultimately leads to arbitration. The contract will set out a process involving a series of structured meetings during which the parties can negotiate a settlement. If a settlement is not reached, the matter is submitted to an arbitrator (or panel of arbitrators), who will hold a hearing and make a decision that is binding on both parties. This grievance process is used to resolve disputes not only over the interpretation of the contract provisions, but also to respond to individual employees' complaints of violations of their rights by the employer.

> **Decision of arbitrator is binding**
>
> **Interpretation of contract disputes to be arbitrated through the grievance process**

While both arbitration and mediation/conciliation involve the intervention of an outside third party, the distinction is that the parties are not required to follow the recommendations of a mediator/conciliator, but the decision of an arbitrator is binding. Arbitration, therefore, is a substitute for court action. Each party is given an opportunity to put forth its position and present its evidence before the arbitrator makes a decision. Arbitrators are not required to follow the stringent rules of evidence that normally surround judicial proceedings, and their decisions can, in some jurisdictions, be appealed to the labour relations board or to the courts. Some provinces, on the other hand, do not permit appeals, so the decision of the arbitrator is final. In all jurisdictions, an arbitrator's decision is subject to judicial review when the arbitrator has exceeded the authority given or when the decision is unreasonable. The collective agreement replaces any individual contract that may have existed previously between the employer and employee, so all disputes between the parties relating to the workplace must be handled by the grievance process. This method of dispute resolution is compulsory. It is not permissible for the parties to indulge in strikes or lockouts or to use the courts to resolve a dispute over the terms of the contract once a collective agreement is in force.

> **No strike when contract is in force**

OTHER TERMS

In addition to the terms specifically relating to conditions of work, rates of pay, vacations, termination, and the like (which are the main objectives of the collective bargaining process), there are various other terms that often appear in collective agreements. The federal government and some provinces have passed legislation requiring collective agreements to cover how technological changes in the industry will be handled.[128] Throughout Canada, the parties can agree to terms that provide for union security. One example is the **union shop** clause, which requires that new employees join the union within a specified period of time. A second arrangement, used particularly in such industries as construction or longshoring, requires that the employee be a member of the union before getting a job. This is a **closed shop** clause. A third option enables employees to retain the right not to join a union, but they must still pay union dues. This arrangement is referred to as the **Rand formula**, or an **agency shop**. Fourth, the collective agreement may contain a **check-off provision**, which means that the parties have agreed that the employer will deduct union dues from the payroll. A fifth option, **maintenance of membership**, requires those who are already union members to pay dues and to maintain their membership, though new employees need not join the union.

> **Agreement must provide for technological change**
>
> **Agency shop, check-off, and maintenance of membership provisions**
>
> **Union shop and closed shop provisions**

---

128. *Canada Labour Code, supra* note 12, ss. 51–55.

Strikes and Lockouts

Job action may involve lockout, strike, or work to rule

Some sort of job action will probably result if the parties cannot agree on what terms to include in the collective agreement. A **lockout** is action taken by the employer to prevent employees from working and earning wages. A **strike** is the withdrawal of services by employees. Although a strike usually consists of refusing to come to work or intentional slowdowns other forms of interference with production may also be classified as strikes. For example, postal employees announced just before Christmas 1983 that they would process Christmas cards with 10-cent stamps on them despite the fact that the appropriate rate was 32 cents per letter. This action was taken to draw attention to the fact that certain commercial users of the postal system got a preferential bulk rate not available to the public. The courts declared that the action was a strike. Since a strike would have been illegal under the circumstances, the union reversed its position. Employees can pressure an employer by strictly adhering to the terms of their agreement or by doing no more than is minimally required. This behaviour is called **work to rule** and will often prompt a lockout. Strikes and lockouts are both **work stoppages**.

CASE SUMMARY 12.16

Is There a Guaranteed Right to Strike? *Ontario Hospital Assn. v. Ontario Public Service Employees Union*[129]; *Saskatchewan Federation of Labour v. Saskatchewan*[130]

Health workers in Ontario had been without a contract for over 300 days when they decided to hold a day of protest. On this day, the employees would not work but would hold rallies and do other things to bring their plight to the public's attention, including picketing at various health-related institutional locations. The employer claimed this was an illegal strike, as health employees in Ontario were prohibited from striking under the *Hospital Labour Disputes Arbitration Act*.[131] The union claimed that this was a political protest rather than a strike, and that its right to strike and to picket was protected under the *Charter of Rights and Freedoms*. The board held that this was indeed an illegal withdrawal of services amounting to a prohibited strike. While the union's political communications were protected under section 2(b) of the *Charter* (freedom of expression), its right to strike was not. The board asserted that there is no guaranteed right to strike under the *Charter*, and that even the right to freely express opinions can be curtailed when associated with an illegal strike.

But a different position was taken by the Supreme Court in the challenge made to Saskatchewan's *Public Service Essential Services Act (PSESA)*.[132] This legislation would allow the work of certain public sector employees to be deemed "essential" and prevented work stoppages of essential employees during a strike or lockout. In this manner the government ensured that essential services, such as patient care in hospitals, would continue if there was a work stoppage involving unionized public sector employees in those hospitals.

Boldly, the Supreme Court declared that circumstances warranted departure from its own earlier precedents that rejected finding a constitutional right to strike. The Court found that the ability to strike was an integral component to meaningful collective bargaining and was constitutionally protected under freedom of association.

[129.] 2003 CanLII 45957 (ON LRB).

[130.] 2015 SCC 4 (CanLII).

[131.] R.S.O. 1990, C. H.14.

[132.] S.S. 2008 c. P-42.2.

The *PSESA* limited the ability of unionized public employees to strike and substantially interfered with collective bargaining; it was an infringement of freedom of association. Further, the infringement was not justifiable, primarily because there was no meaningful dispute resolution mechanism for determining which services were essential. The *PSESA* was thus declared unconstitutional, with the declaration of invalidity suspended for one year until January 30, 2016.

SMALL BUSINESS PERSPECTIVE

Although the Saskatchewan case determined that freedom of association provides a right to strike for unionized employees, this decision does not create a freestanding right to strike in the workplace. Strikes are only available in unionized workplaces, and they continue to be regulated by various provincial and federal statutes.

One may well ask: Should there be a right to strike? Should governments be free to legislate restrictions on this right? The decision outlined in Case Summary 12.16 suggests that if employees are to be effective in bargaining collectively and exercising their freedom of association, they must also have the right to strike.

Since the main objective of modern collective bargaining legislation is to reduce conflict, the right to strike and the right to lock employees out have been regulated. It is unlawful for a strike or lockout to occur while an agreement is in force. Strikes and lockouts can take place only after an agreement has expired and before the next one comes into effect.[133] Any strike or lockout associated with the recognition process or involving jurisdictional disputes between two unions is also illegal and must be dealt with through the certification process described above. Only when the old collective agreement has expired and the dispute is part of an interest dispute involving the negotiation of the terms to be included in a new collective agreement is a strike or lockout legal.

Strike or lockout can occur only between contracts in an interest dispute

If a collective agreement is in place and a dispute arises as to the terms (a rights dispute), it must be resolved through the grievance and arbitration process. Any strike associated with such a dispute is illegal.

Even when a dispute concerns what will go into the new agreement (an interest dispute), there are still some limitations on strike action. The old contract must have expired and the parties must have attempted to bargain in good faith. A vote authorizing strike action must have been taken and a specified period of notice must have been given, for example, 72 hours in Alberta, British Columbia, and under the *Canada Labour Code*.[134] The employer must give the same notice to the employees when a lockout is about to take place. No strike or lockout can take place until a specified period of time has passed after a mediator/conciliator has made a report to the relevant cabinet minister. Even then, in some areas a further cooling-off period may be imposed. In some jurisdictions, the employer is prohibited from hiring replacement workers during a strike. This restriction puts considerably greater pressure on the employer to settle the dispute and goes some way in reducing the violence associated with such labour–management confrontation. The federal government has amended the *Canada Labour Code* to partially prohibit the use of such replacement workers.[135]

Must bargain in good faith first and vote before a strike

Proper strike notice must be given

PICKETING

Once a strike or lockout is underway, one of the most effective techniques available to trade unions is **picketing**. As with striking, the use of picketing is severely limited and controlled. Picketing involves strikers standing near or marching around a

Right to picket is limited by legislation

---

133. *Canada Labour Code, supra* note 12, ss. 88–89.

134. *Labour Relations Code* (Alberta), *supra* note 107, s. 78; *Labour Relations Code* (British Columbia), *supra* note 118, s. 60; *Canada Labour Code*, ibid., s. 87.2.

135. *Supra* note 12, s. 94 (2.1).

place of business trying to dissuade people from doing business there. Picketing is permissible only when a lawful strike or lockout is in progress. Employees who picket before proper notice has been given or somewhere not permitted under the labour legislation are in violation of the law. When the information communicated does not try to discourage people from crossing the picket line or dealing with the employer, the action may not qualify as picketing.

Violence is not permitted

Picketing must be peaceful and merely communicate information. Violence will not be tolerated. Picketers responsible for communicating false information to those who might cross the picket line can be sued for defamation. A tort action for trespass may follow the violation of private property. If violence erupts, the assaulting party may face criminal and civil court actions. When picketing goes beyond the narrow bounds permitted in common law and legislation, the employer can resort to the courts or labour relations boards to get an injunction to limit or prohibit the picketing. Using an excessive number of picketers, as with mass picketing, goes beyond simple information communication and becomes intimidation. The employer can then apply to have the number of picketers restricted.

Strong tradition of union solidarity makes picketing effective

But no legal obligation exists to honour a picket line

Anyone has the legal right to cross a picket line. Customers are free to continue doing business with an employer involved in a strike or lockout, and suppliers are free to continue supplying goods and services to the employer—if they can persuade their employees to cross the picket line. Although picketing may seem to be an ineffectual weapon, there is an extremely strong tradition among union members and many others never to cross a picket line. Others simply wish to avoid the unpleasantness of a confrontation. It eventually becomes very difficult for an employer to continue in business surrounded by a picket line.

Some provinces permit secondary picketing

Which locations can be legally picketed varies with the jurisdiction. Employees in every jurisdiction can picket the plant or factory where they work. In some jurisdictions, such as New Brunswick,[136] **secondary picketing** is allowed, and striking employees are able to picket not just their own workplace but also other locations where the employer carries on business. In any case, unrelated businesses cannot legally be picketed, even if they are located on the same premises as the one struck, as might be the case, for example, in a shopping mall. Since there is some variation with respect to the specific rules relating to picketing, reference should be made to MyBusLawLab to determine what is allowed in the various jurisdictions.

Public Sector and Essential Services

Many people are employed either as part of the public sector or in service industries that are considered essential to society, such as hospitals and police and fire departments. Employees falling into these categories are treated differently than those employed in private industry, and special legislation governs their activities.

CASE SUMMARY 12.17

Freedom to Choose One's Bargaining Agent: *Mounted Police Association of Ontario v. Canada (Attorney General)*[137]

A constitutional challenge was initiated by two private associations of RCMP members. They sought a declaration that the combined effect of the exclusion of RCMP members from the application of the *Public Service Staff Relations Act* (*PSSRA*)[138] and

---

136. *Industrial Relations Act*, R.S.N.B. 1973, c. I-4, s. 104.

137. 2015 SCC 1 (CanLII).

138. R.S.C. 1985, c. P-35.

the imposition of the Staff Relations Representative Program (the SRRP) as a labour relations regime unjustifiably infringed members' freedom of association.

In assessing whether or not the labour relations regime provided to the RCMP employees was sufficient, the Court determined, for the first time, that meaningful collective bargaining requires a process that provides employees with both a degree of choice and independence sufficient to enable them to determine their collective interests and meaningfully pursue them.

The bargaining scheme provided to the RCMP members was not sufficiently independent and did not allow for sufficient employee choice. By imposing a designated body that was to make employee representations, the requirement for employee choice was infringed. Also, the SRRP lacked independence from RCMP management, thus it was not sufficiently independent. As a result, the Court held that the scheme provided to RCMP employees violated section 2(d) of the *Charter*.

DISCUSSION QUESTION

Whereas in the Court's earlier decision in *Canada (Attorney General) v. Fraser*[139] the Court appeared to require "effective impossibility" before a breach of the right to collectively bargain would be found, now the Supreme Court clarified that the test of "substantial interference" is to be implemented. Does this revised test demonstrate an increased willingness to address the balance to be struck between the labour relations interests of employers and employees?

Although labour issues and disputes in the public sector are virtually the same as those in the private sector, governments (and the public) regard the position of public service employees as quite different. Strikes by police officers, firefighters, hospital workers, school teachers, and other public servants are usually considered inappropriate by members of the public.

Public sector employees have limited rights to job action

Every province has special legislation to deal with these groups. Most provinces permit collective bargaining to some extent, but only a few allow public sector employees to participate in strikes and picketing, the others substituting some form of compulsory arbitration of disputes.[140] Of course, in all labour disputes, including private ones, the government retains the right, either by existing statute or by the passage of a specific bill, to impose a settlement or an alternative method of resolving the dispute, such as compulsory arbitration.

REDUCING RISK 12.5

Some employers will feel threatened by the prospect of a union organizing its workforce. Often emotional rather than economic factors come into play, with employers not wanting to give up their right to manage or to surrender any control to trade unions. This is true especially at the organizational stage and is the main reason the employer's role at that level has been minimized. The certification process, supervised by government, has reduced conflict at that stage. Sophisticated clients are well advised to exercise care, especially in a newly unionized situation, to avoid unfair labour practices and other situations that poison the atmosphere because of ill-thought-out tactics and strategies.

Union Organization

Trade unions are democratic organizations in which policy is established by vote. Executives and officers are elected. Members can be expelled or disciplined for misbehaviour, such as crossing picket lines after being instructed not to by the

Unions can expel members for misbehaviour

[139.] *Supra* note 105.

[140.] See, for example, *Canada Labour Code, supra* note 12, s. 80.

Trade unions are overseen by labour relations boards and courts

union executive. Expulsion can be devastating for a worker, since many collective agreements provide for a union shop in which all employees must be members of the union. Some jurisdictions have passed legislation stipulating that a person who loses his union membership for reasons other than failure to pay dues will be able to retain employment.[141] There are some employees whose religious beliefs prevent them from joining or contributing to organizations such as trade unions, which presents a real dilemma in a union shop situation. Some governments have passed legislation exempting such individuals from joining unions; dues are still deducted but are paid to a registered charity. The other terms of the collective agreement still apply.[142]

Trade unions are subject to human rights legislation. In some jurisdictions the labour legislation provides that they can be denied certification or lose their status as a trade union if they discriminate.[143] Unions have an obligation to represent all their members fairly.[144] Employees who feel unfairly treated by the union, or who feel that the union is not properly representing them in disputes with employers, can lodge complaints with the labour relations board. The union may find itself required to compensate the wronged employees.

Trade unions were once considered illegal organizations with no status separate from their membership and therefore no corporate identity. Most provinces have passed legislation giving a recognized trade union the right to sue or be sued on its own behalf, at least for the purposes outlined in the labour legislation.[145]

CASE SUMMARY 12.18

Union Has Duty of Fair Representation: *Dezentje v. Warchow*[146]

The employer usually gave employees extended leaves of absence rather than layoffs. In this case, three employees were laid off by the employer while other employees were given leaves of absence. The three workers went to their union representative for advice about filing a grievance, but the union did not help them very much. Eventually they were told that they had a negligible chance of success. They filed a complaint against the union under a provision that imposed a duty of fair representation on the union.

The Alberta Labour Relations Board found that they had a modest chance of success and that the union had an obligation to represent them and to help them pursue the grievance. In refusing to do so, it had failed its obligation of fair representation. Damages were awarded based on the modest chance of success. This decision was later upheld by the Court of Appeal. There was evidence that the union representatives had not acted with honesty or good faith and that the remedies imposed had been appropriate.

DISCUSSION QUESTIONS

Do you think that giving union members this kind of power puts too many restrictions on the union's ability to effectively manoeuvre in its relations with the employer? Or is it reasonable to expect that if workers have given up their rights to bargain individually their union should be required to represent them fairly?

---

141. *Canada Labour Code, supra* note 12, s. 95(e).

142. Ibid., s. 70(2).

143. Ibid., s. 25(2).

144. Ibid., s. 37.

145. See, for example, Alberta's *Labour Relations Code, supra* note 107, s. 25.

146. 2002 ABCA 249 (CanLII).

SUMMARY

What is employment?

- Must distinguish employees, independent contractors, and agents
- Control and organization tests are used to determine the employment relationship

The law of employment

- Employment law is governed by contract law, common law, and legislation
- Both employers and employees have obligations to fulfill
- Restrictive covenants will be enforced if not too broad and are reasonable
- Employment contracts can be terminated by the giving of reasonable notice, pay in lieu of notice, or just cause
- Just cause includes disobedience, dishonesty, incompetence, and absenteeism
- Reasonable accommodation must be provided to disabled workers
- Damages are awarded for wrongful dismissal (including constructive dismissal)
- Employer is vicariously liable for the acts of the employee during the course of employment
- Employment standards legislation sets minimum standards to protect employees
- Human rights legislation prohibits discrimination and harassment in the workplace
- Many other types of legislation affecting the employment relationship now exist

Collective bargaining

- All Canadian jurisdictions now have collective bargaining legislation
- The legislation governs certification of unions to represent a group of employees
- Unions have exclusive authority to bargain on behalf of employees
- Collective agreements must be ratified by union members
- Mediation and arbitration can be used if negotiations break down
- Legislation requires that certain terms be included in collective agreements, including a grievance process
- Strikes and lockouts cannot take place while a collective agreement is in force
- Picketing can only take place during a strike or lockout
- Public sector and essential service employees may not be allowed to strike or picket
- Unions are democratic organizations with a duty to represent all members fairly

QUESTIONS FOR REVIEW

1. Distinguish among an employee, an independent contractor, and an agent.

2. Explain how a court will determine whether a person is an employee rather than an independent contractor.

3. Summarize the obligations of an employer to its employees, and those of employees to the employer under common law.

4. Explain what is meant by a restrictive covenant. What factors determine whether it is enforceable?

5. What is the proper way to terminate an employment contract that is for an indefinite period of time?

6. How is the appropriate notice period to terminate an employment relationship determined?

7. Under what circumstances can an employee be dismissed without notice? When can an employee leave employment without giving notice?

8. What risk does an employer face who ignores an employee's incompetence over a period of time?

9. What is "constructive dismissal"? Be sure to explain it using a contractual perspective.

10. What factors will a court take into consideration when determining compensation in a wrongful dismissal action? Indicate the various types of remedies that may be available to the plaintiff.

11. Explain what is meant by "vicarious liability." Describe the limitations on its application.

12. Describe how the employment standards legislation protects basic workers' rights.

13. Explain how human rights legislation applies to areas of employment.

14. Explain what is meant by a "duty to accommodate" in the field of human rights and how it can affect employers.

15. Explain the object and purpose of workers' compensation legislation and how those objectives are accomplished. If a worker is injured on the job and is not covered by workers' compensation, what course of action need she take to secure a remedy?

16. What is the significance of the *National Labor Relations Act* (*Wagner Act*) in Canada?

17. Compare and contrast recognition disputes, jurisdiction disputes, interest disputes, and rights disputes.

18. Once a collective agreement is in place, what effect will it have on the individual rights of employees? How will it affect the employer?

19. Explain the difference between mediation/conciliation and arbitration. Describe how these tools are used in Canadian labour disputes.

20. Distinguish among a union shop, a closed shop, and an agency shop.

21. Distinguish between a strike and a lockout. What kind of disputes are strikes and lockouts limited to? How are the other types of disputes between union and employer dealt with?

22. Explain what steps must be taken before a strike or lockout is legal.

23. Explain what is meant by "picketing," when it can take place, and the limitations that have been placed on picketing in different jurisdictions.

24. What is the legal position of a person who wishes to cross a picket line?

25. How is collective bargaining for public sector and essential service employees different from that for people employed in private industry?

CASES AND DISCUSSION QUESTIONS

1. *Lyons v. Multari*, 2000 CanLII 16851 (ON CA); leave to appeal to SCC refused, [2000] S.C.C.A. No. 567

When the plaintiff oral surgeon hired a new associate, Multari, the parties signed a short, handwritten contract containing a non-competition clause. The defendant, Multari, therein agreed not to compete for three years within a five-mile area. After 17 months, he gave the agreed six months' notice and opened his own oral surgery practice in the same city. The plaintiff sought to enforce the restrictive covenant, but the defendant argued that it was not reasonable.

Is it appropriate to enforce a non-competition clause if a non-solicitation clause would adequately protect the employer's interests? What factors will the courts consider when asked to enforce non-competition clauses in employment contracts?

2. *Evans v. Teamsters Local Union No. 31*, 2008 SCC 20 (CanLII)

Evans worked for the union in Whitehorse for 23 years. He was dismissed by a letter faxed to him by the newly elected president. Evans offered to accept 24 months' notice: 12 months of employment, followed by 12 months' salary. Negotiations continued, during which Evans continued to be paid. Four months later the union asked Evans to return to his employment for the balance of the 24-month notice period. Evans refused and the union treated his refusal as just cause. The trial judge awarded Evans 22 months' pay for wrongful dismissal. The Court of Appeal set aside the award, ruling that Evans' refusal to accept the union's offer meant that he failed to mitigate his damages.

The Supreme Court found in favour of the union, holding that a dismissed employee may have to mitigate his damages by returning to work for the same employer. Is this fair to the employee? What factors should a court consider when deciding whether an employee should return to work for the employer who dismissed him?

3. *Brazeau v. International Brotherhood of Electrical Workers*, 2004 BCCA 645 (CanLII)

Brazeau worked as a senior union representative for the union for 25 years. Shortly after his marriage ended, he encouraged a female acquaintance 25 years younger to apply for a job as a union representative and supported her in that application. They went out to dinner, but she thought of him as a mentor. She had no idea that he had sexual interest in her until he sent her cards expressing love for her and bought her gifts. She became uncomfortable and rejected further advances. As a result, Brazeau made negative remarks about her to others, which had a harmful impact on her work. She complained to the union, which had a policy against sexual harassment. When Brazeau refused to retire, he was fired on the basis of the sexual harassment of a co-worker. He brought an action for wrongful dismissal.

Explain the arguments on both sides and the likely outcome. What is the justification for holding the employer responsible when one employee harasses another in situations like these? If he is successful in his wrongful dismissal action, what course of action should the employer have taken instead?

4. *Emerald Foods Ltd. (c.o.b. Bird's Hill Garden Market IGA) v. United Food and Commercial Workers' Union, Local 832*, 2003 MBCA 83 (CanLII)

In Manitoba, the employees of Emerald were in the process of applying for certification when, on the day before the certification vote was to be taken, the president of the company wrote a threatening letter to the employees, hinting that unionization would prevent the implementation of planned wage increases. Only 60 of the 83 employees voted, and they split 30/30 as to supporting certification. The union claimed that the letter intimidated the employees so that the vote actually taken wasn't a true reflection of the employees' feelings. The union made application to the Labour Board.

Indicate the arguments available to both sides, the likely outcome, and what the union could expect if it was successful. Note the restrictions put on an employer in the collective bargaining process and consider whether the statutes in place have allowed unions to become too powerful, placing unfair restrictions on the employers in dealings with such unionized employees.

5. *Goudie v. Ottawa (City)*, 2003 SCC 14 (CanLII)

A number of unionized animal control officers were transferred from the police force to the City of Ottawa. They were to be covered by a new collective agreement. In the process, their work week increased and other provisions of their employment were changed to their disadvantage. They claimed that they were promised prior to their transfer that the terms and conditions of their employment would not change as a result of the transfer. They commenced an action claiming breach of contract and negligent or fraudulent misrepresentation.

Will their claim succeed? Or is this a matter dealing with the collective agreement, demanding that the grievance process be used and the matter arbitrated?

13 Chapter

Intellectual Property

LEARNING OBJECTIVES

1. Identify and distinguish intellectual property from other forms of personal property

2. Review the history of copyright legislation in Canada, including the latest enactment

3. Outline the rights protected by copyright

4. Identify the principal amendments covered by the 2012 legislation

5. Outline the rights protected by patent laws

6. Distinguish between trademarks and industrial designs

7. Describe how the common law protects confidential information and trade secrets

8. Describe how the growth of the Internet and computer technology has impacted intellectual property

INTELLECTUAL PROPERTY

LO ❶

When the products of our mental and artistic efforts were likely to be recorded and distributed on paper, it was relatively easy to determine the source or provenance of that work and to credit its author or creator with any rights or monetary rewards associated with it. With the development of readily available copying equipment and then the advance of digital technology, the creator's rights to intellectual property have become more complicated to enforce and not fully anticipated by legislators who created the law to protect those rights. The Internet and other forms of electronic communication and information manipulation have had a significant impact in the area of copyright, trademarks, and confidential information. A similar problem was created with respect to the physical creations of inventive minds by significant and unexpected technological advances.

Intellectual property must be contrasted to other forms of property. Real property refers to land and things attached to it. Personal property can be tangible or intangible. Tangible personal property consists of movable things in the form of goods or chattels. Intangible personal property refers to rights or claims that one person has that have value and can be enforced in the courts, such as the right to collect a debt. These rights are often referred to as a *chose in action* or a *right to sue*. Real and personal property is the subject of the following chapter. Intellectual property, the subject of this chapter, is a subcategory of intangible personal property referring to ideas, information, and creative works. When a chattel is stolen or destroyed, it is no longer available for use by the original owner. When an idea is taken and used by somebody else or confidential information is wrongfully communicated to another, the idea or information does not change. It is still available to the original holder, although its value might be considerably diminished.

Businesspeople need to protect their intellectual property

As is the case with tangible personal and real property, the rights attached to intangible property are also defined and protected by law. Intellectual property law attempts to balance the protection of the product of a person's mental effort on the one side and the free flow of new and innovative ideas, which stimulate the advancement of the commercial environment, on the other. The attention is on both defending the rights of individuals in relation to their ideas, information, and other creative works, and regulating how others use those products of the mind. These different interests often collide, especially now in the digital information age. In recent years important advances have taken place with respect to the law of intellectual property, especially in the area of copyright. A businessperson must not only appreciate the value of their intellectual property assets and ensure that they are adequately protected, but must also appreciate the legal risks involved when intellectual property legislation is infringed.

Most legislation protecting intellectual property is federal, with copyright and patent legislation being exclusively granted to the federal government in the *Constitution Act, 1867*. The *Copyright Act*, first enacted in 1928 and amended several times since then, is still in place. The most recent amendment to this statute, the *Copyright Modernization Act*[1] that came into force in November 2012, was enacted to bring Canadian copyright law in line with international treaties and to address the issues raised by technological advances in the online storage of and access to copyrightable resources. Canadian copyright law specifically protects computer software and also protects original works published on the Internet. Prior to the 2012 amendments the *Copyright Act* did not adequately address the issues arising from technological change, and it was up to the courts to resolve disputes. The 2012 amendments incorporate several recent Supreme Court of Canada decisions as well as other changes into the *Copyright Act*, thus addressing important contemporary issues.

Ease of digital copying and distribution make intellectual property vulnerable to interference

Other important federal statutes include the *Patent Act*, the *Trade-marks Act*, the *Integrated Circuit Topography Act* (protecting the three-dimensional shapes of integrated circuits),[2] and the *Industrial Design Act* (protecting the unique shape and design of manufactured products).[3] A patent gives rights to the inventor to profit from an invention. Trademark law applies to physical symbols, such as brand names and company logos as well domain names and website logos. Some infractions and abuses in the use of intellectual property have been deemed serious enough to merit response under the *Criminal Code*. Confidential information and trade secrets are protected by common law principles. Passing-off actions provide remedies when parties misrepresent their products or services as those of another, and this protection often overlaps with trademark legislation. These areas will also be discussed in this chapter.

Each of these areas of the law is constantly being challenged as advancements are being made in digital technology. The easy access to information facilitated by the online environment and the enhanced methods for copying not only information but software, music, performances, and inventions makes rights holders vulnerable to those who want to use the products of others for their own personal gain. Personal information is often stored in online databases, and companies holding that information are often asked to share it, thus further denigrating the privacy rights inherent in personal data. Protecting those rights is often up to the holder, who should be aware of the strategies and laws that work in his favour and the tactics of those who want to use that information for their own purposes.

[1.] S.C. 2012, c. 20.

[2.] R.S.C. 1985, c. P-4; R.S.C. 1985, c. T-13; S.C. 1990 c. 37.

[3.] R.S.C., 1985, c.1-9.

COPYRIGHT

LO ❷❸❹

The work is protected, not the idea

Copyright protection is extended to authors and artists for 50 years after their death, and in Canada this protection applies without any formal registration of the copyright. In effect, the owner of the **copyright** controls the reproduction of the work during that period, after which the work becomes part of the **public domain** and is no longer subject to anyone's control. The idea is to give the creator of the intellectual property the exclusive right to profit from and otherwise control her creation for a specified period of time. This period is reduced to just 50 years when a corporation is involved, the author is not known, or the work involves such things as movies, photographs, performances, or sound recordings (with respect to performance if a sound recording is made of it, the period is 50 years from the making or publication of that recording, extending the protection to a maximum of 99 years). Note that there are important exceptions that will be discussed below. The *Copyright Act*[4] gives the owner of the copyright a monopoly over the use of the created work, prohibiting copying or reproduction of the work without permission. Only the actual work itself is protected, not the ideas or thought behind it. Thus, the actual expression of an idea in a book is protected, but someone else is free to express those same ideas in a different way.

Matters Covered

Only original work that is the product of an artist's or author's own mental effort or skill is entitled to copyright protection. Note that it is the *expression* that has to be original, not the idea. In the past only works that were somehow preserved, be it in writing or in some other manner, were subject to copyright. Now, a performer's performance is subject to copyright, whether fixed or not.

The *Copyright Act* gives copyright protection to original works, performer's performances, sound recordings, and communication signals. The categories of copyrightable materials are summarized in Table 13.1.

Table 13.1   Works Protected by the *Copyright Act*

Literary works	"Literary compilations" such as poems, stories, and articles; pamphlets and books; and computer software and hardware
Dramatic works	Movies, videos, television, and theatre productions and performances, including choreography and scenery that are fixed in some permanent form such as writing
Musical works	Musical compositions with or without words
Artistic works	Paintings, drawings, charts, maps, plans, photographs, engravings, sculptures, works of artistic craftsmanship, and architecture

In addition to these works, copyright protection has also been extended to

Performances	Performances by actors, musicians, dancers, and singers
Sound recordings	CDs, tapes, computer memory, and other methods for reproducing sound
Communication signals	Radio, television, cable, and Internet broadcasts

Note that there is considerable overlap, and someone's creative work might qualify for copyright protection in more than one of these categories.

Computer programs are protected

The problem of whether computer programs are protected by copyright or patent law was partially solved by the 1988 amendment to the *Copyright Act* that now specifically provides copyright protection for computer software and hardware.

[4.] R.S.C. 1985, c. C-42.

A particular problem with computer programs is the difficulty in distinguishing between what constitutes the idea behind the software and its expression. Note that, as is the case with other matters covered by copyright, when computer programs are involved it is the expression of the idea not the idea itself that is copyrightable. It is now settled that where one product has the same look and feel in its operation as the other, an infringement of copyright has taken place, even where the actual computer code is completely different. A specific statute, the *Integrated Circuit Topography Act,* has been enacted to protect the design of the integrated circuit expressed in the computer chip itself.[7] The actual three-dimensional design has to be registered, and the protection granted is for a period of 10 years.

CASE SUMMARY 13.1

When Is Copying Considered Fair Dealing? *Society of Composers, Authors and Music Publishers of Canada v. Bell Canada*[5]; *Alberta (Education) v. Canadian Copyright Licensing Agency (Access Copyright)*[6]

Several important cases were handed down by the Supreme Court of Canada in 2012 dealing with fair dealing (see the expanded discussion of this principle later in this chapter). The *SOCAN v. Bell* case dealt with the practice of music suppliers such as Bell and iTunes allowing potential purchasers to preview music selections before actual purchase and digital download. These free previews allowed the listener to listen to the selected file for a period of between 30–90 seconds before deciding to buy. SOCAN applied to the Copyright Board for the right to collect royalties for these previews in addition to royalties paid on the purchased music. The Copyright Board refused, saying that while SOCAN was entitled to royalties for the actual downloads they were not with respect to the previews. The previews were determined to be an example of "fair dealing" and not subject to copyright protection under section 29 of the *Copyright Act.*

The matter went to the Supreme Court of Canada, which upheld the Copyright Board's decision. They held that to find that the previews were covered by the "fair dealing" exception required two steps. First was to determine whether the previews were used for the purpose of "research" or "private study" as set out in section 29 of the Act. (Note that this section has since been amended and now lists research, private study, education, parody, and satire as fair dealing exceptions.) The Court determined that the previews were used for the purpose of research and so satisfied the first step. SOCAN had argued that research should only apply where the object of the research involved some creative purpose, but the Copyright Board and the Supreme Court disagreed. Since the object of the process was the "dissemination" of the work and the preview facilitated that process, it did qualify as research under the Act, thus adopting a broader definition of research than that proposed by SOCAN. The second step was to determine whether the use was "fair." After looking at several factors, the Court decided that since the purpose of the preview was to facilitate the eventual purchase, and since it was short and immediately deleted, it went no further than necessary to fulfill this purpose; therefore it qualified as fair dealing under the Act and was not subject to the collection of royalties.

In the *Alberta v. Access Copyright* case, the minister of education argued that copies of materials compiled by teachers to be used by students in secondary and elementary schools also qualified as fair dealing and should not be subject to royalties. The Copyright Board disagreed. Alberta appealed the decision, and the Federal Court of Appeal upheld the Copyright Board's decision. Alberta then appealed the matter to the Supreme Court of Canada, which overturned the decision of the Federal Court of Appeal and the Copyright Board, holding that the use of these materials in the school

---

5. [2012] 2 SCR 326, 2012 SCC 36 (CanLII).
6. [2012] 2 SCR 345, 2012 SCC 37 (CanLII).

system did fall under the fair dealing exception in section 29 of the *Copyright Act*. Applying the two-step process discussed above, the Supreme Court found that the use of the materials was for the purpose of "research or private study" as required by the Act. They also found that this was an example of "fair dealing" since only parts of text-books and other material were copied, and it would be unfair to require students to purchase the whole textbook to access the portion determined important for study pur-poses. (Note that the amendment to section 29 of the *Copyright Act* also now includes "educational" purposes within the fair dealing exception.)

DISCUSSION QUESTION

Considering the impact on the authors and publishers, has a proper balance been struck between their interests and those of the consumers and students? What would be a better approach?

File Sharing

Copyright law provides the owner of electronic material with the legal right not only to prevent unauthorized copying but also to rent it and otherwise control its use. While the misuse of software causes difficulty, a much greater problem is the unauthorized copying of music, movies, games, and articles found online. The ease of reproducing information has led to massive illegal copying and to dramatic legal steps being taken to stop the process. The ease of downloading free music may have been a boon to music lovers, but it came at a great expense to the producers and musicians. The Napster trial and other high-profile cases have shown that the courts will not tolerate such abuse. The problem, however, continues, with vast amounts of music, movies, and games still being improperly copied. As soon as a more comprehensive regulation or decision is imposed, the copiers try to find ways to get around it, find loopholes, or simply move their operation to a jurisdiction where such regulations or laws can't be enforced.

Copying music is a massive problem that has resulted in serious litigation. In a landmark decision, the Copyright Board of Canada held that peer-to-peer download-ing of music is lawful in Canada under certain circumstances, and it also held that the blank media levy (on recordable CDs, DVDs, tapes, and so on.) should not apply to MP3 players (such as the Apple iPod).[8] Blank media levies are collected by the Canadian Private Copying Collective and distributed to various rights holders (such as the Society of Composers, Authors and Music Publishers of Canada [SOCAN]) to benefit recording artists and musicians. While today downloading a song for private use may not infringe the law, downloading for the purpose of sale, rental, distribu-tion, communication by telecommunication, or performance in public is prohibited.

Copying of music, movies, and games remains a huge problem

CASE SUMMARY 13.2

When Should a Service Provider Have to Provide Information Regarding Its Customers? *Voltage Pictures LLC v. John Doe*[9]

Through investigative research, Voltage Pictures, the producer of several movies, includ-ing the *Hurt Locker* and *Dallas Buyers Club*, managed to obtain the IP addresses of over 2000 subscribers to an Internet service provider, TekSavvy Solutions Inc., which had allegedly improperly downloaded copies of their movies through a peer-to-peer (P2P)

---

7. *Supra* note 2.

8. *Canadian Wireless Telecommunications Assn. v. Society of Composers, Authors and Music Publishers of Canada*, 2008 FCA 6 (CanLII), [2008] 3 FCR 539, 290 DLR (4th) 753.

9. 2014 FC 161 (CanLII).

sharing system using a file-sharing program called BitTorrent. Having the IP addresses didn't help Voltage since they needed the actual names and addresses of these TekSavvy customers to take action against them. Teksavvy, which was not a party to the action, refused to disclose the required information, and this application was brought to force that disclosure.

Since there was no specific defendant to oppose this application, the Court granted intervener status to the Canadian Internet Policy and Public Interest Clinic, which opposed in principle Voltage's application. It took the position that to disclose the requested information would infringe the privacy rights of those parties, and they further argued that Voltage was involved in copyright trolling. This is the practice of companies finding the names of anyone who might remotely be accused of infringement and sending dubious demand letters and launching questionable actions simply to force those individuals to settle to avoid costs, even though they may have a legitimate right to copy the material. This is essentially a business model that uses the courts to earn a profit rather than to advance the purposes of justice.

The order requesting an innocent third party, which is not party to the action, to disclose this sort of information is called a Norwich order, and the judge in this case referred to *BMG Canada Inc. v. Doe*,[10] where the Federal Court of Appeal stated that to succeed the party applying for a Norwich order must show the following:

a. A plaintiff must have a bona fide case

b. A non-party, in this case TekSavvy, must have information on an issue in the proceeding

c. An order of the Court is the only reasonable means of obtaining the information

d. That fairness requires the information be provided prior to trial

e. Any order made will not cause undue delay, inconvenience, or expense to the third party or others

The Court found that Voltage did have a bona fide case, that TekSavvy did have the required information, and that there was no other reasonable method to obtain it other than requiring its disclosure from TekSavvy. The Court also determined that the requirement of fairness was satisfied and that there was no untoward delay or inconvenience caused to TekSavvy. The Court reluctantly issued the Norwich order requiring TekSavvy to disclose the names and addresses of its subscribers. The judges' reluctance was because of the potential abuse by Voltage of the information obtained, and because of this several restrictions were placed on the implementation of the order and any subsequent litigation that followed. The Court would supervise the process, including granting reasonable costs to TekSavvy, vetting any demand letters sent to the subscribers, and otherwise making sure no abuse of the justice system took place.

SMALL BUSINESS PERSPECTIVE

This case is instructive because it illustrates the process of balancing the rights of privacy against the rights of the copyright holder. It also deals with the danger of abuses, such as the copyright or patent troll, and establishes guidelines to ensure that abuse is avoided. Businesspeople should be careful to keep this balance in mind and be aware that even third parties may be subject to such orders.

Creation

As mentioned, in Canada the creation of the work generates copyright protection automatically. There is no need to register or even publish the work. Still, registration may be wise, since it establishes when the copyright was created and the presumption that the person named in the registration is the owner of the

---

10. 2005 FCA 193 (CanLII).

copyright. Registration is now possible online with the Canadian Intellectual Property Office[11] (or by application sent by fax or mail). Although not specified in the Canadian legislation, there is a practice (following the provisions of the Universal Copyright Convention) of notification of copyright that generally takes the following form:

Copyright © 2012 Pearson Canada Inc., Toronto, Ontario

The United States and other countries that are parties to the copyright conventions discussed below recognize valid Canadian copyright, even without registration. However, notification as set out above may still be required. Where the copyright is not registered, the remedies available for infringement may be significantly restricted, so registration, while not required in Canada, is advised. The 2012 amendments to the *Copyright Act* brought the Canadian law into compliance with the World Intellectual Property Organization (WIPO) Copyright Treaty and the WIPO Performances and Phonograms Treaty. For a person to obtain copyright protection in Canada, he must be a citizen or resident of Canada or a citizen, subject, or resident of one of the countries that adhere to the Berne Copyright Convention. Persons whose country is a member of the World Trade Organization can also secure copyright protection through its Agreement on Trade-Related Aspects of Intellectual Property Rights. These international agreements set out common rules of conduct in matters concerning copyright. Note, however, that there are still major concerns over several jurisdictions that continue to resist enforcing intellectual property rights.

> **Copyright is automatic with the creation of a work, but registration ensures availability of remedies**

> **International agreements establish common rules**

Ownership

Copyright belongs to the person who created the work or to the employer where the work was created as part of employment, unless there is an agreement otherwise. Once copyright has been created, its owner can assign or license it, all or in part, to someone else. Courts will presume the creator holds the copyright unless there is evidence to show otherwise. The owner of the copyright can assign it to someone else, but even then the author will continue to have moral rights in the work. These **moral rights** allow the artist, author, or performer to demand that her name continue to be associated with the work as its author, and that the new owner not distort, mutilate, or otherwise change the work in such a way as to degrade it and bring harm to the reputation of the author. For anyone involved in the production of copyrightable material with others, whether employee, partner, or contractor, it is vital to set out in the contract creating the relationship who is entitled to the copyright of the work created.

> **Copyright can be assigned, but moral rights are retained after assignment**

CASE SUMMARY 13.3

Injunctions Protect Moral Rights: *Pollock v. CFCN Productions Limited*[12]; *Snow v. The Eaton Centre Ltd.*[13]; *Patsalas v. National Ballet of Canada*[14]

The *Copyright Act* gives the author the right to restrain any distortion, mutilation, or other modification of his work that would be prejudicial to his honour or reputation.[15] In the *Pollock* case, the plaintiff, a playwright and recipient of the Governor General's

---

11. To register online, go to www.cipo.ic.gc.ca. The fee for online application filing was $250 as of April 2012.
12. 1983 CanLII 1061 (AB QB), 26 Alta LR (2d) 93.
13. [1982] O.J. No. 3645 (H.C.J.).
14. [1986] O.J. No. 1135 (H.C.J.).
15. *Supra* note 4, s. 28.2.

Award, sought an interim injunction restraining CFCN Productions Limited from televising a movie made specifically for television based on Pollock's play *Blood Relations*. This play deals with the gruesome story of Lizzie Borden and the axe murder case of her father and stepmother in the United States. Pollock claimed that the screenplay, written by J. Barclay and filmed by CFCN, seriously distorted, violated, and mutilated Pollock's play to the extent that her reputation would be damaged if the film were televised. The injunction was granted.

In the *Snow* case, the plaintiff sculptor claimed that his naturalistic composition composed of 60 geese in flight near the entrance of a Toronto mall had been made to look ridiculous by the addition of Christmas ribbons tied around their necks. He suggested, "it is not unlike dangling earrings from the Venus de Milo." The Court agreed that the work had been distorted and modified in a prejudicial manner and ordered removal of the decorations. These cases illustrate that one must ensure that an author's moral rights are respected if one hopes to adapt or alter his or her work.

But an injunction will not necessarily be available if the author grants a licence to others to perform her work and later claims irreparable harm if someone else is allowed to choreograph it. In the *Patsalas* case, the Court concluded that if the ballet proceeded to rehearse, stage, and produce *Concerto* as proposed, the plaintiff would not suffer irreparable harm to his reputation. Thus an injunction stopping future performances was denied.

DISCUSSION QUESTION

When dealing with artistic works, how will the courts determine if a modification or performance causes the author of the work irreparable harm? (Note: See section 28.2 [2] of the *Copyright Act*.)

In addition, the work may not be used in association with a product, service, cause, or institution that is prejudicial to the reputation of the author and without the author's permission. For example, Sarah McLachlan demanded that her song "I Will Remember You" be removed from a video that was put together for police-training purposes but which was later made available to the public. McLachlan claimed copyright infringement and asserted that permission would never have been granted because of the "exploitative nature" of the video. The film features aerial images of the Columbine High School in Littleton, Colorado, where two teenagers killed 13 other people and themselves. The song is played while images of the blood-splattered school library are depicted.[16]

Moral rights of authors and artists have been incorporated into the *Copyright Act*. While the Act prohibits the assignment of moral rights, the author of the work can waive them. Provided the author has not waived these moral rights, the author can seek compensation or obtain an injunction even though someone else owns the copyright. Moral rights exist for the same length of time as copyright and can be passed to the author's heirs, even when those heirs do not inherit ownership of the copyright itself.

Copyright holder has complete control over rights for the author's life plus 50 years

Copyright gives the owner control over the work. No one else can perform, copy, publish, broadcast, translate, or otherwise reproduce the work without the permission of the owner of the copyright. As explained above, this protection extends for the life of the author plus 50 years, with some exceptions. At the expiration of this time, the work becomes part of the public domain and anyone can use it. Note that in the United States the protection period is now for life plus 70 years, which will provide added protection for Canadian works being used in the United States. Refer to MyBusLawLab for further details regarding copyright.

[16.] Herald News Services, "McLachlan Song on Columbine Tape: Singer Demands Removal," *Calgary Herald*, April 28, 2000, p. A7.

2012 Amendments to the *Copyright Act*

Prior to the passage of the 2012 *Copyright Act* amendments,[17] several significant Supreme Court of Canada decisions as well as much debate among interested parties took place. These rulings were among the changes incorporated into the Act by the 2012 amendments, but there are several matters that remain the subject of serious debate.[18]

Digital locks, which attempt to secure online content from unauthorized access and use, were not protected prior to the 2012 amendments. Now it is against the law to circumvent access control locks. Software and content distribution companies can now protect what they create and sell. Even where the material is downloaded for personal use, research, or study purposes (which are fair dealing exceptions), the user will be in violation of this provision if he circumvents the locks to gain access. Users must first buy such works before they use them. The new law penalizes commercial infringers by imposing a $20 000 fine per infringement and puts a $5000 cap on fines for an individual who circumvents a lock or shares a prohibited file. A rights holder who notices unauthorized downloading can send a notice to the Internet service provider, who then must forward a notice to its subscriber indicating that they are performing an illegal act. After that notice is served, the Internet service provider is required to provide the offending user's identity and other information to the copyright holder so that further action can be taken.

> **It is illegal to circumvent digital locks**

> **ISPs are required to provide notice to and information about infringers**

> **Fines are reduced for non-commercial infringers**

The new law is seen as frustrating the right to copy for personal use, so some exceptions are provided to the general rule. Non-commercial users are permitted to use copyrighted content in remixed musical performances, mashup videos (where some copyrighted material is incorporated into a new video), or home movies set to commercial music. This is sometimes referred to as the "YouTube exception." The user must identify the source of the original, and the result must not substantially affect the commercial value of the underlying work. The Act also clears the way for many formerly illegal activities that have become commonplace, such as time shifting or recording television shows for later viewing, copying for private purposes, transferring content to portable devices, and creating backup copies, provided they don't override the digital lock if one is present.

> **YouTube exception**

FAIR DEALING

The 2012 amendments also broaden the **fair dealing** exception, expanding the right to use copyrighted work under certain conditions. The Supreme Court of Canada established a standard for fair dealing in *CCH Canadian Ltd. v. Law Society of Upper Canada*.[19] In that case, a law society library offered a service to lawyers: photocopying reports of court cases to assist them in their research. The publishers of those reports challenged the practice as a breach of copyright, and the matter went to the Supreme Court of Canada. The Court held that, because the publisher added headnotes and other annotated material, this additional material was protected by copyright even though the actual judicial report was not. Still, the Court found that no copyright was infringed, as this was an example of fair dealing exempted under the Act. The Court's decision has been incorporated into the Act.

> **Fair dealing rules have been expanded**

The 2012 amendments also added education, satire, and parody to the allowable fair dealing circumstances set out in the *Copyright Act* (research, private study, news reporting, criticism, and review). There is no infringement of copyright if the copyrighted work is used for any of these purposes, provided the use also meets the

---

[17] *Copyright Modernization Act, supra* note 1.

[18] *Entertainment Software Association v. Society of Composers, Authors and Music Publishers of Canada,* 2012 SCC 34; *Rogers Communications Inc. v. Society of Composers, Authors and Music Publishers of Canada,* 2012 SCC 35; *Society of Composers, Authors and Music Publishers of Canada v. Bell Canada, supra* note 5; *Alberta (Education) v. Canadian Copyright Licensing Agency, supra* note 6, *Re: Sound v. Motion Picture Theatre Associations of Canada,* 2012 SCC 38.

[19] 2004 SCC 13.

"fairness factors" established by the Court that take into account the purpose, nature, amount, the alternatives, and the effect of the dealing in the work. Thus, the amended Act expands the fair dealing defences, allowing more freely the use of copyrighted materials for educational purposes, parody, and satire without paying royalties.

For education the amended Act sets out a more structured approach to fair dealing, specifying a number of situations in which such fair dealing is allowed. Educational institutions may now reproduce, display, and distribute protected works in any form of media. For example, teachers may copy materials onto blackboards or flipcharts or incorporate materials into exam questions without infringing copyright. But if overhead projection slides have been made available by the publisher, those commercially produced alternatives are to be used. Educators can also record and keep, for a limited period of time, radio, newspaper, and television material. Generally, the exceptions require that students receiving such materials destroy them within a certain period after the course is finished.[20]

Copyright Infringement

As explained earlier, infringing copyright includes situations where a person tries to obtain a benefit from the sale, reproduction, distribution, performance, broadcast, or other commercial use of the work. Plagiarism (copying another's work and claiming it as your own) is also a violation of copyright. The moral rights of an author are infringed when someone else asserts authorship[21] or if the work is mutilated or modified in such a way that the reputation of the author is harmed. Regardless of who owns the copyright, where moral rights have been infringed the author can seek an injunction or compensation.[22]

CASE SUMMARY 13.4

Students Are Entitled to Copyright Protection: *Boudreau v. Lin*[23]

Paul Boudreau was a part-time MBA student who was working for a high-tech firm. He wrote a paper for a course based on information gathered at his place of employment and incorporated suggestions from his professor. The professor and a colleague published the paper under a different title with only a few revisions, naming themselves as authors. Boudreau discovered his paper published in a casebook and brought forward an action for copyright infringement against the professor and the university.

The Court found that the student was the author and holder of the copyright. The Court rejected the professor's claim that the student's name had been omitted in error. The university was deemed to have knowledge of the infringement, and thus shared liability with its employee. The removal of the student's name and changed title blocked the professor's claim of fair dealing. The inclusion of the paper in a casebook defeated the university's claim that it was for use in private study. Also, the author's moral rights were infringed because they had interfered with the integrity of the work. The Court noted, "Plagiarism is a form of academic dishonesty which strikes at the heart of our educational system. It is not to be tolerated from the students, and the university has made this quite clear. It follows that it most certainly should not be tolerated from the professors, who should be sterling examples of intellectual rigour and honesty."

---

20. *Copyright Modernization Act, supra* note 1.

21. See *Dolmage v. Erskine,* 2003 CanLII 8350 (ON SC), 23 CPR (4th) 495, in which a contract lecturer prepared a case during a school of business case preparation workshop. His moral rights were violated when the case was improperly attributed to others. Damages of $3000 were awarded.

22. *Copyright Act, supra* note 4, ss. 28.1, 34(2).

23. 1997 CanLII 12369 (ON SC), 150 DLR (4th) 324.

DISCUSSION QUESTION

In the academic environment it is not always clear who can claim copyright. This is especially true where university facilities and grants are involved. But in this case there was no doubt that others had taken credit for the student's work. So what steps should an author take who wishes to include, within her own work, the written work of another?

From a business perspective the *Boudreau* case raises a troubling issue, namely that of vicarious liability. If an employee infringes the copyright of a third party, will the employer be held vicariously liable? According to Justice Metivier

Vicarious liability for copyright infringement

the University cannot stand idly by while its professors blatantly breach copyright laws. At the very least, the University is a passive participant. As employer of the professor—it is the duty of the University to set policies for the conduct of its employees and to accept responsibility for monitoring, or failing to monitor, the strict observation of these policies and, in this case, of copyright laws.[24]

Case law both here and in the United States indicates that vicarious liability for infringement of copyright will be imposed.[25] In the case brought by MGM against Grokster Ltd., Justice Souter observed that a person "infringes vicariously by profiting from direct infringement while declining to exercise a right to stop or limit it."[26]

 REDUCING RISK 13.1

Should sophisticated employers implement a copyright policy? Will the existence of a policy relieve an employer from liability if its employees infringe copyright while at work?

In light of the fact that vicarious liability is a form of strict liability, even due diligence by the employer will not shield it from liability. So what is the point of implementing a copyright policy? Even if your policy does not exempt you from your employees' copyright liability, it will help educate those in your enterprise about copyright. In doing so, the policy may lower the occurrences when copyright-protected material is used without permission, and where it is used provides a basis for disciplinary action where appropriate.

Other Exceptions

There are a variety of exceptions and specific rules. Laws enacted by the federal government and decisions and reasons for decisions of federal courts and tribunals can be copied without permission and without a fee. Here the only condition is that due diligence be exercised in ensuring that the copy is accurate and is not represented as being an official version. Be careful here; remember that summaries, annotations, and references contained in compilations of these reports that are added by the publisher will be subject to copyright.

Legislation and case law can be copied without a fee

Exception for fair dealing

Another Supreme Court ruling, discussed in Case Summary 13.1 above, involved photocopying excerpts from textbooks for use in classroom teaching. The Copyright Board found that this was not "fair dealing" under the Act, and the Federal Court of Appeal supported that decision. But this was overturned in the Supreme Court of Canada, and copying for educational purposes has been incorporated into the Act as a separate exception to copyright infringement with specific provisions setting out what is permissible and what is not.

Quotations from the work that are not extensive and are attributed to the author do not amount to an infringement of copyright. Even where fair dealing applies in

Exception for educators

24. Ibid., at para. 52.

25. *Flag Works Inc. v. Sign Craft Digital (1978) Inc.*, 2007 ABQB 434 (CanLII), 427 AR 206.

26. *Metro-Goldwyn-Mayer Studios Inc. v. Grokster, Ltd.*, (2005) 125 S.Ct. 2764, at 2776 (citing *Shapiro, Bernstein & Co. v. H.L. Green Co.*, 316 F.2d 304, 307 (C.A.2 1963)).

the case of criticism, review, or news reporting, the user is required to give the source and the name of the author, performer, sound recorder, or broadcaster. (Recall that in the *Boudreau* case the removal of the student's name was fatal to the professor's claim of fair dealing.)

Further exceptions

Other categories of users to whom exceptions are granted are (1) libraries, archives, and museums; (2) persons with perceptual disabilities; and (3) people making private copies of commercially recorded music or sound recordings. People who have reading or hearing disabilities can make copies to help themselves access the material, for example, by converting the work to Braille. And, interestingly, anyone can make a recording of music tapes, records, and CDs for his own private use. Royalties are charged on blank tapes and other recording media to compensate artists and producers for this exception, but the individuals can't override any digital locks to do so.

Remedies

Interlocutory injunctions may be granted before trial

The remedies normally available in a civil action, including an injunction, are available when a copyright is violated. Sometimes, an **interlocutory injunction** is given before the actual trial to prevent further damage. This is an interim measure, and a permanent injunction may or may not be granted at trial. Often, the effect of the interim remedy is so devastating to the offender that no further action is needed. To obtain an interlocutory injunction, the plaintiff must establish a *prima facie* case: (1) that there has been an infringement of copyright; (2) that if the injunction is not granted, irreparable harm will be suffered that could not properly be compensated for by an award of damages at the trial; and (3) that the **balance of convenience** is also in the plaintiff's favour. This refers to which side will suffer the greatest damage if the injunction is granted. Where the plaintiff seeks an order to stop a much larger operation from producing and selling a work in which they claim a copyright, it will normally not be granted if the order would cause that larger business more damage than the plaintiff would suffer if the injunction were not granted.

Anton Piller order provides for seizure of goods

Sometimes a court will make an order, even before trial, that the offending material be seized. This is called an **Anton Piller order**. Typically, the application is made without notice to the offending party, because the evidence must be seized by surprise before the goods or relevant documentation can be hidden or destroyed. The court will only issue such an order where there is clear and compelling evidence of the infringement of copyright, the danger of significant damage to the plaintiff, and some indication that surprise is needed to protect the evidence. The seizure of the offending works before trial is provided for in the *Copyright Act*.[27]

Permanent injunction may be granted at trial

Delivery up order is often sought

One of the most important remedies is the **permanent injunction** prohibiting the production, sale, or distribution of any of the infringing products. If the defendants were unaware they were violating copyright, the only remedy under the *Copyright Act* is an injunction. This restriction does not apply, however, if at the date of infringement the copyright was duly registered under the Act. Thus, while registering is not required for copyright protection in Canada, there are significant advantages in doing so. Often sought together with an injunction is a **delivery up** order, directing the defendant to deliver all copies of the infringing items in her possession or control to the copyright owner.

Damages can compensate for loss

Accounting requires handing over profits

Punitive damages may be available to punish the wrongdoer

Where the infringement took place knowingly, damages or an accounting may be obtained. An award of *damages* is calculated to compensate the victim for the losses suffered, including the lost profits that would have been earned had the copyright not been infringed. An *accounting* is often given where it would be difficult to determine what actual damages have been suffered. This remedy requires that any profits made from the sale or rental of the offending product be paid over to the victim, even if this amount exceeds the damages suffered by the plaintiff. The court may also award *punitive damages* in cases of flagrant violation to punish the offender rather than simply to compensate the victim of the infringement. In any case, it must

---

27. *Supra* note 4, s. 38.

be noted that the limitation period in which an action should be commenced is three years. But if the plaintiff did not or could not have reasonably known of the infringement, that limitation period may be extended to three years from the date the plaintiff discovered or ought reasonably to have discovered the infringement rather than the date of infringement.[28]

The 2012 amendments to the *Copyright Act* provide a new tool to deal with online infringements. Rights holders can sue any service provider whose primary purpose is to enable online infringers and service providers, including websites, web hosts, or peer-to-peer file-sharing networks.

Damages flowing from copyright infringement can be significant. Consider the case commenced by Viacom and Paramount Pictures against YouTube and Google,[29] where the plaintiffs were seeking damages in excess of US$1billion. The plaintiffs alleged that YouTube had harnessed technology to infringe the copyright of writers, composers, and performers on a vast scale without payment or permission. The plaintiffs identified more than 150 000 unauthorized clips of their copyrighted programming on YouTube that had been viewed an astounding 1.5 billion times. Note that at trial the Court determined copyright had not been infringed, but the case does indicate the potential exposure faced by copyright infringers in this digital age.

The *Copyright Act* also provides a copyright owner with three additional remedies. The first, **statutory damages**, enables a court to award damages that it "considers just" in the circumstances, with a general limit of between $500 and $20 000. This remedy was introduced to alleviate difficulties encountered in proving the exact losses suffered by the plaintiff or the net gain reaped by the wrongdoer. The newly amended Act dramatically reduces the damages that can be awarded against a non-commercial infringer of copyrighted material, limiting them to a range of $100 to $5000.

Statutory damages are now available

The second addition is a wide or **enhanced injunction**. It allows the court to order a wrongdoer to refrain from future infringements of copyright in other works owned by the plaintiff copyright owner. It even applies to works later acquired by that plaintiff. This remedy saves the plaintiff the time and expense of future litigation and can be obtained if the plaintiff shows it is likely the wrongdoer will engage in such future infringements. Finally, **summary procedures** are more expedient and less expensive than full court trials, since the court can make a decision based on affidavit evidence.

Enhanced injunctions prevent repeat infringements

In addition to these civil remedies, the *Copyright Act* provides for penalties of up to $1 million in fines and five years in jail for the most serious cases. The provisions set out in the *Criminal Code,* such as those sections prohibiting theft and fraud, may also apply to infringement of copyright cases.[30]

Fine and imprisonment are available for infringement

Criminal Code *may apply*

CASE SUMMARY 13.5

Statutory Damages Available for Copyright Infringements: *Trout Point Lodge Ltd. v. Handshoe*[31]

Charles Leary and Vaughn Perret own Trout Point Lodge in Nova Scotia and were the victims of a vicious and unjustifiable attack by Mississippi resident, Douglas Handshoe, in his blog, Slabbed.org. In that blog, Handshoe relentlessly and consistently accused Leary and Perret of various crimes and improper conduct. In 2012 Leary and Perret launched a successful civil action alleging defamation and other torts, but when they sought to enforce the judgment the State Court determined that the Handshoe attacks were protected by the Fifth Amendment of the US Constitution.

---

28. Ibid., s. 41(1)(b).
29. *Viacom International Inc. v. YouTube, Inc.,* Dist. Court, SD New York 2010.
30. *Criminal Code,* R.S.C. 1985, c. C-46.
31. 2014 NSSC 62 (CanLII).

In this unopposed action, further claims of defamation were advanced. In addition, Leary and Perret have included a claim of copyright infringement and a demand for statutory damages. Handshoe included four pictures of Leary and Perret and Trout Point Lodge in his blog accompanying his vitriolic and defamatory statements. The photos were taken by various photographers, but Leary and Perret have acquired the copyright through assignment and sought statutory damages in this action for the Handshoe infringement.

Of interest for us is the application by the Court of section 38.1(1) of the *Copyright Act*, which allows the parties to claim statutory damages rather than try to establish the actual damages that have been suffered. In addition to other damages for defamation, the judge awarded statutory damages for copyright infringement. The judge took into consideration the fact that Handshoe had ignored a Nova Scotia court order to stop the defamatory activity and found that Handshoe "snubbed his nose" at all judicial officers and institutions of Nova Scotia." Further, Handshoe's conduct toward the applicants over the years amounted to "outrageous and highly reprehensible" conduct. The Court also determined that the blog, Slabbed.org, where the photos and defamation took place was a commercial activity that used the attack on Leary and Perret to further Handshoe's own commercial purposes. Section 38.1(5) of the *Copyright Act* states that in awarding statutory damages the court must consider all relevant factors, including:

a. the good faith or bad faith of the defendant

b. the conduct of the parties before and during the proceedings

c. the need to deter other infringements of the copyright in question

After considering these factors the damages awarded were $20 000 for each picture (if it had been non-commercial usage, the total maximum would have been only $5000).

The Act further states that the award of statutory damages will not affect the court's ability to award punitive damages. Accordingly, the Court awarded a further $100 000 in punitive damages and a total of $180 000 for copyright infringement. It is doubtful that the additional $245 000 damages awarded for defamation can be enforced in Mississippi, given the lack of success in enforcing the 2012 award. But it may well be a different result with respect to damages for infringing copyright.

SMALL BUSINESS PERSPECTIVE

The case is instructive in that it is the first case where we have a judge quantifying and awarding statutory damages under the newly amended *Copyright Act*. Given the difficulty in establishing actual loss in such cases, it is likely that there will be many more such cases. Businesspeople should remain diligent to avoid this kind of risk.

The Copyright Board

Copyright Board handles disputes and levies fees

SOCAN and Access Copyright collect fees and royalties

A Copyright Board with broad powers to handle disputes between individuals and to otherwise supervise and regulate the industry was established under the *Copyright Act*. It arbitrates tariffs if there is a disagreement between a licensing body and another party, it sets levies on blank audio recording devices (CDs, DVDs, and so on), and it reviews and approves fees for public performance or telecommunication of sound recordings. *Tariffs* are set fees that users must pay for using certain copyrighted material. Criticisms about how the board functions in light of the new legislation may lead to some modification of how the board applies its regulations. Cable companies pay tariffs for permission to transmit programs. Royalties are sums paid as commission for sales of a work or permission to use it. Royalties are paid to musicians when radio stations play their songs. Several collective societies have been created to represent the owners of copyright in licensing arrangements with others and to assist in the collection of tariffs and royalties. A collective may also commence a civil action on behalf of a member seeking compensation for copyright infringement. SOCAN performs this service in the music industry. Access

Copyright (Canadian Copyright Licensing Agency, formerly CANCOPY) serves a similar function in the literary field. Refer to MyBusLawLab for further information concerning the Copyright Board and copyright collective societies.

PATENTS

A **patent** is a government-granted monopoly that gives only the inventor the right to produce, sell, or otherwise profit from a specific invention. Unlike copyright, patent protection extends to the *physical embodiment* of the idea or concept. To qualify the invention must be new, in the sense that no one else has been given a patent for it and that it has not been disclosed to the public in Canada or elsewhere more than a year prior to application. This includes disclosure in an academic paper. The invention must also be the original work of the inventor. Thus, a person could not take an invention found in another country and patent it in Canada as his own. The invention must also be unique and distinguishable from other products. It must be a development or improvement that would not have been obvious to others working with the technology involved. It must have some utility or perform some useful function. It must also be possible to construct and use it on the basis of the information supplied to the patent office. This is the problem that caused the Pfizer patent discussed in Case Summary 13.6 to be invalidated.

A new concern for those wanting to protect their patents is 3-D printing machines that allow individuals working on relatively inexpensive equipment to copy physical products or components. The ease of such 3-D printing now poses a similar problem to patent holders as photocopying did to copyright. How do such actions infringe on the rights of the patent holder, and what permission should be required before such copying is allowed? On the other hand, will it be possible to get a patent on objects created by 3-D printing? Is the patent infringed if the printed product is used only for personal, non-commercial use? It is likely that these technological advances will require some major changes to the *Patent Act* in the near future to catch up.

LO

Must be an original invention to be patentable

CASE SUMMARY 13.6

A Patent Must Disclose All Relevant Information:
Teva Canada Ltd. v. Pfizer Canada Inc.[32]

Pfizer received a patent in 1997 for the successful and profitable drug used to overcome erectile dysfunction known as Viagra. This application was originally brought by Teva to the minister of health to obtain a Notice of Compliance (NOC) allowing them to manufacture a generic version of Viagra. Pfizer brought an application before the Federal Court for an order prohibiting the issuance of the NOC. Teva claimed that the original Pfizer patent was invalid because of obviousness, lack of utility, and insufficient disclosure. With respect to the Pfizer disclosure in the original patent application, they listed several ingredients in the formula for Viagra but failed to disclose that the only effective and active ingredient was sildenafil. It was determined that this was known to the company at the time of the patent application, but they chose to withhold the information.

Because of this failure to properly disclose, the Supreme Court of Canada held that the Pfizer patent for Viagra was invalid and overturned the decision of the Federal Court and Federal Court of Appeal. In the process of reaching that decision, Justice Abella stated that the basic function of the *Patent Act* was to strike a balance between disclosure and protection. In exchange for the disclosure of information, the patent gave the inventor an exclusive monopoly to profit from it for a period of time. Here the inventor

---

32. [2012] 3 SCR 625, 2012 SCC 60 (CanLII).

failed to live up to their side of the bargain. They failed to disclose that the active ingredient was sildenafil, and this was fatal to the patent. That failure to disclose invalidated the patent, and Teva was free to manufacture a generic version of the drug.

SMALL BUSINESS PERSPECTIVE

This case is instructive in that it underlines the basic purpose of the *Patent Act*: to disclose the nature of an invention to the extent that it would be possible for someone else relying on the information to manufacture that product. The idea is that the more information that is out there, the better it will be for the economy with other inventors stimulated to make advances encouraged by the disclosed information. Here they intentionally hid the essential ingredients of the invention, defeating the very purpose of the Act, and suffered the consequences. Small businesses are even more likely to make this kind of error as they try to protect their intellectual property.

Theories, concepts, or obvious improvements are not patentable

You cannot patent a scientific principle or abstract theory, such as Newton's discovery of gravity;[33] nor can you patent obvious improvements to other products, inventions designed for illegal purposes, things that cannot work, and things generally covered by copyright law. But a non-obvious improvement on an already existing invention is patentable. It is clear that variations on lower forms of life such as plants and bacteria are patentable, but higher forms of life are not patentable in Canada (see Case Summary 13.7).

CASE SUMMARY 13.7

Mice? Untested Drugs? What Is Patentable?
Harvard College v. Canada (Commissioner of Patents)[34]; *Apotex v. Wellcome Foundation*[35]

Does a genetically altered mouse fall within the *Patent Act* definition of an "invention"? Scientists injected an oncogene into the embryo of a mouse, thereby creating a mouse that was susceptible to cancer. Harvard College sought patent protection, fearing others might buy an oncomouse and breed it, undermining its market among cancer researchers. The Federal Court of Appeal surprised many when it declared that higher life forms were patentable. For a patent to be available, the legislation requires that the subject matter be a non-naturally occurring composition of matter arising from the application of inventiveness or ingenuity. Arguably, an oncomouse is not merely the product of the laws of nature. The Supreme Court of Canada held otherwise. The Court stated that the patentability of higher life forms should be left to Parliament. So unless the *Patent Act* is amended, higher life forms cannot be patented in Canada.

In June 2006, the patent office published an office practice notice regarding the patentability of fertilized eggs, stems cells, organs, and tissues. Animals at any stage of development, from fertilized eggs on, are higher life forms and are thus not patentable subject matter under section 2 of the *Patent Act*.

Totipotent stem cells, which have the same potential as fertilized eggs to develop into an entire animal, are considered to be equivalents of fertilized eggs and are thus higher life forms and are not patentable subject matter. Embryonic, multipotent, and pluripotent stem cells, which do not have the potential to develop into an entire animal,

---

33. *Patent Act, supra* note 2, s. 27(8).
34. 2000 CanLII 16058 (FCA), [2000] 4 FC 528, 189 DLR (4th) 385; overturned on appeal, 2002 SCC 76 (CanLII), [2002] 4 SCR 45, 219 DLR (4th) 577.
35. 2002 SCC 77 (CanLII), [2002] 4 SCR 153, 219 DLR (4th) 660.

are patentable subject matter. Organs and tissues are not compositions of matter for the purposes of the definition of invention under section 2 of the *Patent Act* and are therefore not patentable subject matter.[36]

What about drugs, the effectiveness of which has not yet been tested? In *Apotex v. Wellcome Foundation,* the Supreme Court articulated the doctrine of "sound prediction," which allows a patentee to claim subject matter not made or tested in certain circumstances. Notably, there must be a factual basis for the prediction and a sound line of reasoning from which the desired result can be inferred from the factual basis. Proper disclosure is likewise required.

The main issue in this case was whether there was really an "invention." The drug AZT was a compound initially developed in 1964 to combat cancer. In 1985, scientists presented a sound prediction (educated guess?) in the patent application that AZT would be useful in treating AIDS. The Court held that as long as the "guess" is subsequently demonstrated to work, it will be deemed to have been an invention at the time the patent application was made.

DISCUSSION QUESTION

Can you think of other inventions or products where the application for a patent might be challenged?

In Canada, as a general rule, computer programs cannot be patented and are now covered by copyright legislation, but such patents have been granted in the United States and may be available in limited situations in Canada in the future. In the United States, it is possible to patent business methods (BMPs), which creates a patent monopoly on a particular process or model of carrying on business. Canadian firms doing business in the United States or even selling products there could be sued for patent infringement for their activities in Canada where the method used infringes the US patent. US patents have been issued for business methods including distribution models, inventory management, service delivery models, training methods, financial models, and models for sharing information. In the past, the Commissioner of Patents in Canada has refused to grant a patent on a business method, but the Federal Court of Appeal has reversed this position in *Canada (Attorney General) v.* Amazon.com *Inc.*[37] That case did not go to the Supreme Court of Canada, so until that Court says otherwise business methods should also be patentable in Canada.

What can and cannot be patented

Creation

Unlike copyright, the patent must be registered before conferring rights on the inventor, so it is vital that a patent be applied for right away. If someone else beats you to it, you will not only lose the right to patent but also be prevented from producing or otherwise using or profiting from the invention. Employers are entitled to patent the inventions of their employees unless they have agreed otherwise, and the holder of a patent can assign that patent to others. Joint patents can be obtained when several people have worked on the same invention. This is another area where it is vital to set out in the contract who has the right to a patent.

The process of obtaining a patent is complex. First, the patent records must be searched to see if a patent already exists, and then an application with supporting documentation and the prescribed fee must be submitted to the appropriate patent office. These documents include a petition, specifications, claims statements, an abstract, and drawings that set out not only what the invention is supposed to do but also enough information so that someone looking at them could build and use

Patent must be applied for and registered

---

36. Canadian Intellectual Property Office, "Office Practice Regarding Fertilized Eggs, Stem Cells, Organs and Tissues," June 20, 2006, www.cipo.ic.gc.ca/eic/site/cipointernet-internetopic.nsf/eng/wr00295.html.
37. 2011 FCA 328 (CanLII).

the item. The patent office then assigns an examiner, who may require further submissions from the applicant, and when all conditions have been met the patent will be granted. If there are opposing applications, the patent will be granted to the person who first made an application. This process is usually handled by a registered patent agent with both legal and engineering training and may take two or three years to complete.

Date of application in your own country determines priority

Pursuant to international agreements, once a Canadian patent has been granted, application can be made for patents in other jurisdictions, but priority in those countries will be based on when the application was first made in Canada. The reverse is also true, and the Canadian patent office will grant a patent to a foreign applicant who applies in her own country before the Canadian applicant applies here. There is a limited period of time after obtaining the Canadian patent to make an application for a foreign patent, so this should be done without delay. Recent multilateral agreements have come into effect accelerating the registration in other jurisdictions once the process has been completed in the original country of application. (For further information, refer to MyBusLawLab, where numerous external links on this topic can be accessed.)

Patent grants monopoly for 20 years but requires disclosure

Once the patent has been issued, the patent number should be put on the manufactured item to which it applies. The use of "patent pending" has no legal effect, but the phrase is put on goods to warn that a patent has been applied for. A patent gives its holder a monopoly for a maximum period of 20 years from the date of application, but it requires that the inventor publicly disclose how to make the item in documents that are open to public inspection. Secrecy is surrendered in exchange for the 20-year protection, the idea being that others will be stimulated to produce new inventions because of the disclosure of that information. The granting of the patent gives the patent holder exclusive rights to manufacture, sell, and profit from the invention for those 20 years. A patent will even protect someone who merely develops a variation of the product, providing that variation satisfies the three basic criteria for patentability: (1) it must be new and original; (2) it must be useful, functional, and operational; and (3) it must be inventive, displaying ingenuity on the inventor's part and not simply an obvious improvement.

Because a patent protects the idea rather than its expression, another person would not be able to produce a simple variation of the product without breaching the patent. An infringement of patent may take place if an unauthorized person were to manufacture, import, sell, or otherwise deal with or use the invention. The patent holder is entitled to the same remedies that would be available in any civil action, including injunction, damages, and accounting, as discussed under the heading "Copyright."

CASE SUMMARY 13.8

How Far Should Patent Protection Go? *Monsanto Canada Inc. v. Schmeiser*[38]

Using genetic engineering, Monsanto developed a specific strain of canola seed that was resistant to Roundup, a herbicide also produced by Monsanto. Farmers planting "Roundup Ready Canola" would also use Roundup, which would kill all other plant forms but leave the modified canola plants unscathed. Monsanto licensed farmers to use its Roundup Ready Canola for a fee of $15 per acre, and licensees agreed to purchase new seeds every year and not plant seeds from last year's crop.

[38.] (CanLII), [2003] 2 FC 165, 2002 FCA 309 (CanLII), 218 DLR (4th) 31; appeal allowed in part, 2004 SCC 34 (CanLII), [2004] 1 SCR 902, 239 DLR (4th) 271.

Schmeiser did not purchase Roundup Ready Canola but noticed that some of his crop was resistant to Roundup. He collected seeds from that section and planted them the next year, giving his entire crop this resistance to Roundup. Through tests on the canola crop grown on Schmeiser's farm, Monsanto determined that his plants contained the genetically engineered genes it had developed and sued him for patent infringement. Even though Schmeiser used seeds from plants growing on his field, the Federal Court of Appeal held that he was infringing on the Monsanto patent and ordered an injunction and damages. It didn't matter how the Roundup Ready Canola had originally gotten on his property or even whether he actually used the herbicide Roundup to take advantage of it.

Schmeiser appealed to the Supreme Court of Canada, but was only partially successful. While the Supreme Court confirmed that the farmer, by collecting, saving, and planting the seeds, infringed the *Patent Act*, it also found that the trial judge erred by awarding an amount for improper profits (as Schmeiser did not make any greater profit as a result of planting Roundup Ready rather than ordinary canola). In essence, the Court confirmed that one can patent genetically altered plant forms. It also warned plaintiffs that if an accounting for improper profits is sought as the remedy, an award will only be made if improper profits are actually made.

Note that a similar case happened in Australia where one farmer growing canola organically (Farmer A) was located beside a farmer (Farmer B) who used genetically modified canola resistant to Roundup. Because of heavy wind during harvest some of the genetically modified seeds escaped and contaminated the field of Farmer A. Because of this contamination that farmer lost his certification for an organically grown crop. He sued, claiming among other things negligence and nuisance. The Supreme Court of Australia found against him, determining that there was no negligence on the part of Farmer B and that because there was no evidence that the genetically modified seeds were in any way harmful there was no damage. If any damage did take place it was purely economic and was not actionable. They observed that the standards imposed by the certification authority were too stringent, and if anyone was negligent it was that organization.[39]

Note that the *Monsanto* decision significantly expands the concept of patent infringement. Whereas in the *Harvard College* case regarding the oncomouse (Case Summary 13.7) the Supreme Court held that higher life forms were not patentable, in *Monsanto* the Court held that the unlicensed cultivation of plants containing a patented gene infringed the patent. Thus, so long as the gene or cell is patented, use of the organism in which the gene or cell is contained can constitute violation of the patent, arguably accomplishing indirectly what couldn't be done directly.

Patent of a gene can prohibit the use of a higher life form containing the gene

Often, the holder of the patent does not have the resources to manufacture or otherwise exploit the invention and will license its manufacture to another company. Where an important invention is involved, there is provision for compulsory licences to be granted by the Commissioner of Patents with the payment of royalties, even over the objections of the inventor.

A 1987 amendment to the *Patent Act* gave drug manufacturers more control over the production and sale of their products. This was aimed at preventing competitors from capitalizing on the research and development of those manufacturers and producing much cheaper "generic drugs." A Patented Medicine Prices Review Board was also established with broad powers, including the power to reduce the sales price of patented medicines. Pharmaceuticals obtained increased patent protection, with exclusive control extended to 20 years.[40] However, in 2005, Bill C-9 (known as the Jean Chrétien Pledge to Africa [JCPA]) came into force. It facilitates

39. *Marsh v. Baxter* [2014] WASC 187 Supreme Court of Western Australia.
40. *Patent Act Amendments*, R.S.C. 1985 (3d Supp.), c. 33.

access to pharmaceuticals in the developing world, to address public health problems, especially those resulting from HIV/AIDS, tuberculosis, malaria, and other epidemics.[41] In September 2007, Apotex Inc., a generic drug manufacturer, was granted authorization under Canada's Access to Medicines Regime to manufacture a pharmaceutical product used in the treatment of HIV/AIDS for export to Rwanda.[42] See links on MyBusLawLab for further details.

The *Patent Act* is a very old statute and is hard pressed to adequately deal with modern advancements in technology. Former Supreme Court of Canada Justice Binnie described the process of dealing with new science in the old Act as putting "new wine in very old bottles."[43]

REDUCING RISK 13.2

Sophisticated clients should take great care to protect their intellectual property. Whether a process or product is developed by an independent contractor, a consultant, or an employee, a provision in the contract creating that relationship should designate who is entitled to the patent, copyright, or other form of intellectual property developed. Otherwise, when the relationship ends it is quite possible to find that process being given to and used by a competitor. Equally important is the need to ensure that one is not infringing the copyright or patent held by another. Research In Motion (RIM) agreed to pay US$612.5 million to settle its BlackBerry patent dispute with NTP.[44] The US Court of Appeal for the Federal Circuit had earlier declared that RIM infringed upon US patents owned by NTP even though RIM located its equipment and performed its activities in Canada. The case leads Canadian businesses to ask: To what degree are Canadian companies exposed to liability if ecommerce or business method patents issued in the United States are infringed? Could one be infringing a foreign patent if serving a foreign customer over the Internet?[45]

LO ❻ # TRADEMARKS

A **trademark** is any term, symbol, design, or combination of these that identifies a business service or product and distinguishes it from a competitor. A trademark identifies the source or manufacturer of the goods rather than the product itself. Registered trademarks are protected by the federal *Trade-marks Act*.[46] Examples of protected trademarks are such words as "Kodak" and "Xerox"; symbols such as the arm and hammer used on that company's baking soda box; combinations of words and symbols such as the Apple logo on computers; and even the distinctive design of a product's container such as the Coca-Cola bottle. The Apple logo, the Nike swoosh, and the McDonald's arches are memorable examples of symbols that quickly and positively identify brands. Trademarks also include the special marks used by some organizations, such as the Canadian Standards Association, to indicate quality or certification.

Symbols or designs of business are protected as trademarks

A major area of confrontation involves the use of trademarks on the Internet. Brand names and company logos are important company assets and have become even more important as they continually flash across a computer screen. Keeping them in the conscious or subconscious mind of the web browser is a key marketing tool. These assets are protected by trademark, and unauthorized use of a name or mark is prohibited. The posting of material on a website invites viewing, so merely

Viewing a website is not a violation, but downloading information from it may be

---

[41]. *An Act to Amend the Patent Act*, S.C. 2005, c. 18.

[42]. For information on Canada's Access to Medicines Regime, see www.camr-rcam.gc.ca/index-eng.php.

[43]. From remarks given in the sixth Fox Moot's introductory lecture as reported in the *Lawyers Weekly*, March 7, 2014, p. 1: "Law is lagging genetic research, warns former SCC Judge Binnie." This is another area where we can expect significant revision in the future.

[44]. See Rob Kelley, "BlackBerry Maker, NTP Ink $612 Million Settlement," *CNN Money*, March 3, 2006, http://money.cnn.com/2006/03/03/technology/rimm_ntp.

[45]. James Longwell, "Court Applies American Patent Law to Canadian Business," *Lawyers Weekly* 24, no. 37 (February 11, 2005).

[46]. *Supra* note 2.

accessing such sites does not violate the trademark. Communication by itself is not an infringement, but when the viewer downloads the visual or sound sequence and prints it, creates a link, or otherwise *uses* it to enhance her own website without permission an actionable infringement has taken place. While people thought the freewheeling nature of the web allowed them to use information in any way they wanted, it is now clear that the traditional rules of trademark and copyright law apply. As always, the problem is with enforcement.

The ease with which people can transfer material from one website to another—or link to other websites, even bypassing that website's home page—is also a cause for concern. Information on the linked site may be connected, in the viewer's mind, to the host site.

A business may be worth more than the total of its *tangible* assets. Its reputation, ongoing relations with customers, and product identification, collectively known as its **goodwill**, also have value. The name and trademarks associated with the business largely embody that goodwill. The object of trademarks is to protect the value of the goodwill and prevent other parties from misleading the public by using the trademarked words or symbols for their own purposes. Ultimately, businesses seek to prevent the trademark's value from being diminished through association with other, usually inferior, products.

Purpose is to protect consumers from deception

For a trademark to be protected under the Act it must be registered. As part of the registration process it is published in the *Trade-marks Journal,* and if any parties believe that it does not qualify they can oppose the registration. Once registered, the trademark gives its owner an exclusive right to use it throughout Canada for 15 years (renewable). The registration also establishes a presumption of ownership so that in an action for infringement, a defendant claiming otherwise must produce strong evidence to that effect. (Using a trademark for a certain length of time can establish your ownership through common law, but use of an unregistered trademark can lead to lengthy litigation.)

Registration protects trademark

Recent changes included in the government omnibus Bill C-31 (Economic Action Plan 2014) will, when the accompanying legislative changes come into force, impact the trademark law in three ways. First, it brings the Canadian trademark law in line with international treaties, which means that Canadian applicants will have to meet more stringent classification requirements and they will have to renew the registration every 10 years. Second, and most significantly, the registrant will no longer need to state that the mark has been used in Canada or that there is an intention to use it in Canada. While this simplifies the registration process, it means that anyone can register a mark even when it has been used or is being used by someone else. The only recourse would be for the original or legitimate user to take steps to oppose the registration, incurring costs in the process. Third, the Bill will also remove the hyphen so that the *Trade-marks Act* becomes the *Trademarks Act.*

Proposed legislation will reduce protection period to 10 years

A trademark can be any word, design, symbol, or packaging that distinctively identifies a business or product. It cannot be obscene or scandalous, but the prohibition of registering sounds as trademarks has recently been changed.[47] Colour, at least at the present time, also cannot be registered, although a colour may be part of the trademark. Nor can it be anything that resembles the insignia, crests, or other symbols of royalty; the government or government agencies (such as the RCMP); service organizations (such as the Red Cross); or even names, portraits, or signatures of individuals (without their consent). There is also a prohibition against using any marks, symbols, or designs that resemble a well-known one, which would cause confusion with the products or services of that other body.

Trademarks must be distinctive

So what about "knock-offs"? Who is to stop a person from imitating another's product? Evidently, it is up to the party aggrieved by the imitator to take legal action.

Injunctions are available against imitators

[47.] The Canadian Intellectual Property office has reversed its opposition and is now inviting registration of sound trademarks. (See the practice notice issued by the registrar on March 28, 2012, at www.ic.gc.ca/eic/site/cipointernet-internetopic.nsf/eng/wr03439.html.)

See, for example, *Hermès Canada Inc. v. Henry High Class Kelly Retail Store*.[48] Hermès was in the process of applying for a trademark for its bags when it discovered a store selling imitation Hermès-style purses. Hermès was successful in obtaining an injunction in this passing-off situation.

CASE SUMMARY 13.9

What's in a Name? *Louis Vuitton Malletier S.A. v. Singga Enterprises (Canada) Inc.*[49]

On several occasions in 2008 and 2009, representatives of the plaintiffs and investigators hired by them attended the Singga warehouse in British Columbia and another in Alberta and found a number of counterfeit handbags and other products bearing the Louis Vuitton trademarks and other trademarks that were confusingly similar. Several infringing products were purchased, and more were subsequently ordered and received. There was also a website where similar infringing products were offered for sale and were ordered and received. These products were either look-alike products bearing the Louis Vuitton trademark or one similar, or were actual counterfeits with patterns infringing the Louis Vuitton copyright.

Orders were also placed and received from the Altec warehouse in Toronto for even greater numbers of similarly infringing products. The same process was followed dealing with Burberry products, with similar proof of substantial infringement established. The defendants in this action are the corporations involved and the principals of those corporations. Follow-up investigations determined that these parties were continuing to sell infringing products in 2010. Note that the defendant, Go, operated a retail store that was also involved in selling products infringing both the Louis Vuitton and Burberry trademarks.

After a summary trial, the Court was satisfied that the plaintiffs had established there had been an infringement of the Louis Vuitton trademark and copyright as well as the Burberry trademark. This infringement took place through the importation, manufacture, advertisement, and sale of the offending products. The Court determined that the public had been misled by this offending conduct and that several sections of the *Trade-marks* and *Copyright Acts* had been infringed and the reputation of the plaintiffs seriously damaged.

The Court ordered first that any inventory of the offending goods be delivered up to be destroyed and issued an injunction requiring that the infringing conduct must end. In addition, the Court ordered damages against the defendants totalling $1 872 000, plus punitive damages for a further $500 000, as well as prejudgment interest and costs.

SMALL BUSINESS PERSPECTIVE

This case is a good example of how much trouble an unsophisticated small businessperson can get into by ignoring trademark and copyright restrictions. Here, all parties knew they were doing wrong and continued to ignore the law and paid the consequences. Where there is any doubt, a wise businessperson can check the trademarks database. The Canadian Trade-marks Database can be accessed online at www.cipo.ic.gc.ca/app/opic-cipo/trdmrks/srch/bscSrch.do?lang=eng.

Surnames may not qualify as trademarks

Normally, simple surnames cannot be registered, so people can use their own surnames in their business without fear of violation. Only where the name has become associated with another product (such as McDonald's hamburgers,

---

48. 2004 BCSC 1694 (CanLII), 37 CPR (4th) 244.
49. 2011 FC 776 (CanLII).

Campbell's soup, or Coach handbags) will the applicant run into problems. Traditionally, a word that is descriptive of what the product is used for, such as "food" or "cleaner," cannot constitute the trademark because it does not distinguish the product. Like a surname, a domain name identifies the user, but because of their descriptive nature, domain names have been subject to considerable abuse. This has led to numerous conflicts over the acquisition and use of the same or a similar name. To make matters worse, cybersquatters (users who buy up certain names just to sell them to others) have tied up domain names that a browser would associate with well-known companies. For example, shortly after Vancouver was granted the 2010 Olympic Games, several domain names (including www.2010-wintergames.com and www.Vancouver2010-Olympicgames. com) were registered and put up for sale on eBay. The organizing committee commenced legal action to protect the domain names, to which they claimed a right. It is important to remember that the registration of domain names and their use on the Internet will not overrule trademark law. In other words, where trademarks are infringed, it will be no defence to show that one registered a domain name first. This is another example of the Internet being subject to general legal principles and statutes.

Domain name disputes are often solved by trademark law

 REDUCING RISK 13.3

Private companies, such as Network Solutions Inc., have been given the responsibility of issuing domain names to applicants on a first-come, first-served basis. A helpful article, "How to Get and Register Domain Names," is available from About.com: Small Business Canada.[50] To facilitate browsing, these names should be closely related to the product or service provided, with the attendant danger that competitors will acquire the name or a similar one first and will divert browsers to their own site. One of the first things a sophisticated client should do in establishing a business is to apply not only for trademark registration but also for all variations of domain names that are likely to be associated with one's service, product, or website.

CASE SUMMARY 13.10

Bad Faith Established with Demand for Money: *Google Inc. v. Fraser*[51]

This dispute was resolved under the CIRA Domain Name Dispute Resolution Policy. Google Inc. announced its "froogle" services and "froogle.com" website in December 2002. Coincidentally, the very next day Fraser registered the domain name "froogle.ca." It was not until months later that Fraser activated a froogle.ca website containing recipes. Nonetheless, she claimed that her domain name had nothing to do with Google's activities. Google Inc. contacted Fraser and advised that legal action would be taken; it alleged bad faith on Fraser's part in registering the domain name. Fraser retorted that she had acted in good faith, but that she was willing to sell the domain name to Google Inc. for $25 000. By requesting money from the complainant for the transfer of the registration, it was inferred that the purpose of registering the domain name in the first place was to extort monies from Google Inc. Bad faith was established. Consequently, the domain name was directed to be transferred to the complainant.

---

50. Susan Ward, "How to Get and Register a Domain Name," About Money, http://sbinfocanada.about. com/od/domainregistration/a/domainname.htm. A list of certified companies issuing such domain names is available through the Canadian Internet Registration Authority at www.cira.ca.

51. (2005), 42 C.P.R. (4th) 560 (CIRA).

> **SMALL BUSINESS PERSPECTIVE**
>
> A prudent businessperson must take steps to secure appropriate domain names in a timely fashion. Failure to act quickly may mean that one will have to bring costly legal proceedings alleging "passing-off" or "bad faith" by those deliberately registering confusingly similar domain names to protect one's presence in the marketplace.

A trademark cannot be a functional aspect of the design of the product. For example, the studs on the tops of LEGO blocks are functional in that they are used to connect one block to another. Because they were functional rather than a distinctive mark, the Supreme Court of Canada refused to recognize them as an unregistered trademark.[52] LEGO's manufacturer had held a patent for LEGO construction sets. Those patents expired and Ritvik, a Canadian toy manufacturer, began selling toy bricks (Micro Mega Bloks) that were interchangeable with LEGO's product. Justice Lebel clarified that "despite its connection with a product, a mark must not be confused with the product—it is something else, a symbol of a connection between a source of a product and the product itself."[53] One cannot trademark the product itself; to do so would be akin to granting a perpetual patent.

Trademark is lost through common usage

Trademarks can lose their status through common use. Aspirin, trampoline, kleenex, and linoleum are examples of terms that have lost their unique status because people use them to describe the general type of product. When a trademark becomes generic it can be a two-edged sword. Initially it has the effect of making the product name very valuable since it is so well known. This is especially valuable for a small growing company. However, as it becomes the common generic term applied to that type of product, including those of competitors, it usually results in not only a loss of value for the original product, but also the loss of the ability of the original rights holder to protect those rights. An example is Twitter Inc. when they did their initial public offering. In the documents filed with the US Securities and Exchange Commission they noted the value of their name and the term "tweet" becoming commonly used, but also stated the danger of it becoming generic and being used with reference to similar competing websites. They noted that this risk, if realized, would cause a devaluation of their shares.[54]

Registration and use of a trademark

Applying for trademark registration is a complicated process requiring the services of an expert, and once registered, a trademark must be used. Failure to do so can result in the loss of the trademark through abandonment. Also, whenever the trademark appears it should be marked with the symbol "®" (indicating that the trademark has been registered). An unregistered trademark can be marked with "TM."

The object of trademark protection is to preserve the value of the goodwill associated with it by preventing someone from using the mark to mislead others into thinking they are dealing with the owner of the trademark when they are not. To enforce that right, the plaintiff must show not only that he is the owner of the trademark, but also that the public would likely be confused by the wrongful use of the trademark, causing damage to the plaintiff. This process would be both facilitated and made more complex if Bill C-31 passes.

Remedies are the same as copyright infringement

If the action to protect a trademark is successful, the types of civil remedies available are the standard ones discussed under copyrights and patents. An effective remedy in the appropriate circumstances is an order giving the owner of the trademark custody of the offending goods. An action can be brought in the Federal Court when the infringed trademark has been properly registered under the Act, but it may be

---

52. A purely functional design cannot be the basis of a trademark. See *Kirkbi AG v. Ritvik Holdings Inc.*, 2005 SCC 65 (CanLII), [2005] 3 SCR 302, 259 DLR (4th) 577.

53. Ibid.

54. As reported in John Simpson, "A Revealing Look at 'Gericide,'" *Lawyers Weekly*, January 24, 2014, 10.

more effective to bring the matter before the appropriate provincial court. Such courts are not limited to enforcing the statute (as is the Federal Court) but may rely on common law principles as well.

CASE SUMMARY 13.11

If a Trademark Confuses the Public It May Be an Infringement: *BBM Canada v. Research In Motion Limited*[55]; *Reynolds Presto Products Inc. v. P.R.S. Mediterranean Ltd.*[56]

The Bureau of Broadcast Measurement provides impartial services to the broadcast industry related to statistical analysis and data collection. These services were not provided or offered to the public and involve no media advertising. The name was changed to BBM Canada, and several trademarks were registered using the BBM Canada name. They also own the registered domain name bbm.ca. These services had been in place for years before RIM started promoting their BlackBerry wireless handheld device, software, and services using BBM (standing for BlackBerry Messenger) in its promotional activities and advertising. BBM Canada brought this application to stop RIM's infringement of their trademark.

In deciding that there was no infringement the Court looked at the degree of confusion that would be caused by both parties using the BBM acronym. Since BBM Canada offered services only to the broadcast industry and had been doing so for some time, and there was no advertising to the public, there was no likelihood that RIM's use of BBM would be confused with BBM Canada. The application was dismissed, and RIM was free to continue to use BBM in marketing the BlackBerry Messenger product. (Note that BBM Canada has since changed their name to Numeris.)

On the other hand, in the *Reynolds Presto* case Reynolds manufactured a honeycomb-shaped polyethylene product using the GEOWEB name. The product was used to stabilize ground and keep it from eroding. When P.R.S. Mediterranean started manufacturing a similar product used for the same purpose in the same market called NEOWEB an application was brought by Reynolds Presto to strike out the NEOWEB entry in the trademark registry. That application was refused, and Reynolds appealed. The Federal Court of Appeal found in their favour. Both companies were in the same business offering the same services. Only one letter of the names used was different, with the N in NEOWEB likely to lead people to think that it was simply a new version of GEOWEB. Because of this the use of NEOWEB would likely cause confusion in the mind of the public and the NEOWEB trademark was struck out.

SMALL BUSINESS PERSPECTIVE

These two cases illustrate when the court will determine infringement of a trademark. The most important factor is whether the use of the trademark will likely cause the public to confuse the trademarks with respect to whose product is being promoted. This principle should guide all businesspeople, especially those involved in marketing products and services where trademarks may be involved.

Passing-off

In addition to the federal *Trade-marks Act*, this area is also covered by common law in the form of a passing-off action. A **passing-off** action is founded in tort law and prevents a person from misleading the public into thinking it is dealing with some

Common law passing-off action gives similar protection

[55.] 2012 FC 666 (CanLII).
[56.] 2013 FCA 119 (CanLII).

Public must have been misled

other business or person when it is not. The court can order compensation be paid or that the offending conduct stop. This remedy is available even when an unregistered trademark is involved.

For a passing-off action to succeed, it is necessary to establish that the public was likely to be misled. The plaintiff must show that its mark, name, or other feature associated with its business was used by the offending party in association with its own operation, causing confusion in the minds of the public. It would be an actionable passing-off for an independent hamburger stand operator to put golden arches in front of her place of business so that people would assume it was part of the McDonald's chain. But if a person were to use an attractive logo developed by someone else who had not yet registered or used it in association with any business, a passing-off action would not succeed because the logo had not become associated with any business and, therefore, the public could not be misled. Finally, the onus is on the plaintiff to establish that actual or potential damage was caused. Note, however, that if the defendant has registered a trademark, it may operate as a complete defence to a passing-off action.[57]

CASE SUMMARY 13.12

Failure to Use Trademark Fatal: *Scott Paper Limited v. Smart & Biggar*[58]

Scott Paper had not used the trademark "Vanity" for 13 years when, in response to a request from others wanting to use it, the registrar of trademarks served notice requiring information as to when it had last been used and for an explanation. Scott Paper responded with no explanation as to why it had not been used for the prior 13 years; rather, they stated that there were definite plans to use the trademark in the near future and, in fact, at the time of the hearing sales on a new line of products under that name had begun. With no explanation forthcoming, the hearing officer concluded that their failure to use it "was the result of a deliberate and voluntary decision of the registered owner."

In effect, they had no excuse for their failure to use the trademark over the last 13 years, but because they had plans to use it they argued that their rights in the trademark should be preserved. The hearing officer agreed, finding that this intention was sufficient to qualify as special circumstances within the Act and continued Scott Paper's right to the trademark "Vanity." That decision was appealed to the Federal Court, and Justice Strayer found that a plan to use the mark in the future did not excuse their failure to use it in the past and overturned the hearing officer's decision to preserve Scott Paper's right in the trademark. The matter was further appealed to the Federal Court of Appeal, which upheld that decision in dismissing the appeal, noting the aptness of Justice Strayer's statement: "Would one excuse a truant schoolboy for an absence of a month because, when confronted, he demonstrated that although he had no explanation for his past absences he genuinely intended to go to school the next week?"

SMALL BUSINESS PERSPECTIVE

A sophisticated businessperson must remember that when a trademark is developed and registered, it must be used.

Industrial Designs and Integrated Circuit Topography

Artistic designs must be registered to have protection

Two other federal acts protect intellectual property. Through registration under the federal *Industrial Design Act*[59] an inventor can protect a unique design, shape, or pattern that distinguishes a manufactured article, such as the Coca-Cola bottle.

---

57. *Molson Canada v. Oland Breweries Ltd.*, 2002 CanLII 44947 (ON CA), 214 DLR (4th) 473.

58. 2008 FCA 129 (CanLII), 291 DLR (4th) 660; 65 CPR (4th) 303.

59. *Supra* note 3.

Registration is particularly important, because unlike trademark and copyright protection, there is no legal protection against imitation unless an industrial design is registered. Registration must take place within one year of the design being published, and items (or their labels or packaging) should be marked with the capital letter "D" enclosed in a circle followed by the proprietor's name or an abbreviation thereof. Damages are available for infringement if the design is marked; otherwise, only an injunction forbidding others from using the design is available. The Act gives the proprietor protection for a period of up to 10 years, but unless a maintenance fee is paid within five years from the date of registration, the protection expires after five years.

The Act is intended to protect attractive and distinctive patterns or shapes as opposed to useful ones. For example, in the *Benchmade Furniture* case, a uniquely designed sofa was protected by an industrial design registration.[60]

As with copyrights, patents, and trademarks, the product involved must be original and not a copy of some product already on the market. Industrial designs can also be assigned to others, or licences allowing usage can be granted, typically for a fee.

The *Integrated Circuit Topography Act*,[61] on the other hand is specifically intended to protect the 3-D design of integrated circuits. These are at the heart of most products manufactured in our increasingly digitized world, and proper registration assures the registrant against copying for a period of 10 years in this and other countries. Remedies available against infringers include, in addition to damages and injunction, the payment of royalties, punitive damages, and the seizure and destruction of the offending product. Registration takes place through the appropriate division of the Canadian Intellectual Property Office.

REDUCING RISK 13.4

Intellectual property is fast becoming the most important asset of many businesses, yet many businesses fail to properly protect or exploit these assets. The right to use such resources can also be abused. A party who recognizes the value a name, a domain name, a logo, or a concept might have for an established business might be tempted to register it himself if he discovers that registration has been overlooked. He may then attempt to sell the rights to use the name, domain name, logo, or concept back to the business for a price. A business's exclusive right to a logo can also be lost through lack of use or not exercising proper control over its use. It is vital that sophisticated clients turn their attention to their intellectual property resources, determining the extent of those resources and taking steps to protect and benefit from them.

CONFIDENTIAL INFORMATION

LO ❼

Duty to keep confidence

Confidential information is given in circumstances where it is clear that the information is intended to remain confidential and not be disclosed. In business, it may be necessary that insiders, such as managers, investors, and employees, as well as outsiders, such as contractors, consultants, and suppliers, keep confidences. The disclosure of confidential information can prove as devastating to a company as interference with other forms of intellectual property, so its protection is a vital concern of business. For example, keeping confidential the fact that a manager or key employee in a business is terminally ill might be vitally important to a business with shares selling on the stock exchange. For information to be confidential it must not be generally known and must not already be disclosed to others.

In fiduciary and other trust relationships, there is a common law duty not to disclose such information or to use it for personal benefit. Such a duty usually arises because of a special relationship, such as that between a principal and agent, between

Duty may arise because of the parties' relationship

60. *Cimon Ltd. v. Benchmade Furniture Corp.* (1965), 1 Ex. C.R. 811.
61. *Supra* note 2.

partners, in some cases between employer and employee or contractor,[62] between business and consultant, or between officers and their corporation. The duty not to disclose or misuse confidential information is not restricted to fiduciary relationships. It can also arise in other situations, for example, pursuant to express or implied contracts between the parties.

CASE SUMMARY 13.13

Ordinary Ex-Employees Free to Compete:
Boehmer Box L.P. v. Ellis Packaging Limited[63]

Kurt Harfst was employed as a senior sales account executive and Ralph Spittal as a sales representative when they left their employment with Boehmer Box L.P. and went to work for a direct competitor. Despite their titles, both were simply highly paid salespersons with no management responsibility. Boehmer was in the business of manufacturing cardboard boxes for the grocery industry, and these employees had important information about marketing and its customers. Boehmer had obtained an interim injunction restraining them from soliciting any of their customers and from misusing any confidential information obtained while at Boehmer. This action involved an application from Boehmer to continue that injunction.

The Court refused to continue the injunction. Although these employees were highly paid, it was because of their skill in dealing with customers, not because they had any management responsibility. It is true that management employees after leaving their employ may continue to have a fiduciary duty not to compete, but ordinary employees have no such duty. They do have a duty not to disclose any confidential information they may have learned while there, but there was no evidence before the Court that they had made any such disclosure. They had in fact returned any documents that may have contained such information, such as customer lists, to Boehmer. They did declare their intention of soliciting the former customers they serviced at Boehmer, and since they were no longer employed there they were free to do so for their new employer. In the absence of a restrictive covenant preventing them from doing so, these former employees were free to directly compete with their former employer and solicit any of their customers.

SMALL BUSINESS PERSPECTIVE

A careful employer with important employees would be wise to include a restrictive covenant in their employment contract so that this kind of problem is avoided. Note that the result in this case may have been different if the two employees had been the "exclusive face" of the company when dealing with customers, but they were not. After they had made the sale, others in the company supplied the service to the customer.

One of the most significant legal settlements in Canada arose out of such a duty by LAC Minerals Ltd. not to use information obtained in confidence from International Corona Resources Ltd.[64] Essentially, Corona had obtained land claims in the Hemlo district of northwestern Ontario. Representatives of LAC entered into discussions with representatives of Corona with the prospect of a joint venture or partnership. In the process, information was given in confidence to LAC to the effect that Corona did not own the surrounding gold claims but was in the process of negotiating for them.

[62.] *Gertz v. Meda Ltd.*, 2002 CanLII 49608 (ON SC), 16 CCEL (3d) 79, involves the duties of an employee. In this case, the information in question was found not to be confidential, no fiduciary duty was found to exist, and since no confidentiality agreement existed, no liability was imposed.

[63.] 2007 CanLII 14619 (ON SC).

[64.] *LAC Minerals Ltd. v. International Corona Resources Ltd.*, 1989 CanLII 34 (SCC), [1989] 2 SCR 574, 61 DLR (4th) 14.

When negotiations broke down between LAC and Corona, LAC independently purchased the surrounding claims and made huge profits from the resulting mines. The Court held that LAC violated its duty (which arose as a result of the special circumstances in which it was obtained) not to disclose or use the information for its own benefit. A trust relationship had been established; the information gained because of it was intended to remain confidential. When the information was used for LAC's gain at Corona's expense, the duty of confidentiality was breached. In that case, the courts found that the duty to keep information confidential arose when information was disclosed in circumstances that showed it was to remain confidential. The unauthorized use of that information was a breach of that duty of confidentiality.

Trade Secrets

A **trade secret** is a particular kind of confidential information that gives a businessperson a competitive advantage. Customer lists, formulas, processes, patterns, jigs, and other unique features unknown to competitors are trade secrets. Successful actions for the wrongful disclosure of trade secrets have been brought in such varied matters as recipes for fried chicken and soft drinks, formulas for rat poison, methods to flavour mouthwash, processes for making orchestral cymbals, and even the techniques prescribed in a seminar to help people quit smoking. A trade secret has the additional requirement that it be valuable to the business and not readily available to any other user or manufacturer. Customer lists available through government publication cannot be classed as trade secrets, nor can a process involved in the manufacturing of a product that is plainly discoverable simply by examining or disassembling the product.

> **Duty of confidentiality covers trade secrets as well**

It is the conveying of the private information that is wrongful. There is no proprietary right in the idea or information itself. If Deng operated a company manufacturing tiddlywinks and had a secret process by which they could be produced more cost effectively, which she failed to patent, and one of Deng's employees were to give that information to a competitor, it would be a wrongful disclosure of a trade secret. But if the competitor were to develop the same or a similar procedure independently, Deng would have no complaint since she has no proprietary right in the idea or process.

While an employee may be required, either expressly in the employment contract or by implication, not to disclose trade secrets and confidential information that he acquires in the process of employment, the employee can use the general skills and knowledge he gains on the job in another employment situation.[65] An employee working in a guitar-manufacturing factory who acquires the skills of a luthier would not be expected to refrain from using any of those skills if he were to work for another manufacturer. However, specific processes or jigs used to make guitars might qualify as a trade secret, and these he could not use in his new employment. It is sometimes difficult to draw the line, and in such circumstances it would be wise for the first manufacturer to include a **restrictive covenant** in the employment contract (a non-competition clause).

Although the courts are reluctant to enforce such covenants against employees, if the covenant is reasonable it may be enforceable, discouraging an employee from seeking subsequent employment with a competitor. In any case, it is good policy to specifically include in the employment contract prohibitions and consequences dealing with the disclosure of confidential information and other forms of intellectual property of the employer. Consultants and independent contractors should also be required to sign such an agreement. The owner of secret information can best maintain its confidentiality by informing the employee or other confidant that she is in a position of confidence and is expected to keep the information private. A person cannot be expected to keep a confidence that she doesn't know is secret.

> **Employers should impose covenant not to disclose trade secrets or confidential information**
>
> **Employees, consultants, and contractors should sign non-disclosure agreements**
>
> **Specify what is confidential**

---

65. *Gertz v. Meda Ltd.*, *supra* note 62.

A person cannot be accused of wrongful disclosure of information if it has been widely distributed and is no longer confidential. While Canada's law related to trade secrets is founded on common law and equity, in some parts of the United States statutes have been passed to govern this area. Whenever foreign jurisdictions are involved, care should be taken to be aware of and comply with the appropriate statutes.

Remedies

Where someone wrongfully discloses information causing harm, the remedies of injunction, damages, and accounting may be available. The court, however, is reluctant to grant an injunction that will prevent an employee from earning a living, unless it is clear that the injunction is necessary to prevent the disclosure of confidential information. This usually happens when the employee goes to work for a competitor. Damages or an accounting are also available when confidences have been breached in this way. Even punitive damages have been awarded.

Non-disclosure provisions in employment contracts

Contract and tort law may be used to give increased protection to the various forms of intellectual property. Non-disclosure provisions in employment and service agreements will provide grounds for remedies such as dismissal, damages, accounting, or an injunction in the event of breach. While it may not be worth the trouble to seek damages from an employee, when the employee has been enticed away or persuaded to disclose the information to a rival business, the employer can sue the competitor for the tort of inducing breach of contract. To succeed in such an action, the plaintiff is not required to establish malice on the part of the defendant, but it must be clear that the interference was intentional (see Chapter 4).

Suing for inducing breach of contract

The confidant who uses the information personally, and possibly the recipient who induces its disclosure, can be sued if confidential information is disclosed or used to the detriment of the owner.

REDUCING RISK 13.5

When sophisticated clients have trade secrets and other forms of confidential information to protect, they should impress upon their employees and those with whom they do business the importance of keeping information confidential. The company should reiterate that duty to keep material confidential in its written contracts with such parties. It may require recipients to sign a non-disclosure statement identifying just what is to be kept confidential. Marking documents as "Confidential" is a good idea, but it should not be taken too far or the notification loses its effect. It is also important to remind employees of their obligations with respect to confidentiality when their employment comes to an end.

LO ⑧ REGULATING INFORMATION TECHNOLOGY

The enforcement of intellectual property rights has been complicated by the ease with which people can transfer material from one computer to another through website links. Information on the linked site may be connected, in the viewer's mind, to the host site. This was the problem addressed by the Federal Court in the *Imax Corp. v. Showmax* case,[66] when Showmax promoted the grand opening of their large-format theatre and created a link on their website to the Old Port of Montreal website, which in turn included a link and other information to an Imax theatre located at their site. The Federal Court agreed that this caused confusion by linking the Showmax promotion to the Imax site and granted an interlocutory injunction to Imax.

[66.] 2000 CanLII 14748 (FC), 182 FTR 180.

CASE SUMMARY 13.14

Computer Linking Muddies Jurisdictional Claims:
Equustek Solutions Inc. v. Google Inc.[67]

Equustek produced devices that allowed complicated interactions and communication to take place between industrial equipment made by different manufacturers. Equustek alleged that the defendant in the main action, Morgan Jack and Datalink Technologies Gateways Inc., manufactured a competing product with the help of former employees of Equustek, thus improperly using trade secrets of Equustek. This product is known as GW 100. Further, Equustek alleged that Jack sold Equustek's products passing them off as their own by covering Equustek's name and logo on the product. In addition, Equustek alleged that Jack, while advertising Equustek's products on their website, delivered their own product after an order was received instead of Equustek's. Note that Jack no longer does business in Vancouver but does business as a virtual company operating through various websites where they advertise and sell their products.

An injunction was issued ordering Jack to refrain from selling the GW 100 and Equustek's product on any website, but the order was ignored. Google, the respondent in this action, voluntarily removed webpages used by Jack with respect to products sold in Canada but refused to remove Jack's mother sites from the Google worldwide search process. Since most of Equustek's products were sold outside Canada, they brought this application for an interim injunction to order Google to remove all Jack's websites and any reference that includes the GW 100 for sale from Google's worldwide search engine.

A major problem the BC Court faced was jurisdiction. Google is a California company. Is it subject to a BC court order? The Court determined that since Google advertised in British Columbia and sold products here they were subject to the BC Court's jurisdiction, and after determining that the balance of convenience was in favour of Equustek the Court issued the order.

DISCUSSION QUESTIONS

Do you think that a large corporation like Google should be subject to this kind of order having extraterritorial effect from a BC Court? Remember that there has been no trial of the main issues, only that Equustek was able to show a *prima facie* case when they obtained an interim injunction. The Court observed that it would be inequitable to force a small company like Equustek to commence litigation in California against such a huge company like Google, which has extensive legal resources. They also noted that Google already had resources in place allowing them to easily comply with the order. Do you agree that this should justify the order?

Controls have been introduced to try to stop domain name and other forms of Internet abuses. A person wishing to claim a particular domain name or web address applies to the Domain Name Registry operated by the Canadian Internet Registration Authority (CIRA), which for a small annual fee will issue the name if it is available. If someone else already owns it, the parties can negotiate its purchase; an alternative is to bring an application to reverse the original registration on the basis that this new claimant has a better right to the name. Dispute resolution mechanisms are now in place to resolve these conflicts, and a name issued to one party can be rescinded on the basis that the registration was improper because of bad faith. The CIRA, which handles such disputes in Canada, defines bad faith

Issued domain names may be reversed because of bad faith

[67.] 2014 BCCA 295 (CanLII).

as obtaining the name to resell at a profit, to prevent someone who has a greater right from using it, or to disrupt another's business.[68]

The *Personal Information Protection and Electronic Documents Act* (*PIPEDA*)[69] necessitated that the CIRA introduce a new privacy policy in 2008, protecting the rights of domain name registrants. Under the new policy, the personal information of individual (as opposed to corporate) domain name registrants, including registrant name, home address, phone number, and email address, is now protected. Exceptions, however, do exist, allowing contact information to be disclosed in situations arising from child endangerment offences, intellectual property disputes (e.g., cybersquatting), threats to the Internet, and identity theft. These rules attempt to strike a balance between privacy and disclosure, but trademark holders may find these new rules an obstacle, making it more difficult to effectively protect intellectual property rights.

Protecting Private Information

Private information about individuals is now subject to widespread abuse because personal data is collected, stored, and shared through online resources. Privacy protection legislation goes some way to ensure that such information is regulated. The *Privacy Act*[70] protects information held by government institutions, limits its collection, and provides for limited access where appropriate. The more recent *PIPEDA* covers all areas of federal jurisdiction and the provinces as well, unless they have passed similar legislation. The acts restrict the use of all health-related information, customer lists, consumer purchasing habits, credit and entertainment information, information gathered from websites, subscriptions to magazines and Internet services, or any other personal information held by a company that relates to identifiable individuals. The federal Act requires companies to develop privacy policies that ensure information they hold on their employees and customers is not improperly disclosed to others.

Apart from government regulation, the onus is still primarily on the company or individual to secure confidential information. Information held in databases, whether on paper or stored in a digital cloud or distributed by email, must use all preservation techniques available to protect it from destruction or disclosure, whether intentional or accidental, including backups, encryption devices, digital locks, and anti-virus and anti-malware software. A company must protect not only its employees from the unlawful release of private information, but also access to its confidential records by unscrupulous or careless employees. Banking information, passwords, electronic signatures, and records that disclose identity can be subject to theft and fraud if they are not properly protected. A company can be held criminally responsible or have civil liability if they do not exercise due diligence in this respect.

Additional Challenges

The massive expansion of the Internet has led to increasing problems of abuse. These problems range from increasing spam and privacy and security concerns to outright fraud. There have been some attempts to impose regulations to deal with these problems, including the changes to the statutes discussed above. A notable addition is Bill C-56, the *Combating Counterfeit Products Act*.[71] This Bill, in addition to expanding the definition of trademark, creates additional criminal offences, increases penalties, and also expands the powers of those involved in enforcement.

---

[68]. For more information on the CIRA, go to www.cira.ca, and for the dispute resolution policy, see http://cira.ca/content/cdrp. The approach used by the CIRA to handle disputes is similar to the Uniform Domain Name Dispute Resolution Policy for dot-com domain name disputes, but with some differences.

[69]. S.C. 2000, c-5.

[70]. R.S.C. 1985, c. P-21.

[71]. S.C. 2014, c. 32.

Primarily because of the impossibility of enforcement, the Canadian content rules, generally administered by the Canadian Radio-television and Telecommunications Commission, have been temporarily set aside with regard to the Internet. In areas such as gaming and lotteries, however, federal and provincial regulations are applied, and both the originator of the contest and the Internet service provider (ISP) will be held liable if it is found to infringe these regulations. These services are, however, usually provided by companies operating from offshore locations, making enforcement extremely difficult. Although there are several examples of statutes that apply to companies doing business on the Internet, many Internet transactions and communications remain unregulated.

Difficult to enforce such regulations

Another major problem is determining who is subject to these controls and who can be held responsible for violations. An Internet-based business can involve many players—including the retailer or business providing the service, the website developers and operators, the ISPs, and even the advertisers, product manufacturers, and deliverers. The *Nexx Online* case[72] serves as an example of an ISP responding to non-legal pressure. A home furnishing company attempted to advertise by sending out bulk emails. This practice was thwarted when its ISP deactivated the company's website after receiving complaints from other users who received the unsolicited emails. When the home furnishing company, claiming irreparable harm, sought an injunction to force the ISP to reinstate the service, the Court refused. It found that the ISP had included a term in the contract restricting this kind of activity. When, after notification, the home furnishing company refused to stop, the ISP acted within its rights by discontinuing the company's account. Today this activity would be controlled by the anti-spam legislation and regulations just recently enacted (Canadian Anti-Spam Legislation, CASL,[73] and the *Electronic Commerce Protection Regulations*[74]), which essentially require a business to acquire the consent of the recipient before sending them advertising material. It will likely take a combination of government regulation, the application of traditional law, and this kind of self-regulation by the major players to finally strike the appropriate balance in these new and challenging areas of electronic communication.

Determining jurisdiction is a difficult problem with respect to information technology and the Internet. When an abuse has taken place, such as defamation or infringing copyright or trademark, it is often impossible to determine who committed the act or where they are located. Even were the offender can be located, often they are in another country where accountability is difficult to enforce. This has proved especially true with respect to the improper downloading of music, games, and movies. In the past it was difficult to obtain information from the ISP so that such perpetrators could be identified and pursued. Today the courts have shown a willingness to require disclosure of such information, and legislation such as the *Copyright Act* has been amended to require the disclosure of the identities of those infringing the Act in this way.

ISP may be responsible to stop abuses

From the point of view of someone offering such services, especially gambling and pornography, they may be operating in a jurisdiction where the activity is legal but still be in violation of the law and subject to prosecution because that activity is illegal where they are received or where customers taking advantage of the service reside. Web messages go into every jurisdiction in the world, but it is now generally accepted that there has to be something more than information delivery or mere advertising to give a particular court jurisdiction to hear a complaint. A passive website will usually not create a problem in any particular jurisdiction where it is viewed. There must be a special link or connection or *degree of interactivity* to have a local court take jurisdiction. Without that special connection, the courts in a particular

---

72. *1267623 Ontario Inc. v. Nexx Online*, 1999 CanLII 15070 (ON SC), 45 OR (3d) 40.
73. S.C. 2014.
74. SOR/2012-36.

province may refuse to hear a case. This principle has now been incorporated into legislation in several jurisdictions.[75]

Still it would be wise for a business providing such services to include a message in their home page statements to the effect that the service is only available where legal and include in any contracts a declaration that the laws of a particular friendly jurisdiction will apply to the transaction. The problem of jurisdiction has become particularly important where goods and services are being sold over the Internet. This subject will be treated in more detail in Chapter 16.

Dispute Resolution

ADR can be used to settle Internet disputes

It has been suggested that problems with monitoring the Internet make it a prime area for the use of alternative dispute resolution (ADR) mechanisms, thereby avoiding the bureaucratic red tape that would come with government regulatory bodies. Independent dispute resolution processes have already been used with success. For example, the National Arbitration Forum has been very effective in handling domain name disputes, as has the CIRA, which handles disputes through British Columbia International Commercial Arbitration Centre and Resolution Canada Inc. Also, negotiation and mediation services such as World Intellectual Property Organization (WIPO) or Cybersettle are now available online, offering the same savings in time and money that have characterized the ADR forums discussed in Chapter 3. These services are intended to handle not only domain name disputes, but also all disputes arising from the use of the Internet.

Regulatory Trends

Web users often impose sanctions on each other and report offenders to ISPs or groups who patrol illegal activities on the net. This is one aspect of **netiquette** and is a form of self-regulation used by applications such as Usenet (which distributes news posted by users, but also enables users to request the removal of a posting). Another example of self-regulation is the code of ethics and standards of practice established by the Canadian Direct Marketing Association, with which its members must comply.

Complete self-regulation is a failed dream, and governments will continue to impose ever more effective regulations. There will be more comprehensive international treaties, leading to a more unified approach to law creation and enforcement. To avoid pitfalls that could be disadvantageous, astute businesspeople need to understand the law with respect to electronic commerce and Internet communication.

Criminal Activity and Other Abuses

Criminal offences proliferate on the Internet

In addition to the problems related to the fraudulent uses of electronic technologies and the outright piracy of computer programs, businesses must contend with computer viruses that interfere with the operation of programs and corrupt or destroy data. Hackers can steal telephone services and access confidential or secret information through misuse of the telecommunications systems and computers of other businesses. Outright piracy of computer programs, music, and videos is a huge problem. Other common Internet and computer offences include pornography, theft, gambling, criminal defamation and harassment, pedophilia, hate literature, and other human rights violations.

General *Criminal Code* provisions such as theft and fraud, specialized provisions prohibiting the unauthorized use of computers (section 342.1), mischief relating to computer data (section 430 [1.1]), and the specific offences included in the

---

[75.] For example, BC's *Court Jurisdiction and Proceedings Transfer Act*, S.B.C. 2003 c. 28, s. 3, 4, and 10.

Copyright Act and *Trade-marks Act* are used to deal with these problems. *R. v. Cheung*[76] is a good example of a criminal prosecution under the *Competition Act* and the *Criminal Code*. In that case, those charged participated in a telemarketing scheme directed toward US residents in which several misleading and deceptive statements were made about the product being sold, and they also falsely led the customers to believe that a prior business relationship existed between them and the sellers. It is interesting to note that just because the victims of the deceptive marketing scheme were in the United States, this didn't make it any less of a crime in Canada. Also note that sections 183 and 184 of the *Criminal Code* prohibiting the interception of private communications apply to the Internet as well as to more traditional methods of communication. But relying on criminal prosecution is not a very reliable way to protect a business from these activities. Matters are made worse by the global nature of the web and other forms of electronic communication and data transfer, which require international cooperation to prosecute. It is hoped that the recommendations made in an international treaty on cybercrime now being implemented in various jurisdictions (Canada signed on in 2005) will eventually lead to much greater control and regulation of electronic communication.[77]

The authorities are to be commended for several successful prosecutions, extending from hackers to numerous child pornography convictions. The most significant breach of US government security, of course, was the WikiLeaks scandal involving disclosure of a huge amount of highly sensitive government information. Julian Assange, the creator of WikiLeaks, was subsequently arrested in the United Kingdom for extradition to Sweden where he faces investigation on sex-related charges. Some say that this is simply a method to get him to a country from which he can be extradited to the United States where he will face serious charges with respect to the WikiLeaks disclosure. When released, still facing extradition to Sweden, he took refuge in the Ecuadorean Embassy where he still remains at the time of writing. His prosecution has been applauded by many, but caused outrage in others. Assange was not the hacker or source of the government leaks; rather, he was the publisher who made that information available on his website. His arrest and extradition (some say persecution) is a matter of considerable controversy, balancing the interests of privacy and security against the interests of freedom of speech and free access to information on the Internet. Many opposed the government response, with some committing crimes themselves in support. For example, Visa and PayPal were hacked and shut down for a period of time because those companies refused to continue to support the WikiLeaks website and operation.

Despite their many successes, law-enforcement agencies are overwhelmed, and businesses cannot count on help from that quarter for effective prevention. Civil litigation is often not much more attractive. Although the person bringing the action is in control of the process, there are still many inherent disadvantages. For example, determining the identity of perpetrators is often impossible, and even then they usually have limited resources, making a civil action a waste of time and money.

Encryption of data and other defences are the best protection

---

REDUCING RISK 13.6

Usually, the best solution is a defensive one. Internet technology continues to outstrip the law, and businesses must take active steps to protect their data and their communications. Effective security is vital, but this measure must go further than simply changing passwords frequently. A sophisticated client will use **encryption coding** of data and other special software to protect against viruses and hackers; these programs also require constant updating.

---

76. 2011 ABQB 225 (CanLII).

77. Cristin Schmitz, "Government Plans Massive Expansion of 'Lawful Access,'" *Lawyers Weekly* 22 (September 13, 2002), 18. Canada was the first non-European country to sign the Council of Europe's Cybercrime Treaty Protocol (focusing on Internet hate). This protocol is a side agreement to the larger COE Cybercrime Treaty.

SUMMARY

Intellectual property

- Protected by both federal legislation and common law
- Comparison of the Five Main Types:

Type	Copyright	Trademarks	Patents	Industrial Designs	Confidential Information
What is protected	Original works	Marks used to differentiate	Inventions	Shapes and patterns	Trade secrets and other private information
Registration required	No	Recommended	Yes	Yes	N/A
Length of protection	Life of author plus 50 years	Renewable, so long as being used	20 years	10 years	Indefinitely, if secrecy is maintained

- Copyright:
  - Protects literary, artistic, dramatic, and musical works, as well as performers' performances, sound recordings, and communication signals, from being copied or used by unauthorized parties
  - Generally lasts for the author's life to the end of the calendar year, plus 50 years
  - Producing the work creates the copyright
  - Registration ensures international protection
  - Remedies include injunctions, Anton Piller orders, damages, and accounting of profits
  - *Copyright Modernization Act* changes rules on digital locks, making it illegal to circumvent them
  - The amendments impose new penalties for infringement and requires ISPs to provide notice to and information about infringers
  - Fines for non-commercial infringers have been reduced
  - Fair dealing rules expanded to include education, satire, and parody
  - Fairness factors are established by court decisions
- Patents: Registration gives international monopoly protection on the use of an invention for 20 years
- Trademarks: Registration protects certain terms, symbols, and designs associated with a business or product; prevents deception of consumer; and protects goodwill. Passing-off action may provide similar protection
- Industrial designs: Visual appeal of an object is protected by federal legislation
- Confidential information:
  - Trade secrets and other private or sensitive information can be protected contractually
  - In common law, an employee or associate under a fiduciary obligation is prohibited from disclosing confidential information, including trade secrets

- Damages or an injunction may be awarded when such confidences are breached
- Current copyright and other intellectual property statutes apply to the Internet
- Measures to protect private information online should be undertaken
- *Criminal Code* can be applied to copyright infractions online

QUESTIONS FOR REVIEW

1. What two principles does the law of intellectual property try to balance?

2. Explain how a copyright is obtained and the qualifications that must be met to obtain such protection.

3. Summarize the nature of the protection given to the holder of a copyright and indicate what remedies are available to enforce such rights.

4. How long does copyright protection last?

5. Discuss under what circumstances an Anton Piller order would be given and indicate how this remedy might be more valuable than other remedies that might be available.

6. What is the purpose of patent law, and why is registration required for protection?

7. How long does patent protection last?

8. What kinds of things are protected by trademark legislation, and how is that protection obtained or lost?

9. What options are available when someone registers a domain name that conflicts with your trademark?

10. How long does trademark protection last?

11. Explain what constitutes passing-off and what course of action is available to the victim.

12. What type of protection extends to industrial designs? How is this protection obtained?

13. What steps should an employer undertake to protect confidential information?

14. How does the duty of confidentiality arise, and what protection or remedies are available to the confider?

15. What federal statutes have been enacted to protect privacy rights?

16. What are some of the problems related to enforcing copyright and trademark law when the medium for transmitting information is the Internet?

17. What steps should a company take to protect itself and its data from internal and external threats?

18. Indicate how criminal law, tort law, and contract law can be used to protect intellectual property. How effective are such alternatives when dealing with online infractions?

CASES AND DISCUSSION QUESTIONS

1. *Mars Canada Inc. v. M&M Meat Shops Ltd.*, 2008 CanLII 4982 (ON SC)
Mars, the manufacturer of M&M candies, had held its trademark in Canada since the 1950s. M&M Meats operated a retail chain across Canada selling specialty foods, including desserts. In 1991, M&M Meats applied to register a new logo with just the letters

M&M. Mars opposed the application largely because M&M Meats had dropped the words "Meat Shops" from its logo. Eventually, the parties reached an agreement under which Mars agreed to withdraw opposition in exchange for M&M Meats' promise not to use marks in association with candy or toys and not to use letters in a style similar to that used by Mars for M&M candies. Subsequent amendments to the agreement resulted in M&M Meats agreeing to restrict the sale of ice cream and baked goods to company-owned or franchised stores trading under the name M&M Meat Shops. M&M Meats entered into an arrangement with Mac's Convenience stores in 2001, whereby Mac's became an M&M Meats franchisee. When Mars learned of the arrangement, it took the position that the sale of M&M Meats ice cream and dessert products in Mac's stores breached the agreement between Mars and M&M Meats.

Should M&M Meats be allowed to continue selling its ice cream and baked goods through Mac's outlets? In each Mac's franchise, M&M Meat Shops had separate signs, counters, displays, fixtures, and equipment. Does this additional information have any impact on your opinion?

2. *Black v. Molson Canada*, 2002 CanLII 49493 (ON SC), 60 OR (3d) 457

Black obtained the use of the domain name *Canadian.biz* through proper registration with the intention of using it for a website catering to Canadian businesses and entrepreneurs. This site was not yet established as it awaited resolution of the dispute over who had the right to use this domain name. Molson, which produces a product called "Molson Canadian," claimed the exclusive right to the use of the domain name on the basis that it was identical to its trademark. The brewer demanded its transfer from Black, and when he refused Molson complained to the National Arbitration Forum, the body that deals with these kinds of issues. The forum agreed with Molson, concluding that the name had been registered in bad faith by Black, who had no legitimate claim to its use, and ordered its transfer to Molson. Black brought this application to the Court to have that decision overturned.

Who do you think should be entitled to use this domain name?

3. *Rains v. Molea*, 2013 ONSC 5016 (CanLII)

Rains is a Canadian artist who has created a series of images that depict crumpled paper in various guises. Molea is also a Canadian artist who, quite independently, also created a series of works depicting crumpled paper in various forms. Rains claimed that he has copyright in the whole (the series of crumpled paper works he has created) and that Molea was in violation of that copyright.

What do you think? Does Rain have a copyright in the series or only in each individual work? Would it affect your answer to know that Rains claims that his series, consisting of over 200 works, is a reflection of Greek and Roman architecture; that the series is entitled the "classical series"; and that each work features crumpled paper against a dark background? Also, each work is titled with a reference to a specific Mediterranean location. On the other hand, Molea produced his work, "The Molea crumpled paper works," as a process of using simple material to create drama by contrasting light, shadow, and volume.

4. *Wenzel Downhole Tools Ltd. v. National-Oilwell Canada Ltd.*, 2012 FCA 333 (CanLII)

Wenzel was an inventor who had patented and produced a tool containing bearings that could better handle the download in well-drilling operations. National-Oilwell manufactured an identical product, and Wenzel sued for patent infringement.

Explain the appropriate remedies available to Wenzel. How would it affect your answer to know that Wenzel manufactured a tool sold to the industry that contained the bearing at the time of the patent application? Note as well that National-Oilwell also claimed that the development of the bearings was an obvious development to anyone in the industry.

14

Chapter

Real and Personal Property and Protection of the Environment

LEARNING OBJECTIVES

① Distinguish real and personal property

② Describe the various estates in land

③ Outline the unique properties of mortgages and the rights of the parties

④ Compare the rights and obligations of landlords and tenants

⑤ Outline the special rules applicable to fixtures

⑥ List the rights and obligations associated with bailment

⑦ Outline legal issues relating to the protection of the environment

⑧ Discuss the competing interests of economic growth and environmental protection

⑨ Describe how to resolve conflicts in environmental law

REAL VERSUS PERSONAL PROPERTY

This chapter focuses on property rights and how they are protected in Canada. The two types of property—real and personal—are examined. The related subject of environmental protection is the final subject in this chapter.

    While people usually think of property as a physical object, such as a boat, car, or land, "property" more correctly refers to the relationship existing between the item and the individual who owns it. When a person says he owns a boat, it is descriptive of the nature of the interest he has in the boat rather than the boat itself. This distinction must be kept in mind as we examine the nature of the different interests in property.

LO **①**

Ownership describes one's interest in property

Ownership and possession are separate

Although ownership or title is the highest form of property right to a particular item, other lesser forms of interest are also possible. In our legal system, ownership or title can be separate from possession. Thus, one person might be in possession of something that belongs to someone else.

The term **real property** refers to land and things permanently attached to the land, such as buildings. The essential characteristic of real property is that it is fixed and immovable. **Personal property**, on the other hand, is movable and can be divided into two categories. **Chattels** (or **goods**) are tangible personal property, consisting of movables that can be measured and weighed. An intangible right is a claim one person has against another, such as a claim for debt, and is called a **chose in action**, which is, in effect, a right to sue. Bonds, share certificates, and negotiable instruments are examples of choses in action. Note that different aspects of personal property are dealt with in other sections of this text. For example, personal property security and the sale of goods are dealt with in Chapters 15 and 16, respectively. A special category of intangible personal property dealing with ideas and creative works is now called *intellectual property* and encompasses such topics as copyright, patents, and trademarks. Intellectual property was dealt with in Chapter 13.

This chapter will first focus on real property and then on tangible personal property (goods or chattels).

Real property—land and buildings

Chattels—goods

Chose in action—intangible property

Intellectual property deals with ideas and creative work

LO ❷   REAL PROPERTY

Real property is land or anything attached to land

Whether shelter is obtained through ownership, rental, or even squatting, the relationships created are governed by real property law. The following examination is necessarily abbreviated, but it will serve as an introduction to certain significant aspects of the law of real property. To understand this body of law, one must first acquaint oneself with unique concepts of ownership, estates in land, and rights to possession. We shall begin by examining interests in land and their transfer, followed by an examination of the landlord and tenant relationship.

Interests in Land

Real property owners face restrictions on use

The term "real property" includes land and anything affixed to it, such as buildings and chattels that are permanently attached. As far as the areas above and below the surface are concerned, only the portion that the owner can permanently use or occupy is now considered part of that property. Even to this space, an owner's rights will probably be restricted by local zoning regulations, which may limit the type or size of building that can be erected as well as the activity that can take place on that land.

Mineral rights may be separate from surface rights

A landowner has no actionable complaint when an airplane flies over the property, but power lines or an overhanging building that permanently intrudes into this air space and is unsupported by some legal right such as an easement would give rise to a right to sue for trespass. As for the subsurface rights, usually the Crown has retained the mineral and oil and gas rights. Property owners generally have no complaint when these rights are granted to others and mine shafts or oil wells are developed under their property. In these cases, the property owner is entitled to compensation for surface disturbance, in the form of access roads, shafts, and so on, but not to a share of the profits coming from the minerals, oil, or gas. Mineral and oil and gas rights are important topics with their own body of law, and no attempt will be made to deal with them in this text.

Estates in Land

The current law of real property is rooted in the ancient feudal system of England, in which people held rather than owned their land. The king actually owned the land; the right to possession of it, called an **estate in land**, was granted on the basis of some obligation of service to the king. Today in Canada these estates in land have been reduced to a few significant types known as *estates in fee simple*, *life estates*, and *leasehold estates*.

FEE SIMPLE

The greatest interest a person can have in land today (and what we think of as ownership) is an estate in **fee simple**. Although the Crown, federal or provincial, technically still owns the land, a fee simple estate gives the holder all of the rights that we normally associate with ownership, including the right to use the land in any way the "owner" sees fit and the right to sell it, subject only to restrictions imposed by agreement or legislation. Those restrictions may include government and municipal regulations with respect to what the property can be used for and the nature and description of the buildings that can be erected on it. The health, sanitary, and appearance standards to be maintained may also be prescribed. The property may even be expropriated under certain circumstances.

All land is owned by the Crown

Fee simple is comparable with ownership

LIFE ESTATE

Whereas a fee simple estate can be inherited, a **life estate** is more restrictive and cannot be willed to others. Both types of estate give exclusive possession of the property to the holder, but upon the death of the life tenant, the property reverts back to the original owner of the fee simple or that owner's heirs. This right to take back the property or **reversionary interest** may be transferred to a third party, who is then called the **remainderman**. The remainderman holds the right to the remainder of the fee simple after the death of the life tenant. Life estates are not particularly common in Canada. The holder of a life estate has special responsibilities and must pay for normal upkeep, pay fees and taxes, and not commit "waste"—that is, not do anything to harm the value of the reversionary interest, such as cut down trees or damage the house. The uncertainty associated with them makes a life estate unattractive from a business point of view. Recently, however, life estates have been used to market accommodation for seniors.

Life estate divides fee simple

In many provinces, interests similar to life estates are created through the operation of law. **Dower rights** provided the wife a one-third interest in the husband's land as a matter of right while they remained married, but this also interfered with the free transferability of property. Today, dower rights have been modified or replaced by other statutory protections.[1] Now these claims are protected in most provinces by **homestead rights**[2] or in family law statutes that give the spouse a claim to a substantial portion of all family assets in the case of marriage breakdown.[3]

Dower and homestead rights protect spouse

LEASEHOLD ESTATES

Fee simple estates and life estates are described as freehold estates because a person has exclusive possession of the property for an indeterminate time. **Leasehold estates** or leases are limited to a specific period of time, after which the property reverts back to the landowner. These leases may be short term or long term (99 years) or may take the form of a periodic tenancy. With a periodic tenancy, there is no definite termination date; rather, the term is for some recurring period (usually month to month) that continues until terminated by notice. For example, a person may rent an apartment on a month-to-month basis until the landlord or tenant gives notice for it to end. (Landlord and tenant law will be discussed in a separate section of this chapter.)

Leasehold estates are determined by time . . .

. . . but may also be periodic

Lesser Interests in Land

Unlike freehold and leasehold, there are several lesser interests in land that do not convey the right to exclusive possession of the property. An **easement** gives a person the right to use a portion of another's land, usually for a particular purpose. The **right of way** gives a right to cross another's land, usually to get to their own property,

---

1. *Dower Act*, R.S.A 2000, c. D-15.
2. *Homesteads Act, 1989*, S.S. 1989–90, c. H-5.1.
3. *Family Relations Act*, R.S.B.C. 1996, c. 128, s. 56.

Easement gives right to use land, but not possession

Must be a dominant and servient tenement

but does not give that person the right to stop, park her car, or build some permanent structure on that property. The property that has the advantage of the right of way is called the **dominant tenement**, and the property subject to it is called the **servient tenement**. An easement can also involve a permanent incursion onto the property, such as giving the right to have part of a building hang over onto a neighbour's property. **Statutory easements** give utilities or other bodies similar rights to run power lines or sewer lines across private property.

A **licence** gives a person permission to use another's land. Examples include allowing the public to shop in a mall or a patron to rent a hotel room. Such a licence is not a true interest in the property and does not run with the land.

Property rights may be acquired by prescription . . .

In some provinces a right to land can be acquired by use. Acquiring such a right over property is called an **easement acquired by prescription**. To prevent such an easement from arising, the landowner must periodically exercise some control over the portion of land in question, such as blocking off public access from time to time.

. . . or by adverse possession

A right to actual possession of land can be gained in a similar manner. Acquiring possession through **adverse possession** occurs when someone has had possession of the land for a significant number of years with the knowledge and toleration of the owner (see Case Summary 14.1). The actual number of years needed varies with the jurisdiction. Several Canadian jurisdictions, specifically those using a land titles system, have abolished both the right to an easement by prescription and the right to acquire land by adverse possession. Refer to MyBusLawLab for details.

CASE SUMMARY 14.1

Adverse Possession Applied in Land Titles Jurisdiction: *Cantera v. Leah Eller*[4]

Laura Cantera purchased her home in 1997, and her neighbours (Wendy Eller and Paul White) purchased theirs in 2004. A post and wire fence that had been there for over 50 years divided the properties. When Eller and Wright purchased their property they did so intending to tear it down and build a new home. In the process they discovered that the fence had been misplaced, so they tore it down and built a construction fence in a new location on what Cantera thought was her property. Although only a small strip of property was involved, Eller and Wright were concerned that even a small reduction in their overall property area might affect what they were allowed to build. The Court decided in favour of Cantera.

The original fence had been there long enough to establish a right to the disputed strip of property by adverse possession. Although this is a land titles jurisdiction, when the change-over from the registration system took place the *Land Titles Act*[5] made it clear that although no new rights could be created by adverse possession, any rights obtained by adverse possession before the land titles system was put in place were preserved.

SMALL BUSINESS PERSPECTIVE

Today most jurisdictions have moved to a land titles system. This case shows how careful a prudent businessperson must be when dealing with land titles to ensure that there are no pre-existing rights unrecorded on the title.

Restrictive covenants may bind future owners

Another important right is a **restrictive covenant**. When land is sold a restriction on the use of that land can be included that will bind all subsequent holders. Restrictive covenants may impose restrictions as to what type of building can be put on the land or how the property may be used, such as for residential, commercial, or light industrial use. Normally a contractual provision only applies to the parties to that

---

4. 2007 CanLII 17024 (ON SC).

5. R.S.O. 1990, c. L.5 s. 51.

contract, but with a restrictive covenant and other interests in land the restriction applies not only to the purchaser but also to any subsequent purchasers of that land. They are better viewed as an interest in land rather than as a simple contract; the rule of privity of contract thus does not apply.

For restrictive covenants to bind subsequent owners of the property they must be expressed as negative rather than positive obligations. Thus, a requirement that no building over three storeys be constructed on the property is a negative covenant and will bind future owners. But requiring that a building be built within a certain time period imposes a positive obligation to do something and will bind only the initial purchaser. A **building scheme** involves placing the same restrictive covenants on all the properties in a large development. Building schemes take on many of the attributes of zoning bylaws because the developers have imposed basic rules governing the construction and use of property in the development, just as a municipality would normally do through zoning bylaws.

To bind future owners these covenants must be negative

CASE SUMMARY 14.2

When a Positive Obligation Is Not Binding on Subsequent Purchasers: *Brennan v. Dole*[6]

This action involved a number of townhouse owners who were in a dispute with respect to who should pay for snow removal on the adjacent common right of way. There was an agreement registered against the properties stating that such costs were to be shared by the owners and that all such disputes were to be taken to arbitration. Dole purchased her townhouse from a prior owner and claimed that she was not bound by that agreement. The issue before the Court was whether the requirement that the snow removal costs be shared and that such disputes be arbitrated was binding on her. The Court decided that she was not bound by the agreement. As a successor in title, she was not a party to the original agreement, and for such an agreement to be binding on her it must flow with the land. To do so it had to be worded in the negative and be registered. This agreement placed a positive obligation on the parties to it, so it was not binding on a successor in title.

SMALL BUSINESS PERSPECTIVE

Registering one's interests does not guarantee that those interests are adequately protected. For a restrictive covenant to flow with the land and be binding on subsequent owners it must not only be registered but must also be worded in the negative. The case also illustrates how important it is to have issues that commonly arise between condominium and cooperative owners handled by arbitration. This provision should have been incorporated into the bylaws of the condominium.

Tenancy in Common and Joint Tenancy

When people own property together in a **tenancy in common**, they each have an undivided interest in the land, although they may be entitled to a different percentage of the proceeds on sale. "Undivided," in this sense, means that neither owner can point to any one portion of the property as theirs. The co-owners share the property, and if one dies that person's heirs inherit his interest. Where a will is involved, the terms of the will prevail and the named beneficiary will obtain that person's interest in the property. Estate taxes and probate fees with respect to that property must also be paid.

Owning property together may be joint or in common

People can also share ownership of property in a **joint tenancy** relationship, but here, if one dies the others will be left with the whole property. In effect, the joint

Only joint ownership creates right of survivorship

---

6. 2005 CanLII 33122 (ON CA).

tenants own the entire property outright, and when one dies the survivors continue to own the entire property. This right of survivorship has many advantages. Where a husband and wife own property jointly and one dies, the other continues to own all of the property. There is no inheritance. The property does not go through the estate, and there are no estate taxes, probate fees, or other expenses. This is why joint tenancy is so attractive to families holding property together. Note that other interests such as bank accounts can also be held jointly.

Joint tenancy can be severed

Where property is owned jointly and one of the parties does not want the others to get her interest, it is possible to sever the joint tenancy. This will often be a consequence of marriage breakdown. **Severance** must take place before the death of the party seeking severance and is accomplished by one of the parties acting toward the property in some way that is inconsistent with the joint tenancy continuing. Selling one's interest in the property to a third party, for instance, would sever the joint tenancy, creating a tenancy in common between the other party and that purchaser. But a joint tenant will sometimes try to hide her intention to sever by bequeathing the joint interest to someone else in a will. This does not work, since the will operates after death and after the rights of the survivor have been established. In some jurisdictions, legislation prevents registration of a transfer that would have the effect of severing a joint tenancy unless that transfer is executed or consented to by all the joint tenants, or proof is submitted that a written notice of the intention to register such a transfer was served on all joint tenants.[7] Creditors can also bring applications to the court to partition or sever a joint tenancy so that the debtor's interest in the property can be sold to pay the debt.

To avoid the creation of a joint tenancy, terms such as "held jointly" or "joint ownership" should not be used in the title document. When such words do not appear, the creation of a tenancy in common is presumed.

CASE SUMMARY 14.3

What Can Sever a Joint Tenancy? *DeLong v. Lewis Estate*[8]

John DeLong held property in joint tenancy with Helen Lewis in Nova Scotia. Without the knowledge of DeLong, Lewis attempted to sever the joint tenancy by transferring the property to herself through a quitclaim deed (a document whereby one person surrenders their interest in property, often to a bank). This was properly filed in the appropriate land registry with the notation that its purpose was to sever the joint tenancy. Lewis died 18 months before DeLong and it was only upon her death that he learned of the attempt to sever the joint tenancy. The issue before the Court was to determine whether the quitclaim deed was effective in severing the joint tenancy. If it was, DeLong was only entitled to a half interest as a tenant in common. If it was not effective, he would be entitled to the whole property as survivor in a joint tenancy.

The trial court made it clear that it was established law that one party transferring that property to himself without the knowledge of the other party could not sever a joint tenancy. That was upheld on appeal. The result is that no severance of the joint tenancy had taken place, and DeLong acquired the full interest in the property through the right of survivorship.

The case is interesting in that it illustrates the operation of the right of survivorship, the effect of severance, and the fact that conveying the property to one's self will not accomplish the severance of a joint tenancy. Note that it was the lawyer who advised Lewis with respect to the quitclaim deed and was given status as a party at the trial that appealed the lower court decision.

---

7. See, for example, s. 65 of Alberta's *Land Titles Act*, R.S.A. 2000, c. L-4.
8. 2012 NSSC 369 (CanLII); appeal, *Penny v. DeLong Estate*, 2013 NSCA 74 (CanLII).

REDUCING RISK 14.1

Shared property can be both a boon and a thorn in the side of the people who own it and those they deal with. Partners may find it efficient to own business property jointly so that if one dies the other acquires the whole property without having to deal with the estate and thus reducing taxes. Still, the consequences of this decision must be fully understood. If a joint owner dies, that property does not go to her estate and is not available to her heirs. This may be an appropriate result if planned for by a sophisticated client and other arrangements are made to provide for the family, but it may be a tragedy if the implications of joint ownership have not been fully appreciated.

Other Interests in Land

Normally, an offer can be revoked at any point before acceptance. Such an offer can be made irrevocable when the offeree pays some additional consideration to keep the offer open for a specified period. This is called an **option agreement**, and when land is involved it conveys with it significant rights, giving the offeree a right to purchase the land at a specified price, which can, in turn, be sold to someone else. Land speculators often use the option to purchase to acquire a right to purchase land at a given price and then search out another buyer and sell that option to them at a significant premium. In the process the land never comes into their possession. Leases also often contain an option to purchase. Such options to purchase must be registered against the title to bind subsequent purchasers of the property. Registration is discussed below.

> An option gives the right to purchase

When a person purchases land, paying for it by a series of instalments, this is secured by either a mortgage or less commonly by an **agreement for sale**. An agreement for sale is like a conditional sale of personal property of the seller providing the financing. The sale takes place in two stages: Possession goes first and the title transfers when the last payment is made. In the event of a default, the seller can reclaim the land that he has title to. The agreement for sale also must be properly registered to protect the interest against subsequent claims against the property.

> Security is given through mortgage or agreement for sale

A more common way of financing the purchase of property is through a mortgage, which will be discussed below.

Transfer and Registration of an Interest in Land

The first stage in the purchase of property, commercial or residential, involves the creation of an **agreement of purchase and sale** between the vendor and purchaser. It is important to understand that this is the contract governing the transaction, and great care must be taken in its creation. This agreement is sometimes referred to as an **interim agreement**, an unfortunate term since this is the binding contract for the sale of the property. All of the terms and special conditions must be properly set out in the agreement of purchase and sale, which governs the relationship between vendor and purchaser. If the purchaser wishes to avoid being bound until acceptable financing is arranged, until her existing house is sold, or until the house passes a proper inspection, that must be carefully stated as a **condition precedent** in the contract. It will be too late to insist on it later. The purchaser's lawyer will search the title to ensure all is in order and at the appropriate time, when all conditions

> An agreement of purchase and sale is binding on parties

have been satisfied or removed, the transaction will "close"—at that point the property transfers from vendor to purchaser.

Historically, land was transferred by grant. The document used to accomplish this transfer had to be under seal and was called a **deed of conveyance**, now shortened simply to *deed*. A problem with this system was that there was no way to keep track of the various deeds that would accumulate with respect to a particular property over the years. It was impossible to be certain that good title to the property had been transferred by the most current deed without inspection of all the past documents. Two different solutions to this problem were developed, and either one or the other has been adopted in all Canadian jurisdictions.

Both systems require the registration of documents, but in the **registration system** the rights of the parties are determined by the registered documents, rather than the process. The registry is merely a repository of documents that provides assurance to the parties that they will not be affected by any unregistered documents. The purchaser's lawyer must still "search the title" by examining the title documents and establishing a chain of valid deeds to determine whether the seller has good title. This usually means going back over the documents for a set period of time (40 years) to make sure no mistakes have been made. Anything before that period is presumed to be correct. Confusion may arise, however, since many interests in land may exist at the same time, all needing registration, including the fee simple, lease interests, easements, and judgments.

The western provinces, the territories, more recently New Brunswick and Nova Scotia,[9] and some areas of Ontario and Manitoba have taken the registry system one step further and adopted a **land titles system**, where the title to real property is guaranteed. In this system, once registration has taken place in a central registry a certificate of title is created and registered that is binding on all parties. The government guarantees that the information on that certificate of title is correct. This information sets out the declared owner of the property as well as any mortgages, easements, judgments, or other interests that might be held by others. The key to understanding this system is that the certificate of title determines the interest of the parties listed on it to the land specified.

For example, in Alberta the *Land Titles Act*[10] states that the **certificate of title** is conclusive evidence in any court that the person named on the certificate is the holder in fee simple of that property and that is the end of the matter. Both systems require registration, but in the registration system it is up to the parties to sort out the legal relationships derived from those registered documents, whereas in the land titles system the certificate of title determines the interests. The Liu case summarized in Case Summary 14.4 illustrates the difference between the land titles system and the system of land registry used in other parts of the country, where the validity of a forged document could be challenged and a person in Liu's position would have retained the home. Prince Edward Island and Newfoundland and Labrador remain the only Canadian jurisdictions that have exclusively deed registry systems.

Registration system: registration is imposed to assist in ascertaining title

Land titles system: provincial government guarantees title

CASE SUMMARY 14.4

Certificate of Title Final: *Household Realty Corporation Ltd. v. Liu*[11]

Mr. Liu and Mrs. Chan were married, and prior to immigrating to Canada in 1993 they purchased a house in Richmond Hill, Ontario. Chan stayed in Canada, but Liu returned to Hong Kong to work in the jewellery business and made periodic trips to Canada.

---

9. For a good summary of recent developments, see "Nova Scotia Land Registry," www.novascotia.ca/sns/access/land/land-services-information/land-registry.asp.

10. *Supra* note 6, s. 62; see also British Columbia's *Land Title Act*, R.S.B.C. 1996, c. 250, s.23(2).

11. 2005 CanLII 43402 (ON CA), 261 DLR (4th) 679.

Chan had a gambling habit and, after losing a considerable amount of money, borrowed first from the TD Bank, which she paid off, and subsequently from CIBC and Household Realty. The loans were secured by mortgages that she was able to obtain by forging a power of attorney purporting to be by her husband authorizing her to take out mortgages against the Richmond Hill property. She defaulted on the mortgages, and in this action Liu disputed the validity of those mortgages.

The trial court found, and the Court of Appeal agreed, that both banks were innocent and had not acted negligently in any way. Although the transactions were based on a fraudulent instrument, the registration was not fraudulent, making the mortgages properly registered and valid under the land titles system and binding on Liu. In the words of the trial judge:

> Both the policy underlying the *Land Titles Act* and the language of s. 78(4) reflect the principle that an instrument, once registered, is effective. In the result, the two mortgages in this case, having been given for valuable consideration and without notice of a fraud are, once registered, effective and can be relied on.

This case illustrates the nature of the land titles system and the overriding effect of registration under it. Note that had the Court determined that there was negligence on the part of the bank or that they were in a position to avoid the fraud, the result would likely have been different.[12]

DISCUSSION QUESTION

Note the differences between the two systems and consider whether the changes imposed with the land titles legislation is an improvement. What do you think was the purpose of moving toward a land titles system?

Since governments guarantee title in a land titles system, parties who sustain a loss (through an omission, mistake, or misfeasance of the registrar, or who are deprived of their land by the registration of another person as owner) can bring an action against the registrar for damages. In Alberta, for example, every time land is transferred assurance fees are paid and deposited into a fund. The party who suffers a loss can then bring an action against the registrar and any other party whose wrongful conduct caused the loss. The registrar can be found liable for any part of the judgment that remains unsatisfied, and recovery is then available out of the province's General Revenue Fund, where these assurance fees are pooled. Note, however, that any such action must be brought within a relatively short "limitation period."

In both registry and land titles systems, great strides are being made to modernize the process using advanced data compilation technologies. One very important change is in the process of filing the documents, which now can be done electronically in many jurisdictions, including British Columbia, Saskatchewan, Ontario, New Brunswick, Nova Scotia, and Newfoundland and Labrador.[13] Refer to MyBusLawLab for details.

Electronic registration systems have advantages and disadvantages. One advantage is increased access to information. Searches can be conducted online, reducing the need to personally attend a local registry or land titles office to complete a title search. Larger volumes of searches and registrations can be processed, and physical storage requirements should be reduced with the reduction of paper. However, electronic systems can crash, and fraud remains a serious threat. Title fraud may be simpler in a system that eliminates signatures, witnessing of documents, and paper itself.

---

12. See, for example, *Reviczky v. Meleknia*, 2007 CanLII 56494 (ON SC), 287 DLR (4th) 193.

13. See British Columbia's *Land Titles Act*, *supra* note 9; Saskatchewan's *Land Titles Act 2000*, S.S. 2000, c L-5.1; Ontario's *Land Registration Reform Act*, R.S.O. 1990, c. L-4; New Brunswick's *Land Titles Act*, S.N.B. 1981, c. L-1.1; Nova Scotia's *Land Registration Act*, S.N.S. 2001, c. 6; and Newfoundland and Labrador's *Registration of Deeds Act*, 2009, SNL 2009, c R-10.01.

REDUCING RISK 14.2

The purchase of real estate, be it residential or commercial, constitutes one of the most important transactions a person will be involved in. Both vendor and purchaser should have their own lawyer involved at an early stage. Remember that the purchase agreement ("interim agreement") is the contract governing the transaction and is binding on the parties. Great care should be taken with the terms of that contract; all conditions should be fully understood and carefully worded. The actual transfer documents that are completed later are just the execution of that contract.

Often it will be necessary for a sophisticated client to have the property surveyed to determine its proper boundaries. It is also important to have the buildings properly inspected by a competent independent professional so that any problems can be factored into the purchase price. In some jurisdictions title insurance is recommended to protect mortgage lenders and consumers against fraud; but where a land titles system is used, the need for such insurance is minimal.

Condominiums and Cooperatives

Condominium legislation allows vertical title

Condominium interest involves some shared property

Because traditional real property law did not recognize the difference between the land and the buildings affixed to it, it was incapable of handling the modern practice of creating ownership in suites stacked vertically in an apartment building or attached townhouses. All Canadian provinces have passed legislation allowing fee simple interest in individual units in a condominium structure. But because condominium ownership involves a combination of unit and common ownership, many unique rights and responsibilities apply. Although individuals may own their separate units, all common areas, such as the halls, reception areas, and laundry facilities, are owned in common.

The condominium association is a corporate body and functions in a way similar to a company or society, holding regular meetings where each member (those owning units in the development) has a vote. Bylaws are passed that outline the rights and duties of members. Although these bylaws must conform with statutory requirements, they can still create hardship where rules are put in place that interfere with what would normally be considered a right of ownership, such as prohibitions on pets or children.

Rules must be obeyed and fees paid

Liens can be registered for non-payment of fees

The condominium association will levy a fee on each member to pay for such things as repairs, the cost of management, and other services. If these fees are not paid, the condominium corporation has a right to place a lien or caveat on the title of the member and force a sale, if necessary, to recover the funds.[14] When unexpected repairs occur, these fees or levies can be substantial. In British Columbia, there has been a particular problem with "leaky condos," the repair of which has required many condominium owners to pay levies sometimes in excess of $50 000, causing many to lose their homes. Each member of the condominium owns his own suite, and the normal rules of real property apply; the suites can be sold, mortgaged, or rented (although rental can be restricted by condominium rules). Note that the interest the member has in the common areas goes with the conveyance and so do the responsibilities associated with it. The condominium structure is not limited to residential apartments but can be applied to commercial properties, townhouses, or even separate, physically unconnected units or vacation properties.

Apartments can be owned through cooperatives

A **cooperative** is a less common method of shared ownership. As with condominiums, cooperatives offer members shared amenities and individual entitlements. Members also cooperate in the administration of the project. Cooperatives may differ in their structure. The real property interest may be held in common, with leases granted in favour of the members. Alternatively, the entire property might be owned by a corporation, with individual units being leased to shareholders. In either case, the real property interest in all the suites and the common areas is held by the cooperative, and the members do not have title to the specific suite that they occupy but have shares in the cooperative.

---

14. Ontario's *Condominium Act, 1998*, S.O. 1998, c. 19, grants condominium liens priority over every registered and unregistered encumbrance, even pre-existing encumbrances.

The property may be covered by a blanket mortgage, since the title to the whole is placed in the cooperative. Members usually assume a portion of the mortgage obligation and a levy for operating expenses. Problems can develop if some members fail to contribute to the mortgage. This will affect everyone, even those who have paid their share. Accordingly, cooperative agreements often provide for a claim against a member's corporate interest in the event of a failure to contribute as agreed.[15]

There are some disadvantages to condominium and cooperative ownership, such as submission to the bylaws and the monthly fee, but there are also significant advantages. This form of ownership is the only viable alternative to renting an apartment. Also, members can share facilities such as swimming pools and other recreational areas that normally would not be available to an individual homeowner. In condominiums or cooperatives, residents can be required to leave if they violate the bylaws. For example, buildings can be designated as adults only or pet free, and couples can be required to leave if they have pets or children (although such provisions may violate human rights legislation).

MORTGAGES

LO ③

Mortgage transfers title to creditor as security

The purchase of a home is one of the most important transactions an individual will make, and a mortgage is almost always associated with such a purchase. Most people understand that a **mortgage** involves the debtor borrowing money and giving the creditor a claim against her property (land and buildings) as added security in the event of default. Historically, the mortgage transaction involved the mortgagor (debtor) transferring title to the property to the mortgagee (creditor) as security for the loan. But only the title was transferred; possession of the property remained with the debtor—hence the term "mort-gage," or "dead transfer." If the debt was repaid the title was returned, but in the event of default the mortgagee (creditor) kept title and took possession of the property as well. Today, in a land titles jurisdiction, both title and possession remain with the debtor, but the rights created in a mortgage transaction remain the same, including the creditor's right to take title and possession of the property in the event of default.

Long amortization periods but short duration

Usually, a mortgage agreement is calculated on repayment of the debt over a long period of time (25 or 30 years). This allows for a relatively modest regular monthly payment. That is referred to as the amortization period. However, the mortgage agreement itself usually has a fixed duration of a much shorter time where the whole amount of the mortgage debt becomes payable in, for instance, five years. In effect this requires the mortgage to be renewed every five years, allowing the parties to adjust the interest rate payable and other terms to reflect changing rates and the value of the property as they fluctuate.

Equity of Redemption

Equity of redemption gives mortgagee the right to redeem property

Although title was transferred to the creditor, the Court of Chancery recognized that the mortgagor (debtor) still retained a right to redeem the property even after default by paying all that was owed. This is still the case today and is referred to as the **equity of redemption**. It has a value that can be the subject of further transactions by the mortgagor. This is the origin of the term "equity" in common use to describe the value of property after all debts and claims owing on it are deducted. It is common today for a mortgagor, needing more funds, to transfer this equity of redemption to another creditor (the second mortgagee) as security for a further loan. This gives that second mortgagee (in the event of default) the right to take the property, but only after paying all that is still owing to the first mortgagee. This places the second mortgagee in a much more dangerous position, which explains why the interest rates on second mortgages are much higher than on the first. Again

---

15. B. Ziff, *Principles of Property Law*, 3rd ed. (Toronto: Carswell, 2000), at 332.

the mortgagor retains a right to redeem the second mortgage and can use this to create a third mortgage, and so on, with each level assuming more risk—making third and fourth mortgages extremely rare.

For example, if your property was worth $200 000 and you borrowed $80 000 secured by a first mortgage against that property, your equity of redemption would be valued at $120 000. You could then borrow a further $50 000 from a second mortgagee by transferring that equity of redemption to him as security. In the event of a default, in order to get his $50 000 back that second mortgagee can't simply take the property. He only has the right to redeem the property by paying out the $80 000 owing on the first mortgage. Remember that the amount owing would also include unpaid interest and the costs associated with the process. Thus, the second mortgagee, in order to realize on his security in the event of a default, must be prepared to pay out the first mortgage, including interest and expenses, as well as take over the property.

Foreclosure

Foreclosure ends equity of redemption

To create balance, the mortgagee has a right to apply to the court to set a time limit within which that equity of redemption must be exercised. After that time, it will be too late and the right to redeem will be forever lost. This process takes place in two stages. After the default and pursuant to an application by the mortgagee, the court issues a preliminary order of **foreclosure**, setting a time limit (e.g., six months) within which time the mortgage must be redeemed by paying what is owed. After that redemption period expires without payment, the mortgagor returns to court and obtains a final order of foreclosure giving her an uncontestable right to both title and possession of the property.

Right to Sell

Other creditors can have property sold before final foreclosure

Mortgagor is responsible for shortfall

Other creditors, including a second mortgagee, will take steps to ensure that they don't lose out. They have the right to bring an application to the court (done at the same time as the initial application for foreclosure) to have the property sold. This is called an **order for judicial sale**, and an attempt is then made during the redemption period to sell the property before that period expires. Note that mortgagors faced with these proceedings often think that they have the full redemption period to reorganize their finances. But this order for judicial sale means that the property could be sold within weeks, leaving the mortgagor in bewilderment saying, "But I thought I had six months." If the property is sold for less than what is owed, the mortgagor will still be responsible to repay the deficit. In some jurisdictions, such as British Columbia, the first mortgagee is limited to the remedy of foreclosure, and if after obtaining title he sells the property for less than what was owed, he cannot claim a deficit—he has had his remedy. In Ontario, however, in the event of default the mortgagee will normally have the property sold under the power of sale in the mortgage contract, and in the event of a shortfall he can claim a deficiency, as illustrated in Case Summary 14.5. See the mortgage appendix on MyBusLawLab for a more detailed discussion of mortgages.

CASE SUMMARY 14.5

Mortgagor Must Pay Shortfall: *Meridian Credit Union Limited v. Hancock*[16]

The Hancocks had a mortgage with Meridian for two years before it fell into default in 2009. At that time the amount owing was $236 193.04. Meridian, relying on the power of sale in the mortgage agreement, listed it for sale and after nine days received an offer of $226 000, which they accepted. This offer was $1000 over the 2009 assessed value of the

16. 2009 CanLII 60093 (ON SC).

property. This action was brought by Meridian for an order requiring the Hancocks to pay a shortfall of $24 474. The Hancocks argued that they shouldn't have to pay the shortfall because Meridian failed to take reasonable steps to get a fair market price for the property. They claimed that leaving it on the market for only nine days and jumping at the first offer made this an improvident sale.

The Court disagreed. The Hancocks had separated and had previously listed the property for sale, dropping the price several times to eventually ask $255 000. They had received no offers. While nine days was short for a listing, given the economic environment of the day, accepting an offer that was over the appraised value was not improvident. The Hancocks were therefore liable for the shortfall, which was much more than the difference between the amount owing and the price obtained (the difference accounted for the unpaid interest and the costs associated with the process).

Note that in some jurisdictions, such as British Columbia, the first mortgagee could not conduct a sale in this way. Their only remedy would be foreclosure, and if there was a shortfall after a subsequent sale the first mortgagee would be out of luck. If there was another creditor involved, such as a second mortgagee or judgment creditor, and they obtained a court order to sell the property, then if there was a shortfall after the sale all would have a claim against the mortgagor for any shortfall, including the first mortgagee.

SMALL BUSINESS PERSPECTIVE

This case shows the process involved when a mortgage is defaulted on and also the responsibility of the debtor to pay any difference between what is still owing on the debt and what is obtained from the sale of the property. It also shows how careful a prudent mortgagee has to be to ensure she follows accepted procedures to get a good price when acting on a power of sale. The effect is the same in the western provinces where a second mortgagee conducts the sale pursuant to a court order. This area of law varies considerably from province to province, and the reader is encouraged to check the legislation in place in the applicable jurisdiction.

THE LANDLORD–TENANT RELATIONSHIP

LO ❹

Leasehold Estates

A leasehold estate lasts for a specific or determinable period of time, usually ending on a specified day or at the end of a specified period. It also may take the form of a **periodic tenancy**, where the specific period (usually a month) is automatically renewed. Unlike a licence, which does not convey an exclusive right to the property, the lease gives the tenant the right to use the property to the exclusion of all others for the period of time stated in the lease agreement. If Jones were to rent a hotel room for a month, this would normally be a licence since the hotelkeeper has the right to come into the room, make the beds, clean the room, do any repairs, and even move Jones to another location if it is deemed appropriate. But if Jones were to lease an apartment for a month he would have the exclusive use of it and the landlord could not enter without permission unless some arrangement to do so had been set out in the lease agreement or by statute (residential tenancies).

Tenant has the right to exclusive possession during the period of the lease

As with other business relationships, the general requirements of contract law apply to leasehold estates. Even though it is wise to put a lease in writing, one need not do so with a lease for three years or less. In most jurisdictions, however, leases over three years must be evidenced in writing to satisfy the *Statute of Frauds* or its equivalent.[17] The written evidence must specify the premises covered by the lease, the parties to it, the consideration or rent to be given by the tenant, the duration of the lease, and any other special provisions the parties may have agreed to. In the

Terms of the lease can modify obligations

---

17. *Statute of Frauds*, 1677 (29 Car. 2) c. 3, s. 4; see Ontario's *Statute of Frauds*, R.S.O. 1990, c. S.19, s. 3.

absence of written evidence, part performance, such as the occupation of the premises by the tenant, may satisfy this requirement.

Leases, like freehold estates, are interests that run with the land, and as explained above any subsequent owner or mortgagee taking the property after a default will take it subject to that lease, which must still be honoured. Many jurisdictions require long-term leases to be registered along with other claims affecting the title of the property.[18] Shorter-term leases, although not registered, are still enforceable by the tenant as against the new owner of the property.

As in other contracts, a landlord who contracts with an infant, a drunk, or a mentally incompetent person runs into all the problems associated with incapacity, as discussed in Chapter 7; the resulting contract may not be binding. Historically, frustration, as discussed in Chapter 9, did not apply to land.[19] Many jurisdictions have changed this with respect to residential tenancies so that if the property is destroyed or damaged, rendering it unusable, the contract will be discharged by frustration and the tenant's obligation to pay rent will cease. Only British Columbia has applied its *Frustrated Contracts Act* to commercial tenancies.[20]

Most jurisdictions have introduced special legislative provisions determining the rights and obligations of landlords and tenants in residential relationships. Commercial tenancy law has also been modified by statute to a lesser extent. This legislation varies from province to province, so refer to MyBusLawLab for local details. What follow are statements concerning tenancies in general.

Types of Tenancies

Property may be leased for a specific period of time, such as for "one year" or "ending September 5," or it may be a periodic tenancy with no set duration. When a lease has a set duration, it is called a "term lease," entitling the tenant to exclusive possession of the property for the specified period. Where the lease allows the tenant to *assign* the lease and she does so, all rights and claims in relationship to the property are given up to the new tenant. However, if the property is **sublet**, the tenant retains a reversionary interest, giving the tenant the right to retake possession at the expiration of the sublease. Usually, leases contain provisions allowing for such assignment or subletting with the permission of the landlord, "which shall not be unreasonably withheld." This gives the landlord some say in who takes possession of the property but does not allow unreasonable interference.

A periodic tenancy has no specific termination date; rather, it involves a specific lease period that is automatically renewed in the absence of notice to the contrary. The period involved can be weekly, monthly, or yearly, but the most common is the month-to-month tenancy. Without notice bringing the relationship to a close, a periodic tenancy will continue indefinitely. Notice to end the periodic tenancy must be given at least one clear period in advance (unless otherwise specified in the lease). Thus, in a month-to-month tenancy, notice must be given before the end of one month to take effect at the end of the next. If Jookie rents a store from Politichny in a month-to-month tenancy and pays his rent on the first of each month, the lease period ends at the end of the month. Notice to terminate must be given on or before the last day of the month to take effect at the end of the next month. The temptation is to give notice when the rent is paid for termination at the end of that month. In these circumstances that notice would not be effective. This requirement has caused considerable problems and has thus been modified by statute with respect to residential tenancies in many jurisdictions.

Registration and written requirements for leases

Leasehold interests run with the land

Statutes apply frustration to some tenancies

Property may be sublet

Periodic tenancy is usually month to month

Notice period is one clear rental period

---

18. See, for example, Alberta's *Land Titles Act, supra* note 6, s. 95.

19. *Paradine v. Jane* (1647), Aleyn 26 (K.B.).

20. *Commercial Tenancy Act*, R.S.B.C. 1996, c 57, s. 30. Note that Ontario, the Northwest Territories, and Nunavut also have commercial tenancy acts, but they do not have provisions included relating to the doctrine of frustration.

Rights and Obligations of the Parties

In common law, commercial and residential tenancies are treated in the same way, but all provinces have passed statutes modifying these rules. These changes apply primarily to residential tenancies; reference to the specific legislation in effect in your jurisdiction is advised. The following comments apply primarily to commercial tenancies.

Obligations may be modified by statute

It is important to remember that a lease is a contract, and it is common for the parties to include unique terms and modify normally included rights and obligations. Normally a lease will set out a description of the premises, the parties, the rent to be paid, and the term of the lease. Other terms that are often included in commercial leases relate to what use the property can be put to and who is responsible for the payment of utilities, taxes, repairs, and insurance. In special situations, such as services or retail stores in shopping malls, provisions may prohibit the operation of a similar business close to the tenant. In the shopping mall situation, rent is sometimes fixed as a percentage of sales. Long-term commercial leases often include an option for the review of the rent at set periods or at its renewal.

Lease sets out the rights of the parties

VACANT POSSESSION

The landowner has an obligation to ensure that the premises are vacant and ready for occupancy at the time the lease period is to start. A failure to deliver **vacant possession** is often caused by construction delays or an overholding prior tenant, and compensation is normally based on how much it costs the tenant to find other accommodation in the interim.

Landowner must provide vacant premises

QUIET ENJOYMENT

A landlord is obligated to give a tenant quiet enjoyment of the premises. This does not mean that the tenant has to be happy or like the premises, only that the landlord must ensure that nothing happens to interfere with the tenant's use of the property. Tenants have the right to be protected against interference by the landlord or those claiming under the landlord. Where Labuda leases office space in a new building to Telzerow, but the construction is not complete, causing noise and vibration that interferes with Telzerow's business, this would be a breach of her right to quiet enjoyment of the lease. Where Telzerow's office is on the tenth floor and the elevator is not yet installed, where the entranceway is blocked by construction, or where the central heating is not yet working in the winter, a breach of quiet enjoyment also occurs.

Landlord must not interfere with the tenant's use of the property

REPAIR OF PREMISES

The landlord has no general obligation to deliver premises that are clean or in good repair. The tenant takes the property the way it comes, and if he wants it in better condition the cost is the responsibility of the tenant. Only when the premises are in such disrepair that it amounts to a breach of quiet enjoyment can the landlord be held responsible. In the example above, Telzerow would have no complaint if the premises were not painted or the carpet was threadbare when she moved in, unless a provision to provide better facilities were in the lease. But if the structure of the building were in such poor repair that it was no longer capable of supporting a wall or a floor and a resulting cave-in would make the office unusable, this would be a breach of the covenant of quiet enjoyment. Usually the parties specify changes to these obligations in the lease agreement, but there are also many situations in which the courts will imply contractual obligations because of the circumstances. For example, when a tenant rents only part of a building the court will assume that the landlord has an obligation to provide heat, unless otherwise stated in the lease. But when the tenant leases the entire building, that obligation may be assumed to fall on the tenant.

There is no general obligation to repair

TERMINATION

A lease that ends on a specific date or one that is for a specified period of time ends when specified unless there is an agreement to extend it. But when a periodic

Proper notice must be given for periodic tenancy

tenancy is involved notice to terminate must be given.[21] If the tenant fails to leave after the lease has expired or after being given the appropriate notice, a **tenancy at sufferance** relationship is established. When this happens, the landlord is entitled to compensation; but if the normal rent payment is made and accepted, there is a danger of creating a periodic tenancy requiring more notice before the tenant can be ejected.

TENANTS' OBLIGATIONS

Tenant must pay rent

The tenant's primary obligation is to pay the rent when it is due. In fact, in one case a commercial landlord who accidentally charged a tenant lower rent than demanded by the lease was able to recover substantial back rent.[22] The obligation of paying the rent at the appropriate time is independent of any special obligations that the landlord may have agreed to in the lease contract, such as a duty to make repairs. As a result, when the landlord fails in her obligation to make repairs, the tenant cannot withhold rent until the repairs are made. In these circumstances, the tenant can ask the court for an order of **abatement** that will reduce the rent to be paid as compensation for the landlord's breach of the lease obligation.

Tenants are not responsible for normal wear and tear

The tenant has no obligation to repair normal wear and tear or even to make serious repairs when they occur unless caused by the tenant (waste). The landlord should be notified of any serious problems, but in common law the landlord has no obligation to make these repairs unless failure to do so would interfere with the quiet enjoyment of the tenancy. If Telzerow rents an office from Labuda and the rug on the floor wears out over the years, Telzerow would be under no obligation to replace it. But neither would Labuda, since the landlord is not required to provide premises of any standard of fitness for the tenant. It is common in the lease agreement for one of the parties to assume the responsibility for keeping the property in good repair.

When the premises are used in a manner not anticipated in the lease and undue wear and tear takes place, a tenant does have an obligation to make repairs, and the landlord may also be able to evict the tenant. If Telzerow rents premises from Labuda to be used as an office and instead it is used for manufacturing furniture, Labuda could demand payment for any excessive wear and tear, and require Telzerow to vacate the premises, no matter how long the lease had left to run.

CASE SUMMARY 14.6

Is This a Residential or Commercial Tenancy? *Rossmore Enterprises Ltd. v. Ingram*[23]

Gordon Ingram leased premises from Rossmore Enterprises Ltd. to use as a live-in studio. He lived and worked there with his partner for many years but periodically sublet part of the premises to others. The lease did not permit subletting, and when the landlord found out he served notice to terminate the lease. This was disputed, and both were surprised when the residential hearing officer determined that this was a commercial rather than a residential tenancy and declined jurisdiction.

Rossmore then served one-month notice demanding possession and terminating the lease. Ingram failed to leave, and Rossmore brought this application for an order for a writ of possession. Ingram in turn made an application requesting judicial review of

---

21. Landlords should err on the side of generosity in terminating commercial leases. Landlords may be required to show a legitimate business reason for terminating or not renewing a lease. See *Tannous (c.o.b. Tannous Produce) v. Ontario (Food Terminal Board)*, 2003 CanLII 31783 (ON SC).

22. See *Meadowvale Industrial Mall Ltd. v. Becquerel Laboratories Inc.*, [1999] O.J. No. 5199 (Sup. Ct. J.).

23. 2013 BCSC 894 (CanLII).

the decision of the dispute resolution officer that the premises were not covered by the *Residential Tenancy Act*.

Both applications were combined and the Court determined that the decision of the dispute resolution officer was correct: This was a commercial rather than a residential tenancy. The Court also determined that Ingram subletting to others had breached the lease. Since Ingram refused to leave, he was found to be a wrongfully overholding tenant and Rossmore's application for a writ of possession was granted, requiring Ingram to vacate the premises. Rossmore was also entitled to damages for the non-payment of rent for the overholding period amounting to $23 268.

SMALL BUSINESS PERSPECTIVE

This case shows the importance of the difference between a commercial and residential tenancy and the procedure to follow when a lease is breached and the tenant refuses to leave. Failure to follow the appropriate procedure is a common error made by landlords and their tenants.

A tenant's normal obligation to clean and repair the property is determined by the condition of the premises when occupied and the nature of the business carried on in the premises. A tenant is not responsible for normal wear and tear but will be responsible for consequential damage. For example, the tenant will not be responsible for a tile that blows off a roof, but will be responsible for any damage done to the premises when the landlord is not notified and the hole caused by its loss is left open to the weather.

When tenants attach something (a fixture) in such a way that it is clearly intended to become a permanent part of the building or will cause damage to remove it, they are not permitted to remove it when they leave. If Telzerow installed modern wiring and added a staircase to the second floor of her rented office, these fixtures would become permanent and she could not remove them when she leaves. Trade fixtures, on the other hand, such as shelving, display counters, machinery, decorative artwork, and signs, can be taken away by the tenant who attached them. But they must be removed when the tenant leaves; if they are left by the tenant, they become part of the real property and the tenant cannot come back later to recover them.

Tenant can remove her fixtures before the termination of a lease

Remedies

When the rent is not paid, the landlord can sue for the overdue rent. When some other breach occurs, the landlord may sue for damages and, in serious cases, may require the tenants to vacate the premises. This is called **forfeiture**, and when unpaid rent in a commercial lease is involved, no court order is needed and forfeiture may be accomplished by the landlord simply changing the locks. When the tenant is in breach of some other term of the lease, such as in the manner of use of the premises, the landlord must first give the tenant notice to end the breach and time to do so. When eviction is necessary, the services of law-enforcement officers (such as sheriffs or civil enforcement bailiffs) must be obtained, which can be a costly and time-consuming process. Residential tenancy statutes usually limit the availability of eviction as a remedy; landlords may be restricted to terminating a tenancy by giving a prescribed amount of notice or by seeking a court order. Refer to the legislation in effect in a particular jurisdiction for details.

Landlord can sue for compensation when lease is breached

When the landlord does retake the property for failure to pay rent prior to the end of the lease term, the tenant can pay the arrears and apply to the court to have the lease reinstated. This **relief against forfeiture** is an equitable principle. When the tenant abandons the premises, the landlord retains the right to payment of rent for the duration of the lease period. It should be noted that the landlord is normally not obligated to mitigate this loss, at least in commercial tenancies, by finding a new occupant for the premises until the expiration of the lease period.

Landlord can seize the tenant's property when lease is breached

The landlord of commercial premises also has the right to seize the tenant's property and hold it until the rent is paid or sell it to pay the rent owing. This is called **distress** or distraint. Written notice of distress is given the tenant setting out the amount owing. Should the tenant deny the landlord access, a court order can be obtained. In some jurisdictions where a tenant surreptitiously removes goods to avoid distress the court may award damages.[24] The landlord can either remove the tenant's property to a secure location or separate and mark the property subject to distress. That property is then appraised, and once the prescribed period (allowing the tenant to satisfy the indebtedness) expires, the property can be sold to satisfy the outstanding debt. Distraint often causes confusion, because the sale of property may result in the rent being paid and the continuation of the lease. The landlord cannot treat the lease as ended and also distrain the tenant's property. This power to seize the tenant's property is usually significantly limited or eliminated in residential tenancy legislation.

Monetary compensation is available for breach of lease

The landlord can also seek contractual remedies in the form of damages when the lease is breached. This usually amounts to the rent due but may also be compensation for the cost of repairs when damage is done to the premises.

Injunctions are also available in some limited circumstances

The courts will also issue an injunction when either the tenant or landlord carries on some activity that is inconsistent with the terms of the lease. Thus, when a tenant uses the premises for a purpose different from that contemplated in the lease, the landlord can get an injunction to prevent the misuse of the property.

Tenant has limited remedies

The remedies available to the tenant for the landlord's breach of the lease are more limited. The tenant is generally entitled either to sue the landlord for compensation for any injury suffered because of the breach or to seek an injunction. The tenant is not entitled to withhold rent to force the landlord's compliance with the lease obligations. But if the landlord's breach is significant enough to qualify as a breach of a major contractual term, the tenant may be entitled to treat the lease agreement as discharged and vacate the premises voluntarily, thus terminating the lease. For example, if the lease agreement requires the landlord to provide heat and water and those services are turned off, this would probably be a significant enough breach for the tenant to terminate the agreement. In such circumstances a more prudent course would be for the tenant to seek a court order declaring the lease ended or reducing the rent the tenant must pay because of the landlord's breach.

Occupier's liability is imposed on tenants

It is a principle of tort law under the *Occupier's Liability Act* that the occupier of property is responsible for any injury caused to people using the property. The occupier here is the tenant and usually not the landlord. However, the landlord may also be liable if the landlord is responsible for repairs under the lease and the tenant has notified the landlord but the repairs are not made. The landlord may also be responsible for injuries to the tenant or the tenant's employees when such repairs are not made and injury results.

CASE SUMMARY 14.7

A Lease Must Be Registered to Ensure the Rights of the Lessor: *Canada Mortgage and Housing Corporation v. Seetarram*[25]

Huang leased his residence to Jasmin Seetarram for a term of five years before returning to China. During that five-year period he defaulted on a mortgage from the Royal Bank secured against the property. The Canada Mortgage and Housing Corporation (CMHC)

---

24. See *1268227 Ontario Ltd. (c.o.b. Seamus O'Briens) v. 1178605 Ontario Inc.*, [2001] O.J. No. 3642, aff'd 2003 CanLII 44935 (ON CA).

25. 2008 CanLII 10379 (ON SC).

paid out the Royal Bank and took over the mortgage. They wanted to exercise their power of sale but were faced with a claim by Seetarram that he had a valid five-year lease and that any rights of the mortgage holder were subject to that lease. In this action, CMHC sought a declaration that it should not be subject to the lease. An application had already been brought before the Landlord and Tenant Board that determined that the lease was valid and the Court would not review that decision.

The question remaining was whether that lease affected CMHC's right to deal with the property. The *Land Titles Act* requires that a lease for over three years must be registered, and this five-year lease was not. As a result, CMHC was not deemed to have notice of the lease and its rights were not restricted by the lease. CMHC could sell the property, and that sale would not be subject to the unregistered lease.

SMALL BUSINESS PERSPECTIVE

As this case illustrates, it is important for both landlords and tenants to be aware of and to comply with the statutory provisions applying to their relationships.

 REDUCING RISK 14.3

Businesses typically require physical space to carry on their activities. Whether it is office space, a manufacturing plant, or a warehouse, the space is usually leased rather than purchased outright. It is vitally important that a sophisticated client understand the terms of the lease agreement. Legal advice should be sought to ensure that appropriate modifications are made to any standard form lease agreement before it is signed. Does the lease provide for the possibility that the facility needs of the business might change in the future?

A common failing for tenants is to commit themselves for an extensive period without the flexibility to change as the business grows or declines. When entering into these commercial leases, legal advice should be sought to ensure that provisions are added or modified, providing for as much flexibility as possible.

Residential Tenancies

Most jurisdictions have introduced statutes that significantly modify the common law where the tenancy involves residential premises. Like consumer protection legislation, residential tenancy statutes alter the rights and obligations of the parties. Areas that are typically changed with residential tenancy statutes include the following:

- A requirement that the parties use a standard form lease specified in legislation with the tenant being given a copy within a limited time

- The landlord is also made responsible for any repairs other than normal wear and tear, while the tenants are responsible to maintain minimal standards of cleanliness and pay for any damage they create

Residential tenancy rules have been modified by statute

- The period of notice required when a landlord terminates a tenant or increases the rent has been extended in residential tenancies, and any security deposit taken is strictly controlled

- How often a rent increase can be imposed is usually restricted, and in some cases the amount of that increase is restricted as well

- The landlord is required to not eliminate any services in place such as laundry facilities, storage, and parking during the tenancy

- If when the tenant leaves there is unpaid rent or damage, the landlord has no right of distress in a residential tenancy.

The specific provisions in place in each jurisdiction vary considerably, and reference should be made to MyBusLawLab for further details.

LO ❺ ❻ PERSONAL PROPERTY

Chattels

Chattels are movable things

Chattels are movables, such as electronic devices, clothes, animals, and motor vehicles. Even construction cranes, boats, and locomotives are chattels. Real property, on the other hand, is land and things fixed or attached to the land, like a building. A chattel can become part of the real property when it is attached to the land. "The test is whether the purpose of the attachment was (a) to enhance the land (which leads to the conclusion that a fixture exists); or (b) for the better use of the chattel as a chattel."[26]

Things fixed to the land become real property

This transformation from chattel to fixture can lead to conflict with respect to who has first claim to it. Assume Bowen buys and installs a hot water heater in his cottage. On installation, the item that was a chattel becomes a fixture. If Bowen later loses the cottage because he defaults on his mortgage payments, the mortgagee may have a claim to the hot water tank. If Bowen bought the water tank on credit, then two creditors may have conflicting claims, namely the mortgagee and the party that provided financing for the water tank. The *Personal Property Security Act*[27] discussed in Chapter 15 aims to resolve such competing claims.

Trade fixtures can be removed by the tenant

The owner of the land is free to remove a chattel that has become a fixture (severance) just as she was able to fix the chattel to the land in the first place. Difficulty arises when third parties, such as creditors or tenants, become involved and claim the property. Generally, when a chattel has been affixed to real property it becomes part of that real property and cannot be removed. However, if a tenant of a commercial property attaches fixtures to enhance trade or carry on a business, he has the right to remove those trade fixtures when leaving. In residential or commercial tenancies, non-trade fixtures attached for the comfort, convenience, or taste of the tenant, such as mirrors, paintings, or entertainment equipment, can also be removed. Of course, when those fixtures have been incorporated into the property in such a way that they clearly are intended to stay or where their removal will cause damage, they must stay. This would be the case with Bowen's hot water tank described above.

In any event, these fixtures can be removed only during the term of the tenancy. When the tenant moves out at the end of the tenancy and takes the mirrors, light fixtures, rugs, and display cases that had been installed by the tenant, the landlord has no complaint unless the property is damaged. But if the tenant comes back for them after the landlord has retaken possession, it is too late. Those fixtures have become part of the property of the landowner. Of course, any provisions in the lease to the contrary override these general provisions.

Finders Keepers

A finder gets good title against all but the original owner

When a person finds a watch or a ring in a park, she has the right to that item against everyone except a prior owner. If that finder were to hand it to the police or the lost-and-found centre and the rightful owner could not be found, that finder would be entitled to it. Only the rightful owner or someone having a proprietary interest in it, such as a secured creditor, could demand it from the finder. In *Thomas v. Canada (Attorney General)*,[28] for example, the plaintiff inadvertently opened mail delivered to his address by mistake and discovered $18 000 inside. The police were unable to discover the true owner. Canada Post claimed ownership, arguing that the money remained its property as undeliverable mail. Canada Post's claim for ownership failed, thus the attorney general was ordered to return the money to the plaintiff.

---

26. Ziff, *Principles of Property Law*, *supra* note 14, at 106.

27. R.S.O. 1990, c. P.10; refer to MyBusLawLab for citations to similar legislation in other provinces.

28. 2006 ABQB 730 (CanLII), [2006] 12 WWR 742.

If the goods are found on private property, however, the owner of that property normally has a right to the item. If the finder is an employee of the occupier or owner of that property, the employer gets the item subject to the claim by the original owner. Only if the item is found on a public portion of that property, such as the public part of a restaurant, store, or shopping mall, will the finder (other than an employee) have first claim. In *Trachuk v. Olinek*,[29] four oilfield workers dug up a bundle containing $75 000 when working on a well site. The farmer who had a grazing lease on the land claimed the money. The Court determined that the farmer was not in actual possession of the site, since a surface lease had been given to the oil company. The finders thus had a better claim, and the money was directed to them. Here the "finders" were eventually the "keepers."

CASE SUMMARY 14.8

Where the Finder Was Not the Keeper: *Weitzner v. Herman*[30]

Mrs. Weitzner's husband died suddenly in a fire. She sold their home of 38 years to the Hermans, who had the house demolished. During demolition, the contractor found a fire extinguisher hidden in the basement crawl space containing $130 000. Mr. Weitzner had operated a scrap business from the home, often taking cash but making no deposits in the bank. The Court found that he had put the money there. His sudden death prevented him from telling anyone about the hidden funds. The contractor had no claim to the money, since he was working for the Hermans and they had not given up any claim they had to the demolition materials. The Hermans were entitled to the funds against all except the original owner. As his heir, Mrs. Weitzner was entitled to all of the $130 000. "Finders keepers" is not always the case.

DISCUSSION QUESTIONS

Evidently "losers" are not always weepers. How about finders? When are they entitled to be keepers?

Note that whether it is the owner of the property where the goods are found or the finder who eventually gets the goods, there is an obligation owed to the owner to exercise care in looking after them. This obligation is based on the law of bailment.

Bailment

A **bailment** exists when one person takes temporary possession of personal property owned by another. The owner giving up possession is called the **bailor** and the person acquiring possession is the **bailee**. Although chattels are usually involved, intangibles such as bonds, share certificates, or negotiable instruments can also be the subjects of a bailment. "Bailments require a transfer of possession and a voluntary acceptance of the common law duty of safekeeping, while licenses amount to no more than a grant of permission to the user of the chattel to leave it upon the licensor's land on the understanding that neither possession shall be transferred, nor responsibility for guarding the chattel accepted."[31] With bailment, the possession is only temporary, with the chattel to be returned at the end of the bailment period. Examples of bailment include leasing and rentals of vehicles and equipment; goods left for repair, storage, or transport; and simple borrowing of goods.

Bailment is created by giving goods to a bailee

---

29. 1995 CanLII 9251 (AB QB).
30. [2000] O.J. No. 906 (S.C.J.).
31. N.E. Palmer, *Bailment*, 2nd ed. (London: Law Book Co. Ltd., 1991), at 382.

Determining whether the goods have been *delivered* (where possession is temporarily transferred to and accepted by the bailee) is not as easy as it may seem. When a car is left in a parking lot and the keys are given to the attendant, a bailment has taken place because control and possession have been given to the car lot. But when a person drives onto a lot, parks the car, and takes the keys with him there is no bailment. This is just a licence to use the parking space, and the control and possession of the car stay with the driver. During a bailment, the title to the goods remains with the bailor; only the possession goes to the bailee. Normally, a bailee cannot give the goods to someone else (a sub-bailment), unless there is permission to do so or where it is the custom of the industry, as might be the case where an automobile needing repairs is left with one mechanic who then transfers it to other specialists as needed.

With fungibles, the same goods need not be returned

When **fungibles**, such as timber, oil, and wheat, are placed in the care of a bailee, they can become indistinguishable from similar items being stored for others. In fact, the exact goods need not be returned, only goods of a similar quality and quantity. This situation is still a bailment and is treated under bailment law.

Bailee has a duty to care for the goods

The primary concern of bailment law is the liability of bailees for damage done to goods in their care. Bailees are responsible for any wilful, negligent, or fraudulent acts of themselves or their employees that cause injury or damage to the goods. They may also be responsible for the damage or loss caused by third parties. Today the degree of care required of a bailee of goods has changed in most jurisdictions and is now based on ordinary negligence or on the terms in the contract where one is present; see Case Summary 14.9.

CASE SUMMARY 14.9

Duty Owed to Bailee: *Gaudreau v. Belter*[32]

Gaudreau and Belter were golfing companions. When Gaudreau went on a vacation with his family, Belter agreed to take care of his clubs for him while he was gone. He stored them in his garage, which was usually kept locked, but on this occasion he left it open and the clubs were stolen. This is clearly a case of gratuitous bailment for the benefit of the bailor, and historically the bailor would only be liable if gross negligence could be shown. The judge in this case, however, observed that a change in the law had developed and that today the standard to apply in these cases was what was "reasonable in the circumstances." In this case, it was not reasonable to leave the garage door open knowing that there were valuable golf clubs stored therein, so Belter was liable for the loss of the clubs.

In another Alberta case, *Guarantee Company of North America v. Century Services Inc.*,[33] Guarantee left goods on consignment with Century Services Inc. to be sold at auction. Unfortunately, a thief broke into the secured premises and stole the goods. This is clearly a bailment for reward situation, but the Court applied exactly the same test as that applied in the *Gaudreau* case—that the bailee must take reasonable care of the goods in the circumstances. The company had changed the locks and had an eight-foot chain link fence surrounding the premises. However, the theft took place after entry had been gained by cutting the padlock securing the gate. The Court determined that the degree of care exercised by Century in securing the premises had been reasonable and that they were not responsible for the loss of the goods.

These two cases illustrate the trend today toward imposing a single standard on bailment, thus blurring the different categories of bailment. Because the circumstances are taken into consideration it is still possible to consider who benefits, but it is clear that it will be the reasonableness of the care exercised that will be the predominant consideration. Note that in some jurisdictions the historical approach is still in place.

[32.] 2001 ABQB 101 (CanLII).

[33.] 2004 ABQB 446 (CanLII).

SMALL BUSINESS PERSPECTIVE

These cases illustrate how the historical differences between types of bailment are being blurred at least with respect to the duty owed. Still they show how careful we have to be when caring for the goods of others.

BAILMENT FOR VALUE

Bailments are either gratuitous or for value (or reward). **Bailment for value** involves a mutual benefit or consideration flowing between the parties. Usually the relationship is commercial, and the bailor pays the bailee to repair, store, or transport the goods. But a bailment for value can also arise where a friend stores something, such as a piano, for another in exchange for the right to use it. The standard of care required in such circumstances is simply the ordinary standard for negligence—that is, the amount of care that would be expected from a prudent person looking after such goods in similar circumstances.[34]

The amount of care that should be exercised will vary with both the value of the goods and their nature. More care would be expected where delicate or valuable items were involved, such as china or a rare violin, but where heavy-duty machines were being stored, the standard of care would be much lower.

Of course, if the relationship is commercial the contract will prevail, but where the contract fails to specify liability the bailee will be required to exercise the care that would be expected from a reasonable person in the circumstances. Circumstances to be considered may include the value and delicacy of the goods and industry custom and practice.

Bailment for value—both parties receive benefit

Duty may be determined by contract or common practice

Exemption Clauses

Contracts of bailment often contain exculpatory or exemption clauses, which limit the liability of the bailee. An example of such a clause is, "Goods left on the premises are left entirely at the risk of the owner. The proprietor assumes no responsibility for any loss, whether caused by damage, loss, or theft of those goods." The parties are free to include such clauses, but courts interpret them narrowly, since they favour one side. To be enforceable, such clauses must be clear and brought to the attention of the customer at the time she enters into the contract. Any exemption clauses added to a contract after it is formed must be supported by new consideration or they will not be enforceable.

Exculpatory clauses may limit liability

COMMON CARRIERS

A particularly onerous standard of care is imposed on innkeepers and "common carriers" (trucking and bus companies, railroads, airlines, and even pipelines). Common carriers must be distinguished from private companies or individuals that transport for a particular bailor. These private carriers are merely bailees, as described above. A common carrier offers general transport services to the public and undertakes the standard of an insurer. This means that if the goods are damaged or destroyed while in its care, the carrier is liable even when the damage was not caused by its negligence. But even a common carrier will not be liable when the damage was beyond its control, as when the goods deteriorate because of some inherent problem with them or because the packaging provided by the shipper is inadequate. If an animal dies in transit because of a previously contracted disease or goods are destroyed by spontaneous combustion, there is no liability. A common carrier is also not liable where the damage is caused by an act of war or "act of nature," such as a flood or an earthquake. Most common carriers limit their liability by contract and include a term like "Not responsible for lost or stolen goods or damage over $500." Again, to be valid and binding on both parties such a provision must be clearly brought to the attention of the shipper at the time the contract is entered into. Common carriers are usually controlled by statutory provisions regulating their industry.

Common carrier has duty of insurer

---

[34] *Luider v. Nguyen*, [1994] A.J. No. 494 (Prov.Ct.).

REDUCING RISK 14.4

The law of bailment involves all those situations where one person's property is left in the care of another. From a business point of view, this affects not only service industries, such as restaurants and hotels, but also repairers, mechanics, and transporters of goods. A duty of care is owed to the owner of these goods. It is thus wise for a sophisticated client to both *insure* against loss and *limit liability* through the use of an exculpatory clause included in the service contract and specifically brought to the attention of the bailor. Furthermore, notices that risk remains with the bailor ("property left at own risk") should be posted where clearly visible on the bailee's premises.

INNKEEPERS' LIABILITY

Innkeeper has the duty of an insurer

In common law, innkeepers are also treated like insurers and are responsible for lost or stolen goods of a guest, unless it can be shown that they were lost because of some "act of nature" or negligence on the part of the guest. To succeed, the guest must show that the establishment qualifies as an inn, offering both food and temporary lodging (transient-type accommodation).

Liability may be reduced by statute

Most jurisdictions have significantly reduced the innkeepers' liability by statute so that they are liable only when it can be proven that they or their employees were at fault. To obtain such protection most provinces require a notice to be posted in the guest's room and other designated areas stating the extent of the innkeeper's liability and any options available to the guest.

GRATUITOUS BAILMENT

Gratuitous bailment when only one side receives benefit

Liability today is based on the reasonable person test

A gratuitous bailment occurs when only one side receives a benefit. Historically, when the bailee received the benefit (as when a friend borrows your car), the standard of care imposed was high and liability would be imposed even when the bailee had been only slightly careless. On the other hand, when it was the bailor who received the benefit (as when the bailee stored a bicycle as a favour for a friend), the bailee would be liable only if there had been gross negligence. If the bailment was of mutual benefit, ordinary diligence applied. As mentioned, the courts in most jurisdictions are now imposing the ordinary tests for negligence for all bailments, asking simply whether the bailee was careful enough considering all the circumstances, including who benefits and the value of the item. Thus, in *Gaudreau v. Belter*, discussed in Case Summary 14.9, where Belter had voluntarily stored golf clubs for Gaudreau, the ordinary test of negligence was applied (instead of requiring gross negligence) and he was liable for the loss.

In a bailment action, unlike a normal negligence action, the onus of proof shifts to the bailee. Thus, once the bailment has been established and damage to the goods has been shown, a presumption of negligence arises, which the bailee must rebut to avoid liability. For example, in *Evans v. Northsite Security Services Ltd.*,[35] the plaintiff placed his cellphone and camera in a bowl in the screening area at airport security as instructed and the items went missing. The presumption of negligence arose, and since the defendant failed to explain how the items went missing, judgment was given to the plaintiff.

INVOLUNTARY BAILMENT

Involuntary bailment—duty to keep goods safe and return them

When someone puts away a coat left behind in a restaurant or at a friend's house, or picks up a watch found on the sidewalk, an involuntary bailment has been created. Exercising control by putting away the coat or picking up the watch creates the bailment. You have no obligation until you pick up the item. As soon as you exercise that control, the obligations of a gratuitous bailee for the benefit of the bailor arise—now there is a duty to take care of those goods. The responsibility as bailee is to keep the coat safe and return it to the bailor. Generally speaking, if the goods are returned

---

35. [2002] N.W.T.J. No. 95 (Terr. Ct.).

to the wrong person or discarded, the bailee is responsible. Although strict liability is not applied, the bailee is liable if his actions were negligent in the circumstances.

ADDITIONAL RIGHTS AND OBLIGATIONS

The terms set out in a contract govern a bailment for value. Such provisions as the terms of payment, the requirement of insurance, and any exculpatory clauses are binding if they have been properly brought to the attention of the parties. An unpaid bailee has a common law right to a lien if she has repaired or otherwise worked on the goods, but there is no corresponding common law lien where the goods are just transported or stored, as with a warehouse. Today, statutes give common carriers, repairpeople, storage facilities, and other bailees for value the right to retain the goods until payment is arranged. This statutory lien includes a right to resell the items after giving the bailor appropriate notice and an opportunity to reclaim the goods. Refer to MyBusLawLab for further details about the legislation in effect in your jurisdiction. When it is the bailor who has not been paid (as when rent for tools used is unpaid), he can reclaim the goods and seek normal contractual remedies. Where no price has been agreed upon, the bailor is entitled to recover a reasonable payment on the basis of the principle of *quantum meruit* (meaning "as much as is deserved").

Contract terms prevail except where modified by statute

PROTECTION OF THE ENVIRONMENT

LO ❼ ❽ ❾

A growing area of concern closely associated with the law of property relates to natural resources development and protection of the environment. In addition to the common law applicable in this area, there is considerable government intervention in the form of legislation and government regulatory bodies. This is one area where all levels of government—federal, territorial, provincial, and municipal—have overlapping authority. Business activity has historically ignored the impact on the environment. Forests are cleared; fish stocks are depleted; mineral, oil, and gas reserves are exhausted; and great scars are left on the earth in the process of extracting valuable natural resources. Species of animal life are decimated because they are either directly consumed or their environment is destroyed around them. The byproducts of all of this, in the form of waste materials, are discharged into the atmosphere, into the seas, and onto the lands, further degrading the environment. Industries such as mining, oil development, fishing, forestry, farming, construction, transportation, and manufacturing have all greatly contributed to Canada's environmental problems.

It has been only in the last few decades that our legislators have considered it necessary to create statutes to introduce some balance into the system. Statutes and enforcement bodies have imposed stringent rules imposing difficult, sometimes impossible, burdens on industries that harvest natural resources or pollute the land, air, and water.

Common law and statutes are used to protect the environment

CASE SUMMARY 14.10

Fines and Jail Terms for Environmental Violations:
Ontario (Environment) v. Aqua-tech Blue et al.[36]; *R. v. Whitley*[37]

Aqua-Tech Blue Inc. operated a liquid industrial and hazardous waste site. The Ontario Ministry of the Environment laid 125 charges under the *Ontario Water Resources Act* and the *Environmental Protection Act* against Aqua-Tech, two numbered corporations, and four individuals. The charges were related to illegal handling, storage, and disposal of

---

36. Ontario Ministry of the Environment, News Release, June 9 and August 4, 2000.

37. [2000] O.J. No. 5799 (Ont. C.J.).

waste, as well as to the furnishing of false information to government officials. The charges were laid after oil was found in sewers near the site.

The operating manager of Aqua-Tech pleaded guilty to four offences relating to illegal hazardous waste discharges into the Don River. He was sentenced to 90 days in jail. At trial, the president of the corporation was convicted on 12 counts and received a six-month jail term and fines totalling $193 000. The plant manager was also convicted on 12 counts and sent to jail for six months; his fine was $40 000. A director was convicted on 13 counts and received a four-month jail sentence and fines totalling $100 000. Aqua-Tech was convicted on 17 counts and fined a total of $720 000. One of the other corporations was convicted on one count and fined $50 000.

SMALL BUSINESS PERSPECTIVE

This case shows an increased willingness of various levels of government to punish environmental regulations violators. Businesspeople should keep this growing willingness on the part of all levels of government to punish even minor violators of environmental protection regulations in mind.

Common Law

Riparian right protect water quality

The common law has always had some provisions that relate to the preservation of the environment. These generally take the form of individual rights associated with a person's right to property. **Riparian rights** give people living near rivers and streams the right to have the water come to them in undiminished quantity and quality, subject to limited domestic usage such as washing, drinking, and normal sewage disposal. These rights are, however, fragile. The government commonly overrides them by issuing permits allowing for the withdrawal of large quantities of water for irrigation or other uses, or for the discharge of waste into those rivers and streams.

CASE SUMMARY 14.11

Interference with Riparian Rights: *Neuman v. Parkland County*[38]

Neuman resided on acreage with a creek running though it from which she drew water for domestic purposes and to fill holding ponds constructed on her property. Parkland County, in an effort to control flooding in other areas, capped certain culverts, redirecting water from that creek, which had the effect of diminishing the flow of water in the creek and thus interfering with her domestic needs. She sued the county, claiming they had interfered with her riparian rights. The judge carefully examined the legislation in place to determine whether those rights had been overridden by the statutes or whether the right to sue had been statute barred. He found that in her particular case the riparian rights remained. The judge found that the interference with her riparian rights amounted to a private nuisance. He also held that the complete capping of the culverts that was the ultimate cause of the reduction in flow had been done without consultation and against expert advice and was therefore negligent. The plaintiff was awarded over $5000 in damages.

SMALL BUSINESS PERSPECTIVE

The case illustrates the nature of riparian rights but also shows that those rights are commonly modified or eliminated by legislation and government interference. All landowners on water courses should be aware of these rights, but also keep in mind that they are often modified by statute. Neuman was fortunate to escape the effects of the statutes in place in Alberta overriding these riparian rights.

[38.] 2004 ABPC 58 (CanLII).

Tort law has also been used, with some significant limitations, to control environmental damage. When a person's use of her property interferes with her neighbour's use of his property (through the escape of noise, fumes, or other substances), the tort of "private nuisance" gives that neighbour the right to sue for compensation and to put a stop to the offending conduct.

The torts of negligence and trespass can also be used to enforce a person's right not to be interfered with in this way by others. The problem is that all of these common law remedies require personal involvement. An individual must bear the costs of litigation and, as a prerequisite, must show that she personally suffered damage from the offending conduct. Some modern statutes give individuals the right to sue in tort under the statute and receive private compensation for personal loss, but this still requires the personal involvement and commitment of that individual in the litigation process. One of the main advantages of the modern approach of statutory control and regulation is that a government agency is specifically charged to enforce the legislative framework. Such agencies can use various methods to ensure compliance, before applying sanctions and penalties. These methods include education, cooperation, and negotiation.

The Federal Government

Forests, minerals, air, and water are all local matters and under the jurisdiction of provincial governments. But when activities involving such resources become interprovincial or international in scope, or when they take place on federal lands or in coastal waters, the federal government then has jurisdiction. It also has the power to enact environmental protection laws under its criminal law power and also to exercise a considerable amount of indirect control by requiring that provincial environmental projects satisfy federal standards to qualify for federal funding.

The *Canadian Environmental Protection Act, 1999*[39] (*CEPA*) is the principal federal statute dealing with the environment. This is a comprehensive statute meant to prevent pollution. It also provides for research and development, investigation and measurement of pollution levels, the monitoring of industry, and the investigation and punishment of offences. It has become a model for other levels of government to follow.

Under the Act the federal government is empowered to negotiate with provincial governments or Aboriginal peoples. Where there are provincial equivalent provisions in place the federal provisions of the Act do not apply. The Act also mandates the federal government to provide for appropriate research and monitoring processes and to establish appropriate information, objectives, guidelines, and codes of practice. Registries of documents are kept, and there is provision for the protection of "whistleblowers" who provide information with respect to environmental offences. An important provision allows individuals to make complaints about offences and, if dissatisfied, to apply to a court for an order to prevent an environmental offence and receive compensation for individual damage. Any release of pollutants into the environment must be reported, and pollution prevention plans can be required of businesses as well as a list of toxic substances used, created, and regulated.

In addition, *CEPA* contains provisions relating to nutrients; the disposal of substances at sea; the production, importation, and selling of fuels; vehicle emissions; engines and equipment; international air and water pollution; and the movement of hazardous waste and recyclable material. The Act also contains provisions dealing with environmental emergencies, such as accidental discharge of pollutants.

The Act contains important enforcement provisions, including empowering enforcement officers to enter and inspect premises and, with a court order, to seize evidence and even make arrests in certain circumstances. The officers also have the power to issue an Environmental Protection Compliance Order with respect to any contravention to require compliance with the statute. Significant fines and other

Tort of nuisance protects a person from their neighbour's use of property

Individual must pursue a tort claim

CEPA mandates environmental protection

Enforcement officer can issue a compliance order

Due diligence is an effective defence

---

[39] S.C. 1999, c. 33.

penalties can be imposed for offences committed, including supplying false or misleading information. The nature of the penalties that can be imposed is quite broad, even allowing for a fine equal to the benefit received by committing the offence. The offender can also be ordered to take remedial or preventative action or post a bond to ensure compliance. Note that the defence of "due diligence" is available to most offences listed in the Act. Many other federal government regulations, including those enacted under other statutes, are enforceable through the *CEPA* provisions and agencies.

CASE SUMMARY 14.12

Criminal Prosecution under the *Canadian Environmental Protection Act*: *R. v. Canadian Tire Corp. Ltd.*[40]

Canadian Tire imported bar fridges containing Freon from China. In order to prevent damage to the ozone layer of the atmosphere, new regulations were introduced in Canada prohibiting the importation of any product containing Freon after January 1, 1999. Canadian Tire continued to import the fridges, and when an investigator determined the continued import of the offending product they were charged under the *Canadian Environmental Protection Act*. The company introduced evidence showing that they were a good corporate citizen and had good environmental policies and practices in place, but the facts indicated that even after they were informed about the violation further fridges were imported. Because of this the defence of due diligence failed. At the appeal level the judge said, "The Corporation was found guilty because it was clearly negligent and had taken no meaningful steps to comply with the relevant regulatory law." Instead they had relied on the supplier to comply with the regulations, and that was not good enough. The original conviction and fine of $25 000 was upheld on appeal.

SMALL BUSINESS PERSPECTIVE

The case not only shows the enforcement power under the *Canadian Environmental Protection Act*, but also indicates what is required for the defence of "due diligence." It also shows how easy it is for businesspeople to run afoul of those regulations.

It is important to emphasize that the Act permits the parties to make arrangements and negotiate solutions that bring them into compliance with the legislation, thus avoiding prosecution and punishment. This non-litigious approach is becoming an effective method of obtaining compliance. As mentioned, due diligence is an effective defence, and when a business takes reasonable steps to avoid committing an offence under the Act, such as establishing a compliance audit and training programs for employees, not only will the elements necessary to establish due diligence be established but the possibility of committing such an offence through carelessness will be significantly reduced.

Canadian Environmental Assessment Act requires project proposals for certain activities

An important aspect of the federal legislation is the requirement of an environmental review process on projects and activities that might affect the environment. This is mandated in the *Canadian Environmental Assessment Act*.[41] This Act made significant changes to the prior environmental review process, reducing the number of projects subject to review and streamlining the process. Now the *Regulations Designating Physical Activities*[42] sets out a detailed list of the kinds of activities that are caught and require the submission of a project proposal. Further, the minister can identify additional projects that must submit a project proposal. The type of information that must be included in the project proposal includes which category in

Regulations Designating Physical Activities lists activities, as designated by the minister, that require a project proposal to be filed

---

40. 2004 CanLII 4462 (ON SC).

41. S.C. 2012, c. 19, s. 52.

42. SOR/2012-147.

the *Regulations Designating Physical Activities* the project falls under, where it is to be located, the nature of the work to be undertaken, any infrastructure buildings and construction to take place, the waste to be generated and how it will be managed, and any other impact that might be made on the environment.

On the basis of that submission a decision will be made whether the project will be subject to environmental review. If an environmental assessment is required there are two different types of review that can take place: a standard environmental review or a simple assessment before a review panel. Note that if there is an equivalent provincial assessment process in place the federal process need not take place. Once the environmental assessment has taken place a report is prepared, indicating any significant adverse effects, and a decision is made on the basis of that report. Where there are significant adverse effects indicated, the report is then submitted to the federal cabinet, which will then decide if the project should go ahead.

Project proposal is reviewed to determine if further steps are necessary

The report made by those proposing the project must meet specified requirements, depending on the size and complexity of the project and its potential impact on the environment. The report will normally consist of a justification for the project, an assessment of its potential impact on the environment, a plan for minimizing that impact, and an indication of any potential alternatives. The simplest level is referred to as a screening, but a more comprehensive study may be required depending on the nature and size of the project. The report is then filed with the appropriate government agency, which then studies it and, in appropriate cases, arranges for public input. The supervising body may negotiate changes and then, if appropriate, gives permission for the activity to go ahead.

Other important federal legislation dealing with the environment includes the *Transportation of Dangerous Goods Act, 1992,*[43] which controls the transporting of dangerous goods between provinces or internationally, and the *Fisheries Act,*[44] which attempts to protect fish habitat. It prohibits the discharge of any "deleterious" substance into waterways, lakes, and oceans and does not allow any activity (with specified exceptions) that will harm fish or fish habitat. Some other important federal legislation in this area includes the *Canada Shipping Act,*[45] the *Arctic Waters Pollution Prevention Act,*[46] the *Navigation Protection Act,*[47] the *Nuclear Fuel Waste Act,*[48] the *Hazardous Products Act,*[49] the *Canada Wildlife Act,*[50] and the *Species at Risk Act.*[51]

Other federal statutes dealing with the environment

Provincial Legislation

All of the provinces have some form of legislation dealing with environmental issues within provincial jurisdiction. This legislation varies from province to province. Like the federal government, each of the provinces has one general environmental statute that is supplemented by issue-specific legislation. Examples of general environmental statutes include British Columbia's *Environment Management Act,*[52] Alberta's *Environmental Protection and Enhancement Act,*[53] Ontario's *Environment Protection Act,*[54] and Nova Scotia's *Environment Act.*[55] Often, statutory changes will follow

Provincial legislation also provides important environmental protection tools

---

43. S.C. 1992, c. 34.

44. R.S.C. 1985, c. F-14.

45. S.C. 2001, c. 26.

46. R.S.C. 1985, c. A-12.

47. R.S.C. 1985, c. N-22.

48. S.C. 2002, c. 23.

49. R.S.C. 1985, c. H-3.

50. R.S.C. 1985, c. W-9.

51. S.C. 2002, c. 29

52. S.B.C. 2003, c. 53.

53. R.S.A. 2000, c. E-12.

54. R.S.O. 1990, c. E-19.

55. S.N.S. 1994-95, c. 1.

Municipal bylaws can also have environmental protection aspects

serious environmental tragedy. For example, after hundreds of people became sick and several people died after drinking contaminated water in Walkerton, Ontario, in spring 2000, a public inquiry was held and the government, following its recommendations, passed the *Ontario Safe Drinking Water Act 2002*.[56]

While the federal and provincial governments are the prime players in the environmental field, the municipalities and other local governments can also have a significant impact as they exercise their licensing and permit powers with respect to specific projects. They also have important powers in enforcing local health and sanitary standards.

CASE SUMMARY 14.13

The Polluter Does Not Always Pay: *Kawartha Lakes (City) v. Ontario (Environment)*[57]

Fuel oil was spilled during a delivery to the private residence of the Gendron family. The oil escaped from their property across a road allowance and into a lake. The Ministry of the Environment (Ontario) ordered the Gendrons to clean up the pollution, but their insurance money ran out before they were able to clean up the city property. The Ministry then ordered the city to remediate the problem. The city appealed to the Environmental Review Tribunal, claiming they were innocent of any wrongdoing and should not have to pay for the clean up. The tribunal affirmed the order, and the city appealed to the Divisional Court and then to the Ontario Court of Appeal. All found that there was no requirement of fault in the act and that the city was responsible for the cleanup even though they were completely innocent of any wrongdoing.

In another Ontario case *Baker v. Director (Minister of Environment)*,[58] Northstar Aerospace Canada was a large operation that had several companies. However, Northstar ran into financial troubles, and in the process of reorganizing abandoned some remedial operations they were involved in on one of their properties. The Ministry of the Environment took over cleanup of the contaminated site but looked for someone else to pay. The contamination had occurred under a previous owner, and Northstar was innocent and had no knowledge of the contamination when they bought the property. Northstar and its parent company were unable to pay because of insolvency, so the Ministry, applying section 18 of the *Environmental Protection Act* (Ontario), ordered the former directors to personally assume the costs of the cleanup. Under the Act the directors face unlimited liability for the costs of any cleanup. Their innocence was no defence, nor was the defence of due diligence available under the Act. They appealed to the Environmental Review Tribunal, but in the meantime they had to pay and, facing costs upwards of $100 000 per month in a claim that could take years to resolve, they were forced to settle for a lump sum payment of $4.5 million.[59]

SMALL BUSINESS PERSPECTIVE

These two cases illustrate the principle in place in many jurisdictions that it is not always the polluters who pay. In fact, anyone who can be shown to have an interest can often be required to pay for remediation of a site even though they are completely innocent of any wrongdoing.

---

56. S.O. 2002, c. 32.

57. 2013 ONCA 310 (CanLII).

58. Ontario Environmental Review Tribunal (ERT) case number 12-158.

59. See Dianne Saxe Meredith James, "Where Innocence Is No Defence," *Lawyers Weekly*, January 24, 2014, 15.

REDUCING RISK 14.5

The environment is an important area where the interests of business and government often collide. As environmental regulations and requirements expand, the costs imposed on businesses become oppressive. It is imperative that those embarking on any project that can have an impact on land or the environment make a careful assessment of these costs and risks before embarking on the project. Even the simple construction of an apartment complex will have an environmental impact that must be considered. And there may be hidden costs as well. If such a project is to be built on prior industrial land or even in a location where a corner gas station stood, the lands may be contaminated and the business might incur significant cleanup costs. Who is to bear that cost? Several jurisdictions have passed legislation called "Brownfields" statutes that try to spread the costs, making it easier for a developer to construct on those lands. Still, the obligation to clean them up may be imposed on that developer, and it is vitally important that those costs be determined at the outset. Another factor that must be considered is that liability for environmental offences usually extend beyond the corporation to the directors and managers of those corporations.

OTHER IMPORTANT ISSUES IN ENVIRONMENTAL PROJECTS

While environmental concerns arise in local activities and projects, it is in the development of natural resources, where large projects such as mining, oil and gas fields, forestry, pipelines, and transmission lines are involved, that the environmental concerns discussed above become prominent, requiring the most sophisticated environmental planning proposals and significant public input.

Another important obstacle has arisen in recent times that often causes delays and in some cases prevents projects from moving forward altogether. First Nations peoples make claim to large tracts of rural land based on reservation and treaty rights. In British Columbia, where a number of treaties were never signed, they have claim to traditional land covering a significant portion of the province. Historically, these claims were simply ignored as the provinces granted mining, forestry, and development permits, but in a series of cases starting in 2004 the Supreme Court of Canada developed the requirement that First Nations peoples had to be consulted with respect to these projects on their traditional or reserve lands. But what does consultation mean? This generally was interpreted to mean that they had to tell the First Nations group what they were doing and then simply go ahead with the project despite any objection. Recently, however, in *Tsilhqot'in Nation v. British Columbia,*[60] the Supreme Court of Canada held that consultation requires obtaining the consent of the First Nations group, in effect giving them a veto over any such project. How far this decision is applied is yet to be seen, but most First Nations peoples feel that this has significantly empowered them in these negotiations. Most do agree, however, that this decision will mark a watershed in establishing the rights of First Nations peoples to what happens on their lands.

First Nations peoples must be consulted with respect to projects in their territories

MyBusLawLab

Be sure to visit the MyBusLawLab that accompanies this book to find practice quizzes, province-specific content, simulations and much more!

---

60. [2014] S.C.J. No. 4.

SUMMARY

Real property

- Land and things attached to it
- Estates in land grant right to exclusive use of the land
- Fee simple estate is the closest concept to complete ownership of the land
- Life estate is the right to the land for life; reversionary interest or remainder is held by others
- Leasehold estate is the right to the land for a specific period of time, either for a fixed term or a renewable periodic term
- Lesser interests include easements, rights of way, licences, restrictive covenants and building schemes, option agreements, agreements for sale, and mortgages
- Joint tenancy means that when one of the parties dies, the others take the whole property by right of survivorship
- Tenancy in common is a form of co-ownership where separate interests remain apart
- Land registry system is where provinces keep a depository of documents that affect title
- Land titles system is where the government provides a certificate of title that is conclusive proof of the interests affecting the title of the land
- Condominium owners have fee simple estate in individual units and own common areas in common
- Cooperatives is where ownership of individual units and common areas is held by the cooperative

Mortgages

- Mortgages use land as security for a loan
- Title no longer goes to mortgagee in land titles jurisdiction
- Equity of redemption allows debtor to redeem property even after default
- Second or third mortgages are riskier
- Foreclosure sets a time limit on the right to redeem
- Power of sale or judicial sale gives the creditor the right to have the property sold
- When property is sold after a default, the mortgagor is still responsible for the shortfall

Leasehold estates

- Leasehold estates, or leases, involve landlord and tenant relationships
- Commercial tenancies are governed primarily by common law, with the rights of the parties set out in the lease
- Residential tenancies have been significantly modified by statute
- Notice must be given by the landlord to increase rent or terminate a lease
- Similar notice must be given by the tenant with respect to termination of the tenancy
- Parties have limited obligations to repair and to pay security deposits

Personal property

- Chattels are tangible, movable property
- Chose in action is intangible property; one may have to sue to realize this property
- Fixtures are chattels that have become fixed to real property
- Trade or tenant fixtures can be removed when the tenant leaves, if this can be done without damage
- Bailment is when property that is owned by one person is placed temporarily in the possession of another
- A duty to look after that property is imposed on the bailee; the nature of the duty depends on the contractual terms
- Where no bailment contract exists, extent of duty may depend on several factors, including who benefits from the bailment

Environment protection

- Common law protection found in riparian rights and tort law
- *Canadian Environmental Protection Act* sets standards and requires compliance

- *Canadian Environmental Assessment Act* requires new projects affecting the environment to be assessed
- *Regulations Designating Physical Activities* sets out activities where a project proposal must be filed
- There are similar provincial legislative requirements
- Municipal bylaws may also affect businesses that impact the environment
- Goals of statute law are to prohibit environmental offences, assess the damage of the proposed projects, levy fines and penalties for violations, and encourage good environmental practices
- First Nations peoples must be consulted with respect to activities carried on in their territories

QUESTIONS FOR REVIEW

1. How does personal property become real property? Discuss why a determination of when this has happened may be important.

2. What is a fixture? Under what circumstances can someone other than the owner of real property, such as a tenant, remove fixtures?

3. What interest in land does the purchaser get when he buys a house?

4. What is meant by a fee simple estate in land?

5. Explain the rights and obligations of reversion and remainder when discussing a life estate.

6. Contrast life estates and leasehold estates.

7. What is meant by an easement? Give examples, and explain why an easement is called a lesser interest in land.

8. Explain the significance of dominant and servient tenements when dealing with easements.

9. What is meant by a restrictive covenant? Under what circumstances will such a covenant be binding on subsequent landowners? How does this relate to a building scheme?

10. Contrast a tenancy in common with a joint tenancy and indicate how one can be changed to another. Why is the distinction important?

11. How may failure to properly register a mortgage or deed affect the initial parties to an instrument in a registration jurisdiction? What happens when an innocent third party becomes involved? How is this different in a land titles jurisdiction?

12. How are rights under a lease different from the rights of a resident created under a licence agreement?

13. Under what circumstances must a leasehold interest be evidenced in writing? Why?

14. What is a periodic tenancy? What special problems come into play with periodic tenancies that are not present with term leases?

15. Explain what is meant by a landlord's obligation to ensure a tenant's "quiet enjoyment."

16. Explain what is meant by the saying "finders keepers" in terms of who is entitled to property that has been found.

17. Discuss the different ways in which a bailment may be created. What duty is imposed on a gratuitous bailee? What duty is imposed on a bailee for value?

18. Distinguish between the obligation placed on a bailee for value and that imposed on a common carrier or innkeeper.

19. What common law provisions protect the environment? Why was it necessary to pass federal and provincial legislation?

20. Describe the federal statutes in place designed to protect the environment. What are the provincial statutes in place in your jurisdiction protecting the environment?

21. What is the purpose of a project proposal? When is it required and how is it used?

22. How would you recommend that businesses deal with environmental issues and regulations?

CASES AND DISCUSSION QUESTIONS

1. *Paramount Life Insurance Co. v. Hill* [1986] A.J. No. 1111 (C.A.)

Hill had been turned down by Paramount Life Insurance Company when he tried to obtain a loan to be secured by a mortgage on the house that his wife owned. He then sold the property to his business partner and had his partner arrange for a loan with Paramount to be secured by a mortgage on the property. This mortgage was granted. The problem was that he had not obtained his wife's consent for the sale, but had forged her signature on the documents. Neither the partner nor the insurance company knew this fact.

When Mr. Hill died, Paramount foreclosed, as it was no longer receiving mortgage payments. Mrs. Hill now discovered what her husband had done; she fought the foreclosure action, claiming she was still entitled to the property because of the fraudulent sale. Assuming this took place in a land titles jurisdiction, will she be liable for the mortgage payments? What if it were in a jurisdiction with a registration system? Explain.

2. *Letourneau v. Otto Mobiles Edmonton (1984) Ltd.*, 2002 ABQB 609 (CanLII), [2003] 3 WWR 389

Letourneau's trailer was in need of repair, so he took it to Otto Mobiles and was directed to park the trailer in the adjacent parking lot. Otto Mobiles agreed to repair the trailer the following day. Overnight, the trailer was stolen. Letourneau sued Otto Mobiles for damages, alleging a bailment existed that was negligently breached. The defendant denied liability, relying on a waiver that was contained in a previous work order signed by Letourneau. No work order for the requested service on the trailer was created on this occasion.

Identify the issues in this case. If a bailment does exist, what duty of care arises? What weight will be given to the waiver? Explain the likely outcome of this case.

3. *Waterloo (City) v. 379621 Ontario Ltd.*, [2014] O.J. No. 1416

The City of Waterloo passed a new statute in its Property Standards By-Law prohibiting the distribution of light that disturbed adjacent inhabitants or trespassed on their property. An order to desist such light distribution was issued to 379621 Ontario Ltd. They disputed the order, claiming that the bylaw was too vague and retrospective.

What do you think? Was it being applied retrospectively? Can such a bylaw regulating the distribution of light be clear, or is it necessarily vague?

4. *Dunn Estate v. Dunn*, 1994 CanLII 9136 (AB QB), 2 RFL (4th) 106

The Dunns owned their matrimonial home as joint tenants. During their marriage, Mr. Dunn demanded on several occasions that Mrs. Dunn and his stepchildren leave, only to later reconcile. Prior to his death, the husband obtained a divorce and applied for division of the matrimonial home pursuant to the *Matrimonial Property Act*, but Mr. Dunn died before the property division was effected. The administrator of the estate, the public trustee, applied for division of the matrimonial property under the Act. The issue then arose as to whether the home formed part of the estate or whether it passed by survivorship to Mrs. Dunn.

What do you think? Has the joint tenancy been severed? Is this a reasonable result given the intention and actions of the parties?

15 Chapter

Priority of Creditors

LEARNING OBJECTIVES

1. Outline the process of securing debt by using personal property
2. Outline the process of securing debt by using guarantees
3. Outline the process of securing debt by using other forms of security
4. Review other laws related to creditors
5. Explain the process of bankruptcy
6. Distinguish the priorities among creditors in a bankruptcy
7. Present the bankruptcy offences
8. Describe the situation after discharge from bankruptcy
9. Describe the alternatives to bankruptcy

A considerable industry has developed around the practices of lending money and granting credit. This chapter will examine the various methods that have been developed to ensure that money owed is paid, the legislation that has been created to control such transactions, and federal bankruptcy and insolvency legislation. Other than this federal statute, creditors' rights are generally a matter of provincial jurisdiction. The common principles embodied in the relevant provincial statutes will be the primary area of concentration in this chapter.

METHODS OF SECURING DEBT

LO **1 2 3 4**

Obtaining a claim on a debtor's property will help a creditor get paid

When a debtor borrows money or is extended credit, the creditor is at risk that the debtor cannot or will not pay the debt. Usually, she requires the debtor to take steps to reduce this risk by ensuring that she will be paid first, before other creditors, even in the event of bankruptcy or insolvency. Several methods have been developed to provide the creditor with this protection. One way to do this is to obtain a claim on property of the debtor and become a **secured creditor**.

Personal Property

Real property can be taken as security using a mortgage

Both real property and personal property have been used as security. **Real property** includes land, buildings attached to the land, and **fixtures**—that is, items attached to the land or to anything attached to the land. **Mortgages**, the most common method of using real property as security, were discussed in Chapter 14.

Personal property can also be used as security

Personal property is also used extensively to secure debt. **Personal property** can be divided into **chattels**, which are tangible, movable things, and **choses in action**, which are intangible rights that are legally enforceable claims. Cheques and promissory notes are examples of choses in action.[1] For a chose in action, the relevant document merely represents an obligation that can be legally enforced. Although a chose in action is often used to secure debt, it is much more common to take real property or chattels as security.

Debtor can pledge property to secure a loan

When a pawnbroker lends money, the borrower leaves an item, like a watch or a ring, with the pawnbroker who holds the item until the loan is repaid. The borrower (debtor) still owns the item. The pawnbroker (creditor) only gains the right to sell the item if the borrower does not repay the loan. This type of transaction is referred to as a **pledge**.

Personal property security involves the right to take possession upon default

In most situations, however, the debtor needs the use of the goods cited as security. When, for example, you borrow money to buy a new car, the assumption is that you will have the use of the car while you are repaying the loan. In such cases, the security of the creditor is the right to take the car and sell it if you fail to repay the loan. In the past, the creditor assumed ownership of the goods used as security, while the debtor had possession of the goods. In the event of default, the creditor would simply take possession of the goods based on this ownership. Under modern legislation, the creditor usually does not actually assume ownership of the goods, but the effect is the same. The creditor has first claim to the goods in the event of a default by the debtor. Note that a default may occur not only when a payment is missed, but also when the debtor fails to meet any obligation (such as maintaining sufficient insurance coverage) that increases the creditor's risk or that threatens the value of the assets used as security.

THE TRADITIONAL APPROACH

Conditional seller retains title until last payment

Historically, conditional sales agreements, chattel mortgages, and assignments of accounts receivable were the common methods of using personal property as security. A **conditional sale** involves a two-step process. First, possession of the goods is given to the buyer. The seller, who is also the creditor, retains the title (that is, ownership) as security. Second, after the final payment is made, title to the goods is conveyed to the buyer. It should be noted that the *Sale of Goods Act* applies to conditional sales even though the sale takes place over a protracted period of time.[2]

Chattel mortgages involve transfer of title to goods to secure loan

A **chattel mortgage** differs from a conditional sale in that the creditor is not the seller of the goods. Typically, the debtor approaches a bank to borrow money. The bank requires the debtor to secure the loan by transferring the title of some good (such as a car or a boat) to the bank as **collateral**. Throughout the duration of the loan transaction, chattel mortgages, like conditional sales, involve the creditor having title to the goods as security while the debtor has possession of the goods. With a chattel mortgage, when the last payment is made title of the goods used as collateral is returned to the debtor. Even though a **bill of sale** is often used to create the security, since no actual sale is contemplated the *Sale of Goods Act* does not apply to a chattel mortgage transaction.

Accounts receivable can be used as security for a loan

The assignment of **book accounts** involves using a chose in action as security rather than goods. Often, a business will have few tangible assets, but will have considerable funds owed to it for goods or services provided to customers. These claims are called **accounts receivable**. If the debtor assigns his accounts receivable as security and then defaults, the creditor has the right to intercept the payment of the accounts receivable. The loan is thereby secured.

[1.] For a case that held that taxi licences were "property" that could be used to secure a loan under the personal property legislation, see *Re Foster* (1992), 8 O.R. (3d) 514 (Ont. Gen. Div.), 1992 CanLII 7428 (ON SC). For a case that held that seismic data was "property," see *Re Gauntlet Energy Corporation* (2003), 336 A.R. 302 (Q.B.), 2003 ABQB 718 (CanLII).

[2.] See, for example, Saskatchewan's *Sale of Goods Act*, R.S.S. 1978, c. S-1, which states in s. 2(1)(c) that a contract of sale includes an agreement to sell, and then defines in s. 3(4) an "agreement to sell" as a contract in which the transfer of property to goods is to take place at a future time or is subject to some conditions to be fulfilled in the future.

Leases are also a common method of creating a secured relationship between a creditor and a debtor. The most common type of lease is an **operating lease**, in which goods are simply rented to the lessee to use during the lease period, after which the goods are returned to the lessor. Today, a **lease to purchase** is being used more frequently. A lease to purchase involves, essentially, a credit purchase. Title to the goods will be transferred to the lessee at the end of the lease period, with the lease simply providing security. In both an operating lease and a lease to purchase, possession of the goods goes to the lessee while the title to the goods remains with the lessor, providing the lessor with security for the transaction.

When the manufacturer or the supplier of goods leases them to the lessee using a lease to purchase, the transaction is much like a conditional sale. The lessee can make claims against the manufacturer or the supplier for the quality and fitness of the goods supplied. But when the goods are sold to a financial institution and then leased to the lessee, the relationship is more like a chattel mortgage, as there is only a financial arrangement between the lessee and the financial institution. The lessee has to deal with the manufacturer or the supplier with respect to problems relating to the goods themselves. This may be difficult because of the lack of a contract with them.

In the past, separate statutes with different provisions governed the various ways of using personal property as security. To further confuse things, when other forms of personal property such as negotiable instruments, shares, or bonds were used as security, there was no legislation at all. Today, personal property security acts are in place in most jurisdictions and govern all situations where personal property is used as security.

THE *PERSONAL PROPERTY SECURITY ACT*

The *Personal Property Security Act* (*PPSA*) is now used in all jurisdictions in Canada. It creates a unified approach toward the use of personal property as security. (The details of the provincial statutes do vary significantly, however, so businesspeople should be familiar with the legislation of any province in which they do business.) As a result, the *PPSA* is more complicated than legislation used previously, but because it uses one set of rules and a common approach to cover both tangible and intangible forms of personal property and the various ways that security can be taken, its application is simpler. A **secured transaction** is still created by contract in the traditional forms of conditional sales, chattel mortgages, and assignments of accounts receivable, but other forms, such as leases, can also be used, depending on the property used as security. The formal requirements and procedures for all these types of securities are now the same. As well, the *PPSA* allows other, less common, forms of personal property, such as licences, shares, bonds, and even intellectual property (including copyright, patents, and trademarks), to be used as security and to be treated in a uniform way. The *PPSA* provides for some or all of the assets of a particular debtor to be used as security. It also provides rules to determine the ranking of various claims when several secured creditors have claims against those assets.

The right to take possession of the goods used as security, even when they get into the hands of an innocent purchaser, is the essential nature of a secured transaction. Thus, when Lee purchases her car under a conditional sale agreement and then defaults, the creditor must have the right to retake the car even if it has been resold or if Lee has become bankrupt. In the past, this was accomplished by the creditor's retaining title to the goods and retaking them in the event of default. To protect an innocent third party who might be misled by the debtor having possession of the goods, the secured creditor was required to register his secured claim against the goods at the designated government agency. A would-be purchaser or a potential creditor wanting to use the goods as security could search the title to the goods and would be forewarned of the prior claim of the secured creditor. Under the *PPSA*, the process is a little more involved but it accomplishes the same purpose.

Lessee gets possession while lessor retains ownership

Lease to purchase is like a conditional sale

Personal property security acts are now in place

PPSA creates a common process for using personal property as security

Most personal property can be used as security

Registration of claim protects secured creditors and others

CASE SUMMARY 15.1

Is Predictability More Important than Fairness?
KBA Canada, Inc. v. Supreme Graphics Limited[3]

KBA had a registered security interest in a printing press. A third party discharged the registration without authorization through inadvertence. By the time KBA became aware of the discharge and re-registered its interest, it had lost its priority under the *PPSA*. It sought equitable relief to restore its priority. It was successful at trial; the judge held that another creditor would be unjustly enriched if KBA's priority was not restored and that the principles of equity could be applied to remedy the situation.

The Court of Appeal held that the overriding goal of the *PPSA* is to provide commercial certainty and predictability to personal property financing. As the legislation includes clear rules for registration of financing statements and for priorities among secured creditors, equitable principles have a limited role. They can only be used to cover areas that are beyond the scope of the legislation. Clear statutory rules must be followed, and they cannot be overridden if they result in unfairness. The appeal was therefore allowed, and KBA's priority was not restored.

SMALL BUSINESS PERSPECTIVE

Should the desire to provide commercial certainty and predictability to personal property financing be more important than achieving fairness? In light of the importance of the provisions of the *PPSA*, what approach should a sophisticated creditor follow to ensure that she obtains and maintains her priority?

Creating a Secured Relationship

The method of creating a secured relationship under the *PPSA* is unique. There are three stages. First, the parties must enter into the contractual agreement. Second, the secured interest must attach to the collateral that has been identified to provide the security. Third, the secured interest must be perfected.

Contract must be a security agreement

The parties must have entered into a contract that created a secured relationship. While the *PPSA* may deem some relationships to be secured, it does not create security agreements. In an Alberta case,[4] a lender claimed that it had a perfected security interest in the "capital account" of the borrower, a lawyer in a law firm. The Court ruled that the documents obtained (a loan agreement and a comfort letter from the law firm) did not contain the language required by the *PPSA*. Regardless of the lender's intention, the Court would not accept the lender's claim that a security interest had been taken in the absence of appropriate documentation.

Security must attach to collateral

Assuming there is a security agreement in place, **attachment** takes place when the debtor receives some value under the contract. That is, if a person borrowing funds uses his car as collateral security for the loan, that security attaches to the car only when the bank makes the money available to the debtor pursuant to the agreement. Attachment gives the creditor a claim against the security in the event of default by the debtor. This is normally a right to take possession, if so stated in the contract. It is important to remember that the obligations and the remedies of the parties must be set out in the contract. The purpose of the *PPSA* is to give effect to the contractual obligations entered into by the parties.

Provisions of contract prevail

Perfection is required to prevail against outsiders

It is vital to understand that attachment gives the creditor rights against the debtor only. To protect the creditor's claim if the goods are sold, or if another

---

3. 2014 BCCA 117 (CanLII).
4. *Re Hupfer* (2003), 41 C.B.R. (4th) 187 (Alta. Q.B.), 2003 ABQB 267 (CanLII).

creditor becomes involved, the secured transaction must not only be attached, it must also be perfected. This **perfection** can be accomplished in one of two ways.

The first way perfection occurs is by the registration of the security obligation at the appropriate government agency, as was the case under the old system. This process has been simplified so that the actual contractual documents no longer have to be filed. A single form (a financing statement) is now used to provide notice of the security arrangement. There are some provincial variations but, in general, a financing statement requires the complete name and address of the parties, the type and description (including the serial number) of the security used, and the date and time of registration. When a motor vehicle is used as security, its year, make, model, and vehicle identification number must also be set out. There may also be specific requirements when consumer goods are involved.

Perfection through registration

The second, and less common, way of perfecting a secured transaction is for the creditor to obtain physical possession of the collateral used. Whether possession or registration is used depends on the nature of the security. When promissory notes or shares are involved, there is no need for the debtor to keep them, and perfection by possession is appropriate. Note that the original note or certificate must be taken into possession, not a photocopy. When tangible property is involved, such as a car, a truck, or equipment that is required for use by the debtor, registration is the more appropriate process. The purpose of registration is to ensure that others are alerted that the goods have been used as security and that the debtor is not in a position to deal with them. When perfection by possession is involved, this is not necessary, since the goods are not in the possession of the debtor and third parties cannot be misled with respect to them.

Perfection through possession

Priority of Secured Creditors

If more than one security interest is perfected by registering different financing statements against the same collateral, the **priority** of those secured parties is generally determined by the date that registration takes place. But this is not always the case. For example, sometimes a merchant will secure a loan by granting a security on all of her assets, including after-acquired assets. This can cause a problem if a supplier of goods also claims a security interest in the future acquired goods. The secured creditor selling those goods will have priority with respect to them providing that his security interest is registered within a specified time (for example, 15 days in Nova Scotia). This is called a **purchase money security interest**, or PMSI. A PMSI will prevail over a general security agreement covering all of a merchant's assets if it is registered within the specified time period.

First to perfect usually prevails

But PMSIs are an exception . . .

Similarly, if customers purchase goods from that merchant in the normal course of business, the goods will normally be free of any secured interest of the creditor. If you purchase a car from a dealership, you would get good title even though the assets of the dealership had been used to secure a general loan to operate the business. Since the creditor knows that the inventory will be sold in the normal course of business, an innocent buyer will not be affected by that security.

. . . and buyers in the normal course of business are not bound

 REDUCING RISK 15.1

For a creditor, it is vitally important that a security interest be properly perfected. Legislation in most jurisdictions has registration requirements that must be carefully followed, including the exact recording of serial numbers and names. Sometimes errors in registration can be corrected, but not if the interests of other parties have been affected. Creditors usually register their security interest first, before advancing their credit. In such cases, perfection takes place at the same time that credit is actually advanced (the point of attachment). There are not, therefore, any problems with intervening interests arising or with subsequent errors that affect the validity of the perfection taking place. A sophisticated client will be aware of the process that should be followed when taking security, will ensure that appropriate steps are taken to enter into a contract creating a secured relationship, and will ensure that attachment and perfection of the security interest occur in a timely manner.

CASE SUMMARY 15.2

When Possession Takes Priority over Registration:
Inland Contracting Ltd. v. Bakken[5]

Inland leased equipment to Mike Dery Holdings Ltd. and Giants Head Excavating Ltd. in British Columbia in April 2008. The equipment was moved to Saskatchewan in the fall of 2008. In February 2009 it was sold to 101138096 Saskatchewan Ltd., which registered a security agreement in Saskatchewan on May 5, 2009. 101138096 rented the equipment to Giants Head. Giants Head and Mike Dery defaulted on their payments to Inland and Giants Head defaulted on its payments to 101138096, which then seized the equipment. No tenders were received for its sale, so 101138096 elected to retain it as payment for the debt on October 19, 2009. Inland registered a security interest in British Columbia and Saskatchewan on October 20, 2009. Inland registered by serial number, while 101138096 registered a general security interest without serial numbers.

The Court ruled that 101138096 perfected its security by taking possession of the equipment. It only had to give notice to Giants Head of its election to take the collateral as satisfaction of the debt, as Inland did not register its security interest until the day after the notice was given.

SMALL BUSINESS PERSPECTIVE

This case shows how failure to register security interest can be costly. It also illustrates that failure to keep track of assets that have been given as security can lead to a loss of priority. What should a business in Inland's position do to protect its security interest, besides registering a security agreement as soon as possible?

Rights and Remedies upon Default

Upon default, a creditor can take possession and sell the collateral

In the event of a default by the debtor, the creditor has recourse as set out in the contract and as provided in the *PPSA*. This usually involves taking possession of the goods and selling them to recover the amount owed. In doing so, the creditor not only must comply with the contract, but also must not otherwise violate the law in the process.

Bailiff seizes goods

Usually, when taking possession of goods, the creditor must hire a bailiff, who has authority to go onto the debtor's property and seize the goods. The relevant legislation usually requires that the bailiff not use force when seizing property. (At least one province, however, allows bailiffs to use reasonable force when entering premises other than the debtor's residence.[6]) If the debtor won't allow a bailiff access to the premises, the bailiff can apply for a court order. If such an order is not obeyed, the debtor may be guilty of contempt of court. The police will assist a bailiff only when required to by court order or when the bailiff has reasonable grounds to believe that an attempt to seize is likely to lead to a serious breach of the peace.

Creditor must take reasonable care of goods in possession

Note that some provinces will not permit the creditor to take possession of the collateral without a court order when consumer goods are involved and a significant amount of the debt has been paid. With respect to goods (consumer or commercial) that the creditor has taken possession of, the creditor must take "commercially reasonable" care to protect the goods and keep them in good repair. If the goods require repairs to sell them, such "commercially reasonable" expenses will be added to the amount the debtor owes.

Debtor must be given notice and opportunity to redeem

Before a sale of the seized goods can take place, interested parties (usually the debtor and other creditors) must be given a chance to redeem the goods by paying any money owing. Notice must be given setting out a description of the goods and the amount owing, that the party receiving the notice has the **right to redeem**, and

---

5. 2010 SKQB 122 (CanLII).

6. See Alberta's *Civil Enforcement Act*, R.S.A. 2000, c. C-15, s. 13(2).

that failure to do so will result in the sale of the goods. The notice should also declare, when appropriate, that the debtor will be liable for any shortfall between the amount owing plus expenses and the amount realized from the sale. Sometimes only the missed payments plus expenses need be paid, but there is often an acceleration clause requiring that the entire debt plus expenses be paid to redeem the goods. Some provinces prohibit such acceleration clauses.

After possession of the goods has been taken and the notice period has expired, the goods are usually sold, by private or public sale, to satisfy the debt. Under the *PPSA*, the method chosen must be commercially reasonable.

Sale—goods taken into possession can be sold to satisfy debt

If the proceeds from the sale do not cover the debt, additional costs, and interest, the debtor will usually have to make up the difference. Thus, not only may the debtor lose her collateral, she may also still owe the creditor a considerable amount of money to pay for the shortfall. In several jurisdictions, this right to sue for a deficiency is lost as soon as the creditor chooses to take possession of the goods. In some provinces, this rule applies only when consumer goods are involved. For example, in British Columbia, if Jones defaulted on a consumer car loan owing $15 000, and only $10 000 was realized from the sale of that car after the creditor took possession of it, the creditor would lose not only the $5000 shortfall on the loan but also any costs and interest incurred.[7]

Debtor may be liable for deficiency

Because this was a consumer loan in British Columbia, the creditor exhausted his remedies against Jones when he took possession of the car. The creditor must therefore take great care in these circumstances to balance the risks of suing (and possibly getting nothing) against taking possession of the collateral (and getting at least something). The creditor can also lose the right to a deficiency by failing to properly look after the goods or by failing to get a fair price because of an improvident sale.

Creditor must consider alternatives

REDUCING RISK 15.2

When a debtor defaults, creditors are often quick to seize property used as security. In some jurisdictions, however, this might prevent the creditor from pursuing other more effective remedies. Even in those jurisdictions in which it is possible to sue for a shortfall after the goods have been sold, that right may be lost if the goods are not properly cared for and sold in a commercially reasonable manner. On the other hand, if the debtor defaulted on the original debt, it is likely that any attempt to sue and seize other assets will not result in a significant recovery. Another issue involves the question of whether the debtor can be rehabilitated and kept as a good customer. All of these factors should be carefully considered before deciding to take possession of the collateral. Just because you have the legal right to do something doesn't mean it is always a good idea for you to do it. A sophisticated client will therefore consider all relevant factors before making a decision on how to proceed against a debtor who has defaulted.

Note that, in all jurisdictions, when there is a surplus from the sale, the debtor is entitled to that surplus. In the example above, if the car was sold for $20 000, and costs and interest brought the entire debt up to $17 000, Jones would be entitled to the $3000 surplus from the sale.

Debtor is entitled to surplus

In some jurisdictions, instead of taking possession and selling the goods, the creditor can take the goods and simply keep them, in full satisfaction of the debt. This ends any claim the debtor may have to a surplus and any claim the creditor may have to a deficiency. Notice must be given to all interested parties. If someone files an objection, the goods must be sold in the usual way.

Option to retain the collateral

The procedures under the *PPSA* may appear cumbersome, and the legislation itself is complex, but in actual practice the process outlined by the *PPSA* works quite well. When a person borrows money from a credit union using a car as security, attachment takes place once the contract has been entered into and the money has been advanced. Perfection takes place when the credit union files the financing

PPSA process works well

[7.] *Personal Property Security Act*, R.S.B.C. 1996, c. 359, s. 67.

statement with the appropriate registry. A buyer or subsequent creditor interested in the car would search the registry and, finding the registered security against the vehicle, would be forewarned to avoid any dealings with the car. If the car is purchased and a default takes place, the credit union can recover the vehicle even from the innocent third party. This is the essence of the creditor's security. Once there is a default, the credit union has the option of either pursuing its normal breach-of-contract remedies or taking possession of the vehicle and selling it. If it chooses the latter option, it must follow the proper procedures.

CASE SUMMARY 15.3

If You Elect to Keep the Goods, You Can't Sue: *241301 Alberta Ltd. v. 482176 B.C. Ltd.*[8]

241301 Alberta Ltd. (241) loaned money to one of the defendants, 765918 Alberta Ltd. (765). The loan was to enable 765 to buy equipment and set up a restaurant. The restaurant had only operated for two months when 241 gave notice of its intention to enforce its security on the restaurant's assets. 241 then appointed a receiver for 765, without providing notice. 241 took possession of the assets of the restaurant and operated it for 10 months. It then sold the assets, and sued for the deficiency.

The Court dismissed 241's action. It held that 241 breached the *PPSA* by failing to provide proper notice of the receivership to 765. The notice it gave of its intention to enforce its security was not sufficient to comply with the legislative requirements. The Court also ruled that, because 241 used the assets to operate the restaurant for 10 months before selling them, there was no deficiency owing. 241 had elected to take the collateral in full satisfaction of the debt. The *PPSA* specifically states that if such an election is made, a deficiency judgment may not be obtained.

SMALL BUSINESS PERSPECTIVE

This case illustrates how important it is to understand and to follow the procedures set out in the *PPSA*. Would 241 have used the assets to operate the restaurant if it knew that doing so would prevent it from obtaining a deficiency judgment? The provisions of the *PPSA* are designed to protect both the rights of the debtor and the rights of the secured creditor. How can creditors (such as merchants who take security interests from their customers) ensure that they are in compliance with the legislation so that they can realize the benefits of the legislation, rather than suffer its penalties?

Guarantees

Guarantor must pay when debtor defaults

Another method creditors use to ensure the repayment of a debt is the **guarantee**. When corporations are involved, the use of guarantees is very common as a means of circumventing the limited liability characteristic of incorporation, making the principals of a corporation ultimately responsible for loans and other obligations. In consumer transactions, guarantees are used to make another, more substantial, debtor liable to pay a loan or other debt. A **guarantor** ensures that the debt will be paid even when the debtor defaults. When Der borrows $5000 from the bank with his mother as a guarantor and then fails to pay, his mother is responsible to repay the $5000 debt.

Indemnity involves primary obligation

A guarantee involves a secondary, or conditional, obligation that arises only in the event of a default. In contrast, when a person agrees to be directly responsible for paying the debt of another, the obligation is not secondary but primary, with the debtors sharing the responsibility. This is referred to as an **indemnity**.

---

8. (2003), 341 A.R. 172 (Q.B.), 2003 ABQB 711 (CanLII).

The distinction between a guarantee and an indemnity, although subtle, can be important. As discussed in Chapter 7, the *Statute of Frauds* requires that some agreements must be evidenced in writing to be enforceable. In most provinces, only guarantees must be evidenced in writing, but in British Columbia both guarantees and indemnities must be evidenced in writing.[9] In Alberta, a guarantor must appear before a notary public, acknowledge that she signed the guarantee, and sign a certificate.[10]

Evidence in writing of guarantee required

Since a guarantee is a separate contract, all of the elements of a contract must be present. Consideration can sometimes be a problem. Because the creditor would not advance funds without the guarantee, the advancement of those funds amounts to consideration supporting the guarantee. When the guarantee is given after default on a loan, the consideration is the creditor's refraining from suing the debtor.

Elements of a contract must be present

When a guarantee is given after the funds are advanced, there can be a serious problem. If Kotsalis borrows money from the Business Bank and the loans officer fails to obtain a guarantee as required by bank policy, he will face difficulties if he tries to get it later. Since the funds have already been advanced, there is no consideration to support the subsequent guarantee. To avoid any problem with consideration, lending institutions usually require that all guarantees be placed under seal. As discussed in Chapter 6, when a seal is present, consideration is conclusively presumed.

Guarantees are often given under seal

REDUCING RISK 15.3

People are often persuaded to sign a guarantee thinking that it is just a formality and that no serious obligations are incurred, since the primary debtor will pay the debt. This is a dangerous assumption to make! Whether in business or in your personal affairs, you should never sign a guarantee without first carefully weighing the risks. The creditor is insisting on a guarantee because she doesn't have confidence that the debt will be paid by the primary debtor. She wants someone else to also be responsible. You are adding your credit to the transaction, and there is a good chance that you will be required to honour your commitment. Many bankruptcies result from people signing guarantees without realizing the risks they may face. A sophisticated client will carefully assess these risks before deciding whether to sign a guarantee of another's debt.

RIGHTS AND OBLIGATIONS OF THE PARTIES

The creditor has significant duties to protect the interests of the guarantor. At the outset, the creditor should make sure that the guarantor understands the full nature of the guarantee he is signing. Guarantors often escape their obligation by claiming misrepresentation, *non est factum*, or undue influence. When in doubt, the creditor should insist that the guarantor obtain independent legal advice.

Creditor should ensure guarantor understands the guarantee

The creditor should also avoid any subsequent dealings that may weaken the position of the guarantor. Any substantial change in the nature of the contract between the creditor and debtor without the guarantor's consent will relieve the guarantor of any obligation. If the creditor advances more funds, or even extends the terms of repayment at a higher interest rate, without the consent of the guarantor, the guarantor will usually be discharged from the guarantee. Note that a creditor simply deciding not to sue and giving the debtor more time to pay will not be considered a substantial change. Such actions will therefore not discharge the guarantee. In any subsequent dealings with the debtor independent of the guarantor, the creditor should obtain the consent of the guarantor to any material change. The effect will then be that the guarantor will continue to be bound by the original guarantee.[11]

Creditors must not weaken the position of the guarantor

Significant changes may release the guarantor

Creditor should obtain the consent of the guarantor

---

9. *Law and Equity Act*, R.S.B.C. 1996, c. 253, s. 59.

10. *Guarantees Acknowledgement Act*, R.S.A. 2000, c. G-11.

11. For a case in which the Court held that a guarantee was clear in stating that a renewal agreement did not require the explicit approval of the guarantor, see *A.G.F. Trust Co. v. Muhammad* (2005), 73 O.R. (3d) 767 (C.A.), 2005 CanLII 6 (ON CA); leave to appeal to S.C.C. refused, [2005] S.C.C.A. No. 139.

Releasing security may release the guarantor

A guarantor is also released from her obligation when other forms of security, such as chattel mortgages, are released. For example, if Kotsalis obtained a loan from the Business Bank, with the bank taking a guarantee from Bruno and a chattel mortgage against Kotsalis' car as security, such an arrangement would cease to be binding on Bruno if the bank subsequently allowed Kotsalis to sell the car without Bruno's consent.

Withholding information may release the guarantor

The withholding of important information from the guarantor by the creditor may also be enough to discharge the guarantee. The information withheld must be of some substantial and unusual nature, not simply the usual kind of information that would pass between business associates. A creditor is obligated, for example, to advise a guarantor of a priority agreement that reduced the assets available in the event of a default.[12]

Contract can modify rights and obligations

Because the basic rights and obligations of the creditor and the guarantor are determined by contract, they can be modified by contract as well. It is common for creditors to include provisions that attempt to exempt the creditor from the basic obligations discussed above. Like all exemption clauses, exemption clauses in guarantees are interpreted by the courts very carefully. It is becoming common for a guarantee to contain clauses creating a **continuing guarantee**, allowing the creditor to continue to advance funds up to a preset limit without affecting the obligation of the guarantor to pay in the event of default. Clauses that allow the creditor to discharge and otherwise deal with security, and to otherwise change the terms of the agreement (including changing terms of repayment and increasing interest rates) are now often included in guarantees. These clauses can be effective if they are carefully worded. They then significantly limit the protection normally enjoyed by a guarantor.

Guarantor assumes the rights of creditor upon payment

When a default occurs, the creditor is not required to demand payment from the debtor or to take steps to seize any other security before seeking payment from the guarantor, unless that has been agreed to in the contract. A guarantor who pays the debt is subrogated to the rights of the creditor, which means, in effect, that the guarantor steps into the creditor's shoes. Any remedy or right available to the creditor after payment is assumed by the guarantor, including the right to seize a chattel used as security for the debt or to sue the debtor and take advantage of the processes available to assist in collecting the debt.

Defences of debtor are available to the guarantor

In addition, any defences that are available to the debtor are also available to the guarantor. If breach of contract, fraud, or misrepresentation on the part of the creditor has barred an action against the debtor, it also bars an action against the guarantor. Note, however, that if the reason the guarantee was required was because of the infancy of the debtor or some other factor known to all parties at the time of the guarantee, the guarantor will normally not be allowed to use that reason as a defence against the creditor.

CASE SUMMARY 15.4

Listen to Your Lawyer! *Royal Bank of Canada v. Samson Management & Solutions Ltd.*[13]

Cusack signed a $150 000 continuing guarantee in 2005 for the indebtedness of Brasseur's business, Samson. The guarantee covered present and future liabilities of Samson. Cusack received independent legal advice before signing the guarantee. The bank increased Samson's operating line of credit in 2006, from $150 000 to $250 000. Cusack gave a new guarantee for $250 000, which also covered Samson's present and future liabilities. She again received independent legal advice.

---

12. *Collum v. Bank of Montreal* (2004), 47 B.L.R. (3d) 39, (2004), 29 B.C.L.R. (4th) 18 (C.A.), 2004 BCCA 358 (CanLII).

13. 2013 ONCA 313 (CanLII).

In 2008, the amount of the loan from the bank to Samson was increased to $500 000. The new loan agreement changed some of the loan terms. The bank obtained a new guarantee from Brasseur for $500 000. In 2009, the loan amount was increased to $750 000 and Brasseur signed a new guarantee for that amount.

Samson failed in 2011. The bank made demands on Brasseur and Cusack under their guarantees. It was granted summary judgment against Brasseur, but not against Cusack. The issue on appeal was whether her guarantee should be enforced.

The Court of Appeal allowed the appeal and granted the bank summary judgment against Cusack for $250 000 plus interest, as determined by her guarantee. The changes in the loan agreements between the bank and Samson increased the risk to Cusack even though her financial exposure under her guarantee was capped at $250 000. The terms of the guarantee were clear, however, in ensuring that Cusack would remain liable even if the bank increased the amount of the loan or took other actions such as giving more time for payment, increasing the interest rate, or introducing new terms and conditions to allow the bank and Brasseur to change their business arrangements without having to involve guarantors of the loan, including Cusack.

SMALL BUSINESS PERSPECTIVE

Those who lend funds to small businesses often require guarantees of those loans from the principals of the business and other individuals. Individuals who are asked to provide guarantees should be extremely careful. Before signing a personal guarantee, a sophisticated client will obtain independent legal advice and heed that advice, especially if it confirms that there will be liability under the guarantee even if there are material changes to the loan agreement.

Other Forms of Security

THE *BANK ACT*

This federal statute predates the passage of the *PPSAs*. It allows banks flexibility in what they can take as security. Under the *Bank Act*[14], growing crops, inventories, and goods in the process of manufacture can be taken as security by the banks, despite the fact that the nature of the goods changes in the process. For this type of security, it must be possible to sell the collateral during the course of business without affecting the nature of the security. Sections 426 and 427 of the *Bank Act* allow this to happen.

The *Bank Act* is still an important federal statute, but under the provincial *PPSAs* other lenders now have similar flexibility. There is therefore now more potential conflict between the *Bank Act* and the provincial legislation. Businesspeople must now learn two sets of rules. For example, under the *Bank Act*, security must be registered with the Bank of Canada, creating duplication and confusion. This confusion is compounded because the *Bank Act* enables the banks to continue to use the usual types of secured transactions available to other lenders, such as chattel mortgages, real property mortgages, assignment of debts, guarantees, and so on.

Anticipated crops, inventory, and goods in process of manufacture can be used as security

Conflict and confusion between Bank Act and PPSA

FLOATING CHARGES

Floating charges are used by creditors when dealing with corporations that must be free to buy and sell, without interference, the assets used as security for the loan. When a corporation borrows funds, it may issue bonds or debentures. In Canada, bonds are usually secured by a floating charge. In effect, they involve a mortgage of corporate assets. Debentures are usually unsecured. Bonds and debentures are commonly sold on the open market.

Bonds are usually secured by floating charges

---

14. S.C. 1991, c. 46.

Floating charge provides priority, but allows business to continue

When a bond is issued, the security granted often takes the form of a floating charge against the general assets of the corporation, including inventory and the goods in the process of manufacturing. This allows the corporation to continue to deal with those goods, buying and selling in the normal course of business, unaffected by the floating charge. Customers, for example, take the goods they buy free and clear of the floating charge. It is only upon default, or some other specified event (such as the payment of unauthorized dividends or the sale of a valuable asset), that the floating charge crystallizes by descending, attaching to the specific goods, and becoming a fixed charge. The advantage of a floating charge is that it does not interfere with the ongoing business while still providing a priority over unsecured creditors. Because the various *PPSAs* now allow inventory and other changing assets to be used as security, the floating charge is of diminishing importance. It is, however, still a common aspect of corporate financing.

BUILDERS' LIENS

Suppliers of goods and services can file a lien

Builders' liens were created to overcome a problem in the construction industry. The suppliers of goods and services (such as merchants selling building supplies or electricians wiring a house) often dealt with a general contractor rather than with the owner of the land or building that was to be enhanced by their goods and services. If they were not paid, their recourse was limited to the contractor. They had no claim against the owner or the land or building that was enhanced. Statutes in all provinces—variously called a *Builders' Lien Act, Construction Lien Act,* or *Mechanics' Lien Act*—now give these suppliers of materials and work a claim for payment against the actual land and buildings enhanced by their goods and services. Once the goods or services are provided, the suppliers and workers can register a lien, giving them a claim against the land and buildings. This puts considerable pressure on the owner of the property to ensure that they are paid. The effect of the legislation is to prevent the owner of property from unjustly benefiting from the goods and services that enhance the value of the property without paying for them.

Holdback fulfills the obligation of the owner

Under the various acts, the owner of the property retains a percentage of what he would otherwise pay to the general contractor. This is the **holdback**, which in most provinces is set at 10 percent. After a relatively short period of time, within which any liens must be registered, the owner checks the land registry and, if there are no liens registered, pays out the holdback to the general contractor. If liens have been filed, the amount of the lien is retained and made available to the lien claimants. The owner's obligation is usually limited to the amount of the holdback, even when the total claimed in the liens exceeds that amount. In such a case, the lien claimants will get a proportional share of the amount held back, based on what they are owed.

All in chain must hold back

This requirement of holdback applies to anyone in the construction chain. Thus, the general contractor in turn must hold back from the payment to subcontractors to cover claims by their employees or suppliers of goods and services. The times, percentages, and amounts vary from jurisdiction to jurisdiction, but the general approach is the same. This system provides a form of security to those supplying material and work in the construction industry. In most jurisdictions, similar liens are created by statute against property stored in a warehouse and for maintenance people working on vehicles, machinery, and other goods.[15]

NEGOTIABLE INSTRUMENTS

Negotiable instruments in the form of cheques, bills of exchange, and promissory notes are often associated with secured transactions. For example, debtors are

---

[15.] See, for example, Alberta's *Garage Keepers' Lien Act*, R.S.A. 2000, c. G-2, *Possessory Liens Act*, R.S.A. 2000, c. P-19, *Warehousemen's Lien Act*, R.S.A. 2000, c. W-2, and *Woodmen's Lien Act*, R.S.A. 2000, c. W-14; Saskatchewan's *Threshers' Lien Act*, R.S.S. 1978, c. T-13; and British Columbia's *Tugboat Worker Lien Act*, R.S.B.C. 1996, c. 466.

usually required to sign promissory notes in credit transactions. Negotiable instruments are briefly discussed in Chapter 16.

LETTERS OF CREDIT

Similarly to negotiable instruments, the **letter of credit** is used in commercial relationships, especially in international trade. The letter of credit is a commitment by the importer's bank to pay the stated price upon presentation of appropriate documentation confirming delivery. This provides assurance to the exporter, from the financial institution, that she will be paid. This letter of credit is normally delivered to the exporter by the importer. Upon delivery of the goods, the exporter submits the appropriate documentation (relating to shipment, insurance, customs declarations, etc.) to the importer's bank and receives payment.

Letters of credit are used in international trade

Sometimes, especially when the importer's bank is in a foreign country, the exporter will require that a bank he has confidence in, usually in his own country, become involved as a confirming bank. The importer's bank and the exporter's bank communicate with each other, and both commit to honour the **confirmed letter of credit** upon receiving the appropriate documentation. The confirming bank plays a role similar to endorsing a negotiable instrument in that it adds its commitment to honour the letter of credit. The exporter then simply submits the appropriate documents indicating performance to his bank and receives payment. In effect, the two traders choose banks that they trust to hold and transfer the funds. The effect is quite similar to that of a bank draft, but this process is often more convenient and more flexible.

Role of confirming bank

Letters of credit are used primarily in international trade but, because they are very flexible, it is not uncommon to find them being used in domestic business transactions as well. Letters of credit are also used in other ways. They can, for example, guarantee that one party to a contract will properly perform. If there is a breach, the victim has recourse to the bank that has issued the letter of credit. This is referred to as a **standby letter of credit**.

Also used in domestic transactions

Related Laws

BULK SALES

Other legislation has been enacted to protect creditors against frauds committed by debtors. Most provinces formerly had a *Bulk Sales Act* in place, but Ontario is now the only province to have such legislation.[16] It is designed to prevent merchants from selling all, or almost all, of their business's assets before a creditor can take action to stop them. Creditors expect a business to sell inventory in the normal course of operations, but when all or most of the inventory, equipment, or other assets needed for the ongoing operation is sold, that is an indication that the merchant is going out of business. The *Bulk Sales Act* operates in these circumstances to protect the creditors. The purchaser must obtain a list of creditors, notify them of the sale, and pay the proceeds directly to them, if they so wish. Great care must be taken to comply with the legislative requirements. Failure to comply will make the sale void as against the creditors, requiring the purchaser to account to the creditors for the value of the goods.

Creditors are protected when a merchant sells bulk of business

LANDLORD'S RIGHT TO DISTRAIN FOR RENT

When a tenant fails to pay rent on a leased property, an ancient common law right called *distress* is available to the landlord of the property. The landlord has the right to seize and hold the tenant's assets that are on the rented premises and, eventually, to sell them to pay for the rent owed. There are several restrictions on the right of distraint and many procedural requirements that must be carefully complied with,

Landlord has the right to distrain

[16.] *Bulk Sales Act*, R.S.O. 1990, c. B.14.

especially with respect to residential tenancies. The nature of residential and commercial tenancies and the rights of the parties were discussed in Chapter 14.

FRAUDULENT TRANSFERS AND PREFERENCES

Fraudulent conveyances are void

Sometimes, desperate debtors are tempted to hide property or otherwise protect it from the claims of creditors. Giving or selling property to a friend or relative to avoid the debt is a **fraudulent transfer**. Such a transaction is void. The creditor can seek out the fraudulently transferred property and get it back from the current owner. If the transfer is a valid arm's length sale at a fair price to an innocent third party (a **bona fide purchaser for value**), the transaction is valid and cannot be reversed.

Fraudulent preferences are void

Sometimes, a debtor will seek an advantage by paying one creditor in preference to another. This is also a prohibited transaction, called a **fraudulent preference**. Fraudulent preferences can also be reversed.

Provincial legislation restricts debtor's transactions

Legislation embodying these provisions varies from province to province; the statutes are variously called *Assignment and Preferences Act, Fraudulent Conveyances Act,* and *Fraudulent Preferences Act.* This sort of legislation is designed primarily to prevent debtors from unfairly making payments or transferring property in such a way as to keep the money or property away from the creditors. See Section 3 of the Saskatchewan *Fraudulent Preferences Act,* for example.[18]

Similar restrictions in bankruptcy legislation

The federal *Bankruptcy and Insolvency Act* discussed below also has provisions prohibiting settlements (transfers for nominal or no consideration) and fraudulent

---

CASE SUMMARY 15.5

A Transfer of a Home to a Spouse for No Consideration Can Be Fraudulent! *Mitchell Jenner & Associates v. Saunders*[17]

Jenner was hired by Ladco Display Inc. to help sell the business. Michael Saunders was the president and sole shareholder of Ladco. He sold his shares for $1.1 million. Jenner sued for its commission and won judgment of $241 875. After Jenner commenced his lawsuit, Michael and his wife, Maxine, transferred their matrimonial home into the name of Maxine, for no consideration. The home was later sold.

The Court ruled that there were several "badges of fraud," such as a non-arm's length transfer for no consideration when the Saunders knew about Jenner's lawsuit, there was no approval by the mortgagee, there was no reporting letter completed, the transfer was completed in haste, and Michael continued to use the property. There was, therefore, a fraudulent conveyance. Jenner asked for judgment for the full payment of its claim, but the Court ordered that it receive only Michael's share of the proceeds of the sale of the home.

DISCUSSION QUESTIONS

This case illustrates the danger of ignoring legislation regarding fraudulent transfers and preferences. Many married couples own their homes together, as joint tenants. If one of the spouses has a judgment entered against him or her, the creditor may be able to obtain a court order requiring the joint tenancy to be severed so that the debtor's half of the property can be sold to pay the debt. Is this a fair result? Should spouses be exempt from fraudulent transfers and preferences legislation?

---

17. 2011 ONSC 2930 (CanLII), aff'd on this issue, 2012 ONCA 290 (CanLII).
18. R.S.S. 1978, c. F-21.

preferences. These provisions apply uniformly throughout Canada. While the general intent of the provisions in the bankruptcy legislation is the same as that of the provincial statutes, it should be noted that the wording used in the bankruptcy legislation is quite different than that found in the provincial statutes.

REDUCING RISK 15.4

Businesspeople are sometimes so focused on closing a deal that they miss complying with related statutory requirements. This can come back to haunt them later. In Ontario, where there is a bulk sales statute in place, businesspeople must take great care to comply with it whenever the sale of a significant portion of a business's assets is involved. Failure to do so can result in having to pay twice. Similarly, whenever dealing with an insolvent debtor, creditors must take care to comply with fraudulent conveyance, fraudulent preference, and other legislation that may affect the validity of the transaction. Sophisticated clients will be aware of the dangers that exist when dealing with debtors and will take steps to minimize or eliminate the associated risks.

BANKRUPTCY

Introduction

As discussed above, debtors will sometimes find themselves in a position where they cannot repay their debts. For that reason, wise creditors take steps at the outset of a relationship to ensure repayment. They may take an asset belonging to the debtor as security or get someone else, such as a guarantor, to also be responsible for the debt.

Creditors should protect themselves

Unpaid unsecured creditors have all of the usual remedies available when someone breaches a legal obligation, including the right to proceed to a civil judgment. A judgment creditor can seize the debtor's assets and sell them to recover the judgment, or she can garnish wages and other debts, as discussed in Chapter 3. Such action is often ineffective. There may be many creditors with claims outstanding. Secured creditors will have priority with respect to any secured asset that they might claim, or the debtor may have limited resources with which to pay. Furthermore, in such a situation the debtor may choose to declare bankruptcy or may be forced into bankruptcy.

Unsecured creditors can sue and try to collect . . .

. . . but debtor may declare bankruptcy

The *Bankruptcy and Insolvency Act*[19] (*BIA*) is a federal statute that is uniformly applicable throughout Canada. It has two purposes. The first is to preserve as many of the debtor's assets as possible for the benefit of the creditors. The second is to rehabilitate the debtor by forgiving the unpaid debt, thus removing an insurmountable burden and restoring the debtor as a productive member of society.

People are often confused by the terms used to describe bankruptcy. **Insolvency** simply means that a person is unable to pay his debts as they become due. **Bankruptcy**, on the other hand, is the process by which a debtor's assets are transferred to a trustee in bankruptcy, who then deals with them for the benefit of the creditors. When the debtor makes the transfer voluntarily it is called an **assignment in bankruptcy**. Bankruptcy can be forced on the debtor by a creditor obtaining a **bankruptcy order** from the court. The *BIA* does not apply to banks, insurance companies, trust companies, loan companies, or railways. Farmers and fishers cannot be forced into bankruptcy, but they can make a voluntary assignment.

Purposes of bankruptcy legislation

Bankruptcy involves transfer of assets to a trustee

The government official responsible for bankruptcy for all of Canada is the superintendent of bankruptcy. The superintendent, in turn, appoints official receivers for the bankruptcy districts throughout the country (there must be at least one in each province). A **trustee in bankruptcy** is a licensed private professional who, for a fee, assists the debtor in the bankruptcy process—administering the **bankrupt**'s estate for the benefit of the creditors, filing various documents with the official receiver, and otherwise shepherding the bankrupt through the process from initiation to

Superintendent of bankruptcy is responsible

Superintendent appoints official receivers

Trustees in bankruptcy administer the process

[19.] R.S.C. 1985, c. B-3.

discharge. A trustee serves the same purpose when a proposal is involved. A trustee is called an administrator when dealing with consumer proposals. The courts become involved when a bankruptcy order is requested and when other types of disputes arise. The superior trial court of each province and territory is designated as a bankruptcy court for the purposes of the *BIA*. Although these are courts of the provinces or territories, they have national jurisdiction when administering the *BIA* and related legislation because these are federal statutes.

The Process

Bankruptcy can be forced by creditors . . .

In an involuntary bankruptcy, a creditor petitions the court to force the debtor into bankruptcy. In granting the petition, the court makes a bankruptcy order. This results in a statutory assignment of the debtor's assets to the trustee in bankruptcy, ensuring that the assets will be preserved and distributed fairly so that the creditors will recover as much as possible of what they are owed.

. . . if a creditor is owed more than $1000 and debtor committed an act of bankruptcy

To obtain a bankruptcy order, the creditor must specify in the petition that the debtor owes more than $1000 in debt and has committed an act of bankruptcy during the previous six months. Significant acts of bankruptcy include the voluntary assignment of assets to a trustee in bankruptcy, fraudulent transfers of money or assets to keep them out of the hands of the trustee, the giving of a fraudulent preference to one of the creditors, an attempt to leave the jurisdiction without paying debts, and general insolvency. It is usually the failure to pay debts as they become due that is the specified act of bankruptcy. A sworn affidavit must also be filed with the registrar in bankruptcy in the district in which the debtor is located, verifying the facts alleged in the petition. If the debtor opposes the petition, as is often the case, a hearing before a judge will take place. If she is satisfied, the judge can issue a bankruptcy order, designating a trustee in bankruptcy (normally chosen by the creditors) to receive the assets of the bankrupt. When the petition is unopposed, the hearing can be held before the registrar.

CASE SUMMARY 15.6

No Act of Bankruptcy, No Bankruptcy! *American Bullion Minerals Ltd. (Re)*[20]

The Court granted the petition of the controlling shareholder of ABML, bcMetals Corporation (bcM), asking for a bankruptcy order for ABML. The minority shareholders of ABML applied for an order annulling the bankruptcy. They claimed that bcM made a number of misrepresentations when it petitioned ABML into bankruptcy, that the sole director of ABML failed to oppose the petition or alert ABML shareholders of it, and that bcM petitioned ABML into bankruptcy to facilitate bcM's acquisition of ABML's interest in mineral claims without compensating ABML's minority shareholders.

The Court found that the petition, the affidavit in support, and the submissions of counsel did not inform the Court of the real relationship between ABML and bcM, fully disclose the circumstances of some of the liabilities of ABML, or provide any information relevant to some of its liabilities. The Court found that bcM was the only creditor of ABML, and that bcM could not prove that there were special circumstances that warranted a bankruptcy order. Also, there was no evidence that ABML had committed an act of bankruptcy. The Court concluded that if the bankruptcy court had been fully informed, it would not have made the bankruptcy order. The bankruptcy was therefore annulled.

---

20. (2008), 43 C.B.R. (5th) 210 (B.C.S.C.), 2008 BCSC 639 (CanLII).

DISCUSSION QUESTION
A creditor must prove that the debtor has committed an act of bankruptcy, or the petition will be refused. In such a case, the creditor may be liable for any losses suffered by the debtor. In the ABML case, what remedy may the minority shareholders be able to seek?

Petitioning a debtor into bankruptcy is an involved process, normally requiring the assistance of a lawyer. Caution should be exercised before using this approach. Great damage can be done to the business and reputation of the debtor. If the application is refused, the creditor may be liable to pay compensation for the losses incurred by the debtor. See Figure 15.1 for an illustration of the bankruptcy order process.

Creditor must be careful when petitioning

Figure 15.1 Bankruptcy Order Process

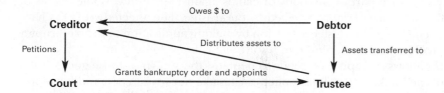

In a **voluntary assignment in bankruptcy**, the debtor must make an "assignment for the general benefit of his creditors," using the prescribed form. The debtor must also prepare a "statement of affairs," summarizing his property and listing all of his creditors, showing the amounts and nature of their claims (whether they are secured, preferred, or unsecured). These documents are filed with the official receiver, who then appoints a trustee in bankruptcy. The trustee will receive the debtor's assets and administer the estate. In practice, debtors will first seek out a trustee in bankruptcy to counsel them, advising of the various alternatives and, if appropriate, assisting them in the preparation of the documents and their filing with the official receiver. When larger estates are involved, the debtor will usually also involve the services of a lawyer. The voluntary assignment process is illustrated in Figure 15.2.

Bankruptcy can be voluntary by debtor

Figure 15.2 Voluntary Assignment

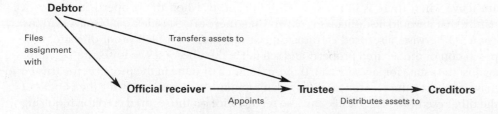

It should be noted that not all of the debtor's property is transferred to the trustee in bankruptcy. The exempt property is determined by the provincial legislation, so it varies from province to province. It usually includes medical and dental aids, food, clothing, furniture and appliances, and tools and other items used to earn an income, up to a limited value. A vehicle of limited value and a personal residence where the debtor has a limited equity may also be protected. The trustee will not take property of little value or property that she considers to be worth less than what it will cost to liquidate.

Exempt property is protected

The trustee in bankruptcy holds the debtor's property in trust for the creditors. She therefore owes them a duty to preserve the property and to sell it for as much as is reasonably possible. The debtor must cooperate with the trustee, disclosing all

Trustee holds property in trust for creditors

assets, documentation, and tax receipts. Often a meeting of the creditors will take place. The debtor must attend, answer the creditors' questions, and otherwise cooperate in the process. The creditors may ask to appoint up to five inspectors to supervise the trustee and the process to ensure their interests are protected. The debtor may also be required to meet with and answer the questions of the official receiver.

Priority among Creditors

Once the trustee in bankruptcy has been given the property of a bankrupt debtor (referred to as the bankrupt's **estate**), she holds those assets in trust for the benefit of the creditors. The trustee has the right and responsibility to lease, repair, receive rents, or otherwise deal with those assets to preserve their value. The trustee will eventually sell the assets and distribute the proceeds fairly to the creditors.

Each of the creditors must establish the validity of his claim by filing a **proof of claim** with the trustee. This document sets out the nature of the debt, how much remains owing, and any claims the debtor might have in return. An important function of the trustee is to evaluate the claims of the creditors. If they are accepted as valid, they will form part of the body of claims against the estate. Some claims of questionable legitimacy may be rejected by the trustee. The affected creditors have the right to challenge the trustee's decision by making application to the bankruptcy court. Mediation is often employed to resolve these and other disputes.

The *BIA* allows a supplier of goods to demand the return of those goods upon learning of the bankruptcy. The supplier must make her written demand for repossession within 15 days of the debtor becoming bankrupt, and the goods must have been delivered within 30 days before that date. The debtor (or the trustee) must still have possession of the goods. Even suppliers of goods that become commingled and lose their identity, such as crops, produce, and fish, have a prior claim. Such suppliers become secured creditors with respect to the value of those goods, provided that the goods were delivered within 15 days preceding the bankruptcy and their claims are filed within 30 days after.

Secured creditors retain their priority position, having a prior claim to at least the value of the property used as security. Most creditors are prevented from taking any further independent action once the assignment or bankruptcy order has been made. (Note that this stay does not apply to criminal prosecutions or matrimonial disputes, which can continue.) A secured creditor, on the other hand, retains a right to take possession of or otherwise proceed against the property used as security without waiting, unless the court orders otherwise. A secured creditor can choose to file a proof of claim for all of what he is owed, giving up any claim for the secured property. He will then be treated as an unsecured creditor for the entire amount. This tactic may be attractive when there is little value in the property, when the property is of such a nature that it would be difficult to sell, or when there are considerable resources in the estate. Otherwise, a secured creditor can, on the basis of a filed proof of claim, take possession of the secured property and sell it. He then becomes an unsecured creditor against the estate for any shortfall. If there is sufficient value in the property, the trustee may simply pay the secured creditor's claim, retaining that property for the benefit of the other creditors. The trustee can also serve notice on the secured creditor, requiring him to place a value on the property and deal with it on the basis of that value or, if the trustee is dissatisfied with the value provided, require the creditor to sell the property.

After the secured creditors have received what they are entitled to, the trustee distributes the remaining assets, or the proceeds from the sales of those assets, to the other creditors. **Preferred creditors** are paid first, pursuant to section 136 of the *BIA*. This section indicates that the following are to be paid, in this order: funeral expenses; costs associated with the bankruptcy process; claims for arrears in wages for a limited amount and time period; arrears in maintenance or alimony; municipal taxes; arrears in rent for a limited period; some direct costs incurred by creditors in the execution process; amounts owed for workers' compensation, employment insurance, and income tax that should have been deducted from salaries; and other claims of the Crown. Unsecured creditors, usually suppliers of goods and services,

---

Trustee must preserve value of the estate

Each creditor must file a proof of claim

Trustee must evaluate the claims of creditors

Suppliers of goods can reclaim goods from bankrupt or trustee

Secured creditors have prior claim to secured property

Preferred creditors paid before unsecured creditors

are paid only after all of these obligations have been satisfied. The unsecured creditors will receive a share on a pro rata basis (a share of the remaining estate determined by the percentage of overall claims their particular claim represents).

The federal government has passed legislation that gives it priority over all other creditors, including secured creditors, in certain situations. Examples include section 224 of the *Income Tax Act*[21] and section 317 of the *Excise Tax Act*.[22] These sections essentially create a trust in situations where there are unremitted source deductions or GST. This gives the government a "super priority." When a requirement to pay (the equivalent of a garnishee summons) is served by the government on a person who owes the debtor money, any amount that is owed, and which would normally be paid to the tax debtor, becomes the property of the government. It never becomes the property of the tax debtor and is therefore not available to its creditors. The courts have held that this gives the government priority over secured creditors of the tax debtor in the case of a bankruptcy of the tax debtor.[23]

> **Government sometimes has priority over secured creditors**

Offences

As discussed above, debtors often attempt to keep their property out of the hands of creditors by transferring it to friends or relatives. Debtors also sometimes try to pay one creditor and not others. Fraudulent transfers and preferences often take place in bankruptcy situations. The trustee in bankruptcy can reverse such transactions.

CASE SUMMARY 15.7

Transferring House to Wife Is Prohibited: *Re Fancy*[24]

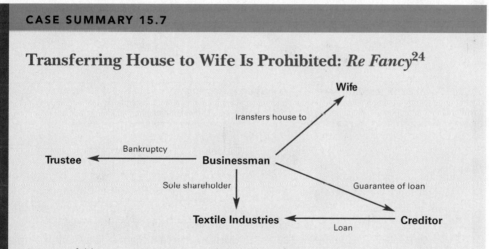

A successful businessman guaranteed the debts of his corporation, Textile Industries, making him personally responsible if it ran into financial difficulties. An action against the corporation resulted in a judgment, causing the corporation to fail and forcing him into bankruptcy. Shortly before his bankruptcy, he transferred his interest in the matrimonial home to his wife. At the time of the transfer, it was clear that the litigation would go to trial and that he was facing substantial losses.

The Court reversed the transfer, determining that the transfer of the house to the wife amounted to a prohibited settlement under the provisions of the *BIA*. A settlement can occur when a person transfers property to another to preserve some benefit for himself, which is exactly what was done in this case.

SMALL BUSINESS PERSPECTIVE

Would the result have been the same if the businessman had transferred his interest in the home to his wife before he incorporated his business?

---

21. R.S.C. 1985, c. 1 (5th Supp.).

22. R.S.C. 1985, c. E-15.

23. See, for example, *Alberta (Treasury Branches) v. Canada (M.N.R.)*, [1996] 1 S.C.R. 963.

24. (1984), 46 O.R. (2d) 153 (H.C.J.), 1984 CanLII 2031 (ON SC).

Settlements are prohibited

Settlements involve the transfer of assets for nominal or no consideration. A settlement is void if it took place within one year of bankruptcy. This period can be extended to up to five years if it can be proven that, at the time of the settlement, the bankrupt knew that she was insolvent.

Fraudulent preferences are prohibited

A payment made in preference to one creditor over the others is also void. The trustee can force the return of those funds so that they can be fairly distributed to all of the creditors. This is the situation in the *Speedy Roofing* case discussed in Case Summary 15.8. There is a presumption that a payment was made to create a preference if it was made within three months of the bankruptcy. Such payments can be challenged even if they were made earlier than that, if it can be shown that the debtor was attempting to avoid other creditors.

CASE SUMMARY 15.8

Preferring One Creditor Is Prohibited: *Re Speedy Roofing Ltd.*[25]

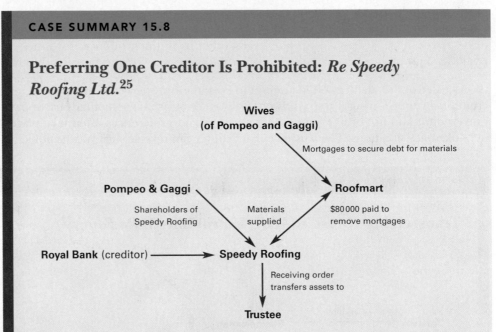

Roofmart supplied materials to Speedy Roofing. As Speedy Roofing was not paying its account, mortgages were given to Roofmart as security for the debt. The mortgages were on the homes of Pompeo and Gaggi, the wives of the principal shareholders of Speedy Roofing. Shortly before the Royal Bank, another creditor, forced it into bankruptcy, Speedy Roofing paid Roofmart $80 000 to discharge the mortgages. The Court had to determine whether that payment was a fraudulent preference and therefore prohibited under the *BIA*. Since the payment was made within three months of the bankruptcy, it amounted to a fraudulent preference. The Court ordered Roofmart to repay the $80 000 it received from Speedy Roofing to the trustee in bankruptcy.

SMALL BUSINESS PERSPECTIVE

A debtor cannot choose to pay one creditor over another or transfer property to a creditor to escape a debt. Do you agree with this policy? Should the debtor be able to choose which creditors will be paid and which will not be paid? If a debtor chooses to pay money owed to one creditor, should the other creditors be able to complain even if a legitimate debt has been properly paid?

Bankrupt has many duties, including swearing an affidavit about financial information

At the beginning of the bankruptcy process, the debtor is required to file an affidavit setting out all of his debts, creditors, and assets. He must provide a summary of all of the transactions that have taken place regarding these assets over

---

25. (1987), 62 O.R. (2d) 312 (H.C.J.), 1987 CanLII 4225 (ON SC), aff'd (1990), 74 O.R. (2d) 633 (C.A.), 1990 CanLII 6792 (ON CA).

the last year (or longer if so ordered). He must disclose any settlements he has made during the previous five years. A bankrupt also has an obligation to cooperate with the trustee by disclosing all relevant information and answering any relevant questions. The bankrupt may also be required to attend before the official receiver, or the court, to answer questions about how he got into financial trouble, as well as questions regarding his debts, creditors, and assets and what he has done with them. The bankrupt has many other duties, including transferring his assets to the trustee; delivering his credit cards, records, and documents to the trustee; and keeping the trustee advised of his address. The bankrupt must "generally do all such acts and things in relation to his property and the distribution of the proceeds among his creditors as may be reasonably required by the trustee, or may be prescribed by the General Rules, or may be directed by the court."[26]

In addition to settlements, fraudulent preferences, and a failure to fulfill the duties of a bankrupt, the *BIA* sets out several other bankruptcy offences for which a bankrupt may be punished. These include refusing to answer questions truthfully; hiding, falsifying, or destroying records; failing to keep proper records; and hiding or concealing property. If a bankrupt is convicted of a bankruptcy offence, she may be fined up to $10 000 or be imprisoned for up to three years or both.[27]

Bankruptcy offences

Once the assets have been transferred to a trustee by voluntary assignment or through a bankruptcy order, the debtor is a bankrupt. A bankrupt is subject to several restrictions. If he is involved in any business transaction or borrows more than $1000 he must disclose his status. He cannot be a director of a corporation.[28] He may also be restricted from carrying on some professions, such as accounting, depending on the particular rules of the professional body in question.[29]

Restrictions on bankrupts

Once the bankruptcy process is completed and the estate has been distributed, the bankrupt may apply to the court to be discharged. This application is automatic after nine months for an individual involved in her first bankruptcy, unless a creditor or the trustee opposes the discharge or if the bankrupt had been required to pay "surplus income" to her estate. If the bankrupt was required to pay surplus income, her discharge would be automatic after 21 months, unless the discharge is opposed. A second-time bankrupt is automatically discharged after 24 months if he did not have to pay surplus income, or after 36 months if he did. A bankrupt may apply for a discharge before he would otherwise be automatically discharged. An application for a discharge from bankruptcy may be granted unconditionally, it may be granted subject to certain conditions, or it may be denied.

Discharge from bankruptcy

Let's look at an example. A lawyer became bankrupt when a business in which he was involved failed. He maintained a very high lifestyle while going through the bankruptcy process. He was looking forward to a reasonable income after his discharge as well. He had not made any payments to the trustee. Given these circumstances, the Court ordered that his discharge be conditional on his paying a significant amount to his creditors.[30] A court has the discretion to place such conditions on the discharge of a bankrupt.

Discharge may be conditional ...

On the other hand, the same Court dealt with another lawyer in a different manner. He was 53 years old when he ran into financial difficulties. He did all he could to repay his creditors, including significantly reducing his lifestyle. It was only after his honest efforts failed, through no fault of his own, that he was forced

... or it may be unconditional, depending on the circumstances

26. *Bankruptcy and Insolvency Act, supra* note 19, s. 158 (o).

27. Ibid., s. 198.

28. See, for example, *Canada Business Corporations Act*, R.S.C. 1985, c. C-44, s. 105.

29. See, for example, Rule 601.1 of the "Rules of Professional Conduct" of the Institute of Chartered Accountants of Alberta, www.albertacas.ca/docs/governing-documents/combined-rulesguidelines-2013-pol.pdf?sfvrsn=6.

30. *McAfee v. Westmore* (1988), 23 B.C.L.R. (2d) 273 (C.A.), (1988), 49 D.L.R. (4th) 401, 1988 CanLII 187 (BC CA).

to make an assignment in bankruptcy. In this case, the Court had no hesitation in finding that the bankrupt was entitled to an unconditional discharge and a fresh start, even though his assets were not sufficient to pay back 50 cents on the dollar. In reaching this conclusion, the Court considered the bankrupt's honesty, his struggle for nine years to pay back his creditors, and his need to be free to prepare for his retirement.[31]

Reasons for conditional discharges

These two cases illustrate the power of the bankruptcy court to place significant conditions on a discharge and the factors that might affect such a decision. Debtors who commit bankruptcy offences will normally not be unconditionally discharged; they may even be imprisoned. The court will also be reluctant to unconditionally discharge bankrupts who have not fulfilled their duties or whose behaviour has not been reasonable. As shown by the *McAfee* case (see footnote 30), in such cases the court can grant a conditional discharge, putting conditions or restrictions on the bankrupt. Justice Estey commented on the purpose of the bankruptcy process as follows: "The purpose and object of the *Bankruptcy Act* [now the *BIA*] is to equitably distribute the assets of the debtor and to permit his rehabilitation as a citizen, unfettered by past debts. The discharge, however, is not a matter of right, and the provisions of Sections 142 and 143 [now sections 172 and 173 of the *BIA*] plainly indicate that in certain cases the debtor should suffer a period of probation."[32]

CASE SUMMARY 15.9

Conditional or Unconditional Discharge? *McRudden (Re)*[33]

This case involves an application for the discharge of a first-time bankrupt. At the time of his assignment into bankruptcy, the bankrupt was indebted to the federal government with respect to income tax, GST, and unpaid source deductions. Prior to the assignment, the government had conducted an audit of the bankrupt and had disallowed several items that had been claimed as business expenses for his dental practice. The items included a hot tub, a tanning bed, plastic surgery, a tractor lawn mower, improvements to his personal residence, a car stereo, and a barbecue. The bankrupt was reassessed and made no voluntary payments on the income tax owing. Collection actions (garnishment and seizure) were taken. The bankrupt then disposed of assets and did not disclose to his trustee a transfer of funds to his sister. At the time of his assignment, the bankrupt owed $150 000 to the government, $50 000 for arrears in child support, and $200 000 to the College of Dental Surgeons for a fine and costs of his appeal from disciplinary proceedings. His licence to practise dentistry was suspended, and he was making no effort to earn money. He pled guilty to two counts under the *BIA* and one count under the *Criminal Code*, for making a false entry or knowingly making a material omission in a statement or accounting. He was given a conditional sentence of 16 months, including six months of house arrest.

The registrar noted that the bankrupt was 65 years old, was not working, was living on a monthly payment from his sister, was depressed, and was "self-medicating" with alcohol, but that he had not changed his lavish lifestyle. The bankrupt asked for an absolute discharge, while the trustee asked that there be no discharge or that there be a discharge conditional on the bankrupt paying a large portion of his debt.

---

31. *Re Irwin* (1994), 89 B.C.L.R. (2d) 114 (C.A.), (1994), 112 D.L.R. (4th) 164, 1994 CanLII 1723 (BC CA).

32. *Industrial Acceptance Corp. v. Lalonde*, [1952] 2 S.C.R. 109, 1952 CanLII 2 (SCC), at 120.

33. 2014 BCSC 217 (CanLII).

The registrar said that, based on the facts, the case "cried out for deterrence," not to punish the bankrupt but to send a message to others who might be tempted to evade income tax liability through bankruptcy. He ordered a discharge conditional on the bankrupt paying $200 000 into the estate and on him filing income tax returns (and paying any income tax owing) every year until he had repaid the $200 000.

DISCUSSION QUESTIONS

Should relieving the bankrupt from the burden of his debts be given priority over him paying his creditors the amount they are owed? What factors should the courts consider when resolving this dilemma?

 REDUCING RISK 15.5

Debtors sometimes use bankruptcy as a convenient way to avoid paying their debts. Some even declare bankruptcy several times. While this is obviously an abuse of the process, sophisticated clients will be ever-vigilant to avoid doing business with such people. Use of credit checks can be a great help, even when goods or services are being supplied. On the other hand, debtors who are tempted to abuse the process should realize that, as a rule, committing a bankruptcy offence will likely result in fines, imprisonment, or both. Furthermore, the courts will generally not grant an unconditional discharge when faced with abuses such as the debtor failing to cooperate with officials, trying to hide assets, or otherwise abusing the process.

After Discharge

During the bankruptcy process, the bankrupt is required to continue to make regular payments (surplus income payments) to the trustee to be distributed to the creditors. Any windfall she receives, such as an inheritance or a lottery win, will go to the trustee for distribution. That all changes upon discharge from bankruptcy (assuming that the discharge is unconditional). When discharged, the debtor is freed from most previous claims by creditors and is in a position to start over. Any assets subsequently obtained by the discharged bankrupt are hers to do with as she wishes; unpaid creditors cannot claim against them. Pursuant to the *BIA*, some obligations do survive discharge, such as fines, alimony and maintenance payments, and some civil damage awards. Student loans also survive bankruptcy. They are payable for up to seven years after the debtor ceases to be a student.[34]

Effect of absolute discharge is to end most debts

The discussion above focused primarily on the bankruptcy of an individual. The primary difference with a bankruptcy of a corporation is that there will not be a discharge after the bankruptcy unless the corporation has been able to repay all of the money owing. That, of course, is highly unlikely, there being little likelihood of a bankruptcy in the first place in those circumstances. A Division II consumer proposal under the *BIA* is not available to a corporation, but corporations often try to restructure using Division I commercial proposals (see the discussion of these proposals below). Larger corporations also often restructure using the *Companies' Creditors Arrangement Act*.[35] If a corporation's proposal is approved, or if it reaches an arrangement with its creditors and it properly fulfills its obligations, the corporation will be free to carry on its business, avoiding bankruptcy

Corporations are not discharged after bankruptcy

Corporations may use proposals and arrangements to avoid bankruptcy

---

34. *Bankruptcy and Insolvency Act, supra* note 19, s. 178. This was changed from 10 years on July 7, 2008. Also, the period before which an application may be made to request a discharge on the basis of hardship was reduced from 10 years to 5 years.

35. R.S.C. 1985, c. C-36.

altogether. The obligations of the debtor to supply appropriate information and documents apply to corporations as well. A corporation must provide someone who is familiar with the situation to answer the questions that would otherwise have been put to an individual debtor by the trustee, the creditors in a creditor meeting, the official receiver, or the court.

Creditors and shareholders may have other remedies

A corporation will often face dissolution after the bankruptcy process, although this is usually not worth the trouble. Still, disgruntled shareholders and creditors may have further rights under winding-up acts or the various business corporations' legislation in place at both the provincial and federal levels. They also may have claims against the directors and other officers of the corporation under those statutes. In this regard, the Supreme Court of Canada recently held that, in certain circumstances, directors owe a duty of care to creditors of the corporation, but the duty does not give rise to a fiduciary duty. The directors owe a fiduciary duty to the corporation only.[36]

Directors of corporations owe creditors a duty of care

Receivers may be appointed by creditors pursuant to security agreement

Corporations that go into **receivership** are usually not involved in bankruptcy at all. When a creditor lends a corporation significant funds, the security agreement usually gives the creditor the right, in the event of default or some other triggering event, to appoint a receiver to take possession of the assets given as security, without the necessity of going through the bankruptcy procedure. Such an assignment of assets to a receiver is not a bankruptcy, but the effect can be every bit as devastating to the business. Some of the rights and responsibilities of receivers are set out in Part XI of the *BIA*. A secured creditor must give the debtor reasonable notice before the appointment of a receiver or taking possession of the goods used as security. Whether the receiver is appointed by the creditor directly or it obtains a court order allowing the appointment, failure to give reasonable notice can be devastating to the debtor. This will result in significant liability to the creditor when it is improperly done.[37]

Reasonable notice must be given

Two purposes of the *BIA*

It must be remembered that there are two main purposes of the *BIA*. The first is to ensure that the creditors realize as much of the amount owed as possible. The second is to facilitate the rehabilitation of the debtor. We will continue to see legislative changes as the debate over the proper balance of these two objectives continues.

Alternatives to Bankruptcy

Debtor should try to avoid bankruptcy

The debtor should, of course, do all he can to avoid bankruptcy. If he becomes bankrupt, he will lose most of his property. He will also find it difficult in the future to conduct business or to make personal credit purchases due to a poor credit rating. A personal bankruptcy will remain on an individual's credit record for about six years. Even after that period of time, it will be obvious to a credit grantor that there must have been serious financial problems because of the lack of credit transactions during that six-year period. If a corporation becomes bankrupt, it will not be discharged and will therefore not survive.

There are several possible informal solutions

For a debtor who is having financial problems, the first step should be to talk to the creditors involved to try to make alternative arrangements for paying the debt. Creditors are usually quite responsive to reasonable arrangements for avoiding both commercial and personal bankruptcies, because they will often get much less if bankruptcy is forced. There are also many tangible and intangible advantages for creditors to keep their debtor as a functioning customer. Another option, especially when significant credit card debt is involved, is to obtain a consolidation loan from a bank or other lending institution. A consolidation loan enables the debtor to consolidate the various debts he owes. There will then be only one creditor and a more manageable payment schedule, often at a lower rate of interest. Individual creditors

---

36. *Peoples Department Stores Inc. (Trustee of) v. Wise*, [2004] 3 S.C.R. 461, 2004 SCC 68 (CanLII).

37. See, for example, *Royal Bank of Canada v. W. Got and Associates Electric Ltd.*, [1999] 3 S.C.R. 408, 1999 CanLII 714 (SCC).

will sometimes agree to take less to pay off the debt. They realize that they will be better off accepting less rather than risking getting nothing by continuing to demand full payment and thus forcing bankruptcy.

If these informal negotiations fail, the *BIA* still provides for an alternative to bankruptcy. Two separate procedures are involved; both allow the debtor to reorganize her affairs and make proposals for partial payment that will satisfy her creditors sufficiently to avoid actual bankruptcy. **Division I proposals** usually involve commercial debtors in the form of corporations or individual debtors with significant claims against them (more than $250 000). The process is started by filing a proposal or a notice of intention to file a proposal with the official receiver. The filing should be done with the help of a professional licensed to provide these services (a trustee in bankruptcy). Within 10 days of filing a notice of intention, a statement of projected cash flow must also be filed, followed within 30 days by the filing of the proposal itself (although this time limit may be extended). A meeting with the creditors is then held, and the proposal is discussed and voted upon. For the proposal to be approved, two-thirds of the unsecured creditors by value and a majority by number must vote to accept it. (Note that they may be divided into classes of creditors and then vote within that class.) The same approach applies to each class of secured creditors to which the proposal was made. The court also must approve the proposal.

If the unsecured creditors approve the proposal, all of them are bound by it. If the unsecured creditors (or the court) reject the proposal, the debtor is deemed to have made an assignment in bankruptcy from the day of the meeting of the creditors. Normal bankruptcy procedures will follow. Secured creditors whose class gave its approval are also bound by the proposal. Secured creditors not included in the proposal, or whose class rejected the proposal, can still realize on their security.

Division I proposals are very flexible. They may include anything from arranging to reduce the debt to devising a new payment structure to helping the creditors wind up the corporation. An important effect of starting this process by filing a proposal or a notice of intention is that creditors, including secured creditors who have been included in the proposal process, are prevented from taking action against the debtor or her assets until the vote takes place, at least two months later. In effect, the insolvent debtor is protected from the creditors. If the proposal is accepted, that protection continues.

> **Debtors can make a proposal and avoid bankruptcy**

> **Division I proposals for corporations and people with debts over $250 000**

> **If proposal is rejected, debtor goes into bankruptcy**

> **Proposals are flexible and they stay proceedings**

CASE SUMMARY 15.10

Proposal Abused: *Janodee Investments Ltd. v. Pellegrini*[38]

Pellegrini had two mortgages on his home. When he defaulted on them, the mortgagees/creditors proceeded to judgment and obtained an order to take possession of the house. Before the order could be enforced, Pellegrini served notice of intention to make a proposal under the *BIA*. Normally, such a notice would result in a stay of proceedings, delaying enforcement of the order. However, in this case the Court held that Pellegrini was using the notice as a delaying tactic. He had no serious intention of reordering his affairs. No other secured creditors were involved, and the mortgagees would not be responsive to such a proposal in any event.

This case is instructive in that it shows not only the normal operation of a proposal but also how such a proposal can be abused. In this case, the Court refused to order the stay, thus preventing such abuse. The difficulty with the operation of such proposals—as well as with the whole bankruptcy process—is that it interferes with the creditors' rights to proceed against the debtor and enforce full payment in a timely manner. The justification for this is that, in the long run, the creditors get more and that, after discharge,

---

38. (2001), 25 C.B.R. (4th) 47 (Ont. S.C.J.), 2001 CanLII 28455 (ON SC).

the bankrupt is able to carry on without overwhelming debt. But, in fact, many creditors get very little or nothing and are barred from further proceedings after discharge.

SMALL BUSINESS PERSPECTIVE

Does the Division 1 proposal process in the *BIA* provide too much protection for insolvent people and businesses, at the expense of legitimate creditors?

Consumer proposals are available for people with debts less than $250 000

Consumer debtors with less than $250 000 in claims against them (excluding a mortgage on their home) are similarly protected when they make a consumer proposal under Division II of Part III of the *BIA*. The insolvent debtor must hire an administrator (a trustee in bankruptcy or a person appointed to administer consumer proposals). The administrator examines the debtor's finances, prepares the consumer proposal and any reports required, provides counselling for the debtor, and files the consumer proposal. This is a simpler process than filing a Division I proposal. No actual meeting is required unless demanded by the creditors. If the creditors reject a consumer proposal, the debtor is not automatically bankrupt. A consumer proposal must contain a commitment by the debtor that the performance of the consumer proposal will be completed within five years. Payments under a consumer proposal are paid to the administrator, who distributes the funds to the creditors.

Consumer proposals stop all legal actions by unsecured creditors

As long as the debtor complies with the obligations in the consumer proposal, acts honestly, and participates in any mandatory counselling required, action cannot be taken against him by unsecured creditors. Even those supplying ongoing services, such as public utilities and landlords, must continue supplying them. But if the debtor defaults on his commitments, the consumer proposal is annulled and the debtor may face the normal bankruptcy procedures. Court approval of Division II proposals is not required.

Secured debts are not affected if not in proposal

For both Division I proposals and consumer proposals, if a proposal is accepted and then properly performed a certificate is issued and the debtor's obligation is complete with respect to those matters covered by the proposal. There are some matters that cannot be included in a proposal, just as some types of obligations cannot be discharged though bankruptcy; these will be discussed below. If a secured debt was not included in the proposal, then that obligation remains and is not affected by the completed performance of the proposal or the certificate issued.

Orderly Payment of Debts program is available in some provinces

In some provinces, individual debtors may also use Part X of the *BIA*, Orderly Payment of Debts (OPD). If the amount the debtor owes is less than $1000 or if the debtor obtains the consent of the creditors, she can apply to the court for a consolidation order. She must provide an affidavit, setting out her relevant financial and personal situation. The application will be approved, unless a creditor objects to it. If there is an objection, there will be a hearing in front of the clerk of the court to determine the validity of the objection.

Consolidation order acts as a stay

A consolidation order requires the debtor to make the stipulated payments into court, such that all of his debts will be paid in full within three years unless the creditors consent to a longer period. Such an order acts as a stay with respect to the debts covered by the order, except for secured debts. If the debtor defaults, the creditors can enforce the consolidation order like any other court order, subject to the court's approval. The OPD program is administered by various public and private agencies in the provinces where it is available. In Alberta, for example, Money Mentors (the successor to Credit Counselling Services of Alberta Ltd.) administers the OPD program.[39]

[39.] See Money Mentors, www.moneymentors.ca. Also, for an explanation of OPD, see Bankruptcy Canada, "Orderly Payment of Debts," www.bankruptcy-canada.ca/alternatives-to-bankruptcy/orderly-payment-of-debts.htm.

For corporations owing more than $5 million, there is an alternative process available that enables them to restructure their affairs and avoid bankruptcy. This alternative is available under the *Companies' Creditors Arrangement Act (CCAA)*.[40] This is a federal statute providing protection to debtors with some advantages over the *BIA*. The attraction of the *CCAA* is in the protection given to debtors from their creditors. This may provide more flexibility to the debtor corporation in its restructuring efforts, since it will be protected from its creditors, both secured and unsecured, for a longer period of time. A judge will often combine the flexibility provided under the *CCAA* with the power under section 47 of the *BIA* to appoint an interim receiver to supervise the restructuring process. Many corporations have filed for bankruptcy protection under the *CCAA* in recent years,[41] including Air Canada and Sino-Forest Corporation.[42]

Large corporations can ask the court for bankruptcy protection

Commercial and consumer proposals under the *BIA*, consolidation orders in the OPD program, and arrangements under the *CCAA* all enable a debtor to avoid the bankruptcy process. Bankruptcy will occur, however, if the creditors reject a proposal or if the debtor defaults on her obligations under a proposal. Businesspeople should be aware of bankruptcy and its alternatives, from both a consumer and a commercial perspective. Consumer bankruptcies are much more numerous than commercial bankruptcies. Any business dealing with the public must therefore factor this risk into its business considerations. Commercial bankruptcies may be less common than consumer bankruptcies, but they generally involve much more money and have a greater impact on the businesses with which the debtor is dealing. Even high profile businesses (e.g., General Motors Corp.) have faced bankruptcy or restructuring in these difficult economic times. A businessperson ignores these risks at his peril.

Be aware of credit risks

 REDUCING RISK 15.6

Bankruptcy is a serious and drastic step. Both creditors and debtors should do all they can to avoid it. Often negotiation between the parties, perhaps with a mediator, will result in an acceptable alternative. The creditors get more than they would get by forcing bankruptcy, and a valued customer is preserved.

If these informal steps fail and proposals are presented, they should be treated seriously. Bankruptcy should be used only as a last resort. It is to the advantage of both creditors and debtors to take a sophisticated approach to situations involving defaults on financial obligations.

MyBusLawLab Be sure to visit the MyBusLawLab that accompanies this book to find practice quizzes, province-specific content, simulations and much more!

---

[40] *Supra* note 35.

[41] The Office of the Superintendent of Bankruptcy Canada provides a list of companies that have been granted protection under the *CCAA* since September 18, 2009; see www.ic.gc.ca/eic/site/bsf-osb.nsf/eng/h_br02281.html.

[42] For an interesting article that explains the *CCAA* and how it is different from "Chapter 11" bankruptcy, see "When a Company Tries to Reorganize," *CBC News*, October 6, 2009, www.cbc.ca/news/business/story/2009/01/14/f-bankruptcyprotection.html.

SUMMARY

Methods of securing debt—personal property

- Real and personal property may be used as security, giving a creditor some assurance that she will be paid even when other creditors are not
- In a conditional sale, the debtor has possession of the goods while the seller retains title until final payment is made
- In a chattel mortgage, the debtor has possession of the goods but gives title to the creditor until final payment is made
- Assignment of book accounts gives a creditor the right to intercept payments upon default

Personal Property Security Act

- The *PPSA* allows both tangible and intangible forms of personal property to be used as security
- The security must first attach to the collateral, but priority is established through perfection, either by registration or by taking possession of the collateral
- Priority is usually determined by date of registration, but PMSIs and sales in the normal course of business are exceptions
- In the event of default, the creditor can take possession of the goods and sell them. The creditor can usually sue for deficiency, but sometimes must make a decision to either take possession or sue
- The debtor has the right to be notified of the sale and to redeem the property

Guarantees

- A guarantee is a contingent liability in which someone agrees to be responsible when a debtor fails to pay; an indemnity involves co-responsibility for the debt
- The creditor must protect the interests of the guarantor, but this protection can be limited by the terms of the guarantee
- If a guarantor is required to pay the creditor, he steps into the shoes of the creditor and can seek repayment from the debtor
- The guarantor usually has the same defences as the debtor

Other forms of security

- *Bank Act* security enables growing crops and goods being manufactured to be used as security
- Floating charges are used by creditors of corporations to allow inventory to be free of a floating charge until it crystallizes
- Builders' liens protect contractors and subcontractors by enabling them to file a lien against the land and by forcing the owner to hold back a portion of what is paid
- Certified cheques, bank drafts, bills of exchange, and promissory notes are often used in credit transactions
- Letters of credit are used to secure credit in international trade

Related laws

- Bulk sales acts protect unsecured creditors from the sale of all the assets of a business
- Fraudulent transfers and preferences are void

Bankruptcy—introduction

- Two main objectives of bankruptcy legislation are to protect creditors and to enable rehabilitation of the bankrupt

The process of bankruptcy

- Bankruptcy can take place voluntarily through assignment or involuntarily through a bankruptcy order
- Involves the transfer of the debtor's non-exempt assets to a trustee in bankruptcy, who sells the assets and distributes the proceeds to the creditors

Priority among creditors in bankruptcy

- Creditors must file proof of claim with the trustee
- Assets go first to secured creditors, then to preferred creditors, and then to unsecured creditors, unless the government has passed legislation giving it top priority
- Suppliers of goods can reclaim them if they make a demand within the time limits

Bankruptcy offences

- Fraudulent transfers and preferences may be reversed by the trustee
- Bankrupt has many duties; if she fails to fulfill them or commits another bankruptcy offence she can be fined, imprisoned, or both
- Once the process is complete, the bankrupt can apply for discharge; discharge is automatic for first-time bankrupts unless an objection is made or the bankrupt had to pay surplus income
- Discharge may be granted unconditionally, subject to conditions, or denied

After discharge from bankruptcy

- Absolute discharge relieves responsibility for most prior debts
- A corporation will not survive bankruptcy, but it can make a *BIA* Division II proposal or a *CCAA* arrangement instead of making an assignment into bankruptcy
- Receivership involves a receiver taking possession of the secured assets

Alternatives to bankruptcy

- Debtors should try to avoid bankruptcy through informal negotiations
- Division I proposal is used to protect commercial debtors and individuals with significant debts from action by creditors, until the proposal is accepted or rejected
- Division II proposal is used to protect consumers with debts less than $250 000
- The Orderly Payment of Debts program gives individuals protection so they can avoid bankruptcy, if they pay off their debts within three years
- Large corporations can ask courts for protection from creditors under the *Companies' Creditors Arrangements Act*

QUESTIONS FOR REVIEW

1. Distinguish between the following:
   a. Real property and personal property
   b. Choses in action and chattels
   c. A chattel mortgage and a conditional sale
   d. A chattel mortgage and a mortgage on real estate

2. What kinds of property can be used as collateral under the *PPSA*?

3. What are the advantages of using the *PPSA* to govern all transactions involving the use of personal property as security?

4. What significant problem associated with the practice of taking goods as security is alleviated by the registration requirements introduced by legislation? Describe the resulting obligations on all parties.

5. Distinguish among security agreement, attachment, and perfection. Explain the significance of each of them and how each is accomplished.

6. How is the priority of secured parties determined? What are two exceptions to this general approach?

7. What are the rights of a secured party when there is a default by the debtor? What determines the limitations of those rights?

8. What obligations are imposed on a secured creditor who takes possession of goods used as security after a debtor defaults?

9. Explain the rights of a debtor after he has defaulted and the secured party has taken possession of the collateral.

10. "The debtor is always liable to the creditor for any deficiency after the goods used as security have been sold." True or false? Explain your answer.

11. What is the difference between a guarantee and an indemnity? Why is the distinction important?

12. What duties does the creditor owe the guarantor before and after the guarantee is given?

13. If the debtor defaults, what steps does the creditor have to take before she is entitled to demand payment from the guarantor? If the guarantor pays the creditor, what rights does he have against the debtor?

14. What is the main advantage of the provisions of the *Bank Act* that allow the banks to take security for the loans they grant? Why may these provisions cause confusion?

15. What happens upon default when a floating charge has been used to secure a debt? What is the main advantage of using floating charges?

16. What significant difficulty facing suppliers of goods and services in the construction industry is overcome by the creation of the builders' lien? How can suppliers protect themselves? Explain the role of the holdback.

17. Explain the nature and use of a letter of credit. Distinguish between a standby letter of credit and a normal letter of credit.

18. How does the *Bulk Sales Act* protect creditors when a business is selling all or almost all of its assets?

19. Explain the difference between a fraudulent transfer and a fraudulent preference. What is the legal effect of both of these types of transactions?

20. Define the objectives of bankruptcy legislation.

21. Distinguish between bankruptcy and insolvency.

22. Distinguish between an assignment in bankruptcy and a bankruptcy order. Explain the process involved in each case.

23. Explain the role of the trustee in the bankruptcy process.

24. Who files a proof of claim? What is its purpose? Who evaluates the validity of a filed proof of claim?

25. Describe the order of distribution of the assets and the proceeds from the sale of assets of the bankrupt. How does a "super priority" affect the order of distribution?

26. How are fraudulent transfers and fraudulent preferences dealt with by the *BIA*?

27. What are the duties of a debtor in the bankruptcy process?

28. Explain what is meant by a bankruptcy offence and the possible consequences of committing one.

29. What restrictions are bankrupts subject to?

30. "An application for discharge by a first-time bankrupt will automatically be granted." True or false? Explain your answer.

31. What factors will a court consider when determining what conditions, if any, to place on a discharge from bankruptcy?

32. What changes for a bankrupt after an absolute discharge?

33. Why is it unlikely that there will not be a discharge after the bankruptcy of a corporation?

34. What can a corporation in financial difficulty do to avoid bankruptcy?

35. When could a creditor who has appointed a receiver to take possession of a debtor's assets face liability for making the appointment?

36. Discuss the informal options that are available to debtors who are experiencing financial difficulties.

37. Distinguish between Division I and Division II proposals. Explain the advantages of making a proposal.

38. "A consolidation order under the Orderly Payment of Debts program requires the debtor to pay her debts in full." True or false? Explain your answer.

39. What legislation is used by large corporations to obtain bankruptcy protection? What is the main advantage of using this legislation?

CASES AND DISCUSSION QUESTIONS

1. *Chartier v. MNP Ltd.*, **2013 MBCA 41 (CanLII)**

Lucy declared bankruptcy in 2007. MNP was the trustee of her estate. Later in 2007, Chartier purchased a home. He married Lucy in 2009. Under Manitoba law, the home became their "homestead property." In 2011, Chartier listed the home for sale. Lucy agreed with this decision and did not want to exercise her right to veto the sale. MNP had registered a notice against the title to the home. It argued that Lucy was an undischarged bankrupt when she married and acquired the homestead interest. The veto right was therefore after-acquired property to which the trustee was entitled.

Chartier accepted an offer to purchase the property. The prospective purchaser offered the trustee $20 000 for its consent to the sale and a discharge of the homestead notice. The trustee accepted the offer, but Chartier did not. The judge decided that the veto right did not vest in the trustee and that it had no value. The trustee appealed.

Is a veto right owned by a bankrupt "property" under the *BIA*? If it is, then the *BIA* would override the interests of the legislation that is meant to protect the family through the provision of a life estate interest in the homestead. Is this an appropriate result?

2. *Hoskins (Re)*, **2014 CanLII 2318 (NL SCTD)**

Honda Canada Finance Inc. sold an automobile to Hoskins. It registered a financing statement showing the name of the debtor as "Hoskins, Thomas E." and the correct serial number of the vehicle. Hoskins filed an assignment in bankruptcy. The trustee in bankruptcy disallowed the security interest on the grounds of an invalid registration because the legislation required that the name be entered as "Hoskins, Edgar Thomas." A registry search under this name did not disclose the registered document, but a search under the serial number did.

Is the security interest invalid as against the trustee in bankruptcy because the name on the financing statement is incorrect? Is there a requirement to conduct a "dual search," using both the name of the debtor and the serial number of a vehicle, in your province? Should there be?

3. *Carevest Capital Inc. v. Belle Harbour Developments Inc.*, **[2009] O.J. No. 1386 (S.C.), 2009 CanLII 15439 (ON SC)**

Carevest asked for summary judgment against the principal debtor of a commercial mortgage and the guarantors of the debt. The guarantors claimed that their guarantees were not binding for several reasons, including the expiry of the mortgage letter, the failure to convey certain leases, the purchase of a contaminated property, and a reduction of the purchase price.

The Court held that even if these defences were valid, the guarantors had to pay the debt of the principal debtor. Why would the Court make such a decision?

4. *Bank of Montreal v. Canada (Attorney General)* (2003), 66 O.R. (3d) 161 (C.A.), 2003 CanLII 52158 (ON CA)

The bank was a secured creditor of the debtor, Vita Pharm. Canada Customs sent a notice to pay GST to the debtors of Vita Pharm. On February 22, 2001, the bank applied for a bankruptcy order against Vita Pharm. On February 23, Canada Customs sent another notice to pay GST to the debtors. On March 8, Vita Pharm was declared bankrupt.

Should the notices to pay issued by Canada Customs take priority over the bank's secured claim? In light of the "super priority" of the government in certain situations, what will lenders do to ensure that they will be repaid? What effect will this have on the availability of credit, especially to small businesses?

5. *On the Vine Meat and Produce BIA Proposal (Re)*, 2012 NBQB 86 (CanLII)

The debtor signed a loan agreement with the Royal Bank of Canada (RBC). The debt was secured by a general security agreement and a security agreement. The debtor filed a notice of intention to make a proposal under the *BIA*. The debtor obtained an order extending the stay of proceedings for an extra 30 days. RBC applied to have the stay lifted; it had been concerned about questionable activities of the debtor relating to the operation of its account. The judge agreed that the activity was questionable, but that it had never created an overdraft and had only put RBC at risk for a moment in time. There was no material prejudice to RBC.

Should the stay be lifted because the debtor had not acted in good faith? When should a stay be lifted by a court?

16 Chapter

Sales and Consumer Protection

LEARNING OBJECTIVES

1. Describe the scope of the *Sale of Goods Act*
2. Explain the relationship between title and risk and outline the rules for determining who has title
3. Examine the rights and obligations of buyers and sellers
4. Describe the remedies of buyers and sellers upon default
5. Explain what consumer protection legislation is and why it exists
6. Review the *Competition Act* and other federal consumer protection legislation
7. Review the areas of consumer protection covered by provincial legislation
8. Identify the main forms of negotiable instruments and explain their basic characteristics

Basic contract law was discussed earlier in Chapters 6 to 9. There are, however, several important areas where legislation has been enacted that profoundly affects the contractual relationship. This chapter is devoted to an examination of sale of goods legislation, various consumer protection provisions, and negotiable instruments. While the *Competition Act* and *Bills of Exchange Act*[1] are federal statutes, most topics in this chapter deal with provincial legislation. There are considerable variations among provinces. Refer to MyBusLawLab to access the unique provisions in place in your jurisdiction.

THE SALE OF GOODS   LO ❶❷❸❹

Scope of the *Sale of Goods Act*

The *Sale of Goods Act* has been adopted with only minor variations by every common law province in Canada. Refer to MyBusLawLab, where the various provincial *Sale of Goods Acts* are linked and described.

---

[1]. *Competition Act*, R.S.C. 1985, c. C-34; *Bills of Exchange Act*, R.S.C. 1985, c B-4.

Sale of Goods Act **implies terms into contract**

All other contract rules must be complied with

The primary purpose of the Act is to imply the terms that the parties to sale of goods transactions often leave out. For example, the parties may fail to specify a date for payment or time of delivery, and the Act will imply the missing terms into the contract. But it will only imply *missing* terms, so the parties are free to override its provisions by clearly stating a different intention in their contract. Note as well that the Act supplements the common law, so the normal rules of contract still apply. The *Sale of Goods Act* is not restricted to retail and consumer transactions; it also applies to commercial transactions, even those involving the sale of large machinery such as railway locomotives.

GOODS AND SERVICES

The Act applies only to the sale of goods

The *Sale of Goods Act* affects only those contracts involving goods. Goods are tangible items, such as watches, televisions, books, and even animals, seeds, and growing crops. Buildings and building materials are subject to the *Sale of Goods Act* until they become attached to the land, at which time they are treated as part of the real property and are not covered by the Act. Nor does the Act cover contracts for intangibles, such as services, negotiable instruments, stocks, bonds, and other documents representing rights or claims (referred to as *choses in action*). Where both goods and services are involved the Act does not apply unless the sale primarily involves the delivery of goods, as when a restaurant serves a meal selected from a menu or where the labour and parts can be separated. Thus, when an artist paints a portrait or a lawyer drafts a will the Act will not apply, but where automobile repairs are involved the Act will apply to the parts component of the bill. Note that if the artist's client were to resell the portrait, the Act would apply to that transaction. Even where the Act doesn't apply there may still be a remedy, though. In *Borek v. Hooper,*[2] an artist painted a portrait using defective materials that caused the painting to deteriorate. The Court refused to apply the *Sale of Goods Act* since the contract was primarily for a service but still granted remedy for breach of an implied warranty of fitness based on common law.

TRANSFER OF GOODS FOR MONETARY CONSIDERATION

Goods must be transferred

The *Sale of Goods Act* applies only when it can be demonstrated that the parties intended that the actual possession and property of the goods would transfer to the buyer. The *Sale of Goods Act* will not apply when goods are used to secure a loan except where that security is actually part of the sales transaction. Thus, if you use your car to secure a loan to obtain funds to pay tuition, the Act would not apply even though the creditor might use a **bill of sale** to create the security. But if you purchase that car, paying for it over time with the seller providing the credit, the Act would apply since there eventually is an actual change of possession. Secured transactions were discussed in Chapter 15.

The Act does not apply to barter situations

Some provinces also require evidence in writing

It is also necessary that the sale involve the actual payment of some money, as illustrated in Case Summary 16.1. The Act will not apply to goods that are traded or bartered unless some money is also exchanged. Several jurisdictions also require that there be a written memorandum if the sale exceeds a specified amount. For example, that amount is $50 in Alberta and $40 in Nova Scotia. Alternatively, part performance will also satisfy this requirement.

CASE SUMMARY 16.1

Is There a Sale of Goods in This Case? *Hearns v. Rizzolo*[3]

Rizzolo exchanged his Jeep for Hearns's Dodge. Unfortunately, the Jeep had a lien against it that Rizzolo had no knowledge about when he bought the car. The finance company learned that the Jeep was in the possession of Hearns and demanded payment

---

2. (1994), 114 D.L.R. (4th) 570 (Ont. Div. Ct.).
3. 2012 NSSC 256 (CanLII).

on threat of repossession. Hearns paid the finance company $10 738.18 to clear the title and then sued Rizzolo for compensation in Small Claims Court, relying on section 13 of the Nova Scotia *Sale of Goods Act*. That section imposes an implied warranty that the goods be free and clear of any charge or encumbrance in favour of a third party.

The Small Claims Court "adjudicator" found that the *Sale of Goods Act* did not apply, as this was a trade of goods rather than a sale. No funds were exchanged. Therefore, the implied terms set out in the *Sale of Goods Act,* including section 13, did not apply. There was no implied warranty that the goods be free of charge or encumbrance. Also, there was no fraud involved as Rizzolo knew nothing about the lien. Applying the principle of *caveat emptor,* Rizzolo was not liable to Hearns for the amount he had to pay to clear the title. The decision was appealed to the Supreme Court of Nova Scotia, but the judge agreed that the *Sale of Goods Act* did not apply to the transaction and dismissed the appeal.

This case is instructive because it illustrates that the *Sale of Goods Act* does not apply to all transactions where goods are exchanged, only where money is involved.

DISCUSSION QUESTIONS

Do you think that this is just a technicality? Should the *Sale of Goods Act* apply to this transaction? Should Rizzolo be responsible in simple contract law? Should Hearns have recourse against anyone else?

Title and Risk

As illustrated in the previous chapter with respect to conditional sales, the transfer of title and possession do not always take place at the same time. When title is to transfer some time in the future, this is called an **agreement to sell**. Determining who has title at any given time is important, because under the *Sale of Goods Act* whoever has the title bears the **risk** of damage or destruction to the goods—unless the parties have agreed otherwise.

Several common methods are used in contracts to specify who will bear the risk. In **CIF (cost, insurance, and freight) contracts** the parties specify who will bear the risk by assigning one party the responsibility to bear the costs of and arrange for insurance and freight. In **FOB (free on board) contracts** the parties specify at what point title and responsibility for the goods will pass. For example, where the goods are to be delivered FOB the purchaser's loading dock, the buyer assumes title and risk at that point. The third method involves **COD (cash on delivery) contracts**. Here the seller assumes all responsibility until the goods are delivered to the purchaser, at which point the goods are paid for and title and risk transfer. It is also possible to control title and risk through a **bill of lading**. When goods are shipped the carrier issues a receipt (the bill of lading), and where the seller specifies themselves as the recipient at the destination, they retain effective control as well as title and risk until those goods are actually transferred to the purchaser. The bill of lading is then assigned to the purchaser who presents it to the shipper at the destination, at which point title and risk transfer.

Distinction between sale and agreement to sell

Normally, risk follows title

 ### REDUCING RISK 16.1

There are many opportunities to exercise control over the various legal aspects of business transactions, such as who bears the risk and when title transfers. While there have been many restrictions imposed when consumers are involved, there are still many options available where a sophisticated client can reduce risk, especially in commercial transactions.

TRANSFER OF TITLE

Who has title can not only determine who bears the risk, but also affect which remedies are available in the event of a breach. If title is transferred, the seller can sue for the entire price; otherwise, only damages for breach of contract are available.

Remedy may depend on who has title

Rules for determining title

Who has title can also determine who has first claim to the goods in the event of default or bankruptcy. The rules for determining who has title as found in the *Sale of Goods Act* are set out below.[4] But remember, these rules apply only if the parties have not specified otherwise in their contract.

Rule 1

Unconditional contract—title transfers immediately

Where there is an unconditional contract for the sale of specific goods in a deliverable state, the property in the goods passes to the buyer when the contract is made; it is immaterial whether the time of payment or the time of delivery or both is postponed.

If the goods are identified and nothing more has to be done to them, the buyer gets title at the point of contracting to purchase. Thus, if Christina accepts an offer from Miles to sell her a car "as is," title would transfer at that point, even though she might take delivery and pay at a later date. Were the car damaged through no fault of Miles before she picked it up; the loss would be Christina's.

Rule 2

If the seller is required to do something to put goods in a deliverable state—title transfers when the task is completed and notice is given

Where there is a contract for the sale of specific goods and the seller is bound to do something to the goods for the purpose of putting them into a deliverable state, the property does not pass until such thing is done and the buyer has notice thereof.

If some repair were required in the previous example, title and risk would pass to the buyer only after the repair was done and Christina was notified the car was ready. If the car were damaged before the notice, Miles would bear the loss.

Rule 3

If the seller is required to weigh or measure to ascertain price—title transferred when purchaser is notified

Where there is a contract for the sale of specific goods in a deliverable state but the seller is bound to weigh, measure, test, or do some other act or thing with reference to the goods for the purpose of ascertaining the price, the property does not pass until such act or thing is done and the buyer has notice thereof.

If Schmidt bought a truckload of potatoes from Naslund, title would not pass until the potatoes were weighed to determine the price and Schmidt was notified.

Rule 4

When goods are delivered to the buyer on approval or "on sale or return" or other similar terms, the property therein passes to the buyer under one of these circumstances:

1. When the buyer signifies approval or acceptance to the seller or does any other act adopting the transaction

Goods delivered subject to buyer's approval—title passes when approval by acceptance is signified or a reasonable time has passed

2. If the buyer does not signify approval or acceptance to the seller but retains the goods without giving notice of rejection, then if a time has been fixed for the return of the goods, title passes on the expiration of such time, and if no time has been fixed, title passes on the expiration of a reasonable time; what is a reasonable time is a question of fact.

This rule covers situations in which goods are taken by the buyer to test for a trial period before deciding to keep them. To modify our earlier example, if Miles had allowed Christina to take the car home for two days, to test drive it and have it inspected by a mechanic, title and risk would not transfer to Christina until the expiration of those two days unless Christina notified Miles before that time that she was happy with the car. Title would also pass earlier if Christina tried to resell or had repairs done on the car.

[4.] These provisions are taken from s. 19 of the Ontario *Sale of Goods Act*, R.S.O. 1990, c. S.1. Every province has a similar Act, although the wording of the provisions may vary. Refer to MyBusLawLab, where these statutes are identified and linked.

Rule 5

1.   Where there is a contract for the sale of unascertained or future goods by description and goods of that description and in a deliverable state are unconditionally appropriated to the contract, either by the seller with the assent of the buyer or by the buyer with the assent of the seller, the property in the goods passes to the buyer, and such assent may be expressed or implied and may be given either before or after the appropriation is made.

2.   Where in pursuance of the contract the seller delivers the goods to the buyer or to a carrier or other bailee (whether named by the buyer or not) for the purpose of transmission to the buyer and does not reserve the right of disposal, the seller shall be deemed to have unconditionally appropriated the goods to the contract.

> **When goods are not manufactured or identifiable as goods in question, title passes upon unconditional appropriation and assent**

The goods covered by Rule 5 are those that have not been manufactured at the time the contract is entered into or that exist but have not yet been separated out and identified as the particular goods to be used in a given transaction. If a chair is purchased from a furniture store, title does not pass until the specific chair is selected from several like it stored in the warehouse. Rule 5 would also apply when a buyer orders a chair that has not yet been manufactured.

Only when the goods have been manufactured or separated out and unconditionally committed to the buyer with the buyer's assent does title pass. While notice to the buyer that the goods are ready may be the most common method of satisfying the assent or approval provision, assent is often implied from the circumstances. Thus, if a person were to leave her car with a dealer for the installation of a specified make and model of tires, she will be taken to have assented to the selection of the particular tires installed since she left her car there for that purpose.

It must always be remembered that the parties can specify a contrary intention in the contract, overriding these rules with respect to title and risk. The wise purchaser should carefully examine the terms of the contract to determine whether this has been done.

CASE SUMMARY 16.2

Did Property in the Fire Truck Pass before the Anderson Bankruptcy? *Re Anderson's Engineering Ltd. (Trustee of)*[5]

Anderson's contracted with Online to build and deliver a fire truck. Online paid Anderson's two advances toward the total purchase price of the truck. Anderson's viewed these billings as advances against the full contract price, consistent with Anderson's procedure on other contracts and with industry practice. Anderson's made an assignment into bankruptcy before the work on the fire truck was complete and listed the chassis and pump that were to be part of the fire truck as assets owned at the time of the bankruptcy. Online claimed ownership of the chassis and pump, the cumulative value of which was approximately equal to the amount paid in advances. An application was brought to determine whether Online's claim to a property interest in these assets was defeated on the grounds that property did not pass to it prior to bankruptcy. The Court applied the provisions of the *Sale of Goods Act* in determining who had title to the disputed goods. It was determined that there was nothing in the conduct of the parties or the contract to indicate otherwise, so Rule 5 of the *Sale of Goods Act* did not apply since the truck was not completed; hence the truck was not in a deliverable state and title had not yet passed at the time of the bankruptcy.

---

5.   2002 BCSC 504 (CanLII), 26 BLR (3d) 62.

Rights and Obligations of the Parties

Conditions and warranties under *Sale of Goods Act*

Acceptance causes victims of breach to lose the right of discharge

The *Sale of Goods Act* implies both conditions and warranties into the contract. This difference is important. An implied warranty is a minor term that, when breached, does not discharge the victim from the rest of his contractual obligations. On the other hand, a breach of an implied condition allows the victim to treat the contract and his obligations under it as ended. The victim may, however, choose to ignore the breach or treat it as a breach of warranty. Also, if the victim accepts the goods knowing of the breach he can no longer treat it as a breach of condition. Thus if Jones purchased a TV with a remote and it was delivered without the remote it would likely be a breach of a condition and he could demand his money back. But if he used it over the weekend that is acceptance, and he could only sue for a breach of warranty for the reduced value without the remote.

Parties may be free to contract out

Manufacturers and retailers often try to override the implied conditions and warranties set out in the Act, especially in the areas related to fitness and quality. They do this by including "limited warranties" that are, in effect, exemption clauses attempting to limit their liability. If such clauses are carefully worded they can override the provisions of the Act unless prohibited by statute. Sometimes parties try to contract out of all obligations and responsibilities. In the *Hunter Engineering* case (discussed in Case Summary 16.3), the Supreme Court of Canada made it clear that a properly worded exemption clause can overcome even fundamental contractual obligations—particularly where sophisticated businesspeople are involved in commercial transactions. Still, courts are reluctant to allow such comprehensive exemption clauses and interpret them very narrowly, only giving them effect where they are crystal clear and both parties should have understood the effect.

CASE SUMMARY 16.3

Suppliers of Defective Gears Fail to Protect Themselves: *Hunter Engineering Co. v. Syncrude Canada Ltd.*[6]

As part of its oil sands extraction project, Syncrude operated a large conveyor belt to carry sand over long distances. Syncrude ordered a number of gearboxes for this system from two different companies. Both companies, Hunter Engineering and Allis Chalmers, obtained the gears from the same manufacturer. All of the gears were made according to the same design and specifications. After several gears failed, it was determined that all would have to be repaired. Syncrude sued both suppliers. Both companies claimed that they were protected by clauses in their contracts limiting their responsibility to a specific period of time that had expired. Although the *Sale of Goods Act* applied, requiring the goods to be fit for their intended purpose, the Court had to determine whether the exemption clauses contained in the contracts overrode the operation of the Act.

The Hunter Engineering contract did have a clause limiting its liability, but it failed to include a clause exempting the operation of the *Sale of Goods Act* provisions that,

---

[6] 1989 CanLII 129 (SCC), [1989] 1 SCR 426, 57 DLR (4th) 321.

still being in force, imposed liability on it. The Allis Chalmers contract specifically excluded all statutory warranties or conditions, so there was no liability. Syncrude also argued that if the breach were fundamental, this exemption clause could not stand. But the Supreme Court of Canada held that even in the face of such a fundamental breach it was still possible for the parties to exempt themselves from liability, as Allis Chalmers had effectively done in this case. (*Fundamental breach* is discussed in more detail in Chapter 9.)

SMALL BUSINESS PERSPECTIVE

This case illustrates how important it is even for a small business to include carefully worded exemption clauses in their contracts of sale or to make sure, as purchaser, such clauses are clearly understood. Usually the services of a lawyer are required to draw up an effective exemption clause.

Several provinces have enacted legislation prohibiting the seller from excluding or limiting these provisions relating to fitness and quality in consumer sales transactions. Others will allow parties to a sales contract to exclude any implied terms. Refer to MyBusLawLab for specific provincial variations.

RIGHT TO CONVEY CLEAR TITLE

The *Sale of Goods Act* implies several terms into sales agreements that cover a seller's right to sell goods to a buyer. Section 13(a) of the Ontario *Sale of Goods Act* makes it a condition that the seller has the right to sell the goods or will have the right at the time title is to be transferred. Thus, Miles breaches a condition of the contract if he cannot deliver good title to the car at delivery. Christina would then be free from any further obligation under the contract.

Seller must convey good title . . .

Section 13(b) requires that the seller provide **quiet possession** of the goods as a warranty of the contract. This means that the goods must be in a condition such that they can be used and enjoyed in the way intended. If the car sold to Christina was subsequently ordered off the road because it was a European model that does not comply with Canadian safety or emission requirements, this would constitute a breach of the covenant of quiet possession. Note that since this is a breach of warranty rather than a breach of condition she would only be entitled to damages

. . . and quiet possession . . .

Section 13(c) implies a warranty that the goods will be free from any charge or encumbrance that has not been disclosed to the buyer. Such a **lien** gives the lien holder (a secured creditor) the right to retake the goods if not paid. (Secured transactions were discussed in Chapter 15.)

. . . and goods that are free from charge or encumbrance

If the car sold to Christina was subsequently seized by one of Miles's creditors and Christina was not aware of the lien this would constitute a breach of the implied warranty and Christina would have to pay off the amount owing or surrender the car. Since this is a breach of warranty, she could seek compensation from the seller.

GOODS MUST MATCH DESCRIPTION

Goods sold on the Internet, by catalogue, by mail order, or through other forms of distance shopping, usually with a picture and accompanying text, are being sold by description. Under section 14 of Ontario *Sale of Goods Act* there is an implied condition that the goods delivered must match that description. If Afsari ordered an iPod touch and an iPod nano was delivered, there has been a breach of the implied condition that the goods match the description. This is also the case when an odometer in a used car has been tampered with.[7]

Delivered goods must match description

[7.] See, for example, *Frey v. Sarvajc*, 2000 SKQB 281 (CanLII), [2000] 8 WWR 74.

Sales of manufactured goods are by description

In fact, the sale of any manufactured good today is a sale by description, one item being indistinguishable from another of the same model. When we buy, we are relying on the manufacturer's description, whether that description is found on the box, a specification sheet, a brochure, a catalogue, or on the Internet. All goods delivered must match that description.

GOODS MUST BE OF MERCHANTABLE QUALITY AND FIT FOR PURPOSE

The *Sale of Goods Act* applies to both small and large transactions, whether they are consumer or commercial in nature. But the parties can contract out of its provisions if they wish. Even fundamental obligations can be overcome by a very carefully and specifically worded exemption clause. The "limited warranties" associated with most manufactured goods are attempts to limit the seller and manufacturer's liability under these provisions of the Act. Remember that the right to contract out of such limited warranties is significantly restricted by legislation in many jurisdictions where consumer transactions are involved.

Goods must be of merchantable quality

The *Sale of Goods Act* requires, as a condition, that when goods are sold by description they must be of **merchantable quality** (section 15 of the Ontario Act). This means that the goods must be free of any defect that is not apparent on examination that would have persuaded the buyer not to purchase had she known of the defect. Because most manufactured goods today are sold by description this provision has become much more important.

Goods must be suitable for the purpose of purchase when a salesperson is relied upon

Sometimes a buyer with a particular need will rely on a seller's recommendation as to what product to use. In these circumstances there is an implied condition that the goods will be reasonably fit for that specified purpose. Thus there is liability, not only where the goods are used in the normal way, but also where those goods are used for some other unique purpose as recommended by the seller. (This is the section of the Act applied in the *Hunter Engineering* case discussed in Case Summary 16.3.)

This protection does not apply when the goods are purchased by trade name in such a way that it is clear that the skill of the seller is not being relied on, or when it is not in the normal course of the seller's business to supply the goods. For example, if Florio asked a sales clerk at McGregor's paint company to recommend a product to paint his cement floor, and after applying it the paint peeled off, this would be a breach of the implied condition that the product be reasonably fit for the intended purpose and Florio could seek compensation. However, if he bought it by trade name, disregarding any recommendations from the sales staff, he would have only himself to blame.

In British Columbia, goods leased or sold must be durable

In British Columbia this protection has been extended to leased goods, and a provision has been added that the goods be "durable for a reasonable period of time."[8] While these provisions do not relieve the buyer of the obligation to be cautious, they do provide for a certain minimum level of protection and quality.

The provisions related to fitness and quality apply in most sale of goods situations. The principle of *caveat emptor* also applies to these situations. The end result is that while the buyer is required to be careful when buying goods, he still has the right to expect a certain level of quality and protection when such care has been shown. There are many examples where courts have found products not reasonably fit for their purpose: for example, when a sandwich was sold containing a piece of wood[9] or a farm dealership was found liable because a tractor had mechanical problems.[10]

GOODS MUST MATCH SAMPLE

Goods must match sample and be free of hidden defects

The *Sale of Goods Act* uses a similar approach for goods purchased after a sample has been examined. There is an implied condition that the bulk of the goods must match the sample provided and be free of any hidden defects. For example, if

8. *Sale of Goods Act*, R.S.B.C. 1996 c. 410, s. 18(c).
9. *Coote v. Hudson's Bay Company* (1977), 6 A.R. 59 (Dist. Ct.).
10. *Pentagon Farm Centre Ltd. v. 228687 Holdings Ltd*, 2006 ABPC 127 (CanLII).

Tsang, after examining a sample Fuji apple, bought a load of those apples from Cashin and what was delivered was a mixture of Fuji and Ambrosia apples, the delivered goods would not have matched the sample, breaching an implied condition of the contract.

OTHER IMPLIED TERMS

There are several other terms that are implied by the *Sale of Goods Act* unless otherwise specified by the parties. Where no price is stated, a reasonable price must be paid for goods. Delivery must take place within a reasonable time, and payment is due upon delivery. The time of payment will be treated as a warranty, unless the parties state time is of the essence. Whether the time of delivery will be treated as a condition or a warranty will be implied from the conduct of the parties. When bulk goods such as grains, lumber, and ore are involved, if significantly too little or too much is delivered the buyer is free to either reject the goods or keep them and pay for them at the contracted rate. Note that the provisions affecting delivery, place, time, and quantity of the goods are usually made conditions by the parties.

Where price is omitted reasonable price prevails

Time, payment, and place for delivery are implied terms

CASE SUMMARY 16.4

Fraud Overrides Exemption Clause: *Loder v. Crocker*[11]

Denise and Ronald Crocker sold Colleen Loder a 2000 Dodge truck for $2900 with the specific provision that it was sold "as is where is." After the sale was complete, Loder had the truck inspected by a mechanic who declared it unfit to drive. In fact, a nail had been inserted into the brake line giving the impression that there was adequate pressure in the lines when in fact the back brakes were not working at all. Crocker had told Loder that $2000 work had been done on the truck, that everything was new, and that no inspection was necessary. The mechanic, after looking at the truck, stated that in fact "no major work" had been done on the truck for some time. The judge found that there had been deliberate misrepresentation by the Crockers. Loder had to pay a further $2900 to repair the vehicle and brought this action in Small Claims Court for compensation.

Because this is a used vehicle the "as is where is" statement on the bill of sale would normally exclude the *Sale of Goods Act* implied conditions with respect to fitness and quality. However, such a statement would not protect the seller from liability where there has been deliberate and fraudulent misrepresentation. The purchaser had been specifically informed that the truck was roadworthy when the sellers knew that it was not. The insertion of the nail in the brake line was a dangerous and reckless act intended to mislead the purchaser with respect to the truck's roadworthiness. Loder was successful in her action and obtained the appropriate compensation.

SMALL BUSINESS PERSPECTIVE

People sometimes rely too much on the inclusion of an exemption clause in a contract to protect them from responsibility for goods sold. No such clause will remove liability where a business or its representative has engaged in misrepresentation, especially where that misrepresentation was fraudulent.

Remedies on Default

SELLER'S REMEDIES

When the buyer defaults, the seller has an unpaid **seller's lien** against the goods. This gives the seller the right to retain goods that have not yet been delivered until appropriate payment has been made, even though title may have transferred.

---

11. 2012 CanLII 20694 (NL PC).

Right of stoppage in transit

Seller protected in case of bankruptcy

Similarly, if the goods are en route to the buyer and the buyer defaults, the seller has the right to intercept the goods and retake possession from the transporter, as long as the goods have not yet reached the buyer. This is referred to as the seller's right of **stoppage in transit**. Reference to the specific provincial legislation is necessary to ascertain when this right arises. Refer to MyBusLawLab for specific provincial variations. The *Bankruptcy and Insolvency Act*[12] also allows a seller of goods to recover those goods even after they are delivered to the buyer if, within 30 days of delivery, the buyer has become bankrupt or a receiver has been appointed and, of course, provided the buyer, receiver, or trustee still has them. This gives the seller priority over the bankrupt's other creditors.

When the seller exercises this power to retake the goods sold that, after appropriate notice, remain unpaid for, the goods can be sold to recover the loss. Such notice of resale is not required when perishable goods are involved.

Seller can sue for price in cases of default or refusal of delivery once title has passed

In the event of a breach of contract, the seller retains all of the normal remedies that were discussed in Chapter 9, namely, the right to sue for the price of the goods when title has passed to the buyer. In such a case, if the buyer refuses to accept delivery of the goods, she is rejecting her own goods and may still be required to pay the purchase price. If the time specified for payment passes the seller can sue for the purchase price even if title has not yet passed to the buyer. Buyers would be wise to refuse delivery only when the seller has breached a condition of the contract. Otherwise, by refusing delivery, the buyer takes the risk of not getting the goods but still being required to pay full price for them. But the seller must be careful and do nothing inconsistent with his continued willingness to perform. If he tries to sell the goods to someone else, for example, he will no longer be able to sue for the whole price, just for what he has lost on the sale.

Where the seller's remedy is limited to damages this can include the costs involved in restocking and resale. When the goods are resold at a lower price, that loss will be included as well. The seller also has an obligation to mitigate losses, which usually requires the seller to take steps to resell the goods immediately. When a deposit is involved, the seller can keep the deposit. This is not the case when the prepayment is a down payment only. In fact, it may not be worth the effort to sue for damages if it is not possible to sue for the actual price of the goods.

BUYER'S REMEDIES

Buyer's remedies are those of contract law

The remedies available to the buyer if the seller defaults are those provided by general contract law. Where misrepresentation is involved, the buyer may be able to rescind the contract or seek damages when there has been fraud or negligence. When a condition of the contract is breached, the buyer may refuse to perform or demand return of any money paid. If only a warranty is breached, the buyer must go through with the deal, subject to a right for damages. When the seller fails to deliver the goods, the damages will usually be based on the difference between what the buyer had agreed to pay for the goods and the cost of obtaining similar goods from another source. But when there are additional losses suffered because of the delay in obtaining the goods or the defect involved, the buyer will be able to claim those losses as well.

Extent of damages depends on the circumstances

Where the buyer's remedy is limited to damages this can include the costs to bring the goods up to the specifications in the original contract or the amount of their reduction in value because of the breach. When defective goods have caused physical injury or damage to other property, those damages are also recoverable, provided they were reasonably within the contemplation of the parties at the time the contract was entered into. Thus, people who suffer food poisoning because of poor-quality food at a restaurant can seek compensation for their injuries under the *Sale of Goods Act* provisions, and those damages can be substantial. When unique goods are involved, the buyer may also be able to claim a remedy of specific performance and

---

12. R.S.C. 1985, c. B-3, s. 81.1.

force the seller to go through with the sale rather than pay damages in compensation. Note that buyers' rights have been augmented with respect to consumer transactions by consumer protection legislation (discussed below).

Online Sales and International Transactions

ONLINE PURCHASES

As was the case with normal sale of goods transactions, the basic provisions of contract law also apply to Internet sales, but distance, anonymity, and jurisdictional problems cause unique challenges. Specifically, one of the problems often arising deals with the formation of the contract. Who makes the offer? Who accepts? When and where does the contract come into existence? Refer to Chapters 6 to 9 of the text for a review of these problems. Another major difficulty dealing with online transactions is the problem of determining jurisdiction. Jurisdiction is discussed in Chapter 3, and it may be helpful to review that topic at this stage.

Normal contract rules apply to online transactions

INTERNATIONAL TRANSACTIONS

All jurisdictions in Canada have enacted an *International Sale of Goods Act,* fulfilling Canada's obligations under the UN Convention on Contracts for the International Sales of Goods. Refer to the links on MyBusLawLab to review these statutes. A great deal of trading today is done in the international arena, and these statutes are intended to bring the same kind of structure and certainty to import and export dealings as the *Sale of Goods Acts* provide domestically.

For example, Ontario's *International Sale of Goods Act*[13] states that an offer arises when a sufficiently detailed proposal to contract is directed to one or more specific people and there is an intention to be bound if accepted. It is effective when it reaches the offeree. The offer can be withdrawn any time before acceptance unless stated as irrevocable. A rejection terminates the offer when it reaches the offeror, and silence is not an acceptance. The acceptance is effective when it reaches the offeror and must do so within the time specified. If it doesn't get there in time it can still be effective if the offeror notifies the offeree to that effect. It is interesting that the acceptance can also be withdrawn provided the withdrawal reaches the offeror before or at the same time as the acceptance.

International Sale of Goods Act applies to international commercial transactions

These provisions summarize the basic rules of forming a contract in common law. Note, however, that the post box rule exception to when a contract is accepted (discussed in Chapter 6) seems to be eliminated, and several other principles have been clarified or in some cases modified. Most of the provisions of the *Sale of Goods Act* relating to performance of the contract, including delivery of title, goods matching the description, and their fitness for the purpose, have corresponding provisions in the *International Sale of Goods Act.* Other provisions relate to transfer of risk and remedies available to the buyer or seller in the event of a breach. Remember that, as was the case with the *Sale of Goods Act,* the parties are free to override the provisions of the *International Sale of Goods Act* by including different terms in their contract.

It is important to note here that the *International Sale of Goods Act* is limited to international commercial transactions and has no application to online consumer purchases. Such consumer transactions are governed by the provincial *Sale of Goods Act* and consumer protection legislation in place in the local area that has jurisdiction of over the sale. These *Sale of Goods Acts* vary, and in many jurisdictions where consumer sales are involved, it is still possible for the parties to agree to override even the requirements with respect to fitness and quality. Of course, where commercial sales are involved, those provisions can be overridden in all jurisdictions. Remember that whether the sale is made online or across a counter, it is normal practice to include terms (usually called "limited warranties") that override or otherwise limit these provisions.

Contract provisions override *International Sale of Goods Act*

---

13. R.S.O. 1990, c. I.10.

Clicking the "I Accept" button accepts the terms

An Internet ad with a "click-wrap" may be an offer

A wise purchaser, whether a prudent businessperson or a cautious consumer, will be extremely careful to look for such provisions and understand their effects. Some sellers may fail to make those exemptions clear to the buyer by burying them at the end of the site or in pages that most buyers skim or neglect to read at all. Generally, all retailers are required to take reasonable measures to draw such terms to the attention of the other party, and if they fail to do so these terms do not bind the buyer. But if a retailer directs the buyer to those terms and the buyer fails to read them, the buyer will typically be bound. As discussed in Chapter 6, online sales are often accomplished by requiring the purchaser to click on an "I Accept" button, usually after acknowledging that she has read all of the terms of the contract, making it exceedingly difficult to claim not having read these provisions. This is called "click-wrap," and the contract is binding as soon as that button is clicked.

REDUCING RISK 16.2

Businesspeople should always be aware of the operation of the *Sale of Goods Act*, especially the provisions related to fitness and quality. Whether your business is large or small, to avoid unwanted terms from being implied into a contract, it is important to specify the nature and limits of the obligations of the parties in commercial transactions. It is also important in consumer sales to understand just what obligations you cannot contract out of. As seen in the *Hunter Engineering* case (Case Summary 16.3), the failure of one supplier to exclude the operation of the *Sale of Goods Act* made that supplier responsible for substantial damages. Whether buyer or seller, it is important for the sophisticated client to keep the *Sale of Goods Act* in mind whenever goods are being transferred for money and to seek legal advice where appropriate.

LO **⑤⑥⑦**

CONSUMER PROTECTION

Consumer transaction involves purchases for personal consumption rather than business use

Statutes prevent abuse

Freedom of contract has been significantly affected by legislation in the context of consumer transactions. **Consumer transactions** involve goods or services purchased by individuals for personal use and not for resale or for business purposes.

Consumer protection legislation imposes standards and responsibilities on manufacturers and suppliers of goods and services. It controls the use and disclosure of information and advertising. It controls the safety and quality of the goods sold. This legislation also controls unethical or otherwise unacceptable business practices. The next part of this chapter will examine this area and consider the regulatory bodies created to enforce the legislation. There are both federal and provincial statutes involved, with considerable variety among provincial jurisdictions. Once again, refer to MyBusLawLab for details pertaining to a particular jurisdiction. Depending on the jurisdiction, the legislation may be contained in one statute or several.[14] Although there has been some limited form of consumer protection in our law for centuries, modern statutes have significantly expanded and modified the law in this area. Until recently, the common contractual themes of *caveat emptor* and freedom of contract dominated consumer transactions. But because of the vulnerability of consumers to abuse and their weakened bargaining position given modern business practices, limits have been placed on those principles. The ever-expanding world of online marketing has added new challenges, and there have been many legislated attempts to impose consumer protection into this new arena with varying degrees of success.

Federal Legislation

Federal department enforces statutes, educates, and protects consumers

Although the developments in consumer protection legislation with the most impact have taken place provincially in recent years, there are some significant and effective federal statutes as well. Industry Canada was established under the

---

14. Ontario and British Columbia have each consolidated a collection of consumer protection laws into a single statute. See Ontario's *Consumer Protection Act, 2002*, S.O. 2002, c. 30, Sch. A; and British Columbia's *Business Practices and Consumer Protection Act*, S.B.C. 2004, c. 2.

Department of Industry Act.[15] Industry Canada, through its various offices, such as Consumer Affairs, the Competition Bureau, and the Office of the Superintendent of Bankruptcy, regulates the various areas of concern. The mission of Industry Canada is to foster a growing, competitive, knowledge-based Canadian economy. Its mandate includes three strategic objectives—a fair, efficient, and competitive marketplace; an innovative economy; and competitive industry and sustainable communities. Product safety is now overseen by Health Canada, which was established under the *Department of Health Act.*[16] Information about these and other consumer-oriented agencies can be found in the *Canadian Consumer Handbook* (www.consumerhandbook.ca/en).

COMPETITION

The mission of the Competition Bureau "is to protect and promote competitive markets and enable informed consumer choice in Canada."[17] The Competition Bureau is an independent law-enforcement agency that administers and enforces the *Competition Act.*[18] This legislation has both civil and criminal aspects to it. The objective is to maintain and encourage competition in Canada so that Canadians can benefit from product choice, competitive prices, and quality services. Hearings pursuant to the *Competition Act* are conducted before the Competition Tribunal, which functions much like a criminal or civil court, depending on the nature of the matter before it. The competition commissioner functions like a prosecutor, bringing matters before the Competition Tribunal. Note that the *Competition Act* was significantly amended in 2009.

The *Competition Act* controls abuses in the free market

One practice that can interfere with competitive markets is through the creation of monopolies, so a major purpose of the *Competition Act* is to control mergers. Mergers are no longer treated as inherently bad, since mergers may reduce prices because of enhanced efficiency in the industry, but they may also increase prices because of a reduction in competition. Today, the Competition Tribunal reviews mergers to determine whether they will have the effect of substantially limiting or lessening competition. When foreign investment is involved, the *Investment Canada Act*[19] requires that the investment be reviewed to determine if it will be of net benefit to Canada and not injurious to our national security.

Mergers are controlled

The *Competition Act* criminalizes some anticompetitive practices, and it is here that a significant change took place with the 2009 amendments. Prior to the changes, the specified conduct was only a criminal offence where it had the effect of "unduly" lessening competition. Now the listed offences are prohibited even if they have no effect on competition, thus making it much easier to prosecute since proof of interference with competition is no longer required. The penalties have also been significantly increased so that fines may be up to $25 million and imprisonment up to 14 years. A few of the prohibited criminal offences include bid rigging, misleading advertising, deceptive marketing practices, pyramid selling, double ticketing, and conspiracy to fix prices among suppliers. Criminal prosecutions must be proven beyond a reasonable doubt. Penalties upon conviction include fines, imprisonment, and injunctions ordering the offender to cease and desist its anticompetitive behaviour. Other decisions made by corporations may have the effect of lessening competition and can be challenged, but in those cases the court will consider both the effect on competition as well as the increased efficiencies created. The Competition Bureau has a leniency program in place that encourages violators to co-operate and agree on fines. Those fines, however, can still be significant. For instance, a recently agreed-upon fine for bid rigging (which

Abusive trade practices are prohibited

---

[15] S.C. 1995, c. 1.

[16] S.C. 1996, c. 8.

[17] See the website for the Competition Bureau, www.competitionbureau.gc.ca.

[18] *Supra* note 1.

[19] R.S.C. 1985, c. 28 (1st Supp) as amended in S.C. 2009, c. 2, s. 445.

took place between offshore suppliers outside of Canada) in the automotive industry totalled $30 million.[20]

Another important change with the 2009 amendments was to enhance a civil option as opposed to a criminal approach to deal with less serious arrangements that tend to lessen competition. A civil action requires a lower standard of proof, making the process much less onerous. Conduct that can be controlled through this civil process includes conspiracies and other arrangements between competitors that have the effect of lessening competition, as well as unilateral anticompetitive practices. Examples include the following:

- Refusal to deal: Substantially affecting a business by refusing to supply product on the usual terms
- Tied selling: Inducing a buyer to purchase a second product as a condition of supplying a particular product
- Exclusive dealing: Restricting the purchaser's right to carry competitors' products
- Market restriction: Requiring a customer to deal only or mostly in certain products, or requiring a customer to sell specific products in a defined market
- Delivered pricing: Bait-and-switch selling, selling above the advertised price, or advertising a "bargain price" that is actually the original price
- Abuse of a dominant position: Essentially any action that puts pressure on a customer, supplier, or competitor, reducing their ability to compete

Both civil and criminal processes control anticompetitive conduct

Even though a civil process is used, the Act now provides for significant "administrative penalties," allowing for considerable penalties to be imposed while avoiding the more onerous criminal process. Note that many of these prohibited practices, including false or misleading representations and conspiracies that affect competition, can be challenged under either a civil or criminal process but not both.

In June 2002, the *Competition Act* was amended to create a new right of "private access," which was retained with the 2009 amendments. This enabled private persons or businesses to seek a legal remedy against another's anticompetitive conduct without laying a complaint with the commissioner of competition. Now competitors, when faced with anticompetitive conduct such as a supplier refusing to supply a product at the regular price, can bring an action directly against that supplier. Cease-and-desist orders can also be obtained to counter exclusive dealing, tied selling, and market restriction when such practices have resulted or are likely to result in a lessening of competition.

Misleading representations stopped

It is expected that making these remedies available to those most affected by anticompetitive practices will lead to more effective enforcement of the *Competition Act*. The Competition Bureau may now focus on business practices that affect the public generally. For example, in March 2009 the Competition Bureau announced it had reached an agreement with offenders in two important misleading advertising schemes. Moore's Clothing for Men agreed to amend its advertising regarding a two-for-one suit sale that failed to disclose that it only applied to selected labels.[21] Also, the Brick Warehouse LP agreed to cancel all advertising related to a national mail-in rebate promotion, which implied a cash rebate when actually the purchaser only received a Brick gift certificate.[22]

---

[20]. Julius Melnitzer, "Competition Bureau Imposes Record Fine for Honda Parts Bid-Rigging," *Financial Post*, April 24, 2013, http://business.financialpost.com/legal-post/competition-bureau-imposes-record-fine-for-honda-parts-bid-rigging.

[21]. Competition Bureau, "Moores Clarifies Advertising to Resolve Competition Bureau Concerns," *Market Wired*, March 6, 2009, www.marketwired.com/press-release/moores-clarifies-advertising-to-resolve-competition-bureau-concerns-958256.htm.

[22]. Competition Bureau, "Furniture Chain Cancels Rebate Promotion to Resolve Competition Bureau Concerns," *Market Wired*, March 26, 2009, www.marketwired.com/press-release/furniture-chain-cancels-rebate-promotion-to-resolve-competition-bureau-concerns-966570.htm.

It is important to note that the prohibited conduct and offences listed in the *Competition Act* will apply whatever form of communication is used. A serious problem associated with Internet communications and sales deal with jurisdiction. Today we are dealing more and more with a global market, and a website may be designed and administered in Canada, but staffed in India or the Philippines. When a customer in Vancouver clicks "I Accept," she may be responding to an offer made in Canada by sending the response to the Philippines where an order is then sent to India where the product is shipped from to be delivered to the customer in Vancouver. What law applies? Refer to Chapter 3 of this text for a more detailed discussion of jurisdiction.

Competition Act applies to online sales depending on jurisdiction

OTHER FEDERAL LEGISLATION

The Competition Bureau also enforces and administers several other federal statutes that have a consumer protection aspect to them. The *Consumer Packaging and Labelling Act*,[23] the *Precious Metals Marking Act*,[24] and the *Textile Labelling Act*[25] are criminal statutes intended to force proper disclosure of information to help consumers make comparisons among products.

There are several statutes, both federal and provincial, designed to protect the consumer from dangerous products. The federal *Food and Drugs Act*[26] is intended primarily to control the sale of food, drugs, and cosmetics that are unfit for consumption or use. The legislation also prohibits misleading or deceptive claims associated with the sale, labelling, and advertising of these products. Several categories of drugs are created. Unsafe drugs, such as thalidomide, are prohibited from sale in Canada. Under the *Controlled Drugs and Substances Act*,[27] certain *dangerous drugs* that are useful are allowed to be sold under controlled conditions. The Act makes it an offence to traffic in certain *controlled drugs*, such as amphetamines and steroids. Strong and effective enforcement provisions are included. One of the problems associated with the labelling regulation on Canadian products, especially food and drugs, is the complicated language used. There is a movement now taking place to introduce plain, easily understood language. For example, where a product may cause indigestion, companies are now required to use that word rather than "dyspepsia" on the label.

The *Food and Drugs Act* carries strict penalties

The federal *Hazardous Products Act*[28] has been significantly modified and works hand in hand with the *Canada Consumer Product Safety Act*.[29] Together these Acts control the manufacture, import, and sale of products that are inherently dangerous. Products such as inflammable clothing or dangerous toys are prohibited from sale in Canada, while the sale of other potentially dangerous products is allowed provided that companies comply with the enacted regulations. Examples are cradles, cribs, carpets, kettles, toys, and pacifiers. The statutes also contain important inspection, analysis, and enforcement provisions. There are new regulations requiring those who manufacture, import, and sell these products to keep more detailed records and to complete incident reports. These records and reporting standards are intended to facilitate the government-instituted recall of products found to be hazardous. Some hazardous products are covered by their own legislation, such as the *Explosives Act*,[30] the *Pest Control Products Act*,[31] the *Motor Vehicle Safety Act*,[32] and the *Organic Products Regulation, 2009*.[33]

Hazardous products are controlled

23. R.S.C. 1985, c. C-38.
24. R.S.C. 1985, c. P-19.
25. R.S.C. 1985, c. T-10.
26. R.S.C. 1985, c. F-27.
27. S.C. 1996, c. 19.
28. R.S.C. 1985, c. H-3.
29. S.C. 2010, c 21.
30. R.S.C. 1985, c. E-17.
31. S.C. 2002, c. 28.
32. S.C. 1993, c. 16.
33. SOR/2009-176, enacted pursuant to the Canada *Agricultural Products Act*, R.S.C. 1985, c. 20 (4th Supp.), c. 0.4.

Of course, consumers injured by dangerous products retain their common law right to seek compensation from the seller or manufacturer whether they bought the goods directly or over the Internet. This may be done in the form of a contract action (usually under the fitness and quality provision of the *Sale of Goods Act* or consumer protection legislation). It can also be done in a negligence action, but the plaintiff would be required to demonstrate that the injury was reasonably foreseeable and that the retailer or manufacturer failed to take reasonable care.

REDUCING RISK 16.3

It is important for businesspeople dealing with the public to keep up with statutory changes in the area of consumer protection, including those within federal jurisdiction. The enforcement sections of consumer protection legislation have become stronger. Abusive practices that may have gone unchallenged in the past are now much more likely to result in bad publicity, censure, fines, or even the loss of a business licence—consequences a sophisticated client can avoid by staying abreast of legislative changes and obtaining appropriate and timely legal advice.

Identity Theft

Identity theft is a growing problem, especially with the ease of access to personal information on the Internet. The problem involves a person wrongfully obtaining enough personal information about someone else so that the perpetrator can impersonate the victim, obtaining credit cards, access to banking and other financial services, and making purchases or obtaining cash or other assets against the victim's credit. Identity theft occurs when the personal information is obtained for criminal purposes, and the misuse of that information is referred to as *identity fraud.*

The *Criminal Code* has recently been amended to include three specific offences related to identity theft. Section 402.2(1) makes it an offence to obtain or possess a person's personal information for criminal purposes. Section 402.2(2) makes it an offence to transmit that information to others knowing that it will be used to commit a fraud. Section 402.2(3) lists a number of other sections that constitute the criminal offences that this wrongfully obtained information can be used to commit. These listed sections of the *Criminal Code* constitute another 10 types of offences that can be applied in identity theft circumstances, such as fraud, forgery, and theft. Section 403 makes it an offence to fraudulently impersonate another and to misuse wrongfully obtained information. The penalty imposed on conviction can be up to 10 years in prison.

These criminal law provisions are the primary tools used to deal with the problem of identity theft, but some provinces are taking steps to include provisions dealing with identity theft in their provincial legislation. Alberta, for instance, has included a provision in its *Fair Trading Act*[34] authorizing the creation of regulations specifically aimed at combating identity theft. Finally, it should be noted that identity theft is a broad term, and many other provisions of consumer protection legislation and criminal law can be applied in such situations.

Provincial Legislation

RESPONSIBILITY FOR GOODS

When products are defective and cause injury or loss, consumers have recourse in either contract or negligence. As we learned in Chapter 5, the problem with suing in negligence is that there must be a failure on the defendant's part to live up to a demonstrated standard of care. This carelessness is often difficult to prove. Another problem is that often only the manufacturer can be sued for negligence, since the

---

34. R.S.A. 2000, c. F-2, s. 51 (m).

wholesalers and retailers don't deal with or even inspect the prepackaged goods they sell. An action based on contract law is much simpler, since the consumer need only show that the product delivered was defective and caused loss or injury. But, because of the principle of privity, any action for breach of contract is limited to the actual purchaser suing the merchant that sold the defective product.

Statutes overcome problems in contract and tort

The sections of the *Sale of Goods Act* requiring the delivery of good title, that goods correspond to the description and sample, and that the goods supplied be fit and of merchantable quality have one serious drawback. In commercial transactions, these can be overridden by properly drafted exemption clauses. Many provinces in Canada have enacted legislation removing the right to override these provisions in consumer transactions. British Columbia does this in its *Sale of Goods Act,* making void any attempt to change certain provisions where retail sales are involved. Other provinces include provisions having similar effect in their consumer protection legislation. Alberta, however, still allows sellers to contract out by including an appropriate exemption clause, even in consumer transactions.[35] Some jurisdictions also require these goods to be "durable," while some have also extended the protection to leased goods. Again, refer to MyBusLawLab for specific provincial variations.

Effect of exemption clauses is limited by statute

Manufacturers usually include a "limited warranty" with their products stating the extent of their responsibility for fitness and quality. These are, in fact, exemption clauses that attempt to limit the liability of the manufacturer and retailer for the product. As mentioned, with recent legislative changes manufacturers and retailers may not be able to rely on such exemption clauses to relieve themselves of the obligation to deliver fit and quality goods to the consumer. In many jurisdictions, consumers can now sue not only sellers but wholesalers and manufacturers as well for breach of contract, and receive significant compensation for their losses when products are unfit, even after the expiration of a stated warranty period. This may also apply to online consumer transactions depending on the legislation in place in the particular jurisdiction. For example, if Joyce bought a new vehicle for her family use from Ace Dealership in such a jurisdiction and the engine seized three days after the expiration of the three-year warranty period, Ace would not be allowed to claim that the stated "limited warranty" had expired and refuse to fix it. The three-year warranty is an exemption clause that is void in a consumer transaction. The vehicle must be of merchantable quality. Since most people would expect a transmission in a modern car to last longer than three years, it is likely that Ace would be required to be responsible for its product and make (or pay for) the repairs in these circumstances.

As mentioned, there are several advantages to suing in contract—as is the case when proceeding under the *Sale of Goods Act*—rather than basing a lawsuit in tort. The plaintiff does not need to prove that the defendants failed in their duty of care, and the damages awarded in breach of contract cases (like in cases based on negligence) can go far beyond a refund of the purchase price. This was the case in *Gee v. White Spot*.[36] In that case a customer was served a sandwich contaminated with botulism poison. The damages awarded under the fitness provisions of the *Sale of Goods Act* went far beyond the value of the contaminated sandwich. However, the principle of privity can pose a significant obstacle to suing in contract, since only the parties to an agreement can sue for breach. In the case of *Donoghue v. Stevenson*, discussed in Chapter 5, Donoghue consumed a contaminated bottle of ginger beer given to her by a friend. She could not sue the seller for breach, not being "privy" to the contract. She had to sue the manufacturer for negligence instead.

Privity problem overcome by statute

Some provinces have extended the requirements of fitness and quality discussed above to anyone the seller could reasonably foresee might use the product. Through their consumer protection statutes, other provinces have eliminated privity as a

---

35. British Columbia's *Sale of Goods Act*, R.S.B.C. 1996, c. 410, s. 20; Alberta's *Sale of Goods Act*, R.S.A. 2000, c. S-2, s. 54.
36. *Gee v. White Spot Ltd.*, 1986 CanLII 776 (BC SC), 32 DLR (4th) 238.

Privity problem overcome by the courts

defence when warranties of fitness are implied. The result in those jurisdictions is that anyone injured or suffering a loss because of a defective product can sue the seller or manufacturer for breach of the implied conditions, whether he is the purchaser or not. The courts have also shown a willingness to get around the privity problem. In *Murray v. Sperry Rand Corp.*,[37] the manufacturer was found liable to the consumer in contract even though the purchase was made from a retailer. Because false claims were included in the advertising brochures produced by the manufacturer, the Court found that there was a subsidiary, or collateral, contract between the manufacturer and the consumer that allowed the consumer to sue the manufacturer directly in contract. This is consistent with the tendency of the courts to abandon the privity principle. It should be mentioned, however, that although exemption clauses in warranties may not protect the seller in consumer transactions, they might still be effective in limiting the liability of the manufacturer, depending on the nature of the contract and the legislation in place in the particular jurisdiction.

CASE SUMMARY 16.5

Defective Bottle Cap Causes Injury: *Morse v. Cott Beverages West Ltd.*[38]

Morse sustained a serious eye injury when she used a nutcracker to remove a difficult bottle cap, which exploded in the process. She sued, relying on Saskatchewan's *Consumer Products Warranties Act*,[39] claiming that the manufacturer's poor quality control caused the accident. The corporation's records showed that on the day the subject bottle was manufactured, more than half of the bottles produced required a pressure greater than that recommended. The judge therefore concluded that the caps were defective because they were too tight. He awarded damages to Morse, including punitive damages because the corporation, given its own test results, had wilfully jeopardized the safety of the public by distributing a dangerous product.

Note that the Act imposed contractual obligations with respect to fitness and quality, eliminating the need to prove negligence. It also removed the barrier of privity of contract, allowing the consumer to sue the manufacturer in contract.

DISCUSSION QUESTIONS

How would you change this legislation to achieve a better balance? From a business perspective, explain what steps, if any, a careful manufacturer should take to avoid liability in these circumstances.

 REDUCING RISK 16.4

Most salespeople don't understand the merchant's liability beyond the manufacturer's limited warranty included with the product sold. It is important, however, for merchants to understand their potential liability for defective products. The obligations imposed by these statutes rest primarily on the seller and less on the manufacturer. As consumers become more aware of their rights and become more aggressive in enforcing them, a

merchant's very existence may depend upon whether appropriate steps were taken to eliminate or reduce such potential liability. Sophisticated clients will not only take what steps they can to limit their legal exposure, but will, through training, inspection, and policy, do all they can to lessen the risk in injury or damage in the first place.

[37.] (1979), 23 O.R. (2d) 456 (H.C.).

[38.] 2001 SKQB 550 (CanLII), [2002] 4 WWR 281.

[39.] This legislation has been replaced by the *Consumer Protection Act*, S.S. 1996, c. C-30.1, which likewise augments the buyer's ability to sue the retailer and manufacturer.

Some useful products, by their very nature, are hazardous. The obligation of the manufacturer and seller of such products is to make them as safe as reasonably possible, to warn the potential user of the dangers, and to provide information on their proper use. An injured consumer can successfully sue in contract or negligence when these steps are not followed. Except when the danger is obvious, a warning incorporated into the product label must alert the consumer to the hazards associated with the product. If the warning is inadequate, the manufacturer and seller may be liable for the injuries that result. Even when such dangers are obvious, as with a sharp knife, the practice is growing for manufacturers to include a warning out of an abundance of caution. Federal legislation dealing with the merchandising of dangerous products was covered earlier in this chapter.

Duty to warn when a product is hazardous

Unacceptable Business Practices

FALSE OR EXAGGERATED CLAIMS

Another major thrust of consumer protection legislation is to prohibit or control certain unacceptable business practices such as making misleading or false statements to persuade people to buy a product. Under the common law, these statements normally do not form part of the contract and generally are dismissed as mere advertising puffs, leaving the purchaser with little recourse. Further, contracts of sale often contain clauses stating that there are no representations other than those contained in the written document, making any false or misleading claims by salespeople not actionable unless they are actually included in the written contract. Today these statements are controlled by statute, with most provinces incorporating them into the contract and making any attempt to override them void. As a result, when a salesperson makes a false or exaggerated claim or when one is included in an advertisement it becomes a term of the contract and is actionable as a breach if it proves incorrect or is not honoured. If Holberg, the purchaser of a used car from Affleck's Fine Car Company, was informed by the salesperson that the car had been driven "only to church on Sundays," that statement would, under these provisions, be incorporated into the contract, even if it were not contained in the written document. If Holberg could convince the court that a false statement had been made, he could successfully sue for breach of contract when the statement proved false. The actual statutes used to accomplish this vary considerably from province to province. Greater detail as to the specific legislation and relevant case law is found in MyBusLawLab.

Legislation incorporates misleading statements into the contract

Typically, this type of statute lists several different kinds of misleading and deceptive statements that are deemed to be unfair practices. For example, taking advantage of a consumer and exerting undue pressure on a consumer are deemed to be unfair practices in Alberta.[40] In addition to the penalties imposed by governments for violations, the consumer is given the right to have the contract rescinded or specifically performed, or to sue for damages. Any attempt to override these provisions or to declare in a contract that there are no other representations other than what appears on the written document will be void, leaving the purchaser free to sue. This is true even when the parties involved have been relatively innocent, for negligence or fraud on the seller's part need not be shown. Innocent but misleading statements may still qualify as deceptive practices under the relevant legislation, bringing with them serious consequences. Other provinces have similar provisions.

Unfair practices are identified in statute

The government department involved is typically given considerable powers to investigate complaints and to deal with complaints against offending merchandisers, including the powers to impose fines, to suspend licences, and in some provinces to pursue a civil action on behalf of the consumer.

Government bodies have been given significant powers

---

40. See, for example, Alberta's *Fair Trading Act, supra* note 34.

Some of the most effective provisions controlling misleading advertising and other deceptive business practices are contained in the federal *Competition Act,* as discussed above. These statutory provisions have considerably strengthened the common law provisions concerning false and misleading claims in consumer transactions.

CASE SUMMARY 16.6

Even Implied Misrepresentation Is Actionable: *Richard v. Time Inc.*[41]

Jean-Marc Richard received a letter in the mail indicating that he had won a sweepstakes prize. In fact it was a letter carefully worded to give that impression but was rather was an entry to the contest, which required him to subscribe to *Time* magazine. He did so, thinking he had won the prize, and when he learned that he had not he brought this action. The Quebec Superior Court found that the document violated the Quebec *Consumer Protection Act* as a prohibited business practice or a misleading representation and awarded $1000 fixed damages and $100000 in punitive damages. This was overturned at the appeal level, and that decision was in turn appealed to the Supreme Court of Canada. The Supreme Court determined that although there had been no specific false statements in the document, the general impression was that Richard had won the prize and only had to submit the application to claim his prize. This general impression was enough to constitute a misleading representation under the Quebec Act. The Court confirmed the compensation award of $1000 but reduced the punitive damages award to $15000.

SMALL BUSINESS PERSPECTIVE

Although this case took place in Quebec, which has a civil law system rather than a common law system, it is helpful in that it shows that even though there may be no specific falsehood in the advertisement or document, it can still be a violation of this type of statute if it gives a misleading "general impression" to an average consumer. The same principle should be applied to the legislation in place in other provinces.

UNCONSCIONABLE TRANSACTIONS

Unconscionable transactions or unfair bargains are controlled

Consumers sometimes are taken advantage of because of some vulnerability, such as desperation, poverty, lack of sophistication, or intellectual weakness. To prevent unscrupulous merchants from taking advantage of such vulnerable individuals, legislation has been enacted, either in consumer protection legislation or in separate Acts (e.g., an *Unconscionable Transactions Act*). Refer to MyBusLawLab for specific provincial variations.

In some provinces this legislation is restricted to situations involving the borrowing of money. For a transaction to be found unconscionable when money is loaned, the actual cost of borrowing must be excessive in the circumstances. If the risk justifies the high rate of interest, it is not an unconscionable transaction, even when the consumer is of weak intellect or in desperate straits. When unconscionability is demonstrated, the courts can set the contract aside, modify its terms, or order the return of money paid.

Some statutes do not limit unconscionability to loan transactions

Common law developments

In several other provinces the legislation goes further, extending the concept of unconscionability beyond loan transactions to also cover unacceptable business practices. In these provinces, the courts can look at factors such as physical infirmity, illiteracy, inability to understand the language of an agreement, undue influence, a price that grossly exceeds the value of the goods, and the lack of reasonable benefit to the consumer in establishing unconscionability. Remedies such as rescission, damages, and punitive damages are available. In some provinces, the government agency

---

41. [2012] 1 SCR 265.

may assist in or even initiate an action on behalf of the consumer. In addition to these legislative provisions, the common law doctrine of unconscionability in contract law, as discussed in Chapter 8, has become much more accepted. It can also be applied in these consumer situations. In Case Summary 16.7, Knuude was able to escape her contractual obligations because she was taken advantage of and unreasonably pressured by the salesperson. The key to unconscionability is that there must be an inequality of bargaining power.

CASE SUMMARY 16.7

Aged Homeowner Protected from Unscrupulous Salesperson: *Dominion Home Improvements Ltd. v. Knuude*[42]

A door-to-door salesperson using intense tactics persuaded Knuude, an 80-year-old homeowner, to purchase a number of home improvements that she didn't need. After four hours of extremely high-pressured selling, including a refusal to leave unless the contract was signed, Knuude agreed to have the renovations done. She signed a $300 cheque as a deposit, but stopped payment on it immediately after the salesperson left.

The next day, workers from the company came to do the work. Knuude insisted that they leave. This brought back the salesperson who, by devious means, persuaded Knuude to reinstate the contract. The work was done. Knuude refused to pay. The company sued for the money owed under the contract.

The judge determined that the contract was not binding on Knuude as it was fraudulent and unconscionable, and did not conform to the requirements set out in the provincial consumer protection legislation. This kind of unscrupulous business practice has led to the increase in consumer protection legislation.

More recently, in *R v. Parkes*,[43] a care-home operator was convicted of cheating a partially incapacitated World War II veteran out of $179 439.15 and sentenced to three years in jail for fraud. She was also required to make restitution of the funds.

DISCUSSION QUESTIONS

Has such legislation gone too far? Should consumers assume more responsibility for their own mistakes? Are there occasions when protection is necessary? What could have been done by the salesperson's employer, Dominion Home Improvement, to better handle this situation? Do you think the criminal penalty is too harsh?

PREPAID CARDS

Gift cards and other prepaid cards are increasingly popular in North America; after sales of these cards fell during the economic downturn, they are again on the rise, with estimated sales of $100 billion in 2012.[44] Gift cards do not involve credit. The purchaser pays in advance to "load" a card, which can then be used up to the amount that has been loaded onto the card. The key issues involving gift cards relate to expiry dates and fees. A monthly fee could, for example, eventually consume the entire value of the card. General provisions in consumer protection statutes go some way in protecting consumers from these abuses, but in Alberta specific legislation has been enacted to cover gift cards. The *Gift Card Regulation*[45] came into force on November 1, 2008. It stipulates that gift cards may not have expiry dates, that only

Laws governing prepaid cards are becoming more common

[42.] (1986), 20 C.L.R. 192 (Ont. Dist. Ct.).

[43.] 2014 SKCA 37 (CanLII).

[44.] Ylan Q. Mui, "Gift-Card Sales Rise After Falling for Two Years," *Washington Post*, December 27, 2010 www.washingtonpost.com/wp-dyn/content/article/2010/12/27/AR2010122703438.html.

[45.] Alta. Reg. 146/2008.

certain fees can be charged with respect to gift cards, and that certain activities (such as refusing to accept a gift card as partial payment on a purchase) are unfair practices under the *Fair Trading Act*.[46] Several other provinces have similar legislation, and the federal government has also introduced prepaid card regulations covering federally regulated institutions such as banks.

Controlled Business Practices

Door-to-door sales are controlled

Consumer protection legislation also places controls on several specific kinds of business activities. All provinces restrict **door-to-door sales**, also known as **direct sales**. The main method of doing this is by imposing a **cooling-off period**, which allows a purchaser a given period of time to change her mind and to rescind the contract. Some jurisdictions also require the disclosure of certain information, that the contract be in writing, and provide for an extended cooling-off period. Refer to MyBusLawLab for specific provincial variations.

Other activities controlled including referral selling

Other types of potentially abusive business activities prohibited or controlled in various jurisdictions are unsolicited goods and services or credit cards, discounted income tax returns, prearranged funeral services, inappropriate debt collection activities, prepaid contracting, timeshare contracts, and referral selling. **Referral selling** involves a purchaser supplying a seller with a list of friends or acquaintances. When sales are made to any of those people, the purchaser is given a benefit, such as a reduction of the purchase price.

METHODS OF CONTROL

Several methods are used to control abusive activity

Controlling these potentially abusive activities through legislation is accomplished by several methods. One method involves requiring that the party supplying these goods and services be licensed. This gives the government an effective control mechanism since licences can be suspended or revoked. Legislation may also impose fines or imprisonment in the event of abusive behaviour. In addition to the powers to investigate, to seize records, and to impose penalties for violations, government bodies are often given the power to initiate actions on behalf of victimized consumers or to help them start their own actions.

Loan Transactions

True cost of borrowing must be disclosed

In addition to unconscionable transactions legislation, every province has enacted legislation requiring that the true cost of borrowing be disclosed, thus prohibiting excessive rates of interest and costs in loan transactions. The federal *Interest Act*[47] has similar requirements. The *Criminal Code*[48] also prohibits the charging of excessive rates of interest.

Legislative provisions aim to prevent the practice of hiding excessive interest rates in the payment of a bonus or through some other form of subterfuge. Statutes demand that all this information be fully disclosed to the borrower at the outset. They usually prohibit misleading information in advertisements about the cost of borrowing, require the cost of borrowing to be stated in a standard format, and require moneylenders to be registered, which makes them subject to suspension by the governing body for misbehaviour or incompetence.

The "unconscionability" of the transaction has an impact on the severity of the penalty imposed by the courts. When it is shown that the parties' bargaining positions were relatively equal and that each had independent legal advice, the reduction in the eventual interest deemed payable may be less.[49] But when the borrower is less

---

[46.] *Supra* note 34.

[47.] R.S.C. 1985, c. I-15.

[48.] R.S.C. 1985, c. C-46, s. 347.

[49.] *Transport North American Express Inc. v. New Solutions Financial Corp.*, 2004 SCC 7 (CanLII), [2004] 1 SCR 249, 235 DLR (4th) 385.

sophisticated and the transaction smacks of unconscionability, the court may refuse to enforce the indebtedness in its entirety or apply a low rate of interest and require the payment of a rebate as in the *Consumers' Gas Co.* case discussed in Case Summary 16.8.

CASE SUMMARY 16.8

Excessive Interest Costly for All Concerned: *Garland v. Consumers' Gas Co.*[50]

In a stunning class action suit, Garland brought an action on behalf of over 500 000 customers of Consumers' Gas (now Enbridge Gas Distribution Inc.). He demonstrated that the 5 percent late payment penalties charged on unpaid accounts constituted a criminal rate of interest. Garland established that when a late payment penalty was charged and the actual bill and late payment were paid within 38 days, the actual annual interest rate was over 60 percent, contrary to section 347 of the *Criminal Code*.

The case went to the Supreme Court of Canada—twice! In the first instance, the Court found that the late payment penalties were collected in contravention of the *Criminal Code* and, as a matter of public policy, criminals should not be permitted to keep the proceeds of their crime. The Court thus ordered Consumers' Gas to repay the late payment penalties collected from the representative class in excess of the interest limit stipulated by the *Criminal Code*.

The issue of restitution brought the matter back to the Supreme Court. It decided that, although late payment penalties had been collected since 1981, only those penalties imposed after the class action was commenced (in 1994) had to be repaid. Prior to 1994, reliance on the Ontario Energy Board's orders gave Consumers' Gas justification for the enrichment; but once Garland's action was commenced, Consumers' Gas was put on notice that it was violating the *Criminal Code*. Collecting excessive interest from that point on constituted unjust enrichment.

DISCUSSION QUESTIONS

Consider other situations where consumers must pay late payment penalties. Should it be left to consumers to challenge these in court? This is fair warning to the perceptive businessperson to avoid charging such penalties.

To deal with abusive payday loan practices, Manitoba amended its *Consumer Protection Act*[51] by adding Part XVIII, "Payday Loans." Among other things, these provisions require the Public Utilities Board to hold hearings when it is setting the maximum interest rates that may be charged for payday loans. The *Payday Loans Regulation*[52] provides for the licensing of payday lenders. Because of this statutory framework, Manitoba was the first province to receive designation under section 347.1 of the *Criminal Code* allowing it to regulate the rates that can be charged for payday loans.[53] Now, most provinces in Canada have some provisions in place regulating the payday loan business.

DEBT COLLECTION PROCESSES

Unpaid creditors often turn to debt collection agencies to assist in the collection process. The actual debts owed are usually assigned to these agencies for a fee. The practices used by such agencies are sometimes abusive, so legislation has been

Abusive debt collection practices are controlled

---

50. 2004 SCC 25 (CanLII), [2004] 1 SCR 629, 237 DLR (4th) 385.

51. C.C.S.M. c. C200.

52. Man. Reg. 99/2007.

53. See *Order Designating Manitoba for the Purposes of the Criminal Interest Rate Provisions of the Criminal Code*, S.O.R./2008-212.

enacted to control their activities. Common law remedies for abusive debt collection practices such as defamation, assault and battery, trespass, and even false imprisonment are usually ineffective. The legislation enacted requires these agencies to be licensed, adding the threat of a suspended or revoked licence in the event of infractions. These statutes set out specific unacceptable collection practices, such as excessive phone calls, calls at unreasonable hours, or collect calls; threats of legal action with no foundation; issuing letters of collection that resemble official court documents; making deceptive or misleading statements; communicating with employers, friends, or relatives; and putting pressure on innocent relatives to pay the debt.

Some provinces require that debt collection agencies use only previously approved form letters in their demands for payment. In British Columbia, a collector must not communicate with a debtor; a member of the debtor's family or household; a relative, neighbour, friend, or acquaintance of the debtor; or the debtor's employer in a manner or with a frequency as to constitute harassment. Any use of undue, excessive, or unreasonable pressure constitutes harassment.[54] The punishment for a party engaged in such activities may range from the loss of its licence to prosecution and a fine. Some provinces give debtors the right to civil action for any damages suffered because of the abusive practices. The threat of criminal prosecution to pressure a debtor to pay is a violation of the *Criminal Code*[55] and can result in prosecution for extortion against the person making the threat.

Credit-reporting practices are controlled

Legislation to control credit-reporting agencies is also in place. While providing a valuable service to the lender, these businesses sometimes cause great harm to the borrower through carelessness or indifference. The relevant statutes usually require such bodies to be registered, limit the type of information that they can disclose, make it an offence for them to knowingly include false information in a credit file, give the individual the right to inspect the file and to correct or remove erroneous information, and in some jurisdictions prohibit an agency from making any report to a lender without the written permission of the borrower. Case Summary 16.9 is an example of such an abuse. Refer to MyBusLawLab for specific provincial variations.

CASE SUMMARY 16.9

Credit Information Disclosure Restricted: *Trans Union of Canada, Inc. v. Business Practices and Consumer Protection Authority of British Columbia*[56]

Trans Union of Canada Inc. was a credit-reporting agency and as such was required to adhere to the provisions of the *Business Practices and Consumer Protection Act* of British Columbia. That Act required that no information that was over six years old and was adverse to the individual being reported on could be included in a report. Thus outstanding debts over six years old could not be referred to. Trans Union followed a practice of including information in such a report of any inquiries made by a debt collection agency relating to such debts prior to that six-year period. Although the inquiry by the debt collection agency was made within the six-year period, referring to such inquiries implied the existence of financial difficulties, such as uncollected debts of bankruptcy prior to the six-year period, thus defeating the six-year prohibition.

---

54. *Business Practices and Consumer Protection Act, supra* note 14, s. 114.

55. *Supra* note 48, s. 346.

56. 2014 BCSC 74 (CanLII).

A compliance order was issued pursuant to the *Business Practices and Consumer Protection Act* requiring them to stop the practice and mask the information so that the inquiries by such debt collection agencies could only be seen by the individual who was the subject of the report.

This application to the Supreme Court of British Columbia is made by way of judicial review rather than appeal, so the merits of the decision have not been reviewed. The Court determined that the procedure was fair and reasonable and upheld the validity of the order.

SMALL BUSINESS PERSPECTIVE

For our purposes the decision illustrates how such consumer reporting companies are limited in what they can report. Other provinces impose similar restrictions. Note that the applicable provision relied on in the *Business Practices and Consumer Protection Act* was section 109(1)(0), which prohibited the disclosure of "any other information adverse to the individuals interest" related to an event prior to six years past.

Businesspeople should also be aware of the *2001 Internet Sales Contract Harmonization Template*[57] that has been implemented with some variation by all provinces and Nunavut.[58] New formalities for online and other distance sellers have thus been imposed. Merchants must disclose specific information items prominently, bringing them expressly to the consumer's attention. The consumer must be able to print and retain this information. The Ontario *Consumer Protection Act, 2002*, for example, and the *Regulation* under that Act require that the supplier disclose to the consumer (before the consumer enters into an Internet agreement) detailed information, including the following:

Consumer protection statutes can apply to Internet transactions

1. The name of the supplier and, if different, the name under which the supplier carries on business

2. The telephone number of the supplier, their business address, and information respecting other ways the supplier can be contacted

3. A fair and accurate description of the goods and services to be supplied to the consumer, including the technical requirements related to the use of the goods or services

4. An itemized list of the prices for the goods and services, including taxes and shipping charges

5. A description of each additional charge that may apply, such as customs duties or brokerage fees[59]

Consumers must also be notified of any cancellation, return, exchange, or refund conditions. The merchant must further give the consumer an express opportunity to accept or decline the proposal, such as by clicking on an "I Accept" button, which when clicked would send an email back to the merchant. Finally, the merchant must send a copy of the contract to the consumer within a set time (typically 15 days). Consumers have the right to cancel contracts if the above

[57.] Office of Consumer Affairs, Industry Canada, *Internet Sales Contract Harmonization Template*, www.ic.gc.ca/epic/site/oca-bc.nsf/en/ca01642e.html.

[58.] These regulations are incorporated into various provincial regulations. Refer to MyBusLawLab for provincial variations.

[59.] Refer to the *Regulation* for a full list of the disclosures required: *Consumer Protection Act, 2002*, S.O. 2002, c. 30, Sch. A; General, O. Reg. 17/05, art. 32.

information requirements are not met. A right to cancel also arises if the merchant fails to begin performing its obligation within a prescribed time frame.

Additional consumer protection legislation to guard against technology misuse has been enacted by the Canadian government. The *Fighting Internet and Wireless Spam Act (FISA)*[60] is usually thought of as simply restricting spam, but it also contains provisions to control the inclusion of hidden programs in downloaded or purchased programs that act like a "Trojan horse," communicating information back to another source without the knowledge of the consumer.

Consumer Service Bodies

In most jurisdictions, government departments have been empowered to implement and enforce these consumer protection statutes. The authority given to such departments usually includes the right to hear and investigate complaints, seize records, search premises, suspend licences, impose fines or some other corrective action, and initiate civil actions on behalf of the consumer.

In some jurisdictions these bodies have become clearinghouses of consumer information with a mandate to collect and disseminate that information to the public. Consumer bureaus can collect information on dangerous products, consumer business scams, or unacceptable practices. They may get involved in advertising to educate the consumer.[61]

Representatives of the federal government and of each of the provinces and territories belong to the Consumer Measures Committee (CMC). The aim of the CMC is to provide, through national cooperation, an improved marketplace for Canadian consumers. To create public awareness, the CMC has published an electronic version of the *Canadian Consumer Handbook*.[62] This publication provides advice and information on a wide range of consumer issues. It includes a Canada-wide directory of names, addresses, and telephone numbers for contacts in government, business, and consumer associations.

Private organizations, such as the Better Business Bureau (BBB), are also designed to be clearinghouses for such information. It must be remembered, however, that the BBB is supported and sustained by the business community. It thus has a vested interest in serving that community. The theory is that it is in the best interests of the business community to maintain high standards by weeding out disreputable businesses. The BBB and similar organizations serve that function for members of the business community who join them. Specialized bodies have also been set up to deal with disputes in unique industries. In particular, there are several organizations that are available to arbitrate disputes arising from the sale and repair of automobiles in Canada. The Canadian Motor Vehicle Arbitration Plan (CAMVAP) is a prime example.[63]

Finally, it should be noted that in addition to those mentioned above, there are other statutes aimed at specialized industries and professions that have a consumer protection function. For example, trading in securities (the stock market) is controlled primarily by provincial legislation. Also, most professionals, such as doctors, lawyers, and dentists, are governed by provincial legislation largely designed to protect clients.

[60.] This Act has a very long title that is normally shortened to FISA: *An Act to Promote the Efficiency and Adaptability of the Canadian Economy by Regulating Certain Activities that Discourage Reliance on Electronic Means of Carrying out Commercial Activities, and to Amend the Canadian Radio-television and Telecommunications Commission Act, the Competition Act, the Personal Information Protection and Electronic Documents Act and the Telecommunications Act*, S.C. 2010, c. 23.

[61.] See, for example, services provided by the government of Alberta: www.servicealberta.gov.ab.ca/Consumer_Info.cfm, www.servicealberta.gov.ab.ca/548.cfm, and www.servicealberta.gov.ab.ca/ConsumerTipsheets.cfm.

[62.] Available online at www.consumerhandbook.ca/en.

[63.] Check out CAMVAP online at www.camvap.ca.

REDUCING RISK 16.5

For businesspeople, it is important to understand that the operation of the consumer protection legislation has shifted the balance. The old principle of *caveat emptor* required the consumers of products or services to be careful in their dealings. Now that principle is often downplayed. Instead, responsibility has shifted to the merchant to exercise care. But even though these consumer protection statutes may *seem* strong, they will be ineffective if they are poorly enforced. Still, a sophisticated client must be aware that the nature of their responsibility has changed and has become much more onerous.

NEGOTIABLE INSTRUMENTS

LO **8**

Negotiable instruments are often associated with consumer and commercial transactions. They take many different forms, but are primarily *cheques, bills of exchange* (sometimes called *drafts*), and *promissory notes*, as set out in the federal *Bills of Exchange Act*.[64] They are particularly important in transactions because of their unique characteristics of free transferability and the favoured position of an innocent third party acquiring possession of the instrument, referred to as a **holder in due course**.

Negotiable instruments are controlled by federal statute. They include . . .

A cheque (see Figure 16.1) is an order made by the **drawer** to his bank to pay funds to a third party called the *payee;* these funds must be paid as soon as the cheque is presented for payment (on demand). A **cheque** is defined as a bill of exchange drawn on a bank that is payable on demand.

. . . cheques

Figure 16.1 Cheque

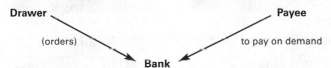

The drawer physically hands the cheque to the payee, who later presents it to the bank.

A **bill of exchange** or draft (see Figure 16.2) also involves three parties The *drawer* orders the *drawee* to pay the *payee* a certain sum of money. But unlike the cheque, the drawee need not be a bank, and the instrument may be made payable at some future time. Bills of exchange are more likely to be used in sophisticated financial transactions.

. . . bills of exchange

Figure 16.2 Bills of Exchange

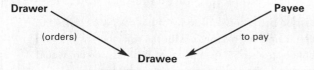

The drawer physically hands the instrument to the payee, who then presents it to the drawee for payment or acceptance.

With these kinds of instruments, the drawer retains the power to countermand even after she has given the cheque or bill of exchange to the payee. To overcome this problem, the payee will often take the instrument directly to the drawee to determine if the latter will honour it. If the drawee "accepts" the instrument, a direct obligation is created on the drawee to pay the payee, ensuring payment. Having a cheque certified has a similar result.

---

64. *Supra* note 1.

... promissory notes

A **promissory note** (see Figure 16.3) involves only two parties. The *maker* promises to pay a certain sum to the *payee* at a specified future date or on demand. Because of their nature, promissory notes are always associated with a creditor–debtor relationship.

Figure 16.3 Promissory Note

Maker ——————————————————————▶ Payee
(promises to pay a certain sum on a future date or on demand)

The maker hands the note to the payee, who later presents it to the maker for payment.

Stop payment order may not protect the drawer where cheque is certified

Cheques are used primarily as a convenient means of transferring funds. Their use has been largely replaced by tools associated with electronic banking, such as debit and credit cards. Cheques are still used, however, and astute businesspeople should be familiar with their unique qualities. Often sellers will require payment by **certified cheque**, which is extremely secure because payment is in effect guaranteed by the bank. Once the certified cheque has been transferred to the payee, the bank will no longer honour an order to stop payment. Instead of certifying a cheque, many banks now issue a bank draft in the name of the payee. It will be given by the customer to the payee at the appropriate time. When a number of regular payments are to be made, another common practice is to give the creditor a series of postdated cheques that are subsequently deposited on the appropriate dates. Negotiable instruments are also regularly used to bolster secured transactions.

CASE SUMMARY 16.10

Drawer Must Honour Cheque Despite Stop Payment: *422885 BC Ltd. (Cashplan) v. 482915 BC Ltd. (End Roll)*[65]

This is a small claims action. End Roll paid a tradesman for service, who then took the cheque to Cashplan for payment. Cashplan was in the commercial cheque-cashing business and paid out on the cheque. Only later did End Roll discover that the work had been improperly done and stopped payment on the cheque. Cashplan, as a holder in due course of a negotiable instrument, brought this action against End Roll for payment on the cheque. The Court had no choice but to find that Cashplan was a holder in due course and to enforce the cheque. The case is interesting in that the judge took it upon himself to observe strongly that he was not happy with the law. He made it clear that these commercial cheque-cashing firms ought to bear more of the risks associated with their business.

DISCUSSION QUESTIONS

What do you think? Would business be better served if some of the risks were shifted to such firms or even to banks, making them more responsible for the risk inherent in taking such cheques and other negotiable instruments? As a prudent businessperson, would you like more or less certainty associated with such cheques and promissory notes?

Holder in due course can enforce a negotiable instrument independent of problems

This unique transferability of negotiable instruments also makes their use particularly attractive for secured transactions. When a negotiable instrument such as a promissory note or cheque is transferred (negotiated) to some innocent third party, the latter can enforce that instrument despite any difficulties that arise under the original transaction (short of forgery or alteration of the instrument). As contrasted to assignment, which was discussed in Chapter 8, the holder of a negotiable instrument can be in a better position than the person from whom she obtained the instrument. Any defence that the original contracting party has against the person assigning those contractual rights can also be used against the assignee. If James purchased a truck from Sam to be used in his business, agreeing to pay for it in 12 payments over a year and he was the victim of misrepresentation, he wouldn't have to pay Sam, and if sued he would have a good defence. If Sam assigned that claim to Ace Finance Company, James would still not have to pay since any defence he had against James would be effective against Ace as well. On the other hand, when a negotiable instrument is signed and passes into the hands of an innocent third party—the holder in due course—the maker almost certainly will be required to honour it. Thus, if Sam signed a promissory note and that also went to the innocent Ace Finance Company, Sam would have to honour the note. Note that in a consumer transaction the result would be different because of changes to the *Bills of Exchange Act*. See the discussion of consumer notes below.

To qualify as a holder in due course, the person receiving the negotiable instrument must be innocent in that she must have had no knowledge of the problems with the original transaction. There must also be no indication of alteration or irregularity on the instrument itself. Consideration must have been given for the instrument by someone during the process, and she must have otherwise received the instrument in good faith. For the instrument to be negotiable, it must meet several requirements, including that it be an unconditional promise to pay a specific amount at some future date or on demand.

 REDUCING RISK 16.6

People often write cheques or sign promissory notes as simply one aspect of the transactions in which they are involved. If they think about a deal going sour at all, they assume that they can either stop payment on the cheque they wrote or simply not pay the promissory note they signed. But negotiable instruments are much more dangerous than simple contractual obligations. If they get into the hands of an innocent third party they can be enforced. When you write a cheque or a promissory note you will likely have to pay. You may think you can stop payment on a cheque, but once it gets into the hands of a holder in due course that is no longer an option. Even a bank can be a holder in due course. A sophisticated client will take care when dealing with negotiable instruments, keeping in mind the potential for danger even in an apparently innocent situation.

Endorser can be liable for payment

Another important feature of negotiable instruments involves the need for free transferability. As the instruments transfer from holder to holder, others not party to the original instrument will normally be required to sign or endorse the back of the instrument. There are several different forms of endorsement, but the usual purpose of an endorsement is for the **endorser** to add its credit to the instrument. This means that if the instrument is not honoured when it is presented for collection, the holder can then turn to the endorser for payment, provided that the holder gave proper notice of dishonour to that endorser immediately after payment was refused.

Promissory notes are often part of a loan transaction

In most credit transactions, debtors are required to sign promissory notes as part of the process. This may seem redundant, given the commitment to pay in the primary contract, but remember that promissory notes provide a great deal of flexibility, making them much more attractive to third parties to whom the creditor may wish to assign the proceeds of the transaction. Merchants supplying goods or services on credit will often assign the debt to a finance company. With the promissory note, the finance company becomes a holder in due course, able to enforce the promissory note independent of any problems that might arise from the original transaction or with the product sold.

Advantages are reduced in consumer transactions

An exception is made for consumer transactions. Pursuant to the *Bills of Exchange Act*,[66] any negotiable instrument used to advance credit in a consumer transaction must be marked "Consumer Purchase." This is notice to any third party that the

---

66. *Supra* note 1, Part V.

instrument does not convey the usual rights and that a holder in due course would in fact be subject to the same defences that the drawer would have against the original payee. Thus, most of the advantages of being a holder in due course are lost. This applies only to consumer transactions, however; when negotiable instruments are used in business transactions, the advantages of being a holder in due course still exist.

Electronic Money

Credit cards, debit cards, and other forms of electronic money are replacing negotiable instruments

Third parties assist with online transactions

Negotiable instruments cannot be created or transferred online since their essential nature is a unique written document. There are, however, electronic substitutes. Credit and debit cards have to a considerable extent replaced the use of negotiable instruments in both commercial and consumer transactions. Access and stored-value cards, which have value embedded in a chip on the card that diminishes as it is used, are increasingly available. Many credit card transactions and most debit cards no longer require a signature, substituting a PIN (personal identification number) or a chip as the essential element of identification. A key electronic substitute for direct payment involves using the services of a third-party Internet business. The most notable is PayPal, managing over 148 million active accounts.[67] These Internet businesses are designed to allow efficient exchange of money between Internet users and merchants. PayPal, for example, considers itself to be an "electronic money transmitter"; since it is not subject to standard banking regulations, users' rights are not as well protected. Note, however, that it is registered as a bank in Europe.

Unregulated virtual money is becoming more common

One step further involves nongovernment-backed online digital currencies, such as Bitcoins. These are used as a medium of exchange and have most of the features of currency but are virtual, lack security, and are not protected by any form of consumer protection legislation. Still, their use is growing and will likely be subjected to increased regulation in the future. Virtual vaults and wallets have been created for storage of these funds, and many online businesses accept Bitcoins as a form of payment along with credit cards, debit cards, and PayPal.

While automated and online banking, along with credit, debit, and access cards have made life more convenient, they have also provided ample opportunity for criminals to gain access to our funds. Many jurisdictions have passed consumer protection legislation limiting a cardholder's liability, placing most of the responsibility for credit card loss on the banks. Cards with embedded security chips have gone some way toward preventing thefts, but with clever new schemes for intercepting our personal data appearing daily, we must use extra caution in protecting our PIN and other personal information, for it is clear that the cost of these losses will be passed on to the bank's customers in one way or another.

Fraud is becoming an increasing problem for online transactions

The issue of fraud relating to electronic funds is a serious one that affects consumers and businesses alike. As the incidents increase in frequency and magnitude, everyone must take precautions. In the case of *R. v. Beauchamp et al.*,[68] the Ontario Superior Court was dealing with a number of forged credit card offences, and the judge noted that losses from credit card fraud were over $500 million each year in Canada and that $300 million of this amount was due to counterfeit credit cards. He took that into consideration when imposing sentences ranging from 15 months to 7 years for credit card fraud, with the lengthier sentences imposed when those offences were committed for the benefit of a criminal organization.

MyBusLawLab Be sure to visit the MyBusLawLab that accompanies this book to find practice quizzes, province-specific content, simulations and much more!

[67.] See Wikipedia, "PayPal," http://en.wikipedia.org/wiki/PayPal.
[68.] 2010 ONSC 1973 (CanLII).

SUMMARY

Sale of Goods Act

- Implies certain terms into a contract unless the parties have agreed otherwise
- Applies only when goods are being sold
- Except where there is agreement to the contrary, risk follows title; the Act supplies five rules to determine when title is transferred:
  - Seller must convey good title and quiet possession
  - Goods must be free of any lien or charge
  - Goods must be fit for communicated purpose
  - Goods must be of merchantable quality
  - Goods must match the sample or description
- In the event of a default, where the goods are not yet in the hands of the purchaser, the seller has an unpaid seller's lien and has the right of stoppage in transit

Consumer protection

- The federal *Competition Act* controls practices that unduly lessen competition
- The federal *Food and Drug Act* and *Hazardous Products Act* control dangerous products
- The *Criminal Code* controls identity theft
- Many other federal statutes protect customers
- Various provincial statutes require that goods be of acceptable quality
- A number of other statutes are in place to protect consumers, including *Consumer Protection Acts*, *Trade Practices Acts*, and *Unconscionable Transactions Acts*—check MyBusLawLab for details
- These statutes control unacceptable business practices, such as misrepresentation and other forms of misleading advertising, unconscionable transactions (i.e., when a merchant takes advantage of a weak-willed or otherwise unequal customer), and specific activities such as door-to-door and referral selling
- Moneylenders are required to disclose the true cost of borrowing to their customers
- Abusive debt collection practices are restricted

Negotiable instruments

- Negotiable instruments are cheques, bills of exchange, and promissory notes
- They are freely transferable without notice to the maker/drawer
- Holders in due course may be in a better position to enforce the negotiable instrument than the original parties
- An endorser is liable on default by the original drawer/maker only if he is properly notified of default
- The use of credit, debit, and stored-value cards continues to expand
- PINs replace signatures
- Online sales are often facilitated by third-party payment businesses
- Consumer protection legislation limits liability for credit card fraud

QUESTIONS FOR REVIEW

1. Explain the purpose of the *Sale of Goods Act* in relation to the obligations of the parties to a sale of goods transaction.

2. What three conditions must be met before the *Sale of Goods Act* applies to a transaction?

3. What is the distinction between a sale and an agreement to sell? What is the significance of that distinction?

4. When does the risk transfer to the buyer in a sale of goods transaction? Explain the exceptions to this general rule.

5. What is a bill of lading? How can it affect who bears the risk in a sale of goods transaction?

6. Indicate when title transfers in the following situations:
   a. When the contract for sale is unconditional and the goods involved are in a deliverable state at the time the purchase is made
   b. When the subject of the contract involves specific goods to which the seller is obligated to do something, such as repair, clean, or modify to get them into a deliverable state
   c. When the contract for sale involves specific, identified goods that must be weighed or measured before being given to the buyer
   d. When the goods are delivered to the buyer on approval
   e. When goods purchased by description have not been selected, separated out, or manufactured at the time the sales contract is entered into.

7. The *Sale of Goods Act* imposes terms relating to goods matching samples or descriptions and meeting standards of fitness, quality, and title. Explain the nature of these implied terms and their effect on the parties. Indicate which terms are conditions and which are warranties. Explain the significance of the distinction.

8. Explain what "merchantable quality" means.

9. Explain the effect of an exemption clause included in a contract that is inconsistent with the terms set out in the *Sale of Goods Act*.

10. Explain the rights of the seller when the buyer of goods:
    a. becomes insolvent
    b. defaults on the contract of sale while the goods are still in the hands of the seller
    c. defaults after the goods have been given to a third party to deliver but before they are received by the buyer
    d. becomes bankrupt after the goods have been delivered

11. Explain why a seller of goods might be less likely to sue for damages than for price.

12. Under what circumstances may a buyer refuse delivery of goods?

13. The *Sale of Goods Act* in each province implies certain terms into contracts of sale relating to the fitness and quality of the product. Some Canadian jurisdictions make these provisions mandatory in consumer transactions. Explain the situation in your jurisdiction.

14. Describe the practices controlled by the *Competition Act* and explain how that control is accomplished.

15. How does the concept of privity of contract limit the effectiveness of many consumer protection provisions? How have some jurisdictions overcome this problem?

16. What common law provisions are available to protect consumers from unscrupulous business practices?

17. Describe the methods outlined in federal and provincial consumer protection statutes to control businesses with a tendency to use abusive practices. Discuss the effectiveness of these tactics.

18. Identify the legislation in effect in your jurisdiction that offers relief to victims of unconscionable transactions.

19. What statutory provisions have been introduced throughout Canada to control door-to-door selling, referral selling, and other potentially abusive practices?

20. What services are provided to consumers through organizations set up by the federal and provincial governments? Discuss whether these services are adequate.

21. Distinguish among a cheque, a bill of exchange, and a promissory note.

22. Explain how the position of a holder in due course compares to the position of an assignee of contractual rights.

23. Explain the nature of an endorsement and its significance on a negotiable instrument.

24. Explain why online transactions do not involve negotiable instruments. What has taken their place?

CASES AND DISCUSSION QUESTIONS

1. *Resch v. Canadian Tire Corporation*, 2006 CanLII 11930 (ON SC), 17 BLR (4th) 301
Resch purchased a bicycle for his stepson from a Canadian Tire dealership owned by Mills-Roy Enterprises Ltd. Because of a defective fork on the bike, the stepson was seriously injured in an accident, and he and his family brought this action against Canadian Tire, Mills-Roy (the dealership), and Procycle Group Inc. (the manufacturer).

Explain what course of action the various parties would have against each of the defendants and any arguments that could be raised in their defence. Explain the likely outcome. Would it make any difference to your answer to know that the stepson paid some funds toward the purchase of the bike?

2. *R. v. Stucky*, Ont. C.A., per Weiler and Gillese J.J.A., 2009 ONCA 151 (CanLII), 240 CCC (3d) 141
Stucky was involved in a direct mailing scheme centred in Ontario and aimed at subjects in the United States. These direct mailings contained false and misleading representations contrary to section 52(1) of the *Competition Act*. He was charged under that section in this action.

Explain any arguments that he might be able to raise in his defence. Does it make any difference where his potential victims reside? If this prosecution were unsuccessful under the *Competition Act*, is there any other legislation that can be used against him?

3. *Behiel v. Primco Limited*, 2011 SKQB 65 (CanLII)
When the Behiels bought flooring from Primco they informed the salesman, Lee, that they had young children and needed a product that would resist scratching, be durable, and be pleasing to the eye. He recommended the product ultimately purchased, stating it would meet or exceed those requirements. In fact, the floor was seriously scratched when furniture was moved on it. The Behiels complained and, when the supplier and manufacturer would do nothing, brought this action.

Assuming there was a restrictive covenant included prohibiting recovery for this type of damage, what would be the likelihood of success of this action? Note that this action was brought in Saskatchewan where there is a *Sale of Goods Act* and a *Consumer Protection Act* in place.

4. *321665 Alberta Ltd. v. Husky Oil Operations Ltd.*, 2013 ABCA 221 (CanLII)
Husky Oil and ExxonMobile were joint owners of oil-and-gas-producing operations in Alberta north of Edmonton. They stood to save about 20 percent of the cost if they switched to one company to provide oil field fluid-handling services instead of two, as was past practice. They choose to use Cardusty Trucking, and the decision in effect drove Kolt (321665 Alberta Ltd.), the other company formerly used, out of business. They sued.

What would be the basis of their complaint, and what would be the expected outcome? Would it affect your answer to know that before choosing Cardusty the oil companies carefully examined each of the service providers giving both a fair opportunity to argue that they should be selected? There was no question that the choice was made after careful and thorough assessment.

Glossary

A

abatement a court order to reduce the rent to be paid to compensate for a breach of the lease by the landlord

absolute privilege exemption from liability for defamatory statements made in some settings (such as legislatures and courts), without reference to the speaker's motives or the truth or falsity of the statement

abuse of power an action by a tribunal beyond the jurisdiction set out in the legislation governing it, or in making an unreasonable decision

acceleration clause a contractual term that comes into effect when there is a failure to make an instalment payment and which requires that the entire debt plus expenses be paid

acceptance an agreement by one party to the terms of the offer made by another

accord agreement by both parties on some change in the contract

accord and satisfaction agreement to end a contract with extra consideration to be supplied by the party benefiting from the discharge

accounting a court-ordered determination of the injuries suffered; the agent must pay over money or property collected on behalf of the principal; a court order that any profits made from wrongdoing be paid over to the victim

accounts receivable funds owed to a business for goods or services provided to customers

actual authority authority given to an agent expressly or by implication

adjusters representatives of the insurer who are charged with investigating and settling claims after the insured-against event occurs

administrative law the rules and regulations governing the function and powers of the executive branch of government

administrative tribunals government decision makers (committees, commissions, tribunals, or individuals) who act with quasi-judicial powers

adverse possession a right to actual possession, which can be acquired by non-contested use of the land

affidavit a written statement made by a witness out of court but under oath

affirmative action programs intended to correct racial, gender, or other imbalances in the workplace

agency the service an agent performs on behalf of a principal

agency agreement an agreement creating an agency relationship between principal and agent

agency by necessity consent to act as an agent that is implied when there is an urgent reason

agency shop *see* **Rand formula**

agent a person authorized to represent or act on behalf of a principal in dealings with others

agreement for sale an agreement where title will be transferred at some time in the future, typically once the property is fully paid for; an agreement that grants possession of property to the purchaser pending full payment of the price

agreement of purchase and sale the first stage in the purchase of real property; also referred to as an *interim agreement* between the vendor and purchaser

agreement to sell an agreement that title will be transferred at some time in the future

alternative dispute resolution (ADR) the use of processes such as negotiation, mediation, and arbitration to resolve disputes instead of court action

annual general meeting a meeting where shareholders elect directors and vote on other important resolutions

anticipatory breach repudiation of a contract before performance is due

Anton Piller order a court order to seize offending material before trial; name derives from a prominent English case where the order was first used

apparent authority authority as suggested to a third party by the conduct of a principal; may exist even when there is no actual authority

appeal a formal process whereby a higher court will re-examine a decision made by a lower court

applications for directions interim applications and questions that are brought before a judge (before the actual trial) for a ruling

arbitration the submission of parties in a dispute to having an arbitrator make a binding decision on their claims

arbitrator a panel or other third party that has been given the authority to make a binding decision on a dispute between parties

articles of association internal regulations setting out the procedures for governing a corporation in a registration jurisdiction

articles of incorporation a method of incorporating based on a US approach and used in some jurisdictions in Canada

assault a verbal or physical threat; an action that makes a person fear physical interference

assignment the transfer of rights under a contract to another party

assignment in bankruptcy the voluntary transfer of a debtor's assets to a trustee in bankruptcy so that they can be administered for the benefit of the creditors

attachment under the *Personal Property Security Act*, the situation in which value has been given pursuant to the contract, giving the creditor a claim against the assets used as security if there is a default by the debtor

attachment of debt a court order that monies owed to the judgment debtor (defendant) be intercepted and paid to the judgment creditor (plaintiff)

auditor a party responsible for ensuring that an organization's financial statements have been properly prepared

authority the right or power to act or to make a decision

B

bailee the person acquiring possession of personal property in a bailment

bailment temporary possession by one person of chattels owned by another

bailment for value a bailment involving a mutual benefit or consideration flowing between the parties

bailor the owner giving up possession of property in a bailment

balance of convenience determination of who will suffer the greatest injury if the damage were allowed to continue

bankrupt a person who has made an assignment in bankruptcy or been forced into bankruptcy through a court order obtained by a creditor, and who has not been discharged from bankruptcy

bankruptcy the process by which an insolvent person voluntarily or involuntarily transfers assets to a trustee for distribution to creditors

bankruptcy order a statutory assignment of a debtor's assets to a trustee in bankruptcy

bargaining agent a body certified to act on behalf of a group of employees or employers

bargaining unit a group of employees who have been certified

battery unwelcome physical contact; non-consensual physical interference with one's body

bias prejudice against or partiality toward one party, for example, based on a decision maker's personal interest in the decision

bilateral contract a contract in which there is an exchange of promises: both parties assume an obligation

bilateral discharge agreement by both sides to terminate the contract or to disregard a term of the contract

bill a draft of a proposed law introduced before Parliament or a legislature

bill of exchange a negotiable instrument by which the drawer directs the drawee to pay out money to the payee; drawee need not be a bank, and the instrument may be made payable in the future

bill of lading a receipt for goods in the care of the shipper accompanied by an undertaking to move the goods or deliver identical goods to a designated place

bill of sale a written agreement that conveys title from seller to buyer

bona fide purchaser for value an innocent third party who has paid a fair price for goods under claim by a creditor

bond a share interest in the indebtedness of a corporation; often used synonymously with "debenture," though a bond is normally secured against specific assets, while a debenture is likely not

book accounts accounts receivable that can be used as security for a loan

breach of contract failure to live up to the conditions of a contract

breach of trust misuse of property held in trust for another by a trustee

broadly held corporations corporations that are publicly traded on the stock market; also called "distributing corporations" in some jurisdictions

brokers persons engaged, for a fee, to negotiate a contract for another; a party hired to ascertain an insured's insurance needs and secure the necessary coverage

builder's risk policy insurance against liability and other forms of loss taking place during the construction process

building scheme a set of restrictions placed on all the properties in a large development

business interruption insurance a form of insurance that compensates the insured for continuing expenses incurred while the business is not earning income

"but for" test a test for causation used in negligence actions to determine whether the injury would have occurred had it not been for the act of the defendant

C

canon or church law the legal system of the Catholic Church, from which common law drew principles relating to families and estates

capacity an element of a valid contract; the freedom to enter into a contract, which is sometimes limited by law as is the case, for example, with minors, the insane, the intoxicated, aliens, bankrupts, and Aboriginal peoples

causation the fact of being the cause of something happening

caveat emptor "let the buyer beware"; a principle that the purchaser must examine, judge, and test for herself

certificate of title conclusive evidence as to the ownership of a property

certified cheque a means of transferring funds by cheque where payment is, in effect, guaranteed by the bank

certiorari a court order overturning a decision and making it null and void

chattel mortgage a loan for which a creditor provides credit to the debtor, securing the loan by taking title of a good such as a car

chattels tangible, movable personal property that can be measured and weighed; also known as *goods*

check-off provision a provision in a collective agreement whereby employees agree to have the employer deduct union dues from their payroll

cheque a negotiable instrument consisting of a bill of exchange drawn on a bank, payable on demand

chose in action the thing or benefit that is transferred in an assignment; intangible personal property, such as a claim or the right to sue

CIF (cost, insurance, and freight) contracts sales contracts in which one of the parties has been designated as being responsible for paying the costs involved in the shipping the goods as well as arranging insurance

circumstantial evidence testimony not based on actual observation or personal knowledge; evidence that leads one to infer the existence of other facts

civil law legal system the legal system used in most of Europe based on a central code, which is a list of rules stated as broad principles of law that judges apply to the cases that come before them

civil litigation the process of one party's suing another in a private action, conducted in a trial court

class action where one or more plaintiffs launch a legal action on behalf of themselves and others with the same interest

clean hands absence of wrongdoing on the part of a person seeking an equitable remedy

closed shop a workplace where only workers who are already members of the union can be hired

closely held corporations corporations in which there are relatively few shareholders; referred to as "non-distributing corporations" in some jurisdictions

COD (cash on delivery) contracts sales contracts in which the seller maintains the proprietary rights or title as well as control over the possession of those goods until they are delivered to the buyer's premises and paid for

code of business conduct a formal statement that sets out the values and standards of business practices of an organization

co-insurance clauses requirements that the insured bear some risk

collateral goods or property used to secure a debt

collateral contract a separate contractual obligation that can stand alone, independent of the written contract

collective bargaining a procedure for settling terms and conditions of employment by negotiation between an employer and its employees as expressed through representatives chosen by them

common law legal system the legal system developed in England based on judges applying the customs and traditions of the people and then following each other's decisions

common law courts the three historical English courts (the Court of Common Pleas, the Court of King's Bench, and the Exchequer Court), where in theory law was discovered in the customs and traditions of the people

common shareholders holders of common shares who do not have any preferential rights or privileges

common shares shares to which no preferential rights or privileges are attached

comprehensive policy property insurance covering all losses not specifically excluded

conditional sale a sale in which the seller provides credit to the purchaser, holding title until the goods are paid for

conditions major terms of a contract

condition precedent a condition under which the obligations of a contract will begin; also called "subject-to" clause

condition subsequent a condition under which the obligations of a contract will end

Confederation the process that united the British colonies in North America as the Dominion of Canada in 1867

confidential information private information, the disclosure of which would be injurious to a business; a type of intellectual property

confirmed letter of credit a document, ratified by the lender, that secures or guarantees the financial aspects of a trade transaction

conflict of laws rules used to resolve questions as to which jurisdiction's laws are to be applied to a particular issue

consensus an element of a valid contract; both parties must objectively know and agree to its terms through an offer and an acceptance

consent permission or assent to conduct that would otherwise constitute a tort such as assault and battery; can be expressed or implied; informed consent constitutes a defence to torts such as assault and battery

consideration an element of a valid contract; the price one is willing to pay for the promise set out in the offer

conspiracy to injure the coordinated action of two or more persons using illegal methods to harm the business or other interests of another

constructive dismissal unilaterally demoting or changing the duties of an employee, contrary to what was agreed to in the employment contract; conduct that essentially terminates a pre-existing contractual relationship, which could be treated as dismissal

constructive trust a trust inferred by the courts to benefit a third party to a contract

consumer transactions purchases by individuals of goods or services for personal use and not for resale or for business purposes

contingency fee a fee paid to a lawyer that is based on a percentage of the sum recovered by the client

continuing guarantee a provision in a guarantee allowing the creditor to advance further funds without affecting the obligation of the guarantor to pay in the event of default

continuing trespass a permanent incursion onto the property of another

contract a voluntary exchange of promises creating obligations that, if defaulted on, can be enforced and remedied in the courts

***contra proferentum* rule** a rule of interpretation; ambiguous provisions in a written contract are to be construed against the party that drafted the agreement

contributory negligence a failure to take reasonable care, which contributes to the injury complained of

control test a test of whether an employment relationship exists based on whether the person being paid for work is told how, when, and where to do it

conversion intentional appropriation of the goods of another person for the appropriator's own purposes

cooling-off period a statutorily defined period during which purchasers in door-to-door sales may change their minds and rescind a contract

cooperative a company composed of members holding shares in it; a method of acquiring residential accommodation

copyright control over the use and reproduction of the expression of creative work; type of intellectual property

corporate myth a corporation is a legal fiction

corporate social responsibility a corporation's environmental, social, and economic performance and the impact of the corporation on its internal and external stakeholders

corporation a business organization that is a separate legal entity from its shareholders

counterclaim a statement of claim by the defendant alleging that the plaintiff is responsible for the losses suffered and claiming back against the plaintiff for those losses

counteroffer a new offer, the proposal of which rejects and terminates the offer available until then

Court of Chancery a court administering equity and proceeding according to the forms and principles of equity; sometimes referred to as the Court of Equity

Court of Equity a court administering equity and proceeding according to the forms and principles of equity; sometimes referred to as the Court of Chancery

crimes wrongs that affect society as a whole and are punishable by the state

crumbling skull rule a tort law principle that the defendant is not liable for losses that were inevitable; used in conjunction with the thin skull rule

D

damages monetary compensation to a victim

debenture an acknowledgment of debts by a corporation normally involving more than one creditor; often used interchangeably with "bond," but whereas a bond is typically secured against a specific asset, a debenture may be unsecured or secured by a floating charge against inventory

deceit the fraudulent and intentional misleading of another person causing injury

declaration an official statement by the court on the law applicable to a particular case as an outcome of a trial

declaratory judgment a declaration by the court as to what the law is in any matter brought before it

deed of conveyance a document transferring an interest in property

deeds of settlement contracts used historically for setting up a company

defamation a false statement published to a person's detriment

delegation entrusting someone else to act in one's place; an agent normally cannot turn his responsibilities over to someone else

delivery up an order directing the defendant to deliver all copies of the infringing items in her possession or control to the copyright owner

deposit money prepaid with the provision that the funds are to be forfeited in the event of a breach

derivative action a lawsuit where certain shareholders are given the right to launch a civil action against the directors on behalf of an injured company; sometimes called *representative action*

detinue wrongful retention of goods legally obtained but subsequently not returned in response to a proper request

direct sales sales made to consumers at their dwellings or places of business; also known as door-to-door sales

disbursements out-of-pocket costs incurred by the lawyer on the client's behalf

discharge by agreement agreement by the parties that a contract is ended

discovery pre-trial disclosure of information, consisting of discovery of documents and examination for discovery

discovery of documents pre-trial inspection of any document that is held by the other party and may be used as evidence

dissent and appraisal the right of minority shareholders who are adversely affected by major changes to indicate their opposition and force the company to buy back their shares at a fair price

distinguishing the facts the process judges use to decide which case is the binding precedent; involves comparing the facts relevant to the issues being determined

distress seizure by a landlord of any property left by a tenant and holding it until the rent is paid or selling it to pay rent owing

dividend a payment to shareholders out of company profits

Division I proposal an alternative to bankruptcy, created by the *Bankruptcy and Insolvency Act*, whereby the debtor secures some time to reorganize his affairs and make a proposal for partial payment that will satisfy his creditors; if the creditors reject the proposal, the insolvent debtor is deemed to have made an assignment in bankruptcy from the day of the meeting of the creditors, and the normal bankruptcy procedures follow

dominant tenement property that has the advantage of an easement

door-to-door sales an example of direct sales

dower rights protection of the rights of a spouse in certain matrimonial property; have been modified or abolished in most jurisdictions

down payment a portion of the purchase price paid to the seller at the time of sale

drawer the person creating the negotiable instrument

due diligence doing everything reasonable to avoid a problem leading to legal liability

duress force or pressure to enter into a contract

duty in a negligence action, an obligation to live up to a reasonable standard

duty of care an obligation to take steps to avoid foreseeable harm; an essential element for establishing liability in the tort of negligence

E

easement the right of a person other than the owner to use a portion of private property

easement acquired by prescription a right to the use of land that is acquired through free use of that land without interference over a number of years

ecommerce (or electronic commerce) commercial activity using electronic communication

employee a person working for another who is told what to do and how to do it

employers' organizations bargaining agents representing groups of employers

employment equity the correction of employment situations where there has been a tradition of racial or gender imbalance

encryption coding technological innovations to protect privacy and security on the Internet

endorser the person who signs the back of a cheque, usually assuming the obligation to pay it if the drawee or maker defaults

enduring power of attorney the power to act as the donor's trustee or representative following the donor's lack of capacity

enhanced injunction a new remedy allowing a court to order a wrongdoer to refrain from future infringements of copyright in other works owned by the plaintiff copyright owner

equality rights basic rights enumerated in the *Canadian Charter of Rights and Freedoms*, including the right not to be discriminated against on the basis of grounds such as gender, age, religion, race, or colour, and the guarantee of equal benefit of and protection by the law

equitable estoppel the principle that when a gratuitous promise to do something in the future causes a person who relies on that promise to incur an expense, the promisor will not be allowed to enforce other contractual rights that are inconstant with that promise; the promise can only be used as a defence by the promisee; also known as *promissory estoppel*

equity legal principles founded upon fairness, as developed in the Court of Chancery to relieve the harshness of the common law; also the value left in an asset after subtracting what the owner owes

equity of redemption an interest in land retained by the mortgagor even after default

error of law when a decision maker incorrectly states the legal interpretation or effect of the statute or common law

errors and omissions insurance insurance to protect the holder should she cause injury by negligence

estate all the property the owner has power to dispose of, less any related debt; also an interest in land; also the property of a bankrupt given to the trustee in bankruptcy

estate in land the right to uninterrupted possession of land for a period of time. The amount of time is determined by the nature of the estate

estoppel an equitable remedy that stops a party from trying to establish a position or deny something that, if allowed, would create an injustice

ethics a system of moral principles governing the appropriate conduct for an individual or a group

evidence in writing any document that provides information or proof

examination for discovery a pre-trial meeting in which lawyers from opposing sides question the plaintiff and defendant in a civil suit under oath—their responses can be entered as evidence; a method of making all relevant information known to both sides before trial

examination in aid of execution a court-ordered review of the judgment debtor's finances to arrange for payment of the judgment; called an examination in aid of enforcement in Alberta

executed contract a fully performed contract; a contract at the stage when both parties have performed or fulfilled their obligations

executive branch the part of the government composed of the Queen acting through the prime minister, cabinet, deputy ministers, and government departments and officials; also known as the Crown

executory contract a contract yet to be performed; a contract at the stage when an agreement has been made but before performance is due

exemplary damages damages in excess of the plaintiff's actual losses, intended to punish the wrongdoer for outrageous or extreme behaviour; also known as *punitive damages*

exemption clause an attempt to limit liability under an agreement (also called an exclusion or exculpatory clause)

express authority the authority of the agent as actually stated by the principal

express contract a contract in which the parties have expressly stated their agreement, either verbally or in writing

F

fair comment a defence available when defamatory statements are made about public figures or works put before the public

fair dealing use of copyrighted material (as permitted under Canadian law) for the purposes of research or private study, criticism or review, or news reporting

fair hearing a hearing conducted in accordance with the rules of procedural fairness; the person affected negatively by a decision has the right to receive proper and timely notice of all the matters affecting the case and be given a chance to put forward his side

false imprisonment holding people against their will and without lawful authority

fee simple the highest interest in land, equivalent to ownership; an estate granting possession for an infinite time

fidelity bond an employer's insurance against an employee's wrongful conduct

fiduciary duty a duty to act in the best interests of another; such duty may arise between directors and officers and the corporation they serve, between business associates including senior employees and their employer, between agents and their principals, and between partners

fixed fee a predetermined fee paid to a lawyer for completing a specific task

fixture a thing attached to land or to a building or to another fixture attached to the land

floating charge a security not fixed on any particular assets until default or some other specified event

FOB (free on board) contracts sales contracts in which the parties have agreed that the seller will bear the risk until a specified point in the transport process

force majeure clause a contract term anticipating some catastrophic event usually exempting liability when such an event interferes with performance of the contract

foreclosure a court process ending the mortgagor's right to redeem

forfeiture the requirement by a landlord that a tenant who breached the lease vacate the property

forfeiture rule the principle that a criminal should not be permitted to profit from a crime

formal contract an agreement under seal

franchising arrangements based on contracts of service and the supply of products between larger and smaller units of one organization

fraud the tort of intentionally or recklessly misleading another person or making statements without belief in their truth

fraudulent misrepresentation misleading (false) words said knowingly, without belief in their truth, or recklessly, causing injury

fraudulent preference a debtor's payment of money to one creditor to give that creditor preference over the other creditors

fraudulent transfer a debtor's transfer of property in an attempt to keep it out of the hands of creditors; not a valid sale at a fair price to an innocent third party

frustration interference with a contract by some outside, unforeseen event that makes performance impossible or essentially different in nature

full disclosure the obligation to reveal all details of a transaction

fundamental breach a breach of a fundamental aspect of the contract that is not covered by an exclusion clause; a breach that goes to the very root of the contract

fundamental freedoms basic rights enumerated in the *Canadian Charter of Rights and Freedoms*, including freedom of conscience and religion, of thought and belief, of opinion and expression, and of assembly and association

fungibles goods being of such a nature that one part or quantity may be replaced by another equal part or quantity of similar quality

G

garnishment when the court orders that monies owed to the judgment debtor by third parties be paid into court and applied toward judgment debts; a portion of the defendant's wages may be so directed to payment of the judgment

general damages compensation for future pecuniary losses and incalculable losses such as pain and suffering

good faith the decision maker must act with honesty and integrity

goodwill a business's reputation and ongoing relations with customers and product identification

goods tangible, movable personal property that can be measured and weighed; also known as *chattels*

gratuitous promise a one-sided agreement that the courts will not enforce

grievance process a procedure for settling disputes arising under a collective agreement

guarantee a written commitment whereby a guarantor agrees to pay a debt if the debtor does not

guarantor a person assuming obligation to pay if the debtor does not

H

holdback a specified percentage that a person owing funds on a construction contract must retain for a specified period to protect against claims made by the suppliers of goods and services

holder in due course an innocent third party entitled to collect on a negotiable instrument despite any claims of the original parties

holding corporation a corporation that owns shares in other corporations

homestead rights rights giving a spouse a claim to a substantial portion of family property

I

illegal consideration a promise to commit an unlawful act or to do something against public policy, which is not valid consideration and will not be enforced by a court

illegal contract a contract that is void because it involves the performance of an unlawful act

implied authority when the authority of the agent as implied from surrounding circumstances, such as the position or title given (by the principal) to the agent

implied contract an agreement inferred from the conduct of the parties

in-camera hearings part of a trial proceeding that is closed to the public

in good faith a characteristic of bargaining that makes every reasonable effort to reach an agreement

indemnity a primary obligation of a third party to pay a debt along with the debtor

independent contractor a person working for himself who contracts to provide specific services to another

inducing breach of contract encouraging someone to break her contract with another

infants persons under the age of majority (also called minors)

injunction a court order to stop some offending conduct

injurious falsehood defamation with respect to another's product or business; also known as *product defamation* or *trade slander*

innocent misrepresentation a false statement made honestly and without carelessness by a person who believed it to be true

innuendo an implied statement that is detrimental to another

insanity when a person cannot understand the nature or consequences of his acts

insider knowledge information that affects share pricing that is not publicly known; directors, officers, and large shareholders, among others, cannot profit by improperly using confidential knowledge about the company or corporation

insolvency inability of a person to pay her debts as they become due

insurable interest a real and substantial interest in specific property or in someone's life

insurance agents persons acting on behalf of an insurer to handle policies

intellectual property personal property in the form of ideas and creative work

intention an element of a valid contract; the parties must objectively intend for an agreement to be legally binding

intentional infliction of mental suffering a tort constituted by harassment or prank causing nervous shock

interest dispute a disagreement about the terms to be included in a new collective agreement

interim agreement a binding contract that will subsequently be put into a more formal document; usually referred to as an *agreement of purchase and sale* in a real estate transaction

interlocutory injunction a court order issued before a trial to stop an ongoing injury

interpretation statute a statute that directs the court to interpret legislation in a specific way

intimidation a threat to perform an illegal act that is used to force a party to act against its own interest

invitation to treat an invitation to engage in the bargaining process

invitee a person coming on a property for a business purpose

involuntary assignment assignment of rights that takes place involuntarily, as in the cases of death and bankruptcy

issue estoppel a principle preventing an issue from being litigated again on grounds that it has already been determined in an earlier trial or hearing

J

joint tenancy shared property ownership with a right of survivorship

joint venture the collaboration of several businesses to accomplish a major project

jointly liable under joint liability, all parties must be sued together; partners may face joint liability for debts of the firm

judicial branch the part of the government composed of courts and officers of the court

judicial review power held by the courts to review decisions made by administrative decision makers

judgment creditor the person to whom a court awards damages or costs

judgment debtor the person ordered by a court to pay damages or costs

jurisdiction legal authority and scope of power; the *Constitution Act, 1867* delegated responsibility for matters to federal or provincial governments, thus giving them distinct jurisdiction to create laws in those areas. Also refers to the province whose courts have the right to hear and resolve a dispute

jurisdictional dispute a disagreement over who has authority; in the labour context, a dispute between two unions over which one should represent a group of employees, or over which union members ought to do a particular job

just cause a valid reason to dismiss an employee without notice

justification the truth of a statement, applied as a defence to a defamation action

L

laches undue delay; neglect or omission to assert a right or claim

land titles system a registration system that guarantees title to real property

last clear chance doctrine a largely outdated principle of torts that the last person capable of avoiding the accident is wholly responsible

law made by government or the courts and can be enforced by the courts or by other government agencies

law of equity a system of law collateral to the common law, developed by the Court of Chancery

law merchant laws developed by the merchant guilds and the source of common law relating to negotiable instruments such as cheques and promissory notes

law society a self-governing body whose mandate involves regulating the legal profession in the public interest; law societies set and enforce ethical and professional standards for lawyers

lease a secured arrangement whereby possession of the goods goes to the lessee, while the title to the goods remains with the lessor

lease to purchase a lease in which title to the goods is transferred to the lessee at the end of the lease period

leasehold estate an interest in land that grants the tenant exclusive possession until a specific date

legal aid the provision of legal services to persons in financial need

legal rights basic rights enumerated in the *Canadian Charter of Rights and Freedoms*, such as the right to life, liberty, and security of the person; and security against unreasonable search and seizure or arbitrary imprisonment or detention

legality an element of a valid contract; the object and consideration of the contract must be legal and not against public policy

legislation laws enacted by Parliament or legislatures; also known as *statutes*

legislative branch the part of government empowered with enacting laws; Parliament and legislatures

letter of credit a commitment by the importer's bank that the price stated will be paid upon presentation of documentation confirming delivery

letters patent a method of incorporating used in some jurisdictions in Canada whereby the government grants recognition to the company as a separate legal entity

liability insurance insurance covering loss caused by the negligence of oneself or one's employees

libel the written or more permanent form of a defamatory statement

licence a non-exclusive right to use property; revocable permission to use another's land

licensee a person on property with permission but for his own purpose

lien a claim registered against property, such as a mortgage; a charge giving the creditor the right to retain what is in her possession until her demands for payment are satisfied

life estate an interest in land ending at death

limitation period the period of time within which legal action must be taken

limited liability liability is restricted to capital contributed; shareholders are shielded from liability for the corporation's debts

limited liability partnership (LLP) a new form of partnership where only the partner responsible for the loss faces unlimited liability

limited partnership a partnership with general and limited partners; limited partners are liable only to the extent of their original investment

liquidated damages a remedy requiring the party responsible for a breach to pay an amount specified in the contract

lockout an action in which the employer prevents employees from working

M

maintenance of membership a requirement in a collective agreement that union members pay dues and maintain their membership, though new employees need not join the union

malicious prosecution a tort action based on criminal or quasi-criminal prosecution motivated by ill will toward the accused and lacking reasonable evidential grounds for proceeding

mandamus a court order directing that a specific act be performed

mandatory retirement forced retirement from employment, generally at 65 years

mediation a discussion between the parties to a dispute that is facilitated by a mediator in an effort to encourage and assist them in coming to an agreement

mediator a neutral third party who facilitates discussion between parties to a dispute to encourage and assist their coming to an agreement; also known as a *conciliator*

memorandum of association the constitution of a corporation in a registration jurisdiction

merchantable quality freedom of goods from defects that, if known, would impact the price

minors persons under the age of majority (also called infants)

misfeasance wrongful conduct

misrepresentation an untrue statement of fact; an incorrect or false representation

mistake an error about some aspect of a contract that destroys consensus

mitigate to lessen a loss, for example, by victims of a breach, who have a duty to take all reasonable steps to minimize losses suffered

moral rights an author's right to prohibit others, including any new owner of a creative work, from distorting or degrading it

mortgage a means of securing loans; title of property is held by the money-lender as security in some jurisdictions; in other jurisdictions, a mortgage is simply a charge against title

N

necessaries the essential goods or services required to function in society, such as food, clothing, and shelter

negligence an unintentional, careless act or omission that causes injury to another person or his property

negligent misrepresentation an incorrect or false statement of fact, made without the required care, that misleads the recipient thus causing injury

negligent statements failure to live up to a duty not to communicate misleading words causing economic loss

negotiable instruments substitutes for money that bestow unique benefits; vehicles for conveniently transferring funds or advancing credit

negotiation direct communication between the parties to a dispute in an effort to resolve the problems without third-party intervention; transferring negotiable instruments to third parties

netiquette a code of conduct for online activities

"no fault" programs insurance programs compensating people for their injuries whether they were at fault or not

non-disclosure a failure to reveal facts; if a duty to disclose exists, silence may constitute misrepresentation

non est factum "it is not my act"—grounds for a court to declare a contract void because a party is unaware of the nature of the contract

nonfeasance failure to act; such failure is actionable in tort only where there is a specific duty to act, as with a guardian, parent, or lifeguard

non-pecuniary damages damages based on non-monetary factors such as pain and suffering

non-profit society a separate legal entity with different rules for incorporation than corporations

notice of civil claim a statement of claim in British Columbia

novation the creation of a new contract through the substitution of a third party for one of the original parties to a contract by the consent of all

O

offer a tentative promise to do something if another party consents to do what the first party requests

offer to settle a formal offer by either party to modify or compromise its claim to settle the matter before trial, refusal of which offer may affect costs

operating lease a lease in which the goods are returned to the lessor at the end of the lease period

oppression action an action against the directors who have allegedly offended the rights of creditors or minority shareholders

option agreement a subsidiary contract creating an obligation to hold an offer open for acceptance until the expiration of a specified time

order for judicial sale a court order that property be sold during the redemption period

organization test a test used to establish whether a worker is an employee or independent contractor; examines whether the worker is providing services integral to the organization's business

P

paramountcy the principle that when a matter is addressed by both valid federal and provincial legislation and there is a conflict, the federal legislation takes precedence

par-value shares a share with a stated value at issuance (most shares are now no par value)

parliamentary supremacy the principle that the primary law-making body is Parliament or the provincial legislatures in their respective jurisdictions, and that statutes take priority over the common law

parol contract a simple contract that may be verbal or written but is not under seal

parol evidence rule a principle that courts will not permit outside evidence to contradict clear wording of a contract

partially executed contract a contract at the stage when one party has performed and the other has not

partnership when the ownership and responsibilities of a business are shared by two or more people with a view toward profit

party and party costs court costs determined by a tariff establishing what opposing parties in a civil action ought to pay

passing-off the tort of misleading the public about the identity of a business or product

past consideration something completed before an agreement is made; it is not valid consideration

patent a government-granted monopoly prohibiting anyone but the inventor from profiting from the invention; gives inventors the right to profit from their inventions

pay equity a principle or statute requiring equal pay for work of equal value

pay in lieu of notice an amount paid to a dismissed employee rather than notice to terminate

perfection protection of a secured creditor's claim, either by registering the secured obligation or by taking possession of the collateral

performance completion by both parties of the terms of a contract

periodic tenancy automatically renewing tenancy with no specific termination date

permanent injunction a court order prohibiting offending conduct

personal guarantee a guarantee of payment for another's obligation

personal property tangible, movable goods (chattels) and intangible claims (choses in action)

picketing job action during a legal strike when employees circulate at the periphery of the job site to persuade others not to do business with the struck employer

pleadings the documents used to initiate a civil action, including the statement of claim, the statement of defence and counterclaim, and any clarification associated with them

pledge an item that a creditor (like a pawnbroker) takes possession of as security and holds until repayment

postbox rule a principle that a mailed acceptance is effective when and where it is dropped into a mailbox

power of attorney an agency agreement in writing and under seal

precedent an earlier court decision; in a common law system, judges are required to follow a decision made in a higher court in the same jurisdiction

pre-emptive right the right of a shareholder to buy new shares in the same proportion as her current ownership of shares

preferred creditors creditors who, by legislation, must be paid before other unsecured creditors

preferred shareholders holders of preferred shares who may have a right to vote arising if dividends are not paid

preferred shares shares giving the shareholder preference over other classes of shares; that preference often pertains to the payment of dividends

prerogative writ one of the remedies the court may apply if it finds that an administrator has acted beyond his jurisdiction, made an unreasonable decision, or not followed the rules of natural justice

prima facie a judicial finding that circumstantial evidence establishes a case "on the face of it," which prevails until contradicted and overcome by evidence to the contrary

principles of fundamental justice principles set by tradition and convention that protect the right to a fair hearing by an impartial decision maker acting in good faith to implement a valid law

priority when there are two or more creditors, the one entitled to be paid first has priority; for example, a registered lien usually has first claim (over other interests) to goods used as security

privacy the right to be let alone; to protect private personal information; and to be free of physical intrusion, surveillance, and misuse of an image or name

private law the rules that govern our personal, social, and business relations, which are enforced by one person's suing another in a private or civil action

private nuisance the use of property in such a way that it foreseeably interferes with a neighbour's enjoyment of her property

privative clause terms in a statute that attempt to restrict the right of judicial review

privity of contract a principle that contract terms apply only to the actual parties to the contract

probate courts specialized courts dealing with wills and estates; also known as *surrogate courts*

procedural fairness rules of natural justice that a hearing must follow

procedural law the law determining how the substantive laws will be enforced— for example, the rules governing arrest and criminal investigation, or pre-trial and court processes in both criminal and civil cases

product defamation defamation with respect to another's product; also known as *injurious falsehood* or *trade slander*

product liability the legal liability of the manufacturer or vendor to compensate buyers, users, and others injured because of product defects

professional associations organizations empowered to regulate educational qualifications and professional standards for their members; they may also have disciplinary powers over members

professional liability liability owed by persons failing to live up to the standard expected of a reasonable member of a group with special expertise

professional liability insurance specialty insurance for lawyers, doctors, and other professionals designed to cover risks occurring in their practices

prohibition an order not to proceed with a hearing or other administrative process

promissory estoppel the principle that when a gratuitous promise to do something in the future causes a person who relies on that promise to incur an expense, the promisor will not be allowed to enforce other contractual rights that are inconstant with that promise; the promise can only be used as a defence by the promisee; also known as *equitable estoppel*

promissory note a promise to pay the amount stated on the instrument

promoter a person who participates in the initial setting up of a corporation or who assists the corporation in making a public share offering

proof of claim a document filed with the trustee in bankruptcy establishing the validity of a creditor's claim

prospectus a public document disclosing relevant information about a corporation

proximity nearness in place, time, occurrence, or relation

proxy when shareholders designate another person to vote on their behalf at an annual general meeting

public domain the category of works that are no longer copyrighted and may be used by anyone

public interest responsible journalism defence a defence to defamation excusing incorrect statements on matters of public interest where conclusions were reached following responsible investigation

public law the public good; law concerning the government and individuals' relationships with it, including criminal law and the regulations created by government agencies

public nuisance unreasonable interference with public property or creating conditions that negatively affect a considerable number of people

public policy the public good; some acts, although not illegal, will not be enforced by the courts because they are socially distasteful (against public policy)

punitive damages damages in excess of the plaintiff's actual losses, intended to punish the wrongdoer for outrageous or extreme behaviour; also known as *exemplary damages*

purchase money security interest (PMSI) a security interest on specific goods that has priority over a general security agreement provided it is registered within a specified time

Q

qualified privilege exemption from liability for defamatory statements made pursuant to a duty or special interest, so long as the statement was made honestly and without malice and was circulated only to those having a right to know

quantum meruit ("as much as is deserved") a reasonable price paid for requested services; sometimes called a *quasi-contract*

quasi-contract a contractual relationship involving a request for goods and services where there is no agreement on price before the service is performed; courts impose an obligation to pay a reasonable price in these situations; also known as *quantum meruit*

quiet possession a condition that the seller, or anyone claiming through the seller, will not interfere with the buyer's use and enjoyment of the property

R

Rand formula an option in a collective agreement enabling employees to retain the right not to join the union, though they are still required to pay union dues; also known as an *agency shop*

ratification when the majority agrees with the terms of a collective bargain; when a principal confirms a contract entered into by his agent

real property land, buildings attached to the land, and items called fixtures, that is, items that are attached to the land or to a building or to another fixture attached to the land

reasonable foreseeability test a test of whether a duty of care is owed, based on what a person should have anticipated would be the consequences of his action

reasonable notice length of notice to be given to an employee to terminate an employment contract of indefinite term; determined with reference to length of service and the nature of the employee's position, among other factors

reasonable person test in a negligence action, the judicial standard of socially acceptable behaviour; the standard used to determine the existence of apparent authority of an agent

receivership a proceeding in which a receiver is appointed for an insolvent corporation, partnership, or individual to take possession of its assets for ultimate sale and distribution to creditors

recognition dispute a dispute arising between a union and employer while the union is being organized

rectification a correction, by the court, of the wording of a mistake in a contract

referral selling a type of sales practice in which the purchaser supplies a seller with a list of friends or acquaintances and receives a benefit when sales are made to those people

registration a legislated requirement for incorporating a company in some jurisdictions in Canada

registration system a means of registering and tracking property deeds

regulations supplementary rules passed under the authority of a statute and having the status of law

regulators government agencies including ministries, departments, boards, commissions, agencies, tribunals, and individual bureaucrats at the federal, provincial, and municipal levels

relief against forfeiture an equitable principle that when a landlord retakes a property because of a failure to pay rent prior to the end of the lease term, the tenant can pay the arrears and apply in the court to have the lease reinstated

remainderman a third party with the right to the remainder of the fee simple after the death of a life tenant

remoteness test determining whether the damages were too far removed from the original negligent act; a breaching party is only responsible for reasonably expected losses

representative action a lawsuit where certain shareholders are given the right to launch a civil action against the directors on behalf of an injured company; sometimes called a *derivative action*

repudiation an indication by one party to the other that there will be a failure to honour the contract (the expression of which can be expressed or implied)

res ipsa loquitur a principle of establishing negligence based on facts that "speak for themselves"; this no longer applies in Canadian tort law

rescission amounts to the undoing of a contract, returning the parties to the positions they were in before the contract

response to civil claim a statement of defence in British Columbia

restrictive covenant in property law, a condition imposed by the seller as to what the purchaser can use the land for; in employment law, a commitment not to work in a certain geographical area for a designated period of time

retainer a deposit paid by a client to a lawyer before the lawyer commences work on behalf of the client

reverse discrimination prejudice or bias exercised against a person or class to correct a pattern of discrimination against another person or class

reversionary interest the right of the original owner to retake possession of property upon the death of the life tenant

revocation withdrawal of an offer before acceptance (must be communicated to the offeree)

right of salvage an insurer's right after paying the insured to sell damaged or recovered goods to recover losses

right of way a type of easement that allows the crossing of another's land

right to redeem after a creditor has taken possession of collateral, the right of the debtor to reclaim it on payment of any money owing

rights dispute a disagreement about the meaning of a term in a collective agreement

riparian rights the common law right given to people living near rivers and streams to have the water come to them in undiminished quantity and quality

risk potential loss from destruction or damage to goods, injury, or other eventuality

Roman civil law the law of the Roman Empire, from which the common law drew its concepts of property and possessions

royal assent the final approval of the representative of the British Crown by which a bill becomes law in Canada

rule of law an unwritten convention inherited from Britain that recognizes that although Parliament is supreme and can create any law considered appropriate, citizens are protected from the arbitrary actions of the government

rules of evidence rules governing the kinds of evidence that will be accepted by the courts

rules of natural justice basic standards of procedural fairness

S

satisfaction a substitute in consideration accepted by both parties

secondary picketing picketing by striking employees not just of their own workplace but also of other locations where the employer carries on business

secured creditor a creditor who has a claim on property of the debtor, giving him priority on that property over other creditors

secured transaction a collateral right to debt giving the creditor the right to take back the goods or intercept the debt owing used as security in the event of default

securities commission a provincial agency that serves as a watchdog for the stock market

seizure when the court authorizes property of the defendant to be seized and sold to satisfy a judgment

self-defence the right to respond to an assault with as much force as is reasonable in the circumstances

self-induced frustration frustration arising when one of the parties to a contract causes or fails to prevent a frustrating event; treated as a breach of contract

seller's lien a seller who holds the goods has a lien against a defaulting purchaser

sentencing circles meetings to suggest sentences in cases involving Aboriginal offenders and victims

separate legal entity the principle that a corporation exists separately from the people who created it

servient tenement the property subject to an easement

settlement transfer of assets where nominal or no consideration is involved

severally liable under several liabilities, each partner can be sued separately

severance an owner's removal of chattel that he has affixed; separation or division of joint ownership; action by one of the co-owners that is inconsistent with joint tenancy

share the means of acquiring funds from a large number of sources to run a corporation; an interest in a corporation held by an investor

shared mistake the same mistake made by both parties to a contract

shareholder agreement an agreement among the shareholders of a corporation that sets out the terms of their relationship

simple contract a written or verbal contract not under seal; also called a *parol contract*

slander spoken defamation

sole proprietorship an individual carrying on business alone

solicitor and client costs costs based on what a lawyer ought to actually charge his client

solicitor–client privilege the duty of the lawyer to keep the information provided by the client confidential

sophisticated client a person who understands and appreciates the importance of the law and the role of a lawyer in making good decisions

special damages monetary compensation awarded by a court to cover actual expenses and calculable pre-trial losses

specific performance an order by a court to a breaching party that it live up to the terms of an agreement

standard form contract a contract with fixed terms prepared by a business

standby letter of credit a commitment by the importer's bank that the price stated will be paid upon presentation of documentation confirming delivery; used as a guarantee

statement of claim the document setting out the nature of complaint and the facts alleged that form the basis of the action

statement of defence response by the defendant to a statement of claim

statutes law in the form of legislation passed by Parliament

statutory assignment an assignment that meets certain qualifications and under which the assignee can enforce a claim directly without involving the assignor

statutory damages a new remedy enabling a court to award damages that it "considers just" under the circumstances

statutory easements easements giving utilities or other bodies rights to run power or sewer lines across private property

stoppage in transit the seller's right to stop the shipment during transit in event of default

strict liability liability even in the absence of fault

strike withdrawal of services by employees

subject-to clause a term making a contract conditional on future events

sublet a lease executed by the lessee of land or premises to a third party for a shorter term than that which the lessee holds

subrogation the right of the insurer upon payment to take over the rights of the insured in relation to whoever caused the injury

substantial performance performance of a contract in all but a minor aspect of it

substantive law the law establishing both the rights an individual has in society and also the limits on her conduct

summary procedures an arrangement allowing a court to make a decision based on affidavit evidence

surety bond insurance arranged in case a party to a contract fails to perform

surrogate courts specialized courts dealing with wills and estates; also known as *probate courts*

T

tenancy at sufferance a situation in which a tenant fails to leave after a lease has expired and owes compensation to the landlord

tenancy in common ownership of land by two or more people with equal, undivided interests in it

tender of performance an unsuccessful (because it is rejected or prevented by the other party) attempt by one of the parties to a contract to perform its obligations under the contract

thin skull rule a principle of torts that we take our victims as we find them, even those with unique physical or mental conditions

tort an action that causes harm or injury to another person

trade secret confidential information that gives a business competitive advantage

trade slander defamation with respect to another's product or business; also known as *injurious falsehood* or *product defamation*

trademark any term, symbol, design, or combination of these that identifies a business service or product and distinguishes it from a competitor

trespass to chattels direct, intentional interference with another's rights to possess his personal property

trespass to land an unauthorized, intentional intrusion upon or direct breach of the boundaries of another's land

trespass to person intentional physical interference with another person; also known as *assault* and *battery*

trespasser a person who intentionally and without consent or privilege enters another's property

trust a provision in equity whereby one person transfers property to a second person obligated to use it to the benefit of a third person

trustee in bankruptcy the licensed professional appointed to administer the estate of a bankrupt for the benefit of the creditors

truth the accuracy of a statement, applied as a defence to a defamation action; also known as the defence of justification

U

umbrella liability a package of several kinds of insurance

unconscionable transaction an equitable principle allowing courts to set aside a contract in which a party in a superior bargaining position took advantage of the other party and the consideration was grossly unfair

undisclosed principal a principal whose identity is concealed from the third parties with whom the agent is dealing; the rights and obligations of the parties depend on whether the agent makes it clear that she is representing an undisclosed principal rather than operating on his own behalf

undue influence pressure from a dominant, trusted person that makes it impossible for a party to bargain the terms of a contract freely

unenforceable contract an otherwise binding contract that the courts will not enforce, such as a contract that does not satisfy the *Statute of Frauds*

unilateral contract a contract formed when one party performs what has been requested by the other party; there is a promise followed by an act, but not an exchange of promises

unilateral mistake a mistake made by only one of the parties about the terms of a contract

union shop a workplace where new employees must join the union

unjust enrichment a windfall that one party to a contract stands to make at the expense of the other

unlawful interference with economic relations a tort consisting of unlawful competitive practices, such as inducing breach of contract

unlimited liability the liability of the business owner or partners for all debts incurred by the business to the extent of their personal resources

utmost good faith another term for fiduciary duty

V

vacant possession an obligation to deliver possession of vacant premises to a tenant at the beginning of a lease period

valid contract an agreement that is legally binding on both parties

vicarious liability liability of an employer for injuries caused by employees while carrying out their employment duties

vicarious performance performance by another designated person of the obligations under a contract rather than the actual contracting party

void contract an agreement that is not legally binding because an essential element is missing

voidable contract an agreement that has legal effect but that one of the parties has the option to end

volenti non fit injuria a defence in torts based on the plaintiff's voluntarily assuming a clear legal risk

voluntary assignment in bankruptcy an assignment of assets to a trustee in bankruptcy for the benefit of creditors made voluntarily by a debtor

W

warranties minor terms of a contract

without prejudice words that, when used during negotiation, are a declaration that concessions, compromises, and admissions made by a party cannot be used against that party in subsequent litigation

work stoppages strikes (initiated by employees) and lockouts (initiated by employers)

work to rule job action in which employees perform no more than what is minimally required so as to pressure an employer

writ of summons the written judicial order by which legal actions are commenced in some jurisdictions

wrongful dismissal dismissal without reasonable cause or notice

Table of Statutes

Table of Cases

Index

The suffix -*f* indicates a figure, -*t* indicates a table, and -*n* indicates a note.